AMERICAN
STATECRAFT

ALSO BY J. ROBERT MOSKIN

Mr. Truman's War

The U.S. Marine Corps Story

Among Lions

Turncoat

Morality in America

The Marines (coauthor)

The Decline of the American Male (coauthor)

The Executive's Book of Quotations (coauthor)

AMERICAN STATECRAFT

THE STORY OF THE U.S. FOREIGN SERVICE

J. ROBERT MOSKIN

Thomas Dunne Books
St. Martin's Press ☙ New York

THOMAS DUNNE BOOKS.
An imprint of St. Martin's Press.

AMERICAN STATECRAFT. Copyright © 2013 by J. Robert Moskin. All rights reserved.
Printed in the United States of America. For information, address
St. Martin's Press, 175 Fifth Avenue, New York, N.Y. 10010.

www.thomasdunnebooks.com
www.stmartins.com

Library of Congress Cataloging-in-Publication Data

Moskin, J. Robert.
    American statecraft : the story of the U.S. Foreign Service / J. Robert Moskin.
        pages. cm.
    Includes bibliographical references and index.
    ISBN 978-1-250-03745-9 (hardcover)
    ISBN 978-1-250-03746-6 (e-book)
    1. United States. Foreign Service.   2. Diplomatic and consular service, American.
    3. Diplomacy.   I. Title.
    JZ1480.M665 2013
    327.73—dc23

                                                                    2013024053

St. Martin's Press books may be purchased for educational, business, or promotional use.
For information on bulk purchases, please contact Macmillan Corporate and Premium Sales
Department at 1-800-221-7945, extension 5442, or write specialmarkets@macmillan.com.

First Edition: November 2013

10 9 8 7 6 5 4 3 2 1

FOR LYNN

partner, personal and professional

Contents

Diplomacy's work is turning challenges into opportunities.
—*Ambassador Thomas R Pickering*

U.S. Ambassador Clarence Gauss crosses a river to Chungking, China, en route to present his credentials, May 26, 1941. Photo courtesy of the Association for Diplomatic Studies and Training. (The Library of Congress)

Introduction

Closing Pandora's Box

W e Americans glorify our warriors and ignore our diplomats. Yet our diplomats are the ones whose job it is to keep us out of war, to keep the nation at peace. They have other functions, of course; they shape and sell the nation's foreign policy, rescue American citizens who get into trouble abroad, find markets for American business—but avoiding war is the crucial function. The men and women of the U.S. Foreign Service see themselves as "America's first line of defense."

How did diplomats get this often-desperate job? French diplomat and historian Jean Jules Jusserand, who served as France's envoy to the United States for twenty-three years, gave us this answer: Diplomats, he said in 1921 when he was elected president of the American Historical Association, "became a necessity among men at the moment . . . when Pandora's fateful box having been opened, evils were scattered throughout the world, and prospered."

"To an ambassador, the safety of the republic must be the supreme law," Ambassador Jusserand said, quoting Aristotle. He must be "rather the maker of peace and concord than of discord and war." Only three years after the horrors of World War I had come to an end, Jusserand, who was awarded the first Pulitzer Prize for history, pleaded, "The fate of nations must depend in the future on something else than force and falsehood."

• • •

The world is now again experiencing what historian Arnold Toynbee called a "time of troubles," when the elements of civilization (nations and extranational elements) battle one another. Diplomacy is their least deadly weapon.

Unlike the military, Foreign Service officers do not rush out to meet a crisis; they are already there. Permanent embassies have existed since the fifteenth century. (The British had a permanent embassy in Constantinople in 1583.) Jusserand quoted François de Callières, a powerful French diplomat of the eighteenth century: "There are temporary embassies for mere ostentation, for the fulfilling of which nothing is needed but a great name and much wealth, like those for the ceremony of a marriage or a baptism. . . . But when affairs have to be negotiated, a man is needed, not an idol."

The people in the Department of State in Washington, D.C., call Benjamin Franklin the father of the U.S. Foreign Service. In Franklin's day, American diplomats were amateurs, members of a small circle of leaders among the colonials rebelling against their British rulers. They had to negotiate with seasoned and sometimes duplicitous European court diplomats. Later, the amateurs were celebrated as the "militiamen of diplomacy."

The United States Foreign Service needed years to acquire a semblance of professionalism. Along the way, its members included many dedicated and courageous public servants, and also some political spoilsmen and rogues.

At first, American diplomats were very much on their own. An American envoy would send an inquiry from his post in Europe to Washington and then wait weeks or months to receive instructions. The functions and responsibilities of American diplomats have evolved dramatically over the more than two hundred years during which the United States has sent the Foreign Service abroad. Time and distance have been squeezed by ever-swifter communications. Even so, the heart of the diplomats' job is still to report home what is being thought and done overseas and to bring the American story to distant regimes and peoples.

For the United States, the conduct of foreign affairs has a built-in difficulty. After serving for forty years, Ambassador Charles E. Bohlen described it, "... The American system of separation of powers was not designed for the conduct of foreign affairs. It was designed for the conduct of non-foreign affairs, really."

Today, the United States Foreign Service consists of a community of men and women who sign up to spend a substantial part of their lives in foreign lands working for the benefit of their fellow Americans. They are the nation's eyes and ears, constantly collecting information and perceptions and, ideally, teaching their hosts how to understand the United States.

Ambassador Jusserand was convinced that "there is no kind of knowledge, science, or accomplishment that cannot happen to be of use in such a profession." He added, "I should have been greatly surprised ... had any one told me, when in boyhood days I was swimming in rivers and climbing rocks, that this 'accomplishment' would be of service years later, when, as an ambassador in far-off America, in order to keep company with the chief of state, President (Theodore) Roosevelt, I swam the Potomac and climbed quarries south of the stream." The President and the ambassador became close tennis-playing friends; in 1906 TR wrote Ambassador Whitelaw Reid that Jusserand was "one of the best men I have ever met."

Today, U.S. Foreign Service members and retirees of the Department of State belong to an organization of more than 58,000 men and women. American Foreign Service officers serve at some 268 posts in 190 of the world's 192 nations. They are honed to a professional proficiency.

Inside the State Department lobby as of May 2013 are plaques honoring the 244 American diplomats who have died in the line of duty. In the 180 years between 1780 and 1960, eighty-one died. And the pace has quickened. In the half century since 1960, 163 have died.

Under Secretary of State R. Nicholas Burns said plainly at a Foreign Service Day in Washington, "Diplomacy has always been a hazardous occupation." And today it has become more dangerous than ever, as the members of the U.S. Foreign Service keep trying to shut Pandora's box.

In awarding President Barack Obama the 2009 Nobel Peace Prize, the Norwegian Nobel Committee said, "Dialogue and negotiations are preferred as instruments for resolving even the most difficult international conflicts." This is hardly a new idea but, I hope, it is a renewed one

PART ONE

I

Making a Difference

Today, many Americans cannot identify the U.S. Foreign Service, even though it is the nation's first line of defense. It is both a highly trained organization stationed in 190 countries and also a community of 58,000 men and women who spend most of their lives in foreign lands serving their fellow Americans.

The members of the Foreign Service—and thousands more who do not pass its tough entrance tests—are motivated, more than anything else, by the desire to "make a difference." They want to create and carry out American foreign policy in creative, effective ways.

To make a difference, a Foreign Service officer must have both the ability and the authority to make decisions and take action—often under the pressure of crisis and danger. Here, for example, are the stories of two modern American diplomats who made a difference.

"HE WAS ONE OF A KIND, UNIQUE"

William A. Eddy masterminded the historic meeting between President Franklin D. Roosevelt and King Ibn Saud of Saudi Arabia during World War II.

Eddy was born in Syria to Presbyterian missionary parents and grandparents. During boyhood summers, his father sent him to live in the desert with the nomadic Bedouins and learn their language and culture. He played varsity basketball at Princeton, and, after graduating in June 1917, he was sent to France with the Sixth Marines.

Eddy led daring reconnaissance patrols, and, within a few months, received the Distinguished Service Cross, the Navy Cross, and two Silver Stars, all for valor, before he was seriously wounded in the battle for Belleau Wood. His regimental commander, Colonel Albertus W. Catlin, a Medal of Honor winner himself, called Eddy "a daredevil who loved nothing better than to stalk German sentries in Indian fashion."

After World War I, Eddy earned a Ph.D. at Princeton, taught at the American University in Cairo and at Dartmouth College, and then became president of Hobart and William Smith Colleges. He rejoined the Marine Corps in World War II and served as a naval attaché in Tangier before the Allies landed in French North Africa on November 8, 1942. The attaché title was a cover; he headed the Office of Strategic Services (OSS) for North Africa, working with Ambassador Robert Murphy, who represented the State Department, and Brigadier General William J. Donovan, who led the OSS. Ambassador Murphy said of Eddy: "He was one of a kind, unique; we could have used a hundred like him."

In November 1943, the State Department asked the OSS to return Colonel Eddy for temporary duty, and President Roosevelt sent him to Saudi Arabia as the American minister. When FDR decided to meet with Ibn Saud on his way home from the Yalta Conference in February 1945, Colonel Eddy organized the secret meeting between the self-taught warrior-hunter Saudi king and the sophisticated, Harvard-educated American president.

Eddy was charged to bring them together aboard the brand-new heavy cruiser USS *Quincy* on the Great Bitter Lake in the middle of the Suez Canal. If word of the meeting leaked out, *Quincy* would be a stunning target for German bomber pilots.

Eddy arranged for the destroyer USS *Murphy* to drop anchor in Jeddah harbor on Sunday, February 11. It was supposed to look like a routine visit, but no American warship had ever stopped at Jeddah. Meanwhile, Ibn Saud and his entourage traveled overland from Mecca to Jeddah. And Eddy convinced the king to reduce his party on board from a hundred to forty-eight (still exceeding the dozen visitors the destroyer had room for).

When the *Murphy* sailed for Suez the next day, some Saudis ashore feared their king had abdicated, others that he had been kidnapped. The ladies of the harem dressed in mourning clothes.

To steam to Suez took two nights and a day. The king insisted on sleeping on deck; a tent was raised and rugs spread over the gray steel. His cooks prepared his traditional lamb and rice. At ten o'clock on Wednesday morning, February 14, Valentine's Day, *Murphy* tied up alongside the USS *Quincy*; and the king, three princes, and two ministers crossed the gangplank to meet with President Roosevelt, who was sitting in his wheelchair on the cruiser's deck. The President and king talked for more than an hour. Eddy was their sole interpreter; dressed in his U.S. Marine uniform, he worked kneeling on one knee between the heads of state.

Eddy then escorted the king to FDR's private suite and to lunch. The only other Americans at the table were Roosevelt; Admiral William D. Leahy, chief of staff to the commander in chief; and Foreign Service officer Charles "Chip" Bohlen, FDR's Russian interpreter at Yalta.

After lunch, the king and President resumed their talk, joined by the Saudi foreign minister and Eddy. The two most significant topics they discussed were American access to Saudi Arabian oil and the settlement of more Jewish survivors of the Holocaust in Palestine. The king favored the first and strongly opposed the second.

Eddy later said that Roosevelt assured the king that "(1) he personally, as president, would never do anything which might prove hostile to the Arabs; and (2) the U.S. Government would make no change in its basic policy in Palestine without full and prior consultation with both Jews and Arabs." Eddy always believed that the meeting on the Great Bitter Lake enabled "the leader of Islam to face West and bind his fortunes to ours."

A DARING ESCAPE

A second story of an American diplomat who made a difference is that of U.S. Consul General J. Hall Paxton. When Mao Tse-tung's Communist armies swept across China in August 1949, Paxton led out the people of the American consulate at Tihwa in China's remote northwestern corner. The Chinese had already cut the escape routes to the east and halted all air and rail traffic. Paxton had no choice but to flee by the ancient and precarious Leh caravan route over the Himalayas into India.

The son of a missionary, Paxton had first come to China when he was two. He graduated from Yale; he entered the Foreign Service in 1925 and was serving as a vice consul in Nanking in 1927. Ten years later, he was aboard the gunboat USS *Panay* when Japanese bombers sank her in the Yangtze River. During World War II the Japanese interned him. By 1949, he was fifty years old and in charge at the walled city of Tihwa, only 150 miles from the Russian and Mongolian borders. The primitive consulate had no indoor plumbing, and whitewashed stables served as guest rooms. The Americans were stationed at Tihwa detecting Soviet atomic bomb activity.

Consul General Paxton's party of ten adults and six children left Tihwa on August 16, just ahead of the Chinese armies. The party included three Americans (Paxton; his wife, Vincoe, who had been a missionary nurse; and Vice Consul Robert B. Dreessen, a former U.S. Marine) and two White Russian drivers; their families; and an interpreter, his wife, and their three-month-old baby.

They left behind Vice Consul Douglas S. Mackiernan, who was actually an undercover CIA agent. A skilled meteorologist trained at MIT, he had been stationed at Tihwa during World War II. Now, the CIA ordered Mackiernan, the last American in Tihwa, to stay where he was.

Two weeks after Paxton left, the Russians exploded their first atomic bomb. Eleven days later, twenty-eight-year-old Frank B. Bessac, who had served in the OSS and CIA, arrived in Tihwa. And on September 27, Mackiernan closed the consulate. On October 1, Mao Tse-tung established the People's Republic of China.

Mackiernan and Bessac tried to escape China through Tibet. They traveled for months, mostly riding Asian ponies. Mackiernan kept in touch by radio with his CIA handler and with W. Walton Butterworth, assistant secretary for Far Eastern affairs at the State Department. Mackiernan's biographer, Thomas Laird, says that the State Department and CIA were feuding and failed to ask the Tibetans for permission for the Mackiernan party to pass through Tibet.

At the border on April 29, Tibetan border guards shot and killed Mackiernan. Permission to let the Americans pass reached the border guards two days after Mackiernan had been killed. He was the first CIA man killed in action and was thus honored by the State Department. Frank Bessac and one White Russian in their party survived and finally made their way home.

After leaving Mackiernan at Tihwa, Consul General Paxton drove an ancient jeep carrying his wife and Vice Consul Dreessen; the others piled into an army truck. They covered nearly a thousand miles, crossing the edge of a vast desert in 108-degree heat. At Kashgar, an oasis on the Russian border, they abandoned their vehicles and hired a caravan.

Five weeks after leaving Tihwa, they reached the last Chinese border outpost. The Chinese border guards allowed Paxton's party to go on. They entered the Himalayas, climbed through treacherous three-mile-high Karakoram Pass, crossed and recrossed icy rapids, and suffered frostbite and high-altitude nausea. Breathing was painful. Nine packhorses died. For sixteen days they did not see another human being. Near the end, Paxton's party had to slog ahead and leave the pack train behind.

The terrain on the India side of the mountains was even more difficult, with deep canyons and steep narrow paths. They reached altitudes above seventeen thousand feet and gasped for oxygen in the thin air. When they came to the first tiny Indian settlement, they still had to pick their way over a perilous four-hundred-foot glacier.

After their ten-week ordeal, they staggered into Leh, the capital of Ladakh. A U.S. embassy plane arrived and flew them to New Delhi. Paxton died in 1962 while serving as consul in Isfahan, Iran. His feat of leadership became a Foreign Service legend, encouraging others to take tremendous risks to achieve their goals.

2

The Militiamen of Diplomacy

1776–80

T he story of the Foreign Service begins on March 3, 1776, four
months before the American colonies declared their independence from Great Britain. The Second Continental Congress'
Committee of Secret Correspondence, with Benjamin Franklin in the
chair, sent Silas Deane, a delegate to the Congress from Connecticut, to
Paris as its covert representative to the court of Louis XVI. Deane's orders
said ambiguously that he was to "transact such business commercial and
political, as we have committed to his Care, in access & by Authority of
the Congress of the thirteen united Colonies." He was the first diplomat
sent overseas to represent the united British colonies of North America.

Thirty-eight years old, Silas Deane was the son of a blacksmith. He had
graduated from Yale, taught school, and practiced law. After his wife died
of tuberculosis, he had married Elizabeth Saltonstall, a daughter of a former governor of Connecticut, and gained entree to the leaders of society.

Deane sailed from Chester, Pennsylvania, in the brig *Rachell,* but an
accident forced *Rachell* to return to Philadelphia, and Deane finally sailed
for Bermuda in the sloop *Betsey* on April 3. From there he sailed to Spain;
crossed over the Pyrenees; and, although British intelligence was alerted
to him, he arrived safely in Paris on July 7.

In Paris, he posed as a merchant from Bermuda buying goods to trade
with the Indians in America. He and a group of colonial merchants were
to be paid 5 percent of the value of the goods purchased.

Deane knew no French nor much about France. Paris was bustling with British agents, and Deane sensed he was surrounded by enemies. He communicated in cipher and invisible ink. Not until November did he receive the official copy of the Declaration of Independence he was to present to the French government.

His orders were to ask the French minister of foreign affairs, Charles Gravier, comte de Vergennes, "Whether, if the Colonies should form themselves into an Independent State, France would probably acknowledge them as such, receive their Ambassadors, enter into any Treaty or Alliance with them, for Commerce, or defense, or both?"

De Vergennes cordially assured Deane he should regard himself under the protection of the French court. Deane stressed the political and commercial advantages of a treaty for France and suggested that without such an agreement the new nation might be forced to establish some kind of reunion with Britain.

Deane arranged through Pierre-Augustin Caron de Beaumarchais, a secret agent well connected at court, for loans to buy a hundred artillery guns, fifteen thousand muskets, ammunition, and clothing to equip twenty-five thousand men. By fall, the first shipment of weapons was on its way. Those arms helped the Americans win their victory at Saratoga.

Deane also recruited European officers, including France's twenty-year-old marquis de Lafayette, who became General George Washington's favorite; the German Baron Johann de Kalb, and Polish Count Kazimierz Pulaski.

Deane was not above turning a dollar for himself on the arms and supplies he acquired. He had speculated with men like Benjamin Franklin, who invested in the vast Vandalia land scheme based around the Ohio River; and Deane had organized a company with the merchant Robert Morris in order to buy supplies from London. Deane also accumulated a small fortune speculating on the London stock exchange. Few risk-taking Americans of the revolutionary era overlooked the opportunity to profit personally from a public assignment. The lines between public service and private gain were ill defined.

BENJAMIN FRANKLIN'S STATECRAFT

The thirteen English colonies in America had been working together for eighteen months, ever since the First Continental Congress assembled in

Carpenters' Hall, Philadelphia, on September 5, 1774. That first Congress sent a message to King George III asking to be relieved of Parliament's taxes. The message went through "Friends of American Liberty" in England, who represented the individual colonies. That fall, for the first time, these agents were asked to act for the United Colonies. Only William Bollan, Arthur Lee, and Benjamin Franklin accepted the assignment. These men had no diplomatic status since there was no national entity to represent. And they were not successful.

The nation being born would be defined both by the trial of arms that George Washington led and by Benjamin Franklin's statecraft. There was no executive; the nation was run by committees of Congress.

On November 29, 1775, the Second Continental Congress created the five-man Committee of Secret Correspondence to deal with foreign policy. Franklin was its chair, and pamphleteer Thomas Paine, the committee's first secretary. Its most active member was James Lovell, an eccentric Harvard graduate and schoolteacher whom the British arrested for spying after the battle of Bunker Hill. The Americans would need three years to win France's support.

At first, efforts to manage a new political entity and fight a desperate war were disorganized. At the end of 1775, the Committee of Secret Correspondence arranged to pay Arthur Lee in London two hundred pounds to keep Congress informed of the attitudes of the European powers toward the colonies. And the committee engaged Charles W. F. Dumas, a scholarly, energetic Swiss who lived at The Hague, as its secret agent to the powerful and potentially crucial Dutch Republic.

The Committee of Secret Correspondence directed Silas Deane to be in touch with his former student, Dr. Edward Bancroft, a Massachusetts-born physician living in London who was a friend of Franklin. Deane paid Bancroft's way to Paris, and when the doctor returned to London, he sold Deane's confidences to the British. Neither Deane nor Franklin suspected his double-dealing.

On September 26, 1776, Congress enlarged Deane's secret mission to France into a formal diplomatic commission made up of Deane, Franklin, and Thomas Jefferson. They were the colonies' first full-fledged diplomatic representatives, and their mission was to rally European support. Of the three, only Franklin had diplomatic experience; his biographer, Stacy Schiff, summed him up, "Franklin was a natural diplomat, genial and ruthless."

The commissioners received no salaries, but they were supposed to be paid "a handsome allowance" for their expenses, effort, and "risque." And, three years later, the commissioners were paid $11,111 and their secretaries $4,444 a year. But as the Revolutionary War drained Congress' purse, their salaries shrank.

Jefferson declined to join the commission abroad because his wife, Martha, was ill, so Arthur Lee was moved over from London to Paris in his place. Lee, the cantankerous, quarrelsome youngest son of a Virginia planter family, had been educated at Eton and Edinburgh. A member of the English bar, he had been living in London for nearly ten years. An ambitious man with an unhappy streak of jealousy, he had met Beaumarchais in London. The French secret agent, who was also the author of the comic play *The Marriage of Figaro,* established a fictitious trading company, Roderigue Hortalez & Cie, to do what today would be called "laundering" French and Spanish government funds for the rebellion in America. The first arms were shipped clandestinely from French arsenals in Haiti and Martinique and from gunpowder stores on the tiny Dutch island of St. Eustatius.

The other commissioner, Benjamin Franklin, was the best-known American after George Washington. He held honorary degrees from Harvard, Yale, and Oxford and the Copley Medal from the Royal Society.

The revolutionaries' treasonous affairs of state required secrecy, until the Declaration of Independence made that unnecessary. On April 17, 1777, the Committee of Secret Correspondence was renamed the Committee of Foreign Affairs, and it became the forerunner of the U.S. Department of State.

Meanwhile, Deane's presence in Paris aroused Lee's jealousy. Lee felt that he had been superseded, and he disliked the prospect of working with the newcomer. Lee became convinced that Deane and Franklin were plotting to cheat Congress. Two years later, Lee denounced Deane and precipitated his recall. Beaumarchais, who knew them both, thought Deane honest and Lee an "insidious politician."

Thomas Paine also attacked Deane for profiting from the Revolution and leaked to a newspaper the information that Louis XVI had given the colonies support in secret. Since this was enough to cause a war with England, the French demanded, and obtained, Paine's resignation as the secretary of the Committee of Foreign Affairs.

. . .

Franklin had spent the decade of 1764 to 1775 in London promoting the colonists' cause. But still he condemned the Boston Tea Party as "an Act of violent Injustice on our part." In 1774, the British Privy Council for Plantation Affairs tried Franklin on the charge of circulating stolen letters in order to incite the colonies to break from Britain. The attack on Franklin aroused support for him in the colonies, but London's social circles ostracized him. For the rest of his life, he resented the humiliation of the Privy Council hearing.

In 1775, when Franklin learned that his wife had died in America, he slipped out of London and sailed for home. While he was at sea on the six-week journey, Patrick Henry in Virginia was asking for "liberty or death," and a skirmish in Lexington and Concord, Massachusetts, left ninety-nine British soldiers dead and 174 wounded. Franklin arrived in Philadelphia to find men drilling in the use of arms. In Boston, militiamen lay siege to the British army.

Now just short of seventy, Franklin was a generation older than Washington, Jefferson, and John Adams. He was fat and square-built; his hair was gray and thin. His body was tortured by gout caused by his indulgent lifestyle. But his charm and magnetism were still powerful, his eyes were bright, and his mind as quick as ever. Like Deane, he worked on the side for his own account; Franklin speculated in vast tracts of land acquired from the British government west of the Alleghenies.

Franklin was promptly chosen a delegate to the Second Continental Congress and served on the committee that drafted the Declaration of Independence. After the British victory on Long Island, he led a delegation to a futile talk with Lord Howe, who was in command at New York.

The American revolutionaries distrusted a strong executive—with good reason. As a consequence, their foreign affairs were conducted by a committee that often lacked authority and continuity. The committee had no permanent chairman. Its members changed as the membership of Congress fluctuated. It was nearly another four years before the need for a more permanent institution was acted on.

The Continental Congress sent Franklin to Paris secretly; he left Philadelphia on October 26, 1776, taking with him his two young grandsons. After a brutal month's voyage, they landed in a forlorn corner of Brittany, and it was late in December before they arrived at the same hotel in the rue de l'Université where Deane was lodging. The next day, Lee arrived from London. The British soon grasped the difficulties these American commissioners, and especially the popular Franklin, could cause them.

The three Americans immediately wrote to the comte de Vergennes that they were empowered to negotiate a treaty of amity and commerce between the United States and France. Five days later, the foreign minister received Franklin and Deane in secret. An experienced diplomat, Vergennes used secrecy as a weapon. When the Americans presented their credentials and proposed articles for a treaty, Vergennes sharply warned them not to deal with anyone else in the French court. And when they proposed to buy eight ships of the line completely manned, he politely turned them down. They reported to Congress that the French would not negotiate formally for fear of angering the British but that French ports were open to American ships and Americans could buy and export French goods.

DIPLOMACY AS THEATER

In March 1777, Franklin moved to Passy, at that time a lovely village a mile outside Paris and seven from Louis XVI's palace at Versailles. He and Deane were put up in the Hotel de Valentinois, an extensive estate with formal gardens, owned by a friendly French entrepreneur who sold supplies for the American army. Franklin made this estate his home and headquarters for the next eight years, during which he never left Paris and its suburbs.

From this peaceful base Franklin used his considerable skills to twist help from a sympathetic but class-conscious and corrupt ancien régime that itself would soon prove ripe for revolution. Although Franklin's French was imperfect, he was a consummate actor, marshaling his amazing charisma and even his plain dress, a brown coat with a fur collar, bifocals, and a fur cap. He understood that politics and diplomacy were, in significant part, theater.

Britain's capable spymaster, William Eden, planted a man inside Franklin's headquarters; he was the same Dr. Edward Bancroft with whom Deane had dealt earlier. This amoral young physician, a fellow of the Royal Society, and a purported friend of Franklin's, was a double agent. Dr. Bancroft stayed in Passy for nearly a decade, passing information to the British and interrupting shipments of supplies to the colonies. Franklin's casual style of living made Bancroft's job simple; Franklin left papers strewn about and found codes too tedious to bother with. George III received information from Franklin's desk before the Congress it was intended for.

In fact, codes were not very effective. British agents intercepting messages had no trouble with the American ciphers. And communication across the Atlantic took so long that secrets quickly became obsolete. On average, an exchange of correspondence between Philadelphia and Paris required two months. It was common to send four copies of a document by different routes in the hope that one would arrive safely. Important documents were delivered by special courier. Most of the time, American diplomats abroad depended on their own devices and judgment.

THE COMMITTEE OF FOREIGN AFFAIRS

By the spring of 1777, General Washington's forces had won battles at Trenton and Princeton, and Congress returned to Philadelphia from a frightened three-month exile in Baltimore. The Committee of Foreign Affairs decided to expand its efforts in Europe.

Many capitals did not welcome representatives from the breakaway colonies. When Arthur Lee was appointed to the Spanish court, he was authorized to offer Pensacola, in Florida, to Spain in return for a declaration of war against Britain. But the Spaniards would not even allow him to enter Madrid. And he had no more success with Frederick II of Prussia. Rejected by both courts, he spent as much of his time as possible in Paris.

Francis Dana was appointed commissioner to Russia and spent two fruitless, embarrassing years being ignored in Saint Petersburg. Ralph Izard, a political leader from South Carolina, was appointed commissioner to the grand duchy of Tuscany, but he never left Paris. And William Lee, Arthur's brother, was sent as commissioner to Vienna and Berlin. He and a Dutch banker drafted a treaty between the thirteen "united states" and the seven provinces of Holland, but it merely vouched for Dutch interest in trade with America in case she did win independence.

William Lee spent months in Vienna, even though the British ambassador prevented his gaining an audience with Empress Maria Theresa. Her son, the arrogant, brilliant Joseph II, who succeeded her in 1780, hated all rebels and supported George III in his battle against his impudent subjects. Both Lee brothers were recalled in 1779. Years later, John Adams ran across William Lee in Antwerp, "a forgotten man of Revolutionary diplomacy."

The truth is that the embryonic United States, fighting its British masters, was dispatching amateurs as envoys. John Adams was probably the first to call them "a sort of militia." Later, Dr. Francis Wharton, a Department of State editor, named them "militia diplomatists" and historian Richard Morris tagged them "militiamen of diplomacy." They preferred to do business in the open rather than in secret; they had little tolerance for the fancies of court life and courtier diplomacy; they could lean on neither diplomatic training nor traditions. They were often quite undiplomatic.

The amateurishness of American diplomacy in this period was demonstrated by the feud between Arthur Lee and Silas Deane. Lee attacked both Deane and Franklin over the first secret arms shipments. Were they gifts or should they be paid for? Did Deane profit personally from them? The answers were not clear, because the arms were procured surreptitiously, and the lines between public responsibility and private gain were shadowy.

A MAJOR DIPLOMATIC VICTORY

On December 4, 1777, the American commissioners in Paris received word that, although the British had occupied Philadelphia and Congress had fled to York, Pennsylvania, British General John Burgoyne had on October 17 surrendered his army of 5,700 men at Saratoga in the Hudson River Valley. In appreciable part, the Americans who fought and triumphed there were armed and clothed by France. This was the first significant American victory, and potential allies began offering support.

The American commissioners promptly wrote Vergennes asking that he act on their year-old proposal for a treaty of amity and commerce. Eight days later, the Americans stole off to a rendezvous outside Versailles. A coach met them and whisked them to a house where Vergennes and Conrad-Alexandre Gérard de Rayneval, the future French envoy to Philadelphia, were waiting. In this hideaway, the foreign minister encouraged the Americans but insisted that nothing could be done openly until Spain joined their cause against Britain. Eighteenth-century diplomacy demanded patience.

After receiving the news of the Americans' victory at Saratoga, King George III could no longer hold out against his government. Frederick, Lord North, the British prime minister, fashioned offers of reconciliation. Victory in battle had an undeniable impact on diplomacy. A historian quoted Franklin, "Diplomacy can convert military victory into political gain."

By year's end, the British were trying to prevent an alliance between the Americans and the French. Various emissaries from London visited the American commissioners and tried to persuade Franklin that Britain and America, acting as one, could make the strongest empire on earth. But their proposals would not guarantee independence, and Franklin was blunt: The Americans would be satisfied with nothing but independence.

This was the terrible winter of Valley Forge, where the American army camped without enough food or shoes. Franklin and Deane were promised safe-conduct passes if they would come to London and discuss peace terms short of independence. Franklin refused. But he used the new British attitude to worry the French with the prospect of an accommodation between Britain and the United States. Only then did Louis XVI's council inform the Americans that it was prepared to recognize the colonies' independence. Franklin had won a diplomatic victory.

On February 5, 1778, Conrad-Alexandre Gérard, who was representing the French, was in bed with a cold, and negotiations were put off. The next evening, Franklin, Deane, Arthur Lee, and Gérard signed a treaty of amity and commerce, as well as a military alliance in case of war between France and Britain. France thus became the first nation to recognize the United States of America. It would take the British another five years.

France pledged to maintain the independence of the United States. Both parties promised not to stop fighting the British without the consent of the other. The United States was given a free hand to seize Canada and Bermuda, and France could take the British West Indies.

Now, things moved more rapidly. France sent Gérard to Philadelphia as minister plenipotentiary and consul general to the United States. He lodged with General Benedict Arnold, then still the respected commandant of the city.

Louis XVI, twenty-four-years old, weak, and facing bankruptcy, received Franklin, Deane, and Arthur Lee for the first time at Versailles on

March 20. They were accompanied by Ralph Izard and William Lee. Franklin chose to dress severely plain for this formal and colorful occasion. An observer wrote of him, "But for his noble face I should have taken him for a big farmer, so great was his contrast with the other diplomats, who were all powdered, in full dress, and splashed all over with gold and ribbons."

When the Americans were introduced, Louis XVI said graciously, "Assure Congress of my friendship. I hope this will be for the good of the two nations."

Franklin thanked him in the name of the United States and added, "Your Majesty may count on the gratitude of Congress and its faithful observance of the pledges it now takes." As the departing Americans crossed the courtyard, an assembled crowd greeted them with cheers.

Congress ratified the treaties on May 4. By June, Britain and France were at war.

"WE HAVE KNOWN A MEANER SIDE"

The few American representatives abroad, even the aging Ben Franklin, performed the functions of both diplomats and consuls. As consuls they acted not government to government but served and protected their fellow individual citizens. (The roots of consular duties went back into antiquity. And, later, the city-state of Venice and the Hanseatic League placed consuls in foreign ports to help their citizens abroad.) Among the Americans' consular duties were the protection of seamen and the disposition of prize vessels seized by the Continental navy and American privateers.

The principle has not changed much since then. Maura Harty, a twenty-first-century assistant secretary of state for Consular Affairs, has explained, "From our very beginnings, we have known a meaner side of a countryman's trip abroad—an arrest, a death, destitution or illness. We are ready to be at an American's side for all those things and others not foreseen. It almost, sometimes, feels like a marriage!"

During the American Revolution, the Philadelphia firm of Willing, Morris, and Company controlled much of this nonofficial business. In one case, Thomas Morris, the illegitimate half-brother of the Revolution's leading financier, Robert Morris, was sent as a "commercial agent" to handle consular matters at the French port of Nantes. Thomas Morris proved to be a hard-drinking, free-spending failure; and Silas Deane and Benjamin Franklin dispatched Franklin's grandnephew, Jonathan Williams, later a superintendent of the U.S. Military Academy at West Point, to Nantes to replace him.

This maneuvering ended in a shambles. William Lee sided with Thomas Morris against Jonathan Williams; and when Deane was recalled, the commissioners simply left the matter in Lee's hands. Then, Thomas Morris died, and Lee appointed his allies as commercial agents in Nantes and Bordeaux. It was an ugly mess of commissioners appointing relatives, manipulating political influence, and slicing commissions off government goods passing through their hands.

When John Adams reached Paris in April 1778, he complained to Congress' Committee of Commerce about the chaos and waste he saw. He wrote, "I find that the American affairs are in a state of disorder." Franklin and Adams wrote the president of Congress on July 20, urging that Congress finally appoint consuls and separate diplomatic and consular work. Since the treasury had no money to pay consuls, they suggested that the consuls should be allowed to take commissions and conduct private business.

THE TRAGEDY OF SILAS DEANE

Just days after being received at court and under attack by Lee, Silas Deane sailed for America with the French fleet that also carried Conrad-Alexandre Gérard to his post as minister to the American government. Deane carried a letter from Franklin to the president of Congress, Henry Laurens, praising Deane's contribution to his country. Through Deane's yearlong political hearing, he was supported by Franklin, Robert Morris, Gouverneur Morris, and John Jay. Nothing wrong was proved against him, and he was dismissed without censure. Congress voted him $10,500 but did not settle his financial accounts. He was ruined.

During the following years, Deane grew embittered and outspokenly critical of the United States. His friends tired of this and deserted him. He returned to Europe, but in the summer of 1789, ill and impoverished, he set out for home again. In September, he died suddenly on board a Boston packet homeward bound and was buried in Deal, on the coast of Kent. He was fifty-four. Conspiracy devotees whispered that Dr. Bancroft poisoned him to conceal his own misdeeds. In 1842, long after Deane's death, Congress cleared his name, and the House of Representatives finally awarded Deane's heirs $37,000 on the grounds that an earlier audit was "a gross injustice to Silas Deane."

Deane's departure left two antagonistic commissioners in Paris. Lee attacked Franklin throughout the rest of his life, and Franklin called Lee "the most malicious enemy I ever had." Deane was replaced in Paris by sober, blunt John Adams, a Boston lawyer and a member of both Continental Congresses.

Adams and his ten-year-old son, John Quincy, traveled for nearly six weeks to reach Paris. On his first evening in Paris, Adams discussed with Franklin the treaties of commerce and alliance that France and the United States had previously signed. The commissioners' work seemed finished.

Adams accepted Franklin's invitation to stay with him in Passy; before long, the straitlaced Adams came to loathe Franklin's easygoing lifestyle. Adams, about five foot seven, portly and physically awkward, could seem aloof and pompous, and lacked small talk. He had an explosive temper as well as serious doubts about his own abilities. But he had the facility to see a problem whole, and he worked hard. He respected capable women, especially his wife, Abigail, on whom he laid endless responsibilities.

Adams' crucial principle was that government must be based on the consent of the governed. "Adams was a conservative," one historian concluded, "a great conservator of what had been achieved in America before the onset of the troubles with the parent state." But another differed, "As an American agent in France, he was worse than useless. . . . He was a complete egotist who suspected himself to be a universal genius."

Franklin took Adams to meet Vergennes, and then Adams criticized Franklin's handling of the French and announced he would deal with them more forcefully. Adams became the commission's de facto administrator, drafting correspondence and keeping its books. And the three Americans oversaw the safety of American shipping, as well as complaints concerning American businessmen, the Barbary Coast pirates, and prisoners-of-war exchanges.

Appalled by the continuing feud between Franklin and Lee, Adams decided that a single representative would care better for the nation's affairs than three quarreling commissioners. He repeatedly cast the deciding vote between the two antagonists and came to dislike them both. He wrote, "I wish Congress would separate us." He judged Lee to be an inadequate diplomat, and complained that the seventy-two-year-old Franklin, nearly thirty years his elder, never found time for work. Adams' harping became so infuriating that Lafayette wrote George Washington begging him to intervene. Adams, the newcomer, tried to compete with Franklin's popularity through hard work, a strategy that was not always persuasive in decadent prerevolutionary France.

England's ships attacked France's ships, and the two powers went into an undeclared war in June 1778. The American commissioners set out to convince the French to destroy the British whaling fleet and to support more privateering. Vergennes lost all patience with Adams and wrote him archly, "The King has no need of your solicitation in order to occupy himself with the interests of the United States."

When Lafayette returned to France in mid-February 1779, the commissioners were shocked to learn that the previous September Congress had dissolved the commission and replaced them with the United States' first minister plenipotentiary to the court of Versailles. And he was Franklin.

From this, Franklin is regarded officially as the first United States diplomat abroad, and Paris as its first diplomatic post. Congress gave Adams no new assignment, and so, on June 17, 1779, he and John Quincy sailed for home in *La Sensible*, the same French frigate that carried the Chevalier de la Luzerne, France's new minister, to the United States. They arrived at Braintree, Massachusetts, on August 2.

The clumsiness of having a legislature manage foreign affairs was demonstrated when, on September 27, 1779, Congress changed its collective mind and decided unanimously to send John Adams back to Paris. This time he would go as minister plenipotentiary to negotiate a peace treaty with Great Britain. He had been home exactly eight weeks.

FIRST FEELERS FOR CONCILIATION

In March 1781, at age seventy-five, Franklin offered his resignation. Congress insisted that he serve another four years. Despite his age and painful gout, his rank as minister plenipotentiary required Franklin to appear in court every Tuesday and to attend assorted tedious ceremonies. And at Passy he had to take care of endless bureaucratic tasks.

The British began to explore conciliation, and unofficial envoys from London came to talk with him about peace. He would not discuss it until the colonies were granted full independence. The British government repealed some of the laws to which Americans objected and offered them the equivalent of home rule—everything but independence.

The war in America had now dragged on for five years. With difficulty, the Congress tried to define its war aims. A committee chaired by Gouverneur Morris drew up instructions for Minister Adams, and they were adopted by Congress. They specified the terms that Britain must include, in addition, of course, to independence: acceptable boundaries on the Mississippi River and the 31st parallel, including southern Canada; access to the Newfoundland fisheries; and a commercial treaty with Britain.

Adams had no forewarning of his new assignment. He was given his own official secretary, Francis Dana, of Boston, a future chief justice of Massachusetts. With his two older sons, Adams set sail again back to Europe. After a terrible midwinter journey in a leaking ship, they landed in Spain and then, by mule, reached Paris two months later, on the afternoon of February 9, 1780. Adams immediately paid Franklin a visit but, ever distrustful, did not tell him the purpose of this second crossing of the wintry and dangerous Atlantic.

Franklin and Adams called on Vergennes at Versailles, and Adams, to avoid speaking in front of Franklin, asked permission to write the foreign minister about his mission. Adams' letter disturbed Vergennes, who told Adams that if he initiated a bid for peace, the British would think the Americans were weakening. Vergennes also feared the possibility of a separate peace between America and Britain. He prohibited Adams from having any contact with Britain and permitted his publishing only a vague statement about a future peace.

Vergennes, a starchy, old-style diplomat, was unhappy with Congress' choice of this blunt, rough-hewn lawyer. He wished the Americans had appointed the more experienced and diplomatic Franklin. And he offended Adams by making his displeasure apparent.

The inactivity that Vergennes imposed discouraged Adams; he found the war interminable and doubted that Britain was ready to make peace. He carped about France's lack of effort for peace but did not ask Franklin to press the French. Frustrated, Adams wrote to friends in England and anonymous articles for British newspapers. French intelligence informed Vergennes of these activities, and Adams became engaged in an intense letter-writing debate with Vergennes, who then used Adams' letters to try to have him recalled.

Finding he was powerless in Paris, Adams moved to Amsterdam to seek Dutch support for the United States. He hoped that Dutch aid would dilute France's hold over the United States. Economic statecraft was a crucial part of American foreign relations.

Congress, its finances overextended, desperately needed loans and sent another "militiaman of diplomacy," Henry Laurens, to the Netherlands in the summer of 1780 to secure a $10 million loan and a treaty of commerce. Laurens, a wealthy South Carolina planter and merchant who had served as president of the Continental Congress, was short, swarthy, wealthy, and abrasively self-assured. Earlier, he had made a fortune in the slave trade.

Laurens' voyage was marred by an event that was dreaded by all Americans crossing the Atlantic. The British frigate HMS *Vestal* intercepted his ship off Newfoundland. The Americans threw all their papers overboard, but Laurens refused to part with his personal trunk. The trunk was finally cast over in a bag weighted with iron shot, but it failed to sink quickly, and British sailors recovered it. Inside, they found the draft of a treaty with Holland. The British used this draft treaty as a pretext for declaring war on Holland.

Ignoring Laurens' plea of diplomatic immunity, the British imprisoned him in the Tower of London. Franklin tried through Edmund Burke, a leader of the parliamentary opposition, to exchange Laurens for General Burgoyne, who had been captured at Saratoga. The British turned him down. Franklin wrote Burke, "Since the foolish part of mankind will make wars from time to time with each other, not having sense enough otherwise to settle their differences, it certainly becomes the wiser part, who cannot prevent those wars, to alleviate as much as possible the calamities attending them." Burke supported Franklin by reading his letter to a hostile House of Commons.

Learning that the British had captured Laurens, Congress named Adams commissioner to the Netherlands. He approached the Dutch government despite French and British efforts to prevent him. But it took months before he could meet a significant Dutch official.

He found more interest among the businessmen of Amsterdam than the politicians in The Hague. The Dutch businessmen suffered from the rivalry with Britain. Adams did an energetic job of what today would be called public diplomacy, seeking the support of the Dutch elite instead of their government. In time, riding a wave of colonial battlefield victories and the sympathies of the anti-British businessmen, Adams secured aid from leading Dutch bankers. As expected, Britain responded with reprisals against Dutch ships, thwarting any possibility that Dutch merchants would openly support the United States.

A year after war began between Britain and France, Spain also declared war on Great Britain. Spain still refused to recognize the United States' independence; but France and Spain agreed that neither would quit fighting until Spain recovered Gibraltar and France, the port of Dunkirk. They actually sent a combined fleet to invade Britain, but the flotilla dawdled until gales swept its ships out of the English Channel.

France and Spain had contradictory agendas: France wanted a strong America to stand against Britain; Spain wanted a feeble America too weak to threaten her in the Western Hemisphere, where Spain ruled three-fourths of the land as well as the wealthiest of the West Indies. Charles III, the uncle of France's Louis XVI, would do what he could to curtail British imperial power; but unlike his nephew, he was not prepared to support rebellion, not even against the British. Charles feared the American rebellion's contagion in his own colonies. He proposed a truce between America and Great Britain, which would have left the British in control in New York City, Long Island, Rhode Island, and parts of Georgia. Surprisingly, the British rejected the proposal. The Americans in Europe were learning lessons in diplomacy.

The Continental Congress sent its president, John Jay, to Madrid in 1779 as minister plenipotentiary. He had also served as chief justice of the state of New York. Of Huguenot descent, he disliked Catholics; but he would stay in Madrid for more than two years, with very little to show for them. The tall, thin, sallow Jay, a meticulous lawyer, had originally opposed the Declaration of Independence. But once it was adopted, he worked for independence, while wistfully continuing to hope for reconciliation with Britain.

Jay took to Madrid as his secretary William Carmichael, a controversial character who three years earlier had volunteered to help Silas Deane in Paris. Jay was instructed to bring Spain into the Franco-American alliance and to obtain a loan for the United States at no more than 6 percent interest. The loan was imperative; the new country teetered on the edge of bankruptcy.

On April 5, 1780, Jay called on the Spanish secretary of state for foreign affairs, Conde de Floridablanca, a shrewd master of duplicity who opposed American independence and who was negotiating with the British so Spain would not recognize independence until Britain did.

Jay was snubbed in Madrid; he was never received officially. Floridablanca told him that the chief obstacle between them was the navigation of the Mississippi River. Spain had driven Britain off the river, but King Charles had replaced one enemy with another, more dangerous one. The Americans envisioned the Mississippi as their western border and a common waterway.

Floridablanca declined to provide funds for the Americans. He told Jay that money would be forthcoming only if the United States gave Spain frigates loaded with tobacco and provisions.

Floridablanca was stonewalling. The French were alarmed to learn that Spain was negotiating a separate peace with Britain, and they were upset by Jay's eagerness to conclude peace with the British and bring the American war to an end.

Jay dropped the diplomatic niceties, angrily telling the Count of Montmorin, the French minister to Madrid, "Your Excellency, I was sent to Spain by Congress to make propositions, not supplications. . . . I consider America as being, and to continue, independent in fact. . . . In my opinion, America ought to rest content with her alliance with France." He was ready to go home.

Isolated, Jay complained to James Lovell about the Committee of Foreign Affairs, "Till now I have received but one letter from them, and that not worth a farthing . . ." He was mortified to receive news from home through Spanish officials, who intercepted letters intended for him.

After a long year, by the summer of 1781, Jay began to show some flexibility. He notified Floridablanca that Congress was prepared to make major concessions for a treaty. The Americans would, indeed, give up their claim to navigate the Mississippi below the 31st-degree latitude if they could have a free port below that line. When he received no reply from the Spaniards, Jay told Gouverneur Morris he had given up all hope of obtaining Spanish assistance.

The British conducted their war against France and the American colonies with startling incompetence. Both Britain and France had been beggared by the prolonged wars that had enabled Britain to dominate so much of North America. John Adams perceived Britain's victory over France for the North American continent back in 1763 had been the first round of the American Revolution because, after that, the colonists no longer needed Britain to defend them against the French. In addition, as the war's winner, Britain had to bear the cost of keeping troops in North America and taxed the colonists to support them.

Propaganda played a role. Franklin was not above perpetrating a nasty hoax. At Passy, in April 1780, he published a false *Supplement to the Boston Independent Chronicle,* which reported that eight large packages of American scalps had been sent by the Seneca Indians to the governor of Canada for the British king and queen. But most of Franklin's propaganda came from his ability to charm people with his old-fashioned ways.

By June, Britain's unpopular, expensive war, managed by a manic-depressive king and an unstable prime minister, caused rioting in London. And in Paris, Jacques Necker, the Swiss-born director general of the French treasury, now opposed great-power diplomacy. Horrified by the mountain of public debt, he demanded the war be ended. In December, Necker wrote directly to Lord North in London, offering to end the fighting on the basis of the status quo. George III turned him down.

3

"The Sword Was Sheathed"

1781–85

As the Revolution dragged on, Congress' Committee of Foreign Affairs collapsed. James Lovell wrote Arthur Lee, "But there is really no such thing as a committee of foreign affairs existing, no secretary or clerk, further than I persevere to be one and the other."

Some members of Congress sought more efficient governance, and, finally, on January 10, 1781, Congress created a Department of Foreign Affairs, transferring the conduct of foreign affairs to the executive branch. The Articles of Confederation were ratified on March 1, 1781, and Article IX began, "The united states in congress assembled, shall have the sole and exclusive right and power of determining on peace and war . . . of sending and receiving ambassadors, entering into treaties and alliances. . . ."

That summer, Robert R. Livingston defeated Arthur Lee to become the first Secretary of Foreign Affairs. Livingston, then thirty-five years old, was the scion of a great Hudson Valley landowning family and a friend and law partner of John Jay. After carefully examining the extent of his powers, Livingston accepted the post on September 23, not quite a month before the American-French victory at Yorktown.

Livingston was charged with the handling of American foreign policy. He was to correspond with American ministers posted at foreign courts and with the representatives of foreign powers coming to America. He dealt only with America's friends; other nations wanted nothing to do with revolutionaries.

Livingston soon brought some order to the conduct of foreign relations. The men in the Department of Foreign Affairs had to write out by hand five copies of every foreign letter received and every document sent out; they were swamped with paperwork. Livingston employed a first undersecretary, Lewis R. Morris; a second undersecretary, Pierre-Etienne Du Ponceau; a translator of French, Jean Petard; and a clerk, Walter Stone. He was allowed to correspond personally, not just on behalf of Congress. He was authorized to advise Congress, settle private complaints against foreign powers, and have access to congressional records. In May 1782, he reported to Congress on the condition of the U.S. missions.

Livingston set up offices in a small three-story brick house owned by Du Ponceau at 13 South Sixth Street near Chestnut Street, Philadelphia. Livingston worked in the front room on the second floor, the undersecretaries in the back room, and the clerks and interpreters on the ground floor. That was the entire department while he was in charge.

When Livingston resigned on June 4, 1783, he sealed his papers and turned them over to Charles Thomson, the secretary of Congress, who was not authorized to open them. They were held for Livingston's successor.

The post of Secretary remained vacant, and there was some doubt that it would be continued; but in May Congress appointed John Jay. Jay returned from Europe in midsummer 1784 and did not take office until December 21. There seemed to be no rush.

When Congress moved to New York City in the new year, Jay tucked the Department of Foreign Affairs into a one-room office in City Hall. Then, the entire department consisted of Jay, an assistant, and a clerk. Before long, the department moved into two rooms in Samuel Fraunces' tavern at the corner of Broad and Pearl streets (and the site of General Washington's farewell to his generals). The department remained there until 1788, when Jay moved it to a house on the west side of Broadway, near the Battery.

Jay held office for more than six years throughout the Confederation period, and as Congress grew poorer, his salary slid steadily downward.

ORGANIZING THE PEACE COMMISSION

The solid block of ice that was Anglo-American relations began to crack. In December 1780, the Netherlands joined the secret League of Armed

Neutrality, formed by Russia's Catherine the Great to protect neutral commerce from British warships seeking to disrupt trade with France. Britain promptly made war against the league, while Congress, of course, supported the league.

However, the British still refused to consider an armistice unless the American colonies declared their allegiance to the Crown. Britain continued to act as if time was on its side.

Vergennes was prepared to settle for a twenty- or thirty-year truce, which would give the colonies de facto recognition and end the war. But at the same time he was also secretly prepared to allow the British to remain in Georgia and South Carolina to divide the colonies.

In response to a call from Vergennes to discuss ending the war, John Adams traveled from Amsterdam to Paris in July 1781. He was determined to secure recognition of American independence. But after two weeks in Paris, Adams returned to his house on the Keizersgracht in Amsterdam, suffering severely from what may have been a nervous breakdown.

Then came the final straw: Congress informed Adams that it had withdrawn his authority to negotiate a commercial treaty with Britain and had enlarged the peace commission to five members, by adding Benjamin Franklin, John Jay, Thomas Jefferson, and Henry Laurens. Adams was shocked. Instead of holding his young country's most important diplomatic assignment, he was suddenly one of five equals. He asked to be recalled. Jefferson again turned down the overseas appointment because of his wife's illness. And Congress did not know that Laurens was still imprisoned in the Tower of London. It was a discouraging beginning.

Congress gave the commission freedom of action with only two essential demands: independence and sovereignty. On all other matters the commissioners were to listen to the French and were directed "to undertake nothing in the negotiations for peace or truce without their knowledge and concurrence. . . ." Both Jay and Adams found the requirement to consult with France unacceptable. Franklin did not mind the restriction; he was always convinced that the United States needed France.

Four long, painful years after the American victory at Saratoga, on October 18, 1781, at Yorktown, Virginia, Lord Cornwallis surrendered, unconditionally, his entire army of seven thousand men to a combined force of Americans and French. As Franklin had insisted all along, the alliance with France proved decisive.

Word of the British defeat at Yorktown reached Lord North in London on November 22. He grasped its importance instantly, even though King George III insisted it made no difference. On February 27, 1782, the House of Commons voted against continuing the war; and on March 20, Lord North resigned. The war was over.

THE LEGATION AT FLUWELEN BURGWAL 18

A new British government came to power, led by Lord Rockingham, who had repealed the Stamp Act sixteen years before. It was a momentous change. William Fitzmaurice, the Earl of Shelburne and a friend of Franklin's, became secretary of state for home, colonial, and Irish affairs. His aims were to separate France and America and to keep the United States in a loose union with Great Britain. Charles James Fox, Shelburne's rival and a proponent of American independence, became Secretary of State for Foreign Affairs.

The British sent a secret agent, the American-born Thomas Digges, to Amsterdam in 1780 to discuss a separate peace with Adams. They met but came to no agreement. Then, at long last, the Dutch recognized Adams as minister plenipotentiary of the United States of America. The Dutch were the second nation to recognize the United States.

To celebrate his victory, Adams proposed a treaty of trade and friendship with the Netherlands and opened the world's first United States legation at Fluwelen Burgwal 18.

The new British government opened direct negotiations with the American peace commissioners. Lord Shelburne sent to Paris Richard Oswald, a widely respected Scottish arms merchant, seventy-five years of age and blind in one eye. And the British released Henry Laurens from prison.

Laurens crossed the Channel with his friend Oswald. While Oswald headed for Paris and Franklin, Laurens went on to the Netherlands, where he and Adams met at the Golden Lion in Haarlem. The meeting was a disaster: Adams told Laurens he would not support reconciliation with Britain, and, fearful of being replaced by Laurens, he made it clear that Laurens was not needed in the Netherlands. Adams had found life in The Hague delightful; he lived well and entertained lavishly. The infuriated Laurens returned to England.

NEGOTIATIONS AND CHICANERY

Months of complicated negotiations began in the spring of 1782. Still trying to divide the Americans from the French, Oswald proposed that the commissioners negotiate with the British separately and that, once independence was resolved, they should not be detained by issues involving France. Franklin disagreed, and they both went to Versailles to meet with Vergennes, who emphasized that a separate peace was impossible; peace required a general treaty involving France, Spain, and the Netherlands.

Franklin sent for Jay, saying, "Spain has taken four years to consider whether she should treat with us or not. Give her forty, and let us in the meantime mind our own business." Jay had no reason to remain in Madrid.

The British hoped that Jay might be easier to deal with, but he proved even more of a stickler for procedure than Franklin. Jay demanded that independence should be granted by Parliament, or by proclamation of the king, and not as a price for peace. The humorless, honest Jay wanted to keep fighting until independence was actually secured. He did not want the colonies to disarm with British garrisons still present in America. Oswald returned to Paris to see Franklin. When they met again, on May 4, Franklin's position was simple: independence was not a subject for negotiation; the United States was already independent.

Twenty-six-year-old Thomas Grenville, representing Secretary of State Fox, now arrived in Paris. Fox had instructed him to be prepared to accept American independence. Oswald took Grenville to meet Franklin on May 8, and Franklin escorted him to Vergennes. Grenville proposed giving the colonies their independence.

Independence was now on the table, although neither George III nor Shelburne was reconciled to it. Vergennes understood that the British, above all, were trying to separate the Americans from the French. His counterproposal was that the Americans and the French should each make their own treaty with Britain, but both documents should be signed on the same day.

The summer was filled with complicated negotiations, suspicions, and chicanery. Adams and Jay both insisted bluntly that they would not treat with a British representative unless he was authorized to deal not with "colonies or plantations" but with the "United States of America."

The most intensely disputed points were whether independence was to be tied to a peace treaty and where the western boundary of the American states would be drawn. Oswald wanted independence to be the first article of the peace treaty, but Jay was determined that independence precede the treaty, because then the United States could negotiate with Great Britain as an equal.

The majority of the British cabinet stood for the principle of combining independence and a treaty ending the war. Then, on July 1, Prime Minister Rockingham died in an influenza outbreak. Shelburne succeeded him, and Fox resigned from the government. This left Franklin and Oswald free to work toward an accommodation. The pace of negotiations picked up.

Ten days later, Shelburne declared that American independence would be a great blow to the nation, but he assured the House that he would not renew the war in America. He said, "The sword was sheathed, never to be drawn again."

In Paris, Jay was bedridden for three weeks in the same influenza epidemic that killed Rockingham. So, Franklin met with Oswald and specified the articles "necessary" to a peace treaty. They were: complete independence, the removal of British troops, settlement of the boundaries of the United States and the boundaries of Canada, and the right to fish freely in Canadian waters. In addition, Franklin listed "advisable" articles: indemnification of those who had suffered losses to the British; acknowledgment of British error in bringing distress to her former subjects; reciprocal shipping privileges; and the surrender of all of Canada, which Britain had taken from France in 1763. The commissioners, despite their instructions, shared none of this discussion with Vergennes.

The next day, Franklin informed Oswald that he was halting further discussions until Shelburne's position on independence was clarified. On July 27 Shelburne notified Oswald that Britain would recognize independence in advance, instead of as a condition for a general peace, if the colonies would end the war.

Shelburne, meanwhile, opened a new channel of communication to the commissioners by sending to Paris thirty-one-year-old Benjamin Vaughan, whose father was a West Indian planter and whose mother was a Hallowell of Boston. Vaughan, related to Henry Laurens by marriage, was another longtime friend of Franklin's.

Finally, on August 19, Jay and Franklin drove out to Versailles to talk with Vergennes. The French diplomat was clearly dragging his feet. He did not want the British to recognize independence before the treaties were signed, nor did he want the Americans to end the war. This confirmed Jay's conviction that the Americans must free themselves from France and follow their own judgment.

Franklin was now incapacitated for weeks, suffering from a painful bladder stone as well as his chronic gout. This strengthened the hand of Jay, who was prepared to violate the instructions that he should act under French direction. Oswald promised him that the independence of the United States would be recognized in the first article of the treaty.

Time was running out for Shelburne; he had to act before Parliament returned. On the evening of August 29, the British cabinet decided that if all the American commissioners agreed to Franklin's necessary points, the cabinet would sponsor legislation in Parliament acknowledging "the independence of the thirteen colonies." The ministers could still not bring themselves to use the word "states."

The cabinet proposed that Canada be confined to its 1774 boundaries, British troops be removed from American territory, and Americans be admitted to the Newfoundland and Labrador fisheries. (They could fish but not dry fish on the shore, because Franklin had not thought to include that. No concessions were being volunteered.)

Fearing that the Americans would defect and leave France exposed to Britain's might, Vergennes now switched suddenly from delaying negotiations to seeking a quick settlement with the British. He could not afford to be left behind.

Meanwhile, Jay had been negotiating with the conde de Aranda, the Spanish ambassador to Paris, over the western boundaries of the United States. They were deadlocked. Aranda was determined to keep the Americans away from the Mississippi, while Jay demanded the Mississippi as the nation's western boundary. Jay would not compromise; he asserted, "We are bound by the Mississippi."

Vergennes proved too clever for his own cause. He tried to keep the Americans away from the Great Lakes. He claimed the Declaration of Independence meant they had lost their right to participate in the Canadian fisheries. Catching wind of this, Jay broke off his negotiations with Aranda.

Shelburne threatened that he would treat for peace with Vergennes and cut out the Americans, hinting at an Anglo-French entente; the two powers would dominate Europe. But privately he was warning George III that the troubles in Ireland were overextending Britain.

Expecting that Vergennes and Shelburne would delay independence until they had arrived at a general peace, Jay took a daring step. Without informing Franklin, he sent Benjamin Vaughan, Shelburne's own agent, back to England with instructions to make sure that Shelburne understood that independence must be unconditional. And without authority to do so, Jay held out a vision of future lucrative commerce between Britain and America. Then, on September 2, Jay saw how to overcome the impasse: simply make independence a fact by referring in the preamble of the treaty to "the United States of America." Although Franklin refused to join him in this presumption, Jay gave Oswald a letter proposing this solution. Jay announced he would accept a treaty with no declaration of independence other than one as an article in the treaty. To his government in London, Oswald pleaded that the Americans had made a great compromise.

When the British cabinet met on the evening of September 18, it changed Oswald's commission to allow him to meet with the representatives of "the thirteen united states of America." Ten days later, Vaughan brought his new commission to Paris. This simple act made American independence a de facto reality, and it made serious negotiations possible.

Jay wrote Adams that the British agreed to negotiate with the "Commissioners of the United States of America" and summoned Adams from Holland to help him in the negotiations.

Then, the allies fighting Britain miscalculated. A French-Spanish armada attempted to invade Gibraltar, and failed. Their successful defense stiffened the British will to resist.

With Franklin still ill, Jay settled the peculiar matter of the West Florida boundary with a secret article specifying that, should Britain hold Florida at the end of the war, the British would receive a more advantageous northern boundary in West Florida than Spain would have granted. Jay urged Oswald to persuade the British to send troops from New York and Charleston to take Florida from the Spaniards. But it was eventually decided that Spain would keep West Florida, and the secret article was nullified.

"FREE AND INDEPENDENT STATES"

On October 5, Jay presented Oswald the draft of a treaty in his own hand. A covering letter provided that the treaty would not go into effect until France agreed to peace terms with Great Britain. This point was essential to Vergennes.

The commissioners did not show Jay's draft to Vergennes, although it became the basis of the final treaty. On October 8, when Jay sent it to London, it shocked Shelburne and the cabinet. On the seventeenth, the cabinet instructed Oswald to secure better terms. And Henry Strachey, undersecretary of state in the Home Office, was sent back to Paris to strengthen Oswald's resolve. Shelburne had to arrange peace before Parliament reconvened on November 26.

Meanwhile, John Adams obtained a loan from a group of three Dutch banking houses and, after months of squabbling over details, settled a treaty of commerce and friendship with the government of the Netherlands.

After a leisurely ten-day trip from The Hague in a carriage drawn by six horses, Adams joined Jay and Franklin in Paris on Saturday, October 26. On Monday, he visited the Jays at the Hotel d'Orleans, in the rue des Petits Augustins, and agreed with everything Jay had been doing.

Adams and Jay found they held views in common, agreeing, for instance, that the French were immoral and atheistic. On Tuesday, Adams, still angry at Franklin's attack on him two years before, reluctantly rode out to see him in Passy. When Adams told Franklin that he supported Jay, Franklin said nothing. He was not happy about Jay's independent negotiating, and he was not at all fond of the always assertive, always jealous Mr. Adams.

The three Americans met informally with Oswald and Strachey, now the most experienced of the British delegation, and Franklin at last stated flatly that he was prepared to proceed without consulting the French.

Negotiations followed for a week, sessions rotating between Oswald's lodgings at Passy and Adams' lodgings (now in the Hotel du Roi in Place du Carrousel), all in good humor and punctuated with hearty meals. Although they differed on many points, the three Americans showed a united front.

The Americans gave up Jay's proposed northern boundary on the 45th parallel and drew a line through the St. Lawrence and the middle of the Great Lakes. This line would go to the Lake of the Woods, thus including within the United States what is now Minnesota.

The northeast boundary was more difficult. The British wanted it at the Penobscot River, while the Americans insisted on the St. John's River. They finally agreed to let a special boundary commission settle this matter.

With his usual precision, Jay drafted a new set of proposed articles; and both parties agreed to them. The British cabinet made minor changes, obtained the king's grudging approval, and gave Strachey a revised set of articles to carry back to Paris.

The negotiators started another round of talks at Oswald's lodgings on Monday, November 25. And the next morning, Franklin and Adams met over breakfast at the Jays' and discussed whether the loyalists who had been driven from America should be paid compensation. Franklin warned that if the British pressed the loyalists' claims, he would demand reparations for the damages suffered in the burning of Charleston, Norfolk, and other cities, as well as the loss of Franklin's library in Philadelphia.

On a lovely autumn day, Friday, November 29, the discussions stalled over counterclaims on reparations and fishing. Tempers rose, and a recess was called. When the British returned to the table, they settled the matters of the fisheries and the loyalists: the United States had the "right" to take fish on the Grand Bank and the "liberty" to fish along the coast of Newfoundland.

It was finished. More than six years had passed since Silas Deane had been sent to Paris.

It snowed on Saturday, when the two teams gathered in Oswald's lodgings in the Grand Hotel Moscovite. Two last-minute points were added at the Americans' insistence: a twelve-month limit on Loyalists' stay in the United States to recover their estates and a clause, pushed by Laurens, forbidding the departing British forces from carrying off slaves or other American property.

They signed duplicates of the preliminary treaty and the secret article on the West Florida boundary. (The American copy of the secret article has disappeared; the British copy is in London's Public Record Office.) And then they all rode out to Passy to celebrate this triumph for the new American nation.

The French, left out of this entire process, resented the Americans' audacity. When Franklin traveled to Versailles to bring Vergennes a copy of the treaty (but not the secret article), the French foreign minister was shocked by the extent of Britain's concessions. He reprimanded the commissioners, and Franklin especially, for signing without consulting him and told the Americans not to send the treaty to Congress.

Franklin sought to reassure Vergennes that the treaty was merely preliminary, that nothing had been agreed to that would harm France, and that peace would not take effect until the French concluded their treaty with Britain. Franklin depreciated the Americans' unilateral action as this "single indiscretion" and "this little misunderstanding." Ever the consummate diplomat, he gently warned Vergennes that the British believed they had divided the United States and France, and he hoped they would be proved mistaken. Franklin offered a model of diplomatic apologies.

The two wily diplomats understood each other. They recognized that what had happened was a matter of American statecraft. And Vergennes could not afford to break with the Americans. In fact, Franklin asked for, and received, another loan for his country.

At home, Secretary of State Livingston criticized the peace commissioners for failing to consult the French and for negotiating a secret article that he was sure could not be kept secret. He praised their results but not their methods. The achievement of the three American "militiaman diplomats" was historic.

George III opened Parliament on December 5, 1782, with a speech from the throne. He ordered the war in North America stopped and, with visible distaste, declared the American colonies "free and independent States, by an article to be inserted in the peace treaty." Within weeks, Britain also achieved armistice terms with France and Spain.

Vergennes directed Franklin to be at Versailles at ten o'clock on Monday, January 20, 1783. At eleven, in the presence of the Americans, the British signed preliminary articles of peace and armistice with France and Spain. Franklin, accompanied by Adams, exchanged the declaration of an armistice with Great Britain. Years of diplomacy were completed.

The agreed-to preliminaries with the United States were presented to both houses of Parliament. The House of Commons accepted the grant of American independence but criticized Shelburne for his concessions. He resigned. In the new government headed by the Duke of Portland, Charles James Fox served as foreign secretary. Fox, whom the king despised as a hard-drinking gambler, dominated the new government but failed to have the preliminary agreements changed to any significant degree. On April 12, 1783, the United States government proclaimed the end of hostilities.

Independence had many costs. American diplomats could no longer enjoy the commercial benefits the Americans had within the British system. Independence also ended the protection of American ships by the British navy. This was a calamity for the United States.

The Anglo-American peace treaty was finally signed on September 3, 1783, in the Hotel d'York, in what is now Paris' 56 rue Jacob in the second-floor lodgings of David Hartley, an eccentric member of Parliament and an opponent of the American war. With simple ceremony, Hartley and Oswald signed for George III, and Franklin, Jay, and Adams for the United States. And that same day at Versailles, France and Spain signed treaties with the Duke of Manchester.

The Peace Treaty of 1783 ended the American Revolution and gave the colonies their independence, but it left unresolved a host of major problems, including the settlement of the debts owed to Loyalists, control of the fur trade, the fate of the Indians who had aided the British against the Americans, the path of the border between the United States and Canada, the fate of seven of the eight forts controlling the Great Lakes, and the mutual use of the fisheries.

When Laurens predicted that Franklin would be blessed for defying their government's instructions, Franklin replied: "I have never yet known of a peace that did not occasion a great deal of popular discontent, clamour, and censure on both sides." This, he explained, was because statesmen of warring powers always raised expectations beyond what is attainable.

The treaty required that it be ratified within six months, but until the following January Congress could not assemble a quorum in Annapolis, the nation's temporary capital, where it sought to escape army mutineers. The peace treaty was ratified by nine states on January 14, 1784, and there were only six weeks left to transmit it to Paris. This would be a formidable feat in midwinter. Three agents were given copies, and Colonel Josiah Harmar of the army was the first to reach Paris at the end of March. Technically, the ratifications arrived after the deadline; but on May 12,

Franklin and Jay for the United States and Hartley for Great Britain exchanged ratified documents in Paris.

Jay and Laurens returned home that summer of 1784. After an absence of more than eight years, Jay came back to a New York City devastated by the British occupation and two huge fires. On his arrival, he learned he had been named Secretary of Foreign Affairs, an office he would hold for five years, when he became the Chief Justice of the Supreme Court; he then finished his career with two terms as governor of New York.

Laurens found his plantations in South Carolina destroyed. Prematurely aged by his imprisonment, he died in 1792 and was buried next to his son, Colonel John Laurens, who had been a Revolutionary War hero and was killed in battle.

Adams traveled to Bath to regain his health, which had been damaged by the influenza epidemic. He detoured to Amsterdam to obtain more loans from the Dutch bankers, most of them, to his annoyance, at high rates of interest. The young country was not an attractive credit risk.

In that summer of 1784, Abigail Adams joined her husband in a spacious mansion in rural Auteuil, the village next to Passy. Franklin stayed on as minister in Paris, suffering from age and illness. His burden was eased only when Thomas Barclay, of Pennsylvania, finally arrived and took over his consular duties. In March 1785, Adams was appointed minister to the court of George III; Jefferson, to the court of Louis XVI; and Franklin was released to come home.

4

Of Consuls, Commerce, and Confidence

1784–1810

In the summer heat of Friday, August 6, 1784, Thomas Jefferson, tall and athletic at forty-one, rode in his phaeton across the Pont de Neuilly, which he thought "the most beautiful bridge in the world," and up the Champs-Élysées to the Hotel d'Orleans in rue de Richelieu. He was coming to replace Benjamin Franklin as one of the three American commissioners in Paris.

This was Jefferson's first trip abroad. Two years before, his wife, Martha, had taken seriously ill after the birth of their third child, Lucy, her seventh pregnancy in their ten years of marriage. Her husband stayed at her bedside day after day throughout the summer. When she died at age thirty-three, he could not be consoled. He never married again.

Jefferson brought with him to Paris his twelve-year-old eldest daughter, also named Martha, whom he called Patsy, and a nineteen-year-old mulatto slave, James Hemings, whom he planned to have trained as a chef. Patsy was placed in the fashionable convent school of Abbaye Royale de Penthemont.

Joining Jefferson in Paris as secretaries were two young protégés: Colonel David Humphreys, a tall, stout, thirty-two-year-old Yale graduate and poet, who had served devotedly on Washington's staff during the war, and William Short, a slim, congenial twenty-five-year-old lawyer and an in-law of Jefferson. He was an early member of Phi Beta Kappa, and Jefferson called him his adoptive son. Both Humphreys and Short would serve as American diplomats.

Short became the first diplomatic officer appointed by President Washington, and his commission established the form that was followed for decades. It began, "Reposing special trust and confidence in your Integrity, Prudence and Ability, I have nominated, and by and with the advice and consent of the Senate do appoint you Envoy Extraordinary and Minister Plenipotentiary of the United States of America to . . ."

Jefferson's fellow leaders of the Revolution turned to him repeatedly as one of the brightest intellects in their cause. Born in the foothills of Virginia's Blue Ridge, he was the son of a small-scale planter who owned sixty slaves. His mother was a Randolph, and that lineage opened many doors for her son. He stood on the radical side of the Revolution, along with John and Samuel Adams up in Boston. They sought independence from imperial Great Britain, not accommodation.

After his wife's death, Jefferson welcomed the appointment as a commissioner in Paris. Then, for a glorious moment, the United States was represented there by the diplomatic team of Benjamin Franklin, John Adams, and Thomas Jefferson. The trio had last collaborated on the Declaration of Independence and was now charged with negotiating treaties of amity and commerce with as many European nations as they could. For the infant United States to survive, it required opening markets for its surplus agricultural production and arranging sources for importing manufactured goods.

The three commissioners recognized that European governments had little enthusiasm for commercial relations with the United States. The foreign governments maintained closed economic systems and were reluctant to engage in business with the United States because, under the Articles of Confederation, any single state could refuse to recognize the treaty. Jefferson wrote home, "There is a want of confidence in us."

Thomas Barclay, the American consul general in Paris, brought Jefferson and Adams together. Despite their differences, they grew to be close friends. Seven years younger and six inches taller than Adams, Jefferson was gracious and sophisticated, an excellent horseman and violinist who enjoyed a range of cultivated interests. The Adamses' mansion in Auteuil became Jefferson's second home. Adams called the Virginian a "wise and prudent Man and Steady Patriot." Theirs was a strange friendship of two men who were to become the leaders of opposing political factions. They grew even closer after Lafayette brought Jefferson word that his two-year-old Lucy had died of whooping cough in Virginia. It took two years for

Jefferson to bring his six-year-old daughter, Polly, to Paris. He insisted she sail in an English or French ship to avoid the risk of capture by Barbary pirates. She finally arrived from Monticello in the care of a fourteen-year-old slave girl, Sally Hemings, who would play a very close role in Jefferson's life.

The government placed the three Paris-based diplomats on limited budgets, restricting their diplomatic entertainment. Jefferson was soon in debt. Still, after a year, he rented a spacious mansion, Hotel de Langeac, near today's Arc de Triomphe.

Prior to the adoption of the Treaty of Amity and Commerce with France in 1778, little distinction was made between diplomatic and consular functions. Consular duties, those related to private American citizens rather than to governments, were handled haphazardly, even though often by men with diplomatic standing and titles. But by 1779 the French had consuls in Boston, Philadelphia, Baltimore, and the Carolinas. (New York was occupied by the British, and Washington, D.C., did not yet exist.) The peace treaty sought to make things more orderly. Article 29 stated that each nation could station consuls in the other's ports.

The first consul sent overseas by the Continental Congress after the adoption of the treaty with France never reached Paris. Lieutenant Colonel William Palfrey, of Massachusetts, a former aide to General Washington and then paymaster of the Continental army, was sent as "consul in France" on November 4, 1780. En route to Europe, the ship simply disappeared. The Atlantic in winter devoured many a sailing vessel.

Not knowing Palfrey's fate, Congress appointed Thomas Barclay as vice consul in Paris, and on October 5, 1781, he was officially given Palfrey's title and salary. Ireland-born, Barclay had arrived in Philadelphia in about 1764 and had become a successful merchant; he was the first American consul to serve abroad. In 1782, Barclay was promoted to consul general and made a commissioner to settle the public accounts of the United States in Europe.

Palfrey and Barclay were Congress' only consular appointments until the peace treaty of 1783 with Britain. But Congress did appoint unsalaried "commercial agents" to assist merchants and other U.S. citizens abroad.

CONFLICT ON THE MISSISSIPPI

The United States' neighbor, Spain, discouraged American commerce. But on Robert Morris' recommendation, Congress named Robert Smith as commercial agent in Havana, the center of Spanish rule in the Caribbean and the only city in the area where Spain would allow a consul. Smith died two years later and was replaced by Oliver Pollock, who had been an advisor to the Spanish governor of Louisiana. Congress terminated Pollock's appointment as consul in 1784; he later spent eighteen months in debtors' prison in New Orleans before Congress helped pay the debts he had amassed in its service.

Trouble also erupted in 1784, when a Royal Spanish proclamation ended Americans' free navigation of the Mississippi. The frontier settlers in Kentucky and Tennessee were outraged; their numbers were growing, and they depended on the river to carry their products to market. In May 1785, Don Diego de Gardoqui, the Spanish minister to the United States, was instructed to make no concessions regarding navigation on the Mississippi. Still, he wined and dined congressmen and presented John Jay with a Spanish stallion, which Congress permitted him to accept.

Congress authorized Jay to negotiate a treaty that would secure navigation of the Mississippi and establish a boundary with Spain at the 31st parallel. In 1786, Jay designed a subtle compromise: America might give up her *use* of the river during the thirty years of a treaty, but not give up her *right* to the river. Jay's proposal ignited an enormous controversy, and the treaty failed to get the two-thirds vote needed to ratify.

Soon after Jay became Secretary of Foreign Affairs, John Adams was sent to London as minister, and Jefferson went to take Franklin's place in Paris. Jefferson famously said that he could not replace Dr. Franklin, only succeed him.

In May 1785, Jefferson presented his letter of credence to Louis XVI in a private audience, and then had his first meeting with the king, Marie Antoinette, and the royal family. As minister plenipotentiary of the United States to the court of His Most Christian Majesty, he now had diplomatic standing. He attended the king's levee each Tuesday, dining afterward with the diplomatic corps. He did not especially enjoy the diplomats, preferring the liberal aristocrats to whom Lafayette, his closest French friend, introduced him.

Franklin finally left Passy for home on July 12, 1785, after having been abroad for a total of thirty years. On Franklin's departure, Vergennes said, "The United States will never have a more zealous and more useful servant than Mr. Franklin." Because of Franklin's painful bladder stone, he was lent a royal litter, and, swaying between two large Spanish mules, he made the slow, painful six-day journey to the port of Le Havre. Then, he endured a forty-eight-day sea voyage to Philadelphia.

Although now in his eightieth year, Franklin was named president of the Executive Council of Pennsylvania, and two years later represented Pennsylvania at the U.S. Constitutional Convention. There, he proposed that the convention open with prayers each day, but his motion was rejected. His last public act before his death on April 17, 1790, was to sign a memorial to Congress for the abolition of slavery.

SEEKING MARKETS IN CHINA

Stymied in their efforts to trade with the Europeans, American entrepreneurs began looking for new markets farther afield. In 1784, the surprisingly small merchantman *Empress of China* sailed from New York by way of the Cape of Good Hope to the port of Canton, a six-month voyage. When she returned to New York in May 1785, loaded with tea, silks, and porcelains, she brought a 25 percent profit and glowing tales of the Far East. This gave birth to a great China trade.

Secretary Jay recommended that Congress send representatives to Canton, and in January 1786 Congress appointed as consul tall, portly Samuel Shaw, who on *Empress*' first voyage had served as supercargo, in charge of the cargo for its owners. He had been a Revolutionary War artillery captain; his nephew was Robert Gould Shaw, of Boston, the famous colonel of the African-American Fifty-fourth Massachusetts Volunteer Infantry in the Civil War. Samuel Shaw's friend and fellow artillery officer, Thomas Randall, of Pennsylvania, was named vice consul.

Shaw and Randall arrived in Canton on August 15, 1786, and spent all of 1787 in Canton and Portuguese Macao. After they returned to Newport, President Washington reappointed Shaw, thus making him the first consular officer selected under the Constitution.

Although the Chinese never allowed Shaw to deal with their government, he served as a consul de facto to the potentially huge Chinese market. In 1794, on his fourth voyage to Canton, Shaw, then thirty-nine, became seriously ill in Bombay, and he died at sea trying to return home.

American diplomatic activity abroad contracted in the period between the Treaty of Paris (1783) and the adoption of the United States Constitution (1789). Permanent missions were maintained only in Paris, London, and Madrid. Adams was still accredited to The Hague, where Charles Dumas served as the American agent. The only secretaries of legation during the period were William Carmichael, in Madrid, and William S. Smith (who became John Adams' son-in-law), in London.

In the summer of 1785, Congress ordered Secretary Jay to recommend the number of consuls and vice consuls that should be appointed in Europe. Jay suggested that five consul generals were essential, to be located in Amsterdam, London, Paris, Madrid, and Lisbon. Each consul general, he asserted, should nominate consuls for as many ports as necessary, and they should be commissioned by Congress. His plan called for consuls in eighteen European ports and Canton. Congress wanted Jay's proposal revised, and so, in his second report, he omitted the separate consuls general.

On October 28, Congress adopted this plan, conferring the powers of consuls general on the ministers, and where there were no ministers, on the chargés d'affaires. In effect, Congress created a consular service but attached it to the diplomatic service. Years later, historian Emory R. Johnson wrote, "In this course Congress cannot be said to have acted wisely."

TOWARD A STRONGER GOVERNMENT

The weakness of the United States' central government made it difficult to obtain commercial agreements with foreign nations. The British ambassador in Paris said that Britain would not enter into a treaty with Congress as long as an individual state could reject it. States enacted discriminatory duties against imports in British ships and even against goods imported by ships from countries other than the United States. States also imposed high protective tariffs. These actions all emphasized the need for a stronger central government.

James Monroe chaired a congressional committee concerned with commercial treaties; he believed they were necessary only with countries that had colonies and operated within closed economic systems. Jefferson, on the other hand, wanted commercial treaties with all countries so that the American national government could gain control over commerce.

When Congress chose John Adams to be the United States minister to the Court of St. James's, the choice aroused considerable opposition; Adams' blunt, acerbic style had won him scores of enemies. But he received the post because of his hard work and the support of the representatives from New England. Jonathan Sewall, a longtime Loyalist friend of Adams in London, noted that Adams lacked the talents for diplomacy:

> He cannot dance, drink, game, flatter, promise, dress, swear with gentlemen, and small talk and flirt with ladies, in short, he has none of the essential arts or ornaments which make a courtier, there are thousands who with a tenth part of his understanding, and without a spark of his honesty, would distance him infinitely in any court in Europe.

Adams was instructed to be in attendance at George III's birthday on June 4, 1785. The Adams family settled into a large town house at 9 Grosvenor Square, which served as both legation and residence.

On June 1, the young Marquis of Carmarthen, Britain's foreign secretary, presented Adams to the king. It was the first time for an American diplomat. Adams assured the king of the United States' friendship. The king replied that since he could not prevent the separation, he too hoped for mutual friendship. The meeting was brief, and the king dismissed the minister with a stiff bow. Following protocol, Adams bowed three times as he backed out of the hall.

For the next three years, Adams' home was the center of the American community in London, while the British, in the main, treated him with indifference. Most urgently, Adams tried to open British ports to American ships by threatening to keep British goods out of the United States. But Congress refused to go along with that threat, and three quarters of the exports from the eight northern states still went to Britain. America's dependency on Britain continued.

Adams kept Jay informed of events in Europe and began negotiating commercial treaties with Portugal and Prussia. The resulting treaties outlawed privateers and endorsed the principle that "free ships make free goods."

In March 1786, Jefferson traveled to London to improve commercial relations with Britain. The trip was fruitless except for Jefferson's endless shopping and viewing of art and architecture. He harbored a long-standing aversion to Britain, possibly dating back to when Cornwallis' soldiers had burned his crops and killed his animals.

While in London, Adams presented Jefferson at court, where George III is said to have deliberately turned his back on the two ministers from the United States. Jefferson commented on the British court, "They require to be kicked into common good manners."

Adams demanded of Lord Carmarthen that the British withdraw the troops from their seven remaining forts in the American Northwest. After waiting months for a reply, he was told candidly that the British would not uphold the Treaty of Paris until the United States honored its commitment to pay British creditors. Adams agreed that those debts should be paid, but he had no authority to make it happen. Individual states refused to require that the debts be collected, and Congress had no power to demand anything from the states.

Adams, frustrated by his failure to build relations with Britain, asked that his successor be chosen. Before he closed the legation and left London in April 1788, he traveled once more to Amsterdam and obtained another loan from a group of Dutch bankers. He sailed home to become George Washington's Vice President and then President of the United States. The United States had no representative in London for the next four years.

JEFFERSON AND ANOTHER REVOLUTION

Jefferson loved France. He admired its revolution and excused even its inexcusable excesses. At the same time, he found Paris society extravagant, empty, and purposeless.

Jefferson told Vergennes that the United States could not buy from France unless it could sell to France, and Vergennes agreed. In truth, France welcomed U.S. commerce no more enthusiastically than did the other European powers. Attempts to open trading markets were countered by the French system, which protected its farmers as well as its colonies.

Over time, France eased some of its economic restrictions. A French decree of August 30, 1784, had permitted Americans to conduct trade with the French West Indies, even though it angered French merchants. Lafayette managed to reduce the duty on whale oil, in appreciation for which the citizens of Nantucket Island collected one full day's milk production of their cows and sent him a five-hundred-pound cheese.

Building on Adams' work, Jefferson obtained another loan from Dutch bankers, enabling the United States to consolidate its debts, ransom American captives in Algiers, and make payments to French veterans of the American Revolution. But he was embarrassed by the United States' foreign debt, two-thirds of which was owed to France. As France's finances became increasingly desperate, the American debt bred ill will in France, a situation the United States could not afford.

Unlike Jay and Adams, Jefferson found Vergennes agreeable and reasonable. Jefferson judged that as long as Vergennes feared Britain, he would be useful to the Americans. Then, on February 13, 1787, he died; the French diplomat had played a major part in forming the alliance between the nation being born and the French empire. He was succeeded as foreign minister by the Comte de Montmorin, who had been the French ambassador in Madrid.

That summer, France's massive national debt drove it to the edge of bankruptcy. Louis XVI convened the Assembly of Notables at Versailles and began the disassembling that ended in revolution. At the same time, the Constitutional Convention in Philadelphia was pursuing quite a different course.

Jefferson himself was too much the optimist to forecast accurately one of the great bloodbaths of the age. He expected the French Revolution would spark political reform. He was convinced that the American Revolution had awakened the French people, and he predicted they would settle their differences peacefully. He even drafted a charter of rights, which Lafayette modified and presented to the National Assembly.

On July 11, Jefferson wrote Thomas Paine that the revolution in France was virtually over. The very next day, the people of Paris exploded into five days of rioting, during which they stormed the Bastille. So much for diplomats' predictions.

Seeking to limit consuls' activities to the fields of commerce and navigation, Jefferson wrote Comte de Montmorin a tactful letter on June 20,

1788, informing him that Congress wished to modify the consular convention that Congress had never formally accepted.

It has been said that Jefferson negotiated in the style of a benevolent
plantation patriarch. Still, that November, at Versailles, Jefferson and
Montmorin signed a new consular convention that eliminated most of the
Americans' objections. Jefferson succeeded in reducing the powers and
immunities of French consuls but left them jurisdiction over civil cases
between French citizens in America. And, as the Americans wanted, the
French agreed to limit the new convention to twelve years.

In his first three years, President Washington appointed seventeen consuls and five vice consuls. Under the revised convention, consuls had both
civil and criminal jurisdiction, particularly over ships' captains and merchants. When broader questions arose involving the United States, they
were to call a meeting of all local American merchants and the captains
who happened to be in port. And if an American behaved scandalously,
the consul could demand he leave the city and could force a ship's captain
sailing for the United States to take him home.

"The crowning achievement of Jefferson as a diplomat in France was
his negotiation of a consular convention with that country," wrote his biographer, Dumas Malone. This became, except for some treaties with Indian tribes, the first treaty submitted to the Senate under the Constitution.
The Senate ratified it immediately and unanimously on July 29, 1789. The
consular convention became the basis of an act of Congress defining the
duties of consuls and vice consuls, which was passed April 14, 1792, and
remained U.S. law for the next sixty-four years.

After transmitting the revised convention to Jay, Jefferson asked for a
leave of five or six months to go home to take care of personal business.
He made the request in November 1788; and with the typical speed of
communication of that day, Jay replied the following March, and the letter granting his leave reached Jefferson in late July.

During that spring and summer of 1789, Jefferson was engrossed in
the dramatic events in Paris. He attended the elaborate opening of the
Estates-General on May 5 and listened to the debates in the National Assembly on June 17. He met repeatedly with Lafayette. Sometimes, he may

have exceeded diplomatic proprieties in offering political advice to his French friend.

Jefferson witnessed how the threat of the use of royal force, and the scarcity of bread, triggered an uprising in the city. On Sunday, July 12, he rode in his carriage through what is now the Place de la Concorde and saw German cavalry and Swiss Guards drawn up, facing an angry crowd. The people gathered behind a large pile of stones and attacked the cavalrymen, forcing them to retire. Two days later, the crowd took arms from the Bastille and carried off and beheaded its governor and the chief officer of the city.

Jefferson watched the entry of King Louis XVI into Paris, led by Lafayette on horseback and flanked by two rows of deputies on foot. Thousands of shouting Parisians armed with muskets, swords, and pikes lined the streets and cheered the king. But Jefferson wrote insightfully of the mob, "Their hatred is stronger than their love."

In late July, a committee appointed to draw up a constitution for France invited Jefferson to a meeting. He declined, but at Lafayette's request, he did play host to a dinner in late August for representatives of two antagonistic groups, royalists and republicans, both of which wanted a constitution for France. Jefferson said later he remained a silent witness to the discussion, but he believed the meeting had saved the French constitution.

STARTING A CONSULAR SERVICE

After five years in France, Jefferson returned and took charge of the Department of State on March 22, 1790, the first Secretary of State under the Constitution. At the time, the United States had only two diplomatic posts and ten consular ones. His first consular appointment was John Marsden Pintard, of New York, a merchant living on the island of Madeira. Pintard was the second consul to be appointed under the United States Constitution, preceded only by Samuel Shaw at Canton. By the end of August, Jefferson had appointed six consuls and ten vice consuls, none of whom received a salary. He opened the first consulate in Paradise Street, in the important port of Liverpool with James Maury, Jr., as consul; he would remain there until 1829.

Since Congress was slow to develop guidelines for American consular officers, Jefferson created his own: Consuls would report every six months on American ships and cargoes and local military activities, as well as supply political intelligence. They were allowed to wear the blue uniform of the U.S. Navy, with red facings, a black cockade, and a small sword.

Under the law of April 14, 1792, consuls could receive protests regarding American shipping, take possession of estates of Americans who died abroad, assume charge of stranded American ships until their owners could act, and collect specified fees for various functions. The law spelled out the earlier convention between the King of the French, and the United States of America. It gave American officials authority to assist French consuls in saving the wreck of a French vessel. Salaries were provided for consuls to the Barbary states, presumably because they would not have time to trade on their own account.

The consuls were authorized to care for the needs of American seamen left impoverished in foreign ports in cases of sickness, shipwreck, or captivity. The act did not instruct consuls to assist Americans abroad other than seamen, judging that they were the group most vulnerable to abuse. It was not uncommon during European wars for American ships to be seized and their crews left on a strange shore, destitute. From July 1796 to June 1797, the French seized 316 American merchant ships. In these practical areas, consuls' judgments superseded even those of American ministers abroad.

When Britain and France were warring, they both seized American ships and confiscated their cargoes. Jefferson reacted to these assaults with an embargo, but that soon proved damaging to American farmers, merchants, and shippers, and after a year it was repealed. In its place a more limited law prohibited trade with ports under British and French control.

The naval powers, and Britain in particular, were stopping American merchantmen on the high seas and kidnapping seamen for their navies. The British claimed they were impressing only British citizens, but many American seamen were British-born, and Britain justified shanghaiing these unwilling men as needed to meet its Navy's manpower requirements. It empowered its naval captains to decide whether a man on a ship stopped at sea could be impressed. Some of those impressed were even given false names so they could not be traced.

As early as 1796, the United States Act for the Relief and Protection of American Seamen provided for two agents to be stationed overseas, one in England and the other in Kingston, Jamaica, to inquire about American sailors impressed or detained by a foreign power. The first agent in London was David Lenox, a former comptroller of the United States Treasury, and in Kingston was Silas Talbot, a former officer in the Continental navy.

Further acts of February 28, 1803; April 20, 1818; and March 1, 1823, spelled out additional duties and set standards under which consular officers were to operate.

The consular side of the Department of State expanded much more rapidly than the diplomatic. By 1830, there were 130 consular posts in existence and only fifteen diplomatic posts. Most of the consular posts were located in European seaports. Others were at Smyrna (now Izmir), Turkey, and more remotely in Canton, Calcutta, Cape Town, and Batavia (Jakarta). Bordeaux in 1778 had become the first U.S. consular post because it was the site of a busy market in seamen. In 1797, President Adams sent William Willis to be the first consul in Barcelona and to promote trade from there.

President Adams commissioned the first consul to the Papal States, Giovanni Sartori, in 1797, and Rome became an American listening post. Fifty years later, it was converted from a consular to a diplomatic assignment.

Most of the early consuls were American citizens, and most served in a single city, where they were already established in business. Unusual was the British Quaker family of Robert Were Fox, which continued over four generations to man the consulate at Falmouth, England, from 1794 almost continually until the post was closed in 1905. And three generations of the Sprague family, originally from Boston, served as consuls in Gibraltar between 1832 and 1934.

The department gave consuls little guidance on how to perform their duties. And in 1801 Consul Isaac Cox Barnet, based in Paris, complained that he had not heard from the Department of State for twenty-one months. One dramatic example was the letter that Secretary of State James Madison wrote the consul at LaGuaira, Venezuela, on April 18, 1807, complaining that the State Department had not received a single communication from him since his appointment in 1800. (This may have been the source of the diplomatic legend about Secretary of State Jefferson, who said that he had not heard from a certain envoy for a couple of years, and if he did not hear from him for another year, he would write to him.)

"WE SHALL BE THE MURDERERS OF OUR CHILDREN"

Spain did not permit direct trade with her colonies and accepted a consul only at Cuba; but as its colonies won independence, they welcomed American consuls and commercial agents.

In 1810, Joel Roberts Poinsett, a wealthy young South Carolinian, was appointed special agent to South America, and the next year he was made consul general at Buenos Aires. He traveled into Chile to help the revolutionaries, but was forced to flee when the Spanish retook Santiago. A decade later, Poinsett became the first American minister to the Republic of Mexico, and still later he served as secretary of war under President Martin Van Buren.

Robert K. Lowry, of Baltimore, was the first U.S. citizen to serve as a commercial agent at Caracas' port of La Guaira; he served there off and on from 1810 until his death in 1824. When an earthquake destroyed most of Caracas and La Guaira in 1812, Lowry was appointed consul, and Secretary of State Monroe sent Alexander Scott to work in Caracas. Congress authorized the purchase of supplies for the earthquake victims. When the Spanish forced Lowry and Scott to leave, they chartered a boat and fled to Curaçao, but the British governor there would not let them land. Eventually, they made their way home.

Earlier, in the summer of 1791, a more fearsome Latin American crisis arose when slaves revolted on the sugarcane plantations of French-ruled Haiti, the world's single most lucrative colony. The slaves defeated French, British, and Spanish forces, virtually wiping out the white planters on the island. The bloodshed aroused fears of slave revolts in the United States.

On Haiti, Secretary of State Timothy Pickering favored working with the revolt's leader, Toussaint-Louverture. In 1799, President John Adams sent Dr. Edward Stevens, Alexander Hamilton's personal physician, to negotiate with Haiti's leaders. He reached an agreement with Toussaint-Louverture that reopened trade.

As a Southerner, Jefferson was less eager to work with the rebellious slaves; his priority was to maintain relations with France. Although he hoped privately that the revolt in Haiti would encourage emancipation in the United States, he too worried about a slave revolt at home. He warned, "If something is not done, and soon done, we shall be the murderers of our children."

On becoming President in 1801, Jefferson replaced Dr. Stevens with Tobias Lear, a Harvard graduate who had been George Washington's personal secretary. Lear arrived without a personal letter from President Jefferson to Toussaint-Louverture, which the Haitian leader took as an insult. Lear described the scene to Secretary of State James Madison:

> He immediately returned my Commission without opening it, expressing his disappointment and disgust in strong terms, saying his Colour was the cause of his being neglected, and not thought worthy of the Usual attentions.

The following year, France's first consul, Napoleon Bonaparte, sent a veteran 44,000-man army against the rebellious blacks of Saint Dominque (Haiti). Only seven thousand of this French force, the survivors of battle and yellow fever, left the island. This expensive defeat was one reason Bonaparte would sell the Louisiana Territory to the United States in 1803.

After Toussaint-Louverture was duped and taken prisoner, General Jean-Jacques Dessalines slaughtered the remaining French on the island and declared Haiti an independent republic. Because of this massacre, on January 1, 1804, Jefferson refused to recognize the new Haitian republic, and Congress embargoed trade with it. And the U.S. government, in a show of racist Southern power, refused to send consuls to Haiti. The revolt had aroused U.S. slaveholders' worst fears, and full diplomatic relations were not reestablished until 1862, when Southerners were absent from the U.S. Congress.

5

Paying Off the Pirates

1785–1805

T
he Revolution cost the Americans the protection of the British Navy. By 1785, pirates sailing out of Algiers, Tripoli, Tunis, and Morocco were seizing American merchant ships in the Mediterranean and enslaving their crews. These pirates worked under avaricious local sheikhs along the Barbary Coast of North Africa and might more accurately be called corsairs because they were freelance operatives.

In Paris, Thomas Jefferson and John Adams agreed that negotiation was impossible. They pleaded with Congress to take action against those small states that had long lived off piracy and were holding European and American seamen for ransom. Jefferson reacted to the pirates with what he called a combination of "indignation and impotence."

The United States had neither a navy to protect its ships nor money to buy back prisoners. At first, Jefferson opposed paying ransoms; he proposed building a half dozen frigates, giving their command to naval hero Commodore John Paul Jones, and rescuing the captured seamen. He then changed his mind, recommending instead that a fleet of the European powers clean up the piracy. Adams thought that paying ransoms would be less expensive.

Among the Barbary rulers, only Sultan Sidi Mohammed ben Abdullah of Morocco made peaceful overtures to the Americans. Starting as early as December 1777, he allowed American ships to enter Moroccan ports; he was interested in increasing his nation's overseas trade. The Americans, however, ignored him and sent the sultan no reply for three years. Finally, on May 7, 1784, Congress authorized the commissioners in Paris to negotiate treaties.

Progress was so slow that when, on October 11, 1784, the sultan's corsairs captured the American merchant ship *Betsey* and brought it and its crew into Tangier, the sultan announced he would hold the ship, cargo, and crew until he had a treaty with the United States. That finally won the Americans' attention.

The following spring, Congress gave the commissioners in Paris $80,000 (almost $2 million in 2010 dollars) to buy peace in Barbary. Since no American consuls were stationed there, Thomas Barclay, the consul general in Paris, was sent to Morocco, and John Lamb, a knowledgeable merchant-ship captain, went to Algiers, the most militant of the Barbary states.

In June 1786, Barclay concluded a Treaty of Friendship and Amity. Under this Treaty of Marrakesh, the sultan freed his prisoners for $30,000 (about $712,000 in 2010 dollars) and promised to protect American shipping and encourage commerce between the two countries. Barclay insisted that there would be no annual tribute. Ratified by Congress on July 18, 1787, this was the first treaty between the United States and an African, Arab, or Muslim nation.

Accompanying Barclay in Marrakesh was the vice consul from Marseilles, Lieutenant Colonel David Salisbury Franks, believed to be the first Jew to serve in the American foreign service. During the Revolution, Franks, then a major, who spoke French fluently, had been liaison to the comte d'Estaing and later was an aide to Benedict Arnold. (A court-martial exonerated Franks of having any part in Arnold's treason.) And in the spring of 1784, Franks had been one of the three men who carried the official copies of the peace treaty to Paris.

Barclay appointed three Italians living in Morocco to serve as deputy consular agents there. On Secretary Jay's recommendation, Congress confirmed them, specifically exempting them from the requirement that they be United States citizens. Congress had decreed on March 16, 1784: "That it is inconsistent with the interest of the United States to appoint any person not a citizen thereof, to the office of Minister, chargé des affaires, consul, vice-consul, or any other civil department in a foreign country." In general, diplomatic appointments followed this rule, but it was not always practical with the more numerous and scattered consular appointments.

Captain Lamb failed in Algiers, partially because he was less skillful and partly because the dey of Algiers demanded more than the $200 per captive ($5,000 in 2010 dollars) he was authorized to pay. The dey asked $6,000 ($14,000) for a master, $4,000 (nearly $10,000) for a mate, and $1,500 ($9,500) for each sailor released from hard labor.

In February 1786, Abdrahaman, Tripoli's ambassador to London, demanded of John Adams $200,000 (nearly $5 million) to arrange treaties and protect U.S. commerce. Jefferson tried to organize a concerted response from the European countries that were suffering from the pirates' attacks. But in that era of economic warfare such cooperation proved beyond reach. For the moment, the Americans had no choice but to pay the ransoms demanded.

President Washington sent David Humphreys, who in 1791 was named the U.S. minister to Portugal, to try to free Algiers' captives; like John Lamb, he failed. So, on June 1, 1792, Washington and Secretary Jefferson signed a commission empowering Commodore John Paul Jones, who was living in Paris, to make a treaty with the dey and ransom his prisoners. A second commission appointed Jones as U.S. consul to Algiers. Jefferson was prepared to pay $27,000 ($600,000) for the thirteen captives still alive of the twenty-one whom the Algerians had captured and to pay $25,000 ($588,000) more for a treaty.

Jefferson instructed South Carolina's Thomas Pinckney, who was to become the American minister in London, to deliver John Paul Jones' commissions. But Pinckney did not sail until mid-July. By the time he reached Paris, Jones was dead.

Jones' assignment to Algiers was transferred to Thomas Barclay, who had been successful in Morocco. But Barclay died in Lisbon in January 1793, on his way to Algiers. Colonel Humphreys was the next to inherit the ill-fated task. He, too, failed to bring the dey to terms because, it was explained, the dey was trying to make peace with the Dutch and the Portuguese and could not accept the additional loss of income that peace with the United States would cost him.

In 1794, Humphreys tried again. This time he was authorized to spend as much as $800,000 ($6 million in 2010 dollars) to gain a treaty and free the captives. Humphreys arranged with Joseph Donaldson, Jr., of Philadelphia, to conduct the negotiations. They sailed in April 1795. When Donaldson finally reached Algiers in September, he was suffering from gout and walked with a crutch, his right foot swathed in a large velvet slipper.

James Cathcart, an American who had been a captive of the Algerians for a decade, made the connection between Donaldson and the dey. Cathcart had learned Arabic, rising to be the dey's chief Christian secretary. Within three days, Donaldson negotiated a treaty with the dey to free the captives, open Algerine ports to American commerce, and make U.S. ships immune to search or seizure. The United States paid $992,463.25 (nearly $20 million), of which $522,500 ($10 million) was to ransom the captives.

In Paris in the summer of 1795, Humphreys met with his Yale friend, Joel Barlow. Humphreys, the U.S. minister to Portugal, and James Monroe, the minister in Paris, wanted Barlow to negotiate treaties with Algiers, Tunis, and Tripoli and to free the 150 Americans who had been enslaved as long as ten years, working in quarries, building roads, and unloading ships.

Joel Barlow had graduated from Yale in 1778 and spent three years in the revolutionary army, fighting in the battles of Long Island and White Plains. He also served as a chaplain in Poor's Brigade of the Massachusetts Line and witnessed the execution of British Major John Andre as a British spy. After the Revolution, Barlow and his wife, Ruth, settled in Hartford, where in 1784 he started a weekly, *The American Mercury*. He became one of America's most widely read authors and poets.

In 1788, Barlow went to Europe as an agent for a speculation company recruiting settlers to buy land along the Ohio River. A large, imposing man, Barlow became a social lion in France. He arranged for six hundred immigrants to sail for America to escape the chaos of the French Revolution. But the land company did not hold title to the land Barlow sold, and the U.S. government had to give the settlers other land. Barlow was blamed, but somehow remained popular, and for his support of the French Revolution was granted French citizenship, an honor only also accorded to Washington, Hamilton, Madison, and Paine.

When Barlow arrived in Algiers in March 1796, the dey was in a fury. He had been waiting months for the money promised him by the treaty with Donaldson, and he threatened to start seizing American ships again. Although the Senate had ratified the treaty, the dey would not let it take effect until he had the funds in hand. He sent another Arabic-speaking American prisoner, Richard O'Brien, to collect the money from Barings, the British bankers, and when they did not have enough specie, Humphreys sent O'Brien to Italian bankers.

In May, the plague struck Algiers and killed five of the prisoners. Barlow was desperate to save the surviving Americans. In June, a new French consul arrived and paid the dey $200,000 ($3.4 million), which he deposited with a local banker. Then, Barlow borrowed the dey's own money to save the Americans from the plague, ransoming the American prisoners and promising to pay the balance. He promptly shipped the prisoners to America.

Barlow had been in "this cursed country," as he wrote his wife, for seven months when O'Brien appeared in October with some of the money that Barlow owed the dey. O'Brien explained that he had been aboard a ship that was captured by a Tripolitan corsair and had been released after three weeks only because the bey of Tripoli was afraid of the dey of Algiers.

Barlow stayed in Algiers awaiting the balance of the money from the United States with which to repay the dey. In the face of the dey's impatience, Barlow promised him a twenty-gun frigate in exchange for a six-month delay. The dey was delighted but demanded a thirty-six-gun frigate. The United States naval bill of 1794 had called for building four forty-four-gun and two thirty-six-gun frigates, which represented the entire American navy. It was January 1797 before Barlow was able to pay the debt, and a precedent was set for offering warships as gifts. With his money finally in hand, the dey was pleased to help Barlow settle with the beys of Tunis and Tripoli, and even sent troops to Tunis to enforce his will.

Humphreys had also been commissioned to negotiate a treaty with the ruler of Tripoli, and he had delegated that job to Donaldson and Barlow. They hired Captain O'Brien, now released from slavery, and, because Tripoli was the weakest of the pirate powers and had the fewest prisoners to ransom, O'Brien was able to arrange a treaty in 1796 for $57,000 (just under $1 million today), with no annual tribute.

In June 1797, President Adams asked Congress to advance funds to build two ships for the dey of Algiers and informed Congress that he wished to post a consul in Algiers. The man would have to act frequently on his own discretion. Of this mission, Adams said, "That country is so remote as to rend it impracticable for the consul to ask and receive instructions in sudden emergencies." While a salary of $2,000 ($35,000 in 2010 dollars) a year seemed adequate for the consuls in Tripoli and Tunis, the consul in Algiers would require twice as much.

After many delays, Barlow sailed for Marseilles, where he spent forty days in quarantine after having been exposed to the plague in Algiers. He finally reached Paris in mid-September.

Meanwhile, the friendly sultan of Morocco had died, and James Simpson, the U.S. consul at Gibraltar, was sent to deal with his successor. Simpson appeared in Tangier, across the straits, armed with cannon, small arms, and gunpowder, and established the United States' first consulate in the Arab world. He stayed there as consul for twenty-four years.

At the conclusion of Simpson's tour in 1821, Sultan Moulay Suliman presented the United States with a handsome stone building for its consulate, the first property acquired abroad by the United States government. Expanded over the years, the building was the seat of the U.S. representative to Morocco until 1956, when Morocco gained its independence from France and moved its capital to Rabat. Later, it became the American Legation Museum, the site of seminars and exhibitions supported by former American diplomats. Today, it houses the American Institute for Maghrib Studies.

During this same period, the United States had to pay attention to the so-called Quasi-War with France, during which the French seized more than three hundred American merchant ships, making the rampages of the Barbary piracy seem minor.

By the turn of the century, the United States had consuls in Morocco, Tripoli, Algiers, and Tunis. The Americans made a tense team: At Algiers, Captain O'Brien was a rough-and-ready sailor; at Tunis, William Eaton, a Dartmouth College graduate and former army captain, was better educated and looked down on O'Brien. The Barbary rulers constantly tested the consuls against each other, trying to gain advantages for themselves.

The rule of force continued to govern relations with the Barbary chieftains. In September 1800, the dey of Algiers demanded that the United States frigate *George Washington* carry his ambassador with gifts to the sultan in Constantinople. Consul General O'Brien and Captain William Bainbridge of the frigate at first refused. But the ship lay under the dey's guns, and eventually they had to accede. When the *George Washington* returned from her mission, the Secretary of the Navy reprimanded Captain Bainbridge for his earlier carelessness, and the ship was anchored out of range of the guns.

The following spring, the first United States naval squadron, consisting of four ships commanded by Commodore Richard Dale, was sent to the Mediterranean. At Gibraltar, Dale learned that the pasha of Tripoli had declared war on the United States and cut down the flagstaff at the consulate. The squadron blockaded Tripoli rather ineffectually.

In 1802, Cathcart was to replace O'Brien as consul in Algiers, but the dey would not accept him, presumably because he was too familiar with Algerian ways and could trump the dey's tricks. Tobias Lear, who had served as consul in Santo Domingo until the French general there kicked him out, was sent instead as consul general to Algiers.

When William Eaton, the American consul at Tunis, was ordered to leave after an argument with the dey over money, he designated George Davis, a doctor on a U.S. Navy ship, to serve as acting consul. (In 1807, Davis became the consul at Tripoli.)

In October 1803, the thirty-six-gun frigate *Philadelphia* was chasing a pirate ship when it ran aground under the guns of Tripoli. This mistake handed Pasha Yusuf Karamanli more than three hundred American prisoners. The following February, in a feat of memorable daring, the navy's Lieutenant Stephen Decatur destroyed the frigate. But someone had to free the American captives.

Eaton obtained Jefferson's permission to try to free them and replace Pasha Yusuf with his brother Hamet. For the first time, but certainly not the last, the United States would attempt through a covert agent to overthrow a foreign government.

Eaton landed at Alexandria, Egypt, and on March 5, 1805, started a formidable march to the shores of Tripoli, across six hundred miles of the Great Libyan Desert. He led five hundred Arabs, seventy-five European mercenaries, and a detachment of eight U.S. Marines, led by Lieutenant Presley Neville O'Bannon. They would attack Tripoli from the rear. On April 27, after a terrible march with little food and water, they assaulted the port of Derna. The Marines, bayonets fixed, led the charge. Two Marines were killed and Eaton and one Marine were wounded. Lieutenant O'Bannon raised the flag over the harbor fort, the first time the American flag had been lifted in battle in the Eastern Hemisphere.

Yusuf's Arab forces fought Eaton's unit almost daily until the Americans won decisively on June 10. The very next day, *Constellation* arrived with the news that Consul General Lear and Joseph Pulis, a controversial American consul to Malta, had already agreed to a treaty, exchanging all the prisoners from *Philadelphia* for payment to Tripoli of $60,000 ($1.1 million dollars in 2010).

Eaton was infuriated; his entire military action was for naught. Although the ransom-bought peace was regarded as a disgrace, since the American navy was standing off Tripoli in force, the American captives were freed. And the United States finally had a naval presence on hand to resolve quarrels with the Barbary states.

6

"One Nation as to Foreign Concerns"

1787—95

J ust as the young nation's leaders were organizing their Constitutional
Convention in Philadelphia, Thomas Jefferson set off from Paris on
a thousand-mile, three-month tour of France and Italy. The historic
political activity back home did not deter him.

Jefferson followed his colleagues' progress toward a constitution through
his correspondence with James Madison and James Monroe, the youthful
disciples who resembled a Virginia dynasty. Replying to Monroe's description of the political drama at home, Jefferson wrote wryly, "I have
nothing to give you in return but the history of the follies of nations in
their dotage."

He left Paris on the last day of February 1787, right after the funeral of
the comte de Vergennes, and on June 10 arrived back in Paris, a grand tour
for the observant diplomat.

The delegates the states sent to Philadelphia that summer hoped the
Constitution would weld the thirteen states into a stronger nation. It did
radically change the United States' approach to foreign relations. Article
II, Section 2, of the new Constitution shifted to the President the power,
with the advice and consent of the Senate, to make treaties and appoint
ambassadors, public ministers, and consuls. And under Section 3 he could
"receive Ambassadors and other public Ministers."

The Constitution did not detail the conduct of foreign affairs. Jefferson
asserted that the Senate could determine whether a candidate for the for-

eign service was fit, but it could not decide his assignment or grade. And Congress held onto the ultimate powers to appropriate money and declare war. The executive's powers still had to be debated and resolved.

For one example, the Constitution did not provide for the dismissal of the Secretary of Foreign Affairs. Did the President require the advice and consent of the Senate if he wished to remove a secretary? James Madison, the principal driving force behind the Constitutional Convention, held that if the President was to be responsible, he must also have the power of removal.

The most irreconcilable issue was slavery. The Constitution provided for a twenty-year extension of the slave trade, and its three-fifths clause—counting slaves as three-fifths of a person for purposes of taxation and representation—left ugly sores.

Jefferson did not approve of all the powers given the federal government under the new Constitution. And he still wanted a Bill of Rights to protect the individual, as well as a limit on the President's tenure. He had experienced the weak conduct of foreign affairs and wrote Madison, "To make us one nation as to foreign concerns, and keep us distinct in Domestic ones gives the outline of the proper division of powers between the General and the particular governments." He was proud that the United States could modify its government without bloodshed.

Nine states ratified the Constitution by May 23, 1788, and it became the supreme law of the land. Congress met the following March in New York City, then a city of twenty-five thousand people. In April, the Electoral College named George Washington President and John Adams, Vice President.

On September 15, 1789, Washington signed an act enlarging the Department of Foreign Affairs' functions to include keeping the acts and records of Congress, publishing the acts of Congress, and serving as custodian of the Seal of the United States. The department's name was changed to the Department of State, and its chief officer became the secretary of state.

The Department of State was now the most important office of the government. Its Secretary was responsible for all governmental administration, domestic as well as foreign, except for that specifically assigned to the treasury and war departments. The Secretary and the other Executive department heads reported to the President; they could speak only in his name and act only with his approval, and he could remove them.

THE FIRST SECRETARY OF STATE

Jefferson left Paris with his two motherless daughters on September 26, 1789, eleven days after the Department of State was born, on what he thought was a six-month home leave. His secretary, William Short, took charge in Paris; he negotiated a commercial treaty with France, handled crucial loans from Amsterdam, and shipped home Jefferson's possessions.

Jefferson landed at Norfolk on November 23 and headed for his Palladian estate, Monticello, for Christmas and his daughter Patsy's wedding. En route, he learned that President Washington had offered him the brand-new post of Secretary of State. On February 14 he halfheartedly accepted Washington's offer.

He reached New York City on March 21, 1790, and, even though it was Sunday, reported to President Washington. The next day, he officially took charge of the department; it consisted of two principal clerks, three subordinate clerks, a French translator, and two messengers.

In a small rented house at 57 Maiden Lane, Jefferson conducted foreign affairs and was responsible for the safekeeping of the great seal, a small engraved metal plate used to seal documents and presidential commissions. His principal clerks were Henry Remsen, Jr., in charge of the foreign office, and Roger Alden, in charge of the home office. Alden soon resigned because his salary was inadequate, and Remsen resigned in 1792 to become the first teller of the new United States Bank. To succeed him, Jefferson chose George Taylor rather than Jacob Blackwell, in good part because Taylor had a family to support.

An act of July 1, 1790, put a ceiling of $40,000 ($984,000 in 2010 dollars) on the total the President could spend on pay (and expenses) for all diplomats serving abroad. Six years later, the ceiling was raised to $60,000 (just over a million dollars in 2010) a year. These funds were to come from duties on imports and ships' tonnage.

That autumn, the federal government moved from New York City to Philadelphia, where it would stay until the new capital city near the Falls of the Potomac was ready.

The management of foreign relations under the new Constitution had to be built brick by brick. No precedents were in place for the Americans to draw on. No cadre existed from which to select ministers and consuls. Some choices worked out superbly, others, naturally, did not.

In April 1790, Washington asked Chief Justice John Jay a crucial question: Under the Constitution, should the President consult the Senate as to where diplomats are to be sent, as well as their ranks? The chief justice advised him that the Senate had no right to interfere and it would be unwise to create a precedent.

The thirteen-year-old nation had little experience with foreign affairs when Jefferson took office. The Great Powers were across a huge ocean that could be traversed only by sail. The United States had ministers in six capitals (Paris, London, Berlin, The Hague, Lisbon, and Madrid) and treaties with only France, the Netherlands, Great Britain, Sweden, Prussia, and Morocco.

However, the United States already had consuls or vice consuls in sixty-nine cities around the world, including Canton, Calcutta, Naples, Barcelona, and Cape Town. There were no consuls in Canada or Britain's island possessions. Latin America and most of the Middle East were inaccessible. Only the Dutch were permitted posts in Japan.

Secretary Jefferson faced three major diplomatic concerns immediately: the first, regarded commerce, especially with Britain; the second, setting the nation's borders; and third, defining the nation's position in case of a European war, especially one involving the United States' ally, France.

The issue over trade with Britain centered on London's aversion to making a commercial treaty with the United States. Americans agreed among themselves that the British monopoly in the West Indies had to be broken but disagreed on tactics. Jefferson advised that if the British could keep their markets to themselves, the Americans could keep the carrying trade to themselves. If the British could impose restrictions and duties, so could the Americans.

Jefferson and Madison wanted to retaliate for Britain's refusal to make a trade treaty. The U.S. Treasury Secretary, Alexander Hamilton, on the other hand, warned that a commercial war would shrink tariff income and undermine his economic plans for the nation. He wanted to persuade Britain, rather than to threaten. In the end, Hamilton dominated the argument.

The chief border issues were Spain's domination of the Mississippi, which was the lifeline of the American interior, and Britain's continuing occupation of the forts in the American northwest. Jefferson contended that people living on the upper stretches of a river, such as the Mississippi, had the right to use the river freely for its entire length. And he asserted to President Washington that the 31st parallel was a legal boundary with Spain, since it was based on lines set by the king of England before the American Revolution.

Jefferson sent David Humphreys to Madrid with a secret letter for William Carmichael suggesting that the United States was willing to go to war to assure free navigation of the Mississippi. He proposed that Spain surrender all its holdings east of the river in exchange for a guarantee of Spain's rule west of the Mississippi.

In 1791, Jefferson found an excuse to press his insistent campaign for use of the Mississippi. Four years earlier, Spanish soldiers, who were under orders to confiscate all foreign property along both sides of the river, had detained the clerk of an American citizen, Joseph St. Marie, and seized St. Marie's goods. Jefferson wanted the soldiers punished, and he wanted indemnification. And, most important, he wanted undisturbed navigation of the Mississippi. He warned that if Spain failed to acknowledge Americans' rights on the Mississippi, the United States government would retaliate. But Spain still refused to negotiate.

Jefferson had little faith in Carmichael in Madrid, regarding him as lazy. (John Jay said Carmichael "mistook cunning for wisdom.") Jefferson, therefore, asked the French foreign minister, Montmorin, to help him with Spain. Montmorin simply sent their correspondence on to Madrid, and Spain, surprisingly, then agreed to negotiate.

William Short was sent from Paris to reinforce Carmichael in Madrid, but the Spanish government declared that the two Americans did not have enough rank to be taken seriously. Thomas Pinckney, America's minister in London, was then sent to pin down the negotiations. Despite the Spanish snub, Pinckney's Treaty, signed on October 27, 1795, gave the United States navigation rights on the Mississippi.

Jefferson also asked Gouverneur Morris, whom Washington was sending on a mission to London, to inform the British that the Americans would not stand by if Britain seized Louisiana and the Floridas.

EXPANDING REPRESENTATION ABROAD

Jefferson's earlier experience in France became invaluable for him as Secretary of State. In the summer of 1791, Jean Baptiste Ternant arrived as the French monarchy's last minister to the United States; as an officer in the American Revolution, he had won praise from Lafayette. That same year, George Hammond, age twenty-eight, arrived as the first British minister to the United States. His instructions prohibited him from even discussing a commercial treaty. But he did propose creating an independent Indian nation between Canada and the United States in exchange for Britain's abandoning her military posts in the northwest. The Americans found this eccentric idea beyond consideration.

Jefferson separated alleged infractions of the peace treaty from those resulting from the conduct of the war. Misdeeds during the war, he asserted, were not violations of the peace treaty. The U.S. government recommended that the state legislatures pay restitution for confiscated Loyalist property. Making a recommendation was the most Congress could do.

Jefferson resented that Hamilton and Jay had the President's ear on foreign policy, while the Hamiltonians thought Jefferson "unsound and dangerous." Jefferson did everything possible to stay in constant touch with George Washington, and on May 1, 1791, even wrote him:

> I write to day indeed merely as the Watchman cries, to prove himself awake, and that all is well, for the last week has scarcely furnished anything foreign or domestic worthy of your notice.

Washington increased the number of representatives overseas, despite the Senate's thinking it not in the interest of the United States to have ministers plenipotentiary reside in foreign courts. The senators created a select committee to investigate the matter. Jefferson, annoyed, asserted that the President was the sole judge of the grade and placement of ministers and that the Senate could only grant or withhold its approval of those nominated. His accurate but tactless paper was never sent to the Senate.

In January 1792, Jefferson appeared before the Senate's select committee and explained that the administration felt it needed diplomatic missions only in Britain, France, Spain, Portugal, and the Netherlands, and that the administration would send the lowest-grade—and least expensive—envoys possible to those posts. With those assurances, the Senate approved the nominations.

Jefferson appointed sixteen consuls to France during his first year in office. And he named David Humphreys minister resident in Lisbon. The original plan had been to send him as a less expensive chargé d'affaires, but the Portuguese government objected, and Humphreys was raised to the rank of minister resident, at no increase in salary.

Although Jefferson wanted the ministry at Paris given to William Short, Washington chose Gouverneur Morris. The disappointed Short was named minister at The Hague. Washington also sent Thomas Pinckney as minister to London. And he had Gouverneur Morris travel to London specifically to sound out British intentions on various unfinished business. Morris found the British foreign secretary unwilling to focus on the issues, and it did not help that Alexander Hamilton undermined his mission. After futile months, Morris returned to Paris, where he poked into the French Revolution, on the side of royalty. Jefferson called him "a high flying monarchy-man."

Gouverneur Morris had come to France three years earlier as a business-man representing Robert Morris (no relation), who was scheming to buy up the United States' debt to France at fifty cents on the dollar. Rich and con-servative, Gouverneur Morris was a tall, imposing man with a quick wit. He had lost his left leg to an overeager surgeon after breaking it in a carriage accident. In Paris, he enjoyed the society of aristocrats, even though France was now bankrupt from wars, extravagance, and its support of the Ameri-can Revolution. He now witnessed the riots and assassinations of the French Revolution. One night, revolutionary militiamen invaded Morris' Paris home; he ejected them firmly. After enduring repeated searches of his home, Morris moved to a safer house farther from Paris.

On July 18, Morris received word that John Paul Jones, whom he had long known, was seriously ill. The minister rushed to Jones' Paris home at 52 rue de Tournon, where Jones dictated to him a simple will. After dinner, Morris, accompanied by his mistress and a French physician, returned to Jones' third-floor apartment and found him sprawled facedown on his bed, dead. The slight, soft-spoken naval hero was barely forty-five.

To save expense, Morris had the commodore's body placed in a pau-per's grave. That infuriated the French, who preserved his body in alcohol in a sealed lead coffin and buried it in a little cemetery for foreign Protes-tants. Morris did not attend the funeral, saying he was giving a dinner party that evening. In his stead he sent an attaché from the legation.

Morris displayed the same coldness when, on Christmas Day 1793, the Jacobin radicals imprisoned Thomas Paine, despite his enthusiastic support of the Revolution and his membership in the French National Convention. Paine demanded his freedom on the grounds that he was an American citizen, but Morris did nothing to help him. Paine never forgave him. In contrast, when the Austrians captured and imprisoned the noble-born Lafayette, Morris saw fit to supply him and his wife with funds.

In 1905, after a dedicated search, General Horace Porter, then the U.S. ambassador in Paris, located John Paul Jones' body in its forgotten grave. President Theodore Roosevelt sent four warships to France and brought Jones' body home. It now rests in the crypt of the chapel of the U.S. Naval Academy at Annapolis.

"A DIPLOMATIC REVOLUTION"

Americans had conflicting ideas about how their country should conduct itself under the new Constitution. In a letter to President Washington on September 9, 1792, Jefferson protested Hamilton's interference in foreign affairs. The skittish Hamilton felt that Jefferson's admiration for France and dislike of Britain were damaging the United States. Washington wrote his warring secretaries that they should not rip the fabric of the young nation while trying to mend it.

Jefferson was determined to quit as Secretary after the elections of 1792, but, instead, the outbreak of a general European war that spring began an intense period of policy making.

Louis XVI was beheaded on January 21, 1793. How should the United States treat the ever-changing governments of France? Jefferson stated a rule that became a guide to American diplomatic practice:

It accords with our principles to acknowledge any government to be rightful which is formed by the will of the nation substantially declared.

The war that radical France declared against Britain, Holland, and Spain was in good part a struggle between revolution and legitimacy. On April 22, President Washington, pressed by Hamilton and opposed by Jefferson, proclaimed the United States' neutrality. But many Americans felt sympathy for revolutionary France. Jefferson called France's opponents "conspirators against human liberty."

On May 9, the French National Assembly decreed that neutral ships carrying food would be taken to French ports. British goods would be seized; American goods were exempt. But in practice it did not happen that way. A British Order-in-Council instructed commanders to seize all ships carrying foodstuff to French ports. The European war now reached across the Atlantic.

THE "AFFAIR CITIZEN GENÊT"

Revolutionary France recalled Minister Jean Baptiste Ternant, who had been commissioned by the monarchy, and sent Edmond-Charles Genêt to America as the first minister from the French republic. He was instructed to procure military equipment and financial aid.

Redheaded Genêt, a brilliant, headstrong young man, age thirty, advocated his cause with energy and bombast. He fiercely attacked President Washington's policy of neutrality; he insisted on arming privateers and ordered them to bring their prizes into American ports, where French consuls set up prize courts. He did France more harm than good.

"Affair Citizen Genêt" came to a head in the summer of 1793. Washington declared that the admission of French warships to American ports violated American neutrality. Hamilton informed Jefferson that Genêt was equipping a French prize ship, *Little Sarah,* as a privateer with twenty guns. When the President ordered the ship not to sail, Genêt appealed directly to the American people over Washington's head. Although the Frenchman's case was helped by the British seizure of some two hundred and fifty American ships trading in the Caribbean, Genêt's attempt at a primitive form of "public diplomacy" was hardly diplomatic.

When Genêt planned to attack Spanish-held Louisiana, Washington denounced the expedition, and Congress made it a crime to enlist Americans in the adventure. Jefferson charged that Genêt was maneuvering the United States into the European war.

Genêt ordered *Little Sarah* to sail, and, on Washington's order, Gouverneur Morris demanded Genêt's recall. The French government was pleased to ask that Morris, no friend of the Revolution, be recalled in turn. Genêt's successor, Joseph Fauchet, arrived with orders to arrest him and return him to France to face the guillotine. He retreated to a farm on Long Island, where, subsequently, he married the daughter of New York Governor George Clinton.

During that summer of 1793, yellow fever struck Philadelphia, driving the populace and the government out of the city. Jefferson stayed in Monticello for six weeks, until Washington asked all his associates to gather in Germantown. Jefferson settled the Department of State in a tavern in the town of King of Prussia; Thomas Lapsley, a messenger, was his only staff member. For several weeks Jefferson was the sole executive continuously present at the seat of government. Then, Chief Clerk George Taylor brought his family back to Philadelphia and, with a few clerks, reestablished the department in a freshly whitewashed office.

Britain arranged a truce between Portugal and Algiers. Guarding the Straits of Gibraltar, Portugal had kept the pirates bottled up in the Mediterranean. The truce freed the pirates to prey once again on U.S. shipping in the Atlantic.

Opposed to Washington's neutrality policy, Jefferson resigned as Secretary of State at the end of 1793 and retired to Monticello. As his successor, Washington wanted Madison, but he declined the post. He had just, at the age of forty-five, married Dolley Payne Todd. Finally, Edmund Randolph, former governor of Virginia and U.S. attorney general, became Washington's reluctant choice as Secretary. Monroe's biographer, historian Harry Ammon, criticized Randolph, "Whatever logical powers Randolph had previously shown at the bar, they were singularly absent during his tenure in the State Department."

By now, Americans were divided politically into factions or parties: the Federalists pro-British and the Republicans pro-French. The Republicans demanded an embargo on commerce with Great Britain until it paid indemnities for carrying off American slaves at the end of the Revolution and until it surrendered the military posts in the northwest. The Federalists sent Chief Justice John Jay as minister extraordinary to Great Britain. And the embargo was defeated when Vice President John Adams broke a tie in the Senate.

On May 26, 1794, President Washington replaced Federalist Gouverneur

Morris as minister to France with Republican James Monroe. Monroe had expected Aaron Burr to receive the assignment and was astonished when it was offered to him.

Monroe arrived in Paris in August, just days after the execution of Robespierre, the leader of the Terror. At Burr's request, he brought along Burr's stepson, John B. Prevost, as his secretary. Also aboard the ship was Jefferson's wife's young nephew, Fulwar Skipwith, who was to serve as the secretary of legation.

In Paris, Monroe was received with enthusiasm by the seven-hundred-member National Convention. (The convention voted to display an American flag next to France's, and Monroe purchased a silk flag with his own money.) The Federalists were upset by the warm reception Monroe received; in London Jay said angrily that it jeopardized his mission.

Monroe was forbidden to negotiate any trade agreement, but he reported fully on political and economic conditions in France. He presented the French government with a list of grievances, especially the seizure of American cargoes contrary to the Treaty of 1778. He was able to gain the release of all Americans still in French prisons. And he helped to get Lafayette's wife out of prison. Monroe's wife, Elizabeth, drove to the prison and asked to see her. Madame Lafayette was brought to the iron gate, where she pleaded for help; her mother and grandmother had just been taken from the same prison and beheaded. The dramatic meeting upset the French public, and she was released. Monroe obtained a passport so she could join her husband in prison at Olmütz in Austria.

That summer, Monroe bought an elegant residence with formal gardens known as the Folie de la Bourexire, in rue de Clichy. There, the Monroes entertained French officials and visiting Americans, as well as English radicals and Irish revolutionaries. Monroe helped restore French appreciation of the United States, but the Jay Treaty with Great Britain would soon destroy it.

7

"To Prepare for War Will Be Wise"

1793–1811

Thomas Pinckney, the U.S. minister in London, discovered toward the end of December 1793 that the British had adopted two Orders-in-Council damaging to the United States. The first order, issued in secret on November 6, directed British naval captains to seize and bring into port all neutral vessels carrying corn, flour, or meal to France. The second ordered the seizure of all ships carrying goods made in a French colony. As a result, more than a hundred and fifty American ships were taken in the Caribbean. And at the same time, in the northwest country, British officials were prodding the Indian nations to fight the American settlers.

Now, barely seventeen years after independence, the leaders of the young nation were demanding that Great Britain treat the United States with respect. Congress decreed a thirty-day general embargo, ordered six frigates built, and added 25,000 troops to the 3,861-man army.

In March, the Order-in-Council of November 6 was revoked, and President Washington tried to avoid war by sending an envoy to London. Alexander Hamilton, his first choice, declined and recommended Chief Justice John Jay. The Republicans, led by Aaron Burr, vigorously opposed Jay, but Washington and Jay met on the morning of April 15 and talked for hours. Jay agreed to undertake the mission.

Secretary of State Randolph, following advice from Hamilton, drew up Jay's instructions: He should not negotiate either a treaty that conflicted with the United States' treaty with France or a treaty that failed to give American ships access to the British West Indies. All else was discretionary. Jay himself desired, above all, to avoid a war.

Jay sailed from New York on May 12 to the cheers of a sizable crowd. At Falmouth, England, on June 8, Robert Were Fox, the American consul there, was at the dock to welcome him. In London, Jay met with Lord Grenville, the secretary of state for foreign affairs, with whom he was to negotiate. Grenville was preoccupied with defeating France.

He and Jay agreed to keep no record of their talks. Jay brought his complaints to the table, and Grenville promised to deal with them sympathetically, while Jay, sensitive to British pride, spoke with deference. His cordiality, his pro-British feelings, and his wish for conciliation did not make him a tough negotiator.

They talked through most of the summer. Jay's list of issues included the capturing of American ships, the impressments of seamen, violations of the Treaty of 1783, and the carrying off of American slaves. (Jay "quietly rejoiced that the negroes had been given their freedom.") In early August, Grenville asked him for proposals for a treaty.

By September 18, Jay wrote Secretary Randolph advising patience. He added, with cautious wisdom, "To continue to prepare for War will be wise. To avoid unnecessary Asperities and Indications of ill-will, would be equally so."

Throughout the fall, Jay retreated, step by step. In the end, he did not win on many points, but he kept the peace, and on November 19 signed a treaty of amity, commerce, and navigation. John Quincy Adams, whom Washington had appointed minister resident to the Netherlands, examined the treaty before Jay signed it, and Adams declared it preferable to war. With an unusual spark, Jay wrote Grenville, "To use an Indian figure, may the hatchet henceforth be buried for ever, and with it all the animosities which sharpened, and which threatened to redden it."

Under the treaty, Britain agreed to vacate the western forts and remove its troops from American soil by June 1796, and the United States repudiated Secretary of State Jefferson's effort to impose discriminatory duties on Britain. The British were assured that they could trap and trade in the Northwest Territory. The United States would compensate British creditors for prerevolutionary claims, most of which were owed by Virginia planters. Jay also obtained the right for American ships of less than seventy tons to trade with the British West Indies. (The treaty's British opponents felt that this last provision was the most injurious.)

Jay was immediately (and eternally) criticized; many Americans believed he had paid too high a price. But the Jay Treaty avoided war while the United States was young and weak.

The British neither made trade concessions nor recognized American principles of neutral rights. British ports were not opened to American commerce. The issues of the impressment of American seamen and the seizure of American slaves during the American Revolution were not resolved. (It was estimated that the British had taken more than 3,500 slaves.) And the treaty was ambiguous on the principle that "free ships make free goods." But Jay assured the President it was all he could wrangle out of the British.

When Jay arrived back in New York on May 28, 1795, having been away more than a year, the treaty's provisions were kept secret from the American public. Over time, they leaked into the newspapers and started a heated political dispute. Partisan critics asserted that the Jay Treaty tied the future of the United States to England, not France, to imperialism, not revolution. Burr even moved to renegotiate it. Jefferson called it a shameful surrender to the British and a "monument of folly or venality." Alexander Hamilton led the treaty's defenders. The debate turned vicious, and the Senate approved it on strict party lines.

President Washington finally signed the Jay Treaty on August 14, although even some Federalists admitted it was disappointing. When finally published, it created a terrible commotion. Jay had just been inaugurated as governor of New York State, but mass meetings and riots took place in Boston and New York. In some towns, Jay was hung in effigy.

The French, of course, also found the treaty threatening. James Monroe, the U.S. minister to France, castigated both it and the President. The French retaliated by placing commercial restrictions on the United States, and the French Foreign Office even suggested that the treaty annulled the treaty of alliance between France and the United States.

In truth, the treaty was a victory for mercantile America—America's merchants and bankers who desired to avoid a war with Britain and to make America's future dependent on British naval power. And as another historic effect, the removal of British troops from the northwest frontier opened the Mississippi Valley and the West to a vast American expansion.

Then, in October 1795, Thomas Pinckney, the minister to Britain and, briefly, to Spain, completed the negotiation of the Treaty of San Lorenzo (or Pinckney's Treaty). Under it, Spain agreed to the southern boundary of the United States at the 31st parallel and free navigation of the Mississippi with the vital "right of deposit" (that is, the right to warehouse goods barged down the river until the oceangoing ships arrived) at New Orleans. Some of the pressing problems of America's early foreign relations were solved.

"INSULTS AND INJURIES" FROM FRANCE AND BRITAIN

A British warship captured a French ship carrying dispatches from Joseph Fauchet, the French minister to the United States. One of the documents implied that Secretary of State Randolph had requested money from Fauchet. In August 1795, Washington confronted Randolph in the presence of his cabinet with the suspicion of treason. Randolph protested and resigned.

Secretary of War Timothy Pickering, a stern, thin-lipped ultra-Federalist, replaced Randolph as Secretary of State. Pickering dumped Monroe as minister to France; and upon his return to Philadelphia the following year, Monroe angrily demanded an explanation. But Pickering claimed that an official explanation was improper. This led to it becoming de rigueur for U.S. diplomats to be changed when administrations changed.

Charles Cotesworth Pinckney, an aristocratic older brother of Thomas, was named to replace Monroe, but the French refused to receive him. Responding to the Jay Treaty, French warships seized American ships that carried British goods or touched at a British port. The United States did not have the strength to stop them, and the rumble of war could be heard.

George Washington had announced, in his Farewell Address, that he would retire after his second term, and the United States' first contested (and abusive) election campaign in 1796 made John Adams President and Jefferson, from the opposing party, his Vice President.

President Adams sent his thirty-two-year-old son, John Quincy Adams, in the fall of 1797 as the United States' first minister to the Prussian court in remote Berlin. The austere young man obeyed the President's orders, but he found little to do in Berlin.

President Adams reacted slowly to the looming crisis with France. He insisted that the United States as a neutral could trade with whomever it wished, and he offered France the same commercial advantages given Britain. He sent to Paris a team of Charles Pinckney, of South Carolina; Elbridge Gerry, of Massachusetts; and John Marshall, of Virginia. And Congress strengthened the army and navy. But in the spring of 1797, Vice President Jefferson wrote Gerry, "The insults and injuries committed on us by both the belligerent parties, from the beginning of 1793 to this day, and still continuing, cannot now be wiped off by engaging in war with one of them."

XYZ AND ALIEN-SEDITION LAWS

On March 4, 1798, shocking news arrived from Adams' envoys to Paris. Secretary Pickering read their first message and, angry and bristling for a fight, carried it himself from the Department of State, now at Fifth and Chestnut streets, to the President's House. The new foreign minister, Charles Maurice de Talleyrand-Périgord, had refused to negotiate with the American diplomats, and four French secret agents had approached them for large bribes in order to begin discussions.

Pickering was indignant. Congress demanded to know everything the envoys had communicated. Adams told what he knew, but identified the four French agents only as W, X, Y, and Z. Public reaction to this "XYZ Affair" was outrage.

In June, John Marshall, the first of the commissioners to return, was met outside Philadelphia by the Secretary of State and three corps of cavalry and escorted into town. Marshall counseled caution with France, but Federalists were determined to keep the pot boiling.

The French Directory decreed that neutral ships carrying British goods should be seized; free ships did not make free goods. French warships seized American merchantmen off New York harbor. President Adams told Congress that the nation should prepare to defend itself, and he donned a military uniform with a sword at his side. Suddenly, the President saw himself as a warrior.

Congress authorized building twelve new frigates, fortifying harbors, and mustering an army of ten thousand, and it canceled commercial ties with France. George Washington was persuaded to be the "Commander in Chief of all the Armies raised" for this undeclared war.

The country became hysterical with war fever aimed against France. The Federalist-controlled Congress passed the restrictive Alien and Sedition laws, which silenced dissent. President Adams did not object, and the Secretary of State led the hunt for seditionists. Pickering prepared massive deportations of aliens; many French citizens simply left the country. Five of the six leading Republican newspapers were indicted.

Madison and Jefferson answered the hysteria by surreptitiously preparing the Virginia and Kentucky Resolutions. These asserted that the states had delegated to the central government certain definite powers and had the right to nullify federal laws that exceeded those limits. Jefferson's assertion that the states could "nullify" federal acts anticipated one basis of the Confederacy's ideology half a century later.

But when Elbridge Gerry returned from Paris in October 1798, he reported that the French did not want war. The specter of the "Quasi-War" with France faded.

After the XYZ insult, Adams insisted on assurances that a U.S. minister to France would be treated with respect. Six months later, Adams accepted assurances from Talleyrand-Périgord, and on his son's advice, chose William Vans Murray, a young congressman from Maryland who was the minister at The Hague and a longtime friend of the Adams family. The Federalists supported young Murray and agreed to send Chief Justice Oliver Ellsworth and William Davie, the Federalist governor of North Carolina, as a commission to France.

Secretary of State Pickering, speaking for Hamilton and clearly disloyal to Adams, tried to delay the departure of Ellsworth and Davie. Adams postponed their sailing. The President and Hamilton engaged in a highly charged argument over the commission, which Hamilton's biographer Ron Chernow called "a total loss of perspective by Hamilton, the nadir of his judgment."

In the end, the envoys shipped out of Newport, Rhode Island, in November 1799. When they landed at Lisbon, they learned that Napoleon Bonaparte had come to power in France as First Consul. They reached Paris on March 2, 1800; the winter journey had taken them a wearying four months.

Slowly and reluctantly, the President became aware of his Secretary of State's double-dealing. Adams condemned Pickering for duplicity, but when he asked for Pickering's resignation, he refused. Within the hour, Adams fired him and replaced him as Secretary of State with Congressman John Marshall.

THE MOVE TO FOGGY BOTTOM

During the summer of 1800, the government moved to the banks of the Potomac River. The new Federal District was raw and unfinished; the states of Virginia and Maryland had given over lowlands known as Foggy Bottom. Eventually, that name attached itself to the Department of State, sometimes out of fondness but more often out of ridicule. The department shared the neighborhood with immigrants who lived close to the gasworks and the Old Heurich Brewery.

The department could not put down roots; it soon moved to Pennsylvania Avenue and Twentieth Street. From May 1801 until 1820 it was housed in the War Office in Seventeenth Street, and afterward, until 1866, in the north wing of the Treasury Department building at Pennsylvania Avenue and Fifteenth Street. And then it was moved again to the Washington City Orphan Asylum at Fourteenth and S Streets, where it remained until 1895.

The mission of Adams' envoys to France still had to be resolved. When Ellsworth and Davie joined Murray in Paris in March 1800, they were promptly received by First Consul Napoleon Bonaparte at the Tuileries Palace. But it was October 3 before the Convention of Peace, Commerce and Navigation was signed. The event was celebrated with a state dinner attended by eight hundred dignitaries and friends of the First Consul.

President Adams read of the treaty in a newspaper. He welcomed the diplomatic solution, which confirmed peace and recognized Americans' right to trade with belligerents in noncontraband articles. Most important, it ended the unofficial war with France. It was the proudest act of Adams' life.

On January 23, 1801, the Senate voted on ratification, but its vote of 16 to 14 fell four short of the number needed. The shortfall resulted from the treaty's failure to provide indemnification for American property seized by the French during the Quasi-War. Then, having second thoughts, the Federalists reconsidered the treaty, and the Senate passed it with reservations, 22 to 9.

Adams nominated James A. Bayard, a Federalist senator from Delaware, as minister plenipotentiary to France to complete the negotiations that the imperfect ratification had made necessary. In its final form, the treaty ended the alliance of 1778 and excused France from paying indemnities. Adams had forestalled a war with France, but he could not head off a war with Great Britain, which continued to impress American seamen and attempted to crush American trade with the world.

When Republicans Jefferson and Burr defeated Adams for reelection in 1800, it was the first successful revolt against the bloc that had held power since the Revolution. Jefferson and Burr won an identical number of electoral votes, and the House of Representatives required thirty-six ballots over six days before it awarded the presidency to Jefferson and the vice presidency to Burr. A disappointed, sullen John Adams turned over the President's House to Jefferson. On March 4, 1801, Adams left for Quincy, Massachusetts, by public stage before dawn to avoid riding in the inauguration with his former friend. It was the era's bitter end.

BARGAINING FOR LOUISIANA

Jefferson chose his confidant, James Madison, to be his Secretary of State. Charles Pinckney, who had delivered every electoral vote in South Carolina for the Republicans, was rewarded with the diplomatic post in Madrid. As minister plenipotentiary in Paris, the President named former Secretary of Foreign Affairs Robert R. Livingston. The wealthy New Yorker had never been to Europe, and when he finally sailed for France in October, he was accompanied by his wife, two daughters, and their husbands, personal servants, and Thomas Sumter, a pompous young man who was to be his secretary of legation. He also shipped over a variety of livestock and a handsome carriage lashed to the quarterdeck. Off Belle Isle, their ship *Boston* was almost driven onto the rocks by a fierce storm.

Lafayette welcomed Livingston to Paris. And the American then paid a visit to the foreign minister, Charles Maurice de Talleyrand-Périgord, and was formally presented to Bonaparte. Talleyrand was a short man, impassive, with a decided limp; he was shamelessly corrupt. He had spent two years in exile in the United States and disliked Americans. The dislike was mutual.

The American writer Joel Barlow introduced Livingston to inventor Robert Fulton, who had been experimenting with a submarine. Fulton built, and Livingston financed, their first boat, which broke in two and sank in the Seine. Eventually, their steamboat made its maiden voyage triumphantly up the Hudson River.

As Livingston settled into the legation in rue Trudon, he was charged to settle the status of Louisiana and West Florida. President Jefferson had his minister notify the French, in the least offensive way possible, that France's ambition for New Orleans could precipitate a partnership between the United States and Great Britain.

Rufus King, the minister to the Court of St. James's, determined that Louisiana had already been transferred secretly from Spain to France in 1800 by the Treaty of St. Idlefonso. But Talleyrand would not even admit that such a treaty existed.

Livingston had instructions to persuade France to leave the mouth of the Mississippi. Livingston tried to skirt the duplicitous Talleyrand, approaching Napoleon through his older brother, Joseph. Livingston argued that Louisiana would drain France financially for years to come, but that if the United States were to acquire Louisiana, France would gain all the advantages of possessing New Orleans without the expense of maintaining it.

As a consequence of this maneuvering, and to prove his commitment to the American settlers in the west, President Jefferson sent James Monroe, the retiring governor of Virginia, to France in 1803 as a special envoy to work with Livingston. Congress appropriated $2 million ($40 million in 2010 dollars) for the purchase of Louisiana, and Monroe was authorized to spend a total of 50 million francs (more than $9 million—$180 million in modern dollars).

After Mass on Easter Sunday, April 10, 1803, Napoleon summoned his ministers to Saint-Cloud outside Paris and told them that war was imminent. He expected that the British would seize Louisiana. He knew the Americans wanted only New Orleans, but it would be wiser if he sold them all of Louisiana.

The next day, the day before Monroe arrived in Paris, Talleyrand summoned Livingston and asked him whether the United States would purchase all of Louisiana. Livingston replied that the United States was only interested in New Orleans and Florida. Talleyrand asserted that Louisiana was valueless to France without New Orleans and pressed Livingston to make an offer. Livingston wanted to complete an agreement before Monroe arrived. But when Livingston returned on Tuesday, Talleyrand suddenly turned evasive.

Monroe and Livingston sat down to dinner on Monroe's first day in Paris, and they saw, walking in the U.S. legation garden, the French minister of finance, François de Barbé-Marbois, a longtime friend of both Americans from the days when Barbé-Marbois had been the secretary of the French legation in Philadelphia. Livingston invited him to have coffee. But Livingston and Barbé-Marbois had no opportunity to talk privately. So Barbé-Marbois suggested that after his guests left, Livingston visit him.

When Livingston did so, Barbé-Marbois told him that, if the Americans would assume all claims against France, Napoleon would sell them all of Louisiana for 125 million francs, the equivalent of $22.5 million (nearly $450 million in modern dollars). Barbé-Marbois was negotiating. Napoleon had already indicated to him that half that amount would be acceptable.

Livingston was shocked by the price and insisted that the United States was not interested in the western side of the Mississippi. When Barbé-Marbois indicated he would accept 60 million francs, plus 20 million in American claims, Livingston replied that it was more than his country could pay. At midnight, the two men parted.

Livingston sent a dispatch to Secretary of State Madison, urging the purchase of Louisiana and suggesting that the United States could always sell off the land west of the river to a European power. At the same time, Fulwar Skipwith, now the consul general, told Monroe that Livingston was trying to turn everything to his own credit. Monroe complained to Secretary Madison about Livingston. Each man was out to seize credit for himself.

After some jockeying, the two Americans agreed that they would purchase all of Louisiana. The French held firm at their price and demanded that the United States pay at once. Since this exceeded the United States' resources, they decided that stock, which France could sell on the open market, would be issued at 6 percent interest, giving Dutch and British bankers a handsome profit.

By April 29, 1803, Livingston, Monroe, and Barbé-Marbois agreed on 80 million francs ($11,250,000 for Louisiana and $3,750,000 for the American claims). The treaty for Louisiana was signed on May 2, and on December 20 the U.S. Army raised the Stars and Stripes over New Orleans. The fate of West Florida would be settled with Spain sixteen years later.

On New Year's Day 1804, Livingston asked Madison to relieve him; he was replaced with his brother-in-law, the pugnacious General John Armstrong. He had left Princeton to fight in the Revolution and, by marrying Livingston's sister, had become a landowner and a U.S. senator.

The Louisiana Purchase raised several major issues that affected the United States' future. Jefferson's executive action, by a President who was a protector of states' rights, strengthened Federal jurisdiction over the expansion westward and opened the question whether the newly acquired western territories were to be slave states or free states. And there was also the question of what the Americans had bought. They had certainly bought the west bank of the Mississippi, from Lake of the Woods to New Orleans. But what beyond that?

Most disruptive was the dispute over Spain's claims to Florida. President Madison wanted all of Florida, if he could get it without pushing Spain into a war. What then occurred has been called "an embarrassing and shameful moment" in early American history. Madison and the State Department sent George Mathews, a former governor of Georgia, to incite the residents of East Florida to revolt against Spain and join the United States. In March 1812, Mathews led a small force of Spaniards and Georgia volunteers to take East Florida, which they would not return to Spain. The United States was now matched not against the power of Spain, but against a handful of local settlers.

Completing his tenure in Paris in June 1803, Monroe replaced Rufus King as minister to the Court of St. James's. George III received him with great courtesy. But Monroe found Britain's ruling classes still resented America as too democratic and too pro-French.

He made a side trip to Paris to try to win Talleyrand support for the United States' annexation of West Florida, but Talleyrand stonewalled him. Monroe wrote caustically in his journal, "The respect which one power has for another is in exact proportion of the means which they respectively have of injuring each other with the least detriment to themselves."

Monroe and John Armstrong, now the American minister in Paris, were both convinced that the United States would have to take Florida by force. On New Year's Day 1805, Monroe visited Madrid to begin negotiations; but in the midst of these talks, Talleyrand suddenly denied that West Florida had ever been a part of Louisiana.

Monroe accused Livingston of encouraging Napoleon to expect that the United States would pay handsomely for Florida. But in October, Armstrong reported that France was willing to accept the acquisition of Florida by the United States if Spain were paid $7 million.

On July 23, 1805, when Monroe was back at his post in London, a British Admiralty Court decided that cargo carried in neutral (American) ships between an enemy and her colonies was subject to seizure. Monroe protested that this ruling threatened a significant part of U.S. commerce. He waited two months for a reply while the British seized more than fifty American ships. Only with the death of Prime Minister William Pitt the following January did a reform government in Britain relax the policy under which the American ships were being seized.

Now, impressment became the paramount issue. The key problem was that the British did not accept the idea that a person born in Britain could become a naturalized American citizen. Also, the British Navy needed thousands of new sailors each year to man its huge fleet.

Congress sent over as a special envoy to London William Pinkney, a brilliant Baltimore lawyer who had served eight years in London on a Jay Treaty commission. On May 17, 1806, Secretary Madison proposed to Monroe that, in exchange for curtailing impressment, the United States return all Royal Navy deserters. Negotiations were almost scotched when Napoleon imposed the Berlin Decree, which created a blockade of the British Isles, and the British demanded that the United States resist the French decree.

Then came a naval crisis. Men of HMS *Leopard* boarded the frigate USS *Chesapeake* off Norfolk, Virginia, in order to seize three British deserters believed to be aboard. Three Americans were killed and eighteen wounded. Monroe received instructions for the British to send an apology and reparations, as well as a promise to end impressment. The crisis was resolved when the British sent an emissary to Washington to settle the matter.

Monroe went home to oppose Secretary Madison for the nomination for the presidency. Madison, a master of parliamentary maneuvering, won easily. Historian Joseph Ellis wrote, "Madison seldom left footprints."

President Jefferson named the former navy secretary Robert Smith as Secretary of State. Smith proved to be incompetent. Monroe had served for only three months as governor of Virginia when, on March 14, 1811, Madison chose him to replace Smith as Secretary of State.

Monroe's appointment made certain that the difficulties with Britain would be resolved. He pressed France to stop seizing American ships and to open its ports to American ships. Madison restored nonintercourse with Great Britain. He did so because Napoleon's foreign minister, the duc de Cadore, had handed John Armstrong, the American minister in Paris, a letter that Armstrong believed indicated that the Berlin and Milan Decrees were no longer applicable to American ships. But Armstrong had not read the letter carefully. He overlooked the condition that lifting the decrees depended on Britain's taking similar steps. Madison gambled that Britain would use Cadore's letter to relax the Orders-in-Council. But the French still seized American ships, and Madison's gamble led directly to the War of 1812.

As soon as he was in office, Monroe asked Jonathan Russell, the American chargé in Paris, to seek a clarification of the Cadore letter. When Russell was unable to do so, Monroe called in the young French minister in Washington, Louis Serurier, to ask why Americans were still being restricted. The United States was embarrassed, Monroe said coldly. His bluntness shocked the French diplomat, who reacted by complaining that no American minister had been assigned to Paris. Joel Barlow had been appointed but had not been allowed to assume his post.

A new British minister, Augustus J. Foster, arrived in Washington with instructions to settle the *Chesapeake* incident. He recognized the need to repeal the Order-in-Council, but he underestimated Madison's willingness to go to war if American demands were ignored.

Instead of trying quietly to settle the *Chesapeake* affair, Foster went on the attack, demanding an explanation for why Commodore John Rodgers had recently disabled the British sloop *Little Belt,* killing ten sailors aboard her. Monroe asked Foster how he expected to seek satisfaction in this matter when he had not settled the earlier *Chesapeake* incident.

Serurier warned his government that a break seemed likely. But tension eased when France released the American ships that it had held since November 1, 1810, the date of Madison's proclamation. The American government accepted this compromise as sufficient to permit Joel Barlow to begin his tour in Paris.

The President and Secretary of State, squeezed between the conflicting interests of the two Great Powers, drove to their homes in Virginia for the summer.

8

Drive for Identity and Respect

1811–23

Т he diplomat and poet Joel Barlow; his wife, Ruth; her half sister, Clara; and his nephew Thomas, who had left Yale to accompany him, sailed from Annapolis on August 1, 1811, aboard USS *Constitution*, commanded by Captain Isaac Hull, whose fame was then still in the future. Barlow was on his way to Paris to negotiate compensation for the French seizure of American ships and to arrange for American ships to enter French ports. Secretary of State James Monroe instructed Barlow regarding France, "If she wishes to profit of neutral commerce she must become the advocate of neutral rights, as well by her practice as her theory."

Locked in a major struggle, France and England had each declared the other's ports closed to neutral vessels. The United States treaty with France prohibited such restrictions, but Napoleon ignored this fine point. The still-immature United States toyed with the fantasy of going to war against both England and France.

Barlow was chosen to change Napoleon's mind because he had served in France; he knew the people and the language and had written a history of the French Revolution. He was one of the handful of Americans to whom revolutionary France had granted the honor of citizenship.

In Paris, Barlow presented his credentials to the duc de Bassano, now the French foreign minister. His timing was terrible. Although Barlow managed to have two meetings with Napoleon, the emperor was preoccupied with mounting a million-man army to invade Russia. Barlow's negotiations stretched out interminably. He did arrange for the French to release American ships they were holding, but he was unable to bring the emperor and his ministers to sign a treaty. He wrote Secretary Monroe that he thought Napoleon had no intention of keeping his promises. Then, the French seized seventeen more American ships, and Monroe told Barlow only the hope that he could negotiate a treaty stopped Congress from declaring war.

TRAGEDY AT ZARNOWIEC

After a year of delays, on October 11, 1812, the duc de Bassano wrote Barlow from Wilna, the ancient capital of Lithuania, stating that if he would come there, they could complete the arrangement Barlow desired. On the twenty-fifth Barlow replied that he would leave Paris the next day.

The journey was horrendous. Young Thomas accompanied his uncle, who taught him German along the journey. Also with them went Jean Baptiste Petry from the French foreign ministry. Their coach drawn by six horses took them through Frankfurt am Main, the battlefield at Jena, and Berlin and Königsberg. Often, they did not stop until after midnight and started again at daybreak. The roads were rutted, the mud deep, the rains incessant. They passed hundreds of wagons loaded with wounded and invalided French soldiers slogging back from the war, as Joel Barlow wrote, "covered with glory, rags and mud."

They needed three weeks to reach Wilna. The warring armies had devastated the countryside. It snowed, and the ground and rivers froze. Along the road they saw countless dead horses and dying and dead soldiers. Half-naked, half-frozen, the soldiers begged to be taken into shelter to die.

In Wilna, Barlow learned that Napoleon had retreated from Moscow and would make Wilna his winter headquarters. Barlow wrote on November 22, "The Russians have an army on each side of him, and are trying to cut off his retreat."

A half-frozen French courier arrived on December 4, with news that Napoleon's army was in full flight. The emperor was being driven in a closed carriage on sleigh runners, surrounded by a square battalion protecting him on all sides from attacks by Cossack horsemen. Discussion of a treaty was impossible.

The next morning, Barlow and his party left Wilna in haste. The emperor passed them on the road. They traveled day and night; the temperature at night fell to twelve degrees below zero Fahrenheit. They covered a hundred and fifty miles; the bridge at Grodno had been smashed, and they had to cross on the ice. It snowed heavily; they had no place to rest.

The fierce cold persisted, and on the seventeenth they reached Warsaw. Their exhausted horses did not have the strength to draw them out of town again, so the governor gave them six artillery horses. They slipped out of Warsaw at 4:00 A.M. and followed the Vistula River valley.

Inside the carriage, the cold was bone-shaking. Barlow became ill; and beyond Krakow, in the little Jewish village of Zarnowiec on the Pilica River, they had to stop and seek medical help. Petry found them refuge with the mayor's family. A doctor was summoned from a neighboring town. But it was too late. Barlow had developed pneumonia. He died at Zarnowiec. He was fifty-eight.

Thomas wanted to bring his uncle's body home. But the Cossacks held all the surrounding country and were killing whomever they caught. They buried Barlow in a nearby churchyard and fled. The Americans in Paris held a memorial service, and on March 9 the *Hartford Courant* reported Barlow's death in the United States.

His unexpected death had a bureaucratic epilogue. He had failed to designate Thomas as secretary of legation, which would have entitled him to succeed Barlow. A brouhaha ensued.

Thomas Barlow made an insistent claim, but the consul resident in Paris, David Bailie Warden, declared himself the consul general and demanded that the French foreign ministry deal only with him. William Lee, the consul in Bordeaux, said he had served for months as Barlow's secretary of legation. Isaac Cox Barnet, the consul for Le Havre with his office in Paris, asserted he was the senior American in length of service. And Barlow's widow asserted she would hold all official correspondence until she heard from Washington.

In the confusion, the French decided to work only with Warden until William H. Crawford, a former senator from Georgia, arrived as minister. Crawford promptly dismissed Warden and gave the consulate to Barnet. It did not matter much, but it demonstrated the strains that could develop in a young foreign service that lacked rules and traditions.

"RESOLVED NO LONGER TO SUBMIT"

In August 1811, while Joel Barlow was on the Atlantic sailing for France, Secretary James Monroe had ridden the eighty miles from Oak Hill near Leesburg, Virginia, to Montpelier, near Charlottesville, to confer with President Madison. They discussed the British seizure of American ships and impressment of seamen and the possibility of going to war with Britain.

In October, British Minister Foster pressed Monroe to settle the *Chesapeake* affair, but the Americans demanded a general settlement. President Madison asked Congress to raise a military force and enlarge the Navy. Secretary Monroe told the House Committee on Foreign Affairs that President Madison favored a declaration of war in the spring if Britain had not conceded by then. The Madison administration felt it had to show the British government that the young, frail United States would stand up for its rights. At the same time, the Federalists were assuring Foster that in the next election the belligerent Republicans would be overthrown. Foster advised London to keep the Orders-in-Council in effect.

His government told Foster to inform the United States that the orders would not be repealed unless the United States could produce a copy of the document revoking the French decree. Monroe was indignant: He had already proclaimed the French decrees repealed. There was nothing more to discuss.

Then, French frigates destroyed two American ships carrying grain to Wellington's army. Monroe berated Louis Serurier, the French minister in Washington, who argued that the American ships had been doing something forbidden by American law. Monroe replied that was irrelevant; they were neutral ships carrying noncontraband.

On April 1, 1812, President Madison asked Congress for a sixty-day embargo against Britain. And Monroe told the press that the embargo showed that the nation was "resolved no longer to submit to the oppression and degradation which heretofore been inflicted on us." He assured the American people that Britain was too busy fighting France to attack the United States. Jonathan Russell, then the chargé in London, reported that Viscount Castlereagh, who now headed the Foreign Office, was not likely to change British policy. Foster even brought a conciliatory proposal from Castlereagh: If the United States suspended nonintercourse,

Britain would stop requiring American ships in the Continental trade to be licensed. His proposal was rejected.

Despite Britain's mollification, anti-French sentiment spread in the United States until Napoleon formally repealed the restrictive edict. His Decree of Saint-Cloud was supposed to provide the justification that the British government needed to repeal the Orders-in-Council. But the French continued to seize American ships, and the British refused to stop impressment. Nothing had been solved.

WAR WITH GREAT BRITAIN

Knowing Great Britain had its hands full with Napoleon, the Americans felt they could talk tough. President Madison delivered a war message to Congress on June 1, and the House promptly declared war, 79 to 49. The Senate needed until June 17 to agree, 19 to 13. And, amazingly, the Senate defeated a declaration of war against France by only two votes. Americans would have been less bellicose if the Europeans had not been busy warring with each other.

Foster, trying to delay war with the United States, asked Monroe to suspend hostilities until the news reached England. Indignantly, Madison rejected the idea, but he invited Foster to tea at the end of their final meeting. The British minister cheerfully accepted.

On June 23, the British cabinet belatedly repealed the detested Orders-in-Council. But the British navy still refused to abandon impressment.

Once war was declared, Secretary Monroe, the only cabinet member with military experience, found the State Department too quiet. He had served as an energetic officer at Harlem Heights, been severely wounded at Trenton, and endured the winter at Valley Forge.

Since the Senate felt that too many Virginians were running the country and would not confirm Monroe, Madison appointed him acting secretary of war. The State Department was left in the capable hands of Richard Rush, son of Benjamin Rush, M.D., a respected signer of the Declaration of Independence.

In February, Monroe returned to the State Department, and Madison chose General John Armstrong, Robert Livingston's brother-in-law, to run the War Department. He was a deplorable choice. American and British consuls left for home, although Reuben Beasley, the U.S. agent for seamen, was permitted to stay in London to help with the exchange of prisoners of war. The U.S. consul at Falmouth, Robert Were Fox, was a British subject, and he simply took down the American flag until the fighting was over.

Charles Stuart Kennedy, the historian of American consuls, tells the story of a cargo of codfish aboard the British brig *Maria* that was captured by the U.S. frigate *President* in June 1813 and sent with a prize crew to Bordeaux. Despite the destructive summer heat, French officials would not give William Lee, the American consul there, permission to sell the codfish. The French director of customs insisted that Consul General David Bailie Warden in Paris controlled such sales. The British had offered Irish-born Warden, an advocate of Irish independence, a choice of jail or exile. He had immigrated to the United States and became the private secretary of Armstrong in Paris. After Armstrong left Paris in 1810, William Crawford succeeded him and fired Armstrong. The early foreign service could be chaotic.

EFFORTS TO MAKE PEACE

In the spring of 1813, John Quincy Adams notified Secretary of State Monroe that Czar Alexander I had offered to mediate between Great Britain and the United States. John Quincy Adams was the first American minister in Saint Petersburg. (Levett Harris, of Philadelphia, had been there as consul since 1803.) When Adams had arrived in mid-October 1809, the Neva River was already solid ice; and through the long, brutal winter, Saint Petersburg was isolated until the ice broke up again in early May. He and the young czar became walking companions, using French as a lingua franca. Adams stayed in Saint Petersburg while Napoleon invaded Russia, occupied Moscow, and disastrously retreated.

President Madison accepted the czar's mediation and nominated as peace commissioners Albert Gallatin, the secretary of the Department of Treasury; James A. Bayard, a Federalist; and Adams. The commissioners were told to continue demanding the end of impressment; that was the essential condition. After the commissioners sailed for Europe, the Senate rejected Gallatin by one vote. But in the end Britain refused the mediation, and the commissioners returned home.

Late in December 1813, Secretary Monroe was offered direct negotiations by Viscount Castlereagh. The U.S. government accepted, and this time Congressman Henry Clay and diplomat Jonathan Russell were added to the commission. Gallatin, meanwhile, had resigned from the Treasury Department, which meant his Senate enemies found him acceptable for the commission.

But hopes for an early peace faded when the British defeated and exiled Napoleon in the spring of 1814. Wellington's veterans were then free to sail for America. As a result, the United States softened its demand to end impressments, and Madison was asking that the embargo be canceled except for those parts referring to trading with the enemy.

THE INVASION OF WASHINGTON

On August 16, 1814, a British naval squadron appeared at the mouth of the Potomac, threatening the District of Columbia. Having no intelligence service, Secretary Monroe saddled up his roan horse on the eighteenth and, escorted by a troop of dragoons, rode out to find the enemy.

They spotted the British army marching on Washington, and Monroe continued his surveillance ahead of them. The approach of the veteran Redcoats forced the American army to retreat toward Washington. By Wednesday morning, the twenty-fourth, the British were approaching Bladensburg on the road to the capital. Secretary Monroe, without great skill and any authority, shifted regiments around in defensive positions. President Madison rode out to join the three thousand assorted soldiers awaiting the British invaders.

It was still a time when the President of the United States and his Secretary of State could ride out to war. But they could not prevent the battle at Bladensburg from becoming a disorganized rout. The British marched into the capital and sacked and burned all public property, and a lot more. Soldiers of the British 1st Brigade blew up the brick building that housed the State, War, and Navy departments.

Just in time, State Department clerks Stephen Pleasanton, John Graham, and Josias W. King stuffed the Declaration of Independence, the Constitution, the papers of the revolutionary government, and other treasures into linen sacks, loaded them on carts, and hid them in a deserted gristmill two miles above Georgetown. They were later moved another thirty-five miles to Leesburg. Monroe told Congress that "many of the books belonging to the library of the Department . . . were unavoidably left, and shared the fate, it is presumed, of the building in which they were deposited." Joel Barlow's widow cleverly stored her furniture with the French minister, who had diplomatic immunity.

Government officials scattered, and not until Saturday the twenty-seventh was Secretary Monroe able to suggest to the President that they return to the capital. Late that afternoon they rode back into the scorched city. Looters had taken over. The only public building saved was the combined post office and patent office. Dr. William Thornton, the State Department clerk in charge of patents, had convinced the British that the patent models were private property.

The next day, with Secretary of War Armstrong still in Frederick, Maryland, Madison asked Monroe to take command of the capital's defenses. Some officials wanted to surrender the city; but Monroe, determined, said he would bayonet anyone seen giving in to the enemy.

Much of the blame for the disaster in Washington was placed on Secretary Armstrong. Fortunately, he resigned in a huff, and President Madison renamed Monroe acting secretary of war. Monroe pressed the President until, in September, the Senate confirmed him. He helped assemble men and supplies to defend Baltimore and also continued as acting Secretary of State.

The "insult" of the "Bladensburg Races" and the trashing of the nation's capital rallied Americans. Volunteers dug entrenchments, and when the British landed at North Point, Fort McHenry stopped their attack on Baltimore. Two days later, the death of the British ground forces commander marked the end to the fighting at Baltimore. The British army went on to New Orleans.

The burning of Washington hardened the British, but their failure to take Baltimore and their defeats at Plattsburgh, New York, and on Lake Champlain turned the tables again. Back home, the British were not proud of the destruction wrought in Washington, and this war across the Atlantic seemed costly and endless. The British government offered the command in America to the Duke of Wellington, who declined and sensibly recommended making peace.

By now, British and American negotiators were meeting at Ghent. The American delegation was led by John Quincy Adams, who left Consul Levett Harris in charge in Saint Petersburg. Just before Christmas, the two sides in Ghent agreed on a draft treaty. On December 24, the U.S. commissioners rode over to Chartreuse, a former monastery, where the British were staying, and, at six o'clock, signed the Treaty of Peace and Amity. It was a simple document: end the war, return all territory except several small islands, restore the Indians to their prewar status, and set up commissions to settle Canadian border questions. The two intense issues that had provoked the war, impressment and restrictions on trade, were totally ignored.

The Treaty of Ghent would not take effect until unconditionally ratified by both parties. For the first time since the rise of Napoleon, Britain was at peace.

But not quite: On December 23, as the peacemakers finished their work in Ghent, the British fleet, with forces led by Major General Sir Edward Pakenham, Wellington's brother-in-law, approached New Orleans. With a victory there, Britain would command the mouth of the Mississippi.

Not knowing peace had already been signed, the British regulars, on New Year's Day 1815, were thrown against Major General Andrew Jackson's men, who were firing from behind a high embankment. The British lost that battle and the war.

Copies of the peace treaty arrived at New York on February 11. The Senate unanimously ratified it on the seventeenth. The next day, church bells rang and cannons boomed across the country. But on the last day of February, Napoleon escaped from Elba. Britain still faced the Hundred Days until Waterloo.

Although the peace treaty had not addressed the Americans' war aims of free trade and the end of impressment, they felt a renewed sense of self-respect. They had stood up to British power; they had fought for their country. Secretary Monroe told the Senate Committee on Military Affairs, "The demonstration is satisfactory that our Union has gained strength, our troops honor, and the nation character, by the contest." The war convinced the Republicans that they needed an army and a navy to support foreign policy. Monroe too now believed in diplomacy based on strength. More cynically, Thomas Jefferson called diplomacy "the workshop in which all the wars of Europe are manufactured."

ANOTHER WAR WITH ALGIERS

Monroe resigned as secretary of war and returned to the Department of State on March 15, 1815. He was succeeded by William Crawford, who had been serving as minister to France since 1813. John Quincy Adams finished his work in Ghent and became the minister to London.

During the war, Omar Bashaw, the dey of Algiers, had expelled the U.S. consul, Tobias Lear. Thus President Madison asked Congress to declare war on Algiers and sent a small squadron commanded by Commodore Stephen Decatur to the Mediterranean. One of Monroe's first jobs as Secretary of State was to draft instructions for the peace commissioners being sent to Algiers, William Shaler, William Bainbridge, and Decatur.

Shaler was the new consul general to the Barbary states. He had served in Havana as the consul and in Louisiana as a secret agent. He had been involved in covert attempts to gain Texas independence from Spain and to establish a U.S. presence in the Floridas and Mexico.

Monroe ordered his peace commissioners to obtain security for American ships and sailors without paying an annual tribute. They were to demand that all American prisoners be released without ransom, that all tribute cease, and that the dey pay ten thousand dollars for having seized an American ship. The dey, faced at last with superior American power, had no choice. Decatur and Shaler reported from USS *Guerriere* in the Bay of Algiers on July 4, 1815, that they had negotiated a treaty with the dey based on Tobias Lear's 1805 treaty with Tripoli.

The following year, the dey of Algiers expelled Consul General Shaler until a British-Dutch fleet bombarded the port and forced the dey to abolish Christian slavery. Shaler returned to Algiers with the U.S. Navy and brought an end, at last, to the Barbary pirates' atrocities. He served in Algiers for twelve years altogether, and in 1833 died in Havana of cholera.

Decatur, his business in Algiers finished, sailed for Tunis and, when he arrived off Cape Carthage, invited the American consul, Mordecai Noah, to his cabin. He handed Noah an official dispatch that he requested Noah read immediately. Noah broke the seal and read the message from Secretary Monroe. It recalled him because he was Jewish. In the dispatch, dated April 15, 1815, Monroe wrote, "At the time of your appointment, as Consul at Tunis, it was not known that the religion which you profess would form any obstacle to the exercise of our Consular functions. Recent information, however on which entire reliance may be placed, proves it would produce a very unfavorable effect. In consequence of which, the President has deemed it expedient to revoke your commission."

Noah was a former Charleston, South Carolina, newspaperman and a friend of Joel Barlow and Robert Morris. He had arrived in Tunis two years earlier just as the prime minister there had his throat slit. Noah had watched from the consulate terrace as the prime minister's mutilated body was dragged through the streets.

Since Decatur did not know the contents of the dispatch, Noah stuffed it in his pocket. Instead, he persuaded Decatur to force the bey of Tunis to pay the United States $46,000. Noah left for home and became a strong political figure and newspaper editor in New York City.

THE LAST OF THE REVOLUTION GENERATION

In 1816, Monroe was the last of the Revolution generation to be elected to the presidency. After considering William Crawford, whom he had defeated for the nomination, Monroe selected John Quincy Adams as his Secretary of State. Crawford became the secretary of the treasury and a major figure in Monroe's administration.

John Quincy Adams took office on September 22, 1817, and the able Richard Rush succeeded him in London. Rush was still the acting Secretary of State when notes were exchanged for the Rush-Bagot Agreement. It limited naval armaments on the Great Lakes to four ships on each side, and they would be used for customs. Both sides continued to maintain forts and garrisons on the shores.

John Quincy Adams turned out to be a superb choice for Secretary of State. The son of a President and member of the moderate wing of the Federalist Party, he had started his diplomatic career as the first U.S. minister to Russia in 1809. He and his family spent nine years abroad; he was present when Napoleon invaded Russia and helped negotiate the end to the War of 1812. He was in Paris in 1815 and served as minister to Britain until he became Secretary of State.

By now, Adams was, like his father, a short, fat, balding man; his manner was cold and reserved, even forbidding. But in small groups, he shined, and he spoke with exceptional clarity and persuasiveness. He respected the President and believed that the function of cabinet officers was to carry out presidential policy.

When Monroe assumed office, the President's House was still unfinished; the stone facing, scorched by the wartime fire, had been painted white, and people began referring to "The White House." Monroe brought back the formality of George Washington's era. He criticized Jefferson's and Madison's informality for lowering the nation in the sight of foreign diplomats. During Monroe's presidency, diplomats saw the President chiefly on state occasions. At a formal reception, the President would stand in the middle of the room next to the Secretary of State. The Secretary presented each new minister to the President; the minister would hand him his letter of credence, which the President would hand to the Secretary without reading it. The President made a set reply to the ministers' remarks; the ceremony was over in ten minutes.

When John Quincy Adams became Secretary, the Department of State numbered fifteen men with salaries totaling $21,160. He found the department inefficient and began to put some additional order into its procedures. He inaugurated the practice of dividing into two parts the instructions to diplomats and consuls going abroad. The first section covered general instructions that were pretty much alike for all. It covered the envoy's work rules and the subjects on which he had to report to the department. The second part was written specifically for the individual, telling him the objectives and issues of his particular mission. Both parts were exhaustive and required careful preparation. Adams also reestablished the State Department library.

Many Americans in the capital frowned on Monroe's European-style formality. But the nation's increasing sophistication, its postwar awareness of the world, and its demographic growth were developments that required change. The President worked out systems for the treatment of cabinet officers and diplomats at formal dinners. He even discussed etiquette with his cabinet members; they did not agree on much. Change was the order of the day, and these efforts were expressions of the drive for national respect.

DIPLOMACY SOUTH OF THE BORDER

The Treaty of Ghent closed the opening diplomatic chapter for the United States, in which it molded a relationship with its former parent. Now that this was pretty much resolved, the United States hungered to expand, in both trade and possessions. And it found that Spain, whose colonies covered most of the Western Hemisphere, blocked its path. The turmoil in Europe, the French Revolution, Great Power conflicts, the Napoleonic wars—all had jarred loose Spain's ties to its colonies. The British helped free the Rio de La Plata in 1806; Mexico won independence in 1821. Soon, Spain's colonial structure was a shambles.

Americans persuaded themselves that the War of 1812 had been a triumph, and they turned an expansive eye southward toward this teetering Spanish empire. Napoleon's defeat brought the Latin American revolutions to the United States' attention. And, in truth, the United States harbored its own acquisitive intentions. It would pull the Floridas, and much else, into its own orbit when it could. Monroe started planning forays to the geographic corners at Galveston and Amelia Island.

First, in 1810, Madison sent William Shaler as a commercial agent to Veracruz, Mexico, where he worked quietly for Mexican independence. Then, Robert K. Lowry was sent to LaGuaira, Venezuela, and Joel R. Poinsett of South Carolina went to the United Provinces of the Rio de La Plata, as Chile, Peru, and Buenos Aires were known. Poinsett informed the revolutionaries that the United States would help, but they would have to keep it unofficial.

Late in 1817, Monroe sent three agents to South America to judge the viability of the newly independent regimes. They were Caesar A. Rodney, of Delaware; Theodorick Bland, who was connected to Baltimore privateers; and John Graham, who had been the chargé in Madrid and chief clerk of the State Department since 1807. Only Graham spoke Spanish. When they returned, they were unable to agree even on a joint report.

More aggressive U.S. intervention came from an unexpected source. Piratical outlaws based on Amelia Island, off Florida's east coast, had become so troublesome that in early 1818 Andrew Jackson, the popular hero of New Orleans, was charged with leading an expedition against them. Jackson was told also to eliminate the raids from Spanish territory by Seminole Indians. He took this as an opportunity to seize East Florida. Much later, Jackson claimed that Monroe had authorized him to take Florida, but that was unlikely since Monroe believed that, with the slightest pressure, Spain would cede Florida.

Jackson occupied Amelia Island without a shot fired, but then Monroe and his cabinet did not know what to do with the island. They finally decided to keep American troops in Florida, and American ministers abroad were told that the United States would regard as hostile any European interference with Spanish America. However, Jackson's invasion did break open the negotiations by George W. Erving, the experienced U.S. minister in Madrid, which had been deadlocked for nearly three years. The Spanish foreign minister thought he might trade Florida for a more favorable boundary of Louisiana.

Jackson did not stop there. He ordered the execution of two British subjects for helping the Seminoles against the Americans. He occupied Pensacola and forced the Spanish governor and garrison to flee to Havana. Secretary of War John C. Calhoun and Secretary of the Treasury Crawford wanted Jackson censured. The House Committee on Military Affairs condemned his execution of the two British men, but Secretary of State Adams advised holding on to what Jackson had seized of Florida. In the end, Monroe insisted that the Spanish posts be returned. Jackson's nerve made him more popular than ever.

The Spanish minister in Washington negotiated the northern boundary of the Louisiana territory. Spain wanted to control the Pacific coast as far north as the Columbia River and compromised at the 42nd parallel. The negotiators also agreed to draw borders along the western banks of the rivers, rather than in the middle, as was customary.

President Monroe signed the Transcontinental Treaty in February 1819. But Spain, hoping to alter it in its favor, ratified it only after two years, when a new regime came to power. Secretary Adams regarded its approval as the "most important event" of his life, but the Missouri Compromise of 1820 made the prospect of adding Florida as slave territory less attractive to Northerners.

Recognizing that Latin America was changing, Monroe sent Congress a special message on March 8, 1822, accepting five Latin American states as seeking independence from Spain: Colombia, Buenos Aires, Chile, Peru, and Mexico. Joel Poinsett met with Mexico's Emperor Agustin I, and Charles S. Todd, of Kentucky, met with the Colombian secretary of foreign affairs. Both brought the news that the United States was recognizing their countries' independence.

These temporary envoys were followed by formal diplomatic agents. In all, the United States established legations in seven Latin American states, starting when Richard C. Anderson, of Kentucky, opened the first legation in Bogotá on December 10, 1823. And at the same time, Congress named Caesar Rodney minister to Buenos Aires. Both Anderson and Rodney died at their posts, as did James Cooley, of Ohio, the chargé who reached Lima, Peru, in 1827.

Heman Allen, of Vermont, was assigned to Chile in January 1823 but did not reach Santiago until April 1824. A legation in Mexico City was delayed because the government there was not eager to send an envoy to Washington. By the end of the 1820s, Mexico had ten American consuls.

The first envoy to Central America, John Williams, was given his instructions on February 10, 1826. From the beginning, he was directed to explore the possibility of cutting a trans-isthmus canal through the province of Nicaragua.

The United States had had a legation in Rio de Janeiro since 1809, when Brazil was still part of Portugal. Recognition of Brazil's independence from Portugal also ran into delays until, on March 5, 1825, Condy Raguet was appointed chargé to the empire of Brazil.

William Tudor, a Boston-born Harvard graduate who had started the *North American Review,* arrived at Callao, Peru, as consul in early 1824. He found the Spanish still in charge of the port and presented his credentials to them. The nationalists were blockading the port and demanding 25 percent of all cargoes. Tudor called in the U.S. Navy to escort American merchantmen. The local revolutionaries took over the city, and in late 1824 Simon Bolivar, the "liberator" of northern South America, entered Callao with his army and recognized Tudor, who became chargé to Brazil.

Another consul got into trouble for calling on the Navy for help. George W. Slacum, although not an accredited diplomat, was in 1832 the top American official in Buenos Aires. Chargé John M. Forbes had died, and Slacum had to object when Argentina seized the American schooner *Harriet,* which was killing seals in the Falkland Islands. He brought it to Buenos Aires and had a U.S. Navy frigate sail to the Falklands, put a landing party ashore, and arrest almost everyone. When the outraged Argentine government protested, the American government backed off and revoked Slacum's commission.

By the mid 1830s, the United States had forty-four consular posts in Latin America and the Caribbean islands.

. . .

In the northwest, British Foreign Secretary Castlereagh, initiated negotiations for the Columbia River area. Pressured by Richard Rush, the U.S. minister in London, Castlereagh returned to the American fur-trading base at Astoria. Adams sent Albert Gallatin, then the minister to Paris, to London to assist those negotiations. The resulting Convention of 1818 also dealt with the fisheries problem created by the British stance that the War of 1812 had canceled all previous agreements. The negotiators drew a line from the Lake of the Woods along the 49th parallel to the Rockies. But the parties could agree only to permit people of both nations to have access to the Oregon region.

The British refused to make concessions on the knotty dispute over West Indies trade, so they settled on extending the agreement of 1815 for ten years. And some small progress was made on impressment when the Americans restricted serving on American warships to native-born citizens. In January 1819, the Senate ratified that convention unanimously.

Efforts to eliminate the slave trade were stalled by the American policy that searches of slave ships were violations of the freedom of the seas. The slave trade had been forbidden to American citizens since 1794, and now the American public was beginning to accept the idea that the British could search American ships looking for slavers. A compromise in 1824 declared that the slave trade was piracy, and pirates were not protected by any nation.

The British foreign secretary, George Canning, accepted classifying the slave trade as piracy, but the U.S. Senate objected. It was adopted only by restricting searches to African coastal waters. Canning felt the Americans had broken their word since they had initiated the slave-trade convention, and he refused to accept this restriction. That ended Anglo-American cooperation to suppress the slave trade.

Canning took office after Lord Castlereagh committed suicide by cutting his own throat, and he was determined to arrange a general agreement between the two countries. After Monroe entered his second term without opposition, Canning suggested to U.S. Minister Rush in London on August 20, 1823, that they join in a public statement opposing any effort by the European powers to restore former colonies to Spain. Secretary Adams expected that Cuba would eventually become part of the United States, and he rejected Canning's proposal that U.S. and European governments agree not to repossess any of those former colonies.

Canning lost interest in the idea when he obtained from France an agreement (the Polignac Memorandum) that it would not annex any of Spain's colonies. Still, Spain again became a problem when Andrew Jackson, as the governor of Florida, arrested a former Spanish governor and refused to acknowledge the writ of habeas corpus issued by a Federal judge. The incident also angered President Monroe, and the administration argued that the former governor did not have diplomatic immunity.

On some points, progress was made. In the spring of 1822, Gallatin, the minister in Paris, negotiated a commercial treaty with France; and, just two years later, Henry Middleton, a former governor of South Carolina who served as the effective American minister in Saint Petersburg for ten years, concluded a treaty, under which the czar limited his activities in North America to territory north of 54° 40′. This was easily ratified by the Senate.

At this same time, Baron de Tuyll, the Russian minister to Washington, delivered a message to Adams from the Russian foreign minister expressing the czar's pleasure that the allied powers had protected Europe from the perils of revolution. Adams was assured that this, indeed, did include the independence of Spain's colonies in the Americas. This gave Adams the basis for making a statement of principle, which he did on the Fourth of July 1821. Following up on Adams' initiative, Monroe wrote into his annual message to Congress a statement of principles; before doing so, he read it to the cabinet on November 25, 1823. It went to Congress a week later and became known as the Monroe Doctrine.

Monroe declared that the Americas "are henceforth not to be considered as the subjects for future colonization by any European powers. . . . It is impossible that the allied powers should extend their political system to any portion of either continent without endangering our peace and happiness." Harry Ammon, Monroe's biographer, said, "It seemed as if the nation had finally reached the point seen so distant in 1776; it had achieved an American identity."

9

An Early Professional

1825–42

The evolution from Revolutionary-era "militiamen" to foreign service professionals was a slow, stumbling process. One early practical step was taken when Secretary of State John Quincy Adams realized his department was handicapped by a paucity of men able to work in Arabic or Turkish. The outrages by the Barbary states forced the Americans to do business with those piratical entities and with the Sublime Porte in Constantinople. And, simultaneously, the United States was reaching into the Mediterranean world for raw materials and markets. But no one in the department could actually read the treaties being negotiated with the Arabic-speaking world.

So, in February 1825, after Adams became President, he was pleased to be introduced to twenty-four-year-old William Brown Hodgson, a well-connected Georgetown resident looking for a job as a clerk-translator. In a conscious attempt to add some professionalism to an "amateurish foreign service," Hodgson was hired, and he quickly revealed a prodigious talent for languages.

His career illustrates the failings of the U.S. Foreign Service even at its best in the first half of the nineteenth century. Henry Clay, Adams' Secretary of State, sent Hodgson to Algiers to learn Arabic and the North African dialect. Algiers was chosen because the consul there, William Shaler, was a scholar of languages and ideal to train the first official American language student. Hodgson was given tenure for three years at six hundred dollars a year. When his sailing for Algiers was delayed, he conscientiously assured Daniel Brent, the department's chief clerk, that he was using the time industriously to study Italian and German.

When he reached Algiers, Hodgson was intrigued by the old walled city facing the spacious bay, which the Ottoman Turks had ruled for some three hundred years. By day Algiers' whitewashed houses sparkled in the tropical sun; at night, the city gates were locked and the citadel's guns protected the fifty thousand inhabitants.

When Hodgson had been in Algiers a year, Shaler wrote Secretary Clay praising the young linguist, who had made more progress than he had thought possible, and predicting he would "probably rank among the first philologists of his time." Shaler had a paper Hodgson wrote on the Berber language read to the American Philosophical Society in Philadelphia.

Hodgson served as chargé d'affaires when Shaler was away; and in 1828 he became the acting consul when Shaler transferred to Havana. Hodgson reported to Secretary Clay on the war between France and Algiers and prophesied that France would colonize Algiers. (In 1830, French troops marched into the city.)

When his three years were up, Hodgson was glad to leave Algiers; his health, too, was suffering. He desired a foreign service career, and, since there was no professional career path, he had to find political connections. He was replaced in Algiers by Major Henry Lee, a half brother of Robert E. Lee and a pamphleteer for President Jackson. When the Senate rejected Lee's appointment, President Jackson sent out Commodore David Porter of the U.S. Navy. At that time out came a second language student, George F. Brown. These were small but vital beginnings.

FOCUS ON THE OTTOMAN EMPIRE

After Jackson was elected President, Martin Van Buren rode the stagecoach down from New York in early April 1829 and took office as his Secretary of State. Van Buren had served briefly as governor of New York State, resigning to join the cabinet. He arrived in Washington late at night, exhausted. A crowd of men seeking jobs followed him into his hotel room, and, while he stretched out on a sofa, they raucously made their bids for offices. The retiring President, Adams, called them the "wolves of the antechamber."

Van Buren was known for being shrewd and for always keeping his options open. He paid a call on Adams and later wrote in his *Autobiography*: "When I left him he said he would give me a hint that I might find useful which was that no secrets could be kept in the State Department, but that on the contrary the foreign Ministers were always certain in one way or another to get information of any negotiation going on there in which their Governments felt an interest."

Van Buren invited the members of the diplomatic corps, whom he sensed distrusted the new Democratic president, to meet in the Executive Mansion in Washington on April 5. One by one, each minister was presented to the President and was given a copy of Jackson's remarks to pass on to his government.

Secretary Van Buren's first venture into foreign affairs was to establish commercial relations with the Ottoman Empire, giving American ships access to the Black Sea. During these negotiations, Van Buren kept all the relevant papers securely in his private room.

In February 1830, Congress created the Office of Translator of Foreign Languages and Oriental Interpreter at a salary of a thousand dollars a year. Van Buren gave William Hodgson the position. The young man disliked the raw primitiveness and intrigues of Washington, but he made important friends there and was elected to the American Philosophical Society and the Royal Asiatic Society of London. He translated into Berber the Book of Genesis and the four Gospels.

In his official role, Hodgson concluded a Treaty of Amity and Commerce with the Ottoman Empire. The United States gained most-favored-nation status and the right of extraterritoriality, and American consuls were posted in Egypt, the Holy Land, Syria, and Turkey. A secret article promised that the U.S. minister would help the Turks obtain shipbuilding contracts in the United States. The Senate approved the treaty but rejected the secret article. Now, American merchantmen could carry Turkish opium to China and rum to the Turks.

Of course, the most important post in the Ottoman Empire was Constantinople, where an American consulate had existed since 1832. It lasted only until the Crimean War in 1853 and was reopened as a consulate general in 1857. By 1914, twenty-two consuls and consuls general served there. The fourteen posts under their jurisdiction included Beirut, Baghdad, and Jerusalem.

Trading between the United States and the Ottomans grew slowly, hampered by distances and the lack of direct shipping lines between America and the ports of the coast of Palestine. As late as 1894, Gottlieb Schumacher, the U.S. consular agent in Haifa, was still complaining that the absence of a shipping line between the United States and the eastern Mediterranean coast made American products uncompetitive. An exception—kerosene—was introduced about 1865 in five-gallon tins for home use; but by the 1890s Russian kerosene had taken over the market.

All of Palestine came under Beirut from 1835 until a consulate was firmly established in Jerusalem. Consuls and consuls general in the Ottoman Empire were often of questionable character, according to Dabney S. Carr, the U.S. minister in Constantinople from 1843 to 1849. Consul generals were repeatedly dismissed and agencies closed until reforms were made in 1857. A noteworthy exception was Gabriel Bie Ravndal, a Norwegian-born politician from South Dakota, who served with distinction in Beirut and later in Constantinople.

In 1835, A. Durighello, a local Levantine, was appointed consul at Aleppo, and Jasper Chasseud was appointed at Beirut. The consular agency established at Aleppo in 1847 was upgraded to a consulate in 1908. Jesse B. Jackson, a Spanish-American War veteran, served there as well until 1923, except during World War I.

At Damascus, Dr. Michael Meshaka, a scholar and native of Corfu, was appointed U.S. vice consul in 1859 and was caught in riots, during which Muslim mobs destroyed the city's Christian quarter. Dr. Meshaka was attacked in his consulate and fled into the street. He was shot at and struck by clubs and axes until some Muslims rescued him and took him, bloody and nearly stripped naked, to the house of a Muslim friend. He stayed there for a month until his wounds healed. He served as vice consul until 1870 and then was succeeded by his son, Nasif.

Once the 1830 treaty, which Hodgson had negotiated, was in place, the President moved Commodore Porter to be the American chargé d'affaires in Constantinople. Porter had had a dramatic naval career: He had been imprisoned in Tripoli when *Philadelphia* was captured; and during the War of 1812, he commanded *Essex* on its historic cruise destroying the British whaling fleet in the Pacific.

Van Buren assigned Hodgson to help Porter establish diplomatic relations with the Ottomans and to carry the treaty and letters to the sultan and to Reis Effendi, the Turkish foreign minister. Aboard USS *John Adams* in April 1831, Hodgson met up with Porter at Port Mahon, Minorca. The two men, who were to become enemies, shared a cabin to Constantinople.

On reaching that port, Commodore Porter stirred up two international crises. The Turks required all warships passing through the Dardanelles to dismount their guns. Porter refused to let *John Adams'* captain dismantle his. And Porter demanded that the Turks salute his ship. These became causes célèbres.

Porter and Hodgson needed almost two months to gain an audience with the sultan. After that, Porter wrote praising Hodgson to Secretary of State Edward Livingston (Robert's younger brother), who had succeeded Van Buren. Hodgson applied for the job of the Legation's First Dragoman, the official in direct touch with the local government. He returned to Boston in 1832, and when he learned that he had been confirmed for the post, he hurried back to Constantinople.

There, he persuaded the foreign minister to stop charging American ships a duty of 15 percent while ships of other nations paid only 3 percent. When Reis Effendi agreed, Hodgson translated the document into English, signing it "Secretary of Legation and Interpreter."

Hodgson modernized the legation's record keeping and requests to the Turks to allow U.S. ships to sail. But Porter demanded that he make no innovations without his approval. By year's end, Hodgson was complaining to the department about Porter's abuses of his office. Chief among them was that Porter had put two of his nephews on the payroll. One, John Porter Brown, became a specialist in Oriental languages and served in Constantinople for forty years until he died, penniless. A friend had to pay his widow's passage home.

Commodore Porter was a martinet and ran the legation like a man of war. A small, weather-beaten man, he made enemies. He and Hodgson argued repeatedly. The following year, Hodgson accused Porter of charging American merchants excessive fees to cover the cost of employing his two nephews. Hodgson asked to be transferred to Algiers or given one of the Barbary consulates.

When Porter removed Hodgson as secretary of the legation, Hodgson protested to Washington that he had been assigned to the post by the Secretary of State. Porter also removed him from the post of dragoman and criticized his Turkish language skills to the Secretary.

By the fall of 1833, Hodgson wrote Secretary Louis McLane, who had replaced Edward Livingston, that Porter had removed him from office, stopped his pay, and would no longer meet with him. Hodgson also reported that Porter was acting as an agent for the heirs of a merchant in Turkish-American trade. Secretary McLane wrote Porter that the President "desires that you dissolve the connection and confine yourself strictly to your official duties."

The two men's final argument was over a horse, worth forty dollars. In a written statement to the U.S. consul, William N. Churchill, Hodgson claimed he had bought the horse; Porter insisted the horse was supposed to have been a gift to him. Porter asked Commodore D. L. Patterson, the senior American naval officer at Constantinople, to imprison Hodgson. Patterson refused because, he said, Hodgson had committed no crime. Porter signed a statement that the horse was his property and Hodgson was a swindler. Commodore Patterson responded that Hodgson was known to the officers of his frigate, USS *United States,* as a man of honor. Finally, Porter's son, a midshipman, assaulted Hodgson and kicked him when he was on the ground. Midshipman Porter was not punished but had to pay Hodgson thirty-five dollars for damage to his clothes.

This increasingly bitter confrontation ended when Secretary McLane wrote Hodgson that, without judging his dispute with Porter, he wanted Hodgson to leave the legation in Constantinople and undertake a mission of importance. He was sending Hodgson to Egypt as a confidential agent to determine whether the United States could form commercial relations directly with Muhammed Ali, who had risen from a tobacco vendor to become the viceroy of Egypt and the Ottoman sultan's vassal. Since Muhammed Ali was in revolt against the sultan, it was a delicate mission.

Hodgson was ordered to proceed to Egypt immediately, collect his information, and report in person to the State Department in Washington within three months. He was told to acquire Porter's cipher so he could communicate with the department in secret and to draw seven hundred dollars from Porter for his expenses. Continuing their feud, Porter would let him take only five hundred dollars.

Hodgson was thrilled with the department's continued confidence in him despite his disputes with Porter. Hodgson reached Alexandria on August 24, 1834, and, with the help of John Gliddon, an English merchant serving as the American consul general, had two meetings with Muhammed Ali. The pasha told Hodgson he wanted closer ties with the United States.

Hodgson traveled to Cairo and up the Nile, visiting several cotton factories and the sugar refinery at Radamon. He prepared two astute reports about conditions in the Middle East, explaining that Muhammed Ali was trying to control the area's Arabic-speaking people as opposed to the Turkish-speaking. He reported that potential trading products were salt, dates, opium, and ostrich feathers.

Back in the United States, Hodgson filed his formal report on March 2, 1835. He informed the department that the viceroy had signed a commercial treaty with Britain and a railroad was to be built soon between Cairo and Suez. He concluded that a separate treaty with Egypt was necessary only if Egypt became independent from the Ottoman Empire. But he recommended that the United States upgrade its representative in Egypt significantly from consular agent to consul general. In fact, John Gliddon was promoted to consul and held the post until his death, when his Scottish-born son-in-law succeeded him. After that, the post at Alexandria was occupied by American-born consuls and was elevated to a consulate general.

THE LACK OF A CAREER SYSTEM

At home, Hodgson could find no post open for him in the diplomatic service. The U.S. foreign service lacked any structure, or even any concept, that allowed a diplomat to build a career. Hodgson had to fill in with odd jobs that often did not match his abilities.

Secretary of State John Forsyth sent him out as a special agent. He sailed on the USS *Constitution* with dispatches for James R. Leib, the U.S. consul at Tangier, and with presents for the emperor of Morocco. He helped renew the treaty with Morocco and returned to Washington.

In 1837, Secretary Forsyth sent him to Lima, Peru, to deliver to the chargé, James B. Thornton, the Treaty of Peace, Friendship, Commerce, and Navigation with the new confederation of Peru and Bolivia, as ratified by the United States.

Hodgson's journey to Lima was adventurous. He left Washington on October 15, traveled to New York, and sailed on a packet to Kingston, Jamaica. There, he caught a small boat hoping to overtake a schooner sailing for Panama. The boat overturned at sea, and a passing Spanish ship picked Hodgson out of the ocean and returned him to Point Royal, near Kingston. After resupplying himself, he took an odiferous cattle boat to Cartagena, on the Caribbean coast of Colombia; from there, sailed to Portobello, Panama; and caught another small boat to Chargeres, struggling through the isthmus' jungles. He spent Christmas Eve with the American consul at a cockfight. But then his health gave out. He could go no farther. He gave the treaty to an American doctor to deliver to Thornton.

On February 5, Hodgson sailed on the USS *Enterprise* for Callao, where he learned that Thornton had died the previous week. He reported to the American consul Edwin Bartlett, stationed at Lima, who informed him that he had to obtain the special permission of General Andrew Santa Cruz, the protector of the confederation, who was at La Paz. The USS *Falmouth* carried him to Islay, and on May 2 he and a Peruvian colonel, José Romera, set out on mule back with an English traveler going to La Paz. In the Andes, Hodgson became very ill, and at Arequipa he turned over his dispatches and the treaty to Colonel Romera. He made his way to the coast and sailed back to Callao. A month later, the colonel appeared but had not had the treaty ratified by the confederation. Consul Bartlett finally completed the exchange and gave the ratified treaty to Hodgson to carry back to Washington.

In mid-July, Hodgson had a run-in with Commodore Henry Ballard, senior American naval officer on the Pacific coast of South America. Ballard broke the seal on a letter written by Hodgson and read it before, he claimed, realizing his mistake. Ballard and Hodgson had a heated argument aboard the commodore's flagship USS *North Carolina*. Hodgson brought charges against Ballard, who was tried by court-martial, found guilty of conduct unbecoming an officer and a gentleman, and suspended of all pay and allowances for a year.

Back home, Hodgson kept applying to the department for a position. In 1840, Secretary Forsyth had him deliver the ratified Treaty of Commerce and Navigation with Hannover to Henry Wheaton, the American minister in Berlin. Finally, in the fall of 1841, his political friends obtained for him an interview with Secretary of State Daniel Webster, who appointed him consul at Tunis. He was to replace Samuel D. Heap, Commodore Porter's brother-in-law, who became the dragoman at Constantinople.

In Paris, on his way to Tunis, Hodgson met and fell in love with Margaret Telfair, the daughter of a former governor of Georgia and a wealthy heiress. She agreed to marry him if he left the consular service.

Hodgson reached Tunis on February 11, 1842; was met by Guiseppe Gaspary, the U.S. vice consul; and was taken by Samuel Heap to meet Ahmed Bey. He assured Secretary Webster that the treaty with the United

States was being observed. In May, Hodgson resigned; turned over his responsibilities to W. R. B. Gale, son of a New Orleans merchant; and left Tunis to meet Margaret Telfair in Florence. Secretary Webster replaced him in Tunis with John Howard Payne, an actor and the author of the lyrics of "Home, Sweet Home."

Hodgson and Margaret Telfair were married in London and settled in the Telfair mansion on Saint James Square in Savannah, where he lived splendidly and managed the family plantation. Unlike most overseers, he could talk with many of his slaves in their native languages. The Civil War bankrupted the family, but he continued working in philology, for which he was honored, until his death in 1871.

Hodgson came to understand that, in the absence of a professional career system, he could survive in the foreign service only through political connections. This experiment in professionalizing the U.S. foreign service soon surrendered to patronage and nepotism.

10

The Spoils System

1829–48

Andrew Jackson's administration ended the dominance of the planter aristocracy personified by Washington and Jefferson and brought to power new leaders from industry and business. They found the sixty-one-year-old military hero Jackson attractive. It was a time of a surging spirit of expansion and a drive westward, fueled by wider enfranchisement, the strengthening of political parties, and a technological revolution featuring the telegraph and the railroad.

Jackson "rotated" new people into government jobs to squeeze out entrenched officeholders and to give more people a chance to participate. His "rotation" began as reform but degenerated in a dozen years into an ugly spoils system.

President Jackson and Secretary of State Van Buren appointed new ministers to London, Paris, Madrid, The Hague, and Saint Petersburg. Not all of their decisions involved hard-nosed political firings. For example, Van Buren kept Daniel Brent as chief clerk of the State Department, although he was a Federalist.

"Rotation" stimulated complaints about the cost and quality of the foreign service. The finances of nonsalaried consuls were a particular headache. On January 2, 1830, Secretary Van Buren received a request from the Senate Committee on Commerce to analyze the consular service and the fees consuls were charging.

Van Buren wrote the committee that various consuls charged different fees for the same services, and this led to "endless criminations and re-criminations." Consuls were not required to account for the money they took in; discrepancies were discovered mainly when people complained that they had been bilked.

Van Buren wanted "a fixed and uniform standard for the regulation of consular fees, charges and commissions." He instructed the consuls to list the fees they were charging and asked Daniel Strobel, of South Carolina, the longtime consul in Bordeaux, who happened to be in Washington, to prepare recommendations for Congress.

Strobel's report in January 1831 was the first thorough analysis of the consular service. Strobel explained that there were two kinds of consular systems. The British system employed salaried consuls and prohibited them from doing business on their own account. The Dutch model engaged successful merchants residing in foreign ports and allowed them to charge fees for their services. Since the Americans could not afford a paid consular system, they tried to follow the Dutch system, but they did not have enough established merchants living abroad. Many less than affluent American consuls, whether serving on fees or salaries, were embarrassed that they could not make ends meet and afford to mix socially with local leaders.

Strobel believed that the functions of a consul and a merchant were in conflict. He favored a uniform schedule of fees from which consuls would be paid salaries. He also wanted the State Department to appoint an official in Washington to provide consuls with better supervision and oversight.

Strobel wanted to end the abuses of the law enacted in February 28, 1803, which, he charged, left destitute American seamen in foreign countries on the consuls' hands. He advocated giving consuls the authority to settle disputes between seamen and ships' masters. Congress never acted on his study. Although his landmark examination of the consular service did not change the law, it influenced future thinking about that service.

THE EATON SCANDAL

Van Buren's term as Secretary of State was cut short by a scandal that he called the Eaton imbroglio. Secretary of War John Henry Eaton was married to a beautiful young widow, Peggy O'Neale, and gossips spread titillating rumors about the couple's behavior while she was still married to her first husband. Wives of the President's private secretary, the secretary of the treasury, the attorney general, and the secretary of the navy sniffed that Mrs. Eaton was an unsuitable cabinet wife. The affronted ladies hosted three parties and did not invite the Eatons.

The last straw came on the evening that the Russian ambassador to Washington gave a ball and took Mrs. Eaton's arm into supper as the ranking lady present. The wife of the Dutch ambassador believed herself insulted. Regarding these slights as attempts to drive Eaton out of his cabinet, Jackson angrily ordered Van Buren to give the Dutch ambassador his passports. To avoid an international incident, Van Buren called on the Dutch ambassador and was assured by his wife that she never meant to ostracize Mrs. Eaton.

The Eaton affair caused tensions between Jackson and Vice President John C. Calhoun. In addition, Calhoun admitted to Jackson that during the Seminole War in 1827, when he was secretary of war, he had felt that Jackson had exceeded his orders by occupying Spanish-held Saint Marks and Pensacola. Calhoun's admission produced a full rupture with Jackson. It was said (apparently, with some reason) that Van Buren had designed the break in order to replace Calhoun as Vice President at the next election.

Van Buren decided to resign and informed Jackson on one of their frequent horseback rides together into the countryside. They finally agreed that Eaton and Van Buren would resign at the same time. Eaton became governor of Florida, and, two years later, minister to Spain.

When Van Buren resigned in April 1831, Jackson appointed him minister to the Court of St. James's. He replaced Louis McLane, who had negotiated the agreement allowing the United States to trade with British colonies in the West Indies. McLane became secretary of the treasury. When he differed with Jackson over the Second Bank of the United States, he was shifted to Secretary of State. Jackson saw the secretaries as his interchangeable subordinates.

Van Buren sailed for London with his son, John, and Aaron Vail, who would become the secretary of the legation. After they had been in London a couple of months, Washington Irving, the already-famous novelist who was then the secretary of the legation, brought Van Buren the awkward news that the Senate had refused to confirm him. The vote had been

23 to 23 and a vengeful Vice President Calhoun had broken the tie by voting against confirmation. Irving immediately predicted this would make Van Buren vice president, and, a year later, it did. Washington Irving became minister to Spain, serving from 1842 to 1846.

Britain's eccentric King William IV went out of his way to show that he understood the politics of Van Buren's departure and invited him to Windsor Castle, where he spent two pleasant days. Van Buren wrote, "His Majesty also took the keys and shewed me many of the most interesting parts of that venerable and noble pile." He arrived back in the States in July 1832.

When Van Buren left London, Aaron Vail, who had succeeded Irving as secretary of legation, was named chargé d'affaires. Vail's father had been an American consul in France; now, his son would hold the London post ably for four years while the Senate blocked Jackson's appointment of another minister. When a friendlier Senate in 1836 approved Speaker of the House Andrew Stevenson as minister to Great Britain, Vail became the U.S. minister to Spain.

"THE WORST CONSULAR SYSTEM IN THE WORLD"

Edward Livingston, who succeeded Van Buren as Secretary of State, called the United States consular service "the worst consular system in the world" and sent Jackson recommendations for reform. He proposed that consuls' duties be specified; they should write the department at least four times a year and promote American commerce and navigation.

Livingston had a capable legal mind and was the younger brother of Robert, who had served as Secretary of Foreign Affairs. Earlier, while Edward Livingston served as mayor of New York City, a clerk stole federal funds in Livingston's safekeeping; he moved to New Orleans, and started life anew. During the battle of New Orleans, he served as Jackson's interpreter and advisor. And he was a U.S. senator until Jackson called him to his cabinet.

Led by Edward Livingston, the State Department issued its first comprehensive instructions to consuls. Among the duties stated were those involving marine protests and declarations, settling estates of Americans who died without legal heirs, conserving wrecked American ships and their cargoes, repatriating American seamen, issuing passports to American citizens, and certifying invoices of goods shipped to the United States.

Consuls were warned to keep out of the political disputes of the country in which they were stationed. Services for which they could charge fees were listed and the fees designated. They began to have responsibilities to report on foreign commercial laws and regulations; but not until after the Civil War did they develop responsibilities to promote trade.

Secretary Livingston also recommended, again, that consuls be paid salaries and prohibited from engaging in business. And if that could not be done, he said, then fees should be standardized. He wrote, "According to the present system, our consuls, with very few exceptions, are commission merchants, anxious, like all other merchants, to increase their business and obtain consignments." He admitted that the supervision of these far-flung representatives overseas was unsatisfactory.

Livingston listed 156 consuls, vice consuls, and commercial agents; and he calculated that by paying the consuls salaries of an average of $2,000, and the other classes an average of $1,000, the total cost would be $186,000. He judged that "customs alone produce more than sufficient for the payment of all the expenses of Government." The President sent Livingston's report to the Senate, but once again Congress did not find time or the desire for consular reform. That would take another twenty-three years.

Secretary Livingston also sent President Jackson a comprehensive and masterful report on the diplomatic service. It warned that salaries were seriously inadequate. He said that the work of the nation's representatives abroad was little appreciated by the American people, and he pointed out that the United States had no diplomatic relations at all in European nations with a total population of seventy-five million. In others, he added, American representatives had to work and live in shameful conditions. He asserted that no minister the United States had sent abroad was able to live on his salary. He concluded, "If the mission is useful, it ought to be supported at the public, not at private expense." Congress ignored him.

By no means did all American diplomatic representation abroad invite complaints. Henry Wheaton was one respected diplomat of the era. He was appointed chargé d'affaires in Denmark in 1827 and in Prussia in 1835. He was raised to ministerial rank in 1837 and negotiated treaties with the new German customs union that reduced tariffs reciprocally.

Substantial moves to reorganize the State Department came in 1833. Secretary of State Louis McLane established a separate Diplomatic Bureau with three clerks for nineteen representatives overseas; the clerks divided the work geographically and communicated with each mission weekly.

McLane also created a Consular Bureau with two clerks for 152 officers overseas. A third clerk was added three years later. McLane's changes were inadequate; such a small staff could not manage the now-widespread foreign service.

And then, in April 1838, the first steam-propelled ship from Liverpool docked in New York. It shrunk the globe.

WRITERS REWARDED WITH CONSULATES

As a notable by-product of the "spoils system," consular assignments were on occasion handed out to reward Americans distinguished in the arts. As early as 1826, New York's Governor DeWitt Clinton proposed James Fenimore Cooper for an assignment. Cooper declined the post of minister to Sweden but accepted the sinecure of consul at Lyons, France. (Evidence that he actually served in Lyons is extremely thin.)

In the summer of 1829, Washington Irving, the most popular American writer of his time, was living and writing in the Alhambra in Spain at the behest of U.S. Minister Alexander H. Everett. He had finished his *Life of Columbus,* when he was appointed secretary of the legation in London. He spent three enjoyable years there; and in 1842, Secretary of State Daniel Webster appointed him minister to Spain. He served four years in that country, of which he was particularly fond.

A generation later, in 1877, James Russell Lowell, poet, satirist, and Harvard professor, followed Irving as minister to Spain. Lowell, a Boston Brahman, was admired, but his most historic achievement was interrupting the shipments of oil that were brought into Spain by smugglers who hid them in tins worn on the chests of skinny women. They were discovered when one admiring inspector tapped on a chest and produced a tinkling sound. Lowell served in Madrid for four years and then had a tour as minister to London.

Bret Harte, who wrote about the American West, sought a post as a consul. He was sent to Krefeld, Germany, as a commercial agent, which carried none of a consul's allowances. So he was delighted to be reassigned to the busy port of Glasgow as a full-fledged consul. But after five years, he was replaced for not paying enough attention to consular business.

Nathaniel Hawthorne was a more serious diplomat. He had been President Franklin Pierce's roommate at Bowdoin College and wrote his campaign biography. At Liverpool, he ran the busiest consulate in Europe from 1853 to 1857, on fees running about fifteen thousand dollars a year. He did not particularly like consular work. He wrote that the pleasantest incident of the day was when Samuel Pierce, the venerable Englishman who was his vice consul, came in with a roll of the queen's coins and deposited on his desk the day's receipts. Hawthorne was pleased that he was making more money than he ever had from his writings.

His consulate was a moderate-size apartment facing the brick wall of a cotton warehouse and decorated with a bust of General Zachary Taylor and steel engravings of a Hudson River steamer and the Tennessee State House. It reminded him of an old-fashioned American barbershop. He said, "For a man, with a natural tendency to meddle in other people's business, there could not possibly be a more congenial sphere than the Liverpool Consulate."

Hawthorne had his hands full during his first Christmas in Liverpool. The new steamship *San Francisco* was battered in a fierce Atlantic storm and had to be abandoned. Three hundred of its passengers and crew perished. Ships picked up the survivors and brought them to Liverpool. They included two hundred men from an American artillery regiment. Hawthorne brought the officers to his home and provided for the enlisted men out of his own pocket. The minister in London, James Buchanan, opened a line of credit at the Barings Bank for the soldiers; and when American steamship lines refused to carry them home, Buchanan chartered a Cunard steamship to take them.

Hawthorne enjoyed telling how he was visited at the consulate by an American clergyman who said he had spent an entire week in an English brothel and was broke. Hawthorne took pleasure in reprimanding him and gave him money to get home to New Orleans.

Some consuls ran into trouble, especially in Italy, which was then torn by revolution and upheaval. John M. Marston, of Massachusetts, was reprimanded for recognizing an insurgent government at Palermo, although he risked his life to arrange a truce so that civilians could escape the battle. William S. Sparks, of South Carolina, greeted the citizens of Venice, who declared themselves a republic in 1848; so, when the Austrians regained power, he had to leave. In 1849, Consul Joseph Binda told the citizens of Leghorn, Tuscany, that the United States would not interfere in the internal affairs of their country. The Austrians remained in power there for a decade, after which the Tuscans removed Binda.

President Theodore Roosevelt, in 1902, appointed as consul at Guaya-quil, Ecuador, the cartoonist Thomas Nast, who had helped destroy Tam-many Hall's corrupt Boss Tweed. But after a few months at his post, Nast died of yellow fever.

During the period of turmoil on the Italian Peninsula, President James K. Polk raised U.S. representation with the Papal States in 1848 from a consul to a chargé d'affaires. This precipitated a dispute in the U.S. Senate that ended with the American representative dealing with the Vatican as a sovereign state, not as a religious entity. Jacob L. Martin, the first chargé there, refused to support the Italian revolutionaries. He served at the Holy See for only four months before his death; by then, the nationalists had pushed Pope Pius IX out of Rome.

The pope's exile spawned a footnote to history. The U.S. chargé in Na-ples, John Rowan, visited King Ferdinand II of the Kingdom of the Two Sicilies while Pius IX was also there. The USS *Constitution* stood in Gaeta Harbor, north of Naples, and the king asked if he could visit the frigate. Rowan invited him aboard and invited the pope as well. Unknown to Rowan, the warship's captain, John Gwinn, had been instructed not to take the two sovereigns aboard because the United States was trying to remain neutral in the dispute between the rulers and the revolutionaries.

Captain Gwinn welcomed them, and they spent three hours aboard; the pope distributed rosaries to Catholic sailors and gave a benediction. The pope became seasick, and after he recovered, departed to a twenty-one-gun salute. As a result of the incident, Captain Gwinn was court-martialed, but he died before he could be tried. This incident aboard the warship was considered the first time a pope set foot on what was legally American ter-ritory.

SLOW FIRST STEPS TOWARD REFORM

Reforming the consular system took a long time. During Van Buren's presidency, Secretary of State John Forsyth made a few changes, mostly affecting how consuls dealt with seamen in foreign ports. Forsyth, a one-time Georgia congressman, had served as minister to Madrid until he of-fended the Spaniards by daring to lecture the king. Forsyth spoke neither Spanish nor French, had a temper, and had come to dislike the Spaniards. An act dated July 20, 1840, asserted the rights of seamen to put their complaints before a consul or commercial agent. It also granted consuls un-limited discretion over the requirement, dating back to 1803, that ships' masters must advance three months' extra wages to seamen discharged in foreign ports to enable them to pay their passage home.

After James Buchanan became Secretary of State in March 1845, Con-gress finally pressed for reforms in the consular service. Buchanan adopted Strobel's ideas of paying salaries and setting fees based on ships' tonnage. But the State Department, with only two consular clerks, did not have enough staff to manage the consuls.

A select committee of the House of Representatives recommended on June 17, 1846, that the consular system undergo "radical changes." The committee sought to establish a consular bureau to supervise the consuls abroad. It pointed out that U.S. commerce was already four-fifths as large as that of Great Britain and "will ere long be even greater than hers."

The committee supported most of Livingston's dormant recommenda-tions: Fees should be charged, based on the size of a vessel. They should be paid into the Treasury, and those funds would be used to pay consuls fixed salaries.

The select committee wanted representatives of the United States abroad to be "intelligent American citizens . . . having no connexion with commerce themselves." Such men, it assumed, would have only the inter-est of the country in mind. The committee also felt that a consul should at least be assured "that while in the faithful discharge of these duties no change of parties at home will lead to his removal, at least for a limited time." Like its predecessors, this bill died in Congress. Political and per-sonal connections continued to rule the selection of American diplomats.

II

Expansion Westward

1821–45

As the United States drove persistently westward, the question that loomed larger and larger was whether slavery would expand along with the nation. In less than two decades, the unstable mixture of expansion and the politics of slavery would explode into civil war.

Of course, Mexico, which had become independent from Spain in 1821, lay directly in the United States' westward path. American consuls began arriving there that year: William Taylor, at the port of Veracruz, followed by James Smith Wilcocks, at Mexico City, and Nathaniel Ingraham, at Tampico. David G. Burnet, who was named the consul in Galveston in 1834, became, briefly, the first president of the Republic of Texas, until Sam Houston replaced him.

In March 1824, Ninian Edwards, a bad-tempered former governor and senator from Illinois, was named the first U.S. minister to independent Mexico. He traveled as far as New Orleans but never reached his post. When he confessed to having written an anonymous attack on Secretary of the Treasury William Crawford, President Monroe forced him to resign. He was replaced by Joel R. Poinsett, who was instructed to bring the Mexican government's attention to the 1823 statement announcing the Monroe Doctrine. (Poinsett was an amateur botanist, and a colorful result of his tour in Mexico was to bring home the scarlet flower named for him.)

The aggressive pressure to possess the vast "empty" continent was by no means supported by all the American people, or all its leaders. In March 1841, the newly elected President, William Henry Harrison, appointed as his Secretary of State Daniel Webster, a New Hampshire farmer's son who had become a great lawyer and orator. Webster opposed annexing Oregon and Texas. He did not want a war with Britain over the border of Oregon; and, as he told a meeting in Springfield, Massachusetts, on August 9, 1844, "The great, fundamental, everlasting objection to the annexation of Texas is that it is a scheme for the extension of the slavery of the African race." He feared slavery's expansion would lead to violence.

President Harrison died of pneumonia a month after his inauguration, and his successor, Vice President John Tyler, a strong supporter of states' rights, declared that even Hawaii and the Pacific Ocean were in the United States' sphere of influence. Webster maneuvered to be appointed minister to the Court of St. James's. President Tyler said he would move Edward Everett from being the minister in London to commissioner and minister plenipotentiary in China. But Everett insisted on staying at his prominent and comfortable post in London.

Two noteworthy events marked Webster's brief term as Secretary of State: He announced that political partisanship by State Department employees would be cause for removal—and he failed to appoint as chargé d'affaires at Bogotá a young Illinois lawyer named Abraham Lincoln. Webster did negotiate the Webster-Ashburton Treaty, which settled several boundary disputes.

Webster tried to discuss the impressment of American seamen with Lord Ashburton, who said he was not authorized to treat that delicate subject. So, Webster wrote him a strong letter saying baldly that the United States would not hereafter allow the impressment of seamen from American vessels. With Webster's stand, impressment was never again a significant issue.

When Webster resigned and returned to his Boston law practice, President Tyler selected as his Secretary of State, Abel P. Upshur. The new Secretary wrote that "few calamities could befall this country more to be deplored than the abolition of slavery in Texas." Upshur was killed on February 28, 1844, by the accidental explosion of a large naval gun aboard USS *Princeton*, and President Tyler brought in John C. Calhoun to run the State Department. Calhoun made certain that, in 1845, Congress passed a joint resolution inviting Texas to join the Union. Polk made it no secret that he also intended to acquire Oregon and California from Mexico.

COMPETING FOR CALIFORNIA

The nation's westward drive reached California's coast in 1842, when Consul John Parrott sent word from Mazatlán, the main port on Mexico's Pacific coast, to the U.S. East Pacific Naval Squadron at Callao, Peru, that British and French squadrons were moving toward California and that war with Mexico was imminent. Commodore Thomas ap Catesby Jones, who had been a hero in the battle for New Orleans back in 1814, sailed the American squadron north to Monterey, and on October 20 he put ashore a hundred and fifty marines and seamen. He demanded that the twenty-nine Spanish soldiers in the fort surrender and raised the American flag. Then, he discovered there was no war. He sheepishly had the flag taken down, fired an apologetic salute, and joined the Californians in their peaceful festivities. Parrott and Jones were four years too early.

Thomas O. Larkin, a merchant in Monterey, was appointed consul there in 1844. An enthusiastic California booster, he sent word back East that California was rich and Mexican rule was crumbling. He appointed William A. Leidesdorff as vice consul in Yerba Buena, which became San Francisco. Leidesdorff's father was a Danish planter of Jewish heritage, and his mother a slave on Saint Croix in the Danish West Indies. He is regarded as the first black to hold the title of American consul.

An energetic businessman who welcomed Americans to his city, Leidesdorff launched the first steamer in San Francisco Bay and chaired the school board that opened California's first public school. He died of typhus in 1848 at the age of thirty-eight. After his death, gold was discovered on his land, which adjoined that of William Sutter, of Gold Rush fame.

On October 11, 1845, Consul Larkin wrote Washington that Britain's Hudson's Bay Company was arming Mexicans in California to revolt against Mexico. That inspired Secretary of State James Buchanan to send Larkin the only letter he received from Washington during the entire crucial year of 1845, the year Texas joined the Union. The letter was carried to Larkin by a presidential secret agent, tough, cocky First Lieutenant Archibald H. Gillespie, U.S. Marine Corps, who had to sail to Veracruz, cross Mexico to Mazatlán, and catch a whaling ship to Hawaii and then a U.S. warship to Monterey. Polk ordered Larkin to prevent the British from seizing California and to encourage the Californians to revolt against

Mexico. Buchanan added, "If the people [of California] should unite their destiny with ours, they would be received as brethren, whenever this can be done without affording Mexico just cause for complaint." The intentions of the United States were clear.

REACHING OUT AROUND THE WORLD

Between 1830 and 1860, the number of U.S. diplomatic posts around the globe doubled, rather haphazardly, from fifteen to thirty-three. Both a legation in Naples and a mission in Constantinople opened in 1831. A mission was started in Venezuela in 1835, and a commissioner with the rank of minister resident was appointed to China in 1843.

Consular posts fanned out even faster. In 1830, the United States had 62 consular posts in Europe and 141 worldwide. By 1860, there were 89 in Europe and 282 worldwide. They had doubled in thirty years.

In Africa, John Elmslie had established in 1799 a consulate at Cape Town, on the route of the East Indies trade. Elmslie left in 1806, and the post reopened only in 1834. A consulate also opened in Constantinople in 1832, and Richard P. Waters set up a consulate on the busy spice island of Zanzibar in 1836.

Pushing outward, the United States bumped up against British power. Jackson's administration wanted a representative in strategic Singapore despite the presence of the British East India Company. At first, the U.S. consul, Joseph Balestier, was appointed to Rhiau, forty miles across the straits, and in 1837 he was recognized as the consul to Singapore. (His wife, Maria, was Paul Revere's daughter.)

The British government, working with the East India Company, stifled early attempts to station American representatives in Calcutta and Bombay. Despite this, Philemon S. Parker opened a consulate at Bombay in 1838. He gave up after less than two years, and the post remained vacant until 1849, when Samuel Simpson tried to work for both the U.S. government and the East India Company. When he told the State Department he wanted his U.S. salary increased to match the $5,800 a year he received from the East India Company, he was dismissed.

In 1832 the House of Representatives, disturbed by the cost of the foreign service, asked its Committee on Foreign Affairs to reduce the number of American diplomats abroad to three: in England, France, and Russia.

The committee refused on the grounds that such congressional action would invade the President's constitutional authority.

Few consular posts produced fees sufficient to support a foreign service officer and his family. In 1842, the most expensive was Havana, followed by Liverpool, Rio de Janeiro, Le Havre, Paris, and London, in that order. When a new appointee found that his post did not meet his needs financially, he often quit and returned home, if he could afford the passage.

A select committee of the House in 1846 again looked into the inadequacies of the consular service. Its highly critical report resurrected Edward Livingston's recommendations, specifically that all fees go into the Treasury and consuls receive salaries. But, again, Congress was not ready to act.

One controversial issue was that all consuls needed clear authority to deal with American citizens, particularly sailors who broke local laws. On August 11, 1848, Congress passed a bill empowering consuls to arraign, try, and punish American citizens. If a judgment was for no more than one hundred dollars or sixty days in jail, the consul could handle it without any right to appeal. Up to five hundred dollars or ninety days, the defendant could appeal to the minister or commissioner. For more complex cases, the consul would create a committee of local American citizens to help him determine the law and the penalty, including the death penalty. Consuls in Chinese ports and the Ottoman Empire were paid one thousand dollars a year for such judicial duties. It was a primitive arrangement, but there were remarkably few abuses.

By 1860, American consular posts, usually manned by unsalaried merchants, studded the Pacific from Honolulu and Manila to Guam and Fiji. In Hawaii, Consul Peter A. Brinsmade, of Maine, made a great deal of money as a land developer. Charles Bunker, of Nantucket, a Harvard graduate, who in 1852 was the consul at Lahaina on Maui, made a fortune by submitting to the Treasury vastly inflated bills for caring for stranded American seamen. When questions were raised, he simply skipped and disappeared.

LEARNING TO LIVE WITH CHINA

Americans found China the most complicated to deal with, and merchants there repeatedly petitioned their government for support. An incident in 1821, while Benjamin Wilcocks was the consul in Canton, dramatized the need for an American diplomatic presence. The Chinese authorities accused a seaman, Joseph (or Francis) Terranova, aboard the American merchant ship *Emily*, of throwing a jar off his ship and killing a Chinese woman on a bumboat (which carries goods from ship to shore). Chinese officials demanded that Terranova be tried under their law of a life for a life. The Americans refused, until the Chinese threatened to cut off all trade, and then a committee of American sea captains, supercargoes, and merchants decided to permit the trial. Terranova was found guilty and strangled by Canton's executioner.

During the Opium War of 1839–42, the British tried to force the Chinese to accept the illicit drug trade. Americans joined the British in the opium trade that addicted large numbers of Chinese and drained the country of hard currency. To stop this profitable but destructive drug traffic, the Chinese closed the port of Canton for a time and executed Chinese opium dealers in front of the foreign quarter. The British retreated to the then-unoccupied island of Hong Kong, while the American consul, Peter W. Snow, who disliked the British tactics, tried without much success to separate American interests from the British. The British-Chinese Treaty of Nanking ended the Opium War but still allowed the British to conduct their opium trade at Canton.

In 1843, after Edward Everett had refused to move from London to China, President Tyler and Secretary Webster named Caleb Cushing, of Massachusetts, chair of the House Committee on Foreign Affairs, the first American minister to China. Cushing came from an old shipping family, and in Congress he carried out the wishes of his constituents who had grown wealthy in overseas trade.

As minister to China, he negotiated the Treaty of Wanghia, which gave the United States most-favored-nation status and extraterritorial rights and opened five ports to American merchants. Cushing was a stickler for protocol. When the Chinese sent him a document with the United States listed on a line below the Chinese Empire, he protested and received an apology.

During the negotiations on the Treaty of Wanghia, Cushing's chief interpreter was Peter Parker, a Yale graduate who in 1834 became the first Protestant medical missionary in China. He founded the Ophthalmic Hospital in Canton and served the legation, which opened in 1845, as a secretary and interpreter. The treaty was renewed in 1856.

It was a tumultuous time in China, with sporadic rioting between foreigners and Chinese. Cushing arranged for an American accused of shooting and killing a Chinese to be tried by an American jury under American law. He was acquitted, and the case served as a precedent for establishing extraterritorial jurisdiction in China. Cushing had a less favorable result when he gave a large flagstaff to Consul Paul S. Forbes at Canton. At its top was a weather vane in the shape of an arrow. The revolving arrow frightened superstitious Chinese, who feared it was predicting disasters and death in the sections of the city the arrow pointed to. A mob broke into the American compound and had to be ejected by force. Forbes had the arrow taken down.

James K. Polk, Andrew Jackson's hard-driving protégé and a tough political operator, won the presidency in 1844 and gave charge of the State Department to James Buchanan after he promised the President his loyalty. Before the year was out, Buchanan was asking Polk to move him to the Supreme Court. But Polk believed that the Secretary of State opposed his positions and was leaking information to the press. Polk said Buchanan was able but "sometimes acts like an old maid."

Polk's inauguration brought a change of party and a redistribution of patronage and jobs. The spoils system was still at work. He gave the lucrative post of consul in Liverpool to General Robert Armstrong, who had served him long and well. Polk's younger brother William went to Naples as chargé d'affaires. And Polk sent Romulus Saunders, a prominent North Carolina politician, as minister to Spain to replace Washington Irving. When Andrew Jackson's longtime supporter Amos Kendall asked to be the minister to Spain, saying "I need rest and money," Polk turned him down.

DRAWING A LINE IN OREGON

Since 1827, Britain and the United States shared the "joint occupation" of Oregon, and Polk's claim on all the Oregon Territory in his inaugural address disturbed the British. There was talk of war, and a diplomatic dance began over Oregon.

U.S. Minister Edward Everett, at the end of 1843, suggested a compromise on Oregon to the Earl of Aberdeen, the British Foreign Secretary: Place the border on the 49th parallel as far west as Vancouver Island and give Britain all of Vancouver. Polk insisted that the United States should have all of Oregon to the line of 54°40′, but privately he was prepared to accept the border at the 49th parallel. That would still give the United States the great harbor of Puget Sound. The British wanted the border even farther south, at the mouth of the Columbia River.

One problem was, unsurprisingly, that many more Americans than British were settling in the Oregon Territory. Another problem was that Polk had difficulties filling the diplomatic post in London. He first offered it to Calhoun, whom he had dropped as Secretary of State. Calhoun was troubled by what a war with Britain would do to the economy of the South, and he was wounded by the loss of his cabinet seat. He turned down London. Polk offered the post to five more men; they all declined. Finally, he asked, successfully, Louis McLane, who had held the post once and was now the president of the Baltimore and Ohio Railroad. He would play a key role in the final negotiations over the Oregon border.

On January 15, 1845, the new British minister in Washington, Richard Pakenham, proposed arbitration over Oregon, and Polk started to maneuver the British into concessions he wanted. This led to a cabinet battle, because Secretary Buchanan dreaded the possibility of simultaneous wars with the British and the Mexicans.

Polk pointed out to Buchanan that a letter prepared by the Department of State for the President's signature violated diplomatic usage. Buchanan disagreed with him, and Polk bet him a basket of champagne. Buchanan failed to find a precedent and offered to deliver the champagne to Polk, but the President insisted he had been jesting. He was satisfied that Buchanan had been embarrassed.

President Polk also had to endure visits like one from two elegant young diplomats who spent their whole time with him talking about the fine paintings and sculpture they had seen and the glamorous people they had met in Europe. That wasn't Polk's style. He spoke to Buchanan about one of the two, Dabney S. Carr, the minister resident at Constantinople, and he wrote in his diary, "I thought it was almost time for him to let some other take his place." Later, the State Department instituted a limit on the time foreign service officers could spend at one post.

By the fall of 1845, Polk's aggressive claims and the prospect of war over Oregon alarmed conservative American businessmen. British and U.S. leaders conducted a verbal battle, offering peace but threatening war. *The Times* of London suggested reassuringly that Polk's jingoistic excesses would be thwarted "by the prudence of New England, and the reluctance of the South." But Polk was convinced that only by going to the very edge of war could he force Britain to compromise.

At the end of the year, the British offered arbitration, expecting a counteroffer to negotiate. Instead, Polk sent them a flat turndown and a demand for the entire Oregon Territory. The British prepared their fleet for action. Ambassador McLane sensed a British willingness to compromise at the 49th parallel, but he could not convince Polk.

Polk was driving toward his unstated goal of the border on the 49th parallel despite the danger of war. On February 25, 1846, the U.S. cabinet agreed on making the border the 49th parallel and allowing the British free navigation of the Columbia River for a limited time. The British rejected that. In March, McLane warned Polk that the British were preparing for war.

WARM-UP IN MEXICO

Events far away on the Rio Grande in Mexico now came into play. Polk worried that the British might persuade the Republic of Texas to remain independent of the United States. Andrew Jackson Donelson, former President Jackson's nephew, was the United States' able representative to Texas. He was authorized to promise the Texas president, Anson Jones, federal funding after annexation, and he helped persuade Texas' leaders to join the United States.

In the spring of 1845, Polk covertly sent to Texas another envoy, Charles A. Wickliffe, Tyler's ex–postmaster general, to strengthen the Texan leaders' desire for annexation. Polk and Buchanan wanted the U.S. border on the Rio Grande and were prepared both to absorb Texas and to seize the disputed territory between the Nueces and the Rio Grande to the west, even if it meant war with Mexico. Donelson convinced Texas' secretary of state to request that U.S. troops be moved to the Texas border and, on Secretary Buchanan's instructions, warned the Texans not to pursue the Mexicans beyond the Rio Grande.

General Zachary Taylor brought four thousand soldiers to the Rio Grande on March 28, 1846. Polk sent him reinforcements and ordered Taylor to regard any Mexican force that crossed the Rio Grande as commencing hostilities.

On taking office, Secretary of State Buchanan had recalled Wilson

Shannon, the U.S. minister who had been conducting an angry correspondence with the Mexican foreign minister. The secretary told Shannon that the President wanted to restore peace and harmony with Mexico. Unfortunately, he sent in Shannon's place Dr. William S. Parrott, a Virginia dentist who had business interests in Mexico and had filed claims totaling $690,000 against Mexico. Because diplomatic relations had been broken off when Texas was annexed, he was sent as a special agent. He shipped back dispatches assuring the government in Washington that the issues with Mexico could be settled peacefully. But on Saturday, May 9, President Polk impatiently told his cabinet he could wait no longer; on Tuesday, he would send Congress a war message.

Just then, word had reached Washington that two weeks earlier a large detachment of Mexican cavalry had crossed the Rio Grande and ambushed two companies of General Taylor's dragoons, causing sixteen casualties and capturing the rest. Polk beat the war drums, contending that Mexico had shed American blood on American soil. On Monday, he had his war.

Before news that the United States and Mexico were at war reached London, McLane persuaded Lord Aberdeen to make another proposal on Oregon. Aberdeen now suggested extending the 49th parallel to the middle of the channel separating Vancouver Island from the mainland and then southward to give Britain all of Vancouver Island and navigation of the Columbia River. The offer was sent from Liverpool by steamer on May 19. Had the British known that the United States was already at war with Mexico, it is unlikely that they would have made any offer.

McLane's efforts to effect a compromise over Oregon succeeded; the American government, with one war on its hands, was now willing to accept the British offer without changes. Buchanan and Pakenham signed a treaty on June 15, based on the British terms. The Senate ratified it swiftly.

Meanwhile, in case of war with Mexico, Secretary of the Navy George Bancroft had already ordered the American warships off the California coast to seize any ports they could. Everyone was in place.

12

War with Mexico

1845–46

Even while the United States was converting Texas into the twenty-eighth state, President Polk began to repair diplomatic relations with Mexico. Secretary of State James Buchanan alerted Congressman John Slidell, of Louisiana, to stand ready in New Orleans and instructed Consul John Black, who remained in Mexico City, to make it possible for Slidell to meet with the foreign minister. Slidell had the status of an envoy extraordinary and minister plenipotentiary and was authorized to assume the claims of American citizens against Mexico, plus $25 million more for most of California and New Mexico and a border with Texas at the Rio Grande. Polk wrote Slidell privately that he was prepared to go to war to acquire California. He would not compromise with what his Secretary of State called "so feeble and degraded a Power as Mexico." Polk was certain Mexico would buckle.

Slidell had landed at Veracruz on November 29, 1845, and found the Mexican government tottering. Foreign Minister Manuel Pea y Pea tried to persuade Consul Black to keep Slidell away from the capital. That infuriated Slidell.

Slidell remained in Mexico for five months, but no official would receive him. He grew increasingly belligerent. As American historian Charles Sellers put it, "The Polk-Slidell policy of combined bullying and bribery was precisely what no Mexican regime could submit to and survive." The Mexican government fell soon after 1846 began, and Slidell was instructed to give its successor a chance to receive him; if he would not be received, he was to come home.

Incredibly, President Polk received a representative from the exiled Mexican dictator Santa Anna, who urged him to march the American army to the Rio Grande and send a naval force to Veracruz.

Polk sent Navy Commander Alexander Slidell Mackenzie (John Slidell's nephew) to Havana to meet with Santa Anna. With the help of U.S. Consul Robert B. Campbell, a former congressman from South Carolina, they met, and the former dictator told Mackenzie he would settle all boundary problems for $30 million. He was allowed to pass through the U.S. Navy's blockade and reenter Mexico. Soon, he was running the country again and fighting against the United States. Santa Anna's goal always was to assure Mexico's independence.

Polk had acquired Texas and Oregon by nerve and manipulation. Now, he faced war. The Mexicans insisted that the land between the Nueces and Rio Grande rivers belonged to them. Because Mexican cavalry had crossed the Rio Grande and ambushed a detachment of American dragoons, Polk dared claim that Mexico had declared war on the United States. On Monday, May 11, 1846, he sent a war message to Congress, which, faced with an apparent fait accompli, voted overwhelmingly to fight. By the time Polk signed the declaration of war on Wednesday, American artillery had already destroyed the Mexican army along the Rio Grande, and the Secretary of State had ordered Commodore John D. Sloat to take possession of California.

Secretary Buchanan suggested notifying the world, falsely, that the United States did not intend to acquire California or New Mexico. Polk argued for two hours and then exploded that he would rather fight a war with "all the powers of Christendom" than make such a pledge.

CONSUL LARKIN AND THE BEAR FLAG REPUBLIC

Consul Thomas Larkin at Monterey learned that the American settlers around Sonoma, north of San Francisco Bay, were rebelling against Mexico and had set up their own "Bear Flag Republic." He sailed there with the American naval squadron, landed fifteen Marines on July 9, and occupied the town without resistance. The Bear Flag Republic became American. The U.S. Navy then "seized" San Francisco and Monterey. When the

British Navy reached Monterey, northern California was solidly in American hands.

The American squadron sailed south, and on August 3, Larkin accepted Los Angeles' surrender. By the end of summer, all California was American. But it did not last. In the fall, the Californians revolted against American rule, retook control of most of their towns, and a guerrilla band even captured Consul Larkin and held him for nearly two months. In January 1847, the U.S. Marines marched back into Los Angeles, and this time conquered California for good.

The Mexicans expelled all the American consuls except John Black in Mexico City. He stayed and reported to Washington until, on March 9, Major General Winfield Scott's army invaded Mexico at Veracruz.

The invasion at Veracruz was well planned. President Polk summoned Francis M. Dimond, who had served as U.S. consul at Port-au-Prince and Veracruz, to come to Washington from his home in Rhode Island. The question for Dimond: Would the army's plan succeed?

Dimond met with the President, Secretary of State, and Secretary of War and assured them that their plan was practical. The troops could land out of range of the guns in the castle of Veracruz. Dimond made a sketch of the scene, and the attack was planned for a force of three to four thousand men. The U.S. Army invested the town from the rear and forced its surrender.

Polk asked Congress for $2 million with which to buy peace and a chunk of Mexico. The bill passed after a debate over the so-called Wilmot Proviso, which said that slavery would not be permitted in any territory acquired from the war with Mexico. Congressman David Wilmot, of Pennsylvania, was no abolitionist, but he did not want white free men to have to compete against slave labor. The House narrowly passed the proviso, and then it was defeated in the Senate.

In view of Mexico's stubborn refusal to surrender and of disapproval of the war at home, Polk secretly sent Nicholas P. Trist, chief clerk of the State Department, to discuss peace with the Mexicans. Trist had gone to West Point and married Thomas Jefferson's granddaughter. After the election of 1828, Henry Clay had offered Trist a clerkship in the Department of State; and in 1833, Secretary Livingston appointed him consul to Havana. He served there for eight years, during which British diplomats accused him of abetting the slave trade. The Whigs removed him in 1840, and Polk named him chief clerk in 1845.

Trist was given full diplomatic powers and arrived at Veracruz on May 6, 1847. Tall, lean, and pugnacious, he promptly got into a prolonged spat with General Scott, who took umbrage at what he thought were orders placing him under the authority of a State Department clerk. He and Scott refused to call on each other until they were chastised by their superiors in Washington. Then, they exchanged conciliatory notes, and Scott sent Trist, who had become ill, a gift of guava marmalade. Because of that gesture, they became fast friends.

General Scott's army conquered Mexico City on September 14. Still, the Mexican foreign minister demanded that the United States pay for Texas and draw the border at the Nueces River, not the Rio Grande. Trist made the mistake of forwarding the demand for the Nueces boundary to Polk. The President presumed that Trist had bungled the negotiations and recalled him.

Trist ignored his recall and went ahead bullheadedly. Although he no longer had any authority, he negotiated the peace treaty of Guadalupe Hidalgo, which achieved Polk's main war aims. The United States gained California, New Mexico, and the border on the Rio Grande. When Mexico approved the treaty, John Black returned to Mexico City, John Parrott went back to Mazatlán, and Francis M. Dimond went to Veracruz. The United States was enlarged by six hundred thousand square miles and fronted on the Pacific. But with these gains came the cancer of slavery.

Americans from Ralph Waldo Emerson to Ulysses S. Grant condemned Polk's action as unprovoked aggression, and in the North it was regarded as a conspiracy to expand the part of the country dependent on slavery. Young Abraham Lincoln, in 1848, wrote a friend that the Mexican War set a precedent that allowed any President "to make war at pleasure."

GOLD

Consul Thomas Larkin wrote Secretary of State Buchanan from San Francisco on June 1, 1848, "to report to the State Department one of the most astonishing excitements and state of affairs now existing in this country, that, perhaps, has ever been brought to the notice of the Government. On the American fork of the Sacramento and Feather River, another branch of the same, and the adjoining lands, there has been within the present year discovered a placer, a vast tract of land containing gold, in small particles." Hordes of men rushed to the goldfields; San Francisco was almost emptied, and crews deserted their ships. Larkin reported that two thousand people were hunting gold by the rivers.

President Zachary Taylor died after taking ill during Independence Day ceremonies in 1850 at the Washington Monument, and Vice President Millard Fillmore assumed the presidency. He brought back Daniel Webster as Secretary of State, replacing John Middleton Clayton. Clayton had concluded the Clayton-Bulwer Treaty to construct a canal across Nicaragua; it was an unpopular treaty.

Webster managed a number of international crises. He supported Lajos Kossuth's attempt to gain Hungarian independence from Austria and told Minister George Perkins Marsh in Constantinople to send Kossuth to the United States in an American frigate. And despite his disgust with the Fugitive Slave Act, when fleeing slaves were seized in Boston, he prosecuted their cases. Known as the "defender of the Constitution," Webster put the law ahead of morality. But his hatred of slavery was never in doubt.

There were still problems to solve. After one of the major debates in American history, the Compromise of 1850 admitted California as a free state and settled, on the basis of "popular sovereignty," the other territory acquired from Mexico. The Bidlack-Mallarino Treaty, signed in 1846 by Benjamin A. Bidlack, the U.S. chargé d'affaires in Bogotá, gave the United States the right of transit across the isthmus of Panama. Americans built the first railroad across the isthmus, and Britain and the United States agreed to keep any canal open for each other.

And in 1853, James Gadsden, a railroad man then serving as the minister to Mexico, fit into place the last piece of the continental jigsaw puzzle. He negotiated the Gadsden Purchase, which cleared the way for a southern railroad route. The United States was still pressing outward.

13

Consular Reform

1853–65

The 1850s saw the nation slip to the brink. The nation divided over slavery in the new territories. President Franklin Pierce said, in 1853, "I believe that involuntary servitude, as it exists in different States of this Confederacy, is recognized by the Constitution. . . . I believe that the constituted authorities of this Republic are bound to regard the rights of the South in this respect as they would view any other legal and constitutional right."

Not everyone agreed.

That same year, President Pierce selected as his minister to France John Y. Mason, of Virginia, and as minister to Spain, Pierre Soulé, of Louisiana, both members of an organization called Young America. It preached that if the Southern states could not replace their tired cotton soil by expanding westward, they would turn south and expand into Cuba and South America.

Secretary of State William Marcy instructed the hotheaded Soulé to try to purchase Cuba from Spain for $150 million. Soulé, Mason, and James Buchanan, now the U.S. minister to Great Britain, met at Ostend, Belgium, in October 1854 to plot a strategy that became known as the Ostend Manifesto. If Cuba could not be purchased, the "manifesto" proposed "wresting it from Spain if we possess the power." Northerners condemned this as a plot to expand slavery, and President Pierce had to disown the idea that had he conceived.

This possibility of expansion was accelerated by technological advances. During the late 1840s, the steamship, railroad, and telegraph were revolutionizing how Americans conducted diplomacy, business, and even warfare. As historian Daniel Walker Howe pointed out, the telegraph "decoupled" communications from travel. No longer was communication limited to the speed of a man or a horse or sail. And only two decades later, the first transatlantic telegraph cable connected Europe and America.

By midcentury, the industrial revolution, the growth of cities, and the increase of population (more than four million immigrants entered the United States between 1840 and 1860) raised the pressure to acquire new lands for growing cotton and to find new markets for the production of American industries.

These advances in communication and the expansion of trade made inadequate the loose structure of the foreign service and the paucity of State Department supervision. The first comprehensive law to try to reshape the consular service was the Consular Reform Act of March 1, 1855. It directed the appointment of twenty-eight ministers, twenty-six secretaries of legation, and a long list of consuls. The act specified where they would serve, what they would be paid, and what would be their duties.

President Pierce and Secretary Marcy protested that the act interfered with the President's constitutional prerogative to make diplomatic and consular appointments. So, Congress replaced the 1855 law with the Reform Act of August 18, 1856. Instead of declaring that the President "shall appoint," the new version carefully said, "If the President shall think proper to appoint . . ." This law directed the American foreign service for the next fifty years.

The wide-ranging 1856 law contained three salary schedules: Schedule A applied to diplomatic posts, and schedules B and C to consular posts. Schedule A salaries rose to a top of $17,500 for "ministers plenipotentiary" stationed in Great Britain, France, Russia, and Germany. "Ministers resident" would receive 75 percent of that. The new salaries represented significant increases and would remain in effect until 1946.

The salaries established in schedule B and C were based on a man's post rather than his personal rank. Consular schedule B applied to the ninety-two larger consular posts with annual salaries from $1,000 to $7,500, and schedule C to forty smaller ones with annual salaries from $500 to $1,000. Consuls in B could neither engage in commerce nor keep the official fees they collected, while consuls in C could profit from private trade but could not keep fees. Officers in charge of some forty others, the smallest posts, could both engage in business and keep their official fees.

The 1856 act introduced the beginning of a badly needed merit system and provided for twenty-five "consular pupils," who were to be the seed of a professional consular service. But this provision for consular pupils was repealed the following year. Henry Adams explained candidly that, with the creation of consular pupils, "The President will then have fewer offices to divide among members of Congress." Those in power wanted to continue filling consular jobs on a political basis.

The Act of 1856 also made it illegal for anyone but the Secretary of State to issue passports and confirmed the President's authority to regulate fees and provide supervision of the men in the field. But the appointment and tenure of consuls still remained largely a matter of political influence and personal connections. And the consular service continued to suffer from a large personnel turnover, caused in good part by the inadequacy of consular salaries.

Secretary of State Lewis Cass sent to the House Committee on Foreign Affairs dispatches from consular officers asking for enough money to live on. The consul at Liverpool, which had been the most remunerative post, said his income under the fee system had averaged $15,000, while now his salary was set at $7,500. Out of that he had to spend $4,000 to hire clerks. The consul at Bremen found his salary of $2,000 entirely inadequate. Robert H. Hamilton, who served twenty years as consul at Montevideo, resigned because his salary was $1,000, while his house rent was $800.

Such inadequate salaries were slowly adjusted one by one until after the Civil War. Congress made broader adjustments in 1874 and 1893. The allowance for rent was increased in 1873, and for hiring clerks in 1874, 1881, and 1896. But provisions for salary levels, rent, and hiring clerks continued to lag behind those of other countries.

Under the 1856 act, consuls were required to make commercial reports annually. These started the following year with a series called Commercial Relations of the United States, which emphasized the trade of foreign countries with the United States.

These consular reports were just one sign of change. The Mexican War had shattered the delicate balance of power in the Senate between slave states and free states, and the increase in northern voters upset the balance in the House.

The cash-crop South was hurt economically by its impoverished soil and its uneducated enslaved population. Cotton growers no longer had the political strength to acquire new lands for a slave-based economy. Ralph Waldo Emerson wrote, "Patriotism for holidays and summer evenings, with music and rockets, but cotton thread is the union."

14

Japan's First American Consul

1856–62

On Monday morning, August 25, 1856 (a week after Congress passed the Reform Act), a stout, round-faced, fifty-one-year-old American with gray hair, sideburns, and a determined chin climbed onto a dock at the small, isolated Japanese town of Shimoda. Offshore, the frigate USS *San Jacinto,* which had brought him there, fired a thirteen-gun salute.

The Japanese government dreaded Townsend Harris' arrival. They did not know how to treat the first consul from the United States. Two years earlier, Commodore Matthew Perry had negotiated the Treaty of Kanagawa, allowing American ships to reprovision at two Japanese ports, one in the far north on Hokkaido island, and the other at Shimoda, south of Edo (later known as Tokyo). The treaty also allowed the United States to station a consul at Shimoda.

Shimoda sat on the tip of the Izu Peninsula, which was fifty miles long and isolated by mountains from the main travel routes. In this remote place, the Japanese exiled undesirables. Perry had been allowed to anchor his ships there; and at the fishing village of Kakizaki, across the bay, he had buried several of his men. Townsend Harris, the man who had landed at Shimoda, had been a successful merchant in New York; his brother bought wholesale chinaware in England, and Townsend sold it in New York. He was a member of Tammany Hall, and as president of the Board of Education helped develop free education, which became the City College of

New York. When the chinaware business failed, Harris spent five years roaming the Pacific, living on gifts from his brother. Harris was unable to persuade President Franklin Pierce to appoint him to a consular post in China, but his friends convinced Secretary of State Marcy to offer him the consular post Perry had created in Japan. Harris was no diplomat, but he was a Democrat and a bachelor; the Americans in power required the former, and the Japanese, the latter.

President Pierce had reservations about Harris, who had developed a drinking problem. Pierce first offered the post to John R. Brodhead, who had served in the legations at The Hague and London and spoke Dutch, the western language used by Japanese interpreters; but Brodhead turned down the post. Harris spoke no Dutch and hired as his interpreter Henry C. J. Heusken, a twenty-three-year-old from Amsterdam.

Pierce's doubts were justified. On the way to Japan, Harris made a drunken fool of himself in Paris, parading in elaborate court dress and handing out cards identifying him as "envoy extraordinary and minister plenipotentiary," when he was neither. But Harris was also capable, and en route to Japan, he negotiated a commercial treaty with Siam.

Landing at Shimoda, Harris, the frigate's captain, and ten others walked two miles to the spacious house of Governor Okada. They did not know enough to remove their boots before stepping on the governor's fine white matting. But Harris was impressive and pompous enough to awe his hosts.

When the governor tried to convince Harris to leave, he threatened to sail to Edo. Perry had told him that would worry the Japanese. They finally let him stay in the temple of Gyokusenji in the village of Kakizaki, where Perry's men were buried. The temple became the first U.S. consulate in Japan. On September 4, sailors from the warship raised an eighty-foot flagstaff and the American flag. Then, within hours, *San Jacinto* steamed out of the bay. Harris and Heusken were alone.

The Great Council in Edo had accepted Commodore Perry because he wanted to negotiate a treaty of friendship and provide care for American sailors shipwrecked on Japanese shores, and he had come with a powerful fleet. But Harris came for trade. The Japanese feared that this would enrich the merchant class and weaken the power of their own samurai, the xenophobic, feudal, landowning class, and were afraid that Harris would bring Christianity to Japan. Many of the conservative noble families wanted the foreigners treated harshly.

Harris found Japan attractive, despite its earthquakes and typhoons, and liked the Japanese people. After two months, he sent the minister of foreign affairs a message that he wanted to come to Edo to deliver a letter from the President of the United States. He would not tell the Japanese at Shimoda what the letter contained.

When officials from Edo came to meet with Harris, he told them he resented not being allowed to deliver the President's letter. His negotiations demonstrated a clash of cultures. Harris felt the Japanese were lying to him, and he repeatedly lost his temper, at which point the Japanese would just politely end the meeting.

On February 25, 1857, Harris was presented with a scroll five feet long bearing the signatures and seals of the members of the Great Council. Heusken received a copy in Dutch. The scroll declared that Harris should deal with the governors in Shimoda. The Japanese insisted this was a great honor; only twice before had the Great Council written to a foreigner: the king of the Netherlands and the prime minister of Russia. But Harris would negotiate only in Edo.

He made progress slowly. On June 26, the Convention of Shimoda was signed, opening Nagasaki to American ships and allowing Americans to reside at Shimoda and Hakodate. Americans would be under the control of their consul, and the consul could go where he pleased.

At Harris' request, the Japanese sent him a seventeen-year-old girl, Okichi, in the role of a nurse, and to Heusken they sent a girl named Ofuku. Okichi had previously been employed "attending seamen when they drank." Thus began a legend of Japanese womanhood sacrificing itself to foreigners' lust for the sake of the country.

On August 18, the Great Council finally agreed that Harris could travel to Edo, but not leave immediately. There was a long argument over to whom he would deliver the President's letter. Harris, angry and frustrated, wrote in his diary that he was ill and weighed only 130 pounds.

An official finally brought Harris the news that his demand had been granted. But he was asked if he would now reveal the important things the letter contained before going to Edo. Harris refused. If the letter's content was revealed, he knew he would not be allowed into Edo.

On September 3, the anniversary of the day when Harris and Heusken had come ashore, they received a package of letters and newspapers, their first. Harris was angered when he learned the Japanese had made a new commercial treaty with the Dutch, which continued government-to-government trade and opened trade between merchants under government supervision. The Dutch were permitted to practice Christianity in their own buildings. Then, a Russian admiral appeared and signed a similar agreement. Harris was losing face.

The deadlock soon broke, and Harris was permitted to set out for the capital. Plans were made with great precision. The entourage of nearly two hundred and fifty men made a procession a mile and a half long and covered fifteen to twenty miles a day. Guards and bearers wore the seal of the United States. For the last seven miles, Harris and Heusken traveled in their *norimono,* carried by twelve men, surrounded by ten guards, and preceded by the United States flag. Following Harris came his umbrella bearer, his shoe bearer, and his horse, led by a stable boy. They moved through a silent throng five deep on both sides of the road. Finally, the bearers entered the castle at a full run.

Harris had a single audience with the Shogun and presented the President's letter, which simply requested a commercial treaty. Ceremonies and discussions went on for weeks, and in February a treaty was finally agreed to, permitting full trade. An American diplomat could reside in Edo and a Japanese in Washington. Five Japanese ports would be opened by 1863. The Americans could practice their religions. The agreement went into effect on July 4, 1859, a date chosen by Harris.

The head of the Great Council set out for Kyoto to obtain the emperor's approval for the treaty, taking along gold in case bribes were needed. Back in Shimoda, an exhausted Harris became delirious and lay in a coma for several days. The Japanese and Heusken thought he was dying. After a week, the crisis passed, but he refused to take medicine or food, preferring to smoke opium. In April, he was well enough to return to Edo aboard the USS *Powhatan.* On July 29, 1858, the treaty was finally signed. Aboard USS *Powhatan,* American and Japanese flags were hoisted side by side, a salute of twenty-one guns fired, and Americans and Japanese toasted each other with champagne. The emperor's approval came through in November, with a disclaimer that the treaty was a stain on Japan, but the emperor understood that the Great Council had no choice.

The next April Harris left Shimoda, while Heusken remained in charge of the consulate. In China, Harris learned that he had been promoted to the rank of minister and that he was to establish a legation in Edo. He closed the consulate at Shimoda and opened a legation in a temple in Edo.

After the Americans left Shimoda, the parishioners did not have money to rebuild the temple Gyokusenji, which they said stank of barbarians, so the whole village turned out and scrubbed it clean. Harris' concubine, Okichi, went on to a life of drunkenness, eventually committing suicide in the river. Her grave is a Shimoda tourist attraction. Ofuku married into a respected family and is buried in Gyokusenji's cemetery.

Antiforeign feeling increased when imports threatened the livelihood of Japanese producers of cheap cotton textiles. Several foreigners were murdered. Harris displayed courage in the face of this violence and won the respect of the Japanese.

On the evening of January 15, 1861, Henry Heusken left the Prussian Legation, where he was helping officials learn how to negotiate a treaty. He was escorted by three mounted officers and four footmen bearing lanterns. Seven assassins attacked them. Heusken was seriously wounded. Trying to escape on his horse, he fell to the ground. The assassins fled.

Heusken was carried to the U.S. Legation and died just after midnight. Fearing Harris would be attacked, the Japanese asked him not to attend the funeral, but he insisted. There was no trouble. He also persuaded the Japanese to send ten thousand dollars to Heusken's mother and erect a monument on his grave.

As a result of Heusken's brutal death, the foreign envoys moved from Edo to Yokohama, where they had ships and men to protect them. When Harris refused to go, the Japanese declared that he was displaying the spirit of a samurai.

Harris was replaced in Edo in 1862, when the United States was fighting the Civil War. He lived in New York City for fifteen more years; because he loved to talk about Japan, he was known at the Union Club by the Japanese word for a powerful man "the old Tycoon."

15

The Nation at War with Itself

1861–65

Between President Abraham Lincoln's election and his inauguration, Southern states began leaving the Union. The foreign service, like the military services, lost men who felt their first loyalty was to their state. The State Department was already quite small, with forty-two employees in Washington and thirty-seven missions abroad that had forty-five diplomats and 282 consulates.

Southerners had controlled much of the federal patronage and held many key positions. The two most important consular posts were in Liverpool and Havana. Beverly Tucker, of Virginia, the U.S. consul at Liverpool, chose to stay in Britain as a Confederate agent. He was later accused of playing a role in the conspiracy that led to Lincoln's assassination. Lincoln had immediately replaced Tucker with Mark H. Dunnell, of Maine; and the former congressman Freeman H. Morse, also of Maine, was given the post of former Congressman Robert Campbell of South Carolina, the outspoken consul in London.

President Jefferson Davis, of the Confederacy, ordered Charles Helm, of Kentucky, back to Havana, where he had been the consul general. In his place to represent the United States, Lincoln assigned Robert Wilson Shufeldt, of Connecticut, a former U.S. Navy officer.

President Davis sent Edwin DeLeon, of South Carolina, the U.S. consul at Alexandria, Egypt, to Europe to persuade and bribe the French press to support the Southern cause. John T. Pickett, of Kentucky, the consul at

Veracruz, covered Mexico for the Confederacy without much success. Other consuls who joined the Confederacy included Ambrose Dudley Mann, who had been at Bremen, and Duncan McRae, recently at Paris, both from North Carolina.

Lincoln appointed writer William Dean Howells, age twenty-four, as consul in Venice. Howells had written a successful campaign biography of Lincoln. Over the next four years, he studied the Venetians and discovered his own abilities as a novelist. Venice was surely the only American consulate with a gondola and a gondolier.

Secretary of State Lewis Cass, after seven years in office, resigned suddenly on December 15, 1860, because President Buchanan would not reinforce the Federal forts in the South. Lincoln asked William H. Seward, his able opponent for the presidential nomination, to be his Secretary of State. Seward, a slight, short, stooped man with penetrating eyes and a good sense of humor, had been governor of New York and a United States senator. Historian Doris Kearns Goodwin quotes Lincoln as saying, on meeting Seward, "Governor Seward, there is one part of my work that I shall have to leave entirely to you. I shall have to depend upon you for taking care of these matters of foreign affairs, of which I know so little, and with which I reckon you are familiar."

Seward wanted to save the Union more than he wanted to destroy slavery. He favored some kind of compromise between North and South, and he had been widely expected to win the Republican nomination. As Southerners left Congress, Senator Charles Sumner, of Massachusetts, assumed the chair of the Committee on Foreign Relations. He believed the Union and slavery could not survive together and demanded emancipation. He also advocated strong representation abroad and opposed giving posts overseas as rewards for political service.

Seward's small Department of State had to cover its diplomatic and consular responsibilities and to serve as custodian of the United States Seal, archivist, and commissioner of patents. In the early months of the war, Seward also imprisoned Southern spies and sympathizers.

The department was housed in a two-story brick building on the corner of Fifteenth Street and Pennsylvania Avenue. The Secretary occupied two rooms on the corner of the second floor overlooking the avenue. The staff consisted of an assistant secretary, a chief clerk, twenty-three other clerks, two messengers, and four watchmen. Chief Clerk William Hunter had been with the department since John Quincy Adams. Assistant Secretary of

State William Prescott had joined the Confederacy, so Seward appointed his own thirty-year-old son, Frederick William Seward, to be assistant secretary, with responsibility for the consular service.

The European nations' reactions to the moral and practical issues around slavery had a major impact on the war in America. The Confederacy needed markets for its cotton and sources for arms and munitions, and the British economy was built in good part on textile mills. The U.S. Navy blockaded Southern ports because Northern leaders knew that if the South was isolated, she would have difficulty withstanding the North's industrial power.

President Davis also understood Europe's importance, and Confederate agents waged a tireless struggle overseas with the Union's representatives. In April 1861, Davis rushed three men over to Britain and France to speak for the South. Their leader was the proponent of secession and defender of slavery William L. Yancey, of Alabama; the others were Judge Pierre A. Rost and Ambrose Dudley Mann.

SEWARD'S MAN IN LONDON

On the whole, Lincoln's and Seward's diplomatic appointments were astute, even though the young Republican Party had few men with foreign experience and Lincoln did make some appointments to reward supporters. But the urgency of the moment and Secretary Seward's diplomatic skills, in the words of Charles Francis Adams Sr., saw that "from a state of utter demoralization at the outset, the foreign service rapidly became the most energetic and united organization thus far made abroad."

Of course, political pressures persisted. Frederick Van Dyne, of the State Department, told this story:

A Congressional delegation once importuned President Lincoln to appoint a certain man as Minister to Hawaii, urging among other reasons for his appointment his ill health and the probability that his health would be benefited by the Hawaiian climate. Mr. Lincoln replied: "Gentlemen, you're too late. There are nine candidates for the place ahead of you, and every one of them is sicker than yours."

Lincoln proposed sending William L. Dayton to London as minister; he had been the Republicans' vice presidential candidate in the unsuccessful 1856 election. But when Secretary Seward pressed Lincoln to send Charles Francis Adams, Lincoln shifted Dayton to Paris and named Adams minister to England. Adams came to Washington for instructions and thanked Lincoln, who candidly replied, "Very kind of you to say so, Mr. Adams, but you are not my choice. You are Seward's man."

Charles Francis Adams was, it is fair to say, their most important foreign service appointment; his effect on the war was crucial. Son and grandson of presidents, he was a short, ruddy heir of a Revolutionary War family. His mother was the daughter of Joshua Johnson, who had been the American consul in London and a governor of Maryland.

Charles Francis Adams was conservative, cautious, and without flagrant ambitions. He despised slavery but believed that the Constitution guaranteed the South certain rights in regard to slavery and that they should be respected. He fought for a law to prevent a state from returning runaway slaves to the South and opposed the annexation of Texas. At the Court of St. James's, he would replace George Mifflin Dallas, who had served as Vice President to Polk. Adams sailed from Boston for London on May 1, 1861, with his wife and their children Mary, Brooks, and Henry, who served as his father's private secretary. On board ship, the only person Adams knew was the eccentric Cassius M. Clay, sailing to become minister to Russia; Adams did not like Clay and spent his time reading Macauley's *History of England*.

When they landed at Liverpool on May 13—steam power sped up the Atlantic crossing dramatically—Adams learned that the British had issued a proclamation of neutrality, which gave the Confederacy the equivalent of belligerent rights. By recognizing a state of war, Britain tried to stay neutral and to thus remain a market for Southern cotton. However, the United States insisted the South had begun not a war but an insurrection.

Adams had to deal with a British government that could at any time become a participant in the war because it had commercial and cultural interests or because it believed that having two nations across the Atlantic would be more advantageous for Britain. Eventually, the Union victory at Antietam and the Emancipation Proclamation cooled British ardor for the South.

The governing British neutrality law of 1819 contained a serious loophole. Although it prohibited arming ships that intended to attack friendly powers, it did not prohibit Britain from building such vessels.

British officials, if generally sympathetic to the South, were courteous to Adams. They arranged a special presentation to Queen Victoria, even though all rituals had been canceled out of respect for the recent death of her mother. While his American predecessors had irritated the British establishment by appearing in court in plain black suits, he carefully dressed in silk stockings and gold lace. The queen said, "I am thankful we shall have no more American funerals."

As Britain's supply of cotton began to run out, some manufacturers turned to India for cotton while others urged the government to support the Confederacy. Lord Palmerston, the prime minister, was actively antagonistic to the United States, but the foreign secretary, John Russell, opposed slavery. He and Adams worked well together; both were direct, formal, and reserved. Adams assumed that events would control what happened. But ever cautious, he rented his house in London by the month.

Adams had a minimal staff in the new legation at 54 Portland Place. In addition to his son Henry, Charles Lush Wilson, owner of the Chicago *Daily Journal,* was a secretary in the legation; he was inexperienced and inefficient. Benjamin Moran, the assistant secretary of legation, was hardworking and knowledgeable, but he was sensitive to slights, making him an awkward match with the aloof Adams.

Freeman H. Morse, the U.S. consul in London, tried to gather information on the Confederates. Energetic and imaginative, he built an invaluable network of informers. But he found he was competing with Henry S. Sanford, the American minister to Belgium, who came to London frequently, built his own spy network, and bought information from British detectives and factory workers.

British cooperation with the Confederacy so frustrated Secretary Seward that he sent Adams blunt instructions in what became known as Dispatch No. 10. It said that the United States expected Britain to honor the Union's blockade of the South. If the British insisted on having relations with the Confederate representatives in London, Adams should cut off all diplomatic contact with the foreign ministry.

Seward wanted Adams to read this confrontational message aloud to Russell. But Adams, appalled by the dispatch, told Russell only its gist. And Seward, he explained accurately, was writing for home consumption.

When the rather reckless statement was published a year later, it did nothing to help the Union cause.

After the Confederate victory at Bull Run in July 1861 stimulated British support for the South, Confederate ships were secretly outfitted and armed in British ports. Adams complained to Russell that British ships were carrying military supplies and clothing to the South, but he was told that the British government could not interfere with private business.

In October, Jefferson Davis reorganized his European team and sent as special commissioners two former U.S. senators, James M. Mason, of Virginia, a fat, pompous, coarse defender of slavery, and John Slidell, of Louisiana, slim, silent, and scheming. Mason was assigned to London and Slidell to Paris. En route to Europe, the two Confederate commissioners ran the U.S. Navy's blockade at Charleston and boarded the British mail packet *Trent* at Havana. Robert W. Shufeldt, now the U.S. consul general in Havana, arranged with Captain Charles Wilkes, commander of the USS *San Jacinto*, to intercept them.

In the Bahama Channel on November 8, Captain Wilkes halted *Trent* with a shot across her bow, sent over a boarding party, and removed the two Confederate agents and their secretaries. They were imprisoned in Fort Warren, in Boston Harbor. Northerners were thrilled, and the House voted Wilkes a gold medal.

The "*Trent* affair" loosed a flood of anti-Union sentiment in Europe, and Britain began girding for war. Lincoln recognized that Wilkes had violated international law, and Adams feared that British opinion would swing against the North.

The French were also demanding that the rights of neutrals be respected, so Secretary Seward sent to Paris his political mentor, Thurlow Weed, and General Winfield Scott. In Paris, the U.S. Consul General John Bigelow, a former New York journalist and politician, wrote a letter explaining the Union view of the *Trent* affair, and General Scott signed it. The letter stressed that the U.S. government had not ordered the seizure of *Trent* and that Britain herself insisted on the right to search neutral vessels for contraband of war. On December 3, Paris newspapers carried the letter, and copies were rushed to London. This was regarded as the most valuable propaganda coup of the war.

By mid-December tempers cooled, although the British press continued to bubble with outrage. Adams informed Russell that Wilkes had acted without government approval. The U.S. cabinet endorsed Seward's new position, and on January 8, 1862, the prisoners were released to a British ship off Provincetown. But no apology was given. The British accepted the compromise, and everyone stepped back from the brink.

ENDING THE OCEANIC SLAVE TRADE

In December 1861, Lincoln told Congress it was time to recognize the black nations of Haiti and Liberia. Senator Sumner brought in a bill to send diplomatic representatives and made sure that it passed. The next summer, Benjamin F. Whidden, of New Hampshire, was sent to Haiti as the first commissioner/consul, and Abraham Hanson, of Wisconsin, went to Liberia. Hanson died at his post in Monrovia in July 1866 at the age of forty-eight of "African fever."

Henry E. Peck, who succeeded Whidden in 1865, was shipwrecked on his way to Haiti; he had to make a second voyage. Peck had been professor of moral philosophy at Oberlin College in Ohio and was a leader in the celebrated rescue of an escaped seventeen-year-old slave, John Price, in 1858, which challenged the Fugitive Slave Act. Professor Peck and twenty-one others were jailed for a month. In Haiti, Peck proved to be an energetic, able envoy and was promoted to the rank of minister resident and consul general. He died in Haiti on June 9, 1867, at the age of forty-five, of yellow fever. Haiti would always be a post of hazards.

In February 1862, Charles Francis Adams proposed to Russell that they work together to suppress the slave trade. With representatives from slaveholding states no longer present in the Senate, Adams told Russell, the United States would welcome British cruisers off the coast of Cuba. Americans well remembered British searching American vessels and impressing American seamen, but the U.S. Navy, blockading the Confederacy, now did not have the resources to stop the slave trade.

As a consequence, on April 7, Seward and Lord Lyons, Britain's minister in Washington, signed a treaty granting the mutual right to search suspected slave ships and creating mixed courts to condemn them. Under the Lyons-Seward Treaty, the number of slaves brought to Cuba dropped from 30,473 in 1859–60 to 143 by 1864–65. Slave-trade traffic was finally smothered. Seward wrote Adams that had the treaty existed in 1808, there would have been no Civil War.

Lincoln thought that the solution for freed slaves might be colonization. James Watson Webb, the U.S. minister to Brazil, suggested that nation's vast land mass as a possible refuge. But Seward took no action, and that idea eventually disappeared.

"IMPECCABLE MANNERS AND GORGEOUS DRESS"

Seward persuaded Congress in March 1863 to pass a bill that permitted privateers to seek out and destroy *Alabama* and other Confederate raiders. And British Foreign Secretary Russell ordered the seizure of *Alexandria,* under construction for the Confederacy. He no longer wanted to be involved in the American war.

According to Doris Kearns Goodwin, the diplomatic corps stuck to tradition and ritual, even in the depths of this war:

> For those fascinated by fashion and etiquette, nothing compared
> to the impeccable manners and gorgeous dress of the diplomats,
> bespangled with ribbons and garters denoting different orders of
> knighthood.

Thomas H. Dudley of New Jersey, the capable consul who replaced Beverly Tucker in Liverpool, took risks to keep Adams informed of the Confederate ships being outfitted there. Liverpool was a bustling center of shipbuilding and international intrigue, and Dudley was a Quaker and an able Republican lawyer with an instinct for espionage and the dangerous. He built his own spy network to replace Sanford's. He engaged Ebenezer S. Eggleston, the consul at Cadiz, Spain, to collect information on the Confederate ships. In a radical move, Eggleston left his consulate in the care of Mrs. H. S. Eggleston. It was a rare early case of a woman having responsibility for an American consulate.

Based on information from Dudley, on March 25, 1862, Adams filed a formal protest with Russell that the British had permitted the seven-hundred-ton steamer *Oreto* to sail and that their claim that she was being built for Italy was false. Adams had simply checked with the Italian minister in London. The Italians supported the Union, and George Perkins Marsh, now the minister at the temporary Italian capital, Turin, worked hard to sustain their endorsement. (Marsh served as the minister to Italy from 1861 to 1882, an exceptional length of time for a chief of mission.)

Oreto was seized in Nassau but then released by the court there. Renamed the CSS *Florida,* she captured or destroyed thirty-two U.S. vessels in the two years before she was finally seized by the American warship *Wachussett.* U.S. Consul Thomas F. Wilson was aboard *Wachussett* when she attacked *Florida* and, to avoid an angry Brazilian crowd, he sailed away in her. The mob attacked the American consulate instead.

Consul Dudley traveled to London in July 1862 and warned Adams that the British were building a gunboat for the Confederates. She was known then as *290,* and most of her crew were British. Adams' protests to the British were ignored until after *290* had sailed. She was the second ship ordered by Captain James Dunwody Bulloch, who ran the Confederacy's shipbuilding program abroad. A Georgia-born former U.S. Navy officer, he was the eldest brother of Theodore Roosevelt's mother.

Adams sent USS *Tuscarora* to intercept *290,* but she eluded the American sloop of war and, under the name *Alabama,* became the most effective Confederate raider, prowling far waters and destroying more than sixty ships.

Alabama's end came when Minister William L. Dayton discovered that she had put into Cherbourg for overhaul. On June 19, 1864, outside French territorial waters off Cherbourg, she was sunk by the USS *Kearsarge.* Those of *Alabama*'s crew who returned to England were interviewed by Consul Freeman Morse. Adams reported to the British Foreign Office and built up bills for damage.

Another distant consul seized an opportunity to play a role in the Civil War. James De Long, the consul at Tangier, had two Confederates arrested when they tried to buy coal for the CSS *Sumter.* He held them prisoner in the consulate and sent them to the United States in a Union warship.

The British refused to interfere with British subjects whose acts of private business were compromising Britain's neutrality. Confederacy-owned vessels sailed under the British flag and were received in British ports. Most of their crews were British subjects.

The Confederates were also active covertly in London. Henry Hotze, a former U.S. foreign service officer, wrote pro-Southern articles for British newspapers and paid British newsmen to place pro-Confederate articles in British and European papers.

Dudley learned that two more ships were being built for the Confederacy at the Laird Brothers' shipyards in Liverpool. The builders insisted they had been ordered by the Egyptian government. These two had underwater iron prows that could smash the Union navy's wooden ships, and they were already nearing completion. Adams understood their value; he wrote on hearing of the *Monitor's* victory over the *Merrimac* that "it dates the commencement of a new era in warfare."

When he learned of the rams, Seward threatened that U.S. warships would follow Confederate ships into British ports and destroy them there. Adams withheld that incendiary note from Russell, but wrote him that if the rams sailed, Britain would no longer be neutral. His statement became famous: "It would be superfluous in me to point out to your lordship that this is war."

Tensions rose. Prime Minister Palmerston condemned Adams' "insolent threats of war." But the British issued orders that the rams were not to leave port until their destination, supposedly Egypt, could be determined. In the end, the British government ducked the whole question by buying them for its own use. The rams were the last wartime problem between the United States and Britain serious enough to lead to war.

Consul Dudley in Liverpool had one final exposure to the Confederate sea raiders. Confederate agent James Bulloch arranged for a British friend to buy a British-built steamer, which was armed for the Confederacy and named CSS *Shenandoah*. She destroyed the New England whaling fleet in the Pacific after General Robert E. Lee had surrendered but before *Shenandoah's* captain received the news. Dudley witnessed her return to Liverpool and her sale by the British.

FRANCE BENEFITS FROM THE WAR

William Dayton, who became the U.S. minister to France in May 1861, cared greatly about appearances; he felt a minister could not properly undertake propaganda and press relations. So, when Napoleon III sought to use the American Civil War to France's advantage, Dayton asked Secretary Seward to send him someone who could write and who knew the European press.

Fortunately, Seward sent him the perfect man. That August, he announced that forty-three-year-old John Bigelow would be the United States consul at Paris. Among Union diplomats and consuls, Bigelow proved second only to Charles Francis Adams in importance to the success of the Union's war effort.

A six-foot farm boy from the Hudson River Valley, Bigelow had graduated from Union College. Coming to New York City when he was eighteen, he made friends with the powerful Sedgwick family, Samuel Tilden, and William Cullen Bryant.

Bigelow was thorough and strong willed, and not at all humble. As a lawyer, he worked for prison reform, universal male suffrage, and the end of the death penalty. But he was more successful as a writer and propagandist than an attorney. In 1848, he became a partner with Bryant at the *New York Evening Post*. Bigelow was a founder of the Republican Party and in 1856 wrote a campaign biography of John Charles Fremont, the Republican candidate for President.

Bigelow expressed disdain for the United States' representatives abroad and recommended closing the foreign service and appointing special commissioners whenever problems arose. He wrote in the *Evening Post* of the diplomatic and consular corps: "If most of them talk abroad as they do at home, the fewer languages at their command the better."

Just before the Civil War, Bigelow sold his one-third interest in the *Evening Post,* and when the consulate in Paris was offered to him, he was glad to take it. In addition to consular work, he would be responsible for creating a favorable French press and keeping France from intervening in the Civil War. Bigelow knew that Napoleon III would censor any dissenting articles and that many French journalists at the time could be bought.

The Bigelows settled in the rue de Rivoli on Saturday, September 14, 1861; he refused to move in the day before because he was superstitious about beginning anything on a Friday. And Friday the thirteenth! The lean, intense Bigelow was not thrilled to be working for the pompous Dayton. And Dayton, who refused to learn French, was disappointed that Bigelow's French was not stronger and that he had to hire an interpreter when he met with the minister of foreign affairs.

Bigelow moved the consulate at his own expense to 47 Champs-Élysées, with three small rooms for his two assistants and himself. He cultivated French journalists, who showed signs of supporting the North. But the only Americans on whose help he could count were Dayton; Henry S. Sanford, the U.S. minister to Belgium, whom Adams was finding such a nuisance; and David Fuller, the black porter at the Paris consulate.

The work of the consulate expanded. In 1861, it had filed 372 invoices. Two years later, trade had increased, and the number of invoices reached 13,000. Bigelow added two men, and they still were not enough. He used part of his salary to add clerks and translators. He spent office hours on consular work and the rest of the day on what he considered his real job. The workload grew so heavy that when Seward asked him for a detailed report on the customhouse system in France, Bigelow lost his temper and offered to resign. Lincoln and Seward dissuaded him.

A FRENCH EMPEROR FOR MEXICO

When John Bigelow arrived in Paris in 1861, he had to face Napoleon III's adventure in Mexico. Mexico had been unable to pay the interest on its $80 million in foreign debts; so Britain, France, and Spain had occupied Mexican ports and were collecting customs duties. Within a few months, Britain and Spain withdrew from Mexico, but Napoleon III's troops occupied Mexico City, overthrew the republican government, and declared young Archduke Maximilian of Austria emperor of Mexico.

At first, Bigelow urged that the United States take action in Mexico, but he came to accept Seward's calmer position that time would solve the problem. Seward worked hard on the Mexican crisis as well as on trying to purchase a Caribbean naval base. It took longer than expected. In April 1866, the French planned their troops' departure, but the new minister of foreign affairs extended the timetable without offering the Americans any explanation.

Bigelow went to Saint-Cloud to meet with Napoleon III. In a tiny smoke-filled room, the emperor said he had advised Maximilian to abdicate and that he would withdraw his troops in the spring. Bigelow reported this to Seward, using the new oceanic cable. Seward at first rejected the new dates, but Bigelow assured him the French would depart peacefully. Their army did so early in 1867, and then a Mexican firing squad executed Maximilian.

JOHN BIGELOW VERSUS JOHN SLIDELL

For three years, Bigelow and the Confederacy's John Slidell locked horns. Both were able and resourceful. With their considerable skills, they both strove to win over the French press. Slidell had the advantage: Bigelow received a salary of $4,800, while Slidell received $12,000 and had a large budget for propaganda.

Bigelow was dogged and persistent. In October 1861, no Paris newspaper supported the North; a year later, only one, *Le Moniteur,* the official government paper, had not carried an article favorable to the Union. Slidell was the more suave and ruthless. As a young man, he had fled New York after fighting a duel over a girl, and he had become a political power in New Orleans. When Charles Francis Adams forced Britain to start closing down the Confederate shipbuilding program, Slidell arranged to build ships in France. Napoleon III is said to have suggested to Slidell that he claim to have the ships built for the Italian government. Slidell checked with the foreign minister, who replied that he wanted to know nothing of such matters.

Bigelow hired a man to go to Le Havre and see what Captain Bulloch was doing in the shipyards there. He found two Confederate warships had been contracted for. Bigelow visited the port of Brest, and when *Florida* put into Brest, despite France's neutrality, Bigelow persuaded a French ship owner to sue for damages to his ship caused by *Florida.* He lost the lawsuit but kept the deadly *Florida* in port for weeks.

In September 1863, Bigelow bought documents from a Frenchman that proved Bulloch was preparing to build two cruisers and two ironclads in France. And L. Arman, a major French shipbuilder, had agreed to build ships for Slidell. Bigelow also learned that the Confederates had ordered four corvettes in France and had received French permission to arm them with fourteen six-inch rifled guns. Arman arranged for Bulloch to transfer the two Laird iron rams from Liverpool to the French company Brav et Cie. Dayton took the documents proving all this deception to the foreign ministry, where he was assured that authority to construct the ships had been withdrawn. But the foreign minister, working both sides, also assured Slidell that the Confederate shipbuilding program could proceed.

Bigelow made the French duplicity public and stopped the rams from going to sea. When Napoleon III's government asserted that the ships were being built for Denmark and Sweden, Bigelow had the French press publish Arman's letter revealing that the ships were being built for the Confederacy.

"GUARANTEE A PERMANENT CAREER"

On the other hand, some of the men who represented the United States abroad during the Civil War gave their country a bad name. Some had no knowledge of the local languages; some sold United States passports; some drank to excess; some were just lazy. At his long-lasting post in Italy, George Perkins Marsh, the U.S. minister to Italy, had to contend with a flourishing trade in fraudulent passports and identity papers. He complained that "the character of the United States Foreign Service has been declining ever since the days of John Quincy Adams."

Toward the end of the war, John Bigelow, at Seward's initiative, wrote a lengthy, thoughtful report advocating reforms for the consular service. He said that the French consular system was the best in the world and should serve as the model for the United States. In his covering letter, he wrote Seward, "I am quite convinced that no reform of our service is worth attempting, which does not raise the standard of qualification and guarantee a permanent career with reasonable prospect of promotion for those embarking in it. Under the system of quadrennial change or even uncertainties an efficient service is simply impossible." He declared that appointments must stop being "the lawful spoils of a triumphing party."

Bigelow quoted Nathaniel Hawthorne, who had been the consul at Liverpool:

It is not too much to say, (of course allowing for a brilliant exception here and there) that an American never is thoroughly qualified for a foreign post, nor has time to make himself so, before the revolution of the political wheel discards him from office.

In his own consulate, Bigelow advised that salaries be increased. He pointed out that he made $4,800 a year while the average consul with a family of four in the French service in Paris was earning $7,422. He said consuls should not engage in private work once salaries were adequate.

. . .

William Dayton, the U.S. minister in Paris, died suddenly on December 1, 1864. Charles Stuart Kennedy, the historian of the consular service, wrote, "Dayton died, supposedly of overeating, in the Parisian apartment of an American lady whose loyalty to the Union cause was suspect."

President Lincoln, without consulting Secretary Seward, offered Dayton's post to James Gordon Bennett, owner of the sensationalist *New York Herald*. When Bennett turned it down, Seward promoted Bigelow, who actually was eager to return home and had put in his letter of resignation. The promotion kept him in Paris for two more years.

After the war ended, Bigelow again resigned. He was succeeded by John A. Dix, a New York politician who had been a U.S. senator and Buchanan's secretary of the treasury. Bigelow had little respect for Dix and said he was tired of keeping a hotel for visiting VIPs. He went home to New York City, where he spent the next forty-five years, until he was ninety-four, as a political and civic leader. If his friend Samuel Tilden had won the disputed election in 1876, Bigelow expected to become his Secretary of State.

16

Public Trust, Private Property

1866—85

On April 5, 1865, two days after Richmond fell, Secretary of State William Seward, then sixty-four years old, went for a carriage ride in Washington, and the horses bolted. Seward was thrown to the ground, unconscious and with a concussion; his right arm and his jaw were broken. Nine days later, Lincoln was assassinated. Within minutes of John Wilkes Booth's attack on the President, Lewis Paine (also known as Powell), a husky former Confederate soldier, invaded Seward's home in Madison Place.

Paine pushed his way to the third floor, where Seward lay bedridden, and stabbed Seward in the throat three times with a large Bowie knife. Seward's soldier-nurse, Private George Robinson, tackled the assassin. Paine struck Robinson, dropped his knife, and fled on a waiting horse. He was captured and hung.

When Seward recovered from his near-fatal knife wounds, he returned to work to realize a goal he had long coveted: the acquisition of Russia's possessions on the North American continent. Seward offered $7 million in gold for Russian America. And then, to ensure the purchase, he added $200,000 to the price. The longtime Russian minister to the United States, Baron Edouard de Stoeckl, whose wife was an American, was delighted with Seward's offer; Stoeckl had been authorized to accept a minimum of

$5 million. At four o'clock in the morning on March 30, 1867, at the State Department, the Baron and the Secretary signed the sale.

A disinterested Senate, in special session, promptly ratified it by a vote of 37 to 2. The House took more than a year to appropriate the money. Without waiting for the appropriation, President Andrew Johnson opened Alaskan ports to American traders. Baron Stoeckl helped by bribing several reluctant politicians, and American speculators also participated in the deal. As part of all this finagling, the baron kept $165,000 for himself.

The Alaska purchase, which shorter-sighted people like editor Horace Greeley and cartoonist Thomas Nast ridiculed as "Seward's Folly," increased the landmass of the United States by 20 percent.

The energized, industrialized United States emerged from the horrific Civil War more involved in the world than ever before. And it needed more markets abroad. For example, U.S. wheat exports rose from $4 million in 1860 to $50 million in 1867. In addition, Secretary Seward supported the United States' desire for bases from which it could control trade routes. The Senate Committee on Foreign Relations rejected Seward's treaty to buy Saint Thomas, but Seward did manage to keep Midway for a naval coaling station.

Seward completed a treaty with Nicaragua for a canal across Central America in 1867, and he sent Caleb Cushing to Bogotá to negotiate a treaty for a canal across the Isthmus of Panama, as William Vanderbilt and Peter Cooper wanted. But Colombia's senate had not been paid off, and it rejected the treaty.

By 1868, it looked as if there was no possibility of settling the *Alabama* claims anytime soon, so Adams resigned as minister at London. The English appreciated his combination of tact and coldness, *The Times* of London praising his "wise discretion and cool judgment." Adams' successor was Reverdy Johnson, a seventy-two-year-old lawyer and U.S. senator.

THE SHAKY GRANT YEARS

Newly elected President, Ulysses S. Grant, chose Hamilton Fish, a former New York governor and senator, to be his Secretary of State in 1869. Fish was no intellectual, but he was hardworking and, as a country gentleman, had few selfish ambitions, a peculiarity that made him distinctive during the Grant years.

While under Grant the Executive Mansion worked on the buddy system, under Fish the State Department was a bit more professional. Bancroft Davis became Fish's assistant secretary, and the veteran William Hunter, his second assistant. Hunter had entered the department as a clerk in 1829, and became its walking memory and the faithful confidant of secretaries.

Secretary Fish faced issues with Canada on the northwest boundaries and on the fishing grounds that had been the subject of controversy since before the founding of the United States. On January 8, 1870, the Canadians abrogated the Reciprocity Treaty of 1854, which had eased restrictions on American fishermen. The fisheries returned to the stricter regulation of the Treaty of 1818. Sizable numbers of American fishermen broke the Canadian law, four hundred American ships were boarded, and American and Canadian fishermen engaged in violent confrontations.

Finally, the whole set of frozen issues between the United States and Britain—fisheries, *Alabama* claims, boundaries, Canadian independence—cracked open on the evening of September 26, 1870, when Secretary of State Fish and the British minister to Washington, Sir Edward Thornton, sat in Fish's study smoking cigars. Fish proposed that all the pending questions be arbitrated at once.

As a result, in February, the two sides accepted a Joint High Commission to discuss the issues. The commissioners met in "the dingy quarters of the State Department in the Old Orphan Asylum Building" and began "the first great arbitration of modern times."

The British-Canadian and the American commissioners spent the first weeks wrangling over the fisheries, the most stubborn issue of all. In a spirit of celebration, Washington society's entertainment of the commissioners was lavish and included a foxhunt in Virginia. They came to a tortuous agreement on definitions of neutrality, but they could not agree on whether the British-built cruisers had prolonged the war.

The treaty of Washington was signed on May 8, 1871, at the State Department. The commissioners celebrated with strawberries and ice cream. And on May 24, the Senate ratified the treaty, 50 to 12. Fish felt euphoric that they had found a new way of settling problems between nations.

The *Alabama* claims still had to be settled by a conference with members named by President Grant, Queen Victoria, the king of Italy, the president of the Swiss Confederation, and the emperor of Brazil. At Secretary Fish's urging, President Grant appointed Charles Francis Adams as the American arbitrator. Adams, of course, knew intimately the history of the cruisers and the British leaders involved. George Bancroft, the U.S. minister to Prussia, and Horace Rublee, the minister to Switzerland, sought the German and Swiss press' support of the conference. John Meredith Read, the consul general at Paris, was less effective until the Americans spent considerable sums to attract the French editors whom the British had not already bought. It was a primitive, antisocial form of "public diplomacy."

As the arbitrators met in the Hotel de Ville in bitter-cold Geneva on December 15, 1871, the Americans began by insisting that the British pay all the costs of the war after the battle of Gettysburg (with 7 percent interest), advancing the rather absurd theory that without British help the South would have quit then. That demand almost destroyed the entire attempt at arbitration.

Secretary Fish argued that if such "indirect claims" were dropped, no agreement could pass the Senate. An emotional debate went on for weeks, and it was June 1872 before the arbitrators agreed that, no matter what the United States demanded, international law provided no basis for awarding compensation for indirect claims.

Only then could the actual arbitration begin. And it concluded on September 14, when the tribunal determined that Britain owed the United States a gross indemnity of $15.5 million for the damage done by the Confederate ships *Alabama, Florida,* and *Shenandoah.* Secretary Fish was pleased.

MANEUVERS WITH SPAIN

Post–Civil War relations with Spain proved at least as difficult as those with Britain. In 1865, American adventurers targeted Santo Domingo after the Spanish army pulled out of the rich but devastated island. The island's wealthier people hoped for an American protectorate or even annexation, but the U.S. government wanted to buy only a naval base and coaling station in Samaná Bay. Secretary Fish, no imperialist, was unenthusiastic about annexing Santo Domingo, but President Grant shared the expansionist fever and became deeply enmeshed in schemes to acquire the island.

In the summer of 1869, Grant sent his young secretary, General Orville E. Babcock, to the island. Babcock carried no diplomatic authority from the State Department, but he returned to Washington with a protocol for the annexation of the Dominican Republic, the eastern half of the island. Fish was furious. Grant called it a "treaty" and was determined to annex the country. He even predicted that in thirty years Mexico City would be the capital of the United States.

The capable American commercial agent in the capital of Santo Domingo, J. Somers Smith, was replaced by the hotheaded Major Raymond H. Perry. And Babcock went back to Santo Domingo to present its leaders with a treaty of annexation and an agreement for a fifty-year lease of Samaná Bay. Perry signed both instruments for the United States.

Despite Grant's vigorous lobbying, the U.S. Senate simply let the treaty lapse. The senators knew that there was serious opposition to annexing tropical areas with dark-skinned, Catholic, Spanish-speaking populations. And many Americans worried that the Dominican Republic would be followed by the acquisition of the black Republic of Haiti next door.

When the deadline for ratifying the treaty was extended, Fish sought amendments to enable the Senate to grant San Domingo its independence if its people so desired. But President Grant, appearing in person at the State Department, told Fish that he opposed a temporary protectorate. The Senate, evenly divided, rejected the treaty.

Grant was vindictive. He demanded the recall of John Lothrop Motley, renowned historian of the Dutch Republic and Senator Sumner's friend, as minister in London. A decade earlier, Sumner had persuaded Lincoln to appoint Motley minister to Austria. He had served ably for half a dozen years until he was accused of criticizing President Andrew Johnson's administration. When questioned by Secretary Seward, Motley had resigned in a huff.

Senator Sumner, loyal to his friend, had urged President Grant to appoint Motley to succeed Reverdy Johnson as minister to London. Grant did not like the way the cultivated Motley assumed what the President felt were superior airs, and parted his hair down the middle. But he wanted to please the powerful chairman of the Senate Foreign Relations Committee.

In London, Motley, echoing the belligerence of his mentor, foolishly accused Britain of having prolonged the South's rebellion. Benjamin Moran, the secretary of the London legation, stayed up into the night transcribing Motley's rash remarks, and he mailed them to Secretary Fish.

When Fish showed them to Grant, he ordered Motley dismissed. Fish pleaded for leniency, and Grant agreed that Fish could ask for Motley's resignation instead.

The historian was very popular in London. When he received Fish's request that he resign, he refused because, he said, it would imply misconduct on his part. In the end, the State Department had to notify Motley that he was being recalled.

Grant wanted to replace Motley with Senator Frederick T. Frelinghuysen, of New Jersey. After he and five other candidates turned down the London post, Motley's eventual successor was bluff, burly Major General Robert C. Schenck, the minister to Brazil. In London, he became best known for teaching draw poker to the "fast set," and it became a great fad. Also, in return for financial consideration, Schenck allowed a Utah silver-mining company to use his name to sell stock in Britain. A House committee found that before the mining company went bankrupt, Schenck dumped his holdings at a high price. In 1876, he resigned in disgrace, returning to Washington to practice law and write a book titled *Draw Poker*.

Fish wanted to replace him with Richard Henry Dana, Jr., a maritime lawyer and author of *Two Years Before the Mast*; but the notorious Civil War general, Ben Butler, and his cronies blocked him. Grant's attorney general, Edwards Pierrepont, assumed the London post.

Grant never quit easily; he proposed that Congress appoint a commission to renegotiate the San Domingo treaty. Although Sumner opposed the plan, Congress authorized sending a commission, and Grant chose its members: Ben Wade, of Ohio; Andrew D. White, president of Cornell University; and Samuel G. Howe, of Massachusetts. Its secretary was Frederick Douglass, the African-American leader. The commission reported that most of the island's inhabitants favored annexation. But that would not happen.

BEGINNING THE STRUGGLE FOR CUBA

The buildup to war with Spain in 1898 was long and bloody. American expansionists focused on the Spanish island of Cuba, where almost half a million Africans were still enslaved. Planters and the military controlled the large, rich island, which, starting in 1868, was wracked by uprisings of

Cubans aided by American "filibusters." A series of filibuster expeditions landed men and arms; the Spanish and even U.S. Federal marshals intercepted others. A landing party of U.S. Marines dispersed one group on Gardiner's Island, off the tip of Long Island.

Most Americans sympathized with the Cuban rebels, but brutality and atrocities were flagrant on both sides. A. E. Phillips, the respected U.S. consul at Santiago, wrote Fish that peaceful citizens were assassinated daily. The governor had three Americans, who landed to help the rebels, shot in public. Phillips protested and received a rare apology. But after he failed to halt the execution of Charles Speakman, a seaman from Indiana, pro-Spanish groups threatened Consul Phillips himself with assassination. When the governor said he could not guarantee the consul's safety, Phillips fled on the USS *Severn* to safety in Jamaica.

In the summer of 1869, a controversial U.S. minister, Daniel E. Sickles, sailed for Spain, along with Paul S. Forbes, a well-connected "special agent" who had secretly supported Cuban freedom. Their goal was to establish U.S. mediation, through which Spain would grant Cuba independence, and Cuba would pay Spain a handsome sum out of customs duties.

Sickles, an aggressive, erratic former army officer with a checkered career of heroism and scandals, had served as secretary of the U.S. Legation in London. He had shot and killed the son of Francis Scott Key, author of "The Star-Spangled Banner," at Lafayette Park for attentions to Sickles' young wife but was acquitted in a sensational trial. At Gettysburg, Sickles commanded a corps and lost half his men before nightfall. Hit by a shell, he had his right leg amputated on the field. After the war, he was military governor of the Carolinas, until he was relieved for overzealotry.

The mission to Madrid came to naught. Secretary Fish proposed an armistice, which the Spanish government rejected outright, ending U.S. attempts at assistance. But in Cuba the Spanish army suffered more than forty thousand casualties, the Cubans, probably three times that number. By April 1872, the Spanish minister in Washington, Don Jos Polo de Bernabe, asked for Sickles' recall. Fish warned Minister Polo that if Sickles left Madrid, he would not be replaced. Alvey A. Adee, age twenty-nine, would remain in Madrid as chargé.

The Spanish government changed, and Fish instructed Sickles to demand the abolition of slavery in Cuba. The order, No. 270, threatened that if Spain did not emancipate the slaves, the country could expect "a marked change in the feeling and in the temper of the people and of the government of the United States." Sickles took it upon himself to moderate the message as he transmitted it, thus neutralizing Fish's threat.

At the suggestion of Consul Henry C. Hall at Matanzas, Fish warned that he would ask Congress for discriminatory duties on goods from slaveholding countries. Since these duties could bankrupt the sugar planters and dealers, the Spanish government was forced to free slaves in Puerto Rico. But Spain was not prepared to apply these reforms to Cuba.

On the evening of February 13, 1873, during a reception at the White House, Minister Polo handed Fish a telegram reporting that Spain's king had abdicated and fled to Portugal. Suddenly, Spain was a republic. Two days later, bands in Madrid were playing "The Star-Spangled Banner." Unknown to Fish, Sickles, again overstepping his orders, had supported the republicans' revolution.

That June, a Spanish warship captured the steamship *Virginius* at Aspinwall, Panama (still part of Colombia). *Virginius* carried American registration papers and flew the American flag but was, in fact, manned by Cuban insurrectionists, and it was running guns to the Cuban rebels. James Torrington, the U.S. consul at Aspinwall, summoned the navy, and USS *Kansas* led *Virginius* safely out to sea.

On November 5, the veteran diplomat Henry Hall, now the American consul general in Havana, telegraphed Secretary Fish that a Spanish warship had captured *Virginius* on the high seas and taken her into Santiago de Cuba. When the ship arrived, the insurgents cut the telegraph line to the capital. The vice consul at Santiago was a tough-minded American businessman, E. G. Schmitt, who resourcefully arranged for the French consul to carry a message to Havana for him.

In Washington, a cabinet meeting was interrupted when an Associated Press correspondent sent in an urgent message saying that four of the prisoners in Santiago, including one American ("General" Ryan), had been shot to death. Vice Consul Schmitt's demand to see the remaining imprisoned American and British citizens was rejected. On November 12, Consul General Hall notified the State Department that the military governor of Santiago had executed forty-nine more of the 155 men aboard *Virginius,* including her captain, Joseph Fry, of Louisiana. Eight Americans now had been killed.

Secretary Fish reported these atrocities to President Grant, arranged for the U.S. Navy to send a warship to Santiago, and instructed Sickles in

Madrid to protest with a virtual ultimatum. Indignant demonstrations were held in American cities. But everyone stopped short of demanding war; the memory of the Civil War was too fresh.

The executions were halted when the British warship *Niobe* sped over from Jamaica; her captain trained his guns on Santiago and prepared to bombard the city. Vice Consul Schmitt brought in the USS *Juanita*.

Meanwhile, in Madrid, the Spanish foreign minister angrily rejected Fish's protest. Sickles, in turn, threatened to close the American legation. By November 26, President Grant, too, had lost his patience; he demanded a satisfactory answer from Madrid by the following day. This led the two governments to an understanding: Spain would surrender the ship and the prisoners, and an inquiry would result in punishing the Spanish officials and saluting the American flag. *Virginius* was delivered to the U.S. Navy, and the prisoners were transferred to *Juanita*. The United States received an eighty-thousand-dollar indemnity for the executions. *Virginius* sank on her voyage to the United States. The brutal Spanish military governor, never tried or punished, was promoted.

The cantankerous Sickles was succeeded in Madrid at the end of 1873 by Caleb Cushing, the antithesis of Sickles. Cushing was a respected lawyer, although to him slavery was not a moral question; he believed that blacks were inferior beings.

Secretary Fish was proud that he had avoided "the terrible evil" of war with Spain. The fact was, he had only postponed war. (Ironically, one of his grandsons would be the first American soldier killed when war finally came twenty-five years later.)

DELIRIUM TREMENS AND SLAVE GIRLS

The post–Civil War period was filled with opportunities for speculation and corruption. The diplomatic and the consular services suffered. President Grant gave relatives and former army cronies attractive posts overseas. Secretary of State Fish busied himself with affairs of state and did not rein in the patronage hunters. Henry Adams wrote scathingly that even the best members of Congress will distribute patronage to "convert a sacred public trust into a private property." He added, tongue in cheek, that Grant should be applauded for giving offices to his relatives and friends and rescuing them from the taint of political corruption.

Michael J. Cramer, Grant's brother-in-law, became the minister to Denmark; his secretary's uncle, the minister to Belgium. Secretary Fish had to persuade Grant not to appoint a Methodist minister as consul in the Muslim-dominated city of Jerusalem. But Grant did appoint Edward Rumsey Wing, of Kentucky, minister to Ecuador. Wing suffered from delirium tremens, and five years later shot himself to death.

George H. Butler was made consul general in Alexandria, Egypt, through his notorious uncle, Ben Butler. The nephew sold jobs and "protection" and purchased young girls until missionaries pressured Fish to recall him. Ben Butler also enabled his brother-in-law to become consul general in Frankfurt.

The nation's diplomatic and consular services grew steadily. In 1859, the U.S. had thirty-one diplomatic missions abroad; by 1891, there were forty-one. The most significant of the new ones were in Persia (Iran), Siam (Thailand), and Korea. Consular posts grew from 282 in 1860 to 323 in 1890. And in that same period, the number of smaller consular agencies increased from 198 to 437.

Shortly after the Civil War, when the State Department was moved from its offices in the shadow of the White House to the dilapidated Orphan Asylum far out on Fourteenth Street, Congress cut the number of State Department clerks from forty-eight to thirty-one as of July 1, 1869. Secretary Fish reorganized the department for the first time since 1833, dividing the department into nine bureaus and two agencies, manned by twenty-nine clerks plus a translator and a telegraph operator. The First Diplomatic Bureau was responsible for eleven European nations, China, and Japan and was headed by the assistant secretary of state. The Second Diplomatic Bureau was responsible for seventeen Latin American countries and an assortment of other states, from Russia to the Hawaiian Islands and was directed by the second assistant secretary. The First and Second Consular Bureaus paralleled the diplomatic bureaus. This would remain the basic organization of the department for the next thirty-nine years.

The consuls were busy with the tens of thousands of Europeans immigrating to the United States each year and with the endless paperwork associated with trade. They were given no training even for these chores. And they were also saddled with diverse responsibilities, ranging from protecting Americans from unjustified arrest to informing businessmen about which goods would find a market in their areas. Consuls in Germany, for example, recommended marketing mouse and rat traps.

William J. Stillman, who served as consul in Rome and on Crete, was critical of some of the men he met in the American foreign service. He wrote of "a minister of the United States of America found drunk in the streets of Berlin by the police and of a chargé d'affaires who, in an outbreak at Constantinople, hoisted the flag over a brothel he frequented. Our representation abroad was a disgrace to America."

17

The Long, Bumpy Road to Professionalism

1864–97

In 1864, a Shanghai consular court declared Irish-born John D. Buckley guilty of murder. Following a dinnertime argument over the Confederate privateers in the Civil War, Buckley had shot to death an American merchant-ship captain. With the agreement of Anson Burlingame, the U.S. minister in Peking, Consul General George F. Seward, the Secretary of State's twenty-four-year-old nephew, had Buckley hanged. Overwhelmed by his part in the hanging, young Seward closed his report, "I have only to say, in conclusion, that I trust no similar duty will be imposed upon me again so long as I remain in this office."

The responsibility to put errant Americans to death demonstrated how foreign cultures could present U.S. diplomats with grim challenges for which they were unprepared. Few American ministers or consuls in China had command of the language; they depended on missionaries and British envoys to read documents for them. (In 1906, Congress created an international court for China that eventually took over many of the consular courts' duties.)

President Lincoln named the able Anson Burlingame minister at Peking in 1861, after the Austro-Hungarian monarchy rejected him because he had supported the revolutionary Lajos Kossuth. Burlingame was a Harvard Law School graduate and an antislavery and early Republican congressman from Massachusetts. When Senator Preston Brooks challenged him to a duel for criticizing Brooks' beating of Senator Charles Sumner in the Senate, Burlingame, an expert shot, chose rifles at Niagara Falls. The belligerent Brooks backed down.

In Peking, Burlingame opposed the foreign powers' treatment of China and worked to build a more equal relationship with the imperial government. Helped by the legation secretary, S. Wells Williams, a scholar and former missionary, he was quite successful.

When, after five years, Burlingame resigned his post, the Chinese government asked him to serve as China's first envoy to the West. He led a Chinese mission to Washington and Europe and negotiated the Burlingame Treaty in 1868 with Secretary Seward, who wanted to develop trade with China.

The treaty expressed respect for China, which the European powers had treated so arrogantly. It amended the Tientsin Treaty of 1858, supported Chinese sovereignty, assured religious freedom for Americans in China, and secured the right of Chinese to emigrate. It became the basis for importing Chinese laborers into the United States. Burlingame and his Chinese colleagues traveled through Europe's capitals, until he died of pneumonia in Saint Petersburg. He was forty-nine.

American traders in 1872 built a railroad line in China with the help of Vice Consul O. B. Bradford at Shanghai. Consul General George Seward warned Bradford that the Chinese were distrustful of foreign efforts to control their railroads and open up the interior, so Bradford had the project sold to a British firm. The Chinese government then bought the railroad and tore up the tracks.

George Seward shaped the American settlement in Shanghai. The British and Chinese had determined the first boundaries of the foreign settlement in 1846 and enclosed an area of some 138 acres. Further negotiations in 1899 enlarged the American settlement to 5,583 acres, in which only Americans could live.

The importation of cheap Chinese labor into the United States soured relations with China. As work on the major railroads in the United States was completed, the demand for cheap labor disappeared and was replaced by discrimination against the peculiar people who worked for "coolie wages." By 1880, Congress was limiting the number of Chinese entering the country. And U.S. consuls reported that the Chinese Exclusion Act of 1882 increased anti-Americanism in China, which in turn spread anti-Chinese sentiment in the western states.

Charles Denby, who replaced John Russell Young as minister to China in 1885, was an admirable diplomat who stayed in Peking for thirteen years. His father had been the consul general in Marseilles, and, although Charles was Virginia-born and a Virginia Military Institute graduate, he had moved to Indiana and had been severely wounded fighting for the Union. In Peking, Denby and Vice Consul William N. Pethick tried to help American entrepreneurs, but increasing Chinese resistance defeated the schemes of many American investors. And in 1891, China refused to accept Henry W. Blair, the proposed U.S. minister, because he had voted to exclude Chinese laborers from the United States. He was not replaced until Edwin H. Conger arrived in 1898.

DEEP WATERS ACROSS THE PACIFIC

During the 1860s, Japan was modernized by the tumultuous Meiji Restoration, which revived the power of the emperor. Resigning as the U.S. consul in Amoy, China, Charles LaGendre became a consultant to the Japanese armed forces and led expeditions to Taiwan. Trade between the United States and Japan expanded, but negotiations for a trade treaty dragged on from 1872, when the Japanese foreign minister led a mission to Washington, until 1894, when the empathetic American minister, Richard D. Hubbard, overcame Japan's demand that the United States give up extraterritoriality.

Increasing American trade with the more isolated kingdom of Korea was also difficult. (The earliest trade was said to be in medicinal ginseng root the Indians found in the Berkshire Hills around Stockbridge, Massachusetts.) The first meaningful, if secret, effort to negotiate a treaty with Korea was made by Commodore Robert W. Shufeldt, who in 1882, with the help of the Chinese government, established tariffs and extraterritoriality, allowed Americans to live in some Korean ports, and recognized Korean independence.

The United States established a short-lived legation in Seoul in 1883, and U.S. Minister Lucius H. Foote arranged for a Korean mission to the United States, as China and Japan had previously done. China and Japan competed for hegemony over Korea, leading to the Sino-Japanese War of 1894–95. U.S. merchants tried to profit from the anticipated Japanese victory, while Secretary of State Walter Q. Gresham pursued the official U.S. policy of neutrality.

During the war, Minister John M. B. Sill had the cruiser *Baltimore* sent to Seoul, and the Chinese called in as advisors John Watson Foster, a former Secretary of State, and former Vice Consul William N. Pethick. But the Japanese conquered Port Arthur and the Shantung Peninsula, which opened access to north China. And, finally, in the spring of 1895, a Chinese delegation, accompanied by Foster and Pethick, accepted the oppressive Treaty of Shimonoseki, by which Japan took over Taiwan and the Liaodong Peninsula. In 1905, the United States recognized Japan's control over Korea and closed its Seoul legation.

That war opened more of China to foreign traders. When Minister Charles Denby in Peking championed particular American firms to the Chinese establishment, he was reined in by the State Department. But at the end of 1896, Richard Olney, the new Secretary of State, gave Denby virtual carte blanche with "reputable" companies and their representatives.

Denby energetically fought for selected railroad developers and other entrepreneurs in China. Most of these schemes failed, and British commerce in China continued to outrun American. The United States was stepping very gingerly into the deep waters on the far side of the Pacific.

During the same outward thrust, several American consuls in the Ottoman and Austro-Hungarian empires became involved in the efforts of local peoples to break free from foreign domination. In 1866, William J. Stillman, the U.S. consul on Crete, supported a local revolt against the Turks. He traveled into the interior of the island to expose Turkish atrocities in Christian villages. Secretary Seward approved his daring.

After two tense years, Stillman and his family moved to Athens. There, his wife, Laura, who had been distressed by the Turkish actions but refused to leave Crete without him, committed suicide. Historian Charles Stuart Kennedy wrote: "Laura Stillman is one of the unrecognized heroines of the U. S. consular service." Despite Stillman's admirable record, he never obtained another post.

President Grant sent Benjamin Franklin Peixotto to Romania under unusual circumstances. Born in New York, Peixotto became a lawyer in

San Francisco and a leader of the Sephardic Jewish community there. In 1870, Grant asked him to go to Turkish Romania in response to pleas from American Jews who feared for the fate of the Jewish community there.

President Grant would not request a congressional appropriation to establish a consulate in Romania, but he offered the prestige of his office if private sources would finance it. Prominent American, British, and French Jews underwrote the consulate. Grant wrote Peixotto:

> The United States, knowing no distinction of her citizens on account of religion or nativity, naturally believes in a civilization the world over which will secure the same universal laws.

Peixotto stayed in Bucharest for six years, fighting anti-Semitic legislation and persuading Romanian Jews to organize modern schools.

Meanwhile, in Bulgaria, Turks killed Christians who were revolting against Ottoman rule. In 1876, Howard Maynard, the U.S. minister at Constantinople, sent the veteran Consul General Eugene Schuyler, a Columbia University lawyer and a linguist, to investigate. He had served as consul at Moscow and Tallinn and as secretary of legation in Saint Petersburg. Shocked by what he saw in Bulgaria, he reported that thousands had been massacred. Men had their eyes torn out and their limbs cut off; women were raped. Britain withdrew its support of Turkey, and Russia attacked the Turks.

The Ottoman envoy in Washington protested Schuyler's report; and Secretary of State Hamilton Fish, unhappy with the trouble Schuyler had stirred up, transferred him, first to Birmingham, England, and then to Rome as consul general. Later, in a remarkable career, Schuyler served as the minister and consul general to Greece, Romania, and Serbia. When he retired, Schuyler publicly criticized both the foreign service and Congress. As a result, when he was proposed in 1889 to be assistant secretary of state, the Senate refused to confirm him. He went to Cairo as consul general and died there, an exceptional figure in a time of mediocrity.

In 1874, Grant decided that General Montgomery C. Meigs should no longer serve as quartermaster general of the army and wanted to send him as minister to Russia. But Secretary Fish finally spoke up. Tired of interference by Grant's "kitchen cabinet" and his cynical and corrupt secretary, Orville Babcock, Fish sent Grant his resignation.

He really hoped that the President would give him control of his own

department. In a face-to-face confrontation, Grant gave Fish the autonomy he demanded and agreed to make appointments only after a cabinet
discussion. Thus, Fish was able to raise the quality of diplomatic appointments: George H. Boker became minister to Russia; John W. Foster was
named minister to Mexico; and Caleb Cushing, a popular choice, replaced
Sickles in Madrid. In the process, young Alvey A. Adee stayed on as Cushing's secretary of legation; his singular service to the department would
cover fifty years.

Several of Grant's own appointments were admirable. He sent Elihu B.
Washburne to replace General Dix in Paris, kept historian George Ban-
croft in Berlin, and, later, appointed John Russell Young as minister to
China.

Elihu Washburne had an imposing career. A tall, impressive man,
rough-hewn and direct, Washburne was the son of a country storekeeper
in Maine. After attending Harvard, he served in Congress for sixteen years
and became friends with Lincoln and Grant (Grant even waited in Washburne's home to learn the results of the presidential election in 1868).

Washburne served as Secretary of State for only eleven days before
becoming the minister to Paris. He distinguished himself during the
Franco-Prussian War of 1870–71, taking responsibility for the thousands
of Americans living in France who now besieged the legation and helping
thirty thousand German civilians leave France.

Washburne was the only foreign envoy who spent courageously long
periods in the chaotic, violent city after German troops withdrew. He also
arranged for the release of American and German prisoners from prison.
He stayed in Paris until 1877, an exceptionally long tour. Secretary Fish
said warmly, "Washburne is entitled to all the honor his friends may wish
to confer upon him."

"THE SYSTEM IS RADICALLY DEFECTIVE"

In the period after the Civil War, many Americans became interested in a
capable foreign service, and the effort of the Reform Act of 1856 to reduce
personal rewards was now considered inadequate. The Congressional Joint
Select Committee on Retrenchment, on July 2, 1868, condemned the arrangement by which a diplomatic or consular officer, as soon as he has
familiarized himself with his duties, "is removed to make room for another

novice, who is likewise superseded as soon as his experience begins to enable him to discharge the duties of his office." The committee report concluded, "The system is radically defective."

The committee proposed that the diplomatic and consular services follow the army and navy, which graded and promoted men by competitive examinations. It also called the consular reports on commercial and industrial activities abroad "imperfect and superficial." It blamed these defects on unqualified consular officers. And it criticized the representation of the United States in the "petty states" of South America, with which commerce was regarded as "insignificant." The report recommended economies in the diplomatic representation in Europe and said American diplomats, "if they find nothing worse to do, remitted to utopian dreams and the solution of sublime and mysterious problems of diplomacy. . . . It might be well to select the best dunces of the land and send them forth to aid in perpetuating the absurdities of an age which demanded harlequins at court." The report even asked "whether the entire diplomatic machinery employed by governments might not be dispensed with."

Nothing came of this burst of congressional indignation; the spoils system stayed firmly in place.

Two years later, Congress did pass a law, under which the Treasury Department assigned De Benneville Randolph Keim to examine the accounts of the entire consular service. This was the only such inspection in the nineteenth century. Keim, a former newspaperman, spent a year visiting posts around the globe. Although he praised a number of consular officers, he said the Reform Act of 1856 had failed to eradicate abuses or to prevent ingenious new ones. He found standards of honesty and efficiency embarrassingly low, and he reported, "Almost every consulate had some defects in its history, owing to the incompetency, low habits or vulgarity of some of its officers, during the endless round of evils incident to official rotation."

In Yokohama, he discovered that Consul Lemuel Lyons was taking bribes. In Shanghai, Consul General George F. Seward was peddling the right to fly the American flag to Chinese owners of junks and selling licenses to bars and so-called boardinghouses. In Hong Kong, consuls demanded a fee for each Chinese emigrating to the United States.

In Alexandria, Keim demanded that Consul General George Butler stop selling the office of vice consul. At the port of Tumbez, Peru, Keim disrupted the activities of Consul Ralph Abercrombie, whom he described as "an utterly hopeless inebriate."

Critical of the State Department's failure to supervise the consular service, Keim recommended moving the entire system to the Treasury Department. And he advised appointing two inspectors with power to investigate consuls. But the House again remained loyal to the patronage system.

One of the strangest assignments for members of the foreign service was the pursuit of William M. Tweed, the corrupt "Boss of New York." The Tweed Ring controlled Tammany Hall, a powerful political club, and stole from the City of New York an estimated $200 million, or $4 billion in modern dollars. Presidential hopeful Samuel Tilden led the fight against the powerful, vulgar Boss Tweed, and, in November 1873, Tweed started serving time in the Ludlow Street Jail, with all the comforts money could buy.

Tweed was given outrageous privileges, and on a visit to his home, Tweed, who had bribed his guards, escaped, aided by conspirators and disguises. State Department and foreign service officers led the pursuit of the fugitive. The search was intense, until Consul General Henry Hall, in Havana, reported that a fisherman had landed two persons with United States passports at Santiago de Cuba. They proved to be Tweed and a colleague, who were using false names and had been arrested by the Spaniards. At Santiago, the youthful U.S. consul, Alfred Young, of Cincinnati, was directed to protect their rights. In fact, he was so helpful that he had to retire from the foreign service.

From Cuba, Tweed and his colleague sailed in a Spanish ship to Vigo, Spain, where Spain had them arrested again. Secretary of State Fish instructed Minister Caleb Cushing in Madrid to apprehend them. Since Cushing was on vacation, Alvey Adee, the young chargé in Madrid, obtained a drawing of Tweed and identified him. The Spanish government was glad to turn him over to the captain of the frigate USS *Franklin,* which brought him back to jail in New York. Thinking he had made a deal for his freedom, Boss Tweed confessed his crimes. But he died in jail on April 12, 1878, at the age of fifty-five.

. . .

By 1875, Secretary Fish increased his staff from twenty-five to forty-five clerks. The shabby Orphan Asylum was supposed to have been a temporary department home, and Secretary Fish forced General Babcock to return money that had been earmarked for a south wing to the new State, War, and Navy Building, where the State Department would be quartered, but that Babcock had used for other work. Babcock was brought to trial for involvement with the Whiskey Ring, which had defrauded the government of taxes due on alcoholic beverages. Grant vouched for Babcock's character, which assured his acquittal, and appointed him Inspector of Lighthouses. The Grant administration's reputation dropped another notch.

AFTER GRANT'S NADIR OF GOVERNANCE

Grant's two terms as President were a nadir of American governance. Then, things turned. After the era of "Grantism," the quality of foreign service appointments improved. President Rutherford B. Hayes supported civil service reform. Among the improvements, he appointed James Russell Lowell as minister to Spain in 1877. After creditable years in Madrid, he served five years as minister in London. (Henry James praised his career as "a tribute to the dominion of style.") Also of note was John A. Kasson, of Iowa, who became minister to Austria-Hungary in 1877 and to Germany in 1884. Major General Lewis Wallace, the author of *Ben-Hur,* was sent to Turkey as minister, and New York banker Levi P. Morton went to France.

Grover Cleveland led the Democrats back into power in 1884, and he replaced the head of every diplomatic mission but one, sending Charles Denby to China, Edward J. Phelps to London, George H. Pendleton to Berlin, and Robert M. McLane to Paris.

Neither the Republicans nor Democrats had much luck in Italy. The Republicans failed there with William Waldorf Astor, whose ideas proved quite adverse to American character and customs. President Chester A. Arthur appointed him as minister and supposedly said, "Go and enjoy yourself, my dear boy." Astor served for three years, and when his father died, he became the richest man in America, but certainly not the most democratic. He was quoted as saying, "America is not a fit place for a gentleman to live." He transformed himself into a British viscount.

In their turn, the Democrats ran into Italian objections against the choice as minister of Anthony M. Keiley, a former Confederate officer and mayor of Richmond, Virginia, for having protested against including Rome in the Italian kingdom. Keiley was then proposed as minister to Austria-Hungary, but its foreign minister notified Secretary of State Thomas F. Bayard that Keiley was unacceptable because his wife was Jewish, which would be "untenable and intolerable in Vienna." To show his and Bayard's displeasure at Austro-Hungarian bigotry, President Cleveland left the Vienna legation under a chargé for the next two years.

In 1887, Cleveland appointed as minister at Constantinople Oscar S. Straus, who had helped him win the nomination and election. Straus had been born in Bavaria and came to the United States in 1854, when he was three. His family settled in Georgia, moving after the Civil War to New York, where the family business, R. H. Macy and Abraham and Straus, flourished. Because Straus was Jewish, Cleveland obtained the approval of his appointment from organizations that sent Christian missionaries to the Ottoman Empire, as well as from the popular preacher Henry Ward Beecher.

Straus was pleased to find the Ottoman authorities tolerant of Jews fleeing from persecution in Russia and Romania. In this, he clashed with the longtime American consul, Selah Merrill, a Yale-educated Congregational minister and a fervent Holy Land archaeologist. Merrill honored the ancient Israelites but reviled contemporary Jews and opposed their settling in Palestine. Merrill also feuded with the Spafford family, Protestants who established the American Colony settlement in Jerusalem.

American consuls had been posted in Jerusalem since 1856, when John Warren Gorham, a Boston physician, became the first salaried consul there. Selah Merrill had then worked hard to get the appointment, and he held the post for sixteen years between 1882 to 1907, with several interruptions.

At the sultan's request, Straus also tried, unsuccessfully, to interest William K. Vanderbilt in taking over the German project of building a railroad from the Persian Gulf to Constantinople. When Straus returned home in 1889, he wrote, "Had diplomacy been a career nothing would have pleased me more than to continue in such service of my country."

Straus approved as his successor Solomon Hirsch, a Republican businessman and political figure from Portland, Oregon, but wrote, "I only regret one fact, that this Mission should be singled out as a prize for Jewish political reward. It has the appearance as if our country only dared appoint or accredit a Jew to a non-Christian country."

"AMERICA HAS NO FUTURE IN THE PACIFIC"

The United States also reached out across the Pacific, where the European powers were already competing. Bismarck had annexed part of New Guinea, Tahiti became a French colony, and the Fijis became British. Germany and Great Britain grappled for control of the peaceful, palm-bedecked Samoan archipelago, four thousand miles beyond San Francisco. There, the Germans had developed extensive copra plantations and dominated the economy.

President Grant sent Albert B. Steinberger as a special agent to study Samoa's prospects, and he recommended that the United States annex the islands or establish an American protectorate. Secretary Fish was totally disinterested, so Steinberger traveled to Germany, where he was hired by the German government and the German company dominating Samoa. Then, without telling the American government of his German arrangement, he accepted a U.S. assignment to report further on Samoa.

In Apia, the capital, Steinberger arranged for a Samoan chief, Malietoa Laupepa, to become king of the archipelago. Steinberger resigned his State Department post and had himself appointed prime minister. He proved an efficient ruler but antagonized both the British and Americans, who persuaded the king to dismiss him. The British transported him in the brig of a warship to Fiji, where the governor quickly freed him.

The Samoans sent a representative to Washington and signed a treaty of friendship in 1878. This gave the United States rights over the magnificent harbor at Pago Pago and a role in the Great Powers' competition for Samoa.

Then, Harold M. Sewall, the twenty-seven-year-old son of a wealthy Bath, Maine, shipbuilding family, went as consul general to Apia. He was left very much on his own; the nearest cable station was in Auckland, New Zealand. "A young man of high spirit and a generous disposition" is how the novelist Robert Louis Stevenson, then living in Samoa, described him.

Shortly after Sewall arrived at Apia, the German consul arranged a coup d'état, replacing King Malietoa Laupepa with a chief named Tamasese Titimaea and giving him a German, Captain Eugen Brandeis, as prime minister. The coup was enforced by five German warships in Apia Bay. Several hundred German marines were landed, and they carried Malietoa into exile. When two British warships showed up in October 1888, tension increased.

Sewall was the only foreign consul who opposed the coup. When Secretary of State Bayard insisted he be neutral, the consul returned to Washington and presented his views to a Senate subcommittee. The Senate voted six hundred thousand dollars to construct a naval base at Pago Pago.

While in Washington, Sewall angered Secretary Bayard, who asked him to resign. As a result, Sewall was absent from Samoa during a naval incident in which the Samoans, in opéra bouffe style, "defeated" the Germans. In mid-March 1889, the United States and Germany each had three warships jammed into Apia Bay, and the prospect of war loomed. Then, on March 16, a hurricane destroyed or beached every warship in the harbor except for one British cruiser, drowning Germans, British, and Americans alike, despite the Samoans' heroic rescue efforts.

Not all Americans wanted the United States involved in Samoa. Secretary of State Walter Q. Gresham told President Cleveland that the United States was better off not competing in the South Pacific. Henry Adams toured the area and wrote Senator Henry Cabot Lodge, "On the whole, I am satisfied that America has no future in the Pacific."

Sewall returned to Apia as consul general. During the next two years, he acquired Pago Pago for a U.S. naval base. Afterward, Sewall served as the minister to Hawaii, and returned to Bath in 1900, a rich man. An agreement was worked out in which the Germans controlled Samoa's main islands and the United States kept what it wanted most: the harbor at Pago Pago.

A SURPRISING FORCE FOR REFORM

A surprising force for consular reform turned out to be a small, enterprising lawyer named John S. Mosby, who had been one of the Confederacy's most effective guerrilla fighters, terrorizing northern Virginia and Washington, D.C., during the Civil War.

In 1876, Colonel Mosby helped elect Rutherford B. Hayes, who rewarded him with the appointment as consul at Hong Kong, which by then had become a commercial center. Mosby found that his predecessor,

David H. Bailey, had defrauded the United States by pocketing thirty thousand dollars in fees, mostly by certifying Chinese wanting to immigrate to the United States. Mosby's report also implicated George F. Seward, the U.S. minister at Peking. Seward had previously been cited for owning forty houses of prostitution in Shanghai. Mosby sent his report to his superior, who happened to be Assistant Secretary Frederick W. Seward, son of the former Secretary of State and George Seward's cousin. Fred chose not to act on Mosby's report.

A House committee recommended that George Seward be impeached. He was never tried, but he left Peking in August 1880, returning to private life. Later, when Mosby uncovered corruption by David B. Sickels, the U.S. consul at Bangkok, he reported this directly to President Hayes. Sickels resigned before the State Department could dismiss him.

To investigate Mosby's charges against his predecessor, David Bailey, Assistant Secretary Frederick Seward sent former Major General Julius H. Stahel, the American consul at Osaka, Japan, to Hong Kong. As a Union cavalryman in the Civil War, he had been Mosby's adversary in Virginia and had been awarded the Congressional Medal of Honor. To Seward's chagrin, the two former enemies became friends. Stahel confirmed Mosby's charges against Bailey, and Secretary of State William M. Evarts tried unsuccessfully to squash his report.

This became a public scandal, and George Seward, David Bailey, and Frederick Seward were all urged to resign. Although Mosby's pugnacity was unpopular at the State Department, he remained in Hong Kong, fighting increasing racism against Chinese immigration to the United States. Most Chinese came through Hong Kong, and Mosby had to certify them as appropriate. When he was attacked for allowing Chinese prostitutes to enter Hong Kong, he protested to Assistant Secretary of State C. Bancroft Davis, arguing that he had to rely on Chinese testimony when judging women applicants and that he presumed a woman's virtue until the opposite was proved. On May 9, 1882, in a burst of temper, he wrote the U.S. collector of customs in San Francisco:

> The women who get my certificates are much better than a majority of the white women who come from San Francisco to Hong Kong. The China coast is overrun with California prostitutes who are much more demoralizing in China than Chinese cheap labor and lewd women in California. . . . I am no more responsible for the

number of Chinese going to the United States than you are for the number of San Francisco whores continually coming to Hong Kong.

In 1885, President Cleveland recalled Mosby, who returned home to become a lawyer for the Southern Pacific Railroad.

ASSASSINATION RAISES HOPE FOR REFORM

A tragic incident in the story of the spoils system resulted from the persistent attempts of Charles J. Guiteau, a failed Chicago lawyer and evangelist, to obtain the post of consul general in Paris. He harassed Secretary of State James G. Blaine until Blaine banned him from his office. On Saturday morning, July 2, 1881, Guiteau shadowed Blaine and President James A. Garfield into Washington's railroad station; Garfield was en route to commencement exercises at Williams College. Guiteau shot Garfield, who died two months later (because of less than competent medical care). Guiteau was tried and hanged. Reformers used the case of Guiteau, the *diplomat manqué*, to dramatize their cause.

Prodded by the presidential assassination, Congress passed the crucial Civil Service Act of 1883, known also as the Pendleton Act, establishing competitive Civil Service examinations. Many hoped it would also help reform the foreign service, but the opposite happened. Basing Civil Service jobs on merit put more pressure on the foreign service to supply patronage jobs.

Several more attempts were made by Congress to abolish the fee system and put consular officers on salary. The American business community favored such changes, because, as foreign trade grew, consular work became more complex, and consuls needed to be better equipped to help business effectively.

Beginning in the 1850s, the State Department collected and circulated commercial information from abroad to help American businessmen. In 1874, the Bureau of Statistics began issuing reports. Once Frederic Emory, a former Baltimore newspaperman, was appointed its chief in April 1894, the bureau began efforts to make the United States competitive internationally. By July 1897, renamed the Bureau of Foreign Commerce, it published reports from consuls around the globe, ranging from uses for iron slag to the cultivation of exotic fruits. Who knew from which odd product some enterprising American could profit? Emory published daily summaries of commercial information and tried to post a commercial attaché in every embassy and legation.

In 1903, the bureau was moved over to the new Department of Commerce and Labor. But the consuls abroad remained attached to the State Department and continued to collect and disseminate business information. State also created its own Bureau of Trade Relations with Emory in charge. Essentially, the State Department collected information abroad and Commerce and Labor disseminated it in the United States, creating extreme rivalry.

Commerce and Labor wanted to receive consular reports without going through State's Bureau of Trade Relations. Wilbur Carr, head of the consular bureau, counterattacked by recommending that Commerce's agents overseas be transferred to State. After heated debates, State lost the appropriation for its Bureau of Trade Relations, but State's consuls continued to report to Commerce and Labor through the State Department.

To replace its Bureau of Trade Relations without arousing congressional anger, State's Francis Mairs Huntington Wilson created the Office of Foreign Trade Advisers in September 1912. It helped businessmen find foreign markets, win contracts, negotiate commercial treaties, and study tariff provisions. Charles Pepper and Evan Young, former head of the Near Eastern Division, became the first trade advisors. Soon the new office was doing all that the bureau had previously done, and more.

TOO EXALTED A TITLE

The United States used the title of ambassador for its envoys for the first time in 1893. "Ambassador" had been thought too exalted and European, but American ministers had often been disadvantaged when dealing with foreigners with ambassadorial rank. For example, when George Perkins Marsh served as U.S. minister in Constantinople in 1849, he was placed seventy-second at official dinners. He protested to the State Department that this lowered his country in the eyes of the Turks.

Congress decided that the President could designate a U.S. ambassador to a foreign country that was represented in the United States by an ambassador. Great Britain, France, Italy, and Germany gave the title to their representatives in Washington, and President Cleveland did the same for American envoys to those countries. Thomas F. Bayard, the first ambassador, had served as Cleveland's Secretary of State and presented his new credentials on June 22, 1893, to the Court of St. James's.

The three decades between the Civil War and the Spanish-American War saw a continual struggle between patronage and reform. As American foreign trade grew, President Cleveland repeatedly spoke up for consular reform, but to little avail. Chairman Senator John T. Morgan, of Alabama, chairman of the Committee on Foreign Relations, introduced a bill to improve the efficiency of the consular service because the cotton industry needed help to export. That bill was designed by Francois S. Jones based on his study of the French foreign service and declared that only those who passed an examination were eligible for appointment or promotion. But the Senate rejected it on a point of order.

The editors of the influential magazine *The Century* gathered views from former ministers about the consular service and the spoils system and published their replies in June 1894. Edward Burd Grubb, a former minister to Spain, warned that the American consul, although he was not as well equipped as the trained consuls of other countries, "goes to the wall as surely as does the raw, unarmed recruit before the veteran soldier." William L. Scruggs, former minister to Colombia and Venezuela, said colorfully:

> As civilization advances, nations seek higher methods of adjusting their differences than those usually adopted by ants and beetles. Friendly arbitration takes the place of war, and the services of the professional soldier are discounted by those of the trained and skillful diplomat. . . . When (a consul) is thus equipped for his work, and proves himself honest and faithful, it is extremely detrimental to the service, and to our interests abroad, to dismiss him for some half-educated and vulgar politician who claims the office as a reward for work at the primaries.

But Thomas W. Palmer, who had been briefly the minister to Spain, disagreed, concluding, "We have been well served under the present system; why change?" Clearly, the consensus was that the consular service needed attention.

To improve the consular service, Secretary of State Richard Olney, in 1895, sent President Cleveland a draft of an Executive Order prepared by Walter Faison, chief of the Consular Bureau; the draft was based on the 1871 Civil Service Act. The Executive Order decreed that any consular position with an annual salary between $1,000 and $2,500 could be filled only by an officer of the State Department or by a presidential nominee who had passed an oral and written examination. The test would include consular regulations and a foreign language. At the first one, held in March 1896, eight candidates passed and five failed.

Cleveland initiated an inspection of consular posts. In 1896 and 1897, Robert S. Chilton, Jr., chief of the Consular Bureau, made a global inspection tour. Among the abuses he found were the misuse of funds in Shanghai and fee splitting in Mexico and England.

At this stage, reform contained more than a touch of hypocrisy. Before issuing his Executive Order, Cleveland replaced many consular officers with Democrats. And two years later, William McKinley replaced 259 of the 320 consuls with Republicans. His cousin, William McKinley Osborne, was made consul general in London. Jim Boyle, McKinley's personal secretary when he was governor of Ohio, became the consul in Liverpool. His friend, Bellamy Storer, of Cincinnati, was made ambassador to Belgium. McKinley did not rescind Cleveland's Executive Order; he ignored it.

PART TWO

18

First Steps to Empire

1898–99

As the twentieth century approached, United States foreign policy making experienced a paradigm shift that Robert L. Beisner, a historian of foreign relations, compared to the change of perception that Thomas S. Kuhn identified in writing of the history of science. Under the old paradigm, foreign relations had been passive or reactive and "ambivalent about the use of governmental power." The new paradigm, according to Beisner, recognized the United States as a world power and required a foreign policy initiated and conducted by government. Under this change, the foreign service began to refocus, timidly at first, from assuring payment of duties on imported goods to the grander goal of finding markets for American goods abroad.

The change was energized by an enormous surge of American population, from thirty-nine million in 1870 to sixty-three million in 1890; the expansion of American cities; and the confrontation of trusts and labor unions. The geographic frontier was replaced by "a frontier of export markets and colonies."

HAWAII ACQUIRED WITHOUT FORCE

Foreign service officers and politicians, not soldiers and Marines, acquired Hawaii for the United States in 1893. This early venture into overseas empire was protracted and controversial, but not especially bloody. Some Americans had wanted to annex Hawaii in the 1850s; and American Commissioner David L. Gregg, a Chicago lawyer, persuaded Hawaii's native rulers that it was in their interest. But at that time President Franklin Pierce was more interested in Cuba.

Four decades later, interest in Hawaii had increased. Native insurrectionists had destroyed Cuba's sugar crop, and American refiners looked to Hawaii for a new supply. United States trade with Asia increased, also fanning interest in the islands. The U.S. Navy switched from sail to coal and needed coaling stations on the sea routes to Asia. And, finally, Japan's interest in the islands also spurred the drive for American annexation.

At first, the rivalry over Hawaii had been between the United States and Britain. President Zachary Taylor sent to the "Sandwich Islands," as commissioner, Luther Severance, of Maine, a former congressman and a founder of the *Kennebec Journal*. He negotiated an agreement with King Kamehameha III to give the United States a protectorate over Hawaii, but Secretary of State Daniel Webster refused to support the idea.

During the Civil War, the Hawaiian sugar planters, mostly white men from the mainland, prospered. Western diseases decimated the native Hawaiians, and the white planters imported Japanese laborers to replace them in the cane fields. Right after the war, Secretary of State William H. Seward sent Edward M. McCook, a former Union cavalry general, as minister, charging him to oppose any British presence.

In 1875, the Kingdom of Hawaii and the United States concluded a Treaty of Reciprocity, which specified that Hawaii give up its rights to the potential naval base at Pearl Harbor while the U.S. give up tariff revenues on the islands' sugar. Now, Hawaiian sugar could enter the continental United States duty free. The islands' sugar industry boomed.

The treaty had to be renewed after seven years, but it was not accepted by the U.S. Senate until 1887. A cabal of sugar planters and the powerful white minority, led by Sanford Dole and refiner Claus Spreckels, forced Hawaii's king to accept the aptly named "Bayonet Constitution," disenfranchising most Hawaiians.

In 1889, Secretary of State James G. Blaine named as the American minister to Hawaii John L. Stevens, Blaine's former partner on the *Kennebec Journal*. As minister to Paraguay, Uruguay, and Sweden, Stevens had worked hard for U.S. business. He went to Hawaii knowing that Blaine wanted annexation.

But disaster hit the Hawaiian sugar planters in the form of the McKinley Tariff of 1890. It protected mainland sugar producers and eliminated the Hawaiian planters' price advantage, dumping the islands into an economic depression that lifted the planters' desire for annexation.

The king died during a visit to San Francisco and was succeeded by his sister Queen Liliuokalani. Minister Stevens warned her not to overturn the Bayonet Constitution. But in 1893, she proposed a constitution that would restore her and Hawaiians to power by giving only those born in Hawaii the right to vote.

Encouraged by Stevens, on January 16, the planters staged a coup d'état to install a white-dominated provisional government led by Sanford Dole. They landed a force from the cruiser USS *Boston*. When the queen protested, Stevens made it clear that the U.S. forces supported the coup. The next day, without authorization, he recognized the Dole government. That night, Queen Liliuokalani surrendered, as she said, "to the superior force of the United States of America."

A delegation from Dole's government reached Washington just weeks before the end of President Benjamin Harrison's term, and Secretary of State John Watson Foster quickly drafted a treaty. But as soon as President Cleveland was inaugurated, he and his antiexpansionist Secretary of State, Walter Q. Gresham, denounced the way the Republicans had overthrown the Hawaiian government, and they refused to annex Hawaii.

In March 1893, Cleveland sent James H. Blount to Hawaii with extraordinary powers. Blount had a reputation for integrity; he was a ten-term congressman from Macon, Georgia, and former chairman of the House Foreign Relations Committee. He was critical of U.S. diplomats, even telling Congress in 1878; "If there is any service that is of questionable value to the country it is our diplomatic service."

Blount declared that Stevens had overstepped the limits of diplomacy and rescinded the American protectorate. Cleveland recalled Stevens and withdrew the treaty. Henry Cabot Lodge opposed him in the Senate, on grounds that Britain and Japan threatened Hawaii.

Cleveland told Congress that "a substantial wrong has been done" by a diplomatic representative of the United States, and he replaced Stevens with Albert S. Willis, a Kentucky congressman, who was instructed to restore the queen to her throne. But Dole refused to step down. Cleveland

castigated the provisional government but would not use force to remove it.

On July 4, 1894, Sanford Dole proclaimed the birth of the Republic of
Hawaii. Cleveland, his view reversed by the panic of 1893, recognized it,
even though it disenfranchised most Hawaiians, Chinese, and Japanese
residents of Hawaii. Then the Wilson-Gorman Tariff put Hawaiian sugar
growers back in competition with domestic U.S. growers.

Early in 1895, the Hawaiians rallied again to try to overthrow the
white-dominated republic. In a brief fight near Diamond Head, the forces
of the republic, better armed and trained, easily dispersed the Hawaiians.
One man on each side was killed. The native rebels were tried by a military court, and Hawaiian newspapers were shut down and their editors
jailed. Queen Liliuokalani was arrested and convicted of misprision. She
was isolated for eight months and forced to abdicate.

Once the Wilson-Gorman Tariff restored their prosperity, the annex-
ationists had no economic issue to rally round, so they envisioned a threat
that Japan was taking over the islands. This illusion was given some substance when the rehabilitation of the sugar plantations sparked an inflow
of Japanese labor. By 1896, nearly half of the islands' population was Asian.

McKinley sent as minster Harold M. Sewall, who echoed the planters'
story of a Japanese invasion. And Assistant Secretary William Day let
Sewall use the U.S. Navy to establish a protectorate over Hawaii. When
the Dole government kept out newly arrived immigrant laborers, Japan
sent a warship to Hawaii. But from Tokyo, two successive American ministers, Edwin Dun and A. E. Buck, reported calmly that Japan had no intention of seizing the islands.

On June 12, 1897, William Day handed the cabal's representative a draft
treaty of annexation. Secretary of State John Sherman signed it in the reception room of the Department of State. The surprise treaty met resistance
in the U.S. Senate, but concern over Japanese intervention ended when the
Japanese simply withdrew their objection to the treaty.

Still, the native Hawaiians fought back, bringing to Congress a petition with twenty thousand signatures opposing annexation. Their protest
weakened the support for annexation in the Senate. Queen Liliuokalani
warned that the Hawaiian people were going to be reduced to the status of
the American Indian.

The sinking of the *Maine* changed everything. And when the U.S.

Army was sent to the Philippines, the annexation of Hawaii, on the Pacific sea lanes, became inevitable. Three days after the United States destroyed the Spanish fleet off Cuba, the Senate voted for annexation. McKinley approved it the next day.

On August 12, in front of 'Iolani Palace in Honolulu, President Sanford Dole turned over the sovereignty and property of the Republic of Hawaii to the U.S. minister Harold Sewall. He swore in Dole as the territorial governor. The American flag was raised over the palace. Almost no native Hawaiians attended the ceremonies. Promptly, Congress gave the Hawaiians American citizenship minus the right to vote in presidential elections. Diplomat and historian Warren Zimmermann, former ambassador to Yugoslavia, called it "imperialism in its purest form."

BRINGING UP THE GUNS

Fitzhugh Lee, the bearded, florid, heavyset U.S. consul general at Havana, had been, thirty years earlier, a fighting general of Confederate cavalry. The son of Robert E. Lee's older brother, he had graduated forty-fifth of the forty-nine cadets in his West Point class. But he was a hero at Chancellorsville and Winchester and, after the war, a governor of Virginia. In 1896, President Cleveland sent him, now sixty-two, to Havana.

Consul General Lee condemned the brutality of the Spanish suppression of the Cuban rebellion and defended Americans accused of aiding the insurgents. Peasants who did not hesitate to burn American-owned sugar plantations had taken over the civil war. In December 1897, fearing for the safety of Americans in Cuba, Lee asked that the battleship USS *Maine* stand by at Key West.

On January 24, Judge William R. Day, first assistant secretary of state, and John D. Long, the secretary of the navy, walked over to the Executive Mansion and asked President McKinley to send the USS *Maine* and the cruiser USS *Montgomery* to Cuban waters. Judge Day was supporting Secretary of State John Sherman, the seventy-four-year-old brother of General William Tecumseh Sherman and a longtime senator. (Sherman, at that time often confused and forgetful, was moved to the State Department and gave Mark Hanna his Senate seat.)

The *Maine* steamed to Havana, although Lee had, in the meantime, asked that its visit be postponed. He was surprised when the battleship appeared. Lee had helped bring Spain and the United States to the brink of war.

The danger had been building. McKinley, in addition to sending Lee to Havana, had named General Stewart L. Woodford, a vigorous New York lawyer, minister to Spain. He was to make sure that Spain gave up the island.

Before Woodford reached Madrid, Spain's hard-line premier was assassinated, and a government formed with men who promised reforms and home rule for Cuba. From Madrid, Woodford reported that the Spanish "want peace if they can keep peace and save the dynasty."

The new Spanish government recalled Cuba's brutal governor, General Valeriano Weyler y Nicolau. More than a hundred thousand Cubans were said to have died in his concentration camps; the American "yellow press" called him "the Butcher." The new governor, General Ramón Blanco y Arenas, was instructed to help the rural Cubans. Woodford showed surprising negotiating skill, but it was too late. The Cubans now demanded their independence.

Once *Maine* was at Havana, Consul General Lee recommended that it extend its stay a week; he feared its early departure would be seen as a sign of weakness. Then, at 9:40 on the night of February 15, *Maine* exploded, and 266 of her crew were killed.

The Spanish government denied responsibility for the explosion and warned that it would repel with force U.S. intervention in Cuba. On March 29, Minister Woodford presented the Spanish government with an ultimatum to establish an armistice in Cuba within forty-eight hours. A French diplomat said Woodford had "claws under his gloves."

The Spanish government retorted that it would grant the Cubans an immediate armistice, but not independence. By then, the American people, aroused by the warmongering of the Hearst newspapers, were inflamed enough to demand war.

Lee had a declaration of war delayed until Americans in Cuba could be evacuated. Congress, on April 19, called for Cuban independence and renounced any wish to annex Cuba. Two days later, Woodford and the U.S. legation staff in Madrid entrained for Paris. McKinley ordered a blockade of Cuba and replaced Secretary of State Sherman, who was fragile, with Judge Day.

. . .

The war, which was centered on Cuba, actually began in the far Pacific. McKinley ordered Commodore George Dewey, commanding the U.S. Asiatic Squadron of four old light cruisers and three gunboats, hurriedly painted battle gray, to sail from Hong Kong and destroy the Spanish fleet at Manila.

An insurgency was already bloodying the Philippines. American Consul General Oscar F. Williams, staying in Manila despite threats to his life, reported violence there. Dewey delayed sailing from Hong Kong until Williams could convey information on Manila's defenses to the flagship *Olympia*.

On May 1, Dewey attacked the Spanish squadron. The battle was so one-sided that Dewey interrupted the fighting to have his men served breakfast and to redistribute ammunition. Then, they destroyed the Spanish ships. Nine Americans were wounded but none killed; the Spanish suffered 381 casualties. The Spanish army in Manila was isolated.

Washington received no word of the outcome of Dewey's battle, so the State Department, impatiently, cabled Consul Rounsevelle Wildman at Hong Kong for news. A vigil was mounted at State. Cots were set up and Second Assistant Secretary Alvey A. Adee and Third Assistant Secretary Thomas W. Cridler divided the watches. But Commodore Dewey, to prevent interference from headquarters, did not send word to Hong Kong until four days after the battle.

At dawn on May 7, a terse alert roused Assistant Secretary Cridler at the State Department: "Hong Kong McCulloch Wildman." Then, Western Union delivered a message in code to the navy. Over the shoulder of the code clerk, Assistant Navy Secretary Theodore Roosevelt read aloud the names of the Spanish ships destroyed. The crowd outside the Executive Mansion cheered.

"TELL AGUINALDO TO COME"

Even before Dewey's victory in Manila Bay, Consul Wildman, an experienced East Asia hand, was working from Hong Kong to convince the Filipino leader Emilio Aguinaldo to help the Americans defeat Spain.

Wildman spoke no Tagalog, and Aguinaldo had little Spanish. The Spaniards had sent Aguinaldo, still in his twenties, into exile with four hundred thousand pesos. At Hong Kong he bought substantial arms for the revolution.

Aguinaldo next turned up in Singapore and met with U.S. Consul General E. Spencer Pratt, a former minister to Persia. Pratt persuaded him to return to Hong Kong, cabled Dewey that Aguinaldo would collaborate, and sent the State Department word that Aguinaldo expected independence for his islands. Dewey replied: "Tell Aguinaldo to come as soon as possible."

Consul Wildman arranged for Aguinaldo to meet with Dewey, who put him ashore at Cavite, on the island of Luzon. Aguinaldo rallied the Filipinos and soon controlled all of the Philippines except Manila. Wildman supplied them with rifles.

Aguinaldo thought he had American assurance of independence, but the American consuls on the scene had annexation, not independence, in mind. The government in Washington had not decided on the Philippines' future. So, in June, Aguinaldo simply declared independence and took charge of the Filipino government.

Oscar Williams reopened the consulate in Manila in August and recommended that Aguinaldo and his fighters be granted recognition and pay, but his advice was ignored. In December, the Treaty of Paris gave the islands to the United States. The consulate was closed. On their voyage home, Consul Rounsevelle Wildman and his family were lost at sea.

Meanwhile, USS *Charleston* seized Guam in the Marianas, on the trade routes to Asia, without shedding blood. And Congress passed a joint resolution to annex Hawaii, which was now a way station to the Philippines.

Major General Wesley Merritt brought to the Philippines a force that would grow to twenty thousand soldiers. He and his staff had little respect for the guerrilla fighters, and U.S. army officers would not let Aguinaldo's men enter Manila. The Americans believed they ruled the Philippines. And so it appeared.

THE WAR IN THE ATLANTIC

On May 12, a squadron of Spanish armored cruisers commanded by Admiral Pascual Cervera y Topete reached the Caribbean island of Martinique. The U.S. Navy, lacking swift scout ships, depended for information on American consuls ashore in the West Indies. U.S. Marines captured Cuba's Guantánamo Bay in mid-June. And when the army arrived, three-hundred-pound General William Shafter bungled the attack on Santiago de Cuba; and Teddy Roosevelt, who had surrendered his Navy post to seek frontline glory, led the charge up San Juan Hill, a polka-dot handker-chief waving conspicuously in his campaign hat.

On Sunday morning, July 3, four Spanish cruisers tried to break out of Santiago's harbor, but blockading American warships disabled them, one by one. Cuba was isolated, and Spain had lost the war. Fortunately, Spain had proved to be a third-rate opponent; the U.S. Army was unprepared to fight a real war.

French Ambassador Jules Cambon called on McKinley and Secretary of State Day to inquire whether the United States was ready to reach an agreement. On July 29, Day presented the cabinet the draft of a note prepared with the help of First Assistant Secretary John Bassett Moore, on leave from the chair of international law at Columbia University. Under it, the United States would not occupy or rule Cuba, but Spain would have to leave. The United States would hold on to Puerto Rico and other Spanish islands in the Caribbean and one in the Marianas.

Philip C. Hanna, the U.S. consul, notified the State Department that the Puerto Ricans welcomed the autonomy that Spain had already granted them. Led by journalist Luis Muñoz Rivera, the Puerto Ricans set up a government; but a week later, U.S. Marines and sailors landed at Gunica and raised the American flag. Puerto Rico would be American.

CONFRONTATION IN CONSTANTINOPLE

While McKinley was occupied by the war with Spain, he also faced a confrontation in Constantinople between the Ottoman government and the American minister, Dr. James B. Angell, former president of the University of Michigan, who had aroused the sultan's anger. Angell asked the president to send warships to Constantinople to "rattle the Sultan's windows."

McKinley replaced Angell with Oscar S. Straus, who opposed sending warships to Turkey. Because Straus had served there earlier under the Democrat Cleveland, the press speculated that his appointment by a Republican promised a merit system in the foreign service.

For a year, Straus tried to resolve the indemnities due to Christian missionaries for damage to their property during the Armenian massacres. After months of talks, the sultan, who would not publicly admit the massacres had taken place, agreed to buy an American cruiser and hide the indemnities in its price. But Ottoman credit was so poor that it took years before the agreed-upon amount was paid.

Straus also persuaded the sultan in Constantinople, as the religious leader of Islam, to instruct the sultan of the Sulu Islands, who had always opposed Spanish rule, to cooperate with American military forces in the Philippines. The sultan in the Sulus was convinced when Straus produced a translation of a section of the treaty between the United States and Tripoli negotiated by Joel Barlow in 1796. It said:

> As the Government of the United States of America is not in any sense founded on the Christian Religion; as it has in itself no character of enmity against the laws, religion, or tranquility of Musselman; and as the said States have never entered into any war or act of hostility against any Mehomitan nation, it is declared by the parties, that no pretext arising from religious opinions shall ever produce an interruption of the harmony existing between the two countries.

The Americans promised that they would not interfere with the Muslim religion, and that won the Sulu sultan's agreement not to join Aguinaldo's insurrection.

The war with Spain was over, but McKinley could not decide whether to keep just Manila or the whole Philippine archipelago. He said plaintively, "If old Dewey had just sailed away when he smashed that Spanish fleet, what a lot of trouble he would have saved us."

The cabinet was divided. Three members wanted to keep the entire island group, and three wanted to keep only Manila. Judge Day, in the latter group, cited "the consent of the governed." Senator Lodge and Captain Alfred T. Mahan, the spokesman of sea power, wanted to keep the Philippines, Cuba, and Hawaii for their strategic value.

Negotiations continued until Ambassador Cambon, of France, and Day signed the protocol in the tatty Cabinet Room of the Executive Mansion, on August 12. Cuba would be independent, and Puerto Rico and Guam, American. For the time being, Cuba would be ruled by the American military led, fortunately, by Brigadier General Leonard Wood, M.D., a humanitarian.

But the Filipino tragedy was not finished. Fighting broke out between the Americans and Aguinaldo in February 1899. When it ended two years later, two hundred thousand Filipinos had died. In March 1901, Aguinaldo was captured in his mountain hideout, and two years later he pledged his allegiance to the United States.

THE GREATEST DEBATE

The Spanish-American War led to one of the greatest foreign affairs debates in United States history. It was about empire. Did the Constitution allow for second-class (nonslave) people? Would dark-skinned tropical people wreck American civilization? Imperialism entailed a sizable element of racism. The prevailing attitude was that Americans' racial and moral superiority permitted them to do as they pleased.

Powerful voices preached on both sides. One group argued that the United States should confine itself to developing its vast continent. The other side—and it would prevail—wanted to reach beyond the continent and seek markets and bases for the coal-burning navy and to propagate democracy and Christianity. Thus, the United States inched closer to the world's violent confrontations. World War I was less than two decades away.

The opponents of imperialism included industrialist Andrew Carnegie, writer Mark Twain, and a goodly number of intellectuals. They spoke of principles: Government required the consent of the governed. The Former minister to Spain, Carl Schurz, wrote heatedly that this small war in the Philippines was supposed to have been "a war of deliverance and not one of greedy ambition, conquest, self-aggrandizement."

The imperialists asserted that, in reality, the future of Spain's former colonies was not self-government but domination by Germany or Japan. It was not then foreseen that forty-three years later the Philippines would suffer under Japanese rule and that, on July 4, 1946, the United States would finally grant the Philippines independence.

19

Three Diplomatic Friends

1898–1905

Among the American diplomats debating American imperialism were three good friends who lived interlocking lives. All three came from small towns: Xenia, Ohio; Salem, Indiana; and Clinton, New York. All three were self-made, and all three married wealthy women who helped their husbands gain access to the salons of wealth and power.

Whitelaw Reid became a hard-driving New York newspaper editor, an effective peacemaker at the end of the Spanish-American War, and finally the U.S. ambassador to the Court of St. James's. John Hay and Elihu Root both served as Secretary of State. Hay, fragile, retiring, a poet, died on the job. Root, the best of corporation lawyers and a lover of the outdoors, brilliant and ruthless, reshaped both the War Department and the Department of State.

WHITELAW REID

Diplomacy was not Whitelaw Reid's first passion. He had been born on a frontier farm that his father had chopped out of the Ohio forest. As a young man, Reid wrote and set type, and with his brother and a friend bought their hometown newspaper, the *Xenia News*. When Reid died in

London, at seventy-five, representing the United States, King George V paid him honor.

Reid opposed slavery and supported Abraham Lincoln. During the Civil War, he made his byline, "Agate," famous by reporting for the *Cincinnati Gazette,* vividly and candidly, the fierce battles at Pittsburg Landing, Shiloh, and Gettysburg. In 1869, Horace Greeley made him the editor of his *New York Tribune.* John Hay also joined Greeley's newspaper and wrote editorials, and Mark Twain, Bret Harte, and Henry James contributed to the paper.

Young Reid was tall and slender with a drooping mustache and a shock of black hair. In New York, he knew the powerful people, joined the Union League Club and The Century Association, and was elected the longtime president of The Lotos Club. He boosted Grant until his attempted annexation of Santo Domingo; Reid then became Grant's opponent. In 1872, Reid had a major part in making Greeley the Liberal Republican and Democratic candidate for President. Greeley lost badly to Grant and died that November. Reid bought the *Tribune* with a loan from Jay Gould, a speculator who welcomed a friendly connection in the press.

Reid was an elegant political wheeler-dealer. In December 1878, his friend, Secretary of State William M. Evarts, wanted him to replace Bayard Taylor, who had died in Berlin, where he was the U.S. minister. Reid declined. But Evarts asked him to help persuade John Hay to join the State Department, and he did that. Reid also helped appoint James G. Blaine as Secretary of State.

A turning point in Reid's life came on April 26, 1881, when he married Elizabeth "Lizzie" Mills, the daughter of Darius Ogden Mills, who as a poor twenty-three-year old had joined the California Gold Rush and made a fortune. Reid now had, in addition to ambition and power, access to great wealth. The couple bought the Villard mansion at Madison Avenue and Fiftieth Street in New York City and a thousand-acre estate (since 1952 the site of Manhattanville College) in Westchester County.

President Benjamin Harrison named Reid minister at Paris in 1889 and sent Robert Todd Lincoln to London, a post that Reid coveted. John Bigelow wrote, "Going into diplomacy is much like experiencing a shipwreck or going into a battle, a very good thing when it is safely over."

Reid's most pressing diplomatic chore in Paris was to eliminate France's protectionism against American petroleum exports and reverse its refusal to allow American pork to be sold in France. French imports of American pork had dropped from $3.9 million to $5,000, and Reid's predecessors were unable to improve imports.

The problem was solved when Reid's *Tribune* simply predicted American retaliation on French wines. Reid's retaliatory vinous spin worked. The French repealed their ban on American pork, and Reid wrote Harrison he was ready to resign. He delayed his departure to complete an extradition treaty, and then ran for Vice President on the Republican ticket with Harrison, who was seeking a second term. They lost to Grover Cleveland and Adlai E. Stevenson.

Four years later, Reid supported McKinley's candidacy, and as a reward represented the President at the celebration of the sixtieth anniversary of Queen Victoria's accession to the throne. Reid had ambitions to be Secretary of State, but he had made too many political enemies. Still, some said that if he had become Secretary, there might have been no Spanish-American War. Reid's *Tribune* editorialized that it was ridiculous to go to war over a battleship.

JOHN HAY

John Hay, the second of the three friends, was the son of a frontier doctor in Salem, Indiana, just north of the Ohio River. At school in Pittsfield, Illinois, he befriended a boy six years older named John Nicolay. Hay graduated from Brown University as a member of Phi Beta Kappa and class poet. Returning to Illinois, he read law with his uncle in Springfield. Abraham Lincoln had been a partner of the firm and still had an office there. In 1860, Hay enabled Nicolay to be Lincoln's secretary during the presidential campaign. Lincoln took Nicolay to Washington as his private secretary, and Nicolay brought twenty-two-year-old Hay as his assistant. The two young men lived and worked in the Executive Mansion.

After Lincoln was shot, Hay stood at the head of his bed as Lincoln weakened and died. Secretary of State Seward sent Hay to Paris as secretary to the U.S. legation. John Nicolay was stationed there as consul; they both served under Minister John Bigelow. A year later, when John A. Dix, who had a reputation for avarice, replaced Bigelow, Seward made Hay the chargé d'affaires ad interim at Vienna, to replace John Lothrop Motley.

He enjoyed Vienna, but after a year he became first secretary of legation at Madrid under the controversial Daniel Sickles.

Hay was a handsome, complicated man with a neat, trim beard, long mustache, and deep brows. There was devilment in his eyes, but he was always under control. Now thirty-two, he was a bit too dignified, a bit too shy, but surely a young man of the world.

After leaving Madrid, Hay stayed away from diplomacy. Until he married the daughter of a wealthy Cleveland railroad builder, he worked for Whitelaw Reid at the *New York Tribune*. Reid sent Hay, an excellent reporter, to report on the Chicago fire in October 1871. He interviewed the husband of the woman who had milked the cow, as Hay wrote, "that kicked over the lamp that spilled the kerosene, that fired the straw, that burned Chicago." He and Nicolay wrote a ten-volume life of Lincoln. He shuttled back and forth between journalism and diplomacy. In 1879, Secretary of State William M. Evarts brought Hay to Washington to replace Frederick W. Seward, the former Secretary's son, as assistant secretary. When Garfield became President in 1881, Hay returned to the *Tribune*.

President McKinley appointed Hay ambassador to the Court of St. James's, a post Hay had worked hard to persuade McKinley to offer him. When Hay arrived with his friend Henry Adams, Henry White and American-born novelist Henry James met them at Southampton. White, an exceptionally able young diplomat, was Hay's first secretary at the embassy, which was then at 5 Carlton House Terrace. They served together congenially for a year and a half, until a surprising cablegram cut short Hay's tenure.

In February 1898, Hay and Henry Adams were returning from a trip up the Nile when the battleship *Maine* exploded. Hay wrote a friend, "I detest war, and had hoped I might never see another, but this was as necessary as it was righteous."

Hay never found his London responsibilities strenuous, and he detested the horde of visitors who came begging favors. Life brightened a bit one evening when Queen Victoria seated him next to her at a Windsor Castle dinner, and she proved to be a fascinating partner.

Relaxing in the countryside on August 14 that wartime summer, Hay was shocked when White brought him a cablegram:

It gives me exceptional pleasure to tender to you the office of Secretary of state, vice Day, who will resign to take service on the Paris

Commission, to negotiate peace. It is important that you should assume duties here not later than the first of September. Cable answer. William McKinley.

The President left him no choice. And Hay's decision was assured once Henry Adams wrote him, "No serious statesman could accept a favor or refuse a service." Although Hay was sixty and his health was delicate, he started at the Department of State on October 1, 1898, and stayed to oversee the blooming of the United States as a world power. His father-in-law's wealth made him more sympathetic than ever to the needs of American business.

Secretary Hay was fortunate to have two adept professionals at his elbow: Henry White, in London, and Alvey A. Adee, in the department. The tiny, hardworking Adee, a Yale graduate and Shakespeare scholar, had already been with the State Department for nearly three decades and knew its policies and routines intimately. His memos in red ink on green slips signed A A had become legendary. So had his "quacking falsetto voice" and his sense of humor. The story was told that when Adee reviewed a document with the sentence, "Our entering wedge appears to be bearing fruit," he wrote on it, "Not fruit but wedgetables."

ELIHU ROOT

The third of this trio was Elihu Root, whom Theodore Roosevelt described to Andrew Carnegie as "the greatest Secretary of State we have ever had."

Hay and Root were an intriguing contrast. Hay was literary, intellectually creative, and quotable, but neither skillful at administrating nor at working with Congress to achieve the administration's international program. Root was a superb administrator and effective at bringing congressmen to his point of view. He kept them informed, he listened to them, and he compromised. He got himself invited to the Foreign Relations Committee's Wednesday-morning meetings. While Hay cursed senatorial obstructionism, Root scouted imaginative ways around it.

This man, who became one of the great secretaries of state, had origins in America going back to 1639. His ancestors fought at Concord Bridge and helped stop Burgoyne and the British army coming down the Hudson Valley. One jovial forbearer had a tavern in Great Barrington, Massachusetts; his father's father, Elihu, ran an inn near Utica, New York. Root's own father, Oren, went to Hamilton College and became a teacher. His mother, Nancy Buttrick, was the granddaughter of the man who ordered "the shot heard round the world." His father and older brother taught mathematics at Hamilton, where they were known, respectively, as "Cube" Root and "Square" Root.

Root was rail-thin and had a prominent nose and a high-pitched voice. When Lincoln called for volunteers in the fall of 1860, Root tried to enlist but was rejected as too frail. He went to New York City, studied law, and was admitted to the bar in 1867. In time, he and Alexander T. Compton formed a law partnership; and when New York's "Boss" Tweed was indicted, Root, then twenty-eight, defended one of Tweed's codefendants, a cousin of Compton's wife. His client was sentenced to five years in prison, and Root was paid with four lots on West Eighty-fourth Street. Years later, after Root helped defeat William Randolph Hearst for governor of New York, Hearst's newspapers relished labeling him as a defender of Boss Tweed.

In 1878, Root married Clara Wales, whose father was a leading banker and managing editor of *Scientific American*. He became involved in the Union League Club and Republican politics. Root was friendly with Joseph H. Choate and Chester A. Arthur and was an early supporter of young Theodore Roosevelt, working with him when he became president of the New York Police Board. Root had, according to Hay, a "frank and murderous smile."

As a lawyer, Root was hugely successful. President Arthur appointed him U.S. attorney for the Southern District of New York. But he made an enemy of the New York State boss, Senator Thomas C. Platt, a man who did not forget grudges.

In the summer of 1899, McKinley asked Root to replace the widely criticized Russell A. Alger as his secretary of war, in order to manage the nation's new overseas possessions. The army was still occupying Cuba and fighting Aguinaldo in the Philippines, but the department Root took over was riddled with inefficiency, red tape, and corruption. Setting out to change all that, he ended the army's tradition of promotion by seniority. He came to work at 9:00 A.M. when most of the men in government started at least an hour later. He had lunch at his desk, a sandwich and coffee sent over from the Metropolitan Club.

When Hay was ill, Root took charge of the troubles with the so-called

Boxer Rebellion in China. He reduced the politically powerful post of commanding general to a chief of staff. And after having an immense impact on the U.S. Army, he resigned in 1904 and returned to his law practice. He was widely regarded as the nation's best-ever secretary of war.

And Elihu Root was not finished. He still had ahead of him the assignment of Secretary of State. The country was lucky to have these three remarkable friends to guide it through one of its most transforming eras.

20

Practicing Imperialism

1898–1905

U ntil 1898, the United States possessed no territory farther offshore than Nantucket and Martha's Vineyard. The Spanish-
American War changed that. It was the nation's passport into
the troubled world of the Great Powers.

President McKinley asked Judge William R. Day to resign as Secretary
of State and to head the Paris Peace Commission, realizing that after the
war he would need a more effective diplomat as Secretary of State. To assure
the treaty's ratification, he named to the Peace Commission two Republican
members of the Senate Foreign Relations Committee: Cushman K. Davis,
of Minnesota, and William P. Frye, of Maine, both of whom favored annexing the Philippines. He also appointed Whitelaw Reid of the *New York Tribune,* and a token Democrat, Senator George Gray, of Delaware. First
Assistant Secretary of State John Bassett Moore would be its secretary.

McKinley counseled the commissioners to be magnanimous. In Paris
on October 1, 1898, Judge Day and Senator Gray opposed keeping any of
the Philippines except for a naval coaling station. Reid, who proved to be
the most effective negotiator, sided with the majority in favor of keeping
all the islands because the navy needed bases.

Reid wanted to hold the Philippines as a territory, not a state that would
threaten the nation, as he said, "with so large a half-breed citizenship, and
with a further deluge of new States and senators." His was a racist position
but a popular one. Accordingly, McKinley instructed the commissioners

to annex all the Philippines. The commissioners offered Spain $20 million as compensation, and the Treaty of Paris squeaked through the Senate by one vote.

After the treaty negotiations, Reid badgered Hay for the diplomatic post in London, but the President selected Joseph H. Choate for London, General Horace Porter for Paris, and William F. Draper for Rome. Reid's cause was wrecked when New York's "boss," Thomas Platt, threatened to fight his nomination.

The Filipinos, who had expected their independence, rebelled. Emilio Aguinaldo led the struggle, which produced Filipino and American casualties over the next three painful years. Historian Margaret Leech called the insurgency "the muddle produced by three effusively annexationist consuls [Pratt, Wildman, and Williams], a fatuously complacent admiral, and four overbearing military commanders." The fighting was marked by barbaric atrocities on both sides.

McKinley also sent to Manila a fractious five-man Philippine commission chaired by Jacob Gould Schurman, president of Cornell University. Its only member from the foreign service was Charles Denby, the veteran minister to China.

McKinley wanted the American forces in the Philippines to win the respect of the Filipino people, but the war grew vicious, and the self-reliant Filipinos, defending their homeland, were hard to defeat. By early 1900, haughty, elderly General Elwell S. Otis commanded sixty-five thousand troops in the islands. He was succeeded by General Arthur MacArthur, "the precise, arrogant, dandified General who would finally tranquilize the islands by a policy of relentless subjugation."

After Aguinaldo was captured by a ruse, McKinley sent William Howard Taft to head a second commission in Manila. And to moderate the islands' government, on July 4, 1901, he replaced General MacArthur as governor with the civilian Taft.

Shortly before McKinley was assassinated, he directed Secretary Hay to establish the Bureau of Insular Affairs in the State Department and planned to place Charles H. Allen, the governor of Puerto Rico, in charge of it. But with McKinley's death, the nation's colonial governance remained under the War Department.

Secretary of War Root sought to reduce American troops' use of brutality and torture on the Filipinos. When the press publicized the atrocities, public outrage forced a congressional hearing. People were horrified by the trial of Major Littleton Waller Tazewell Waller of the U.S. Marine Corps for murdering Filipinos on the island of Samar. The army's General Jacob Smith said he wanted Samar made "a howling wilderness" and was court-martialed for his excesses.

Root denied American atrocities publicly, but Congress made him bring the accused officers to trial. Years later he admitted, "There is a moral law which prevents the Government doing certain things to any man whatever. We haven't always stuck to it."

On the Fourth of July 1902, President Theodore Roosevelt declared the war over. More than four thousand Americans and tens of thousands of Filipinos had been killed. Taft remained as governor for four years, improving people's lives but ignoring their desire for independence.

MANNING UP FOR THE WORLD

During the decade after the war with Spain, the foreign service, still staffed mostly by political appointment, tried to catch up to the evolution of the United States into a world power. The number of people working at the State Department doubled, from 87 to 167. Congress permitted the number of diplomatic secretaries overseas to increase between 1898 and 1908 from 24 to 60, and by 1918 double again to 122. The consular corps, of course, outnumbered the diplomatic by a large number. And still, all these additions were not enough to deal with the expansion in trade, investment, and immigration.

Americans who needed relationships abroad still found the clubby foreign service inadequate and pressed to change the way the nation's representatives abroad were selected, trained, and organized.

Of course, the familiar ways had their successes. Henry White was a superb example of how the personal influence dominating the American foreign service during the Gilded Age worked at its best. White was the heir of two old, affluent Baltimore families; his father died when he was three, and he was reared by a mother who insisted on schooling him at home and speaking with him only in Italian. After the defeat of the Confederacy, she married a prominent physician, and with some bitterness they moved to Europe.

Six foot three, handsome, affable, always helpful, and congenial company, Harry White was not an intellectual or a great wit, but he was dependable. He grew up learning languages and foxhunting with the landed aristocrats of Europe. His was a comfortable life of privilege and idleness. Then, in 1879, he married Margaret Rutherfurd, a handsome and strong-minded woman who wanted him to do something useful with his life. Diplomacy was the field chosen, and the Rutherfurds' friend, courtly Secretary of State Frederick T. Frelinghuysen, found him a secretaryship in the Vienna legation.

White received the telegram telling him of his appointment while his elegant wife and he were attending a house party along with the Prince of Wales, the Duchess of Manchester, and other lords and ladies, at the home of Ferdinand de Rothschild, in Buckinghamshire. And a telegram urging him to accept the post arrived from Alphonso Taft, the U.S. minister in Vienna and father of the future President.

White reached his post in July 1883 and found the Viennese narrow-minded and boring. He did not complain, because he expected the job would end when a new administration came to office in Washington. It ended even sooner, when he received a better offer, to be second secretary to the legation in London, where his friend James Russell Lowell was now the minister.

President Cleveland replaced Lowell in 1885, and White stayed in London under Edward J. Phelps, a stout, stubborn Yale law professor. The next year, White became first secretary. Phelps moved the legation to 123 Victoria Street, and he and White pressed Congress to give the legation the status of an embassy. White contended that in Vienna minister Alphonso Taft was seated below the ambassador from Monaco.

When White prepared to go on home leave in September 1893, Ambassador Thomas Bayard told him that President Cleveland had asked for his resignation. Cleveland was persuaded that White had spoken disparagingly of him. Secretary of State Walter Q. Gresham tried to defend White, but the President replaced White with a Democrat.

White's mother died, and he became a man of means. He devoted his new free time to building contacts in London and Washington and to promoting a nonpolitical, professional foreign service. In a long article in the influential *North American Review* (December 1894), White charged that "the present system of appointments and removals for political reasons is very prejudicial to our commercial interests." He was critical of the "Consular Debauch," in which Cleveland had replaced 30 of 35 consuls general and 133 of 183 consuls. White was also appalled that U.S. consuls in Latin America did not have to know Spanish, and he pilloried a consular agent in Seville who had deluged a Catholic religious procession with Protestant tracts.

White wanted to follow the British consular service, in which appointments required passing an examination in English, French, and the language of the place to which the consul was being sent, as well as an examination in British mercantile law; and, he added admiringly in his article, the French realized "the absolute necessity of keeping 'politics' out of their Consular Service, and devoting its energies exclusively to the interests of French trade." The French held an examination to fill vacancies at the lowest level, that of "pupil consuls" (*elve consuls*). To sit for this examination, a man had to have served for a three-year probationary period. The exam covered international law, English or German, and political economy or political or commercial geography. Those who passed had to take an oral examination and work for a year in a chamber of commerce. Only after three years as pupil consuls were they eligible for a vice consulship. White admired what he called "the elaborate precautions taken by the French."

He proposed that the United States organize its consular service as it did its military services. A candidate would be examined and admitted as a vice consul. Removal would be only for cause. The chief sacrifice would be that the political party coming into power would have to leave men of the opposite party in office. But, he predicted, it would not object because "most of our diplomatic and consular officials long to be servants of their country and not of a political party." He predicted a career service would come into being.

At a Washington dinner in May 1896, Henry White talked candidly with Secretary of State Richard Olney. He told Olney that he thought President Cleveland's treatment of the consular service was "disgraceful" and that no one in the London embassy was able to "see much of the leading men of England in private life." When White sailed for England a few weeks later, Secretary Olney told him to report what the leading men were thinking. White's mixture of intelligence and charm made him ideal for the assignment.

The American business community was demanding consular reform. In 1894, the Boston Chamber of Commerce asked Congress to put the consular service on a merit basis. Boston was joined by the New York State

Chamber of Commerce and by the National Civil Service Reform League. Four years later, Harry Garfield, oldest son of the assassinated President, became president of the Cleveland Chamber of Commerce and was brought into the movement for consular reform by Gaillard Hunt, a former foreign service officer who despised the spoils system. Gustav Schwab, head of the American office of the North German Lloyd Steamship Co., read in the *New York Post* of the Cleveland chamber's efforts, wrote to Garfield, and they joined forces. By 1900, Senator Lodge and Congressman Theodore E. Burton, of Cleveland, sponsored a bill to transform the consular service. The Lodge-Burton bill rallied little public support, and, as always, Congress' desire to distribute patronage ruled. The bill for consular reform died.

THE CANAL

The expansion of international business, the search for new markets abroad, and the acquisition of overseas possessions all gave fresh urgency to the old wish to connect the two great oceans. Benjamin A. Bidlack, U.S. chargé d'affaires in Bogotá, had negotiated the Bidlack-Mallarino Treaty of 1846, which made it possible to build a railroad across Panama. And the United States was willing to share a neutralized canal with Great Britain under the Clayton-Bulwer Treaty of 1850. In the war with Spain, the USS *Oregon* dramatized the difficulty of steaming between the oceans when she raced around Cape Horn to meet the Spanish fleet.

In December 1898, Secretary Hay asked Henry White in London to see whether Lord Salisbury would be willing to discuss a new canal treaty. Lord Salisbury was not an easy man to see. He went into his London office only once a week and did not welcome having his country life disturbed. But he knew and liked White and invited him down to his estate, Hatfield. After breakfast, and before they went shooting together, they talked in the library, and Salisbury amiably agreed to discuss a new treaty. He required that all nations should pay the same tolls and that the negotiations should take place in Washington.

On February 5, 1900, Secretary Hay and British Ambassador Lord Pauncefote, signed a convention that gave the United States the exclusive right to build and control an isthmian canal. It stipulated that the United

States would not fortify the canal and would keep it open to all nations even in time of war.

For the United States, this was a major improvement over the 1850 treaty, but Hay had failed to consult the powerful leaders of the Senate before agreeing to a neutralized canal. The convention sparked a power struggle between the Executive branch and the Senate. Senator Lodge did not want to allow an enemy fleet to pass through the canal in wartime, so Senator Cushman K. Davis offered an amendment that made the treaty inapplicable in times of war. Furious, Hay attacked opponents of the treaty and handed the President his resignation, which was rejected. Hay felt the senators were intruding on the President's role, and he condemned their action as "an exhibition of craven cowardice, ignorance, and prejudice." It was not an attitude to win a senator's heart.

Although Hay believed in a strong presidency as epitomized by Lincoln, he was no street fighter. He had to draft a revised canal treaty, which omitted the prohibition against fortifications and wartime neutralization. Joseph H. Choate, the ambassador in London, talked with Salisbury, who, preoccupied with the Second Boer War, agreed. And in November 1901, Lodge made sure that this second Hay-Pauncefote Treaty sailed through the Senate, 72 to 6.

OPEN DOOR AND VIOLENT BOXERS

Japan's defeat of China in 1895 led to a feeding frenzy, during which the aggressive Great Powers snapped up parts of China. Germany, Russia, and Britain chopped China into spheres of influence, squeezing out the United States. American diplomats Ethan A. Hitchcock, in Saint Petersburg, and Charles Denby, in Peking, were confident that U.S. business could turn these aggressions to its advantage.

By the summer of 1898, McKinley sent to Peking as minister his friend Edwin H. Conger, a genial former Iowa congressman who had been serving as minister to Brazil. He was given no preparation for the Chinese post and had no appreciation of China's traditions. He held the idea that he could Westernize the Chinese.

Expertise in Far Eastern affairs was scarce in Washington, so, in early 1899, Secretary Hay brought in his friend William W. Rockhill to advise him on Asia. The six-foot-four scion of a wealthy Philadelphia family, Rockhill was a brilliant but austere and rather tyrannical young man. He had grown up in Europe, graduated with honors from the French military academy at Saint Cyr, and served in Algeria with the French Foreign Legion. He had become second secretary of legation in Peking, but four years later Minister Charles Denby dismissed him for devoting himself to his scholarly passions for Sanskrit and ancient Buddhism. Denby's son got his job.

Unemployed, Rockhill made daring scientific expeditions into Mongolia and Tibet for the Smithsonian Institution. He returned to the State Department in 1893 as chief clerk and then third assistant secretary. But McKinley sent him out again as minister to Greece, Romania, and Serbia until Secretary Hay brought him back to Washington.

Rockhill guided U.S. policy during the Boxer Rebellion and, later, became the U.S. minister to China and, successively, ambassador to Saint Petersburg and Constantinople. Secretary Hay regarded Henry White and William Rockhill as the best American diplomats of the era. White may have been the most distinguished. Certainly, Rockhill was one of the most colorful.

During the summer of 1899, a friend of Rockhill's, Alfred E. Hippisley, an Englishman who served in China's Maritime Customs and was a China scholar, stopped in Washington because his American-born wife wanted to visit her family in Baltimore. Hippisley proposed to Rockhill the scheme that became the Open Door policy. He recommended that the United States obtain from each European power a commitment to apply treaty tariffs and to open treaty ports in its spheres of influence without discrimination. A rather modest proposal, it replaced competition with cooperation.

Some historians have judged "Open Door imperialism" the dominant form of American empire building. It did not create repressed third world colonies like the Belgian Congo; it kept doors open for American trade, financing, mining, and communications. And it helped sustain third world governments that accepted such a relationship.

Secretary Hay had Rockhill draft a memorandum based on Hippisley's thoughts. The proposed policy was inadequate because it preserved the existing spheres of influence, and it was radical in that it sought from other powers commitments to the United States. In September, Secretary Hay proposed to six Western nations that their spheres of influence in

China not interfere with commercial treaties and asked them to assure the United States that they would honor equal rights for all parties.

On March 20, 1900, Hay sent out a circular announcing simply that the six governments had agreed; and the State Department leaked, as news, word that all the powers had agreed to the American proposition. In fact, their answers were complicated and evasive. None of them wanted to go along; none dared not to. Charlemagne Tower, the U.S. ambassador at Saint Petersburg, wrote Hay, "The truth is the Russian Government did not wish to answer your propositions at all." This rather dicey business contained a great element of bluff. Hay wrote Henry Adams, "I would rather, I think, be the dupe of China, than the chum of the Kaiser." In the United States and Britain, however, Hay's brazen Open Door policy was widely praised and gained him great respect.

At the same time, the Chinese were facing crop failures and rising taxes, and they were mounting quite a different response to the invading powers. A secret, militant patriotic group, the Boxers, reacted violently against the foreigners in north China. From Peking, Minister Conger cabled Hay that Boxers and rampaging government troops had him under siege. Fifty Marines and seamen from USS *Newark* went ashore to serve as a legation guard. And Consul William Pethick, guarded by U.S. Marines, ventured out and rescued several Christian missionaries.

Although Rockhill doubted that the Boxer situation was serious, an international force of two thousand men, including a hundred Americans, left Tientsin for Peking on June 10, 1900. They soon lost touch with their base, the multinational fleet anchored at Tientsin's port of Taku.

After June 20, nothing was heard from the American minister in Peking, and Secretary Hay cabled Conger to report. The Chinese legation in Washington was in touch with Peking, and on July 11 Hay asked Minister Wu Ting Fang to send a coded message requesting information. Finally, on July 20, after a month of silence, Conger was able to send a message asking for help to prevent a massacre in Peking. Hay doubted whether this unnerving message was authentic and requested the Chinese to send another message asking Conger to confirm his message by sending Conger's sister's name. Back came the correct answer: Alta.

In Peking the situation was precarious. The foreigners were gathered in the besieged British legation compound. Sixty had been killed and one hundred and twenty wounded; the survivors were living on horsemeat. On Rockhill's order, Conger warned China's foreign office that they had a responsibility to protect foreigners. The Chinese ignored him. The international relief force took until August 14 to battle through to Peking and relieve the foreign legations.

Hay sent Rockhill to China with the title of commissioner. He visited the local rulers in Nanking and Hankow and sailed up the Yangtze River in the USS *Nashville*. Then he returned to Peking for an international conference on China that lasted for a year. The United States was handicapped because Conger did not speak French, the language of the conference, and only one representative from a country could be present at any time. When Conger went on leave, Rockhill took over the negotiations more effectively. A protocol was signed on September 1, 1901, and Rockhill left Peking the next day.

Capitulating to the stress of the Boxer attacks, Hay withdrew to his summer place on Lake Sunapee in New Hampshire. Second Assistant Secretary Alvey A. Adee became acting Secretary of State. From his retreat, Hay wrote to Henry White of the Boxers, "We have killed ten for one at least; we have looted and destroyed many millions of property. The story is enough to sicken a Zulu."

One positive spin-off of these stormy events in China was that in 1902 Congress authorized the posting of ten student interpreters at the legation in Peking to study Chinese. The department requested that these interpreters be chosen on a nonpartisan merit basis. And the program was later expanded also to train six students at Tokyo in the Japanese language.

The nasty Boxer emergency had a light side. McKinley came to depend on Secretary of War Elihu Root for advice on China. Root, who stayed in constant touch with Acting Secretary Adee, complained to his wife that he had to shout at Adee, who was very deaf, and then go to the Executive Mansion and shout at the President over the telephone to his home in Canton, Ohio.

Root and Adee had offices at opposite ends of the State, War and Navy Building. Root wrote Adee, "I notice that your people are still sending copies of dispatches to me by mail. As I have already told you, I found that they were doing the same thing here, but I think I have stopped that. If it would be a comfort to your people to continue mailing communications to me, I will get the Postmaster General to put a mail box in my office, and they can come over and put the communications in it, but if they would hand them to my Private Secretary it would save expense."

The President wanted to remove American troops from China; he wrote Hay, "I know of no way to get out but to come out." Minister Conger urged that the troops stay in Peking, and he demanded that pro-Boxer Chinese authorities be punished. Still, at Hay's suggestion, the United States returned to China its share of the indemnity collected, minus actual expenses, and the Chinese created a $12 million fund for the education of Chinese students in the United States.

President Roosevelt appointed Rockhill to succeed Conger in 1905. On the way to his post in Peking, the new minister stopped in Shanghai and was shocked to meet a surge of anti-Americanism. And in Peking, the American consul, Rockhill's friend, Fleming Duncan Cheshire, briefed him on a boycott against American goods. The cause was the growing hostility in the United States against Chinese immigrants. The consul in Canton, Julius Lay, cabled the department to send a warship as a show of force against the protests. But Rockhill advised Secretary Root against that move, believing that Congress should face up to Chinese grievances.

The controversy grew so violent that several missionaries were killed and a riot ripped through Shanghai's International Settlement. Foreign sailors were landed to keep order, and Rockhill agreed that a U.S. warship should be kept at Shanghai to protect Americans. But when the British wanted the Chinese to pay for the damage caused in the riots, Rockhill argued that he did not see how they could be held responsible since they were not allowed to have police or soldiers in the International Settlement.

After the Russo-Japanese War broke out in February 1904, Rockhill, like his superiors in Washington, was more concerned about Russia's ambitions than Japan's. The Americans were slow to recognize Japan's expansionism; the Japanese took over Inner Manchuria from Russia and stood toe-to-toe with China. By 1907, Rockhill appreciated the threat Japan presented.

When William Howard Taft became President in 1909, he appointed Rockhill ambassador to Saint Petersburg. The Chinese foreign office gave him an elaborate farewell dinner to express their high regard for him.

Following the Russo-Japanese War, the United States became the first nation to close its legation in Seoul as Japan demanded. This upset Secretary of Legation Willard Straight. He had worked for the Chinese Maritime

Customs Service, covered the Russo-Japanese War for Reuters, and then joined the U.S. foreign service. He served as vice consul in Seoul and later as consul general at Mukden in Manchuria, where he witnessed early Japanese aggressions.

When Rockhill was transferred to Constantinople, he was glad to be free of Taft's business ambitions in China. But his sympathy for the views of the people among whom he was posted continued to make trouble. In April 1912, the Turks sank a ship, the *Texas,* which was flying the American flag, and saved and arrested the captain, a Greek. The American consul general in Smyrna (Izmir) protested the captain's imprisonment and claimed he came under American consular jurisdiction. The Turks asserted that since they had pulled him out of the water, he came under Turkish jurisdiction. Rockhill agreed with the Turks. The State Department disagreed and told Rockhill to ask the Ottoman authorities to free the man. Rockhill did as he was instructed, but the Turks refused; the captain was sentenced to eighteen months in prison.

When Woodrow Wilson was inaugurated, Rockhill, after thirty years of service, was replaced in Constantinople by Henry Morgenthau, a major contributor to Wilson's campaign. Rockhill became an advisor to the Chinese republican government. In November 1914, traveling to Peking, Rockhill had a heart attack in Honolulu and died there. He was praised as a diplomat and a thoughtful expert on Asian affairs. He had formed American foreign policy toward China, but his first loves always were scholarship and the study of ancient cultures.

TEDDY ROOSEVELT INVIGORATES
FOREIGN RELATIONS

President McKinley, age fifty-eight, died of an anarchist's bullet on September 14, 1901, in Buffalo, New York. When Vice President Roosevelt received the telegram from Elihu Root notifying him that McKinley had died of his wounds, Roosevelt made a midnight dash from the Adirondack Mountains, where he had been hiking, and took the oath of office in the library of a friend's home in Buffalo. At forty-two, Roosevelt was at the time the youngest President to have served. Secretary Hay met the new President at Washington's Union Station, and Roosevelt asked him to stay on. Hay, although tired and depressed, was now first in line for the presidency.

Hay had to deal with Roosevelt's brash reaction when Canada, wanting an entryway to the Yukon gold mines, requested a connection to the Pacific through the Alaska panhandle. Hay was prepared to lease Canada a strip of land and a port, and McKinley had agreed to this solution. But the new President caustically said Hay was giving away too much.

Hay negotiated an agreement in 1903, by which a Canadian Boundary Tribunal of six reputedly impartial jurists settled the matter. Although emotions ran high, the issue ended peacefully when the lord chief justice of England, one of the British jurists, graciously cast his vote for the American position.

The vigorous Roosevelt was determined to see a trans-isthmus canal completed. At first, Nicaragua had the advantage because a government commission, the Walker Commission, favored a route through that country. In response, the New Panama Canal Company dropped the price of its assets from $109 million to $40. And it hired William Nelson Cromwell, a New York lawyer-lobbyist, who arranged a $60,000 contribution to the Republican Party's campaign. That helped Senator Mark Hanna support the Panama route. Congress passed a bill to buy from the French canal company and from Colombia rights to a strip six miles wide across the isthmus.

On January 22, 1903, the United States and Colombia signed the Hay-Herrán Treaty, which gave Colombia $10 million for the company's rights and the country's land. After nine years, Colombia would also receive $250,000 annually. The experienced American minister in Bogotá, Arthur M. Beaupre, reported that the Colombians angrily claimed they had been cheated. Hay cabled back that if Colombia did not ratify the treaty, Congress would do things "which every friend of Colombia might regret."

Beaupre, urbane and courtly, had been consul general to Guatemala-Honduras, and President Roosevelt had promoted him to minister, a rare switch for a consul at that time. Roosevelt charged him to have the Colombian congress ratify the treaty.

The Colombians were trying to squeeze better financial terms out of the United States; and in August, Beaupre informed the State Department that the Colombian senate had unanimously rejected the treaty. Enraged crowds threatened Beaupre with violence. Assistant Secretary Francis B. Loomis delivered to Roosevelt a State Department statement that no single nation could veto a canal that would benefit all the world.

Philippe-Jean Bunau-Varilla, a dapper stockholder in the French effort to build a Panama canal, suggested to Roosevelt and Hay that the province of Panama be separated from Colombia. Roosevelt ordered the navy to prevent armed forces (presumably Colombian) from landing within fifty miles of Panama. USS *Nashville* showed up at Colón in time to do that.

Bunau-Varilla arranged for a revolution to take place on November 3. Vice Consul Felix Ehrman, in charge at Panama, cabled the State Department, "Uprising occurred tonight. Six. No bloodshed." The next day the Republic of Panama was proclaimed and hundreds of U.S. Marines went ashore to prevent the revolution from unraveling. On November 6, the United States cabinet recognized the instant nation.

Bunau-Varilla returned to Washington, this time, rather incredibly, as the envoy from Panama; and on November 18 he and Hay signed a treaty in the little blue drawing room of the White House (as Theodore Roosevelt had officially renamed the Executive Mansion). The treaty contained the same terms as the Hay-Herrán Treaty, except the Canal Zone was now ten miles wide instead of six. The U.S. Senate ratified the treaty. Panama received its $10 million and the stockholders of the canal company took $40 million.

General Rafael Reyes, Colombia's representative, asked Hay to reconsider. Hay told him that it was too late. Hay reported this to Roosevelt and added with a twinkle, "I have a complaint to make of Root. I told him I was going to see Reyes. He replied, 'Better look out. Ex-Reyes are dangerous.' Do you think that, on my salary, I can afford to bear such things?"

The shameless action in Panama aroused a storm of long-lasting distrust in Latin America. But Hay was proud of what had been accomplished, and Roosevelt disdainfully said he had been prepared to take the Canal Zone by force if necessary. The bloodless revolution was a better solution. The President called his indignant congressional critics "a small body of shrill eunuchs."

OTHER DRAMATIC CRISES

Even while the activist President was "liberating" the province of Panama, he tackled other dramatic foreign policy crises. On June 15, 1903, six leaders of the American Jewish community asked him to condemn a pogrom in Kishinev, Russia, during which forty-nine Jews had been killed and hundreds injured. Roosevelt did not want to confront Czar Nicholas II, but when the czar refused the petition, the President advised the Jewish leaders to make it public.

The following May, Samuel R. Gummer, the American consul general in Tangier, notified the State Department that a Moroccan "bandit" named Malay Hamid el Raisuli had kidnapped an American named Ion H. Perdicaris and his stepson and was holding them out in the desert for a seventy-thousand-dollar ransom. Gummer was a longtime friend of Perdicaris, whose Greek father had been the U.S. consul in Athens. Actually, Raisuli wanted to force the sultan of Morocco to pay the ransom. A rather sophisticated (and vengeful) brigand, Raisuli wanted to get even because the sultan had once caused Raisuli to be chained to a dungeon wall.

During long negotiations, President Roosevelt threatened to land the U.S. Marines. And Secretary Hay vividly cabled Gummer, "We want Perdicaris alive or Raisuli dead." French diplomats finally persuaded the sultan to meet Raisuli's demands, and Gummer cabled that Perdicaris would be returned that evening. The next day, Perdicaris wired Hay his thanks. Raisuli had gotten his revenge.

This colorful story was told at the Republican National Convention, and Secretary Hay's macho message became wildly popular across the country. Hay commended Gummer and made him the first American minister to Morocco.

In March 1905, Roosevelt wanted to settle the war between Russia and Japan. He transferred George von Lengerke Meyer, the ambassador in Rome, to Saint Petersburg and directed him to talk to Czar Nicholas II. The ambassador, a skilled bridge player, cut through the czarist bureaucracy and delivered Roosevelt's message to the czar. The President also had Lloyd C. Griscom, the minister in Tokyo, inform the Japanese government he wanted to help end the war.

Since Secretary of War Taft was on his way to Manila with the President's daughter, Alice, and a group of congressmen and their wives, Roosevelt asked him to stop in Tokyo. Premier Taro Katsura assured Taft that the Japanese government did not intend to interfere with the Philippines or Hawaii but said that it must control Korea. Taft and Roosevelt agreed that, as Root said, Korea was better off under "the liberal and progressive constitutional Empire of Japan."

In late April, Roosevelt was hunting black bears in Colorado's mountains when he received a coded cable from Taft informing him that the Japanese foreign minister wished him to initiate peace negotiations. But first the Japanese navy destroyed Russia's Baltic Fleet in the battle of Tsushima; it was the beginning of the end for the Romanovs.

Ambassador George Meyer met with Nicholas on June 7, and the czar agreed to talk with the Japanese in secret. Meyer was effective with royalty; he had all the right connections. Born on Boston's Beacon Hill, he had graduated from Harvard, been Speaker of the Massachusetts House of Representatives, and served four years as ambassador in Italy.

Both parties agreed to meet at Portsmouth, New Hampshire, and by the end of August, the victorious Japanese agreed to compromises: They took only half of Sakhalin, and the Russians did not have to pay an indemnity. They signed the Peace of Portsmouth, and Roosevelt was awarded the Nobel Peace Prize.

"THE ROPE OF SAND"

By the spring of 1905, Hay was exhausted. Frail and a hypochondriac, he no longer had the stamina to continue as secretary. He was worn out, he said, "twisting the rope of sand which is American diplomacy."

Beginning his second term, Roosevelt served more and more as his own Secretary of State. Hay and his wife and Henry Adams sailed to Europe. Hay, weak and ailing, was lifted aboard ship in a wheelchair. He visited doctors in Italy and Germany. Henry White, on his way to the embassy in Rome, visited them in the seaside resort of Nervi, and they had lunch together in nearby Genoa. They would never see each other again.

From Nervi, Hay wrote the sculptor Augustus Saint-Gaudens, "My doctor here says there is nothing the matter with me except old age, the Senate, and two or three other mortal maladies." Hay was too ill to accept a degree from the University of Cambridge or a visit from the kaiser, but King Leopold of Belgium arrived unannounced. Henry Adams drove Hay around Paris in his new Mercedes; he visited King Edward at Buckingham Palace and sailed for the United States. He was taken to his home in New Hampshire, and he died there on July 1. His funeral was held in Cleveland, his wife's hometown. The President and his entire cabinet attended.

Hay had been a beloved Secretary. *The New York Times* praised him for doing "so much to raise the standard of American diplomacy and endow it with a prestige among the nations of the earth."

Elihu Root wrote Roosevelt, "Ah me! The old times are passing."

21

"The Main Object of Diplomacy"

1905–12

President Theodore Roosevelt and Elihu Root rode together on the train to Secretary of State John Hay's funeral in Cleveland. Root had resigned from the War Department more than a year before and returned to his remunerative law practice, where his clients included financier J. P. Morgan, railroad owner James J. Hill, and insurance tycoon Thomas Fortune Ryan.

After the train left Jersey City, the President asked Root to become his Secretary of State. And during the train ride home, Root accepted. When reporters asked him why he had left a $200,000 law practice for an $8,000 job, he said he was happy to return to public life. The *New York Times* said Republicans assumed Root would run for President in 1908. Roosevelt gave a more innocent explanation, "I am extremely fond of him and prize his companionship as well as his advice."

On the brutally hot morning of July 19, 1905, Elihu Root came back to the massive, ornate State, War and Navy Building, where he had served so capably as secretary of war. He walked to the south end of the building, where the Department of State had its offices, and took the oath of office from William McNair, the department's assistant librarian. He spent a week working at the department and then left on a fishing vacation in Newfoundland, during which he studied the endless controversy over fishing rights. Root wrote his friend, John St. Leo Strachey, editor of *The Spectator,* that he could not replace Hay, "But I shall try to keep the country out of trouble, which after all, when it is done in the right way, is the main object of diplomacy."

Root had an enormous effect on the Department of State and the foreign service. First, he created an efficiency rating for consuls and made promotions based on it. This trimmed back the spoils system in the foreign service, although in the department itself he replaced First Assistant Secretary Francis B. Loomis with Robert Bacon, tennis-playing friend of Roosevelt and a partner of J. P. Morgan. Bacon would do what Root wanted done. Root retained the veteran Alvey A. Adee as second assistant secretary and brought in Francis Mairs Huntington Wilson from the embassy in Tokyo as third assistant secretary. Huntington Wilson was self-centered and lacked a sense of humor, but Root found him invaluable on East Asian policy.

When Wilson graduated from Yale, his father arranged an appointment for him as second secretary in Tokyo. Young Wilson was capable and ambitious, and after nine years in Tokyo he sent his attractive wife Lucy to make a personal appeal to her friend, Secretary of War William Howard Taft. Taft took her by the arm into Secretary Root's office at the other end of the building; Root, who enjoyed feminine beauty, soon named Lucy's husband the third assistant secretary of state.

Wilson antagonized people and clashed with Wilbur Carr. Wilson had oversight of the consular bureau and was appalled to find the clerks were assigned to countries alphabetically rather than geographically; the same clerk handled China and Cuba.

Root was open to fresh ideas. He allowed Wilson to reorganize the department into geographically based divisions with a diplomatic and a consular section in each division. Although both he and Carr preferred more control and less delegation, Root recognized that the mounting workload made it impossible to run the department on the old relaxed basis. As a first step, he gave Wilson command of the informal Far Eastern Bureau.

When he returned to Washington, Wilson was one of only three men in the whole department who had served in the foreign service. The rules allowed bringing foreign service officers to Washington only on temporary duty. William Phillips, second secretary at Peking, agreed to a job in Washington's lowly messenger service on the promise of interesting work.

And Percival Heintzleman, vice consul general at Canton, came back as a clerk third class.

On March 20, 1908, Root created the Division of Far Eastern Affairs, with Phillips as its chief and Heintzleman as his assistant. These two young men set up their office behind a screen in Huntington Wilson's office and began reorganizing the department. It was an immediate success with diplomats and businessmen, who needed expert information.

William Phillips, the man chosen to direct the first geographic division, was another elite Bostonian and not quite thirty years of age. In 1900, during his senior year at Harvard, he had traveled to Washington with a proper letter of introduction and coolly knocked on the door of Secretary of State Hay's home. Hay advised the self-confident young man to go to Harvard Law School. He followed that advice. But during his second year, at a house party on the Vanderbilt estate in North Carolina, he met and charmed Joseph H. Choate, then the ambassador to the Court of St. James's. Choate invited him to come to London as his private secretary, without pay. This was the high end of the spoils system at work.

By April 1903, Phillips was posted in the London embassy and costumed, like everyone else, in cutaway coat, striped trousers, and silk hat. His main responsibilities were to keep the ambassador's calendar and accompany him to his many engagements. Then, in 1905, he met William Rockhill, who invited him to join the legation in Peking. As Phillips later told the story:

> I replied with enthusiasm, but never expected favorable results as I had no pull politically and no friends in the State Department. In those days there was no foreign service in the present accepted sense. The President appointed at his pleasure, with the consent of the Senate, not only Ambassadors and Ministers but also Secretaries of Embassy and Legation. With a change of party all chiefs of mission resigned, and nearly always Secretaries were replaced by political appointments from the party in power. There was no stability whatsoever in our missions abroad and naturally no incentive to a young man to adopt diplomacy as a career.

In Peking, Phillips soon replaced Henry P. Fletcher as second secretary. Phillips' first assignment was to chair a meeting in Nanking at which officials of the Standard Oil Company of America and local Chinese hammered out an agreement on land the company wanted to acquire. Then, Phillips maneuvered to return to the State Department, and Root made him chief of the new Division of Far Eastern Affairs.

One day, through a well-placed contact, Phillips was invited by President Roosevelt to join a small group on a hike in Rock Creek Park, including a rugged climb up a steep cliff. That was an informal form of diplomatic examination of the day. Phillips, forewarned to wear rubber-soled shoes, performed well. And it led to invitations to play tennis with the President on the White House court. The matches were followed by tea for the "Tennis Cabinet."

Phillips became a guest at Roosevelt's Oyster Bay, Long Island, home and was invited to luncheon at Henry Adams' home. By the end of 1908, the bright young diplomat succeeded Wilson as third assistant secretary of state. But after TR left office and under pressure from a senator with clout, Phillips was transferred out to be secretary of the embassy in London under Ambassador Whitelaw Reid. Political interference continued to flourish.

AN EARLY VICTORY FOR CONSULAR REFORM

Since Root detested the spoils system, when he took charge of the State Department in 1905, he had Roosevelt sign executive orders requiring all consular positions with salaries over one thousand dollars a year and all diplomatic vacancies at the level of secretary of embassy or legation and above be filled by examination, transfer, or promotion. A politician could no longer force the direct appointment of an ineffectual constituent.

The charge that with those executive orders Roosevelt gave away his patronage rights was not true. His Executive Order 367, of November 10, 1905, based consular promotions on merit and consular appointments to the junior grades on examinations. And Executive Order 368, of the same date, appointed all diplomatic secretaries on a merit basis. And the President continued to appoint ambassadors and ministers.

The results of the early consular examinations were disappointing; before World War I American universities were not teaching international relations. When Root looked into the examination system, he wrote the President with candid irony: "In view of the character of the examination, a rejection would practically be an imputation of idiocy."

But exams, even if of dubious quality, were now in place. On the same day as those executive orders were issued, Root created a board of the third assistant secretary, the chief of the consular bureau, and an officer from the Civil Service Commission to raise examination standards.

One thing Root did not do was to accede to Roosevelt's suggestion that the diplomatic corps accommodate his love of pomp and uniforms. Root said the only appropriate uniform for American diplomats was a coat with a tail pinned with a sprig of mistletoe.

In a move that did have a lasting effect, Root switched the supervision of the consular service from the third assistant secretary to Wilbur Carr. Two years later, Root promoted Carr to chief clerk of the department and kept the Consular Bureau under him. Carr was a reliable subordinate and believed in gradual reform. He liked to say that if you gain an inch a day, at year's end you will have gained 365 inches. He stayed in charge of the consular service until 1937; by then, he had served for forty-five years under seventeen secretaries of state.

Within six months of taking office, Root helped draft, and had Senator Lodge introduce to the Senate, a comprehensive bill to reform the entire foreign service. Root appeared before the Senate Committee on Foreign Relations and won its cooperation. He operated on the idea that, as he said, people "tend to trade with their friends." Of the 103 treaties Root signed as Secretary, the Senate failed to ratify only three. He was said to have a "mind packed in ice."

Root's foreign service reform bill was emasculated before it passed on April 5, 1906, but it accomplished a great deal: It reorganized the consular service. For all posts below chief of mission, appointments and promotions were based on merit, and tenure was guaranteed during good behavior. American citizens would fill all clerkships with salaries of one thousand dollars or more. Consular fees were eliminated, and all consuls put on salary. Consuls with annual salaries of more than a thousand dollars could not engage in business. Five inspectors would spread out and check each consular office every two years. Consular agents, a position in place since the Revolution, were eliminated. Here were major pieces of a modern consular corps. After eighty years, the spoils system, if not dead, was at least grievously wounded.

The act did not require examinations for entry to the lower consular grades or for junior consuls' promotion. That June, Root summoned five of the best consuls to serve as an advisory consular reorganization board. Frank H. Mason, the consul general at Paris, presided. The board recommended creating five consular districts, each with an inspector (called a consul general at large). This board also decided that the development of U.S. export trade should be the consuls' major responsibility. No attention was given to imports necessary to maintain a trade balance.

Root and Carr drafted another Executive Order on the basis of the board's recommendations, and President Roosevelt signed it on June 27, 1906. It based consular appointment on examinations, both written and oral, and would cover diplomatic usage, international law, and language. Above the lower ranks, promotion would depend on a man's record rather than on examination.

Eighteen applicants sat for the first exams the following March, and ten passed. During Root's secretaryship 171 men were examined and 75 were accepted. By 1909, the United States had 64 U.S. consuls general, 229 consuls, and 700 consular officers of lower rank.

It was a time of important change. The arrival of a Republican administration in 1897, followed by the nation's taking giant steps toward overseas involvements, led to a surge of applicants for government jobs. And this was the first period during which African-Americans had a chance to win some of these positions. President McKinley appointed Mifflin Wistar Gibbs, an African-American graduate of Oberlin, as U.S. consul to Tamatave, Madagascar, and Richard Theodore Greener, a Harvard College graduate and a recognized intellectual, as consul at Vladivostok. President Roosevelt named James Weldon Johnson, a respected black Florida lawyer, as consul at Puerto Cabello, Venezuela, and Corinto, Nicaragua. At least twenty African-American consuls served in the foreign service during this period.

It was also found politically necessary to give greater representation to the Southern states. In 1906, only nine consular officers out of 274 came from the South, while sixteen came from Senator Lodge's state alone. During the next five years, 63 consuls were added, 31 from the South and 32 from the North. All candidates now had to be identified by the President and had to have their senators' support. The reforms were far from perfect, but they were steps forward.

This intense attention was paid to the consular service because it was taking on, as a key function, the overseas needs of American business.

During the financial panic of 1907, Edward Ozmun, consul general at Constantinople, urged the department to bring consuls home to show American manufacturers how to replace shrinking domestic markets with foreign markets. The idea was adopted, and Julius Lay, then the consul general at Cape Town, was the first to add six weeks to his home leave to visit American manufacturers. As one example, he showed them that the Germans were selling a superior plow in South Africa.

Change usually has a downside, and consular reform was no different. The twin factors of size and a call for efficiency led to the growth of a bureaucracy. As one observer put it, "Like the officers themselves, the consulates were also beginning to resemble interchangeable parts in a large mechanism." And what was to be done with the below-standard, ineffective consular officer? Inspector Charles M. Dickenson told a consul in Jerusalem that his archaeological scholarship could not replace his failure to promote trade and recommended that he be transferred. A consul in Algeria, where France was developing agriculture, was criticized for failing to promote American equipment; it was said he still thought like a New Jersey sheriff, not a consul. If an unfit consular officer had influential friends to protect him, he would be moved to a quieter post or his office would simply be closed. No one wanted to embarrass the powerful.

The link between the consular service and business affected the entire State Department; American business was becoming the consular service's constituency.

REFORMING THE DIPLOMATIC SERVICE

Reforming the diplomatic service was much more difficult than reforming the consular. Diplomatic salaries were low and personal expenses were high, and only affluent men could accept such conditions. Some diplomats were not eager to work hard, and, in truth, at some posts there was not much to do.

Various diplomats were content to keep the elitist way things were. Henry P. Fletcher, now first secretary of the legation in Peking, said salaries should remain low to keep out "a lot of cheap sports of the country prize speller type." Root countered by trying to build a professional substructure beneath the political appointees. He had efficiency records kept on every subordinate foreign service officer to guide promotions and retention. Examinations became more sophisticated and probing. Root's energy, vision, and political skills made his administration of the State Department a historic landmark, even though the new rules did not cover the entire diplomatic service until Taft's Executive Order 1143, of November 26, 1909.

LATIN AMERICA DEMANDS ATTENTION

In November 1905, Secretary Root received from John Barrett, the U.S. minister to Colombia, a memo that convinced him that the United States was taking a self-defeating attitude toward Latin America. Official Washington tended to regard Latin America as a backwater and simply sought to shelter its countries from outsiders, even if they did not want protection.

Root decided to attend the Third International Conference of American States in Rio de Janeiro during the summer of 1906. A Secretary of State had never traveled outside the United States on official business. That was not yet considered part of his duties.

Root and his wife sailed on the cruiser USS *Charleston* to Puerto Rico and then on to Brazil. At Rio, they were ceremoniously rowed ashore in the sixty-four-oared barge in which Don Joao VI of Portugal had landed in 1808 while fleeing from Napoleon's armies. Root served as honorary president of the conference, and when he departed Rio on August 3, he trailed a torchlight parade of thousands of students. He visited São Paulo, a coffee plantation, a community of Civil War Confederate veterans, and Montevideo and sailed through the Strait of Magellan and up the west coast to Chile, Peru, Panama, and Colombia. He hoped the elaborate trip would strengthen diplomatic and commercial relations, but it was slow going.

While Root was on this tour, Consul General Frank Steinhart in Havana notified the department that the Cuban government had asked that two warships be sent to snuff out an uprising against President Tomás Estrada Palma. President Roosevelt insisted that the American force not intervene until the Cubans had tried every means of their own to put down the rebellion.

When Estrada Palma asked for more troops, Roosevelt sent a force of U.S. Marines. On September 12, a hundred men and three field pieces of artillery from USS *Denver* were landed and took positions covering

Havana's main thoroughfares. Roosevelt had not ordered the force landed and cabled the Havana consulate: "You had no business to direct the landing of those troops without specific authority from here."

The men were promptly withdrawn, and Estrada Palma resigned. Roosevelt appealed to him to stay in office and sent Secretary of War Taft and Acting Secretary of State Robert Bacon to Havana. He appointed Taft as provisional governor of Cuba.

By now, Secretary Root was back in Washington. The Cuban intervention had taken the bloom off his tour and angered South Americans, who feared the United States intended to stay in Cuba. When Judge Charles E. Magoon, a former governor of the Panama Canal Zone, replaced Taft as provisional governor of Cuba, he declared that his purpose in taking office was to preserve Cuban independence.

Root had to continue devoting attention to relations with South and Central America. The U.S. minister at Caracas, Herbert W. Bowen, a career foreign service officer, recommended sending warships to force Venezuela's dictatorial president, Cipriano Castro, to repay his loans to European bankers. But Castro was bankrupt, and Bowen's demanding style was not Root's. William W. Russell replaced Bowen in order to reestablish friendlier relations.

Then, Castro made trouble for a French company and was told France had broken relations with Venezuela. That frightened him. Britain and Germany threatened that they were going to blockade Venezuela's ports. Although the crisis was over money and debt, Roosevelt, typically, felt sure that the Germans intended to acquire bases in anticipation of an isthmian canal. When the German commander fired on a Venezuelan fort and sank several gunboats, Roosevelt gave Admiral Dewey command of a flotilla and pugnaciously told him to prevent the kaiser from occupying the country. In Berlin, Ambassador Charlemagne Tower, Jr., less militantly, persuaded the German government to ease its debt-collection methods. And in London, Henry White encouraged the British to arbitrate the dispute.

Roosevelt gave the kaiser ten days to accept arbitration. Otherwise, the American flotilla would move to protect Venezuela. Four days before the deadline, the German ambassador announced that in answer to a Roosevelt question, the kaiser still would not arbitrate. In response, Roosevelt shortened the deadline by twenty-four hours. Roosevelt was threatening war. Up against the deadline, the Germans accepted arbitration. The blockade was lifted peacefully.

In Central America, the United States had only two representatives, one accredited to Guatemala and Honduras and the other to Costa Rica, Nicaragua, and Salvador. Root established separate legations in each country. He also helped create the Central American Conference and a Central American court of justice, and he persuaded Andrew Carnegie to build a palace for the court at Cartagena, Colombia.

In 1907, Italy threatened to seize a customs port of the bankrupt Dominican Republic. Root had the Dominicans appoint a collector of duties but said he would intervene only if its government could not protect the lives and property of American citizens. The following year, on the same island, Root instructed the American minister to Haiti, Dr. Henry Watson Furniss, an African-American physician from Indiana, that the United States would not grant asylum in American legations to political refugees. Even after five refugees expelled from a U.S. consulate were shot to death, Root held to his legalistic position. Asylum, he said, was a custom and not recognized under international law.

In 1909, Root sought to smooth the strained relationships between Colombia and Panama. This seemed possible because General Reyes, who had represented Colombia in Washington, was now its president. Three treaties were negotiated over two weekend meetings at Root's home. But an uprising in Colombia removed Reyes and ended that hope of reconciliation.

With the nations of the Western Hemisphere, Root preferred to use the carrot rather than Roosevelt's "big stick." In 1907, he first used a term that became well-known years later: "the Good Neighbor Policy." But during the interval, the Taft presidency resorted to Dollar Diplomacy, often backed up by armed force and intervention.

A RACIST GENTLEMEN'S AGREEMENT

Root walked into an ugly foreign relations problem right at home. Especially on the West Coast, American racism mixed with competition for low-paying jobs. Americans tried to prevent Asian laborers from immigrating and discriminated against those who did reach the United States. Root compared the treatment of the Chinese to that of African-Americans and Indians.

This tension was not new. In October 1871, a mob had rampaged through Los Angeles's Chinatown, hanged fifteen Chinese, and shot and wounded four. And eleven years later, a federal exclusion law prohibited Chinese laborers from entering the United States. Enforcing the law was complex, especially "section six," which defined those, mostly businessmen and students, who were exempt. American consuls abroad were increasingly called on to enforce exclusion once an 1884 law required visas on section-six-exemption certificates. Consuls felt tightening such exemptions interfered with their job of improving international trade. Consul Wildman at Hong Kong criticized the rules defining exempt classes, and Consul Robert McWade at Canton admitted he issued visas only to Chinese endorsed by bankers he knew.

President Roosevelt asked that all exclusion laws be handled fairly and pressed the State Department to set consistent procedures. And the changes made Chinese applicants bitter at being given what they felt were humiliating medical examinations. Deception became the rule. In 1911, at Hong Kong, Consul George Anderson judged that three-quarters of the visas he issued went to fraudulent applicants.

Japanese immigrants received similarly severe treatment. Root explained to the Japanese ambassador that Japanese laborers were "a formidable competitor" because they worked hard for little money. The ambassador asked Root, "Then you would exclude us for our virtues?" "Exactly so," Root replied.

Employers welcomed the cheap labor; labor unions did not. Railroad builder James J. Hill wrote the Japanese ambassador that the Great Northern Railroad employed twelve hundred Japanese laborers and could use another five thousand. California fruit growers also wanted many more Japanese.

Although Japan voluntarily stopped giving workers passports for the mainland United States, there were still no limits on immigration to Hawaii, where the sugar industry needed workers. And the U.S. government could not stop immigrants from traveling to the mainland once they were inside the country. The 1907 financial depression intensified the competition for jobs, and Root had the law amended to keep out aliens who held passports to travel in the islands, Canada, or Mexico, and he obtained the Japanese government's approval.

Root worried about war with Japan. He thought the Japanese could easily seize Hawaii and the Canal Zone. Roosevelt shifted the "Great White Fleet" to the Pacific (the Canal was not yet ready), just in case. Taft visited Japan again and reported that the Japanese did not want war. At Root's request, Ambassador Thomas J. O'Brien in Tokyo invited Japan to help solve the immigration problem. Out of this came an informal Gentlemen's Agreement: The Japanese would stop exporting laborers, and the United States would stop discriminating against Japanese already in the United States.

Under the Root-Takahira Agreement of November 30, 1908, Japan agreed to recognize America's control of the Philippines and Hawaii, and the United States recognized Japan's rule over Korea. Willard Straight, the U.S. consul general at Mukden, added a statement supporting the independence of China. And Minister Rockhill at Peking obtained the concurrence of the Chinese government. Ambassadors Whitelaw Reid, in London; David J. Hill, in Berlin; and Henry White, in Paris, also negotiated endorsements in support of the Agreement.

Eventually, however, the U.S. Senate passed the National Origins Act of 1924, excluding both Japanese and Chinese; and that, Root always believed, ended Japan's friendly relations with the United States and led, seventeen years later, to the attack on Pearl Harbor.

THE CONFERENCE IN ALGECIRAS

Signs of the future could be seen as early as January 1906, when Kaiser Wilhelm II sought to share in controlling Morocco. France was the dominant power in Morocco under a 1904 deal that gave Britain a reciprocal free hand in Egypt. Refusing to be left out, the kaiser confronted France while her ally Russia was occupied fighting the Japanese, and he forced an international conference at Algeciras, Spain. Germany, Austria-Hungary, France, and Great Britain all participated; Austria-Hungary aligned with Germany, and Britain sided with France. Henry White, now the ambassador to Italy, represented the United States.

The ostensible questions at Algeciras concerned who would police the ports of Morocco and who would control the international bank managing the country's finances. But the real issue was power. The conference deadlocked. At Roosevelt's request, White conferred with the delegates and came up with detailed proposals. The kaiser rejected the key ones, but Roosevelt would not compromise. White continued his adroit diplomacy, and the kaiser gave way. By the end of March 1906, perceptive Americans could see the black cloud of a European war.

AN AMBASSADOR OF THE OLD SCHOOL

Pre–World War I Europe was a golden realm of processions and ritual, crowns and tiaras. London developed this splendor at its most elaborate. To it in 1905 came United States Ambassador Extraordinary and Plenipotentiary Whitelaw Reid, the able and ambitious boy from Xenia, Ohio. Finally, at age sixty-seven, he had obtained the diplomatic post he had so long pursued. And he proved to be a perfect fit.

Ambassador Reid and his family made their home in Dorchester House, one of Mayfair's most impressive mansions, on the site where The Dorchester Hotel, now stands. They also delighted in Wrest Park, a country estate with a deer park, a lake, and forty-four servants. They entertained lavishly. When the ambassador was criticized for his expensive lifestyle, Roosevelt wrote him, "I think a man should live in such a position as he has been accustomed to live."

Before the Reids arrived, Henry White, the first secretary at London, was promoted to Rome as minister; and John Ridgely Carter, whose wife, Alice Morgan, was related to J. P. Morgan banking interests, became Reid's first secretary. White did not find his two years in Italy onerous. On one hunting trip with the king, he shot five ibex and fifteen chamois. In 1907, White was transferred to Paris. He moved the embassy to 4 rue François-Premier and was occupied with commercial issues like the Payne-Aldrich Tariff and the price of coffee from Puerto Rico.

When William Howard Taft became President, White expected to be kept on; but in April he received a letter from an assistant secretary of state saying that his resignation would be accepted as of January 1, 1910. It was a total shock.

Roosevelt wrote only that White's dismissal had been "for reasons unconnected with the good of the service." Senator Lodge, White's longtime friend, recounted that when William and Helen Taft had been in London on their honeymoon in 1886, Taft had asked White for tickets to an important debate in Parliament. The tickets were impossible to obtain, and White instead produced tickets for a visit to the Royal Stables. Taft, or more likely Helen Taft, saw it as a personal affront and took revenge twenty-three years later.

London's First Secretary John Ridgely Carter was appointed minister to Romania in 1909 and was replaced in Victoria Street by William Phillips. Much later, Phillips wrote this portrait:

> Mr. Whitelaw Reid was an Ambassador of the old school and looked the part. He was handsome, his manners were perfect, and he was always immaculately dressed. At the same time there was something artificial about his personality. He had little genuine warmth, and at times his studied politeness was annoying. But he was the perfect host and people liked him at the first approach. . . . He was, in his way, a highly successful Ambassador. However, much of this success was due, in my opinion, to Mrs. Reid. . . . She was truly a remarkable woman and a great Ambassadress.

As expected, Whitelaw Reid was an active and effective ambassador. The British treated him with respect and honors. But during dinners and shooting parties at Wrest Park, he witnessed the private squabbling that accentuated the international discord.

Reid negotiated the dispute over the Newfoundland fisheries that had been reignited when Newfoundland imposed new restrictions on American fishing vessels. Even so, both sides were still disgruntled, and not until Root and the British submitted seven issues to the Permanent Court of Arbitration at The Hague was the dispute settled, a triumph for Secretary Root.

Ambassador Reid urged Roosevelt to give priority to his relations with England. He also sought Sir Edward Grey's participation in a conference to control the opium trade, which resulted in the Opium Convention of 1912. And he worked toward assembling a Second Peace Conference at The Hague. Ever the perceptive reporter, in 1908 Reid wrote Mrs. Theodore Roosevelt, "Europe is at this moment like a powder magazine."

At the age of seventy-five, Ambassador Reid went hiking in Wales and became ill. Two months later, on December 15, 1912, he died in Dorchester

House, just as the world, which he had observed for so long as journalist and diplomat, was beginning to stagger.

King George V personally notified President Taft of Reid's death. The memorial service for the United States ambassador extraordinary and plenipotentiary was held in Westminster Abbey. Reid's flag-draped coffin on a caisson traveled to Victoria Station and then to Portsmouth, from where the armored cruiser HMS *Natal* took Whitelaw Reid home.

Six U.S. Navy warships met *Natal* off Nantucket Light. With a guard of U.S. Marines, his body was carried to New York's Cathedral of Saint John the Divine; Presidents Taft and Roosevelt were among the hundreds present. His had been an extraordinary career that reached from the Civil War to the very rim of World War I.

22

Warm-up for a World War

1899–1914

T he drumbeat of small wars, the Spanish-American, the Boer, the Russo-Japanese, the Philippine-American, and others less justifying of the term, energized men who knew the horrors of war to seek more civilized ways to solve problems between nations. They did what little they could: They met and they talked.

On May 17, 1899, the six American commissioners to the Peace Conference at The Hague gathered at the home of Stanford Newel, the U.S. minister to The Hague. They chose Andrew D. White as their leader; he had already been the first president of Cornell University, minister to Russia, and the first ambassador to Germany.

The next day, delegates from twenty-six countries opened the conference in the palace called Huis ten Bosch (The House in the Wood). They organized themselves into three committees with the responsibility to limit armaments and war budgets, to extend Geneva Red Cross Rules to include warfare at sea, and to use mediation and arbitration to prevent wars.

The Americans said their policy "expresses a determination to refrain from enunciating opinions on matters into which, as concerning Europe alone, the United States has no claim to enter." This cautious renunciation of Europe's problems seems in retrospect unrealistically optimistic.

The U.S. delegates signed, as the final act of the Peace Conference on July 29, 1899, "a Declaration prohibiting throwing projectiles and explosives from balloons or by other new analogous means." But the Americans did not sign a "declaration prohibiting the use of projectiles having as their sole object the diffusion of asphyxiating or deleterious gases" or "a declaration prohibiting the use of bullets which expand or flatten easily in the human body." The conference established the Permanent Court of Arbitration but could not agree on a limitation of armaments. It left plenty of problems unsolved.

A second conference did not actually convene until 1907, this time with forty-four countries present. The Americans were now led by Joseph H. Choate, Hay's successor in London. The conference agreed on the rights of neutrals and rules for naval bombardment and for the use of submarine contact mines. It also proposed a third peace conference. But World War I, which historian Fritz Stern termed "the Ur-catastrophe" of the century, arrived first.

Kaiser Wilhelm II summoned the capable American ambassador Charlemagne Tower, Jr., in January 1908 and asked him to warn President Roosevelt that the Japanese were trying to provoke a racial war against the United States. The kaiser advised Ambassador Tower that Japanese soldiers by the thousands had landed in Mexico disguised as workers.

After the Japanese had humiliated the kaiser's cousin, Czar Nicholas II, in the Russo-Japanese War, the kaiser fantasized that the Panama Canal was the object of Japanese intrigue and that Mexico would be the next battlefield. The kaiser told William Bayard Hale of *The New York Times* that the United States would have to fight Japan's "yellow menace" to save the white race. The *Times'* publisher killed the story.

MEXICO: TEMPLATE FOR TROUBLE

By 1910, Mexico had become a real concern for the government in Washington, when Francisco Madero, son of a wealthy banking and mining family, led a revolt against Mexico's dictator, Porfirio Díaz. In Mexico City, U.S. Ambassador Henry Lane Wilson, a "dollar diplomacy" diplomat, continued to support Díaz.

Ambassador Wilson cared about U.S. business interests; and Díaz, who had ruled Mexico for sixteen years, was supposed to supply the stability that business needed. Actually, Madero organized his revolt because Díaz stole another term as president in the rigged election of 1910. Madero, a five-foot-two, well-educated white man, rode into Mexico City on a white horse at the head of a determined band of impoverished macho Indians. By May 1911, Madero forced Díaz into exile in Paris and became Mexico's president. Less than two years later, General Victoriano Huerta, a full-blooded Aztec and Madero's military chief, organized with Félix Díaz, nephew of the deposed dictator, a counterrevolt for the ruling classes. The State Department ordered Ambassador Wilson to stay out of the dispute. He did not.

The ambassador had only contempt for Madero. On the evening of February 18, 1913, he invited Huerta and Félix Díaz to the U.S. embassy and negotiated the "Embassy Pact." As a result, General Huerta had President Madero arrested and proclaimed himself president. Madero's wife appealed to Ambassador Wilson to protect her husband, and he told her, with a straight face, that he could not interfere in Mexico's internal affairs. Huerta pledged that Madero and his foreign minister could go safely into exile. But while they were being transferred between prisons, they were shot to death.

The murders shocked the world, and President Taft rejected his ambassador's persistent requests that the United States recognize Huerta's government. Madero's assassination made that impossible. Within days, on March 4, Woodrow Wilson became the President of the United States, and the crisis in Mexico became a trial run for him. How he handled affairs there would forecast how he would act on the larger European stage.

Venustiano Carranza, a cautious, gray-bearded provincial governor, rebelled against Huerta and demanded a constitutional government. Carranza led local warlords Álvaro Obregón, Pancho Villa, and Emiliano Zapata, all of whom were to become legendary heroes of the Mexican Revolution.

President Wilson distrusted both the Republican-built State Department and the ambassador in Mexico. He instructed Ambassador Wilson to set free elections and amnesty as conditions for Mexico's recognition. (Later, he would withhold recognition of Russia.) President Wilson's test was "constitutional legitimacy." He offered to mediate between Huerta and his enemies. (He would do this later in Europe.) And he sent his own special agent to Mexico with orders to report directly to him. (He would do this in Europe with Colonel House.)

The agent he sent to Mexico was William Bayard Hale, the one-time Episcopal minister turned *New York Times* reporter who had interviewed the kaiser. Hale had also written President Wilson's 1912 campaign biography. He would become a German agent, at least until the United States entered the war. To make matters even more complex, Secretary of State William Jennings Bryan, popular but uninformed, sent his own man, Reginald del Valle, to Mexico. When Hale reported to President Wilson that Ambassador Wilson had been deeply involved in the Huerta coup, he was recalled.

President Wilson felt that if he sent a new ambassador to Mexico he would be recognizing Huerta's regime, which he privately called "a government of butchers." Instead, in August 1913, the President dispatched yet another agent, John Lind, and hoped he could peacefully get rid of Huerta, whom the President called a "desperate brute."

Tall, wiry Lind had been born in Sweden and brought to the United States as a boy; he served four terms as a congressman and also as the governor of Minnesota. When Lind offered Huerta a loan, the general, knowing he could not obligate himself to the Americans, turned him down. Carranza formed his own government, and President Wilson sent Hale to him. But Carranza, like Huerta, could not afford to accept Wilson's mediation, or his interference.

Huerta and his opponents next prepared to do battle at Tampico, the site of European oil-storage facilities. The Europeans, fearing Tampico would explode, sent naval ships. And the United States rushed to Tampico a naval force that outgunned all the European navies present.

Then, an incident upset everyone's plans. At Tampico, in April 1914, General Huerta's men threw seven sailors from the gunboat USS *Dolphin* into jail (for less than an hour). Admiral Henry Mayo, of the navy, pompously demanded the Mexicans apologize and fire a twenty-one-gun salute to the American flag. Mayo claimed the Mexican action was a casus belli. Huerta waffled.

At the same time, William Canada, the American consul at Veracruz, Mexico's principal port, sent word that the German merchantman *Ypiranga* was bringing two hundred machine guns and fifteen million bullets to Veracruz for Huerta. President Wilson ordered the arms seized. It had to be done after they left the German ship and before they reached Huerta. Seven thousand armed Americans were put ashore at Veracruz; they cleared out Huerta's snipers in house-to-house fighting. Seventeen Americans were killed and seventy-one wounded; three hundred Mexicans were killed. In the United States, no one knew whether the country was at war or not; patriotic volunteers flooded recruiting stations. The whole exercise was a disaster.

Mexico fell into civil war, and Woodrow Wilson sent Paul Fuller, a partner in the New York law firm of Coudert Brothers, to persuade the Mexicans to settle their differences. He was unsuccessful. As war broke out in Europe, Wilson brought his troops home from Veracruz.

Robert Lansing, the meticulous but colorless counselor of the State Department, replaced Bryan as Secretary of State in June 1916, and the department took over relations with Mexico from the White House. A leading New York Democrat, Lansing was the first to recommend to the President that the United States should not recognize the Bolshevik government in Russia.

The Germans brought Huerta to New York's Ansonia Hotel, from which he made his way, under American surveillance, to El Paso. The Germans planned to set up a pro-German government in Mexico. Huerta was arrested in New Mexico, and while in custody he died of cirrhosis of the liver.

At Santa Ysabel on January 10, 1916, Mexicans led by Pancho Villa killed sixteen American mining engineers. And during the night of March 16, four hundred of his men galloped into Columbus, New Mexico, and shot up the town. The U.S. ambassador in Berlin, James Gerard, asserted that the Germans had chosen Pancho Villa to instigate a war between the United States and Mexico. President Wilson sent Brigadier General John J. Pershing and 6,600 soldiers into Mexico. Villa holed up in the mountains; Pershing could not catch him.

President Wilson sent down a new ambassador, Henry P. Fletcher, to stop Carranza from nationalizing the Mexican oil industry. Fletcher had served in Cuba, China, and Portugal and as the first American ambassador to Chile. But he could not prevent the Mexicans from nationalizing their "subsoil" resources—that is, oil.

BIG CHANGES IN THE DEPARTMENT

By 1910, the State Department comprised 35 officers, 135 clerks, and 40 messengers and custodians, a total of 210 people. This was more than double its payroll of 1898. The number of clerks increased from twenty-five in 1870 to 156 forty years later. And the department's workload grew so oppressive that when the Tariff Act of 1909 piled on even more tasks, Secretary of State Philander C. Knox asked Congress for an additional hundred thousand dollars in the budget.

Secretary Knox admitted he did not want to work too hard, but he had a quick mind. The able assistant secretary Huntington Wilson became Knox's right-hand man, and William Phillips his third assistant secretary. But Phillips did not last long. Knox could not obtain his hundred thousand dollars unless he appointed the son of the powerful Senator Eugene Hale of Maine as third assistant secretary. So Phillips was shipped to the London legation—and Knox got his hundred thousand dollars.

The funds enabled Knox and Huntington Wilson to rebuild the department. The diplomatic service was put under the third assistant secretary and the consular service under a director of the consular service. Wilbur Carr, now a seventeen-year department mainstay, became the first director.

They also created senior positions of counselor and resident diplomatic officer to advise the secretary on foreign policy. The resident diplomatic officer came from the foreign service and brought field experience to headquarters. The first resident diplomatic officer in 1911 was Thomas C. Dawson, the department's leading expert on Latin America, who had served as the chief of the Division of Latin American Affairs and as minister to Panama.

The department was set up along geographic lines, building on the model of the Far Eastern Division. The new divisions covered Western Europe, the Near East, and Latin America, and foreign service officers were brought in to lead them. A new Division of Information published news on diplomatic, political, and economic issues.

Huntington Wilson amassed influence throughout the foreign service. Obsessed with structure and organization, he strove to become the department's number two. He wisely brought in Hugh S. Gibson from London as his private secretary. Huntington Wilson tended to be short-tempered, while Gibson was witty and personable. Joseph C. Grew wrote privately of Gibson, "that wild Indian . . . is a crackerjack."

Despite all this attention on headquarters, conditions for foreign service officers abroad were neglected. Just weeks before World War I began, Ambassador Walter Hines Page in London wrote President Woodrow

Wilson that he would have to resign because he could not afford to do his job on the same salary as was paid the American ambassador to Mexico. Wilson sent Page an allowance for two years from a special fund.

The law of April 5, 1906, was too limited to eliminate the spoils system. One obstacle to building a foreign service based on merit was that the appointments of diplomats and their pay and promotions were tied to their posts, not their grades. In order to promote an officer, the department might have to move him to another post, even when that was undesirable.

The outbreak of war in Europe multiplied the demands on U.S. representatives abroad. Embassies and consulates were besieged by Americans seeking help, and, as neutrals, American foreign service officers accepted responsibility for the interests of belligerent nations in their enemies' territories. They also took on the responsibility to inspect camps for prisoners of war and civilian internees.

Wilbur Carr testified that the consul general at Buenos Aires received $4,500 a year, but to fill the post properly needed a salary of $8,000. Bringing up to date the salaries post by post would take years.

The Stone-Flood Act of 1915 was finally passed as "an act for the improvement of the foreign service." It was the first act to use the term "the foreign service" to cover both the diplomatic and consular services. It provided that all secretaries in the diplomatic service and consuls and consuls general would be commissioned to a grade and not a post. They could be transferred between posts as required. These were liberating improvements.

Until then, a foreign service officer asked to serve in the department had to resign from the foreign service, and in Washington he could be paid only as a clerk. The new act allowed him to serve for three years in the State Department without loss of salary or class. As the department needed more men with field experience abroad, this change became invaluable.

Another move toward a merit-based service was the restoration of living allowances. In the past, salaried consuls were given a small stipend for office rent, and diplomatic officers were given "outfits," a sum equal to a year's salary, to establish themselves. In 1856, "outfits" had been eliminated; officers had to be wealthy enough to provide their own outfits

In July 1916, Congress appropriated $150,000 to help foreign service officers meet the rising cost of wartime living. They received small allowances for serving in countries at war; and in 1919, these allowances were extended throughout the foreign service.

A diplomat's largest expense was rent. Cleveland was the first President to propose the purchase of residences for diplomats in the more important capitals. Until then, the United States owned diplomatic residences only in Tangier, Bangkok, and Tahiti, which had been received as official gifts, and in Amoy, Seoul, and Tokyo, which had been purchased.

In 1911, Congress enacted the Lowden Act, authorizing the Secretary to buy sites and buildings for which Congress appropriated funding. The Lowden Act said that no more than $500,000 could be spent in one year and no more than $150,000 could be spent on any one place. Representative Frank O. Lowden, of Illinois, said, "Let us either withdraw from the capitals of the earth, or let us enable our foreign representatives to serve their country abroad on something like equal terms with the rest of the world." Only seven buildings and one site were bought until the Foreign Service Buildings Act of 1926 eased the rules.

INEXPERIENCED CHIEFS OF MISSION

President Cleveland had interrupted the Republican succession, and, again, Woodrow Wilson ended the Republican Gilded Age. Although patronage continued to rule at the chief-of-mission level, President Wilson did moderate Secretary of State Bryan's desire to reward Democrats with jobs in the diplomatic and consular services. As chiefs of mission, Wilson wanted men who could communicate his message, but he enabled fewer than a half dozen consuls to circumvent the examination process.

Critical of the Wilson-Bryan record, Representative John J. Rogers, a Republican of Massachusetts, told the House after the war that in 1913 the United States' forty-one ambassadors and ministers included only twenty-three with previous experience. And by 1919, only four of the forty-one were still serving. Since 1913, he said, fifty-one new ambassadors or ministers had been named, of whom only two had diplomatic experience. They were assigned to Colombia and Haiti. Although many appointments were sound, Rogers was shocked at the absence of demand for merit or experience.

Wilson and Bryan, for instance, replaced the very professional William Rockhill, then the ambassador to the Ottoman Empire, with Henry

Morgenthau, a New York real estate investor and chairman of the Democratic National Committee. John B. Jackson, a diplomat with twenty years' experience, was replaced with Charles Vopicka, a Chicago politician, as minister to Romania, Serbia, and Bulgaria. And the veteran Arthur M. Beaupre was replaced as minister to Cuba by William E. Gonzales, an editor from Columbia, South Carolina.

Wilson kept a few experienced diplomats and made some noteworthy new appointments, including Walter Hines Page to Britain, James W. Gerard to Germany, and Paul S. Reinsch to China. In general, however, the Wilson appointments represented a setback to the career principle.

The United States' envoys in the warring capitals, Page at London, Myron T. Herrick at Paris, and Gerard at Berlin, were without diplomatic experience. So was Brand Whitlock, who filled the crucial post at Brussels. (Frederic C. Penfield, minister to Austria-Hungary, was an exception; he had served in Egypt.) Fortunately, all the new men proved to be capable.

The man at the Court of St. James's, Walter Hines Page, came from small-town North Carolina and had attended three colleges without ever completing a degree. In Atlanta, in 1881, the young journalist Page had met Woodrow Wilson, the young lawyer. Page was twenty-six, Wilson twenty-five. Page would become editor of *The Atlantic Monthly* and a partner in the book publisher Doubleday, Page and Company.

Page became an early booster of Wilson, who, in March 1913, selected him for London. He was met on his arrival in Liverpool by First Secretary Irwin B. Laughlin, who had fifteen years' service and would be Page's able assistant for Page's five hectic years in London.

A tall, gaunt, animated, candid man, Walter Page became a controversial ambassador. Wilson's and Page's ideas were often fundamentally at odds, and Page believed that he should make certain the President appreciated Page's own wise views.

Page was kindly and humorous. He had a lifelong love of England and English literature and believed the British were of "the right stock" and "the right blood." He admired their courage and their stoicism. As he put it in 1916, "already the land is full of young widows."

Page's faith in Anglo-American cooperation influenced Wilson. And Colonel Edward M. House, the small, dapper Texan who had been an architect of Wilson's political victory in 1912 and became his powerful foreign policy advisor, often supported Page's ideas. Historian Barbara Tuchman called Colonel House a "self-conceived, if naive, Machiavelli."

Like Page, James Gerard at Berlin was untried as a diplomat. He had grown up in Geneseo in western New York State and graduated from Columbia University. As a lawyer, he was closely tied to Tammany Hall. To accept appointment as ambassador to Berlin in the fall of 1913, Gerard resigned as a justice of the New York State Supreme Court.

On the way to Berlin, Gerard sized up Ambassador Page in London. These two crucially placed diplomats were a contrast. Page, cultured and conservative, had a freewheeling mind not limited by his employer's thought. Judge "Jimmy" Gerard was an institutional man, absorbed by process and detail. He took a serious interest in Germany's economic and industrial development.

Although Gerard was already in Berlin at the time, he (and Tammany Hall) defeated Franklin Delano Roosevelt in the 1914 Democratic primary for U.S. senator, and then Gerard lost the election to Republican James W. Wadsworth.

Gerard's embassy was in a shell of a rented white-stone mansion on the Wilhelm Platz, opposite the Foreign Office. Each week while he was in Berlin, he wrote a confidential letter to Secretary Lansing, a practice that distressed his more bureaucracy-sensitive aides. He enjoyed the colorful pageantry of the German court, where Kaiser Wilhelm II appeared theatrically in the black uniform of the Death's Head Hussars. But Gerard was appalled by the arrogance of the Prussian officer class.

Paul Reinsch, whom President Wilson sent to China, had earned his Ph.D. at the University of Wisconsin under Frederick Jackson Turner, the historian of the American frontier. Reinsch himself became a brilliant professor of history at Wisconsin, with a special interest in East Asia. He preached that the United States needed to compete with the Great Powers for world markets in order to avoid choking on its surplus of manufactured products. During six years as minister to China, he obtained concessions for U.S. firms, opposed Japan's invasions of China, and tried to bring China into the war on the side of the Allies. Despite his efforts, the war in Europe allowed Japan to ransack China.

In retrospect, that Germany was becoming a world power had been apparent for a generation. The Germans threatened to overturn the European balance of power. Ambitious, rapidly industrializing, and containing part of Europe's expanding population, Germany frightened her neighbors, and with good reason. Now that military victory depended on conscripting the masses, the choice between diplomacy and war could no longer be left to the aristocrats.

Germany's conquest of France in 1871 had shocked Europe, and afterward Germany competed for overseas markets and colonies and built a navy to protect them. The United States stumbled across Germany's presence at Samoa in 1888, Manila Bay in 1898, Venezuela in 1902, and Morocco in 1905. Henry White, the first secretary in London, had confronted the emerging Germany in 1899 when he tried unsuccessfully to buy the Danish Virgin Islands. When the Danes did not nibble, he was sure the kaiser had disrupted the deal.

23

"Well, the Roof Has Fallen In"

1914–16

On the summery Sunday afternoon of June 28, 1914, American Ambassador James W. Gerard and his wife were enjoying the yacht races at Kiel aboard the yacht *Utowana,* as guests of Allison Armour of the Chicago meatpacking family. Armour was a longtime friend of the kaiser. Frederic W. Wile, a correspondent for *The New York Times* and the *Daily Mail,* drew alongside in a launch to inform them that Archduke Franz Ferdinand, heir to the Austrian throne, and his wife had been assassinated that morning at Sarajevo. The kaiser left for Berlin, but the Kiel yachting party never stopped. On Tuesday, Ambassador Gerard sailed on the kaiser's yacht *Meteor,* which won the Kiel-to-Eckernfjord race. He felt no need to rush back to Berlin.

In Brussels on this same peaceful Sunday, the exceedingly tall, frail U.S. Minister Brand Whitlock sat at his desk in his home at 74 rue de Tréves, working on his novel, which was set in a small town like Urbana, Ohio, where he had grown up. He had welcomed his appointment to serene Brussels, which promised to allow him time to write. Now, the ringing of the telephone interrupted him, and an aide told him that the archduke had been assassinated. Whitlock, who was new to diplomacy and had been at his post for barely four months, had not heard of Sarajevo. No one was unduly disturbed about the death of the Austrian nobleman.

Whitlock, forty-six, was a former Toledo and Chicago newspaperman. He had never gone to college, but he had read law and been admitted to the bar. His friend, the already-famous civil rights lawyer Clarence Darrow, asked him to join his Chicago law firm, but Whitlock wanted to be free to write, which he called "my first and only love." After Toledo's mayor died in office in July 1904, Whitlock served four terms as a reform mayor.

From that Sunday, the tension in Europe built. A month later, Austria declared war on Serbia. On July 28, Ambassador Walter Hines Page in London, on his own initiative, called on the foreign secretary, Sir Edward Grey, and asked him how the United States could help restore peace.

Hundreds of Americans crowded the London embassy. American bankers, lawyers, and businessmen set up offices in the Savoy Hotel's ball-rooms to help Americans who needed funds, transportation, and pass-ports. Ambassador Page sent over several clerks, and he chose a young mining engineer, Herbert Hoover, to manage the stranded Americans.

At the same time in Washington, President Woodrow Wilson, at the bedside of his dying wife, Ellen, received a cable from Ambassador Myron T. Herrick in Paris. The message: "Situation in Europe is regarded here as the gravest in history." President Taft had appointed Herrick in 1912, and Wilson had not gotten around to replacing him. A banker and one-term Republican governor of Ohio, Herrick advised Wilson to work for mod-eration. His cable alerted Secretary of State William Jennings Bryan to the seriousness of the crisis. President Wilson wired Page for his guidance and waited until August 4 before sending a note offering help.

Secretary Bryan also asked Page how the United States could help stop the war. Page, the amateur, sent a romantic description of Sir Edward as "this always solitary man. . . . He looked ten years older than he looked a month ago . . . a sort of sad and wise idealist . . . a grave philosopher who feels the prodigious responsibility he carries." But Page offered no advice.

On July 31, Ambassador Gerard in Berlin cabled the State Department that a European war was inevitable. Crowds eager for war were marching in the streets cheering. Russia had mobilized its huge, primitive army, and Germany sent Russia an ultimatum. Gerard also sent a note to Chancellor Theodore von Bethmann-Hollweg of Germany, asking what the United States could do "towards stopping this dreadful war?" He received no reply. The next day, Germany declared war on Russia. What diplomat and historian George Kennan called the "self-destructive madness" had be-gun. At the Berlin embassy, Americans were advised to drive out through

Holland, but no automobiles were permitted to leave Germany. The embassy staff ran out of cash to distribute. Years afterward, First Secretary Joseph Grew wrote that it had been "an end to those days of diplomatic serenity, a fool's paradise."

Several nights later, Grew learned that Frederic Wile and S. Miles Bouton of the Associated Press had been mistaken for spies and arrested at the luxurious Hotel Adlon. Grew and three staff members drove to the Adlon, confirmed the report, and raced on to the Foreign Office to find the reporters. Grew met German Under Secretary Dr. Arthur F. M. Zimmermann, who apologized profusely. At police headquarters, Grew found the newsmen and drove them to the embassy. Grew mused, "Berlin is no longer a civilized city; the inherent barbarity of the German race never showed itself so strongly."

The war came to Belgium swiftly, and a neutral diplomat had a lot to do. Hugh Gibson, the legation's energetic and fun-loving secretary, and Vice Consul General Roy Nasmith, with the help of Dr. Henry Van Dyke, the finicky new American minister at The Hague, assisted thousands of German civilians in returning home across the Dutch border.

The previous March, the thirty-year-old Hugh Gibson had been pleased to come to Brussels, "this quiet post . . . where nothing ever happens," and he said he "wallowed in the luxury of having time to play." The legation consisted only of Minister Whitlock, Gibson, and a clerk. Gibson grew bored and asked the department to find him a post where there was more to do.

The war began on July 28. Gibson wrote, "Well, the roof has fallen in. War has been declared by Austria this afternoon. Everybody here is greatly excited. Nobody can foresee what will come of it all. England is trying to localize the conflict and has the help of Italy. If she does not succeed, the result may be terrible." No longer bored, he wrote, "I would not be anywhere else for anything on earth."

On Sunday evening, August 2, the German ambassador in Brussels charged that intelligence said French forces intended to march through Belgian territory against Germany. Therefore, German forces would have to move into Belgium. That same evening in Paris, Ambassador Herrick, his voice garbled by tears, telephoned Premier Ren Viviani and told him he had just been asked to take responsibility for the German embassy. Germany was going to war. In minutes, the German ambassador notified the French premier that their countries were at war.

Ambassador Herrick stayed in Paris after he had bid the French government an emotional farewell as it had departed for Bordeaux. Since the Germans warned that whole quarters of Paris might be bombed, Herrick, an excellent organizer, set up an ambulance system and added to the American Hospital at Neuilly the so-called American Ambulance, itself a hospital for the care of the war's wounded. The French appreciated his skills and his courage.

Minister Whitlock found space for as many Americans as possible on ships crossing the Channel to England. War correspondents appeared at the legation, eager to get to the front. "You only have to wait a few hours," Whitlock told them, "and the front will come to you."

The next morning, the German army invaded Belgium. The Belgians' six infantry divisions could delay but not stop the Germans' thirty-four divisions. Whitlock and Gibson listened to King Albert address Parliament. Then, Whitlock accepted a request to take charge of France's affairs in Belgium.

On Tuesday, the German legation made the same request. At five o'clock, Whitlock and Gibson went over to the German legation and found the minister and his secretary slumped in their chairs, making no effort to pack. Whitlock oversaw the sealing of the cabinets containing the archives; and by seven, the German diplomats boarded the train that took them through Holland to Germany. The British diplomats leaving Brussels also asked Whitlock to represent them.

This war would be fought, through conscription, by the nation as a whole. And large enlistments required elaborate planning, vast mobilizations, and interlocking diplomatic activity before war was ever declared. Warfare in the early twentieth century might have appeared to be more instantaneous than in the past, but, in fact, it needed a longer time for preparation and commitment, and it reduced options for peace.

King Albert and the Belgian government had already withdrawn to Antwerp when the German commander demanded the surrender of Brussels. The Belgian military commandant said his honor required that he defend the city. Brand Whitlock and the Marquis of Villalobar, the physically handicapped yet capable Spanish ambassador whom Whitlock had known in the United States, went to the city hall to dissuade the mayor from defending Brussels with the civil guard of boys and old men. If he fought, the Germans would destroy the city, as they had done repeatedly across Belgium. But the mayor refused to surrender until King Albert ordered him to. The king later thanked the two diplomats for helping to save Brussels.

On August 20, the Americans found that the telegraph and telephone wires to the embassy had been cut. Trains had stopped running. The people of Brussels were isolated. Whitlock watched from the windows of the Italian legation as the long columns of the gray-clad conquering German army marched through the undefended streets, ranks closed, bayonets fixed, artillery in tow. Their numbers, weaponry, and discipline overwhelmed the dogged French, Belgian, and British forces trying to stop them short of Paris.

The Germans horrified Whitlock. They burned villages and executed Belgian hostages. He said that he would always remember "that almost savage chant and those grey horsemen pouring down out of the Middle Ages into modern civilization." He wrote that the occupation of Brussels "became terrible, oppressive, unendurable, monstrous." He was to stay behind German lines for two years.

The Brussels legation no longer was able to communicate with Washington, so Hugh Gibson and a driver set out on August 27 in a little racing car to try to drive through the battle lines and reach Antwerp. Gibson carried letters allowing him passage signed by the German general occupying Brussels and by Burgomaster Adolphe Max. After a series of close calls as they sped through the two battling armies, they drove into Antwerp, found diplomats they knew, and made their way to the American consulate general to send cables. Gibson was summoned to the Grand Hotel to meet with the Belgian prime minister, and he reassured the Cabinet Council about the condition of their capital.

That night, a Zeppelin soared silently overhead and dropped bombs on sleeping Antwerp. One landed within two hundred yards of the Americans and killed many civilians. Another bomb nearly hit the palace. Here was a new dimension to warfare: an early "strategic" bombing attack from the air, aimed at terrorizing the civilian population. War had changed.

After meetings with the king's secretary (the king was at the front), the foreign minister, and the American consul general, Gibson and his driver left Antwerp and sped through small towns they had admired two days before, now totally destroyed, arriving back at the legation in Brussels safely.

Ten days later, Gibson made another daring trip to Antwerp. This time, he heard the story of how Julius Van Hee, the American vice consul in Ghent, saved that city from destruction.

The Germans had agreed to march around Ghent; but if attacked, they would annihilate the town. An hour later, in front of the American consulate, a Belgian armored car, armed with a machine gun, its occupants unaware of the agreement, fired on a German military car and wounded its two men. Van Hee, who witnessed what happened, jumped in his car, found the mayor, and drove him to the Germans' army headquarters to plead that no reprisals be made.

The general in charge finally accepted Van Hee's word but demanded that the Americans guarantee the wounded Germans' safety and produce vast amounts of supplies. Vice Consul Van Hee gave his word of honor that the supplies would arrive. But Antwerp's military governor refused to send them; the Ghent authorities had to appeal to the national government. The citizens of Ghent praised Van Hee for saving their town.

Driving back on this second trip, Hugh Gibson was unable to find a route through the battle lines to Brussels and had to return to Antwerp. Starting again, he stopped at a battery of French howitzers and met King Albert, accompanied only by an aide, walking through a field of cabbages to inspect the guns. The king asked Gibson about conditions in Brussels, and as shrapnel bursts fell across the road, they climbed on a pile of manure to watch the French guns in action. Gibson spent time under fire before getting through to Brussels.

By that fall, the war of movement was over on the Western Front. The armies dug in and began the long stalemate of trenches and attrition. Gibson traveled to London to find food for the Belgian people. He and Ambassador Page and the Spanish ambassador met with Sir Edward Grey. Also present was Herbert Hoover, who would organize the American Relief Committee to send food to Belgium. Hoover impressed Gibson, who wrote, "I was astonished to see how clearly he grasped all the essentials of the situation." George Kennan said, "Hoover had succeeded in surrounding himself with a group of able and energetic men, who surely contrasted favorably with the regular diplomatic staffs in Europe, weighed down as they were by the routine pressures of war work and oppressed, as always, by the strictures of governmental routine."

On New Year's Day 1915, the Germans prohibited any celebrations in Brussels. But that morning several Belgian policemen appeared at the American legation in their great blue capes and kepis and set a leather-bound book with blank pages on a table just inside the door. A steady stream of Belgians came down the rue de Tréves, signed the book, left their cards, and walked away. Some also left letters or baskets of flowers. Thousands of them came all through the day and into the night, expressing their grati-tude for what the Americans were doing for Belgium.

BEHIND GERMAN LINES

When Britain entered the war at midnight on August 4 in response to the German invasion of Belgium, crowds stoned the British Embassy in Ber-lin. Ambassador Gerard drove over to offer the British ambassador refuge in the American Embassy. The offer was declined, and Gerard drove back through the hostile crowd. One man climbed on the running board of Gerard's car, spit at Gerard, and struck the driver with his hat. Gerard jumped out and chased the man, and his footman explained to him that this was the American ambassador. The man, a Berlin lawyer, came to the embassy the next day and apologized.

Americans lined up outside the Berlin embassy, seeking help to return home. Ambassador Gerard arranged for the Dresdner Bank to supply funds and bought hundreds of steerage tickets each week on Holland American Line ships. He also helped Japanese citizens, trapped in Germany, leave through Switzerland.

At the State Department's request, Gerard met with the kaiser on the morning of August 10. Wilhelm II was sitting under a large canvas um-brella in a little garden on the River Spree with two dachshunds at his feet. Gerard brought him a message from President Wilson offering to mediate between the warring powers. The kaiser wrote out his reply in pencil. He blamed England and Russia for starting the war and thanked the Presi-dent for his offer. He wrote that Germany had invaded Belgium because it would not permit passage of German armies into France. He predicted that Britain's coming into the war meant that it would be long.

. . .

German enmity toward Americans was evident from the outset. At midnight on October 7, 1914, Berlin police raided the building from which the American embassy was distributing funds from London to British citizens. Gerard had the approval of the German Foreign Office, but his workers were arrested. In the end, the Foreign Office asked Gerard to forget the incident.

The German press castigated the United States for shipping supplies to the Allies. After August 10, 1914, the kaiser refused to see Gerard, because the United States was supplying the enemy. The standoff continued for a year, until September 25, 1915. Then, Gerard sent the foreign minister a note saying he should no longer bother to try to arrange an appointment for him. That brought a response. Gerard was summoned to Potsdam and saw the kaiser privately for more than an hour. The kaiser told him that, as a gentleman, he would not have permitted the torpedoing of the *Lusitania* if he had known about it. But he spoke bitterly of the United States.

Gerard thought the height of "disgustingly bad taste" was the distribution in Germany of medallions celebrating the sinking of the *Lusitania*. He visited POW camps, where he tried to improve conditions. Other U.S. diplomats in warring countries undertook similar missions, and, at times, this duty became overwhelming. On reaching Russia in April 1916, the U.S. ambassador, David R. Francis, found he had assumed oversight of the treatment of 1.2 million Austrian prisoners of war, 250,000 German prisoners in Russian camps, and 250,000 interned Austrian and German civilians.

WAR SPREADS TO THE MIDDLE EAST

The war stretched beyond western Europe. Henry Morgenthau, President Wilson's ambassador to Constantinople, had arrived at his post on November 27, 1913, and noted that the diplomatic community resembled "expectant legatees of a friendless dying man, sitting at tea in his parlour, and waiting for his last gasp as a signal for a scramble to divide his property among themselves." The sultan was now powerless, fronting for a cabal headed by Talaat Bey, a huge village railroad porter who had risen to be the real ruler of the Ottoman Empire.

The sense of change was prevalent just before Christmas, Morgenthau's daughter, Helen Fox, accompanied him to a dinner at the British embassy and described it to her mother as resembling the last act of a pageant about the elaborate prewar diplomatic life.

Morgenthau told a story to illustrate some aspects of diplomacy in February 1914. At the first dinner he hosted as ambassador, German General Liman von Sanders seemed silent and sulky. After dinner, the German chargé protested to Morgenthau that General von Sanders had not been placed at the table in accordance to the rank due him as the personal representative of the kaiser. The issue was eventually brought to the Turkish cabinet, which decided the general should rank ahead of all the foreign diplomats. After all, the kaiser had personally chosen him to lead the Turkish army. Morgenthau reported this to the State Department as evidence of the growing importance of Germany to Turkey's preparation for the approaching war. And the American military attaché at Constantinople concluded from the incident that Turkey would become Germany's ally and could divert a Russian army corps from the European theater.

The Ottoman Empire, afraid of Russia, sided with Germany. So the British aroused the Arabic-speakers within the empire to overthrow Turkish rule. In contrast, Morgenthau's instructions were to avoid giving advice to the Turkish government and to maintain America's neutrality.

At 4:00 A.M. one November morning in 1914, the Turks tried to occupy a convent school run by the French Sion Soeurs. They found Morgenthau and his wife there, waiting for them. The ambassador prevented the seventy nuns from being locked up and the two hundred young girl students from being left in the streets. Mrs. Morgenthau hid the order's fifty thousand French francs in gold coins in her clothes and locked them in the embassy vault. The Turks took over the school.

In March 1915, Morgenthau toured the Gallipoli Peninsula after the British-French fleet had failed to destroy its defenses. When the Allies landed Australian and New Zealand troops, Turkish leaders opened a concentration camp on the peninsula and planned to fill it with three thousand European civilians. An Allied bombardment would endanger them. Morgenthau objected persistently until the Turks agreed to send only fifty young male hostages to the camp. The embassy's counselor, Hoffman Philip, former minister to Abyssinia, insisted on accompanying them. The hostages stayed a week, until the British fleet finished its bombardment, and then they returned to Constantinople unharmed.

The Turks stepped up their campaign to eradicate the two million Armenians in the Ottoman Empire. Missionaries brought the embassy word of massacres from the American consuls. They told Morgenthau that only American intervention could stop the atrocities. Frustrated, Morgenthau left Constantinople and went home to work on Wilson's 1916 presidential campaign.

Because of the war, the State Department demanded more and more information from diplomats and consuls overseas. Posts in Europe reported daily on the war and on political and economic developments. And foreign service officers still had to supply data useful to manufacturers and merchants and even project expectations for postwar trade. All these duties were handled with no increase of staff.

In August 1914, U.S. diplomatic personnel abroad totaled 121, and in December 1918, there were 124. In the same period, the number of clerks in American diplomatic missions declined from 55 to 48. The number of consuls general and consuls increased slightly from 291 to 300. Each year during the war, new officers were admitted to the foreign service, but, in good bureaucratic fashion, most of them stayed in Washington. The department grew from 208 to 440.

Ambassador Page pressed President Wilson to strengthen the foreign service "from the Department of State to the humblest consul." Page complained that his cables lay in the department unanswered and that the department kept the London embassy in the dark about developments in Washington. When he wrote the department confidentially, Page said, his message could appear in the London newspapers the next day. In anger, he wrote, "There is only one way to reform the State Department. That is to raze the whole building, with its archives and papers, to the ground, and begin all over again."

Page astutely praised Minister Whitlock to President Wilson: "You found the right man the day you chose him. Hold fast to him. He's more than a diplomat: he's a man." When Whitlock admitted to President Wilson that he was heart and soul for the Allies, Wilson, despite his public position of neutrality, replied, "So am I. No decent man could be anything else."

Page clashed with the President's drive to keep the United States out of the war. Wilson saw the war as a selfish struggle for power on both sides, while Page, reflecting the view in London, believed Germany was embarked on world conquest. He bluntly wrote Wilson, "The German military party had deliberately planned the practical conquest of the world."

U.S. officials in both London and Washington disregarded Page's views because of his undisguised support of Britain. Wilson told former President Taft, "Page is really an Englishman and I have to discount whatever he says about the situation in Great Britain." When this reached Page's ears, he told Wilson that in London he was regarded as too pro-German.

During that first fall of the war, the Germans made several undercover approaches to negotiate a peace, on their terms. The first attempt began on Saturday evening, September 5, 1914. In France, the battle of the Marne was raging, and the German drive on Paris had been barely halted. At his home in suburban Scarborough-on-Hudson, New York, pro-German banker James Speyer gathered for dinner his longtime friend, Oscar Straus, the former ambassador to Turkey; Count Johann von Bernstorff, the aristocratic, new German ambassador to Washington; and banker Frank A. Vanderlip and their wives. Ambassador Bernstorff assured the group that Germany wanted peace, and Straus asked if it would be open to mediation. Bernstorff said it would, and Straus asked if he could present this to his government. When Bernstorff agreed, Straus immediately got up from the dinner table, was driven into New York City, and caught the midnight train to Washington.

On Sunday morning, he told the story to Secretary Bryan at his home. Bryan asked Bernstorff to discuss the possibility with him. And he had Straus meet with the British and French ambassadors, Sir Cecil Spring-Rice and Jean Jules Jusserand. They were skeptical about Bernstorff's initiative but decided to take it seriously. Unconvinced, Page wrote Colonel House: "If we are so silly as to play into the hands of the German-Hearst publicity bureau, our chance for real usefulness will be thrown away. Put the President on his guard."

House conferred with President Wilson and then replied to Page that "peace must come only upon condition of disarmament and must be permanent." Germany must not be crushed, he added, because that would leave Russia the dominant military force in Europe. He wrote, "The Kaiser did not want war and was not responsible for it further than his lack of foresight which led him to build up a formidable engine of war which later dominated him."

Page answered House, "The plain fact is that the English people . . . don't care a fig what the Americans think or feel. . . . Why don't they come and help us in our life-and-death struggle?" He added, "If the [German] military party keeps in power, they will try it again in twenty-five or forty years. This is all the English care about or think about."

THE UNITED STATES SLOWLY TURNS TOWARD WAR

President Wilson continued to hope that diplomacy could stop the massive killing. When Robert Lansing became Secretary of State in 1916, he instructed Page to ask Britain to adopt the Declaration of London of 1908, which limited naval warfare and defined controversial terms like "blockade," "contraband," and "neutral trade." Page objected passionately, and the British ambassador to Washington, the foppish, emotional Cecil Spring-Rice, ranted that America's "German-Jewish bankers are toiling in a solid phalanx to compass our destruction."

Page reported that his staff was worn out. He described the civilians killed in London by bombs dropped from Zeppelins and the war-wounded and their nurses he saw in the park as he walked to the embassy. He sent his prewar publishing partner, Frank N. Doubleday, a long Christmas letter that concluded, "And when you take stock of your manifold blessings, don't forget to be thankful for the Atlantic Ocean. That's the best asset of safety that we have." He evoked this blessing repeatedly.

When Wilson instructed Ambassador Gerard to ask the Germans to compromise for the sake of peace, Gerard reported that the Germans defiantly raised the price of a compromise. The kaiser haughtily told Gerard that he and his cousins, George of Britain and Nicholas of Russia, would make peace only when the time was right. Gerard concluded, "The hate here against England is phenomenal." Wilson's diplomatic efforts were useless.

As the casualties piled up, it was clear that the war would not be brief, and both sides, locked in a murderous stalemate, needed the resources of the United States—the Allies needed arms, ammunition, and horses, and the Central Powers, foodstuffs and raw materials. Both sides faced the identical dilemma: how to keep the United States' friendship while stopping it from supplying the enemy. Most Americans displayed two inconsistent wishes: They wanted the Allies to be victorious, and they wanted the United States to stay out of the war.

24

"Slaughterhouse Where Madness Dwells"

1915–17

At about seven o'clock on Friday evening, May 7, 1915, Ambassador Page returned to the America embassy at 6 Grosvenor Square shaken by terrible news: hundreds of men, women, and children had been drowned shortly after two o'clock that afternoon when German submarine U-20 fired a torpedo into the starboard side of the British liner RMS *Lusitania*. The queen of the Cunard Line sank within sight of the Irish coast, with the loss of 1,201 lives. Of 159 Americans aboard, 128 died.

Three months earlier, the Germans had switched their policy from trying to persuade the Americans not to send the Allies war supplies to taking direct action: submarine warfare. They were determined to starve out the British. They drew a zone around the British Isles and announced that any neutral ship entered it at its own risk.

That Friday evening, May 7, the ambassador and Mrs. Page planned to give a dinner at the embassy for Colonel and Mrs. House. The colonel had spent a pleasant day touring Kew Gardens and visiting with the king at Buckingham Palace. The news of the *Lusitania* tragedy came too late for the Pages to cancel the evening. Throughout the dinner, Page was handed bulletins on slips of yellow paper, and he read them aloud to the subdued guests. Colonel House assured them that within a month the United States would be at war with Germany.

The next evening, Page sent President Wilson a telegram marked "Confidential in the extreme." It reported that the British believed the

United States now "must declare war or forfeit European respect. So far as I know, this opinion is universal." Early Sunday morning, Page drove to Euston Station and met the bedraggled Americans who had survived the sinking. He reported that they walked listlessly as through a fog.

Many expected that the Germans would be made to pay for the sinking, but President Wilson, speaking in Philadelphia the following Monday, said: "There is such a thing as a nation being too proud to fight." He received great applause. The Americans were not ready to go to war.

In Berlin, after the *Lusitania* sinking, Under Secretary Zimmermann of the Foreign Office banged on the table with his fist as he warned Ambassador Gerard that the United States would not dare do anything about submarine warfare because there were a half million German reservists living in the States and they would rise in arms if the United States acted against Germany. Gerard snapped back, "We have five hundred and one thousand lampposts in America, and that was where the German reservists would find themselves if they tried any uprising."

Page, outraged by his government's mild response, cabled the President and Secretary of State that the "failure to act definitely will shut the United States out of British and I should guess of all European respect for a generation." He was relieved when he read the President's note that Ambassador Gerard delivered to German Foreign Secretary Gottlieb von Jagow. Wilson demanded that Germany stop unrestricted submarine warfare, disavow the sinking of *Lusitania*, and pay an indemnity. The Germans did none of these things.

At the suggestion of a friend in the German Foreign Office, Gerard cabled the State Department on June 25, proposing that the President send him a message to be delivered to the kaiser personally. The presumption was that the kaiser was isolated by the military and the navy, which backed submarine warfare, and had no access to the Foreign Office and others trying to avoid war with the United States. This message would force the kaiser to see Gerard.

Instead, the Germans stated their position in reply to a second *Lusitania* note from Wilson, "The Imperial Government is unable to admit that the American citizens can protect an enemy ship by mere fact of their presence on board." The United States insisted on the rights of neutrals at sea.

Ambassador Page was now willing to pay with American lives to assure an Allied victory. As Wilson persisted in his policy of neutrality, Page lost faith in his leadership. And Wilson, not surprisingly, started to belittle Page's value as a source of information. Page dared to write House, "The only solution that I see is another *Lusitania* outrage, which would force war."

He was pleased when Secretary of State Bryan resigned, almost exactly a month after *Lusitania* went down. House and others proposed that President Wilson replace Secretary Bryan with Page, but Wilson felt that his friend's strong support of the Allies would make such an appointment seem partisan. In the end, Page praised Wilson's handling of the *Lusitania* crisis, but he warned House that the United States would inevitably go to war and advised him to get the nation ready as rapidly as public opinion would allow.

In Brussels, Minister Whitlock reported that the Germans posted on walls a proclamation blaming England for the sinking, because "England in trying to starve Germany has forced her to take measures of reprisal." The Germans claimed *Lusitania* had been carrying munitions. Expecting that the Americans might have to leave suddenly, Whitlock shipped all important documents in Brussels to The Hague and he and his staff started packing their bags.

Then, without warning, on August 19, a German submarine sank the British liner *Arabic* off Ireland with the loss of forty-four lives, including two Americans. As First Secretary Joseph Grew noted, the sinking infuriated the German Foreign Office, but it was helpless against the Admiralty's power. King George V declared to Page that the Germans, his "kinsmen" he called them, were trying to push the United States into the war; he too would welcome that.

"HAVE PITY ON HER!"

That same August 1915, Ambassador Page cabled Whitlock to look into word that the Germans had secretly arrested and imprisoned an English nurse in Brussels. Whitlock immediately inquired of Baron Oscar von der Lancken-Wakenitz, the veteran Prussian diplomat who headed the German Political Department for Belgium. As a neutral, Whitlock reminded the German, he had accepted responsibility for the affairs of the British legation. The baron replied that the nurse, Edith Cavell, was in solitary confinement in the military prison at Saint Gilles for helping British and Belgian soldiers to escape to neutral Holland and then go on to the front.

On September 21, Whitlock informed Page that Cavell had been arrested on August 5, and the German prosecutor had asked for the death penalty. Whitlock wanted his legation's experienced legal counselor, Maitre Gaston de Leval, to assist Cavell at her trial. The Germans refused.

Cavell, a frail but indomitable woman of about forty, was greatly respected in Brussels; she had nursed there for years and had organized a nursing school. On October 7, the Germans began the court-martial for her, along with thirty-four others, behind closed doors and without keeping a record of the trial. The most damning evidence against her was a postcard that a young man had written from England thanking her for helping him escape and saying he had joined the British army. The Germans had intercepted the postcard.

On October 11, when word came that the trial was over, Hugh Gibson stayed close to the legation telephone. He wrote later that, "We were haunted by a feeling of impending horror that we could not shake off." Eventually, Maitre de Leval appeared at the door of Whitlock's bedroom and reported that the military court had condemned her and seven others to death and she was to be executed at two o'clock in the morning.

Whitlock immediately wrote Baron von der Lancken-Wakenitz, "Have pity on her!" And he wrote to the German governor general in Belgium, the cruel, imposing Baron Moritz von Bissing, asking that her sentence be commuted and she pardoned. Whitlock reminded him that she had nursed German soldiers and her school had trained nurses for Germany and for the world. He remembered later, "The whole proceeding was the veryest travesty and mockery."

On Whitlock's instruction, de Leval and the Marquis de Villalobar worked desperately to find the German officials who could halt the execution. One was at the theater, another out playing bridge. When they located Baron von der Lancken-Wakenitz late that night, he first told them to go home and return in the morning. But after a long argument with Gibson, de Leval, and de Villalobar, the baron personally took Whitlock's appeal for clemency to the newly arrived military governor, General von Sauberzweig, who claimed he alone had the power to intervene. He rejected their appeals. At about seven that morning, a firing squad executed Edith Cavell.

Whitlock sent word to Ambassador Page, who notified the Foreign Office; the British government informed the press of Cavell's execution. Whitlock commented, "The storm of universal loathing and reprobation for the deed was too much even for the Germans." They forced both Leval and Gibson to leave Brussels. They had written the reports given to the press. Much later, Whitlock wrote of Edith Cavell, "And so they slew her, those Generals with stars on their breasts and iron crosses, bestowed for bravery and gallantry, slew the nurse who had cared for their own wounded soldiers." (In June 1940, when Adolf Hitler toured Paris, he ordered the memorial to Edith Cavell destroyed.)

At about the time of Cavell's death, Secretary Lansing ordered the recall of the German military and naval attachés in Washington, Captain Franz von Papen and Captain Karl Boy-Ed. The two overzealous Germans had plotted with General Huerta, of Mexico, against the United States. As Count Bernstorff recognized, their recall marked an American shift toward the Allies.

By now, Hugh Gibson had a record of provoking the Germans. They were suspicious of his cross-border trips, resentful of his spats with border guards, and angry at his open support of the Belgians and his efforts to save Edith Cavell. Admittedly, Whitlock too had become critical of Gibson. Whitlock had concluded, "He is truculent and impetuous, always wishes to rattle the sabre in the scabbard."

Whitlock, still, praised Gibson warmly to Colonel House, "He is entitled, not only by seniority, but by long, devoted and very arduous service, to a promotion to first secretary of embassy . . . if he only had a rich wife he might easily be an ambassador some day."

In fact, Gibson would make his way up the foreign service ladder: secretary at Paris, minister to Poland, minister to Switzerland, ambassador to Belgium, and minister to Luxembourg. He became expert in disarmament issues, and, despite "occasional lapses into anti-Semitism," President Herbert Hoover named him ambassador at large in Europe. In 1933, President Roosevelt sent him to Brazil, where he helped end the Chaco War, between Bolivia and Paraguay. He retired from the foreign service in 1938, after thirty years of exceptional service. Privately during World War II, he sought relief for Belgians and Poles and worked with Herbert Hoover on proposals for peace. (On a lighter side, he reputedly created the Gibson cocktail; at first it was water disguised with an onion; later, it evolved into a gin drink.)

. . .

Under the tensions of the German occupation, it is not surprising that Whitlock also developed problems with some of the people around him. Herbert Hoover thought him a dilettante, and Gibson blamed him for his removal from Brussels. But the people of Brussels greeted Whitlock with affection when he took his walks with his two Pekingese, King Kung and Ta Ta. To the Bruxellois he was an elegant reminder of freedom, conscience, and civilization.

Whitlock experienced more horrors when the Germans shipped thousands of Belgian men in cattle cars to forced labor in German mines and fields. In January 1917, he sent a young American attaché, Christian Herter, who had just graduated from Harvard and was seconded from the Berlin embassy, to witness these atrocities. Herter returned shaken by the cruelties he had seen. Few of the men deported to Germany ever returned to Belgium, except to die. As for Whitlock, Secretary Lansing offered him the post of ambassador to Russia; he turned it down to stay in Belgium.

The United States moved closer to war in late September 1915, when Alexander C. Kirk, third secretary of the U.S. Embassy in Berlin, arrived in London. He brought a package of documents that Ambassador Gerard had felt were too incendiary to send to Washington by any means other than a trusted foreign service officer. Kirk reported to First Secretary Irwin Laughlin, who took him and his parcel to Ambassador Page. The papers contained the names of German agents in the United States and abroad whom Count Bernstorff, the German ambassador in Washington, had employed and the amounts they were paid.

Although Bernstorff was able and charming, he was devoted to efforts, legal and extralegal, to keep America neutral. He had brazenly asked the State Department to deliver the sealed parcel to the German foreign minister. In Berlin, Gerard received the package in the diplomatic pouch and had the bottom flap of the envelope opened without breaking the seals. Reading the documents, he felt they were too dangerous to be sent directly from Berlin to the State Department. So he had Kirk carry them to Page, who forwarded them to Washington.

When the State Department returned the papers to Gerard with instructions to deliver them to the German foreign minister, Page was enraged. He had expected his government to demand that Bernstorff be recalled. But President Wilson still wanted to avoid a break.

The Germans torpedoed the British channel passenger steamer *Sussex* on March 24, 1916. Forty persons, but none of the seventy-five Americans aboard, were killed. The Germans claimed their U-boat captain thought he was sinking a minelayer, but Secretary Lansing wanted to recall Ambassador Gerard immediately. President Wilson still refused to join the endless war. He pocketed Lansing's note and just demanded that Germany stop using submarines against passenger and cargo vessels. This seemed to the American diplomats in Berlin like a sure step toward breaking diplomatic relations.

On April 28, Foreign Minister von Jagow stopped by the American embassy and asked Gerard to go that very evening to visit the kaiser at his field headquarters in France. Gerard brought along First Secretary Joseph C. Grew. He had gone to Groton and Harvard, studied in Paris, and in 1904 had started a foreign service career.

They took the train to the kaiser's headquarters at Charleville in the Ardennes. Grew brought along a codebook so they could receive messages in cipher from the State Department. While waiting to meet with the kaiser, Gerard checked on the distribution of food to the French people by the American Relief Committee. And he protested to the chancellor that the German military was shanghaiing French women from the cities and forcing them to work in the fields.

On Monday, May 1, the chancellor took Gerard and Grew to have lunch with the kaiser. He was walking in a garden and called to Gerard, "Do you come like the great pro-consul bearing peace or war in either hand?" He referred to the historic meeting between Quintus Fabius Maximus and Hannibal during the Second Punic War. Gerard replied, "No, your Majesty, only hoping that the differences between two friendly nations may be adjusted."

The kaiser defended submarine warfare, saying that a person traveling in an enemy ship was like a man traveling behind the battle lines. Gerard disagreed: The man behind the lines was on enemy territory, the man at sea was on free territory. Their discussion went on through lunch and continued into the afternoon.

Grew wrote in his diary, "Whatever the result of our visit may be, this much may be said: Mr. Gerard was the right man in the right place at this important juncture. He does not mince his words, he speaks with force and directness, which is sometimes the only method of talk that carries weight here, and once he sees an issue clearly he rams it home straight from the shoulder. Any apologetic tone or sign of weakness would have been fatal. There was no sign of weakness on the Ambassador's part."

Before entraining back to Berlin, Gerard and the chancellor agreed that submarines would operate under "cruiser rules": a submarine would give a passenger ship warning, at the risk of being sunk itself. A cruiser was visible on the surface and could take aboard passengers from a torpedoed liner. A submarine depended on stealth and had no room to take in rescued passengers. If carried out, this agreement would eliminate the submarine's unique value.

The German Foreign Office agreed that Germany would not sink ships without attempting to save lives. This concession angered the German admirals. If obeyed, it too would destroy the submarine's advantage. The Germans also stated that Germany expected the United States to insist that the British government also "observe the rules." It warned that if the British continued to violate international law at sea, Germany would have to review its position. The debate inside Germany over the untrammeled use of the submarine continued.

"WE ARE PARTICIPANTS"

President Wilson began to shift his stance on staying out of the war. As early as February 1, 1916, in Des Moines, he said, "America cannot be an ostrich with its head in the sand. America cannot shut itself out from the rest of the world." He wrote Colonel House supporting "the concerted action of nations against unjustifiable breaches of the peace of the world."

As the 1916 American election approached, the Democrats rallied under the motto "He kept us out of war." And the Republicans stepped up their attack on Wilson's neutral attitude. Speaking as the temporary chairman of the New York Republican Convention, Elihu Root declared that U.S. "diplomacy was bankrupt."

On May 27, Wilson said publicly, "We are participants, whether we would or not, in the life of the world." He regarded that speech as a foreign policy "turning point"; he gave up isolationism for participation.

Ambassador Page, like many others, did not immediately catch the importance of Wilson's speech. He complained that it made the British feel that Wilson "was speaking only to the gallery filled with peace cranks."

Through the summer of 1916, which for the United States would be the last in a cocoon of peace and war-fed prosperity, the diplomatic front remained as frozen as the European battlefront. Chancellor Bethmann-Hollweg of Germany repeatedly urged Gerard to press President Wilson to arrange a peace quickly before the German military restarted its U-boat campaign. Mrs. Gerard was sailing for the United States in September, and Jagow entreated Gerard to go along to induce the President to seek peace immediately. At the month's end, Gerard left Joseph Grew in charge of the embassy and sailed with his wife via Copenhagen. Aboard ship, Gerard met Herbert Bayard Swope, editor of *The New York World,* and William C. Bullitt, of Philadelphia's *Public Ledger,* and warned them to expect that the Germans would soon resume submarine warfare.

After waiting days for an appointment, Gerard met with President Wilson for four hours at his home in Long Branch, New Jersey. By the time Gerard arrived back in Berlin, Arthur Zimmermann had replaced von Jagow as foreign minister. Jagow had had considerable experience abroad, but Zimmermann's only foreign post had been as consul at Shanghai when he was a young man. And, unlike Jagow, Zimmermann agreed with the navy's desire to use the U-boats. He dreamt up a fantastic idea to counter the United States' anger: He would seduce Mexico and Japan into an alliance to attack the United States.

By now, Page and Wilson differed so strongly that Wilson was not replying to Page's letters. In July 1916, the President summoned Page on a home visit "to get some American atmosphere into him."

Page twice had lunch with Wilson at the White House, but they avoided discussing foreign affairs. He saw Secretary Lansing a number of times, but, again, Lansing did not ask Page about relations with Britain. After waiting impatiently for five weeks, Page was invited to spend the night at Wilson's home in New Jersey. In the morning, the President listened to his old friend at length. Wilson said he had lost his sympathy for England; as he saw it, imperial England had the earth and Germany wanted it. They talked all morning, but the President was unresponsive to Page's appeals. Wilson wanted only to end the war. Afterward, Page told his son, "I think he is the loneliest man I have ever known." They never saw each other again.

Back in London, Page wrote to the reelected President, calling for Germany's defeat and the end of neutrality and saying he wanted to resign. Wilson did not reply. He offered the London post to his wealthy Princeton classmate, Cleveland H. Dodge, who declined, and then had Secretary Lansing tell Page that the President wanted him to stay on. Page agreed to stay for the duration of the war.

A NIGHT FILLED WITH TENSION

One black night in early October 1916, the darkened *City of New York* slipped into Liverpool harbor, already jammed with ships seeking refuge from the German submarines lurking outside. The voyage's last night crossing the Atlantic had been filled with tension. Shortly after dawn, a tender came alongside, and the American consul and British port officers climbed aboard and led Wilbur J. Carr off the steamship.

Secretary Lansing had sent him on a two-month tour of wartime Europe, and Carr was thrilled. He had been the director of the worldwide U.S. consular service for seven years, and he had never been abroad. He confided delightedly to his diary in his tiny pinched scrawl, "Here is the opportunity I have wanted for years. . . . It is a long way to have traveled in 25 years, from the plow to all this!"

In London, Carr visited the consulate general in New Broad Street. The quarters were dingy and cramped, and Carr was shocked to see the staff still wore top hats and long-tailed coats to work. And, worse than that, the office was miles from the embassy. Carr was appalled to see the two branches of the foreign service in locations so distant. It made for trouble, Carr found. He wrote in his diary, "There is some latent feeling between Emb & consulate. No open clash. Emb. evidently . . . has blocked Consulate with FO."

London Consul General Robert P. Skinner wanted to move the consulate to a handsome Christopher Wren building at 18 Cavendish Square, which would be more comfortable and distinguished. Carr approved the move, even though, he noted, the new location would be less convenient for the exporters whom the consulate served.

Carr believed that pressures had built up between embassy and consulate because their men (never women) pursued three very separate career paths. They could become officers in the Department of State in Washington, diplomatic secretaries in capitals abroad, or consular officers in ports and commercial cities. Each was a distinct universe, and crossovers from one to another were difficult and rare. Watching how the system actually worked overseas, Carr came to see vividly the need for change. But that would have to wait until the war was over.

On April 28, 1916, just a year before Vladimir Lenin arrived, a new American ambassador arrived at the Finland Station in Petrograd, as Saint Petersburg was called after 1914. Tall, handsome David R. Francis, age sixty-five, arrived at 2:00 A.M., alone except for his valet; he was met by the embassy staff, who had waited there for three hours. Francis, replacing Ambassador George T. Marye, a Saint Louis banker, was an amateur to diplomacy. But Francis was able and experienced as a self-made wheat broker, "the boy mayor" of Saint Louis, governor of Missouri, and Grover Cleveland's secretary of the interior. He seemed a good choice for Petrograd.

His first assignment was to restore the trade agreement with Russia that, four years earlier, the United States had abrogated, in good part because the czar's government refused to recognize the passports of Jewish Americans or to give them entry visas. But the absence of a treaty had not hampered the growth of sales to Russia of American arms, cotton, food, and agricultural machinery.

Before leaving the United States, Francis met at the Lotos Club in New York with a dozen Jewish leaders, who asked him to renew the trade treaty only if Russia accepted the passports of all Americans. They briefed Francis on Russia's pogroms and persecutions of Jews. One of the men asked him how they could help him. Assured that he could speak candidly, Francis replied, "By not talking so much." Although Francis had Jewish friends in Saint Louis, he wrote of Jews, "They are very aggressive and, at the same time, shrewd and unscrupulous, as you know, but of course such statements must not be publicly made."

Francis took with him to Russia Arthur T. Dailey, from the State Department, as his private secretary and Professor Samuel Harper, a respected young Russian scholar from the University of Chicago, where his father had been president. Sailing via the Orkney Islands, Francis secretly visited Britain's Scapa Flow Naval Base. On the voyage, he struck up an acquaintance with Matilda ("Meta") de Cramm, an attractive Russian woman who, when she reached Petrograd, took an imposing apartment near the U.S. Embassy. She and Francis, whose wife remained in Saint Louis, were soon taking walks and carriage rides together. Russian intelligence suspected she was a German agent.

Francis worked in a large, decrepit building the U.S. government rented at 34 Furstatskaya Street; he lived in a two-room suite on the upper floor. In the wide cobblestone street out front, the Russian army drilled recruits. First Secretary Fred M. Dearing and his wife and other embassy employees lived in the Hotel d'Europe some distance away, and most of the other diplomatic and consular staff worked in leased offices on Nevsky Prospect. Francis felt that the Eastern-bred career diplomats like Dearing looked down on him. Dearing left in less than a year, and Arthur Dailey resigned to work at the local branch of the National City Bank.

The new ambassador knew no Russian and little French. George F. Kennan later would write caustically, "One can attribute this choice only to that unfamiliarity with the requirements and possibilities of diplomatic representation which has so often characterized even the best of American statesmanship." But Kennan did credit "the old gentleman" with "courage and enthusiasm."

Francis' first official visitor was the representative of the Rockefeller-connected National City Bank of New York, which was competing with J. P. Morgan and Company for Russian business. Francis favored National City Bank and recommended that it loan the Russian government $50 million. Oscar Straus, former ambassador to Turkey, warned Francis that it was known that his investment company back in Saint Louis would profit from the deal.

Francis had been in Petrograd just a week when he and ranking members of the staff traveled by special train to Tsarskoye Selo, half an hour south of Petrograd, to be received by Czar Nicholas II and Czarina Alexandra. Francis brought the czar a sealed message from President Wilson, and they talked privately (the czar spoke fluent English) about a trade treaty, Francis' responsibility for German and Austrian prisoners of war, and the United States' neutrality policy.

Russia's persecution of Jews haunted Francis. He wrote Oscar Straus that treatment of Jews in Russia was improving, and Straus replied adamantly that this was not true. Francis wrote Frank L. Polk, counselor of the State Department, that if the Jews in Russia were treated equally they would soon possess the whole Russian empire. He wrote of "the designing, usurious and pitiless Jew."

Francis reported that Russia was exploring a separate peace with Germany. By midsummer, Polk was instructing Francis to drop his pursuit of a trade treaty because Russia was too unstable. Polk also warned Francis to break off his relationship with Meta de Cramm, whose husband was also suspected of being a German agent. Francis answered that, even though she spent a great deal of time at the U.S. embassy, his relationship with her was strictly personal.

The bloodletting did not stop; by 1916 the Austrians had lost two million men, and the Russians four million. In the West, the dead also numbered half a million at Verdun, and the Allies lost six hundred thousand on the Somme. Millions of refugees wandered Europe, desperate for food. Page called Europe the "slaughterhouse where madness dwells."

By that fall, the Allies and the Central Powers were deadlocked on land and blockading each other at sea. Neither side had anyone in power who would accept Wilson's offer to negotiate an end to the war. By the end of 1916, even Wilson felt neutrality was "intolerable."

In Berlin, Joseph Grew, serving as the chargé d'affaires in Ambassador Gerard's absence, notified the State Department on November 17 that William Bayard Hale, now the Hearst correspondent in Berlin, had had an interview with Chancellor Bethmann-Hollweg and come away with a peace suggestion for President Wilson. The State Department told Grew that Bernstorff had tried to stop publication of the interviews. The department timidly did not spell out its own wishes. That frustrated Grew, who thought that if the department agreed with Bernstorff, he could persuade Hale to delay the article. Grew wrote in his diary:

> This was one of those cases where American diplomacy is handi-
> capped beyond the diplomacy of other nations by the failure of the
> Government at Washington to keep its diplomatic officials in inti-
> mate touch with the sentiment, policy and intentions of the Ad-
> ministration. . . . The American diplomatic representatives are too
> generally treated as office boys.

Five days later, Grew discussed with the chancellor the German use of Belgians for forced labor. Then, the chancellor brought the conversation around to peace and warned that if Germany's readiness for peace was ignored, it would have to adopt hard measures in self-defense. Grew repeated Wilson's desire for peace but suggested that the German government had to do more.

On December 12, the chancellor handed Grew a note addressed to the Allies asking for peace negotiations. Ambassador Page brought the proposal to the British Foreign Office, stating sharply that it did not express the opinion of the United States. The Allied leaders turned down the Germans. The British said that they were not interested in "buying a pig in a poke." The Germans had expected that reply; they were preempting Wilson.

Grew delivered another note from Wilson to Zimmermann. In light of the Allied rejections of the German peace proposal, this time President Wilson asked only that the belligerents make known their demands for accepting peace. Nothing came of the whole venture. It was a dead end.

25

"America in Armageddon"

1917—20

U.S. Ambassador James Gerard arrived at the German Foreign Office, as requested, at six o'clock on the evening of January 31, 1917. Foreign Secretary Dr. Arthur F. M. Zimmermann read him a note announcing that at midnight Germany would again begin unrestricted submarine warfare. Gerard made no comment, stuffed the note in his pocket, and returned to his embassy.

Germany's military leaders had decided to revoke the "cruiser rules," which required their U-boats to try to save the passengers from ships they sank. The Imperial German Crown Council was responding to the enormous casualties at Verdun and on the Somme and to the food shortages on the home front. Council members were fully aware that this decision was likely to draw the United States into the war. But they calculated that they could finish the fight before America's military strength could be brought to bear. They were convinced that President Wilson had been reelected to keep the United States out of the war; Wilson himself now spoke of "a peace without victory."

In Washington at four o'clock that same afternoon, Count Johann von Bernstorff, the German ambassador, was ushered in to see Secretary of State Robert Lansing, and informed him that starting the next day German submarines would sink on sight all neutral ships in a zone around Britain and in the Mediterranean. Once a week, the Germans would allow safe passage in each direction between Falmouth, England, and the United States for one American ship, garishly marked.

The meeting was brief. Lansing, shocked, said only that he would convey the information to the President. When he did, Wilson called the abhorrent declaration an attack on humanity.

The U.S. foreign service was not prepared for what was coming. Its officers were not sophisticated about security; the Germans were having little trouble breaking the American codes. And American diplomats were not very skilled at inducing people to accept their views.

Foreign service officers operated under conditions that were virtually obsolete. Inadequate salaries of fifteen hundred to four thousand dollars a year were a major problem. Alfred W. Donegan, who served as consul in Magdeburg, Bern, and Basel, summed up the problem:

> A promotion in the Foreign Service can be an invitation to bankruptcy because a promotion often involves a transfer, and only men with independent incomes can afford to move family and furniture halfway around the world.

The World War was showing that this was no way to run a global diplomatic system.

At two o'clock on Saturday, February 3, 1917, President Wilson announced to a joint session of Congress that he had instructed the Secretary of State to sever diplomatic relations with the imperial German government. He did not ask for a declaration of war, but if more American ships were torpedoed and American lives lost, he said, he would request authority to protect Americans. The President still needed two months to be ready to go to war.

As Wilson spoke, Secretary Lansing was handing Bernstorff his passports, and Assistant Secretary of State William Phillips instructed Ambassador Gerard in Berlin to ask for theirs and to turn over American affairs to the Spanish ambassador. The break had finally come.

That long Saturday, five Americans sat nervously in the ambassador's room of the U.S. Embassy in London. Ambassador and Mrs. Walter Hines Page, First Secretary and Mrs. Irwin B. Laughlin, and Eugene C. Shoecraft, the ambassador's secretary, waited hour after hour for instructions from Washington. At nine o'clock that evening, the bell rang, and Shoecraft rose and met Admiral Sir William Reginald Hall, the short, tough director of British Naval Intelligence, hurrying up the stairs. Seeing Shoecraft, Admiral Hall stopped and said simply, "Thank God!"

In the ambassador's room, Admiral Hall read aloud a succinct message from the British naval attaché in Washington. It said, "Bernstorff has just been given his passports. I shall probably get drunk tonight!"

On Sunday morning, Ambassador Page met with Prime Minister David Lloyd George at 10 Downing Street. Page felt vindicated for his ceaseless preaching against neutrality. He described Europe as "a hellswept continent having endured more suffering in three years than in the preceding three hundred."

In Berlin that Saturday evening after the theater, Ambassador and Mrs. Gerard had supper with Zimmermann, who confidently predicted that America would not retaliate against the resumption of submarine warfare. On Sunday, Gerard read in a Berlin newspaper that his country had broken relations with Germany. When the official dispatch arrived belatedly on Monday, Gerard went to the Foreign Office and requested his passports.

Foreign Office officials pressured him to sign papers that they thought would modify the treaties existing between Germany and the United States. They showed Gerard a copy of a 1799 treaty between Prussia and the United States, to which they had added clauses, and asked him to sign it. If he would not, they threatened, Americans, especially American correspondents, would not be permitted to leave Germany. Gerard refused to be blackmailed.

He turned over the interests of the United States to Polo de Bernabe, the Spanish ambassador, who, ironically, had been the minister to the United States given his passports at the start of the Spanish-American War. Tuesday afternoon, Gerard took a walk alone through Berlin's bleak winter-swept streets. No one disturbed him. On his return, the Foreign Office's officer in charge of American affairs was waiting. Gerard asked why he had not received his passports and was told that the government was waiting to hear what had happened to Ambassador Bernstorff. In fact, Bernstorff and a party of two hundred would leave Washington on February 14 and sail from New York the next day.

As one last grasp at peace, President Wilson instructed Ambassador Page to see whether Britain was willing to seek a separate peace with

Austria-Hungary. The British were too preoccupied to follow that lead, but Prime Minister Lloyd George did say to Page that it was essential that Wilson be present at the eventual peace conference. He explained, "We want him to come into the war not so much for help with the war as for help with peace."

The U.S. embassy in Berlin was cut off from the world for a week. Then, Carl Van Anda, *The New York Times'* managing editor, cabled war correspondent Oscar King Davis that Bernstorff and his staff were being well treated and that German ships in American ports were not being confiscated.

The next Saturday, February 10, First Secretary Grew and the Spanish minister sealed up the U.S. embassy's archives. That evening, Gerard and some hundred and twenty Americans boarded a train at the Potsdam station. In the spirit of gracious prewar diplomacy, Gerard provided those on the train with champagne and cigars. At the Swiss border the next afternoon, Gerard gave the two German army officers serving as escorts engraved gold cigarette cases, and then the Americans traveled on to Zurich and Bern.

At the same time in Brussels, Ambassador Whitlock had the American flag removed from his car. He hoped to continue to help feed the Belgians and to protect the Americans administering that program.

The next day, the Germans handed Whitlock the expected encoded message from the State Department instructing him to turn over American interests to his Spanish friend, the Marquis de Villalobar; to close the four American consulates in Belgium; and to move to Le Havre, which was serving as Belgium's capital. Whitlock refused to leave Brussels until the forty food-relief personnel scattered around the country were safe.

Because young Christian Herter was a member of the Berlin embassy staff and Ambassador Gerard was leaving Berlin that evening, the Germans in Brussels gave Herter his passports and ordered him to leave. Herter caught the early morning train, but en route he was confined for some hours. It took him several days to reach Switzerland.

An agreement was reached enabling Whitlock to stay in Brussels unless the United States entered the war. The Americans working in the relief program began to be replaced by Spaniards and Dutch. On March 25, Secretary Lansing telegraphed Villalobar and asked him to relay to Whitlock instructions to leave Belgium with his staff and the Belgian relief workers.

On April 2, Minister Whitlock paid his respects to General Moritz von Bissing, the detested commander of the German occupation. That evening he was driven through large crowds of silent Belgians waiting at the Gare du Nord. A group of seventy-five entrained for Switzerland, including Whitlock, his wife, his staff, the American consuls, members of the Belgian relief, and the staff of the Chinese legation. (China also had broken relations with Germany.) Whitlock arrived in Le Havre, which he instantly disliked, calling it "a filthy hole . . . might as well be Lima, Ohio." He spent his time writing and taking walks with his wife and their Pekingese.

After the armistice, Whitlock would return to Brussels, where he was regarded as a hero. He was offered the ambassadorship in Rome; but when President Wilson visited Brussels, he raised the legation to an embassy, and Whitlock chose to remain there as Belgium's first American ambassador.

A ZANY CONSPIRACY

Admiral Hall, the director of British Naval Intelligence, on February 22, 1917, showed a decoded German telegram to Edward Bell, whose job at the American embassy in London was to keep in touch with British intelligence. The British had obtained the telegram clandestinely in Mexico; it included Zimmermann's message instructing Heinrich von Eckhardt, his minister in Mexico City, to negotiate a German-Mexican alliance. If the United States entered the war, the cable said, Germany would help Mexico invade the United States and be rewarded with possession of Texas, Arizona, and New Mexico. Von Eckhardt was to persuade President Carranza of Mexico to invite the Japanese to join the scheme.

The Germans sent the "most secret" Zimmermann telegram to Ambassador Bernstorff in Washington by the State Department itself. He forwarded it to Von Eckhardt in Mexico City. To decipher it, British Naval Intelligence used a codebook they had acquired early in the war after the Russians sank the German cruiser *Magdeburg*.

Edward Bell read of this zany scheme with disbelief, but Admiral Hall satisfied him that it was real. They discussed with Ambassador Page and First Secretary Laughlin how this information could be passed on to President Wilson without revealing that the British had broken the German code. They decided that Foreign Secretary Arthur J. Balfour would give the message formally to Page. Admiral Hall suggested that the code-book be brought to the U.S. Embassy so the Americans could say that the telegram had been decoded on American soil by Americans.

Ambassador Page was summoned to the British Foreign Office, and Balfour formally handed him a copy of the Zimmermann Telegram. Lansing was absent over the weekend, so Acting Secretary Frank L. Polk received the message and walked it over to the White House. Wilson was indignant at the German duplicity. Polk asked Ambassador Henry Fletcher in Mexico to get assurances from President Carranza that he would not act on the plan. But the Mexicans were already negotiating with Germany and had approached the Japanese.

Could the telegram be a British forgery? Initially, all those accused denied its authenticity, but on March 3, Zimmermann admitted that he had written the telegram. His stunning confession came during a press conference in answer to a question from William Bayard Hale, the correspondent who was by then a paid German agent and was trying to lead the foreign minister to deny, not confess, his role. Zimmermann's admission that Germany was conspiring to attack the United States destroyed the case of the most die-hard supporters of neutrality.

Then, word arrived that the Germans had sunk the Cunard liner *Laconia* without warning off Ireland; twelve people had died, including two American women who died of exposure in an open boat. That Monday, Wilson asked a joint session of Congress for authority to arm American merchant ships

The next day, the President agreed that the State Department should put the Zimmermann Telegram on the Associated Press wire. Lansing invited E. M. Hood of the AP to his home that evening and gave him a paraphrase of the telegram, pledging him to secrecy on how he had obtained the story. Published across the country on page one with eight-column headlines, the telegram swept the American people to the brink of war.

The House of Representatives overwhelmingly voted Wilson the authority he sought to arm merchant ships, but in the Senate Robert La Follette mounted a filibuster and prevented it from coming to a vote. Wilson famously labeled the filibusters "a little group of willful men." Seventy-five angry senators signed a statement supporting Wilson.

Although Wilson put armed guards on civilian ships, the American *Algonquin* was still sunk without warning. During the next week, three more American ships were torpedoed. Food riots erupted in Petrograd, and on March 19, the czar abdicated. During the night of March 20, President Wilson came to the conclusion that a state of war existed.

"A WAR AGAINST ALL NATIONS"

President Wilson told Congress that unrestricted submarine warfare was "a war against all nations." And to Americans who dreaded the prospect of war and the maiming of their young men, he asserted that Germany was already at war with the United States.

Peace advocates held a rally at New York's Carnegie Hall; and at the Metropolitan Opera, Ambassador Gerard, in the audience, asked the management to announce from the stage the United States' entry into the war and to play "The Star-Spangled Banner." He was turned down. Gerard returned to his box and shouted to the audience to cheer the President. They did so with enthusiasm, and the orchestra on its own broke into what would become the national anthem. On the stage, a German woman singer collapsed and had to be carried off.

The next day in London, Ambassador Page went to see Balfour, who shook his hand and said, "It's a great day for the world." Three days later, Congress declared the United States was at war. The *New York Tribune* ran the headline "America in Armageddon."

Page felt a great weight had been lifted from him. He no longer needed to pretend that he agreed with his President's neutrality. Suddenly, he was welcome again in battle-torn London. For the first time in history, the British and American flags flew together over the Houses of Parliament. King George V invited Ambassador and Mrs. Page to spend the night at Windsor Castle and served them a wartime breakfast of bread, one egg apiece, and lemonade.

Ambassador Page wrote President Wilson from Brighton:

> I suppose I saw one hundred men this afternoon on a single mile of beach who had lost both legs. Through the wall from my house in London is a hospital. A young Texan has been there, whose legs are gone at the thighs and one arm at the elbow. God pity us for not

having organized the world better than this! We'll do it, yet, Mr.
President, you'll do it; and thank God for you.

On both sides of the Atlantic, diplomats began coordinating the war
effort. Page wrote the Secretary of State and the President on April 27, that
the British did not have the strength to defeat the German submarines
and that the British civilian food supply would last less than two months.
He urged the United States to send all possible destroyers to Britain immediately. He was promised thirty-six destroyers "eventually."

Page persuaded Balfour to write the President that the Germans were
building submarines faster than the British could sink them. Page wrote
his son: "The Germans are winning the war, and they are winning it on
the sea." By midsummer, the U.S. Navy was fully in action, and in the
battle of Passchendaele in Belgium, the British suffered, dead and wounded,
another 240,000 men, and the Germans, 200,000. The human tragedy went
on and on.

MIDDLE EAST INTRIGUE—1917 STYLE

Henry Morgenthau, the former ambassador to Turkey, proposed to Secretary Lansing that he try to negotiate a separate peace with Turkey. President Wilson approved a secret mission to explore, but not to negotiate,
peace with Turkey. Morgenthau was to start by going to Palestine under
the guise of inquiring into the situation of the Jewish people there.

Morgenthau had the support of the pro-Ottoman faction in a divided
British Foreign Office. But, indiscreetly, he told too many people in Washington and New York that the purpose of his mission was to get Turkey
out of the war. Both the British government and the Zionists opposed this
and disrupted Morgenthau's attempt to create a separate peace with Turkey. Justice Louis Brandeis persuaded President Wilson to have Professor
Felix Frankfurter of the Harvard Law School join Morgenthau's mission.
And Dr. Chaim Weizmann, a leading Zionist in Britain, dined with Morgenthau on July 4 at the British fortress on Gibraltar and used both persuasion and threats to deter the mission. State Department special agent
William Yale wrote, "Mr. Morgenthau never forgave the Zionist leader,
and some years later publicly announced his opposition to the Zionist
Movement."

Inside a spiderweb of secrecy, the European powers had already agreed on how they would divide up the Ottoman Empire: Russia would get the northern part, Britain would keep Mesopotamia and the area adjacent to Egypt, and France and Italy would receive slices. Colonel House warned Balfour they were creating a breeding ground for future wars. In a series of secret treaties, Allied diplomats picked their way through a morass of war aims. The Russians wanted the Dardanelles. The French wanted to control Syria and recover Alsace-Lorraine. Japan desired Shantung and other German colonies. Romania entered the war on the promise of acquiring territory. The United States stayed aloof from this deal making, which widened the gulf between Wilson and the Allies' leaders.

The first assistance the Americans gave the Allies after joining the war was a billion dollars as credits against loans to the Allied governments. And an Allied purchasing commission coordinated the buying of war materiel. The Allies also created the civilian-dominated Supreme War Council to coordinate their efforts. And in the fall, when the Italian army was defeated at Caporetto and the Bolsheviks took over the Russian government, Wilson sent to Europe another American mission led by Colonel House.

Third Assistant Secretary of State Breckinridge Long, a Wilson appointee, stressed the need to define American war aims and policies. Wilson assigned that task to House, who skipped over the State Department and organized a secret group of academics who called themselves The Inquiry. It included Sidney Mezes, House's brother-in-law and president of the College of the City of New York; Charles Seymour, the future president of Yale; and geographer Isaiah Bowman. Walter Lippmann, significantly, served as the Inquiry's secretary.

When Lippmann went to Washington on Inquiry business and visited the State Department's Near Eastern Division, he was dismayed to find it consisted of one man and a filing cabinet. Lippmann pulled down a large wall map of the Middle East; it was fifty years old and obsolete. The State Department tried to take over The Inquiry but failed, and the department began to lose control over foreign affairs.

The Inquiry worked day and night to supply Wilson with plans for a postwar Europe, plans that would nullify the Allies' autocratic intentions and their secret treaties. On January 8, 1918, the President presented the results to Congress in his Fourteen Points.

Wilson and his colleagues could not wrench from the individual Allied governments agreement on war aims or even support for the President's Fourteen Points. Each Allied government objected to the points that menaced its own ambitions. However, once the German military began to weaken during the summer of 1918, the Fourteen Points took hold and Wilson became their prophet.

Overwhelming American military strength began arriving on the Western Front and made a German victory impossible. The American military buildup, of course, was accompanied by a sudden expansion of the American foreign service overseas. Ambassador Page wrote his sister:

> The Embassy now is a good deal bigger than the whole State Department ever was in times of peace. I have three buildings for offices, and a part of our civil force occupies two other buildings. Even a general supervision of so large a force is in itself a pretty big job.

After the Germans signed the Brest-Litovsk treaty on March 3, 1918, taking Russia out of the war, they tried to finish the war swiftly. They shifted some forty divisions from the Eastern Front to the Western, and the Allies took a stab at reopening a front in northern Russia and Siberia. By then, more than a million American soldiers were in France; they promised the Allies' victory. German General Erich Ludendorff, now a virtual dictator, sprang a massive offensive, and spent nearly half a million men. It was a final failure.

As the Allied summer offensive approached its borders, Germany's manpower resources, military supplies, and even food were exhausted. The German generals began predicting a military disaster and sought an armistice along the four-hundred-mile battlefront.

Ambassador Page, now exhausted and ill, wrote Wilson that he had to resign. He left for the United States in October, and Britain's leaders came to Waterloo Station to see him off. Irwin Laughlin, on one side, and Eugene Shoecraft, on the other, helped him to his seat in the special railway car. He died at his home in North Carolina just before Christmas. In Westminster Abbey years later, Lord Grey unveiled a tablet to Walter Hines Page, paid for by public donations. The inscription concludes, "The Friend of Britain in her Sorest Need."

"SO GLORIOUS A VICTORY"

A new government took over in Berlin, and, pressured by Ludendorff, its leader, Prince Maximilian of Baden, asked President Wilson for an armistice and "the restoration of peace." The Allies, and even U.S. senators, wanted Wilson to reject the offer and demand unconditional surrender. Colonel House pushed the President to demand guarantees from the Germans and the evacuation of France and Belgium. Wilson said he would not reject a sincere offer of peace.

Germany's military leaders recognized their enemies' new strength, and the German people were overwhelmed by the futility of the killing and the violence that, in defeat, ripped every major German city. Wilson and his advisors gave the German government no option but to surrender. On October 20, Germany accepted Wilson's demands.

Planning the armistice, Wilson gave Colonel House only two instructions: It should not be possible for Germany to renew the fighting. And Germany should be treated with moderation. Wilson said that he was "certain that too much severity on the part of the Allies will make a genuine peace settlement exceedingly difficult if not impossible. . . . Foresight is better than immediate advantage."

On the night of October 17, Colonel House and his party, which included foreign service officers Joseph Grew and Gordon Auchincloss, a lawyer and House's son-in-law, sped in a police launch to the Narrows of New York Harbor and boarded *Northern Pacific,* a swift merchant ship that the Navy had armed. Escorted by two destroyers, they sailed for Brest.

In Paris, they were surprised to find crowds of Americans and hordes of American army vehicles. The Place de la Concorde was filled with captured German guns and airplanes. House had the assignment of gathering the views of each of the European leaders; Grew accompanied him and served as gatekeeper. On October 26, Prime Minister Georges Clemenceau, of France, handed House a new statement of the Allied military leaders' terms for an armistice. House slept with it under his pillow, and a U.S. sailor guarded his bedroom door.

Now the arguments began. The Americans in the advance civilian delegation to Paris suspected that the British and French were, as Grew put it, "making strenuous efforts to take the leadership away from the President."

House told Grew he hoped for a "magnanimous" peace and that the fighting would stop quickly. Both men anticipated that the French president, Raymond Poincaré, and Prime Minister Lloyd George would demand a vengeful peace and Germany's destruction.

On October 28, Austria-Hungary surrendered unconditionally, and the end of the war became visible. The next morning, the Allied prime ministers and foreign secretaries (except for Italy's prime minister, Vittorio Orlando, who arrived the next day) met in House's Paris home at 78 rue de l'Université to discuss peace terms. This involved considerable debate and compromise. When harsh terms were proposed, House warned that they could tip the Germans over into Bolshevism. Lloyd George said Britain could not accept the statement in the Fourteen Points that would assure the freedom of the seas in both peace and war. House struck back forcefully, declaring that if the Allies did not accept Wilson's Fourteen Points, the United States would have to consider a separate peace.

House clashed again with Lloyd George the next morning, and the French and Italians voiced objections. The maneuvering and compromising continued for days. The sticking points were the freedom of the seas and the disposition of conquered territories. House warned that if they had too many objections, Wilson would have to explain the Allies' war aims to Congress.

Joseph Grew was named secretary of the United States Commission to the Peace Conference and, with Willard Straight and Walter Lippmann, organized the commission and collected political intelligence. Christian Herter served as Grew's secretary. Then, suddenly, Grew, Straight, and Lippmann were stricken by an epidemic of influenza, which killed Straight.

German delegates met French Marshal Ferdinand Foch, who forced them to ask for an armistice. On November 9, the German generals shipped the kaiser into exile in Holland, and on the following day, the Germans signed the armistice.

November 11 was a day of wild celebration. The four-year horror in which millions of young human beings had died was finished. Walter Lippmann called it "so glorious a victory."

"TRY A SECOND TIME TO CRUSH US"

The United States and the Allies—Wilson was careful to separate the two and to call the United States an "associate" of the Allies—could not coordinate their war aims. They brought to the table different geography, different territorial aspirations, different experiences, and different feuds. Each ally was different from the others and all were different from the Americans. Wilson, sitting thousands of miles away, took an Olympian position above the pain of old wounds and the striving for secret advantages. The Allied leaders resented what they saw as his air of moral superiority and his growing prestige; they distrusted him, while he regarded them as selfish. They all struggled to control the peacemaking and to decide the shape of postwar Germany.

The war was just over when, on November 26, Henry White and Elihu Root sat in a hushed room of Roosevelt Hospital in New York City by the bedside of Theodore Roosevelt. Only weeks from death, he was unable to speak much. White, now a ruddy, energetic, heavyset man with a large white mustache, was on his way to Paris as a member of the U.S. Peace Commission. He took penciled notes on cards as Root spoke about the forthcoming peace treaty. Root emphasized that the peace must be fair to all peoples and that an international organization was essential to prevent wars in the future. (Just before Christmas, Roosevelt left the hospital, and on January 6, he died in his sleep at his home, Sagamore Hill on Long Island. He was only sixty.)

In Washington, Henry White met with Senator Henry Cabot Lodge, who had become the chair of the Foreign Relations Committee when the Republicans won the 1918 midterm election. Lodge handed White a nine-page memorandum to show to the European leaders; it represented, he maintained, the views of the American people. Lodge wanted Germany crippled so it could not make war again, and he warned the peace commissioners to refuse to put the American military at the call of any international body.

Henry White, like Wilson, did not believe in crushing Germany. White's daughter, Countess Muriel Seherr-Thoss, had married a German and lived in Upper Silesia; she convinced him that the German people opposed militarism.

Marshal Foch expressed his concern about France's future security, saying, "We have no idea of attacking Germany and recommencing the war. Democracies like ours never attack. They demand only to live in peace. But who can say that Germany, whose democratic ideas are recent and perhaps a bit superficial, will not recover rapidly from her defeat and not many years from now try a second time to crush us."

White and Lansing, also a peace commissioner, sailed for France on December 4 with President Wilson on the *George Washington,* escorted by the battleship USS *Pennsylvania* and her destroyers. The other two commissioners were Colonel House and General Tasker H. Bliss, who had directed the mobilization of the U.S. Army. White, the only experienced diplomat and the sole Republican among them, had been surprised by his appointment. Many Republicans said that if Wilson had chosen someone more influential from among Republicans, he would have helped the cause of the League of Nations.

In Paris, Wilson was welcomed as a messiah who would bring peace to the world. Europe was burdened with millions of unemployed people facing starvation. White had always loved France and found the French dreaded Germany's ability to recover from the war and threaten France again.

The Peace Conference opened on January 18, 1919, the anniversary of the coronation of Kaiser Wilhelm I. The Great Powers excluded the leaders of the small nations and the new national movements. White briefed the press each morning and listened to the representatives of small nations, who could not reach Wilson directly.

On February 14, Wilson presented the proposed Covenant of the League of Nations to the full Peace Conference. He promised, "It is a definite guaranty of peace." The exhausted, debt-ridden nations accepted Wilson's international organization, which, tragically, the U.S. Senate would reject. Powerful Senator Lodge, who had disagreed with Wilson for years, was indignant that Wilson had not consulted the Senate.

On March 7, Henry White reached out to Lodge and asked him to suggest language that would make the covenant acceptable to the Senate. Not wishing to wait for letters to make a round-trip, White also sent Lodge a cable through the State Department. But Lodge was suspicious of a message coming from the department. And Root destructively advised Lodge not to negotiate with White in order to preserve his own status as Wilson's coequal. White's attempt to soften Lodge's opposition failed. Lodge insisted that the President had to deal with the Senate.

The Allied commissioners debated a multiplicity of issues: New lines crisscrossed the map of Europe like drippings in a Jackson Pollock painting. Hundreds of delegates chewed endlessly over issues that often seemed trivial and punitive. They politicked and they partied. Henry Morgenthau described the scene:

> Instead of men who were freely utilizing their individual attainments for the general good, this was a battle of conflicting interests, petty rivalries and schemes for national aggrandizement.

Lloyd George, who did not hold diplomats in high regard, was quoted as observing, "Diplomats were invented simply to waste time."

In the midst of the peace deliberations, violence spread. Increasingly, Germany was rocked by internal explosions, riots, mutinies, strikes, and calls for martial law. The press criticized Hugh Gibson, now the minister in Warsaw, for denying the existence of pogroms in the reborn state of Poland. House asked Gibson to meet with Louis Brandeis and Felix Frankfurter, who excoriated him for injuring the Jewish people. They made Gibson furious.

President Wilson assigned Morgenthau to a three-man commission to investigate the pogroms. The commissioners toured Poland for two months and listened to leaders of various factions. They focused on anti-Semitic acts reported in eight cities of the postwar Polish state. They visited Pinsk shortly after Polish soldiers lined up thirty-five leading Jews against the cathedral wall and shot them to death. In Minsk, thirty-one Jews were killed while the commissioners were in the city. The commissioners confirmed the reports of violence in Poland and recommended that the League of Nations create a long-term commission to study and improve conditions.

On May 7, the peace treaty was presented to the German envoys at Versailles, and terms were signed in the Hall of Mirrors on June 28, the fifth anniversary of the death of Archduke Franz Ferdinand. For the United States, the treaty was signed by Ellis Loring Dresel, an experienced diplomat who had closed the embassy in Vienna in 1917 and would serve later as the chargé d'affaires for Germany.

Germany was required to surrender its European conquests and overseas colonies, disarm, and pay suffocating reparations. France kept Alsace-Lorraine and the Saar coalfields. The severe peace terms handed Germans the rationale that the Socialists and the Jews had stabbed them in the back. Surrounded by their conquerors and determined to regain their dignity and power, the Germans soon turned away from democracy and economic liberalism to statism and fascism. In little more than a decade, they would hand their leadership to Adolf Hitler.

Wilson and Lansing sailed for home. White stayed in Paris and represented the United States on the Council of Five until Assistant Secretary of State Frank L. Polk arrived to head the truncated U.S. Peace Commission.

On November 19, 1919, the U.S. Senate rejected the peace treaty, eradicating the State Department's ability to negotiate under the treaty's authority. The United States and its occupation forces in Germany continued to operate under the terms of the armistice for almost two more years. Then, in August 1921, the United States made its own peace with Germany.

A DAZZLING DIPLOMATIC CAREER

In December 1919, White, Polk, and General Bliss sailed for home aboard a slow army transport. It was the end of Henry White's dazzling diplomatic career. Joseph H. Choate, the former ambassador to the Court of St. James's, summed up White's qualities:

> Mr. White set up a school of diplomacy in London. He took fresh, green ambassadors and put them to school. What a group they were! Phelps, Lincoln, Bayard, Hay, and last of all myself. He was a wonderful diplomatist. . . . You can imagine, with Harry White in the back room, how much of the responsibility they turned over to him.

Henry White had sought to professionalize the foreign service. He told the Navy League in 1916, "The Diplomatic Service is the outer bulwark, the forefront, of a country's national security and defense." And he warned, "Unless we are prepared to sacrifice local political interests whenever they clash with the Nation's welfare, we shall, as certainly as the globe revolves upon its axis, find ourselves before long in the position of a second-rate Power."

On standards for the foreign service, White was an absolutist. He preached "the entire elimination of Party politics from our relations with the other nations of the world." And he argued forcefully that "the most important branch of the Service, the Chief of Embassies and Legations . . . should be men of training. . . . Their appointments are still largely based upon Party services, financial and otherwise. . . ." He urged "doing away with this pernicious system."

White told the American Historical Association that the recurrent political turnover of ministers and ambassadors damaged the nation, and he cited comparisons: Between the Civil War and 1916, Britain sent eight ministers or ambassadors to the United States. During that same period, the United States had fifteen ministers or ambassadors at London. In that half century, Britain had six ambassadors in Paris, while the United States had five ambassadors there in ten years. Over thirty-four years, Switzerland had six ministers to the United States, and the United States had fifteen at Bern. White did not favor appointing ambassadors exclusively from the service, but none should be removed when an administration changed "unless for some very serious non-partisan reason."

He pointed to the example of Myron Herrick, the American ambassador to Paris. President Wilson had retained Herrick, a Republican; and when the war broke out, the president of France moved the government to Bordeaux and told Herrick he was leaving Paris practically in his charge. Herrick, White said, endeared himself to the citizens of Paris, but because of the "pernicious" American system, he was recalled.

White enumerated the essentials of a professional service. He had high standards. A "diplomatist," he emphasized, must "keep out of the limelight and particularly out of the newspapers." In order to be trusted, a diplomat must not seek credit for what he did. He believed nonpartisan professional diplomats would support a new administration's changes in policy.

In 1921, at the request of Nicholas Murray Butler, the president of Columbia University, White wrote a report on the discontinuity of the United States foreign service and the inability of capable men to make a career in the service. He noted that during the twenty-three years that Jean Jules Jusserand served alone as the French ambassador in Washington, the United States had seven ambassadors in Paris.

Henry White died on July 15, 1927, in Pittsfield, Massachusetts, soon after surgery. He had served effectively under five presidents and both parties. His ashes were interred in the National Cathedral in Washington. His biographer, Allan Nevins, concluded simply, "He was a great gentleman."

26

The Russian "Terror"

1917—20

From the American embassy in Petrograd, Ambassador David R. Francis watched saber-wielding mounted Cossacks disperse a hungry crowd of thousands. Francis knew no Russian, but with the help of his foreign service officers, he grasped the shocking scene played out about him. He was witnessing the beginnings of the revolution in Russia that would overthrow the czar, remove Russia from the world war, and open a new front extending as far away as Vladivostok. It would bring American soldiers and diplomats to the fighting.

In the abnormally cold, subzero winter of early 1917, Russian casualties piled up in vast numbers, breadlines grew long, and the Russian people became more and more desperate. On March 8, tens of thousands of ordinary Russians, striking workers and housewives (it was International Women's Day), crossed the ice-covered Neva River and, just three blocks from the U.S. Embassy, marched toward the Winter Palace, shouting: "Bread! Bread!"

A regiment mutinied nearby the embassy and killed their commanding officer. Francis sent the State Department descriptions of the chaos. When night came, he and his new secretary, Earl M. Johnston, a twenty-six-year-old Missourian, walked around the area to see for themselves. They did not get far before threatening armed revolutionaries made them decide to return. Francis wrote the department optimistically: "This is undoubtedly a revolution, but it is the best managed revolution that has ever taken place, for its magnitude."

When the czar abdicated on March 15 and a revolutionary provisional government took over, Francis' staff urged him to be cautious. He received no guidance from Washington, and on the eighteenth he decided to do what he thought was right. His horse-drawn sleigh drove him to the mansion that was the home of the president of the Duma, Mikhail Rodzianko. Then, he rode to the Foreign Office and met with the dynamic new foreign minister, Paul Miliukov. Both officials assured him they would continue to fight the Germans.

Back at the embassy, Francis dictated to Johnston a cable for the State Department. While it was encoded, Francis read it to his top staff members. They were stunned by what he had done without clearing it with the department. His cable requested that the United States be the first to recognize the new Russian government as the champion of "government by consent of the governed." Francis asked his aides whether any of them wished to accompany him to take the cable to Miliukov, who had said he would forward it to Washington. Only young Norman Armour offered to go.

Secretary of State Robert Lansing's reply directed Francis to affirm that "the United States recognizes the new Government of Russia." So, that very next afternoon, Francis and his staff, all in formal dress, were driven to the Mariinsky Palace and made the United States' recognition official. An officer wrote in his diary:

This afternoon the Ambassador and his entire official staff, ten secretaries of embassy and attachés, drove up the Nevsky and through the business centre to the Palace of the Imperial Council; the ambassadorial sleigh was decked with two large American flags and in one of the following sleighs rode the military and naval attachés in the striking uniforms of staff officers. At the palace the entire Council of Ministers was waiting for them. Miliukoff introduced them, and the Ambassador read the cable of the Secretary of State and said a few appropriate words. Prince Lvoff answered most cordially and simply, thanking the United States for this first recognition of the new government.

Two days later, the British, French, and Italian governments also recognized the new government. And shortly after, President Wilson asked Congress for a declaration of war against Germany. Francis believed that the United States' prompt recognition, closely followed by the declaration of war, were "vastly strengthening to the Provisional Government."

Francis wrote his wife explaining his direct action, "As I am six thousand miles away from home and communication is slow and unsatisfactory, and as I am better acquainted with the local situation than anyone in Washington can be, I will take responsibility of acting and reporting to the Department instead of asking for instructions."

If the ambassador had sought instructions, the State Department could not have anticipated the cataclysm that was to happen next in Russia. But North Winship, a young American consul in Petrograd, did write directly to Secretary Lansing, advising him that if the food shortages continued, the revolution would turn to more violence and more radical Socialism. And from Moscow, Consul General Maddin Summers informed Francis that the Russian army was disintegrating and the provinces were disrupted by riots and murders.

Francis recommended that the United States provide a line of credit for Russia to buy American products. The Stevens Railway Commission arrived at Vladivostok in June to upgrade the Trans-Siberian Railway, which had become ever more important since German submarines made the Atlantic dangerous. And the Root Commission, led by seventy-three-year-old Elihu Root, joined Francis in recommending that, to keep Russia in the war, the United States lend $15 million to pay the Russian army in Finland, which was threatening to revolt.

Francis wanted to help the provisional government and its prime minister, Alexander Kerensky, survive. Kerensky appointed Lavr Kornilov, a tough Cossack, as head of the army, and Francis proposed the United States loan Russia another $60 million. But Prime Minister Kerensky and General Kornilov fell out, opening a gap for the Bolsheviks to climb through.

Francis' reputation came to depend on the provisional government's survival. His reputation was also vulnerable because of his relationship with Madame de Cramm. He shared sensitive diplomatic matters with her, and diplomats began to avoid discussing confidential issues with him. A British espionage officer named Somerset Maugham arrived in Petrograd, and it is said that among his assignments was one to determine whether the American ambassador was having an affair with a German spy. His conclusion: Francis was having an affair, but the lady was not a German spy.

Francis complained to his friend and fellow Missourian, Third Assistant Secretary of State Breckinridge Long, that personal rumors were circulating about him. Long wrote that he understood the strains Francis was under. He urged Francis to do everything he could to keep Russia in the war.

THE BOLSHEVIKS "HAVE CONTROL OF EVERYTHING"

By summer, the Bolsheviks made an aborted attempt to seize control of the country. Francis recalled later, "Had the Provisional Government at this time arraigned Lenin and Trotsky and the other Bolshevik leaders, tried them for treason and executed them, Russia probably would not have been compelled to go through another revolution, would have been spared the reign of terror, and the loss from famine and murder of millions of her sons and daughters."

One July evening, a belligerent mob moved toward the embassy. A Russian official interrupted Francis' dinner party to warn his guests to leave. They dispersed in haste. Francis grabbed a shotgun and, with an embassy servant, stood at the entrance as the crowd pounded on the door. Cradling his shotgun, Francis announced this was American soil and he would shoot the first man who crossed the threshold. The crowd hesitated and slowly pulled back. The next day, the American ambassador was called a hero.

Early on the morning of November 7, Prime Minister Kerensky commandeered from Second Secretary Sheldon Whitehouse, of the United States, a Renault touring car belonging to Assistant Military Attaché Captain E. Francis Riggs, and, with its American flag flying, he was driven out of Petrograd at high speed. He was going to try to locate and rally loyal troops.

The next night armed Bolsheviks stormed the vast, ornate Winter Palace and arrested the ministers of the provisional government. Lenin assumed the title of chairman of the Council of People's Commissars, and Leon Trotsky became commissar of foreign affairs. Francis wrote Consul General Summers in Moscow, "Disgusting! but . . . the more ridiculous the situation the sooner the remedy." And Francis cabled the State Department: "Bolsheviki appear to have control of everything here."

Street fighting confined Consul General Summers to his home in the

Bryusovski Pereulok for four days. Bullets and shrapnel struck the building. Three of his colleagues, DeWitt Clinton Poole, Jr.; David B. Macgowan; and Arthur Bullard, were trapped in the consulate. The four hundred yards between the consulate and Summers' home became a battle zone. Summers saw artillery killing civilians; murders and looting reenforced his loathing of the Bolsheviks.

Various consuls came to his house seeking protection for their nationals. The Bolsheviks' War Revolutionary Committee, meeting with Summers and the Swedish consul general, agreed to treat foreigners by the rules of international law. The American Red Cross representatives demanded special cars in which to flee Moscow until Summers threatened to call the President. But he praised the YMCA's representatives.

This time, Francis was in no hurry to recognize the new men in power. He admonished his staff to do nothing that would acknowledge a Bolshevik government. Some of the staff started carrying arms to protect the embassy if necessary.

In the middle of all this, Francis received an American cable marked that it must be deciphered by the ambassador himself. Actually, J. Butler Wright, the experienced counselor of embassy and Francis' second in command, decoded it and brought it to Francis. It ordered him to sever Madame de Cramm's employment at the embassy. The ambassador was outraged: She was not employed by the embassy. Francis defended his friend and denied that she was a German agent, but he advised her to stop coming to the embassy.

Ambassador Francis avoided the Bolsheviks. The American who had the closest contact with Trotsky was Colonel Raymond Robins, a man of energy and intensity, if not always judgment. Robins headed the American Red Cross in Petrograd. His aide, Russian-born Alexander Gumberg, had known Trotsky in New York. The Red Cross men criticized Francis; one wrote that during his ambassadorship, "spies slipped in and out under his nose and diplomats made a monkey of him."

Brigadier General William V. Judson, the embassy's capable military attaché and chief of the American Military Mission to Russia, met with Trotsky on December 1. Judson had been an observer on the Russian side in the Russo-Japanese War. The Bolsheviks were already negotiating a separate peace with the Germans, and Judson, unrealistically, tried to persuade them to include a provision that the Germans would not transfer troops to the West. He also opposed helping the White Russians and other anti-Bolsheviks to reestablish an eastern front. That would, he predicted, only start a civil war.

At the same time, F. Willoughby Smith, the U.S. consul in Tiflis, was giving the State Department the opposite advice and supporting the anti-Bolsheviks in southern Russia. Smith's parents lived in Transcaucasia, and he knew the local players. He cabled the State Department, asking that $10 million in financial aid be sent to General A. M. Kaledin, the leader of the Don Cossacks, who opposed both the provisional government and the Bolsheviks. Smith's ideas were received in Washington with considerable caution, but when Consul General Summers in Moscow sent in similar recommendations, Lansing and President Wilson decided to send financial support secretly to General Kaledin through Britain and France to avoid congressional accountability. In the end, the British covertly supplied the finances.

In mid-December, anti-Bolsheviks captured the city of Rostov, and studious Consul DeWitt C. Poole was sent to meet with General Kaledin. Poole reported that the Cossacks were too weak to stand up to the Germans, but he recommended that financial aid be sent immediately in order to keep as many Germans as possible in the east. When Kaledin shot himself through the heart, the Communists took Rostov back, marking the end of Cossack resistance. Consul Douglas Jenkins, who was posted at Riga, was sent to check on the situation in the Ukraine. But when German forces approached, he had to work his way back to Moscow.

SHAPING AN AMERICAN ATTITUDE

It took time to unscramble an official American attitude toward the Bolsheviks. Secretary Lansing depended on Arthur Bullard, a specialist on Russia now in Moscow, who asserted that the Bolsheviks could hold power only through terror. Lansing wrote, "Russia will fairly swim in blood, prey to lawlessness and violence" and recommended doing nothing until "the black period of terrorism comes to an end." Nonrecognition of the Bolshevik government became American policy.

Some of Francis' staff began to oppose him behind his back. Edgar G. Sisson, a journalist developing propaganda to influence the Bolsheviks, even asked that Francis be recalled. Sisson had a reputation for energy and suspicion, and he tried to send his message to the Committee on Public Information in Washington without the State Department's knowledge. But State's cryptographers decoded it, and President Wilson ordered Sisson to stay out of political and personal matters. The following May, the Committee on Public Information ordered Bullard and Sisson to leave Russia posthaste. No reason was given.

The Allied and American intelligence services cooperated in monitoring the disorderly Russian scene. Summers engaged Xenophon Dmitrivich de Blumenthal Kalamatiano, an American businessman who had sold farm machinery in Russia and was married to a well-placed Russian woman, to organize a network of about thirty Russians. Their reports were passed to Assistant Secretary Frank Polk in Washington.

DOES THE AMBASSADOR NEED TO KNOW?

On Christmas Eve 1917, without consulting his staff, Ambassador Francis cabled the department that he was revising his recommendation and now wanted relations to be established with the Bolshevik government. The department turned down his recommendation. But he did obtain permission for Robins to continue meeting with Trotsky (which Francis had not known about), as long as Robins said he represented the Red Cross and not the embassy.

Failures of communication worsened the confusion between the embassy and the department. George Kennan offered the following insight:

It should not be thought that Francis' experience in this respect was unique. The assumption that the Ambassador abroad has no need to be fully informed of the thoughts and aims of his superiors at home is, after all, a frequent feature of American statesmanship. Posterity will never know how much confusion has been occasioned, how much effort wasted, as a result of this complacent assumption. The annals of American diplomacy are studded with mistakes and lost opportunities, some major, some minor, over the memory of which might well be placed the epitaph: "The Ambassador doesn't need to know."

It can be assumed that Kennan knew whereof he spoke.

Ambassador Francis was at the Mariinsky Ballet on the evening of January 14, 1918, when he was informed that Bolsheviks had arrested the Romanian ambassador, Count Constantine Diamandi. The following afternoon, Francis led twenty Allied and neutral ambassadors in a procession of limousines to Bolshevik headquarters in the Smolny Institute. Deep in the vast building, the diplomats confronted Lenin. (This was the only time Francis ever saw Lenin.) With the embassy secretary Livingston Phelps interpreting, Francis said he had not come to discuss the ambassador's arrest, only the violation of the principle of diplomatic immunity. The French ambassador spoke up, and the Belgian minister and the Serbian minister followed. Lenin, staying cool, said he would reconsider the arrest.

At midnight, Lenin telephoned Francis to tell him the Romanian ambassador would be released but ordered to leave the city. Francis went to the station to see him off. Although threats continued against the embassies, Lansing assured Francis that his informal contacts with the Bolsheviks were appreciated in Washington.

The peace talks between the Russians and Germans at Brest-Litovsk broke down (again) on February 10, 1918, and the German army, advancing toward Petrograd, met little resistance. Francis cabled that he was considering leaving the capital. On February 21, the five Allied ambassadors met and decided to leave Petrograd. Robins saw Lenin and obtained railway accommodations. A lead party of twenty-three left by train on February 24 for Vladivostok. Francis decided to stay in Russia and help any Russians who would continue to fight.

At the beginning of March, John K. Caldwell, the consul at Vladivostok, wrote the department that the Bolsheviks controlled the city and the Trans-Siberian Railway line. The British proposed that the Japanese land at Vladivostok to discourage more Germans from transferring to the Western Front. Some of President Wilson's advisors warned that if the Japanese did come in, they would be difficult to remove. But they came anyway, arriving in April, eager to take over the railroad. The United States sent the cruiser *Brooklyn* to Vladivostok to emphasize its objection.

The prospect that Japan would invade Siberia with or without Allied approval threw the State Department into a turmoil, which was intensified when the British and French supported the Japanese presence. But in the absence of American agreement, the Japanese pulled back.

VOLOGDA AND VLADIVOSTOK

Ambassador Francis decided to move the U.S. Embassy to Vologda, a strategic railway junction 350 miles directly east of Petrograd and thus farther away from the advancing German army. He had the embassy's confidential papers burned in the courtyard and handed over the building to Norway for safekeeping. Francis also recommended to Lansing that the United States take control of Vladivostok and that the British and French seize Murmansk and Archangel.

Francis and the embassy staff traveled in two special trains. The first left on February 24, 1918; the second, including Ambassador Francis, was delayed. Two days later, Francis, bringing along his golf clubs but abandoning, for the moment, his Model-T Ford and his stock of good wines, was driven by horse-drawn sleigh to Petrograd's Nikolai Station. The Germans were now 150 miles away.

For ten nerve-racking hours the ambassador's train sat in the station. The Bolsheviks had changed their minds. Robins rushed back to their headquarters, faced Lenin, huddled behind his desk, and argued that it made good sense to let the diplomats go. Finally, at 2:00 A.M. on February 27, Lenin allowed the train to start for Vologda.

Only the Japanese and Chinese joined the Americans at Vologda; most of the Europeans chose to leave Russia. And on March 6 Lenin's government decided to move to Moscow. The Germans pressed the Bolsheviks to order Francis out of Russia. They ignored the demand.

President Wilson resisted opening a new front in Siberia; it was too far away. But David B. Macgowan, the American consul at Irkutsk, a Bolshevik military center some forty miles west of Lake Baikal, wired Francis that trainloads of German prisoners of war, heavily armed, were traveling eastward to seize the Trans-Siberian Railway. Massive stores of munitions, coal, and war supplies were stockpiled along the railroad at Archangel and Vladivostok.

Francis ordered Chapin Huntington, the commercial attaché at Irkutsk, to check on rumors of attempts to start a Siberian republic that would refuse to accept peace with Germany. Consul Macgowan's report on the trains filled with German POWs proved incorrect, but it helped convince the United States to send two regiments to Siberia.

Japan and the United States were both nervous that the other would unilaterally seize control of the Russian Far East. The Bolsheviks seized Vladivostok toward the end of March and began shipping inland the munitions stored there. The British, French, and Italians all pressed President Wilson to support a Japanese intervention. House and Lansing opposed it; J. Butler Wright at the embassy and Charles Moser, the consul in Harbin, favored a joint intervention.

On April 4, three Japanese civilians were killed at Vladivostok, and the Japanese put five hundred men ashore to protect Japanese lives and property. The British landed fifty men to guard their consulate. The Japanese and British Marines stayed ashore, ignoring the Russians' resentment. The American navy had orders not to get involved.

The Czechoslovak Legion, which had been formed to fight the Germans on the now-dead eastern front, was traveling by train to Vladivostok and planned then to go around by ship to the western front. The legion had grown to a force two divisions strong. Wary of Bolshevik good faith, the thirty-five thousand Czechs prepared to fight their way into Vladivostok if necessary. Francis, in Volgoda, opposed a Bolshevik demand that the Czechs be disarmed.

By the third week in May, relations between the Russians and Czechs broke down, and fighting erupted along the Trans-Siberian Railway. West of Omsk, the American vice counsel L. S. Gray participated in a conference between Bolsheviks and Czechs. The meeting failed, and the Czechs continued to fight eastward despite Bolshevik resistance. By the end of June, the Czechs occupied Vladivostok.

To the American diplomats in the old provincial town of Vologda, the war seemed far away. They lived on their train until the Bolshevik mayor gave them use of a large empty wooden building. When they learned that Russia was out of the war, Francis sent Counselor Wright home via Vladivostok to check on the railroad and military forces en route. And Francis cut his staff down to fifteen. Most senior in Vologda now was Norman Armour, a thirty-one-year-old Princeton graduate with a Harvard law degree. There was not much for them to do, but their presence was important.

Raymond Robins and Consul Roger C. Tredwell returned from Vologda to Petrograd, where Trotsky told Robins he feared Japan would invade Siberia. And Francis asked John F. Stevens to send him twenty engineers from his Railway Mission to repair the railroad.

Consul General Summers, in Moscow, with State Department concurrence, appointed Americans already in Russia to serve as consuls in eight Siberian towns, which, if the Germans took Moscow, would become centers of American activity in Russia. Notable among the new consuls was Ernest L. Harris, who, until 1916, had served for years in the consular service. He was now sent to Irkutsk as consul general.

A raging quarrel broke out between Robins and Summers. Robins believed the Allies should collaborate with the Bolsheviks, and Summers disagreed. Summers wanted Francis to remove Robins, and Robins asked for Francis' recall. Lansing concluded that Robins' unofficial contacts with the Soviet leaders were disrupting the foreign service and ordered him home for consultation. The dispute ended when Summers, after being ill only twenty-four hours, died on May 4 of a brain hemorrhage. Francis went to Moscow and, at the funeral in the English Church, lavishly praised Summers.

Summers was succeeded by DeWitt C. Poole, Jr., an astute observer, an able former newspaperman, and the son of an army officer. Young, energetic, and cheerful, he became the primary American diplomat in contact with the Russian Foreign Office. He was more objective than either Summers or Robins, and Francis felt comfortable with him. But Robins' departure reduced American access to Lenin and Trotsky. Although Poole clearly opposed Bolshevism, he believed that only forces from the outside could dislodge the Bolshevik government.

Trotsky repudiated diplomacy, but Bolshevik leaders found they had to stay informed about other governments' designs and that they needed to have lines of diplomatic communication in place. They abolished diplomatic ranks and wiped out distinctions between diplomatic and consular officers, but otherwise they continued to work inside diplomacy's traditional framework. All this disruption did not make for an efficient diplomatic service.

Trotsky was replaced in March by the eccentric, university-educated Georgi V. Chicherin as the people's commissar for foreign affairs. His job was to execute Russian foreign policy, and he saw that his most useful weapons were the disagreements among the capitalist powers.

At Summers' funeral, the Russian Foreign Office asked Francis to move the American embassy to Moscow. They repeated this in Vologda. But Francis wanted to stay out of the Germans' reach and to hold together the reduced corps of diplomats. He also worried that the Bolsheviks might take foreign diplomats hostage.

While in Moscow, Francis arranged a variety of information-collecting and espionage activities with representatives of the Czech Legion and counterrevolutionaries. To carry out these activities, he chose Poole, the consul general in Moscow; Robert W. Imbrie, a vice consul in Petrograd; F. Willoughby Smith, the consul in Tiflis; and Felix Cole, the consul in Archangel.

In June, Francis reported to State that the Bolshevik government might collapse. And Acting Secretary of State Polk said the United States did not recognize the Russian government or any of its acts. Francis told the Russians, "We do not observe the Brest-Litovsk peace. Surely no Russian who loves his country and looks with pride upon her greatness is going to submit tamely to her dismemberment and humiliation."

British Marines went ashore at Murmansk by agreement with the local Soviet. Murmansk was a new port built on the Barents Sea and was ice-free all year. The Germans, of course, protested the landings; the Russians simply denied they had taken place.

The British decided that instead of using British soldiers, the Allies should send elements of the Czech Legion to defend Archangel and Murmansk. The successes of Germany's spring offensive made it crucial to stop the flow of German troops to the Western Front.

At the same time, Lieutenant Hugh S. Martin, an intelligence officer who was the American representative at Murmansk, arranged for a warship to be sent there. Ambassador Francis endorsed the idea to the State Department, and USS *Olympia* showed up at Murmansk.

Except for Allen Wardwell, a levelheaded New York lawyer who was on Robins' American Red Cross staff, Lieutenant Martin was the only American official to reach Murmansk. He had arrived in a freight car in

February, when the temperature was thirty below zero, and he took supplies back west as quickly as he could.

Martin had an affinity for adventure. Late in April, he set out for Vologda
to meet with Ambassador Francis. He took along in his private railroad
car the commander of a Russian warship, whose life had been threatened
by Bolshevik sailors. Martin had the local Soviet's approval to transport
the naval captain, but still angry sailors encircled the train and demanded
that Martin turn him over. Brandishing a revolver in the door of his car,
Martin kept them at a distance. The next morning, the train hit a barricade of railroad ties laid across the track. Russians in the car next to Martin's were killed; Martin's car landed upside down, and he was hospitalized.

By the time Martin was released from the hospital and reached Vologda,
Francis had changed his mind and favored Allied intervention in the Far
East without Bolshevik agreement. He told the State Department, "In my
judgment, the time for Allied intervention has arrived."

Francis had known since March that the Russians were seizing Allied
munitions stored at Archangel and shipping them inland for their own
purposes. And he had grown concerned that the Germans would occupy
Murmansk. He now advocated an Allied intervention, whatever the Bolsheviks' attitude.

Lenin, on May 14, made a speech predicting that capitalist economics
made "inevitable a desperate conflict between these two powers [Japan
and the United States] for mastery of the Pacific Ocean and its shores."
That evening, Robins started home via Vladivostok in a private railroad
car with Alexander Gumberg and a small party. He carried in his pocket
a detailed proposal from Lenin on how American-Russian commercial
relations could develop and how the United States could exploit the mineral wealth of eastern Siberia. When the train stopped at Vologda, Robins
met on the platform with Francis, but he did not mention the message he
carried from Lenin. When Francis discovered this, he was infuriated. The
Red Cross representative was carrying out in secret the State Department
function of enabling American companies to develop commercial relations in a foreign country. He never forgave Robins.

Francis had become convinced, he later told a Senate committee, that
"the best answer to Bolshevik Russia is economic cooperation, food,
friendliness on the part of America." He proposed sending an economic
commission to Russia to help the peasants avoid starvation and to initiate
trade with the West. That same day, Consul General DeWitt C. Poole;

Chapin Huntington, the commercial attaché; and Vice Consul John Lehrs met with Foreign Minister Chicherin, and they agreed on a protocol for regular meetings and candid talk.

On May 27, President Wilson agreed to support military action at Murmansk and Archangel. The official American view now was that the Bolsheviks had acquired power by the use of force, and they did not speak for the Russian people. The Americans explained that they were not trying to reopen an Eastern Front or force the Russians back into the fighting. The war would be decided on the Western Front.

On June 1, President Wilson told Lansing that he would send American troops to Murmansk if Marshal Foch, commander in chief of the Allied armies, approved. And Hugh Martin returned to Murmansk with an order from Ambassador Francis for the captain of *Olympia* to land 150 Marines; they were the first American military unit to operate on Russian soil.

Once the Czech Legion broke with the Bolsheviks, it seized major portions of the Trans-Siberian Railway. When Consul General Harris, at Irkutsk, realized the Czechs and Bolsheviks were battling not out of misunderstandings but as part of a civil war, he asserted again that he was under orders not to mix in Russia's partisan politics. And in mid-June, Consul General Poole, with no time to consult Ambassador Francis, instructed George W. Williams, the vice consul in Samara in western Siberia, where the Trans-Siberian Railway crossed the Volga, to tell the Czech leaders that the Allies would prefer it if they just held the railroad. Francis was delighted with Poole's initiative, but he warned him the department might object.

THE AMERICANS INTERVENE

Even though Siberia still seemed distant and forbidding, Wilson and Lansing decided to keep the northern ports of Murmansk and Archangel out of German hands. And officials of Murmansk's local Soviet were desperate for Allied help. On June 23, the British landed six hundred men, who turned back Russian Red Guard detachments trying to reach the port. But the Murmansk officials faced Lenin's and Chicherin's anger at their insubordination.

Four days later, Jean Jules Jusserand, the longtime French ambassador in Washington, informed the State Department that Marshal Foch approved directing American soldiers to defend Murmansk. President Wilson, against his military advisors' judgment, sent three battalions of infantry and three companies of engineers.

News that the Czechs were fighting the Bolsheviks along the railroad sparked the idea of using them in place rather than moving them on to the war in France. U.S. foreign service officers differed on this. Although Paul S. Reinsch, the professorial minister in Peking, wanted to use the Czechs against the Germans, at Archangel, Consul Felix Cole, a young Harvard graduate with a command of Russian, told the State Department that to expect the Russians to join the Czechs was unrealistic.

John Caldwell, the consul in Vladivostok, reported that fifteen thousand Czechs were determined to stay and help their countrymen fight the Bolsheviks. Three days later, these Czechs took over Vladivostok by force.

As soon as that happened, more Japanese and British forces landed. And thirty Marines from the *Brooklyn* came ashore under Captain Archie F. Howard, of the U.S. Marine Corps and a young Annapolis graduate, to guard the U.S consulate and help patrol the city. (The story was told that local Bolsheviks half-expected a revolt among the crew of *Brooklyn* because three times a day a red flag was raised on the cruiser. It was, in fact, the navy meal pennant.)

On July Fourth, at Vologda, Francis hosted a makeshift reception with punch and sandwiches and dancing to music from a Victrola. He gave a talk promising the Russian people that America would never let the Germans exploit them. Two days later, Count Wilhelm von Mirbach-Harff, the powerful German ambassador to Moscow, was assassinated in his legation. Fears rose that the Germans would retaliate, and Francis urged his government to land troops at Archangel.

In Washington, July Fourth was beastly hot, so Wilson and Lansing cooled off by sailing on the Potomac River to Mount Vernon. Aboard the presidential yacht *Mayflower,* the Secretary drafted a memorandum asserting that the United States had an obligation to fight the Germans by contributing both soldiers and military supplies.

President Wilson's cautious wavering now came to an end. On July 6, he summoned his chief aides and read to them his decision proposing to send seven thousand Americans and approving seven thousand Japanese "to guard the line of communication of the Czecho-Slovaks proceeding toward Irkutsk." American and Allied forces would also land at Vladivostok.

Wilson implied that the Czechs were fighting German war prisoners. No mention was made of either the Bolsheviks, the actual opponents of the Czechs, or the White Russians, the Czechs' allies. George Kennan called Wilson's views "delusions." And years later, Justice Brandeis suggested that these decisions were the first signs of Wilson's mental disintegration.

The Allies' reaction was hardly what Wilson and Lansing had expected. The British unilaterally sent a battalion from Hong Kong to Vladivostok. And White Russian forces also tried to move into the Asian port. In Tokyo, the general staff persuaded the government to seize northern Manchuria and dominate eastern Siberia. The Japanese decided to send not seven thousand men but an entire division of twelve thousand. Wilson was shocked.

The Allies were now on Russian soil uninvited; and, on July 29, the Bolsheviks informed Consul General Poole that Allied military personnel who wanted to leave Russia would not be allowed to. They were hostages. Lenin blamed the Allies for the Czech revolt, for landing at Murmansk, and for conspiring with anti-Bolsheviks. On August 2, the British and French seized Archangel, and the next day British and Japanese soldiers landed at Vladivostok. An Allied force from Murmansk (including Marines from *Olympia*) came to Archangel. The British advanced them two hundred miles inland to fight the Red Army, which infuriated Wilson.

AMERICANS ARRIVE IN STRENGTH

In August, the first of nine thousand soldiers of the American Expeditionary Force Siberia arrived at Vladivostok, and 5,500 Americans of the North Russia Expeditionary Force arrived at Archangel from England. On September 4, 4,500 more landed at Archangel. The Bolsheviks used their arrival to stir up the fear that the old regimes were returning. The American soldiers had orders to defend the port and its massive stores of supplies and to assist the Czechs, but they were not to make war on the Russians. And they certainly had no intention of going into the interior.

The War Department objected when Wilson gave Ambassador Francis

control of U.S. troops at Archangel. Major General William S. Graves, a
Texan and a West Point graduate, arrived at Vladivostok on September 1
to command the American Expeditionary Force Siberia. His orders were
to avoid advancing west of Lake Baikal and to stay out of Russia's internal
conflicts.

But Czech and other anti-Communist troops were driving the Bolsheviks out of the towns on the railway. Consul General Harris tried to mediate between Czechs and Bolsheviks.

Battle lines began to form. The Japanese poured in 72,000 men and
forced the Bolsheviks back from Vladivostok. Wilson worried why the
Japanese sent so many men. The Czechs ruled Siberia from Vladivostok to
Irkutsk and fought the Bolsheviks. The Bolsheviks negotiated an agree-
ment with the Germans to release more Russians to take on the Czechs.
Although the British, French, and Japanese supported the anti-Bolsheviks,
Major General Graves insisted that "as far as American troops were con-
cerned, the United States was not at War with any part of Russia."

Consul General Harris was scornful of the anti-Bolshevik political islands across Siberia. He looked for a "strong man" who could take charge,
and by November the Americans were backing the Cossack leader Admiral Aleksandr V. Kolchak in Omsk. The so-called Whites controlled all
the local governments in Siberia.

American troops in Siberia were vilified because Graves would not
permit them to help either the Russian Whites or Reds, but General Pey-
ton C. March, the U.S. chief of staff, supported Graves' policy. He wrote
Graves a personal note saying, "Keep a stiff upper lip. I am going to stand
by you until——freezes over."

Chicherin continued to press the Allied diplomats to come to Moscow.
Francis insisted they felt safer in Vologda than they would in Moscow,
and he shrewdly released his statement to the press. Then, on July 17, the
Bolsheviks murdered the czar and his family.

The Allied diplomats at Vologda, knowing of the impending Allied
landing at Archangel, decided to move to that remote port. But on July 23,
Chicherin impatiently demanded they move to Moscow at once. The Allies packed in haste and boarded a waiting train but did not say where they
intended to go. The local Russians refused to release a locomotive without
permission from Moscow. Messages sped back and forth until, at 2:00

A.M. on July 25, the train started for Archangel, carrying Francis and about 140 Americans and other diplomats. Twenty Americans who were with the YMCA and National City Bank stayed in Vologda under the charge of Second Secretary Norman Armour.

When Ambassador Francis and the Allied diplomats arrived across the river from Archangel, the local Soviet leaders had a boat waiting to take them out of Russia. Francis refused to leave Russia and insisted they would stay on the train until they could communicate with their government. Cable connections had been down for weeks. A battle seemed imminent between the Bolsheviks and counterrevolutionaries, so the diplomats crossed the White Sea in two ships to Kandalaksha. From there, Francis led a party of fifteen in boxcars 150 miles further north to Murmansk. They were greatly cheered to see in the harbor British and French warships and USS *Olympia*.

THE BOLSHEVIKS RETALIATE

The Bolshevik government again ordered Norman Armour to move from Vologda to Moscow. He burned the official files and found an old top hat that had been left behind. He put the hat in the empty embassy safe and sealed it with official red tape. Later, he was delighted to hear that the Russians worked for hours to open the safe and finally blew it up.

In the middle of the night of August 3, Bolsheviks armed with machine guns invaded the embassy at Vologda and forcibly moved Armour and the other Americans to Moscow under guard. The Americans found the capital a chaos of violence, fighting, and executions. Incidentally, Armour had a romantic personal adventure. Using a false Norwegian passport and pretending to be a courier, he precariously stole back into Petrograd and enabled the Russian princess Myra Koudacheff to escape to Sweden; after the war, they were married.

On August 25, Poole organized a meeting of Allied diplomats and spies. The businessman Kalamatiano represented the Americans. Afterward, he traveled across Siberia on an information-gathering mission, during which he learned that the Bolsheviks had rolled up his spy network. The British and French agents escaped or were exchanged, and ninety-five Americans were cleared to leave Moscow.

Courageously, Poole and Allen Wardwell stayed behind to do what they could. Armour wanted to stay, but he was ordered to lead out the others. The fleeing Allies were stopping on a train in Petrograd's rail yards on August 30 when anti-Bolsheviks assassinated the chief of Petrograd's Cheka secret police, and in Moscow they shot Lenin in the neck and chest.

The Bolsheviks reacted with fury. They tortured and executed hundreds, invaded the British embassy, shot the senior British official, and imprisoned the rest. The Americans were not arrested, but their consulate general was surrounded by police, and water and electricity were cut off. The siege went on for ten days. Through the Norwegians, Poole reported their predicament to the State Department.

Poole tried to warn Kalamatiano not to return to Moscow. He avoided Cheka agents waiting for him in his home, but when he showed up at the consulate general, they seized him. He claimed he had only been collecting commercial information, but inside his cane the secret police found codes and messages that made his interest in military information obvious. They locked him up in Lubianka Prison and sentenced him to death.

By radio broadcast, the only form of communication possible, the American embassy in Paris ordered Consul General Poole to leave Russia by any means he could find. On the morning of September 18, he slipped out of the consulate. He hid all day among the throng at the railroad station and, that evening, went by train to the Norwegians in Petrograd. A Norwegian vice consul took him to the Finnish border, where a Russian officer, who had been bribed, let him cross.

Allen Wardwell and members of the American Red Cross mission were the only Americans with official status still in Moscow. They took great risks to get out in mid-October. At Archangel, Ambassador Francis was stricken with a prostate infection and confined to bed in great pain.

Kalamatiano was brought to trial in November. Others, including Poole, were tried in absentia. Kalamatiano's agents were executed, but the Bolshevik Central Committee kept him alive to exchange for Russian prisoners. During the summer of 1921, when the American army was long gone, he was released in exchange for food during the Great Famine, which affected 35 million people. Herbert Hoover, director of the American Relief Administration (ARA), insisted that eight Americans still in Soviet custody be released before he would help the Bolsheviks cope with the famine.

The ARA food program fed some ten million Russians, mostly children, but could not overcome the starvation sweeping across Russia. The ARA relief workers in the field were a mixed bag of mostly young college graduates. One, James Rives Childs, of Lynchburg, Virginia, caught typhus at Kazan in Tartarstan, recovered, and became the ARA chief in Kazan. Later, he married a widowed White Russian aristocrat and, in 1923, became a U.S. consular officer, launching a thirty-year diplomatic career. He wound up as ambassador to Saudi Arabia, Yemen, and Ethiopia and an ardent Arabist.

The United States' refusal to recognize the Bolshevik government made exchange of hostages extremely difficult. Consul Thornwell Haynes negotiated the recovery of a hundred Allied prisoners in exchange for a quarter of a million dollars' worth of pharmaceuticals. But Acting Secretary Polk turned down that proposal because Consul Roger C. Tredwell was still being held in violation of international law. Tredwell and twenty-one other prisoners were eventually released on April 25, 1919, without any quid pro quo.

At this time, Robert W. Imbrie, a vice consul at Petrograd, organized a dozen anti-Bolshevik officers to track German activity in the Baltic area, as well as Bolshevik movements around Archangel and Murmansk. Imbrie was forced to leave Russia in 1919 and then operated out of Finland, from where his network gathered political and military information inside Russia. As vice consul at Vyborg, Imbrie bizarrely organized an anti-Bolshevik attack from Finland and even schemed to capture Petrograd and Moscow. Acting Secretary Polk tried to discourage some of his schemes. The Cheka broke up the network, imprisoned and tortured the spies, and sent word that Imbrie, when caught, would be executed. But he managed to stay alive for five more years.

Ambassador Francis asked for more American troops and condemned the Bolsheviks' executions of their enemies. The Germans were now losing the war, and Wilson refused to send more troops. But he had Lansing commend Ambassador Francis. When his illness grew still more serious, Lansing advised him to go to London for surgery. Eight sailors carried Francis aboard the cruiser *Olympia*; and by the time *Olympia* coaled and left Murmansk on November 13, the war was over. Francis traveled via Scotland to London for his surgery.

DeWitt Poole, who was now serving as chief of the Russia bureau at the State Department, was sent to take charge at Archangel.

Early in February 1919, Francis traveled to Paris, hoping to see President Wilson during the Peace Conference. He was able to talk with Secretary Lansing, Colonel House, and General Pershing, but the President never made time for him. After waiting two weeks, the persistent ambassador booked passage on the *George Washington,* on which Wilson was returning to the United States.

Aboard ship, Wilson came to Francis' cabin for a long talk. Francis proposed to the President that the Allied diplomatic missions return to Petrograd with a hundred thousand Allied troops, not to fight the Bolsheviks, he said, but to restore order. Wilson replied that this would be unpopular at home and that Lloyd George and Clemenceau agreed with him. Wilson and Francis differed. They met again socially aboard the ship but never had another substantive discussion.

The ambassador became the target of attacks in the House of Representatives because of his role in Russia. And Francis himself testified for several hours before a subcommittee of the Senate Judiciary Committee. As he told *The Boston Globe,* he believed that Lenin and Trotsky did not represent the Russian people and that Bolshevism is "neither democracy nor Socialism." He wrote the American Peace Commission in Paris, "Lenin is a fanatic. . . . Trotzky is an adventurer, absolutely without conviction and saturated with personal ambitions." Francis consistently recommended that the United States refuse to recognize the Bolshevik regime.

In Washington and in Paris, American officials bickered into 1919 over Russia's future. The Bolsheviks tried to use their faith in economic motivation to persuade American businessmen to trade in Russia. Lenin set up a Soviet Bureau in New York to build business contacts. It lasted only a few months before U.S. government agents raided the Bureau's office, and its director, Ludwig Martens, fled to Moscow.

Even though Francis returned to the United States, he remained the ambassador to Russia. The State Department felt that if he resigned, he would have to be replaced, which would amount to recognizing the Bolshevik government. In June 1919, American troops left Archangel. And in July, the deserted American embassy in Petrograd was trashed and the Finnish woman caring for it was arrested and sent to Moscow. In September, the interim chargé d'affaires Felix Cole and all embassy personnel left Archangel, and the Bolsheviks took over.

BULLITT'S MISSION

The American peace commissioners in Paris sent a covert mission to Moscow in February 1919 to study political and economic conditions. It was led by William C. Bullitt, a highly self-confident twenty-eight-year-old Philadelphian. The charming, intellectually arrogant son of a wealthy West Virginia coal operator, Bullitt had studied at Yale, traveled extensively in Europe, worked as a foreign correspondent for Philadelphia's *Public Ledger,* and served as chief of the State Department's Bureau of Central European Information in the Division of Western European Affairs under Joseph Grew.

He traveled to the Paris Peace Conference on the same ship as President Wilson and kept busy informing the peace commissioners about what was taking place. At the end of January, he wrote Colonel House a bold memorandum recommending that the American and Allied troops at Archangel be sent home immediately.

Secretary Lansing asked Bullitt to inquire about the fate of Roger C. Tredwell, the American consul in Petrograd whom the Bolsheviks still detained in Tashkent. Bullitt was armed with questions from Colonel House and Lloyd George's secretary, Philip Kerr.

Journalist Lincoln Steffens went with Bullitt to Petrograd and Moscow. The two Americans were in Russia for one week and convinced themselves that they were supposed to negotiate peace terms with the Bolsheviks. On March 14, they met with Lenin, and he impressed them as straightforward and liberal. Lenin, for his part, came to think he could do business with the United States, if not the other capitalist nations. And the Russians agreed to release Tredwell.

Back in Paris, Bullitt submitted a report that was comprehensive and detailed for one having been in Russia so briefly. He wrote, "The destructive phase of the revolution is over and all the energy of the Government is turned to constructive work. The terror has ceased."

He had meetings with House, Lansing, Henry White, Lloyd George, and Balfour, among others. But President Wilson would not meet with him and refused to make his report public. Nevertheless, Bullitt himself made the report public by presenting it to the U.S. Senate Committee on Foreign Relations. Lloyd George said that if Bullitt's report had value it was up to the President to bring it to the Peace Conference. Wilson never did.

Dramatically, Bullitt resigned from the State Department. In his anger, Bullitt wrote that the United States should not sign the peace treaty and should not join the League of Nations. He was severely criticized, especially for repeating private conversations with Lansing and others. Lincoln Steffens classified him with "those conscientious, high-bred, mostly rich young gentlemen and their wives, who wanted to do right." Joseph Grew, who had worked closely with Bullitt, wrote in his diary long afterward: "This testimony of course carried great influence in the defeat of the Treaty of Versailles by the American Senate, and Bullitt was branded throughout the country by the press, the public and his friends as disloyal to his former chief."

AFTER THE ARMISTICE

"The Armistice had absolutely no effect in Siberia," said Major General Graves. That was true from his command viewpoint, because the end of World War I had eliminated most of the public reasons for the American intervention.

In March 1919, the governments concerned divided up the Trans-Siberian Railway. U.S. troops guarded one section. On the other hand, Graves, following his orders uncompromisingly, stuck to neutrality. Graves wondered how the State Department could send arms to the Cossacks and still claim to stand for "non-interference in Russian internal affairs." In a discouraged moment, he admitted, "It is difficult to understand diplomatic language."

The President and State Department wanted Graves to relax his neutrality and to aid the anti-Bolsheviks, but the War Department and both congressional and public opinion prevented that. Graves wrote later, "As a result, the representatives of the War Department and the State Department were carrying out entirely different policies at the same time and in the same place." He felt that the State Department officials involved had no sympathy for "the so-called submerged class." He was critical of Harris, Macgowan, and Poole and was particularly angry at General Alfred Knox of the British Army for persuading John K. Caldwell, the consul in Vladivostok, to cable the department that Graves was misinterpreting American policy and should be relieved.

After President Wilson suffered a stroke on October 2, 1919, Secretary Lansing stopped sending aid to the Cossack leader Kolchak. His White Russian regime disintegrated, and the Bolsheviks eventually executed him.

Major General Graves left Siberia with the last echelon of Americans on April 1, 1920. Three nights later, the Japanese opened fire in the streets of Vladivostok. By the end of that year, the Russian civil war was over, and the Bolsheviks ruled the vast area that had been the czar's unhappy empire. A pragmatic Britain negotiated a trade agreement with the Soviet Union. The United States adamantly refused.

Graves was always uncertain why the United States had intervened in Siberia. The United States had declared its neutrality in Siberia and, in contradiction, supported the dictatorial Kolchak. Graves agreed with those who called the American intervention a blunder and a dismal failure.

27

The New Diplomacy of Oil

1919–38

The brutal death of Vice Consul Robert W. Imbrie in Tehran on the afternoon of July 18, 1924, was a warning of violence to come. Imbrie, with another American, Melvin Seymour, and a legation messenger, stood on Agha Sheikh Hadi Street preparing to photograph a drinking fountain that Tehran's Muslim faithful regarded as sacred. In the street, the crowd began shouting that the men were members of the Baha'i religion. The mob stoned and beat them. The men tried to flee in their carriage, and the mob chased them, crying that the infidels had poisoned the fountain. The crowd surrounded them near police headquarters, and, as Minister Joseph S. Kornfeld wrote the State Department, "dragged the Americans from their carriage and attacked them savagely."

Inexplicably, Persian army soldiers also hacked at the three with swords and bayonets. A saber blow cut Imbrie's head to the bone. As he lay on the ground unconscious, a stone smashed his jaw. The police carried the men to their headquarters hospital nearby. The mob stormed the hospital, pushed into the operating room, and beat Vice Consul Imbrie to death.

Imbrie was forty-one. A Yale graduate with a law degree, he had led an adventurous life, big-game hunting in Africa and crossing Asia Minor on horseback. During World War I, he drove in the American Ambulance Field Service at the Somme and Verdun and in Albania, and he was decorated with the Croix de Guerre. Because he was stricken with fever at Salonika, he was unable to join the U.S. Army. He entered the consular service and was posted to Petrograd, where he became deeply involved in anti-Bolshevik intrigue and built a network of spies. He served at Viborg, Finland; Ankara; and Constantinople and was commissioned a major in the U.S. Army Reserve. When Imbrie was posted to Tehran, *National Geographic* magazine asked him to take photographs, a fateful assignment.

His battered body was brought home aboard the USS *Trenton* and buried in Arlington National Cemetery. Seymour, who was also attacked when Imbrie was killed, was an American oil-well driller who was being punished for fighting with Persian oil-field workers and who at the time was paroled to the U.S. consulate.

Although the crowd apparently killed Imbrie with religious zeal, Legation Second Secretary W. Smith Murray wrote the State Department that the violence had been provoked not solely by the fanaticism of the street. He reported that men involved in the intense competition in Persia between British and American oil companies had stirred up the street crowd. Imbrie's earlier intelligence activities gave credence to this hypothesis.

Murray told the department that "the recrudescence of clerical power in Persia in the last two years has supplied the background and, in large part, the motivation for the tragedy that has just occurred." The mullahs had regained power when the prime minister rallied them against Reza Khan, who as Persia's war minister had promoted the separation of church and state. In 1923, the British had installed the tough, anticlerical Reza Khan as prime minister.

At the time of Imbrie's murder, Reza Khan was steering a bill through the parliament (Mejlis) in favor of the American Sinclair Oil Company. Second Secretary Murray predicted that once the oil bill was passed, Reza Khan would "assume dictatorial powers." The next year, he did, in fact, declare himself His Majesty, Reza Shah Pahlavi.

Murray, who in 1945 would become the American ambassador to Iran, concluded his 1924 report with a perceptive warning:

Viewing the tragedy, in its larger issue, one is led to the inevitable conclusion that, unless Reza Khan is able and willing to purge the military of its criminal lawlessness, and, unless the malign power of the clergy can be broken forever in the land, there is every reason that the killing of Imbrie is but a foretaste of more terrible events to come.

OIL MEANS "MASTERY"

In 1909, the year after oil was discovered in Mesopotamia (Iraq), the U.S. State Department had created its Near Eastern Division. John D. Rockefeller, founder of Standard Oil, wrote, "One of our greatest helpers has been the State Department. . . . Our ambassadors and ministers and consuls have aided to push our way into new markets in the utmost corners of the world."

World War I increased everyone's dependence on oil. Britain had to capture Basra and Baghdad to protect its Persian oil fields and refinery. Increasingly, the United States was providing most of the oil that the Allies required for their navies and their automobiles, trucks, and tanks. The United States competed for foreign sources of oil.

The global battle royal over petroleum resources continued into the postwar years. Britain concentrated on controlling oil sources in the Middle East, while the Netherlands secured Southeast Asia. In Persia (which became Iran), the British government fought American investment; while in Mesopotamia, a consortium of American companies negotiated with British Petroleum, the dominant company. First Lord of the Admiralty Winston Churchill declared that oil meant "mastery."

Whether its direct cause was religious fanaticism or petroleum competition, Imbrie's murder was a consequence of this new importance of oil. Oil became a crucial component of world diplomacy, and the Middle East became a cockpit of the power struggle.

Before the dependency on oil, this vast Muslim area had been fought over because of its strategic location; the Christian British Empire had to secure its hold on the routes to India. "The Great Game," as the British called the tussle for the heart of Central Asia, was played out between Russia and Britain. It consisted of controlling an Islamic buffer between the two countries.

Growing German interest in the Middle East drove Britain and Russia to share the rights to Persian oil: Russia took over the northern oil fields, and Britain, the southern. The British created the publicly owned Anglo-Persian Oil Company. In June 1914, the British Parliament, pressed by Winston Churchill, acquired 51 percent of the company. That was less than two weeks before Archduke Franz Ferdinand was assassinated at Sarajevo.

. . .

The Russian Revolution and the severe terms of the Treaty of Brest-Litovsk sidelined Russia from the "Great Game." But the British still wanted a buffer zone running from Egypt to India that was secure from Russian encroachment. Britain and France tried to divide up the Middle East with the secret 1916 Sykes-Picot Agreement; France was to receive Syria, and Britain, Mesopotamia. Palestine would be internationalized. The route to India would then be defined, and the two allies would control the Middle East's oil.

The demand for oil and the simultaneous rise of Zionism stimulated America's involvement in the Middle East. President Wilson and Congress tended to support Jewish aspirations, while the State Department gave greater weight to Arab objectives—and oil. The State Department's position was based on a combination of hardheaded concerns about Western access to Middle East oil and, in some cases, emotional feelings approaching anti-Semitism.

At the Peace Conference in Paris, President Wilson assured the British and the French that he understood their interests, but he insisted that Britain and France not rule over other peoples unless those people desired it. Frustrated by the Allies' web of secret treaties, Wilson formed an international commission to gather information on the Middle East. Britain and France refused to participate, fearing that an objective study might derail their agendas. Undeterred, the Americans formed a unilateral commission. Wilson named to it not seasoned diplomats but a college president and a plumbing-supply millionaire: Dr. Henry C. King, the president of Oberlin College, and Charles R. Crane of Chicago. Secretary Lansing privately said Wilson's attraction to appointing inexperienced men was "amazing." (In 1909, President Taft had appointed Charles Crane as minister to China, but he was never sent because Taft was shocked by his dislike of "Japs and Jews.")

During the summer of 1919, King and Crane spent forty-two days in the Middle East, interviewing a variety of people and receiving petitions. They submitted to Under Secretary of State Frank Polk a voluminous report recommending that the League of Nations' mandates govern the Arabic-speaking areas of the former Ottoman Empire, a greater Syria, Mesopotamia, a separate Armenia, a "Constantinopolitan State," and a state in Asia Minor. King and Crane recommended that the United States should be the single mandatory power over all these lands. They declaimed "the injustice of the Zionist program" and demanded that the idea of a Jewish state in Palestine "should be given up."

King and Crane's report was not made public for years. And later, Crane supported Hitler. He told William E. Dodd, the ambassador to Germany, that he was going to propose to the pope an agreement with the Islamic world to protect Muslims against the Jews who were taking over Palestine. Dodd thought Crane, with his extreme ideas, seemed in his dotage. Introduced to Ibn Saud by H. St. John B. Philby, father of the future notorious British spy Kim Philby, Crane befriended the king of Arabia and also tried to persuade the Grand Mufti of Jerusalem to join the Vatican in an anti-Jewish campaign.

On September 11, 1922, Congress passed a joint resolution favoring a Jewish homeland in Palestine, but the State Department downplayed it as merely a statement of sympathy. Zionists charged anti-Semitism, but the department was certain that Zionism angered Arabs, who controlled sources of Middle Eastern oil, and that was not in the United States' interest.

THE OPEN DOOR REVISITED

After World War I, the British dominated the Middle East. Although the massive Standard Oil Company of New York (Socony) clandestinely sent geologists to Mesopotamia in the fall of 1919, the British government prevented them from prospecting. In Palestine before the war, Socony had bought from the Ottomans seven tracts of land; but after the war, the British would not let the Americans search for oil. When Socony was allowed to analyze the sites, it was dismayed that it had to inform the British fully of its findings.

Persia emerged from World War I in chaos. Britain sought to monopolize oil rights there by jamming through the Anglo-Persian Agreement of August 1919. The State Department protested to the British; and John L. Caldwell, now the American minister in Tehran, made sure the Persians were informed of America's interest. The Iranian parliament, expecting that U.S. companies would step in, refused to ratify the agreement with Britain.

Violence began in Egypt and spread to Afghanistan, Transjordan, Palestine, and Iraq. In Iraq, both Shi'ite and Sunni Muslims rose up against British rule in 1920, and suppressing that revolt cost Britain almost two thousand casualties, including 450 killed.

Colonel Reza Khan took command of a force of six thousand Persian soldiers and, in 1921, marched on Tehran and seized power. But he soon disowned the Anglo-Persian Agreement and signed a treaty with Soviet Russia.

The United States reverted to a strategy that had served it well in East Asia, establishing an Open Door policy in the Middle East. "Open-door imperialism" avoided the burdens and immoralities of traditional colonialism but still hung onto a share of resources and markets. Historian Robert Buzzanco wrote, "Pursuing open doors globally, the ruling class [of the U.S.] overwhelmed weaker peoples, people of color, peasants and farmers; it denied self-determination and national sovereignty and diminished and crushed movements for broader or participatory forms of democracy."

Lewis Heck, the American commissioner at Constantinople, told the Peace Conference in Paris that the Turks continued to mistreat Christians returning to Turkey's interior. He urged that consulates be reopened in Smyrna and Aleppo to protect them. Turkish leaders could not control the havoc in the interior, where Mustafa Kemal, the hero of Gallipoli, had begun building a nationalist base. (In 1934, he would be given the honorific title Ataturk, "Father of the Turks.")

The American mission in Turkey was upgraded under the leadership of Rear Admiral Mark L. Bristol, commander of U.S. naval forces in the Levant, who opposed the United States' accepting a mandate over any part of Turkey. Whether the United States should accept a mandate to guard the Armenians also was seriously debated, but after the Senate refused to ratify the Treaty of Versailles, any American mandate in the Middle East became impossible.

The European powers met at San Remo, Italy, in April 1920 and carved up the Arab-speaking parts of the defeated Ottoman Empire. Robert Underwood Johnson, the American ambassador to Italy, a poet, and formerly the editor of *The Century* magazine, helped Britain and France quietly divide the oil resources between themselves.

As planned all along, the French took Syria, and Britain, Mesopotamia.

The British gave France 25 percent of the oil that the Turkish Petroleum Company discovered in Mesopotamia. This enabled the U.S. oil companies to work with the Turkish company, which was already exploiting Iraq's oil fields.

A treaty signed at Sevres on August 10, 1920, in effect abolished the Ottoman Empire. And once the government in Constantinople was forced to sign that severe treaty, the Soviets' Georgi Chicherin developed diplomatic relations with the Turks to counteract Britain. The Russians fed arms and supplies to Mustafa Kemal's Nationalists at Angora (Ankara). And invasions of Turkey, by Greece in 1919 and by Britain the next year, entrenched Kemal.

The San Remo agreement was leaked to the Standard Oil Company of New Jersey, and as a result the State Department demanded that American oil companies be allowed to participate. But American claims were dismissed on the grounds that the United States already produced 80 percent of the world's oil. Consequently, Congress passed an act denying drilling rights to foreign companies whose governments denied them to Americans.

Rear Admiral Bristol opposed partitioning Turkey and creating an independent Armenia, although consuls in the area reported that thousands of Armenians were being massacred. In March 1921, Bristol wrote of reports that the Turks massacred thousands of Armenians in the Caucasus, "Such Armenian reports are absolutely false. . . . The Near East is a cesspool that should be drained and cleaned out without any halfway measures."

An American from the high commission at Constantinople, Cornelius van H. Engert, disputed Bristol's statements that no Armenians were being massacred. The State Department found it difficult to discern the truth in these conflicting reports. Engert investigated the chaos in Syria and recommended that the Europeans should either send large forces to the Middle East or leave. In April, the United States recognized an independent Armenia, and the Supreme Council in Paris asked the United States to accept a mandate over it.

Arab leaders wanted independence from both Turks and Europeans, but the area's Christians and Jews dreaded a separate Arab kingdom. The Allies, led by the British, put troops ashore at Constantinople and arrested Turkish nationalists, while the French marched into Damascus. Arab forces fled.

In June 1922, Congress passed a joint resolution expressing sympathy for a national home for the Jews. But the State Department refused to act on it, saying American policy was to avoid intervening in these issues. Historian Bernard Lewis wrote, "By 1920, it seemed that the triumph of Europe over Islam was complete. . . . It seemed that the long struggle between Islam and Christendom, between the Islamic empire and Europe, had ended in a decisive victory for the West. But the victory was illusory and of brief duration."

POKER GAME IN LAUSANNE

Throughout this period, Rear Admiral Bristol stubbornly stood up for American rights against British attempts to rule the Middle East. Bristol protested to Mustafa Kemal that the Turks were deporting young Greek men to the interior with a great loss of lives. The Near Eastern Division of the State Department, in the best bureaucratic style, told the Secretary of State that Bristol should not have protested to Kemal because the United States did not recognize him. But, added the division, perhaps saving ten thousand lives made his action appropriate.

In January 1921, representatives of the Ankara government of Mustafa Kemal sought out the captain of an American destroyer at Samsun to open relations with the United States. The Ankara government organized most of Turkey, and Julian Gillespie, the assistant trade commissioner at Constantinople and an official of the Department of Commerce, reported that the Turks wanted closer economic ties with the United States. Then, as a result of Gillespie's visit, Foreign Service Officer Robert W. Imbrie was sent to Ankara officially, and after four months there, he warned that American companies should not invest in Turkey without precautions.

The Allied foreign ministers conferred in Paris in March 1922 on the future of the Near East. Ambassador Myron T. Herrick, now back at Paris, watched out for American interests. From Constantinople, Rear Admiral Bristol cabled that the Allies' peace proposals were in "the most authentic traditions of the worst kind of temporizing and ambiguous diplomacy."

The nationalist Turks defeated the Greek army, burned Smyrna, and slaughtered thousands of Greeks. The Nationalists then controlled Anatolia except the region around the straits. In October, Bristol asked that USS

Utah be sent to Constantinople to protect the Turkish threat against the straits. This led to an armistice and a new conference at Lausanne.

Secretary of State Charles Evans Hughes refused to accept British charges that American policies were to blame for the war between Turkey and Greece. He asserted, "Diplomacy in Europe for the last year and a half was responsible for the late disaster."

Acting through George B. McC. Harvey, the U.S. ambassador to the Court of St. James's, the British foreign secretary, Lord George N. Curzon, asked the United States to participate in the Lausanne conference, at least as far as the freedom of the straits was concerned. State's Near Eastern Division, under Allen Dulles, defined broader American interests, including the rights of individual Americans, the protection of charitable and educational institutions, commercial rights, protection of minorities, and the freedom of the straits.

The Lausanne conference opened on November 20, 1922. Richard W. Child, the U.S. ambassador to Italy, led the American delegation, with Admiral Mark Bristol, high commissioner to Turkey, and Joseph C. Grew, minister to Switzerland, as his deputies. The sultan's departure in a British warship from Constantinople, which the Turks had conquered back in 1453, marked the end of the old empire.

Ambassador Richard Child was a self-confident young man who knew little about the Middle East. Grew noted in his diary that Child regarded the conference as a poker game and studied delegates' expressions to read their minds. Grew said admiringly, "It is surprising how often this becomes possible. Old world diplomacy is by no means a thing of the past. We are running up against it every day."

Child and Grew visited privately with Benito Mussolini, the premier of Italy, in his hotel room and briefed him on the United States' goals at the conference. Mussolini assured them he wanted cooperation between Italy and the United States. Grew's impression was that Mussolini was "a simple, open, direct, strong man of the people, the patriot rather than the statesman."

Ambassador Child reasserted the United States' interest in an Open Door policy, speaking at length on the importance of keeping the straits open at all times for the commerce of the world.

In January 1923, the British and Turks deadlocked over the disposition and boundaries of the vilayet of Mosul, which was rich in oil and which the British considered the military core of Persia. Child, Bristol, and Grew all tried to help the Turks and the British locate some common ground on the issues that divided them. But the Americans insisted that any treaty achieved at Lausanne omit mention of the Turkish Petroleum Company, because the United States had an interest in participating in that enterprise.

At the last moment, the conference broke down when Turkey refused to sign the treaty drafted by the Allies. After the Turks walked out, Child, Bristol, and Grew made one final effort to bring the Turkish leaders around. They won some concessions, but by the time they drove to the railroad station to bring them to Lord Curzon, leader of the British delegation, his train had left Lausanne. Frustrated, Grew noted, "Patience was the necessary element which Curzon lacked and now I know that without that quality it is useless to try to deal with the Turk."

The conference reopened on April 23, 1923, with Grew now leading the American delegation. The British did their best to prevent his active participation in the conference. And the Greeks and Turks threatened to go to war against each other over a demand for reparations. Another issue that was never formally discussed but hung in the air was the so-called Chester concession. Admiral Colby M. Chester, U.S. Navy, and his business partners in the Ottoman-American Development Company had, before World War I, sought oil and railroad concessions in Mesopotamia. After the war, Grew worked to make sure that the French, who opposed the concession to the Americans, would not discuss it at Lausanne. Grew wanted the issue settled by arbitration, not by negotiation. With Secretary of State Hughes' encouragement, he sided with the Turks against the Allies until they granted the Chester Concession.

On July 24, the Allies and Turkey agreed on the Treaty of Lausanne, by which Turkey gained its independence as a nation. Although not all American individual rights were assured, an Open Door policy was agreed to. The straits were demilitarized, and an International Straits Commission was created under the League of Nations, which prevented American membership.

Climaxing two months of negotiations, Joseph Grew and thirty-eight-year-old Ismet Pasha, the able leader of the Turkish delegation at Lausanne, signed a treaty of amity and commerce. But the U.S. Senate rejected it in a close vote, partly because it did not provide privileges for Christians or for an independent Armenia. Grew's experience in Lausanne made him realize how important it was for the United States to "avoid getting mixed up in the political schemes of Europe."

. . .

The Warren Harding administration was, unsurprisingly, much more amenable than Wilson's to promoting American oil interests east of Suez. In 1923, Britain granted seven American oil companies, led by Standard Oil of New Jersey, a 20 percent share in Mesopotamia's oil.

Four years later, a gusher named Baba Gurgur demonstrated that oil in great quantities could be obtained from Mesopotamia. In 1928, a combine of British, French, Dutch, and American interests created the Iraq Petroleum Company. And in 1933, Standard Oil of California won an exclusive concession in the Kingdom of Saudi Arabia, which was not under British control. The United States was now fully engaged in the Middle East.

Persia offered the United States oil concessions in its five northern provinces in order to block British expansion. But the Harding administration required that private petroleum companies, not the government, make the arrangements. Even though American diplomats in Persia were directed to help U.S. companies gain oil rights, the American companies were reluctant to invest their capital in such an unstable country, a reluctance the British understood.

When two American companies, Standard Oil and Sinclair, did begin competing for concessions in the north, Secretary Hughes instructed the American consul in Tehran to remain strictly impartial. These two principles, government avoidance and equality of commercial opportunity, undermined the United States' ability to compete.

By 1921–24, British-American competition in Persia was at its peak. Persia tried to keep the Anglo-Persian Oil Company out of the northern provinces, offering Standard Oil of New Jersey a fifty-year oil concession in exchange for a $5 million loan secured by royalties from the Anglo-Persian Oil Company in the south. The British squashed that scheme by stopping payments of the royalties.

Standard Oil then sought a cooperative agreement with Anglo-Persian Oil that would include participation in Turkish Petroleum in Mesopotamia and Palestine. This interested the British because it would help keep out the Russians. The State Department supported cooperation between the British and American companies, both nations deciding that teamwork was preferable to a destabilizing competition. But the Persians objected to the deal, and Bernard Gottlieb, the American consul at Tehran, informed Washington that the Russians would challenge British interests in taking any oil from what the Russians regarded as their sphere of influence.

In 1922, the Sinclair Oil Company arrived in Persia and doubled the ante, offering a $10 million loan in return for oil concessions in the north. But the British again prevented the use of their royalties to secure the loan. Upon the death of Robert Imbrie, Sinclair's representative immediately left Tehran for Moscow, and the British regained the initiative for Persian oil. In 1998, Mamed Abbasov wrote in the *Journal of Azerbaijani Studies*:

> There were different versions of Imbrie's murder. Most of them pointed in the direction of the Anglo-Persian Oil Company's intrigues. Whether Imbrie was killed by the British or another group, the result of the assassination served the cause of the Anglo-Persian Oil Company. This incident won a negative victory for the British, just as they wished. . . . Having been left tete-a-tete with the government supported Anglo-Persian Oil Company, the American oil corporations were unable to achieve any victory in obtaining oil concessions in Iran, and were thus forced to withdraw.

JOSEPH GREW AND KEMAL ATATURK

The bilateral treaty between the United States and Turkey, which had been negotiated at Lausanne, was rejected by the U.S. Senate in January 1927. Admiral Mark Bristol did restore diplomatic relations with Turkey, and Joseph Grew went to Constantinople as ambassador. He and his family were accompanied on the dock in New York City by a Secret Service agent and a member of the New York bomb squad. An Armenian activist had threatened to kill either the Turkish ambassador to the United States or Ambassador Grew. But the Grews sailed without incident.

Their arrival at Constantinople was more elaborate. The embassy launch brought the entire diplomatic staff out to meet their ship. The Grews' Cadillac, shipped over from Washington, was waiting with a Turkish chauffeur and a *Kavass,* an embassy guard, and drove them up the steep hill into the Pera section to the embassy. Seduced by the beauty of the place,

Grew wrote in his diary at sunset, "The water nearly approached, I think, the color of lapis lazuli and the tops of the waves were very nearly carmine. That sounds crazy but it didn't look so. It took my breath away for sheer beauty."

Three days after his arrival, Ambassador Grew took the night train to Ankara and met with the minister of foreign affairs, setting up relations with Turkey's new government in its new capital. Grew had to manage an embassy that functioned in two cities more than two hundred miles apart. And there were other challenges. After some time in Turkey, he observed, "In this country, more than at any post at which I have served, the facts necessary to present a subject adequately are often not available and no amount of industry can elicit them. In Turkey, the borderline between fact, fiction and rumor and gossip is often untraceable."

Grew's most controversial task was to persuade Kemal Ataturk's government, which detested foreign influences, to reopen American schools that had been closed. When Grew left Turkey five years later, he was given a farewell luncheon at which he said, with obvious satisfaction, "The practical and eminently successful working out of a new policy of international friendship to take the place of the old policy of international bickering, suspicion and enmity, has been one of the most inspiring experiences in history."

By the mid-1930s, the discovery of oil in Bahrain, Kuwait, and Saudi Arabia; a frenzy of exploration and exploitation; and the Great Depression transformed a world shortage of oil into a surplus. Britain turned over its interest in Kuwait's oil to United States interests.

Andrew Mellon, the seventy-seven-year-old U.S. ambassador to London and one of the richest Americans, won a Kuwait concession for his Gulf Oil Company. His conflict, acting as both diplomat and businessman, was so flagrant that the State Department had to warn him. The answer was a joint venture between Anglo-Persian and Gulf called the Kuwait Oil Company with a seventy-five-year concession.

In 1936, two powerful New York investment bankers, James Forrestal and Paul Nitze, designed a strategy by which Standard Oil of California (Socal) and Texaco, under the name Caltex, could combine their oil efforts in Bahrain and Saudi Arabia. Although Socal moved quickly, the United States was slow to recognize the importance of Saudi Arabia. It did not accredit Bert Fish, FDR's Florida campaign manager, as its minister to Saudi Arabia until 1939, and it did not open a one-man legation there until 1942. By then, World War II had interrupted the worldwide competition over oil.

THE UNITED STATES STRIKES SAUDI OIL

The United States was late in entering the Great Game. Only in 1931 did the United States and the kingdom of Abdul Aziz bin Abdul Rahman al Saud realize that they both could benefit if they strengthened their bilateral relations.

Saudi Arabia granted an oil concession to Standard Oil of California, and on February 18, 1943, under Executive Order 8926, President Roosevelt declared the defense of Saudi Arabia vital to the defense of the United States.

On September 26, 1945, President Harry Truman forcefully advocated admitting a hundred thousand more Jewish displaced persons into Palestine. Abdul Aziz was shocked. And when Congress adopted unlimited Jewish immigration into Palestine, Abdul Aziz called it a "betrayal." But, always fearful of Hashemite rivalry, he had nowhere to turn except to the United States. Although he saw American support of Zionism as unfriendly to the Arabs, he continued to seek American military and economic aid. In the end, the United States, Saudi Arabia, and Israel forged a lasting combine.

THE WESTERN HEMISPHERE DISCOVERS OIL

In 1925, Mexico's congress passed laws that endangered American property rights. The State Department had the laws interpreted so they would not be applied retroactively. Ambassador James R. Sheffield, a New York corporate lawyer and reform Republican, visited President Plutarco Calles, of Mexico, who vilified the United States and said he planned to expropriate American land and mineral rights. Sheffield was determined to protect American interests from "the Bolshevik tendencies" of the men ruling Mexico and recommended the use of force if necessary. The American business community in Mexico supported Sheffield, but his vigorous stance aroused opposition among Mexicans and among Americans at home. When he resigned in 1927, he was succeeded by his friend and President Coolidge's Amherst classmate, Dwight Morrow.

By the 1930s, Mexico was supplying 20 percent of U.S. oil. But Mexican oil required foreign capital, and violence made Mexico most unattractive to investors.

Franklin Roosevelt's Good Neighbor policy toward Latin America undercut political support for the Western Hemisphere oil companies. In March 1938, President Lázaro Cárdenas expropriated the Mexican oil industry, initiating a prolonged struggle for control. Mexico broke diplomatic relations with Britain. When U.S. Ambassador Josephus Daniels tried to cool the crisis, a British embargo on Mexican oil left the Fascist nations as its main remaining markets.

With the onset of World War II, the United States no longer allowed Mexican oil to reach the Axis powers. And after Pearl Harbor, Mexico broke relations with the Axis; Ambassador George S. Messersmith wrote, "Japan could have done us no better service." The Mexican company, Pemex, became the world's first state-owned oil company.

The war could have been an opportunity, but the State Department missed it. Secretary Hull and Assistant Secretary Breckinridge Long fired Germans working for U.S. companies. After Pearl Harbor, some four thousand Germans were confined in U.S. internment camps. And the pressure for reliable supplies of energy led to the exploration for alternative sources. The diplomacy of oil is endlessly changing and endlessly challenging.

28

"A Single Unified Service"

1920–45

aving experienced the nightmare of World War I, the battered world could no longer depend on the luxury of what had been called "courtier diplomacy" or "aristocratic statecraft." Traditional diplomacy had long been conducted by aristocrats and members of the elite, whose elaborate rituals and bemedaled uniforms made visible a service that carried out much of its work in secret.

The catastrophe of World War I woke great populations to the monstrous price paid when leaders failed to solve problems diplomatically and people failed to participate in their governance. Many blamed an enigmatic diplomacy conducted by the elite for the horrendous war. Although Britain attempted to democratize its foreign service, in France diplomacy remained a career for aristocrats.

Postwar America, willing or not, was a world power, a burgeoning empire, and a global trader, interacting with other nations. Communications and transport accelerated, and American diplomats abroad informed their government that conditions had changed and time had contracted. Diplomats and consuls had to ensure that American businessmen, who needed foreign markets and resources, had opportunities to compete. And American diplomats noticed that European foreign services helped their businessmen.

The United States was now a creditor nation, which aroused the attention of several of its better-placed diplomats. Ambassador George B. McC.

Harvey in London was the most astounding example. A protégé of Joseph Pulitzer, friend of Henry Clay Frick, and intimate of Warren Harding, Harvey was a prominent editor and publisher with a wide streak of ambition and self-publicity. In 1923, when Secretary of State Charles Evans Hughes was trying to persuade the British government to accept 3 percent interest on its debt to the United States, he discovered that Ambassador Harvey had already, on his own, offered the British an interest rate of 1.5 percent. Secretary Hughes ordered Harvey to stop discussing terms being negotiated. Harvey also promised the British a tax-free loan in New York and shocked London insiders by presuming to write a speech for Stanley Baldwin, the chancellor of the exchequer. As soon as President Harding died, Harvey prudently volunteered to resign from the State Department.

American traders, tourists, students, and seamen were now traveling abroad in greater numbers than ever, loading the consular service with crushing responsibilities. In addition to meeting new passport and visa requirements, the consuls administered quarantine laws, safeguarded public health on ships heading for United States ports, and performed a variety of legal services. By one count, in 1921 alone, "consuls performed 235,194 notarial acts."

Although American diplomats still came mostly from an educated elite, they were already more representative of their nation than were many of their European counterparts. The world had become faster-moving and more complex and contained more nation-states, and diplomats faced new challenges. But Americans were frequently assigned posts for reasons other than their diplomatic skills.

One of those challenges could not have been foreseen. The dictatorships of Mussolini, Hitler, Stalin, and Franco spurned both the traditional prewar diplomacy and the more open diplomacy that emerged from the war. Dictators would negotiate treaties with no intention of living up to them. Historian Maurice Pearton wrote that with Mussolini, "diplomacy ceases to be concerned with reconciling opposites; its primary task is to exploit them. . . . The Old Diplomacy had the virtue of attempting to convince; the New addressed itself to the fears of the people."

Some of the most observant American diplomats recognized that the United States foreign service was not ready to operate in the postwar world. At the Paris Peace Conference, Joseph Grew, for one, became discouraged because he saw the post of American minister handed to "out-siders" in countries created since the war. He expressed to Secretary of State Robert Lansing the hope that at least 30 to 40 percent of those lega-tions would be headed by career foreign service officers. Lansing told Grew frankly that was unlikely because the administration was under pressure to appoint influential Democrats.

Grew shared Lansing's views with J. Butler Wright, counselor of the U.S. embassy at London:

> He [Lansing] also said that, in his opinion, long service abroad as Secretary of Embassy or Legation did not, as a rule, fit a man to be a Minister or Ambassador, as it tended to narrow his point of view and render him bureaucratic.

Grew, on the contrary, believed that men were enriched by experience abroad.

Wright, Grew, and Assistant Secretary William Phillips carried on a three-way correspondence about the future of the foreign service. Grew wrote Wright that the American public believes "that the Diplomatic Ser-vice was instituted for the purpose of permitting the gilded youth of the country to shine in foreign society and to afford comfortable berths for undesirable or decayed politicians." He proposed that diplomats persuade neither the department nor the Congress but the public itself of the worth of the diplomatic service.

Public opinion, he went on, would be swayed not by skillful handling of the political situation in Silesia or Lithuania but by "the ability of the [Diplomatic] Service to ensure business, better business, bigger busi-ness." The diplomatic service must show it could help business through its contacts with "the high Government officials who alone can turn the trick."

Grew was appointed the American minister to Denmark, in part to keep an eye on what was happening in Russia. He would also later become the ambassador to Japan and undersecretary of state. On a trip home, he blamed some of the diplomats' dissatisfaction on the State Department. He wrote:

> But there is little incentive for initiative just now: the Department seems to take no interest; we never receive comments on our work

and many of our questions to governmental policy remain unanswered. When in Washington, I brought up some of these questions, but nobody seemed to know or care anything about them, and the only constructive criticism I received was: "Don't send in too much stuff." Let us hope that things will be different after March 4th (the inauguration of President Harding) and that we shall have a reorganized Department, thirsting for information, which it will be a pleasure to supply knowing that it will be appreciated, and put to use. . . .

Before World War I, the majority of young men entered the United States' diplomatic service from society's affluent, fashionably educated East Coast elements. Hugh Gibson, now the acerbic, outspoken U.S. minister to Poland, called them "the boys with the white spats, the tea drinkers, the cookie pushers."

Another observer said, "For example, Leland Harrison, Eton, Harvard (Porcellian Club), Knickerbocker Club, served in Washington as assistant secretary of state for several years, where his accent, his spats, Rolls Royce, and aloofness even among social equals were not likely to appease democratic instincts. He was an extreme case, but extremes establish popular stereotypes."

Low salaries and the lack of a reasonable retirement system meant that only a young man with a private income could aspire to a diplomatic career. It also meant that elderly diplomats often could not afford to retire and make room for younger people. Diplomat Robert Murphy later remembered, "When I first went to work in Washington (in 1917) the federal civil service had no pension plan, and every morning I would see employees hobbling on crutches to their offices or even being pushed along in wheel chairs. It was said in those days: 'Few die and none resign!'"

Hugh Gibson boldly told a congressional committee, "We are far too largely dependent upon the class of men who are not only incompetent in the service, but who could not make a decent living in private business if they had to."

THE PAIRING OF ROGERS AND CARR

In the spring of 1919, the National Civil Service Reform League identified the changes needed to fight patronage: entrance by examination, merit promotions, higher salaries, and paid transfers between the diplomatic and consular services. In London, the British were abolishing the provision that foreign service candidates meet a property qualification, and they were modernizing methods of appointments and promotions.

Wilbur J. Carr, director of the U. S. Consular Service, felt that the service that he led was better organized than the U.S. Diplomatic Service. But his long experience in office and his 1916 European tour also had made him aware of the consular service's shortcomings. He circulated all consular officers, asking for recommendations on how to improve their own service.

That summer, Congressman John Jacob Rogers, a young Republican from Massachusetts, dined in London with his Harvard Law School friend Keith Merrill and his superior, Consul General Robert P. Skinner. Over dinner, Skinner persuaded Rogers to initiate legislation folding the Diplomatic Service into the Consular Service. Back home, Rogers naively introduced a bill that would recommission all diplomatic secretaries as consular officers. Career diplomats were horrified.

Wilbur Carr may have relished the idea of giving his Consular Service dominance, but he suggested a more practical program: Combine the two services into a single Foreign Service identical for pay and promotion. Of course, such unity could work only if salaries were equalized.

So Rogers introduced a second bill, and thus began the long, embattled journey that Rogers and Carr traveled together. Rogers became the driving force bringing reform of the foreign services before Congress. Carr was the architect who shaped each new version to fit his vision of what the foreign services might become. Revisions of the Rogers bill were written and rewritten in Carr's office at the State Department.

Rogers, thirty-seven years old, was just back from a brief wartime duty in the army. He had been intrigued by international affairs since his undergraduate days at Harvard, in the same class (1904) as Franklin D. Roosevelt. He became a determined advocate of career diplomats and professional diplomacy. (He would die at age forty-five, and his wife, Edith Nourse Rogers, would replace him in Congress.)

In contrast, Carr had grown up on a farm near Taylorsville, Ohio, and now, at forty-nine, was a veteran of thirty years in the State Department, twenty of them as director of the consular service and its three hundred posts. A small, bespectacled, balding man with a neat mustache, he seemed awkward with his colleagues. He was weak on foreign policy, but he was a canny, ambitious bureaucrat, dedicated to professionalism at a time when the spoils system was in flower. And he earnestly wanted his consuls to receive the same respect as diplomats. If colleges would produce "gentlemen," he said, the State Department would turn them into diplomats. One observer portrayed him as "punctual, methodical, prudent, and disciplined, he was the typical bureaucrat. . . . He almost never lost his temper. . . . Carr amassed extraordinary power."

John Rogers and Wilbur Carr became the fathers of the modern U.S. Foreign Service. And it is quite to the point that neither of them was a member of the Diplomatic Service.

Rogers' first two bills went nowhere, but he assured the House of Representatives that if his proposals were adopted, "We shall have laid the foundation of a thoroughly progressive, modern, and businesslike foreign service. We shall go far to eliminate from the diplomatic side the idle rich young man who thinks in terms of silk hats . . . and afternoon teas."

Post–World War I events swung in Rogers' favor. In January 1920, only twelve candidates sat for the diplomatic service entrance examination. And that next October, only eighteen took the test. Secretary Lansing agreed for the first time that the two overseas services should be brought closer together and made interchangeable, and diplomatic service salaries should be raised. Lansing confessed to Rogers, "The machinery of government now provided for dealing with our foreign relations is in need of complete repair and reorganization."

President Harding declared, "American diplomatic appointments should not be regarded as mere temporary results of political football in the United States." Of course, the foreign service had been organized for political football from the beginning. Article II, section 2, of the Constitution clearly says the President alone shall "nominate, and by and with the Advice and Consent of the Senate, shall appoint Ambassadors, other public Ministers and Consuls."

Not surprisingly, a spoils system had soon developed; and in 1856, Congress started to attempt to control the worst of the spoils system's abuses with a law establishing salary scales. In 1906, President Theodore Roosevelt had condemned the spoils system as "wholly and unmixedly evil"; he said it was "primarily designed for partisan plunder." He created a board of examiners to vet the qualifications of candidates for the consular service and required that all fees consuls collected be accounted for by attaching adhesive stamps to documents. Three years later, President Taft extended civil service status to the diplomatic service.

These steps were not enough. Secretary Lansing wrote the chairman of the House Committee on Foreign Affairs, "The European war came upon the United States in 1914 as a surprise chiefly because its Department of State through inadequate equipment had been unable to gather information and interpret it in a manner which would reveal the hidden purposes of the government by which hostilities were precipitated. . . . No reasonable effort must be spared to make a similar surprise impossible in the future."

In 1915, Congress had tied promotions to men's commissions rather than to their post assignments, reordered the classes and salaries, and made other reforms. But four major institutional problems remained to be solved: First, the diplomatic service had to attract the best and the brightest, not only the best of the wealthiest. Second, the separate boxes in which the diplomatic service and the consular service operated had to be unlocked. Third, their two salary structures had to be brought into sync so that officers could be shifted between diplomatic and consular assignments. Finally, the "brain drain" had to be slowed; able men had to be kept from leaving for better-paying jobs in the private sector, and older men who could not afford to retire needed to be dislodged.

By the summer of 1922, Rogers and Carr fashioned a bill to which Secretary of State Charles Evans Hughes gave his crucial support. And when Hughes obtained President Harding's endorsement, Rogers introduced the new bill, which began, "That hereafter the Diplomatic and Consular Service of the United States shall be known as the Foreign Service of the United States."

CREATING "FOREIGN SERVICE OFFICERS"

This was the key. Rather than being designated as Diplomatic officers or Consular officers, all of those below the rank of minister would be commissioned and paid as Foreign Service officers. However, no such title existed under the international rules by which nations had agreed, in 1815, to send envoys abroad. So, the President assigned the "Foreign Service officers" to duty as either a diplomatic officer or a consular officer or both.

This "interchangeability" was new—and controversial. Rogers' revised bill proposed either to recommission all 120 diplomatic secretaries and 521 career consular officers (below the grade of minister) as Foreign Service officers, or to retire them. If adopted, the United States, for the first time, would have a formal and unified Foreign Service.

Even though the proposal would raise both diplomats' and consuls' salaries, diplomats disliked being grouped with consular personnel. Among those who spoke up in opposition were Under Secretary William Phillips; Lewis Einstein, minister to Czechoslovakia; Ulysses Grant-Smith, minister to Albania; and DeWitt Poole, a consular officer who had served in Russia and later became director of the School of Public and International Affairs at Princeton University. William R. Castle, chief of the Division of Western European Affairs and scion of a wealthy family on Hawaii, continued to preach that no one without a large income should be admitted to the diplomatic service; to succeed, he said, diplomats needed an affluent upbringing.

These men cherished the prewar diplomacy. They thought intellect was less important than personality, social status, and poise. They revered breeding and background. And they dreaded being assigned pedestrian consular work in ugly industrial cities and unhealthy ports. One diplomat joked that the definition of "a man in a sweat" was a consul at an embassy dinner.

Lansing had another criticism. Rogers' bill failed to cover officers of the State Department in Washington, who belonged to neither overseas service.

Striking a narrower, more political note, Joseph Grew expressed concern that Wilbur Carr would "bureaucratize" the Diplomatic Service, which would be swallowed up by Carr's larger and better-organized Consular Service. Grew, Castle, and Hugh Gibson met privately and schemed to counter this threat to the Diplomatic Service by proposing the whole system be led by a powerful chief of personnel identified with neither branch.

Critics grew edgy. Hugh Gibson in Switzerland tried to talk Grew into appearing before the House Committee on Foreign Affairs. Gibson said Grew would have to show that American diplomats spoke "American" and could "find their way in and out of a drawing room without the use of a monocle." With a touch of humor, Grew declined, writing Gibson that "people who talk through their nose and spit on the floor will cut a lot more ice than those who try and talk like Englishmen." In the end, Gibson himself sailed home and testified.

In December 1922, the House Committee on Foreign Affairs, which included John Rogers, held hearings. Secretary Hughes made the opening argument, "Low salaries are keeping out men who might invigorate the Diplomatic Service." He said, "The days of intrigue to support dynastic ambitions, to promote the immediate concerns of ruling houses, are over."

Wilbur Carr acknowledged that the President already had the authority to move a man between the diplomatic and consular services, but pointed out their salary scales were so disparate that this could almost never be done.

As to the "cookie pushers," Rogers told the committee, "I have seen some of these young secretaries, who have had exceptional social opportunities and advantages in the capitals abroad, become the most abject followers of the social regime in the foreign capital. One of the things that I hope is going to follow from this bill is to send some of these de-Americanized secretaries to Singapore as vice consul, or to force them out of the service." Carr agreed with Rogers.

Consul General Skinner, who had arrived the night before from London, took another tack to win over the Republican-dominated Congress. He began, "Mr. Chairman, this bill is a business bill." He promised the bill would assist international commerce in a businesslike way.

Congressman Tom Connally, Democrat from Texas and a veteran of two wars, asked skeptically, "What is the matter with our foreign service?"

Skinner answered him directly:

> It lacks stability; it lacks unification; it lacks special training among the higher diplomatic officers where such training and experience are most necessary. It is not properly housed, and in the higher diplomatic offices the rate of pay is such that only rich men can accept the positions.

Carr shrewdly emphasized that while Congress could not tie the President's hand in appointing or promoting diplomatic secretaries and consuls, it could regulate the new class of Foreign Service officers.

When the committee met the following week, John W. Davis, former ambassador to London, pleaded for reform of the entire foreign service, saying that in London serious young diplomatic officers often came to ask his advice about staying in the service. And he had to tell them that, in justice to themselves, they should get out because there were no incentives, salaries were inadequate to support a family, and they faced the "fear of a dependent and penniless old age." Davis said that his expenses in London were nearly three times his salary.

The committee reported out an amended bill on January 7, 1923. Rogers told the House triumphantly, "We shall get rid of the caste system, of a system where the diplomatic side of the service sometimes looks down on the consular side. We shall create a spirit of loyalty to a single unified service."

Significantly, his bill closed the gap between diplomatic and consular salaries. The then existing scale for diplomatic officers rose in four steps from $2,500 to $4,000; the scale for consuls had twenty-five levels, climbing from $1,500 to $12,000. (The lowest living wage for a day laborer in New York City at the time was $2,600.) Rogers protested the existing number of steps: "Four is too few, just as 25 is . . . absurd."

He proposed that the Foreign Service have one scale with nine steps for both diplomats and consuls alike. The scale would start at $3,000 a year (class 9) and climb to $9,000 (class 1) for the rank just below that of minister. Rogers asserted that the nine-rung ladder would be "one of true merit, an American ladder."

The main way his proposed bill would touch diplomats of the rank of minister or above was in the so-called "representation allowance" that embassies would receive to help pay entertainment expenses. Also, officers who served as chiefs of missions could return to their career track. New appointments would be based on examination and a period of probation or by transfer from the State Department after five years' service.

Tom Connally rose to attack the bill. He contended that other countries did not use the term "Foreign Service officer." He declared the designation was meaningless "the moment the foreign-service officer leaves the shores of the United States and comes in contact with the diplomatic or consular officers of other countries."

Connally condemned the bill's retirement plan as more generous than the government could afford. And salary increases would cost the government an additional $528,000 annually.

The ranking Democrat on the Committee on Foreign Affairs, Congressman J. Charles Linthicum of Maryland, spoke in favor of the bill. He admonished that "the turnover in the diplomatic service is tremendous and extremely injurious to the service and to the country." Diplomats often returned poorer than when they went overseas. Rogers cited one diplomat who had resigned after sixteen years because he wanted to leave something for his wife when he died.

Linthicum emphasized that older men who did not retire clogged up the rolls, blocking the promotions of younger men. Under present salaries, he said, young men could not hope to raise a family. He asked, "Shall our Government be a party to a service which compels celibacy?"

THE LAST BATTLE

On February 8, 1923, the House passed the Rogers bill by 203 to 27. The Senate's Committee on Foreign Relations swiftly and unanimously reported it out without amendment. The Senate was ready to pass it by unanimous consent, but Senator Thomas Sterling of South Dakota objected, and even a letter from President Harding could not change his mind. The 67th Congress adjourned on March 4 without the Senate having acted on the bill.

Its sponsors had to start over. The following October, Secretary of State Hughes obtained President Coolidge's endorsement of the bill, and Rogers introduced it again. Senator Henry Cabot Lodge, also of Massachusetts, introduced an identical bill in the Senate.

The House Committee on Foreign Affairs held hearings, and the House debated the bill on April 30, 1924. This time, each side had one hour. Connally claimed the hour against the bill. The fight was still on.

Rogers assured the House that the proposed reforms were affordable. For the previous fiscal year, he said, Department of State expenditures totaled $8,435,000, and receipts totaled $7,981,000. The net cost to the taxpayers was less than a million. He predicted his bill would increase that cost by only $345,000 a year. Observing that a coast-defense gun cost $2 million, he said, "We must have proper defense, but, gentlemen, in my judgment, if you can give us the best foreign service that the country can provide, you are doing a lot more toward peace insurance than you are by multiplying munitions of war." Applause greeted that.

"What are we going to do under this bill?" Rogers asked. "Every young man, when he is originally appointed to the unified foreign service, is going to be sent to a consulate. He is going to be sent to Singapore, perhaps, or to the West Coast of Africa or to some point in the Transvaal or to Saigon. He will not find social opportunities awaiting him in those cities. He will rather find an opportunity for the hardest kind of work." And he will become a better public servant.

Rogers defended the proposed retirement program; under it, he said, the career Foreign Service would for the first time be treated like the Army and Navy and the Federal judiciary. He added that Civil Service employees were taxed 2.5 percent of their annual salaries for retirement, but under the proposed law Foreign Service officers would contribute 5 percent of theirs.

Congressman Ross A. Collins, a lawyer from Meridian, Mississippi, spoke in opposition, "It is a pay increase bill, and that is all there is to it."

Linthicum responded that the British ambassador to Portugal receives $19,466 and the British ambassador to Uruguay was paid $29,439, while in both cases the American ambassador received $10,000.

Connally attacked again. He said his greatest objection was to the proposed retirement pay. Under it, a secretary of embassy could retire after thirty years' service with $5,400 a year. "That is too high, gentlemen."

Henry W. Temple, Republican of Pennsylvania, came to the bill's final defense, saying that the government spent $300 million for the Army and a similar amount for the Navy and only $8 million for the conduct of foreign affairs.

After a motion to recommit was defeated 201–110, the House passed the bill, again with twenty-seven negative votes. Two days later, the Senate approved it by unanimous consent. The House agreed to four minor Senate amendments.

DIPLOMACY BECOMES A PROFESSION

On the sunny Saturday afternoon of May 24, 1924, President Coolidge signed the Rogers Act into law; it took effect on July 1 and brought the

United States Foreign Service to life. American diplomacy was now a profession, not as mature as law or medicine, certainly, and still open primarily to an elite, but nonetheless professional.

On July 3, *The New York Times* played up a different point. Its headline read: "Record Shake-Up in Foreign Service: 60 Are Out or Reduced" and "Merit Now Has a Chance." The article began, "The greatest shake-up the Foreign Service of the United States has ever experienced was announced today by Secretary Hughes. Sixty persons have been dropped from the Diplomatic and Consular Services, or reduced in rank."

The Rogers Act accomplished the most fundamental reforms in American history of the system by which the United States is represented abroad. It established a single Foreign Service that allowed officers to be assigned on an interchangeable basis between diplomatic and consular branches. It created the first uniform salary scale for both branches, making interchangeability feasible and reducing the need for private income. It granted American missions abroad representation allowances to reduce the demand on the private resources of ambassadors and ministers, making it possible to promote more trained career people to the top. And, finally, it initiated a program of retirement payments that retained able career officers and facilitated the retirement of career people at age sixty-five.

The American Consular Association, which was formed in 1918 to represent the interests of the consular corps, now was reorganized into the American Foreign Service Association (AFSA) to serve both diplomats and consuls and to begin publication of the *Foreign Service Journal*. In 1972, AFSA would also become the exclusive bargaining representative for Foreign Service employees.

President Coolidge signed Executive Order 4022 on June 7, 1924, setting rules for Foreign Service examinations and for the governance of the new Foreign Service. All admissions to the Foreign Service would be at the lowest grade, and all promotions would be filled from the lower classes. Officers and employees of the department were eligible for appointment to the Foreign Service after five years of continuous service. A Foreign Service Personnel Board would manage personnel, and a Board of Examiners would conduct examinations for appointments. A Foreign Service School would develop new appointees.

Now, newly appointed officers would serve a period of probation, during which they would undergo training in Washington before going to their first posts. The nature of this training would be determined by the Foreign Service School Board, headed by the undersecretary of state. Lectures ranged from foreign policy to consular responsibilities. For practical application, students were assigned to a geographic division of the department. All this was soon modified so that, before going through the school, new probationary officers spent at least six months at a post and gained some on-the-job experience.

THE REFORM STRUGGLES CONTINUE

The adoption of the Rogers Act did not end the struggles over reform. How the act would be administered within the State Department still had to be resolved. Two plans emerged, one developed by Wilbur Carr and Tracy Lay, head of the State Department's Budget Office, and the other by Hugh Wilson, chief of the Division of Current Information, and Joseph Grew, the Under Secretary. Grew was particularly worried that the Carr plan would, as he put it, "tend to bureaucratize the whole Foreign Service, which would take much of the spirit and morale out of the diplomatic branch at least." Grew worried that the act would have the men in the department, rather than the men in the field, control the administration of the Foreign Service.

Instead, Wilson and Grew proposed that the system be headed by a single director of personnel, who would be a member of neither branch. Secretary Hughes rejected that idea, saying that some future Secretary of State might abuse the system and appoint a politician. They ended up with a compromise executive committee of three Foreign Service officers and the Under Secretary and two assistant secretaries. The Secretary of State would break any ties. Grew pushed through this version with an executive order, over Carr's strong objections. The diplomats won that important argument; the consuls felt cheated.

All this internal maneuvering did not eliminate politics from the system. Individual senators continued to push their own candidates as ambassadors and ministers. Under Secretary Grew, still playing the game, believed, for example, that Peter Jay should be promoted from minister to Romania to ambassador to Argentina. He called on Senator Jesse Metcalf of Rhode Island, pointing out to him that only one man from his state was a chief of mission and urging him to talk to the President. Senator Walter Edge of New Jersey boosted real estate broker Ogden Hammond, who was eventually sent as ambassador to Spain. George L. Kreeck of Kansas was appointed to Paraguay to satisfy Kansas' Senator Charles Curtis.

The Rogers Act made an enormous difference. It set new standards. Two years after its passage, Under Secretary Grew read that a certain Foreign Service officer had contributed one thousand dollars to the reelection campaign of New York's Senator James Wadsworth. Grew wrote his colleague a tactful but firm letter, saying in part:

> The Rogers Act and previous legislation have aimed to take the Foreign Service out of politics and have effectively done so. The whole spirit of this legislation aims at continuous tenure of office regardless of political considerations. Foreign Service officers are to be retained and promoted on the basis of efficiency without regard to the Party in power. However, the moment a Foreign Service officer publicly and materially supports a political candidate of one party as opposed to the candidate of the other Party, he places not only himself but the whole Foreign Service, of which he is a member, in an anomalous position.

This moved a long way from the spoils system. But not all the way. Just a month later, Grew wrote a stiff note to Secretary Frank B. Kellogg, complaining about the failure to appoint more career officers as Chiefs of Mission. He charged that the administration had filled only six of fourteen vacancies for Chief of Mission with career officers. And four of those were to small Central American countries. Only one, Robert Skinner, was appointed to Europe (Greece). In summary, Grew concluded, of fifty chiefs of mission then in office, only nineteen, or about 40 percent, were career men.

He admonished the Secretary that if only a small percent of career officers could hope to be chiefs of mission, "the best young men of the country" would not choose the Foreign Service as a career. Still, the Rogers Act's career possibilities, overall, attracted larger numbers of candidates to the entrance examinations. Just after World War I, thirteen applicants applied for the Diplomatic Service exam. In January 1925, 172 candidates sat for the first examinations under the Rogers Act. And as a result, that

September the Foreign Service School graduated its first class of seventeen, including one woman.

It was not all clear sailing. At first, the Foreign Service Personnel Board established two separate promotion lists for former diplomatic and consular officers. Former diplomatic officers received what former consular officers regarded as a disproportionate share of the promotions. During the first two and a half years, 63 percent of all diplomatic officers and only 37 percent of the consular officers were promoted. In 1927, Congressman Charles Edwards of Georgia charged that "promotions and plums" were going to diplomatic officers on the basis of social position and wealth, and consular officers were being "neglected and robbed."

Grew and J. Butler Wright were accused of being the leaders of the "social diplomats" and the "tea hounds." Secretary of State Kellogg tried to calm the waters by promising to promote an equal number of former consular officers. The Senate Committee on Foreign Relations called for an investigation of the Foreign Service Personnel Board, and a Senate subcommittee found that the two-list system violated the intent of the Rogers Act. It also found that members of the personnel board themselves turned up inappropriately high on the promotion lists. The committee proposed that promotions be based on salary gradations within each class and that the board stop recommending its own members for promotion.

As a result, in 1927, the personnel board, under pressure from Congress, promoted forty-four consular officers who had been passed over since 1924. And the personnel board started using a single promotion list of both diplomatic and consular officers.

Growing pains were eased by the Moses-Linthicum Act of 1931, which placed the Foreign Service Personnel Board under the assistant secretary in charge of personnel and limited its members to Class 1 Foreign Service Officers (FSOs), the top class. No class 1 FSO was eligible to become a minister or ambassador while serving on the board or during the next three years.

The 1931 act also improved pay and allowances. It reorganized FSOs into eight classes, increasing salaries in each class, and it raised Class 1 salaries to a cap of ten thousand dollars. Small automatic annual pay increases were established, and an FSO with thirty years' service was allowed to retire before age sixty-five. The Moses-Linthicum Act went a good distance toward making workable the great changes in the Foreign Service that the Rogers Act had achieved.

The new acts gave added stature to the career Foreign Service. And Secretary Hughes stimulated President Harding to promote experienced men like Joseph C. Grew, Henry P. Fletcher, Hugh Gibson, and Ira N. Morris. President Coolidge tended to follow Secretary Hughes' lead. Still, the career heads of mission did not surpass 53 percent of the total until 1940.

State Department morale was stung by the failure of Congress to appropriate funds for the efficient running of the Foreign Service. By 1929, 37 percent of Foreign Service officers entitled to promotions had not received them for as long as six years. Secretary of State Henry L. Stimson finally persuaded Congress to fund promotions of all officers due for them.

Another regulation reduced the Foreign Service's flexibility. At the end of World War I, 18 percent of Foreign Service officers were married to women who had been born in other countries. But a President Franklin Roosevelt Executive Order in November 1936 ruled, with State Department approval, that an FSO could not marry an alien without permission.

The Great Depression required economies and wiped out some of the improvements that had been made. All promotions of Foreign Service officers were stopped, salaries cut by 15 percent, allowances eliminated, and living-cost stipends reduced by more than half. These Depression setbacks dominated the U.S. Foreign Service until the rise of international tensions in the 1930s and the approach of World War II again increased the need for Foreign Service officers. Then, some of the recently established standards were recovered.

29

Between World Wars

1920–39

On March 3, 1920, just six weeks before the payroll robbery in South Braintree, Massachusetts, that led to the executions of Nicola Sacco and Bartolomeo Vanzetti, Italian immigrants with anarchistic beliefs, a bomb exploded at the entrance to the American consulate in Zurich. And on September 16, a bomb killed thirty-eight people at midday in New York's Wall Street. In October 1921, a package addressed to Ambassador Myron T. Herrick in Paris exploded and nearly killed his valet. These violent incidents frightened many around the world, who feared that the Soviet Union's Bolsheviks were out to destroy their way of life.

General John J. Pershing, commander in chief of the American Expeditionary Forces, had announced to his troops on November 11, 1918, that "hostilities were suspended." The word "suspended" was well chosen. This peace was only a pause; in two decades, the fighting would begin again.

The two world wars were really one massive upheaval with more than twenty-two million battle deaths. The years between the two spasms of carnage were rocked by international explosions resulting from the enormous recent changes on the world's map. World War I's bloody victories and defeats, the ripping apart of empires, the destruction of homes and livelihoods, and the disruption of traditional societies stirred up instability and retribution.

Many Americans wanted to pull back into isolationism and ultranationalism, which certainly decreased the attractiveness of a Foreign Service career and damaged the morale of those already committed to one. Presidents Warren Harding and Calvin Coolidge preached "normalcy" and a return to business as the United States' business. Numerous Americans rejected the League of Nations and the World Court and tried to raise a wall of tariffs. When Adolf Hitler started to rearm Germany and Japan swallowed Manchuria, many Americans felt those events did not affect them. They feared repeating the horrors of the initial experience of worldwide war.

At a two-year-long disarmament conference, beginning in Geneva in 1932, Ambassador Hugh Gibson warned that the machinery of war again threatened civilization. In October 1933, Germany's new Nazi government walked out of that conference. And from Berlin, U.S. Consul General George S. Messersmith notified the State Department that the Nazis were rearming.

The spirit of the times was given voice on January 10, 1937, when the House of Representatives rejected, by only 209 to 188, a constitutional amendment requiring a popular referendum before Congress could declare war. That same year, in that same spirit, the State Department eliminated its Eastern European Division. But, in truth, the United States could never again excuse itself from the world's quarrels and belligerent passions.

A second stage of world war approached surprisingly fast. Hitler withdrew from the League of Nations in 1933 and began rearming in violation of the Versailles Treaty in 1934. Mussolini attacked Ethiopia in 1935. Hitler took over the demilitarized Rhineland, and civil war erupted in Spain in 1936. The Nazis invaded Austria and the Sudetenland section of Czechoslovakia in 1938. Through it all, some U.S. Foreign Service officers hobnobbed with Nazis and German industrialists; they approved Italy's invasion of Ethiopia or Franco's bringing order to Spain. They agreed with Hitler that Bolshevism was the real danger.

FDR'S DIPLOMATIC TEAM

President Franklin D. Roosevelt appointed Cordell Hull as his Secretary of State for the old wrong reasons: Hull had supported FDR's candidacy for the presidency. Roosevelt owed him for that, and he owed the South for its part in his 1932 victory. Cordell Hull was competent, but he was inexperienced in foreign affairs and in managing a government department. He was better known for his croquet parties. Still, by 1945 he would receive the Nobel Peace Prize for helping to organize the United Nations.

Roosevelt buttressed Hull with three sophisticated diplomats who shared FDR's patrician background. Elements of the spoils system were still alive at these high levels. Even before he was inaugurated, Roosevelt telephoned William Phillips and asked him to become Under Secretary of state. And he promptly sought out Sumner Welles and William C. Bullitt, both of whom were strikingly urbane, charming, and arrogant. Welles and Roosevelt had been friends since childhood, and, like FDR, Welles went to Groton and Harvard; Welles and Eleanor Roosevelt shared the same godmother. He was brilliant and capable and developed an internationalist's long view of America's active role in the world.

But he had a personal side that would bring about his downfall; he was attracted to intimacies with both women and men. (Most scandalous was his drunken pursuit of Pullman porters on the presidential train in September 1940.) Both Hull and Bullitt demanded that Roosevelt fire Welles. He refused. But when Hull threatened to resign, FDR eased Welles out.

Welles had joined the Foreign Service in 1915 with recommendations from then Assistant Secretary of State William Phillips and Roosevelt, who was then assistant secretary of the Navy. The young Welles passed the examinations with high marks. He served in Tokyo and Buenos Aires and then as commissioner to the Dominican Republic. He was a fledgling star, but his personal life alienated President Coolidge. When Coolidge refused to give him ambassadorial rank, Welles resigned.

FDR had first brought in Welles as assistant secretary of state for Latin America, and assigned him to crush violence in Cuba. Welles helped get rid of dictator Gerardo Machado. But when Cuba removed Welles' friend Carlos Manuel de Céspedes and Welles angrily recommended sending in U.S. troops, Welles was burned in effigy in Havana. His successor in Cuba, career diplomat Jefferson Caffery, was left to work with army strongman Sergeant Fulgencio Batista.

Welles' closeness to the President, and Roosevelt's growing dissatisfaction with Secretary Hull, enlarged Welles' influence. He shared Roosevelt's desire for the United States to play a larger role in world affairs, and he energetically built his own power base in the department and among newsmen.

By 1936, Under Secretary Phillips replaced Ambassador Breckinridge Long in Rome, and Welles moved into Phillips' post in Washington. Welles supplied the energy and hard work that were beyond Hull.

In Rome, Ambassador Phillips was to replace the outdated 1871 Treaty of Friendship, Commerce and Navigation. The Italians insisted that a new treaty refer to the sovereign as the king of Italy and emperor of Ethiopia. The Americans refused, and that killed the new treaty.

Phillips was not yet disillusioned with the Fascists. In April 1937, he wrote Roosevelt about Mussolini, "Through his dynamic personality and great human qualities, he has created a new and vigorous race throughout Italy. He is essentially interested in bettering conditions of the masses and his accomplishments in this direction are astounding and are a source of constant amazement to me." But Phillips grew more troubled as he dealt with Count Galeazzo Ciano, Mussolini's tough-talking son-in-law, and the German and Japanese ambassadors to Rome. Phillips felt the Fascists were closing ranks, and Munich and the *Anschluss* heightened his concern. Other Foreign Service officers also turned, slowly; Charles E. Bohlen and James C. Dunn held on to their faith in neutrality. It was not a time of daring or intellectual independence. George Kennan said it was "an unhappy time."

As Under Secretary, Sumner Welles wielded immense power on foreign policy at a crucial moment. He reorganized the State Department and ran it day by day. He created the American Republics Division and gave its direction to his assistant, Laurence Duggan. The new Division of European Affairs went to his Groton friend, Jay Pierrepont Moffat, a conservative career officer and Joseph Grew's son-in-law. And Welles found key jobs for his allies, Adolf Berle and the former undersecretary Norman Davis. He built a power center.

When World War II began, Welles attended an inter-American conference at Panama, led the State Department's postwar planning, and agreed with Roosevelt's goal of eliminating colonialism. And Welles, copying the World War I "Inquiry," set up an Advisory Committee on Problems of Foreign Relations. This time, the committee was kept within the State Department.

"DEAR BILL BUDDHA"

In November 1933, the Soviets sent over Maxim Litvinov to negotiate recognition (which the other Great Powers had already granted). Believe it or not, the U.S. delegation greeting the Soviet party at the railroad station did not wear their top hats because the men they were meeting did not represent a government they had recognized.

Roosevelt was determined to open diplomatic relations with the Soviet Union, despite the opposition of Robert F. Kelley, chief of the State Department's Division of Eastern European Affairs. Roosevelt chose for this job William Bullitt, another diplomat he found congenial; he ignored Bullitt's disastrous mission to Russia in 1919. In the meanwhile, Bullitt had married the widow of the American radical John Reed, and he had become a close friend and perhaps a patient of Sigmund Freud, with whom he wrote a book about Woodrow Wilson.

As with Sumner Welles, Bullitt's access to FDR gave him clout. While Roosevelt was still President Elect, he sent Bullitt on two secret missions in Europe. The information he gathered there must have been helpful, but at times he was grandly off the mark. After talking with a half dozen German leaders, he wrote, "Hitler is finished." Adolf Hitler became chancellor of Germany a month later.

With similar lack of prescience, on December 7, 1937 (an ironic date), Bullitt wrote FDR, "The Japanese will have their hands full with China and the Soviet Union and their one hope will be to avoid war with us."

FDR appointed Bullitt as special assistant to the Secretary of State to study the conditions needed for the recognition of the Soviet Union. And then Bullitt was named ambassador to the Soviet Union, an appointment that was controversial from the start. The British ambassador to Washington said of Bullitt, "He may be regarded as thoroughly untrustworthy, and completely unscrupulous where there is a question of taking his objective."

In Washington preparing for Moscow, Bullitt met a young Foreign Service officer, George F. Kennan, who spoke Russian and had studied the Soviet economy. He engaged Kennan as his interpreter and diplomatic secretary.

A native of Milwaukee and a graduate of Princeton, Kennan was one of the first officers to join the Foreign Service after passage of the Rogers Act. Following tours in Geneva and Hamburg, he chose Russian language study and served as a vice consul at Tallinn, Estonia, and at Riga, Latvia. In 1929, he did postgraduate study in Russian language and culture at the University of Berlin, and then he returned to the Russian section of the U.S. legation at Riga. From there he watched the Soviets. The U.S. minister in Riga was Robert Skinner, who had been so effective as consul general in London during World War I. Within two decades, Kennan would be a department expert on the Soviet Union. He would be respected and honored for his understanding and insights until his death in March 2005, at the age of a hundred and one.

A few days after engaging Kennan, Bullitt sailed for Moscow to present his credentials and locate possible quarters in Spaso House. He took along Kennan and Joseph Flack, the first secretary in Berlin. The young Kennan was thrilled. Bullitt found that the Soviet leaders feared an attack by Japan, as well as a combined attack by Germany and Poland. The Russians wanted to join the League of Nations and form an alliance with France.

Bullitt had to return home, leaving George Kennan in charge in Moscow. At the National Hotel bar, he met a bored but not boring young American, Charles W. Thayer, a polo-playing West Pointer, and put him on the payroll as a messenger. They located an old Harley-Davidson motorcycle, on which Thayer raced about the city on embassy business. They both had a wonderful unbureaucratic time until the embassy staff began arriving in March 1934 and Kennan reverted to his ordained role as a diplomatic secretary.

From Moscow, Bullitt discussed political affairs with President Roosevelt directly by telephone or letter. They chatted up each other. FDR might address him as "Dear Bill Buddha," and Bullitt would sign his letters "Yours affectionately" or "Yours permanently" and add such sycophantic comments as, "I cannot tell you how glad I shall be to see you" or "and don't forget that in Moscow there is a fellow who is very fond of you."

Bullitt wrote FDR:

If we send men [to the USSR] who will be absolutely on the level with the Soviet Government and will refrain from spying and dirty tricks of every variety we can establish a relationship which may be very useful in the future. . . . The men at the head of the Soviet Government today are really intelligent, sophisticated, vigorous human beings and they cannot be persuaded to waste their time with the ordinary conventional diplomatist.

FDR urged Bullitt to bring to Moscow only men who spoke or who could quickly learn Russian. He also wrote Bullitt, "As you will be thrown into extraordinarily close contact with all the members of your little community, you should exercise exceptional care in selecting men of congenial character and should keep a weather eye out for uncongenial wives." Bullitt collected as his associates in Moscow such future ambassadors as Kennan, Loy W. Henderson, Charles E. Bohlen, John Cooper Wiley, and Elbridge Durbrow.

Bullitt recognized early the danger of the rise of Hitler and Nazism. He gave due weight to the formation of the German air force, the adoption of universal conscription, and Britain's agreement that Germany could build submarines openly. As early as 1935, he wrote FDR, "No one in Europe is any longer thinking of peace but that everyone is thinking furiously about obtaining as many allies as possible for the next war."

The men in the U.S. Embassy at Moscow believed that the Bolshevik regime was incompetent. One of the few who disagreed was Major Philip R. Faymonville, the first American military attaché to the Soviet Union. A West Point graduate and fluent in Russian, Faymonville had served in Siberia with General Graves during World War I. Arriving in Moscow in June 1934, he developed a respect for the Red Army's modern armored and aviation forces that was not shared in the embassy. Ambassador Joseph E. Davies valued his judgments. When Germany invaded the Soviet Union in June 1941, Faymonville, now a colonel heading the Lend-Lease program for the Soviet Union, was one of the few who expected the Russians to resist successfully. He met such fierce disagreement, especially from the current military attaché, Ivan Yeaton, a passionate anti-Communist, that it required intervention by Harry Hopkins to keep Faymonville in Moscow. Retiring from the army in 1948, he became an advisor to the State Department. He had shown courage in predicting, correctly, that the German Wehrmacht could not crush the Red Army.

Soon, Bullitt and his colleagues in the State Department became convinced that the Russians' enthusiasm for cooperation with the United States was based solely on their desire for American recognition. Bullitt was horrified by Stalin's paranoid imprisonment and exile of anyone he suspected of disloyalty. And Kennan regarded Stalin as "a man of absolutely diseased suspiciousness."

During the Third Congress of the Communist International, Bullitt, bypassing the State Department, sent FDR word that U.S. secret messages and codes were being sent through Nazi Germany by open mail. He advised boldly, "I feel that it will be impossible to handle secret matters in a secret way until you decide that a 1935 Foreign Service is just as essential as a 1935 fleet and ordain a full reorganization and reconstruction [of the State Department], on the ground that a Merrimac-Monitor Department and Foreign Service, in 1935, is dangerous. It is." FDR shrewdly replied that he would not act on this until he knew that Bullitt had informed the State Department, "for I do not want them to think you are telling tales out of school! Let me know."

When the Russians asserted that their government was not responsible for actions of the Communist International, Bullitt's growing distrust of the Soviet government intensified. By the time he was ready to leave Moscow, Bullitt had reversed his view of the Bolsheviks. He wrote Secretary Hull, "Yet it must be recognized that communists are agents of a foreign power whose aim is not only to destroy the institutions and liberties of our country, but also to kill millions of Americans." Kennan observed that, as Bullitt's line hardened toward the Soviet Union, FDR turned away from him when he needed advice on Russia.

Kennan early placed Bolshevism in the continuum of Russia's ruthless oppression, which was based on mass poverty. In the Great Purges of the mid-1930s, Soviet citizens who had been friendly to Americans were liquidated, and even U.S. embassy servants and gardeners disappeared. Kennan followed the purge trials and sat through one set. He said it was "a terrible spectacle" that convinced him that the xenophobic Soviet Union was a greater danger than Nazi Germany.

By the time Bullitt moved on to be the ambassador in Paris in 1936, he was bitter toward the Soviet regime. In France, he felt totally at home, speaking French fluently (he knew no Russian). And he found in sophisticated Parisian circles a popularity that he relished. Some American diplomats criticized him for being too close to the French. He fell in love with France all over again. He asserted that only French-German harmony could prevent the Soviets from sweeping the world. Because of this view, the British secretary of state wrote, "Nobody, not even Lady Astor, now takes Mr. Bullitt seriously."

Once Bullitt left for Paris, the U.S. Embassy in Moscow carried on under career diplomat and chargé Loy Henderson. George Kennan concluded, "By the end of 1936 it was developing, we felt, into one of the best informed and most highly respected diplomatic missions in Moscow, rivaled only by the German." This sense of professionalism was upset when Bullitt's replacement proved to be Joseph E. Davies, a Democratic millionaire lawyer married to cereal heiress Marjorie Merriweather Post. At the end of Davies's first day at the embassy, the staff met in Loy Henderson's quarters and discussed resigning en masse.

The professionals despised what they regarded as Davies' ignorance of Russia and his judgments of events there. Davies even reported to Washington that the purge trials were necessary and useful. Bohlen found him superficial and Kennan considered quitting.

Davies did not think the embassy was as good as its staff did and wrote a colleague that he had found it "in a terrible condition." On May 5, 1937, Bullitt wrote FDR from Paris: "For cat's sake put through Howland Shaw as Chief of Foreign Service Personnel. The morale of the Service is becoming more demoralized every day."

Bullitt approved of FDR's appointment of Joseph P. Kennedy as ambassador to the Court of St. James's, and he asked the President to be sure to warn Kennedy that the British had all the American codes and had bugged the embassy and residence.

Bullitt came to see that Hitler's aggressions were disasters for France and England, and he argued for supporting the Allies as much as possible, but always without taking the United States into war. Like many others, Bullitt wanted peace if he did not have to fight for it.

German troops marched into Czechoslovakia on March 15, 1939. Bullitt usefully reported on French armaments and airpower, as well as Nazi military maneuvers and invasions. In August, Germany and Russia signed the treaty that freed Germany from worrying about an attack from the rear if Hitler struck France. It was the final step to war.

Hitler attacked in the west. The Belgians surrendered, and at Dunkirk the British withdrew their army from the continent. France was defeated. The Axis was triumphant.

In 1940, FDR sent Welles on a tour of Europe's warring capitals, although Hull, Bullitt, and the isolationists opposed the mission. He talked with the major leaders to see whether the war could be settled. Bullitt, who regarded himself as the President's man in Europe, had not been consulted about it, and Welles had to face Bullitt's lasting and fatal resentment. He snubbed Welles by leaving Paris before he arrived.

THE FOREIGN SERVICE CENTRALIZES

During the interwar years, the U.S. Foreign Service moved toward centralization and the implementation of the principles of the Rogers Act. By the start of World War II, most American embassies and legations included both diplomatic and consular personnel and functions. Whenever possible, the separate elements were drawn together into a single building or complex and served under one chief of mission. Consular offices outside a capital city were connected to the embassy through the head of the consular section there.

At the State Department, oversight of the Foreign Service was now in the hands of the Foreign Service Personnel Board, which controlled transfers, promotions, and discipline. The Division of Foreign Service Personnel was the board's executive arm. The board approved the rating list by which promotions were determined, and it prepared for the White House the names of Foreign Service officers judged fit to become chiefs of mission. Throughout the 1930s, approximately half of the chiefs of mission were career officers.

At the end of 1937, the Foreign Service had 703 Foreign Service officers and 733 American clerks. The clerks did not have to sit for an examination; their top pay was $4,000 a year, and they rarely could advance to become officers. The Foreign Service employed 919 non-American clerks in consular posts; in diplomatic posts, aliens could serve only as interpreters.

The process for entering the Foreign Service now started with an application, and approved candidates took written examinations over three days, covering a wide range of subjects including a foreign language. A candidate who scored 70 or better was given a half-hour oral examination designed to bring out his personal qualities. The examiners were looking mostly for "congeniality." A candidate with a total score of 80 percent was put on an eligible list. Fewer than 5 percent of those who took the written exam made it into the Foreign Service.

GETTING TO KNOW THE NAZIS

When he appointed chiefs of mission, President Franklin Roosevelt tended to shun career Foreign Service officers. He believed that they had been hired in good part for their social skills and were inclined to be too cautious and ambitious. He saw "a lot of dead wood" in the higher Foreign Service grades; he had more confidence in the men he personally chose to represent him.

FDR had a difficult time finding a replacement when Frederic M. Sackett, a wealthy businessman friend of Herbert Hoover, and a former senator from Kentucky, resigned as ambassador to Berlin in March 1933. At that crucial post, Sackett had been undistinguished; his fear was that Hitler's radicalism would push Germany to become a Communist state.

Roosevelt offered the Berlin embassy in turn to James M. Cox, his 1920 running mate; former Secretary of War Newton D. Baker; businessman Owen D. Young; and even New York Democratic boss Ed Flynn. Each one turned him down. At noon on June 8, 1933, he hurriedly telephoned William E. Dodd, chair of the University of Chicago history department, and offered him the post. He asked Dodd to decide in two hours, and the Senate took just two days to approve him. Among the few who knew Dodd, he was a popular choice.

Sixty-three-year-old Dodd was a distinguished historian but had no diplomatic experience. He was proudly a Jeffersonian Democrat. Born on a North Carolina farm, he had managed to study for his Ph.D. at the University of Leipzig, where he familiarized himself with Germany's ambitions and militarism.

During World War I, Dodd had been an early member of The Inquiry, which analyzed postwar foreign policy problems. But he came to feel that the Inquiry was confused about its purposes and withdrew. He wrote a paper warning that great corporations and rich men would try to sabotage Wilson's program for free trade and national self-determination.

A slender little man, Dodd was brilliant and both parsimonious and abstemious. He worked for FDR's nomination in 1932. When Secretary of State Hull, whom he believed to be "one of the most competent men in the government," offered him some minor diplomatic posts, he had turned them down. He told his wife they were too expensive and "my objection is to the fuss and feathers and the daily absorption with petit detail." He felt differently about the President's offer of Berlin.

Before sailing for Germany, Dodd met with Jewish leaders at the Century Association and lunched with FDR at his desk in the White House. The President spelled out his goals: to get the Germans to repay all private American loans, moderate their persecution of Jews, and agree to trade arrangements that would enable the Germans to meet their debt payments. He also reiterated that disarmament was essential if war was to be avoided. Such a program was too much to hope for.

A footnote to the Dodd story was the presence in Berlin of his daughter Martha, a former assistant literary editor of the *Chicago Tribune,* who proceeded to have affairs with assorted Nazis and a Russian intelligence officer.

Just before Dodd arrived in Berlin on July 13, 1933, George S. Messersmith, the blunt, German-speaking Pennsylvania Dutchman serving there as the consul general, wrote Under Secretary Phillips that the Nazis were converting Germany into "the most capable instrument of war that there has ever existed. . . . With few exceptions, the men who are running this Government are of a mentality that you and I cannot understand. Some of them are psychopathic cases and would ordinarily be receiving treatment somewhere. Others are exalted and in a frame of mind that knows no reason."

Messersmith, a disciplinarian in steel-rimmed glasses, had been a schoolteacher and, in 1913, decided to enter the foreign service. He failed the consular exam and then passed the diplomatic exam. But John Bassett Moore and Wilbur Carr both advised him he could not live on a diplomat's salary. He repeated the consular exam, passed, and made a name for himself as hardworking, efficient, and economizing.

By 1930, he was the consul general at the Berlin embassy, and two years later found himself in the middle of a flap not of his own making. Albert Einstein had been invited to leave Germany and do research in the United States, but right-wing organizations in the United States accused him of being a Communist and demanded that the State Department certify him. While Messersmith was away from Berlin, Wilbur Carr, chief of the consular service, ordered Consul Raymond H. Geist in Berlin to call in the Einsteins and question them. When Geist asked the Einsteins about their political views, Elsa Einstein protectively refused to answer, stormed out with her husband, and told the newspapers they demanded an apology. Walter Lippmann called for Messersmith's recall, and the American Civil Liberties Union began an investigation. But the whole matter quieted down when Secretary Stimson supported Messersmith, and Lippmann apologized.

Messersmith tried to persuade the United States to boycott the 1936 Olympics in Berlin because Hitler would not let German-Jewish athletes participate. His appeals to the State Department were ignored, but his persistence strengthened his reputation.

He gained an ally in his disgust with the Nazi regime when Ambassador Dodd reached Berlin on July 13, 1933. On his first evening in Berlin, Dodd took a stroll up the Bellevuestrasse and along the Sieges Allee in the Tiergarten among the statues of Prussian kings. He was entranced with the serenity of Berlin and optimistic about his new responsibilities. At first, Dodd was hopeful that he would find the National Socialist leaders, who had been running Germany for barely six months, reasonable men. He grew close to Messersmith, until Messersmith was promoted to minister in Austria. (That was an unusual move for a consul; and he went on to become ambassador to Cuba, Mexico, and Argentina and assistant secretary of state.)

But Dodd was soon swamped with requests to help persecuted intellectuals and Jews and decided the Nazi leaders were "adolescents in the great game of international leadership and even national guidance." Like many others, he believed that leading German conservatives could control Hitler.

Dodd warned FDR and Hull that American isolationism would lead to war. He proposed that the United States organize a British and French boycott of the Nazi Party Congress at Nuremberg in September. When Under Secretary Phillips rejected the boycott, Dodd arranged a boycott on his own. And he cautioned the foreign minister, Baron Konstantin von Neurath, who had served pre-Hitler Germany as ambassador to Rome and London, that street violence, persecution of Jews, and beating Americans for not giving the Nazi salute were hurting Germany abroad. He told the department that Neurath did not promise any changes but had seemed embarrassed.

The Nazis came to dislike the straight-talking American ambassador. They tapped Dodd's telephone and opened his mail. In order to confer, he and the British ambassador had to stroll in the Tiergarten. Dodd still hoped the Nazis could be reasoned with.

Dodd reported that some major German businessmen expected to govern through the Nazis and received large tax exemptions for their support. He tried to obtain repayment of hundreds of millions of dollars loaned to Germans by American banks, often represented by John Foster Dulles, the grandson of Secretary of State John Watson Foster.

Dodd could not stop Nazi brutality against Germans, but when they attacked American citizens and damaged American businesses, he spoke up. The wife and son of prominent American radio commentator H. V. Kaltenborn were beaten bloody in the street while the police stood by. Secretary Hull, outraged, ordered Dodd to protest personally to Hitler.

Dodd first met with Hitler on October 17, 1933, only days after he had withdrawn Germany from the League of Nations. The chancellor "ranted" about Germany's defenselessness but promised that attacks against individual Americans would be punished and that foreigners would not be expected to give the Nazi salute. Dodd described Hitler in his diary: "My final impression was of his belligerence and self-confidence."

On March 7, 1934, before leaving on a trip home, Dodd met secretly again with Hitler. This appointment was arranged by foreign press chief Ernst "Putzi" Hanfstaengl, a pre-1923 Nazi who was a Harvard graduate and whose mother was a Boston Sedgwick. Dodd and Hitler talked for almost an hour, and Dodd found Der Führer unyielding on every point he brought up. When Dodd criticized pamphlets advising German-Americans that they must always remain Germans, Hitler replied emotionally, "Ach, that is all Jewish lies."

Hitler seemed convinced that the United States was weak and could be ignored. Dodd wrote in his diary that evening, "A unique triumvirate! Hitler, less educated, more romantic, with a semi-criminal record; Goebbels and Goering, both Doctors of Philosophy, both animated by intense class and foreign hatreds and both willing to resort to the most ruthless methods. They do not love each other, but in order to maintain their power, they have to sit down together."

Dodd went home at that time, in part because he wanted to persuade Roosevelt to modernize the Foreign Service. Dodd was disturbed by what he regarded as inefficiency and profligate spending in the Berlin embassy. He was appalled by the endless diplomatic parties and complained that his wealthy staff members were attracted to cocktail parties and card playing, while he found it hard to exist on his $17,500 salary. He complained about those who came to work at ten or eleven, spent two hours in the office, took a break for lunch, and then went home at four o'clock. He identified them as Ivy League graduates and sons of rich men.

On shipboard, he wrote in his diary, "The further I go in my study of State Department policies, the more evidence there is that a clique of kins-people connected with certain rich families are bent on exploiting the Foreign Service for their set, many of them Harvard graduates who are not even well informed. Snobbery and personal gratification are the main objects with them." His attitude won him no friends at the State Department.

In Washington, he spent a week working at the State Department and met with the State Department's personnel board: Assistant Secretaries R. Walton Moore, Wilbur J. Carr, Sumner Welles ("of doubtful Cuban fame"), and Hugh R. Wilson. Dodd told them extravagant diplomacy was obsolete and urged them to make merit rather than social class the prerequisite for recruits. Under Secretary Phillips; Jay Pierrepont Moffat, chief of the Western European Division; and Wilbur Carr were known to dislike Jews and to want to keep them out of the United States. Phillips was called "a social antisemite."

Before returning to Germany, Dodd met with FDR, who asked him to greet Hitler for him "but be sure to imply no political approval of his policies." At the State Department's suggestion, he spoke at lunch with twenty newspaper editors and executives at the Century Association in New York and had dinner with Colonel and Mrs. House.

He sailed on May 9, still hoping to achieve better relations with the Nazis. But en route he read a speech by Goebbels declaring that the Jews were "the syphilis of all European peoples." And in Berlin, anti-Semitism had grown more intense. This and his meeting with Hitler drained him of any hope that the Nazis could be reasoned with. He considered resigning.

Dodd repeatedly confronted Nazi brutality. Dr. Daniel A. Mulvilhill, an American medical researcher, was knocked unconscious in the street for not saluting SA troops marching by. Violinist Fritz Kreisler was prohibited from giving concerts because he was Jewish. At a dinner at Joachim von Ribbentrop's house in Dahlem, he sat next to the wife of Count Wolf Heinrich von Helldorf, the Nazis' chief of police of Potsdam, who told him that all black people in the United States should be sterilized. Helldorf would lead the Berlin police on Kristallnacht.

At the end of June 1934, Hitler and his Nazi colleagues killed or imprisoned scores of their opponents, including Hitler's old comrade in arms, SA leader Ernst Röhm. It was politics by murder. Dodd wrote in his diary, "I decided . . . that I would never again attend an address of the Chancellor or seek an interview for myself except upon official grounds. I have a sense of horror when I look at the man."

In Vienna, George Messersmith had been the U.S. minister for barely two months when, on July 25, 1934, Austrian Nazis murdered Engelbert Dollfuss, the anti-Nazi chancellor. That evening, Messersmith cabled the State Department and described the 150 Austrian Nazis occupying the Ballhausplatz. The Austrian army arrested the Nazis. A million people turned out for Dollfuss' funeral.

Dollfuss' death was followed on August 2 by the death of Field Marshal Paul von Hindenburg, the president of Germany. Hitler promptly seized the presidency as well as the chancellorship. His command of Germany was now total.

Dodd collected information from his consuls around Germany and reported on Nazi preparations for war. Dr. Hjalmar Schacht, president of the Reichsbank, admitted to him that Hitler was preparing for war but predicted it would not happen for ten years. Dodd urged him to speak out against war, but he never did. In his diary, Dodd wrote, "The arms manufacturers over the world are the cause of most of this trouble in Europe."

At this time, the Berlin consul, Raymond Geist, wrote Jay Pierrepont Moffat at the State Department, "Many of the young Nazis are enthusiastic with regard to the military prospects. They speak of gas war, of bacteriological war, of the use of death-dealing rays. They boast that airplanes will not pass the German frontiers. Their ideas of Germany's invincibility and Germany's power in 'the next war' are really phantastic." Dodd believed the United States needed to intervene to restrain the dictators. He wrote Roosevelt, "If we had entered the League in 1919, Mussolini and Hitler would not be in existence today."

Under Secretary Phillips, in London for the five-power International Naval Conference, came over to Berlin after Christmas 1935 and asked Dodd to arrange a meeting for him with Hitler. But the chancellor was at Berchtesgaden in Bavaria for the holidays. Phillips predicted to Dodd the almost certain failure of the naval conference. (Japan and Italy did walk out.) The military attaché and Phillips drove around several German army bases but were not permitted inside them. And the American commercial attaché warned, "In two years Germany will be manufacturing oil and gas enough out of soft coal for a long war, the Standard Oil Company of New York furnishing millions of dollars to help." Phillips was amazed and distressed.

Dodd held innumerable meetings with Nazis, anti-Nazis, visiting Americans, diplomats of other nations, journalists, bankers, ministers, priests, and rabbis. He tried to say nothing that would give the Nazis an excuse to attack him. He argued over the debts that the Germans owed to American banks and the tariffs that the Nazis claimed prevented them from earning income to pay their debts. But they found ample funds to buy military aircraft, arms, and munitions.

30

Early Aggressions

1934–39

Germany possessed no monopoly on violence. On September 28, 1934, Ambassador Breckinridge Long cabled Secretary Hull that Italy was sending two hundred thousand men to Africa with tanks, artillery, aircraft bombs, machine guns, barbed wire, and five hundred thousand sun helmets. Long admired Mussolini, but for more than a year he had been advising the State Department that Italy was mobilizing to attack Ethiopia (called Abyssinia).

The department transferred a senior Foreign Service officer, George C. Hanson, the consul general in Moscow, to Addis Ababa in February 1935. While traveling to his post, Hanson was taken seriously ill, and, sailing home for treatment, he shot and killed himself.

Cornelius van H. Engert, a veteran career officer, was rushed over from Cairo to serve as the chargé d'affaires in Addis Ababa. Emperor Haile Selassie immediately berated him, charging that Secretary Hull had persuaded the Standard Vacuum Oil Company to cancel an agreement the emperor had signed with British promoter Francis Rickett for the development of Ethiopia's vast oil resources. Rickett had promised the emperor that, if he signed the oil concession, the United States would defend Ethiopia. The chairman of Standard Vacuum Oil appeared before an indignant Secretary Hull, who afterward told the press that the oil concession was a "great embarrassment" to the U.S. government. Hull punctured Rickett's scam.

Ambassador Long, in Rome, warned Hull that if Mussolini conquered Ethiopia he would send "millions of colonists" there, threatening British control over Egypt and the Suez Canal. Long counseled that Italy must be stopped. He also urged Roosevelt not to impose an oil embargo on Italy, and when he was reprimanded for bypassing the State Department, he resigned.

Mussolini, dreaming of a new Roman empire, invaded Ethiopia on October 3, 1935. Haile Selassie's primitive army was armed with obsolete rifles and had only seven flyable planes. The American chargé in Addis, Cornelius Engert, was an unusual member of the American diplomatic service. He found that to advance in the Foreign Service, he had to fit in. And he worked at it. Secretive, slight, and bespectacled, he obfuscated his ancestry, birth, and youth. He said he had been born in Vienna to Dutch parents who moved to California when he was a child. But his granddaughter, Jane Morrison Engert, wrote that his father was a Russian citizen and his mother was from Hungary.

Cornelius Engert had arrived in New York in 1904, when he was sixteen. He went to college and law school at the University of California, Berkeley, and won a fellowship to Harvard. Reinventing himself, he planned a diplomatic career, but Wilbur Carr steered him into the consular service as more fitting his financial resources. Marrying a wealthy woman helped; his wife, Sara Morrison Cunningham, was a cousin of Whitelaw Reid's wife.

Engert started as a student interpreter in Turkey in 1912 and, during World War I, advanced to legation secretary at The Hague. He also served in Tehran and Kabul, followed by four Latin American countries. And he was posted in Beijing and Cairo before Addis Ababa.

Since war was imminent in Ethiopia and reporters poured in and overwhelmed his communications, Engert imported a U.S. Navy team of four radiomen with equipment from an abandoned submarine to keep communications open. He was promoted to minister resident in April 1936, just as the emperor was forced to leave Ethiopia. On May 1, Haile Selassie and his entourage entrained for exile in Bath, England. He addressed the League of Nations in June, describing how Ethiopians were sprayed with Italian mustard gas from airplanes: "a fine, death-dealing rain." He asked for help but received none.

After the emperor left Addis Ababa, it was swept by looting and indiscriminate shooting. The city was in flames. The American legation was fired on repeatedly. Sir Sidney Barton, the British minister, moved American women and children, including Engert's two children, to the British compound, guarded by Sikh. Eighteen hundred people took refuge there.

Engert and his wife and a dozen others stayed behind and armed themselves to defend the U.S. legation. They gathered nine rifles, two shotguns, and ten revolvers, and a fleeing policeman brought in a submachine gun. Firing on the legation intensified, and on May 4 a band of Ethiopians tried to break in. Native servants rushed to guard the gates with swords and spears until staff members brought shotguns and pistols. Engert radioed State: "After brisk exchange of shots, in course of which one bandit was either killed or wounded, they were driven off."

By morning, Engert and his crew were running out of ammunition, just as four British trucks pulled up with Sikh guards and took them to the British legation. That afternoon, the Italian army arrived and began to impose order. Elsewhere, the Italians still bombed undefended towns and spread poison gas.

On May 9, President Roosevelt cabled Engert, his wife, and the staff his appreciation for their "courage and devotion to duty." Representative Edith Nourse Rogers proposed that Congress award Sara Engert the Medal of Honor.

The United States refused to recognize the Italian conquest, and Engert left for home in May 1937. After that, he served as consul in the Middle East and as the first American minister to reside in Kabul. Despite his length of service and skills, he never "fit in" well enough to be given the rank of ambassador. And Italy's brutal conquest failed to rouse the democracies. The dictators seemed stronger and more aggressive than ever.

MOVE INTO THE RHINELAND

In January 1936, Secretary Hull received a warning from Hugh Wilson, the U.S. minister to Switzerland, that Germany was rearming on a scale that "can be designed only for the purposes of aggression."

Ambassador William E. Dodd arrived at his Berlin office at 9:30 on Saturday morning, March 7, and met with Counselor Ferdinand L. Mayer. Earlier that morning, Mayer, an experienced career Foreign Service officer originally from Indianapolis, had been summoned to the German Foreign Office. Hitler was to speak to the nation and the world at noon.

Mayer brought back a summary of Hitler's message: He was sending thirty thousand troops into the demilitarized zone of the Rhineland. The embassy informed the newspapers, and the news sped around the world. Dodd and Mayer went to the jam-packed Kroll theater to hear Hitler speak.

Two weeks later, a coerced plebiscite gave Hitler's invasion of the Rhineland a 95 percent vote of approval. And from Berlin, Ambassador Dodd wrote the President, "Germany's dictatorship is now stronger than ever. If she keeps the pace three more years, she can beat the whole of Europe in a war."

In retrospect, these early aggressions were recognized as decisive moments when the Allies could have avoided World War II. But Hitler learned that he could succeed with fait accompli.

Dodd and Messersmith were among the American diplomats who stopped believing the Nazi movement would self-destroy. Hitler was going to be around for a while. If they only knew: Ahead stretched a steep, three-year-long slippery slope and then, once again, Armageddon.

That spring, Dodd returned to the United States, enjoyed a rest on his farm, and gave speeches that most newspapers ignored: He wanted the United States to stop shipping arms and fuel to Italy. He declared that Germany and Italy would be helpless without the oil that Standard Oil and Shell Oil were sending the dictators. Under Secretary Williams Phillips and Jay Pierrepont Moffat belittled his reports. Moffat said Dodd "would be hopeless if war should break out," and Phillips asked FDR to replace Dodd in Berlin.

Ambassador Bullitt, in Paris, also urged Roosevelt to drop Dodd. He said, "Dodd has many admirable and likable qualities, but he is almost ideally ill equipped for his present job. He hates the Nazis too much to be able to do anything with them or get anything out of them. We need in Berlin someone who can at least be civil to the Nazis and speaks German perfectly."

Dodd was by then openly expressing his hatred for National Socialism. He saw no possibility of living with the Nazis. He criticized Counselor Mayer's attempt to build closer relations with Göring, and he called Hitler "the monstrous specimen of a debased humanity."

Washington columnist Drew Pearson wrote a front-page article reporting that President Roosevelt wanted to replace Dodd with Bullitt, who was less antagonistic to the Nazi regime. This apparently reflected the State Department's view but not the President's. Dodd retorted that after such an indictment he could not resign as he had planned. Assistant Secretary Moore wrote him that Pearson's column was "both truthless and ruthless."

Dodd experienced a personal frustration. He tried to save Helmut Hirsch, a twenty-year-old Stuttgart-born Jew who claimed American citizenship and was accused of plotting to blow up Nazi headquarters in Nuremberg. Although Hirsch had not actually done anything, the Germans refused to recognize his American citizenship and charged him with treason. They said he had admitted his guilt before a secret people's court. Dodd carried his protest to Hitler's office and was told by his private secretary that no leniency was possible. Hirsch was beheaded.

SPAIN—"A WAR AGAINST DEMOCRACY"

The Spanish Civil War broke out on July 17, 1936, and Germany's three-year-old Nazi regime participated in a war for the first time. A military coup d'état had tried to overturn Spain's leftist government. Civil war followed and brought in the Fascist powers. At the U.S. Embassy in Madrid, Third Secretary Eric C. Windelin and Consul John D. Johnson provided food and shelter to scores of Americans until they could escape in U.S. Navy ships.

Although Ambassador Dodd, in Berlin, had not foreseen the Spanish war, he expected that Hitler and Mussolini would help the Spanish rightists and that Britain and France would not support the Spanish republicans. He asserted that if the United States had stayed involved with Europe after World War I, it would now not have to face "a solid dictatorship front which in due time will give serious trouble. How unwise our minority Senators were and have continued to be!"

On Christmas 1936, Dodd noted that Germany, Italy, and France were sending tens of thousands of troops into Spain. And a month later, he wrote, "Recently reports have come to me that American banks are contemplating large new credits and loans to Italy and Germany whose war machines are already large enough to threaten the peace of the world. I have even heard, but it seems unbelievable to me, that Mr. Bullitt is lending encouragement to these schemes."

Ambassador Claude G. Bowers, in Madrid, thought much as Dodd did. Bowers had been a newspaper editor in Indiana and later had joined *The New York World* as a columnist. Like Dodd, he came from a poor family and like Dodd he was a historian and an active Democrat, but Bowers had not gone to college.

During the halcyon days in 1933, when Ambassador Bowers first arrived in Madrid, he fell in love with Spain. He traveled over much of the country and reported astutely on the complicated political choreography that would lead to the finale of armed violence. In the fall of 1934, shooting erupted in Madrid, and all Spain was put under martial law. Bowers telephoned Secretary Hull and discussed the safety of Americans. On October 9, Jay Allen of the *Chicago Tribune* told Bowers that King Alexander I of Yugoslavia and the French foreign minister had been assassinated. The Yugoslavs were certain they had been murdered by Mussolini's Fascists.

Bowers judged that the leftist Spanish government contained not one Left extremist. But the new government's attempt at land reform infuriated the great landowners. The country became polarized. Bowers favored the Republicans and warned the State Department that the civil war would be long, because it was a struggle between a professional army and a people.

Military forces opposed the Left government and took possession of many of Spain's cities, but they failed in Barcelona and Madrid. Bowers, like most of the diplomatic community, set up a summer embassy in the Continental Hotel at San Sebastián, a Basque city on the coast of the Bay of Biscay, east of Bilbao. When Hallet Johnson, counselor of the embassy, drove to San Sebastián, he found the roads guarded by armed men and the wires to Madrid cut. Basque fishermen fought in San Sebastián's streets, and the diplomats were confined in the hotel.

One morning, Bowers sighted the U.S. Coast Guard cutter *Cayuga* two miles offshore. The cutter sent a boat, and aboard the cutter Bowers was persuaded to cross the border into the safety of France at Saint-Jean-de-Luz. Some American reporters criticized him for leaving Spain, but President Roosevelt reassured him some members of the press make "us boiling mad."

Assistant Secretary Wilbur Carr telephoned Bowers at the hotel in Saint-Jean-de-Luz and had him go aboard *Cayuga* and evacuate Americans from ports along the coast. With First Secretary Walter Schoellkopf and Biddle Garrison, Bowers made the cutter his floating embassy.

At Bilbao, they encountered the German battleship *Deutschland* and learned that the Axis was shipping warplanes to Spain. Consul William E. Chapman came aboard *Cayuga* for dinner, and the next day he brought word that the Basque government intended to take possession of Bilbao's American Firestone plant and seize its formulas. Bowers and his staff went ashore and, escorted by two Spanish armored cars, called on the local governor, who said he wanted tires from the plant but, despite the rumors, had no intention of taking its formulas.

At the silent town of Vigo, Consul William Cochran came on board *Cayuga* and reported that the local garrison had fired into a group of unarmed citizens, killing several and imprisoning three hundred. Because Cochran had refused to participate in rebel activities, he was confronted in the street. Bowers had him transferred out of danger.

The ambassador was irritated by three traveling Bryn Mawr girls who, he said, "were unable to understand the gravity of the situation" and had made friends with some young Fascist soldiers. And *Cayuga* took refugees aboard at Gijn. After its ten-day cruise, *Cayuga* returned to San Sebastián, and Bowers established the embassy in the spacious Eskualduna Hotel at Hendaye, on the French side, overlooking the sea.

On August 7, 1936, Acting Secretary William Phillips distributed to all U.S. diplomatic and consular officers in Spain a circular telegram signed "CH," declaring, "This Government will, of course, scrupulously refrain from any interference whatsoever in the unfortunate Spanish situation." And Secretary Hull declared publicly, "These present warlike tendencies can only lead to a world holocaust. Are we in this supposedly enlightened age so stupid that we cannot read this awful lesson of history?"

In September, the diplomatic corps reassembled at Saint-Jean-de-Luz. Bowers set up his embassy in the Villa Eche Soua, on the edge of the golf course and with a grand view of the Pyrenees. He later wrote bitterly of those days, "I observed that while the diplomatic representatives of totalitarian states were aggressively Fascist, . . . it was rather lonely for democrats in the bizarre capital of Saint-Jean-de-Luz."

. . .

By October, General Francisco Franco set up a government at Burgos, and Bowers reported that this was "a war against democracy . . . the dress rehearsal for the totalitarian war on liberty and democracy." Bowers described Franco as a small, forceful man with a colossal vanity, who took command of the rebel (Nationalist) forces and their Fascist supporters.

Franco's Nationalists fought to the edge of Madrid but could not penetrate the capital. During the winter of 1936–37, Madrid's population froze and survived on rations. Italian soldiers and German specialists joined the war on Franco's side; American correspondents met Italian officers they had known in Abyssinia. The next summer, Franco overran the Basque country and bombed Durango and Guernica.

By the spring of 1938, Roosevelt realized that an evenhanded embargo was a grave mistake. He planned covert aid to the Republicans, but it was now too late. Spain was divided.

Starting on March 16, bombers from Germany and Italy struck Barcelona repeatedly, killing nine hundred civilians. Bowers's military attaché, General Stephen Fuqua, was on the telephone in the consulate when he was blown across the room but not hurt. Bowers was appalled at the failure of Neville Chamberlain's government to stop the killing.

When, at the end of September 1938, the Munich agreement gave Germany the Sudetenland section of Czechoslovakia, Bowers attended a party in Biarritz, at which, he said, everyone applauded Chamberlain's triumph. Bowers disagreed, writing, "To me the Munich bargain seemed the greatest British tragedy since Austerlitz."

Bowers arranged for the first prisoner exchange, trading young Americans who had fought with the Abraham Lincoln Brigade for an equal number of Italian prisoners. He met the Americans at Hendaye and sent them home in the *Queen Mary*.

He wrote Roosevelt that the American embargo made the United States a collaborator of the Axis powers, which were destroying democratic Spain. Barcelona, the Republican capital, fell in heavy fighting early in 1939. Thousands, including members of the Republican government, fled into France. But Britain and France recognized Franco's government.

Secretary Hull and the State Department differed with their man in Madrid. Bowers condemned the fatal imbalance that the Germans and Italians imposed on the struggle, while officials in Washington feared that the "civil war" in Spain would spread across Europe. Bowers was sure that appeasing the Fascists made World War II inevitable and would kill democracy in Europe. He wrote, "With these views constantly sent to the State Department for more than two years, I never received any comment from the department. Now we know that there was a cleavage there even in the higher strata."

Secretary Hull recommended that FDR recall Bowers; and on March 1, 1939, he was ordered home, as Hull explained, to free the American government to deal with Franco. The government wanted to be represented by ambassadors who got along with Fascists.

While Bowers was sailing home aboard the *Queen Mary*, Madrid surrendered. Bowers wrote passionately, "The marvelous fight to save democracy in Spain was over." He met with FDR in the White House, and the President told him solemnly, "We have made a mistake; you have been right all along."

Bowers was replaced by the aging Alexander W. Weddell, and the embassy moved from France to Burgos in Spain. When Weddell retired in 1942, Roosevelt appointed Carlton J. H. Hayes, a distinguished history professor at Columbia University and a Catholic convert sympathetic to Franco. His mission was to keep Spain out of the world war, and his attitudes toward Franco and the refugees from Nazism were the subject of endless controversy. At the end of 1944, the Spanish ambassadorship was given to Foreign Service officer Norman Armour, who had served in Russia during World War I and whom *Time* magazine called "astute, aristocratic." He had no affinity for dictatorships, but he lasted less than a year before the United Nations decreed the recall of all ambassadors from Spain.

Spain was without an American ambassador until 1951, when the Korean War began and the Cold War reshaped American foreign policy. The new U.S. ambassador, investment banker Stanton Griffis, negotiated with Franco for air and naval bases on Spanish territory. Franco had not changed; the world around him had.

"BACKWARD TOWARD MEDIEVALISM"

By the mid-1930s, Ambassador Dodd could no longer bear to entertain the Nazi leaders, whom he regarded as "known and confessed murderers."

Dodd asked to be replaced by someone who knew Germany, and he vehemently opposed assigning the post to any of the wealthy career Foreign Service officers, whom he viewed as "the kind of Ambassadors who have injured our Service [for] forty years."

Dodd wrote President Roosevelt acrimoniously, "I am not so sure that diplomats are worth anything like what they cost our country. When I see how many Ambassadors we have and how little they can actually do, it seems something of a waste to continue them in service."

George Messersmith, while en route from Vienna to Washington to succeed Wilbur Carr as assistant secretary of state in the summer of 1937, called on Dodd and warned him that the Austrians were expecting Hitler to try to take over their country.

With new responsibility over budgets and salaries, Messersmith had the chance to democratize the system. He was hampered by the power struggle between the executive and legislative branches, and he had little experience working with Congress. And he had to learn to swallow petty congressional complaints—for example, that said the State Department changed typewriter ribbons too often.

Messersmith participated in a major departmental shake-up directed by Under Secretary Sumner Welles. The political leaders decided that, with war looming, the Foreign Service must become more professional and merit-based. Traditionalists and conservatives would be shipped out or retired. But, of course, the Old Guard was still firmly connected to power, and the shake-up was never truly effective.

The department and the Foreign Service that Messersmith now oversaw embraced 713 Foreign Service officers and more than 4,000 clerks at 312 installations overseas. The State Department's operating budget was only $14.2 million, and State had to struggle to keep that. (The War Department budget at the time was $600 million.)

Messersmith concluded that the reason State was underfinanced was because it had no organized constituency. He pointed out the absurdity of spending $60 million per battleship and scrimping on the department charged with making such weapons unnecessary.

He also fought in the battle between State and the Department of Commerce over the status of Commerce's attachés, who had been given the functions of business reporting and promoting, which traditionally had been State's responsibilities. Messersmith determined that the senior commercial attachés preferred to be integrated with State. Therefore, when Congress made commercial attachés a permanent part of the Commerce Department, he and Sumner Welles were able to persuade Roosevelt to veto it.

Dodd went home at the end of July 1937, but FDR asked him to return to Berlin for three months to enable him to shift from Moscow to Berlin Ambassador Joseph E. Davies, whose appointment Hull had opposed. While in New York, Dodd read in the newspapers part of a confidential letter he had written advising Secretary Hull not to send Prentiss Gilbert, the chargé d'affaires in Berlin, to join the British and French ambassadors attending the Nazi Party Congress in Nuremberg. Dodd blamed Under Secretary Welles for leaking the story.

Gilbert was familiar with controversy. In September 1931, after the Japanese attacked the Chinese in Manchuria, Secretary Stimson had sent Gilbert to sit with the League of Nations council investigating the event. The Japanese objected to a representative from a nonmember nation sitting in those meetings. The council had then formally invited Gilbert to participate.

Before Dodd returned to Berlin, FDR brought him to his home at Hyde Park, New York, to get his views on how to halt Japan and the European dictators. Dodd took the opportunity to urge the President to send, as ambassador to Berlin, Professor James T. Shotwell, of Columbia University. Roosevelt said he would appoint either Shotwell or Hugh Wilson of State.

Back in Berlin, Dodd collected information and rumors from a variety of diplomats, but he was unable to influence Germany's rulers. He noted, "All people are so afraid of another war that Hitler and Mussolini think they can keep everybody scared and seize what areas they want. I am afraid they are right in their appraisals." And he added, "How our modern civilization drifts backward toward medievalism!"

Then came a surprising message from Hull: Dodd had to retire by December 31 and would be succeeded by Hugh Gibson, the ambassador to Belgium. Dodd was shocked at this "violation of my understanding with the President." He attributed this also to Welles.

But Hugh Gibson declined the post, and Assistant Secretary of State Hugh R. Wilson, who spoke German fluently and whom Bullitt favored, succeeded Dodd. Wilson, a Yale graduate and every bit the bureaucratic diplomat, had joined the Foreign Service in 1912; had served effectively in Latin America, Berlin, Bern, and Tokyo; and had been the American minister to Switzerland for ten years. He held the Berlin post for less than a year during 1938 because Roosevelt ordered him home after Kristallnacht.

At year's end, Dodd left Berlin, sixty-eight, frustrated, and worn out. He regarded his tour in Nazi Germany a failure. He died two years later on his farm in Virginia. By then, the war he long feared had begun.

JOSEPH KENNEDY TO LONDON

President Roosevelt, who sent anti-Fascists like Dodd to Berlin and Bowers to Madrid, chose Joseph P. Kennedy, Sr., for London. By the time he appointed Kennedy in January 1938, most Americans understood what the dictators promised. The Rhineland, Munich, the Sudetenland, Ethiopia, and Guernica had all made clear where Hitler and Mussolini were taking the world. But Roosevelt dispatched, as his personal representative to hard-pressed Britain, a man who still found good in the Fascist myth, a man who did not grasp the Fascists' true danger, who wanted to keep the peace but saw no responsibility for his country in that challenge.

Joe Kennedy, a self-made millionaire businessman, had become rich in the stock market, the movie industry, and reputedly in bootlegging during Prohibition. He contributed heftily to Roosevelt's campaign, and when FDR was in the White House, Kennedy introduced him to such notables as William Randolph Hearst, the future Pope Pius XII, and the pro-Fascist Father Charles Coughlin.

Kennedy had pressed Roosevelt to appoint him ambassador to London. Both men were amused at the idea of an Irishman at the Court of St. James's. There, Kennedy preached appeasement; and when Chamberlain returned from Munich, Kennedy cabled him simply, "Good man." He said, "I have four boys and I don't want them to be killed in a foreign war."

When Hitler seized the Sudetenland, Kennedy asserted that it was nothing worth getting upset about. And after Charles Lindbergh visited German airfields and proclaimed the Luftwaffe unbeatable, Kennedy had the flier-hero relate his doomsday story to British officials.

The result was predictable. Roosevelt sidestepped his ambassador in London. The President did not want to have Kennedy come home and make trouble. Roosevelt began to do his own negotiating and sent abroad missions that bypassed the London embassy. He was determined that Britain would not fall.

All that time, Kennedy was sure Britain would be defeated. He wanted America to stay out of the war, even though he admitted openly he did not know what the war was all about. He confessed that he did not understand what had happened to the world since 1914. The destruction of a European generation and the ambiguous defeat of the kaiser's Germany had shifted power from the landed elites to the industrialists and to whomever could mobilize the mass of workers. Kennedy was one of the politicians unable to grasp the magnitude of that change.

When Hitler and Stalin signed their nonaggression pact on August 23, 1939, Kennedy advised the powers in Washington to press Poland to back down. He believed Ambassador Bullitt in Paris had convinced Roosevelt to insist that Poland stand up to Germany, and only that pressure had forced France and Britain to make Poland the cause of the war. Years later, over a golf game, Kennedy said to Secretary of the Navy James Forrestal that Prime Minister Chamberlain had told him that America and the Jews had forced Britain into war. Until Germany attacked Poland, Kennedy misjudged both the character and consequences of Adolf Hitler.

THE FINAL STEPS TO WAR

While Kennedy was taking charge of the embassy in London, Hugh Wilson presented his credentials to Hitler and then described the experience to the President. He summed up Hitler:

He was clad, as I was, in a dress suit, and wore only one Order, the Iron Cross. He is a more healthy looking man than I had anticipated, more solid, more erect, the complexion is pale, but there is more character in the face than I had anticipated from photographs. He speaks with a strong Austrian accent, but was quite easy to follow. He is a man who does not look at you steadily but gives you an occasional glance as he talks. His hands are fine, artistic. In our conversation, at least, he was restrained and made no gestures of any kind. I had met and had a talk with Mussolini, and felt the astonishing charm of that man, as well as a vivid impression of

force. I remember, when leaving Mussolini, I wished that I could
invite him out to dinner and sit over a beer and talk things over
with him. I had no such desire on leaving Hitler.

Ten days later, the German Eighth Army crossed the border into Austria. Hitler's home became a province, the Ostmark, of the Third Reich.
The American minister at Vienna, John Cooper Wiley, a career Foreign
Service officer, was now accredited to a country that no longer existed;
his legation became a consulate general reporting through the embassy
in Berlin.

Following the Anschluss, thousands of Austrian Jews surrounded the
U.S. mission in Vienna, desperately seeking visas to save their lives. Minister George Messersmith, who had preceded Wiley, strictly obeyed the
immigration laws. He did not want these refugees in the United States,
fearing they would create a nativist backlash. He worried that Hitler would
use the refugees to wheedle trade advantages from the United States. He
wanted the United States to remain the domain of native-born citizens.
John Wiley, succeeding Messersmith in Vienna in 1937, was more sympathetic to the Jews' plight. From Washington, Messersmith advised Wiley
not to relax the immigration laws. At a world conference on refugees at
Évian-les-Bains in 1938, only the Netherlands and Denmark were willing
to accept Jewish refugees.

Shortly thereafter, Hugh Wilson had an interview with Reich Minister
for Propaganda Joseph Goebbels, who condemned "libels" in the American press about the Reich Chancellor. He said every German venerated
Hitler as "*heilig*" (holy). Wilson reported that Goebbels and he agreed "that
what took place within Germany was a matter for Germany and what took
place within America was a matter for Americans." When Wilson brought
up Nazi treatment of the Jews, Goebbels said that he hoped responsible
American officials would stop the publication of lies in the American press.
Wilson said he concluded by telling Goebbels "that I feared that we had a
difficult road in front of us."

Hitler was gathering Germanic people into the Third Reich and wanted
security in the west so he could hunt for Lebensraum in the east. In September 1938, Ambassador William Phillips in Rome received a ciphered
message from President Roosevelt, which he was instructed to deliver to
Mussolini. Mussolini's son-in-law, Count Galeazzo Ciano, drove Phillips
to Il Duce's massive office in the Palazzo Venezia, where the ambassador

slowly read aloud the message asking Mussolini to prevent Hitler's threatened attack on Czechoslovakia. Il Duce thanked the President and informed Phillips that he had already received from Hitler a twenty-four-hour delay and a four-power meeting. Phillips later learned that the Italians had decoded the President's message and Mussolini had read it before Phillips ever arrived.

In Berlin, Hugh Wilson continued to entertain and conciliate the Nazis. He and Messersmith differed. Wilson emphasized the good side of Nazi Germany, but Messersmith said there was none. Wilson, fearing Bolshevism more than Nazism, praised Hitler's achievements and denounced the Jewish-owned press in America for criticizing Germany.

Ostensibly in retaliation for the murder of a third secretary of the German embassy in Paris by a young Polish Jew, the Nazis staged Kristallnacht ("The Night of Broken Glass") at 2:00 A.M. on November 10, 1938. They smashed Jewish life in Germany. Twenty thousand Jewish Germans were rounded up and shipped to concentration camps. Hundreds were killed. The American consul in Stuttgart reported that "a mass of seething, panic-stricken humanity" deluged the consulate day after day. The American consul general in Vienna protested to the police that Nazis were beating Jews lined up outside the consulate general. Their viciousness aroused anger around the world.

After the Kristallnacht pogrom, Roosevelt, at Assistant Secretary Messersmith's instigation, abruptly summoned Ambassador Wilson home to report in person. It was a symbolic act condemning Nazi brutality. The Germans responded by recalling their ambassador from Washington. Wilson left his wife in Berlin, expecting to return. He never did.

In January 1939, Ambassador Phillips presented Mussolini another letter from President Roosevelt, as well as a memorandum suggesting that Jews seized by the Nazis be settled in southern Ethiopia and Kenya. Mussolini said he had offered a better area northwest of Addis Ababa and had been rejected. He said there would be no room for Jews in Europe; they could go to Russia and North America.

From Warsaw, U.S. Ambassador Anthony J. Drexel Biddle, Jr., cautioned Secretary Hull that the Nazi killing of Jews would spread to Hungary, Romania, and Poland. He urged a response to Kristallnacht, which he called a "challenge to modern civilization." His warnings went unheeded. In his annual message to Congress, Roosevelt still sat on the fence. He said, "A war which threatened to envelop the world in flames has been averted, but it has become increasingly clear that peace is not assured."

ONE INVASION TOO FAR, PRAGUE

Hitler marched into Prague on March 15, 1939, and erased the twenty-year-old nation. Three weeks after that, on Good Friday, Mussolini took over Albania. Neither the French nor the British raised a finger.

George Kennan, the secretary of legation in Prague, was awakened at 6:00 A.M. on that March 15 and made his way in the dark through a raging snowstorm to the chancery. Then, Kennan drove around town, in what had become a blizzard, to see what was happening. Minister Wilbur Carr rushed off a cable to the State Department, and his staff turned away terrified Czechs seeking asylum from the Gestapo. All day, German troops, tanks, and military vehicles pounded over the cobblestones. At eight o'clock that evening, a curfew emptied Prague's streets.

Prague was one invasion too far. On the radio two days later, Prime Minister Chamberlain told the world quite candidly that Hitler had deceived him; Hitler's assurances that the Sudetenland would be his last conquest had been false.

The U.S. legation in Prague was closed, but Kennan and Consul General Irving Linnell stayed behind to report what they could from the shutdown city. Kennan kept watch on the German occupiers and reported to Washington on Nazi murders and arrests, looting and corruption. He decided that Germany was not fit to dominate Europe.

Because Hitler sought Lebensraum for the German people in the East, most everyone, including the British prime minister, now expected that Der Führer's next target would be Poland. Chamberlain told the House of Commons that both Britain and France were, finally, prepared to give the Polish government all possible support if Polish independence was threatened.

In Washington, the approach of war enabled Assistant Secretary Messersmith in May to win approval for increasing the State Department budget by $1.3 million and adding 120 new positions. When Harry Hopkins became secretary of commerce, he and Messersmith arranged to give the State Department jurisdiction over trade promotion abroad. On July 1,

114 commercial and agricultural attachés were commissioned as Foreign Service officers.

The turbulent interval between two great wars was nearly over. Once Stalin and Hitler signed their nonaggression treaty, Hitler could ignore the Russian giant to his East. There were no more barriers blocking the Nazis. Messersmith ordered the roofs of American missions throughout Europe painted black with brilliant chrome-yellow letters seven feet high: U.S.A.

31

"The Sands Are Running Fast"

1931–41

I n Peking, American Minister Nelson T. Johnson was sleeping soundly at 2:30 A.M. on September 19, 1931, when his houseboy switched on the bedroom light and shouted at him in Chinese. Mr. Johnson was wanted on the telephone.

William H. Donald, an Australian newsman and advisor to Chang Hsueh-liang, the drug-addicted Chinese marshal, was calling to inform Johnson that the Japanese army was moving into the Manchurian city of Mukden. Johnson cabled the State Department and the embassy in Tokyo. Myrl S. Myers, the American consul general at Mukden, checked in and reported that the Japanese were occupying all the major cities of Manchuria. Johnson notified the department of this "aggressive act by Japan," as he called it—the first shooting aggression leading directly to World War II and, eventually, the attack on Pearl Harbor.

Nelson Johnson, shrewd and gregarious, was not surprised by the Japanese invasion of Manchuria. He knew that Japan was hunting for natural resources and land for the people on its crowded islands. He wanted the United States to apply pressure to stop Japan. But the policy in Washington was to play down any aggressions. The United States was unprepared to intervene.

The League of Nations tried to convince Japan to withdraw from Manchuria, and Secretary of State Henry L. Stimson instructed Prentiss Gilbert, the American consul at Geneva, to absent himself as an observer at the League. The League gave the Japanese a deadline of November 16; the date came and went, and the Japanese stayed in Manchuria. President Hoover and Secretary Stimson opposed sanctions; they would damage American trade with Japan.

In Tokyo, the relatively liberal civilian government fell, and the army put together a more aggressive government, which finished occupying Manchuria and set up the puppet state of Manchukuo. In January, the Japanese attacked Shanghai. Minister Johnson and Councilor Cornelius van H. Engert went there to keep watch on what the Japanese were doing.

Nelson Johnson had served in China for most of twenty-four years. Descended from an old New England family, he had been reared in Oklahoma, where, he liked to say, he had learned that only armed citizens willing to shoot could clear out the bad men. After a year at George Washington University, the sociable redheaded youth took the Foreign Service examination for student interpreters and was sent to Peking for language study. He served as interpreter and consul in a half-dozen Manchurian and Chinese cities.

Witnessing the Chinese Revolution on October 10, 1911, he appreciated that Chinese nationalism was stimulated by the desire to get rid of foreign powers. In 1925, Johnson came home to be the chief of the State Department's Division of Far Eastern Affairs. He influenced Secretary of State Frank Kellogg to take the liberal position that China should be granted tariff autonomy and that foreign nations should give up extraterritoriality. The other powers disagreed. In 1927, Johnson, by now an acknowledged China expert, became an assistant secretary of state. And the next year the United States recognized the Nationalist (Kuomintang) government of Chiang Kai-shek.

President Hoover appointed Johnson to replace John V. A. MacMurray as minister to China. Arriving in Peking in January 1930, Johnson soon became popular with the Chinese for his informality and for traveling around China unescorted. Observing the commotion inside China and Japan's aggression, Johnson predicted to Ambassador Joseph C. Grew, who had recently arrived in Tokyo, that eventually the United States would have to fight Japan.

"A DICTATORSHIP OF TERRORISM"

Ambassador Grew was en route to his new post in Tokyo when military extremists assassinated Japan's prime minister and minister of finance on May 15, 1932. Japan was divided over how it would establish its place in the world. Ever since the Russian Revolution and the Russo-Japanese War, the Imperial Japanese Army had been moving into mainland East Asia. The United States was the most important remaining obstacle to what Secretary of State Charles Evans Hughes called Japan's "aggressive" policies.

A decade earlier, John V. A. MacMurray, then chief of the State Department's Far Eastern Division, had devised an American counterstrategy based on the Open Door principles. Elihu Root, with a different view, acknowledged Japan's interests in the mainland, and President Hoover's administration did not want to provoke Japan's military. The result was a compromise that relaxed relations between Japan and the United States, for the time being.

Japan's admirals and generals insisted that the naval-limitation treaties lowered Japan to a status inferior to the western nations and that the 1924 American prohibition on Japanese immigration had humiliated Japan.

The tension was still there. Culver B. Chamberlain, the consul at Harbin, was severely beaten by Japanese sentries at Mukden in January 1932, and a month later Vice Consul Arthur R. Ringwalt, while escorting Chinese with American citizenship to Shanghai's International Settlement, was attacked in the street by Koreans hired by the Japanese.

Despite such violence, Grew found Tokyo delightful, if fraught with the potential for trouble. The embassy's four white buildings were shielded by great trees and surrounded by carefully tended lawns. Grew was fascinated with the tea ceremony and geisha entertainment. And he enjoyed defeating his Japanese peers at poker. He found that Japan was steeped in tradition, even though, in contrast, its diplomatic service was less than forty years old.

Grew understood tradition; he was a tall, sophisticated Boston Brahmin, a graduate of Groton and Harvard, and a cousin by marriage of J. P. Morgan. In 1904, he started his foreign service career as a clerk in Cairo; he always remembered that when he arrived, the temperature hit 118 degrees. He worked in turn for the consuls general John W. Riddle, who had served in Turkey and Russia, and Lewis Iddings, a one-time New York newspaperman. In Cairo, Grew's hearing failed him, a handicap he had to cope with the rest of his life.

His wife, Alice Perry Grew, was a descendant of Commodore Matthew Perry and had lived in Tokyo for three years as a girl. Now, she charmed the Japanese. After the couple had been in Tokyo about two years, their daughter Elsie married Cecil B. Lyon, third secretary of the Tokyo embassy, who went on to a long and successful Foreign Service career, climaxing as ambassador to Chile and Sri Lanka.

Young Grew was adventurous; during a world tour, he shot a tiger in a cave in China. That, President Theodore Roosevelt declared in 1906, qualified him for the Foreign Service, and TR appointed him third secretary of embassy in Mexico City. His stay there was brief because his wife became seriously ill and had to return to Boston. Grew arranged a transfer to Saint Petersburg as third secretary. He later remembered, "We didn't have to keep very long hours in the office in those comparatively idle days." Young diplomats filled a great deal of their time copying documents by hand.

When he moved on to Berlin as second secretary in 1908, he was captivated by the elaborate social life of the European courts, the show of wealth, and the formality. And in 1911, he became first secretary in Vienna. That embassy, at Heugasse 26, was in a mansion built for a young Rothschild who shot himself when his parents would not let him marry the girl he loved.

In Vienna, Grew made himself invaluable to Ambassador Richard C. Kerens, a Missouri railroad builder who knew little about either foreign policy or diplomatic niceties and who spoke only English. Grew valued Kerens as a businessman representing the United States, but he was appalled by the way Kerens ran the embassy and by the failure of the ambassador and his inflexible wife to entertain as the Europeans expected them to.

Back to Berlin as first secretary in 1912, Grew admired Ambassador John G. A. Leishman, former president of the Carnegie Steel Company, who already had served fifteen years in the Foreign Service. When Grew felt threatened by President Wilson's political-based turnover of the Foreign Service, he sought support from Franklin D. Roosevelt, whom he had befriended at both Groton and Harvard and who was now assistant secretary of the Navy. The Old Boy network worked.

Grew was enthralled by the grand wedding of the kaiser's daughter, which was attended by the czar of Russia and the king and queen of England and some fifty-seven royal personages. That gala event turned out to be the last elaborate gathering of European royalty before World War I destroyed their world.

At the Paris Peace Conference after the war, Grew gained a reputation for being tactful and evenhanded. He was appointed minister to Denmark, served a tour as Under Secretary of State until he clashed with Secretary Kellogg, and in 1927 he was named ambassador to Turkey, where he spent the next five years.

In 1932, Grew brought with him to Tokyo as his private secretary twenty-five-year-old J. Graham Parsons, who had been recommended by their Groton headmaster and was just beginning a distinguished if controversial Foreign Service career. Grew was offered the use of Prime Minister Inukai's Lincoln until his own Cadillac arrived, but the prime minister was assassinated before he could take delivery.

Grew was an optimist and a conciliator; he believed in the possibilities of diplomacy after many diplomats had lost faith. He hoped that each new Japanese cabinet would strengthen the forces for peace and civility. And he was repeatedly disappointed. Stanley K. Hornbeck, chief of the Division of Far Eastern Affairs, thought him an appeaser. More accurately, Grew saw the dangers. He wrote, "The military are still supreme and still form a dictatorship of terrorism."

Through speeches, interviews, and articles in the Japanese press, Grew worked to show the Japanese that their actions and ambitions shocked the world. In *The Japan Times,* he wrote, "Diplomatic agents nowadays rarely endeavor to negotiate secret agreements. . . . Today the world has become so small, with the development of communications, and there is such a constant interchange of peoples, and such close commercial and financial relations between states, that the relations of any one nation with another are of deep concern to all nations." But the men who ruled Japan had other priorities.

When the Grews had been in Tokyo nearly two years, Alice and the ambassador sailed on a Japanese destroyer to Shimoda to mark the eightieth anniversary of Commodore Perry's signing Japan's first treaty with the United States. The party visited the village of Kakizaki, where Consul Townsend Harris had lived before he was allowed to go to the capital.

At Kakizaka, the Grews burned incense at the graves of the five sailors from Perry's ships who were buried there and to Harris' memory. Grew was deeply affected by the little ceremony. The Americans were driven to Shimoda through solid rows of schoolchildren waving American and Japanese flags and shouting, "Banzai!" Grew noted, "It was a really grand day."

Most of his days were less grand; he called them "days of political intensity." The Japanese government wanted no interference with its hegemony over China. And it had to overcome its shortage of oil. Grew described to Secretary Hull Japan's "swashbuckling temper" and warned, "We would be reprehensibly somnolent if we were to trust to the security of treaty restraints or international comity to safeguard our own interests or, indeed, our own property."

There were lighter moments, too, such as the day he escorted Babe Ruth and Lefty O'Doul to play at the Tokyo Golf Club. Grew, an ardent golfer, had a delightful time but he was not impressed with the Babe's golf game. Between 1931 and 1935, the American baseball stars made three tours in Japan and were received with large cheering crowds, shouting "Banzai Bambino." The outpouring of baseball goodwill ended when the Japanese newspaper publisher promoting the tour barely survived an assassination attempt. Apparently, not all Japanese appreciated Americanization through baseball.

Following a five-month home leave, Grew plunged into "a dreadful time." On Tuesday evening, February 25, 1936, the Grews gave a dinner for thirty-six in honor of the aged Viscount Saitō Makoto and his wife. Saitō, an admiral, had been the moderate prime minister when Grew first arrived in 1932. Grew called the older man, who much earlier had attended the U.S. Naval Academy, "lovable, gentle, charming, courtly." After dinner, the Grews showed the film *Naughty Marietta,* with Jeanette MacDonald and Nelson Eddy. The Saitōs left at about 11:30 P.M.

At about 5:00 A.M., Viscount Saitō was murdered in his home by young military radicals. Well-organized and disciplined, they also assassinated the grand chamberlain, the finance minister, the home minister, the former war minister, and the inspector general of military education. And they seriously wounded the chief of the Metropolitan Police Board. They tried to kill the prime minister, Admiral Okada Keisuke, but when the alarms went off in the official residence, Okada stopped to dress while his brother-in-law Matsuo immediately ran downstairs and into the garden shouting "Banzai!" The assassins mistook him for the prime minister and killed him. Okada was rushed into the servants' area and hidden in a closet. He remained there until nightfall, when he was disguised and walked out among the mourners.

Ambassador Grew was awakened early Wednesday morning and told of the assassinations. By ten o'clock he had dispatched a telegram to "Secstate Washington," but it took six hours for the message to be acknowledged. He went to the Saitō home. Viscountess Saitō had been wounded; she had placed herself in front of her husband with her hand over the machine-gun muzzle aimed at him. She and Grew knelt together before the viscount's body.

That night, the Grews slept in a different room than usual and nearer their baby daughter; the next day, the embassy was guarded by loyal Japanese troops behind sandbag barricades. The leaders of the revolt surrendered four days later, and the government granted them two hours to commit hara-kiri. When they did not, they were tried by court-martial, and thirteen officers and four civilians were shot. The emperor ordered Koki Hirota, the foreign minister who was acceptable to the army, to form a new cabinet. Violence had paid off for the military.

Grew reported to Washington that the ruling Japanese, determined to expand beyond the home islands, debated whether the expansion should be westward into northern China and Mongolia or southward to New Guinea, Borneo, and the oil-rich Dutch East Indies. In August 1936, the cabinet secretly adopted the military's preference to drive southward.

Toward the end of the year, Japan and Nazi Germany signed an anti-Comintern pact. And in February, the Chinese Communists, based in remote Yen'an province, sought a common front with Chiang Kai-shek against the Japanese.

Emboldened by its partnership with Germany, on the night of July 7, 1937, Japan attacked Chinese troops at the Marco Polo Bridge, twelve miles north of Peking. In the capital, American Foreign Service officer O. Edmund Clubb stood at a Chinese-manned barrier and helped Americans scramble to safety in the city. A few days later, Ambassador Johnson advised Washington that the Japanese army was moving through the Great Wall. Chiang Kai-shek tried to stand firm. In the view of many, this was really the start of World War II.

On orders from Washington, Grew covertly visited Koki Hirota at his home and offered the United States' good offices to halt the Sino-Japanese

War. Most Westerners in Tokyo retreated to the countryside in the summer, but Grew stayed at his post, playing a lot of golf.

When a Japanese naval officer was murdered in Shanghai, the Japanese bombarded the city. Bombers hit the foreign concessions as well as USS *Augusta,* waiting to evacuate women and children, and the liner *President Hoover,* also trying to rescue American refugees.

Secretary Hull cabled Grew, "I consider it desirable for you . . . to suggest to Japanese officials that Japan, by the course it is pursuing, is destroying the good will of the world. . . ." The Secretary authorized Leland Harrison, the minister to Switzerland, to sit with the League of Nations committees studying the Japanese aggression. But the United States was not ready to participate in any joint action to end the fighting. When Hull asked Ambassador Johnson whether the United States should invoke its neutrality law, Johnson counseled him that, if the law hurt China, China would simply blame the United States for its own failures. The neutrality law was not applied.

In September 1937, Grew learned that the Japanese planned to bomb Nanking, which was now Chiang Kai-shek's capital. Grew met with Koki Hirota and protested. The Japanese bombed the well-marked American missionary hospital at Waichow and undefended foreign universities and churches. Americans were killed.

On September 19, the commander of the Japanese Third Fleet advised the foreign diplomatic missions to leave Nanking because he was about to bombard the city. *Time* magazine perceptively wrote, four years before the attack on Pearl Harbor, "In modern times accepted Japanese strategy has been a knife-in-the-back thrust without warning."

The Great Powers appealed to Japan to spare defenseless Nanking. On the twentieth, Ambassador Johnson and his staff boarded the gunboat USS *Luzon* at anchor in the Yangtze River off the Nanking Bund. The Japanese did not attack on the twenty-first as announced, and the following morning Johnson prepared to return to the embassy. But at 10:35 A.M., about forty Japanese planes began to dive-bomb and firebomb the city. Wave after wave of bombers attacked for four hours. When the all clear sounded, Johnson went back to the embassy. It had hardly been damaged. The next day, the Japanese bombers returned.

The Chinese and some Americans, including missionaries and the *New York Times'* editors, charged that, by boarding the gunboat, Johnson had left his post and demonstrated that the United States would not stand firm against Japanese aggression. Actually, Johnson had recommended to the State Department that the United States should help the Chinese resist.

Chiang Kai-shek's government moved five hundred miles upriver to Hankow, and Ambassador Johnson and his staff followed. A small group, including Secretaries J. Hall Paxton and George Atcheson Jr.; Captain Frank N. Roberts, the assistant military attaché; and the embassy clerk Emile Gassie, stayed with the gunboat USS *Panay* at Nanking to watch over Americans and American interests there.

Meanwhile, at the beginning of November, in Brussels, Norman H. Davis represented the United States at a conference of nineteen nations trying to halt the Asian war. Ambassador Johnson thought the conference might inform public opinion about what the Japanese were doing, but he did not expect that it could end the war. Grew and the new British ambassador to Tokyo, Sir Robert Craigie, urged the Brussels conference to remain impartial so it could mediate.

Japan refused to participate in the conference, and Koki Hirota politely warned Grew not to allow the Western nations to gang up on Japan. Hirota hoped that the United States would persuade Chiang Kai-shek to negotiate for peace.

The Japanese army marched on Nanking, and in the infamous "rape of Nanking" tortured, raped, and killed some three hundred thousand civilians and prisoners of war. The killing and looting went on for six weeks. The Japanese closed the city's exits, and when Chinese soldiers surrendered, the Japanese executed them en masse. The invaders killed the defenders of the last escape route, Hsiakwan Gate, and piled up the dead, "forming a mound six feet high." F. Tillman Durdin of *The New York Times* wrote, "Nanking's streets were littered with dead."

SINKING THE *PANAY*

As the Japanese army approached Nanking, the four members of the U.S. embassy still in the city boarded the gunboat USS *Panay* on Wednesday night, December 8, 1937. By Sunday morning, the twelfth, the flat-bottom, shallow-draft *Panay* had moved some twenty-six miles up the Yangtze River. She was escorting three Standard Oil barges carrying American refugees away from the fighting.

On that sunny Sunday morning, the Nanking embassy's Secretary George Atcheson, Jr., asked Shanghai's able Consul General Clarence E. Gauss to notify the Japanese embassy of the neutral U.S. Navy *Panay*'s position. Gauss did so at 12:15. An hour and twenty-three minutes later, Japanese twin-engine bombers and single-engine fighters bombed and strafed the *Panay* repeatedly. The gunboat rocked from the blasts. Its captain, Lieutenant Commander James J. Hughes, U.S. Navy, and his executive officer were badly wounded. The sailors fired their antiquated Lewis machine guns at the planes. With the main deck awash, Hughes gave the order to abandon ship.

The Japanese strafed *Panay*'s two outboard-powered sampans, which were chugging repeatedly toward shore carrying survivors, and machine-gunned the men trying to hide in the marsh reeds along the riverbank. Atcheson, a doctor's son, helped carry Hughes, whose leg was broken, to safety. While he hid Hughes in the reeds, Japanese soldiers in two patrol boats machine-gunned the now-abandoned *Panay*, sinking it and two of the three oil barges. Three men were killed, and eleven seriously wounded.

That Sunday, Ambassador Johnson was visiting a friend in Hankow's hospital. He was notified that radio contact with *Panay* had been broken. He had the British gunboat *Bee* ask for *Panay*'s whereabouts and learned that *Bee* had been fired on. Alarmed, he told Washington that he could not reach *Panay*. He did not know until Monday that *Panay* had been sunk and Americans killed and wounded. He wrote Stanley Hornbeck, "We must be prepared to fight if we want to be respected." But, instead, many in the United States asked what an American warship was doing on the Yangtze.

On the riverbank, Atcheson and Hughes gave charge of the party ashore to Assistant Military Attaché Captain Frank N. Roberts, a West Point graduate from Kansas. Atcheson, Paxton, and Roberts all knew the Chinese language and enabled the party to survive during their two days ashore. Paxton, a missionary's son from Danville, Virginia, was sent inland alone to get out a message; he had not revealed that he was wounded in both arms and one knee.

After dark, the Americans scrounged food from farmhouses upriver and improvised stretchers for the thirteen men wounded so badly that they had to be carried the five miles to Hohsien. Local Chinese helped, and the next morning Atcheson made telephone contact with two American missionaries, who telephoned Ambassador Johnson.

Japanese troops flooded into the area, and the Chinese hurried the Americans into junks and hid them up a creek. Then, Atcheson and Roberts walked two miles into Hanshan. After two days, the men from *Panay* found refuge aboard small craft. In his dispatches, Atcheson gave credit to Roberts and Paxton. Paxton had hiked fifty miles from the river seeking help.

At the embassy in Tokyo, Monday morning was quiet because it was Sunday in Washington. Ambassador Grew was going golfing until he learned that the Japanese had attacked American ships on the Yangtze. Secretary Hull told Grew to deliver a note to Hirota. It said, "The Government and people of the United States have been deeply shocked." He demanded a formal expression of regret, indemnifications, and assurance that Americans and their property in China would not again be attacked.

Grew called on Hirota and demanded that such indiscriminate firing be stopped. Hirota replied coolly that all foreigners had been warned to leave Nanking. Grew diplomatically thanked Hirota for sending naval ships to aid the S.S. *President Hoover,* which had been caught in a monsoon and had gone aground off Formosa (Taiwan).

At three o'clock that afternoon, Hirota's office telephoned the American embassy to say he was coming to see Grew, an unusual concession for a foreign minister. Hirota immediately informed Grew that *Panay* had been sunk, and he apologized for the Japanese government.

Grew was horrified by the bombing and machine-gunning of neutral Americans. When Hirota left, Grew began to prepare in case diplomatic relations were broken and the embassy staff had to pack and swiftly depart. The following day, Hirota sent Grew a note of apology, claiming the sinking of *Panay* was "a mistake" and, incredibly, blaming the attack on "poor visibility."

"DIPLOMACY CANNOT STEM THE TIDE"

President Roosevelt proposed economic sanctions to his cabinet. The State Department planned to do little but ask American aircraft manufacturers not to sell to Japan. In Berlin, Ambassador Dodd counseled Roosevelt to establish a boycott.

Grew recognized that there were, as he said, "two Japans." By his own account, he obtained most of his information about what the military was thinking and doing from civilians, colleagues in the diplomatic corps, especially the German ambassador. He had little access to Japan's military leaders, who were determining the nation's course.

On December 22, he did meet for three hours in his study with a group led by Admiral Yamamoto Isoroku, a risk-taking vice minister of the navy. Yamamoto had studied English and economics at Harvard and had been posted as an attaché in Washington. Three years in the future, he would design the attack on Pearl Harbor. Now, they spread maps on the floor and tried to untangle the facts of the *Panay* incident. "But for a good many reasons this has not been easy." Grew closed the meeting by warning them that "another similar incident would bring about the most serious results."

That next summer, the Japanese bombed Hankow and forced the Chinese government to retreat another six hundred miles up the Yangtze to Chungking. Ambassador Johnson alerted Roy Howard, president of the Scripps-Howard newspapers, that he expected Japan to finance its conquest of China in the United States. Howard promised to warn the American people.

Ambassador Johnson and his staff moved to Chungking early in August and set up the embassy on the second floor of the four-story former Standard Oil Company headquarters. They operated a portable radio from the attic. To escape the frequent bombing, Johnson and his staff spent a lot of time in the embassy's bomb shelter. For recreation there was little to do but play cards and write letters. It was a miserable existence.

By the end of 1938, Hankow and Canton fell to the Japanese. And the Japanese government reversed its promises to support the United States' Open Door policy in China. Now Johnson was advocating that the United States send aid to the Chinese. Grew told the Japanese leaders, "A Japanese-American war would be the height of stupidity from every point of view."

Ambassador Johnson made a trip home in 1939. When he returned to China in May, the Japanese had begun moving south. Like Grew, he now urged giving China extensive military aid. He wrote FDR that dictatorships understand nothing but force.

Grew also went home, to New Hampshire, on furlough from May to October 1939, and was surprised to see how much American opinion had hardened against Japan. He advised President Roosevelt to take economic measures against Japan only if the United States was "prepared to see them through to their logical conclusion, and that might mean war."

On his return to Tokyo, Grew addressed the America-Japan Society with new militancy: Influential Japanese should understand the mood of America. Nowadays, he said, "Wars are not only destructive of the wealth, both human and material, of combatants, but they disturb the fine adjustments of world economy." He said frankly that "the people of the United States resent the methods which the Japanese armed forces are employing in China today. . . . American rights and interests in China are being impaired and destroyed by the policies and actions of the Japanese authorities in China. American property is being damaged or destroyed; American nationals are being endangered and subjected to indignities." He warned that Japan and the United States were headed toward a conflict and hoped they would remain friends. It was an important speech.

In December, Admiral Nomura Kichisaburo, now Japan's foreign minister, excused all the affronts to the United States as merely accidents of the massive war. The admiral was cordial, but the Japanese government was not backing down. Grew wrote, "Time, I believe, will play into our hands if we allow nature to take its course unhindered by us. By hindrances I mean steps in the nature of sanctions."

The crisis spread. In January 1940, the United States terminated its 1911 commercial treaty with Japan, and by July, the political winds in Tokyo, energized by Germany's military victories, had swung around. The army made Prince Fumimaro Konoye prime minister. Japan was moving into Southeast Asia and French Indochina, and the Dutch East Indies lay in reach.

Limiting Japan's ambitions, as Tokyo saw it, were the British navy in the Pacific and the Soviet army to the west. Both had to be neutralized. And Germany expected Japan to divert the United States from joining the war in Europe.

Although Grew regarded Konoye as a weakling, he saw Konoye's government "going hell-bent toward the Axis and the establishment of the New Order in East Asia, and of riding roughshod over the rights and interests, and the principles and policies, of the United States and Great Britain." Japanese who favored aggressive policies were now "vastly in the majority."

Would embargoes on strategic supplies backfire and push Japan into war with the United States? The American people were by no means ready for that. By the autumn of 1940, Japan, with Vichy's forced agreement, placed troops in northern French Indochina. That persuaded Secretary of War Henry Stimson and Secretary of the Treasury Henry Morgenthau to favor an embargo on exporting oil to Japan. But Secretary Hull was still determined to avoid a military collision. They reached a compromise that prohibited the sale to Japan of high-grade iron and steel, as well as high-octane aviation gasoline and certain lubricants. But the embargoes were not very efficient, and the United States was reluctant to leave Japan no alternative except to seize oil in Southeast Asia.

Grew summarized his new point of view to Secretary Hull in September 1940. He wrote, "In general, the uses of diplomacy are bankrupt in attempting to deal with such powers [Italy, Germany, and Japan]. Occasionally diplomacy may retard, but it cannot stem the tide effectively. Only by force or the display of force can these powers be prevented from attaining their objectives. Japan is today one of the predatory powers." He concluded that unless the United States demonstrates that it is willing to use its power, the situation is "hopeless."

In December, Grew wrote the President a "Dear Frank" letter predicting that unless the United States showed it would fight, it was headed for a showdown with Japan. In reply, Roosevelt's "Dear Joe" letter emphasized again the global nature of the war and his determination to achieve an Allied victory.

Grew wrote in his diary: "January 27, 1941. There is a lot of talk around town to the effect that the Japanese, in case of a break with the United States, are planning to go all out in a surprise mass attack on Pearl Harbor. Of course I informed our Government." His message to Secretary Hull said, "A member of the Embassy was told by my colleague [apparently Peruvian Ambassador Ricardo Rivera Schreiber] that from many quarters, including a (drunken) Japanese one, he had heard that a surprise mass attack on Pearl Harbor was planned by the Japanese military forces, in case of 'trouble' between Japan and the United States; and that the attack would involve the use of all the Japanese military facilities. My colleague said that he was prompted to pass this on because it had come to him from many sources, although the plan seemed fantastic."

Grew's warning did not trigger alarms in Washington. Much later, Third Secretary Frank A. Schuler, Jr., a Japanese language expert in the Tokyo embassy at the time, charged that Grew's cable had been phrased so that its last sentence made it clear in deft diplomatic style that the ambassador did not endorse the warning. Schuler complained that he had been shunted aside for warning that war was imminent and disagreeing with Ambassador Grew.

The Japanese poured more troops into Indochina, occupied Saigon's airport, and took positions from which they could seize Singapore. On April 14, Foreign Minister Yōsuke Matsuoka and Stalin signed a nonaggression treaty. That freed the Soviet Union to defend itself against Germany and freed Japan to move into Southeast Asia. Roosevelt declared an unlimited national emergency. He felt he was moving as fast as he could bring along the American people. Historian James Chace wrote, "Roosevelt was still playing poker with Tokyo."

Germany attacked the Soviet Union on June 22, and Grew claimed Hitler had "double-crossed Japan by signing a nonaggression pact with Soviet Russia." And the Japanese government decided it would not help Germany by going to war in Siberia. Because the United States had much earlier broken Japan's diplomatic "Purple" code, Tokyo's decision was known in Washington almost immediately. Now, Japan did not appear to be so deeply in Hitler's pocket.

COUNTDOWN TO PEARL HARBOR

President Roosevelt welcomed Ambassador Admiral Nomura Kichisaburo to the Oval Office of the White House at 5:00 P.M. on July 24, 1941. Also present were Acting Secretary of State Sumner Welles and Admiral Harold R. Stark, chief of naval operations. Welles and Stark had met individually with Nomura the day before. Roosevelt began by explaining that the United States had not cut off Japan's supply of oil because it wanted Japan to have no excuse to invade the Dutch East Indies. If Japan seized oil resources there, he said, the Dutch would resist and the British would come to their aid. There would be war in the Pacific.

Actually, the United States was not totally the innocent victim. Japan had become dependent on the United States for strategic materials and oil. But, appalled by the Japanese aggressions in Manchuria and China, the United States had revoked its bilateral trade treaty in January 1940. And it established export restrictions, which one historian called "full-blooded financial warfare against Japan." Consul U. Alexis Johnson, in Mukden, reported that because Japan could not find oil in Manchuria, it would try to procure oil from the Dutch East Indies by force.

Roosevelt said the United States disapproved of Japan's advance into Indochina. He suggested that if Japan refrained from occupying Indochina, its raw materials would remain available to Japan.

Roosevelt's assurances did not deter Japan. That very day, the Vichy French authorities, under duress, allowed Japan to use air facilities and ports throughout Indochina. And two days later, Roosevelt by Executive Order froze Japanese assets in the United States. The British and Dutch followed the American lead. Roosevelt also federalized the Philippines' armed forces under General Douglas MacArthur. Commercial Attaché Frank S. Williams, in Tokyo, cabled: "At last the United States has shown this country that it is no longer bluffing!"

Grew became tougher. On Sunday morning, he received Roosevelt's plan to neutralize Indochina. Without consulting Washington, he visited the new minister of foreign affairs, Admiral Toyoda Teijiro, at home, and emphasized that this was an opportunity Japan should not miss. Grew said, "If the Japanese fail to avail themselves of it, their own position in history will not be enviable."

Four days later, Japanese navy bombers overflew Chungking, now China's capital, and dropped bombs near the Yangtze patrol gunboat USS *Tutuila* and the U.S. Embassy. Americans who witnessed the attack unanimously declared it was intentional. Before Grew could react, Admiral Yamamoto Isoroku, acting vice minister for foreign affairs, appeared at the U.S. Embassy and apologized.

After Roosevelt and Churchill met aboard USS *Augusta* off Newfoundland on August 9, Admiral Toyoda asked Grew over to his office and, in a two-and-a-half-hour conversation, laid out a program to maintain peace. Its high point was that President Roosevelt and Prime Minister Konoye should meet in Honolulu and discuss relations face-to-face. Ten days later, Ambassador Nomura delivered this proposal to Roosevelt. When word leaked out, the Japanese feared that extremists would assassinate the prime minister.

The Japanese proposal of a summit meeting was thoroughly discussed in Washington, and the Americans decided that Konoye and the military leaders could not be trusted. Roosevelt handed the Japanese ambassador a note for Konoye asserting he needed agreement on what was to be discussed.

Konoye invited Ambassador Grew to a private dinner at a friend's home on September 6; present were only the two principals and two aides. At this very time, the Japanese military and naval chiefs of staff were pressing the emperor to accept the possibility of war with the United States. At dinner, the prime minister asked Grew to make sure that his statements about the proposed meeting with Roosevelt were forwarded to the President personally. Grew reported, "Prince Konoye repeatedly stressed the view that time is of the essence." Secretary Hull and the State Department belittled this detour from diplomatic formalities.

Grew, in a report to the Secretary of State, said he now believed that Japan's policy of expansion by force could be halted only by a demonstration of American willingness to use force. He still favored conciliation, that is, diplomacy, rather than "progressive economic strangulation." He judged the risks of failure from meeting were less than the risks if the United States refused to meet. Grew wrote in his diary; "Let us not forget that diplomacy is essentially our first line of national defense."

Grew now described Tokyo as like the "wild West." He started carrying a pistol after four men armed with daggers and short swords jumped on the running board of Prime Minister Konoye's car and attempted to kill him. Grew's own name was known to be on death lists. The embassy guard was increased, and a guardhouse erected at the entrance to the chancery.

As the weather grew colder, the Japanese blocked heating oil from being supplied to the American and British embassies.

Discussions in Tokyo and Washington about a Roosevelt-Konoye meeting seemed interminable until the peace-minded Konoye resigned suddenly on October 16. He clearly had no authority over the military high command. Grew said he was surprised only that this had come so soon. He noted hopefully that the new prime minister, minister of war, and home minister, General Tōjō Hideki, an active-duty general, might control the military extremists. Tōjō had been one of the original members of the Konoye cabinet and had supported direct talks with the United States. Grew wrote in his diary, "This is important."

Tōjō, in fact, supported Nazi Germany and advocated preemptive air strikes against China and the Soviet Union. Secretary Hull described him as "small-bore" and stubborn. Grew was informed that the emperor had told the army's leaders that he wanted no war with the United States. Thus, Grew remained optimistic.

But by November, his view changed radically. Strong editorials against the United States in the semiofficial Japanese press convinced him that time was truly running out. In a cable that Grew said was "on the record for all time," he gave Secretary Hull and Under Secretary Welles his judgment that foreign economic pressures could neither destroy Japan's military nor avert war. German victories and defeats would determine Japan's foreign policy.

But he warned that the United States should not underestimate "Japan's capacity to rush headlong into a suicidal struggle with the United States. While national sanity dictates against such action, Japanese sanity cannot be measured by American standards of logic." If efforts at conciliation failed, Grew said, Japan would adopt a do-or-die policy. He added, "The sands are running fast."

Grew was reassured when, on November 11, Churchill proclaimed that if war began between the United States and Japan, a British declaration of war would follow within the hour. Churchill did not know that Japan's government had already, on November 5, decided to go to war with the United States in early December.

The Japanese government sent diplomat Kurusu Saburo to Washington to assist Ambassador Nomura. Kurusu had been a vice consul in New York in 1914, and, while serving as the consul in Chicago, he had married an American; they had three children. Although Kurusu had later been the ambassador to Rome and Berlin, Grew felt he was not biased toward the Axis.

Now, at the embassy in Tokyo, Eugene Dooman arranged for the State Department to delay by two days the American clipper's departure from Hong Kong so that Kurusu could catch the flight. The next clipper, the Japanese told Dooman, would be too late.

Wheels turned faster and faster as the diplomats approached the abyss. At the end of November, Secretary Hull handed the Japanese a ten-point proposal on a range of Far Eastern problems. It promised Japan access to raw materials, trade, financial support, and the end of freezing assets, if it would halt its aggressions and remove its troops from Indochina.

But Prime Minister Tōjō kept sending troops into Indochina and swore publicly to end Western domination of East Asia with a "vengeance." Grew called Tōjō's speech "utterly childish." On December 1, a friend at the Tokyo Club told Grew that the cabinet had decided to break off the talks with the United States.

Late in the evening on December 7, in Tokyo, Grew received a heads-up message from Hull to expect a message from President Roosevelt that he must take to the emperor instantly. Grew and Counselor Dooman tensely paced the embassy's walnut-paneled library. Although the coded "triple priority" message for the emperor arrived at Tokyo's central telegraph office at noon, the Japanese did not deliver it to the U.S. Embassy until 10:30 P.M. It promised that the United States did not intend to invade Indochina and again asked Japan to remove its troops.

Dooman called the secretary of the foreign minister, Togo Shigenori, and said the ambassador must see the foreign minister immediately. The foreign minister agreed to wait for Grew until midnight. At 11:45 the message was decoded, and Grew sped in Secretary Merrell Benninghoff's Ford across town to Togo's official residence. They dashed up the stairs and into the second-floor drawing room and sat in two blue overstuffed chairs. Grew put on his glasses and read aloud President Roosevelt's message.

Grew left the foreign minister at about 12:30 A.M. The use of diplomacy was suddenly exhausted. It was then about two hours before the Japanese fleet attacked Pearl Harbor.

32

"A Rattlesnake Posed to Strike"

1939–41

Japan had been at war for eight years when, at 2:50 A.M. on September 1, 1939, Ambassador Anthony J. Drexel Biddle, Jr., in Warsaw telephoned President Roosevelt: Germany has invaded Poland! Twenty minutes later, Ambassador William C. Bullitt, in Paris, confirmed the report. Roosevelt replied, "Well, Bill, it's come at last. God help us all."

By 4:00 A.M., Secretary Hull, Under Secretary Sumner Welles, and Assistant Secretaries Adolph A. Berle and George S. Messersmith gathered in Hull's office and listened on the radio to Adolf Hitler shouting in the Reichstag. Ambassador Joseph P. Kennedy in London called Hull and said bleakly, "It's all over."

First, the men in Secretary Hull's office prepared to bring Americans home from Europe. The Secretary summoned Breckinridge Long, the former ambassador to Italy, from Rome to direct the operation, with Hugh Wilson, who was already in Washington, as his deputy. By month's end, they had requisitioned twenty thousand ship berths.

Two days after Germany invaded Poland, France and Britain declared war on Germany. In London that same day, Prime Minister Neville Chamberlain summoned Ambassador Kennedy to 10 Downing Street and showed him the speech he would make to Parliament. Kennedy was spinning into black despair; his eyes filled with tears. Back at the embassy, he telephoned Roosevelt to express his certainty that Britain would lose the war he had so desperately wanted to avoid. His voice choking, Kennedy cried, "It's the end of the world."

Roosevelt comforted him and realized he could no longer turn to Kennedy for objective advice. Although now FDR could act more vigorously, polls showed that most Americans wanted to stay out of the war. He announced that the United States would remain neutral.

Bullitt urged Roosevelt to modify the Neutrality Act in order to supply France and England with arms and warplanes with which to fight Hitler. Otherwise, he wrote, "It would be our turn next." Congress, cautiously, repealed the arms embargo.

Since Italy did not plunge into the fighting, Ambassador William Phillips in Rome was busy at first moving American tourists to safety and trying to convince the Fascists not to send back to Germany the German Jews who had fled to Italy before the war began. Phillips later remembered how frustrated he was:

> We in the Embassy were curiously out of touch with the course of events in the north. The department was not keeping me sufficiently informed of day-to-day operations. Although this was rather typical of its then prevailing attitude toward the Foreign Service, failure to keep the Embassy in Rome properly advised in those critical days was inexcusable, particularly as we had few reliable outside sources of information.

As soon as the war started, George Kennan was sent to Berlin, where he witnessed German barbarity toward Poland. But he evidenced little sympathy for the Poles. He detested Hitler's regime, but he thought that Nazism contained the seeds of its own destruction.

As the Berlin embassy's administrative officer, Kennan handled problems for the veteran chargé d'affaires Alexander Kirk, an old-fashioned diplomat who loathed the Nazis. Kennan's duties multiplied as the Germans closed the ten major U.S. consular offices in Germany. By the time of Pearl Harbor, two years later, the embassy and its staff of ninety-nine Americans and a handful of Germans represented the interests of eleven countries at war.

Kennan was heartened by the ordinary Berliner's dislike of the Nazi war. He never saw the German people "as a mass of inhuman monsters, solidly behind Hitler." But he did speak of the "lust to dominate Europe which are all that most Germans really have in common." Kennan had clandestine meetings with two important anti-Nazis: Count Helmuth von Moltke, a great-nephew of the famous Prussian field marshal and a legal aide to the German general staff, and Gottfried Bismarck, the Iron Chancellor's grandson and governor of Brandenburg. They helped Kennan sustain his belief in the German people's eventual salvation.

Another anti-Nazi was less successful. Adam von Trott zu Solz was a young Prussian aristocrat whose mother was half-American; he had spent a year at Balliol College, Oxford, on a Rhodes Scholarship. (There, he had met an American Rhodes Scholar, Dean Rusk.) In 1937, Trott had visited cousins in New York, Dr. William Schieffelin and his wife, who gave him an introductory note to Secretary Hull; unfortunately, Hull was out of town.

Two years later, Trott visited the United States again. This time, he sought help for those conspiring to get rid of Hitler. On December 20, Trott met with Assistant Secretary of State Messersmith and then with Supreme Court Justice Felix Frankfurter, who recommended that FDR not meet the young German because he might be a Nazi acting as a dissident. Later, Trott actually did join the Nazi Party in order to fight it from within.

Although Messersmith instructed Alexander Kirk to keep the door of the Berlin embassy open for Trott, his visit to America was an opportunity missed. Neither the United States nor the British government imagined that the Resistance inside Nazi Germany could possibly be effective. When, on July 20, 1944, the German conspirators exploded a bomb that wounded Hitler, Trott and Moltke were among thousands tortured and hanged.

"ONE OF THE MOST TERRIBLE MOMENTS
IN HUMAN HISTORY"

In Rome on April 29, 1940, Ambassador William Phillips met with Mussolini and read him a message from President Roosevelt urging Italy to stay out of the war. The President's note politely warned that if the war spread, nations wanting to stay out of it might be forced to come in. Mussolini replied that recent German victories in Norway made the Allied blockade ineffective. Germany was unbeatable, he said, and the consequences of

World War I's defeat had to be wiped clean before Europe would find peace.

In London, Winston Churchill replaced Neville Chamberlain as prime minister. In Paris, the French scheduled their buildup of armaments on the assumption that the German attack would not come for months. They were disastrously wrong.

At 3:00 A.M. on May 10, Hitler began his blitzkrieg, sending tanks and aircraft against Belgium and Holland. Thousands of French men, women, and children fled south. Bullitt cabled Secretary Hull: "We are at one of the most terrible moments in human history."

Despite the madness of war, Roosevelt kept trying to reason with the Fascists. On May 27, Ambassador Phillips delivered another message from the President to the foreign minister, Count Galeazzo Ciano, but Ciano coolly informed him that Italy would soon go to war to fulfill its commitment to Germany. Four days later, Ciano told Phillips that Italy was going to war and he preferred not to receive "any further pressure."

Six days after the evacuation by sea of 338,000 British and French soldiers at Dunkirk, Italy declared war on Britain and France and invaded France. Roosevelt declared, "On this tenth day of June 1940, the hand that held the dagger has struck it into the back of its neighbor."

That same evening, Ambassador Bullitt, in Paris, received a message for Roosevelt from the French premier, Paul Reynaud. It beseeched the United States to send all aid "short of an expeditionary force" to save France. Bullitt had the USS *Vincennes* and two destroyers pick up $250 million worth of French gold at Casablanca and bring it to the United States. At the same time, Ambassador Kennedy, in London, urged the President to accept Hitler's terms because they were better now than they would be in the future. The British made it clear they were disgusted by Ambassador Kennedy's defeatism.

The German blitzkrieg was dramatically successful. Unlike World War I, this became a war of maneuver on the ground and in the air, soon accelerated by jet engines and radar. Strategic bombing made targets of cities and their civilian populations.

Just a month before Germany had invaded Poland, Albert Einstein sent President Roosevelt a warning that Germany might convert the enormous energy locked inside the atom into a military weapon. If a single bomb from a single aircraft could wipe out a city, massed armies would become irrelevant. The human race would be able to commit suicide.

"THE EVENTUAL DEMOCRATIZATION
OF ALL DIPLOMACY"

George Kennan's Norwegian wife, Annelise, and their two small daughters were visiting her family in Kristians when the Germans attacked Denmark and Norway. Kennan brought them back to Germany two days before warships shelled the town. By the end of May 1940, the Germans had subdued Holland, Luxembourg, and Belgium; the British army was escaping the Continent from Dunkirk, and in two more weeks Hitler swept into Paris.

Hitler then turned on his new ally, the Soviet Union. Kennan warned against giving support to the Soviet Union, which had taken over the Baltic states, attacked Finland, shared in the partition of Poland and Romania, and made a compact with Hitler. Kennan broke with American policy for the remainder of the war.

At that time, wives and children of U.S. Foreign Service officers gathered in the American legation at 28 Nobelsgate, Oslo. The wives needed a place to wait for their husbands, whom they had left in the war zone. Florence Jaffray "Daisy" Harriman, the U.S. minister to Oslo, organized twice-weekly meetings of the wives to knit layettes for the wives of the fishermen in the Norwegian north.

"Daisy" Harriman was the sophisticated, articulate widow of a New York banker; she had devoted herself to the better health of children and working conditions for women. President Wilson made her chairperson of the Committee on Women in Industry, and she also organized the Red Cross Motor Corps and served in France.

Franklin Roosevelt appointed her minister to Norway when she was a sixty-seven-year-old grandmother. She enjoyed two idyllic years getting to know Norway, entertaining King Haakon VII and Queen Maud, and fishing for salmon in the River Stryn.

Then, suddenly, the world seemed to turn bloodred, and she and the Norwegian government, both representing nations wishing to stay out of the war, struggled to deal with the chaos. Harriman was responsible for two thousand Americans living in Norway and for tourists trying to make their way home. The State Department wanted no American to become a casus belli.

Her first test came when the State Department and Frederick A. Sterling, the career minister in Stockholm, asked her to help locate the American merchantman *City of Flint*. The ship, though neutral, had been seized on October 9 by the German battleship *Deutschland*. After searching for nearly a month, Harriman and Consul Maurice P. Dunlap, in Bergen, located *City of Flint* at Haugesund, seventy-five miles south of Bergen. The Norwegians interned its German prize crew and escorted the ship to Bergen. The Germans demanded that the Norwegians return the ship to them.

Harriman took the train to Bergen and arranged with *City of Flint*'s Captain Joseph A. Gainard, who had served twenty-nine years in the U.S. Navy, to sail the ship back to the United States. Captain Gainard was awarded the Navy Cross.

On April 8, 1940, a predawn telephone call from the American legation in Copenhagen told Daisy Harriman that a large number of German warships were passing through the Great Belt, the forty-mile-long strait connecting the Baltic with the Kattegat leading into the Oslo fjord. She wrote, "I put on my hat and set off as fast as I could for the Foreign Office."

Sir Cecil Dormer, the British minister in Oslo, called to warn her that Germans were sailing up the fjord and to ask if she, representing a neutral nation, would take over the British legation. Although she should have gotten Washington's permission, she immediately agreed. Then, Ray Cox, secretary of the U.S. legation, cabled the State Department. When the telegraph operator cautioned that the message would not get through, Harriman telephoned the legation in Stockholm, and the message was forwarded from there.

The Norwegian foreign minister, Dr. Halvadan Koht, advised her that the royal court and government were going by special train north to Hamar and he hoped she could go with them. But at 6:40 A.M. she was told the train would leave in twenty minutes, too soon for her staff to be ready.

French legation officials also asked her to take charge of their interests. Wives and children of the legation staff were sent to a little mountain resort above Lillehammer. Harriman could be dropped off at Hamar to join the government.

By 9:45 A.M. the Americans piled into their cars for the trip north. Irja E. Lindgren, a clerk in the legation, drove Harriman's Ford, which was crowded with the minister, a maid, typewriter, codebook, and as many suitcases as could be jammed in. On its roof they tied an American flag.

German bombers began circling, and the Americans watched fighters in aerial combat overhead. Shrapnel hit one car in their convoy, but no one was hurt. They passed Kjeller Airfield, where the hangars were still burning. Nazis parachuted out of the skies and occupied Oslo. Major Vidkun Quisling and his Norwegian Fascists seized Oslo's telephone and radio centrals.

Harriman led her party north after the royal family, first to Hamar and then to Elverum. The German army was not far behind. From Elverum, she could telephone the American minister in Stockholm, but she could not communicate with now-occupied Oslo.

The Norwegians had erected barricades topped with barbed wire across the roads and had laid crisscrossed layers of ships' masts eight feet high and twice as deep. Further north, at Nybersgund, the Germans bombed the hotel, and King Haakon had to flee into the snowy woods.

Harriman and her colleagues spent the night in an isolated farmhouse. The farmer skied through the forests to find a road that was clear. No passable road existed, so he clung to Harriman's running board and guided them back to a barricade they had passed. Soldiers there helped slide the car down to and across the ice-covered river, and they drove back to the now-burned-out town of Elverum. Norwegians guarding wounded Germans urged them on. They passed busloads of German prisoners. Nybersgund was now a smoking ruin. The royal family and government had already gone, and although Harriman's people were obviously Americans, the frightened local people would not admit knowing which road the royal party had taken.

They drove across the Swedish border and telephoned Minister Sterling in Stockholm. Secretary Hull had ordered a young military attaché to join Harriman. Captain Robert M. Losey, an army flier and a member of the West Point class of 1929, replaced the clerk-driver, and they set out again after the Norwegian royal couple and government. Captain Losey and an aide made an all-night dash into Stockholm with dispatches. The young flier made another trip into Norway, where, on April 20, a splinter of German shrapnel pierced his heart and killed him. Ambassador Harriman accompanied his body to Stockholm.

The Germans conquered southern Norway and, aided by a Quisling fifth column, seized Narvik in the far north. At the end of May, French, Polish, and Norwegian troops, supported by British warships, counterattacked and drove out the Germans. Before they left, the Germans burned Narvik's supply of coal for the next winter. In the end, the Nazis occupied all of Norway.

King Haakon and the government were secreted to London, and Norway's Crown Prince Olav asked Harriman to take Crown Princess Märtha and their children to the United States, where they were invited to be guests of President Roosevelt.

The troop transport *American Legion* sailed to Finland's ice-free port of Petsamo on the Barents Sea and picked up the royal party and nearly nine hundred Americans, including three hundred children. Harriman sailed with them to New York. She had performed heroically.

Looking back over her diplomatic service, Harriman wrote:

> It seems to me that the business of the American Foreign Service is to make a great contribution to the eventual democratization of all diplomacy. Our mission everywhere is to convince people of the benefits of our own democracy, to make our connections when we go abroad, not merely with the sovereign, the Government and privileged society, but with the democratic elements wherever we may find them.

"PUT EVERY OBSTACLE IN THE WAY . . ."

Putting Breckinridge Long in charge of the Immigrant Visa Section proved disastrous. Long, a Princeton graduate married to a wealthy woman, enjoyed horses and Democratic politics. For helping Wilson's 1916 presidential campaign, he had been rewarded with the post of third assistant secretary of state; for supporting FDR's 1932 campaign, he was appointed ambassador to Italy. Long was an early admirer of Mussolini, and when Italy invaded Ethiopia, he helped persuade Roosevelt not to embargo oil to Italy. He was reprimanded by the State Department and resigned as ambassador in 1936. Despite this spotty record, once World War II began, he was named assistant secretary of state in charge of refugee affairs.

The restrictive 1924 Johnson-Reed Act allowed an annual quota of 153,774 immigrants to be admitted from outside the Western Hemisphere; the quota was never filled during the war. Long and most of his superiors were not inclined to assist Europeans endangered by the Nazis.

Long was described as "an extreme nativist with a particular suspicion of Eastern Europeans." He called Hitler's *Mein Kampf* "eloquent in opposition to Jewry and to Jews as exponents of Communism and chaos." He vowed he was keeping out Communists, radicals, and spies.

Historians still argue whether Long was anti-Semitic or simply indifferent to the fate that faced Europe's Jews. Either way, the result was the same. Certainly, some American diplomats tried to help Jews and others imperiled by the Nazis. But other American diplomats either despised the victims or felt that helping them would damage the United States' national interest.

The anti-Semitism issue existed long before the Nazis. For example, Selah Merrill was the United States consul in Jerusalem for fifteen years between 1882 and 1907. In 1891, Merrill wrote the State Department a detailed rebuttal to the Blackstone Memorial, by which more than four hundred prominent Americans, mostly Protestants, had petitioned President Benjamin Harrison to support a conference on Jewish claims to Palestine. Merrill opposed the petition and wrote, "The Jew needs to learn that his place in the world will be determined by what he can do for himself, and not much by what Abraham did for himself four thousand years ago."

After World War II, the simultaneous arrival of the Great Depression and Nazi-fanned anti-Semitism made the American restrictions significant—and controversial. President Herbert Hoover directed the State Department to further reduce immigration by enforcing a 1917 law that barred anyone likely to become a public charge. Assistant Secretary Wilbur Carr and A. Dana Hodgdon, head of the visa division, went to Europe to ensure the consuls revised their interpretation of the law to limit visas to 10 percent of each quota. This rule was in effect by 1931, before Hitler ever came to power.

As the Nazis intensified their persecution of German Jews, Carr, Jay Pierrepont Moffat, and William Phillips led the department to enforce the immigration bars against refugees. The dispute centered on whether to allow the use of bonds to provide the guarantee that refugees would not become public charges.

Pressure increased to admit more Jewish refugees when, in mid-1935, the Nazis instituted the infamous Nuremberg Decrees. President Roosevelt finally indicated an interest in the fate of Jewish refugees, but State Department officers said polls showed that the majority of Americans opposed admitting more Jews.

After Germany annexed Austria in March 1938, Nazis intensified their persecution of Jews, and that November Kristallnacht aroused worldwide condemnation of Germany. Still, the chief of the visa division, Avra Warren, went to Europe to tell consuls to stop granting so many visas.

In 1940, the U.S. Embassy in Berlin reported that thousands of Jewish Germans were being shipped to Poland as forced labor. Learning of the deportation of twelve hundred Jews from Stettin, Assistant Secretary Adolf Berle wrote Breckinridge Long that if the reports were only 20 percent true, it was "a problem that ought to enlist our humanitarian interest." He received no reply from Long, so Berle wrote Secretary Hull directly, urging that the United States protest.

That brought a prompt reply from Long; there was no need for a protest, he wrote; everyone knew how Americans felt. It had been understood since *Mein Kampf* was published, Long added, "that these poor people would be subjected to all kinds of improper treatment." The State Department rejected Berle's appeal.

On June 26, 1940, Long sent State a memo describing "effective ways" to block Jews from reaching the United States. He said; "We can delay and effectively stop for a temporary period of indefinite length the number of immigrants into the United States. We could do this by simply advising our consuls, to put every obstacle in the way and require additional evidence and to resort to various administrative devices which would postpone and postpone and postpone the granting of the visas." But a long-term solution would require that an emergency be proclaimed.

Visa applicants were required at the time to have multiple people vouch for them, obtain notarized certificates, and tolerate long interviews, in addition to the barriers against emigration that the Nazis erected. It was reported that only three visas were issued in a month at Stuttgart, and three or four a week at Vienna.

Before the United States entered the war, the State Department repeatedly tightened regulations on admitting refugees. If a refugee left a close relative behind in a country opposed to the American form of government, that prejudiced his application. Each applicant had to produce two American sponsors, one financial, the other moral. In some cases, they needed to produce a clean criminal record from the country they were fleeing, an obviously impossible demand. Certainly, there was a masked anti-Semitism in the State Department. William Phillips in Washington; Hugh Gibson in Warsaw; and Richard C. Beer in Budapest were all known to disparage Jews. Jews found the bureaucratic labyrinth more and more impenetrable.

But not all Foreign Service officers approved these restrictions. The International Raoul Wallenberg Foundation later identified "courageous diplomats" who had saved lives from the Nazis. Among them were six American Foreign Service officials: Hiram Bingham IV, vice consul in Marseilles; Rives Childs, consul general in Tangier; Howard Elting, Jr., vice consul in Geneva; Raymond Herman Geist, consul general in Berlin; Thousands Standish, vice consul in Marseilles; and Stephen B. Vaughan, vice consul in Breslau, who issued visas to seven hundred Jewish families.

Immediately after Germany's surrender, Raymond Geist, then a consul in Mexico City, made a statement for the U.S. Chief Counsel for Prosecution of Axis Criminality describing Nazi attacks in Germany on Americans and some of his efforts to have Americans released from concentration camps. Berlin Consul General Messersmith called Geist, who had been born in Cleveland and earned a Harvard Ph.D., "the most valuable American representative in Berlin." Geist also reported on his ten years of scouting out German military mobilization, during which he was "being disguised as a German and speaking the language."

In 2002, the American Foreign Service Association gave "Harry" Bingham a special posthumous award for "constructive dissent." Bingham's father was a U.S. senator, and his mother, a Tiffany heiress. He had graduated from Yale and the Harvard Law School and joined the Foreign Service in 1929. As a vice consul in Marseilles in 1940 and 1941, Bingham issued visas that saved 2,500 Jews and other enemies of Hitler. Among those he saved were painters Marc Chagall, Max Ernst, and Marcel Duchamp; sculptor Jacques Lipchitz; novelist Lion Feuchtwanger; and Nobel Prize–winning biochemist Otto Meyerhof.

Bingham took risks. He hid people in his home, bought fake documents, and claimed refugees were members of his family. But the only price he paid was to the State Department. A telegram from Secretary Hull on April 26, 1941, cut short his tour at Marseilles, over his protests. He was transferred to Buenos Aires, and after the war he resigned.

"THE UTTER FAILURE OF CERTAIN OFFICIALS"

In January 1942, the Nazis clarified their intentions and ordered a "final solution" for the Jews. Within five months, they murdered five hundred thousand Jews. The U.S. Embassy in Berlin sent a stream of reports to Washington.

On Saturday morning, August 8, 1942, Vice Consul Howard Elting, Jr., greeted in his office at the U.S. consulate in Geneva a "greatly agitated" young man. He was Gerhart Riegner, secretary of the World Jewish Congress in Switzerland, and he had asked to see Paul Chapin Squire, the American consul, whom he knew. Squire was on vacation, so Riegner gave Vice Consul Elting the information he had received from a German businessman, that the Nazis had ordered the death of all the Jews in Europe. At that time, it was still not known that in January the Nazi leaders had adopted the Wannsee protocol, the program to kill Europe's Jews. Elting, a Princeton graduate with more than a decade in the Foreign Service, passed Riegner's report to the State Department with the assurance that Riegner seemed a reliable informant.

Riegner asked that his report be delivered to Rabbi Stephen Wise, president of the American Jewish Congress in New York. But the State Department's Division of European Affairs did not forward Riegner's cable. They said the report was "fantastic." Riegner had taken the precaution of also sending his report through the British Foreign Office to the British section of the World Jewish Congress. Rabbi Wise finally received the cable via London and was immediately in touch with Under Secretary Sumner Welles, who, although long concerned about the fate of Jews in Hitler's Europe, persuaded Wise to refrain from any public announcement until the extermination order could be confirmed.

Myron C. Taylor, President Roosevelt's new personal representative to the Vatican, asked Roman Catholic Church officials to confirm the reports soon flooding into American embassies and consulates about the Jews being moved to their death in the east. Vatican officials answered Taylor's inquiries with careful evasion. Riegner dramatized the horror by bringing to Consul Squire evidence of two factories that were manufacturing soap, glue, and lubricants from Jewish corpses.

At the end of October, Leland Harrison, the American minister at Bern, met with Riegner at Welles' request and detailed the various reports in a personal letter to Welles. He did not send a copy of this communication to the State Department, but affidavits and personal accounts poured in. Welles released Rabbi Wise from his agreement not to make his information public.

Ambassador John C. Winant in London was also deluged with appeals for action. But, despite his repeated inquiries, he received no instructions from Washington. By the time President Roosevelt met with a delegation led by Rabbi Wise on December 8, an estimated two million Jews had died.

On January 16, 1944, President Roosevelt was visited by Secretary of the Treasury Henry Morgenthau, Treasury's general counsel Randolph Paul, and John Pehle, head of the Treasury's Division of Foreign Funds Control. Morgenthau handed FDR a "Personal Report" in which he charged the "utter failure of certain officials in our State Department . . . to take any effective action to prevent the extermination of the Jews in German-controlled Europe." The only State Department official that the report criticized by name was Breckinridge Long. The report said responsible people were beginning to refer to "plain Anti-Semitism motivating the actions of these State Department officials."

After meeting with Morgenthau, Roosevelt created the independent War Refugee Board to counteract foot dragging in the State Department and in the International Committee of the Red Cross. Seventeen months had passed since Gerhart Riegner's first meeting with Vice Consul Elting in Geneva and millions of Jews had died when Secretary Hull finally sent a cable to all U.S. embassies, missions, and consulates ordering that "action be taken to forestall the plot of the Nazis to exterminate the Jews and other persecuted minorities in Europe." It was too little and much too late.

SWASTIKA OVER THE CRILLON

Ambassador Anthony J. Drexel Biddle, Jr., and H. Freeman Matthews, first secretary of the U.S. Embassy, accompanied the French government fleeing Paris for Bordeaux. Ambassador Bullitt insisted—"foolishly," according to journalist William Shirer—on staying in Paris. Bullitt argued that he was acting in the tradition of U.S. ambassadors, citing Gouverneur Morris and his wooden leg, Elihu Washburne and the Paris Commune, and Myron Herrick.

Secretary Cordell Hull and General Charles de Gaulle later criticized Bullitt's decision to stay in Paris because it separated him from the French government. But, Bullitt, knowing that the State Department would oppose him, dealt with FDR directly, and the President supported his decision. By staying in Paris, Bullitt was able to help the French negotiate through the Swiss and prevent the city from being destroyed. But Shirer held Bullitt responsible for "some fanciful reporting" because of his "hysteria about Communism."

The Germans commandeered, for their headquarters, the Hotel Crillon on the Place de la Concorde, near the American embassy. They flew a flag with a giant swastika. U.S. Counselor of Embassy Robert Murphy, with Commander Roscoe Hillenkoetter, the naval attaché, and Colonel Horace Fuller, the military attaché, walked across the street from the embassy to the hotel to meet the German military governor, Lieutenant General Bogislav von Studnitz. Murphy was startled when the German general's aide greeted him by name; they had known each other fifteen years earlier when Murphy was a young vice consul in Munich.

Robert Murphy was the son of a Milwaukee railroad worker and had long experience with the Nazis. Entering the Foreign Service in 1921, he was sent to Munich to help reopen the postwar consulate general there. It was the beginning of an important diplomatic career. He met Hitler and other Nazis when they were obscure young agitators; he experienced the postwar turmoil and runaway inflation on which they rose to power. The Americans then issued as many as four hundred visas a day to Bavarians wishing to escape to the United States. Murphy sent in reports about Hitler's activities but heard nothing from Washington.

At 3:00 A.M. on November 9, 1923, Murphy visited with Hitler, whose men had seized the government buildings, in order to send a telegram in code to Washington. Hours later, he stood in the Odeonsplatz and watched Hitler and General Ludendorff lead their Brown Shirts against the Bavarian police. He saw the two Nazi leaders throw themselves to the ground when the firing started. After Hitler's putsch failed, Murphy watched the trial at which Hitler was sentenced to Landsberg Fortress, where he wrote *Mein Kampf*. In 1930, Murphy was assigned to Paris, and ten years later was sent to Vichy.

General von Studnitz told the three Americans who called on him that Germany would finish with France in ten days and then invade Britain. The general visited Ambassador Bullitt the next day, according to protocol. And the Germans began stringing telephone wire from the Crillon onto the roof of the American embassy, until Bullitt sent word that this was a violation of American soil and threatened to fire on them. The Germans stopped immediately.

At Bordeaux, the French cabinet was torn between asking the Germans for an armistice or continuing the fight from Algeria. First Secretary Matthews, of the United States, said Premier Paul Reynaud was pressured by his mistress, Countess Hélène de Portes, who hysterically pleaded that France surrender.

Biddle and Matthews did what little they could to keep France in the war, but on Sunday evening, June 16, Premier Reynaud told Biddle that France could hold out no longer; masses of French refugees faced starvation and disease. Biddle entreated the exhausted premier to continue the war from abroad and to save the French fleet from the Germans. Reynaud "shrugged again and looked away."

That evening, the French turned over the government to eighty-four-year-old Marshal Henri-Philippe Pétain, knowing he would ask the Germans for terms. And at dawn, the British flew Brigadier General Charles de Gaulle from Bordeaux to London. Churchill called him "the honor of France."

On Monday, the United States government froze France's assets in the United States. And as the German army advanced on Bordeaux, Biddle received a cable from Roosevelt warning the French not to let the Germans seize their fleet. Otherwise, "the French government will permanently lose the friendship and good-will of the Government of the United States."

On July 1, Bullitt and Murphy joined the desperate French government near Vichy and reemphasized that the French fleet must not fall into German hands. Bullitt was profoundly depressed by French defeatism. Marshal Pétain berated Churchill and de Gaulle and French parliamentarians. France's new leaders told Bullitt that France would become a province of Germany and they wished the same fate for Britain.

Feeling useless in this chaos, Bullitt left Murphy as chargé d'affaires of the U.S. Embassy at Vichy and headed home. On January 7, 1941, the president accepted Bullitt's resignation as ambassador, while Murphy settled the U.S. Embassy into a villa owned by Mrs. Jay Gould.

Bullitt said Under Secretary Sumner Welles was a latent homosexual. When his accusations leaked to the press he insisted Welles be dismissed. His ultimatum permanently ruined Bullitt's relationship with FDR, but, nevertheless, two years later, Welles was forced to resign.

In November 1941, Roosevelt sent Bullitt as his personal representative to the Middle East. He was en route there when the Japanese bombed

Pearl Harbor. And three years later, Bullitt served in uniform with France's First Army as it fought its way north to liberate Paris.

Soon after France's defeat, Commander Roscoe Hillenkoetter, the naval attaché at the U.S. Embassy in Vichy, visited Algeria and Morocco and analyzed how France might fight again in North Africa. Hearing this, President Roosevelt sent Robert Murphy to tour French Africa quietly. Murphy flew into Algiers' harbor in an ancient Air France trimotor seaplane. With the help of Felix Cole, the consul general at Algiers, he collected a great deal of confidential information for the President. In Dakar, he and General Maxime Weygand, France's supreme authority in Africa, negotiated an accord that enabled the United States to supply the French in Africa with nonmilitary supplies.

In the months before Pearl Harbor, the United States had consulates in five French-African cities, manned by a dozen Foreign Service officers. When the Murphy-Weygand accord began shipments, Murphy added a dozen vice consuls, who were, in fact, intelligence agents. Though they were carefully chosen, most were inexperienced, and none knew Arabic.

Murphy's network of neophyte spies was resented by State Department career people in North Africa, particularly by J. Rives Child, the tradition-minded minister at Tangier. Consulate staffs did not know what these special vice consuls were up to. They worked with General William J. Donovan's intelligence team, led by Marine Colonel William A. Eddy, who knew the area and was fluent in Arabic. Murphy handled the political side, and Eddy, the espionage.

WARTIME ADJUSTMENTS

In 1939, at the beginning of the war, the U.S. Foreign Service consisted of about four thousand people, of whom 833 were Foreign Service officers. The FSOs included 113 transfers from Commerce and Agriculture.

As the United States inched toward war, work piled up for American officials overseas. Special agencies were created to handle many of their new responsibilities, while the closing of American consulates in Axis and Axis-controlled countries freed about a hundred Foreign Service officers for new assignments.

In 1941, a decision was made to expand the Foreign Service by eliminating formal examinations and making temporary appointments for the duration of the war. These employees became members of the Foreign Service Auxiliary. By the war's end, auxiliaries were stationed all over the globe, and the Foreign Service consisted of 976 auxiliary officers and only 820 career officers.

In December 1941, Foreign Service officers became responsible for international cooperation against the enemy. Chiefs of mission took charge of personnel from other civilian agencies operating in their jurisdictions, adding their functions to usual foreign relations activities such as negotiations, political and economic reporting, protection of U.S. interests, and the range of consular duties.

By 1944, wartime experience led to changes in the way the Foreign Service was managed. A new Office of the Foreign Service was organized into three divisions responsible for planning, training, and reporting. The training division became the precursor of the Foreign Service Institute.

Once the war was over, a basic reorganization of the Foreign Service was needed. And then limits on the percentage of officers in the higher classes were removed, reopening promotion opportunities that the war had destroyed.

"THE GREAT ARSENAL OF DEMOCRACY"

In September 1940, Roosevelt had taken a giant step toward supporting the Allies. He agreed with Britain to exchange fifty overaged destroyers for ninety-nine-year leases on eight naval and air bases at British holdings in the Western Hemisphere from Newfoundland to British Guiana.

That fall, Ambassador Joseph P. Kennedy, Sr., flew home from London on the Atlantic clipper (it took five days), planning to go on the radio and persuade the nation to vote for Republican candidate Wendell Willkie. But Roosevelt shrewdly arranged that Kennedy would talk to no one involved with political questions before Kennedy and he had a chance to talk together. In a masterful display of political wheeling-dealing, over his traditional Sunday-evening family dinner of scrambled eggs and sausages, Kennedy agreed to endorse FDR for reelection on a national broadcast. The decisive but unspoken key was that Kennedy and his wife, Rose, were aware that FDR could affect the political futures of Kennedy and his sons. As a result, both Roosevelt and Kennedy promised the nation, "Your boys are not going to be sent into any foreign wars!" A few weeks later,

Roosevelt was reelected for a third term, and Kennedy resigned. Roosevelt accepted his resignation.

Kennedy stopped at the State Department and advised Assistant Secretary Breckinridge Long to cut a deal with Germany and Japan, anticipating that the United States would have to accept a Fascist form of government. Kennedy never again played a part in the war. He blamed a number of people around Roosevelt, but Supreme Court Justice Felix Frankfurter wrote in his diary, "I don't suppose it ever enters the head of a Joe Kennedy that one who was so hostile to the war effort as he was all over the lot, and so outspoken in his foulmouthed hostility to the President himself, barred his own way to a responsible share in the conduct of the war."

That December, Roosevelt sent retired Admiral William D. Leahy, then the governor of Puerto Rico, to Vichy as the American ambassador with strongly worded instructions to warn the French government that the United States intended to make sure that Britain won the war and would not tolerate any French actions interfering with that goal. As German and Italian armies overran Yugoslavia and Greece, Roosevelt spelled out to the American people what an Axis victory would mean to them. Roosevelt said, "Never before since Jamestown and Plymouth Rock has our American civilization been in such danger as now." He declared, "We must be the great arsenal of democracy." The United States slid inescapably into a fighting role.

Early in 1941, Under Secretary Sumner Welles warned the Soviet ambassador in Washington that Germany was planning to attack the Soviet Union. And on June 22, Hitler's armored divisions struck Russia on a broad front. The United States moved troops to Iceland to keep the North Atlantic sea lanes open and, by fall, began arming its merchant ships so they could defend themselves. President Roosevelt told the American people, "When you see a rattlesnake posed to strike, you do not wait until he has struck before you crush him." Endless rows of war graves planted across Europe would testify to the failure of the diplomats and politicians to stop the rattlesnake from striking.

IN HARM'S WAY

Both before and after the United States' entry, the war brought U.S. Foreign Service people into harm's way. In Warsaw, members of the consulate general staff narrowly escaped when a bombardment destroyed their building. In Chungking, embassy staff were subjected to repeated bombings that damaged their offices. Two consuls at Le Havre barely escaped death when German planes bombed the ferry they were riding. Bombs and fire destroyed consulates in Britain. Before the Allies landed in North Africa, American consuls learned that they were in danger from their contact with the French underground. At some risk, Consul General Sam E. Woods and Consul Robert E. Cowan, in Zurich, helped Allied fliers who escaped Swiss internment camps flee to nearby countries.

One Foreign Service officer who survived an especially hazardous wartime was Walter W. Orebaugh, who escaped from internment in Italy and joined Italian partisans fighting in the mountains. Born in Kansas in 1910, Orebaugh had joined the Foreign Service in 1932, after college. As the American consul in Nice on the French Riviera, he witnessed the police rounding up Jewish families at night and packing them into freight cars.

On November 5, 1942, Pinkney Tuck, the U.S. chargé in Vichy, phoned and warned Orebaugh to leave France and remove his consulate to neutral Monaco. A few days later, the Italian army invaded Monaco, occupied the American consulate, and interned Orebaugh and two women consulate employees.

They spent a miserable winter at Gubbio in Umbria and then were transferred to Perugia. They were still there in September when Italy surrendered. As the Germans in Italy approached, Orebaugh and the two women hid in the home of Margherita Bonucci and her family; they climbed into the attic when German soldiers searched the house.

On January 29, 1944, the athletic, six-foot Orebaugh, having made careful clandestine arrangements, joined a group of Italian partisans called the Band of San Faustino. The two women were transported to the care of Harold Tittman, Myron Taylor's assistant in the Vatican.

Fighting with the partisans, Orebaugh helped ambush a German truck convoy climbing a narrow mountain road. They also hit the German arms depot at Gubbio and later battled SS troops in an all-day firefight in the hills, killing 170 of the enemy.

The partisan band began to run out of ammunition, so Orebaugh volunteered to travel to the Allied lines with one of the partisans. The pair made their way through the mountains, staying ahead of pursuing German soldiers. They then sailed the Adriatic in the leaking hulk of a fishing boat and came ashore at the remains of the port of Ortona, which the

Allies had just liberated. On May 12, 1944, after Orebaugh had spent sixteen months behind enemy lines, British Marines led them through an artillery barrage to the American 12th Air Corps headquarters at Foggia. They met with Ambassador Alexander C. Kirk and Consul General George Brandt at Naples and General Harold Alexander, the Allied commander, at Caserta. Orebaugh arranged with the Office of Strategic Services (OSS) to airdrop ammunition and supplies to the Band of San Faustino.

Later, he reopened the U.S. consulate in Florence. He was granted the Medal of Freedom, the U.S. highest civilian award for valor. The citation said he "displayed courage, resourcefulness and coolness under fire, worthy of the best traditions of the Foreign Service."

33

"A Very Tragic Moment"

1941–45

Having delivered President Roosevelt's message for the emperor of Japan and left the Japanese foreign minister after midnight, Ambassador Joseph C. Grew was awakened by a telephone call at 7:00 A.M., on Monday, December 8, 1941, Tokyo time. He was asked to come back and see Foreign Minister Togo Shigenori, as soon as possible. Grew dressed hurriedly and arrived unshaven at Togo's official residence at 7:30 with Robert Feary, his private secretary. Togo told them that he had seen the emperor at 3:00 A.M. The foreign minister, grim and formal, then handed Ambassador Grew a thirteen-page memorandum stating that Japan had cut off the talks between their two governments in Washington.

Grew returned to his quarters, shaved, ate breakfast, and then learned that Japan was at war with the United States and Great Britain. Togo had not mentioned it. Later in the morning, a Japanese Foreign Office official came to the embassy and read aloud, his hands trembling, the official announcement that war had begun between their two governments. First Secretary Edward S. Crocker said simply, "This is a very tragic moment."

The Japanese police locked the embassy's iron gates; no one was allowed in or out. Grew ordered all codes and confidential communications burned. The Japanese prohibited sending coded telegrams; their radio mechanics came and took away all shortwave radios. Grew intended to notify the department that all the staff were safe, but, in fact, one man,

Randall Jones, was missing. He had gone to Yokohama on his day off and not returned. In short order, he turned up, having heard the news. He climbed a ladder over the wall and made it safely into the embassy compound.

Grew received a jumbled telephone call from Maxwell M. Hamilton, chief of the State Department's Far Eastern Division, who needed to discuss who would handle American interests. Camille Gorgé, the hardheaded Swiss minister to Tokyo, was chosen. That evening, everyone in the embassy, some sixty people, gathered for cocktails, a congenial but exhausted group.

After initial interference by the police, Gorgé was able to visit Grew every two or three days. Police swarmed over the premises, and arrangements were made to get food and fuel oil, although there was never oil enough to heat the buildings more than a few hours a day. Staff members living outside were squeezed into the embassy buildings. The assistant naval attaché laid out a pitch-and-putt golf course, and Charles "Chip" Bohlen won the first-day's tournament.

Christmas was celebrated with caroling, a Virginia sugar-cured ham that Eugene Dooman, counselor of the embassy, had stored away, and two turkeys sent in to Alice Grew by the wife of Vice Foreign Minister Haruhiko Nishi. Japanese employees were allowed visits by their families for the first time. At Easter, the Americans were still interned in the embassy compound while negotiations to repatriate them dragged on. On April 18, just before lunch, the Americans heard planes overhead and saw a half dozen fires burning in various parts of the city. Jimmy Doolittle's B-25 bombers were raiding Tokyo from the carrier USS *Hornet*.

On Memorial Day, the Americans were unable to decorate the American graves in the cemetery at Yokohama, as was their custom. But Ambassador Grew was moved to say to the gathered staff, "We do not, we cannot forget those who gave their lives for our country, whether in the heat of combat or in carrying out other duties aimed to create conditions in which combat might never occur." He read them the Gettysburg Address.

Finally, in mid-June, the American diplomats boarded the Japanese exchange ship *Asama Maru*, which was emblazoned with huge white crosses on its black sides. They sat at anchor in Yokohama harbor for seven long days while negotiations continued. By then the Americans had heard of the U.S. naval victories of the Coral Sea and Midway.

On the night of June 25, *Asama Maru* got under way, picking up internees at Hong Kong and Saigon. During the long voyage, Ambassador Grew amused himself by sitting in on the newspaper correspondents' evening poker game. The Japanese would not let the exchange ships cross the Pacific Ocean, and the American Navy did not want a Japanese ship near Hawaii. Sleepy Lourenco Marques in neutral Portuguese East Africa (now Mozambique) on the Indian Ocean became the designated exchange point. There, nearly a thousand Americans and British men, women, and children transferred from the *Asama* to the blue-and-gold-painted Swedish *Gripsholm*. The two ships were tied up next to each other, nose to stern. And six hundred more from Japanese-occupied China crowded aboard the *Gripsholm* from the *Conte Verde,* which had sailed from Shanghai. The Japanese who had come out on the *Gripsholm* went home aboard the *Asama Maru*. On the dock, Ambassador Grew passed Ambassadors Nomura and Kurusu; Grew merely raised his hat. He said later he had nothing to say to them.

OUT OF BERLIN IMMEDIATELY

In Berlin, George Kennan learned from an American shortwave broadcast on Sunday night that the Japanese had attacked Pearl Harbor. He woke Leland Morris, now the chargé d'affaires, and late that night the staff met at the embassy, expecting the United States would soon be at war with Germany. By Tuesday the Gestapo surrounded and isolated the embassy.

The Americans burned codes and classified correspondence, and on Thursday, while Hitler was addressing the Reichstag, Leland Morris was summoned to hear Foreign Minister Ribbentrop read the declaration of war.

Saturday afternoon, Kennan was told that all American diplomats had to leave Berlin immediately. They were to report to the chancery at eight on Sunday morning with no more than two pieces of hand luggage each.

The Germans shipped them to Bad Nauheim, a resort near Frankfurt am Main, and confined 130 officials and journalists in Jeschke's Grand Hotel, watched over by armed guards. Later, Kennan commented tersely, "Not until the end of April 1942 did the United States government bother to communicate with us, which they could easily have done through the Swiss."

The Americans organized themselves, even created "Badheim University," which offered fifteen courses, and adjusted to the confinement, crowded quarters, and poor food. When they were scheduled to be shipped home, the departure of half the group was postponed to make room aboard ship for Jewish refugees. This was resented by Kennan and his colleagues, who were left behind. They stayed there for five more months and then were sent to Lisbon and home.

"MY MISSION FAILED"

During the months before the United States officially went to war, Ambassador William Phillips, in Rome, the third Axis capital, kept in touch with diplomats and journalists based in the capital or coming back from the battlefields. He talked frequently with Foreign Minister Ciano, but Il Duce would not see him. And he took charge of the affairs of Allied embassies as their staffs departed.

At the end of April 1941, Phillips received new instructions that went to all members of the U.S. Foreign Service. Although America was not then at war, the United States was already determined to oppose the forces of aggression. Phillips advised President Roosevelt to distinguish between the Nazi or Fascist governments and their people.

In June, the Germans sank the American merchant ship *Robin Moor* in the South Atlantic. Phillips told Ciano that the Americans were incensed. The United States closed all German and Italian consulates in the United States; and in response, the Germans and Italians ordered the Americans to shut their consulates.

On October 6, Ambassador Phillips flew to Washington, leaving Counselor George Wadsworth in charge of the Rome embassy. Phillips made reservations to return to Rome on December 12, but that turned out to be too late. He said candidly, "My mission failed. Italy entered the war against the western Allies and the United States."

BAPTISM IN NORTH AFRICA

Two weeks after the attack on Pearl Harbor, Prime Minister Churchill met in the White House with President Roosevelt, Secretary Hull, and Under Secretary Welles. They started planning an offensive in French North Africa, to be called "Torch."

As long as the fighting continued, Roosevelt devoted his entire attention to winning the war and left the troublesome complexities of the postwar world to Hull, Welles, and Vice President Henry Wallace. The State Department was divided over the course of the war, and Hull and Welles feuded face-to-face.

In the August after Pearl Harbor, the United States began to recover from the devastating attack on its Pacific fleet. Robert Murphy was summoned from Algiers to rural Hyde Park, New York, because the President was worried that some French officers would oppose the American landings in Africa. And he admonished Murphy, "Don't tell anybody in the State Department about this. That place is a sieve!"

General George C. Marshall sent Murphy, disguised as a lieutenant colonel because, Marshall said, "Nobody ever pays any attention to a lieutenant colonel," to General Dwight Eisenhower's headquarters in the English countryside. Foreign Service folklore tells that an unexpected problem arose when the chief of the State Department's passport division, Ruth Shipley, refused to give Murphy a passport under a false name.

In England, he conferred at length with Eisenhower and his staff, briefing them on North Africa's political complexities. Back in Washington, Murphy was assigned to work directly with the President and Eisenhower. Murphy described himself as a "a secret agent for Eisenhower . . . a diplomat among warriors."

By mid-October, Murphy was back at the consulate general in Algiers. He brought with him five small radio transmitters and negotiated support from diverse French and native factions for an invasion by a hundred thousand Americans and British. He also had to unravel the maze of French politics involving the British protégé, General Charles de Gaulle. Some of the most powerful French leaders in North Africa opposed American intervention, but Murphy received overtures from Admiral Jean-François Darlan, commander of all French forces in North Africa, and from the American favorite, General Henri Giraud, who had escaped from a German prison.

Eisenhower's deputy, General Mark Clark, led a team that landed secretly in Algeria from a British submarine and met with Giraud's men, despite hair-raising close calls that nearly got them all killed. Giraud demanded the command of all the French and American invading forces. Murphy tried to appease him, and H. Freeman Matthews ultimately persuaded him to visit Eisenhower at Gibraltar. On the eve of the North African invasion, Giraud agreed to help the Americans. He arrived at Algiers after the landings had begun on the night of November 8–9.

The Allied invaders landed at three sites at Casablanca, Oran, and Algeria. If the American GIs thought they were going to war against Germany, they discovered that first they had to fight the French. And the French resisted.

That night, Murphy raced to the villa of General Alphonse Juin, leader of the French army in Morocco. He woke the general, who appeared in his pink-striped pajamas and who insisted on conferring with Admiral Darlan before cooperating with the Americans. And Darlan in turn said he needed the approval of Marshal Pétain in Vichy.

Four hours after meeting with Giraud, Murphy was still waiting for word of the invading force. He stepped out into the garden and had a submachine gun stuck in his back. The regular French army had quietly taken over to protect its commander. Word was received that the American forces had, indeed, landed, but Murphy was forced to stay at Juin's residence until midafternoon, when Darlan asked him to contact the invading American general.

The Americans had come ashore on the wrong beach. Murphy found them, and also came upon the prime minister's son, Randolph Churchill, in a Ranger uniform, who took him to Major General Charles W. Ryder. Ryder drove with Murphy to French headquarters, where he and General Juin signed an agreement to halt the shooting in Algiers.

Murphy could not communicate with Eisenhower's headquarters because of the enormous radio traffic. He continued making his own decisions until General Mark Clark flew into Algiers the next afternoon in the midst of a German air raid. Two days later, Eisenhower arrived and approved the agreement with Darlan, instructing Murphy to keep close to Darlan.

Early on November 10, Clark and Murphy met with Darlan, Giraud, and Juin. Clark threatened Darlan with arrest unless he ordered a general cease-fire. The relationship between Eisenhower and the Vichy admiral became wildly controversial. The Gaullists regarded Darlan as a Nazi collaborator. On the afternoon before Christmas, a young Gaullist shot him at point-blank range and killed him. The twenty-year-old assassin was promptly executed, to protect the not so innocent.

Hal Vaughan, historian of the North African intrigue, wrote, "Nothing can take away from Murphy's bravery, dedication, and dogged perseverance under unbearable pressure." Ten of Murphy's vice consuls (as well as Gordon H. Browne of the OSS and Vice Consul L. Pittman Springs of the State Department) received a medal for covert services at the risk of their lives. (Murphy's ten were John Harvey Boyd, Frederick P. Culbert, David Wooster King, Ridgway B. Knight, John Crawford Knox, Kenneth W. Pendar, W. Stafford Reid, Leland L. Rounds, John E. Utter, and Harry A. Woodruff.)

The Allies needed until May 1943 to clear North Africa of Axis forces and secure the path to Egypt and the Suez Canal. Then, they prepared to invade Sicily.

On January 14, 1943, Roosevelt, Churchill, and the Combined Chiefs of Staff met at Casablanca. Stalin declined to join them. Therefore, the two Western leaders did not bring to the conference any representatives of the State Department or the British Foreign Office. Churchill brought Harold Macmillian as a minister resident, so FDR promoted Murphy to ministerial rank. Murphy and Giraud persuaded the Americans to rearm the French in North Africa. And for the war's end, the conference adopted a policy of unconditional surrender.

They tried to find an arrangement by which Giraud and de Gaulle could work together. But de Gaulle was determined to control French Africa and restore France to power on his own. By summer, with the adroit help of Jean Monnet, an influential member of the French government in exile, de Gaulle had gotten rid of Giraud and controlled French Africa.

At year's end, Churchill and Roosevelt met with Stalin at Tehran, where they agreed that the invasion of Western Europe would be led by Dwight Eisenhower; on the entrance of Russia in the Pacific war once Hitler was defeated; and some ideas about an organization of the postwar world that might prevent World War III.

"A MESSENGER BOY FOR THE PENTAGON"

George Kennan's experience at his next post, neutral Lisbon, intensified his criticism of the State Department. The British had made a secret deal with Portugal's dictator, Antonio Salazar, to build an airfield in the Azores. But when the Americans also wanted a base there in order to shuttle planes from the United States for the Normandy landings, the U.S. Embassy in Lisbon received no directions.

Communications between the department and the embassy were confused enough to baffle Salazar and require Kennan, who was now the chargé d'affaires, to make a frustrating five-night flight to Washington. After having fruitless meetings with Secretary of War Henry Stimson, Secretary of the Navy Frank Knox, Admiral William D. Leahy, the President's chief of staff, and Harry Hopkins, Kennan finally met with President Roosevelt, who gave Kennan a personal note to Salazar, which settled the matter. Kennan was sharply critical of Acting Secretary of State Edward R. Stettinius, Jr., and the State Department "regarding its role at that time as nothing more than that of a messenger boy for the Pentagon and accustomed to sneezing whenever the Pentagon caught cold."

Of course, the State Department was not alone in its confusion over how to deal with the new wartime conditions and relations with enemy and neutral Europe. The managers of a number of major American corporations believed it in their interest to continue to do business in enemy nations. Among the companies charged with maintaining relations with the enemy were IBM, European subsidiaries of Eastman Kodak, Standard Oil, ITT, and Ford. In Switzerland, Vice Consul Howard Elting Jr. met with Kodak's Swiss manager as late as 1943 and recounted, "I pointed out to him that our sole interest is to shut off every possible source of benefit to our enemies, regardless of what American commercial interests might suffer."

Kennan was next assigned to the European Advisory Commission, through which Britain, Russia, and the United States were planning for the German surrender and the occupation of Europe. Kennan, a relatively junior diplomat, met with the President and had him define American policy on the boundary between the Western zone and the Soviet zone. Kennan criticized the State Department for accepting FDR's handling of major questions of foreign policy and "the farcical and near-tragic confusions to which it repeatedly led."

In the spring of 1944, when Kennan was in Washington, Bohlen introduced him to Averell Harriman, the ambassador to Moscow, who was looking for a minister-counselor. Bohlen and Kennan dined with Harriman in his suite at Washington's Mayflower Hotel, and Kennan got the job.

Kennan arrived at Moscow on July 1 and temporarily lived in Spaso House, which had been his and Bullitt's residence back in 1933. The embassy was now divided into two sections, the civilian, which Kennan was to administer, and the military. He came to appreciate Harriman as a hardworking, demanding ambassador who did not overvalue the niceties of diplomatic practice. Although Harriman dealt only with the people at the top, Kennan commented, "His integrity in the performance of his duties was monumental and unchallengeable."

First, Kennan had to concentrate on Poland, which the Soviets had divided up with Germany. Most of the Allies recognized the Polish government in exile in London, while Stalin created the Committee of National Liberation, "the Lublin Poles," to speak for Soviet interests. When the Warsaw uprising occurred, the Russians let the Poles and Germans destroy each other. Kennan believed that was the point when Roosevelt should have forced a showdown with Stalin.

After FDR's death, Harry Hopkins came to Moscow. He met with Stalin and then with Kennan to hear his opinions. Kennan remembered, "He described to me Stalin's terms for a settlement of the Polish problem . . . and asked whether I thought we could do any better. I said I did not. Did I think, then, that we should accept these terms . . . ? I did not; I thought we should accept no share of the responsibility for what the Russians proposed to do in Poland. . . ."

"'I respect your opinion,' Hopkins said sadly. 'But I am not at liberty to accept it.'"

LOOKING BEYOND THE END

Britain and the United States favored contrasting strategies for winning in Europe. Churchill wanted to invade Italy and the Balkans, while Roosevelt wanted to save their best effort for a cross-Channel assault. Meanwhile,

Robert Murphy was given such diverse tasks as informing King Victor Emmanuel that he must abdicate and bringing presidential greetings to Pope Pius XII. He also visited Tito on his hideaway island of Vis off the Adriatic coast.

Murphy was thrown into the complex planning for the occupation of Germany. FDR was convinced that without postwar Soviet-American co-operation, world peace was not possible. The summit conference at Yalta in February 1945 spread hope that cooperation was a real possibility, even though Stalin held to his plan for a security zone in Eastern Europe. Again, the Foreign Service officers in the field were the first to become disillusioned.

Major General Lucius Clay was selected to administer the American zone of occupation, and Murphy, now an ambassador, was appointed his political advisor. After V-E Day, Murphy had to inform Grand Admiral Karl Dönitz, whom Hitler had appointed to succeed himself as Führer, that Eisenhower had ordered his arrest. Murphy's office was responsible for the twenty million defeated, hungry Germans in the American zone of Germany and for relations with the diplomatic missions at the Allied Control Council in Berlin. Hopes of cooperation were soon smothered by the Soviet determination to accept no interference in Eastern Europe and the Balkans.

CELEBRATION IN MOSCOW

The Russians, anticipating that the Germans might surrender to the Americans and British but keep fighting in the East, did not tell their people that the war in Europe was over until the day after V-E Day. That night, the word spread through Moscow, and the city celebrated. From the National Hotel hung an array of Allied flags, and at the U.S. embassy next door flew an American flag. Ambassador Averell Harriman was away, and Kennan obtained from the hotel a Soviet flag to hang with the Stars and Stripes. Crowds of young people waving flags and cheering filled the square in front of the embassy.

Kennan and a sergeant from the embassy's military mission climbed onto the pedestal of one of the large columns in front of the building. The crowd happily ignored the police and surged toward them. Kennan shouted, "Congratulations on the day of victory! All honor to the Soviet allies!"

The crowd roared and passed a Soviet soldier over their heads until he embraced the American sergeant.

This euphoria could not last. President Harry S Truman, unlike Roosevelt, turned to the State Department for help with foreign policy decisions. But by the time the Potsdam Conference closed on August 2, few Foreign Service officers still anticipated a smooth relationship with the Soviets. Then, four days after the Potsdam Conference closed, the first atomic bomb exploded over Hiroshima, and within two weeks the Japanese surrendered.

34

Foreign Service for a New World

1946–51

President Roosevelt had believed it was essential that the victorious Allies cooperate in order to rebuild the postwar world. But as the Soviet armies swept triumphantly westward, the American diplomats watching the Soviets close-up, especially the so-called Riga Group of George Kennan, Charles Bohlen, and Loy W. Henderson, saw how cruelly the Soviet Union treated the peoples of Eastern Europe. The Soviets liquidated political opponents, wrecked local economies, and shipped whole factories beyond the Urals. There were few signs of cooperation or moderation. Some feared that the Soviets planned to dominate all of Europe.

In mid-February 1946, Ambassador Averell Harriman in Moscow received a distressing message from the State Department. The Soviet Union was refusing to work with the World Bank and the International Monetary Fund for the reconstruction of Europe.

Ambassador Harriman was about to leave his post, and the State Department's inquiry was turned over to George Kennan, who was taking charge of the embassy. Kennan was convinced that the United States was already making too many concessions to the Soviet government, but he said that trying to explain his view to the State Department was like "talking to a stone." Now, by chance, his opinion was being asked, and he seized the opportunity. Although he was in bed with the flu, he dictated a telegram of some five thousand words, extraordinarily long, expounding his understanding of the Soviet view of the postwar world and its significance for American policy. He sent it off to Washington on February 22.

He believed the American government could not escape the Russians' historic insecurity and xenophobia, and he made three key points: First, he wrote, "At the bottom of the Kremlin's neurotic view of world affairs is traditional and instinctive Russian sense of insecurity." Second, "We have here a political force committed fanatically to the belief that with US there can be no permanent modus vivendi, that it is desirable and necessary that the internal harmony of our society be disrupted, our traditional way of life be destroyed, the international authority of our state be broken, if Soviet power is to be secure." And third, "World communism is like malignant parasite which feeds only on diseased tissue. . . . Every courageous and incisive measure to solve internal problems of our own society, to improve self-confidence, discipline, morale, and community spirit of our own people, is a diplomatic victory over Moscow worth a thousand diplomatic notes and joint communiques."

Kennan's telegram firmly contradicted Roosevelt's determination to get along with the Soviet leaders. Kennan believed that they intended to hold on to a sphere of control in Eastern Europe. His tough view created a sensation in Washington. President Truman and his cabinet members read it. Kennan was suddenly the center of attention in the topmost circles, listened to as a strategist and philosopher of American foreign policy.

His message, referred to simply as the "Long Telegram," had an extraordinary impact on official Washington because it promised to solve a dilemma. And it also put a name—"containment"—on what appeared to be an inchoate attitude toward the Soviet Union.

During the war, the United States and the Soviet Union had gone to great lengths to cooperate. Research by Hugh De Santis showed that Charles Bohlen in Moscow; H. Freeman Matthews, the chargé in London; Burton Perry, the consul general in Istanbul; and Llewellyn Thompson, in Moscow, all agreed with President Roosevelt's conviction that cooperation among the victorious powers could continue after the war. But Kennan thought Roosevelt was "unrealistic."

American diplomats posted in Eastern Europe and the Balkans had their hopes darkened by Soviet crackdowns on the newly liberated nations. From Bulgaria, U.S. diplomat Maynard B. Barnes angrily complained of the Soviets' ruthless "people's courts" and of efforts to isolate the American mission. When he gave asylum to Georgi Dimitrov, secretary general of the Agrarian Party who was fleeing house arrest, the State Department warned him to use caution. The outspoken Barnes reacted by condemning the "diplomacy of silence."

This was not Barnes' first encounter with crisis. As a young vice consul in Smyrna in 1922 he had been left in charge of the temporary consulate on a pier at the edge of the city, in which tens of thousands of Armenian and Greek Christians were being killed. And he was the chargé in 1940, when the Germans invaded Paris.

Barnes now pressed Washington to react to the Soviets more forcefully. Similarly, Harold Shantz, counselor in Cairo, urged the department to educate the American public about the Communist menace. But the State Department could not turn on a dime. To act on such appeals meant accepting realpolitik spheres of influence in Europe. And that was generally regarded as the road to confrontation, and possibly war, with the Soviet Union.

Stalin stated outright that Communism and capitalism were incompatible. Winston Churchill, out of office and speaking at Fulton, Missouri, declared that an "iron curtain" divided Europe. This echoed Kennan's policy of containment and his idea of an ideologically based "cold war."

After the World War II fighting stopped, more Americans began to recognize that the Soviets' twin intentions were to sell Communism and to construct an Eastern European glacis to protect themselves from attacks. Kennan authenticated the emerging view that their wartime ally was becoming an opponent. In effect, Charles W. Freeman, Jr., ambassador to Saudi Arabia, noted later, "Balance of power is the system in which diplomacy comes to flower."

Unlike Kennan, most Foreign Service officers, whatever they thought in private, did not participate in the debate over how to deal with the Soviet Union. They accepted the policy, of course, and over time worked to make other nations aware of the danger to their freedoms and stability. They brought nations to the West's side in what became the Cold War's forty-year struggle. They frowned on left-leaning governments, pursued funding for economic development, and strengthened military resources and bases.

Roosevelt had been convinced that spheres of influence "have always failed." He said that this kind of traditional nation-state diplomacy created hostile blocs. His hope lay in large-power cooperation. And he was gone by the time the first explosive military reaction occurred, when North

Korea invaded South Korea, and President Truman met that aggression with American power. Force was also the response to the Suez Canal crisis, the Congo, and the Cuban missile crisis. They were "hot" elements of the Cold War.

Kennan disagreed with those who expected that the Soviet Union would take over all of Europe, even the world. He felt that the West could not exert much influence inside the areas the Soviets controlled. But the West could reinforce Western Europe; Soviet power had limits. In fact, he said, local Communist parties would be the instruments that would menace the West.

By 1949, his thinking had evolved—an important point about Kennan. He said, "I did not believe in the reality of a Soviet military threat to Western Europe." Like Bohlen and Churchill, he saw value in negotiations with the Soviet Union. Eisenhower and Dulles did not.

The Cold War of words extended into the Middle East. The Soviet Union refused to remove its troops from Iran by the agreed-on deadline of March 2, 1946. Charles Bohlen had Ambassador Wallace S. Murray ask the shah whether he planned to take the issue to the Security Council. Loy Henderson judged that the Russians were after Middle East oil, and Kennan predicted they would deny those oil resources to the West. Only when the Security Council, at Iran's request, actually put the issue on its agenda did the Soviet Union remove its troops.

Many U.S. diplomats shared in the spreading mistrust of the Soviets. It became difficult to accept Kennan's assurance that Soviet expansion would stop at a line in the heart of Europe. Soviet specialist Elbridge Durbrow, who succeeded Kennan as counselor of the Moscow embassy in July 1947, believed the Soviet leaders felt their former allies were now their enemies.

DEPENDING ON DIPLOMACY

In April 1946, Kennan was appointed the first "deputy for foreign affairs" of the new National War College, and later became a member of a special committee to study aid to Greece and Turkey, chaired by Loy Henderson, director of Near Eastern and African Affairs.

On February 21, 1947, Herbert Sichel, first secretary of the British embassy, called on Henderson with the shocking news that in six weeks Britain had to stop sending aid to Greece and Turkey. World War II had cut Britain's national wealth by one quarter.

And so began a period during which Kennan, until he resigned from the Foreign Service six years later, became one of its more thoughtful and respected officers, as well as one whose ideas were repeatedly rejected by his superiors.

Truman asked a joint session of Congress on March 12, 1947, to support Greece and Turkey with what was called the Truman Doctrine. He said, "This is no more than a frank recognition that totalitarian regimes imposed on free peoples, by direct or indirect aggression, undermine the foundations of international peace and hence the security of the United States."

Before Kennan finished his year at the National War College, Secretary Marshall asked him to return to the State Department and run the Policy Planning Staff. (Marshall gave him one piece of advice: "Avoid trivia.") The Policy Planning Staff would consist of top-flight men like Ware Adams, John Paton Davies, Joseph Johnson, Jacques Reinstein, and Carleton Savage; it was charged with swiftly developing plans for European recovery. The staff, created on May 5, 1947, a month later produced its report, which formed the heart of Marshall's historic speech at Harvard University.

That June an article appeared in *Foreign Affairs* magazine entitled "The Sources of Soviet Conduct," bylined by "X." Kennan, of course, was "X." His friend, Secretary of Navy James Forrestal, had asked Kennan to comment on a paper written by a Smith College professor analyzing Russian objectives. Kennan responded with the article by "X." Of the many commentaries on foreign policy in that establishment magazine, this one produced a storm.

Kennan told a National War College audience that the Soviet Union was "a great political force intent on our destruction." But he insisted such destruction would be attempted by political and economic, not military, means. Kennan advocated the "containment" of Soviet Communism. He was willing even to give up the concept of the United Nations in favor of the traditional system of spheres of influence. He believed that before long Soviet dominance over what it controlled at the end of World War II would collapse.

The esteemed conservative commentator Walter Lippmann attacked the article with fourteen columns of his own. He labeled containment "a strategic monstrosity." It would produce a war on the Eurasian landmass, one the United States could not win. Kennan tried to make clear that he too meant the United States should not meet the political threat with a military response.

Kennan felt validated when the Yugoslavian coalition led by Joseph Broz (Tito) defected from Moscow in 1948 and when differences emerged between Chinese and Russian Communists in 1957. Those developments confirmed for him the Soviet Union's inability to control even the Communist-ruled part of the world. The West had to encourage Communist heresy and support national efforts to rip apart the Soviet monolith. Kennan favored skillful diplomacy and patience.

Patience was essential. It took more than a decade for the United States and the Soviet Union to work out even a consular convention that both countries had desired. The convention was not signed until 1964.

But patience was not red-blooded enough for those who feared Soviet Communism most intensely. Some attacked personally those who would use diplomacy rather than military force. When, in 1947, President Truman nominated John Carter Vincent for promotion to the rank of career minister, Vincent became a victim of McCarthy and was denounced for having handed over China to the Communists. Secretary Acheson had to save him. But later, Secretary John Foster Dulles refused to. When Kennan wanted to add Williams College economics professor Emile Despres to the Policy Planning Staff that same year, and Representative Karl Mundt of the Un-American Activities Committee attacked Despres' loyalty, Kennan withdrew the invitation. Williams College's president James Baxter protested, but Kennan replied that the nation's interests outweighed the individual's. It was a taste of the devastating "Red Scare" that Senator Joseph McCarthy would capitalize on and give his name to.

And when Under Secretary James Webb required the Policy Planning Staff to coordinate its papers with other department elements before submitting them to the Secretary, Kennan quit.

DIPLOMATS VERSUS GENERALS

During World War II, the Pentagon had taken over from State much of the policy making for foreign affairs. The nation had faced military problems that demanded military solutions. But once military victory had been won, the nature of the problems facing the United States and its friends changed. The Pentagon was not eager to surrender its authority, under which the military commanders in the occupied countries were "virtually laws unto themselves."

George Marshall, appointed Secretary of State by President Truman at the beginning of 1947, topped the roster of professional soldiers making foreign policy: General Douglas MacArthur, in Japan and Korea; General Mark Clark, in Austria; General Lucius Clay, in Germany; General Walter Bedell Smith, as ambassador to Moscow; and Admiral Alan G. Kirk, as ambassador to Brussels.

Foreign Service officer Robert Murphy, who accompanied Secretary Marshall to Moscow in order to negotiate a German peace treaty, wrote, "Personally, I appreciated why President Truman felt justified in placing so many military men in important posts abroad. I knew how difficult it had been to get support from Congress for the State Department, how few qualified men our Foreign Service had, and how thin these good ones were spread." One cause of the paucity of qualified civilians was the McCarthy witch hunt that forced some men out of the service and kept others sidelined.

The Foreign Service still contained skilled diplomats. Charles Bohlen was one who won the respect of most everyone. A poll of diplomats ranked him as "the ideal diplomat." He had chosen the Soviet Union as his specialty in 1929 and later had served as interpreter for Roosevelt at Tehran and Yalta and for Truman at Potsdam. Despite the opposition of both Senator McCarthy and Secretary John Foster Dulles, President Eisenhower appointed Bohlen ambassador to Moscow in 1953. Only later did Dulles manage to divert him to Manila.

When Dulles died in 1959, Eisenhower appointed Under Secretary Christian A. Herter to succeed him, and he brought Bohlen back to Washington as his prime Soviet advisor. Herter himself had a varied career. He joined the Foreign Service before World War I and served in Berlin and Brussels and as secretary to the Paris Peace Commission. He left in 1924 to enter journalism and politics, serving in Congress for ten years and as governor of Massachusetts. He returned to the State Department in 1957 and became Secretary of State two years later.

MACARTHUR VERSUS THE FOREIGN SERVICE

Some thoughtful officers regarded the postwar tensions as challenges to the military's professionalism. Already dissatisfied with their peacetime lifestyle and pay rates, they perceived that laymen were invading areas they had grown accustomed to running. Major General Robert N. Ginsburgh, who had been a member of State's Policy Planning Council, wrote in *Foreign Affairs*, "Because of their wartime popularity, prestige and experience, professional military men were called upon to fill influential positions in politics, in industry and in government. . . . The military professional found himself challenged both on his own ground and on non-military grounds as well."

The most difficult relationships between the State Department and the Pentagon developed over the conquered Axis partners, Germany and Japan, where the American proconsuls were Generals Clay and MacArthur.

To Germany, the State Department posted Ambassador Murphy, a career veteran with experience and prestige. There, the overarching objective was to prevent Germany from starting a major war. Kennan came to believe that a reunified and disarmed Germany would keep Europe stable better than would a divided Germany. State Department officials, led by John Hickerson, head of the office of European Affairs, disagreed, and General Clay and Ambassador Murphy resisted removing Western military forces from Germany. By the fall of 1949, the Russians tested their first atomic bomb, and those who most feared Stalin sought safety in a divided Germany. The United States looked to a strong West Germany and NATO.

When Japan surrendered, it had 3.5 million Imperial troops under arms. And MacArthur on his own prerogative announced that U.S. troops in Japan would be reduced from five hundred thousand to two hundred thousand. But Acting Under Secretary Dean Acheson told the press sharply, "the occupation forces are the instruments of policy not the determinants of policy."

The State Department sent to Tokyo as political advisor George Atcheson. He was an established China hand who had been aboard USS *Panay* when she was sunk in 1937 and had served with General Joseph Stillwell in Chungking during the war. MacArthur stuck Atcheson in a remote office and insisted that State send him advice through the War Department and that Foreign Service officers in Japan report to State through MacArthur's headquarters.

Eventually, Atcheson managed to close the gap. But when Atcheson was flying to the United States, the pilot crashed in the ocean and Atcheson was drowned. Some claimed his plane had been sabotaged. Those who thought so quoted him as saying as the plane went down, "Well, it can't be helped."

Atcheson was succeeded by his deputy, William J. Sebald, a lawyer who knew the Japanese language and had spent most of his life in Japan. He had joined the staff of the Office of Naval Intelligence in December 1941 and would become the ambassador to Burma and to Australia. In Tokyo, MacArthur simply did not consult Ambassador Sebald.

The evolution of postwar policy with Japan and Asia was complicated. Japan, like Germany, had to regain its economic footing and be guided toward a peaceful future. China was torn by civil war and then ruled by the Communists, and elsewhere nationalistic urges were surfacing. In the United States, men who could only conceive of primitive responses to these events blamed conspiracy and disloyalty by Americans.

In Tokyo, General MacArthur exercised virtually absolute power. His job, as he saw it, was to bring a feudal society to peaceful, prosperous, democratic, and Christian modernity. Such a grand transformation could be achieved only if the Communists on the one side and the authoritarian militants on the other could both be suppressed. As a young Foreign Service officer in the diplomatic section of MacArthur's headquarters, William Sullivan remembered he had to screen and certify Japanese diplomats who, wedded to the old traditions, "arrived in morning coats and striped trousers smelling of mothballs" for their ordeal.

Secretary of State Marshall sent George Kennan to track how Japan's metamorphosis was progressing, as well as to repair relations among the supreme commander, the Allied powers, and the State Department. With him went Marshall Green, a Foreign Service officer who had been Ambassador Joseph Grew's private secretary in Tokyo before the war.

Kennan did not find working with MacArthur easy. The general and the diplomat started from quite different places. While MacArthur wanted to conclude a multinational peace treaty for Japan, Kennan feared that Japan was not ready to defend itself from external or internal Communist and totalitarian threats. Making the situation even more difficult, as Kennan put it later, MacArthur, who "had a violent prejudice against the State Department, resented any attempt by the State Department to interfere in the conduct of the operation in Japan."

At first, MacArthur turned a cold shoulder to Kennan. But the diplomat understood the challenge. Kennan spent a long evening alone with MacArthur and won him over by treating him with great deference and some flattery. Kennan showed the general a line of reasoning by which he could advance Japan's rehabilitation without needing the approval of the international Far Eastern Commission, with which MacArthur was repeatedly wrestling.

MacArthur saw the United States' Western frontier running along the Asian shore of the Pacific, eight thousand miles west of San Francisco. For Americans, Asia had always been westward; the Far East was a European idea. The Far East was now America's Far West. MacArthur and Kennan agreed that the United States had to assure the integrity of that line.

Kennan disapproved of what he saw as "totalitarian practices" that the American occupiers had imposed on the Japanese: land reform, antitrust rules, and purging in government, education, and business of Japanese who had aided Japan's earlier aggression. He wanted the United States to relax controls over the Japanese government, and by early 1949 his principles were generally accepted in Washington.

One nagging issue was whether to allow Japan's emperor and the imperial institution to continue. MacArthur opposed trying him as a war criminal, and Joseph Grew asserted that Pearl Harbor had been attacked against Hirohito's wishes. He and others repeatedly tried to convince President Truman to relax Roosevelt's policy of unconditional surrender. And James F. Byrnes, the first postwar Secretary of State, wanted the question of whether to retain the emperor left to the Japanese.

Among Japanese officials, Baron Hiranuma Kiichiro, a prewar prime minister, argued the emperor's cause with Foreign Service officer Max W. Bishop (a future ambassador to Thailand). The State Department's Advisory Committee on Postwar Foreign Policy also favored lenient treatment of the emperor, in order to assure Japan's economic recovery and the success of the occupation. Opposition to retaining the emperor came mainly from the War Department's Civil Affairs Division and the

State Department's China specialists. When the Joint Chiefs of Staff approved retention, the issue was essentially settled. The State Department was left to make the imperial institution more democratic.

John Carter Vincent, an experienced China Hand who would later fall victim to Major General Patrick J. Hurley and Senator Joseph McCarthy, represented the State Department on the interagency committee that Truman set up to shape occupation policy. Vincent at first wanted to try Hirohito as a war criminal but came to feel that the emperor could strengthen the stability of the occupation. Hirohito became more and more indispensable to the occupation.

The question was resolved by compromise. When the atomic bomb ended the need to invade Japan, Truman issued the Potsdam Proclamation, which established that the emperor would remain but subject to the supreme commander of the Allied powers—that is, MacArthur.

On New Year's Day 1946, the emperor issued an Imperial Rescript, denying his divinity and urging the Japanese people to accept democratic change. The debate over the retention of the emperor ended with the defeat of those who saw a principle of justice in punishing Hirohito and a victory for those who emphasized the practical benefits of keeping him in place.

Kennan had another conflict with MacArthur when Kennan argued that Japan needed to be able to defend itself against Communist pressures from outside. MacArthur believed he had already made Japan immune to such threats. When MacArthur said that the U.S. military could begin leaving Japan, Dean Acheson and John Foster Dulles both disagreed. Kennan believed the decision to keep a military force in Japan led to the attack instigated by Russia in Korea. But, he admitted candidly, he was the only one who thought this.

When Kennan returned to Washington, he recommended maintaining enough American military strength to protect Japan from external aggressions. He advised that reparations, purges, decartelization, censorship, and war-crimes trials all be discontinued. MacArthur resented these suggestions as personal criticisms, while Kennan felt that the general's boasting of Japan's Christianity and reverence and affection for the United States was vacant rhetoric.

The outbreak of war on the Korean Peninsula in June 1950, and a 1951 Japanese-American security treaty left the United States still responsible for Japan's military safety.

ISRAEL DIVIDES THE DIPLOMATS

Another postwar controversy, over the establishment of the State of Israel in 1948, was so controversial and emotion-filled that the very idea set off fireworks and schisms within the State Department and Foreign Service. President Truman wanted to recognize the new Jewish state as a safe haven for the survivors of the Holocaust. But both Acheson and Marshall saw trouble ahead with the oil-rich Arabs, favoring a single Arab-Jewish state. Critics said Truman weighed Jewish votes over Arab oil.

State Department opponents of a Jewish state in Palestine included Loy Henderson, director for Near Eastern and African Affairs, and his assistant, Edwin Wright. Although they denied that their opposition to Zionism was rooted in anti-Semitism, others debated them. Henderson spoke of "the Zionist juggernaut." And Wright wrote, "I accused the Zionists of using political pressure and even deceit in order to get the U.S. involved in a policy of supporting a Zionist theocratic, ethnically exclusive and ambitious Jewish State." Loy Henderson opposed partition and a Jewish state as being against American interests and the principle of self-determination. His biographer, H. W. Brands, said Henderson was "one of the most criticized individuals in the history of the American foreign service." He was transferred to New Delhi. And on May 15, 1948, Truman prevailed and the State of Israel came into existence. The United States rushed to recognize Israel before the Soviet Union did.

THE COLD WAR TURNS HOT

At eight o'clock on Sunday morning, June 25, 1950, in Seoul, Deputy Chief of Mission Everett F. Drumright telephoned Ambassador John J. Muccio that units of the North Korean army were crossing the 38th parallel into South Korea. They were already within fifty miles of the capital. Muccio, a lean, bespectacled career Foreign Service officer, walked through a torrential monsoon to his office in the Bando Building, and the two men wrote a telegram to the State Department, the first word Washington had of the invasion.

It was then Saturday evening in Washington, and Dean Rusk and his wife, Virginia, were dining at the home of journalist Joseph Alsop. A note reporting the invasion was passed to Rusk, then assistant secretary of state for Far Eastern Affairs. Rusk and Secretary of the Army Frank Pace immediately left for their offices, while the other dinner guests and Alsop speculated on what had happened. In Washington, the invasion was a total surprise.

On Sunday afternoon, the UN's Security Council met in emergency session and voted 9-0 to order North Korea to desist. Historian James A. Field, Jr., said, "Aggression had been committed. The cold war had become hot."

At that moment, the Soviet Union was boycotting the Security Council and unable to veto the resolution. In Seoul, President Syngman Rhee summoned Ambassador Muccio to announce that his government had decided to leave the capital. Muccio protested that it would demoralize the South Korean army. The American occupation army was long gone. Muccio concentrated on sending hundreds of American women and children to safety; by Monday evening, they were on a merchant ship in Inchon harbor on their way to Japan. MacArthur sent planes to remove others. By 4:00 A.M. on Tuesday, Rhee left the capital, and by night the North Korean army entered Seoul.

Muccio later remembered, "I had not been back at the residence since Sunday morning when I left following Drumright's message. I went by the residence, opened up the food and liquor lockers, and told the servants to help themselves and not to be found there at the residence. . . . I picked up my cigars and I told Sergeant Edward, who was my right-hand man, to get a case of Scotch, and I packed a bag with some clean socks, and underwear, a hat and a few shirts, and started down to KMAG headquarters, got there about noon."

As Muccio's party drove south, they came under fire from North Korean aircraft. Told that General MacArthur was trying to call him from Tokyo, Muccio found a telephone in the Suwon post office and talked with General Edward H. Almond, MacArthur's chief of staff. They arranged for MacArthur to fly into Suwon.

Troops of the U.S. 24th Infantry Division stationed in Japan began arriving in Korea on July 2 under the command of Major General William F. Dean. Two days later, they were in combat. The first unit to come directly from the United States, the 1st Marine Provisional Brigade, arrived at Pusan, Korea, on August 2 and went into combat on the seventh.

The United States faced three major decisions in Korea: whether to cross the 38th parallel and invade North Korea, whether to approach the border with China at the Yalu River, and whether to insist on voluntary repatriation of Korean prisoners of war to avoid forcing them to return to the North. MacArthur decided the first two and Truman insisted on the last.

After the war began, Foreign Service officer O. Edmund Clubb warned repeatedly that if U.S. forces crossed the 38th parallel separating North and South Korea, the Chinese were certain to enter the war. Arthur Ringwalt in London reported that the British Foreign Office said that Zhou Enlai had given the ambassador of India to Peking the same warning. And in New Delhi, Ambassador Loy Henderson was given an identical warning after UN forces landed at Inchon on September 15. Many Americans thought Zhou Enlai was bluffing; MacArthur assured the President when they met on Wake Island that the Chinese would not enter the war.

MacArthur moved his forces up toward the Yalu, and on October 25 faced thousands of Chinese soldiers who had crossed the river. Their appearance ignited attacks on China-knowledgeable Foreign Service officers. The State Department ordered Clubb to appear for an investigation of his loyalty.

In April, 1951, President Truman relieved MacArthur of his command. His many admirers lashed out at those in government whom they blamed for losing both China and their favorite general. Dean Acheson said brutally, "MacArthur was a jackass."

35

The Foreign Service Catches Up

1946—88

The United States emerged from World War II a Great Power that could tackle disputes of any size anywhere on the planet. The Foreign Service had to catch up.

From 1941 to 1945, the Foreign Service had held no entry examinations. Positions were filled on a temporary basis, and no career diplomats of military age were recruited. The number of career Foreign Service officers (FSOs) shrank by 10 percent.

The result was a postwar shortage of trained manpower just when the State Department and Foreign Service faced radically new responsibilities. The U.S. Foreign Service struggled to handle unfamiliar duties: managing occupied areas, relief, rehabilitation, and refugees. It was a different and demanding world. (The wartime squeeze on civilians also contributed to the rising role of the American military in foreign affairs.)

A first attempt to ease the postwar constriction was a law of July 3, 1946, which authorized, on an emergency basis, 250 Foreign Service officers. This actually gave the service 166 new officers. But more were needed, and the Foreign Service Act of 1946, which went into effect in November, attempted to supply them.

The Foreign Service Act also established an array of new management systems: a Director General of the Foreign Service, a Board of the Foreign Service, a Board of Examiners for the Foreign Service, and the Foreign Service Institute. The Director General was to be a Foreign Service officer with broad powers to oversee the administration of the service. The Board of the Foreign Service participated in policy issues and personnel management and included representatives of the departments of Agriculture, Commerce, and Labor.

The act reduced the classes of Foreign Service officers from eleven to seven and added a new class of career minister. Salaries ranged from $3,300 to $13,500 to make opportunities for candidates regardless of their means. Categories were also established for specialists as Foreign Service Reserve officers, as well as for administrative, fiscal, and clerical staff.

A Foreign Service officer no longer had to resign from the Foreign Service to accept an appointment as a chief of mission. Chiefs of mission would continue to receive their salaries as Foreign Service officers, in addition to remuneration for their new responsibilities. Maximum salaries for ambassadors and most ministers were increased for the first time since 1855.

Following the military systems, officers who failed to win promotion within a prescribed number of years would be separated. Career ministers were given a mandatory retirement age of sixty-five, and all other officers had to retire at sixty. Among the most important and long-lasting initiatives was the creation of the Foreign Service Institute, in which FSOs were trained for their careers and advancements.

Approval of the 1946 bill was held up because the Bureau of the Budget left specifics to the Secretary of State. And the House Committee on Foreign Affairs gave more weight than did the Bureau to building up the administrative structure of the Foreign Service. Secretary of State James F. Byrnes had to convince President Truman to sign the bill over the Bureau's objections.

The 1946 act brought the Foreign Service to a crossroads. Some Foreign Service officers who served close to the seats of power felt that the new law failed to force the Foreign Service to meet the new challenges. Career diplomat Lucius D. Battle, special assistant to Secretary Acheson (and later to Dean Rusk) and executive secretary of the department, believed that the traditionalists, who wanted the Foreign Service to remain a small elite diplomatic corps, had won. In the eyes of the traditionalists, Battle said:

These newer things, economics and information and intelligence, were not really basic. They were one whack below what a Foreign

Service officer should be dealing with, and the Department refused to really try to gain control of these several emerging agencies in those fields. . . . To me it was the biggest mistake the Service ever made. . . . In the Foreign Service, economics was not regarded as a gentleman's profession; that is, finance and economics and intelligence and information skills were not the things that ambassadors were made of. Ambassadors grew up or trained on the political side, almost without exception, and it's still the case.

In 1947, the so-called Hoover Commission, formally named the Commission on Organization of the Executive Branch of Government and chaired by former President Herbert Hoover, reexamined the entire executive branch. Such a multiagency review was needed because, as the Commission pointed out, more than forty-five executive agencies had become involved in foreign affairs. Overseas missions included more and more specialists from the Treasury, as well as the departments of Agriculture; Commerce; Labor; and Health, Education, and Welfare; and Justice and Interior and agencies such as the Atomic Energy Commission and the Aeronautical and Space Administration. Only about 5 percent of the $7 billion then expended annually for international affairs still went through the State Department, and only 11 percent of the 128,000 civilian Federal employees abroad belonged to the State Department or the Foreign Service.

The Hoover Commission recommended that the State Department concentrate on defining objectives and forming foreign policy and refrain from operating programs. Its report advised the State Department and the Foreign Service to become more closely integrated to reduce jurisdictional squabbles. And since the power of the new Director General seemed to dilute that of the Secretary, an act of May 26, 1949, returned that authority to the Secretary.

The most drastic external change was Congress' creation in 1947 of the National Security Council (NSC) to coordinate from the White House the various agencies influencing foreign policy. In the beginning, there was no National Security Advisor to the President—only an executive secretary, whom John Davies, an original member of the Policy Planning Staff, described scathingly:

He was expected to spend his evenings and Sundays contentedly at his desk or home, not luxuriating in TV talk shows, pontificating at variance with the Secretary of State, broadcasting cacophony in the American government.

But by the time of the Eisenhower administration, the National Security Council had taken on a life of its own. NSC members, rather than State Department officers, chaired interagency committees. By the time of Richard Nixon's administration, the President and his national security advisor, Henry Kissinger, were making end runs around the State Department.

Nixon was direct; he said, "Down in the government are a bunch of sons of bitches. . . . We've checked and found that 96 percent of the bureaucracy are against us; they're bastards who are here to screw us."

Here the contrast between Nixon and Kennedy was virtually absolute. Nixon's Kissinger depended on secrecy that bred distrust. Kennedy's national security advisor, McGeorge Bundy, was trusted as an honest broker.

In 1948, Secretary Dean Acheson appointed the Advisory Committee on Personnel (the Rowe Committee), which recommended a single personnel system for the State Department and the Foreign Service. But many members of the department were reluctant to assume the strict commitment to overseas service. The Rowe Committee's results were generally disappointing.

These attempts at reorganization led Secretary Dulles to appoint the eight-man Public Committee on Personnel, headed by Henry M. Wriston, president of Brown University, and manned chiefly by members of the State Department and the Foreign Service. The resulting Wriston Report, submitted to Dulles on May 18, 1954, criticized the administration of the Foreign Service during the previous eight years. It found morale low and noted the decline in the number of Foreign Service officers in one year (1953), from 1,427 to 1,285. It castigated the separate personnel systems as resulting in injustices and inequalities, censured the failures to bring in Foreign Service officers at the bottom rank and to accept candidates from the Civil Service into the Foreign Service, and asked for improvements in the training of Foreign Service officers.

The Wriston Report candidly found a need overseas for three times the existing number of Foreign Service officers. It proposed that the department's Civil Service employees, if unwilling to meet Foreign Service requirements, should be moved out to other employment.

The Report proved enormously influential. Civil Service employees working in the State Department on foreign affairs were taken into the Foreign Service. This gave the United States an integrated Foreign Service sixty years after Francois S. Jones and his allies had drafted their bill.

Not everyone agreed. A decade later, Ambassador Charles E. Bohlen said, "The so-called Wriston Report merged the Foreign Service Officers and the Home Service Officers which I think, in the opinion of most everybody in the Foreign Service, and still in my opinion, was a great mistake, for the reason that nine-tenths of the people who are in the Home Service don't want to go abroad. They are people who live in Washington and have gotten acquainted with the jungle of this town and know their way around."

A NATIONAL ACADEMY OF FOREIGN AFFAIRS

A decade later, two committees, chaired by James A. Perkins, vice president of the Carnegie Corporation of New York, and by former Secretary of State Christian A. Herter, recommended establishing a National Academy of Foreign Affairs. And in February 1963, President John F. Kennedy had a bill sent to Congress proposing such an academy. It would combine education and training, and it would be independent and interdepartmental. Foreign Service officers who opposed the idea predicted that such an academy, modeled on the military service academies, would compete with the nation's independent academic institutions, which already provided training in diplomacy and foreign policy. They further contended that it would turn out technicians who were unprepared to direct policy making. Ambassador Stephen Low, director of the Foreign Service Institute for five years, preferred that the Foreign Service seek out people educated at colleges and universities across the country.

During the 1980s, Ambassador Low campaigned to improve the Foreign Service Institute's facilities and had strong support from Secretary George P. Shultz and Under Secretary Ronald I. Spiers. Low liked to explain that in his office hung a picture of the beautiful facility where McDonald's trained its personnel, known informally as Hamburger University. He told visitors that the nation's diplomats should be trained in a place at least as suitable as "HU," the place that trained those who made the nation's hamburgers.

In 1993, the Foreign Service Institute moved to a seventy-two-acre campus called the George P. Shultz National Foreign Affairs Training Center. There, the institute offers more than 450 courses, including those in 70 languages, to more than 50,000 students a year from the State Department and 40 other government agencies and the military services. Courses run from a half day to two years; they include language studies abroad and electronic "distance-learning" courses. Its nine-week basic course for incoming diplomats, known as A-100, is the foundation. In addition, at the institute specialists and foreign nationals are prepared for their career tracks; family members are introduced to life abroad; and veteran FSOs learn how the American domestic political scene works.

Virtually all new Foreign Service officers take the A-100 course. Many return to the institute several times during their careers. Officers learn another language or a new skill, or a political appointee might learn how to function as a chief of mission. Ambassador Tom Korologos, in Brussels, said that he had found the chief-of-mission course invaluable. He summed it up by saying, "I learned how to say 'Amazing!' rather than 'Holy shit!'"

At the end of 1954, 3,689 positions at overseas posts and in the department were designated as Foreign Service officer positions. Anyone filling them had to be a member of the Foreign Service officer corps and had to be willing to serve wherever assigned by the Secretary of State. The requirements took time to achieve; in 1960, 326 Civil Service officers still occupied Foreign Service positions.

In 1955, the State Department mounted an exceptional effort to recruit young candidates to the Foreign Service officer corps. Experienced FSOs visited college and university campuses across the country. Only 750 candidates took the written Foreign Service entrance examination in September 1954, but 8,300 candidates sat for the two exams given in 1956. By April 1957, 679 new junior officers had been appointed.

In those days, the entrance process was even more excruciating and prolonged. Brandon Grove remembers taking the written exam in Los Angeles at the end of 1956 and the oral exam nearly a year later in Washington, D.C. And then he had to wait another sixteen months before he could enter the Foreign Service. Finally, in April 1959, Grove was admitted to the A-100 course; most of it, he thought, was boring and ineptly taught. Grove was first assigned to a new consulate in Abidjan, in the French colony of the Ivory Coast. It had taken him nearly three years to become an American diplomat.

Over time, the exams were made more appetizing. The three-and-a-half-day written ordeal, which tried to cover everything from agriculture to zoology, was replaced with a one-day examination. Oral exams, which had been given only in Washington, were now offered in twenty-three U.S. and five foreign cities.

"EVEN WHEN THEY BROUGHT BAD NEWS"

After World War II, a major effort was made to bring diplomacy up-to-date by international agreement. It took two decades to complete the job. In the beginning, the General Assembly of the United Nations, at its four hundredth plenary session on December 5, 1952, asked the International Law Commission to codify "diplomatic intercourse and immunities." Then, it required almost nine years before an international conference met in the Neue Hofburg, the onetime palace of the Hapsburgs and the site of Adolf Hitler's 1938 speech proclaiming the *Anschluss* to cheering Viennese.

During six weeks in the spring of 1961, representatives from eighty-one nations hammered out the Vienna Convention on Diplomatic Relations. The United States was represented by Warde M. Cameron, who had negotiated the consular treaty with the Soviet Union and served as consul general to the Netherlands. The convention sought, its preamble stated, to "contribute to the development of friendly relations among nations, irrespective of their differing constitutional and social systems." Fifty-three articles covered issues from defining "head of mission" to codifying rules that apply if the nation in which a diplomat is stationed goes to war.

The Convention on Diplomatic Relations and the parallel 1963 Convention on Consular Relations paid prime attention to the principle of immunity. A State Department commentary pointed out that the concept of diplomatic immunity dates back to when ancient tribes allowed messengers to travel from tribe to tribe without fear of harm. It said, "They were protected even when they brought bad news."

These principles still hold, fortified and balanced on an armature developed in the Western world over the centuries. But not long after the Vienna conference, the centuries-old principle of immunity was disrupted when diplomats were kidnapped and murdered as targets of terrorist attacks.

By the end of the twentieth century, 177 nations had signed the Vienna Convention on Diplomatic Relations; it was virtually global international law. The United States became a party to the Convention in 1972 with passage of an act to protect diplomats and their families. And U.S. law was brought into line by the Diplomatic Relations Act of 1978 and the Foreign Missions Act of 1982. Both laws emphasized the principle of reciprocity.

British scholar Eileen Denza, former legal counselor to the British government's Foreign and Commonwealth Office and visiting professor at University College London, concluded that the Convention improved the protection of missions but diminished the immunity and privileges of individuals in their private activities.

Protecting diplomatic communications also became more difficult. Sophisticated bugging devices that can intercept an embassy's communications violate the Vienna Convention. In the mid-1960s, the Americans found that the U.S. embassy in Moscow had been bugged in the 1950s and early 1960s. And even after the Convention was adopted, the new U.S. embassy building in Moscow in 1985 was discovered to be fitted with hidden microphones. U.S. diplomat Warren Zimmermann said he discovered that his typewriter in the Moscow embassy was bugged.

The next year, the United States justified air raids on Libya by citing a message it had intercepted between the Libyan embassy in Berlin and Libya's government in Tripoli. And Soviet Communist Party chief Nikita Khrushchev blundered when he told U.S. Ambassador Foy D. Kohler that he had read the ambassador's message opposing the sale of large-diameter pipe to the Soviet Union.

The application of diplomatic immunity to subordinate staff members has proved complicated. A diplomat's family members are granted immunity under the Vienna convention, but the definition of "family members" has been variously interpreted by different countries. In a note to chiefs of mission in 1986, the U.S. State Department defined the term to include a spouse and unmarried children under twenty-one, as well as children who are full-time students to age twenty-three. In exceptional cases, the United States has protected other household members and covered more than one wife of polygamous diplomats. The United Kingdom includes unmarried partners and, in theory, same-sex partners.

Which of a diplomat's duties are official can be hard to establish. In one dramatic case, the Austrian ambassador to Yugoslavia was invited on a hunt by the president of Yugoslavia. The Austrian ambassador accidentally shot and killed the French ambassador. When the widow and children sued, the Supreme Court of Austria held that the ambassador's death occurred while carrying out official duties and that the Austrian government was therefore liable for providing compensation.

Numerous violations of immunity agreements affect American missions—whether they are committed by governments, as, most dramatically, at Tehran in 1979–1981, or by terrorist groups, as in Beirut, Nairobi, Dar es Salaam, and Jeddah.

THE DIMENSIONS OF CHANGE

After World War II, William Phillips, an experienced Foreign Service officer, said, "A great change has come over the thinking of the American people. As never before, they are discussing not only what is best for the United States but what is best for the world."

The State Department and Foreign Service also began two new activities that do not fit easily into traditional diplomacy: economic aid to other countries and international dissemination of information. Initially, both programs were activities of the State Department, but, over time, other agencies ran the programs with policy guidance from State. Both activities have altered the functioning of the Foreign Service.

In 1961, President Kennedy, frustrated with the multiplicity of programs, established by Executive Order the United States Agency for International Development (USAID), to make continuing contributions from the United States to the people in poor countries, and countries savaged by world war. Fowler Hamilton, Rhodes Scholar and lawyer, was USAID's first administrator, holding the rank of undersecretary of state. USAID sought to set up country-by-country planning and long-term development. Its initial program was the Alliance for Progress in the Americas.

During the 1970s, USAID, like the State Department, suffered from

Congress' refusal to appropriate adequate funding. The USAID work-force, which was 4,300 in 1975, decreased to 2,200 by 2007. The war in Vietnam was one crushing reason for this. USAID's response was to con-centrate on the basic problem areas of the poorest sections of the poorest nations: agriculture, family planning, and education.

By the end of the 1970s, management of economic assistance was given to the Secretary of State, but this was not very successful. In 2008, 73 percent of USAID personnel responding to a survey said they wanted to be separated from the State Department, and a majority complained about USAID's "fragmentation of foreign assistance" among government agencies.

Candidates for positions in the USAID are not required to take the Foreign Service examination but must pass a security clearance and meet medical standards. Candidates also must be willing to serve wherever in the world they are needed.

The Office of War Information had closed down in August 1945, and some of its functions were transferred to the Office of International Infor-mation and Cultural Affairs of the State Department. By 1952, this activ-ity had a budget of $85 million and personnel totaling 12,000, of whom 850 were American officers at Foreign Service posts. In 1953, the creation of the U.S. Information Agency (USIA) relieved the State Department of this direct responsibility. Abroad, the principal USIA officer became part of the diplomatic team under the chief of mission. But by the end of 1958, the number that the USIA employed was down to 8,284 people.

Numerous improvements were made in the status and living conditions of Foreign Service personnel. Pay differentials for service at hardship posts were liberalized in 1955, help was given to overseas employees for educating their children, and medical examinations were provided to de-pendents without charge.

On the Wriston Committee's recommendation, the class of career am-bassador was established to reward distinguished service. In 1956, the Foreign Service's class structure was again modified to improve the appeal of the promotion schedule. And in 1960 more fine-tuning was achieved. Knowledge was required of the primary language of the country to which an FSO was assigned, salary increases within a class were authorized for meritorious service, the retirement system was improved, and Foreign Service officers who had retired for age could be reemployed in the Federal service.

Postwar diplomacy also gained a multinational dimension. The Foreign Service established liaison on military and economic aid with such organizations as the North Atlantic Treaty Organization and the Southeast Asia Treaty Organization.

A REVOLUTION IN COMMUNICATIONS

A significant dimension of change since World War II has been technological. Jet aircraft, secure telephone lines, computers, the Internet and e-mail and its descendants are only the most public of the advances that have sped up communication and transportation and altered how diplomacy is conducted.

Ambassador Philip Habib told of a negotiation in which he had a meeting with a foreign principal at 11:00 P.M. They made substantial progress on the issue, so at 3:00 A.M. he went from the meeting directly to the airport and flew to a second country involved. While in flight he asked for a meeting with the president of the second country. He arrived at 7:00 A.M. and was driven directly to meet with the president. Habib said, "You walk in, going from the airport directly to the meeting; you lay it on the line, and then you move on to another place. This happens constantly in this day. It is possible. It's not the most comfortable type of diplomacy, but in certain circumstances it's the most effective."

The 1956 Suez Canal crisis dramatized the effect of technology, in both communications and transportation. A week after Secretary Dulles abruptly withdrew the offer to help Egypt build a high dam at Aswan, Egypt's President Gamal Abdel Nasser declared he needed the canal's income for the dam. He nationalized the canal and closed it to Israeli shipping.

The nations with the most at stake—Britain, France, and Israel—prepared to use force to overcome Nasser's decision. At that moment, Secretary Dulles was in Peru attending a presidential inauguration, and Winthrop W. Aldrich, the ambassador to the Court of St. James's, was vacationing in Maine. President Eisenhower, in transatlantic communication with Prime Minister Anthony Eden, called in Acting Secretary of

State Herbert Hoover, Jr., and rushed Deputy Under Secretary for Political Affairs Robert Murphy to London.

Murphy flew out within hours, and the next morning he was meeting in London with the British foreign secretary and the French foreign minister. That first evening, Murphy's longtime friend Harold Macmillan, now chancellor of the exchequer, had him to dinner along with U.S. Chargé d'Affaires Walworth Barbour and retired British Field Marshal Harold Alexander. Macmillan and Alexander told Murphy that Britain and France were prepared to use armed force to get rid of Nasser. The Suez Canal was vital for the flow of oil to Europe.

President Eisenhower decided that such an attack would violate the United Nations Charter. He sent over Secretary Dulles, who arranged a conference in London of twenty-two nations that used the canal. They sent a committee (Deputy Under Secretary of State Loy W. Henderson represented the United States) to offer Nasser a compromise, which he rejected.

At dusk on October 29, Israel invaded the Sinai Peninsula. Britain and France called for a cease-fire, and two days later they moved in their own forces. The Israeli army reached the Suez Canal in four days. Eisenhower, campaigning for reelection back home, was furious. In the UN's General Assembly, Ambassador Henry Cabot Lodge condemned Israel's attack and demanded a withdrawal. George Kennan wrote in *The Washington Post* that the United States was responsible for the French and British "ill-conceived and pathetic action." And Eisenhower, using a brand-new transatlantic cable, told Eden he wanted an end to the fighting. Overseas cables and telephones and intercontinental aircraft enabled Eisenhower to stay on top of the crisis and direct Murphy as his representative.

Two years later, in another crisis, Eisenhower sent Robert Murphy on short notice to advise the commander of the U.S. forces that were then landing in Lebanon. Eleven hours after leaving Westover Air Force Base in Massachusetts, a nonstop flight in a KC-135 landed Murphy in Beirut.

Fourteen thousand U.S. soldiers and Marines went ashore at the request of the Lebanese government. At some risk, Murphy hunted for the leaders of various warring factions. He arranged for a Lebanon presidential election, which ended the civil war for a time. (The Turkish ambassador in Beirut told Murphy it would have been cheaper to buy off the Lebanese.)

On his way home, Murphy stopped at Jordan, Israel, Iraq, Egypt,

Ethiopia, Greece, England, and France and explained the American interventions. He met in turn with King Hussein; Prime Minister David Ben-Gurion; Premier Abdul Karim Kassim; President Gamal Abdel Nasser; Emperor Haile Selassie; Premier Constantine Karamanlis; Selwyn Lloyd, the foreign secretary; and Couve de Murville, the foreign minister. The next evening, he met with President Eisenhower and Secretary Dulles, who were in New York for a United Nations meeting, and flew to Washington with the President, whom he briefed in flight. A decade earlier, a diplomat would have found such a whirlwind tour impossible.

As communications advanced to computers, the Internet, and e-mail, the impact on diplomacy multiplied. The 1982 crisis in Lebanon was the first international crisis during which a voice signal was beamed from diplomats in the State Department to a satellite and then down to Ambassador Philip Habib, standing on a hill overlooking Beirut.

More recently, an American consul in Istanbul said that she was asked for material needed for a meeting at the embassy in Ankara. She sent it by e-mail in time for the meeting; the cable from the consulate to the embassy arrived two days later. E-mail, and even newer systems, now cut through hierarchical ranks and share information swiftly at lower levels.

Of course, technological advances have their downside. John M. Evans, when consul general in Saint Petersburg, acknowledged that "getting to know people cannot be done by fax machine." And high-speed communications reduce the time the diplomat has for both careful consideration and bureaucratic delays. They increase the danger of instantaneous, less-thoughtful responses. They put more pressure on analysis and decision making. Ambassador William H. Attwood, an able journalist turned diplomat, even came to feel that the new technology "reduces the role of the ambassador to that of a greeter at the airport, an innkeeper, and a kind of a guide."

One example of how new technology can lead to chaos occurred when the United States learned in 1988 that Saudi Arabia had bought medium-range ballistic missiles from China. U.S. Ambassador, Hume A. Horan, an effective Arabist, was instructed to protest strongly to King Fahd in Riyadh. Surprised, Horan called Washington to make certain that officials there understood how such a rebuke would offend the king. Then he delivered the message as ordered.

Back at the embassy, Horan received a new telegram saying that a more polite message had been delivered to the Saudi embassy in Washington. But King Fahd was shocked and insisted that Horan be replaced. Retired Under Secretary of State Habib was rushed to Riyadh to make amends. This would not have happened before diplomacy was conducted at such speeds.

As the issues of foreign relations became more numerous and complex, the officers at the top have had to delegate more decision making to subordinates. Secretary of State Dean Rusk said, "The idea that policy is sent down from on high is just plain wrong. The endless stream of business, the pace of events, and the complexity of the modern world require even junior officers in the department to make high-level decisions."

And Foreign Service officers, of course, come up against human limitations. The quantity of information has increased incalculably, but one's ability to absorb and analyze it has not. An observer who watched the tragedy at Mogadishu in 1993, when eighteen Americans were killed and seventy-eight wounded after a Black Hawk helicopter was downed, commented, "If... there had been some rum-soaked old honorary consul who had been sitting on the veranda of the hotel in the middle of Mogadishu, simply learning about what has been going on in the country for twenty years, he would have been a lot more help to Admiral [Jonathan] Howe [of the UN]."

Technological advances have, at times, also led to the demand for a cutback in the personnel manning embassies and consulates. And such advances have also inspired the idea that the number of personnel abroad can be reduced by extending the coverage of individual envoys. The multiple layers of approvals and clearances built into decision making and taking action open any bureaucracy to challenge. And the ratio of support personnel such as bookkeepers and housing officers to those actually performing the acts of diplomacy is always suspect. But if a mission is staffed efficiently, the expanding of coverage will be counterproductive.

The fundamental problems of a large bureaucracy have not changed. Secretary Rusk, like others, came to see that the core problem is not a struggle for power but the reluctance of bureaucrats to take action and responsibility, or, as Rusk said, "to stick their necks out and live with the results." Like most large organizations, the State Department has more often rewarded long and loyal service rather than risk taking. Rusk found this standard was not attractive to the young, eager bunch he dealt with in the Kennedy White House.

Overall, the positive effect of the new technology is enormous. As the

Center for Strategic and International Studies (CSIS) summarizes, "the world of diplomacy is undergoing unprecedented change." And Arthur Schlesinger, Jr., said: "The shift from a factory-based to a computer-based economy is more traumatic even than our great-grandparents' shift from a farm-based to a factory-based economy." And this is especially true in an organization like the U.S. Foreign Service, where tradition and shared standards are so important.

Benjamin Franklin, here wearing his colorful fur hat, chaired the Second Continental Congress' Committee of Secret Correspondence and sent Silas Deane to Paris as the united colonies' first diplomat. LIBRARY OF CONGRESS, LC-USZ62-45185

Silas Deane of Connecticut, the first covert representative to go abroad for the united colonies, was sent to Europe even before Independence was declared. LIBRARY OF CONGRESS, LC-USZ62-26779

Silas Deane obtained for the Americans French arms that enabled the rebels to win the crucial early victory at Saratoga (*above*) in October 1777. LIBRARY OF CONGRESS, LC-USZ62-39585

Deane also recruited European officers to help fight the American Revolution. Here, Baron DeKalb (*center*) introduces the young Marquis de Lafayette (*left*), who became George Washington's favorite foreign military colleague, to Silas Deane (*right*). THE CONNECTICUT HISTORICAL SOCIETY, HARTFORD, CONNECTICUT

ABOVE: When Thomas Jefferson's wife died at the age of thirty-three, he joined Franklin and Deane in Paris in 1784, forming a diplomatic commission representing the colonies. And in 1790, Jefferson became the first Secretary of State under the U.S. Constitution. LIBRARY OF CONGRESS, LC-USZC4-5179

LEFT: John Quincy Adams was posted for the United States in Saint Petersburg and London before becoming Secretary of State. He expanded the U.S. into Florida and Oregon and led the battle against slavery. LIBRARY OF CONGRESS, LC-D416-28035

In the 1850s, novelist Nathaniel Hawthorne ran the busiest consulate at Liverpool and earned more than he ever did from his writings. LIBRARY OF CONGRESS, LC-DIG-CWPBH-03440

In 1856, Townsend Harris became the first American consul posted to Japan and had to grapple with the enormous cultural gap between the powers on opposite sides of the Pacific. LIBRARY OF CONGRESS, LC-DIG-CWPBH-01611

This cartoon showed young Abraham Lincoln's failure to receive an appointment to the embassy in Bogotá, Colombia, under the "spoils system" that dominated the early U.S. foreign service. LIBRARY OF CONGRESS, CAI-REINHARDT, NO. 32

Charles Francis Adams Sr. played a decisive role in the Civil War as minister to the Court of St. James's and opposed British support of the Confederacy. LIBRARY OF CONGRESS, LC-USZ62-46426

The monstrous State, War, and Navy Departments building was opened in 1888 just west of the White House. Mark Twain called it "the ugliest building in America." LIBRARY OF CONGRESS, LC-USZ62-28206

In 1903, U.S. Minister Arthur M. Beaupre struggled to force the government of Colombia to sell the Panama Canal Zone to the United States. LIBRARY OF CONGRESS, LC-DIG-GGBAIN-06262

U.S. Ambassador George von Lengerke Meyer (top hat), sitting with the wife of President William Howard Taft, negotiated with Russian Czar Nicholas II the Treaty of Portsmouth which ended the Russo-Japanese War in 1905 and won the Nobel Peace Prize for President Theodore Roosevelt. LIBRARY OF CONGRESS, LC-DIG-HEC-00160

President Theodore Roosevelt in 1906 operates an American steam-shovel at the Culebra Cut of the half-finished Panama Canal, which would change global traffic. LIBRARY OF CONGRESS, LC-DIG-STEREO-1S02355

Emotional drawing of a consul telling a story to children drowning aboard British RMS *Lusitania* torpedoed by German submarine U-20 eleven miles off the coast of Ireland on the afternoon of May 7, 1915. The sinking resulted in 1,201 deaths, including 128 Americans. LIBRARY OF CONGRESS, CAI2A14502

Ambassador James W. Gerard, here at his desk in Berlin, had to negotiate with Kaiser Wilhelm II until the United States entered World War I. LIBRARY OF CONGRESS, BIOG FILE

"Have pity on her!" U.S. Ambassador Brand Whitlock told the Germans in Brussels who proposed to execute British nurse Edith Cavell.

LIBRARY OF CONGRESS,

LC-DIG-GGBAIN-05450

Ambassador David R. Francis represented the United States to the Czar and the governments produced by the Russian revolutions. And he oversaw American military intervention in Siberia.

LIBRARY OF CONGRESS,

LC-USZ62-71967

Elihu Root, the capable former Secretary of War and Secretary of State (*civilian in center*), led the Root Mission to Russia in 1917 and tried, unsuccessfully, to keep the Soviet government in the war against Germany. AP IMAGES

Courageous "Daisy" Harriman was a sixty-seven-year-old grandmother when FDR sent her as minister to Norway on the eve of World War II. Here, she returns from war-torn Norway to New York with her dogs Bart (*left*) and Viking. AP IMAGES

American leaders at signing of Treaty of Versailles in Paris in 1919, ending World War I. *Left to right*: Colonel E. M. House, Secretary of State Robert Lansing, President Woodrow Wilson, Peace Commissioner Henry White, and General Tasker H. Bliss. ©BETTMAN/CORBIS

Lucile Atcherson of Columbus, Ohio, helped French wounded during World War I and in 1922 became the first American woman foreign service officer. THE OHIO HISTORICAL SOCIETY

Wilbur J. Carr, the epitome of a Washington bureaucrat, combined with Congressman John J. Rogers in 1924 to merge the diplomatic and consular services into the U.S. Foreign Service. LIBRARY OF CONGRESS, LC-DIG-NPCC-11647

Frances Elizabeth Willis was named the third woman career foreign service officer in 1927. From Stockholm in 1933, she cabled the State Department: "The minister left last night. I have assumed charge. Willis." Secretary of State Henry L. Stimson asked famously: "Who is Willis?" By taking charge, she became the first woman to represent the nation abroad.
AP IMAGES

Minister William A. Eddy, a heroic U.S. Marine colonel, kneels to interpret for King Ibn Saud and President Franklin Roosevelt aboard USS *Quincy* in the Great Bitter Lake, Egypt, on February 14, 1945.
©BETTMAN/CORBIS

Clifton R. Wharton Sr., the first African-American career diplomatic officer to be named an ambassador, was sworn in as envoy to Norway in 1961. AP IMAGES

John Paton Davies (*center*) with, left to right, Chou En-lai, Cheh The, Mao Tse-tung, and Yeh Chien-ying in Yan'an province in October 1944. Davies, who led the so-called Dixie Mission, was accused by Senator Joseph McCarthy of having "lost China" to Mao's Communists. THE DAVIES FAMILY

Author interviews George F. Kennan, one of the U.S. Foreign Service's most respected intellectuals, at the Institute for Advanced Study in Princeton, N.J., in 1963. They talked at length again before Ambassador Kennan died in 2005 at the age of 101. COURTESY OF AUTHOR

ABOVE: The jet age vastly expanded diplomatic travel. Secretary of State Dean Rusk and his wife, Virginia, shop in Helsinki's market in 1966 during an extended official tour of European nations. COURTESY OF AUTHOR

LEFT: Simultaneous terrorist attacks on the American embassies in Nairobi and Dar es Salaam on August 7, 1998, destroyed the U.S. Embassy and bank building in midtown Nairobi. Embassy is five-story building at right. REUTERS/GERADO MAGALLON

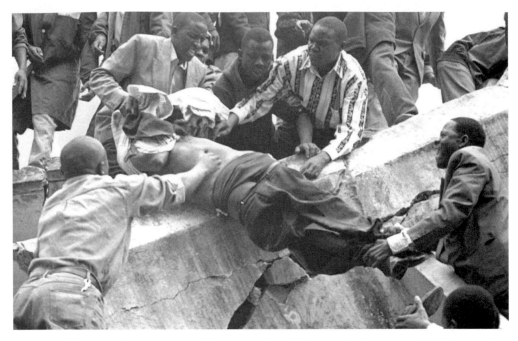

Rescue workers struggle to save one of the 220 people, including twelve Americans, killed by terrorists in 1998 bombing of the U.S. Embassy in Nairobi. AP IMAGES

Consul General Archer K. Blood said President Richard Nixon and National Security Advisor Henry Kissinger silenced his protests against U.S. policy that failed to oppose Pakistan military's massacres in 1971. He said: "I paid for my dissent." AP IMAGES

ABOVE: John Gordon Mein was the first American ambassador ever assassinated when, on August 28, 1968, terrorists in Guatemala City forced his official car to the curb and shot him to death with submachine-gun fire.

RIGHT: Ambassador J. Christopher Stevens, here talking during an event in Tripoli, Libya, was one of four American officials killed when armed men stormed the U.S. consulate in Benghazi on September 11, 2012. ©STRINGER/ EPA/CORBIS

Secretary of State Hillary Rodham Clinton congratulates President Obama after his second inaugural speech on January 24, 2013. During four years as secretary, she visited 112 countries and traveled nearly a million miles. AP IMAGES/EVAN VUCCI

ABOVE: Newly appointed Secretary of State John Kerry jokes with a staff member's daughter at U.S. Embassy in Rome during his first overseas tour in February 2013. AP IMAGES/JACQUELYN MARTIN

LEFT: An international State Banquet, in the grand style of traditional diplomacy, was hosted by Queen Elizabeth II at Windsor Castle in honor of Denmark's Queen and Prince Consort. ROYAL DANISH EMBASSY

PART THREE

36

Diversity Comes to the Elite Service

1922—2011

No woman became a U.S. Foreign Service officer until December 1922. Before that, the Foreign Service was a sanctuary for white, mostly Protestant, males. But by 2005, the Foreign Service consisted of 66 percent males and 34 percent females. And in fiscal 2006, the A-100 course at the Foreign Service Institute enrolled 215 women and 172 men. By that year, women occupied a third of all ambassadorships, although few were assigned to major posts.

Lucile Atcherson, of Columbus, Ohio, was appointed in 1922 as the first woman Foreign Service officer. Bright, independent, and from an affluent family, she had graduated from Smith College, marched for women's suffrage, and during World War I worked in France with the wounded. She had the third highest score of all FSO candidates in her year.

Atcherson was nominated for the Foreign Service by President Warren G. Harding, who came from Marion, Ohio. Although the U.S. Senate turned her down the first time around, she was finally admitted to the club. *The New York Times* reported, "She is the first woman to be selected for an important position in the American diplomatic service."

For nearly 150 years, the Department of State had employed women only to clerk, copy letters and documents, and scrub the department's offices.

Of course, women had always played a significant part as wives of Foreign Service officers. They not only guided and assisted their husbands but were important to the informal diplomacy that is an essential part of the job. A cultivated, socially talented wife was appreciated as an asset for a mission. Assistant Secretary William Castle said, "a clever woman can . . . tone up the whole atmosphere of a mission."

Recognition of this contribution was appreciated when the State Department, in 1906, started the formal inspection of missions abroad. Efforts were then made to democratize the Foreign Service, climaxing with the Rogers Act of 1924, and new financial provisions enabled wives of less affluent diplomats to accompany their husbands at their posts. They were representative of the United States and could move with a freedom their deskbound husbands often could not.

On the other hand, wives judged too independent or aggressive could damage a husband's career. And marrying a foreign woman was controversial until an executive order in 1936 mandated that a Foreign Service officer need the Department's permission to marry a foreign woman.

At the beginning of the nineteenth century, Secretary of the Treasury Albert Gallatin had suggested to President Jefferson that he consider women for public service. In a letter dated January 13, 1807, Jefferson replied, "The appointment of a woman to office is an innovation for which the public is not prepared, nor am I." That opinion prevailed in the State Department.

Before the Civil War, Clara Barton and Rose Greenhow were both State Department copyists. Barton later founded the American Red Cross, and Greenhow became a spy for the Confederacy. The women the State Department did employ were kept in the lower ranks. In 1876 only four women worked full-time in the department, and they were clerks at the lowest salary level. Secretary of State John Hay said no woman was worth more than $1,200 a year.

In 1909, Assistant Secretary Frederick Van Dyne opposed admitting women to the Foreign Service because of "their well-known inability to keep a secret," an attitude that persisted in the department until after World War I.

Cecilia Kieckhoeder Jourdan, the wife of Consul Alexander Jourdan at Algiers, is regarded as the first woman clerk inside the Foreign Service; she served in Algiers from 1882 to 1884. In 1914, Wilbur Carr, director of the consular service, still decreed that the State Department could hire women only as clerks. Not so the Foreign Service. Following World War I, a struggle began over admitting women to the Foreign Service, a battle that took decades to resolve. (Not coincidentally, the Nineteenth Amendment was adopted on August 26, 1920.)

In 1922, Lillie Maie Hubbard, a young African-American woman from Hattiesburg, Mississippi, went with her parents to Liberia, where her father was a Baptist missionary. She was asked to fill in for a clerk in the U.S. Legation at Monrovia for a month, a temporary assignment that grew into a Foreign Service career lasting thirty-eight years. When she resigned in 1961, she was a vice consul in Rio de Janeiro.

Only Lucile Atcherson was accepted as a Foreign Service officer before the landmark Rogers Act became law. Coming home from France in 1921, she worked with determination to pass the Foreign Service examinations. She took courses at several universities in diplomatic practices, commercial geography, statistics, international law, and American treaties.

Between 1921 and 1923, six women took the diplomatic exams and four, the consular exams. Of the ten, four passed the written exams, but only Atcherson rated well enough in the orals to achieve a combined score of 80, which allowed her to be appointed a secretary in the diplomatic service. She was assigned to the Division of Latin American Affairs, researching relations between the United States and Haiti. Most new male officers stayed in such a post at headquarters for only a short time and then were sent overseas. But the Foreign Service Personnel Board never gave Atcherson an overseas assignment.

The most influential voices in the debate over admitting women were those of Wilbur Carr, director of the consular service, and Under Secretary Joseph Grew. Neither of them wanted women in the Foreign Service. Carr said "the most feasible way to deal with the question was to defeat them in the examination." Grew opposed this as a "subterfuge" that could not be sustained. He wanted to persuade the President to sign an executive order openly excluding women. But if that were not possible, he would accept Carr's strategy.

The executive committee of the Foreign Service Personnel Board developed three alternative strategies for dealing with women, African-Americans, and naturalized citizens who tried to join the Foreign Service: say candidly that they were not eligible; assert that because they could not serve in all posts, they rated too low to be admitted; or accept all candidates on an equal basis. Before Grew brought the executive committee's memorandum to Secretary Charles Evans Hughes, Grew made sure that Carr and Third Assistant Secretary J. Butler Wright agreed with the order of the alternatives.

Secretary Hughes refused to recommend that the President sign an order excluding women. He said, "It would only be a question of time before women would take their place in diplomacy and consular work just as in the other professions." He opposed stemming "the inevitable tide temporarily."

Under Secretary Grew had to adjust to the changing attitudes. In January 1925, he wrote confidentially to Hugh Wilson that women had to be treated precisely like men as candidates for the Foreign Service. In his diary he said, "We might as well face the fact that women will be satisfied with nothing less than treatment on complete equality with men with respect to the Foreign Service as Clerks, Foreign Service Officers, Ministers and Ambassadors."

After three years, in April 1925, Lucile Atcherson was finally assigned as the third Secretary of the Legation at Bern, Switzerland. Before she left for Bern, she discussed with Grew issues she would meet abroad and agreed to respond in ways least embarrassing to the Foreign Service. Grew asked what she would do when faced with a dinner of a hundred men smoking cigars and drinking beer; she said the best solution would be her temporary absence from Bern.

Even so, Hugh Gibson, then the minister at Bern, protested to Grew that Atcherson would fit in better at a large embassy. Grew replied that she would be sidetracked in a large embassy and the department would be unable to evaluate her abilities.

Gibson was convinced that women were not suited for diplomatic work. He asked Hughes and Grew confidentially how a woman should handle the variety of problems he anticipated: issues like what were suitable clothes for a woman diplomat and where a female Foreign Service officer would go after dinner, when the men and women traditionally separated.

Gibson's objections were made with a touch of good humor. He wrote, "My wife has already expressed considerable apprehension as to the advent of a charming secretary of the fair sex in the Legation." And he asked whether the department was prepared to pay for a chaperon when it was necessary to work late with the Third Secretary. He signed his letter, "I have the honor to be, Sir, Your obedient servant, Michael J. O'Prune."

Lucile Atcherson served at Bern for almost two years. Then, she was denied a promotion, in part the result of a poor report from Gibson because she was a woman—and she was sent to Panama, still as a Third Secretary. That was too much. She agreed to marry George Curtis, M.D., whom she had met in Bern; and she quit the Foreign Service. Married women could not serve in the Foreign Service. Her resignation was accepted with regret.

"WHO IS WILLIS?"

The first Foreign Service examinations under the Rogers Act were held in January 1925; 199 persons, including eight women, were approved to sit for them. Of the 144 persons who took the tests, twenty passed, including one male African-American, Clifton R. Wharton, who was promptly assigned to Liberia.

Pattie H. Field of Denver became the second female FSO. She studied for several months at the Foreign Service Institute and then was sent to Amsterdam as a vice consul. *Time* magazine greeted her with a laudatory write-up detailing how "good" she looked in a petite Paris wardrobe and "a ravishing orange skin-tight swimming costume."

Amsterdam's consul general, William H. Gale, grumpily wanted Field reassigned to a larger post because she would be "worse than useless" in Amsterdam. She served four years there, and then in 1929, although Gale's successor, Charles L. Hoover, gave her a positive report, she resigned to join the National Broadcasting Company.

Between 1924 and 1929, eighty-four women were allowed to sit for the Foreign Service examinations; seventy-three of them took the written exams, and ten passed. Of these, four were admitted to the Foreign Service.

Frances Elizabeth Willis, who had a Ph.D. from Stanford University and had taught at Goucher and Vassar colleges, became the third woman Foreign Service officer in 1927. She was twenty-nine; her fiancé, an American aviator, had been killed in a train wreck. (She never married.)

When Willis was a young third secretary in Stockholm in 1933, she cabled the State Department to say, "The minister left last night. I have assumed charge. Willis." When the message reached the desk of Secretary of State Henry L. Stimson, he asked famously, "Who is Willis?" By taking charge, she became the first woman to represent the nation abroad.

Willis was outspoken and rarely intimidated, hardworking and self-confident. She never pleaded discrimination or condemned sexism in the department. She wrote, "I went into the Service as an officer, not as a woman." She served in Brussels, Madrid, London, and Helsinki. Helped by such well-placed men as Joseph Grew and Hugh Gibson, both of whom had at first opposed women in the Foreign Service, Willis became the first woman chief of mission from the career service—serving as ambassador to Switzerland and later to Norway and Ceylon (Sri Lanka)—and the first woman named a career ambassador. She served overseas thirty-six years.

Despite discrimination from some of her colleagues and superiors, Willis' career was clearly successful. And she had a number of opportunities to exercise her courage. She was in the U.S. Embassy in Brussels in 1940 when German bombs fell on the embassy grounds. While in Madrid, she helped downed American pilots and Free French agents escape to Gibraltar.

The next post–Rogers Act woman Foreign Service officer was Margaret Warner, who had attended Radcliffe College and entered the Foreign Service in 1929. She was assigned to Geneva and resigned in 1931. Nelle B. Stogsdall, a graduate of Wellesley College with an M.A. from Columbia University, also joined in 1929, and she was assigned to Beirut. She married a British vice consul, and when he was transferred in 1931, she resigned.

Constance Ray Harvey, with degrees from Smith and Columbia, began serving in 1930 as a vice consul in Ottawa, and during World War II she was awarded the Presidential Medal of Freedom for bringing out maps of the German antiaircraft installations around Paris. She was one of the half dozen women serving in France who were interned by the Germans for months. The final post of Harvey's thirty-five years in the Foreign Service was at Strasbourg, where she was the first woman consul general.

After Constance Harvey, no woman was appointed by examination between 1930 and 1941, although examinations were given in nine of those years. Seven women did join the Foreign Service by "lateral transfer." Executive Order 5189 of September 11, 1929, provided that officers and employees with five years of continuous service in the State Department could transfer to the Foreign Service on the recommendation of the Foreign Service Personnel Board and the approval of the Secretary of State. The first woman to be appointed by lateral transfer in 1937 was Margaret M. Hanna, who had served as assistant to Alvey Adee. She had

been in the department for forty-one years and had less than six months
to go until mandatory retirement.

After World War I, foreign services were established in the Departments of Commerce, Agriculture, and Interior. From a State Department point of view, this made for confusion and duplication. So, on May 9, 1939, President Roosevelt proposed, and Congress approved, consolidating the departments' foreign services. Under the so-called Reorganization Plan No. II, Commerce and Agriculture moved 114 foreign service personnel over to State. They included fifteen women, six officers and nine clerks from the Department of Commerce. World War II caused a scarcity of male candidates for the Foreign Service. And by March 1942, G. Howland Shaw, chief of the Division of Foreign Service Personnel, recognized that the wartime Foreign Service needed women and older men as clerks. The following year, eight hundred women were serving on the Foreign Service clerical staff.

Some of these women endured arduous experiences on the fringes of the war. When the Japanese attacked Pearl Harbor, Helen L. Skouland stayed at her post as a clerk at the U.S. Embassy in Tokyo. She helped destroy the embassy's codebooks and was one of the dozen staff women locked in the embassy for the next six months. Exchanged for enemy prisoners, in June, her aircraft crashed while taking off from a Newfoundland field, killing eighteen. She was thrown clear and served the rest of the war in London.

WOMEN IN THE OLD-BOY SYSTEM

Once admitted into the Foreign Service sanctum, women soon proved themselves. Ruth Bryan Owen, the eldest daughter of former Secretary of State William Jennings Bryan, was the first woman to be appointed as a chief of mission. President Roosevelt named her minister to Denmark in 1933. (In the following seventy years, 207 women were appointed as ministers or ambassadors.) Ruth Owen had been elected to Congress in 1929 as a Democrat from Florida. Arriving in Copenhagen as the minister, she appeared at a reception carrying an armful of roses and accompanied by a grandchild. She resigned her diplomatic post in Copenhagen in 1936, when she married a Danish captain of the King's Guard. Ruth Owen's success encouraged the appointment of Florence Jaffray Harriman as minister to Norway in 1937, the second woman chief of mission.

The first American woman to hold the rank of ambassador was political appointee Helen Eugenie Moore Anderson of Red Wing, Minnesota. President Truman named her to Denmark in 1949. The next two women ambassadors—both in 1953—were Clare Boothe Luce, the playwright and wife of the publisher of *Time* and *Life* magazines, who was sent to Italy as a noncareer appointment, and Frances E. Willis.

In 2006, the U.S. Postal Service issued a set of six stamps honoring distinguished U.S. diplomats. Frances Willis was the only woman; the five men were Charles E. Bohlen, Hiram Bingham IV, Philip C. Habib, Robert D. Murphy, and Clifton R. Wharton.

The first African-American woman ambassador was Patricia Robert Harris, a noncareer appointment, to Luxembourg in 1965. The first woman Director General of the Foreign Service was Career Ambassador Carol C. Laise in 1975. Two years earlier, she also was the first female assistant secretary of state. Her husband, Ellsworth Bunker, was ambassador to Vietnam while she was ambassador to Nepal. The first woman Under Secretary was Lucy Wilson Benson in 1977.

The Foreign Service Act of 1946 voiced the principle that the Foreign Service should reflect the makeup of the American people. At first, the change was only "in principle." But even that was progress.

The first two Foreign Service examinations after World War II were open only to candidates already working in the Foreign Service or the State Department. Of the 396 candidates taking the written exam in March 1945, eighteen men and one woman were accepted. The woman was Betty Ann Middleton, the first to be accepted in fifteen years. That November, five more women were admitted; in October 1946, one woman passed, and by the end of 1950, five more women had been appointed officers. It was still a very narrow gateway.

Measures were enacted to ease lateral entry for men and women working on temporary status or in the Civil Service. The first woman to be assigned to the Foreign Service on exchange with the Civil Service was Margaret Joy Tibbetts, a native of Maine, a graduate of Wheaton College, and a veteran of the OSS. In 1964, she was named ambassador to Norway, the first career woman of that rank since Frances Willis. Tibbetts also became the third woman to attain the rank of career ambassador.

The number of women Foreign Service officers more than doubled, from 125 in 1955 to 293 in 1962. But, by 1965, this total had dropped to 254 and by the decade's end was down to 147. In view of this discouraging record, Secretary of State Dean Rusk was determined to treat women and members of minorities as equals, and he invited civil rights leaders to Washington in 1963 to discuss increasing their number. Rusk wondered whether the goal of a meritocracy would be downgraded by diversity or whether opening the ranks to all ensured the meritocracy.

Women began to take a more assertive role on their own behalf. A major reevaluation of the department was begun in January 1970, and thirteen task forces with 256 members were established. Only twenty were women. A few women in the department became concerned about this lack of representation, and at a meeting on May 21 Foreign Service officer Jean Joyce raised questions about promotion rates for women. Thus, on July 14, nine women set up the Ad Hoc Committee to Improve the Status of Women in Foreign Affairs Agencies.

On August 26, the fiftieth anniversary of the Nineteenth Amendment to the Constitution, giving women the right to vote, Deputy Under Secretary of State for Administration William B. Macomber met with eight women officers and agreed to hold an open meeting to discuss women in foreign affairs. Elizabeth J. Harper presided over that meeting, which was attended by more than 150 women and men. At that time, women made up less than five percent of the Foreign Service officer corps and held one percent of its senior positions. The report on the meeting asked for a greater effort "to provide greater justice and equity for female employees." And the ad hoc committee reconstituted itself as the permanent Women's Action Organization, with Mary S. Olmsted, one of its organizers, as president. It set out to make changes from within.

During the next year, radical new regulations decreed that Foreign Service careers and marriage were indeed compatible, and both members of a married couple could be assigned to the same post. After 1972, a female Foreign Service officer did not have to resign when she married, and a married woman could enter the service.

The State Department also agreed that a Foreign Service officer's spouse was not an employee unless he or she wished to be. No FSO's wife had authority over other wives, and a husband would not be judged on his wife's activities. This made it unacceptable for a senior Foreign Service wife to make demands of a junior officer's wife—such as doing laundry or other chores. Such imperious Foreign Service wives were known as "dragons" and were dreaded by junior officers.

In contrast, more chiefs of mission briefed the wives of senior officers on embassy problems and seated them next to a prime minister or foreign minister and encouraged them to talk about something besides children and family. Alfred Leroy Atherton, Jr., entered the service out of Harvard in 1947, and his wife, Betty Atherton, left behind an account of how she had felt when her husband joined the Foreign Service:

> It was Roy who had been hired for the Foreign Service, and . . . as far as the State Department was concerned, I did not exist. Kind of a shock. . . . There was a questionable lecture given to us on proto-col. I learned when to wear white gloves, when to wear hats, which corner of the calling card I should turn down when calling your-self. . . . (When we arrived in Germany) there we were in the For-eign Service; no preparation, no education allowance, no medical allowances. It was 1947; it was the postwar period. It was a very, very traumatic experience all around.

She made clear that the Foreign Service had done much since those days to see that this kind of vacuum did not continue and that spouses could be useful "from day one."

FIGHTING SEX DISCRIMINATION

In August 1971, when less than 2 percent of the Foreign Service was made up of women, a female Foreign Service officer brought a sex-discrimination case against the State Department. Even though Alison Palmer had a de-gree from Brown University and had served in Ghana before passing the Foreign Service exam in 1958, she had been hired as a secretary. She fought for an overseas post as a Foreign Service officer and was sent to the Belgian Congo. Then, she was assigned to study at Boston University, and afterward, although she was now knowledgeable in African affairs, she was rejected by ambassadors in two African countries. U.S. Ambassador

Edward M. Korry wrote of her, "The savages in the labor movement [in Ethiopia] would not be receptive to Miss Palmer except perhaps to her natural endowments."

Palmer charged that she had been discriminated against in her desire for an appointment as a political officer. Other "female junior-level Foreign Service applicants" joined her plea, and in 1976 she filed a class-action suit. This enraged Lawrence Eagleburger, the undersecretary for administration, who was quoted in court as having said, "We are going to get Alison."

In 1983, the United States District Court for the District of Columbia found that the department had been engaged in sex discrimination, and Palmer was awarded a promotion, back pay, and assignment to the National War College.

Court orders in the Palmer case forced a number of changes in the hiring, promoting, and assigning of women. The oral examination was judged to be discriminatory, and the 1989 exam was canceled and future exams redesigned. Twenty-six women who had previously been passed over were given Superior Honor Awards. But still, in 1987, out of a total of 135 promotions, only seven women in the Senior Foreign Service were promoted. Between 1972 and 1983, 586 persons were appointed deputy chiefs of mission, but only nine were women. And in 1989, only 7 percent of ambassadors were women. The department notified 601 women they might be eligible for relief, and, by 1994, more than 200 women received compensation.

Not all female Foreign Service officers were pleased with the class-action suit. Avis T. Bohlen, daughter of Ambassador Charles Bohlen, who herself had a highly successful twenty-five-year career in the Foreign Service, said in an interview:

The class action suit has been very damaging for women in the Foreign Service. The court-ordered corrective action has, in effect, allowed every woman who was part of the class action suit to virtually name her job.

In addition, priority has been given to naming women as consul generals. You now have an absurd situation where of about fifteen such jobs that came open this year [1991], some two thirds were given to women. This creates new distortions and new problems. I have a lot of male colleagues who have been very badly and unfairly disadvantaged by this. It is a question of two wrongs not making a right.

By the 1970s, women were beginning to receive chief of mission assignments in significant numbers. Still, the Women's Action Organization warned its members in 1976, "Old male-dominant attitudes persist, our gains can be lost unless all women and friends of women act together in keeping watch on our continual progress."

Years later, Madeleine K. Albright, the first woman Secretary of State, told the Women's Foreign Policy Group, "It used to be that the only way a woman could truly make her foreign policy views felt was by marrying a diplomat, and then pouring tea on an offending ambassador's lap. Today, however, women are engaged in every facet of global affairs."

In 1972, the same year as the Equal Employment Opportunity Act prohibited discrimination based on gender in hiring, wages, and promotions, Mary Olmsted received the Christian A. Herter Award, named in honor of Secretary of State Herter. The citation respected her leadership and said, "Her intellectual courage is not only evident in the reforms she has been able to help win from a conservative system but in the fact that she is the first senior woman FSO who voluntarily put her name, her rank and her career on the line to help remove discrimination against women." (Three years later, she became ambassador to Papua New Guinea and chief of mission to the Solomon Islands.)

Under Secretary Macomber said, "There's no job out there that a woman can't do as [well as] a man." When asked about women serving in Muslim countries, he said, "Oh, even in a Muslim country. You know, I've been hearing that for a long time. If the human being walking into the office represents the United States of America, you can bet your neck they'll deal with that person. And if she's a good person, they'll like it."

But the stereotypes persisted. Ruth A. Davis, who had a brilliant career as an FSO, wrote a letter to the editor of a magazine who had described American diplomats as men in top hats and striped pants, saying that she was very much a diplomat on active duty overseas and owned neither a pinstripe suit nor a top hat. The editor answered, "At first I thought you were some sort of nut, but then I realized that you were for real and that I had been mistaken in my type casting." Ambassador Davis went on to become ambassador to Benin, director of the Foreign Service Institute, and, in 2001, the first African-American woman Director General of the Foreign Service.

Cyrus Vance, on becoming Secretary of State in 1977, reflected, "I was determined to bring the department and the Foreign Service more fully into the process of developing and implementing policy." He announced that he would bring in qualified women and create an environment equal for all. He said, "The white, male Foreign Service was already on its way out, and I intended to hasten the transformation."

Vance established the Executive Level Task Force on Affirmative Action, chaired by Ambassador Philip C. Habib, to review recruiting and examinations. Congress, dissatisfied with the rate of progress, in the Foreign Service Act of 1980 finally made equal opportunity mandatory. But Mary Olmsted still called improving the status of women "agonizingly slow."

The percentage of women among Foreign Service officers climbed in the 1970s and 1980s. In 1977, there were 337 women among 3,514 Foreign Service officers, or 9.6 percent. That was a new high. In 1987, there were 1,006 women among 4,427 officers, or 22.7 percent. But still, at the higher Foreign Service levels the picture had not changed much. At the end of 1989, in the senior Foreign Service, where the people contributed most directly to making policy, still only 6.9 percent (54 persons) were women.

In the twenty-first century, progress has been more noticeable. In 2003, a third of Foreign Service officers were women, and so were 31 percent of Foreign Service specialists. And women occupied 25 percent of the slots in the Senior Foreign Service.

Complaints of gender discrimination continued to be filed against the State Department. Outside consultants judged that the improvements in regulations and policies did not do much within the department to change attitudes. The Commission on Civil Rights said in 1981, "Recruitment efforts suffered from an image of the Foreign Service as elitist, self-satisfied, a walled-in barony populated by smug white males, an old-boy system in which women and minorities cannot possibly hope to be treated with equity in such matters as promotions and senior level responsibilities."

Some women claimed that the "cone" system, by which Foreign Service officers are trained and organized, discriminated against them. And the decision in the Alison Palmer case echoed this claim. The four areas, or "cones," to which new officers are assigned, and in which they usually remain, are political, economic, consular, and administrative. Women were less likely than men to be assigned to the political cone, which leads to the highest rate of advancement up the career ladder. In 1989, a General Accounting Office survey confirmed that women were most likely to be placed in the administrative and consular cones.

Still, important steps were taken. Jeane Kirkpatrick became permanent representative to the United Nations in 1981, and President Reagan named her the first women on the National Security Council. Sixteen years later, Secretary of State Madeleine K. Albright was the second.

Over the decade ending in 1993, Ann Miller Morin, the wife of a Foreign Service officer, interviewed thirty-four of the forty-four women who had been ministers or ambassadors and came to these conclusions: Political appointees have greater access than career FSOs to the White House and the top of the State Department. Women career FSOs "paid a price in their personal lives." And foreign governments often prefer trained career diplomats over political appointees. None of those findings was surprising.

In 1985, 80 percent of Foreign Service officers and specialists were male; but twenty years later, only 66 percent were, and more women than men were entering the service.

In 1989, two commissions, one named by Congress and one by the State Department, said the department was still not hiring enough women. Progress was being made, but slowly.

Some on the inside had a different perception. Ambassador Langhorne A. Motley, who helped prepare many ambassadors, said, "The Department has gone overboard on Equal Employment Opportunity. If you are a woman of sufficiently high rank, you will be appointed an ambassador. That may sound chauvinistic, but it is that simple. It is a fact. . . . But it is not only women; it is minorities in general. The Department is on a 'quota' system."

ACCEPTING AFRICAN-AMERICANS

Only after the two world wars did the virtually lily-white U.S. Foreign Service find itself being pried open, slowly, reluctantly, to admit significant numbers of African-Americans.

The earliest African-Americans identified in the foreign service were Joseph Warren, an assistant messenger, and his wife, Louisa, a laundress, in 1817, according to research by Marc J. Susser, historian of the State Department, and his colleague, Kathleen B. Rasmussen.

In Reconstruction days after the Civil War, the State Department sent a few black Americans abroad. The first African-American minister, Ebenezer Don Carlos Bassett, born in Litchfield, Connecticut, to a slave father and a Pequot mother, was sent to Haiti. When the United States finally recognized Haiti in 1862 (fifty-eight years after its independence), it sent three white envoys before naming Bassett in 1869 as minister and consul general. Before President Grant chose him, Bassett had studied at Yale and become a distinguished educator. He stayed at his post in Haiti for eleven years.

Two years after Bassett's appointment, James Milton Turner became the minister to Liberia. Turner had been born in slavery and become a respected educator in Missouri. His tour in Monrovia was tumultuous. After seven years, he returned home discouraged about his attempts to encourage economic development and African-American immigration into Liberia.

At first, African-American diplomats were confined to those two black countries. A few candidates rejected these appointments; for example, Joseph Charles Price, the young president of Livingstone College in Salisbury, North Carolina, declined President Cleveland's offer to make him minister to Liberia in 1888. The next year, President Benjamin Harrison appointed the former slave Frederick Douglass minister to Haiti. He was then about seventy-two. He tried to help the U.S. Navy lease a coaling station at the Môle St. Nicolas. When that imperialistic mission failed, he resigned and returned home in disgust.

African-Americans found a somewhat broader range of opportunity in the consular service. The first consul was George Jackson, who passed the examination in 1897 and was assigned to Cognac, France. He was soon followed by Richard Greener, the first African-American Harvard graduate in the consular service; he was sent as consul to Vladivostok. Three other African-Americans became consuls in 1906. But by 1908 there were still only eleven African-Americans in either part of the foreign service.

Woodrow Wilson ran into controversy as a Southerner when he became President in 1913. Under Southern pressure, he replaced Republican African-American physician Henry W. Furness of Indiana as the minister to Haiti with Madison R. Smith, a white former congressman from Missouri, and followed him with another white, Arthur Bailey-Blanchard of Louisiana, an experienced foreign service officer. African-American leaders were outraged.

It required two world wars, the civil rights movement at home, and the decline of colonialism abroad to defeat the old prejudices. The cutting back of colonialism meant that more American diplomats were assigned to the new nations populated by people with darker skins. And the diplomats were expected to practice the democracy and lack of prejudice they preached.

Liberia, which had first been settled by African-Americans in 1822, was a constant source of trouble for the United States, a site of yellow fever and covert forced labor. In the State Department, these problems first fell on Assistant Secretary Robert Woods Bliss and William R. Castle, Jr., chief of the Division of Western European Affairs. A major controversial player was the Firestone Tire and Rubber Company, which in 1926 leased for ninety-nine years sixteen hundred square miles of jungle to produce its own rubber.

African-American Minister William. T. Francis in Monrovia and Secretary of State Henry Stimson continued to wrestle with Liberia's problems. And Dean Acheson reported to President Roosevelt in 1945 that conditions in Liberia were still "scandalous." Forty years later, coups and assassinations were still keeping Liberia in turmoil.

When the Rogers Act combined the diplomatic and consular services, three African-Americans became part of the Foreign Service: James Carter, James Weldon Johnson, and William Yerby. Between 1924 and 1949, only five African-Americans became Foreign Service officers; four of them went to Liberia and the fifth to Haiti. During the time Joseph Grew was chairman of the Foreign Service Personnel Board, most black Americans who tried to join the Foreign Service failed the very subjective oral examination; were confined to the lower, nonprofessional ranks; or were restricted to serving in the "Negro circuit" of Liberia, the Azores, the Canary Islands, and Madagascar.

Clifton R. Wharton, Sr., who was the first African-American to pass the new Foreign Service examination in 1924, had a law degree from Boston University and had already worked in the State Department as a law clerk. In *Black Diplomacy*, historian Michael L. Krenn noted that Wharton, who was light-skinned, was admitted without an interview. Grew made certain he was assigned to Liberia, and Wharton did not leave the "Negro circuit" for more than two decades.

He also was the last black Foreign Service officer appointed during the next twenty years, and by 1942 he was the only one still in the service. He became first secretary and consul in Lisbon in 1948, and then consul general there, a European first. Ten years later, he was named minister to Romania, and in 1961 ambassador to Norway, the first black career officer to attain that rank. Later, he was awarded the rank of career minister. It had been a long struggle.

Ralph Bunche, one of the most distinguished black Americans of the period, served in the Office of Strategic Services (OSS) during World War II as an expert on Africa, transferred to the State Department in 1944, and was loaned to the United Nations two years later. In 1949, President Truman personally asked him to return to the State Department as assistant secretary. He declined because he did not want his children to live in "Jim Crow" Washington. A year later, he received the Nobel Peace Prize. He never returned to the State Department.

In 1950, Professor Rayford Logan, of Howard University, wrote that only thirty-three of the more than thirteen thousand members of the Foreign Service were African-American. Twenty-eight of them were in low-level jobs, and two-thirds were sent to Liberia. Only two served in Europe.

Of the five professional FSOs among the thirty-three, Edward R. Dudley alone then held ambassadorial rank. Dudley had been counsel for the National Association for the Advancement of Colored People and legal aide to the governor of the U.S. Virgin Islands. President Truman elevated him in 1949 to be the first African-American ambassador. When Ambassador Dudley traveled with Assistant Secretary George McGhee in 1950, he had to stay in the consulate in Johannesburg because he was not welcome in a hotel's public rooms.

A number of prominent white diplomats, including Dean Rusk, Chester Bowles, and George McGhee, worked to reduce discrimination. But the dominant culture at the State Department insisted that black Americans were not suitable representatives of the United States, even in a predominately multiracial world. Terence A. Todman, who was born in the Virgin Islands, at first was given a desk job because the personnel department said he did not have an American accent. Despite this, he served as ambassador in six countries over twenty years. He believed the argument against black ambassadors "was concocted within the State Department. It was made out of whole cloth. It was a total lie."

When Dwight Eisenhower became President, the House Appropriations Committee cut the State Department's funding and forced a reduction in employment. That made it more difficult for blacks to keep Foreign Service jobs and for black candidates to find places. And since the Republican Party then attracted relatively few black voters, African-Americans felt that the party did not have the incentive to put much energy into improving their situation. Only seven African-Americans were appointed Foreign Service officers while Eisenhower was President, and of these four were lower-grade holdovers from the Truman presidency. In 1961, the State Department reported it had seventeen black FSOs and three black Foreign Service Representatives out of 4,872.

Secretary Dulles held the perception that some leading blacks could not get full clearance from the Federal Bureau of Investigation because they belonged to organizations that had been "infiltrated" by Communist security risks. Even though the FBI reported it was not true, Dulles stuck to this belief. Biographer William Manchester wrote that Winston Churchill called Dulles "the only bull who brings his own china shop with him."

President Kennedy's appointments of Dean Rusk as Secretary of State and Chester Bowles as undersecretary encouraged African-Americans to expect changes for the better. Kennedy told his new undersecretary: "As you know I have been deeply concerned at the small number of Negroes and members of other minority groups in the foreign service and throughout the foreign affairs operations of the government." Kennedy appointed Carl Rowan as deputy assistant secretary of state for public affairs, Clifton Wharton as ambassador to Norway, and Hugh Smythe as ambassador to Syria. But in 1968, there were still fewer than two dozen African-American FSOs.

Rowan's appointment as deputy assistant secretary of state for public affairs, as ambassador to Finland two years later, and then as director of the USIA in 1964 put flesh on the promises of equality. But still, the United States fielded only two black ambassadors.

To illustrate the state of the nation, Ambassador Rowan told this story: He was mowing his lawn in the Spring Valley section of Washington, D.C., when a Cadillac pulled up, and a white woman in the backseat called out,

"Boy? What do they pay you to cut this grass." Rowan turned to her and replied, "As matter of fact, the lady of the house lets me sleep with her!"

In a heartening step, the Ford Foundation in 1963 allocated $600,000 a year to fund the Foreign Affairs Scholars Program, a summer intern program to improve the skills of forty African-American college students so they could join the Foreign Service and other foreign policy institutions. It did not help. Between 1961 and 1967 only two African-American officers entered the Foreign Service. Of all candidates taking the written exam, 25 percent passed; of African-Americans, 4 percent. The Ford Foundation dropped the scholars program.

A new argument was brought out: that African countries felt sending a black American as ambassador was sending a second-class citizen. William Attwood, a leading white journalist and diplomat, followed a black American, John Morrow, as ambassador to Guinea and wrote later that he found some Africans believed "that Washington is being deviously patronizing, and clearly race-conscious, in sending them more or less dark-skinned ambassadors." Mercer Cook, who was named ambassador to Niger in 1961, pointed to the resistance he received from home and said, "Support was my problem, not acceptance."

Black Americans in the Foreign Service voiced their frustration at the State Department's failure to use them without reference to race. Franklin H. Williams, ambassador to Ghana (1965), wrote that in the Foreign Service "in-breeding is tremendous!" Hugh Smythe, who was the first African-American ambassador to serve in the Middle East—he was appointed to Syria in 1965 (and later to Malta)—wrote in 1968 to John M. Steeves, director general of the Foreign Service, that none of the four black ambassadors then serving believed that they would be given a challenging post as long as he remained in office. Carl Rowan labeled the State Department "a virtual plantation."

In 1965, President Johnson appointed Patricia Roberts Harris, a law professor at Howard University, as ambassador to Luxembourg. She was the first African-American woman to hold that rank. She was the daughter of a railroad-dining-car waiter, and she had graduated summa cum laude from Howard. She said candidly that she figured that the State Department had not been able to find a smaller or less significant post "for a woman who is also black." She said she found the Foreign Service "a pain in the neck." After two years, she returned to academia.

The 1970s saw a more substantial change as President Nixon and President Ford sent thirteen African-Americans to sixteen ambassadorial posts. But the debate over elitism versus diversity continued. Starting in 1977, President Carter and Secretary Cyrus Vance had fourteen black ambassadors. Terence Todman became assistant secretary for inter-American affairs, and Andrew Young and Donald McHenry became ambassadors at the United Nations. But resistance continued to be crippling.

In the Reagan years, the number of black ambassadors slipped again to six. After only a year, Todman was shifted from Washington to the post of ambassador to Spain, leaving no African-Americans at his level in the State Department. He retired in 1993 with the rank of career ambassador.

Another successful black ambassador was Edward J. Perkins, who, after serving in the U.S. Army and the Marine Corps, in 1972 became a staff assistant in the Office of the Director General of the Foreign Service. Then, he served as political affairs counselor at the embassy in Ghana, deputy chief of mission (DCM) in Liberia, ambassador to Liberia and South Africa, and permanent representative to the United Nations. In 1989, he was named the first black Director General of the Foreign Service. Perkins then served as ambassador to Australia and retired as a career ambassador.

Through all the battles over discrimination in the Foreign Service, African-Americans both inside the State Department and in the wider community outside protested that the exclusion of members of minorities damaged the United States around the world. And at the same time, whites complained of reverse discrimination. Eventually, some black FSOs went to court; and in 1996 the State Department paid out nearly $4 million to thirty plaintiffs as compensation for being discriminated against.

Makila James, a young Foreign Service officer who had graduated from Cornell University and Columbia Law School and had served in two African embassies, said of the Foreign Service, "It is a racial institution and not everyone should tackle it. You have to fight the battle and not everyone can do that. . . . There is a backlash from those who feel threatened by us."

She also wrote, "The African slave trade, which led to my becoming an American, bestowed on me advantages that I can use to reconnect with Africa." James persevered; by 2005, she became the first full-time consul general in Juba, the capital of South Sudan, and then the ambassador to Swaziland.

When two secretaries of state in a row were African-Americans, Colin Powell and Condoleezza Rice, the struggle seemed won. In 2002, Secretary Powell presented a $1 million grant from the U.S. government to the Ralph J. Bunche International Affairs Center of Howard University to prepare members of minorities for careers as diplomats. The John D. and Catherine T. MacArthur Foundation added a grant of $1 million for the same purpose.

But prejudices are hard to overcome. During the entire 1990s, only seventy-one African-Americans joined the Foreign Service. By the end of 2005, only 6 percent of FSOs were African-American. The overall picture had not changed fundamentally over a half century.

OTHER DISCRIMINATED GROUPS

It also took time to tear down official barriers against other groups that were discriminated against. The first Hispanic to become a Foreign Service ambassador was Joseph John Jova, a Dartmouth graduate who was appointed to Honduras in 1965. By 1992, only seven Hispanics had served as chiefs of mission.

The first Asian-American ambassadors were Julia Chang Bloch (Nepal in 1989) and William H. Itoh (Thailand in 1996). Bloch had been born in China and brought to San Francisco when she was nine. She could not become a Foreign Service officer, because when she graduated from college one had to be a citizen for nine years before joining the Foreign Service. "I saw no one who remotely looked like me in the Foreign Service, let alone in positions as ambassadors." Instead, she entered diplomacy through the Peace Corps. When she returned to Washington, she said she still found every interview began with "How fast can you type?" She concluded, "My experience has taught me that diplomacy is still very much a man's world."

Gays and lesbians, the physically handicapped, and members of various other groups have been accepted slowly. A dramatic change was the admission of blind persons to the Foreign Service in 1989. The National Federation of the Blind credits Ambassador Edward J. Perkins, then Director General of the Foreign Service, for reversing the State Department's historic attitude of excluding the blind and others.

Homosexuals had a difficult time during the security alarm that accompanied the Cold War and the McCarthy era. Although information here tends to be less transparent than that related to most other areas of discrimination, the State Department dismissed ninety-plus homosexual employees at the beginning of that period as security risks vulnerable to blackmail. Persecution intensified until gays and lesbians turned to the courts, and by the mid-1970s homosexuality was no longer a cause for dismissal.

As recently as 2007, Ambassador Michael E. Guest, a veteran of twenty-six years in the Foreign Service, resigned in protest against rules that discriminated against same-sex partners. He said the Foreign Service gave them fewer benefits than it did family pets. After serving as ambassador to Romania, Guest had worked in Washington to change the rules that deprived same-sex married partners and heterosexual unmarried partners of evacuation rights, foreign language training, diplomatic passports, and medical care. In 2006, he received the Christian A. Herter Award for constructive dissent from the AFSA, but he finally resigned.

Eugene Sweeney, consul general in Lisbon, believed things were changing because in 2009 same-sex partners finally won housing and travel coverage. But health care and pensions were not yet covered. The Foreign Service has certainly moved a significant distance toward reflecting the varieties and diversities of American society, but it still has battles to fight.

37

China Hands

1946–89

The U.S. Foreign Service suffered a devastating trauma on the far side of the world in October 1949 after Mao Tse-tung's Communists took command of mainland China, and some powerful Americans accused U.S. diplomats of "losing China" and even of supporting Communism.

The rivalry inside China had long been building. While the United States' military forces advanced across the Pacific and closed on the Japanese home islands (Manila, February 3, 1945; Iwo Jima, February 19, 1945; Okinawa, April 1, 1945), Japanese forces inside China were winning victory after victory. American diplomats in China concentrated on persuading the Chinese Nationalists and the Communists to fight the Japanese rather than each other.

In China's capital, Chungking, Ambassador Clarence E. Gauss and Foreign Service officer John Carter Vincent met with Generalissimo Chiang Kai-shek, leader of the Nationalists. He brazenly asked the United States for a billion dollars in aid. And Ambassador Gauss sent Foreign Service officer John S. Service, the China-born son of a missionary and himself an Oberlin College graduate, to scout out the Chinese Communists at their base in Yenan in the mountains of northwest China.

John Paton Davies, Jr., had accompanied Lieutenant General Joseph W. Stilwell when he went out to command the new China-Burma-India theater early in 1942. Davies also visited with Communist Premier Zhou

Enlai three times that spring, and he recommended to Stilwell that military and political observers be sent to Yenan. Roosevelt exhorted Chiang to permit such a mission, but the generalissimo stalled.

The situation in East Asia was also aggravated by the contrast between the United States and its British ally over their visions of the postwar world. The British were determined not to have their empire destroyed and not to become a third-rate power, while the United States nurtured the end of colonialism. Such a fundamental difference allowed for little compromise.

Over time, Roosevelt realized that Chiang Kai-shek was unable, or unwilling, to fight the Japanese; by July 1944 (a month after D-Day in Normandy), a frustrated FDR was demanding that Chiang turn over command of his armies to Stilwell "at once." By then, Chiang and Stilwell despised each other, and Chiang was demanding Stilwell's recall.

Relations grew so tense that Vice President Henry A. Wallace flew to Chungking to talk with Chiang. With Wallace came FSO John Carter Vincent and Professor Owen Lattimore of the Johns Hopkins University, who acted as Wallace's interpreter. Chiang resisted, but finally Wallace persuaded Chiang to allow American observers to visit Mao's headquarters. Chiang also asked the President to send a personal representative to Chungking.

Roosevelt sent as his representative Major General Patrick J. Hurley, a hot-tempered Oklahoma Republican who had been the attorney for the Choctaw nation, a Tulsa oil lawyer, and Herbert Hoover's secretary of war. Hurley distrusted the State Department, which he regarded as pro-imperialism, pro-Communism, and pro-Zionism. The egotistical Hurley must have been FDR's most unfortunate diplomatic appointment.

The observer group that reached Yenan in July 1944 was known as the Dixie Mission (the Communists were cast as the Confederates). In charge was Colonel David D. Barrett; John S. Service represented the Foreign Service; and with them came six army officers, an enlisted man, and the astute *Time* journalist Theodore H. White. The Americans lived in mud houses dug into the loess cliffs beside the Yen River; the Communist leaders dwelt on the opposite bank. Living was austere. Service, who in August had an eight-hour meeting with Mao Tse-tung, reported that Chiang's government was "selfish and corrupt" and reported fully on Mao's desire for American aid.

THE ARRIVAL OF PATRICK HURLEY

Patrick Hurley arrived at Chungking in September 1944 and promptly allied himself with the generalissimo against Stilwell. After agonizing consideration, Roosevelt accepted Chiang's legitimacy as head of state. Chiang retained command of his disorganized forces, and General Albert C. Wedemeyer replaced Stilwell. Chiang had gotten what he demanded but at great cost; the Allies now gave priority to their amphibious forces fighting across the Pacific toward Tokyo.

Shocked by Stilwell's recall, John S. Service in a long letter to Stilwell from Yenan on October 10, Double-Ten Day in China, said, "We should end the hollow pretense that China is unified and that we can talk only to Chiang." Hurley accused Service of insubordination.

Meanwhile, FSO Raymond P. Ludden and four U.S. Army men set out on a hike of hundreds of miles through northern China behind Japanese lines to install weather equipment for American fliers and to judge whether the Chinese Communists were, in fact, viable. The Americans judged that most Chinese did support the Communists, while China was undergoing the painful evolution from a traditional to a modern society.

In November, on the day before FDR was reelected for a fourth term, Hurley unexpectedly flew to Communist headquarters in Yenan. He stepped off the plane in the uniform of a major general bedecked with colorful medals, an awkward contrast to his hosts' plain padded jackets, and suddenly he gave a prolonged Choctaw war whoop.

Hurley soon took umbrage at John Davies and shipped him back to Chungking. And Hurley sat down with the Chinese Communist leaders without a Foreign Service officer present who spoke Chinese. They agreed to a unified effort to defeat Japan, and Hurley flew to Chungking with Zhou Enlai. Their plan outraged Chiang, who had expected to be given control of the Communist forces. Zhou Enlai carried Chiang's reaction back to Mao, and Chiang's opposition crushed Hurley's attempt at diplomacy. Both sides were furious with him.

In December, Ambassador Gauss resigned and Hurley was given his title. Although Gauss had spent most of the years since 1907 in China, he had never learned Chinese. But, unlike his successor, he had an orderly mind and a sense of a superior's loyalty toward his subordinates.

Ambassador Hurley issued an order that no word unfavorable to

Chiang Kai-shek was to be sent to Washington. Arthur Ringwalt, the head of the embassy's political section, ignored the order and forwarded reports from the field as they were submitted. Hurley ordered Ringwalt to stop sending derogatory messages about Chiang—and drew a pistol on him.

The gut issue was clear: Was it the responsibility of members of the Foreign Service to report what they saw and heard or to send a "party line" back to Washington? For the next decade this question would be crucial.

In early 1945, John Davies was transferred to Moscow. When he took leave of Hurley, the ambassador called him a Communist and threatened to have the State Department fire him. Hurley also fought with Wedemeyer and Ludden and threatened to destroy John Service if he got in the ambassador's way. The Chinese official Ji Chaozhu characterized Hurley as a "narcissistic blowhard."

Hurley made a trip to Washington, convinced that Foreign Service officers in China were sabotaging his mission. Most of them certainly disagreed with his support of Chiang; they knew Chiang could not win his power struggle with Mao. A year earlier, John Service had reported, "China is in a mess. . . . Chiang, and only Chiang, is responsible." Now, the generalissimo's refusal to cooperate with Mao defeated Hurley's plans. O. Edmund Clubb explained the controversy from the Foreign Service's point of view when he told an interviewer:

> He [Hurley] had come out in favor of working entirely for the one side—for the Nationalists, thus causing the United States to abandon neutrality to a degree. . . . Of course, Hurley had also planted other seeds, because when he suddenly retired in November of 1945, he let out a blast against the Foreign Service charging effectively that the China policy of the United States was being molded by people who had Communist inclinations and all the rest of it. And he suggested likewise that there was a Communist conspiracy that had infected, if you will, the State Department. It was long afterwards that Joe McCarthy got into the act. It was Hurley, Patrick J. Hurley, really, who planted the seed of McCarthyism.

While Hurley was in Washington, Chargé George Atcheson and other Foreign Service officers in Chungking sent a telegram to the State Department urging that the United States supply the Communists, as well as the Nationalists, so both could fight the Japanese. They also advised that

Chiang was corrupt and ineffective and that China was heading toward civil war. In Washington, Hurley saw the message and exploded. He swore he would get Service if it was the last thing he ever did.

General Wedemeyer sent Service north to Yenan in March 1945 to observe the first congress that the Chinese Communist Party had held in a decade. Service had another long talk with Mao, who requested a visit with President Roosevelt and promised to cooperate with the Americans. In Washington, Hurley heard of Service's mission and fantasized that he must be giving secret plans to the Communists. Even though Service reported to Wedemeyer, not Hurley, the ambassador had him recalled from Yenan. Service left Yenan for the last time on April 4 and was sent by plane all the way to Washington. (Hurley also had Atcheson recalled from China and replaced as deputy chief of mission by a political appointee, Virginia banker Walter S. Robertson.)

Hurley convinced Roosevelt to send military aid only to Chiang, not to Mao. And Hurley was sent to explain the China confrontation to Churchill and Stalin. In Moscow, Hurley met with Stalin and Foreign Minister Vyacheslav M. Molotov on April 15, 1945, and sent Washington an optimistic report. Chargé George Kennan and John Davies, by then the Moscow embassy staff member who knew China best, read Hurley's report. Kennan sent Ambassador Averell Harriman a personal note warning him that Hurley had not understood what the Soviet leaders had told him. In his memoirs, Kennan wrote of "the nightmarish quality of that world of fancy into which Washington, and much of our public opinion, can be carried in those times when fear, anger, and emotionalism take over from reason in the conduct of our public life."

John Davies also came under attack, although Kennan vouched that he was brilliant and imaginative and "a rock of strength to us at that time in the Moscow embassy . . . without an ounce of pro-Communist sympathies."

And Kennan was not the only one to find Davies a rock of strength. Back in August 1943, Davies had been one of seventeen passengers on a C-46 two-engine military aircraft flying over the Hump from India to China. Aboard were a dozen GIs and war correspondent Eric Sevareid. As they flew over Burma's mountainous jungle, one of the plane's engines quit and everyone had to strap on a parachute and jump. None of them had ever parachuted before. Davies volunteered to go first.

In the jungle, they were met by naked Naga headhunters, and eventually they needed two weeks to hike out through the rugged mountain wilderness. For his leadership and courage, Davies was awarded the Medal of Freedom.

Years later, when Secretary Dulles fired Davies, alleging he was unreliable, Sevareid recounted over CBS radio, "If ever again I were in deep trouble, the man I would want to be with would be this particular man. . . . [He was] all that a man should be in modesty and thoughtfulness, in resourcefulness and steady strength of character."

On the evening of June 6, 1945, the FBI arrested John Service in Washington for violation of the Espionage Act. They also arrested five Americans associated with the left-wing magazine *Amerasia*. Among those arrested were Lieutenant Andrew Roth, of the Office of Naval Intelligence, and Emmanuel S. Larsen, who had lived in China for many years and had worked in Washington for U.S. Naval Intelligence and briefly for the State Department. Service had given the magazine classified memoranda he himself had written about China.

Service spent a night in jail before he was bailed out. The FBI confiscated the papers in his State Department office. A Federal grand jury indicted three of the men and voted unanimously not to indict Service. Those indicted were Larsen, Roth, and Philip Jaffe of *Amerasia* magazine. Two of those indicted paid fines (Larsen paid $500), and the government dropped the case against Roth.

Service's friends thought his passing classified documents was "recklessly indiscreet," but the Foreign Service Personnel Board cleared him of disloyalty, and he was restored to duty. He, as well as FSOs John Emmerson and James Penfield, both China Hands, joined MacArthur's staff in Tokyo.

Immediately after the atomic bombings of Hiroshima and Nagasaki and the Japanese surrender, General MacArthur issued General Order No. 1, which declared that Chiang Kai-shek would accept the Japanese surrender in China, Formosa, and Indochina north of the 16th parallel. The Nationalists would be recognized as the legitimate government of China.

Chiang invited Mao to Chungking and guaranteed his safety. Ambassador Hurley and a Chinese general flew to Yenan and, on August 28,

1945, escorted Mao and his aides to Chungking. Chiang and Mao were both stubborn; their public declarations left no room for cooperation. When the meeting of the chairman and the generalissimo failed, Hurley blamed the Chinese-speaking American diplomats.

United States armed forces airlifted and "sea-lifted" 400,000 Nationalist troops and 53,000 U.S. Marines to northern China, where the Communists predominated. Thus, the United States took sides in the Chinese civil war while continuing to insist that it was not involved in China's domestic affairs.

Mao and Zhou Enlai flew back from Chungking to Yenan by November 25. And the Nationalists attacked Manchuria, which both sides coveted. The next day, Hurley gave President Truman his resignation, criticizing "the career men who were opposing the American policy in the Chinese Theatre of war." In December Truman sent General George C. Marshall to China as his personal representative to negotiate peace and the unification of China.

Hurley appeared before the Senate Foreign Relations Committee and denounced Foreign Service officers Atcheson, Davies, Emmerson, Freeman, Ludden, Ringwalt, and Vincent. He charged they all were "disloyal to the American policy" and were trying "to destroy the Government of the Republic of China." Secretary Byrnes came to his men's defense, and the Senate committee decided that Hurley's charges were baseless. Byrnes also ordered a departmental investigation, which came to the same conclusion.

The battling parties announced the end of the fighting in China, and after three weeks of negotiations reported agreement of many differences. But Chiang refused to apply the truce to Manchuria. So the Russians did not remove their troops, and the Chinese Communists built up their men and materiel there.

In May 1946, the Nationalists won a full-fledged battle around a railroad junction, Ssuping-kai, but the Communists were now in force in Manchuria. Both sides agreed to a truce, although the expiration of the truce at the end of the month signaled the failure of Marshall's mission. He selected John Leighton Stuart, the China-born president of Yenching University, to serve as ambassador to China and returned home to become Secretary of State.

O. Edmund Clubb had briefed Marshall on China, and Philip Sprouse helped the general write his report. Clubb was transferred out of Manchuria, at the Communists' request, for being too anti-Communist. He became the U.S. consul general in Peking. A rancher's son, he had studied international law, joined the Foreign Service, and, in 1929, was sent to Peking to learn Chinese. In 1942, the invading Japanese held Clubb in Hanoi for eight months, including two months in solitary confinement. Shipped to neutral Lourenço Marques, he and Foreign Service officer Raymond P. Ludden, at the State Department's request, turned around and returned to Chungking. Clubb served much of World War II as consul general in distant Vladivostok. In October 1947, he took charge in Peking from veteran FSO Fulton Freeman.

As the China civil war continued, the Communists gained strength. They scooped up vast amounts of American arms every time they defeated the Nationalists. By the end of 1948, the Nationalists had lost more than four hundred thousand soldiers and mountains of American weapons and supplies. And they had lost Manchuria. John Davies said sarcastically that the United States became the "quartermaster to the Reds."

In Mukden, Manchuria's capital, the Communists beat up Angus Ward, the American consul general, and his staff members and held them in the consular compound for fifteen months. The large, white-goateed Ward also spent a month in solitary confinement. The Chinese refused to recognize the American diplomats. The Communists finally tried Ward and four others for espionage and deported them (Clubb arrived from Peking to accompany them).

On January 21, 1949, after a climactic battle at Huai-Hai in central China, Chiang Kai-shek resigned the presidency. Ten days later, in Peking, Consul General Clubb stood on the sidewalk before the consulate general and watched the Chinese Red Army march triumphantly down Legation Street. Chinese soldiers had not done that since the Boxer Rebellion.

In April, Communist troops took Nanking, the Nationalist capital. At 6:30 A.M. on Sunday, April 24, a squad invaded the bedroom of seventy-three-year-old Ambassador John Leighton Stuart. They were ushered out with no damage done. Shanghai fell on May 27. Even such diehard "mish-kids" (missionary kids) as Henry Luce finally recognized that Chiang's cause was hopeless. In July, the Communists closed the United States Information Agency centers and libraries in Peking and Tientsin. In response, Clubb fired his Chinese employees.

On October 1, the People's Republic of China was formally installed in Peking, and in December the Nationalist government relocated to Formosa. Major General David Barr, head of the U.S. Advisory Group with Chiang, blamed "the world's worst leadership and . . . widespread corruption and dishonesty throughout the Armed Forces." The titanic civil war was over.

The Communist government notified Clubb and the other foreign consuls in Peking, now called Beijing, that diplomatic relations would continue only if they recognized the new government and broke off relations with the Nationalists. The State Department refused. On January 6, 1950, the Chinese posted a sign on the gate of the consulate general in Beijing, saying the property was requisitioned for government use. Clubb dumped tons of equipment in the adjoining lot, had the American flag hauled down, and closed the consulate general.

Clubb became the director of the State Department's Office of Chinese Affairs when the Korean War began. His superior was the new assistant secretary for Far Eastern Affairs, Dean Rusk, who had replaced W. Walton Butterworth. The capable Butterworth had fallen to attacks from McCarthyites, whom Dean Acheson called "the Primitives."

"COMMUNISTS" IN THE STATE DEPARTMENT

During the Chiang Kai-shek government's last days on the mainland, the FBI, the State Department, and committees of the Congress repeatedly investigated the Foreign Service's China experts. And President Truman created the Loyalty Review Board as an appeals court for people judged adversely by their own Federal government departments.

That summer the State Department issued a major White Paper, *United States Relations with China*, which reviewed the whole period since World War II. In its covering letter, Secretary Acheson wrote, "The unfortunate but inescapable fact is that the ominous result of the civil war in China was beyond the control of the government of the United States." That was the prevailing view in the State Department. As Lucius Battle put it, "There wasn't a thing you could do about the fall of China."

Chiang Kai-shek was old and tired. But his sympathizers in the United States immediately attacked. Congressman Walter H. Judd, M.D., of Minnesota, who had been a missionary doctor in China, also lashed out at John Service, and the State Department tried to tuck him away as head of the political section of the embassy in New Delhi.

Communist infiltration was already a national worry. On February 9, 1950, just two months before Clubb arrived back in Washington, Senator Joseph McCarthy, in a speech at Wheeling, West Virginia, opened his windmill crusade against "Communists in the State Department." McCarthy's irresponsible accusations would result in widespread dismissals and resignations from government service.

Three weeks before McCarthy's spellbinder, Alger Hiss, who had worked in the State Department for eleven years, had been found guilty on two counts of perjury and sentenced to five years in prison. He was accused of having lied about being a Communist. In 1936, Hiss had joined the State Department as an assistant to Assistant Secretary of State Francis Sayre and, two years later, became an aide to Stanley Hornbeck, advisor on Far East affairs. During World War II, Hiss served in the Office of Special Political Affairs on postwar planning for international organizations. He rose to become executive secretary of the Dumbarton Oaks Conference, an advisor at the Yalta Conference, and the secretary general of the founding convention of the United Nations. He left the State Department in February 1947 to become president of the Carnegie Endowment for International Peace; its board chairman was John Foster Dulles. The charges against Hiss made him the subject of national controversy and headlines.

The consensus of historians is now that the Soviet Union ran an espionage network in the United States in the 1930s and 1940s but that it was dismantled at the end of World War II. The network is believed to have included Foreign Service members Laurence Duggan, Alger Hiss, and Noel Field. Duggan had led the State Department's Latin American division, had retired in 1944, and committed suicide four years later.

McCarthy's assault was not limited to State Department employees who, according to McCarthy, wanted China to be Communist. Among the Foreign Service officers he targeted, few were still working for State. He attacked John Carter Vincent, the U.S. minister to Switzerland, and John Service, who at the time was on his way by sea to India. The department ordered Service to return to Washington.

Thus began a three-year struggle that threatened to wreck the State Department and the Foreign Service. Senator McCarthy grabbed headlines and aroused emotions, and he was prodded by an assortment of right-wing activists and last-ditch supporters of Chiang Kai-shek. Even his most radical opponents suppressed support through what Nobel Prize laureate Gunnar Myrdal called "false loyalty to what was considered to be the national cause." The damage to the United States was enormous.

McCarthy found support within the State Department through Otto F. Otepka, a protégé of Scott McLeod, who was Dulles' choice as the State Department's chief of the Office of Internal Security. After Otepka had spent ten years hunting down security risks in the department, he refused to clear Walt W. Rostow, President Kennedy's chair of the department's Policy Planning staff. President Kennedy and Secretary Rusk stood up to him. In 1963, Otepka was assigned to an empty office with nothing to do, and then was dismissed for passing classified documents to the Internal Security Subcommittee of the Senate Judiciary Committee. (Years later, President Nixon brought Otepka back into government.)

In 1951, the criteria for dismissing government employees were relaxed from reasonable grounds of disloyalty to "reasonable doubt of loyalty," making it much easier to relieve Clubb of his duties, transfer Vincent from Switzerland to Tangier, and ship Davies off to Germany.

Henry Stimson and George Kennan defended John Service before the State Department's Loyalty Security Board, and the board cleared Service. A subcommittee of the Foreign Relations Committee, chaired by Senator Millard Tydings of Maryland, also exonerated him.

The zealous investigations went on. State's Loyalty Security Board questioned Clubb for months. The House Un-American Activities Committee subpoenaed his diaries. Patrick McCarran, the powerful senator from Nevada and chairman of the Senate Subcommittee on Internal Security, had the former Communist Whittaker Chambers testify that he had met Clubb in New York in 1932; and Louis Budenz, the former managing editor of the Communist *Daily Worker,* denounced Vincent and Service. Vincent was brought back from Tangier, and he stated under oath that Budenz's assertion that he was a Communist was untrue.

The overall Loyalty Review Board decided in December 1951 that, under the new rules, there was reasonable doubt about Service's loyalty and reversed his clearance by the State Department's board. Within hours, Secretary Acheson fired him. On the CBS radio network, Eric Sevareid declared Service was "a completely loyal American citizen" who had made one mistake, giving classified information about China to *Amerasia*.

Service fought his dismissal, and in 1957 the U.S. Supreme Court decided 8 to 0 that the State Department had violated its own rules by dismissing him. His status in the department was restored as of the date Acheson had discharged him six years earlier, and he went back to work for the Foreign Service. In 1959, he finally secured an overseas assignment to Bonn, but only after another ten days of security questioning. The Department of Defense objected to his assignment in Bonn, and he was reassigned to Liverpool. Three years later, he took early retirement at age fifty-three and settled in Berkeley, California.

At the same time that Service was fired, the State Department determined that, although there was no doubt about Clubb's loyalty, he was a security risk and he too should be drummed out of the Foreign Service. He hired Paul A. Porter as his attorney and was cleared. But the department hid him, an officer with twenty-four years of service, at a desk in its Department of Historical Research. At age fifty-one, he took early retirement at less than half pay.

Vincent lasted in Tangier only until December 1952, when the Loyalty Review Board, which had previously cleared him 2 to 1, now enlarged and with new members, reversed itself and recommended 3 to 2 that he be "terminated." The board said it based its new decision on Vincent's "studied praise of Chinese Communists and equally studied criticism of the Chiang Kai-shek Government." The directors of the American Foreign Service Association and the editorial board of its *Foreign Service Journal* protested.

Secretary Acheson was pressed to have another board, headed by the highly respected Judge Learned Hand, review whether Vincent should continue in office. But John Foster Dulles, coming into office, dismissed Hand's panel and gave Vincent the choice of being dismissed or resigning quietly with a pension. He chose the latter.

Senator McCarran also went after Davies. While Davies was serving on State's Policy Planning Staff, Kennan had assigned him to help with a CIA undercover intelligence scheme code-named Tawny Pipit. The CIA needed contacts who knew China's new rulers. Davies suggested some academics and journalists. Word of Tawny Pipit leaked out, and McCarran's supporters wanted Davies to tell all. He regarded anything about the CIA as out of bounds and refused. Kennan got the CIA to fire the agent who had leaked the story, but the State Department exiled Davies to Lima, Peru.

A year later, Senator McCarthy, with bizarre logic, said Davies was "trying to put Communists and espionage agents in key spots in the Central Intelligence Agency." Davies was investigated for the ninth time. Hurley and Wedemeyer testified against him, and in November 1954, Secretary Dulles dismissed him. As Davies left the Secretary's office, Dulles said if he ever needed a character reference for a new job, Dulles would be glad to give him one. Davies went back to Peru, learned to design and make mahogany furniture, and started a new life.

After a long struggle and with the persistence of Secretary Dean Rusk and Under Secretary Nicholas deB. Katzenbach, Davies bypassed the State Department bureaucracy and obtained a security clearance through the Massachusetts Institute of Technology and the Arms Control and Disarmament Agency.

It is impossible to measure the injury to the Foreign Service done by the fantastical battle over who lost China. Foreign Service officers were fired, forced to resign, or transferred far from China. And future officers were discouraged from entering such a vulnerable career.

The reputation and morale of the State Department and its Foreign Service slumped. Many Foreign Service officers felt that the Eisenhower administration failed to defend the State Department and its Foreign Service from ideological attacks. George Kennan said sourly that the Foreign Service had been "weakened beyond real hope of recovery."

In 1954, five retired diplomats with impeccable credentials (Norman Armour, Robert Woods Bliss, Joseph C. Grew, William Phillips, and G. Howland Shaw) published a common letter in *The New York Times* declaring that the attacks were creating a Foreign Service better able to serve a totalitarian government than the United States "as we have heretofore known it."

E. J. Kahn, Jr., reported in his book *The China Hands* on the skilled and experienced Foreign Service officers, experts on China and East Asia, who were stopped from doing what they did best—the China Hands whose careers were destroyed. The State Department was blacklisting its own.

In 1972, just before President Nixon went to the People's Republic of China, Senator J. William Fulbright of Arkansas, longtime chair of the Senate Foreign Relations Committee, summed up, "These Foreign Service officers in China served their country well, but their country did not always serve them well."

The following January, the American Foreign Service Association held a luncheon on the eighth floor of the State Department, at which the association's board chairman, Ambassador William C. Harrop, said, "We will honor those Foreign Service Officers in China during the early 1940's who demonstrated their professionalism and integrity by reporting events as they saw them." Among those attending were Clubb, Emmerson, Ringwalt, Freeman, Robert Barnett, Butterworth, Service, and Vincent's widow. Davies stayed at his home, then in Malaga, Spain.

Introducing John Service, historian Barbara Tuchman explained, "For having been right many of them were persecuted, dismissed, or slowed or blocked in their careers, with whatever damage done to them personally outweighed by damage done to the Foreign Service of the United States." She concluded, "It remains essential to maintain the integrity of Foreign Service reporting."

The luncheon inflamed those who continued to condemn the China Hands. The critics excoriated the State Department for allowing the Foreign Service Association to hold the luncheon in its building. But *The New York Times* ran an editorial saying the luncheon helped vindicate the Foreign Service officers and closed with this warning:

> It would be naive to think that what happened to the "old China hands" in the postwar era could never happen again.

FOLLOWING THE MCCARTHY PANIC

The Foreign Service had to rebuild its China expertise. Until it could, other men from the State Department, the National Security Council, and the CIA filled in. Few of them had firsthand knowledge about China or experience in East Asia.

For two decades, the United States regarded the Republic of China on Taiwan as the government of all China. The United States had no diplomatic representation in mainland China. Attempts to initiate talks between the United States and Communist China began in 1955, ostensibly to recover Americans imprisoned in China. U. Alexis Johnson, the ambassador to Czechoslovakia, was the U.S. liaison. The talks bogged down, especially over Taiwan.

In the 1960s, the Vietnam War and the chaotic Cultural Revolution made it doubly difficult, and important, to understand what was happening inside China. British-run Hong Kong became a major American listening post. From there, Consul General Edward Rice recommended that American policy ease travel and trade restrictions and end opposition to the entry of the People's Republic to the United Nations. In June 1966, Rice cabled State that events of China's Cultural Revolution were both significant and "clouded in obscurity." Walt Rostow called China "a dragon with a bellyache," while Ambassador James Lilley referred to the Cultural Revolution as "Mao's last social engineering experiment gone mad."

All U.S. diplomatic and consular posts abroad were advised, in January 1967, to accent the positive about China and Sino-American relations. The purpose was to mollify China's leaders. Starting in 1968, CIA operatives in Hong Kong began to pick up clues that the People's Republic, then at odds with the Soviet Union and fearing a Soviet invasion, was interested in reopening relations with the United States. And the United States, bogged down in "a war on the mainland of Asia," began to find reasons to explore openings. After North Vietnam's Tet offensive, the United States checked on whether China could help end the war.

During the next year, stimulated by battles between the Soviet Union and China along the Ussuri River, which borders the two countries, U.S. Ambassador John Gronouski in Warsaw moved to resume Sino-U.S. ambassador-level talks. He was not successful, and Johnson and Rusk were discouraged about the prospects of improving relations with China. After talks had been in abeyance for two years, President Nixon cautiously checked with the old China Lobby, and Henry Kissinger, his national security advisor, instructed Ambassador Walter J. Stoessel to restart talks in Warsaw.

Unsurprisingly, that turned out to be difficult. In December 1969, Stoessel tried to make an in-passing contact (in Polish) with the Chinese chargé d'affaires, Lei Yang, as they walked out together from a Warsaw fashion show. The chargé avoided talking with Stoessel, who followed Lei Yang's interpreter into the men's room and there passed the message from Washington.

This unlikely beginning developed into two talks between Stoessel and the Chinese. Ambassador Stoessel arrived at the Chinese embassy for the first meeting in a heavy snowstorm. He and three colleagues sat with Lei Yang and three aides over pots of tea. Stoessel proposed relaxing travel restrictions on journalists, scholars, and students and determining the fate of six Americans still in China. There were no polemics; the meeting lasted only seventy-five minutes. A second meeting was held in the American embassy.

Journalist James H. Mann commented, "These Warsaw talks effectively ended the State Department's role in China policy; they paved the way for what became Kissinger's personalized diplomacy." Thus, Kissinger moved the center of China policy from State to his National Security Council (NSC). When he left for Beijing, Kissinger kept Secretary of State William P. Rogers in the dark. Historian Barbara Keys noted Kissinger's "intense, consuming jealousy of Rogers."

The NSC was not originally conceived as a replacement for the State Department. National Security Advisor Rostow always sent Secretary of State Rusk a copy of any memo in which he commented on a State Department report to the President. And Rusk said of Rostow, "After we'd been in a lot of foxholes together, we became good friends."

The next step in the process of relating to China, peculiarly enough, was "Ping-Pong Diplomacy," which occurred in Japan when the People's Republic invited American Ping-Pong athletes to visit Beijing in 1971.

While the State Department was discouraging high-level contacts, Kissinger was making secret trips to Beijing in July 1971. Joseph S. Farland, the experienced noncareer U.S. ambassador to Pakistan, helped make Kissinger's secrecy possible. In Islamabad, Farland arranged for Kissinger to attend a banquet given by the president of Pakistan, feign a severe stomachache, and be taken to the mountain rest home of dictator Agha Mohammed Yahya Khan to recuperate. Late that night, a Pakistani general drove Kissinger from the rest home to the airport, where the President's plane waited to fly him to China. An overweight member of the security detail at the rest home pretended to be Kissinger. The group going with him included NSC aide Winston Lord, China specialist John Holdridge, Vietnam specialist Richard Smyser, and two Secret Service agents.

Kissinger later wrote, "We were fortunate that our ambassador in Pakistan at the moment was a man outside the regular Foreign Service establishment. A traditionalist would never have responded without first reinsuring himself by a 'personal' communication to his departmental chiefs in Washington."

In Beijing, Kissinger did what he could to encourage the Chinese to negotiate with the United States. He emphasized the Soviet threat to China, offered concessions on Taiwan, and sought Chinese help to end the Vietnam War. And Brigadier General Alexander M. Haig, Jr., then deputy director of the National Security Council, even offered the Chinese intelligence information about Soviet forces in place against China.

To prepare for Nixon to visit China, Haig had two meetings with Zhou Enlai in January 1972. They were disasters. Haig said he was "speaking the blunt language of a soldier." With surprising insensitivity, Haig said the United States would maintain the viability and integrity of China. And although he asserted to Zhou that "unfortunately, most American journalists are shallow idiots," he urged that everything possible be done during the forthcoming visit to "reinforce President Nixon's image as a world leader."

Zhou Enlai contradicted Haig. He said that China did not need foreigners to maintain its integrity and that "the image of a man [Nixon] depends on his own deeds." Zhou denounced the American "invasion" of Vietnam and the bombing of North Vietnam. A red-faced Haig apologized at length. Zhou replied bitingly that it is "not only a matter of terminology but a matter of attitude."

This clumsy maneuvering led to President Nixon's trip to Beijing in February 1972. Nixon and Kissinger sidestepped the State Department. And State Department staff members labeled the National Security Council experts who replaced them "diplomatic scabs." Max Frankel represented *The New York Times* on the trip and wrote much later, "The Nixon trip was essentially just a piece of theater."

The President's trip to Beijing ended the fiction that Chiang Kai-shek's government still ruled China. Nixon hoped that opening diplomatic relations with the People's Republic would, as Kissinger later put it, "give the Soviet Union something else to think about." Nixon hoped that the Chinese would help the United States get out of Vietnam, and Zhou's chief pragmatic objective was to get the Americans out of Taiwan. Although these objectives were approached slowly, Beijing over time replaced Taipei at the United Nations.

In Beijing, Kissinger refused to use State Department translators. Ambassador James Lilley commented, "Until he became Secretary of State in

September 1973, Kissinger often did not allow State Department professionals with the requisite Chinese language skills to attend certain high-level meetings with the Chinese."

George H. W. Bush, while ambassador to the United Nations, wrote in his journal in 1971 about Kissinger:

> The State Department to him is an increasing obsession. He is absolutely obsessed by the idea that they are incompetent and can't get the job done. It comes out all the time. . . . I worry about the system, about this two State Departments thing. . . . Henry is very excitable, very emotional almost. He has a great sense of humor and sometimes is tremendously relaxed and buoyant. Often, however, he hits the ceiling and raises hell. . . . He is arrogant yet he can be charming. He is paranoid about the Department just as he was about the China vote, and yet he is very bright.

"The secret trip was secret even from our State Department," Winston Lord said. When President Nixon toasted Zhou Enlai at the opening banquet in Beijing, the Chinese official, Ji Chaozhu, served as Nixon's interpreter. And Secretary Rogers was left out of the only meeting that Nixon and Kissinger held with Mao Tse-tung. Operating independently from State had been standard procedure for Nixon and Kissinger. When they sent Nelson Rockefeller in 1969 on a tour of the capitals of Latin America, he had been instructed to meet each head of state without the local American ambassador present.

Kissinger was certainly not the only top American diplomat preoccupied with secrecy, but he carried it to the extreme. Secretary Dean Rusk too had his back channel, and he was well known to be unwilling to speak candidly with President Kennedy while others were in the room. Nicholas Katzenbach explained Rusk as "a very private person, very self-controlled person." No one said that of the more volatile Kissinger.

Kissinger returned to Beijing in February 1973, as Nixon began his second term. Over two hours, Mao and Kissinger discussed everything from women to espionage to relations with the Soviet Union. They were switching American foreign policy from a bilateral match with the Soviet Union to a triangular contest including Communist China.

That July, the United States Liaison Office (USLO) opened in Beijing with David Bruce, former ambassador in London, Bonn, and Paris, leading twenty-six carefully picked Americans. The USLO's Foreign Service officers included co-DCMs John Holdridge and Al Jenkins. And James Lilley became a "declared CIA officer," whom the highest Chinese officials knew was a spy. His real job was to provide a back channel for Kissinger with China's leaders.

The State Department had opposed appointing Lilley as a CIA agent in the United States Liaison Office, but Kissinger insisted. And Lilley had the background for the assignment. He had been born in 1928 on the Shandong Peninsula southeast of Peking, where his father worked for John D. Rockefeller's Standard Oil Company of New York. After attending Yale, Lilley had gone back to Asia during the Korean War. He watched Communist China and worked on covert CIA operations in East Asia for more than twenty years, until syndicated columnist Jack Anderson exposed his CIA connection and he had to leave.

RESTORING RELATIONS WITH CHINA

By the end of 1976, the Vietnam War was over. Both Mao Tse-tung and Zhou Enlai were dead; power was held by the more pragmatic Deng Xiaoping. Jimmy Carter was President and Cyrus Vance was his Secretary of State. Just as Kissinger and Rogers had, Vance and Zbigniew Brzezinski, the national security advisor, competed for control of foreign policy.

When Vance visited Beijing in August 1977, he was unable to normalize relations even though Deng wanted to open China to the West in order to modernize the country economically. Brzezinski persuaded Carter to send him to Beijing in May 1978. When Brzezinski talked with Vice Premier Deng, Richard C. Holbrooke, assistant secretary of state for East Asia, was left outside. On Brzezinski's return to Washington, Carter told him that the Chinese had seduced him, but his visit was a breakthrough. Brzezinski and Deng normalized relations on December 15, 1978, even though the sale of arms to Taiwan was still unresolved. U.S. relations with Taiwan remained hostage to domestic American politics.

That January, thirty years after the People's Republic was founded, the United States finally closed its embassy in Taipei, and Beijing and Washington commenced diplomatic relations. Vance was shocked by the news.

Carter sent Deputy Secretary of State Warren Christopher to Taipei to placate the Taiwanese government. The car bringing Christopher and U.S. Ambassador Leonard Unger from the airport was attacked by government-organized demonstrators, who broke the car's windows, injured Christopher, and smashed Unger's glasses. Taiwanese anger was violent.

The Americans replaced their embassy on Taiwan with an "unofficial American Institute," manned by fifty members of the embassy staff. Lilley retired from the CIA in January 1979, and in 1982 President Reagan named him director of the institute. He was saddled with the unenviable job of leading the Republic of China to accept reduced military support. The two factions of Chinese sparred with increasing anger over whether the Americans would set a date to terminate their arming of those on the island.

President Ronald Reagan supported Taiwan and wanted to maintain a balance of power between the Beijing government and the Nationalists across the Taiwan Strait. Secretary of State Haig tried to show Reagan that, although the men in Beijing were Communists, they could be decent human beings. He brought to the White House Ji Chaozhu, the sophisticated Harvard-educated Chinese official who had served as Zhou Enlai's interpreter and would later become Beijing's ambassador to the Court of St. James's.

In 1981, Secretary Haig sought support in Beijing for a scheme by which the United States could arm Taiwan if it sold Beijing high-tech military materiel. James Lilley and Richard L. Armitage, the latter then a Pentagon expert on East Asia, both informed President Reagan that Haig had made the deal public. Reagan immediately disowned him, and the Chinese demanded the United States set a date to cut off all arms sales to Taiwan. In 1982, Haig resigned as Secretary.

His successor, George P. Shultz, changed the debate, by asserting that Japan, not China, was crucial to the Cold War. Japan, he said, was strong economically and was trying to be democratic. He minimized the China-based approach of Kissinger, Brzezinski, and Haig.

James Lilley became the ambassador to South Korea in November 1986. There, he had to deal with the Korean government's crackdown on opposition. Working with Assistant Secretary Gaston Sigur in Washington, he sought to democratize South Korea step-by-step.

In June 1987, President Chun Doo-Hwan was preparing to evict demonstrating students from Myongdong Catholic Cathedral in Seoul. President Reagan sent a letter of protest for Ambassador Lilley to deliver by hand to President Chun, who had put down earlier demonstrations with force. The embassy's political counselor, Harry Dunlop, tried to make an appointment for Lilley with President Chun but was repeatedly turned away. Dunlop finally lost his temper and shouted into the telephone that Chun could not be so stupid to refuse to see the ambassador. That got Lilley his appointment. He delivered Reagan's letter and lectured Chun on the consequences if he used force. Dunlop said losing his temper was the single action in his career that had the most impact on history. President Chun decided not to impose martial law.

TIANANMEN SQUARE

Newly elected President George H. W. Bush attended Emperor Hirohito's funeral in Tokyo in February 1989 and afterward stopped in Beijing. On his second night in Beijing, he planned to host a "Texas-style barbecue" banquet for five hundred guests. Ambassador Winston Lord was instructed to compile a guest list. Lord had been the president of the Council on Foreign Relations, which has been called "the biggest exclusive club in the world"; and as a young diplomat, he had accompanied Nixon and Kissinger to Beijing. Although he never learned Chinese, he was married to Shanghai-born Bette Bao Lord, who spoke impeccable Chinese.

Among the some 275 Chinese on President Bush's guest list for dinner was the astrophysicist Fang Lizhi, a leader of the political reform movement and an outspoken critic of the Communist Party. By inviting Fang and other dissidents, Ambassador Lord intended to demonstrate Bush's concern for human rights in China.

The Chinese government protested Fang Lizhi's appearance on the guest list to Deputy Chief of Mission Peter Tomsen and then, with increasing vehemence, to Ambassador Lord. The Chinese threatened to boycott the President's dinner. But they compromised: Fang could attend the dinner if he sat in the back and Bush did not make the rounds of the tables.

On Sunday night, February 26, while the guests gathered for the dinner in the grand ballroom of the Great Wall Sheraton Hotel, several blocks away security police intercepted Fang Lizhi; his wife Li Shuxian, a physics professor herself; and Perry Link, professor of Chinese literature at Princeton; and Link's wife Jean Wong. The police prevented them from approaching the hotel and stopped them from taking a taxi to the American embassy. They finally walked, accompanied by police, for more than an hour toward Ambassador Lord's residence.

On the street, the four were spotted by Canadian diplomat David Horley, who took them to his apartment nearby. At the end of the evening, Fang Lizhi held a large press conference at the Shangri-La Hotel, on the other side of the city. He told the reporters, "What we are calling for is extremely basic, namely, freedom of speech, press, assembly and travel."

The incident was widely reported in the U.S. press. Speaking from the White House, National Security Advisor Brent Scowcroft criticized Ambassador Lord. *Time* magazine reported, "The Bush administration was left with egg foo yung on its face."

Ambassador Lord felt he had acted in keeping with the changes taking place in China. But political reformers made China's leaders feel threatened. Lord sent Scowcroft a private protest by CIA channels; he never received a reply. And a month later, President H. W. Bush replaced Lord with James Lilley as the ambassador to China.

The incoming ambassador Lilley and the outgoing ambassador Lord had dinner together at Washington's Metropolitan Club just before Lilley flew to Beijing. They both were Yale graduates and had been Kissinger advisors. Lord poured out to Lilley his anger at the way he had been treated.

Lilley and his family arrived in Beijing on May 2, 1989, as thousands were gathering at Tiananmen Square in the center of the capital to protest governmental corruption and nepotism. Tens of thousands more demonstrated across China. The Soviet Union had sent President Mikhail Gorbachev to Beijing, and the United States ordered elements of the Seventh Fleet to Shanghai. As someone said, Ambassador Lilley had stepped into a volcano. On May 17, the Chinese government declared martial law.

Lilley predicted to the State Department that the protests would end in bloodshed. Americans were advised to avoid Tiananmen Square. The embassy stocked food and medical supplies; embassy files were shipped to Hong Kong. The staff and other Western embassies and the Japanese organized to watch over the various sectors of the city. The four U.S. consulates reported on trouble in their outer areas.

Just before midnight on Saturday night, June 3, Chinese-speaking Foreign Service officer James Huskey, observing the violence in Tiananmen Square, telephoned the embassy that firing had begun. Ambassador Lilley told Huskey to get Americans out of harm's way.

The embassy cabled the State Department that the People's Liberation Army was cracking down on the protesters in Tiananmen Square and meeting peaceful protest with live fire. Tanks blasted through civilian barricades. Chinese were killing Chinese. More than a thousand Chinese were dead. Americans back home watched on television in horror.

James Huskey was swept along with the huge mob and saw them build a bonfire around an immobilized armored personnel carrier, burn it, and beat to death one of its crew trying to escape. He witnessed demonstrators being mowed down by machine guns. Inside the embassy, the gruesome events were followed over an ABC-TV walkie-talkie and CNN telecasts. As unarmed Chinese around him were shot to death, Huskey found safety in the Beijing Hotel. Lilley later described Huskey to President Bush: "He is a giant among men."

Lilley himself was, as he said, "badmouthed widely in Peking and throughout the U.S. for failing to set up procedures to safeguard Americans beforehand," but President Bush praised him as "experienced" and "able."

On Monday at noon, Fang Lizhi and his wife came to the American embassy and asked for "physical protection." Fang did not request political asylum because he wanted to remain in China if he could. They were told to leave the embassy while the staff called Washington for instructions. Embassy staff members, following policy but not political common sense, sent them back into streets patrolled by the Chinese army.

At the State Department, distraught officers ordered the embassy to find Fang. The couple and their son were located in a hotel room that Perry Link had obtained for them. Acting Deputy Chief of Mission Raymond Burghardt and McKinney Russell, head of the press and cultural affairs office, took them out the hotel's back door and into an unmarked minivan, hurried them into the embassy compound. In a cable dated July 12, Lilley said of Fang Lizhi, "He is a living symbol of our conflict with China over human rights."

The couple spent more than a full year in a windowless apartment in the embassy compound guarded by Marines before the Chinese permitted them to fly to England. They had to promise "not to engage in activities directed against China." Feng Lizhi ended up teaching at the University of Arizona in Tucson until his death in 2012.

Immediately after the Tiananmen Square massacre, the United States imposed sanctions and embargoed arms sales to China. But the Tiananmen Square violence occurred during the period in which the Berlin Wall came down and the Soviet Union fell apart. The Cold War no longer forced the U.S. President to accommodate Communist China. A new policy was needed.

Tuesday night, military attaché Major Larry Wortzel received a call from a Chinese army officer warning the Americans to stay away from their residence compound. The next morning, Lilley held a meeting of all staff and dependents in the chancery in order to clear out the residences. On the pretext that a sniper was on the roof, the PLA then machine-gunned the embassy residences.

Lilley arranged with United Airlines to fly 350 Americans out of Beijing, and FSO Lyn Edinger led eighty-three more in a convoy of embassy vehicles from Tientsin to the Beijing airport. Only two Americans were injured. At the airport, Ambassador Lilley told the departing Americans, "Go home and tell the world what you have seen."

The United States could no longer ignore human rights in China. President Bill Clinton told President Jiang Zemin that the Chinese government was "on the wrong side of history."

38

Public Diplomacy

1941–2012

One of the most controversial changes in recent American diplomacy has been the growth of what is euphemistically called "public diplomacy." The issue is simple: Traditional diplomacy works government to government, but "public diplomacy" bypasses the foreign government and appeals directly to its people. It challenges the age-old prohibition against diplomats interfering in the internal affairs of a host state. If the People's Republic of China or the Islamic Republic of Iran attempted "public diplomacy" inside the United States, it would unleash a patriotic cry of outrage.

"Public diplomacy" achieved a significant potential once technological advances, particularly electronic communications, enabled governments (and others) to reach large audiences anywhere on the globe. American public diplomacy typically aims "to promote the national interest of the United States through understanding, informing and influencing foreign audiences." Thus, public diplomacy asks what is information and what, propaganda. Totalitarian regimes make no such distinction. But the difference between information and propaganda creates endless problems for a democracy.

It is surprising that a society like the United States, with highly developed advertising and public relations skills, has not been particularly competent at public diplomacy. Daniel Russel, deputy chief of mission at the U.S. Embassy at The Hague, former assistant to Secretary of State

Colin Powell, and a Foreign Service officer for twenty years, explained, "Public diplomacy creates a public environment in which it is easier for other nations to do what we want them to do. . . . It wouldn't be an issue if we were doing a good job of it. But we are not getting traction. We are taking a marketing approach rather than a common interest approach. We don't try to explain what we are doing. We have to convince our partners that we have common goals."

The technological transformation that made it possible to reach vast populations abroad came in two waves: Radio and television were the first, and the computer and Internet, the second. Radio and television carried messages beyond the reach of the printing press and telegraph. Radio, of course, reaches millions of people, significantly, in the developing world.

Secretary of State Madeleine Albright, perhaps optimistically, told the Senate Foreign Relations Committee, "Television's ability to bring graphic images of pain and outrage into our living rooms has heightened the pressure both for immediate engagement in areas of international crisis and immediate disengagement when events do not go according to plan."

The computer and Internet, the second wave, eliminated the media gatekeepers and spoke directly and instantly to multitudes of individuals. To an important extent, they replace hierarchies with networks. The Center for Strategic and International Studies (CSIS) in Washington, D.C., concluded, "Ending the culture of secrecy and exclusivity is a requirement for developing a collaborative relationship with the public."

Paradoxically, these technological advances enabled public diplomacy to reach out to people at precisely the time when the primitive form of warfare called "terrorism" drives embassies and consulates to isolate themselves from the very public they want to reach. Missions have been converted into fortresses shielded by concrete walls and armed guards. Enthusiasts claim that public diplomacy has not only supplemented but replaced government-to-government diplomacy. The CSIS study said, "In this world of instantaneous information, contemporary diplomacy struggles to sustain its relevance."

The center contended that Benjamin Franklin was "America's first practitioner of public diplomacy," on the debatable premise that Franklin's popularity in Paris influenced Louis XVI's government to support the United States. In truth, the French had more powerful reasons to support the American colonies' revolt against Britain.

"WE SHALL TELL YOU THE TRUTH"

During the two world wars, the American government disseminated information and launched propaganda efforts directly to the people of both allies and enemies.

In 1914, the propaganda started as soon as did the killing. When the war began, the British cut the transatlantic cable between Germany and the United States. The British immediately created the Neutral Press Committee, whose prime target was the neutral United States, and the British Foreign Office formed a news department using its own radio transmitters in Wales. Germany set up the German Information Bureau, and the German Foreign Office established the Central Office for Foreign Services. The German Press Bureau and Information Service hired Hearst journalist William Bayard Hale and others to do public relations in the United States.

To counter German propaganda, President Woodrow Wilson created the Committee on Public Information (CPI) with newspaperman George Creel as its chairman. But old-line diplomats watched the CPI with suspicion. In mid-1941, President Roosevelt established the U.S. Foreign Information Service (FIS). Playwright Robert Sherwood and a staff of journalists produced material for FIS broadcasts to Europe over privately owned American shortwave stations and the British Broadcasting Corporation (BBC).

Once the United States entered the war, FIS sent shortwave broadcasts directly to Asia from a studio in San Francisco. On February 24, 1942, eleven weeks after Pearl Harbor, FIS sent its first broadcasts to Europe via BBC transmitters. In perfect German, the American announcer stated, "Here speaks a voice from America. Every day at this time we will bring you the news of the war. The news may be good. The news may be bad. We shall tell you the truth."

From this came the principle and the name: the Voice of America (VOA). Using eleven private shortwave radio stations, it sought to bring reliable news to people in closed and war-torn societies. By June, VOA had a new base, the Office of War Information (OWI), created by Executive Order and guided on policy by the State Department. The OWI, which also became the parent of the FIS, was directed by the respected newsman and Rhodes Scholar Elmer Davis. All these were strictly wartime arrangements.

As World War II ended, VOA's broadcasts were cut back or eliminated. The OWI was scrapped as soon as Japan surrendered. But in 1946, seventy-six U.S. diplomatic missions still had information staffs, and the VOA still broadcast in twenty-five languages. The VOA's Latin America broadcast services were transferred to the State Department. By 1948, programs aiming information at foreign peoples had almost disappeared.

Congressional foot-dragging melted away with the arrival of the Korean War, the Cold War, and the Berlin blockade. Congressmen junketing in Europe and, not coincidentally, experiencing Soviet propaganda are credited with giving birth to the first systematic "peacetime" American effort at overseas propaganda. In 1948, Public Law 402, the Smith-Mundt Act, ordered the U.S. worldwide information program to sell America by telling the truth. That is, the program was to be part of U.S. foreign policy. In 1950, the VOA added language services for the Korean War, bringing "public diplomacy" new life. By the end of 1952, VOA was broadcasting in forty-five languages.

The Smith-Mundt Act established America's international informational and cultural exchange programs on a permanent basis. But the act prohibited aiming VOA's programs at U.S. audiences and thus nullified its second charge—to educate Americans about other countries. One congressman even proposed that a committee of the Daughters of the American Revolution edit all VOA scripts.

Another question emerged: Was the proper role of these governmental international broadcasts to report the news and reflect America, warts and all, or was it to serve as a "weapon" against the Soviet Union?

In 1950, National Security Council Document 68 (NSC-68) attempted to deal with such questions. Incorporating the basic points of Kennan's "X" article, NSC-68 emphasized military strategies against the Soviet Union "in the fields of economic warfare and political and psychological warfare with a view to fomenting and supporting unrest and revolt in selected strategic satellite countries." This tough-minded blueprint intensified the debate.

WINNING HEARTS AND MINDS

In Iran in July 1950, Ambassador Henry Grady made a request, classified as secret, to fund an extensive Information and Education program "influencing the attitude of the Iranian people toward their government, their future and the United States." Grady wrote, "The program must be varied enough to appeal, on the one hand, to an entrenched and sophisticated intellectual elite and, on the other, to a large, illiterate mass concerned with little beyond the struggle for bare existence."

Once Dwight Eisenhower won the presidency in 1952, the United States started retracting again, and Secretary of State Dulles began transferring out of the State Department activities designed to shape public opinion overseas.

In 1953, Senator McCarthy began to decry subversive activity in the State Department. He attacked the Voice of America. Its budget was reduced, transmitter construction was halted, and a number of language services were shut down. It was a shameful episode in the nation's history and the department's.

One Foreign Service officer McCarthy forced out was Reed Harris. He had joined the State Department in 1945 and became a VOA executive. The senator assailed him for having written, while a student back in 1932, that Communists had a right to teach in the schools. Although Harris told the Senate committee he no longer believed Communists should be allowed to teach, McCarthy badgered Harris, and Dulles refused to speak up for him. Harris resigned.

Edward R. Murrow played the video transcript of McCarthy's questioning of Harris on his CBS program *See It Now* and exposed the senator's demagoguery. A decade later, Murrow, then director of the United States Information Agency, rehired Harris as one of his deputies. That happy ending was unusual.

More typical was the case of Beatrice Braude, who had worked for the Office of Strategic Services, the U.S. Embassy in Paris, and the USIA until McCarthy attacked her. She never faced those who accused her of being a security risk, and she never again held a government job.

When McCarthy attacked the U.S. Army, the Senate finally found the courage to censure him. A commission chaired by former President Herbert Hoover decided that all U.S. foreign information activities, including the Voice of America, should be separated from the State Department. Secretary Dulles too wanted to get the State Department out of operations and propaganda, and to concentrate on policy. Many in the State Department had grown wary of foreign information activities.

THE BIRTH OF THE USIA

On August 1, 1953, the United States Information Agency was established as an independent entity taking its policy guidance from the State Department. It became a weapon of the Cold War. The new agency began with its morale depressed by McCarthy's pummeling and by the laggard response of responsible members of the U.S. government to defend those who represented the nation abroad.

The information mandate was transferred to the USIA, but overseas cultural activities remained in the State Department and were assigned to the new Bureau of Educational and Cultural Affairs. The distinctions were often fuzzy and the division of responsibility chaotic, so in 1979 cultural operations were also moved to USIA.

USIA employees not only had a mission different from the diplomats of the State Department but also were part of another culture. State Department people were by tradition and training conditioned to play their cards close to their chests and to deal with their official counterparts. USIA people, in contrast, spread out as far as possible and talked to anyone who would listen. Even though such differences made for clashes, ambassadors like Chester Bowles and Clare Boothe Luce, who came from the civilian communications world, valued the USIA.

The new agency performed its public diplomacy functions abroad through the U.S. Information Service (USIS), which was stationed in nearly three hundred communities around the globe. At first, these USIS posts, overseen by a public affairs officer in each U.S. embassy, were manned by temporary reserve Foreign Service officers who went home when their contracts were up.

The USIS centers worked with local media and organizations and established more than two hundred libraries in eighty countries. Anyone could browse in them and anyone could borrow a book or publication. The libraries enabled foreigners to learn about the United States.

Senator McCarthy sent two zealous young aides overseas to purge the

State Department's libraries; and the department, reacting with fear, removed hundreds of books from the shelves. Some were burned.

USIA did not always win the hearts and minds of other peoples for the United States. But it showed Hollywood films, produced documentaries, created magazines, sent students to the United States, and made use of television. Satellites made live telecasts possible worldwide.

In 1956, when President Gamal Abdel Nasser nationalized the Suez Canal, Israel invaded Egypt, and British and French parachutists landed near the canal, the VOA increased its broadcasts to the Arab world from one hour a day to fourteen. When Poland and Hungary revolted against Soviet domination, Hungarian freedom fighters thought they heard USIS say the Americans would support them. But when Russian troops and tanks crushed the Hungarian revolt, the Americans were nowhere to be found. That was a disaster.

The challenge of communicating directly with people is complex. An audience that is sophisticated and educated requires a certain level of material, while "the street" demands a more simplified approach. Public diplomacy also has to meld the objectives that come out from Washington and the know-how amassed by USIS personnel in Upper Volta, Ouagadougou, Baghdad, or London.

Among the more daunting issues USIA faced was human rights, which repeatedly confounds American diplomats. Should the United States intervene when other governments suppress human rights? Secretary of State Shultz gave one answer: "The cause of human rights is at the core of American foreign policy because it is central to America's conception of itself." And Secretary Vance cautioned that it was an illusion to believe that "a call to the banner of human rights will bring sudden transformations in authoritarian societies. We have embarked on a long journey."

A respected career diplomat, George V. Allen, former ambassador to Iran, Yugoslavia, India, and Greece, was brought in from Athens to be USIA's director in 1957. He developed solid cultural programs with considerable effect overseas and stressed objectivity in his information efforts.

President Kennedy in 1961 appointed as USIA director the great journalist Edward R. Murrow. And Murrow named as his deputies *Time* magazine editor Donald Wilson and Foreign Service officer Thomas C. Sorensen, brother of Kennedy's policy advisor. The agency suddenly basked in the spotlight.

Kennedy and Murrow mobilized public opinion, both domestic and foreign, to counter the Soviet Union's sponsorship of "wars of national liberation" among third-world countries. The USIA built up its programs aimed at African and Asian countries. During the Cuban missile crisis, the U.S. government used its broadcast and media power to tell Cubans, Russians, and the rest of the world what the Soviet Union was doing.

The missile crisis triggered an angry response from Henry Loomis, director of VOA, when the USIA insisted on monitoring the VOA's output. Loomis charged, "We were required to distort and concentrate our program at the expense of credibility and relevance to our audience." Murrow, later backed at CBS by his fighting colleague Fred W. Friendly, promised he would mislead neither the nation's enemies nor its friends.

In February 1963, President Kennedy sent a memorandum to Murrow defining USIA's functions and limits. The agency was instructed to help realize national foreign policy objectives, and it was charged with "influencing public attitudes in other nations." Its mission was defined as not only information but persuasion—psychological warfare.

The Kennedy memorandum directed the USIA overseas to function under the State Department's chiefs of mission. But in general the USIA was seen as diminishing the State Department's expertise on overseas information.

Ed Murrow kept asking that the USIA be in on the takeoffs, the formulation of foreign policy, and not only the crash landings. He told the Senate Committee on Foreign Relations at his appointment hearing, "In the end of the day it may well be that the example of this nation will be more important than its dollars or its words."

It is ironic that the USIA shifted toward short-term propaganda during the directorship of Murrow, who had a global reputation as an objective journalist. But Murrow understood that the USIA was something other than journalism; its function was not only to inform but to persuade. That did not mean that it lied. Murrow told a subcommittee of the House Committee on Foreign Affairs: "To be persuasive we must be believable; to be believable we must be credible; to be credible we must be truthful. It is as simple as that."

. . .

Once the Vietnamese defeated the French at Dien Bien Phu in 1954 and the United States took over the war in Vietnam, the Foreign Service Institute organized a public diplomacy course for Senior Foreign Service officers. And a USIA officer was assigned to the staff of South Vietnam's president. USIA historian Robert E. Elder made a distinction clear: "The commercial press, whether American or foreign, is not interested, and should not be, in attaining the foreign policy objectives of the United States."

Propaganda was the government's responsibility.

After President Kennedy was assassinated, Murrow was succeeded in 1964 by another respected newsman, Carl T. Rowan. Both Murrow and Rowan raised the USIA's image, but the controversies continued over information versus propaganda and USIA control of the VOA. Rowan had to explain to the world the civil rights struggle in America, especially the march on Selma, Alabama, in March 1965. He also had difficulty when President Lyndon Johnson ordered U.S. Marines and soldiers into Santo Domingo. Johnson thought he was preventing a Castro-like takeover; Latin Americans saw it as old-fashioned gunboat diplomacy. The intervention was condemned throughout Latin America.

Henry Loomis, a former CIA officer, resigned as director of the Voice of America in 1965 because he felt that Johnson was sacrificing credibility to propaganda. That may have been true, but the Johnson administration also created the Senior Interdepartmental Group and gave the USIA a seat at the policy table. (Loomis returned in 1969 as a deputy director of the USIA.)

Loomis was succeeded by two esteemed telecasters, John Chancellor, in 1965, and John Charles Daly, Jr., in 1967, both of whom made "honest journalism"—Chancellor's term—their standard. They said only by reporting what both the U.S. government and the opposition were saying could the VOA be credible. This was especially crucial in reporting the war in Vietnam.

In Saigon, the USIS post was converted as early as 1965 into the all-encompassing Joint U.S. Public Affairs Office (JUSPAO), led by the experienced and effective Barry Zorthian. Two years later, JUSPAO was keeping some 250 USIA employees busy. It had both a psychological-warfare and an informational responsibility to brief the American media. In Vietnam, the USIA competed for the "minds of men." When Zorthian left Vietnam in 1968, he had not been able to win his battle, and criticism of the United States covered the globe.

Relations between President Johnson and Carl Rowan cooled after a year and a half, and Johnson chose as Rowan's successor Washington communications attorney Leonard H. Marks, who had helped the Johnsons buy their first radio and television stations in Austin, Texas. Marks used his political clout to persuade Congress to convert USIA officers from the reserve Foreign Service to permanent status.

President Ronald Reagan chose as director of USIA Charles Z. Wick, a former bandleader, Hollywood agent, and close friend of the Reagans. Wick added show business know-how to propaganda activities. Some credited him with coining the phrase "public diplomacy." Others credited that to Edmund A. Gullion, when he was ambassador in the Congo in 1965.

Under Wick, the USIA's budget doubled. It also compiled a blacklist of Americans who disagreed with Reagan's views. Telling the American story became increasingly a hard sell abroad once Reagan labeled the Soviet Union the "evil empire."

This was a period of intense controversies. One was the Iran-Contra scandal. And in 1987 the comptroller general of the United States accused the State Department's Office of Public Diplomacy under Cuban-born Otto Juan Reich, a fervent anti-Castroite, of engaging in "prohibited, covert propaganda activities" inside the United States.

"AN EXPLOSION OF INFORMATION"

The second wave of new communications technology in the 1980s and 1990s, with satellites, computers, the Internet, and so forth, resulted in spectacular advances in public diplomacy. Said one ambassador, "There was an explosion of information."

During the Cold War, the USIA no longer spoke in a monotone. After 1963, VOA broadcasting to the People's Republic of China required experimentation with content, language, and technology to determine how best to speak to the most plausible audiences in mainland China. The

USIA publicized around the planet the story of the American *Apollo 11* landing on the moon in the summer of 1969, hoping to balance the prestige the Russians had gained from their *Sputnik* achievement. Astronauts became stars, and moon rocks, the proof of the landing.

After the scare of the Cuban missile crisis and the tiptoeing into the Helsinki Accords in 1975, the Soviet Union stopped jamming Voice of America broadcasts, and the USIA lowered its stridency.

The Nixon administration made efforts to open doors to both the Soviet Union and Communist China. However, the Chinese showed little interest in accepting American public diplomacy, except for admitting Chinese students at American universities to study subjects useful back home.

USIA Director Frank Shakespeare, a former CBS executive, adopted a more confrontational ideological stance. At one point, Secretary of State William P. Rogers objected to tough VOA commentaries while he was trying to negotiate with the Soviet Union. Shakespeare was gone before the USIA had to report the Watergate scandal in 1972, which resulted in the resignation of the President of the United States. Wilson Dizard headed a panel that reviewed all VOA scripts and USIA stories on Watergate for fairness and accuracy.

On another useful level, embassies staged interactive video press conferences between local foreign reporters abroad and State Department officials in Washington. Italian newspaper reporters in Rome found it intriguing to talk directly with an assistant secretary of state sitting in his office in the State Department. A State Department report said, "More than half of the journalists whom State serves on a daily basis work for foreign media."

Along the way, tension developed between the USIA and the CIA, the former working openly and the latter covertly. The USIA did not do nonattributable propaganda; that was the province of the Central Intelligence Agency. Of course, the exposure of the CIA's clandestine sponsorship of educational and cultural programs and publications that had been assumed-to-be-independent, as well as its disinformation efforts abroad, made actually objective activities suspect.

The disintegration of the Soviet Union forced the USIA to reorient itself again, this time to take advantage of a new openness that made more broadcasts and exchanges possible. But State Department budgets were cut at the same time as embassies were opening in the nineteen countries that came into being with the collapse of the Soviet empire. For three years, the department could not afford to hire a single additional Foreign Service officer.

As former National Security Advisor Anthony Lake put it, "The successor to a doctrine of containment must be a strategy of enlargement, enlargement of the world's free community of market democracies." The promotion of trade and private enterprise became important missions.

The driving force behind the ending of the USIA's independence was Senator Jesse Helms, of North Carolina, the chairman of the Senate Foreign Relations Committee and a perpetual USIA critic. He collected statements of support from Henry A. Kissinger; Alexander M. Haig, Jr.; George P. Shultz; James A. Baker III; Lawrence S. Eagleburger; Brent Scowcroft; and others. But President Clinton said flatly that he would veto the proposed Foreign Relations Revitalization Act of 1995 because it would "undermine the President's authority to conduct our nation's foreign policy."

The dispute resulted in the Foreign Affairs Reform and Restructuring Act of 1998, which abolished the USIA and the United States Arms Control and Disarmament Agency. And it put the Agency for International Development under State Department authority. This added up to what was called "a reinvented Department of State." On October 1, 1999, after forty-six years as an independent agency, USIA was embedded in the State Department. An information bureau was established as the department's organization for electronic communication aimed at overseas populations. USIS libraries were converted into Information Resource Centers. All of these were major, and intensely debated, changes.

By the time the USIA disappeared, it had 190 posts in 142 countries with 6,352 employees, of whom 904 were Foreign Service personnel. Transferred to the State Department were 1,946 U.S. employees—1,294 in the United States and 652 overseas—and 2,080 Foreign Service Nationals. They were called "crosswalkers." Another 2,689 worked for the Broadcasting Board of Governors, which became a separate broadcasting entity that included the Voice of America.

Ruth A. Davis, director of the Foreign Service Institute, organized daylong sessions to acquaint the crosswalkers with the State Department culture. They then operated educational, informational, and cultural programs, including the Fulbright exchange program, varied broadcast services, foreign press centers, and public opinion surveys abroad. But the budgets for such activities were cut deeply.

An undersecretary of state for public diplomacy and public affairs replaced the USIA's director. The new undersecretary was given limited authority over public diplomacy and public affairs activities abroad. Evelyn Lieberman, the first Under Secretary, said, "I believe that the work we do is the future of the Department." But others felt the State Department and an aggressive propaganda effort were incompatible. Edwin J. Feulner, president of the conservative Heritage Foundation and former chairman of the U.S. Advisory Commission on Public Diplomacy, said, "The first thing I learned about public diplomacy is that public diplomacy is too important, and too different, to be left to the very talented State Department professionals who 'earn their stripes' by influencing government-to-government relations directly." Senator Richard Lugar of Indiana, chairman of the Senate Foreign Relations Committee, declared, "American public diplomacy lacks vision."

Cynthia P. Schneider of Georgetown University described in *The Washington Post* how she, while ambassador to the Netherlands, received thousands of man hours of help and many thousands of dollars to persuade the Dutch government to participate in the development of the new Joint Strike Fighter aircraft. However, during those prolonged negotiations, she wrote, "I devoted equal time to cultural diplomacy, communicating ideas about America through its creative achievements. And I had to do so without the benefit of the monetary or strategic support I received for military promotions." She added that after September 11, 2001, "I tried to counter the prevailing Foreign Service officers' attitude that cultural outreach is 'soft,' or tangential to the real business of international relations."

The attacks of September 11, 2001, rallied the State Department, the Department of Defense, and the CIA to mount public diplomacy efforts in the Islamic world. They were run by a White House task force. Important among them was the new Radio Sawa, targeted at Islamic youth. Opposition around the globe to the United States' invasion of Iraq in March 2003 obstructed these efforts.

Discontent with public diplomacy increased. Peter G. Peterson, chairman of the Council on Foreign Relations, even warned that the government could not attract enough "truly creative professionals who could utilize the cutting edge media and communications technology" to make public diplomacy effective.

Under Secretary for Public Diplomacy and Public Affairs Margaret DeBardeleben Tutwiler told a House subcommittee in February 2004, "Audiences may not agree or like what we say and do, but we are communicating our policies to governments and influential elites, including the foreign media. . . . In addition, we must do a better job of reaching beyond the traditional elites and government officials. . . . This must be a priority focus now and in the future." She pointed to the variety of new media that carried the American message to the "non-elites" abroad.

After the USIA was absorbed into the State Department in 1999, international broadcasting activities, which remained outside State, were carried on by a spectrum of individual entities under the Broadcasting Board of Governors (BBG). The board was made up of political appointees, including the Secretary of State. It oversaw the Voice of America (VOA), al-Hurra, Radio Sawa, Radio Farda, Radio Free Europe/Radio Liberty, Radio Free Asia, and Radio and TV Martí. The largest of them, the VOA, broadcast on radio and television in forty-four languages to audiences estimated at 80 to 96 million people.

This panorama of broadcasting fiefdoms led to competition and conflicts, especially between the BBG and the VOA. The board was intended to build a firewall to protect the VOA from political interference. But it did not work out. The board tried to reduce or eliminate broadcasting in Thai, Turkish, Hungarian, and other languages and lowered the priority of broadcasting in English.

In 2002, the board decided to phase out VOA's Arabic service because it used too many Classical Arabic speakers. The BBG launched Radio Sawa in Arabic, as well as Radio Farda to supplement the VOA's Farsi service. And in 2004 it spent $62 million to start the controversial satellite-based television network in Arabic al-Hurra. Surveys showed that its target audiences regarded it as untrustworthy. In some cases, the State Department itself had to step in and prevent ill-advised moves. Sanford J. Ungar, former director of the VOA, wrote regretfully, "The country's best instrument of public diplomacy, the Voice of America broadcast service, is being systematically diminished."

LOW-TECH PUBLIC DIPLOMACY

Public diplomacy is by no means entirely high-tech. The American enterprise includes newspapers, magazines, photographs, and pamphlets. These print activities are varied and numerous and often can treat issues in greater depth than can radio and television.

One dramatic example of the public diplomacy problems faced by the American Government occurred when President Kennedy was assassinated. Nongovernmental wire services commented on the relationship of Lee Harvey Oswald, his alleged killer, with the Soviet Union. But a policy decision forced the USIA to omit reporting this intriguing point to avoid escalating the tragedy into a confrontation with the Soviet Union. Later, photographs of American soldiers abusing prisoners in Abu Ghraib prison in Baghdad were removed from the VOA Web site, even though they were widely disseminated elsewhere. Neither decision improved VOA's credibility.

Foreign Service officers abroad also manage the International Visitors Program (IV) that brings to the United States a variety of people, decision makers, scholars, teachers, and journalists, to meet their counterparts and discuss counteracting terrorism, promoting religious tolerance, and defending freedom of the press. Since September 11, 2001, this program has concentrated on countries with significant Muslim populations. USIS officers select participants, giving priority to young people, who, they think, will make worthwhile use of such exchanges in the future.

Both Foreign Service and USIS employees have been endangered when nongovernment groups abroad have used violence to make a public impact. As of 1985, twelve USIS buildings had been bombed, and American employees were kidnapped in Vietnam and Latin America.

Foreign nationals faced the greatest danger. Some have been held for years in prisons and labor camps. Lubomir Elsner, a Czech translator in the U.S. Embassy in Prague, spent eleven years in Czech Communist prisons and at forced labor in mines for spying for the United States. He was released in 1961, and thirty years later Ambassador Shirley Temple Black, the former child movie star who served in Ghana and Czechoslovakia, was charged with giving Elsner $18,000 in back pay.

For years, USIS provided local populations with books, periodicals, films, and lectures that depict the kind of society Americans believe they have. Since 9/11, vulnerable libraries in industrialized countries have been partly replaced by the American Corners program, a cooperative venture between an embassy and a local library or other institution. Access is free to all citizens of the host country. By 2009, American Corners had more than four hundred sites worldwide.

The global potential for public diplomacy is so enormous that it has proved difficult to identify and reach all important target audiences. Recently, much of the public diplomacy program has attempted to divert Muslim audiences away from recruiters for terrorist organizations. Under Secretary of State for Public Diplomacy and Public Affairs James Glassman, a former magazine publisher, confirmed, "The focus of today's war of ideas is counter terrorism." In the process, it has become clear that public diplomacy aimed at the elites usually does not carry over to the masses in the streets.

Ambassador Tom C. Korologos in Brussels has served on the Broadcasting Board of Governors and as chair of the U.S. Advisory Commission on Public Diplomacy. He says it was "dumb" to kill the USIA: "We have to go out for the people now. We have to have a dialogue, not a monologue." On the other hand, veteran FSO Daniel Russel prefers the integration of USIA into State. He says, "Now their agenda is my agenda. They have a seat at the table."

Some Foreign Service officers declare emphatically that the department has too many other things on its plate and cannot campaign strongly enough for more money for public diplomacy. Others believe just as fervently that public diplomacy must be a part of the diplomatic mission of the department's officers abroad.

Outside evaluators judge that U.S. public diplomacy has been injured by "excessive bureaucratic review" that interferes with public diplomacy's agility and by "misplaced security concerns" that limit travel into hostile areas.

Despite these differences, the newest technologies are able to reach huge audiences abroad. And these technologies also enable the public diplomacy program to train indigenous communicators abroad and to counter the partisanship often perceived in United States–run media.

. . .

At the same time, it also was the Foreign Service's job to show local populations abroad what the United States is like. The frustrations accompanying this mission were demonstrated when Karen Hughes, an energetic television reporter and confidant of President George W. Bush, was appointed undersecretary of state for public diplomacy and public affairs in 2005. She initiated a public diplomacy full-court press on the Muslim world. But after two years of hard work, studies showed no improvement in the U.S. image, and Karen Hughes left the government.

By 2007, 22 percent of public diplomacy positions were still vacant and 30 percent of positions requiring language proficiency were filled by officers who lacked those skills. Many embassies had to close facilities that had been open to the public. The Foreign Affairs Council concluded bitterly, "Those responsible for U.S. public diplomacy are standing tall in a deep hole."

By the end of George W. Bush's administration, the purpose of public diplomacy was shifting to explain American objectives and international actions to the world's population. But the number of Americans employed for this purpose dropped from 1,742 in 1986 to 1,332 in 2008. The American Academy of Diplomacy said the State Department's public diplomacy effort "needs a major infusion of new resources" and must reach out to broader audiences, especially the young "Internet Generation."

Public diplomacy is an optimistic strategy, because it is based on the expectation that it is possible to influence people abroad with information and reason. Perhaps it will eventually be determined that, faced with the potentials of nuclear disaster and unpredictable terrorism, human beings will become more eager to talk to one another rather than to flex muscle. Looked at this way, whether USIA is inside or outside the Department of State will seem less important and will be decided pragmatically, based on whatever proves to work best.

39

Diplomacy for American Dictators

1953–89

The nations of South and Central America have been a special concern for the United States since the country's beginning. U.S. diplomats have assumed the unilateral right to shape the nations of Latin America. In 1823, when the United States was only four decades old, President James Monroe, with surprising self-assurance, declared his doctrine:

> The American continents, by the free and independent condition which they have assumed and maintain, are henceforth not to be considered as subjects for future colonization by any European powers.

The United States' intimate relationship with the multicultural, multiracial nations of Latin America began by being paternalistic, grew to be domineering, and evolved to include the Good Neighbor policy in 1933, Cold War interventions in 1954, and the Alliance for Progress in 1961.

In 1904, President Theodore Roosevelt told Congress that, while the Monroe Doctrine prohibited other nations from intervening when Latin American nations misbehaved or were threatened, this restriction did not apply to the United States. He called this "corollary" to the Monroe Doctrine a "moral mandate."

After World War II, the signatories of the Treaty of Rio Janeiro pledged to use the international police power to meet any armed attack against any American nation. Secretary of State Dean Acheson told the Pan American Society, "We oppose aggression; we do not oppose change. Indeed, we welcome and encourage change where it is in the direction of liberty and democracy." And he added wisely, "The nature of democracy is such that it can be achieved only from within."

United States policy toward authoritarian governments in the Western Hemisphere has usually asserted that dictatorships of the left threatened their neighbors' and the United States' strategic and economic interests, while right-wing dictatorships repeatedly have been found more acceptable. The United States established and supported the Western Hemisphere dictatorships of Somoza, Trujillo, Noriega, and Duvalier. In recent years, the threat of Communism disguised the ugliness of such dictatorships.

Ambassador to the United Nations Jeane Kirkpatrick perceived General Somoza of Nicaragua (and the shah of Iran) benignly as "traditional rulers of semi-traditional societies." In 1977, President Jimmy Carter supported human rights abroad and, with mixed success, placed Patricia Derian, assistant secretary of state for human rights and humanitarian affairs, in charge.

During the half century after World War II, the United States feared, above all, that local Latin forces opposing U.S. domination would align with the Soviet Union in the Cold War. Certainly, the conditions under which Latin American peasants and urban poor lived provided fertile ground for revolutionaries.

In the 1980s, Peter F. Romero, a young desk officer, observed Secretary of State Haig accentuating this anti-Communism and ignoring the local inequities in Latin America. Romero became a perceptive Foreign Service officer, ambassador to Ecuador, and assistant secretary for Western Hemisphere Affairs. As he saw economies grow, the rule of law strengthened, and many Latin Americans make progress on their own. Romero concluded optimistically; "Lots of good things are happening; a sea change is happening."

NICARAGUA "THIS SNAKE NEVER DIED"
IRAN-CONTRA

Starting in 1853, United States Marines repeatedly occupied Nicaragua to protect American business interests. When the Marines pulled out in

1933, they turned over the National Guard they had trained to Anastasio Somoza García. General Somoza arranged the assassination of the nationalist leader Augusto César Sandino. The Somoza family ruled the coffee-growing country for the next forty-three years. The United States appreciated the family's anti-Communism and support of free trade. The family appreciated the opportunity to become immensely wealthy.

Among the groups that confronted Somoza and his sons, the most effective one called themselves Sandinistas. Just after Christmas in 1974, nine Sandinistas crashed a party in a private home in Managua in order to assassinate Anastasio Somoza Debayle and his friend, U.S. ambassador Turner B. Shelton, a career Foreign Service officer. Somoza was not present and Shelton had just left the party. In the melee, the Sandinistas killed four people and took twenty-five hostages. Sixty-two hours later, when Somoza agreed to free fourteen political prisoners and pay the guerrillas $1 million, the Sandinistas released their hostages.

Two years earlier, Ambassador Shelton had escaped another kind of close call when an earthquake destroyed the center of Managua just after noon on December 23, 1972. The embassy building collapsed; his secretary, Rose Marie Orlich, was among some five thousand people who died then. Somoza's forces proved too corrupt and inept to handle the crisis, so Shelton called in six hundred American troops from Panama to restore order.

President Jimmy Carter withdrew U.S. support from the Somozas, and by June 1978 Nicaragua was torn by civil war. Ambassador Lawrence A. Pezzulo came over from Montevideo to try to end the fighting. The United States planned to install a democratic government backed by elements of Somoza's National Guard.

Pezzulo and DCM Thomas O'Donnell met with various factions and negotiated with Somoza. The dictator certainly had supported the United States and done its dirty work. In the end, Somoza escaped during the night of July 13, 1979, to Miami and then Paraguay. When Pezzulo requested his own recall, the Sandinistas took over Nicaragua.

The Sandinistas started a leftist social and economic revolution. The United States would not accept that. At the end of 1981, President Reagan's administration slashed sugar imports, blocked international loans to Nicaragua, and shut down its economy. The CIA mustered armed anti-Sandinista "Contras," including men from Somoza's former National

Guard. But the U.S. Congress passed the so-called Boland amendments, which prohibited funding the Contras.

In the spring of 1985, officials in the Reagan White House, led by National Security Advisor Robert C. "Bud" McFarlane, evaded Congress by organizing other nations and wealthy private donors to supply the Contras with money and arms. For example, the Saudis contributed $32 million. And U.S. National Security Council staff member Lieutenant Colonel Oliver North, U.S. Marine Corps, offered to remove pressure from Manuel Noriega's drug-smuggling operation in Panama if Noriega helped the Contras. Assistant Secretary of State for Inter-American Affairs Elliott Abrams met the defense minister of Brunei and had him deposit $10 million in a Contra bank account. A secret sophomoric cable from the U.S. embassy in Brunei to the State Department read, "Our emissary should telephone [blocked out] at Dorchester Hotel, prior to meeting to make specific arrangements. [Blocked out] probably suggest that they meet in Hyde Park. You may wish to have emissary use a code name, which I can pass." The Sultan of Brunei transferred the $10 million from his bank account to a Swiss bank.

As part of this elaborate scheme, a conspiracy-minded group in the White House fantasized that if the United States supplied arms to Iran, which was then fighting an exhausting war against Iraq, Iran would persuade Hezbollah terrorists in Lebanon to release thirty Western hostages, including seven Americans. To complete this arms-for-hostages deceit, Israel would sell arms to Iran and the United States would replenish Israel's inventory. President Reagan authorized the sale of arms to Iran from Israeli stocks, even though American policy clearly prohibited paying for hostages.

At the same time, another complicated brainstorm was in full flower: The United States government would raise money for the Contras by selling arms to Iran. Income from the illegal arms-for-hostages sales would be surreptitiously diverted to support the Contras, an arrangement that the Boland amendments had made illegal.

Arms for hostages and money for the Contras—they were all illegal. L. Paul Bremer III, a career Foreign Service officer who was then the ambassador at large for counterterrorism, said of the White House, "It's amateur hour over there."

Hawk surface-to-air missiles were shipped by air from Israel to Iran. This was another catastrophe because the deal makers shipped the wrong model of the missile. Eventually, hundreds of TOW missiles went through Israel to Iran. As a result, exactly one American hostage held by the Hezbollah was released.

These activities were, in part, the result of a power battle between the State Department and the White House's National Security Council over who would make foreign policy. Secretary of State Shultz opposed the secret White House program. He gave two reasons: If hostage takers think they could sell hostages, they would simply seize more hostages. And State, not the NSC and CIA, should make counterterrorism policy.

On December 5, 1985, Vice Admiral John Poindexter replaced McFarlane as National Security Council advisor. Two days later, in a meeting with President Reagan, Shultz warned that selling arms to Iran was illegal. The President protested that the American people would not understand if hostages died because "I would not break the law."

Shultz was horrified that Middle East countries would see the United States breaking its own laws to help Iran defeat Iraq. When one participant rationalized that TOW missiles were defensive weapons, a frustrated Shultz snapped, "So's your old man!"

The whole plot was soon exposed as an amateurish attempt at gun-running, drug dealing, money laundering, lying to Congress, document shredding, and random law breaking, all originating in the Reagan White House, its National Security Council, and the CIA.

"Iran-Contra" became one of the messiest international scandals in modern American history. But it unraveled in May 1986, when Ambassador Charles H. Price II in London, formerly a prominent Kansas City banker, called the State Department to ask about rumors of arms-for-hostages sales to Iran. Secretary Shultz demanded that the operation be stopped. And only then did the first State Department document oppose the Iran intrigue. Shultz said later, "But this snake never died, no matter how many times I hacked at it."

That October, a "lethal resupply" flight was shot down over Nicaragua, and the public learned of the conspiracy. The *Los Angeles Times* bared the complex resupply system that was arming the Contras, and the *San Francisco Examiner* reported that Vice President George H. W. Bush was the link between the government and the downed flight. Elliott Abrams told the Senate Foreign Relations Committee that the elaborate supply system was "not our system."

A Lebanese newspaper made the arms-for-hostages story public in November, and Shultz and Paul Bremer were able to stop further arms sales to Iran and to bring counterterrorism policy back to the State Department. Shultz wrote that he believed the buck for the arms-for-hostages deal stopped on the President's desk.

That same month, a White House meeting revealed that millions of dollars from the Iran arms sales had been siphoned off to buy weapons for the Contras in Nicaragua. The plan came tumbling down. The public uproar was deafening. Admiral Poindexter resigned, and Oliver North was fired.

Although the White House schemers had tried to keep the State Department out of the illegal loop, some members of the Foreign Service were caught. The ambassador to Lebanon, John Kelly, confessed to Shultz that he had met repeatedly with the National Security Council staff, including McFarlane and North, about the hostage negotiations; and he had not informed the Secretary. In addition, at least three U.S. ambassadors had been dragged into providing the Contras with "lethal resupply": Ambassador Everett Ellis Briggs in Honduras; Ambassador Edwin G. Corr in El Salvador; and Ambassador Lewis A. Tambs in Costa Rica. Both Briggs and Corr were career Foreign Service officers. Briggs, whose father, Ellis O. Briggs, had been an ambassador to seven countries, did not have his career impeded. Dr. Tambs, a professor of history, resigned from the Foreign Service and returned to teaching.

The court-appointed independent counsel, Lawrence E. Walsh, ultimately decided not to indict Corr, but Walsh spoke of the veteran diplomat's "continuing and unbelievable assertions in the Grand Jury." Corr left to become a professor of political science at the University of Oklahoma. Four CIA officials also were charged with criminal offenses.

Years later, Walsh asserted that Secretary Shultz and his aides, M. Charles Hill and Nicholas Platt, knew all along what was going on. After interviewing Shultz and others in the State Department, Walsh concluded that "central aspects of Shultz's testimony were incorrect." But, Walsh explained, "Independent Counsel declined to prosecute because the evidence did not establish beyond a reasonable doubt that his testimony was willfully false."

Those involved in the scandal were able to protect each other. President George H. W. Bush pardoned various officials, including Assistant Secretary Abrams, who "pleaded guilty to unlawfully withholding material information" from Congress. *The Washington Post* tagged Abrams "one of Washington's most accomplished, and controversial, bureaucratic infighters."

Despite all these machinations, the United States only marginally affected the outcome of the war in Nicaragua. Much of the United States' prolonged effort was staged from poverty-ridden Honduras, where Ambassador John D. Negroponte, a career diplomat, kept watch on the U.S.-owned United Fruit Company and Honduras' CIA-supported military. When Negroponte had a Contra leader to dinner at the residence, Ambassador Anthony C. E. Quainton, then the ambassador to Nicaragua, protested strongly against his "gastronomic diplomacy" with a man seeking to overthrow a neighboring government. Negroponte, the son of a Greek shipping tycoon, went on to become the director of national intelligence and deputy secretary of state.

One Foreign Service officer, William R. Meara, later wrote about the twelve months he spent in Honduras, working from the U.S. Embassy in Tegucigalpa as assistant to Ambassador Everett Ellis Briggs and liaison with the Contras. Shortly after Meara's arrival, a Honduran mob stormed the embassy and set fire to its six-story annex. Honduran authorities were in no hurry to disperse the rioters or put out the flames.

The Contras had their own limitations. A USAID study showed that 70 percent of them were under twenty-four years old and that 87 percent had only one year's education. Meara admired the peasant Contra fighters and scorned their political leaders, living safely in Miami. He wrote, "I didn't want to see U.S. soldiers involved in Nicaragua. . . . I thought we had other, better options. We had the contras."

GUATEMALA: "THERE ARE TWO SORTS OF PEOPLE IN THE WORLD"

When John E. Peurifoy assumed office as U.S. ambassador to Guatemala in October 1953, President Jacobo Arbenz Guzman was expropriating huge landholdings of the United Fruit Company. The company dominated Guatemala's agriculture and railroads and was a powerful political and economic force in Central America.

President Arbenz invited Ambassador Peurifoy and his wife, Betty Jane, to a private dinner in the Casa Presidencial. They talked until two in the morning. Arbenz "bitterly" blamed the dispute on the ruthlessness of the United Fruit Company, while Peurifoy put the blame on the Soviet Communism gnawing at Guatemala. Each man stuck to his preconceptions. Ambassador Peurifoy ended his report by writing, "I came away definitely convinced that if the President is not a Communist he will certainly do until one comes along."

Arbenz, democratically elected president in 1951, had set out to break the foreign monopolies of electricity, railroads, and the United Fruit Company. After Secretary of State Dulles sent Peurifoy to Guatemala, Flora Lewis, of *The New York Times,* wrote, "It was perfectly clear that his instructions and his purpose had one simple theme: 'Get rid of the Reds.'" Dulles' former law firm represented United Fruit.

United Fruit's influence was extensive. Thomas Dudley Cabot, of Boston, was the president of United Fruit in 1948 and 1949. In 1951, President Truman appointed him director of International Security Affairs in the State Department. His younger brother, John Moors Cabot, served as ambassador to five nations and assistant secretary of state for inter-American affairs. Both brothers were longtime stockholders and directors of the company that was known throughout Latin America as El Pulpo (the Octopus).

Much later, Dulles explained his position, stating, "For us there are two sorts of people in the world. There are those who are Christians and support free enterprise, and there are the others."

On January 16, 1954, President Eisenhower told Ambassador Don Guillermo Toriello, who was returning to Guatemala to become foreign minister, that the United States could not help a government that was friendly with Communists. Toriello insisted the problem was not communism but United Fruit.

In May, a secret shipment of arms from Czechoslovakia arrived in Guatemala. Dulles ordered the CIA to overthrow Arbenz for projecting Soviet power into the hemisphere. The CIA went to work, using the threat of U.S.-armed intervention and aggressive propaganda.

Although Deputy Under Secretary for Political Affairs Robert D.

Murphy and Louis J. Halle of the Policy Planning Staff objected, on the evening of June 18, 1954, a CIA-built army crossed from Honduras into Guatemala. President Arbenz called it the "United Fruit Company expeditionary force." CIA planes supported the invasion. When two of the three F-47s failed, William Pawley, a wealthy Florida businessman who had been ambassador to Peru and Brazil, replaced them, with Eisenhower's approval. The United Nations Security Council, pressed by Ambassador Henry Cabot Lodge and John C. Dreier, U.S. ambassador to the Organization of American States, refused to examine the Guatemalan crisis. Britain and France opposed the United States, but Eisenhower persuaded them to abstain from voting, thus squelching the inquiry.

The invading army was easily defeated, but on June 27, five senior colonels met with Ambassador Peurifoy. Afterward, they persuaded Arbenz to resign. He found asylum in the Mexican embassy, and the colonels took charge.

Robert E. White, former ambassador to Paraguay and El Salvador, identified June 27 as the date "when U.S. policy towards Latin America went wrong. . . . The Eisenhower administration gave the green light to the Central Intelligence Agency to overthrow the constitutional order and install a military government, thereby igniting widespread rebellion. Over the next thirty-five years, the CIA bankrolled a war in which torture, murder and the firebombing of rural villages resulted in the deaths of 200,000 people, most of them defenseless Mayan Indians."

By July 5, the United States government placed in office as president of Guatemala the man it really wanted: Colonel Castillo Armas. He reversed Arbenz' land reform, so injurious to United Fruit, and set up death squads. Castillo was assassinated in 1958, and instability and violence racked Guatemala. Arbenz drowned in his bathtub in Mexico City in 1971. Peurifoy (and his nine-year-old son) died in an automobile accident while he served as ambassador to Thailand; he was forty-eight. The overthrow of President Arbenz aroused anti-American feelings throughout Latin America for years.

MURDER, RAPE, AND TORTURE

Political chaos, corruption, and violence continued in Guatemala. The murder, rape, and torture of thousands of Guatemalans attracted little attention in the United States, except when American citizens were the victims.

John Gordon Mein was the first American ambassador ever assassinated. He and his driver were a block from the embassy in Guatemala City at 3:00 P.M. on August 28, 1968, when a green car forced his official Cadillac to the curb. A small red car blocked the limousine from the rear. A young man in fatigues pointed a submachine gun at the two men and ordered them out. The driver obeyed, but Ambassador Mein opened the opposite back door and started to run. The driver of the green car shouted to the armed youth, "Kill him!" He fired and Mein fell, dead.

The terrorists, reported to be Castro-paid guerrillas, left Ambassador Mein's body, soaked in blood, lying on the grassy median of the broad Boulevard La Reforma until U.S. Consul Neil Ruge drove up and identified him. Then, Ruge and the wife of Deputy Chief of Mission Max Krebs drove out to the official residence to inform Mrs. Mein and their young son.

A rebel group that in January had killed two American attachés (Colonel John Webber and Lieutenant Commander Ernest Munro) took responsibility for Ambassador Mein's assassination. It was assumed they were trying to capture Mein and hold him hostage to exchange for a rebel leader.

Two decades later, a series of ugly cases emerged during the tenure of Ambassador Thomas F. Stroock, a classmate and friend of George H. W. Bush at Yale. Stroock, became active in oil exploration and Republican politics in Wyoming.

President George H. W. Bush sent Stroock to Guatemala City in 1989, and he ran into horrendous problems. On November 2, Sister Dianna Ortiz, an Ursuline nun from New Mexico who was teaching indigenous children, was tortured and raped. She told the embassy that the man who abused her apparently was an American citizen, and she accused Ambassador Stroock of having concealed the Guatemalan government's human rights abuses.

In June 1990, American innkeeper Michael DeVine was kidnapped and beheaded. An army captain and six enlisted men were convicted of murdering DeVine, but somehow the captain escaped. Colonel Julio Roberto Alpirez of the Guatemalan army was accused, while on the payroll of the CIA, of covering up DeVine's murder, as well as participating in the torture of a guerrilla leader married to an American citizen.

That September 11, a Guatemalan army intelligence specialist stabbed the respected American anthropologist Myrna Mack Chang twenty-seven times as she left her office. She died in the street. After a perilous campaign by her sister, Helen Mack, a Guatemalan army colonel was found guilty of planning the killing, based partly on classified U.S. government documents.

On August 23, 1992, the fully clothed body of American archaeologist Peter Tiscione was found dead of machete wounds in his bathtub at the Pan American Hotel. His widow interested Congressman Robert G. Torricelli in the case; until then Ambassador Stroock insisted it was a suicide.

During all this bloodshed, Stroock sent a secret cable to the Secretary of State, identifying many of those murdered as "leftists" and the violence as part of the thirty-year war against those supporting the political guerrillas. He called Myrna Mack Chang a "leftist anthropologist" and said Dinora Pérez, who was also shot to death, was a leftist political organizer.

The attacks on Americans grew so infamous that in 1995, at the direction of President Clinton, Anthony Lake, assistant to the president for national security affairs, investigated human rights abuses against Americans in Guatemala. A committee under Anthony S. Harrington, former ambassador to Brazil and chairman of the Intelligence Oversight Board, issued a voluminous, if cautious, report. It reviewed nine cases, in addition to the five Anthony Lake had listed in which Americans in Guatemala were killed, abused, or attacked, and it said: "The human rights records of the Guatemalan security forces were widely known to be reprehensible." It criticized the State Department, the CIA, and the Department of Justice but named no U.S. officials. The violence in Guatemala did not stop.

VENEZUELA: "OUR LATIN POLICIES HAVE BEEN RIDICULOUS"

During the Cold War, Venezuela was officially neglected until Vice President Richard M. Nixon and his wife landed in Caracas on May 13, 1958, on the final stop of an official eight-nation Latin America tour. At the airport, belligerent Venezuelans on a balcony above greeted them with a rain of invective and spit. They were spewing their hatred at United States policy that had supported their brutal military dictator, Marcos Pérez Jiménez, who had welcomed U.S. companies extracting their country's riches of iron ore and oil. Pérez Jiménez had fled into exile and was living luxuriously in Miami Beach.

Neither the new Venezuela government nor the U.S. Embassy in Caracas wanted Nixon to come. But the White House insisted. The embassy's DCM Charles Burrows flew to Bogotá to alert Nixon to trouble ahead and accompany him to Caracas.

As the visitors' cars entered the city streets, a mob attacked them, banged on the cars, dented their sides, and smashed the rear windows of the Vice President's car, covering the passengers with slivers of glass. The convoy changed course and made a run for the American ambassador's residence, situated safely on a hill in a suburban neighborhood. Nixon hunkered down there the rest of his time in Venezuela, guarded by embassy Marines and soldiers from the U.S. military mission. Russ Olson, a young Foreign Service officer, was assigned as a control officer for the visit, and said later, "The decision to flee to the security of the residence saved the Nixons' lives and ours."

Eisenhower ordered troops to the Caribbean to rescue his Vice President, but Nixon radioed Washington that they were safe. Nixon also called Puerto Rico's governor, Luis Muñoz Marín, and asked if he and Mrs. Nixon could come and stay with them overnight. After a long, thoughtful pause, Muñoz agreed. To move the Vice President to the Caracas airport safely (and nine hours early), Venezuelan troops lined the entire twenty-kilometer route. Russ Olson wrote his brother, "Our Latin policies have been ridiculous and some protest was expected and justified. However, this went beyond a civilized demonstration as you know." Venezuela was neglected no longer. Hugo Chavez became its president, and he was intent on separating his country from United States domination.

PARAGUAY: AN AFFRONT TO DECENCY

In Asunción, Paraguay, General Alfredo Stroessner seized power in 1954 and became one of the modern world's longest-ruling dictators. Americans helped him develop his secret police, and Stroessner ruled Paraguay for thirty-five years by relying on torture and murder.

In the late 1970s, his regime harassed U.S. Ambassador Robert E. White for protesting human rights violations, and in the 1980s threatened

Ambassador Clyde D. Taylor, who was protesting press restrictions and human rights violations and encouraging a coalition of opposition parties. Stroessner threatened to set fire to the U.S. Embassy, and in February 1987 his troops actually lobbed tear gas into a reception that the Paraguayan Women for Democracy were giving in Ambassador Taylor's honor. *The New York Times* called the attack an affront to decency.

A *Times* editorial praised Taylor as well as Ambassadors Harry G. Barnes, Jr., in Chile; Deane R. Hinton in Pakistan; and Stephen W. Bosworth in the Philippines, for combining courage with effective diplomacy. Two years later, a bloody military coup overthrew Stroessner, and he fled to exile in Brazil.

CUBA: "ONE MISTAKE CAN MAKE THIS WHOLE THING BLOW UP"

After the Spanish-American War, the United States tried to achieve stability on the island of Cuba. In June 1957, President Eisenhower forced his friend Arthur Gardner to resign as ambassador because he seemed blind toward dictator Fulgencio Batista's excesses. Gardner was replaced with investment banker Earl E. T. Smith, who urged Batista to retire in December 1958. Smith later testified to a U.S. Senate subcommittee that the United States government was responsible for the revolution that brought Fidel Castro to power. Of course, a major cause of the revolution was the Cuban government's own pervasive corruption.

Once Castro took command of Cuba at the beginning of 1959, the CIA tried repeatedly to remove him. The most conspicuous attempt, the landing of fifteen hundred armed Cubans at the Bay of Pigs in April 1961, was a humiliating failure. Sixteen months later, a high-flying American U-2 reconnaissance plane detected ballistic missiles that the Soviet Union had placed in western Cuba.

President Kennedy decided that the Soviet missiles, ninety miles from the United States, must be removed. On Tuesday, October 16, 1962, he organized a powerful ad hoc executive committee of the National Security Council to manage the crisis. The "ExComm" included, from the State Department, Under Secretary George Ball, Deputy Under Secretary U. Alexis Johnson, Assistant Secretary Edward Martin, and Charles Bohlen, the former ambassador to Moscow.

When Bohlen moved on to his new post in Paris, he was replaced on the committee by Ambassador Llewellyn Thompson, just back from Moscow. "Tommy" Thompson knew the Soviets better than anyone else present, and Dean Rusk said he was "the unsung hero of the crisis." Former Secretary of State Dean Acheson and Adlai Stevenson, then the ambassador to the United Nations, also joined the group.

In Moscow that same day, Premier Nikita Khrushchev summoned Ambassador Foy Kohler and told him he did not want to cause the President any embarrassment right before a national election. Kennedy thought he was lying.

The executive committee selected three options: a naval "quarantine" to prevent the arrival of more missiles and nuclear warheads, a surprise air attack to "take out" the missile sites, and an outright invasion of Cuba. The invasion option was soon dropped, and the choices became a naval blockade versus an air strike. The executive committee was divided.

Dean Rusk and Llewellyn Thompson went to the White House on Thursday afternoon and briefed the President before he met with Andrei Gromyko, the Soviet foreign minister. Gromyko reassured Kennedy about the tension in Berlin and said the Soviet Union was only helping Cuba defend itself. Kennedy told him that he would not accept a Soviet strategic base in Cuba.

Thompson advised the executive committee that an air strike was the more dangerous option because it would kill Russians. So, on Friday night the decision was made to begin with a naval quarantine and, if that did not work, to move on to air strikes. Attorney General Robert Kennedy's deputy, Nicholas Katzenbach, prepared a legal brief justifying a blockade. Ships of Navy Task Force 136 steamed into position to make the blockade real.

Although the hub of the crisis was in Washington, Foreign Service officers abroad played significant roles. Anticipating that the Russians would react to the American moves, with the possibility even of nuclear war, allied leaders had to be informed of the plan. Livingston Merchant, former ambassador to Canada, was located at a Princeton football game and rushed to Ottawa to inform Prime Minister John Diefenbaker. Walter Dowling, ambassador to West Germany, reached at home in Georgia, was told to fly with Dean Acheson to deliver a message from Kennedy to Chancellor Konrad Adenauer. Others were informed through a presidential letter sent to the U.S. embassies in their capitals.

Saturday night, Secretary Rusk telephoned Acheson and told him President Kennedy wanted him to fly to Paris to inform President Charles de Gaulle personally of the American plans. At eight o'clock Sunday morning, Acheson flew to Paris. The plane first put down in the dark at a remote air base near Newbury, England, where Ambassador David K. E. Bruce met Acheson with a bottle of Scotch in one raincoat pocket and a revolver in the other. Acheson asked why he brought the revolver. Bruce said, "I don't know. I was told by the Department of State to carry this when I went to meet you." Acheson asked, "There was nothing said about shooting me, was there?" Bruce replied, "No. Would you think it's a good idea?" Acheson gave the ambassador photographs of the Soviet missiles to show to Prime Minister Harold Macmillan.

Acheson next landed at Évreux, France, at 2:30 A.M. local time. He was met by U.S. Chargé d'affaire Cecil Lyon and driven to Lyon's house, where he tried futilely to sleep for a few hours. In careful secrecy, Acheson and Lyon met with de Gaulle at 5:00 P.M. at the Elysées. De Gaulle held out his hand saying, "Your President has done me great honor by sending so distinguished an emissary." After Acheson described the situation, de Gaulle said, "You may tell your President that France will support him in every way in this crisis."

The Americans anticipated the Soviets might try to skirt the naval blockade by flying nuclear warheads into Cuba. The State Department instructed the U.S. ambassadors in Jamaica, Trinidad, Guinea, and Senegal to ask their host governments not to grant landing rights to any Soviet planes heading for Cuba. Since Conakry and Dakar were the only practical refueling sites for Soviet planes on that route, Ambassadors William Attwood in Guinea and Philip Kaiser in Senegal had the most crucial assignments. Both were capable diplomats.

The Russians were already pressing President Sékou Touré of Guinea for landing rights, but Touré promised he would not grant them. Ambassador Kaiser sent his political officer, Stephen Low, with Kennedy's urgent letter to President Senghor of Senegal. Low had him wakened, and he came out in his dressing gown. Later, when Ambassador Kaiser asked Senghor to deny the Soviets landing rights, he replied, "Anything President Kennedy wants."

Stephen Low said the lesson he learned that morning was, "Wherever you are, set up ahead of time a way to get to the chief of state in an emergency."

. . .

Twenty-five Soviet ships were identified sailing toward Cuba. The first two declared they had no weapons aboard and were permitted to pass the quarantine. Twelve others were spotted turning back. U Thant, acting secretary general of the United Nations, proposed exchanging the removal of the missiles for an American pledge not to invade Cuba.

Friday morning at 7:30, the destroyer *Joseph P. Kennedy, Jr.,* forced the freighter *Marucla,* bound for Cuba under Soviet charter, to stop. A party boarded with the captain's permission and determined that *Marucla* carried no weapons. It was permitted to proceed. The purpose of the boarding was to demonstrate to Khrushchev that the United States meant what it said. It would board Soviet ships.

That afternoon, hints began reaching Washington that the Soviets were looking for a way out. Soviet ships began turning back, and Dean Rusk was quoted as saying, "We're eyeball-to-eyeball, and I think the other fellow just blinked." He later admitted, "I was always sorry that leaked out. Those things don't help. When you solve a problem, you ought to thank God and go on to the next one."

On Saturday evening, Kennedy sent Premier Khrushchev a proposal, and Sunday morning the Soviet agreement arrived. There were still critical points to settle, but the Cuban missile crisis was over. Rusk called it a "triumph of both American and Soviet diplomacy." Only years later did the United States learn that at the time the Soviet Union already had 158 nuclear warheads in place on the island.

Kennedy said later on television that the United States never anticipated that the Soviet Union would place offensive missiles in Cuba and the Soviet Union did not expect that the United States would force them to be removed. He said such misjudgments in a nuclear era clearly branded this a dangerous time, noting that "one mistake can make this whole thing blow up."

The United States continued to scheme to get rid of Castro. Plots (some under the silly code name Operation Mongoose) included constructing an exploding seashell, making Castro's hair fall out, poisoning his cigars, converting a ballpoint pen into a hypodermic needle, and even organizing a traditional assassination.

The U.S. embassy in Havana, which had been closed in 1961, remained empty until the U.S. Interests Section opened in 1977 under the Swiss embassy. It was staffed by fifty Americans and some three hundred Cubans chosen by the Cuban government. One chief of the U.S. Interests Section, James Cason, a Dartmouth graduate and veteran Foreign Service officer, introduced ridicule. He built a replica of a jail in his backyard and wore a pink robe after a Cuban cartoon depicted him as a wand-waving fairy. Castro called him "a bully with diplomatic immunity." Neither threats nor ridicule made much difference.

GRENADA: "TO EXPORT TERROR AND UNDERMINE DEMOCRACY"

When Prime Minister Maurice Bishop of the Caribbean island of Grenada was assassinated, Deputy Assistant Secretary of State Charles A. Gillespie, Jr., and U.S. Ambassador to the Eastern Caribbean Milan Bish met on Barbados with six Caribbean prime ministers on October 21, 1983, and persuaded the Organization of Eastern Caribbean States to support a U.S. invasion of tiny Grenada in order to eliminate the military government that had assassinated Bishop. President Reagan had already decided to invade the island. From Augusta, Georgia, where he was enjoying a weekend of golf, Reagan ordered Vice President George H. W. Bush to convene a special situation group to handle the crisis.

The United States announced it was concerned for the safety of six hundred young Americans attending the St. George's University School of Medicine. The medical students did not want to leave the island, and Grenadian army officers vouched for their safety. But that did not deter the U.S. planners.

Planning for Grenada was sidetracked two days later, when a suicide-bomb truck driven by an Iranian terrorist destroyed the headquarters of the 24th Marine Amphibious Unit at Beirut's International Airport and killed 241 Americans. More Marines died that morning than on any single day since D-Day on Iwo Jima. Almost simultaneously, two miles away, another truck blew up the French paratroopers' barracks, killing fifty-eight.

In Beirut, fighting between the United States and various factions in a bitter civil and religious war had been sputtering along for months. On April 18, a pickup truck loaded with explosives had been driven into the lobby of the U.S. Embassy on the Beirut waterfront and blown up. Sixty-three people, including seventeen Americans, died.

Reagan was determined to go ahead in Grenada as planned despite opposition from British Prime Minister Margaret Thatcher and many other leaders. On October 25, U.S. soldiers and Marines landed by helicopter and across Grenada's beach, and sped to the medical school. They found no one to fight. By mistake, a U.S. pilot scored a direct hit on a civilian mental hospital, killing fifteen patients.

The British governor general of the island signed a letter prepared by the State Department and backdated to precede the invasion asking for U.S. help. More than a hundred members of the UN General Assembly voted against this violation of international law.

HAITI: POOREST OF THE POOR

Hispaniola was France's most valuable island colony until Toussaint-Louverture led a slave rebellion. In 1804, Haiti, which occupies half of the island forty-eight miles east of Cuba, became independent but took on a ruinous indebtedness to France. Haiti was the poorest country in the Western Hemisphere.

The United States replaced France in Haitian affairs, and by 1910 the country was hopelessly in debt to American and European banks. The U.S. Marines occupied Haiti from 1915 to 1934, their longest and probably their least successful occupation in Latin America. They organized the Gendarmerie d'Haiti, led by white Marines. Americans ran the country and Assistant Secretary of the Navy Franklin D. Roosevelt drafted a constitution.

Objection to the occupation was so widespread that a Senate committee demanded that someone be appointed to manage Haiti. Brigadier General John H. Russell, commander of the 1st Marine Brigade, was named high commissioner with the rank of ambassador. In 1930, President Herbert Hoover chose as minister to Haiti Dana Gardner Munro, the young chief of Latin America affairs, who after twelve years in the Foreign Service would become a professor of Latin American history at Princeton. He was followed in 1932 by the respected veteran Norman Armour, whose mission was to oversee the departure of the Marines. Before they left, the Gendarmerie became the Garde d'Haiti, with Haitians serving as low-rank officers. By then, most Haitians had come to hate the occupiers.

The Marines returned in 1958 to help Haiti's dictator François "Papa Doc" Duvalier build an army. When he died in 1971, his nineteen-year-old son, Jean-Claude "Baby Doc" Duvalier, ran the country until President Reagan forced him into exile. Brutal military regimes still ruled.

In 1990, Haiti seemed to have a chance for a change. Jean-Bertrand Aristide, a thirty-seven-year-old former Roman Catholic priest, was elected president. He received two-thirds of the votes as a supporter of the poor against the wretched country's military and economic elite. He planned to raise the minimum wage and force business to pay taxes. This frightened the foreign-owned companies, and, after eight months in office, Aristide was forced to leave by a violent military coup. Washington did not interfere. After another period of instability and violence, four years later, President Clinton sent American troops to Haiti to restore Aristide's party to power. But the Republican Congress in Washington denied aid to Haiti.

In 2000 Aristide was again elected by a large majority. President Clinton sent Brian Dean Curran, an experienced Foreign Service officer, as ambassador. He was told to work with Aristide to strengthen democracy in Haiti by seeking compromises with the establishment. In time, the Aristide government lost considerable popularity, and international lenders and President George W. Bush, fearing the ascent of leftists, withdrew U.S. support from Aristide's government.

Ambassador Curran had expected cooperation from the International Republican Institute (IRI), which was funded by USAID, the State Department and private foundations and corporations and chaired by Senator John McCain, of Arizona. The IRI was determined to get rid of Aristide. Curran repeatedly protested to the State Department about the IRI's leaders in Haiti.

During the George W. Bush administration, Curran's cables went to Otto J. Reich, assistant secretary of state for Latin American affairs, his deputy Daniel W. Fisk, and Elliott L. Abrams. Reich and Abrams were veterans of the Iran-Contra affair, and Fisk had worked for Senator Jesse Helms. It was not a group expected to sympathize with Aristide. Reich called Clinton's support of Aristide a "crime."

In the face of growing violence, assassinations, and kidnappings, Ambassador Curran was succeeded by Foreign Service officer James B. Foley. Seven months later, armed rebels based in the Dominican Republic and supported by some Americans deposed Aristide. The United States, again, did not interfere. Leaving the country in an American government plane with an armed guard, Aristide and his wife were dropped in the Central African Republic, where the French military still ruled. The United States had closed its embassy there. Aristide said he had been "kidnapped." The UN reported that Haiti returned to "assassinations, mob violence, torture and arbitrary arrests."

PANAMA: "THE BEST DRUG BUST IN HISTORY"

In March 1973, the Security Council of the United Nations voted that the United States should give full sovereignty over the Canal Zone to Panama. The United States vetoed the resolution but the problem would not go away. Secretary of State William Rogers asked Ambassador Ellsworth Bunker, just back from Saigon, to negotiate. The Pentagon and the U.S. Congress made Bunker's efforts impossible.

President Jimmy Carter took office in 1977 and believed both sides wanted a secure, efficient canal. He sent Sol Linowitz, former ambassador to the Organization of American States, to Panama as a conegotiator after Linowitz refused to replace Bunker. Instead, he reenforced the position of the veteran Bunker, age eighty-two, that control of the Panama Canal should be turned over to the Republic of Panama.

Then the domestic battle in the United States began. Bunker made seventy-five speeches in twenty-one states. Carter wanted to change U.S. "control" over the canal to guaranteed "access" to it. The American people were divided. The U.S. Senate finally ratified the treaty (actually there were two treaties) in March and April by one vote more than the two-thirds required. This concluded Bunker's exceptional diplomatic career.

The treaty did not divorce the United States from Panama and its canal. In 1983, General Manuel Antonio Noriega took command of the Panama Defense Forces and dominated the country, including the canal. The United States depended on General Noriega to keep order in Panama. On the CIA payroll for years, he played a double role with the Medellín drug lords.

Noriega, a brutal man, forced Panama's president, Nicolás Ardito

Barletta, from office. Ambassador Everett E. Briggs, who despised Noriega, informed the State Department of Noriega's involvement in drugs and gunrunning. In December, Briggs traveled to Washington to put pressure on Noriega, but he was thwarted by officials, including Assistant Secretary Elliott Abrams and Colonel Oliver North.

When Briggs' successor, Arthur H. Davis, Jr., a Golden, Colorado, real estate developer, underwent confirmation hearings in Washington, he spoke in favor of a civilian government in Panama. Secretary of State George Shultz had to state publicly that General Noriega did not run a civilian government.

By 1987, Panamanian opponents to Noriega began exposing his many crimes, and demonstrators mobilized against him and his supporters in Washington. On June 26, the U.S. Senate, by a vote of 84 to 2, demanded that he resign. Noriega had the Panamanian assembly declare Ambassador Davis persona non grata and four days later organized a crowd that marched on the white stucco U.S. Embassy and bombarded it with rocks and paint-filled bags. The State Department sent Panama a bill for $106,000 to repair the damage, which Noriega paid with disdain. But that was the first serious attack on the dictator and led eventually to his removal.

By February 1988, a Florida grand jury brought criminal indictments against him for drug trafficking. Encouraged by Ambassador Davis, Panama's President Eric Arturo Delvalle fired General Noriega. Eight hours later, Noriega had the National Assembly fire the president, who went into hiding. Ambassador Davis harbored dissidents seeking safety in his residence.

In Washington, the former assistant secretary of state William D. Rogers, now a partner at Arnold and Porter, saw that Panama's U.S. bank accounts were closed. Noriega short-circuited a military coup, and several large American companies made early tax payments to help him out. But Panama's economy went into a severe decline.

A battle raged between Assistant Secretary Elliott Abrams and the Defense Department. Abrams now wanted Noriega removed, but the Pentagon stonewalled. "They were just throwing in the kitchen sink in an effort to tell you that you couldn't confront Noriega," Abrams told reporter Kevin Buckley. Buckley judged that Abrams' "ineptitude" had helped Noriega survive. President Reagan sent thirteen hundred troops to Panama to protect American citizens, and, finally, Reagan agreed to drop the indictments if Noriega withdrew.

In May 1989, the Panamanian people voted to turn out the dictator. Observers, led by the former President Carter, were flown in from the United States to assure the results; Noriega suffered an overwhelming defeat. But he stole the election by having the army destroy ballots and polling places. The army fired tear gas at demonstrators and at the opposition candidates, and Noriega declared the election nullified.

President George H. W. Bush sent in two thousand American troops to protect Americans and recalled Ambassador Davis. The President said publicly that the Panamanians should get rid of Noriega. But Secretary of Defense Richard Cheney promised U.S. troops would not be used to decide who governs Panama, and he slowed down the dispatch of troops.

That October, Panamanian army Major Moises Giroldi, thinking he had U.S. cooperation, staged a coup and captured Noriega. After arguing with his colleagues, some of whom wanted to kill Noriega on the spot, Giroldi offered to turn over Noriega to U.S. Army headquarters. But the United States Army failed to block the roads against Noriega's forces, which were advancing on the capital. Noriega shot one rebel in the face and had the hands of another cut off. Major Giroldi was tortured and shot to death. Senator Jesse Helms, no friend of Noriega, called President Bush and his associates "a bunch of Keystone Kops."

On Saturday night, December 16, a carload of Marines off duty in Panama City was stopped at a Noriega roadblock, and First Lieutenant Robert Paz was shot and killed. That triggered an invasion three days later by 22,500 U.S. paratroopers and Rangers, who jumped into Panama City with "overwhelming force." Two hundred Panamanians, mostly civilians, were killed. The Panamanian army fired six rocket-propelled grenades into the U.S. Embassy compound. The Americans suffered 347 casualties, 60 percent of them from "friendly fire."

The Americans wrecked Panama City, but Noriega hid out until he could obtain asylum with the Papal Nuncio. On the day before Christmas, in the parking lot of a Dairy Queen ice cream stand, he turned himself over to the priests. Secretary Baker demanded that the Vatican transfer Noriega to the U.S. Army.

Deputy Secretary of State Lawrence Eagleburger arrived from Washington, and Noriega surrendered to American soldiers. He was sentenced to forty years in prison on drug charges. U.S. Ambassador Deane R. Hinton called the operation "the best drug bust in history." But two years later, Colombian drugs were again flowing through Panama to the United States, and "the white elite" was again in control of Panama.

40

Trujillo and Pinochet—Contrast in Violence

1960–2004

Officers of the U.S. Foreign Service played shadowy roles in the fate of two key Latin American dictators during the period after Fidel Castro took over in Cuba. These two affairs were handled with contrasting violence: in the Dominican Republic, the United States landed Marines; in Chile, the CIA acted with stealth.

While United States Marines governed the Dominican Republic from 1916 to 1924, they had trained Rafael Leonidas Trujillo. After the Marines left, he ruled the sugarcane country for thirty years. His dictatorship aroused such revulsion across Latin America that it was feared he would be replaced as had been Cuba's Fulgencio Batista, another made-in-the-U.S. dictator. One American diplomat tagged Trujillo and Batista "the underworld in epaulets."

Trujillo was assassinated in 1961, with some help from the United States. A decade later, President Nixon ordered the removal of Chile's elected president, Dr. Salvador Allende Gossens, who had nationalized the U.S.-owned copper mines. In 1973, General Augusto Pinochet Ugarte led a violent coup that disposed of Allende, and Nixon and his National Security Advisor Henry Kissinger welcomed Pinochet.

First, the Trujillo story.

TRUJILLO: "THE INGREDIENTS FOR THE SALAD"

At a cocktail party in the spring of 1960 in Ciudad Trujillo, the capital of the Dominican Republic, a leader of the political opposition to General Trujillo sidled up to U.S. Ambassador Joseph S. Farland and asked that the United States send him and his comrades rifles with telescopic sights.

The party was being given for Ambassador Farland, who had asked to be transferred when Trujillo insisted that embassy press officer Carl Davis be recalled. Farland, a former West Virginia businessman and wartime FBI agent, carried the request for rifles back to Washington, and President Eisenhower and Secretary of State Herter decided to help those planning a coup against Trujillo. Assistant Secretary for Inter-American Affairs Roy R. Rubottom arranged with the CIA to deliver to the rebels twelve sniper rifles with telescopic sights and five hundred rounds of ammunition. Deputy Chief of Mission Henry Dearborn, in Cuidad Trujillo, was told the rifles would be airdropped.

That June, Trujillo's agents tried to assassinate Venezuela's president, Rómulo Betancourt, and the Organization of American States (OAS) unanimously censured him. The United States broke off diplomatic relations with the Dominican Republic, reduced its embassy to a consulate general, shipped out most of its American staff, and imposed economic sanctions. Dearborn, who stayed on as chargé d'affaires and de facto CIA station chief, said that the only way to get rid of Trujillo was by assassination.

Thomas C. Mann replaced Assistant Secretary Rubottom in September, and Dearborn advised him to have the "Dominicans put an end to Trujillo before he leaves the island." When Kennedy became President, Dearborn wrote the State Department about a plot by Dominican dissidents. He used the metaphor of a picnic and reported that they did not have "the ingredients for the salad." Two .38 caliber pistols were shipped down; and three M1 carbines, which had been left in the naval attaché's office when the United States broke off relations, were passed to the dissidents. Four M3 machine guns were also sent to the Dominican Republic by diplomatic pouch, but they did not reach the dissidents.

When the Bay of Pigs invasion of Cuba failed in mid-April, the State Department and CIA, now suddenly gun-shy, urged the Dominicans to call off their assassination plan. But, if the Dominicans went ahead on their own, Kennedy assured Dearborn, the United States would support them.

Dearborn received instructions, approved by Under Secretary Chester Bowles, to continue to refuse to give out the machine guns. Although U.S. leaders were eager to avoid a "second Cuba," they were timid about being connected to an assassination. Dearborn later testified that he had understood it would be acceptable for the Dominicans to assassinate Trujillo without the United States' participation.

At about 10:15 on Tuesday night, May 30, 1961, the dictator was riding with his tough, well-armed chauffeur, Army Captain Zacaras de la Cruz, along the four-lane coastal highway on his way to San Cristóbal and a rendezvous with his mistress. A black car carrying seven Dominicans, with whom the Americans had been in touch, spotted Trujillo's baby-blue Chevrolet just south of the city. As they passed his car, a marksman aimed his shotgun at the backseat of the Chevy, and his first shot hit Trujillo. Zacaras grabbed a submachine gun and opened fire. Trujillo stumbled out, firing a .38. In minutes, it was over, and the sixty-nine-year-old dictator lay dead with five bullets in him. The assassins stuffed his body in their car's trunk and drove back to Cuidad Trujillo.

That midnight, Consul General Dearborn and his wife left a charity bridge party four miles from the assassination site. When they reached home, Consul General Dearborn received a telephone call informing him laconically in Spanish that Trujillo was dead. Dearborn walked through the gardens to the consulate and cabled the State Department.

In Paris, it was Wednesday evening when President Kennedy told his press secretary, Pierre Salinger, that Secretary of State Dean Rusk had just called from Washington and said Trujillo had been killed and that Rusk would not join them in Paris. A few moments later, Salinger held a press briefing at the Hôtel de Crillon and mentioned the assassination. His remark made headlines around the world because word of Trujillo's death had not yet been released. Secretary Rusk was worried that Salinger's announcement might lead Trujillo's sons to retaliate against Kennedy. All CIA personnel were flown out of the Dominican Republic.

The Dominican Republic was swept again by turmoil and factionalism. Trujillo's playboy older son, General Rafael "Ramfis" Trujillo, Jr., flew home from France in a chartered jet and took charge of the Dominican armed forces. The secret police tortured or killed most of the conspirators. The bloodbath went on for weeks.

On Saturday, November 18, Ramfis had six men who had participated in his father's assassination taken from jail on a ruse. When the wife of one of the prisoners heard they were being transferred, she raced to the U.S. consulate general, and with Consul General John Calvin Hill, Jr., who had replaced Dearborn, rushed to ask President Balaguer for help. But the six had already been taken to a Trujillo estate, where Ramfis and his friends executed them.

That same Saturday afternoon, Consul General Hill telephoned Lieutenant Colonel Edwin H. Simmons, of the U.S. Marine Corps, a decorated combat veteran of World War II and the Korean War. Before Trujillo was killed, Simmons had been the embassy's naval attaché, and now, in September 1961, he had returned as "military liaison officer" to the consulate general; diplomatic relations had been suspended, but not consular relations.

When Consul General Hill called, Simmons was downtown on the terrace of the Hotel Embajador talking with Juan Bosch, head of the Dominican Revolutionary Party. Simmons drove out to the Dominican military headquarters at San Isidro Air Base and met with Major General Fernando Sanchez, the Dominican air force's chief of staff. Petan Trujillo, the dictator's brother, threatened Simmons with a Thompson submachine gun until Sanchez called him off. Simmons warned Sanchez that an amphibious task force lay over the horizon and if needed its Marines would come ashore.

Sunday morning, the surprised citizens of Cuidad Trujillo awoke to see, just outside the three-mile limit, the missile cruiser USS *Little Rock* and three destroyers leading a task force of nearly forty ships, with Marine Expeditionary Unit 14 aboard.

That morning, Trujillo's brothers and their coconspirators flew to Florida. The next day, President Joaquín Balaguer, who had been Trujillo's former handpicked president, restored the capital's name to its original, Santo Domingo. Amidst political jockeying on December 12 and 13, rioting mobs forced the visa office of the U.S. consulate general to close.

The OAS restored diplomatic relations with the Dominican Republic on January 4, 1962. The United States reopened its embassy, and Hill was named chargé d'affaires. A mass demonstration forced President Balaguer to resign, and elections in December chose Juan Bosch, a social democrat, as the first democratically elected president in the country's history. He hung on to office for seven months with the support of U.S. Ambassador John Bartlow Martin.

Bosch was succeeded by Balaguer, which led directly to the bloody events of 1965. And Ambassador Martin was replaced by W. Tapley Bennett, Jr., a veteran Foreign Service officer on his first ambassadorial assignment. Bennett recommended that Washington support Donald J. Reid Cabral, who had opposed Trujillo and favored the big-business interests.

The Santo Domingo CIA station chief asserted that Reid was in trouble because the economy was under severe pressure from strikes, sabotage, and widespread corruption, but Ambassador Bennett continued to support him. Bennett departed on April 23, 1965, to visit his seriously ill mother in Georgia, and the next day bloody rioting began for the purpose of bringing Bosch back in office.

The U.S. chargé d'affaires in Santo Domingo, William B. Connett, Jr., was instructed to work with the Dominican armed forces to prevent Bosch and the Communists seizing power. Bosch's forces captured Radio Santo Domingo and stopped General Elias Wessin y Wessin from bringing his soldiers into the city. Bosch appeared to be the people's choice. On Sunday, April 25, army leaders arrested Reid.

The United States Embassy supported the generals against Bosch. On Sunday afternoon, April 25, the generals ordered the air force to strafe and the navy to shell the National Palace. By nightfall, thousands of Dominicans were demonstrating their willingness to fight for Bosch and against the military. Pro-Bosch leaders asked the U.S. Embassy to help stop further air attacks. They were turned down.

Monday morning, General Wessin y Wessin asked for American troops. The embassy refused the request, and Connett was instructed to start evacuating American citizens, with the help of Marines in a task force offshore. As the fighting spread, more than thirty people were killed, and two hundred were wounded.

Embassy officers felt that a show of force by the anti-Bosch military was needed before political negotiations could be successful. Bennett returned to his embassy Tuesday afternoon and tried to persuade Bosch's men to lay down their arms. The anti-Bosch military strafed and bombarded the city again.

During the night, pro-Bosch forces stopped General Wessin y Wessin's troops; and the next afternoon, Ambassador Bennett recommended to Washington that the Marines be landed immediately because, he claimed, American lives were in danger. By 6:00 P.M., President Johnson approved the landing of five hundred Marines from the helicopter carrier USS *Boxer*.

These were the first combat-ready U.S. forces to invade a Latin American country in more than three decades. U.S. foreign policy, which was intended to improve relations between the United States and her southern neighbors, had been overruled.

By dawn on Friday, April 30, the White House converted the invaders into an OAS-directed Inter-American Peace Force led by a Brazilian general. Meanwhile, Ellsworth Bunker, U.S. ambassador to the OAS, tried to obtain a cease-fire through the Papal Nuncio in Santo Domingo.

Foreign Service officers were sent to Venezuela and Costa Rica to marshal support for the U.S. action. Ambassador Averell Harriman, Under Secretary Mann, and Arthur Schlesinger, Jr., were all instructed to get in touch with Latin American governments. John Bartlow Martin was sent back to Santo Domingo to help Ambassador Bennett. The President ordered Carl Rowan, director of the U.S. Information Agency, to mount a campaign to put the intervention in a good light. But all efforts to establish a cease-fire failed.

The Dominican military was unable to retake the city. The U.S. Marines, advancing eastward, met resistance; one was killed and eight were wounded trying to link up with the 82d Airborne moving westward on the other side of the city. Early Friday afternoon, the U.S. Embassy came under fire, and Bennett had to go into his bathroom to talk with the Papal Nuncio, Emanuele Clarizo. They drove to San Isidro and worked out a cease-fire with the junta, despite the bitterness between the two groups struggling for control of the Dominican Republic. American troops stopped advancing and returned to their positions.

By Sunday afternoon, May 2, it was agreed that the Americans could link up in order to guard the evacuation of some five thousand American and foreign citizens, a purpose the OAS would accept. There were now 2,200 U.S. soldiers and Marines ashore and another ten thousand aboard ships off the coast—an excessive number, for sure.

On May 6, four more Marines were killed and several were wounded. By the end of the month, the first Latin American troops, Brazilians, arrived, and U.S. forces started to withdraw.

The U.S. military intervention was condemned throughout Latin America. And Secretary Rusk agreed that the United States, at the least, had failed to explain its concerns and actions to the American people and the world.

. . .

Ellsworth Bunker represented the United States on a three-man OAS commission, which arrived in Santo Domingo on June 3 to negotiate a settlement. He had developed a reputation as a skillful negotiator when he had moderated between Sukarno's Indonesia and The Netherlands to avoid a war over western New Guinea and again later when he negotiated between Egypt and Saudi Arabia over civil war in Yemen. Bunker had graduated from Yale (where Dean Acheson had been his rowing coach) and had a successful career in his family's sugar-refining business. Then, in 1951, just before his fifty-seventh birthday, he entered public service as ambassador to Juan Perón's Argentina. He was now seventy-one.

Once in Santo Domingo, Bunker appealed directly to the public in order to establish a temporary government that would hold honest elections. Helicopters blanketed the country with seventy thousand copies of the commission's proclamation. Still, even with Bunker's negotiating skills, it took until September to install a government.

In the June 1, 1966, election, Balaguer easily defeated Bosch, allegedly with help from the United States. This time, he stayed in office until 1974. U.S. Ambassador John Hugh Crimmins, who had been Bennett's deputy chief of mission, was ordered to support Balaguer, starting with a $40 million loan. Crimmins knew covert activities. When Trujillo was assassinated, he had eased out the family members who tried to hold on to control. And after the Cuban missile crisis, he had coordinated efforts to prevent freelance invasions of Cuba by Cuban exiles in Miami. Crimmins' purpose now was to prevent the Dominican Republic from becoming "another Cuba."

Throughout Latin America, U.S. armed forces had again aroused the fear of U.S. imperialism. Even former Ambassador Martin called the Dominican intervention "illegal," and Senator J. William Fulbright, chairman of the Senate Foreign Relations Committee, said it was a violation of inter-American law. But Bunker's patient diplomacy restored some of the United States' reputation for fairness.

PINOCHET, A HAND WELL HIDDEN

At times, the U.S. government overturned the results of a reasonably free and fair election abroad. A catastrophic instance of destroying a constitutional government occurred in 1970 in Chile, which had one of the more democratic political systems in the Western Hemisphere and significantly large U.S. economic investments.

U.S. Ambassador Claude G. Bowers had been posted in Santiago from 1939 to 1953, and thoroughly appreciated Chile's democratic roots. Outspokenly anti-Fascist and anti-Communist, Bowers had previously served as the envoy to civil-war-torn Spain from 1933 to 1939. In Chile, he witnessed how World War II divided the country and how it was not until victory seemed fairly certain that it joined the Allies.

Bowers understood that Chile's landed and industrial elite dominated the country. He believed that the United States businessmen who owned the copper mines and nitrate deposits had Chile's interest at heart. In the three presidential elections during his time in Chile, he saw that U.S. entrepreneurs had not intervened. Later, they would.

As early as 1947, Bowers believed that the U.S. would be better off if it gave its Latin American friends economic rather than military assistance. He wrote, "The landing of the marines in Nicaragua and other foolish acts of our adolescence, when Dollar Diplomacy was in full flower, have rendered no service to the friendly relations among nations anywhere in South America." And he added, "Our too great reliance on military might for defense against the encroachment of communism fails to take into consideration the reason for the progress the communists have made in countries in need of economic aid."

In the 1950s, the ascension of Castro and the U.S.-arranged overthrow of the elected president, Jacobo Arbenz Guzman, in Guatemala produced anti-Americanism throughout the hemisphere. These protests made U.S. diplomats suspicious of the intentions of the young Socialist senator Salvador Allende Gossens, suspicions that in time would bear tragic results.

When the demand for copper declined in the 1950s, and U.S. and indigenous companies laid off workers, Americans feared Chile would succumb to Communism. Senator Allende built leftist coalitions and, by 1958, was nominated for the presidency. He almost won then, shocking the State Department. Twelve years later, he was elected president of Chile.

. . .

On August 5, 1970, Deputy Assistant Secretary of State for Inter-American Affairs John Hugh Crimmins (the former ambassador to the Dominican Republic) cabled U.S. ambassador Edward M. Korry in Santiago, asking what should be the U.S. attitude if the Chilean military prevented the inauguration of socialist candidate Allende. Korry, who openly disapproved of Allende, replied that a military coup was impossible.

The CIA had vigorously opposed Allende in the previous presidential election of September 1964. Eduardo Frei of the Christian Democratic party won that election overwhelmingly, and Kissinger, at the time national security advisor, asked State, Defense, and the CIA to study the effect of a coup in Chile. The study, known as NSSM 97, concluded that Allende posed no threat to the United States.

The next election, on September 4, 1970, gave Allende the largest percentage of votes for president. Finishing a close second was Jorge Alessandri Rodríguez, the candidate preferred by the U.S. government and by the international companies doing business in Chile. Chile's constitution said if no candidate had a majority, its congress would choose between the two candidates with the most votes. Traditionally, Chile's congress chose the one with the plurality.

Ambassador Korry sent Washington eighteen reports, which became known as "Korrygrams" because of their length and the prominence of his opinions. To prevent Allende coming to office, Korry proposed earmarking a $250,000 fund to bribe members of the Chilean congress. But after the funds were authorized, Korry decided that if word leaked out, the backlash would be disastrous across the hemisphere.

Even after Allende was elected, President Nixon was determined to prevent him from taking office. He feared Allende would create Latin America's second Communist government, redistribute income, and nationalize major foreign-owned industries. Historian Robert Dallek charged that Nixon's fear was "nothing more than paranoia."

Officers of the large American companies in Chile met repeatedly with high State Department and CIA officials to discuss the threat. International Telephone and Telegraph (ITT), owner of Chile's telephone company, offered to put up $1 million to help the government stop Allende and to serve as a conduit to distribute $8 million to the opposition.

Nixon instructed the CIA to organize a military coup d'état to prevent

Allende's inauguration on November 4; $10 million was allocated for this purpose. Once again, Nixon demonstrated his distrust of the State Department. No one from the State or Defense departments was present at the White House meeting, and no one was told of the proposed coup. Kissinger ensured that the U.S. Embassy in Santiago and Ambassador Korry were not informed.

The U.S. Embassy's military attaché in Santiago was instructed to work with the CIA to deny the presidency to Allende. And he was ordered not to tell the ambassador, his direct superior on the scene, what he was doing. Leaders in Washington were prepared to deceive not only their perceived enemies but also their own colleagues. The Senate Select Committee to Study Governmental Operations with Respect to Intelligence Activities, chaired by Senator Frank F. Church, and known as the Church committee, found the CIA understood that the "American hand [was to] be well hidden."

The U.S. strategy to prevent Allende from occupying the presidency was split into two parts, Track 1 and Track 2. The State Department followed Track 1 to create economic and political chaos, and the White House and CIA moved on Track 2, closely held, which would promote a coup by the Chilean military.

Ambassador Korry later told the Church committee that he had been kept ignorant of the existence of Track 2. But, in fact, he met on September 20 with Chile's defense minister and minister of the economy and discussed "steps that President Frei could take in order to precipitate a constitutional crisis." Korry told the defense minister "a favorable parliamentary solution is no longer in the cards."

Korry advised Charles A. Meyer, assistant secretary of state for inter-American affairs, that General Rene Schneider, commander in chief of Chile's army, had indicated that "under any conditions, he would do nothing to prevent Allende's election by congress." The ambassador warned: "If necessary, General Schneider would have to be neutralized, by displacement if necessary."

By early October, the CIA sent tear gas grenades and submachine guns to Chile in the State Department diplomatic pouch. Colonel Paul Wimert, the embassy's military attaché, delivered them in the middle of the night to a group of Chileans planning the coup.

High Chilean officers opposed to Allende planned to kidnap General Schneider. On October 22, plotters attempted, and botched, the kidnapping. They ambushed, shot, and severely wounded Schneider. He died three days later.

The Chilean people's disgust at Schneider's murder assured Allende of the congress' vote. And this unintended outcome forced the CIA to bring in a new network of agents. The CIA later admitted it had given $35,000 to the group that killed Schneider. Ambassador Korry told the Church committee that the murder was "grotesque and inexcusable."

President Nixon expected that Ambassador Korry would work separately with the generals to organize a military coup that would prevent Allende's inauguration. The generals were to be warned that if Allende took office, U.S. military assistance would dry up.

When Korry did not organize a military coup, he claimed that CIA Station Chief Henry Hecksher confronted him, "shouting at me." Korry gave Hecksher twenty-four hours to accept the fact that he was Hecksher's superior or to leave the country. After that run-in, Korry realized the CIA was hiding things from him.

Other ambassadors have complained about being cut out by the CIA. Ambassador John O. Bell, successor to John J. Muccio in Guatemala, had asserted that Muccio learned only from *The New York Times* that people were being trained in Guatemala for the Bay of Pigs. Bell blamed the assistant secretary of state, who had agreed that the ambassador did not need to know. Bell said, "This I think was unforgivable."

In Washington, the ambiguously named A40 Committee, and its equally disguised predecessors, were assigned the responsibility of making sure covert operations abroad in peacetime were deniable. And in 1954, Eisenhower's administration had imposed some oversight on the CIA with NSC 5412, requiring that the director of central intelligence coordinate the planning and conduct of covert operations with the secretaries of state and defense.

In the case of Chile, it was said that the 40 Committee was not informed of Track-2 activities. But the committee was known to have approved a $1.2 million contingency fund with which Ambassador Korry was to control the Chilean election, purchase a radio station for use against Allende, and pay for a variety of other anti-Allende programs. An ITT cablegram verified that Korry was moving against Allende.

Korry contended that, in opposition to the views of the State Department, an Allende government would be the same as a Communist government and worse than a Castro government. If Korry did know about

Track 2, he lied to the Senate committee; if he did not know, his position as an American ambassador was untenable. Senator Church told him he should have been "outraged."

Nixon and Kissinger's preinauguration intrigue failed. Chile's congress voted for Allende, 153 to 35. He took office and promptly adopted a course that many regarded as Marxist. After Korry said he had been instructed to do anything short of a Dominican-type murder to keep Allende out, the President exclaimed to his press secretary about Korry, as recorded on tape, "But he just failed, the son of a bitch. That was his main problem. He should have kept Allende from getting in." Secretary of State William Rogers considered recalling Korry and forcing him to retire, but Alexander Haig advised finding him another post to keep him quiet.

Two days after Allende's inauguration, the U.S. National Security Council met in the Cabinet Room to review the situation. Both Secretary Rogers and Secretary of Defense Melvin Laird urged that everything possible be done to bring down Allende. President Nixon voiced the strategy: "We'll be very cool and very correct" toward Chile.

Assistance, loans, and credit were quietly blocked to squeeze Chile's economy into decline. The United States covertly helped Allende's opponents. Kissinger issued a top-secret memorandum, NSDM 93, dated November 9, that said the United States will limit Chile's "ability to implement policies contrary to U.S. and hemisphere interests."

Allende proposed expropriating all foreign copper mines and applied "excess profits taxes" retroactively to counteract any compensation negotiated for the United States. He also declared a moratorium on Chile's foreign debt payments.

This U.S. economic offensive against Allende was part of Track 1. Ambassador Korry dreamt up a catalogue of crises to damage Chile's economy and frighten the public. And despite State Department opposition, the CIA urged private groups to incite a military coup. The CIA's Richard Helms wrote that U.S. policy would "make the economy scream."

The New York Times reported that in 1972 the CIA "heavily subsidized" a massive truck shutdown organized by the truck owners. Ambassador Korry declared that "not a nut or bolt will be allowed to reach a Chile under Allende." By late 1972, a significant number of trucks and buses stopped running because of a lack of spare parts. The United States policies created financial chaos, unemployment, and violence, but they failed to dislodge Allende.

Chile's economy was chiefly dependent on foreign-exchange earnings from one product, copper, and U.S. companies controlled 80 percent of Chile's copper. The nationalization of copper was a political issue in Chile as far back as 1932, when the then U.S. ambassador William Culbertson had supported a right-wing coup to bolster U.S. interests. The CIA began covert operations in Chile in 1961, and Korry said that when he first arrived as ambassador in October 1967, after serving as ambassador to Ethiopia, he told Chile's leaders that they had a sovereign right to nationalize copper or anything else they wanted to, as long as they paid for it appropriately. By 1970, Chile's foreign indebtedness reached $3 billion, the price of copper plunged, and the nation's trade deficit rose. Chileans blamed the United States.

Less than a year after taking office, Allende amended the constitution to nationalize the copper mines and other large foreign-owned companies. Every one of the 158 representatives in the Chilean congress voted for the amendment.

Still, nationalization alienated many Chileans, and compensation for the nationalized U.S. companies became a prime economic issue. They could expect none. Companies fought back, transferring abroad capital and technicians, and the U.S. government tried to make it impossible for Allende to govern.

The Allende government also pursued land reform, and by the middle of 1972 it had expropriated almost all estates over about 190 acres (80 hectares). But most farm workers, the campesinos, did not receive land, and rural unemployment remained a problem. Kissinger said Chile "moved toward totalitarianism." But, somehow, he still asserted, "The slide to chaos owed nothing to American intervention."

Ambassador Korry was replaced in October 1971 by Nathaniel Davis, a professional Foreign Service officer who had served as minister to Bulgaria and ambassador to Guatemala. He was told "to aid the opposition by any means possible."

On November 1, 1973, Ambassador Davis was invited to talk with General Augusto Pinochet, leader of the military junta. Davis brought up human rights, and Pinochet said the bloodshed would be worse if the army permitted leftists to obtain arms. Davis reported to the Secretary of State, "I reiterated assurances of the good will of the [U.S. government] and our desire to be helpful." Nearly three years later, Kissinger repeated virtually that same assurance to Pinochet, saying, "We want to help, not undermine you."

While Korry never held another Foreign Service post, Davis went on to become Director General of the Foreign Service and assistant secretary of state for African affairs. Foreign ministers of forty-three African nations opposed Davis' appointment as assistant secretary, and he soon resigned because, he said, Kissinger and William Colby, director of the CIA, authorized sending $10 million worth of arms covertly to factions fighting a civil war in Angola.

How well the United States' role in Chile was hidden and how Ambassador Korry was crushed by the CIA's mandate were demonstrated when Korry told the Church committee that he "did not know about Track II." But Korry was surely disingenuous when he testified that one could not say the United States proposed to overthrow Allende's government because "there was no government at that time. . . . To say overthrow the government, there has to be a government in power. He hadn't even been confirmed in office."

Korry estimated to the Church committee that U.S. investment in Chile amounted to $2 billion "voted mostly by this Congress." In addition, Chile enjoyed great private investments from ITT, Anaconda, Kennecott, Firestone, W. R. Grace, Pepsi-Cola, and other major corporations. And Korry admitted that he had recommended buying the support of the leading opposition newspaper *El Mercurio* for U.S. political purposes. Still, Korry, a former foreign correspondent for the United Press and the European editor of *Look* magazine, claimed that "without our assistance the free press" under Allende "would have collapsed." At the same time, Korry castigated "the idiots in the CIA" and characterized Chile's military as "toy soldiers."

The CIA, especially its Santiago station, were the hard chargers for a military-coup solution in Chile. The CIA reported it "actively supported the military Junta after the overthrow of Allende." Its report went on:

These Cold War attitudes persisted into the Pinochet era. After Pinochet came to power, senior policymakers appeared reluctant to criticize human rights violations, taking to task US diplomats urging greater attention to the problem. US military assistance and sales grew significantly during the years of greatest human rights abuses.

Kissinger's NSC staff aide William J. Jorden reported that the Chilean military was plotting against Allende. Strikes, demonstrations, and violence spread in the cities. Allende declared a state of emergency, and on August 9 he reluctantly brought the military into his cabinet. On August 15, bombs were found outside the homes of three U.S. Embassy officers.

PINOCHET'S SUCCESSFUL COUP

Responding to the mounting pressures, both foreign and domestic, in August 1973, President Allende made a major miscalculation. When the commander in chief of the army resigned as a result of CIA intrigue, Allende promoted Augusto Pinochet Ugarte, the army's second most senior officer, to be its commander in chief. Allende assumed that Pinochet, a professional army officer, would remain neutral in the political battles. He was wrong.

Pinochet headed a group of army leaders who, at 8:00 A.M. on September 11, launched a carefully prepared coup. The fighting centered on La Moneda, the massive two-story stone presidential palace. The army entered it by noon. Allende was killed by gunfire; the political right said he committed suicide and the left charged that the army killed him. The American embassy reported his death as a suicide. By 2:30 P.M. La Moneda surrendered.

The next day, Colonel Carlos Urrutia, military attaché at the U.S. Embassy, met with Pinochet to discuss political plans and recognition. Protesting what he called "political mythology," Henry Kissinger, who became Secretary of State at that time, said that, although Allende had an "implacable ideological hatred of the United States . . . our government had nothing to do with planning his overthrow and no involvement with the plotters."

The military junta arrested Allende's aides and executed at least seventy-two of them. It shut down the congress, banned political parties, censored the press, fired university rectors and teachers, and declared martial law. A new and brutal secret police (DINA) organized assassinations of the junta's opponents at home and in exile abroad. Thousands of Chileans were jailed and tortured; many, including two U.S. citizens, were executed or just disappeared.

Two days after Allende's death, the Nixon White House cabled Ambassador Davis to tell Pinochet that the U.S. government welcomed strengthening ties between Chile and the United States. Privately, Kissinger told his staff, "However unpleasant they act, this government is better for us than Allende was."

When Pinochet was officially appointed president late in 1974, the United States recognized the junta and reinstated financial aid to Chile. The U.S. Embassy and its CIA component helped the new government gain strength and respectability. The Americans appreciated Pinochet's free-market economic policies. Companies that Allende had nationalized were returned to private ownership. But Allende's most ardent leftist adherents continued to believe that a Socialist revolution could flower out of democratic political soil.

President Nixon had achieved his goal of bringing down Allende. But endorsing his successors proved difficult and embarrassing. Seventeen years of horrors began for Chile. The DINA arranged that 3,200 people were executed or disappeared. Some were shot; some imprisoned without charges or trial; some were thrown alive down mine shafts; some were dumped into the ocean from helicopters after their stomachs had been split open while they were still alive so their bodies would not float. The forms of torture were grotesque and sadistic.

Through it all, Pinochet had supporters among Chile's businessmen, whose companies had been taken over, and among landowners, who had lost their estates. Others risked their lives against the Pinochet dictatorship; still others waited until the nightmare was over.

U.S. officials, including Korry, Meyer, and Kissinger continued to insist that the United States had not brought about Allende's downfall and death. A *New York Times* editorial in 1973 said those denials "have encountered worldwide skepticism" but that "there is no evidence of American complicity in the coup." An article in *Foreign Affairs* agreed that there was no proof that the United States had tried to remove Allende. But within a year, the facts began to appear. William Colby, the CIA's director, revealed that the Nixon administration had spent $8 million covertly to "destabilize" Allende's regime.

Kissinger played power-politics hardball. He believed that regimes that supported American interests should be supported. Whether they indulged internally in human rights abuses (torture, assassination, etc.) was irrelevant. But the current of American thinking was flowing in the opposite direction. Under congressional pressure, in mid-1974 Kissinger had to accept a human rights office in the State Department, and Section 502B of the 1974 Foreign Assistance Act required the State Department to report on foreign human rights violations. Deputy Secretary Robert Ingersoll ordered all diplomatic and consular posts to support human rights, but Kissinger still refused to connect aid to human rights. That would require more time and a different administration.

General Vernon Walters, the CIA's deputy director, conferred with Pinochet in Santiago. And the head of Chile's DINA, General Manuel Contreras, traveled to Washington in 1975 and discussed with Walters how the Chile regime could dodge congressional opposition and still obtain U.S. military equipment. Decades later, the CIA acknowledged that for a time Contreras had been in its pay.

OPERATION CONDOR

In May 1975, Ambassador David H. Popper endorsed a report "maintaining and strengthening the present government in Chile." Some Foreign Service officers in Santiago protested Popper's response to Pinochet's violations of human rights, and four Foreign Service officers in the embassy signed a dissent saying tougher measures were needed to change Chile's behavior regarding human rights. The Kissinger-Popper view prevailed but the number of dissenters grew.

That November, the intelligence services of five South American nations (Argentina, Bolivia, Chile, Paraguay, and Uruguay) met in Santiago and organized Operation Condor to eliminate Marxist terrorism and subversion on the continent. (Brazil, Ecuador, and Peru joined later.) The CIA soon knew that Operation Condor planned political assassinations. Over the next five years, Operation Condor agents carried out political murders and disappearances throughout South America. In 1978, Ambassador Robert E. White in Paraguay informed Secretary Vance that Operation Condor was using an American communications installation in the Panama Canal Zone.

Kissinger used an Organization of American States general assembly meeting in Santiago to confer in person with Pinochet on June 8, 1976, and to assure him of U.S. support. And the CIA finally informed the State Department that Operation Condor participated in assassination. A month later, Operation Condor became infamous with a shocking act of terrorism in downtown Washington, D.C. Pinochet's secret police directed anti-Castro Cuban exiles in the murder of Orlando Letelier, who had been Allende's ambassador to the United States and his defense minister. Michael Townley, an American who became a DINA assassin, taped a homemade, remote-controlled bomb under the driver's seat of Letelier's Chevrolet, parked in the driveway of his Bethesda, Maryland, home. Early on the morning of September 21, while Letelier was driving to work around Sheridan Circle near the White House, the Cuban exiles exploded the bomb under his car, blowing off his legs. Letelier's young American colleague, Ronni K. Moffitt, was also killed; her husband, Michael, was thrown clear and survived. When Townley confessed to the FBI, he implicated the Chilean government; but Pinochet brazenly claimed that Townley was run by the CIA.

The killing of Letelier, together with Jimmy Carter's election, frayed the Pinochet regime's relations with Washington. Carter, conditioned by the Vietnam War and Watergate, felt strongly that human rights were important in international affairs. Although his emphasis on human rights was extremely controversial and not always successful, it injected a new dimension into the debate over American foreign policy.

U.S. Ambassador George Landau threatened that the Letelier terrorist act on U.S. soil would not go "unpunished," but after years of haggling, nothing substantive was done. In August 1981, Jeane Kirkpatrick, Ronald Reagan's ambassador to the UN, met with Pinochet in Santiago and announced the desire "to fully normalize our relations with Chile."

Pinochet imposed a constitution that reinforced his power and permitted him to remain in office until 1989. Chile's economy plunged into recession, and political protests multiplied. Before a plebiscite on October 5, 1988, U.S. Ambassador Harry Barnes helped get out the opposition vote and ensured a fair count. Although Pinochet ruthlessly suppressed the opposition, the plebiscite produced a 55 percent vote against continuing his regime. The angry dictator had to accept the results.

At the end of 1989, things began to change. Elections brought Christian Democratic leader Patricio Aylwin to the presidency of Chile. The secret police were disbanded, and its chief was imprisoned for Orlando Letelier's murder. Overall, Chile's security forces were found to be responsible for 1,102 disappearances and 2,095 certain deaths during Pinochet's rule.

Among those victims were at least four American citizens known to have been murdered, three in Chile and Ronni Moffitt in Washington. Embassy personnel in Santiago and some at the State Department were criticized for failing to save the lives of Charles Horman, Frank Teruggi, and Boris Weisfeiler and for failing even to determine who was responsible for their deaths. Foreign Service officers were denounced for ineptness and disinterest.

Pinochet finally surrendered his position as the army's commander in chief in 1998, but he clung to his immunity from prosecution for human rights abuses. When Pinochet was in London for spinal surgery of a herniated disc, Scotland Yard officers arrested him in his hospital bed. He was held under house arrest in Britain during a long trial, and in 2000 he was allowed to return to Chile.

A Chilean court decided on May 28, 2004, that Pinochet no longer could claim immunity. The family of General Rene Schneider announced they would sue the United States government and Henry Kissinger for Schneider's murder. Kissinger denied his involvement; he explained in an interview years later, "Human rights were not an international issue at the time."

By 2004, 311 Chilean military officers had been convicted and sentenced or faced human rights charges. A national commission judged that 28,000 people had been tortured during Pinochet's dictatorship. His hidden fortune was estimated at $27 million. He was pursued through the courts, although he insisted he had saved Chile from Communism. When he died in 2006, more than three hundred criminal charges were still pending against him in Chile.

After the Pinochet experience, a disastrous military coup that sought to upset a democratically elected government would commonly be called "a Chilean solution."

41

Dangerous Diplomacy

1960—78

Today, more career Foreign Service officers than ever serve in the backwaters of the world. As colonies have converted into independent nations, more embassy assignments are regarded as too hazardous to allow wives and families to accompany American diplomats. Some officers serve at "presence posts," where they are the lone representative of the United States.

Harlan Cleveland, assistant secretary for international organization affairs, said, with a touch of irony, "Statesmanship is in direct proportion to one's distance from the problem." It is difficult to stand aloof when one's boots are in the mud.

AFSA vice president Steven Kashkett remembers that when he joined the Foreign Service in 1980 there were only two "hardship posts": Beirut and Bogotá. Beirut was notorious as the scene of an early U.S. consular murder. In 1937, Consul General J. Theodore Marriner, a Foreign Service veteran of nineteen years, was shot to death by a young Armenian who mistakenly believed that Marriner had refused him a visa to return to the United States. And Bogotá was well known as the base of various armed political factions, which were often involved in the violent cocaine trade.

Now, Steven Kashkett estimates, two-thirds of overseas Foreign Service missions earn the rating of hardship posts. This revolution influences the kind of people who are attracted to the Foreign Service, raises questions about the kind of careers they can expect, and reflects the changing role of the Foreign Service. Officers at hardship posts have vastly different stories to tell from the appointees assigned to the more sophisticated capitals of Europe.

Of course, first world posts also have their dangers:

> Laurence A. Steinhardt, ambassador to Canada, was killed in an aircraft crash in 1950. He had already served as minister to Sweden and ambassador to Peru, Turkey, Czechoslovakia, and to Moscow during the Nazi invasion of the Soviet Union.
>
> Douglas R. Smith encountered danger in Sofia, Bulgaria, where he had the "dissident portfolio." He says, "For a year and a half I went to meetings in underpasses and obscure cafés."
>
> U. S. Ambassador Armin H. Meyer was attacked by a knife-wielding Japanese in July 1969 while accompanying Secretary of State William Rogers to the Tokyo airport.

Exemplifying how Foreign Service officers can come in harm's way are two stories of officers serving in hardship posts, one in the Congo in Africa and the other in Guyana on the tropical Atlantic coast of South America.

THE CONGO, AN AVALANCHE TURNS VICIOUS

Men of a ragged rebel army, some led by witch doctors waving wands to protect them from harm, entered Stanleyville on the Congo River on Tuesday, August 4, 1964. They trooped past the white, ground-hugging American consulate; and by evening, these rebels and national troops were firing wildly at each other across the consulate's broad lawn.

Stanleyville sits where the Congo River first becomes navigable on its way to the Atlantic. The site had been "discovered" by Henry Morton Stanley in 1877; and a river boat captain with the pen name of Joseph Conrad stopped there in 1890, witnessed the Belgians' brutal exploitation of the local people, and wrote *Heart of Darkness*.

At Wednesday noon, August 5, a dozen rebels armed with automatic weapons forced their way into the American consulate. To escape their fire, Consul Michael P. E. Hoyt crawled to the CIA's room-size steel communications vault. Four Americans were among those in the vault (a fifth,

Ernie Houle, was still in the staff apartments). The Congolese tried to break into the vault; the Americans feared for their lives.

At nightfall, the attacks stopped; the rebels had found the consulate's whiskey supply. At about nine, in the silent darkness, the burly, thirty-four-year-old Hoyt led the Americans out of the vault, and they radioed the U.S. Embassy in Leopoldville.

Consul Hoyt had been in Stanleyville for only three weeks. He had been sent there from the Leopoldville embassy by Ambassador G. Mc-Murtrie Godley II, a career Foreign Service officer, whom Hoyt served as second secretary. Hoyt had shipped his three older sons home and flown with his wife, Jo, and their two-year-old youngest son, Evans, a thousand miles into the heart of Africa to take temporary charge of the riverbank consulate.

As a consequence of World War II, Africa, in particular, experienced "a great avalanche of decolonization," as Sir Brian Urquhart, a former undersecretary general of the United Nations, called it. The United Nations estimated that 750 million people, almost one-third of the world's population, lived in colonies and dependent trust territories in 1945. Two decades later, more than eighty colonies had gained independence and fewer than two million people still lived in such colonies. In Africa alone, the State Department sent envoys to twenty-one new nations.

The Republic of the Congo was abruptly granted independence from Belgium in July 1960. Although the Congo was one of the largest and potentially richest countries in Africa, the Belgians had not prepared the Congolese for self-governance, and so the new nation immediately began to fall apart. When leftist Prime Minister Patrice Lumumba was assassinated in January 1961, a United Nations intervention sought to restore stability. Then, Brian Urquhart had a major responsibility for rushing peacemaking troops from ten nations to the Congo, until conservatives led by Moise Tshombe could gain control.

When the UN left in 1964, radical nationalist leaders, who distrusted both the Belgians and the Americans, saw another chance to seize control. Lumumba's successors led a rebellion in the eastern Congo, but the United States supported the central government in Leopoldville, and Consul Hoyt was sent to keep the flag flying in Stanleyville.

As the rebels advanced on Stanleyville in August 1964, Belgian companies still operating in the area shipped their employees' wives and children out of danger. At Hoyt's request, the U.S. Embassy agreed to send planes to evacuate Americans.

Ambassador Godley ordered Hoyt; David Grinwis, the CIA representative with the cover of vice consul; and communicator James Stauffer, a former navy radio operator, to stay behind if the rebels seized the city. The evacuation took place on Tuesday. But two staff members, Ernie Houle, a retired navy chief petty officer and now the file clerk, and Donald Parkes, a former navy radio man, did not make it out.

On Thursday, the Americans were cheered by a new plan to rescue them: an armed helicopter would be landed on the consulate lawn. The ambassador had changed his mind and now wanted to remove all the consulate staff. But it was too late.

At about 6:00 P.M., another band of rebels demanded to enter the consulate; they shoved Hoyt and Grinwis around and drove off with the consulate's cars. The rebels calling themselves Simbas, or lions, appeared to be drunk or on drugs. They fired mortars and automatic weapons into the city. The Americans spent most of the night under their steel desks.

On Friday, Hoyt called off the helicopter rescue mission because it would be too dangerous. The Simbas swarmed over the city, beating up Belgians. Unburied bodies lay in the streets. Hoyt wrote later, "We now had to concentrate on diplomacy to extricate ourselves."

By the week's end, Ambassador W. Averell Harriman flew to Brussels to persuade the Belgians to send military aid to the Congo. The result was a compromise; Belgium sent advisors, and the United States sent military equipment.

As things quieted down in Stanleyville, the Americans gathered in the Belgian consulate to meet with consuls of seven other nations. Hoyt and the other consuls met with the rebel general, Nicholas Olenga, on Monday, August 10. The general was conciliatory to the other consuls, but angrily declared the Americans personae non grata.

The next day, a group of militant Simbas invaded the American consulate. One of them struck Hoyt with a rifle butt and ground his eyeglasses into the floor. They forced the Americans to try to eat the American flag, piled them into a truck, and carried them at breakneck speed to rebel headquarters. The Americans were frightened but eventually were returned to the consulate.

On Wednesday afternoon, the Simba "president," Christophe Gbenye, who had been Lumumba's minister of interior, took Hoyt and Grinwis to the Stanleyville central prison. They were dumped into a blood-spattered cell and left there. That evening, another Simba officer arrived and freed them with apologies. The chaos was nerve-racking. The next day, the Americans were placed under what amounted to house arrest until Friday, August 21.

On that day, General Olenga ordered that all Americans would be tried by a military court and executed. Playing for time, Hoyt agreed to send the embassy a telex asking the U.S. government to stop assisting the central Congolese government. Then, the Americans were taken to the airport, where the Simbas forced them to undress, jump, and dance to avoid their bayonets, finally locking them in a toilet overnight. They could hear drums beating outside.

They were moved to a cottage in the Sabena Airline guesthouse complex and locked up again in the filthy airport toilet. It was now thirty-two days since the consulate had been attacked. The Americans were beaten and returned to a bare cell in the central prison for ten more days.

The Organization of African Unity (OAU) created a seven-nation commission to establish a cease-fire and save the hundreds of hostages in Stanleyville. The commission sent a delegation to Washington to cut off American military aid to the Congo. President Johnson and the State Department declined to meet with the mission unless it included members of the Congo government. In Nairobi, Kenya, the scene of the violent Mau Mau rebellion in the 1950s, U.S. Ambassador William Attwood persuaded President Jomo Kenyatta to accept the OAU delegates as his personal envoys, which allowed the Africans to save face.

On Wednesday, September 25, a Red Cross DC-3 arrived at Stanleyville. It was the first airplane to land there since the rebel takeover, and it brought in Swiss doctors and medicines. But the rebels did not permit it to evacuate any of the 1,300 Europeans in Stanleyville, including many women and children. Hoyt hoped the Americans would be allowed to see the Red Cross representative, but the next day the Red Cross plane left. President Gbenye was using the whites as hostages to prevent Stanleyville being bombed. The Americans despaired.

Late Friday night, October 9, they were roughly thrown back into a cell at the central prison. They were still there two weeks later when Dr. Paul Carlson, an American medical missionary, was also put into their cell. He had been seized in mid-September and badly beaten. Secretary of State

Rusk sent Kenyatta a message vouching for Dr. Carlson's innocence. The random violence made the Americans vulnerable to any angry or drunken Simba.

In early November, the consuls of Belgium and Italy joined Hoyt in the central prison. They heard rumors that the army of the central government in Leopoldville, led by white mercenaries, was advancing to retake Stanleyville, and they would all be killed if the rebels lost the city. In Europe, a battalion of Belgian paratroopers was organized to land from American planes, if they would prevent a massacre.

The American hostages were stuffed into jeeps on Wednesday, the eighteenth, and taken to the Lumumba Monument, where the rebels performed their executions. A large, noisily anti-American mob enveloped them, reaching for them, striking them. They were led through the frenzied crowd toward the monument. Then, suddenly, the Americans were ordered back into the jeeps and were driven to the airport and forced to stand on a balcony while a Simba leader exhorted a crowd against American mercenaries. He said the executions had been postponed for four days at the request of President Kenyatta. The Americans were locked back in the prison.

On Friday, Hoyt alone was taken to President Gbenye and told that negotiations had begun in Nairobi. He was ordered to sign an appeal to the Leopoldville embassy asking for a cease-fire in order to save the hostages' lives. Then, the Americans were moved to the Victoria Hotel, where some two hundred hostages were already being held. The Americans picked up rumors by radio that Belgian paratroopers were now on Ascension Island in the South Atlantic.

On Monday, Hoyt was shown an urgent telex from Ambassador Godley, informing President Gbenye that Ambassador Attwood in Nairobi was to discuss the fate of the Americans with President Kenyatta and with Gbenye's negotiator, Thomas Kanza, one of the Congo's few college graduates. The nationalist army was less than two hundred miles from Stanleyville, and 320 Belgian paratroopers were prepared to drop into Stanleyville; the two forces would coordinate the assault. Attwood was told to ask Thomas Kanza whether the rebels would release the hostages and leave the city before the Leopoldville army arrived. Kanza gave no such assurances.

The assault was planned in such secrecy and haste that when it came time to erect tents on Ascension Island for the paratroopers, it was discovered that they had only brought wooden tent pegs, which could not be driven into the island's barren coral. Metal tent pegs had to be rushed from Europe. For the want of a tent peg . . .

At 4:00 A.M. the next morning, November 24, airplanes were overhead, and the Simbas panicked. They removed all the two-hundred-plus hostages from the Victoria Hotel. The rebel leaders started marching the column of prisoners indecisively and arguing whether to shoot them or to take them to the airport and use them as shields.

The prisoners were finally ordered to sit down in Sergeant Ketele Street. Some rebels fired weapons into the crowd of prisoners as the paratroopers were air-dropped from American C-130Es. When the Simbas began firing, Hoyt and Grinwis jumped up and ran into an alley. They heard screams from prisoners and shouts from the Simbas. Hoyt dove behind a low wall.

The 320 paratroopers secured the airfield in thirty-two minutes, and in another forty minutes they had cleared the runways. But the rebels had already killed twenty-eight of the hundreds of hostages crowded into the square. The troops started moving the hostages to the airfield for evacuation to Leopoldville. During the next two days, two thousand hostages were saved. Two Belgian soldiers were killed and eleven wounded.

As the gunfire faded, Hoyt lifted his head and saw a paratrooper wearing a camouflage uniform and a red beret. The soldier pointed his weapon at him. Hoyt identified himself as the American consul and asked to be taken to the soldier's commander. The paratrooper, replying in French, led Hoyt to where his colonel and other officers were studying a map.

Hoyt was promptly reunited with Grinwis, who had been hiding in a toilet. John Clingerman, the consul Hoyt had replaced in Stanleyville, appeared, and Hoyt tried to persuade him to have troops sent to protect the missionaries outside the city. Dr. Carlson's body was found; he had been killed climbing a wall when the rebels started firing. Phyllis Rine, an American missionary nurse, had her leg shot off and bled to death in the street. Bodies were strewn everywhere. Eighteen had been killed and forty were seriously wounded. Five more died during the flights to Leopoldville.

Hoyt and Grinwis were rushed to the airport and into an American C-130 loaded with the badly wounded. The plane took off immediately for Leopoldville. Once in the air, the pilot told them that all the American consulate's staff people were safe. Their ordeal of 111 days of fear and confusion was over. In the Congo, the struggle went on.

GUYANA: MURDER AND VALOR

Richard A. Dwyer arrived at Georgetown, the capital of tropical Guyana on the Atlantic coast of South America, in April 1978. He had already been in the U.S. Foreign Service for twenty years and was to serve as deputy chief of mission to a career officer, Ambassador John R. Burke. Guyana, formerly British Guiana, had been granted its independence in May 1966, after the United States had helped unseat its Chicago-educated Marxist prime minister, Cheddi Jagan.

Shortly after DCM Dwyer arrived, he flew with Richard McCloy, chief of the consular section, 140 miles over tropical forest in a small chartered plane to the river town of Port Kaituma, which served an American-owned manganese mine. From there, they rode a jeep six rough jungle miles to the vast Jonestown settlement, where a thousand U.S. citizens, mostly African-Americans, lived in a cult community called the People's Temple Agricultural Community at Jonestown.

The community had cleared hundreds of acres of jungle. Its leader, the Reverend James W. Jones, a white man born in Indiana, had built his following in California. Jones was particularly influential in San Francisco, where he had served as commissioner of housing.

Among those also concerned about Jonestown was Congressman Leo J. Ryan of California. Some of his constituents were members of the cult, while others were relatives worried that family members were being forced to stay in Guyana. Ryan met with Assistant Secretary of State Viron P. Vaky of the Bureau of Inter-American Affairs and telegraphed Reverend Jones that he planned to fly to Guyana.

The leaders in Jonestown expected that Ryan's visit would be unfriendly. He intended to bring home from Guyana a friend's two granddaughters who were living in Jonestown with their mother. The U.S. Embassy believed the U.S. government could not force them to return to the United States. Their father had defected from the People's Temple and had been killed in a railroad accident in California. Their grandfather suspected he had been murdered.

On Tuesday, November 14, 1978, Congressman Ryan landed in Guyana with James Schollaert, a former Foreign Service officer who was his legislative assistant; Jackie Speier of his personal staff; nine members of the press; eighteen relatives of people at Jonestown; and two People's Temple lawyers.

In Georgetown, Congressman Ryan was put under the charge of Dwyer, who arranged for an eighteen-seat Twin Otter airliner to be taken out of government service on Friday and rented to Ryan. Those on the plane included eleven members of the press and four relatives of people at Jonestown. Dwyer served as Ryan's escort.

When they arrived on the tarmac airstrip at Port Kaituma at about 3:30 P.M., representatives from the People's Temple made it clear that they were not welcome. Finally, it was agreed that Ryan, Dwyer, Jackie Speier, and Neville Annibourne from Guyana's Ministry of Information would be allowed in. They traveled the forty-five minutes to Jonestown in the back of a dump truck.

Reverend Jones permitted Ryan and Speier to interview residents they wanted to talk with and agreed that the press and relatives could come into Jonestown. Because they had started late from Georgetown that morning, everyone had to stay overnight. Jones' people gave them dinner, staged a musical show in the main outdoor pavilion, and found sleeping facilities for the core group. The rest had to stay in Port Kaituma.

During the night, a number of members of Jonestown left the People's Temple and walked to nearby villages in the jungle. The next morning, the NBC television crew interviewed the Reverend Jones, and a dozen people told Congressman Ryan they wanted to leave Jonestown. That upset Jones, but the dissenters remained adamant. Dwyer could locate only one additional five-passenger Cessna aircraft, so he decided the people who wanted to leave would have priority; everyone else would wait for return air trips.

As Dwyer oversaw the loading of the truck, suddenly there were screams and shouts from the pavilion. Dwyer rushed back and found Ryan shaken, his shirt covered with blood. Members of the People's Temple were holding a young man with a knife; he had grabbed the congressman from behind and threatened to kill him

Dwyer insisted that Ryan leave Jonestown immediately. They returned to the airstrip. No planes were there. The truck drove Dwyer into Port Kaituma to locate a shortwave radio, but he could not find one that worked. By the time he returned to the airstrip at about five o'clock, the two planes had arrived.

While the planes were loading, a People's Temple member boarded the Cessna, drew a pistol, and shot two defectors before he was subdued. A farm tractor pulling a cart approached the planes; men in the cart stood up and began firing. Dwyer was shot through the left thigh, the bullet lodging near his spine. He lay in the middle of the tarmac and played dead.

When the shooting stopped, Dwyer located Ryan; he had been shot repeatedly, and part of his face had been blown away. Three members of the press and one defector were also dead, and Speier and nine others were wounded. Others had fled into the bush. Dwyer and Charles Krause, the *Washington Post* reporter, who was also wounded, followed them but soon returned to the airstrip. The smaller plane was gone with both pilots aboard. Dwyer saw that the wounded and other survivors were cared for. Krause praised Dwyer, saying, "He was tireless, firm, and brave." Ambassador Burke later said, "He was a very able FSO. I had absolute confidence in him."

In Georgetown that night, the pilots met with Prime Minister Forbes Burnham, members of his cabinet, and Ambassador Burke. At dawn Sunday a company of 120 Guyanese soldiers arrived at the Jonestown airstrip and were posted around the tarmac. At that point, Dwyer said later, he felt safe for the first time.

All the wounded and dead at the airstrip were shipped out. A television film of the shooting had already been broadcast in the United States, and Dwyer's daughter, who was in college, saw the film and recognized her father. Dwyer was flown back to Georgetown in a small military plane loaded with body bags, one of which held Congressman Ryan. Dwyer was hospitalized in Georgetown to recover from his wound.

After Dwyer's plane took off from Port Kaituma, the Guyanese soldiers went into Jonestown and discovered that more than nine hundred people, including some 260 children, were dead. The Reverend Jones had told his community to drink a red grape punch laced with cyanide. Jones was among the dead, apparently killed by a single bullet.

Although Ryan's staff criticized the State Department for not warning the congressman of the cult's violence, the department sent Dwyer its Award for Valor for his actions and courage at Jonestown.

Years later, Dwyer summed up his Jonestown experience in dangerous diplomacy:

> As far as what happened subsequently, the Department mailed down to me by surface mail a little plaque, a little brown piece of wood with a strip of metal, award for valor on it, not quite mounted squarely,

which I thought was kind of typical. . . . Within two or three years, this was ancient history and there was nobody around who remembered it. There was nobody around who cared, except those of us directly concerned.

42

Terrorists in the Embassies

1968–2009

Nothing prepares you to be called at four in the morning to be told that two embassies in Africa have been bombed within ten minutes of each other. As you drive through the empty streets at that time of the morning, you are praying that by the time you get to the office the number bombed won't be three, four, or five. And then when it is still only two and you are slightly relieved, the actual horror starts to seep in, even as you are putting the other embassies on alert and coordinating rescues or medical supplies.

Thus, Under Secretary of State for Management Bonnie R. Cohen described to a U.S. Senate task force in 1998 her initial reaction to terrorist attacks on two American embassies.

Diplomats are unarmed civilians on missions of conciliation and peace. In recent years they have become the all-too-vulnerable targets for terrorists spewing violence and murder. These outlaws have attacked American diplomats around the globe. Former Under Secretary R. Nicholas Burns says, "Our diplomats are in harm's way every day of the year."

Terrorism is a tactic by which violently dissenting people and destructive religious fundamentalists attack the powerful. Terrorist acts are premeditated; they have political purposes, and they usually target unarmed civilians. Although "terrorist" attacks often appear similar in purpose and even method, they do not originate from a single central command, and the terrorists vary in their objectives and skills. This raises serious doubts about the concept of a "global war on terror."

"I bridle a little bit at the use of the word battle against terrorism, war against terrorism, because terrorism is a tactic," said Deputy Secretary of State Richard Armitage. "I didn't recall in the Second World War that we had a war against kamikazes or a war against snipers."

To a significant degree, contemporary terrorists have distorted Americans' lifestyle. "The 'war on terror' has created a culture of fear in America," Zbigniew Brzezinski wrote in *The Washington Post*. He added, "Terrorism is not an enemy but a technique of warfare, political intimidation through the killing of unarmed civilians." Since terrorists do not have the resources or weapons to fight the top of the power chain straight on, they select noncombatants unequipped to defend themselves or fight back. This form of violence led Ambassador Frank Carlucci to conclude, "I spent many years in diplomacy and diplomacy is very hollow unless it's backed by military strength." Antiterrorist specialist Brian Jenkins of the Rand Corporation sums it up more hopefully: "Terrorism is theater."

American Foreign Service officers have faced violence since the days of the Barbary Coast pirates. In the most recent half century, violations of the traditional respect and immunity granted diplomats have multiplied in number and ferocity. Of the names on the plaques in the State Department lobby honoring men and women who have died overseas in the Foreign Service, the great majority are dated since World War II.

By 1984, the problem had grown so severe that Secretary of State George P. Shultz appointed the Advisory Panel on Overseas Security, chaired by retired Admiral Bobby R. Inman. It led to the fortifying, rebuilding, and relocating of American missions around the world.

The State Department's Bureau of Diplomatic Security analyzes terrorist threats and violence to safeguard U.S. missions abroad, as well as U.S. citizens overseas in thousands of businesses and religious and other nongovernmental organizations.

Americans and local nationals have been wounded and killed, installations damaged and destroyed. Such attacks are usually one-day news stories in the States. Listing them here makes evident their cumulative impact.

And on one summer morning in 1998, terrorists achieved a devastating effect on diplomats and those supporting them. Therefore, the morning of August 7, 1998, appears out of order here and leads this chronology of danger, pain, and death.

"WE CONFRONTED A NEW REALITY"

Bombs exploded nearly simultaneously on the morning of August 7 at the American embassy in Nairobi, Kenya, and at the embassy four hundred miles away in Dar es Salaam, the capital of Tanzania. The bombs killed more than 230 people; thousands were wounded, and both embassies were destroyed.

In Nairobi, a huge bomb exploded at 10:37 A.M., while Ambassador Prudence Bushnell and two U.S. Commerce Department officers were meeting with Kenya's commerce minister in his office, high in the twenty-one-story Cooperative Bank Building behind the U.S. Embassy. The blast knocked Ambassador Bushnell unconscious; flying glass cut her badly. The ceiling had collapsed, and she thought she was going to die.

One of her Commerce Department colleagues helped her slowly down the smoke-filled stairs. When they reached the street, she was driven immediately to a nearby hotel, where she received medical attention. Soon, she was back overseeing the rescue operation. In her previous job as assistant secretary for African affairs, Ambassador Bushnell, the fifty-two-year-old daughter of a career Foreign Service officer, had learned how evacuations were carried out.

Seven hundred men and women, including people from seventeen U.S. government agencies, worked for the embassy in Nairobi. This August 7 morning, among the 220 dead were 12 American government employees and family members, 32 Foreign Service National embassy employees (FSNs), and 247 other Kenyan citizens. Ten Americans, 11 FSNs, and 4,000 Kenyans were wounded. Forty-four were killed inside the embassy, now disintegrated into burning rubble.

The attack on the five-story building, standing with no setback on a busy downtown intersection, began when the embassy's Kenyan perimeter guards refused to open the gates for a truck and the two men in the truck started shooting.

The guards posted outside the chancery were unarmed. They tried to summon the U.S. Marine Security Guard on a handheld radio and from the telephone in a nearby guard booth. The embassy's single radio frequency and the one telephone line were both busy; the Kenyan government had never acted on the ambassador's repeated requests for a second frequency. The rear basement garage door had also been broken for months, and a temporary door was kept open during the day. The guards had no emergency panic alarms with which to warn those inside of danger. The damage to the embassy was "massive."

Highest ranking among the dead Americans was Consul General Julian L. Bartley, Sr. His son, Julian "Jay" Bartley, twenty, also died in the attack. Julian Bartley, Sr., had served in the Foreign Service for twenty-four years and was one of its most respected African-Americans. His son, a sophomore at Nairobi's U.S. International University, was working as a summer intern at the embassy.

Local Kenyans were infuriated when the U.S. Marine Security Guard would not allow local rescuers into the embassy for hours after the bombing. Ambassador Bushnell had to go on television and explain that she was trying to protect the "crime scene" and prevent more civilians from being hurt and killed.

Secretary of State Madeleine Albright flew to Germany and accompanied the flag-covered coffins of ten Americans back to Washington. The Bartleys, father and son, were buried in Arlington National Cemetery. At their funeral, retired Ambassador Terence A. Todman and Ambassador Ruth A. Davis, both distinguished senior African-Americans in the Foreign Service, praised Consul General Bartley's contributions and courage. Deputy Secretary of State Strobe Talbott and Under Secretary Thomas R. Pickering also participated in the service.

The embassy staff moved into the USAID building across town. Years later, Ambassador Bushnell, then the ambassador to Guatemala, wrote sensitively about the effects of terrorism on its living victims. She remembered:

We confronted a new reality. Squeezed with our colleagues in the poorly constructed USAID building, surrounded by barbed wire, sandbags, sniffer dogs and Marines in combat gear, we were constantly reminded of failure. Phones and faxes didn't work, computers, equipment and files had been destroyed, and everything took too long to come together. We dearly missed our dead colleagues and quickly learned just how much the Kenyans, in particular, contributed to the running of the mission.

Analysis that followed showed that the State Department's method of determining threat levels was "seriously flawed," said the department's Accountability Review Board, which studied the tragedy. The embassy staff had feared local crime more than international terrorism. The embassy did not meet the "Inman security standards," although Ambassador Bushnell, with seventeen years of Foreign Service experience, had repeatedly sought Kenyan permission to relocate the chancery. A new Overseas Presence Advisory Panel judged that 85 percent of U.S. diplomatic facilities overseas were vulnerable. One State Department specialist on counterterrorism said that an attack on power grids, for example, could wipe out computer memory.

The State Department's immediate emergency response to the bombing was also inadequate. The interagency, on-call Foreign Emergency Support Team (FEST) did not set out until six hours after it was alerted; its plane broke down in Rota, Spain, and the team's wait for a backup plane caused a fifteen-hour delay. The FEST team arrived in Nairobi almost forty hours after the blast. A second Air Force plane and a medevac plane from Germany were also delayed. The Accountability Review Board criticized the department for bungling its crisis management.

Almost simultaneous to the Nairobi disaster, an attack was mounted by a truck laden with explosives on the U.S. embassy in Dar es Salaam. The reinforced concrete building at 36 Laibon Road had been built originally as an Israeli mission. Responsible for the embassy was Chargé d'affaires John E. Lange, who later would serve as ambassador to Botswana.

Here, at Dar es Salaam, an embassy water tanker blocked the terrorists' truck. They had to detonate their bomb outside the embassy perimeter. It blew a crater ten feet wide but caused fewer casualties than did the bomb in Nairobi. All five unarmed perimeter guards were killed. U.S. Marine Corps embassy guards, pistols in hand, rushed to cordon off the area.

The Dar es Salaam attack came as a total surprise; Tanzania was usually free of political violence. No Americans were killed, but seven FSNs and three civilian Tanzanians died. Eighty-five people were injured, including a number of Americans. The U.S. embassy was wrecked, and the French and German embassies nearby were damaged.

The Accountability Review Board studying the Dar es Salaam attack credited procedural changes introduced by the recently arrived Regional Security Officer John DeCarlo for having contained the damage. The United States blamed the attack on Osama bin Laden, claiming the terrorists had trained in his camps.

The Accountability Review Board also said that State Department criteria did not anticipate a large vehicular bomb attack and that existing safety rules had not been fully applied. The department and the embassies had failed to appreciate the seriousness of transnational terrorism. The board said to correct these failures systemwide would cost $1.4 billion a year for ten years.

The day's bombings caused embassies and other U.S. diplomatic installations to be closed down temporarily from Kampala, Uganda, to Kuala Lumpur, Malaysia. Congress was criticized for failing to fund adequate security for the embassies.

The bombings triggered a major effort to improve embassy security. New buildings were started and "berms, bollards, and barricades" rose at three hundred locations. Shatter-resistant window film was installed in 190 posts. Nine hundred satellite telephones were provided for emergency communication.

In a frustrated attempt to hit back at the terrorists, on August 20, the United States fired cruise missiles at a terrorist training center in Afghanistan and at a pharmaceutical factory in Khartoum, Sudan. The factory was said to be financed by Osama bin Laden to produce nerve gas. Four al-Qaeda agents were tried in New York in 2001 and sentenced to life imprisonment.

The effects of the twin attacks of August 7 were enormous. And they set off a series of terrorist attacks over the next decades that was long and destructive.

Guatemala City, August 28, 1968. One block from the U.S. consulate, members of a rebel faction forced the official car of U.S. Ambassador John Gordon Mein off the road. When he tried to escape, they shot him dead. Mein was the first American ambassador assassinated.

Rio de Janeiro, Brazil, September 3, 1969. Ambassador Charles Burke Elbrick, of Louisville, Kentucky, was kidnapped by the Marxist revolutionary group MR-8 while riding from his official residence to the embassy. The kidnappers left a note demanding he be exchanged for fifteen Brazilian political prisoners. After four days, Brazil's military government agreed to free the political prisoners (or let them escape). The day after the plane carrying the released prisoners flew to Mexico, the terrorists released Ambassador Elbrick. The Brazilian government promptly arrested four thousand leftists.

Haiti, January 23, 1973. Two men and a woman ambushed U.S. Ambassador Clinton E. Knox and took him to the embassy's residence. He was released unharmed twenty-three hours later when the Haitian government agreed to pay a ransom and fly the terrorists and twelve political prisoners to Mexico. Ward Christensen, chief of the consular section, was kidnapped at the same time.

Khartoum, Sudan, March 1, 1973. Newly appointed Ambassador Cleo A. Noel, Jr., and Deputy Chief of Mission George Curtis Moore, both experienced Arabists, were leaving an informal diplomatic party at the Saudi Arabian embassy at about 7:00 P.M., when eight masked Palestinians of the Black September group, which had murdered eleven Israelis at the Munich Olympics, drove up in a pair of Land Rovers firing automatic weapons. Noel and the Belgian Chargé, Guy Eid, who were wounded, and eight others, including Moore, were captured. President Nixon refused to negotiate with the terrorists, so they dragged Noel, Moore, and Eid down to the basement and, reputedly on the order of Yasir Arafat, shot them to death.

Thirty-five years after those murders, early on New Year's Day 2008, AID staff member John M. Granville, thirty-three, of Buffalo, New York, left a party at the British embassy in Khartoum and was almost home when his car was cut off. Two gunmen fired seventeen shots.

Granville and his Sudanese driver, Abdelrahman Abbas Rahama, were killed.

Guadalajara, Mexico, May 4, 1973. Four armed members of the People's Revolutionary Armed Forces kidnapped U.S. Consul General, Terrance Leonhardy, who ironically was driving home alone from a police exhibition on law enforcement. The terrorists demanded that thirty political prisoners be flown to Cuba or they would execute their prisoner. The Mexican government finally agreed, and after seventy-six hours Leonhardy was released in an empty street.

Nicosia, Cyprus, August 19, 1974. U.S. Ambassador Rodger P. Davies was killed by a sniper's bullet while Greeks were demonstrating in Nicosia, the capital of Cyprus, to protest the United States siding with Turkey on the divided island. A Greek-Cypriot embassy secretary, Antoinette Varnava, was killed trying to help Davies. Two Greek-Cypriots were acquitted of murdering Davies and sentenced to prison only on the lesser charge of possessing weapons.

Beirut, Lebanon, June 16, 1976. U.S. Ambassador Francis E. Meloy, Jr.; Robert O. Waring, an economic counselor; and their Lebanese driver, Mohammed Moghrabi, drove across the "green line" separating the Christian and Muslim sectors of Beirut and were shot to death by the Popular Front for the Liberation of Palestine.

Kabul, Afghanistan, February 14, 1979. Adolph "Spike" Dubs, the U.S. ambassador in Kabul, was being driven from his home to the embassy just before 9 A.M., when four men in Afghan police uniform stopped his armored car and persuaded the driver to open his bulletproof window. At gunpoint, they forced the driver to take the ambassador to the Kabul Hotel, where they held him in room 117 on an upper floor. The driver was sent back to the embassy to report the kidnapping.

Weeks earlier, the Soviet Union had invaded Afghanistan, and now Americans at the hotel saw Soviet officers advising the Afghans. At the end of the morning, someone fired a shot, and the Afghan police responded with automatic gunfire into room 117. After a full minute of intense firing, Ambassador Dubs was found slumped in a chair with bullets through his head and heart. He had been killed by shots from a .22 caliber pistol. Ambassador Anthony C. E. Quainton, director of the Office for Combating Terrorism, wrote, "Ambassador Dubs was killed in an assault carried out with Russian advice in a Soviet satrapy."

Tehran, Iran, on November 4, 1979. On Sunday morning, the United States Embassy in Tehran was overrun by radical young Iranians. By the end of the day, sixty-three Americans were being held hostage, three more were trapped in the foreign ministry, and six were in hiding. Fifty-two members of the group were held hostage under appalling conditions for 444 days. When Ronald Reagan became President on January 20, 1981, they were immediately released.

Islamabad, Pakistan, November 20, 1979. At midday, seventeen days after the Americans were taken hostage in Tehran, well-organized young Pakistanis started climbing over the walls of the U.S. Embassy compound in Islamabad. Administrative Counselor David C. Fields and Political Officer David Welch, met students at the gate and took their petition. Then, the students reboarded the buses and headed back to the university.

Within minutes, the buses turned around again and, joined by others, headed back to the U.S. Embassy. Now, some of the rioters were armed. They pulled down part of the compound wall and set the building on fire. Shots were fired. Twenty-year-old Corporal Steven J. Crowley, a six-foot-six U.S. Marine security guard stationed on the chancery roof, was shot above his left ear. Master Sergeant Lloyd G. Miller, commander of the embassy's detachment of seven Marines, and two CIA men carried the unconscious corporal into the building on a plywood board. The Marines tried to turn back the invaders with tear gas.

The embassy personnel, Americans and Pakistanis, took refuge, according to plan, in the steel-lined code room on the third floor. Inside the vault, smoke and tear gas made breathing difficult. Rioters shot at the vault crowded with 137 people. Fran Fields, the embassy nurse and David Fields' wife, cared for Crowley, but he died at 3:35 P.M.

When daylight faded, Master Sergeant Miller led the Marines and several armed diplomats onto the roof. The rioters were gone. All six embassy buildings and more than sixty embassy vehicles were burning. The charred, beaten body of Army Warrant Officer Brian Ellis was found in his apartment in the compound.

Tripoli, Libya, December 2, 1979. In support of Iran's Ayatollah Khomeini and the seizure of the American embassy in Tehran, a mob attacked and set fire to the U.S. Embassy on Mohamed Thabit Street in the center of Tripoli. The United States had recalled its ambassador in 1972, and now it withdrew the rest of its diplomatic staff. Muammar Qaddafi's government was charged with "state-sponsored terrorism." Full diplomatic relations were not restored until 2006, when Qaddafi said he had given up his plans to develop nuclear weapons. At the end of 2008, Gene A. Cretz became the first U.S. ambassador in Tripoli in thirty-six years.

Bogotá, Colombia, February 27, 1980. U.S. Ambassador Diego C. Asencio came out of the Dominican Republic ambassador's residence in downtown Bogotá and headed for his armored limousine. The Independence Day diplomatic reception was breaking up, and the guests were leaving. (The Soviet delegation had already left; later, no one could say whether it was a coincidence.) Outside the compound, a group of young men and women in sweat suits stopped kicking a soccer ball, drew automatic weapons out of their gym bags, and started firing. In a two-hour shootout with police and bodyguards, two young men were killed, and five wounded.

Masked with black kerchiefs, the sixteen guerrillas, from a group called M-19, grabbed at gunpoint thirty-two guests, including fifteen ambassadors. Among them was Ambassador Asencio. Born in Spain and reared in a poor neighborhood of Newark, New Jersey, Asencio, a big, bearded man with a commanding presence and a helpful sense of humor, had joined the Foreign Service in 1957 and most recently served as DCM in Caracas.

When Colombian officers leading trigger-happy troops rejected the guerrillas' demands for the release of 311 M-19 prisoners and payment of a $50 million ransom, the guerrillas were at a loss as to what to do next. Then took place a scenario unique in the annals of terrorists and hostages. Ambassador Asencio created a rapport with his captors. He and the ambassadors from Mexico and Brazil taught the guerrillas how to reply to government negotiating documents and how to end the crisis and still save face.

After sixty-one days, the hostages were released unharmed. The guerrillas won guarantees of fair trials and the inspection of prison conditions for their colleagues. No rebel prisoners were released, and the terrorists settled for a $1.2 million ransom and safe passage to Havana. Together, the guerrillas and twelve ambassadors (including Asencio) boarded a plane that Fidel Castro sent for them.

San Salvador, El Salvador, May 12, 1980. On October 30, 1979, two hundred armed guerrillas entered the U.S. Embassy compound in El Salvador. The U.S. Marine Security Guard drove them off with tear gas. Two Marines were wounded. The United States supported the coalition that overthrew the military government.

On May 12, 1980, hundreds of demonstrators surrounded the home of U.S. Ambassador Robert E. White, and Marines again fired tear gas so that the ambassador could escape. Later, three American nuns and a lay missionary were murdered. The United States suspended $25 million of new military and economic aid. Ambassador White believed the El Salvador security forces were involved in the four women's deaths. The State Department sent down a fact-finding mission, led by former Under Secretary William D. Rogers.

On the evening of June 19, 1985, a dozen men of the Farabunto Marti National Liberation Front (FMLN) insurgency shot to death four unarmed embassy Marines sitting off duty in civilian clothes at a sidewalk cafe. Two U.S. businessmen were also among the thirteen people killed in the attack.

The leftist FMLN opened an all-out urban terrorist campaign against the government in November 1989. Six Jesuits of the local Catholic university were taken from their beds and killed. Subsequently, Ambassador William G. Walker came to the conclusion that the FMLN no longer intended to target Americans. And two years later, El Salvador and the FMLN signed a peace agreement.

Rome, Italy, October 12, 1981. One incident had a happy ending. Maxwell M. Rabb, the American ambassador to Italy, had just given a Columbus Day speech in Milan and returned to his hotel when he received a telephone call from Peter Bridges, his DCM, in Rome: "Don't say anything to me. Just listen and do as I tell you. Take the 11 o'clock plane to the United States. Don't ask anything more. Just go." And he hung up. Rabb caught the plane. He would have been assassinated the next day when he returned to Rome.

Beirut, Lebanon, April 18, 1983. Sixty-three people were killed and 120 injured when, at 1:06 P.M., a four-hundred-pound bomb in a pickup truck exploded in the lobby of the U.S. Embassy on the corniche in Muslim West Beirut. The blast destroyed seven floors in the center section of the chancery. Seventeen of the dead were Americans, including three USAID employees, one Marine Corps Security Guard, and the CIA's Middle East director Robert C. Ames, as well as all eight of the CIA contingent. Within an hour, Marines of the 24th Marine Amphibious Unit, weapons loaded, arrived from the Beirut International Airport and established the embassy's perimeter security.

The path to this tragedy had begun ten months earlier, when Israeli troops attacked Palestinian and Syrian forces in Beirut, ostensibly as revenge for the shooting of the Israeli ambassador in London. Ambassador Robert S. Dillon shut down the U.S. Embassy on the Beirut waterfront and moved its staff to his residence in the hills. Communication was kept flowing through Ambassadors Samuel W. Lewis in Israel and Richard Murphy in Saudi Arabia.

Ambassador Philip C. Habib, who a year earlier had negotiated a cease-fire between Israel and the Palestine Liberation Organization (PLO) in Lebanon, rushed back to Beirut to negotiate another cease-fire. From outside Ambassador Dillon's residence above the city, Habib described the firefights he was witnessing to the State Department. In this early use of satellites, he reported; "The city is progressively being destroyed, and the Lebanese are asking me what there is to negotiate about."

President Reagan cabled the right-wing prime minister of Israel, Menachem Begin, that Israel's attacks were "incomprehensible and unacceptable." Habib needed months to work out an agreement before fifteen thousand Palestinian and Syrian soldiers left Beirut, mostly for Syria.

U.S. Secretary of Defense Caspar Weinberger refused to allow U.S. Marines to deploy into the city, so Habib designed a fresh solution: the French Foreign Legion would replace the Marines. When the last of the PLO left Beirut, President Reagan proclaimed it "one of the unique feats of diplomacy in modern times" and presented Habib with the Medal of Freedom.

But the fragile situation soon fell apart. Within two weeks, the multinational force was withdrawn and Lebanon's prime minister was assassinated. Israeli Defense Minister Ariel Sharon sent troops back into the city to surround the refugee camps filled with Palestinian civilians.

Early on Saturday, September 18, U.S. Foreign Service officer Ryan C. Crocker called the embassy in Beirut on a handheld radio as he walked through the Shatila refugee camp and described how hundreds of its residents had been massacred. And hundreds more had been murdered at the Sabra camp. The Israeli commanders had sent in Lebanese Maronite Christian militia to do the awful job. Philip Habib and the Marines came back to Beirut. On April 18, 1983, the U.S. Embassy was destroyed.

In July, Robert C. McFarlane, who had replaced Habib as the President's chief Middle East negotiator, ordered U.S. naval gunfire to support the Lebanese government troops. That eliminated any pretense that the United States was neutral.

Early in September, U.S. Navy warships silenced artillery firing at Ambassador Dillon's residence. And McFarlane had U.S. naval ships bombard in support of Lebanese government forces at Souk El Gharb, which confirmed the Muslims' perception that the Marines, and all Americans, were partisans of the ruling Maronite Christians.

At 6:22 Sunday morning, October 23, truck bombs blasted both the American and French compounds. A yellow open-bed truck carrying the equivalent of a twelve-thousand-pound bomb crashed into the lobby of, and destroyed, the headquarters of the 1st Battalion, 8th Marines at the Beirut International Airport; 241 Americans died there. And two miles away, a four-hundred-pound bomb destroyed a French base, killing fifty-eight troops. The Islamic Jihad took responsibility. The cost was now too high; the United States pulled its military out of Lebanon.

On March 16, 1984, the Islamic Jihad kidnapped William Francis Buckley, the CIA station chief in Beirut. After fifteen months in brutal captivity, Lieutenant Colonel Buckley, a Silver Star recipient in Vietnam, died from illness and torture.

Southern Lebanon, February 17, 1988. U.S. Marine Corps Lieutenant Colonel William R. Higgins, a decorated veteran of the Vietnam War and a former aide to Defense Secretary Weinberger, was kidnapped and murdered by Iranian-backed Hezbollah terrorists while he was serving as chief military observer of the United Nations Truce Supervision Organization in southern Lebanon. He was driving on a coastal highway near Tyre when armed men pulled him from his car. He was interrogated, tortured, and, a year and a half later, hanged. The U.S. government classified Higgins as a hostage, not a prisoner of war, and thus he was not protected under international rules. His wife, Robin, also a Marine Corps lieutenant colonel, protested, "The State Department, not the Defense Department, had the lead. That meant diplomacy, not military might. It meant no retribution, no retaliation, no rescue."

Athens, June 28, 1988. The defense attaché of the U.S. Embassy in Athens, U.S. Navy Captain William E. Nordeen, was killed when a terrorist group called November 17 detonated a car bomb by remote control as he drove by his home. Ambassador R. Nicholas Burns called the attack "cold-blooded" and "senseless."

The same small but deadly anti-American Greek group was held responsible for assassinating at least two dozen people, including three other Americans: On December 23, 1975, three masked members of the organization had shot and killed Richard S. Welch, the CIA station chief in Athens, as he and his wife returned home from a Christmas party. On November 15, 1983, the same terrorists gunned down U.S. Navy Captain George Tsantes, Jr., and his driver, Nikos Veloutsos. Tsantes, an Annapolis graduate, was the head of the Joint U.S. Military Advisory Group in Greece. And on March 12, 1991, the same gang killed U.S. Air Force Sergeant Ronald O. Stewart with a remote-controlled car bomb that exploded as he entered his home.

A plaque on the Athens embassy honoring those five victims carries this quotation from Thucydides: "But the bravest are surely those who have the clearest vision of what is before them, glory and danger alike, and notwithstanding, go out to meet it."

The Athens embassy continued to attract terrorists. On February 15, 1996, shortly after 11:00 P.M., an antitank rocket hit an outside wall of the embassy compound and damaged buildings and several diplomatic vehicles. Despite intense security efforts, shortly before sunrise on January 12, 2007, an antitank grenade launched from ground level flew over a ten-foot security wall and struck the embassy. This time, damage was minor, and no one was hurt at that hour.

Manila, April 21, 1989. While riding to work in Quezon City in the Philippines, Colonel James N. Rowe was killed by hooded gunmen of the Communist New People's Army. Twenty-one machine-gun bullets struck his car. One hit Rowe in the head, and another wounded his driver. Rowe was a member of the Joint Military Advisory Group training Filipino soldiers. His death aroused a bitter controversy. Although he was known to be a terrorist target, he was not warned because, allegedly, some zealot did not want to lose Rowe's undercover contacts among the terrorists.

"Nick" Rowe was a West Point graduate and a decorated Special Forces veteran of the Vietnam War. In 1963, Viet Cong guerrillas had captured him during a firefight in the Mekong Delta and held him, mostly in a small bamboo cage, for five years before he found a chance to escape.

Indonesia, January 18–19, 1991. Iraqi terrorists planted a bomb in the Indonesian home of Ambassador John Cameron Monjo. They had noted that at 6:00 P.M. each evening Ambassador Monjo, a career Foreign Service officer, sat by a certain window and drank a Scotch and soda. The Iraqis hid a bomb in a flowerpot on the windowsill. An alert gardener spotted a corner of the bomb that the inept terrorists had left exposed. It was detonated, and the plot, foiled.

Karachi, March 8, 1995. While being driven to the consulate at 7:45 A.M., two Americans working for the consulate in Karachi were killed and one was wounded. At a busy downtown intersection, two cars boxed in the white consulate van, and masked gunmen sprayed it with AK-47 fire. Gary C. Durrell, from Alliance, Ohio, an intelligence agent working as a communications technician, died instantly, and Jackie Van Landingham, a secretary from Camden, South Carolina, died in a hospital. Mark McCloy, from Framingham, Massachusetts, survived his wounds. Karachi police in a squad car with a rooftop machine gun, fearing they might get killed, refused to pursue the terrorists.

Moscow, September 13, 1995. A rocket-propelled grenade penetrated the sixth floor of the U.S. embassy in Moscow. Fired from a building across the street, the grenade struck a large copying machine but caused no casualties. The rocket launcher, a ski mask, and a glove were found at the scene.

Dhahran, Saudi Arabia, June 25, 1996. At 10:00 P.M., an enormous bomb inside a sewage truck exploded with the force of twenty thousand pounds of TNT in front of the U.S. Khobar Towers military housing facility in Dhahran. It killed nineteen and wounded 240 U.S. servicemen.

Lima, Peru, December 17, 1996. Fourteen armed members of the Tupac Amaru Revolutionary Movement, arriving in an ambulance, entered the Japanese ambassador's residence during a celebration of the birthday of Emperor Akihito, of Japan. The heavily guarded party was held in a huge red-and-white-striped tent behind the residence. The masked terrorists, dressed in black fatigues, took hostage several hundred people. Among them were seven officials from the U.S. embassy: the political officer, James Wagner; the economic officer, John Riddle; the senior narcotics agent, John Crowe; Donald Boyd, the USAID director; and the USAID officials David Bayer, Michael Maxey, and Kris Merschrod.

Several hostages were released over the next months. On April 22, 1997, 140 Peruvian commandos stormed the ambassador's residence, which was a fortified imitation of Tara from *Gone with the Wind*. They killed all the terrorists and freed seventy-two hostages. (One died of a heart attack.) The Japanese bulldozed the fantastical ambassadorial residence. Ironically, demonstrators across Latin America protested the use of force by the Peruvian armed forces.

Manila, December 30, 2000. Thirteen people were killed and almost a hundred wounded by a series of bombs that exploded at about noon across Manila. One exploded on a park bench across the street from the U.S. Embassy and injured nine persons. That bomb dug a two-foot-deep crater. The building was not damaged, and no embassy staff members were injured. A terrorist group called the Moro Islamic Liberation Front was charged.

Calcutta, January 22, 2002. Shortly after 6:00 A.M., four heavily armed men riding two motorcycles staged a running battle in Jawaharlal Nehru

Road with thirty-two police guards outside the American Center, which housed the U.S. Information Service library and the public affairs section. The gunmen killed four policemen and wounded sixteen others. The attack came as the security guard was being changed and before the Americans arrived for work.

Islamabad, Pakistan, March 17, 2002. During a service attended by diplomatic and local personnel, grenades were thrown into the Protestant International Church in Islamabad. Five persons were killed, including State Department employee Barbara Green and her daughter, Kristen Wormsley. Thirteen U.S. citizens were among the forty-five wounded.

Lima, Peru, March 20, 2002. Three days before President George W. Bush was to visit Peru, a car bomb exploded at a shopping center near Lima's U.S. Embassy. Nine persons were killed and thirty-two wounded. The Shining Path guerrillas were blamed for the attack.

Karachi, Pakistan, June 14, 2002. A car bomb killed eleven persons and wounded forty in the fortified U.S. consulate general at about 11:00 A.M. on the day after Secretary of Defense Donald Rumsfeld completed a visit to Pakistan. The bomb blew a ten-foot hole in the consulate wall. All the dead were Pakistanis, and among the wounded was a U.S. Marine Security Guard. Al-Qaeda was blamed. The previous January, terrorists in Karachi with ties to al-Qaeda had kidnapped and beheaded *Wall Street Journal* reporter Daniel Pearl.

Amman, Jordan, October 28, 2002. A lone gunman killed Laurence Foley, executive officer of the USAID mission in Jordan. He was shot eight times at close range as he left his home in Amman at 7:20 A.M. Neighbors heard no shots, indicating that a silencer was used. The masked gunman escaped. It was the first murder of a Western diplomat in Jordan. The day before Foley's death, Ambassador Edward W. Gnehm Jr. had presented the sixty-year-old diplomat with an award for superior service.

Riyadh, Saudi Arabia, May 12, 2003. Late on the night before the arrival in Riyadh of Secretary of State Colin Powell, thirty-four people were killed when Saudi suicide bombers blew up three residential compounds for foreign workers in Riyadh. Eight Americans were killed and forty injured in the attack, which sheared the fronts off five-story buildings.

Another nighttime attack against a residential compound was staged the following November 8. This time, seventeen were killed and 122 injured. No Westerners were killed, although several were wounded. Analysts said that al-Qaeda did the bombing because the ruling Saud family supported the United States in the war against Iraq.

Baghdad, Iraq, October 12, 2003. At midday on Sunday, Iraqi guards fired on two cars filled with explosives as the vehicles sped toward the concrete-barricaded Baghdad Hotel, where American officials lived. Guards killed the drivers and exploded the bombs before they reached the hotel. A half dozen Iraqis were killed and thirty-two people were wounded, including three American soldiers.

Gaza Strip, October 15, 2003. Three U.S. Embassy guards were killed and one was wounded when a wire-controlled bomb exploded under an armored van in an American diplomatic convoy traveling through the northern Gaza Strip at 10:15 A.M. The Americans were on their way from the embassy in Tel Aviv to Gaza City to interview Palestinian applicants for Fulbright scholarships to study in the United States. The Americans killed were John Branchizio, Mark T. Parson, and John Martin Linde, Jr. American investigators arriving shortly afterward were pelted with stones, and Palestinian police entering a Palestinian refugee camp to investigate the attack came under machine-gun fire.

Baghdad, Iraq, October 26, 2003. On Sunday morning, Lieutenant Colonel Charles H. Buehring was killed and eleven Americans were wounded when Iraqis fired rockets at the fortified al-Rashid Hotel in Baghdad. Deputy Secretary of Defense Paul D. Wolfowitz, who was staying one floor above Buehring's eleventh-floor room, was not injured. Buehring, a Special Forces officer, was serving as an intelligence advisor to L. Paul Bremer, the top U.S. civilian official in Iraq. The next day, the Baghdad office of the International Red Cross was blown up.

Damascus, Syria, September 12, 2006. Just after 10:00 A.M. on the morning after the anniversary of 9/11, four men armed with automatic weapons, grenades, and a car bomb in a pickup truck attacked the walled U.S. Embassy from two sides. Syrian security forces killed the attackers in a fifteen-minute gun battle. A Syrian security guard and a passerby were also killed, and a dozen others were wounded.

Belgrade, Serbia, February 21, 2008. In the spring of 1999, when Christian Serbians tried to remove a million Muslim Albanians from Kosovo, a NATO air campaign drove out the Serbian military, and the United Nations took over the administration of Kosovo. Albanians, seeking revenge, drove out a hundred thousand Serbs from Kosovo.

A government-organized rally of a hundred thousand protestors opposed independence for Kosovo, and during the evening of February 21, 2008, attacked the U.S. Embassy and other nearby embassies. The Belgrade government closed the schools and brought demonstrators into the capital with free train rides. Protestors ripped down the American flag and threw burning flares through the U.S. Embassy windows, burning parts of the chancery.

Under Secretary R. Nicholas Burns demanded that Serbian security forces be sent to the embassy. The riot police moved slowly, but no Americans were killed or injured because Ambassador Cameron Munter, a career Foreign Service officer, had earlier sent home most of the staff and closed the embassy.

Istanbul, Turkey, July 9, 2008. Four young bearded gunmen killed three police officers and wounded two other Turks in a brief gun battle just outside the U.S. Consulate General at about 10:30 A.M. Police killed three gunmen; the fourth escaped. Ambassador Ross Wilson reported that no American was killed or wounded. After that, the venerable consulate building in the city center was replaced with a hilltop fortress protected by fifteen-foot-high walls.

Sanaa, Yemen, September 17, 2008. Sixteen people, none of them American, were killed when the fortified U.S. embassy was fired on at 9:15 A.M. by armed terrorists disguised as soldiers in camouflage uniforms. They also detonated a car bomb at the front gate. The dead included six attackers and six embassy guards. Yemen had been the scene of repeated attacks by Jihadists, including the bombing of the destroyer USS *Cole* in Aden harbor in 2000, during which seventeen American sailors had been killed.

Quetta, Pakistan, February 2, 2009. Gunmen kidnapped John Solecki, an American serving as head of the United Nations refugee office, and shot his driver, Syed Hashim, who died in a hospital. They had been driving to work in the provincial capital, Quetta, near the Afghan border. Solecki was in charge of the United Nations agency that supported four hundred thousand Afghan refugees in ten villages and camps. He was held hostage for sixty-two days and then released.

"A NEW GENERATION OF DIPLOMATS"

Terrorists have become a central life-and-death concern at every American embassy, legation, and consulate around the world. A great part of a senior FSO's time is diverted to anticipating terrorist attacks. Daniel Russel, DCM at the embassy at The Hague, commented, "Now, the issue is to provide for our own safety."

Terrorism has also increased the proliferation of U.S. Federal agencies stationed abroad, which now include even the Treasury and the Coast Guard. Often, these new members of the embassy team have not been trained for overseas duty. But they are all working on the same issue: security and counterterrorism. As the former Assistant Secretary of State for Diplomatic Security Anthony C. E. Quainton put it, "Coping with increasing levels of violence will require a new generation of diplomats, accustomed to living in conditions of instability and violence rather than in the orderly nineteenth-century world of balance-of-power diplomacy."

The epidemic of terrorist attacks has also truncated entry into the United States and has discouraged many people, especially students, from coming to the United States. The consul general in Amsterdam, Michele Bond, pointed out that a State Department's visa only determines entry itself, and the Department of Homeland Security now decides how long a student may stay. A visa permits a foreign citizen to travel to a U.S. port of entry, and there the Department of Homeland Security's U.S. Customs and Border Protection (CBP) immigration inspector decides. Although terrorists have experienced many failures, their attacks on American diplomats and missions overseas have disrupted American diplomacy.

43

A War Too Far—Vietnam

1952—75

American policy toward Indochina was a "muddled hodgepodge" ever since World War II, Secretary of State Dean Acheson has conceded. "I could not think then or later of a better course," he said. It remained a hodgepodge for more than a quarter of a century, until Ho Chi Minh's Viet Minh defeated France and the United States on the battlefield and at the conference table.

At first, the United States opposed the return of French colonial rule to Indochina and supported Ho Chi Minh's ambition for an independent Democratic Republic of Vietnam. But the commerce of Euro-centered colonialism won out over ideals of liberation. The Potsdam Conference assigned the surrender of the Japanese in Vietnam to the Nationalist Chinese in the North and the British in the South. The British brought back the French, and when they arrived, Ho Chi Minh's government disappeared from the South.

France's role in Indochina's nationalist-colonial struggle was regarded as an essential part of winning the global Cold War, of the revival of western Europe, and of the success of the Marshall Plan and NATO. In contrast, of course, the Vietnamese saw the struggle as a civil war for national independence.

South and North Vietnam were scheduled to hold unifying elections two years after the Geneva Agreements, which had ended the French-Vietnamese war with the battle of Dien Bien Phu in 1954. But because

Secretary John Foster Dulles feared the Communist North would win the elections and dominate the entire country, he eliminated the elections. Instead, North Vietnam set out to unify the country by force. As Ji Chaozhu wrote, "Dulles was the reactionary's reactionary, with a reputation for dealing with Communists as if he were killing snakes." Dulles' refusal to shake hands with Premier Zhou Enlai in Geneva became a public scandal.

Dulles sent out Colonel Edward G. Lansdale, of the CIA, to make the devoutly Catholic, anti-Communist Ngo Dinh Diem chief of state in South Vietnam. U.S. Ambassador Frederick Reinhardt had been thrilled when Diem easily won the farcical Southern election in 1955; Diem opposed reunification with the Communist North. By 1961, Secretary of State Dean Rusk believed that Diem's repressive rule had to be reformed to counter the South's growing support for the National Liberation Front (the Viet Cong). Rusk did not want to Americanize the war.

President Kennedy sent General Maxwell Taylor, former army chief of staff, to Vietnam. He returned to warn that without an American military presence, Diem would not make the needed reforms on his own. Rusk said that Diem had to make political reforms first in order for the infusion of American combat troops to be useful. Kennedy agreed.

By 1963, eighteen thousand U.S. military advisors were in South Vietnam. Many took part in combat. U.S. planes bombed the Viet Cong, and Buddhist monks burned themselves to death to protest Diem's brutalities. Kennedy replaced Ambassador Frederick Nolting, who also supported Diem, with Henry Cabot Lodge, Jr. And the United States took over the war.

On Saturday, August 24, the newly arrived ambassador Lodge received a cable from the State Department saying, "We must face the possibility that Diem himself cannot be preserved." The significance of that cable is still disputed. It culminated weeks of debate at Washington's highest levels. On that summer Saturday, President Kennedy, Secretary Rusk, and Secretary of Defense McNamara were all out of town. Roger Hilsman, Jr., the assistant secretary of state for far eastern affairs, who had been director of the State Department's Bureau of Intelligence and Research, sent the cable. Lodge interpreted it as legitimatizing a coup to get rid of Diem.

Afterward, Rusk confirmed that Under Secretary George Ball had telephoned him and that he understood Ball to say that President Kennedy had already approved the cable. The President had actually said he approved the cable if both Rusk and McNamara did. Rusk admitted "the Saturday cable was a snafu to which we all contributed."

On the night of November 2, General Duong Van Minh hunted down and executed Diem and his brother. (Twenty days later, President Kennedy himself was assassinated.)

Ambassador Lodge predicted that the Van Minh coup would shorten the war, but instead the Saigon government disintegrated. Diem, a powerful and ruthless dictator, had held the country together. In time, it was recognized that the United States had actually ended the rule of the Catholic, Frenchified, landowning mandarins.

Barely a year after the coup, McNamara explained why he thought the United States could not simply walk away from Vietnam:

> We saw a world where the Hanoi-supported Pathet Lao continued to push forward in Laos, where Sukarno appeared to be moving Indonesia foment closer to the Communist orbit, where Malaysia faced immense pressure from Communist-supported insurgents, where China had just detonated its first atomic device and continued to trumpet violent revolution, where Khrushchev and his successors in the Kremlin continued to make bellicose statements against the West. In light of all those threats, we viewed unconditional withdrawal as clearly unacceptable.

"A CATASTROPHIC WAR"

At 4:07 P.M. on August 2, 1964, the captain of the destroyer USS *Maddox* radioed from the Gulf of Tonkin that he was under attack. And he soon reported that *Maddox* and aircraft from USS *Ticonderoga* had damaged two North Vietnamese torpedo boats (PT) and left one dead in the water. Maxwell Taylor, the ambassador in Saigon, demanded a stronger reaction:

> Unprovoked attack against U.S. destroyer in international waters by three illegal North Vietnamese torpedo boats will be received dramatically in current atmosphere Saigon. It is not adequate to local minds (not indeed to ours) to state that attack was repelled and that patrol will continue.

Rusk reassured him. "We believe that present OPLAN 34A [secret patrols in the gulf] are beginning to rattle Hanoi, and *Maddox* incident is directly related to their effort to resist these activities. We have no intention [of] yielding to pressure." Two days later, on August 4, at 7:40 P.M., *Maddox* reported that she and destroyer *Turner Joy* faced an imminent attack. This time, President Johnson ordered retaliatory air strikes against North Vietnamese PT bases.

Contradictory reports soon started arriving. *Maddox*'s captain said torpedo firings were doubtful and no PT boats had actually been sighted. But the Joint Chiefs of Staff insisted the destroyers had been attacked. And Rusk asserted, "An immediate and direct reaction by us is necessary. An unprovoked attack on the high seas is an act of war for all practical purposes." USIA Director Carl Rowan was the first to ask whether the attack had actually happened. Secretary McNamara replied: We will know definitely in the morning.

At President Johnson's request, Joint Resolution 1145 overwhelmingly passed the Senate (88 to 2) and the House of Representatives (416 to 0). It supported taking "all necessary measures to repel any armed attack against the forces of the United States and to prevent further aggression." On August 10, Johnson signed it as Public Law 88-408, which empowered the President to conduct military actions in Southeast Asia.

Benjamin H. Read, Secretary Rusk's executive secretary at the time of the Tonkin incidents, said later of the alleged August 4 attack, "I recall there being a great deal of doubt about just exactly what had been approaching those destroyer units." Ten years later, the U.S. National Security Agency declassified an official report that said of August 4: "No attack happened that night." But a decade of war did begin that night.

The Viet Cong attacked American installations in South Vietnam. At 5:45 (the popular "happy hour") on Christmas Eve, two Viet Cong agents blew up Saigon's Brinks Hotel, a billet for U.S. officers. They killed two Americans and wounded fifty-eight.

President Johnson began bombing North Vietnam; and on February 26, 1965, he approved landing two battalions of Marines to secure the South Vietnam air base at Da Nang.

At midmorning on March 29, the Viet Cong exploded a car loaded with explosives outside the U.S. Embassy on the Saigon River waterfront, killing twenty-two people, including American secretary Barbara A.

Robbins, and wounding 188, including Deputy Ambassador U. Alexis Johnson and CIA Station Chief Peer de Silva. Congress promptly assigned a million dollars to build a massive, secure, white-concrete embassy in Saigon.

In July, Rusk told President Johnson he feared that if the United States deserted South Vietnam, it would lead to "a catastrophic war." Under Secretary Ball opposed the rising call for war and urged the United States to stick to diplomacy, even if it meant losing Vietnam.

North Vietnam sent more forces into the South, and President Johnson ordered raising U.S. troop strength there from 23,000 to 175,000. (The total would rise to 500,000.) He also authorized a pause in the bombing of North Vietnam and secret meetings in Paris between former Saigon DCM Edmond Guillion and North Vietnamese Consul General Mai Van Bo. The conversations were brief and accomplished nothing.

Other approaches were explored through a variety of American and UN officials, including White House Press Secretary Pierre Salinger; Ambassador John Gronouski in Warsaw; Ambassador Foy D. Kohler in Moscow; and Ambassador David K. E. Bruce in London. Every attempt crashed on the rocks of intransigence on both sides.

Johnson assembled a panel of elder statesman for their advice. He met one evening with former Secretary Dean Acheson; General of the Army Omar Bradley; John Cowles, publisher of *The Minneapolis Star, and Tribune*, and *Look* magazine; Eisenhower's Korea negotiator, Arthur Dean; former Secretary of Defense Robert Lovett; and former U.S. High Commissioner for Germany John McCloy. They all favored committing whatever forces were necessary to prevent South Vietnam from becoming Communist.

Late in the year, Ambassador Henry A. Byroade in Burma was also instructed to sound out his North Vietnamese counterpart on a discussion of the so-called Christmas bombing pause. The North Vietnamese responded that the American proposal was a trick. By the end of 1965, most authorities felt that military victory was fantasy. The war would drag on for ten more years.

The "mediator" the Americans found most objectionable was Charles de Gaulle, who demanded that the United States remove its troops from South Vietnam so negotiations could begin. Both the Kennedy and Johnson administrations believed de Gaulle's prescription would end with the communization of all Vietnam. On December 31, 1965, Arthur Goldberg, U.S. ambassador to the United Nations, met with de Gaulle in Paris, but they reached no compromise.

In August 1966, Lyndon Johnson, always fearful of looking weak, appointed Averell Harriman his "ambassador for peace" but assigned him to the State Department, rather than the White House. Johnson did not consult Harriman about policy. Harriman, with Chester Cooper, a Vietnam policy veteran, urged Johnson to approve a Christmas bombing pause. But the secret negotiations brought the parties no nearer to the bargaining table. Instead, a year later came the North's Tet offensive, followed at last by Johnson's unilateral bombing pause. Then the North Vietnamese were ready to talk.

A hopeful contact appeared in Paris in June 1967, when two Frenchmen, one of whom was a longtime friend of Ho Chi Minh, approached Henry Kissinger, who was then still a Harvard University professor. At the State Department's request, the two Frenchmen talked with Ho and with Premier Pham Van Dong in Hanoi and reported to Kissinger on their return to Paris. But before they could go back to Hanoi, the United States stepped up its bombing of the North. This kind of disconnect convinced the North Vietnamese to refuse to meet again.

The bombing of the North continued. Although Secretary McNamara and his aides, John T. McNaughton and Adam Yarmolinsky, no longer believed that bombing could decide the outcome, the uniformed chiefs of staff emphatically disagreed. The Pentagon was divided.

As casualties piled up and the draft disrupted young lives, more Americans became convinced that the United States could not win on this battlefield on the other side of the globe. And some, like Senator J. William Fulbright, felt that a Communist and nationalistic regime in Vietnam might, in fact, serve as a barricade against Communist China.

A DIPLOMATIC DIMENSION

In 1968, five years after Diem's assassination, the Communists attempted to expand the war from the rural countryside to the population centers of South Vietnam. To draw American troops away from those cities, the North Vietnamese attacked the Marine Corps base at Khe Sanh in the hills on the northern border of South Vietnam. Then, at the end of January, at the time of the Tet lunar new year, sixty thousand North Vietnamese and Viet Cong soldiers attacked the South's cities and towns. This Tet offensive staggered the American commanders.

Ambassador Ellsworth Bunker, who had replaced Lodge, was sending Washington positive reports based on what the generals told him. President Johnson had drafted Bunker on the urging of Nicholas Katzenbach and former National Security Advisor McGeorge Bundy, and he was determined to prevent South Vietnam falling to the Communists. Katzenbach had succeeded Robert Kennedy as Attorney General at the beginning of 1965 but resigned the following year and replaced George W. Ball as Under Secretary of State, the number two job in the State Department. He left the government on November 8, 1968, three days after Richard Nixon was elected President, and went to work for IBM.

The astonishing Tet offensive started on Wednesday, January 31, 1968. The Communists seized the ancient capital of Hue and held it for twenty-five days. Several thousand Viet Cong penetrated Saigon and devastated the capital. They seized the main radio station and assaulted the presidential palace.

At 2:47 A.M., nineteen black-pajama-clad commandos blew a hole in the compound wall of the new fortresslike U.S. Embassy in the heart of Saigon. Marine guards and Army MPs fought them; Saigon policemen simply fled. The attackers, firing AK-47s and B-40 grenade launchers, killed the two American MPs at the front gate, after the MPs had killed the Viet Cong leader. The commandos blew open the doors of the six-story chancery.

E. Allan Wendt, a junior Foreign Service officer on night duty, locked himself in the code-room stronghold. (Wendt would become the first American ambassador to Slovenia in 1992.) By 3:15 A.M., the Associated Press' Peter Arnett told the world that the U.S. Embassy was under attack. Additional MPs rushed to the main gate, and helicopters tried to land paratroopers of the 101st Airborne Division on the roof. A Viet Cong machine gun held off the paratroopers until it was silenced at dawn.

An MP tossed a .45 and a gas mask up to Colonel George D. Jacobson, of the U.S. military mission, through a second-floor window of the building where he lived. The last Viet Cong invader charged up the stairs firing at Jacobson. He missed, and the colonel's first shot at point-blank range killed him.

The attack on the embassy had more political than military effect. Fought before television cameras, it shocked millions of Americans. In his Pulitzer Prize–winning book on the war, Stanley Karnow wrote, "On the eve of the Tet offensive, therefore, the Communists added a diplomatic dimension to their plan."

The Viet Cong also fired on Ambassador Bunker's residence. His Marine Guard hustled him, in his bathrobe, into an armored personnel carrier and sped to a secret "safe house." At dawn, the Marines flushed his residence with tear gas in case Viet Cong were hiding there, and then took him back to dress and then to the embassy. He sent a reassuring cable to his wife, Carol Laise, who was serving as the ambassador in Kathmandu, the capital of Nepal.

After six and a half hours of fighting, at 9:15 A.M., the embassy was declared secure. Whether the Viet Cong commandos actually penetrated the chancery has been debated ever since. General William C. Westmoreland arrived five minutes later and declared no enemy had entered the embassy. The MPs on the scene said otherwise.

Four U.S. Army MPs and a Marine corporal were killed defending the embassy, and seventeen of the nineteen attackers died. In Hue, Stephen Miller of the USIA was one of the many defenders executed. Three days later, Bunker dared to tell reporters that the Tet attack had outraged the South Vietnamese and that the Viet Cong held no important objectives, although Hue still remained in enemy hands.

The results of the Tet offensive were mixed. The Communists lost a large number of men but demonstrated their ability to carry the war to the cities. In the end, the South Vietnamese people did not rise. Meanwhile, in the United States, two-thirds of those polled no longer supported President Johnson. The tipping of the American opinion against the war was Tet's most important result. Don North, who covered the attack on the embassy for ABC and NBC news, judged that "Tet was the beginning of the end of the Vietnam War."

Robert McNamara, who no longer believed the war could be won, was moved to the World Bank and was succeeded as secretary of defense on March 1 by Clark Clifford. He arrived in Vietnam with a reputation for toughness, but as soon as he examined the situation firsthand, he recommended that the United States stop wasting young men's lives. Secretary Rusk proposed that the bombing of North Vietnam be stopped to encourage the Communists to negotiate an end to the war.

Nicholas Katzenbach sent President Johnson a review drafted for him by his assistant, Richard Holbrooke, saying in part, "Time is the crucial element at this stage of our involvement in Vietnam. Can the tortoise of progress in Vietnam stay ahead of the rabbit of dissent at home?" After Tet, the only eventual answer to that question was: "No!"

FIVE MORE YEARS OF TALK AND WAR

On March 31, 1968, Johnson announced on television that he would decrease the bombing of North Vietnam. And he concluded dramatically, and unexpectedly, "I shall not seek, and I will not accept, the nomination of my party for another term as your President." Within five days, the North Vietnamese offered to negotiate toward peace. The peace talks dragged on for five years.

Averell Harriman and Cyrus Vance, the American representatives, sat down at the table in Paris on May 10, but they made little progress. The Communists wanted the National Liberation Front (Viet Cong) given a place at the peace-talk table, and the Americans demanded that the North's forces leave South Vietnam.

Into the fall, all the negotiators were occupied with a notorious bit of maneuvering that was known in the United States as discussing "the shape of the table." The North Vietnamese wanted the Paris peace talks at the Hotel Majestic to be a four-way conference of the United States, the two governments of Hanoi and Saigon, and the National Liberation Front (NLF). However, the United States insisted that the talks be two-sided; its delegation would include the Republic of Vietnam's delegation. Whether Hanoi included the NLF on its side of the table was up to them. The Saigon government would not participate if the NLF was present "as a separate entity." They compromised on "two separate tables facing each other." Eventually, two rectangular tables were added for the foreign ambassadors, whose troops were to supervise the cease-fire.

Among many procedural issues, the early discussions debated the number of days between the cessation of the bombing of North Vietnam and the date of the first meeting of all four parties at the Hotel Majestic. The United States wanted the meetings to begin the day after the bombing stopped. President Johnson did not want to have to restart bombing. He said, "But after we stop the bombing, I expect them to be ready to move and have their tennis shoes on."

The American presidential election was approaching; and, on October 31, President Johnson announced the end of bombing of North Vietnam. The 1968 election took place amidst a nightmare of deceit and conspiracies; spying and wiretapping; the Tet offensive; bloody riots during the Democratic convention; the assassination of Robert Kennedy; and Richard Nixon's phony secret "plan to win the war." The bartering and trading and stonewalling went on and on, frustrating, contradictory, and baffling.

When Richard Nixon assumed the presidency in January 1969, he named Henry Kissinger his national security advisor and sent a new team led by Henry Cabot Lodge, Jr., to the Paris peace talks. Bunker had expected to come home, but Nixon asked him to stay on in Saigon. The new administration instituted "Vietnamization," a program to hand over the fighting to the South Vietnamese and start bringing U.S. troops home. General Creighton Abrams, then commander of U.S. forces in Vietnam, called Vietnamization "slow surrender."

(Prior to his second trip to Vietnam in 1969, the author interviewed National Security Advisor Kissinger and asked him whether Vietnamization expected to prepare the South Vietnam army to fight the Viet Cong or the stronger North Vietnam forces. Kissinger pushed a button under his desk, and an army colonel appeared. Kissinger repeated the question. Colonel Alexander M. Haig, Jr., said, "I don't know, sir. But I'll find out." Neither of them knew. They were concentrated on the domestic political effect of Vietnamization in the United States, not on foreign policy.)

Bunker wanted to bomb enemy bases in Cambodia and North Vietnam and begin ground operations into Cambodia. Nixon, in his frustration and what Stanley Karnow called his "pugnacious paranoia," widened the war by invading neutral Cambodia in April 1970. The reaction at home was ferocious. Two hundred State Department employees petitioned their opposition to their President. Four students demonstrating at Kent State University in Ohio were killed by National Guard rifle fire. Four of Kissinger's close aides quit, and nearly a hundred thousand demonstrators marched in Washington. The American public's anger cut short the invasion of Cambodia. One analyst wrote, "This may be the real lesson of Vietnam. A free people has to believe in what it is doing."

Bunker thought the opposition irrational. After a 1971 South Vietnam election that gave President Thieu more than 90 percent of the votes, the State Department had to defend Bunker against demands that he be fired. The Communists knew that the Viet Cong, devastated by losses during Tet, could not defeat the South Vietnamese on the battlefield.

After Tet, the United States and South Vietnam governments expanded the covert Phoenix Program, which was designed to destroy the Viet Cong's local leadership in South Vietnam. Tet had brought into the open thousands of Vietnamese who favored the Communists, and they now became the Phoenix Program's targets. The ruthless William F. Colby, who ran Phoenix for the CIA, estimated that by 1971 Phoenix had killed 20,857 Vietnamese.

Nixon and Kissinger were obsessed with secrecy. Ambassador William H. Sullivan later learned that when he was assigned to the State Department, the White House tapped his telephone calls at both his office and home, at least until his loyalty to the Nixon administration had been assured. As the Paris peace talks stretched on, Kissinger began meeting secretly at various places outside Paris with Le Duc Tho, the head of the North Vietnamese delegation to the peace talks. Kissinger played this back-channel activity so close to his vest that not even the Secretary of State knew about their repeated meetings.

Of course, the Russians did. At one point, Brezhnev reportedly joked to Kissinger, "If you get rid of the State Department then we will get rid of the Foreign Office." And Kissinger replied with unintended candor, "With all respect, Mr. General-Secretary, we have made more progress in abolishing the State Department than you have in abolishing the Foreign Office." Helmut Sonnenfeldt, staff member of the National Security Council and State Department counselor, said the State Department "simply felt that they were being made fools of, because the Soviets would know that they didn't know. . . . You have to make sure that you don't demoralize your normal diplomatic establishment." Sonnenfeldt's and Kissinger's visions of Soviet-American relations often clashed, despite their similar backgrounds as native Germans and scholars of international affairs.

. . .

Agreement and peace continued to be elusive. Neither side would compromise. Even when Nixon and Kissinger traveled to Beijing with cameras rolling in February 1972, and both Americans and Chinese wanted the war to end, the trip proved to be yet another dead end to peace in Vietnam.

In March, the North Vietnamese launched their Easter offensive to prove that Vietnamization was an illusion. By then, relatively few U.S. combat troops remained in South Vietnam. The Easter offensive was stopped in September only because B-52s flew thousands of bombing sorties, including massive strikes against targets in North Vietnam. Kissinger went to Moscow (of course, without informing U.S. Ambassador Jacob Beam) to obtain Soviet help in ending the endless war. That trip, too, proved another useless detour.

The secret Kissinger–Le Duc Tho talks continued sporadically through 1972, but by October both North and South Vietnam opposed the American peace proposal. Nixon and Kissinger were now eager to end the war before the U.S. elections. On October 8, Le Duc Tho presented a draft treaty, which did not require replacing the South Vietnamese government, and in four days they hammered out an agreement. John Negroponte, Foreign Service liaison officer to the North Vietnamese in Paris, admitted later that the "draft agreement was essentially the one we signed four months later. But in the process, we really overlooked consulting the government of South Vietnam adequately."

The South Vietnamese government did not participate in the settlement. The draft agreement provided that American forces would withdraw in sixty days and that prisoners of war would be returned, but President Thieu rejected it because the North Vietnamese would remain in the South.

In mid-December (after the American elections), Nixon ordered another massive air offensive against Hanoi and Haiphong. Deputy Assistant Secretary William H. Sullivan, who had been the ambassador to Laos and to the Philippines, said, "We warned them [the North Vietnamese] that our president would resume bombing of the north. They seemed not to believe the nature of this threat." The Washington Post called the air attacks "savage and senseless."

When Thieu realized that Nixon and Kissinger would sign a peace agreement with or without him, he buckled. On January 8, 1973, the two covert negotiators met again and settled their differences in a day. On the eleventh, Kissinger cabled Nixon that the agreement was ready.

The Paris peace talks ended on January 27 in the elaborate grand ballroom of the Hotel Majestic. A cease-fire agreement was signed on the huge round table around which the enemies had castigated each other for years. Foreign Service officer Heywood Isham was the acting head of the U.S. delegation. Two ceremonies were required because the Saigon government refused to imply its recognition of the Viet Cong.

After years of talks, the truce in place proved to be temporary. U.S. forces agreed to go home, but the fighting was not over. Henry Kissinger and Le Duc Tho received the Nobel Peace Prize. Nixon declared the Paris peace accord "peace with honor." Historian Edwin E. Möise called it "a joke."

"WHITE CHRISTMAS" IN VIETNAM

At best, a truce was not peace. Richard M. Moose, who had repeatedly served as a Foreign Service officer, said they had achieved nothing but "a fighting cease fire." The North Vietnamese opened another (and final) offensive in December 1974. They were intent on taking Saigon before the rains came in May. They seized Hue again on March 25 and Da Nang on Easter Sunday (March 28). After they won a ten-day battle at Xuan Loc, thirty miles from Saigon, on April 20, the capital lay helpless before them.

American civilians had already been leaving Saigon. They could get out relatively easily; but the South Vietnamese fleeing before the advancing Northerners depended on a black market for passports and exit visas. The evacuation was managed by the State Department, even though Ambassador A. Graham Martin, who succeeded Bunker in Saigon, claimed the capital could be defended. Some felt his view had been formed when his foster son, a Marine lieutenant in a helicopter gunship, had been killed in Vietnam. Kissinger also opposed full-scale evacuation because it would further weaken the South Vietnam government. Reality seemed hard to grasp.

The job of saving the Americans, military and civilian, scattered around South Vietnam was chaotic. In charge of that effort was Wolfgang J. Lehmann, who had the special title of deputy ambassador and who established an evacuation control center at Saigon's Tan Son Nhut airfield.

Further north in the I Corps area, Foreign Service officer Theresa Tull was in charge at Da Nang. She had managed to qualify for the Foreign Service in 1963 even though she did not have a college degree. She arrived in Saigon as a junior political officer two weeks before the 1968 Tet offensive, went back to the States, and returned in August 1973 as deputy head of the consulate general at Da Nang. By then, most of the U.S. military was gone, and Tull attended and reported on the briefings of the three-star Vietnamese general in charge. She also supervised an overview report that had input from the provincial offices and concluded that I Corps was not viable without a U.S. military presence. Tull's report was killed in Ambassador Martin's embassy. It never reached Washington.

Just before the final North Vietnamese offensive, Consul General Albert A. Francis, Tull's superior, was medevaced to the States, and she was in charge. She learned from the CIA that the South Vietnamese were pulling their best divisions back to Saigon and abandoning I Corps. She organized an evacuation plan to take out families and Vietnamese employees. Since Ambassador Martin was in Washington for what was called "dental work," Wolfgang Lehmann approved Tull's plan. Vietnamese employees and their spouses and children were flown to Saigon.

On March 18, Lehmann instructed Tull to keep her team in Da Nang. Mobs took over the airfield there, and later that month Consul General Francis, who had just returned, had Tull evacuated in the last scheduled Air America flight to Saigon. He escaped with his staff by barge and a Vietnamese frigate. Da Nang was no longer an American base. In Saigon, Tull helped organize the evacuation, and then she was flown to the United States. (She later became chargé d'affaires ad interim in Laos and ambassador to Guyana and Brunei.)

Until the very end, Ambassador Martin believed South Vietnam could survive and he dragged his feet getting cooperative Vietnamese out of the country. He explained to *Time* magazine correspondents Roy Rowan and William Stewart, "You have a nation here that we encouraged to resist, gave assurances to, not in treaty form, but quite precisely. . . . For all sorts of specious reasons we have reneged on every one of these agreements. My only regret is that I did not speak out more openly, to the distaste of the State Department."

. . .

As the North Vietnamese army neared Saigon, their aircraft shot up the flight line at Tan Son Nhut on the evening of April 28. Before dawn, rockets hit the airfield, and two Marine Security Guards were killed. That ended the round-the-clock operation of fixed-wing aircraft.

Early that morning, Major General Homer D. Smith, the defense attaché, reported to Ambassador Martin that the Tan Son Nhut runways were unfit for use and that the evacuation would have to continue with helicopters. Martin insisted on seeing for himself and headed for the airport. Two Marines led in an advance jeep; a driver and escort were in the ambassador's car, and two more Marines rode in a following car. The airbase was in flames. Aircraft were burning on the tarmac, and the runway was cratered by bombs.

A strong believer in symbols, Martin refused to have cut down a giant tamarind tree that dominated the embassy lawn. While it was there, helicopters arriving from aircraft carriers could not land. But as late as April 29, he still insisted that if it were cut down, American prestige would suffer. In the evacuation's final hours, someone chopped down the tree. Then, as the prearranged signal for Americans to proceed to the evacuation points, the American Forces Radio station began to play, over and over again, Bing Crosby's "White Christmas."

A thousand people crowded into the embassy compound, frantically seeking a way out. Martin and Lehmann sent a final message, closing the mission. By nightfall, after eighteen desperate hours, seventy Marine Corps helicopters had helped carry out a thousand Americans and nearly five thousand Vietnamese, two thousand from the U.S. Embassy compound. Marines manned machine guns on the four corners of the embassy roof. Other Marines shoved back Vietnam civilians trying to climb the walls.

During that final night of frightened pandemonium, a helicopter landed on the roof and in the parking lot every ten minutes. The landing zone on the roof was marked only with a barrel of burning oil and rubbish. At 3:45 A.M., Ambassador Martin announced that from then on only Americans would be flown out, although there was an urgent need to evacuate Vietnamese who had worked with the Americans or belonged to families of Vietnamese married to Americans. Martin, ordered to board the last helicopter, went home to get his black poodle, and at 4:30 A.M. he and his wife climbed from the chancery roof into a helicopter named *Lady Ace 09*. The Marine Guard was removed just before seven o'clock. The last helicopter left at 7:53 A.M.

On July 11, 1997, two decades after the dawn when Saigon fell, Congressman Douglas B. Peterson, of Florida, became the first United States ambassador to the Socialist Republic of Vietnam. During the war, Peterson had been a captain in the air force. He and his copilot, Lieutenant Bernard L. Talley, Jr., had been shot down on Peterson's sixty-fifth combat mission and Talley's seventy-sixth. They both had endured as POWs in North Vietnam's "Hanoi Hilton" for six and a half years.

In all, 978 Americans and 1,120 Vietnamese and others were airlifted from the Saigon embassy. The North Vietnamese did not fire at the evacuation helicopters. But they quickly looted the deserted U.S. Embassy.

Lehmann estimated that, in all, 27,000 people were taken out of Vietnam, most of them to Guam and the Philippines. Much later, Robert McNamara wrote of a terrible lesson learned:

> Our misjudgments of friend and foe alike reflected our profound ignorance of the history, culture, and politics of the people in the area, and the personalities and habits of their leaders. We might have made similar misjudgments regarding the Soviets during our frequent confrontations—over Berlin, Cuba, the Middle East, for example, had we not had the advice of Tommy Thompson, Chip Bohlen, and George Kennan. These senior diplomats had spent decades studying the Soviet Union, its people and its leaders, why they behaved as they did, and how they would react to our actions. Their advice proved invaluable in shaping our judgments and decision. No Southeast Asia counterparts existed for senior officials to consult when making decisions on Vietnam.

The long war and its outcome were disillusioning to the entire United States and, of course, its Foreign Service. The lessons that American leaders chose to learn were confusing. Historian Robert Jervis recognized that "for the United States, the Vietnam War was never about Vietnam, but rather about its impact on the Cold War."

When the end came in 1975, Dien Bien Phu was twenty-one years in the past. More than 58,000 Americans, and untold thousands of Vietnamese, were dead. The North Vietnamese Communists owned Saigon, which was now Ho Chi Minh City.

44

Destiny and the Peacock Throne

1951–81

During the afternoon of the Fourth of July 1951, six men sat on the veranda of Averell Harriman's Georgetown home overlooking the Potomac River. Secretary of State Dean Acheson had brought them together to discuss candidly and privately the British government's militant reaction to the government of Iran's nationalization of the Anglo-Iranian Oil Company's (AIOC) facilities and the great refinery at Abadan.

In addition to Acheson and Harriman, the others conferring on the veranda were Under Secretary of State H. Freeman Matthews; Paul Nitze, director of the State Department's Policy Planning Staff; George McGhee, assistant secretary of state for Near Eastern, South Asian, and African affairs; and Sir Oliver Franks, the British ambassador to Washington. But the man at the heart of the controversy was not there—Mohammad Mossadegh, Iran's prime minister, who had persuaded the Majlis, the parliament, to nationalize Iran's oil resources.

Sir Oliver, who had just returned from London, told the Americans that his government and the British people were furious at the "wild men in Iran" who had violated the 1933 agreement by which the oil company had invested millions of British pounds in Iran. British warships were already patrolling off Abadan, he said, and troops were preparing to move out.

The Americans on the veranda agreed that if the British Royal Navy intervened, the Soviet Union would land troops to support its own oil concession in the northern province of Azerbaijan. Iran would be divided into spheres of influence, and Britain would still be unable to recover its oil fields. The Russians would replace the British as the most powerful foreigners in Iran. Acheson summarized: "In short, armed intervention offered nothing except great trouble."

At the end of the afternoon, Acheson proposed sending Harriman to Tehran to try to move negotiations forward. Everyone (except Harriman) was enthusiastic about the idea. The next day, President Harry S Truman cabled Prime Minister Mossadegh, through U.S. Ambassador, Henry F. Grady in Tehran, and asked him to meet with Harriman.

Britain and Russia had vied for control of Iran, which sat on Britain's route to India and on Russia's southern frontier. And in 1907, the two powers had agreed to divide Iran. The very next year, a British explorer discovered great supplies of oil in western Iran; and just before World War I, the British government bought 51 percent of the Anglo-Persian Oil Company for the oil-burning Royal Navy.

After the Bolshevik Revolution, the Soviet Union withdrew from Iran, and the British had control. They turned the so-called Peacock Throne over to Reza Khan, who proved to be a ruthless ruler and who, as Reza Shah Pahlavi, cozied up to the Nazis. In 1941, the British and Russians sent in troops and forced him to abdicate in favor of his eldest son, twenty-one-year-old Shah Mohammad Reza Pahlavi.

The British-dominated company, renamed the Anglo-Iranian Oil Company, exploited Iran, refused to let the Iranians see its books, and housed its "native" workers in hovels. After World War II, Iran stumbled toward chaos. Ambassador Grady had served as assistant secretary of state for economic affairs until he was replaced, in February 1941, by a recruit from the Treasury Department, Dean Acheson. Grady arrived in Iran in 1950, amidst a major Iranian crop failure and raging riots.

By then, the United States had decided that the Arabian-American Oil Company (Aramco) would be the sole developer of oil in Saudi Arabia. George McGhee and Ambassador J. Rives Childs presented the American case to King Ibn Saud. Significantly, Aramco agreed to split profits equally with Saudi Arabia.

When AIOC and the British government refused to match the Aramco policy on revenues, tension in Iran climbed to the boiling point.

Assistant Secretary McGhee was sent to London to persuade the British to negotiate, without success. McGhee was born in Waco, Texas, and had been a Rhodes Scholar and a Louisiana oil wildcatter. Much later, he served as chair of the State Department's Policy Planning Staff, and as Under Secretary for political affairs.

Arriving in Tehran, McGhee found the British ambassador angry at the United States, and the shah impotent. In February 1951, McGhee summoned the chiefs of all U.S. diplomatic missions in the Middle East to a secret meeting in Istanbul. Over three days of discussions, the participants decided their prime job was to prevent the Soviet Union from gaining control of any Middle Eastern country. They also agreed that the obstinacy of the British company (AIOC) was encouraging Communism in Iran.

Assistant Secretary McGhee led another conference in the hill country of Sri Lanka, then called Ceylon. The fifty-seven Foreign Service officers there determined that the Cold War was America's central concern but that the most demanding problem for the underdeveloped nations was poverty. The United States and the smaller countries were focusing on different issues.

On March 7, 1951, Iran's Prime Minister Ali Razmara was assassinated, and Britain posted warships off the Abadan oil refinery. Mohammad Mossadegh became prime minister and set out to nationalize Iran's oil facilities. He would not allow British tankers to sail with Iranian oil. Since Iran had no tankers of its own, the refinery would have to close when its storage tanks were full. Despite this, nationalization was emotionally popular in Tehran.

As a diplomat who knew about oil, McGhee found the shah in Tehran too frightened to oppose nationalization. McGhee advised the State Department that policy on all Middle East oil should be coordinated, mostly based on the equal division that Aramco was offering Saudi Arabia, and that AIOC should continue to operate in Iran.

At the British government's request, he traveled to London and met with Foreign Secretary Herbert Morrison. En route to London, he stopped at other capitals. Hours after he left Damascus for Beirut, the room he had occupied at the U.S. Legation in Damascus was dynamited. Damage was severe, but no one was injured. McGhee said, "I wanted to believe that the perpetrator knew I had gone and wanted only to register a protest."

In May, U.S. Ambassador Walter Gifford in London cabled Secretary

Acheson that the British were preparing to invade Iran. Acheson objected, and Prime Minister Clement Attlee, instead, sent troops to Iraq next door and explored other covert actions.

Fearing that Britain and Iran were playing Russian roulette, Acheson had organized the meeting on the Harriman veranda. When Harriman reached Tehran, he was driven into the city by a circuitous route to avoid angry crowds demonstrating in the streets. To the Iranians, Harriman appeared to be one more foreigner interfering in their affairs.

Touring the Abadan refinery, Harriman was horrified by the slums the Iranian workers lived in. Sitting with Mossadegh in his upstairs bedroom Harriman made practical arguments for compromises. The prime minister was not interested; he wanted only to get rid of the British oil company and foreign influences.

Ambassador Grady cabled Washington that Iran was "explosive." The British imposed sanctions and asked the United States to help overthrow Mossadegh. But President Truman refused, urging the British to compromise with Iran. Acheson described Mossadegh as "a demagogue of considerable shrewdness and ability . . . a great actor and a great gambler."

Tehran newspapers quoted Ambassador Grady as predicting Iran was on the verge either of war with Britain or a Communist takeover. That riled the British so much that Acheson replaced Grady with Ambassador Loy Henderson; and had Chester Bowles succeed Henderson in New Delhi.

Henderson too spent hours at Mossadegh's bedside debating the issues. The distinguished prime minister, educated in Paris and Switzerland, feared the now-fading domination of Britain, but he could not be persuaded that the Soviet Union was even more dangerous.

Mossadegh flew to New York in October 1951, addressed the United Nations Security Council, and visited Truman in Washington. To the UN and to Truman, Mossadegh emphasized the importance of oil as a national resource able to lift Iran's people out of poverty. But the new Churchill-Eden government would not make concessions. Oil was too important and too profitable. Lieutenant Colonel Vernon Walters visited Mossadegh at Walter Reed Hospital and pointed out that Mossadegh was going home empty-handed. Mossadegh said that not being in debt to the United States gave him strength.

In 1952, Mossadegh broke diplomatic relations with Britain, and Foreign Secretary Eden began designing a coup. Acheson decided the United States should start steering its own course and to explore whether American oil companies might purchase $100 million of Iranian oil, an idea President Truman approved. The threat that the United States would go it alone moved the British, as Eden wrote, to look for "alternatives to Mussadig."

Time ran out. In January 1953, President Dwight Eisenhower brought in a more aggressive attitude toward Iran. Secretary of State John Foster Dulles prophesied that if the Soviet Union took over Iran, the rest of the Middle East would follow, and the Russians would control 60 percent of the world's oil. Dulles advised his brother, Allen, director of the young CIA, that Mossadegh was leading Iran toward Communism and must be removed.

Secretary Dulles summoned Henderson home in June; when Eisenhower's advisors heard Henderson's recommendations, they approved a coup, called Operation Ajax, to be organized jointly by the CIA and the British Secret Intelligence Service.

Kermit Roosevelt, chief of the CIA's Near East and African Division and grandson of President Theodore Roosevelt, organized the final stages of Operation Ajax from a basement office in the U.S. Embassy compound in Tehran. Intelligence operatives even brought the shah's dynamic twin sister, Princess Ashraf Pahlavi, from Europe to convince her brother to dump the popular Mossadegh. Iran was engulfed in intrigue, riots, and violence. Late on Saturday, August 15, the coup was launched. It failed.

The careful plotting misfired because a leak allowed the Iranian soldiers loyal to Mossadegh to overwhelm the army unit sent to seize him. The shah, widely disliked for his cruelty and arrogance, flew off to Baghdad and then on to Rome.

Ambassador Henderson returned to his post the next afternoon. He threatened to evacuate Americans if Mossadegh would not protect them. Kermit Roosevelt soon organized a second coup. This time he brought in the mullahs, the Islamic clergy, with cash. The army helped him mobilize pro-shah demonstrations. At Mossadegh's home, a gun battle erupted. As the house burned, he fled over the garden wall in his pajamas and went into hiding. By evening, General Mohammad Fazlollah Zahedi, loyal to the shah and to the Americans, was in control. Ambassador Henderson was thrilled.

The CIA's secret history of the coup explained with a straight face: "By the end of 1952 it had become clear that the Mossadeg government in Iran was incapable of reaching an oil settlement with interested Western countries." The shah flew home from Rome, and Kermit Roosevelt quietly left the country. Mossadegh spent three years in prison and the rest of his life in the countryside under house arrest. The CIA quickly made $5 million available to the government; and the shah, back on the Peacock Throne, treated dissenters with decisive barbarity. In December 1954, Henderson, a single-minded anti-Communist, was brought home and put in charge of reorganizing the State Department, which had been badly wounded by McCarthy's attacks.

A consortium was formed called the National Iranian Oil Company (NIOC). The British-based AIOC, now British Petroleum, owned 40 percent of NIOC, five American companies together owned 40 percent, and the rest was divided between the Dutch and the French. Profits were to be divided evenly between the NIOC and Iran, but the Iranians still could not inspect the NIOC books. The United States was viewed in Iran with intense hostility.

The British shared Iranian oil with the United States and its oil companies. There was plenty of oil to share; Iran was the world's second largest oil exporter after Saudi Arabia. The United States gave Iran substantial economic and military aid. But years later, Ambassador L. Bruce Laingen admitted, "We were wrong. At least history tells we were wrong if events since that time [are] any indication of that."

"OUR DESTINY IS TO WORK WITH THE SHAH"

The shah used his great oil revenues to modernize, secularize, and arm his country. He exhibited monumental displays of extravagance and corruption. In contrast, the ruling family of Saudi Arabia used its great new oil wealth to strengthen its traditional values and systems, rather than to overthrow them.

American diplomats admired the shah's efforts to build village health clinics, improve roads, and establish universities. Nicholas Thacher, the deputy chief of mission in Tehran, said, "We loved to see these tangible accomplishments, the new dam that our aid helped to build created the water supply for Tehran. Here was a modern monarch who wanted these things, who tried to develop his country, trying to raise his people."

The truth was the shah ruled from the Peacock Throne through force and intimidation, while his aides dipped greedily into his vast wealth. Iran was a depressing example of a traditional society attempting unsuccessfully to transform itself into a modern industrialized nation.

Many Iranians of all classes wished for their society to return to the Islamic traditions that governed their lives before oil became supreme. Shiite religious leaders aroused the people against the godless, materialistic West. Both the shah and the United States, now deeply dependent on each other, became the targets of discontent and anger.

Within the Islamic world (not only in Iran), battle lines were drawn between those who wanted to live in the modern world and those who treasured the traditions of an older way of life. Deputy Secretary of State Richard Armitage saw this fundamental conflict as continuing the "aftershocks of the dissolution of the Ottoman Empire." The shah was the United States' instrument for trying to bring stability to the Middle East's oil-rich nations.

The shah met in Tehran at the end of May 1972 with President Nixon and his national security advisor, Henry Kissinger. They gave him a blank check, said some State Department veterans, in exchange for which he would protect U.S. interests in the Persian Gulf area.

But in exile in Paris sat the seventy-year-old Ayatollah Ruholla Khomeini, a powerful Shiite religious leader who opposed the shah's "Westoxication" of Iran and who desired to lead Iran back to its Islamic roots. The shah had first imprisoned him and then, in 1964, had exiled him. He waited; his time would come.

In Iran, problems were already visible. As soon as President Nixon left Tehran, the shah pressured the foreign oil company consortium to give Iran more of the revenues. And by August 1972, Ambassador Joseph S. Farland in Tehran was warning the State Department that unless the shah improved the living conditions of ordinary Iranians, he faced a rebellion.

The shah did not join the Arab oil embargo in 1973, and the United States allowed him to purchase $10 billion more worth of military equipment and to engage military advisors. Carter continued this interdependence and granted the shah another $1.1 billion in military purchases.

William H. Sullivan, who had served as a colorful, hard-bitten ambassador in Laos and the Philippines, became the U.S. ambassador to Tehran in 1977. He raised troublesome questions about the social and economic consequences of the shah's huge arms expenditures.

Ambassador Sullivan managed a mission of two thousand Americans and two thousand Iranians, and he tried harder to understand Iran than had earlier envoys. He expected that the shah's industrialization program would lure young men into the cities, where there were no jobs.

With 1978 came trouble. President and Mrs. Carter celebrated a pleasant if well-guarded New Year's Eve in Tehran, but in January a Shiite revolt against the shah broke out in the religious city of Qom. This uprising was ignited by the death of Khomeini's son. Many Iranians believed he was killed by SAVAK, the shah's secret police, which the Americans had helped set up. Growing out of both fervent nationalism and religious fundamentalism, the revolt threatened the flow of oil to the West. And in April in nearby Afghanistan, a pro-Communist coup replaced the monarchy. The shah was in danger.

Leaders in Washington began searching for options for dealing with the Islamist threat. The State Department looked for political alternatives, and Carter's National Security Advisor Zbigniew Brzezinski hunted for a solution with the Iranian military.

Demonstrations against the shah grew more and more violent; the Islamic revolution tore Iran apart. Ayatollah Khomeini, although still in Paris, assumed the leadership of the opposition, making effective use of the press and television. At the end of Ramadan, on September 6, tens of thousands of well-organized protestors marched through Tehran.

The shah declared martial law. Dependents among the 35,000 Americans in Iran began leaving the country, and American businesses cut back their personnel. Oil production dropped precipitously, and Iran's economy threatened to crumble. Ambassador Sullivan voiced American policy in October 1978: "Our destiny is to work with the Shah." But the future of the United States' relationship with Iran became very much in doubt.

Secretary of State Cyrus Vance called in former Under Secretary George Ball to critique the crisis. And Brzezinski opened a back channel to Tehran without the State Department's knowledge. He even telephoned the shah directly. Vance forced a confrontation with Brzezinski in President Carter's presence and shut down the back channel. By early November, the forces of the shah in Tehran were battling those of Khomeini, who branded the United States "the Great Satan." Strikes in the oil fields threatened to create a worldwide shortage. After one meeting at the prime minister's office, Ambassador Sullivan and British Ambassador Sir Anthony Derrick Parsons had to flee from a mob in Parsons' Rolls-Royce and seek safety in a bank building. Another mob torched the British chancery as part of a wider burning of Tehran.

Sullivan warned that the shah's regime might not survive. And Washington politicians accused the intelligence services of reporting that left them unprepared for the evaporation of the shah's support. Ambassador Sullivan recommended that the United States champion an accommodation between Iran's pro-Western military and the powerful Shiite clergy.

On November 22, Secretary Vance instructed Sullivan to help the shah paste together a new civilian government. Sullivan replied bluntly that the shah no longer believed American assurances of support. Powerful men, including David Rockefeller and Henry Kissinger, recognized the investment the United States had made in the shah over twenty-five years and could not accept the ugly reality that Sullivan was reporting. Rockefeller later said of the shah, "The United States owed him help."

By mid-December, George Ball reviewed the situation in Iran with the help of Harold Saunders, former director of the State Department's Bureau of Intelligence and Research and now the assistant secretary for Near Eastern and South Asian affairs. They recommended that the United States advise the shah to turn his authority over to a civilian government.

Brzezinski entreated President Carter to reject Ball's advice and proposed a pro-shah military coup. Secretary Vance opposed that plan and wanted the shah to stay on as a constitutional monarch. Sullivan was concerned that the army, made up of conscripts, would disintegrate. Vance and Carter now said that if a civilian government failed, the shah should support a military government with the power to end the disorder and bloodshed.

The crisis grew worse. On December 18, Ambassador Sullivan cabled that the shah's downfall was inevitable. On the day before Christmas, demonstrators marched past the American embassy compound. Marines secured the gate just as the driver of an embassy automobile tried to enter. An argument started, and a demonstrator threw a Molotov cocktail into the car, which burst into flames. Ambassador Sullivan called out the Marine Guard, and when the crowd started throwing rocks and bricks, he ordered the Marines to fire tear gas grenades. The Iranian army platoon guarding the embassy fired automatic weapons into the air until reinforcements arrived, blocked all the entrances, and ended the threat.

In the midst of strikes in the oil fields just before Christmas, Paul Grimm, a Texaco executive seconded to the Oil Service Company of Iran, was shot through the head while driving to work. His murder hastened the departure of foreign technicians. By Christmas Day, oil exports from Iran stopped; and by year's end, all American dependents were told to leave Iran.

The Soviet Union admonished the United States not to interfere in Iran's internal affairs. Brzezinski protested Vance's conciliatory reply to the Soviets and demanded they be sent a severe warning. And during all this, the Ayatollah Khomeini urged the Iranian people to overthrow the shah. The United States tried to negotiate with the provisional government, but the real power behind the scenes now lay with Khomeini's Revolutionary Council.

Without informing Ambassador Sullivan, early in January 1979 President Carter sent to Tehran General Robert "Dutch" Huyser, the deputy to General Alexander Haig. Huyser's job was to hold the Iranian armed forces together and to demonstrate American support. Sullivan heard about the plan only from Haig, who opposed it. An angry Sullivan required that Huyser work under him as the chief of mission. Brzezinski wanted Huyser to instigate a coup, but Vance told Sullivan and Huyser that the United States opposed a military coup.

Sullivan now proposed that the State Department send an emissary to Paris to discuss with Khomeini the need for the Iranian army to maintain law and order. Vance chose Theodore L. Eliot, Jr., a retired Farsi-speaking Foreign Service officer. The night before Eliot was to leave, the mission was canceled; Brzezinski had persuaded President Carter to reject the idea. Instead, the President asked President Valéry Giscard d'Estaing, of France, to convince Khomeini to stay out of Iran while the shah prepared to leave. Sullivan declared that this strategy would be a major mistake. He voiced his disagreement with such indignation that the President was ready to fire him. But Sullivan continued to follow his instructions and informed the shah of the Carter-Brzezinski plan.

Carter approved meetings between Warren Zimmermann, the U.S.

political counselor in Paris, and Ibrahim Yazdi, a naturalized American citizen who was close to Khomeini and who had stayed in Waco, Texas, while the shah was in power. They talked in a small restaurant in a Paris suburb, the first official meetings between the Americans and the ayatollah's people.

Sullivan brought the shah word from Washington that it would be best for him to leave Iran, and on January 16, 1979, he flew to Aswan in Egypt. Tehran celebrated. Anti-American incidents multiplied, and Secretary Vance told Sullivan to order nonessential officials and Americans in the business community to leave Iran. The new restrictions were a triumph for what Henry Kissinger called an "almost metaphysical rebellion against modernization."

KHOMEINI TAKES OVER

Ayatollah Khomeini flew into Tehran on February 1 and established an Islamic republic. Delirious crowds greeted him. Ambassador Sullivan was instructed to support the moderate civilian government that was in place. But Khomeini demanded the resignation of that civilian government, which the shah had appointed. Sullivan's orders were not to negotiate with the ayatollah's Revolutionary Council.

Sullivan was convinced the Iranian army would not fire on its own people on the barricades, but he feared that the oil fields would be destroyed. He cabled Washington that the United States should accept the fact that Khomeini had won. He wrote, "We must put the shah behind us and look to our own national interest as foremost in Iran."

On the night of February 9, fighting broke out between factions of the Iranian army at Iran's Doshan Tappeh Air Force Base. U.S. Air Force personnel on the base, caught in the middle, had to be evacuated by helicopter and bus. The next day, an armed mob passed the U.S. Embassy and fought a battle nearby at military police headquarters.

On the eleventh, Brzezinski reluctantly stopped asserting that Iran's military could protect American interests. Gary G. Sick, Brzezinski's National Security Council staff member on Iran, wrote, "When the moment of truth arrived, the military was revealed to be an empty shell."

The next day, the Iranian army was pulled back into its barracks, and troops guarding the U.S. Embassy were withdrawn. Khomeini's Islamist

Revolutionary Council was now the nation's sole power. The Islamist revolution was engulfing the country and bewildering Westerners who had never witnessed a religious-based revolution. Not incidentally, the world's oil market was disrupted. The effect on American economic interests was disastrous.

As the Iranian army disintegrated, Sullivan obtained a verbal agreement from Khomeini's provisional government to protect the embassy but made plans to meet an attack. At 10:30 A.M. on Valentine's Day 1979, the day that U.S. Ambassador Adolph Dubs was killed in Kabul, militant radicals assaulted the embassy in Tehran with automatic fire from taller buildings on all sides. Some seventy-five Iranians climbed the walls and entered the embassy compound. They attacked the residence building and the chancery and damaged the consular facilities across the street.

The Americans in the embassy retreated into the communications vault on the second floor. They destroyed documents there and disassembled communications equipment. The Marine Guard pulled back behind a screen of tear gas. On Ambassador Sullivan's order, the Americans offered no resistance. One by one, they were taken into the courtyard.

Later, Khomeini sent his apologies for the attack. But six Iranians who worked at the embassy, including one Foreign Service National, were killed. And the embassy had to accept revolutionary guards for its "protection"; the Americans referred to them as "thugs." Some Foreign Service officers present thought the embassy should have been closed then.

At the same time, the U.S. consul in Isfahan was beaten, the consulate in Tabriz was set on fire, and the consul there, Michael Metrinko, had a noose thrown around his neck and was threatened with death. The consulate in Shiraz was shut down and the staff moved to the embassy compound. In the streets of Tehran, armed men fought each other. Sullivan's priority was to get as many Americans as possible out of Iran.

The U.S. Embassy searched for a new approach to Iran. The staff cleaned up the aftereffects of the February 14 attack and resolved business contracts worth billions of dollars. The Americans had to establish relations with new political elites, especially the Islamic clergy. On February 21, Sullivan was directed to tell Khomeini that the United States accepted his revolution.

At that moment, the shah, then in exile in Morocco, informed the U.S. ambassador there, Richard B. Parker, that he wished to come to the United

States. But it was too late. Sullivan urged the shah to choose some other place of exile. Sullivan feared that Iranian revolutionaries would imagine that the United States was helping the shah return to the throne and would retaliate against Americans still in Iran. Secretary Vance called turning down the shah "one of the most distasteful recommendations I ever had to make to the president."

Secretary Vance and Under Secretary David Newsom asked David Rockefeller and Henry Kissinger, both friends of the shah, to find him an alternative haven. They refused; they said the shah was a friend of the United States and should be admitted, even if Americans in Iran were put at risk. But, nevertheless, they did find the shah a refuge in the Bahamas, from which he moved on to Mexico in June. His lymphoma, well hidden even from the United States government, worsened, and his entry to the United States became a high-pressure issue.

Ambassador Sullivan flew out from Iran on April 6. He and DCM Charles Naas were identified with the shah's regime and were relieved. It was the end of Sullivan's thirty-five-year diplomatic career.

At the same time, the U.S. Senate was protesting Khomeini's brutal actions against members of earlier governments and of ethnic and religious minorities. This angered the Iranians, who reversed their acceptance of Sullivan's replacement, Walter L. Cutler, an able career Foreign Service officer, giving the excuse that he had served in Iran during the shah's rule.

Therefore, Ambassador L. Bruce Laingen arrived at Tehran on June 16, 1979, as chargé d'affaires ad interim. He said the twenty-seven-acre embassy compound resembled a "used car lot and yard sale lot. . . . The compound was a mess."

A farm boy from Minnesota, Laingen had entered the Foreign Service in 1950, following duty in the Navy in World War II. He had served already as deputy chief of mission in Kabul and, most recently, as ambassador to Malta. He was experienced and knowledgeable.

Things seemed to calm down during the summer, and the United States was able to reopen the consulates at Shiraz and Tabriz. Laingen was instructed to tell the Tehran government that the United States would not try to bring back the shah. Ever an optimist, he said later, "We thought that . . . there was a sufficiently good atmosphere for us to continue to work to try to find a basis for a relationship with this new crowd. Most diplomats, I think, tend to be optimists. Most of us are sort of convinced after long years of service that problems can be resolved, and, of course, we want to resolve problems, that is our job." This time, the optimism was unwarranted.

Early on a brutally hot Sunday morning in mid-August, Laingen, wearing swim trunks and a bathrobe, opened the door of his bedroom on the second floor of the embassy residence and faced the muzzles of Uzi submachine guns in the hands of two soldiers of Iran's Revolutionary Guard.

The Uzi-bearing Iranians had climbed through the rear kitchen window. They brought Laingen downstairs, where the two U.S. Marines on watch had also been seized. After some tense hours, Laingen was released. The Marines again took charge inside the compound, and Iranian police guarded outside. But worse was yet to come.

On October 22, Laingen was at breakfast when the Marine on duty delivered an urgent message from Washington: The U.S. government had decided to admit the shah to the United States for medical treatment, and Laingen should inform the Iranian government at the highest level. He was shocked; the timing of the decision was appalling. But the shah's medical condition had degenerated so severely that his doctors said sophisticated medical attention in the United States alone could save him. The shah underwent surgery in New York.

Laingen warned the State Department that admitting the shah could produce another attack on the embassy. Laingen tightened security at the embassy. Following his instructions, Laingen, along with Henry Precht, State Department country director for Iranian affairs, who was visiting Tehran, met that morning with Prime Minister Mehdi Bazargan, Foreign Minister Yazdi, and other government officials and told them the shah was being admitted to the United States. The Iranians had not known the shah had cancer and distrusted the Americans. The Iranians wanted their own physician to participate in the medical diagnosis. Laingen asked for additional security to protect the embassy, but Bazargan gave no guarantee. He said, "We will do our best."

On November 1, at an international celebration in Algiers, Brzezinski sought out Prime Minister Bazargan and Foreign Minister Yazdi in an effort to patch up relations. But newspaper pictures of them talking together in Algiers angered the radical clerics in Tehran, who saw them as a sign of increased United States' imperial interference. The pictures were the last straw.

FOUR HUNDRED AND FORTY-FOUR DAYS

Sunday, November 4, two weeks after the decision to admit the shah to the United States, was, as usual, a workday in Tehran. Chargé Bruce Laingen; Acting Deputy Chief of Mission Victor Tomseth, who was fluent in Farsi; and security officer Michael Howland drove two miles through the rain to the Foreign Ministry. They wanted to establish diplomatic immunity for the new six-man Defense Liaison Office that would replace the huge military assistance group that had run the giant arms program supporting the shah.

Laingen and Tomseth conferred over traditional cups of tea with the deputy foreign minister and then rejoined Mike Howland in the parking lot. He was talking over his walkie-talkie with his security chief, Alan Golacinski, who reported that hundreds of Iranians were trying to force their way through the motor-pool gate into the U.S. Embassy compound. The three Americans set off for the embassy.

After they drove a couple of blocks, Golacinski radioed them not to try to return to the embassy. They turned around and sped back to the Foreign Ministry to seek help from the provisional government. Laingen raced up the stairs and talked with the embassy by telephone and Howland's radio. He then spent hours next to the foreign minister's desk on a telephone hookup to Washington. But the Iranian government no longer had the power, or the will, to protect the U.S. Embassy.

Since the previous attack in February, the embassy had been reinforced with steel doors, an alarm system, and teargas devices and had been stocked with enough supplies to enable it to hold out until help arrived.

At the embassy, political officer Elizabeth Ann Swift, the senior officer present, stayed on the telephone for two hours describing to officers at State and Defense and in the White House Situation Room how several thousand young Iranians were invading the compound. After talking with Swift, Assistant Secretary Harold Saunders in the State Department's Operations Center took charge of trying to get Iranian officials to control the crowd. He and Laingen ordered the destruction of the embassy's visa stamps and classified materials. Unfortunately, not all of them were wrecked, and the students in time painstakingly pieced back together a lot of shredded documents. As a result, many Iranians were identified and made to suffer.

No one knew whether Khomeini had approved the invasion of the American compound. But the young men and women wore Khomeini photographs around their necks. They broke into the basement and climbed on the roof. They reached the depths of the long, two-story chancery. They threatened to kill Gunnery Sergeant Michael Moeller and his Marine Guards. The students had prepared well and were determined to hand over power to Khomeini's militants.

The embassy staff gathered in the fortlike second floor of the chancery. The Marines tried to keep the attackers at bay with tear gas. But once Laingen realized no Iranian authority was coming to help them, he ordered the staff to surrender.

In three hours it was over. An Iranian grabbed the telephone over which Swift was talking with Washington. Swift led about seventy people downstairs. Bound and blindfolded, they were marched through hordes of young Iranians shouting their hatred of the United States.

Kathryn Koob, at the U.S. Cultural Center three miles from the embassy, also stayed on a telephone to Washington; she destroyed coding equipment and secret documents before she lost contact. She and her assistant William Royer were captured the next day. In all, sixty-six Americans became hostages of the militant students; three more were at the Foreign Ministry, and six had escaped and gone into hiding.

The six in hiding were two young couples and two single men who worked in the consulate building; they had managed to flee the compound through back streets. On the fourth day, Robert Anders, head of the consular section, phoned John Sheardown, the number two official at the Canadian embassy, with whom he played tennis, and asked for help. They began the long process of getting the six Americans out of Iran. Canadian Ambassador Kenneth Taylor was able to visit Laingen at the Foreign Ministry and tell him the missing Americans were with him.

Taylor decided to smuggle the six Americans out of Iran with Canadian passports and Iranian visas forged by the CIA, led by Antonio J. Mendez. They designed a cover story that the six were a Hollywood team scouting locations for a movie named *Argo*. After two and a half months, on January 27, 1980, the six boarded a flight for Zurich and arrived safely. Ambassador Taylor prudently closed his embassy, and he and his staff returned to Canada. The U.S. Congress awarded him the Congressional Gold Medal.

On the first day that the Americans in the U.S. Embassy were made hostages, the Iranians blindfolded their captives and tied their hands. Some of the last holdouts, including State Department communicators Frederick Kupke and Charles Jones, and U.S. Marine Sergeant Kevin Hermening, were severely beaten. The invaders broke the embassy's radio and telephone links to Laingen, who sat at the foreign minister's desk talking with Washington until midnight. An irate Laingen finally was able to confront Yazdi himself, but the foreign minister could not help. For a while, the three Americans at the Foreign Ministry could receive diplomats from other embassies, but that did not last long. The three were put into a third-floor reception room, from which they were able to stay in touch with Washington for a few more days.

In Washington, officials were unfamiliar with the dynamics of the Islamic revolution. Brzezinski told President Carter he "ought to deliberately toughen both the tone and the substance of our foreign policy." Carter stopped shipment of military equipment to Iran and, by November 14, froze Iranian assets in American banks. He also halted importing Iranian oil.

At the State Department, officials soon discovered that they had virtually no way of exerting pressure on Iran's theocratic rulers. They gave priority to rescuing the hostages. And they had to design a response in case Iran refused to continue exporting the seven hundred thousand barrels of oil it sent to the United States daily.

The Vatican, the Palestine Liberation Organization, and the United Nations all made attempts to get the hostages released. President Carter sent former U.S. attorney general Ramsey Clark (who had opposed the shah) and retired Foreign Service officer William Miller, who now directed the staff of a Senate intelligence committee, to negotiate the Americans' release. But Khomeini would not let them fly into Tehran. The provisional government resigned. The Revolutionary Council had achieved its goal.

Secretary Vance and Hal Saunders flew secretly to New York and drove by yellow taxi to the Sutton Place home of UN Secretary General Kurt

Waldheim. They arranged for thirteen hostages, all women and African-Americans, to be released. Among the remaining hostages were only two women, Ann Swift and Kathryn Koob, and one African-American, State Department communicator Charles Jones. Khomeini proclaimed on American TV's *60 Minutes* that the remaining hostages would not be released until the shah was returned to Iran.

In addition, the American embassies in Islamabad and Tripoli and the consulate in Karachi were all attacked. Two Americans and two Pakistanis died in Islamabad.

President Carter worried that the hostage takers would start to execute their prisoners. By the end of November, the men in Washington were deliberating options—from bringing their case to the International Court of Justice to mining Iran's ports.

On December 15, 1979, the shah left the United States for Panama. And on Christmas Eve, the Soviet Union invaded Afghanistan. Even before the Soviet invasion, U.S. representatives, at Brzezinski's initiative, met with Afghan dissidents who did not want the Soviet Union to take over their country. And after the invasion, the Carter administration imposed embargoes and fishing restrictions, to set a price on aggression. Most dramatic was the boycott of the 1980 summer Olympic games.

Secretary Vance warned the Senate Foreign Relations Committee that "to disregard the growth of Soviet military programs and budgets . . . or to explain aggression as a defensive maneuver . . . is to take refuge in illusion." The Soviet aggression tipped the scales away from Secretary Vance's belief in negotiation to the more confrontational course Brzezinski favored.

In January 1980, Waldheim traveled to Tehran to try to free the American hostages, but Khomeini refused to meet with him. And the Soviet Union vetoed the United States' proposal for UN sanctions against Iran. By mid-May 1988, the Soviet Union, faced with U.S. intervention, began to withdraw its hundred thousand troops from Afghanistan. American diplomats believed this withdrawal demoralized the Soviet army and discredited the Soviet leadership. One more round in the Great Game came to an end.

Informal channels of communication were opened with representatives of Iran's leadership. Harold Saunders and Hamilton Jordan, the White House chief of staff, worked out a scheme for an international Commission of Inquiry. Jordan met with Iranian contacts from Paris, who wanted secret negotiations. They met, on one occasion, at the home of Edward Streator, the deputy chief of mission of the U.S. Embassy in London. On February 17, in Paris, Iran's Foreign Minister Sadegh Ghotbzadeh covertly joined the discussion with Jordan and Henry Precht. According to Laingen, Ghotbzadeh had begun to feel that holding the hostages was hurting the revolution. (He was eventually executed by a firing squad.)

Moderates in Tehran were also getting tired of the students and wanted to talk. Signs emerged that the Iranian government would give up its demand that the shah be returned and would settle for the United States promising not to intervene in Iranian affairs. The United States demanded that the hostages be released before any discussions began.

The American goal was to have the radical students place the hostages under the protection of the Iranian government. But obstacles repeatedly appeared even between the Revolutionary Council's government and Khomeini's young militants holding the hostages. And Khomeini stood firmly behind the hostage holders.

The five members of the international commission flew to Tehran on February 23. They had been promised they could talk with the hostages, but the students prevented it. Baffling negotiations continued until, on March 10, Khomeini announced that the commission could meet with the hostages only after it had determined the crimes of the shah. That torpedoed the whole effort, and the commission flew home. The shah moved on to Egypt.

By April 7, the hostages had been held for 157 days, and President Carter broke diplomatic relations with Iran, froze $12 billion in Iranian assets, established economic and political sanctions, and ordered Iran's diplomats to leave the United States.

The hostages' ordeal seemed interminable; they were angry and frightened. They lived in terrible conditions, blindfolded even to be taken to the bathroom, paraded through Tehran, isolated from contact with the world. They were interrogated daily; their questioners regarded them as spies and liars. Some were beaten and threatened with death.

The irrationality of the Islamist students was demonstrated by the case of U.S. political officer John Limbert, Jr. He loved Iran. His father had worked in Tehran for AID; Limbert had learned Farsi, volunteered for the Peace Corps, and taught in Kurdistan, where he met his wife. While earning his Ph.D. at Harvard, he taught at the university in Shiraz and then joined the Foreign Service. He disagreed with U.S. policy supporting the shah and admired the revolution that followed the shah's flight. But now he was a prisoner, accused of being a spy.

More than one Foreign Service officer attempted to escape; none was successful. William Belk was caught and beaten. Political officer Michael Metrinko, who had been the consul in Tabriz and spoke fluent Farsi, survived for months in solitary confinement in a tiny basement room. Bruce Laingen, in letters to his wife and sons that he smuggled out with visitors, stated the heart of the problem: "We must find a way to reduce our dependence [for oil] on uncertain and unstable regimes such as this one." He finished his letters with, "P.S. Save Gas!"

Laingen summed up the lesson he learned from the hostages' experience:

> However secure your embassies and homes may be against terrorist attack, against any kind of security intrusion, if you don't have assurance from the government to which you are accredited that they will come to your protection with force when the crunch comes, then all that security is useless.

DISASTER IN THE DESERT

Secretary Vance was in Florida on a weekend vacation on Friday, April 11, 1980, when the National Security Council and President Carter decided to rescue the hostages. Vance opposed using force to bring them out. He had been a member of the team at the Paris peace talks to end the Vietnam War and had faith in diplomacy. Returning to Washington on Monday, Vance voiced his strong objections to the President; after much discussion, on April 21 he handed Carter his resignation. He could not support the rescue mission. Senator Edmund Muskie of Maine took charge of the State Department.

The rescue mission, code-named Eagle Claw, was a disaster. On April 24, eight Sea Stallion helicopters, with Marine Corps pilots, flew from the carrier USS *Nimitz* five hundred miles across the desert beneath Iran's radar to a site near the town of Tabas. Three helicopters failed because of sandstorms or mechanical trouble, and Delta Force's Colonel Charlie A. Beckwith had to abort the mission. Then, in the desert, a helicopter struck a C-130 loaded with fuel and exploded. Eight servicemen of the Joint Special Operations Group died, and several were severely burned.

To discourage more such rescue efforts, the Iranians scattered the hostages around the country. When the fifteen judges of the International Court of Justice at The Hague demanded that Iran release the hostages immediately, Iran announced that the court had no jurisdiction.

In July, the shah died in Cairo. The Iranians released one of the hostages, Vice Consul Richard I. Queen, who was twenty-eight and from New York and who was seriously ill with multiple sclerosis. For the other Americans, Iran's heat, rising above a hundred degrees, was exhausting.

The value of the hostages to the Iranians had peaked, and in the United States, newspapers and television programs tired of the story. The Carter administration was isolating Iran, and leaders of the Islamic revolution hinted that the hostages' value was diminishing.

In mid-September, MiG-23 bombing attacks on Tehran told the hostages that Saddam Hussein was leading Iraq against Iran. He began an eight-year war in which a million people would die. He hoped the hostage crisis would catch Iran distracted and isolated. As Bruce Laingen judged it, Saddam Hussein set out to "take and hold areas of the south of Iran, oil producing areas, and, of course, in the process strengthen Baghdad's access to the Gulf." Oil again was at center stage. And the outbreak of war again dashed the hostages' hopes of being freed.

The new war damaged Iran's Abadan oil refinery, its ports, and its military. Men close to Khomeini told the German ambassador in Tehran that Iran would, under certain conditions, release the hostages whom they had now held for more than three hundred days. Deputy Secretary of State Warren Christopher met secretly in Bonn with Iranian Minister of State Sadegh Tabatabai in the presence of German Foreign Minister Hans-Dietrich Genscher.

The Iranians were suspicious that the Germans were too close to the Americans, and so they brought in the Algerians. Christopher led a team that repeatedly went to Algiers to negotiate. Jimmy Carter's defeat in the November election created a fresh target date of January 20, when a new American president would be inaugurated. The Iranians feared that Ronald Reagan might prove tougher than Carter, and might even resort to force.

With the approach of their second Christmas in captivity, the three Americans held at the foreign ministry were suddenly moved to join the forty-nine hostages held by the students. The men who came for the three diplomats in the middle of the night tried to seize their flight bags and tie their hands. Mike Howland tackled and kicked one of the students. Laingen shouted at the students that they were diplomats; a student took out a .45 and pointed it at Laingen's head. The students put the three in solitary confinement in a cold Tehran prison. For seventeen days, they were totally cut off from contact with the outside world.

Christopher's bartering through the Algerians was chiefly about how much money would be returned to Iran. It continued right up to January 19, the day before Reagan entered the White House. By January 20, $8 billion had been transferred.

On the morning of January 20, the fifty-two remaining hostages were all piled into an Algerian aircraft. They were free, joyful, and noisy. They had been prisoners for 444 days. They were flown to Algiers and then led into two U.S. Air Force medevac aircraft and flown to Rhein-Main Airport in Germany. There, Vance and Ambassador Walter Stoessel greeted them. The control tower was wrapped with a huge yellow ribbon. They were bused to the U.S. Air Force hospital at Wiesbaden and met by a shouting, flag-waving crowd.

The Republicans had expected the hostages would be released just before the election and thus assure Carter's victory. But it turned out differently. As Bruce Laingen tersely described it later:

> We were released within a half hour after the inauguration of Mr. Reagan and there were, in fact, arms deliveries through Israel that began shortly after the beginning of the Republican administration.

There were reports, notably through NSC staff member Gary Sick, that Reagan's campaign managers had persuaded the Iranians to delay the prisoners' release until after the U.S. election. But two congressional committees found no credible evidence to support charges of a conspiracy. However it happened, the Islamist clerics were now solidly in control of Iran.

45

Shuttling Salesman for Peace

1947–83

When Alfred Leroy Atherton, Jr., was a young consul in Bonn in 1952, he made a decision that changed the rest of his life. He was invited to come to Paris to work with Joseph E. Slater, head of the American section of the international High Commission Secretariat, which was converting West Germany from military occupation to a federal republic. Although Roy Atherton recognized the offer's importance and was fluent in German, he turned down the invitation, choosing instead to be posted to the U.S. embassy in Damascus. He wanted to experience a different culture before settling into his Germanophonic life's work as a Foreign Service officer in Europe.

Unexpectedly, in Damascus he began a thirty-three-year involvement in the insatiable problems of the Middle East. Reflecting later, Atherton said:

> I didn't start out with the conscious decision to become a Middle East specialist. I thought I was going to be a European specialist. I had French and German, but I didn't study Arabic. I went straight to the Middle East from Germany without any area training, except a couple of weeks in the FSI [Foreign Service Institute] studying the history and culture of the area. . . . I just became sort of a Middle East specialist by accident. . . . I got involved in the Arab-Israeli

conflict, and that became the focal point around which everything else centered.

Roy Atherton had begun his Foreign Service career in 1947 as a vice consul at Stuttgart in southern Germany. His three years in Stuttgart were disillusioning for an idealistic twenty-six-year-old who had worked his way through Harvard College on a scholarship and who, during World War II, won the Silver Star as an aerial spotter for artillery while crossing the Rhine. In the Stuttgart consulate general, he was shocked to find some American officers determined to reject visas to Eastern Europeans, especially Jews, who sought refuge in the United States. Despite pressure, he refused to sign the rejection of a visa application, saying, "I just couldn't do this." His refusal was brought to the American consul, who supported him.

When James Wilkinson, whom Atherton described as "a man of many biases," replaced Consul General Dana Hodgdon, Atherton was told that his wife, Betty, who had been a teacher in Washington, D.C., was not allowed to teach English to refugees in a displaced persons camp. Atherton said of Wilkinson, "He did not like the fact that Max Finger, who was the head of the political section, was Jewish. If he had his way, and this was not a secret because everybody that knew him knew this, there would be no Jewish officers in the Foreign Service." Atherton added, "I really began to wonder what kind of service I had gotten into."

Betty Atherton became "very unhappy" and suggested that Roy leave the Foreign Service and teach at a university. She added, "I had a hard time with white gloves." Her reaction was not unique among young Foreign Service couples after World War II. The Athertons were especially close, and when Roy decided to stick it out, wherever he was assigned, Betty found a teaching job or helped local unfortunates.

When the Athertons moved to Damascus, Arabs were already looking to the United States to fulfill their aspirations and felt betrayed by its support of Israel. Atherton found that U.S. diplomatic missions in the area sympathized with the Arabs. It was not necessarily anti-Semitism. Ambassador James S. Moose, Jr., in Damascus, believed, as Ambassador Loy Henderson said, that Israel would destabilize the area.

The Anglo-American Committee of Inquiry recommended to the UN General Assembly in 1946 that a hundred thousand Jews be settled in Palestine, which would become a single binational state. Loy Henderson was called to the White House to explain to President Truman why he opposed the establishment of a Jewish state. Henderson recalled, "I pointed out that the views which I had been expressing were those, not only of myself, but of all our legations and consular offices in the Middle East and of all members of the Department of State who had responsibilities for that area."

In January 1957, Atherton was selected to reestablish a consulate at Aleppo in northern Syria. (A U.S. consulate had originally opened there in 1836.) He found it a congenial assignment until the so-called Eisenhower Doctrine asked the Arabs to regard the Soviet Union as their enemy. The Russians had supported the Arab side in the recent Suez crisis. And revolutions in Baghdad and Beirut, all hostile to the United States, were seen in Washington as Soviet conspiracies. That, Atherton said, was "nonsense."

When U.S. Marines landed in Lebanon in July 1958, a crowd formed in Aleppo to march on the American consulate. Atherton sent Vice Consul Arthur L. Lowrie to ask the chief of police for protection, and they blocked the mob from reaching the consulate.

The problems of the Middle East became the center of Atherton's life. At its core this was a struggle between two stateless people, Palestinians and Jews, each wishing to establish its own national entity on a strip of desert at the eastern end of the Mediterranean. Atherton's abilities were soon recognized, and by the spring of 1967, he was stationed in Washington as the director of Israel and Arab-Israeli affairs just in time for the Six-Day War. He was given charge of the interagency crisis task force in State's Operations Center.

"MY COOK SAYS A WAR IS ON"

In Tel Aviv on Monday, June 5, 1967, Ambassador Walworth Barbour telephoned his deputy chief of mission, William N. Dale, and said, "My cook says a war is on. What does the embassy say? . . . My cook says that the Israeli Air Force has destroyed the Egyptian Air Force on the ground." Dale called the foreign ministry to check the cook's report.

In Cairo, David G. Nes, chargé d'affaires ad interim, was about to accompany the new ambassador, Richard Nolte, to present his credentials when the war struck. The Egyptian Foreign Office canceled the presentation ceremony and instead handed Nolte a note breaking diplomatic relations. The Egyptian government ordered all Americans to leave the country.

When Nes went to his residence, he and a Marine each carried a hand grenade in case they had to deal with violence. Later, Nes commented on lessons learned. Number One was, "Never, ever should the White House send a politically-appointed ambassador with no diplomatic or embassy-country team management experience to his post in the middle of a developing crisis with a war near at hand."

Israel won an overwhelming victory in 1967 and kept the Golan Heights, the West Bank, the Gaza Strip, and the eastern half of Jerusalem. Atherton drafted a letter for President Lyndon Johnson to send to Prime Minister Levi Eshkol, urging that Israel settle for peace rather than territorial expansion. It was the principle that eventually became United Nations Security Council Resolution 242. Arthur Goldberg, the U.S. ambassador to the United Nations, rejected Atherton's letter in the belief that the Israelis and Arabs should work out arrangements themselves. Atherton felt an opportunity was lost. Ahead were years of diplomatic negotiations and threats of war.

In 1968, George Ball replaced Goldberg at the UN and persuaded President Johnson to send him; Joseph J. Sisco, assistant secretary of the Bureau of International Organization Affairs; and Atherton to the Middle East to try to break the stalemate. In the Beirut airport, Ball was hit by a bottle. He kept his sense of humor and punned that he was glad it was a Coca-Cola bottle and not Pepsi "because Pepsi hits the spot."

Their mission failed. And it was the Johnson administration's last significant Arab-Israeli effort before Richard Nixon and Henry Kissinger moved into the White House. The new administration started bilateral talks with the Soviet Union, conducted by Ambassador Anatoly Dobrynin and Joseph Sisco, who was now assistant secretary for Near East and South Asian affairs. Atherton was Sisco's deputy, and Russian-speaking Walter Smith was a crucial member of the team. Their negotiations droned on through the spring and summer and into the fall. As a war of attrition developed, the Soviets armed the Egyptians, and the Americans, the Israelis.

In April 1970, Sisco and Atherton met with Egyptian President Gamal Abdel Nasser. And that summer, Nasser agreed to a cease-fire in place, which held until the 1973 war. But the peace process stalled when Nasser died of a heart attack and was replaced by Anwar el-Sadat, the speaker of the People's Assembly.

Sisco and Atherton accompanied Secretary of State William P. Rogers to Egypt and Israel in early 1971. They met with Sadat and judged him strong and canny. Afterward, in Jerusalem, officials asked them to pass the word to Sadat that the Israelis were ready to receive proposals. Sisco and Atherton carried that message to Cairo. Then, they flew back to Jerusalem with a proposal to mutually withdraw and reopen the Suez Canal. The Israeli government rejected it because it would post Egyptian soldiers east of the Canal.

But the pace picked up: In July 1972, Sadat boldly demanded that Soviet military personnel leave Egypt within a week. And he opened a back channel to the White House for secret meetings between Kissinger and the retired general and diplomat Hafiz Ismail. But Nixon prevented those meetings taking place before he was inaugurated for a second term.

Ismail came to Washington in February 1973, cautiously stopping off in Moscow first. He met with Nixon and the State Department (Kissinger was not included). But after that, Ismail met with Kissinger in a New York suburb, and the State Department was not even informed of those meetings. All the intrigue produced little progress. It was a baffling game.

What a difference from the days of Harry Truman and Dean Acheson. Lucius Battle said that when he first went to work for Secretary Acheson in March 1949, General Harry Vaughan of the White house staff called and asked him to change the Secretary's position on an issue. Battle took the problem to Acheson, who said, "Don't ever tell me that I must do something because the White House says so. If the President says so, that's a different thing. When the White House says something, we won't pay any attention to that."

Kissinger met again with Ismail between Paris and Chartres. And the CIA surreptitiously brought to Paris Harold Saunders, Kissinger's Near East expert on the National Security Council, and Atherton, representing the State Department.

Kissinger, while being briefed by Saunders, turned to Atherton and said, "Now, Atherton, I don't want you sending any separate reports back about these meetings. The reporting will all go from me." Atherton hesitated a second, and Kissinger added sharply, "Is that understood?"

Atherton replied that he would not send back any messages, but when he returned to Washington he had to report to Secretary Rogers and Sisco. Kissinger accepted that.

An all-day meeting with Ismail on May 20 was staged with melodramatic secrecy. Kissinger, Saunders, and Atherton traveled in an unmarked car without an escort to an old farmhouse outside Paris. This meeting also failed because Ismail's demands proved unrealistic, since he knew at the time that Sadat was planning to go to war, and Kissinger did not.

On September 22, Kissinger was named Secretary of State. He realized that he, who had fled the Holocaust as a child, was the first Jew to become Secretary of State. In his remarks, he did not use the word, referring only to "a man of my origin."

Early on Saturday, October 6, 1973, the Jewish holy day of Yom Kippur, Sisco woke Kissinger with a message from Ambassador Kenneth Keating in Israel. Prime Minister Golda Meir had summoned Keating and told him Egyptian and Syrian troops were attacking Israel. She asked Kissinger to assure the Arab leaders that Israel had no intention of attacking them.

Kissinger was shocked that the Arabs were starting a war he believed they could not win. He called the Soviet ambassador and Egyptian foreign minister and gave them the United States' guarantee that Israel would make no preemptive attack. Deputy Assistant Secretary Atherton was the first of the diplomatic insiders to predict the Arabs would resort to an oil embargo.

Within three hours, the Israelis informed Kissinger that the Egyptians were crossing the Suez Canal. Israel's citizens army could not stay mobilized for very long. In the shock of surprise, CIA Director William Colby even claimed the Israelis had started the attack, and the American Secretary of Defense and the chairman of the Joint Chiefs of Staff agreed that was likely. Atherton insisted that Israel could not have "started something."

Kissinger ordered weapons airlifted to Israel to answer the Arab offensive, and Arab oil producers tripled the price of crude oil, shaking the world's economy. Long lines formed at gas stations across the United States. Americans suddenly comprehended what Cyrus Vance called "the perilous dependence of the West on Middle East oil."

Leonid Brezhnev asked Nixon to send Kissinger to Moscow to work out a cease-fire. Atherton accompanied him. In Washington, on October 20, 1973, the evening of the so-called Saturday Night Massacre, the Watergate scandal unraveled. Then, as the Israelis brought more power to bear, the tide of the fighting began to turn. A cease-fire was quickly arranged. The Israelis had won the war but taken heavy casualties. And, significantly, the Arabs no longer believed the Israelis were invincible. Ignoring the cease-fire, the Israelis continued to advance and surrounded the Egyptian Third Army. American pressure on the Israelis broke that menacing confrontation, restored calm, and reestablished the American-brokered cease-fire.

SHUTTLE DIPLOMACY

In November, Kissinger flew to Cairo with his team of Saunders, Sisco, and Atherton; it was Kissinger's first visit to an Arab country. They negotiated a disengagement of forces and an exchange of war prisoners. This opened a productive period in the Arab-Israeli peace process that lasted until the 1979 treaty between Israel and Egypt.

At this moment, Kissinger switched from his Middle East support team to his China support team and sped off to China. The Middle East group flew back to the United States, except for Atherton, who went to China to help Kissinger keep watch on the Israelis and Egyptians. China was followed by quick trips to Damascus, Saudi Arabia, Cairo, and Jordan. And Kissinger put together an international conference at Geneva, hoping that it could ensure a disengagement and also serve as a cover behind which he could hold bilateral Middle East meetings that excluded the Soviet Union.

Before those meetings, Israel's Defense Minister Moshe Dayan brought to Washington a detailed disengagement plan, which had been approved by the Israeli cabinet and which Kissinger believed could be submitted to Sadat. And Kissinger was pleased when it was decided that he should present the Israeli plan to Sadat, even though Kissinger wrote, "In my view, the Secretary of State, should not, as a general rule, go abroad on a serious negotiation unless the odds are heavily in his favor. . . . A Secretary of State who undertakes too many journeys that lead nowhere depreciates his coin."

Kissinger carried the Israeli plan to Sādāt at Aswan, his winter head-quarters in southern Egypt, on January 11, 1974. This was the first leg of what became Kissinger's "shuttle diplomacy." He and his team were based in both Aswan's modern New Cataract Hotel and Jerusalem's classic King David Hotel, flying back and forth, often several round-trips a day. They created a document spelling out a military settlement and a commitment that this was a first step toward "a just and lasting peace." Israel and Egypt signed it on January 18 at a wide place in the Cairo-Suez road known as Kilometer 101.

Then, Kissinger tried to get the oil producers to cancel their embargo in exchange for an agreeable outcome on the Golan Heights. His team undertook a monthlong shuttling to Damascus, Cairo, and Jerusalem. Marathon meetings with Golda Meir or Hafiz al-Assad, the president of Syria, lasted five or six hours. Atherton remembered, "That was the toughest of all the disengagement negotiations."

Kissinger promoted Sisco to Under Secretary for political affairs and replaced him with Atherton as assistant secretary for Near East affairs. This put Atherton in a quandary: He was a Foreign Service officer and had now been based in Washington for nine years; he wanted to go overseas. But Deputy Secretary Kenneth Rush called him in and sternly told him that when the Secretary wants you to do a job, "You stood up, saluted, and did the job."

One reason Atherton hesitated was that he did not want to step over Rodger Davies, his immediate superior and his mentor. He suggested that Davies be given an ambassadorial post. Davies was sent to Cyprus, where he was assassinated.

The shuttle diplomacy continued. Kissinger's negotiating party met with Sadat, and on March 1 they restored full diplomatic relations for the first time in seven years. That evening, Kissinger and Atherton flew to Damascus and met with President Hafiz al-Assad for four hours. Assad demanded that Syria recover all the territory it had lost to Israel, but the two sides could agree only that Israel and Syria would send negotiators to continue the discussion. At last, the Arab governments removed the oil embargo, which Kissinger had insisted precede further discussions.

On this renewed "Damascus shuttle," they visited Algiers, Alexandria, Jerusalem, and Damascus. Kissinger was accompanied by Sisco, Atherton,

Saunders, and Peter W. Rodman. Rodman, the newcomer, was a bright thirty-one-year-old and former student of Kissinger's at Harvard, who was to have a successful career in the State and Defense departments. Ellsworth Bunker, now eighty, also joined them, representing the stalled Geneva Conference.

Atherton served as the American observer while the Syrian and Israeli generals worked out the disengagement. The generals sat on opposite sides of the room, since the Syrians refused to talk directly to the Israelis. A friendly Egyptian general would have coffee with the Israelis and then walk over and have a cup with the Syrians. The charade made nothing easier.

On the night of May 16, a Palestinian attack at Ma'alot killed some Israeli children and took others hostage. That broke off the negotiations. Kissinger believed that the Syrians and Israelis had bargained to the very edge of a peace settlement and had been unable to take the final step. Finally, late in May, the Israelis and Syrians agreed on the details of disengagement.

President Nixon, preoccupied by Watergate and on the verge of calamity, made a grand tour of the Middle East to encourage the peace process. At 6:00 P.M. on August 7, 1974, Atherton, Sisco, and Saunders were conferring with Kissinger at the State Department when the Secretary was summoned to come to the White House immediately. In the Oval Office, Nixon told Kissinger he had decided, in the face of impeachment, to resign. Late that night, as Kissinger was departing, the anguished President asked his Secretary of State to kneel and pray with him. Kissinger, feeling sympathy for Nixon, thought to himself, "Evidently the Deity would not tolerate the presumption that all can be manipulated."

When a deranged relative shot and killed Saudi Arabia's King Faisal on March 25, 1975, President Ford sent Vice President Nelson Rockefeller to the funeral, with Atherton as his political advisor. At the funeral, Sadat urged Rockefeller to ask Kissinger to try again to arrange a troop withdrawal. The prolonged shuttle that followed brought an agreement on the Sinai that both Israel's and Egypt's leaders felt they could sell to their people.

The United States and Israel then faced up to the status of the Palestinians. Atherton stayed up all night negotiating with the Israelis and told them that the United States would not recognize the Palestine Liberation Organization (PLO) until it accepted Security Council Resolution 242 and Israel's right to exist.

The next day, May 1, there was a formal signing ceremony with the Israelis, and then Kissinger and his team flew to Alexandria to get Sadat's signature. To the Americans' surprise, Sadat greeted them with an elaborate lawn party, followed by a banquet. The exhausted diplomats were ready to fall into bed at 1:00 A.M. But Kissinger suddenly called a staff meeting to plan the next day's trip to Syria. Shuttle diplomacy allowed little time for rest.

"THE WHOLE BALL GAME HAD CHANGED"

On Saturday evening, November 12, 1977, Atherton took a telephone call from CBS informing him that Walter Cronkite was going on the air with interviews with Israeli Premier Menachem Begin and Sadat in which both said they were prepared to meet. Sadat had suddenly decided to go to Jerusalem and negotiate directly with the Israelis; he wanted to end the wrangling. Atherton walked over to Vance's office and told him Sadat was going to Jerusalem.

Begin sent word to Sadat through Samuel Lewis, the U.S. ambassador in Tel Aviv, and Ambassador Hermann Eilts in Cairo that he would be welcome in Jerusalem. Sadat flew to Jerusalem on November 19. Begin met one-on-one with him in the King David Hotel. Atherton said, "It took a while for us to accept that the whole ball game had changed."

In Israel, there were two days of ceremonies and celebrations. Sadat addressed the Israeli Knesset, stating, as Christopher Wren reported in *The New York Times*, "Let every girl, let every woman, let every mother here, and there in my country, know that we shall solve our problems through negotiations around the table rather than starting war."

Sadat called a conference in Cairo, but the Syrians, Soviets, Jordanians, and PLO all rejected the invitation. Only the Egyptians, Israelis, and Americans met at the Mena House near the Pyramids. Secretary Vance attended briefly and then left Atherton to lead the delegation. Despite his efforts, this conference could accomplish little.

Sadat took umbrage at remarks Begin made to the Egyptian foreign minister and angrily pulled his delegation back to Cairo. Atherton worked behind the scenes for several days, trying to repair the damage, to no avail. At the end of 1977, Atherton detoured to meet President Carter in Warsaw and continued on with him to Tehran, New Delhi, and Cairo. At the New Year's Eve dinner in Tehran, Carter toasted the shah and praised him as a great leader, an accolade that would haunt him.

AMBASSADOR-AT-LARGE FOR NEGOTIATIONS

Israel invaded Lebanon, creating a period of extreme tension. Begin came to Washington in March and told Carter he was prepared to leave the Sinai and give the Palestinians autonomy in exchange for peace. But in more confrontational meetings, he said that he would not give up the West Bank or Gaza.

Because Secretary Vance was not willing to follow Kissinger's example and spend great chunks of time in the Middle East, Atherton was appointed ambassador-at-large for Middle East negotiations, and Saunders was promoted to assistant secretary. Atherton said, "My job then really became the traveling salesman for a peace process."

Atherton spent the entire spring shuttling endlessly between Jerusalem and Cairo, but negotiations had hit a stone wall. Vance proposed that if they actually sat together, maybe they could agree on some broad principles. As a result, the foreign ministers spent a week together in Leeds Castle, a medieval castle forty miles from London, but they could not break the deadlock. Vance proposed a second meeting and sent Atherton and Ambassador Eilts to Alexandria to obtain Sadat's approval. But as soon as they arrived, Sadat declared that there would be no more meetings until the Israelis accepted the principle of Palestinian self-determination and agreed to withdraw from the occupied territories. Atherton and Eilts left Alexandria quickly. The gap between the Egyptians and Israelis appeared unbridgeable.

Carter now offered a dramatic new approach. He invited Begin and Sadat to meet with him at Camp David, the rural presidential retreat seventy miles north of Washington. The two opposing leaders met there on September 5, 1978, and stiffly avoided each other, while their staffs worked night and day searching for common ground. They drafted a bilateral agreement and a settlement on the issues with other Arab states. Despite the endless talk in venue after venue, two of the most difficult problems, the future of Jerusalem and a freeze on the Israeli settlements on the West Bank, were not solved.

During the second week of negotiations, they reached a partial bilateral agreement; and on September 17, an elaborate signing ceremony was held in the East Room of the White House for what became known as the Camp David Accords.

Vance and his team set out to sell the Arab world on the Camp David Accords. In Beirut, they made little headway; in Damascus, the Syrians would not even talk with them. After a stop in Saudi Arabia, they visited Tehran, where the shah told Ambassador Sullivan and Atherton he would support the accords. The Americans, however, sensed something was wrong; a revolt was building.

Back in Washington, the Egyptian and Israeli negotiators met officially in Blair House. But since the two delegations were staying on adjoining floors at the Madison Hotel, much of the discussion actually took place in their suites there, out of sight of the press.

An Israeli withdrawal from the Sinai would create a serious oil problem. Israel would have to give up the Abu-Rudeis oil fields in the western Sinai, which were one of its major sources of oil. Egypt would neither guarantee to provide Israel with oil nor permit the Texas company exploring for oil on behalf of Israel to continue, so the United States had to step in and make a side agreement with Israel.

Since a number of issues were still not resolved, another Camp David session was organized, without the President. But this did not work, and early in 1979, Atherton and Herbert Hansell, the State Department legal advisor, were again shuttling between Jerusalem and Cairo. They made no progress, and an Egyptian-Israeli treaty seemed dead.

Carter made one last effort. In early March 1979, he went to talk with Begin. After an all-night session, things looked hopeless, and he prepared to leave for home. Israel's foreign minister, Moshe Dayan, took Secretary Vance aside and asked him to try once more. As a result, he moved Begin's position just a bit, enough to give Carter a concession to take to Sadat.

Then, Carter flew to Cairo, met privately with Sadat in the airport building, and emerged on the tarmac to announce that they had an agreement and a date to sign the treaty in Washington. Atherton said, "That was a dramatic moment. For once, the hard-hearted press all cheered and several were seen to weep."

Begin and Sadat met again in Washington. Israel received a most-favored-nation treatment for Egyptian oil, and Israel insisted the treaty took precedence over any other obligations—that is, Egypt promised not to participate in an Arab attack on Israel. This required more negotiation. They finally agreed on a compromise: Egypt would not join in an aggressive war, but if Israel provoked a war, Egypt would join in defending its Arab allies.

On March 26, 1979, the treaty was signed on the White House lawn. Years of shuttling and negotiating had produced at least that. Begin and Sadat shook hands for the cameras and shared the Nobel Peace Prize for the Camp David Accords.

The Egyptian people, in general, were thrilled that peace had arrived. But most other Arab countries, angry at what Sadat had done, broke diplomatic relations with Egypt. And Egypt was suspended from the Arab League, which moved its headquarters from Cairo to Tunis.

AMBASSADORSHIP AND ASSASSINATION

Ambassador Hermann Eilts was leaving Cairo, and President Carter appointed Atherton to replace him. Atherton and his wife, Betty, arrived in Cairo in June 1979. It was the first time since Aleppo in 1957 that Atherton had an overseas post. He and his deputy chief of mission, H. Freeman Matthews, Jr., who had worked with him on the Camp David Accords, took over what was one of the largest embassies in the world at the time. Its staff had more than four hundred people and managed huge AID and military-supply programs.

A decade and a half earlier, the Cairo embassy had been the target of violence. On Thanksgiving Day 1964, it was attacked by a horde of young Africans opposed to the United States' role in the Congo. The library and the Marine barracks were burned down; Ambassador Lucius D. Battle blamed the Egyptian police and fire departments for showing up "unnecessarily late."

Things were quieter now. Without even waiting for Atherton to be accredited, George H. W. Bush, who was campaigning for the presidency, and Henry Kissinger visited him. Betty had taught a Bush daughter at Washington's National Cathedral School.

Ambassador Atherton immersed himself in the problems of Egypt's economy and population explosion. He and Mrs. Sadat conspired to focus President Sadat on these nightmarish problems. And Betty Atherton helped create a support system for the booming American community. This support system became the Community Services Association (CSA), which dealt with everything from drugs to teenage problems and family-stress issues. Egypt's international business community supplied 90 percent of the funding for CSA's counseling and continuing education programs.

Atherton was reappointed by President Ronald Reagan. When his Secretary of State, Alexander Haig, came to Cairo, Atherton had to tell him that the Egyptians had no interest in a "strategic consensus" against the threat Haig perceived from the Soviet Union. Atherton said that Haig had a warmed-over, neo–John Foster Dulles approach to the Middle East.

The ambassador and others in the embassy were aware that forces inside Egypt deeply resented Sadat and his program for the country. Nasser had jailed or executed most of the right-wing Islamic leadership. But when Sadat broke with the Soviet Union, he had released the surviving rightists. Sadat also gave asylum to the shah, and when the shah died soon afterward, Sadat staged a state funeral, at which Atherton represented the United States and Nixon walked in the procession. But most world leaders boycotted the funeral.

Over time, more Egyptians grew disillusioned with Sadat. He jailed Muslim Brotherhood extremists and confined the head of the Coptic Church to a monastery. On October 6, 1981, the Egyptians celebrated the anniversary of their crossing the Suez Canal in the 1973 war. The stands at the parade ground were filled with dignitaries, planes performed fly-bys, paratroopers dropped, the army paraded endlessly.

The ambassadors, including Atherton, were seated together just behind Sadat in the tiered reviewing stands. Toward the end of the parade came the heavy artillery with their crews in the trucks pulling the guns. One of the trucks stopped in front of the reviewing stand. What happened next is as Atherton remembered it:

One of them stopped in front of the reviewing stand. The crew scrambled out. Well, our assumption, and it was certainly Sadat's assumption, was that this was going to be another one of these salutes for the president, as the paratroopers had been. They were going to come up to the stand and salute the president.

The president stood up to take the salute. We all were watching. And at that moment, suddenly, hand grenades were thrown and automatic weapons were being fired. Clearly, this was an assassination attempt at Sadat.

I didn't witness anything else, because, along with all of my colleagues, I was down, hugging the ground as fast and as far as I could. But there was a lot of shooting, and you could hear the shots. I could hear occasional bullets whizzing by. It was just luck who got hit and who didn't. A number of people in the diplomatic reviewing stands did get hit. They were after Sadat, certainly, but they were firing at random to keep down any potential counter-fire from the security forces that might have protected us. As it turned out nobody did, because Sadat's own security had let their guard down, thinking that this was something that the military was in charge of and therefore they didn't have to worry. My security detail was several rows behind me in the reviewing stands. The Israeli ambassador had his security in back of mine, I guess. I had an Egyptian guard at the time, provided by the Egyptian government.

Anyway, it was total chaos. When the firing stopped we all stood up and looked down at the front. There was a jumble of chairs upside down. They had already carried Sadat out and gotten into a helicopter that was standing by, and we heard the helicopter leave. Michael Weir, who was the British ambassador, and I were side by side. With all that training as a political officer I immediately began seeing who was there, comparing notes. . . . Is that Mubarak? Is that the minister of defense? Who isn't there? Who's been hit? Where's Sadat? Sadat was nowhere to be seen. But we did try to get some impression of what the damage had been. We learned sometime later that there had been 8 people killed in addition to Sadat and some 30 people had been wounded, some diplomats, the Belgian ambassador, the Australian commercial officer, and one member of the Chinese or Korean delegation whom I remember seeing as I was leaving. He had been hit in his wrist, bone shattered, his hand dangled. It was a pretty bloody scene.

Well, the assassins ran out of bullets, and they had no escape plan. I guess they expected to be killed in the process. They were all captured, and eventually they were tried, and several of them were executed. It was ascertained that this was an Islamic fundamentalist cell led by an officer in the army.

Atherton did not know whether Sadat was dead or alive. As soon as Atherton reached his car, he called Henry Precht on the radio and asked him to assure Betty he was unharmed. She had turned down an invitation from Mrs. Sadat to sit in the ladies' reviewing section and was watching from the embassy.

Precht's television screen blanked out, and he recognized that something serious had happened. He opened a line to the Operations Center at the State Department. The embassy had to determine which Americans had been killed or wounded. Nancy Reagan called and wanted the ambassador to call Mrs. Sadat. He could only say he would get a message to her. Carter called and Atherton reported that the minister of defense had told him that Sadat was alive. Atherton did not know officially for seven hours that Egypt's president was dead.

Among the injured were two military aides from the U.S. Embassy who had suffered severe injuries. It took time to locate which hospital they had been taken to. They were treated by Egyptian surgeons and flown to U.S. facilities in Europe.

Five days later, Atherton walked in Sadat's funeral procession along with three former presidents of the United States: Nixon, Ford, and Carter. Also in line were Henry Kissinger, UN Representative Jeane Kirkpatrick, and Secretary of State Haig. Among the heads of government was Menachem Begin.

Sadat's assassination derailed the peace process. Many Arab rulers were pleased that he had been killed. Yasir Arafat, leader of the Palestine Liberation Organization, was quoted as saying, "We shake the hand that fired the bullets." In contrast, Begin declared, "President Sadat was murdered by the enemies of peace."

The next year, the peace process was set back further when Israel invaded Lebanon to force the PLO to leave. Egypt's new president, Hosni

Mubarak, stayed out of that crisis until the massacre in the Sabra and Shatila refugee camps, and then he recalled his ambassador to Israel.

THE END OF A SHUTTLING CAREER

When George Shultz replaced Alexander Haig as Secretary of State, he sent Philip Habib to find a refuge for the Palestinians from Lebanon. Habib came out of retirement to serve as the President's special envoy. While negotiating, he lived with the Athertons in Cairo, which had an unexpected consequence.

Habib asked Atherton what he hoped to do when he finished his tour as ambassador, and Atherton thought he might like to serve as Director General of the Foreign Service, as a payback for the satisfying career he had had. Habib apparently mentioned this to Secretary Shultz, and later, while Atherton was in Oregon for the wedding of one of his sons, he received a telephone call from a friend at the State Department saying that career Foreign Service officer Nicholas Veliotes had been appointed ambassador to Egypt. Atherton was stunned. He said, "Well, you can't have two ambassadors to Egypt, can you?" He had received no hint. He let the department know his feelings and promptly received a call from Secretary Shultz apologizing for not informing him in advance. Shultz, as he had intended all along, appointed Atherton Director General of the Foreign Service.

Over thirty years, Roy Atherton had experienced more of Arab-Israeli diplomacy than presidents, secretaries of state, and foreign ministers of the countries involved. He and Harold Saunders had witnessed the replacement of the Arabs' ruling conservative elite with Islamic fundamentalists, which made accommodation ever more elusive.

In addition to appointing Atherton as Director General of the Foreign Service, Secretary Shultz added him to a senior team reviewing how the department was managed. This team included Ronald I. Spiers, the undersecretary for management, who had been ambassador to Turkey and Pakistan, and Ambassador William Harrop, the department's inspector general.

Atherton also originated a study of spouse and child abuse in the Foreign Service, and he set up a task force that would better prepare embassies to handle the chaos when an emergency struck. He retired at the end of 1984 and became the executive director of the Una Chapman Cox Foundation, which is devoted to helping the Foreign Service.

The Arab-Israeli conflict continued to torture the Middle East. The first violent Palestinian intifada began in 1987. After the collapse of the Soviet Union, efforts to solve the Israeli-Palestinian problem included the Madrid conference of 1991, the United States withholding a $100 million loan for Jewish settlements in the West Bank, and the Oslo Accords. A two-state solution became U.S. policy. One historian called it "a peace process of the imagination."

The most intractable issues were the allocation of fresh water, the Israeli settlements on the West Bank, and the future of Jerusalem. Ambassador Edward S. Walker, Jr., in Tel Aviv said he experienced Israel as "a land of rumor."

Mubarak ruled Egypt with increasing repression and corruption until 2011, while the population doubled to 80 million. The resulting tension burst into a massive revolt called the Arab spring, which began in Tunisia and spread rapidly. Many of the protestors were young and jobless, products of the enormous population increase without any hope of work. The United States supported Mubarak, but in January 2011, President Obama sent veteran diplomat Frank G. Wisner II to Egypt to persuade the eighty-two-year-old Mubarak to resign. (Wisner's father had been a cofounder of the CIA.)

Roy Atherton and his Foreign Service colleagues had devoted their careers to bringing sanity and peace to the Middle East, a complicated, confrontational part of the world. But in some cases even diplomacy was not enough.

46

The Very Model of a Modern Foreign Service

1970–2011

When Thomas Jefferson went to work as the first Secretary of State on March 22, 1790, the Department of State consisted of nine men in the small building at 57 Maiden Lane in New York City. Overseas, the United States had a diplomat in six capitals: Paris, London, Berlin, The Hague, Lisbon, and Madrid, and a consul or vice consul at sixty-nine cities round the world.

Jefferson's little department grew until, by 2008, the Secretary of State directed more than 57,906 employees. They included a corps of 11,555 professional Foreign Service diplomats and specialists; a bureaucracy of 37,089 national (local foreign) employees; and 9,262 Civil Service (U.S.) employees (mostly in Washington, D.C.). Of all these, 7,868 Foreign Service and Civil Service employees were stationed at 267 posts in 189 of 191 nations.

Members of the U.S. Foreign Service have had to acquire new skills and solve new problems. The U.S. Foreign Service experienced radical changes in its responsibility to protect Americans and advance their interests abroad. They have had to grasp the global as well as the local.

Ambassador Lawrence P. Taylor, a former director of the Foreign Service Institute, points to the uniqueness of the Foreign Service:

> Marines go to a crisis and leave. But the action does not terminate for the Foreign Service. There is no "Go" or "Stop" order. We have to be out there every day on a full-court press.

And Henry Kissinger, pointing to today's fundamental concern, said, "The object of United States foreign policy today is the big issue we face. . . . We have no clear-cut ideological enemy . . . we are now part of the system."

Foreign Service officers today work in scores of new countries, which present them with novel and sometimes grotesque challenges. George McGhee, when he was assistant secretary for Near Eastern, South Asian, and African affairs, wrote, "We now realize how appallingly little we knew about these people."

One dramatic example took place in Minsk, the capital of Belarus, which sits strategically between Russia and Poland. Secretary of State Condoleezza Rice called Belarus the last "outpost of tyranny" in Europe. Its record on civil rights was abysmal. In March 2008, the Belarus government ordered U.S. Ambassador Karen B. Stewart, an experienced FSO, to go home. Then, Belarus angrily required that the U.S. diplomatic staff be cut. DCM Jonathan M. Moore called it "unreasonable and inconsistent with normal diplomatic practice," but eleven American diplomats and their families had to leave through Lithuania.

The main reason for Belarus' rage were U.S. sanctions for "human rights abuses" that President George W. Bush had imposed. The sanctions froze the assets of Belarus' state-controlled oil refinery. The United States demanded that Belarus release political prisoners, including Emanuel E. Zeltser, a New York lawyer and civil rights activist who had been sentenced in a closed-door trial to three years in prison for "industrial espionage."

Zeltser told Consul Caroline Savage that in prison he was beaten and deprived of his medications. The United States lifted some sanctions, but not those against the oil company. Pressured by both the United States and Russia, Belarus freed Zeltser after sixteen months in jail.

REPRESENTATIVE OF THEIR COUNTRY

As the U.S. Foreign Service's responsibilities changed, its membership was also transformed. It opened its ranks to women, African-Americans, Jews, and men and women who graduated from non–Ivy League colleges. Of course, while the Foreign Service, for the most part, had excluded members of those groups, it represented a country that discriminated against them. Their acceptance into the Foreign Service reflected how American society was slowly opening up.

Ambassador William H. Itoh exemplifies the inclusive nature of the valuable changes. Born in Japan in 1943, his mother was English, and his father was an official in the Japanese Foreign Ministry. They had met at the London School of Economics. After World War II, his parents divorced, and Will Itoh and his mother immigrated to Canada. She married an American and moved to Albuquerque. Will Itoh joined the Foreign Service in 1975. He rose to be executive secretary of the Overseas Presence Advisory Panel, deputy executive secretary of the State Department, executive secretary of the National Security Council, and ambassador to Bangkok. A generation earlier, Itoh would have had little chance for such a career.

Hilarion "Lari" Martinez, another example, was born in Cuba and came to Miami when he was seven years old with his brother on an "Operation Pedro Pan" flight of children without their parents. He became the president of his high school class, graduated from Duke University in mathematics and from the University of Florida law school, and studied international law in Brussels on a Rotary Foundation Fellowship. He joined the Foreign Service and rose to be the first U.S. consul in Sarajevo and the consul general in Florence, Italy.

Martinez felt he made a difference every day. He served in Lima, Peru, at the time of the Shining Path insurgency; in Belfast at the time of the Troubles; and in Bilbao when the Basque terrorists were most active. He preaches that diplomats must get out of their offices, and he adds coolly, "Just as important was my work in Italy urging police to enforce laws that punish those who pirate Gucci and Prada handbags. Sometimes I am a social worker, sometimes a lawyer, sometimes a political scientist, journalist, historian, or lobbyist. . . . I enjoy getting out and meeting people at all levels."

Demographic changes affect today's Foreign Service officers in a variety of ways. One couple who faced a career decision were Benjamin Garcia, an Annapolis graduate, and his wife, Colette, who was born in the Dominican Republic. He wanted to go to Montevideo as the top administrative officer, while she preferred that he accept a post in Jeddah for the extra pay. He said realistically, "Not everyone has to become an ambassador."

It is no longer a given that Foreign Service officers will spend their entire working lives in the service. "It is the only job to have a job hunt every few years," says Douglas R. Smith, consul general in Barcelona. "You can't depend on the system to get what you want. You have to work the system." Ambassador Stephen Low remembers that George Kennan told his recruit class, Never give yourself 100 percent to the Foreign Service. "Always," he said, "hold something back for yourself and your family from this all-consuming commitment."

The change that altered Foreign Service personnel the most vigorously was probably the acceptance of women diplomats. These women have, with good reason, gained self-confidence and usually no longer feel a need to justify themselves. For example Molly Bordonaro, ambassador at Malta, takes pride in being a woman, an ambassador, a wife, and a mother.

D. Kathleen Stephens has also had a brilliant career, a husband, and a son (and a divorce). She started with the Peace Corps in Korea, joined the Foreign Service in 1978, became the consul general in Belfast and the DCM in Lisbon, and after thirty years returned to Korea as ambassador. She admits that family obligations can make the Foreign Service "challenging" and notes, "White men who didn't make it blame women and minorities."

Among all the minority groups, African-Americans have been the most difficult for the State Department to recruit. Either too few have had the preparation necessary to enter the Foreign Service or too few among those who do qualify choose the low-paying Foreign Service for a career. Under Secretary R. Nicholas Burns says he became convinced, "In my generation and younger, we are not getting the best young minds."

One midday early in 1973, white Foreign Service officers coming into the second floor of Washington's Foreign Service Club were surprised to see sixteen African-American Foreign Service officers lunching together. They had never seen that many black officers together and wondered what it meant. The black officers were amused. They were organizing what became the Thursday Luncheon Group to support each other and help recruits get a hold on the career ladder. Soon, the Thursday Luncheon Group numbered more than three hundred.

Ambassador Ruth A. Davis became head of the Thursday Luncheon Group because she was determined to help members of minorities advance in the State Department, as it was said, "with diplomatic readiness." In 1977, she became the director of the Foreign Service Institute.

Should the Foreign Service be a total meritocracy, or should it make room for differences of gender and race? Today, most officers regard diversity as a Foreign Service strength. Daniel Russel, who served in the office of Secretary of State Colin Powell, remembers it took him two years to enter the Foreign Service, and he never found a way to inform the service that he could speak Japanese fluently. Today, he finds the Foreign Service much less bureaucratic.

In 1996, on the grounds of Aspen Institute in Colorado, Professor Edward Thomas Rowe, of the University of Denver's Graduate School of International Studies, began a program, the International Career Advancement Program (ICAP), to help young minority members of the Foreign Service catch up to their better-prepared peers. ICAP was sponsored first by the Andrew W. Mellon Foundation and then by the Ford Foundation and the Fetzer Institute. In its first year, 125 applied for only twenty-five spots.

Mentors and instructors in Rowe's program have included such successful Foreign Service officers as Ambassadors A. Leroy Atherton, Edward J. Perkins, and William H. Itoh. The seminars have no official standing, and the instructors are volunteers. After fifteen years, ICAP had 375 alumni sprinkled among Foreign Service posts around the world. So far, four have achieved the rank of ambassador: Gina Abercrombie-Winstanley, Robin Sanders, Frankie Calhoun Reed, and Makila James. Professor Rowe says, "We realized they are part of a process that represents U.S. interest in a diverse world."

Before women became FSOs, male officers were rated partly on the suitability of their wives for their careers. There were stories of some domineering wives of ambassadors and senior officers making life miserable for the wives of junior officers at their posts.

Today, more FSOs are said to quit the service over issues involving their spouse than any other. "Spouses are becoming a larger problem over the years," said Janice Bay, a thirty-year veteran, when she was the deputy director general of the Foreign Service. Without a career of his or her own, a spouse can become dissatisfied with diplomatic life. Two-career couples face other kinds of problems. One political officer in an embassy in Europe took a year's leave of absence to enable his wife, an ob-gyn, to accept a hospital appointment.

Many Foreign Service spouses are foreign-born and can become "desperately unhappy" when posted to Washington, D.C. Jimmy J. Kolker, deputy chief of mission in Copenhagen, said of his Swedish-born wife, "Going home to Washington wasn't home for her."

Another group now under pressure are "tandem couples," where both are FSOs. One tandem couple solves the problem by taking turns deciding which of the pair will be the "leading member" and which, the "trailing spouse."

When Foreign Service officers Robert A. Bradtke and Marsha Barnes married, he was posted in Moscow as chief analyst of Soviet internal economy and she was in Bonn as chief for German external political affairs. They are a tandem couple who made a serious decision on how to manage their parallel careers; they would not have children. They both achieved the rank of ambassador, he of Croatia, and she of Suriname.

Another tandem couple, Michele and Clifford Bond, both FSOs, were married in Belgrade in 1979. She had graduated from Wellesley College, he from Georgetown University. Once they were married, according to the rules at the time, they could no longer work in the same office. So Michele Bond was given charge of embassy and motor-pool maintenance. She knew nothing about such work. And when he was posted elsewhere, she took a three-year leave without pay.

The Bonds had two girls and two boys, and they feel the department is "family friendly." They served in Prague and Moscow, and eventually Michele Bond became the consul general in Amsterdam, and Clifford Bond became the ambassador to Bosnia and Herzegovina, a hardship post where no diplomatic children were allowed. Michele Bond came to feel that the goal of a Foreign Service career is not to "make ambassador" but to have "terrific experiences." Her evidence: Her husband served in the Foreign Service for thirty-one years, only three of those as an ambassador.

She became the ambassador to Lesotho, in Africa, and others agreed with her view. Veteran Foreign Service officer Virginia Morris never wanted to be an ambassador. Serving as acting consul general in Istanbul, she said, "Ambassadors have a thankless job and spend too much time saying what others tell them to. They have to be nice to a lot of people. I'm nice to people but I don't want it to be part of my job description."

THE CULTURE OF DISSENT

An important, and occasionally more difficult, attribute for a diplomat is the commitment to support the foreign policy of the U.S. government. The modern Foreign Service has found it necessary to build a system for handling dissent in its ranks.

When a diplomat cannot support an official policy, there usually is a price to pay. In 1997, Robert Joseph, undersecretary for arms control and international security, resigned in protest to an agreement that did not require North Korea to surrender nuclear weapons it had already produced.

Several Foreign Service officers resigned in protest against the invasion of Iraq in 2003. One was Mary Ann Wright, the deputy chief of mission at the U.S. Embassy in Mongolia. She had earned a law degree and attained the rank of colonel in the U.S. Army Reserve before she entered the Foreign Service in 1987. The State Department gave her its Award for Heroism in 1997 for evacuating 2,500 people from the civil war in Sierra Leone, and she had served as DCM in Afghanistan after the 2001 U.S. invasion. Despite this record, when she resigned, she wrote Secretary Powell from Ulaanbaatar that she could not "defend or implement" policies she believed were "making the world a more dangerous, not a safer, place."

John Brady Kiesling, a career Foreign Service officer and the political counselor in the U.S. Embassy in Athens, was one of the first to resign to protest the war with Iraq. He acknowledged he had no illusion that his resignation would change the policy. John H. Brown, a twenty-two-year veteran Foreign Service officer and the cultural attaché at the Moscow embassy, also resigned on the invasion of Iraq. None of these who resigned received an award for their dissent.

Other diplomats have voiced opposition to policies and stayed in the Foreign Service. In 1993, twelve Foreign Service officers, all experts on the Balkans, protested the United States' failure to take military action against Serbs killing Muslims in Bosnia. Their petition, known as the Bosnia Dissent letter, was drafted by Marshall Harris, and among the signers were John Brady Kiesling and Eric Rubin, who became the executive assistant to the undersecretary of state for political affairs and then deputy chief of mission in Moscow. Secretary Christopher talked with the diplomats, and an official explained, "This Secretary of State does not consider such sessions a revolt against policy; he considers it a healthy part of the policy-making process."

In another dissent from policy, seventeen retired U.S. ambassadors and six other retired American diplomats asked the U.S. Supreme Court to overturn a 2002 decision of the Court of Appeals for the District of Columbia denying foreign prisoners held at Guantánamo Bay the right to petition for habeas corpus. They argued that the decision "undermines what has long been one of our proudest diplomatic advantages—the nation's Constitutional guaranty, enforced by an independent judiciary, against arbitrary government." The U.S. Supreme Court ruled 6 to 3 to reverse the district court decision.

These retired diplomats did not risk their careers, but by speaking out they made a difference. Another group of former American diplomats took similar action in 2007, in the case of Lakhdar Boumediene, an Algerian who had been held in Guantánamo for seven years. The Supreme Court, by 5 to 4, reversed the lower court.

HONORING CONSTRUCTIVE DISSENT

During 1968, 266 FSOs resigned. Starting the following year, the American Foreign Service Association (AFSA), which had been created as a club in 1924 and converted in 1972 to a combination of professional association and trade union, institutionalized dissent. To encourage constructive dissent in what has often been called a risk-adverse environment, the AFSA has established a hierarchy of awards: the Christian A. Herter Award, for senior officers; William R. Rivkin Award, for midlevel officers; W. Averell Harriman Award, for junior officers; and F. Allen "Tex" Harris Award, for specialists.

These awards are given only to dissenters who neither resign nor go public with their disagreements. As a result, Foreign Service officers know they don't have to resign in order to dissent, and they are encouraged to remain with the service.

Ambassador Anthony C. E. Quainton, who has received both the Rivkin and the Herter awards, said, "Neither dissent affected my long-term career." John Brady Kiesling, a Rivkin award winner before he resigned, explained a bit cynically, "The Service tolerates its modest number of nay-sayers and is happy to reward them with the remote and marginal postings they bid on."

The newest AFSA award, the Harris Award, went to F. Scott Gallo, the Nairobi embassy's regional security officer, in 2005 for his refusal to move embassy personnel into a new residential compound until it was made more secure.

Remarkably, in 1971, the State Department also created its own formal process for dissent, the Dissent Channel, out of the controversies around the Vietnam War. The leak of the Pentagon Papers in mid-1972 created such an atmosphere of distrust that the department used its official Dissent Channel to allow dissenters to let off steam within the system.

President Nixon came to office promising to include dissenters' points of view, but he became convinced that the State Department bureaucracy was sabotaging his foreign policies. Like his predecessor, he reverted to covert activities; he discredited, wiretapped, and even arrested protestors. Dean Rusk recognized such covert activities as "a mean, dirty, back-alley struggle" the United States could not stay out of. For one example, the covert plans to overthrow the Stalinist government of Albania failed repeatedly, surely because the British liaison officer, Harold "Kim" Philby, was a Soviet spy who revealed each scheme to his Communist superiors.

Despite this turmoil, a study of the awards systems published in the *Foreign Service Journal* in 2002 concluded, "After all, the evidence to date indicates that dissent seldom leads to substantive change." But that such awards were seen as necessary is commentary enough.

More conventional, and perhaps even more prized, are the eight State Department "honor awards" that are given for exceptional service or heroism. The Secretary's Distinguished Service Award requires personal authorization by the Secretary of State. The Thomas Jefferson Star for Foreign Service is known as the department's "Purple Heart" medal. There is also a Vietnam Service Award and the Wilbur J. Carr Award for twenty-five years of distinctive service.

"I PAID FOR MY DISSENT"

One well-known American diplomat who dissented and did not resign was Archer K. Blood, who in the spring of 1971 was serving as the U.S.

consul general at Dhaka, East Pakistan. West Pakistan's president and
military dictator, General Agha Muhammad Yahya Khan, was using force
to prevent East Pakistan from breaking off from West Pakistan. At the
same time, President Richard Nixon and his national security advisor,
Kissinger, were cultivating General Yahya to limit Soviet expansion and
to act as a facilitator for the Americans' planned trip to the People's Republic of China. In a handwritten note, Nixon directed, "To all hands:
DON'T squeeze Yahya at this time. RMN."

Consul General Archer Blood witnessed the Pakistan military's murder of many thousands of Bengali and Hindu civilians. He was appalled
by his government's failure to try to stop the butchery. On March 27, 1971,
he sent Washington a telegram beginning, "Here in Decca we are mute
and horrified witnesses to a reign of terror by the Pak[istan] Military."

A week later, twenty Americans at the consulate general signed another telegram to the State Department. Archer Blood did not sign this
second telegram, but he attached a note agreeing with it. This has been
called "one of the most strongly worded demarches ever written by Foreign Service Officers to the State Department." It began:

> Our government has failed to denounce the suppression of democ-
> racy. Our government has failed to denounce atrocities. Our gov-
> ernment has failed to take forceful measures to protect its citizens
> while at the same time bending over backwards to placate the West
> Pakistan dominated government and to lessen any deservedly neg-
> ative international public relations impact against them. Our gov-
> ernment has evidenced what many will consider moral bankrupt. . . .
> We, as professional civil servants, express our dissent with current
> policy and fervently hope that our true and lasting interests can be
> defined and our policies redirected.

In Washington, nine Foreign Service officers, specialists in South
Asian affairs, also signed what is known in Foreign Service lore as "the
Blood telegram." Nixon and Kissinger immediately recalled Blood, who
was tucked away in the State Department's personnel office. He told in-
quirers that he had been silenced.

The killings continued, and millions of Bengalis poured into India.
Ambassador Kenneth Keating, a former U.S. senator from New York, cabled
from New Delhi that he was "deeply shocked at massacre by Pakistani

military," and he urged the government in Washington to "promptly, publicly, and prominently deplore this brutality." Nixon scoffed that Keating had been "taken over by the Indians."

Blood's dissent did not change the Nixon-Kissinger policy, but it gave standing to those who wanted it changed. The AFSA granted Archer Blood the Christian A. Herter Award, for intellectual courage and creative dissent. And in 2005, the U.S. Embassy at Dhaka, now in Bangladesh, opened the Archer K. Blood American Center Library. The State Department gave Blood its highest decoration, the Distinguished Honor Award.

Blood went on to serve as chargé in Afghanistan and in India, but he never became an ambassador. He told *The Washington Post*, "I paid for my dissent. But I had no choice. The line between right and wrong was just too clear."

THE WRONG SIDE OF HISTORY

Constructive dissent failed in the case of experienced Ambassador Robert E. White, who fought for human rights in El Salvador during Carter's presidency. White, who had twenty-five years of service, took office in March 1980; in April, his fortresslike embassy was shelled. On December 3, U.S. Consul Patricia Lansbury notified the police that four Americans, three nuns and a laywoman—Rita Ford, Maura Clarke, Dorothy Kazel, and Jean Donovan—were missing. Two of them had been Ambassador and Mrs. White's overnight guests two nights earlier. The next day, the four bodies were found; they had been raped and shot to death.

In November, Ronald Reagan had been elected President, and in January, Secretary of State Alexander Haig announced that international terrorism would replace human rights as the United States' first concern. Senator Jesse Helms demanded White's resignation, and Secretary Haig recalled Ambassador White to Washington and removed him from his post. Five months later, he was retired because he refused to clear the El Salvador government in their deaths. He later said of the Foreign Service, "You can do a lot of terrible things . . . but you can't dissent."

Constructive dissent also ended painfully for John M. Evans, another respected career diplomat. He resigned over the use of a single word. A Yale graduate skilled in Russian history and language, Evans served as the deputy chief of mission in Prague, consul general in Saint Petersburg, and director of the Office of Russian Affairs and then, in 2004, was appointed ambassador to Armenia. In Yerevan, he was horrified by the story of the murder in 1915 of hundreds of thousands of Armenians in Ottoman Turkey. Speaking before an audience of Armenian-Americans in California, he referred to this tragedy as "genocide." That was a term the Turkish government abhorred and the U.S. government had persistently avoided.

When he reported his misdeed to the State Department, Evans was required to issue a statement saying his use of the term had been "inappropriate." The AFSA withdrew the Christian A. Herter Award that he was scheduled to receive. The association made it clear that the State Department had demanded the reversal. Ambassador Evans was recalled and retired early; his excellent Foreign Service career was finished.

Afterward, he said, "I did it for the United States, not Armenia. The United States ought to be on the right side of history." Ambassador Evans' fate showed that the constructive-dissent system did not always work. But he hoped that in time his sacrifice would make a difference.

That hope gained reality on July 28, 2006, when the then Senator Barack Obama wrote Secretary Condoleezza Rice that the U.S. position on genocide in Armenia "is untenable." He wrote, "That the invocation of a historical fact by a State Department employee could constitute an act of insubordination is deeply troubling. . . . The recall of Ambassador Evans only underscores the need to revisit the official U.S. position on the events of 1915."

As far as is known, Senator Obama never received a reply from Secretary Rice. After Obama became President, the White House did not answer another inquiry. But his letter to Rice gave John Evans hope that the American policy would be changed eventually. In 2007, the House Committee on Foreign Affairs passed a resolution condemning the genocide, but concern over repercussions from Turkey prevented a vote in the House of Representatives. The debate continued; strategic and business issues prevented a resolution.

"A GREAT SENSE OF BEING PROFESSIONALS"

Most Foreign Service officers regard themselves as professionals who are committed to support the foreign policy of the United States. But when Foreign Service officers are asked why they joined the service, they give a variety of reasons: the patriotic say they wanted to serve their country; the practical, that they needed a job. Daniel Russel, for example, recollects, "I really came to believe I owed it to my country to contribute what I knew. I thought it was the right thing to do. And it turned out I liked it."

Avis Bohlen said, "Many of us have a great sense of being professionals, of commitment to our work and the Foreign Service." She remembers her father telling a class of new FSOs, "If you do not want to be aware twenty-four hours a day, don't join the Foreign Service."

Cecil B. Lyon, who became a respected ambassador to Chile and Ceylon, would agree with Russel and Bohlen. After graduating from Harvard, he says, he "spent three miserable years in Wall Street. The day of the big crash in 1929 I went into the toilet at that office, and the senior New York partner came in and he said, 'Cecil, this is a hell of a business. I've been in it twenty years and I have just lost everything I have.' So that made me decide that I was going to go into the Foreign Service."

Unique in a different way was Kyle Scott, who was born in Heidelberg, Germany, the son of a U.S. artillery colonel. One evening, he watched, fascinated, as a Foreign Service officer won the grand prize on the television quiz show *Jeopardy*. Scott decided to take the Foreign Service entrance exam.

He did not learn the results of his examinations for twelve months, and then the State Department required that he report for duty in ten days. He was unable to finish graduate school, and he thought the entrance system "absolutely stinks." But he accepted the appointment and rose to be political minister counselor of the United States Mission to the European Union in Brussels. He concluded, "Europeans are increasingly skeptical about what Americans are saying, and they talk about American arrogance as a hyper-power." He worries that although Americans still have power, they may have lost moral leadership.

Scott believes he has had a great career. He says; "You make a difference. Washington wants to know what you think you can do overseas. Successful FSOs guide Washington on what is achievable. We have to be pro-active."

Some dedicated diplomats have found the bureaucracy stifling. Jimmy J. Kolker, when he served as DCM in Copenhagen (later he was the ambassador to Uganda and Burkina Faso), said, "This is a career I like and would do again in spite of the way employees are treated. They are not letting people rise to their potential. Employees are not trusted. We take in three or four percent of the people who apply and they are not allowed to return a Congressional phone call." Another capable FSO resigned when a superior sent his wife on a lengthy international wild-goose chase to buy a picture frame for the ambassador's wife.

Ambassador Rockwell Schnabel, a noncareer diplomat who headed the United States Mission to the European Union, concluded, "The Foreign Service attracts smart people who are stymied at times by a bureaucracy that is very hierarchal. People are careful not to speak out of their boxes. They can be stifled by the system. The advantage of political appointments is that they can speak out."

Former Under Secretary Nicholas Burns takes umbrage when Foreign Service officers are called "bureaucrats." He says, with a touch of bitterness, "My friend who died at Sarajevo was a bureaucrat." He comments, "We put our families in harm's way and don't get respect."

Ambassador Bruce Laingen, who had been a hostage in Iran, agreed with Burns:

> I am part of that generation that when they made a decision to join the Foreign Service, that was it. It was a lifetime commitment. It didn't enter our minds that we would consider anything else, or leave it. We were so damned happy to be in it. Exceedingly proud. I think then, and I trust still today, that when you pass the Foreign Service examination you have joined an elite.

Laingen envisions a Foreign Service career as a profession, but that commitment is not as universal as it once was. Commonly, members used to put what is best for the service first, but that goal now competes with increased concern for the individual's preferences about assignments, training, and a preferred slot in the cone system. A diplomat from Laingen's generation saw this change as "a decline in professional discipline." More than one officer has found the old-fashioned principle of putting the service first indigestible and resigned. The causes of this important shift range from basic changes in the society to the unionlike functions of the AFSA.

Ambassador Charles W. Freeman, Jr., who served in China and Saudi Arabia, remembers that after prep school, he and two young friends were arrested for sleeping on the beach in Mexico. In the middle of the night, the U.S. consul got them out of jail and let them sleep on his kitchen floor.

At breakfast, Freeman noticed that although the consul and his wife had spent their entire career in Latin America, their Spanish was dreadful. "I thought to myself, as I reviewed that experience, 'My God, if that's what is in the Foreign Service, I can surely excel.'" And he did. He became the director for Chinese affairs at the State Department, principal American interpreter for President Nixon's trip to China, and ambassador to Saudi Arabia during operations Desert Shield and Desert Storm.

Toward the end of his career, Freeman grew critical of the Foreign Service for what he thought was a failure to learn from experience in a systematic way "why things went well or why they went wrong, with a view of improving performance in the future." He decided the core problem was that Foreign Service officers "define themselves not as diplomats but as specialists" on Iran or Latin America or on finance or consular affairs.

Ambassador William Attwood, a noncareer appointee who served in Guinea and Kenya while Kennedy was President, found that State Department people often "had vested interest in [a] policy, whether or not that policy was the right one. They themselves had invested time in argument and effort, and laid their careers on the line for it, and for policy to change implied they had been wrong." But, at the same time, Attwood had a high regard for Foreign Service officers who go out in the field and "have some mud on their boots, so to speak, and they draw on that kind of first-hand experience."

Edward Walker, ambassador to Israel said, "I'm out of the office almost full-time." In addition to consulting his political sources, he had to talk with the country's various religious leaders. For example, he tells of even discussing with the chief rabbi how cows are slaughtered in the United States in order to be imported as kosher beef.

Both Attwood and Walker would have found much to admire in the work of Hume A. Horan, ambassador to the Sudan, who in the 1980s made it possible for thousands of poor black Ethiopian Jews, known as Falashas, to escape from Sudanese refugee camps and go to Israel. Horan, a skillful diplomat who spoke fluent Arabic, and his refugee coordinator, Jerry Weaver, connived with Sudanese and Israeli officials to fly out Falashas night after night. Horan visited the airfield one night to watch their plane load up. He said, "I felt at that moment we were really behaving like Americans should. That this was what the Foreign Service was all about."

MULTILATERAL DIPLOMACY

The shrinking of the world has made more and more issues multilateral, and diplomats have learned that to convince a single foreign minister to agree with a United States position is quite different from persuading representatives of two dozen nations to vote the way the United States would like them to. Tom C. Korologos, U.S. ambassador to Brussels, identified the heart of bilateral diplomacy: "You build up relationships, and then when you need something, you can ask for it." Years earlier, Dean Acheson put it this way: "The best diplomacy is on the personal level. I got along with everybody who was housebroken."

This personal touch becomes more complicated in multilateral diplomacy. And today more issues are global and regional: energy, food supply, population growth, nuclear proliferation, environmental threats, climate change, conflicts between rich and poor (North-South) nations, and human trafficking.

In bilateral diplomacy, each country is likely to know who is responsible for decisions. "Multilateral diplomacy" multiplies the players and diffuses responsibility for decisions. Daniel Russel, deputy chief of mission at the U.S. Embassy at The Hague, compared multilateral diplomacy to three-dimensional chess. And it camouflages the question of responsibility; he says, "It is in their interest to fuzzy up the situation. The fuzzier it is, the harder it is for us to retaliate."

The multilateral institutions that connect nations are of increased importance to U.S. foreign policy. For example, in the West alone, the Marshall Plan, the Organization for Economic Cooperation and Development (OECD), NATO, and the European Community have all pulled the United States into European affairs and changed Western diplomacy.

"If I call Europe, what number do I call?" Secretary of State Henry Kissinger asked famously, and perhaps facetiously, back in the 1970s. By now, his question is passé. The telephone number of the European Union is 32-2-299-1111. American diplomats know it well.

Ambassador Rockwell Schnabel says the United States Mission to the European Union (USEU) in Brussels, where he is stationed, is "one of the key policy posts we have. This is totally an issue shop, all policy-related." Therefore, his book about the European Union is called *The Next Superpower?*

The lobby of the USEU displays a large plaque listing the U.S. government agencies that participate in the USEU: the executive office of the President of the United States; the Departments of State, Defense, Justice, Agriculture, Commerce, and Homeland Security; and the Agency for International Development. Add to these the governments of the twenty-five EU members and the organization of the union itself, and the complexity of "multilateral diplomacy" is plain.

And the United States is not even a member of the European Union.

As the EU expanded beyond its western European core, efforts to give it a viable system of management ran into the tensions between the dream of a united (and peaceful) Europe and the persistent dedication to the competitive traditions of individual nations and national identities. International commentator William Pfaff has written, "The European Union is an amazing accomplishment. The original and early members have made a fifty-year effort to bring about Europe's reconciliation; they did so with generosity and a willingness to pool sovereignty and spend money on one another and on the later members who joined the union. . . . It is a great success."

U.S. diplomats try to make the American government's position clear to the EU when the union takes a significant vote. Richard "Rick" Holtzapple, political officer at the USEU, who has served on the National Security Council, finds the situation confusing but also challenging. A Foreign Service officer has to check with each nation's mission and also with the staff of the EU Commission. "You have to do it all," says Holtzapple. Then, the FSO relays to Washington what has been learned from all the participants. Holtzapple's colleague Kyle Scott finds it highly "frustrating" that EU member governments make decisions and "we are not there."

Norval E. Francis, Jr., the U.S. mission's minister-counselor for agricultural affairs, is responsible for opening and maintaining markets in the European Union for U.S. agricultural products. He finds the EU complex because it is not really representative. Its officers are not elected; they are bureaucrats selected from twenty-five different countries.

Francis notes that the EU has a common agricultural policy and instituted new rules for importing rice from the United States into EU countries, which have made up a major market for U.S. rice. The new rules threatened the competitive position of American growers and exporters of brown rice.

But he works diligently with agricultural officers in the member states. After two years of negotiations, by 2005 they worked out a formula to maintain the same level of U.S. rice imported into the EU countries, plus what they called "a negotiated growth rate," by which the amount of trade would increase over time. The settlement was not as good as the previous arrangement, but it was the best they could get. Francis says, "It's fun to work here."

THE BIG GORILLA IN NATO

A few miles from the EU headquarters, near the Brussels airport, the massive headquarters of the North American Treaty Organization (NATO) gives multinational diplomacy quite a different flavor. Here, the United States is a full-time player. Seventeen European countries plus Canada and the United States are bound by treaty to safeguard their security together. NATO began as an offspring of the Cold War and ties the security of North America to that of Europe, with mutual guarantees. Secretary Rusk said, "If we don't regard an attack on Turkey or Norway as an attack on the United States, we had better watch out, because that is exactly what the NATO Treaty says."

Before the Treaty of Washington established NATO on April 4, 1949, State Department leaders disagreed about the commitment it would involve. Theodore C. Achilles, head of the Office of Western European Affairs, and John D. Hickerson, director of the Office for European Affairs, chaired the group drafting the treaty and had to overcome their superiors' incredulity. George Kennan, in particular, did not want to militarize the Cold War and stressed containment in political and economic terms.

Whether NATO would extend eastward and whether Russia would keep a buffer of Eastern European nations between NATO and itself were endlessly debated. The Soviet Union demanded that NATO expand "not one inch eastward," and the United States wanted a unified Germany in NATO. The essential point was that NATO depended on the United States to defend Europe. Douglas McElhaney, the DCM of the American mission at NATO, said, "We are the big gorilla in the middle of the table."

Of course, all does not run smoothly. NATO operates on consensus, which means all participants have to agree to adopt a new policy. And once decisions are made, they are hard to change. For instance, member nations differ on how much control NATO commanders should have over the troops contributed by member nations. Some governments insist on needing permission even for troops to leave their barracks. But Ian Kelly, when he was public affairs advisor at the U.S. Mission to NATO, said that once the United States approves an operations plan, "We think troops should be answerable to the NATO commander."

As NATO grows more politicized and issues become more multinationalized, NATO increasingly becomes a useful forum for transatlantic political-strategic communication. John M. Koenig, the U.S. mission to NATO's chargé d'affaires, said, "We need places where we can talk about things. We have a strong record of leadership in NATO."

Diplomats posted to NATO have no host country to serve as a base in which they can maneuver. NATO's location in Belgium is virtually irrelevant to the mission of NATO diplomats. Unlike the situation in the EU, the United States is expected to define issues and work out NATO agreements. As the group grows, it is an exciting time there; Koenig says, "We try to use NATO to achieve our objectives."

LAW FOR CROSS-BORDER ISSUES

Multilateral diplomacy also reaches into international law and a collection of international courts. Among them are the International Court of Justice (which Elihu Root helped establish after World War I), the International Tribunal for the Law of the Sea, the International Criminal Tribunal for the Former Yugoslavia, the Iran–United States Claims Tribunal, the Permanent Court of Arbitration, and the International Criminal Court. The United States participates in all but the last of these. That final court, which was established in 1998, deals with three categories of crimes: genocide, crimes against humanity, and war crimes.

Some diplomats regard the American decision to stay out of the International Criminal Court as evidence that the United States considers itself above the law and call the decision "a PR disaster." The United States has doubts about the International Criminal Court, including its jurisdiction over nonparticipants, a lack of checks on politicized prosecutors, and the UN Security Council's reluctance to maintain oversight over the court.

Clifton Johnson, legal advisor to the U.S. Embassy at The Hague, notes

that he does not deal as much with the Dutch as with Iranians and lawyers and judges of all countries of the world. He admires The Hague Conference of Private International Law, which creates treaties for cross-border
matters like the validity of an American's will on a Greek island or an international adoption or a case of child abduction.

As such cross-border issues suggest, multilateral diplomacy is also
an entree into the world of developing nations. Former Secretary of State
Cyrus Vance recognized this years ago. He wrote, "Developing countries
must have a greater chance to join and be deeply involved in critical international institutions." These institutions provide poor and weak nations sounding boards to bring their problems to the attention of the
rich and the powerful. Vance said, "Whenever possible, we must practice
a new kind of diplomacy, an inclusive diplomacy of working together
with others to achieve common goals. Such multilateral efforts are time-
consuming and complex, but they can often be more productive than
going it alone."

"HOLDING IT TO EFFECTIVE PERFORMANCE"

With the end of the Vietnam War, the need for major changes in the U.S.
Foreign Service was obvious. Cyrus Vance, in his overview of American
foreign policy for presidential candidate Jimmy Carter in October 1976,
was outspoken:

> The morale and work product level of the Department of State are
> today in very bad condition. . . . The Department, and the processes
> of the Foreign Service, need complete overhaul in accord with
> modern conditions.

Vance emphasized that this did not mean the State department should
simply be enlarged; the challenge, he said, is "holding it to effective performance."

The rates of change both in the problems the United States faced overseas and in the administration of the foreign policy community itself put
extraordinary demands on the standard of "effective performance." And
the rising desire of other U.S. Federal government agencies to participate
in foreign policy adds to the pressure. And since World War II, the uni-

verse of Foreign Service officers has expanded to include intelligence, propaganda, and other avant-garde areas of responsibility.

The struggle to achieve what would be considered "effective performance" has been a problem the Foreign Service has faced for a long time. One example is from World War II. Vietnam diplomat Robert Murphy was summoned from North Africa to Washington to help deal with French opposition to sending U.S. naval forces to Beirut. On Murphy's arrival, President Roosevelt's chief of staff, Admiral William D. Leahy, informed him that the President had already decided to send the Navy. When Murphy asked whether the State Department had agreed, Leahy replied, "We decided what to do in twenty-five minutes. If we referred this to the Secretary of State, it would take twenty-five days."

This gap between a President and the State Department was still evident when George Shultz followed Alexander Haig as Secretary of State in 1982. Haig, a general who projected a sense of command and his own rightness, had alienated men around Ronald Reagan in the White House and the National Security Council. Zbigniew Brzezinski, who was President Carter's NSC head, had battled with Carter's Secretary of State. But once out of office, he made a candid public statement:

> The secretary of state has not been permitted to run foreign policy. I hope now, with Mr. Shultz coming on, that the president will decide to let the secretary of state run foreign policy and be recognized as the man in charge.

Secretary Shultz saw he had to rebuild the State Department. He filled the political-level positions, but he was warned that the professional civil servants were all Democrats who would give a Republican administration short shrift. He wrote, "That prediction turned out to be absolutely wrong. When career people, whatever their political bent, see serious, responsible effort at the top, they work their hearts out. That has always been my experience." Of the Foreign Service, he added, "Foreign Service officers bring a fund of knowledge and institutional memory not available anywhere else. The selection process is about as rigorous as any in the nation, so the level of talent and energy is first-class. And they possess a skill, a mentality, and an instinct for the record that are exceptional."

But the institutionalization of American diplomacy can also be stulti-fying. The carefully chosen young diplomats working their hearts out run up against a system that, according to some, can crush ambition and offer little incentive. One of the best of the modern era's diplomats, Charles E. Bohlen, observed in 1968, "You see, the Foreign Service of the United States has grown so unbelievably in the last twenty years, and the require-ments for admission are so high, and yet an awful lot of the work, I'd say fully 50-percent of the work in the Foreign Service abroad, is really rou-tine work. And this is something that no one has licked. . . . You get a certain amount of discontent. It's bad for morale."

Ambassador William Attwood, a capable noncareer appointee, often felt free to speak candidly. He said, "I think the worst thing about the De-partment is it doesn't reward, it hesitates to jump a good man over. If you recognize talent, you should be able to move him up through the ranks faster than they do. Now everybody is an FS-04, and they all wait around to be [promoted to] FS-03, and everybody sort of moves forward in these ranks. . . . They're having a hard time attracting really talented young people, the ones who are willing to stick their necks out, because of this long, slow treadmill that you have to go through before you can really feel that you are making a difference."

Henry Kissinger has also criticized the State Department and the Foreign Service. He wrote, "The permanent career service of the State Department has endured so much abuse that its sense of beleaguerment is accompanied by an acute consciousness of bureaucratic prerogative." Kis-singer came to believe that the department "tends toward inertia rather than creativity." He added, in an observation that told as much about Kis-singer as about the Foreign Service:

> In the hands of a determined Secretary, the Foreign Service can be a splendid instrument, staffed by knowledgeable, discreet, and en-ergetic individuals. They do require constant vigilance lest the con-victions that led them into a penurious career tempt them to preempt decision-making.

Two decades later, he was kinder—to a degree. Perhaps the Foreign Service had improved, or perhaps Kissinger had mellowed, or both. He now said, "The U.S. Foreign Service is an incomparable instrument honed by lifetimes of dedicated service. Like every elite service, it does not avoid a certain clannishness. The views of those who did not rise through its ranks are not always taken seriously enough, perhaps on the theory that they could not have passed the Foreign Service exam. Secretaries of State have been frustrated by its complex internal clearances, and Presidents have complained in their memoirs about how slowly it reacts."

Investment banker Felix Rohatyn, after he left the ambassadorship to France, remarked that he found the State Department's culture "extremely risk adverse. . . . I think one of the things that constrains it is this extreme risk adverseness and the fact that the way people are evaluated and the way people are promoted and the way people are viewed is not based on any direct evaluation of what they actually do and how they actually do it. And that there is too much of a penalty, potentially, on somebody making a mistake. . . . For the private sector, the status quo is the enemy. For government, status quo is better."

AFTER THE COLD WAR

With the breakup of the Soviet Union and of Yugoslavia, resources allocated to the State Department were significantly decreased, even though the number of diplomatic and consular posts actually increased by twenty-three. Terrorist attacks on Americans abroad, and in the United States, did not encourage the replacement of those resources.

These developments, of course, also affected the supervisory personnel in Washington. For example, Assistant Secretary Richard Holbrooke had Robert C. Frasure organize the European Bureau and abolish the Office of Eastern European Affairs, which had worked on the problems of the Cold War.

Senator Philip Gramm, of Texas, chairman of the Appropriations Subcommittee, drafted a bill in the fall of 1995 that cut deeply into the appropriations for the State Department. Gramm justified his disastrous program by explaining, "I thought the American people were more interested in law enforcement and fighting drugs than in building marble palaces and renting long coats and high hats." Secretary of State Warren Christopher retorted that Gramm's bill would force him to close more than fifty posts abroad, lay off employees, and withdraw from several peacekeeping operations. Christopher added, "I don't think you can lead on the cheap." His deputy, Strobe Talbott, called the budget cutters "isolationists" who would "turn the American eagle into an ostrich."

Richard N. Gardner, ambassador to Rome and Madrid, blamed the "devastating reductions" in the State Department and Foreign Service budgets on the failure of the people and Congress to grasp the relevance of U.S. foreign policy to the post–Cold War world. He said, "Americans have fallen into the habit of thinking that ambassadors and embassies have become irrelevant luxuries, obsolete frills in an age of instant communications. This is a dangerous illusion indulged in by no other major country.... Diplomacy by fax simply doesn't work."

Gardner warned, "We will be unable to maintain a world-class diplomatic establishment.... Cuts of this magnitude will gravely undermine our ability to influence foreign governments and will severely diminish our leadership role in world affairs."

Between 1994 and 1997, the department replaced only 53 percent of the people it lost through retirement, resignation, and death while on active duty. In 1998, three hundred positions were unfilled worldwide. The candidates were there; the budget wasn't. The State Department operating budget was $2.1 billion, which was less than one percent of the Federal budget. The department maintained some 260 diplomatic and consular posts and engaged 23,000 employees, of whom 14,000 were Americans and 9,000 foreign nationals. Sixty percent of its employees worked overseas. They had to know more than sixty foreign languages.

During the 1990s, the State Department also failed to update its infrastructure and management. A task force of the Foreign Affairs Council, a respected umbrella group of eleven organizations concerned with U.S. diplomacy, asserted, "Their efforts to secure more resources to support the foreign affairs function were frustrated by the Office of Management and Budget and a lack of presidential support."

The department reacted with a drive to attract newcomers. Recruiters visited fifty-three schools seeking young people for an intern program and for Foreign Affairs Fellowships. The effort paid off. In fiscal year 1999, 2,405 candidates were tested; 856 passed the oral exams, and 313 were hired as junior officers. In addition, the department hired 600 specialists— office management specialists, security officers, and technicians. And the following year, 13,460 candidates applied to take the Foreign Service written examination; 28 percent of them were minorities and 40 percent women. The department called it a "record-breaking year."

That claim may have been accurate, but it was overly optimistic. In 2002, some 1,340 positions were still empty. Calls for reform and improvement continued. The next year, after Secretary Colin Powell had been in office for two years, the task force of the Foreign Affairs Council said that he had made improvements but he still needed "a revolution in diplomatic affairs."

Marc Grossman, as director general of the Foreign Service, designed the Diplomatic Readiness Initiative that increased its recruiting budget and shortened the average time needed to hire Foreign Service officers from twenty-seven months to less than twelve, and intensified its drive for minority recruits.

Powell's efforts to improve the quality of chiefs of mission and other top-level officers was limited by "long-standing defects in the Ambassadorial appointment process," especially by the appointment of major campaign contributors unprepared to serve effectively.

The department also failed to keep its information technology up to date. A 2001 study showed that 92 percent of overseas posts were equipped with obsolete classified information networks, which could not connect with the rest of the government. E-mail and telegram systems were also out of date. All in all, it was a period of deplorable neglect for the State Department and its Foreign Service.

47

The First and Second Iraq Wars

1982–2011

One night in the midst of this unsatisfactory era for the Foreign Service, an excited voice on the telephone shouted at Emil M. Skodon, the thirty-six-year-old economics officer of the U.S. Embassy in Kuwait, "They are coming across! They are invading!"

And then the phone went dead. It was about 3:30 on Thursday morning, August 2, 1990, and Skodon recognized the voice as that of an American who worked on the oil rigs near Kuwait's border with Iraq.

Skodon telephoned Ambassador W. Nathaniel Howell, a career Foreign Service officer experienced in the Middle East, who advised him not to try to reach the embassy, across town from Skodon's home. The ambassador told Skodon to take his wife, Dorothea, and their two young daughters to the Japanese embassy a block from his home. Kuwait is small, and Iraqi soldiers were already spreading out and were fighting near the U.S. embassy.

Soon, Americans started coming to their own embassy seeking safety, until the staff, led by Howell and DCM Barbara K. Bodine, telephoned and told them to stay home. As a result, the only Americans captured by the invading Iraqis were those working in the oil fields. Inside the embassy compound, staff members built fires and burned classified papers.

Skodon and his family hurried to the Japanese embassy, where the chargé, Akio Shirota, immediately took them in. He asked no questions. The Skodon family was led to the basement, where they stayed for the next thirteen days with a dozen other Americans, including a senior military advisor, Colonel John Mooneyham, and 295 Japanese refugees. There were two showers and two toilets (one was broken) for the entire group. The Americans were not allowed to go upstairs for fear the Iraqis would spot them. They were permitted one brief telephone call a day to the U.S. Embassy.

On August 14, the Americans were told to drive to their own embassy. They stopped by their homes, filled a suitcase each, and made the perilous trip safely. By then, Iraq president Saddam Hussein had announced that, on August 23, Kuwait would become a province of Iraq and diplomats in Kuwait would lose their immunity. This warning initiated negotiations that allowed the American diplomats and their families to leave Kuwait. Ambassador Howell arranged for 112 Americans with diplomatic passports to form a convoy of thirty cars, which Emil Skodon would lead five hundred miles to Baghdad. The ambassador, a skeleton crew of eight diplomats, and a handful of others would stay to keep the Kuwait embassy open, even though under siege.

Skodon argued against the plan; he did not trust the Iraqis' promise of safe passage. And a summer drive across the desert with women and children was dangerous. But the orders came from the White House. There could be no dispute.

Skodon's convoy was organized into five units of six cars each; the groups would leave five minutes apart, starting at 3:00 A.M. The roof of each car was marked with a large X of tape so it could be tracked by satellite. The Iraqis delayed their getaway for two hours and then permitted a total of only fifty people to go.

With Ambassador Howell leading in his armored limousine, ten cars containing fifty people (actually fifty-one, with one uncounted infant) drove into the baking-hot desert. The others soon followed. When barely out of the city, two cars in Skodon's convoy collided, and an embassy wife dislocated her right hip. Marines in a trailing car found them, and Lieutenant Colonel Tom Funk and Corporal Dan Hudson, at considerable risk, drove her to Amiri Hospital.

At the border, Iraqi troops stopped the convoy. An Iraqi colonel insisted on diplomatic documentation for everyone. Skodon listed all their names on a yellow pad and wrote their job title or, for many, the word "attaché." The Iraqi colonel did not know what "attaché" meant and finally let them go on to Baghdad.

Meanwhile, Ambassador Howell returned to the Kuwait embassy. He had asked to keep fifteen diplomats, but the State Department reduced him to eight. DCM Barbara Bodine later wrote, "By dictating this unrealistic number, the Department of State set up the embassy for failure. A staff of eight could have neither supported or assisted the American community in the city nor even maintained the compound to keep the flag flying as a symbolic defiance."

The Iraqis besieged the embassy for nearly four months. They cut the water line, electricity, and telephones, trying to force the embassy to close. The Americans dug a well that, by October, actually produced water. As best they could, the remaining staff helped the thousands of Americans still in Kuwait. The Canadian embassy helped them organize a dozen flights to take out American women and children.

Skodon's convoy arrived in Baghdad at 1:45 A.M. The Iraqis there told him that all American citizens would be detained until the U.S. Embassy in Kuwait was shut down. But the next day, twenty women and twenty-seven children were allowed to depart through Turkey. All the men except economic-political officer Charles Sidel were kept in Baghdad.

The Iraqis confined them to the city; they were hostages, with a minimum degree of freedom. Joseph C. Wilson IV, the chargé d'affaires in Baghdad since Ambassador April Catherine Glaspie had left at the end of July, put the Americans from Kuwait to work. Skodon served as the embassy's DCM, and Wilson praised him.

Most of the Americans from Kuwait stayed in Baghdad, until, on December 13, the United States closed the Kuwait embassy. Its remaining eight diplomats were then flown to Baghdad. They picked up Skodon and one other from the original convoy and flew to Frankfurt.

On January 17, 1991, the United States began military operations against Iraq. In March, Edward W. Gnehm, Jr., a veteran Middle East hand, was able to land on the Kuwait embassy grounds in a helicopter and, with American Special Forces troops standing guard, became the ambassador in the reopened embassy.

RESHUFFLE IN THE MIDDLE EAST

The Iraqi invasion of Kuwait and its oil fields was no sudden phenomenon. The Middle East had been experiencing a tumultuous reshuffling for nearly half a century, since, at the end of World War II, an exhausted Britain had suspended its aid to Greece and Turkey.

There were hitches. Loy W. Henderson was sent on sudden notice to Athens to work with Ambassador Lincoln McVeigh and to persuade the Greek prime minister, Constantine Tsaldaris, to broaden his one-party, promonarchist government into a coalition. Henderson undertook the assignment despite his conviction that Tsaldaris was the strongman Greece needed to stand up to the Soviet Union.

Britain's postwar exhaustion had also led to its abandoning its mandate over Palestine and to the establishment of the state of Israel in 1948. Britain lost its hegemony in Saudi Arabia to the United States. "We should have a more mature approach to the problem of oil since it is not necessarily a symbol of sinister imperialism but a vitally needed commodity like food," Henderson, then director of the State Department's Office of Near Eastern and African Affairs, said back in 1947.

Henderson, son of a poor Methodist preacher, was from small-town Arkansas and had entered the Foreign Service through consular affairs. He disagreed with FDR's policy of cultivating the Soviet Union; he supported a Cold War confrontation and spent much of his career on petro-centered issues. By 1947, Henderson recognized that the United States would have to guard the area's vast oil reserves from an unfriendly power like the Soviet Union. He had been appointed ambassador to Iran in 1951, when U.S. intelligence services helped the shah gain control of Iranian oil.

His view led, almost a half century later, to what was known as "The First and Second Petroleum Wars." The United States' wars with Iraq, which began on August 2, 1990, coincided with the dissolution of the Soviet Union.

On November 22, 1952, a large demonstration in Baghdad had demanded that the Anglo-American imperialists leave. At noon the next day, a mob burned the United States Information Service library. The police reportedly killed a dozen demonstrators, and the local police station was burned in retaliation. The army declared martial law, but Iraq's police could not promise Ambassador Burton Y. Berry safe passage out of Kuwait until the next day. The crowd harassed them; a "tattoo of blows rained on vehicle as it departed." But once Mossadegh was overthrown, with American collusion, the United States participated in Iran's political affairs.

After Iraq broke relations with the United States during the Arab-Israeli war in 1967, American diplomats rarely visited Baghdad. A United

States interest section in Baghdad was headed by Arabic-speaking William L. Eagleton, Jr., who loved Arab culture but soon despised Saddam Hussein.

In a 1968 coup, the revolutionary and secular Baath Party took control of Iraq, and in the early 1970s Vice President Saddam Hussein nationalized the Iraq Petroleum Company. Through the 1970s, an Islamist revolution, sweeping across the Middle East, overturned the shah in Iran, assassinated Anwar el-Sadat in Egypt, nationalized Iraq's oil resources, attempted to dislodge the ruling family in Saudi Arabia, attacked the Great Mosque in Mecca, and caused the Soviet occupation of Afghanistan. In every case, the Islamists opposed United States policies that had sought to guarantee the region a heavy-handed stability and a steady supply of oil.

Saddam Hussein's aggressiveness had long been a concern. Ambassador Edward L. Peck, who was in charge of U.S. interests in Baghdad when the United States had no direct diplomatic relations with Iraq, described Saddam as "a village thug who wore Pierre Cardin suits and has lovely bridgework and a nice mustache and all that."

Saddam became president in 1979 and invaded Iran on September 22, 1980, encouraged by the American and European governments. By 1982, the United States supported Iraq in this war, and, on November 26, 1983, President Reagan issued a National Security Decision Directive emphasizing the importance of an uninterrupted international flow of oil from the Persian Gulf.

The following month, Reagan sent a special envoy, Donald H. Rumsfeld, who was a past and future secretary of defense, to the Middle East. He was perceived as a defender of the status quo against Iran's Islamist revolution, and he supplied Saddam Hussein with money and weapons.

Rumsfeld was the first senior U.S. official to visit Iraq in more than six years. Although the United States knew that Iraq had used nerve gas against the Iranians, Rumsfeld told Saddam Hussein that the United States wanted to contain Iran and Islamic fundamentalism. He promised that the United States would direct its allies to stop selling arms to Iran. Within months, of course, other members of the Reagan administration were planning to sell arms to Iran and use the proceeds to support the anti-leftist Contras in Nicaragua.

After Rumsfeld and Hussein met, Eagleton checked with Iraqi officials and reported to the State Department that "Ambassador Rumsfeld's visit has elevated U.S.-Iraqi relations to a new level." But this was upset in March when a shipment to Iraq of 22,000 pounds of phosphorous flouride was intercepted at New York's John F. Kennedy Airport.

Secretary of State Shultz reminded the Iraq Foreign Ministry that the United States opposed chemical weapons. But Rumsfeld returned to Baghdad to reassure the Iraqis that U.S. public condemnation of chemical warfare was not aimed at them and to promise financing for a pipeline that would bring Iraqi oil to Aqaba.

By the end of 1984, Iraq and the United States restored diplomatic relations, and David Newton became the first American ambassador to Baghdad in seventeen years. This lasted only a half dozen years until Saddam Hussein invaded Kuwait.

In the same period, Kuwait rejected a chief of mission proposed by the United States because he had served for three years as consul general in Jerusalem. As a result, Philip J. Griffin served as chargé d'affaires for a year until September 1984, and Anthony C. E. Quainton, ambassador to Nicaragua, presented his credentials in Kuwait on September 19, 1984. (During Quainton's term in Nicaragua, the United States had rejected Nora Astorga as ambassador from Nicaragua to Washington on the grounds that she had lured a general of the Nicaraguan national guard to her bedroom, where he was assassinated.)

By the spring of 1990, Saddam Hussein was running out of funds. The Europeans and Chinese were reluctant to lend him money or supply credit, and the price of oil was falling precipitously because Kuwait and the United Arab Emirates were overproducing it. Saddam moved units of the Iraq army to the Kuwait border.

On July 19, Secretary of State James Baker proposed settling disputes by peaceful means, and four days later the State Department warned Iraq against resorting to coercion and intimidation. The State Department instructed April Catherine Glaspie, the U.S. ambassador to Iraq and the first American woman to be an ambassador to an Arab country, to inform Iraq that the United States was beginning a joint military exercise with the United Arab Emirates.

On July 25, Ambassador Glaspie was summoned to the Iraqi Foreign Ministry and, without warning, was driven to Saddam Hussein's presidential palace. She had presented her credentials in Baghdad more than twenty-two months earlier but had never met Hussein privately. Now, she had no chance to obtain instructions from Washington before this unexpected meeting.

Glaspie was an experienced senior Foreign Service officer who was fluent in Arabic and had served as deputy chief of mission in Damascus. Transcripts of her talk with Saddam Hussein show that she asked him why his troops were massed near the Kuwait border. He replied by accusing Kuwait of violating agreements on oil supplies and pricing and claimed Kuwait was stealing oil from Iraq's side of the border. Glaspie told him the United States took no position on Arab-versus-Arab conflicts and hoped disputes between Iraq and Kuwait would be settled peacefully. The transcripts have been interpreted in contradictory ways, and the State Department never confirmed their accuracy.

Eight days after his meeting with Glaspie, Saddam invaded Kuwait. The United States countered with an air campaign, and then followed with an international land offensive that drove Saddam's forces back to Baghdad. The first Iraq war, a thirty-two-nation coalition, began as Operation Desert Storm on January 17, 1991.

Glaspie was blamed for not preventing Saddam Hussein's invasion of Kuwait. When the Senate Foreign Relations Committee asked her how Saddam could have taken her no-interference comment to imply the U.S. would accept his invading Kuwait, she answered, "We foolishly did not realize he was stupid." But others thought the message Glaspie conveyed to Saddam assured him he could invade Kuwait without interference. Glaspie was not given another ambassadorial post; she became consul general in Cape Town until she retired in 2002. The United States had no ambassador in Baghdad until John D. Negroponte went there in June 2004.

EXPORTING JIHAD TO THE UNITED STATES

When Saddam Hussein invaded Kuwait, Secretary of Defense Dick Cheney arrived in Saudi Arabia and proposed stationing American troops there, infidel soldiers in the land of Islam's holy sites. The zealous Osama bin Laden, founder of the terrorist group al-Qaeda, could not accept this. He turned against his homeland's rulers and their allies across the Atlantic.

On September 11, 2001, bin Laden's terrorists, most of them recruited from Saudi Arabia, destroyed the twin towers of the World Trade Center in New York City and severely damaged the Pentagon in Washington, D.C. Another hijacked plane was aimed at the White House, but the bravery of its civilian passengers forced it to crash prematurely. Some 2,974 were killed in the twin towers, 184 at the Pentagon, and 246 aboard the planes. Exporting the jihad to the American superpower led to the United States' retaliatory invasions of Iraq and Afghanistan.

The Afghans had already suffered from the struggle. At Christmastime 1979, the Soviet Union had invaded the primitive but strategically placed Afghanistan and installed its own puppet. This exposed the Persian Gulf oil states to attack by Soviet tactical air forces. Zbigniew Brzezinski flew to Islamabad and coordinated with the Pakistanis a joint response to the Soviet invasion. The United States sent arms to the Afghani resistance, and in 1984 President Reagan brought in the Saudis.

When the Soviet Union withdrew from Afghanistan in 1986, the State Department sent special envoy Peter Thomsen, the DCM in Beijing, to work with the victorious Afghans. The black-turbaned Taliban, puritanical "students of Islam," imposed Islamic rule in Kabul.

As the Soviet Union disintegrated, the United States lost interest in xenophobic Afghanistan. But private American oil companies still wanted to explore for oil and gas. The United States tolerated the Taliban in part because Unocal wanted to build a pipeline across Afghanistan with Taliban help. Thomas W. Simons, Jr., the ambassador to Pakistan, opposed a competing Argentine pipeline. One informed observer called it "a tawdry season in American diplomacy."

General Mohammed Zia-ul-Haq, the Islamic dictator of Pakistan for two decades, was killed when his plane exploded mysteriously in midair shortly after takeoff from Bahawalpur Airport on August 17, 1988. Also killed were U.S. Ambassador Arnold L. Raphel, who had helped release the U.S. hostages from Tehran; the U.S. defense attaché, Brigadier General Herbert M. Wassom; and twenty-eight Pakistani generals. Robert Oakley, the former director of the State Department Office of Combating Terrorism, replaced Raphel in Kabul.

Edmund McWilliams, an army intelligence officer in Vietnam, became the DCM in Kabul and special envoy to the Afghan rebels based in Islamabad. McWilliams visited the tribal areas, but he and Ambassador Oakley disagreed on what policy to recommend for Afghanistan. McWilliams feared the anti-American Afghan Islamists and the Pakistani intelligence organization that supported them. After an intense struggle, Oakley replaced McWilliams as special envoy to the Afghan rebels with Peter Thomsen. For years, the United States assisted the Taliban, hoping to separate them from Osama bin Laden. Assistant Secretary Karl Inderfurth met with the leader of the Northern Alliance opposition, but they could not agree on much.

After the 9/11 terrorist attacks, the United States invaded Afghanistan. Bin Laden's terrorists had trained there after he had been forced out of the Sudan. But why the United States also invaded Iraq remained a controversial mystery. The political reason given was that Saddam had collected weapons of mass destruction. But it wasn't true. Ambassador Joseph C. Wilson IV went to Niger to seek evidence that Saddam had bought uranium there. He returned convinced that this had not happened, but President Bush still included the allegation in his State of the Union address. Wilson wrote in *The New York Times* that the American people were being misled. In reaction, his wife, Valerie Plame Wilson, who had been a CIA operative for more than twenty years, was "outed," sparking a nasty public scandal.

Journalist Nicholas Lemann asked Richard Haas, head of the State Department's Policy Planning Staff, why Iraq had been invaded, and he replied, "I will go to my grave not knowing." Secretary Colin Powell said, "I think the intelligence community let all of us down."

By the end of 2001, the Americans unseated the Taliban, which had been harboring bin Laden and his cohort. Hamid Karzai was installed as head of a new Afghan government with U.S. Ambassador Zalmay Khalilzad at his side. American and American-paid forces chased Bin Laden into the mountains of Tora Bora and Saddam Hussein into a hole in the ground.

In 2003, the Americans tore apart the Iraq that the British had stitched together from three Ottoman Empire provinces. The Americans removed the Sunnis from power but were unable to turn it over to the Shiite majority. On May 1, President George W. Bush foolishly declared, "Mission Accomplished." It wasn't. The Shiites inflamed a bloody civil war.

COMPETING FOR IRAQI OIL

By 2007, Iraq was debating an American-inspired law that would end the nationalization of oil and bring back the Western oil companies. The first agreement was actually made between the Hunt Oil Company and the Kurds' provincial government. This was against American policy, but the State Department was blamed for having encouraged it.

In the spring of 2008, when oil was selling at up to $140 a barrel, the American-sponsored government in Baghdad announced that it was negotiating no-bid contracts with major Western oil companies that had been stripped by Saddam Hussein in 1972. Andrew E. Kramer wrote in *The New York Times*, "There was suspicion among many in the Arab world and among parts of the American public that the United States had gone to war in Iraq precisely to secure the oil wealth these contracts seek to extract." He quoted Charles Reis, economic officer of the U.S. Embassy in Baghdad, who explained that the no-bid contracts were intended to bring modern technology to Iraq's obsolete oil fields.

Whatever the truth, the no-bid contracts lasted less than three months before Iraq's Oil Ministry canceled them. A group of Democratic United States senators had objected. In public, the State Department insisted the contracts were an internal Iraqi affair. The issue became a boiling cauldron, with the United States fighting wars in Afghanistan and Iraq and trying to keep the lid on an unsteady Pakistan.

In the spring of 2008, President Pervez Musharraf, Pakistan's strongman and U.S. ally, lost power, and the United States faced a new power structure. The Iraqi government held a public sale with a take-it-or-leave-it price of $2 a barrel on oil. Iraq could make a deal only with a consortium of BP and the China Natural Petroleum Corporation.

AMERICA'S LARGEST EMBASSY

To handle these serial disruptions, the U.S. Embassy in Baghdad ballooned into the largest installation the Americans had anywhere overseas. A thousand people worked in the embassy, and another four hundred on the twenty-six Provincial Reconstruction Teams in the countryside. They included more than three hundred Foreign Service and Civil Service officers.

Iraqis who dared to work for the Americans were left in harm's way. Not until 2008 did the United States pass a law permitting Iraqis who had worked for the State Department to come to the United States. Then, the United States accepted five thousand Iraqis a year for five years, plus their spouses and children.

At that time, Iraq was designated a hardship post to which Foreign Service officers could not expose their wives and families. Some 750 Foreign Service jobs were now rated as hardship posts, and since assignment to these posts was for one year only, this also created a huge turnover and strained the Foreign Service.

The State Department ran into another headache. Because of troop shortages and increased violence in Iraq, twenty thousand civilian mercenaries were imported to keep order, protect convoys, and perform similar duties. The Special Inspector General for Iraq Reconstruction reported in 2008 that U.S. governmental agencies had contracts with at least three hundred such private companies. Most of them came under the Department of Defense, but at least one group, hired by Blackwater Worldwide, was run by the State Department.

These employees came under the assistant secretary for diplomatic security, in turn, Richard J. Griffin and Gregory Starr, whom the State Department sought to protect from Iraqi accusations. Well-armed Blackwater employees were accused of using excessive force during incidents in which Iraqi civilians were killed.

Despite charges that Blackwater personnel used riot-control gas indiscriminately, State renewed its contract in early 2008, citing the shortage of military personnel to protect diplomats. Accusations forced out of office both Richard Griffin and Howard J. Krongard, the State Department's inspector general.

In 2010, David Farrington, a security agent at the Baghdad embassy, revealed in closed-door hearings that the embassy had tried to help Blackwater guards escape punishment, and the embassy was accused of not seriously investigating the excessive-force charges. When the case against five Blackwater guards was dismissed, the Iraqi government threatened to force the U.S. Justice Department to appeal the dismissal.

By 2007, 20 percent of the Foreign Service had served in Iraq, and Ambassador Ryan C. Crocker, in Baghdad, cabled Secretary of State Rice that more and better political and economic officers were urgently needed in Iraq. Crocker had been on the job for only two months and was already critical. He had been immersed in the Middle East since the bombing of the U.S. embassy in Beirut, twenty-four years earlier. During that attack, he and his wife, Christine, a Foreign Service secretary, were in their offices, and he was slightly injured. Highly respected in the Foreign Service, Crocker had served as ambassador in Lebanon, Kuwait, Syria, and Pakistan. He took particular pride in his role in the American effort after the 2005 earthquake killed seventy thousand Pakistanis.

Crocker, who took charge in Baghdad after L. Paul Bremer III, John D. Negroponte, and Afghan-born Zalmay M. Khalilzad, was admired for his affinity to tough assignments, for his incessant long-distance running, and for his fluent Arabic, which he had learned in part out in the desert with goat-tending Bedouins.

In response to a request from Crocker on June 18, 2007, Secretary Rice ordered eleven more political officers to be added to the fifteen already in Iraq, and the nine economic officers there were increased to twenty-one. She also mandated that diplomatic posts in Iraq be given priority before filling any other State Department openings in Washington or overseas. After rockets killed two American civilians in 2008, the State Department ordered all personnel to wear helmets when they left the policed Green Zone and to sleep in blast-resistant locations.

The department also announced that diplomats wanting to learn Arabic could leave their posts immediately for two years of language training. Locally employed staff members working in embassies around the world were invited to take long-term temporary-duty assignments in Iraq. Their pay would be 50 percent above basic salaries. There was no attempt to sugarcoat the message. It said:

> The U.S. Embassy, regional offices and embedded sites are located in an active combat zone with frequent attacks on facilities and personnel. Types of attacks experienced are indirect fire from rockets or mortars, vehicle-borne improved explosive devices, improvised explosive devices (IEDs), suicide bombers, rocket-propelled grenades, and small arms fire.

"WE'RE NOT COWARDS"

The personnel crunch lit sparks of tension throughout the Foreign Service. Some officers emphasized their understanding that when men and women join the Foreign Service they commit themselves to go wherever they are needed. Others stressed that diplomats traditionally were not forced to serve under enemy fire.

Whispers emerged from Washington of growing resistance to assignments in Iraq. Accusations were made that "antiwar" people in the State Department were sabotaging efforts to staff the embassy and that the dangers for civilians were being exaggerated. Steven Kashkett, vice president of the American Foreign Service Association, testified to Congress that the AFSA had not taken a position on Iraq policy but that it had to represent its members' concerns. That, he said, did not mean the AFSA opposed the Secretary's policy. He told Congress that 40 percent of the diplomats serving in hazardous zones suffered serious mental and emotional problems and that the percentage was even higher in the Green Zone, where FSOs faced incoming fire.

In October 2007, the AFSA distributed a report titled "Telling Our Story" because "a small but growing number of voices are criticizing the State Department and Foreign Service for not 'stepping up to the plate' in Iraq." The report included these facts: The Foreign Service is made up of 11,500 men and women. Another 1,500 are with USAID, the Foreign Commercial Service, the Foreign Agricultural Service, and the International Broadcasting Bureau. Sixty-eight percent of the Foreign Service's members were stationed abroad at 167 embassies and a hundred consulates and other missions in 162 countries. The typical Foreign Service member spent two-thirds of his or her career abroad.

Sixty percent of the members overseas were serving at posts the government classified as hardship posts because of crime, terrorist threats, health risks, harsh climate, and other factors. Since 2001, the number of unaccompanied or limited-accompanied Foreign Service positions had quadrupled. Overall, in September 2007, the report said, 2,094 positions were unfilled worldwide. At the time the report was written, all two thousand career Foreign Service members who served in Iraq had been volunteers. But that was a standard hard to maintain.

Several hundred FSOs attended a department meeting to discuss "directed assignments." Afterward, veteran FSO John K. Naland, president of the AFSA, declared "that directed assignments into the war zone in Iraq would be detrimental to the individual, to the post, and to the Foreign Service as a whole." Already, the transfer of FSOs to Baghdad and Kabul had left nearly a quarter of all diplomat posts vacant. Naland said, "We urge the Administration and the Congress to make sure that every position established in Iraq is necessary."

Steven Kashkett said emphatically, "We're not weenies, we're not cowards, we're not cookie pushers in Europe." In October 2008, he reported with pride that Secretary Rice had announced that the missions in Iraq and Afghanistan would be filled into 2009 exclusively with volunteers. Expressing a more wary view, retired Ambassador James R. Bullington wrote, "At best, this [conflict] is a public relations disaster for the Foreign Service. I fear it may be worse than that.... Ultimately FSOs must go where they are sent."

48

Fortress America: The Embassy

2004—07

Just before seven o'clock on the first Saturday morning in May 2004, the U.S. Marine on post at the American embassy in Rome alerted the duty officer, young Foreign Service officer Elia Tello, at her home that there was an emergency: The Grand Hotel Parco Dei Principi, north of the Villa Borghese, was on fire. An American from Atlanta and two Canadians were dead, and more than two hundred Americans had been evacuated.

The Marine patched through to Tello's home a representative of the Holland America cruise line, which had fourteen passengers staying at the hotel. Tello learned that when smoke engulfed the building, the American who died, James Lawery, fifty-seven, had tied bedsheets together and let himself out of the fifth-floor window. His wife watched him fall to his death.

Tello immediately notified the embassy's consular section and the Operations Office of the State Department in Washington. At that same moment, Rome's Consul General Carolyn Huggins was driving down the *autostrada* south of Naples, heading out for the weekend, when her cell phone buzzed. Huggins listened to the message, whipped her car around, and drove swiftly back to Rome.

Elia Tello also hurried to the embassy in the Via Veneto, a grand old mansion known as Palazzo Margherita. And Emil Skodon, now the Deputy Chief of Mission, and Counselor Minister William J. Haugh rushed there with other Foreign Service officers. People had to be cared for, and thirty-one passports, lost in the fire, had to be replaced. Elia Tello worked until ten that night, especially helping the newly widowed American. "I was impressed with everyone coming together," she said of the experience. "That's why a lot of people join the Foreign Service."

One hundred and thirty-five Americans work in the Rome embassy. Fifty of them are diplomatic and consular officers, and thus members of the U.S. Foreign Service. Two hundred and forty-three staff are locally hired, of whom ten or so are American citizens.

The rest of the Americans in the embassy are specialists: Marine Guard, Seabees, secretaries, technicians. An embassy diplomat said, "Our footprint is so darn big here that we have to ask whether we are becoming part of the scene we are here to report on and watch over." Another diplomat said with a smile, "We spend a lot of time negotiating with ourselves."

The consuls in Rome, consuls general in Milan, Florence, and Naples, as well as consuls in other Italian cities provide a surprising range of help for Americans when they get into trouble. And they answer twelve thousand visa requests a year from Italians who wish to come to the United States.

The American consuls throughout Italy also man a lookout system to inform Washington of terrorist suspects and an emergency warning net of four thousand names of the American community in Italy marked to receive urgent information. Since the terrorist attacks of 9/11, the State Department has slowed down issuing visas, frustrating both individuals and institutions. There are angry complaints that the increased difficulty of obtaining visas by business people, students, scientists, artists, and others diverts them to other countries and deprives the United States of their talents. As an example, the medical school of Cornell University offered one student in its premed program in Qatar, a citizen of Iran, the opportunity to do summer research at its medical college in New York. She had to apply for three years before the United States admitted her.

It was charged that the 9/11 terrorists had entered the United States because of negligent visa screening and that fifteen of the nineteen terrorists held visas approved in Saudi Arabia. Congress' General Accounting Office said that the State Department should have rejected the applications of every one of them.

Consuls also have a responsibility to find missing Americans, some of whom do not want to be found. Peggy A. Gennatiempo, an experienced consul originally from Seattle, says that in such cases the government has to respect a "missing" person's privacy. But more often the consuls bring family and traveler together.

Consuls also advise Americans who want to marry in Italy or to obtain absentee ballots or veterans' benefits. They handle property when an American living in Italy dies, find the next of kin when someone dies while traveling alone, and obtain medical care for tourists who have to be hospitalized.

In addition to the Foreign Service's consuls, several "consular agencies" in Italy are manned by a lone American. In Venice, a port and a tourist destination, Megan Jones, a native of Pensacola, Florida, and a graduate of the University of North Carolina at Chapel Hill, was hired in 2006 at age twenty-nine to work from a one-person office at the airport. Her responsibility reached as far as Trieste, covered by fees from passports, notary services, and reports of births and deaths. She reported to the consul in Milan, but in Venice she was on her own.

Megan Jones must be available twenty-four hours to Americans in trouble, attend Italian civic events, and visit Americans who wind up in Italian hospitals or jails. She regards herself as a permanent-duty officer. For instance, when a young U.S. citizen with pulmonary problems lost his respirator's power cord during a security check at one of Italy's chaotic airports, she replaced it. He could live for only twenty-four hours without it. She also brings food under an arrangement with McDonald's to two American women in jail for importing drugs.

Her job has no health benefits and does not count toward entry into the Foreign Service. But she is dedicated and loves her work, even when the telephone wakes her at midnight.

"EXPORTING OUR ANGER AND FEAR"

Today, the staff of the American embassy in Rome is always concerned about terrorism. One cordon of Rome's police is stationed outside the embassy, and men of a second Italian police force and a detachment of sixteen U.S. Marines guard positions inside the gates. DCM Skodon says he tries to put himself inside terrorists' heads. He admits, "I think every day how I would kill Americans."

An American citizen now seeking entry to the embassy compound in Rome has to surrender his passport and cell phone and is tagged with a yellow-striped badge that declares him a visitor. He is escorted everywhere he goes. A Rome newspaper ran an article about the embassy titled: "La Fortezza USA."

In the past, American embassies reflected the grandeur and freedom of the United States. The Paris embassy (built in 1928), near the Place de la Concorde, resembles an Italian palazzo. The U.S. embassy in Helsinki (1936) was modeled on the mansion of a Virginia plantation.

In 1954, the New Delhi embassy adopted local traditions such as a concrete sunscreen; and the Accra embassy, in 1956, echoed anthills and tribal spears. In London, the ambassador originally wanted the embassy in redbrick Georgian on stylish Grosvenor Square; but as designed by Eero Saarinen, it ended up oversized and melodramatic. In 2010, a new billion-dollar London embassy, designed by the Philadelphia architectural firm of Kieran Timberlake, was announced for a 4.8-acre site in a quieter area, south of the Thames River. It will be a glass cube surrounded by a pond (moat) and two terraced meadows concealing security barriers. *The New York Times* called it "a fascinating study in how architecture can be used as a form of camouflage."

Security has replaced drama, and the buttoned-up embassy is now American policy. Architects design perimeter walls and eliminate vulnerable screens and stilts. The buildings often resemble pillboxes with bulletproof shields and windows far above ground. Remote locations with deep setbacks replace exposed downtown sites. Some of the results have been called prisons.

Ambassador Diego Asencio, who has been a hostage himself, is convinced that "hardening sites" cannot solve the problem. "If you harden a site," he says, "you get a bigger bomb." And he adds, "Diplomacy is the establishment of contacts. . . . Sitting in your bunker, first of all, doesn't allow you to do your job and, second of all, doesn't protect you."

Gone are the days when an American visitor could move around in a U.S. embassy, or even the Department of State, virtually without restraint. Senior Foreign Service officers handle the constraints with aplomb, but many junior officers, afraid of making a mistake and damaging their careers, can be excessively cautious.

Also gone are the days when a citizen of any country could visit an embassy's U.S. Information Service Library and read American newspapers, magazines, and books. The libraries in industrial countries for the most part have been closed because they were vulnerable to attack. But Bonnie R. Cohen, undersecretary of state for management, told a U.S. Senate task force, "It does not make sense to turn our embassies into fortresses, even if we could, which is doubtful, or into places where we put security so far ahead of promoting American ideals that we cannot do our business properly." Secretary of State Colin Powell says, "The important part of diplomacy is listening to the other side and taking into account their fears and concerns." That is difficult to do from behind closed doors.

These restraints have been a long time coming. One early cause was the murder of U.S. Consul General Thomas C. Wasson in Jerusalem on May 22, 1948, probably by an Arab sniper. His successor asked for U.S. Marines to guard the consulate, and this led to the creation in 1967 of the Marine Security Guard Battalion, which now provides guard units for embassies, consulates, and missions. Members of the Marine Security Guard Battalion have been killed in Saigon, Phnom Penh, and Islamabad; others have defended posts in Nicosia, Bangkok, Tripoli, Kuwait, Taipei, and Manila.

By now, tension and fear have tarnished the Foreign Service's sense of public service. This started well before 9/11. The American ambassador at Nicosia was killed in 1974. The ambassador at San Salvador had to be rescued in 1979. American diplomats in Tehran were held hostage for 444 days. The U.S. Embassy in Beirut was blown up in 1983. The embassy in Athens has been attacked more than once. At the Lisbon embassy in 1986, an explosive was discovered underneath a car. The embassies in Nairobi and Dar es Salaam were blown up in 1998. In Rome, a group of Moroccan "tunnelers" were arrested when in possession of explosives and maps of the ancient caverns under the embassy compound.

During the five years after the destruction at the two embassies in Nairobi and Dar es Salaam, Congress appropriated $5.7 billion for embassy security. Three ambassadors, George L. Argyros, Marc Grossman, and Felix G. Rohatyn, led "The Embassy of the Future" project, which tried to resolve the conflict between protecting embassies and still enabling diplomats to function. In the following decade, the State Department built sixty-eight buildings, including forty-nine embassies, and moved twenty thousand employees into safer facilities.

This was not easy. In Madagascar, the government had to be overthrown and most embassy personnel ordered home. In Karachi, terrorists wrecked the consulate. In Jerusalem, seven years were needed to move the consulate.

At the Rome embassy, Regional Security Officer Robert A. Hartung, who was born in London where his father was a Foreign Service officer, was responsible for making security measures effective. He said, "All non-employees are screened. Without that, people are going to die. We always have high-risk areas.... Now, every embassy is a viable target. You can't be surprised if any embassy is hit."

Deputy Secretary of State Richard Armitage said, "We used to export optimism and hope and a welcoming face to the world. And now because of the horror after 9/11, I think, we started exporting our anger and fear.... A foreign leader said: 'Look at your embassy. We call that Alcatraz.' We've got to become more open, more accessible, everywhere."

Deputy Secretary Armitage was not a Foreign Service officer, but as a Naval Academy graduate, he had served in Vietnam and The Pentagon. He managed to get himself involved in Iran-Contra and the outing of CIA agent Valerie Plame.

A VARIETY OF AMBASSADORS

In command of the American diplomatic fortress in Rome at the time of this report was Ambassador Melvin F. Sembler, who made a fortune building shopping malls in the South and who was a fund-raiser for both Presidents Bush. The elder Bush sent him to Canberra as his ambassador, and the second posted him to Rome. Sembler earned both jobs. Of politics, he said, "If you don't have money, you don't have a voice." In Rome, he said, he also contributed "adult supervision" to the Foreign Service personnel.

As ambassador in Rome, Sembler and his wife, Betty, and their staff lived in Villa Taverna, a magnificent thirty five-room Roman villa within seven acres of formal gardens. Villa Taverna has been the home of American ambassadors since 1933. Romans call it one of the city's "pleasure palaces," but stories about it are not exclusively pleasurable. Ambassador Clare Boothe Luce told how her husband, publisher Henry Luce, repeatedly got lost in the tunnels underneath the property. And Ambassador Luce was reported to have been poisoned by arsenic buried in the ceiling of their bedroom. The State Department called that story apocryphal, but *The New York Times,* when she died more than thirty years later, said it was fact.

Over the years, the assignment of a minister or ambassador to Rome has frequently been a problem, starting with William Waldorf Astor in the 1880s. Rome has received its share of capable career Foreign Service officers, but its diplomatic importance and lavish comforts have attracted as ambassadors political appointees like Richard N. Gardner, Maxwell M. Rabb, Clare Boothe Luce, Peter F. Secchia, Congressman Thomas M. Foglietta, and John Volpe, a U.S. secretary of transportation.

Luce was skilled at dealing with the upper echelons of society on both sides of the Atlantic and had easy access to President Eisenhower and the White House. Secchia, a Grand Rapids lumber baron, and Sembler were political-campaign contributors. Earlier, while Graham Martin served as ambassador to Italy from 1969 to 1973, he tried to defeat Italy's Communists by covertly distributing $10 million to their opponents. This included $800,000 to their intelligence arm, whose leader later ran for parliament as a neo-Fascist.

Ambassador Gardner opposed such clandestine interventions into Italian politics. Gardner, a lawyer, arrived in Rome in March 1977 when the Italian Communist Party was winning 34 percent of the vote, and both the president of the Chamber of Deputies and Rome's mayor were party members. Some American leaders worried that local non-Soviet Communists, called Euro-Communists, would win government jobs and infect Western Europe.

The Communists were not an ambassador's only problem; even more pervasive was the corrupt system of "bribery and kickbacks," which long pockmarked Italy's politics and business.

Gardner exemplified the modern American diplomat who tried to influence foreign policy. He even organized meetings of American ambassadors in Western Europe: Arthur Hartman, from Paris; Walter Stoessel, from Bonn; Tapley Bennett, from NATO; Thomas Enders, from the European Community; Brewster King, from London, and Gardner came from Rome. They discussed policy issues and sent the State Department their conclusions.

In 1979, Gardner led efforts to persuade the Italian government to accept American nuclear cruise missiles on its territory to counter the intimidating new Soviet SS-20 missiles. Germany, the only Western European country willing to accept the cruise missiles, had required that at least one other government join it.

Ambassador Gardner and DCM Allen Holmes worked to convince the Italians to join Germany. Embassy political officers briefed political leaders, and John Shirley, the public affairs counselor, rallied newspaper editors and writers. Despite massive demonstrations, the Italian Chamber of Deputies approved the U.S. missiles by 313 to 262. That was just weeks after the seizure of the U.S. embassy in Tehran and before the Soviet Union invaded Afghanistan.

Gardner also pressed the Italians, with some success, not to send helicopters and spare parts to Iran. And he opposed the Italian commitment to sell Iraq equipment for reprocessing plutonium. Assistant Secretary of State Thomas R. Pickering flew to Rome, and he and Gardner asked the Italians to limit what they would send to Iraq. They received no assurances, but the problem was eliminated two years later when Israel bombed the nuclear reactor at Osirak.

A few diplomats tried to redirect the security-above-everything philosophy. Victor H. Ashe, then ambassador to Poland and previously the mayor of Knoxville, Tennessee, opposed the $80 million budget for a new consulate in Krakow, in which only twelve Americans would work. He also argued that facilities in Iceland and New Zealand did not need to be fortresses.

A generation later, Ambassador Sembler sat in his expansive, gold-encrusted corner office at the Rome embassy and described how he had acquired the final building to give the embassy the entire city block facing the Via Veneto. Real estate was a subject Sembler knew. This last nonembassy building on the block was for sale for $110 million. The State Department opposed the purchase. The Four Seasons Hotel wanted to buy the building, and that meant trucks would pull up next to the embassy and the Marines' living quarters. "That was unacceptable," Sembler said. "I got on a crusade."

Sembler went over the State Department's head to Congress. "I understand real estate and I have contacts that career officers don't have," he said confidently. The United States purchased the building in 2003 for $83.5 million.

Ambassador Sembler regarded the consulate general in Florence as the embassy's most vulnerable facility, because the building is tightly surrounded by city streets. One day, he and the mayor stood on a consulate balcony and watched a truck pull up alongside the building. That sight convinced the Italians to close off all four streets around the consulate.

All this, of course, was unrelated to the dark evening in March 2005, when American soldiers without warning shot Guiliana Sgrena, a recently freed Italian journalist who had been held hostage in Iraq, and killed her Italian security guard as their car tried to run a roadblock. Ambassador Sembler was called in by Prime Minister Silvio Berlusconi, who was generally regarded as pro-American and who demanded an explanation. The Italian government started withdrawing its three thousand troops from Iraq.

Ambassador Sembler provoked his own flap when an act of Congress named the final building that he had arranged to purchase in the U.S. Embassy complex the Mel Sembler Building. The decision was widely criticized as an honor that had never before been bestowed on a sitting ambassador.

A DCM TAKES ON TERRORISM

Recently, counterterrorism has led the list of the Rome embassy's concerns. DCM Emil Skodon explained, "There is a war on terrorism and we are part of it."

(Half a century earlier, Senator Joseph McCarthy's junior agents Roy Cohn and G. David Schine were invited to lunch at the residence of Skodon's predecessor, Elbridge Durbrow, and checked over his personal library for books revealing an interest in Communism. Since Durbrow had just served a tour in Moscow, the two McCarthy devotees had a field day.)

When terrorists struck in the United States on September 11, 2001,

Skodon was serving in The Pentagon as a Foreign Service political advisor to the Air Force. He had just returned to his office after a staff meeting when he heard the plane hit. "I knew immediately what had happened. I knew the world had changed, America was under attack. I was scared and frustrated that I could not do more to help."

As a youth, Skodon sold shoes in the back of the Chicago stockyards to pay for earning two degrees at the University of Chicago. To escape the South Side of Chicago, he joined the Foreign Service. He commented, "I found I just loved it. You represent America. You have to want to make things happen, to make a difference."

Skodon has experienced a surprising number of crises; in the embassy at Kuwait when the Iraqis invaded in 1991 and in The Pentagon on 9/11/01. He served for two years in East Berlin, and said, "I saw how a totalitarian government sucked the life out of people." As DCM in Singapore he was exposed to the fierce differences between Chinese and American approaches to human rights. The question he had to answer for himself there was whether the United States should negotiate with a nation that does not agree with America on human rights. He decided the United States should, explaining, "We need to be careful not to fall into single-issue diplomacy. We need to deal across the whole spectrum of issues."

Twenty-seven years of service have given Skodon strong views about the Foreign Service as a career. He observes, "The Foreign Service in the field is different from the Foreign Service in Washington. In Washington it's hard not to be just another bureaucrat. In the field you are doing things." Working in The Pentagon with the Air Force convinced him that the military distributes responsibility, while the Foreign Service requires that decisions be cleared by too many people. He concluded, "Diplomacy is the art of getting other people to do what you want by putting yourself in their shoes."

Skodon credits Frank G. Wisner II for being a mentor early in his career, when he was the State Department's desk officer for Mozambique. "He drove me nuts," he admits, "but he taught me if you apply enough energy, you can solve insoluble problems."

THE ELEPHANT AND THE MOUSE

Rome is special in that it has three American ambassadors. And at any time, all three may be political appointees since career FSOs don't often secure ambassadorships in Europe.

When Ambassador Sembler served at the "big embassy" for Rome, Ambassador R. James Nicholson headed the United States Embassy to the Holy See. He operated from a handsome modern house across the Tiber. Staff members lightly refer to the missions to Rome and the Vatican as "the elephant and the mouse."

The third U.S. ambassador in Rome, Tony P. Hall, had been a Democratic congressman from Dayton, Ohio, for twenty-four years, and he had been a tailback on the Little All-America team at Denison University. In Rome, he led the Mission to the United Nations Agencies, which had offices in the Piazza del Popolo. His charge was to work with six UN agencies, including the Food and Agricultural Organization and the World Food Program. He concentrated on people who are starving; and a decade earlier, he fasted for twenty-two days to draw attention to them.

The U.S. First Amendment was long interpreted as denying full diplomatic relations with the Vatican, although the United States did have a legation there from 1848 to 1867. No reciprocal relations were allowed. In 1940, Franklin Roosevelt sent a personal presidential representative to the Holy See. Myron C. Taylor, chairman of United States Steel, was the first such representative, and he stayed for ten years. In 1947, J. Graham Parsons was sent out by the State Department. Since Parsons was reporting to Taylor's superiors at State, Taylor objected and within the year fired him.

In 1984, Ronald Reagan, impressed by Pope John Paul II's defiance to Communism, opened formal diplomatic relations. When the presidential representative was raised to an ambassador, Ambassador Thomas P. Melady said the relationship offered many opportunities in a world "where the unholy trinity of poverty, illiteracy, and disease affect so many."

Ambassador Nicholson, a trim West Point graduate and Army Ranger, had been the chairman of the Republican National Committee and became the ambassador to the Holy See. He characterized his embassy as a "regular bilateral mission" without military and commercial sections, concentrating on issues of food, health, and religious freedom. He says of the United States and the Vatican, "We have a foundation of shared values. The Pope has repeatedly said that people who kill in the name of God must be stopped."

All three ambassadors in Rome are backed up by carefully selected Foreign Service officers as their Deputy Chiefs of Mission. That is where the Foreign Service expertise comes to bear. In addition to Skodon, Nicholson's DCM, D. Brent Hardt, is a Yale graduate with a Ph.D. from the Fletcher School of International Studies at Tufts University. He had served in East Berlin and The Hague and worked on tough issues like German reunification, NATO arms sales, drug-traffic enforcement, and the technological improvement of food supplies. DCM Hardt said, "We have to be very clear on what is a church matter and what is a state matter." Nicholson and Hardt appreciate that the Vatican can reach around the world, and they have developed their own embassy public-affairs effort. Hardt said, "We are carrying our values to a global audience. The Pope is a political force people listen to." (DCM Hardt went on to become the ambassador to Guyana.)

Before he entered the Foreign Service, DCM (or deputy permanent representative) J. Michael Cleverley of the Mission to the United Nations Agencies had served on a Mormon mission to Finland and as the DCM in Helsinki and Athens. His son, Mikael, became an FSO in Helsinki and sat in the same office that Cleverley occupied twenty-five years earlier.

Of his job in Rome, Michael Cleverley says, "It's satisfying because you are helping people who are starving." He judges that the largest hungry population is in Africa, where AIDs kills farmworkers and leaves the fields untended. Cleverley estimates that 800 million people on earth are hungry and that UN agencies reach only 10 percent of them.

A MULTITUDE OF AGENCIES

In a major embassy like Rome, some twenty-eight agencies of the Federal government are present, from Immigration to the FBI and Secret Service. They can confuse responsibility for the creation and execution of foreign policy.

William Harrop, who has served as ambassador in four countries and as the Foreign Service's inspector general, figures that members of the Foreign Service now comprise less than a third of the total officers in most embassies. Personnel from other departments and agencies complicate the ambassador's job and, as Under Secretary Nicholas Katzenbach put it, "[create] a bureaucracy of horrendous proportions."

When David Bruce became the U.S. ambassador to the Court of St. James's in 1961, he was amazed to find that forty-four U.S. agencies were operating out of his embassy. At the other extreme is the embassy to the Holy See, which has a staff of eighteen, including only four FSOs.

THE WAY AN EMBASSY WORKS

The Foreign Service personnel in the Rome embassy are organized under five minister-level officers. The political minister is the most traditional, working directly with the Italian government on treaties and other inter-governmental arrangements. The economic minister serves as an advisor on trade relations, with emphasis on helping American corporations de-velop markets for their goods and services. The consul (or consul general) serves individual Americans and Italians. The minister for administra-tion or management supervises the needs of the embassy from facilities to personnel. Finally, the minister for public affairs communicates directly with the Italian press and people. Other elements in the embassy, such as security, work immediately under the ambassador.

Foreign Service officers usually stay at a post only for three or four years. This removes them soon after they have learned their job and have had a chance to win their hosts' confidence. But that limit also reduces the danger of being co-opted by the local environment. Rome embassy's man-agement counselor, William J. Haugh, says, "You have to move people around or they forget who they are working for."

The embassy also hires foreign nationals, who may remain in place for twenty years. The fast-revolving Americans need them to maintain con-tacts and to serve as the mission's institutional memory.

The rapid turnover of Foreign Service officers depreciates the quality of life for them and their families and keeps them thinking about their next assignment. The Rome embassy's economic officer, Scott Kilner, says, "You are always laying the groundwork for what comes next." Although this turnover could become very competitive, Foreign Service officers in general respect each other's dignity and privacy. Cutthroat rivalry can backfire and wreck a career.

Another major career concern, of course, is the climb through the ranks. FS-5 and the FS-4 are the junior ranks; FS-3 through FS-1 are the midlevel ranks, with FS-1 the equivalent of a colonel in the army. Above these are four Senior Foreign Service ranks: counselor, minister-counselor, career minister, and, at the top, career ambassador. Their military equivalents would be generals. Senior officers are now able to serve seven years in a rank and then must move up or retire. Their legal retirement age is sixty-five.

Among the Foreign Service officers at Rome, William Haugh is a West Point graduate. He provides management for all three diplomatic entities in Rome. He joined the Foreign Service after seven years in the Army, earned a degree at Harvard's Kennedy School, and served in various State Department crisis centers and the White House Situation Room.

Thomas M. Countryman, Rome's minister-counselor for political affairs, leads thirteen people who monitor Italy's internal politics, Italy's interaction with other nations and with the European Union, and various political-military matters, like the seventeen thousand U.S. troops on Italian bases and the two thousand members of the Italian military whom Italy has sent to the war in Iraq. Countryman comes from Tacoma, Washington, and his sister, Mary Ellen, is a Foreign Service officer in Myanmar (Burma).

At one of Countryman's early posts, Belgrade, he met his wife to be, the daughter of a Yugoslav diplomat. Later, he was assigned to go back to Belgrade as DCM. But when the Kosovo crisis erupted, he did not want to bomb his wife's hometown and turned down the assignment three times. After the bombing stopped in 1999, he accepted the difficult post. Before coming to Rome, he also served in Cairo, digging into terrorism's threats against the Egyptian government. One Egyptian official was gunned down right after talking with him.

Seeking a change after Cairo, Countryman hoped to be sent to the Solomon Islands, a small post where he could be his own boss and do it all. But he was assigned to counterterrorism in Washington and became a Middle East specialist at the United Nations Mission in New York under Madeleine Albright. There, he helped draft the oil-for-food program with Iraq in 1995 and worked on Israeli-Palestinian issues. After this, he worked with the National Security Council under Samuel R. Berger on the Israeli-Palestinian peace process. One perk at the NSC, he says with a smile, was bringing his young sons, Stefan and Andrew, to meet Socks and Buddy,

President Clinton's cat and Lab. He came to Rome in 2001, where he worked on preventing nuclear proliferation and sustaining Italy's support of the Iraq war.

One Foreign Service officer working with Tom Countryman on political-military issues was Kelly Degnan, who came from Detroit and the University of Southern California Law School. She had an exotic professional history. After law school, she and a friend had a forty-two-foot boat built on Taiwan and sailed the Pacific. When they reached the UN trust territory of Truk, they sold the boat, and Degnan worked as a lawyer on Truk for two years and then as a lawyer for the Supreme Court of the independent country of Palau.

This did not make for a typical résumé, and it took ten months to get her security clearance for the Foreign Service. Her first post was the consulate at Peshwar, Pakistan, a few miles from the Khyber Pass. From there, she could monitor Afghanistan. Later, in Washington, she became a special assistant to Secretary of State Albright.

Degnan's responsibilities in Rome included watching Italy's relations with NATO and increasing Italy's effectiveness as a military ally. She was involved with issues of arms control, disarmament, military standardization, and defense-industry cooperation. She says of the Foreign Service, "It's not your job to agree with policy. It's your job to represent it. It's like being a lawyer." She adds that "everyone has a red line" beyond which their conscience won't let them accept a policy.

Rome's DCM Skodon comments, "Our job is to explain American foreign policy that is set by the President and also to make recommendations to go into foreign policy. If you feel you can't do it, resign." Behind closed doors it is right to argue and dissent. "That's how you get good policy, by arguing," he says. But when the doors open, he advises, go out and sell the policy.

Italy's external political relations are the domain of the embassy's first secretary, James E. Donegan, who in Rome worked on the European Union's effort to develop a common foreign policy for twenty-five nations. He says, "More and more is happening in Brussels."

Supporting the economic side of American life has long been among the Foreign Service's functions. In the beginning, it sought foreign loans to pay for the American Revolution and to keep the United States government afloat. Today, the emphasis is on helping manufacturers, bankers, and service providers obtain access to markets abroad. After 1980, the

Commerce Department took over the hands-on work of trade promotion, and State was relegated to defining national policies.

In Rome, the prime economic responsibility is in the hands of economic officer Scott Kilner. He had his difficulties breaking into the Foreign Service. He earned degrees from Stanford and Johns Hopkins and then went into banking. He worked for a San Francisco bank for three years and took the Foreign Service exams. When he was told he had failed them for the third time, he decided that he would make international banking his career.

One morning nine months after that, he was leaving home to catch the bus for work when he received a telephone call from the State Department's Board of Examiners telling him they had discovered an error in his test results. He had, in fact, scored above the cutoff. Was he still interested in joining the Foreign Service? He was stunned. There was a long silence, and the woman calling him finally said that he did not seem very enthusiastic. But after thinking it over, he called back and accepted.

The approval process took Scott Kilner another fifteen months. He was rigorously questioned about his views on the Vietnam War when he was the editor of his high school newspaper and why he had spent a month traveling in Eastern Europe. Finally, he was admitted to the Foreign Service in 1981. He learned Turkish and served three tours in Turkey, and he is now a member of the Senior Foreign Service.

In Rome, Kilner's responsibilities were wide-ranging. He tried to advance U.S. economic policies bilaterally and, through the European Union, multilaterally. He chaired interagency committees and sought to improve the protection of intellectual property, strengthen export controls, and reduce prohibitions on modified foodstuffs. Still, Kilner says, "I spend 30 percent of my time on Homeland Security issues, terrorism, terror financing, aviation security. Ten years ago I didn't do any of this in Paris." What gives him the most satisfaction, he says, are "opportunities you get every day to help Americans."

PUBLIC DIPLOMACY AND THE HARD ROCK CAFE

Diplomacy now puts Foreign Service officers directly in touch with the people of their host countries. Ironically, public diplomacy has burgeoned at a time when USIS libraries have been liquidated, embassies walled in, and consulates closed.

Rome's USIS Library was open to everyone and sat across from the embassy in a site now occupied by the Hard Rock Cafe. The library has been replaced by a computerized Information Resource Center inside the embassy compound. This IRC has two distinct audiences: the American diplomatic mission and preidentified outsiders researching such subjects as trade, terrorism, and human trafficking. To some degree, the IRC still maintains contact between the United States and its host. When Giovanni Guasina, director of Rome's IRC, received the State Department's annual report on terrorism, he sent it out to three hundred Italians before breakfast the next morning. But he works deep inside the embassy, where no Italian passersby can drop in.

John P. Dwyer, the minister-counselor for public affairs, and his associates constantly dream up projects through which they conduct their public diplomacy with the Italian people. In one brief period, they staged a meeting in Venice called America: A Work in Progress, about changes in the United States during the past quarter century; sponsored an Islamic imam's tour of Italy; helped a documentary filmmaker from the States; held live video conferences for Italian reporters and State Department officials sitting in Washington; and selected thirty Italians to visit their counterparts in the United States.

The members of the Italian media were the responsibility of Chicago-born Ian Kelly, the press attaché with a Ph.D. in Russian and nineteen years in the Foreign Service. Italy is the fifth country he has served in. He began as a cultural attaché; and when he shifted to work with the media, the State Department gave him a three-day course and turned him loose. Despite the inadequacy of this, by 2009 he was serving as a State Department spokesman with the rank of minister-counselor.

The cultural side of public diplomacy in Italy was directed by the able Anne Callaghan. She graduated from Colby College and the National War College. At one point she was assigned to organize public diplomacy with Cuba, even though she was not allowed to enter the country. In Italy, she made the younger generation her prime target. She is determined to "tell the world about America, warts and all." And Paula S. Thiede, the press attaché, has also targeted the younger generation with "challenge seminars" aimed at university students.

Jerome J. Oetgen, the assistant cultural attaché, is from Savannah and has a Ph.D. in Medieval Studies. He has charge of outreach programs that put Italians in touch with Americans. For example, he staged a series of conferences on U.S.–European Union relations, explaining he was trying to "get the American voice into the mix." He says frankly that Italians are rapidly adopting American cultural ways but at the same time, "They don't like us."

49

New Challenges for Modern Diplomacy

1970–2012

In the 1970s, the U.S. Foreign Service began to display discouraging signs of wear and tear. Ever since the upheavals of World War II, the Foreign Service had faced extraordinary pressures. It had to serve the United States as it emerged as a global power, met the tensions of the Vietnam War and the Cold War, and coped with revolutionary changes in American society wrought by the changing role of women, the struggle for civil rights, and the dangers of international terrorism, as well as changes within the Foreign Service itself.

The number of applicants wishing to join the Foreign Service declined from twenty thousand in 1963 to eleven thousand in 1979. Persons who were offered Foreign Service appointments in 1979 responded with more rejections than acceptances. Midcareer resignations rose by 69 percent between 1969 and 1979. The American Foreign Service Association (AFSA) surveyed three thousand officers and found that more than five hundred were considering resigning.

The nation was focused abroad on the military demands for the Vietnam War and the Cold War and gave the Foreign Service pitiful support. On a minor but telling level, Bruce Laingen remembered that when he was sworn in as an ambassador for the first time, in 1977, he needled Carol Laise, then Director General of the Foreign Service, because there was no money to provide drinks for his guests.

The Foreign Service also displayed warning signals that could not be analyzed statistically. Some applicants were given Foreign Service status although they would never serve abroad. Personnel categories and complex pay scales created inequities. And a "senior glut" of older officers gridlocked promotions. Since admission was no longer limited to the affluent, pay scales came under pressure. One emotional money issue was whether divorced spouses should receive a share of pensions. That debate grew so heated that during a meeting with management, the AFSA delegation actually walked out. The Foreign Service needed to be reexamined in depth, and calls for reform came from many sources.

While trying to meet such challenges, the State Department acquired some of the characteristics of a bureaucracy. George Kennan, retiring as ambassador to Yugoslavia, explained, "The great difficulty was to get opinion and authority out of Washington, especially when it cost money. The ponderousness of our government institutions works against our best interest." He complained he could not get congressional approval to repair the embassy fence. And when an earthquake devastated Yugoslavia, he said, "The only thing I could do was give blood. No congressional committee could stop me from doing that."

Young Virginia Morris, a junior consul in Barcelona, was denied tenure for several years until she taught herself to work the system. She concluded, "The State Department puts a high priority on conformance. . . . You can buck the system. The system doesn't like it but it accepts it." Once she learned how, she went on to a long, satisfying Foreign Service career.

Later, as a consul in Florence, Morris had a chance to make a modest difference. The United States' visa form asked whether an applicant had ever voted for a Communist party. Many Italians had voted for a Communist candidate but were not Communists and had to lie to get a visa. She persuaded a number of other foreign consuls in Italy to urge applicants to check the box that said they had voted for a Communist. Flooded with these confessions, the immigration service changed the form. She admits, "It was a small victory."

The comprehensive Foreign Service Act of 1980 dealt with problems facing a bureaucracy. It raised salary levels and emphasized training, especially midcareer training. It established "up or out" criteria to reward merit and dump the least able. AFSA leaders met with Under Secretary for Management Benjamin H. Read to find a balance between correcting the underrepresentation of minorities and women while still raising standards for recruitment, promotion, and retention.

Congress handled the 1980 act without attracting much public attention. As noted by Ken Bleakley, president of the AFSA board, there was a "general apathy of most of Congress to this arcane bill." During the congressional debate, Senator Jesse Helms of North Carolina, a frequent critic of the Foreign Service, introduced his own bill as an amendment to the 1946 Act. He told the Senate the 1980 bill

> ... does not recognize that the crisis in the Foreign Service does not arise mainly from such administrative issues as the number of classes of Foreign Service officers, the categories of its personnel, or even the promotion and selection out procedures it employs. It arises instead from confusions as to the proper role of the traditional Foreign Service in foreign policy . . .

Helms wanted to retain strict selection standards even if they reduced opportunities for women and minorities. His bill, which favored maintaining the traditional elite service, was never reported out of the Foreign Relations Committee.

(Four years later, Helms was the center of an open political battle when twenty-two active ambassadors, all Republican political appointees, endorsed his campaign for re-election. In response, thirty-six retired ambassadors, led by former Ambassador Philip M. Kaiser, opposed Helms' re-election, and denounced the entry of active ambassadors into partisan politics.)

The conference report dated September 29, 1980, pointed up what its adherents regarded as most important by opening with this paragraph:

> (The Act) Requires all personnel actions to be made in accordance with merit principles. Directs the Secretary of State to ensure that members of and applicants for the Service are free from discrimination, free from reprisals for specified disclosures, free to submit any report, and free from prohibited personnel practices. Directs

the Secretary to establish a minority recruiting program and report
to Congress annually concerning such program.

On October 17, President Jimmy Carter signed the 1980 act as Public
Law 96-465. It asserted that the Foreign Service should be strengthened
and improved. Its range of instructions was enormous.

Entry and advancement should be open to persons from all segments of
American society, and admission should be through impartial and rigorous
examination. Selection boards would include public members, women, and
members of minorities. Members of the Foreign Service should participate
in the formulation of policies and procedures that affect their conditions of
employment, and a fair system should resolve individual grievances. Salaries, allowances, and benefits should attract and retain qualified personnel,
and incentives should reward exceptional performance.

Entrance into the new Senior Foreign Service should be only through
superior performance, not through seniority. If the contract of a member
of the senior service was not renewed, he or she could not return to the
regular Foreign Service. Chiefs of mission should normally come from
the ranks of career Foreign Service officers, although noncareer appointments were allowed.

All Foreign Service personnel would be on a single pay schedule divided into nine classes. And the act provided for a pay raise of about $27.4
million, or 19 percent.

The mandatory retirement age of all Foreign Service employees was
raised from sixty to sixty-five. Retirement annuities and survivor benefits
would be automatically shared with qualifying divorced spouses only if
they had been married for ten years and if they became "former spouses"
after February 15, 1981.

The Foreign Service Act of 1980 concentrated on the conditions under
which Foreign Service men and women live and develop their careers. It
intended to reverse the decline in the number of applicants and the rise
in the percentage of those who rejected Foreign Service appointments, as
well as the rise in the number of those who resigned in midcareer.

Three points in the massive text of the Foreign Service Act of 1980 were
especially noteworthy:

First, the law omitted any basic consideration of the nature and purposes of the Foreign Service, because, as a mature institution, it seemed no longer to need such definition.

Second, even after two centuries, the Foreign Service and its members still perceived a need to clarify ethical issues. Third, despite its detailed exposition of the Foreign Service's operation, the law had to be amended repeatedly during the following years with sharply focused laws and executive orders.

The up-or-out provision of the new law attracted continuing attention from the State Department and the Foreign Service. At the request of a subcommittee of the House Committee on Government Reform, the State Department's Office of Inspector General (OIG) issued an internal report in 2002. The OIG emphasized that the up-or-out system was designed to provide promotion opportunities for the best officers at every level. This "orderly flow" would be accomplished by establishing the maximum number of years an officer could remain at any one level before being promoted or required to resign.

The OIG study found that more officers were on active-duty status in the very senior ranks than there were positions for them, and this became known as "the senior glut." It produced desperate senior officers walking the corridors of the department looking for jobs. And just below them, middle-level officers had a window of six years to be promoted into the senior service, or they would be involuntarily retired. Some officers with twenty years of service and eligible for promotion were squeezed out. And the up-or-out provision could dilute young officers' commitment to a career. They could find themselves eliminated on the way up. Some middle-grade officers decided not to risk a lifetime commitment to the Foreign Service.

But overall, the Foreign Service was improving. Eric S. Rubin, the DCM in Moscow and former executive assistant to the under secretary for political affairs, said vividly, "When I came in there were many alcoholic middle-aged white guys in the Foreign Service. Now it is more of a meritocracy."

"MOST IN NEED OF REPAIR"

The stresses facing the modern Foreign Service gave birth to a stream of commissions, panels, and committees, which zealously studied what was wrong. "It's been a rough twenty years for the Foreign Service," Eric Rubin observed. "We are really stretched."

Still in *Foreign Affairs* in 1996, two career Foreign Service officers, Lawrence S. Eagleburger, who was briefly Secretary of State, and Robert L. Barry, former ambassador to Indonesia, asserted that State's swollen bureaucracy and Congress' budget cutting were major problems needing solution. They said five under secretaries and nineteen assistant secretaries were too many.

Overseas, the reformers called for a revolutionary revision of the prime function of Foreign Service officers as "hunter-gatherers of information." They recommended that "America's representatives abroad should focus on advocacy." Here were early signs pointing to a new future.

The severest critique came from the U.S. Commission on National Security / 21st Century, known as the Hart-Rudman Commission after its cochairmen, former U.S. senators Gary Hart and Warren B. Rudman. President Clinton appointed this commission in 1998 to examine federal agencies involved with national security and to make recommendations to the President.

In its third and final report, issued in 2001, the commission described the State Department as "a crippled institution" and boldly recommended its "redesign." Among the specific recommendations were these: create an under secretary for global affairs, eliminate the State Department's "functional" bureaus while retaining the "regional" ones, integrate the U.S. Agency for International Development fully into the State Department, and establish an office devoted to strategic planning, assistance, and budgeting.

"Confidence in the Department is at an all-time low," the Hart-Rudman Commission declared. The State Department had surrendered "many of its core functions" to other agencies and developed an "exceedingly complex organizational structure." Foreign assistance is "a bureaucratic morass," and the department's "worldwide informational technology assets must be updated." The department's inefficiencies were blamed as the reasons that Congress consistently underfunded it.

The Foreign Service "is most in need of repair," the commission asserted. It recommended shortening the hiring process dramatically and ending the "blindfolding policy" on the oral exams, under which the examiners know nothing about an applicant. That, it said, runs "completely counter to common sense."

Most recommendations of the Hart-Rudman Commission were never adopted. That was not surprising because its damning analysis might have been accurate but it failed to consider the bureaucrats wedded to their ways of doing things.

More temperate and more effective were the analyses of diplomatic processes in March 2003 and November 2004 by the Foreign Affairs Council, a self-styled "non-partisan umbrella group of eleven organizations concerned about U.S. diplomatic readiness."

In its first report, the Foreign Affairs Council asserted that when Secretary Colin Powell arrived the State Department was "an organization weakened by years of budget cuts and hampered by antiquated operating procedures." Among the pressures damaging Foreign Service morale, the council found, were the requirement to fill posts in war zones and the "ludicrous" requirement that middle-level and junior Foreign Service officers take an 18.6 percent pay cut when they were sent overseas.

The council said the State Department had also been hurt by an absence of presidential support and by a system of political patronage that too often appointed ambassadors lacking experience and expertise. The council judged that Secretaries James A. Baker and Madeleine Albright had turned away from the Foreign Service when seeking policy advice. It quoted studies by the Center for Strategic and International Studies and the Una Chapman Cox Foundation that the Foreign Service had developed a taste for confidentiality and a certain arrogance.

In sharp contrast, twenty months later, the council's second report on Powell's regime was ecstatic, saying he had arrived at the State Department determined to fix "a broken institution" and that during his four years of leadership "the achievements have been extraordinary, even historic."

This 2004 report declared that now "morale is robust." The number of persons taking the Foreign Service officer examination had jumped in four years from eight thousand to twenty thousand. Most staffing goals had been met. Hardware for modern information technology was in place. Leadership and management training were required for midlevel and higher officers.

The Foreign Service turned around. In 2004, a quarter of the Foreign Service corps had been hired since 2001. Two thousand new staff above attrition had been employed during the previous three years. Candidates' rejections of job offers from State had plunged from 25 percent to 2 percent. And the time from success in the oral examination to in-service employment had been reduced from more than two years to less than one year.

The 2004 report said there was still a need to improve performance in several places. Heading that troubled list were relations with Congress, public diplomacy, public affairs, and the creation of an active-duty ready reserve for crises.

Four years later, the Foreign Affairs Council published a parallel analysis of Secretary Condoleezza Rice's first two years in office. This time, its report began with a "key finding": an appeal to fund eleven hundred new positions in order to fill two hundred existing jobs, mostly overseas, and nine hundred training slots.

In August 2007, Foreign Affairs Council President Thomas D. Boyatt spelled out to a Senate subcommittee on homeland security how personnel shortages in the State Department and the Foreign Service had developed over two decades of Democratic and Republican administrations. The shortages had begun when the Soviet Union imploded and Secretary James Baker had to cover more than a dozen new countries with existing Foreign Service personnel. Secretary Powell's Diplomatic Readiness Initiative restored the department almost to 1990 levels, until the wars in Iraq and Afghanistan again wiped out the progress that had been made. Samuel R. Berger, assistant to the president for national security affairs, summarized, "America cannot be a first-rate power on a third-class budget."

This authoritative call for a larger and better-trained Foreign Service occurred as its traditional core functions of reporting and representing were being eclipsed by making leadership and management of human and financial resources as important as traditional reporting and representation." The stress on "managing" sought to answer attacks on the department's and the Foreign Service's inefficiencies.

The council criticized most severely the public-diplomacy program with its turnover of under secretaries and its absence of country-based communication plans after the abolition of the U.S. Information Agency. And the list of criticisms was open-ended.

But the report by no means consisted only of criticism. It noted several improvements. By 2005 the department had modernized much of its laggard information technology system. "Everyone" now had access to the Internet and the State Department's intranet. It also praised consular affairs, saying, "CA prides itself on operating a well-oiled business whose top priority is its customers, especially Americans." And it rated the construction of secure embassies a "huge success."

The stream of studies continued. At the end of 2007, the so-called HELP Commission (standing for the Madison Avenue–type slogan "Helping to Enhance the Livelihood of People around the Globe") looked at America's foreign-assistance programs. The HELP Commission concentrated on what the private sectors of developing countries could achieve. It proposed a "super-State" department under which "development" would be coequal with diplomacy and defense. The report said giving primacy to diplomacy is "fundamentally flawed." If adopted, this new approach would turn the Foreign Service's course 180 degrees.

TRANSFORMATIONAL DIPLOMACY

Condoleezza Rice moved from national security advisor to become Secretary of State in 2005, when President George W. Bush began his second term. The nation was fighting its first Afghan and second Iraq wars, and the most pressing Foreign Service issues were counterterrorism and nuclear proliferation. And along with Rice came the beginnings of a shift from dependence on military resources to diplomatic.

The State Department switched 280 midlevel Foreign Service officers from Europe and Washington to countries that were now a high priority. The number of unaccompanied and limited-accompanied positions multiplied from fewer than two hundred to more than nine hundred.

To pay for this, Congress in 2005 raised State's diplomatic and consular programs from $2.76 billion in 2001 to $3.52 billion (plus $374 million for Iraq operations). And FSOs were now required to have served in a hardship post to be considered for promotion into the Senior Foreign Service. John K. Naland, AFSA past president, said, "For better or worse, this is not your father's (or mother's) Foreign Service."

Secretary Rice began to reform the Foreign Service under the impressive neologism of "transformational diplomacy," defined as aiming U.S. diplomatic resources to "create a more secure, democratic, and prosperous world for the benefit of the American people and the international community." Sometimes, the department's goal was proclaimed with even greater hubris: the State Department titled its financial report for fiscal year 2007 "Transforming the World Through Diplomacy."

Secretary Rice appointed the Advisory Committee on Transformational Diplomacy, which issued the report "A Call to Action" in January 2008, proposing to

> transfer personnel from comfortable European posts to places where the current action is and to double the diplomatic workforce in the next ten years,
>
> seek greater cooperation between foreign affairs and national security agencies,
>
> involve private-sector organizations in foreign affairs operations, and
>
> increase the efficiency and speed of the foreign affairs community.

The advisory committee gave as the reason for this program "a fundamental shift from the bi-polar world of the Cold War towards one characterized by the rise of new global powers, notably China and India; the increasing power of non-state actors; and ever more agile and adaptive adversaries."

The committee asked to add 1,030 new positions to the department and 350 positions in the U.S. Agency for International Development (USAID) Foreign Service Officer Corps. The committee made no effort to conceal the department's own concern, warning that it was still necessary that "the President make an explicit statement underscoring the Department of State's role as the lead foreign affairs agency."

The committee proposed establishing a cadre of stabilization professionals that could be deployed to meet a disaster abroad. It sought to train more FSOs in difficult languages such as Arabic, Farsi, and Chinese, as well as in basic business and organizational skills.

The report also rather boldly criticized the department's structure as "a fragmented, rigid, and inefficient bureaucratic design" that resisted measuring performance and long-range planning. The new structure should reduce the number of persons reporting directly to the Secretary, "driving more decision-making down into the organization." It affirmed its intention to "strengthen the role of the ambassador; and improve the distribution of decision-making authority." And that meant improving how ambassadorial candidates are identified and vetted.

The Advisory Committee on Transformational Diplomacy was organized into five working groups. Looking furthest into the future was the State Department in 2025 Working Group, cochaired by Career Ambassador Thomas R. Pickering and Dr. Barry M. Blechman, a former State Department officer and founder of the Henry L. Stimson Center in Washington, D.C. The 2025 working group predicted that resorting to force by that date would cause enormous casualties and physical damage and that, therefore, the United States would more than ever need trained, experienced diplomats.

During approximately the same period, the AFSA conducted annual electronic opinion polls to see what issues were most troubling its members. The results, published in early 2008, were based on responses from nearly 4,300 active-duty Foreign Service members.

Not surprisingly, the Foreign Service respondents felt most strongly about bread-and-butter issues, such as receiving tax exemptions for warzone service and shortening the length of unaccompanied tours. Nearly half voiced the wish for career FSOs to have a larger role in policy making, and hundreds even urged the downsizing of the mammoth Baghdad mission. In fact, shrinking Baghdad's Foreign Service organization seemed unlikely. In January 2009, the American embassy's staff moved out of the Republican Palace and into a brand-new peach-colored complex nearby.

That April, Christopher R. Hill, veteran of Kosovo, the Bosnia peace settlement, and the North Korean nuclear talks, assumed the ambassadorship in Baghdad. The multitude of issues he faced ran from resettling refugees to determining how oil resources would be managed and, of course, to the "draw down" of U.S. military forces. Ambassador Hill told a Senate committee before he left for Baghdad, "Diplomacy is a team sport." In this case, it called for a strong team.

SOFT POWER VERSUS HARD POWER

Critics became increasingly blunt. J. Anthony Holmes, a retired ambassador and past president of the AFSA, said the Foreign Service "is simply not able to do its job. . . . To do what is expected of it, the Foreign Service needs two to three times as many people as the 11,555 it currently has." Holmes also charged that the Bush administration tried "to publicly embarrass the diplomatic corps." Most diplomats regarded the personnel shortage as their most significant, and solvable, problem. They called for the United States to turn away from "militarization" and "staff up for diplomacy."

Harry W. Kopp, a former Foreign Service officer and author of *Career Diplomacy,* said:

> The Foreign Service is traditionally not very good at planning ahead, for what's needed ten years from now. . . . This is partly because the service has never had the luxury to plan; they've always been putting out the fires and not doing enough strategic planning.

Two years after Secretary Rice set up the Advisory Committee on Transformational Diplomacy, she was still requesting funds for eleven hundred more diplomats. This shortage was felt most urgently during and after an armed conflict, when the State Department found itself unable to provide a sufficient number of trained personnel to take charge of rebuilding a failed or destabilized state. And Under Secretary R. Nicholas Burns noted that the world's big problems have no military solutions. They are solvable not by force "but by patient long-term diplomacy."

Ambassador John E. Herbst, an expert on Russia and the Middle East who had been the consul general in Jerusalem and ambassador to Uzbekistan and to the Ukraine, was assigned to fashion a component of trained civilians who could be deployed to a "hot spot." He understood the problems of rebuilding cities and nations and was well fitted to head the State Department's new Office of Reconstruction and Stabilization.

Among the office's goals were reducing the rivalry between the Defense and State departments and preventing management failures like those that stained the early years of the Second Iraq War. With the forthright cooperation of Defense Secretary Robert M. Gates, Herbst's office planned to organize and train personnel from fifteen civilian and military agencies and to establish the Active Response Corps of 250 "first responders" from civilian federal agencies. They were to be ready to move in forty-eight to seventy-two hours.

Backing up these first responders would be two additional echelons: the Standby Response Corps, composed of two thousand government officials, and the Civilian Reserve Corps, consisting of private sector and state and local government personnel. They would be trained in public administration, economics, public health, and city planning. Some called the scheme grandiose and "ludicrously ambitious." By 2008, two years after it was established, the Active Response Corps had only eleven members and was still waiting for congressional funding.

President Bush presented a Civilian Stabilization Initiative in the 2009 budget. Under it, the State Department would deploy its "soft power" resource as a partner of the Department of Defense's "hard power" military intervention. Secretary Gates declared, "I am here to make the case for strengthening our capacity to use 'soft power' and for better integrating it with 'hard power.'" He was ready to synchronize diplomacy with warfare.

The American Academy of Diplomacy, with the support of the Una Chapman Cox Foundation, issued a report in the fall of 2008 ominously called "A Foreign Affairs Budget for the Future: Fixing the Crisis in Diplomatic Readiness." Among the participants in the study were retired ambassadors Thomas Boyatt, Ronald Neumann, Thomas Pickering, Edward Rowell, and Clyde Taylor. It proposed solutions for challenges that the incoming President, Barack Obama, would meet "with inadequate diplomatic personnel and resources to carry out policy effectively."

The study's report began, "There must be enough diplomatic, public diplomacy, and foreign assistance professionals overseas and they cannot remain behind walls of fortress embassies." It proposed increases in staffing and funding in the international affairs portion of the federal budget. It divided foreign-affairs activity into four major categories (core diplomacy, public diplomacy, economic assistance, and reconstruction/stabilization) and found "critical personnel shortages in each of them." Under "Fixing the Crisis," the report made four major recommendations:

Increase staffing in the four categories by 4,735, an increase of 46 percent, by 2014. Those additions, with training and locally hired staff overseas, would increase costs by $2 billion annually by 2014.

Fund ambassadors to meet humanitarian and political emergencies by an increased $125 million in 2010 and $75 million annually thereafter.

Expand public diplomacy programs, especially exchanges of personnel, at a cost of $455.2 million annually by 2014.

Shift authority over selected security assistance programs, totaling $785 million annually, from the Defense to the State Department.

Although the academy's report did not say so, the whole proposed annual package to repair American diplomacy would cost less than the new aircraft carrier USS *Ronald Reagan*.

NUCLEAR DIPLOMACY IN A TIME OF TROUBLES

Once the Cold War was over, the United States could no longer treat an international problem simply as a threat from the Soviet Union. Third-world nations would have to be dealt with in terms of their own problems, ambitions, and fanaticisms. No longer, for example, could discontent in Guatemala be blamed on Communism. No longer could the Balkans be viewed as an unstable borderland that must choose between East and West.

After the Cold War deteriorated, the dominant concerns holding center stage were terrorism and nuclear proliferation. Terrorism, on the front burner everywhere, was much more difficult to oppose than the single-minded Cold War. And nuclear proliferation had been a worldwide worry ever since the atomic bombing of Hiroshima. Attempts to stop nuclear testing involved so many concerns—moral, scientific, national security, international mistrust—that a comprehensive ban on nuclear testing proved impossible. As one example, in 1952, the State Department refused to give Linus Pauling a passport, until he received the Nobel Prize for Chemistry two years later.

During the Eisenhower administration, many Americans believed that U.S. atomic superiority was the chief hope for peace. But the launch of *Sputnik* confirmed the need for a nuclear test ban, and the Cuban missile crisis pushed both sides toward at least a partial arms control agreement.

In 1963, the United States and the Soviet Union signed the Limited Test Ban Treaty. But, paradoxically, the prolonged emotional debate accelerated the nuclear arms race.

In the 1970s, India refused to participate in the nuclear-nonproliferation treaty, and for the next three decades India lived under sanctions. Despite some tough-minded reactions by the rest of the world, India still developed nuclear weapons. When Prime Minister Manmohan Singh came to Washington in July 2005, President Bush moved to a new strategy. The United States would help build power plants and provide nuclear fuel and technology. India would submit its civil program to international inspection. Its weapons program was ignored.

Under Secretary of State R. Nicholas Burns became the point man in what he called a "diplomatic marathon of negotiations." In March 2006, Prime Minister Singh and President Bush created the U.S.-India Civil Nuclear Cooperation Initiative and developed a bilateral agreement for peaceful civil nuclear cooperation. And Congress passed the Hyde Act, which approved the initiative. Under Secretary Burns said, "These steps marked a huge change in U.S. and global thinking about how to work with India."

ENDLESS TALK WITH NORTH KOREA

To apply this development to North Korea and Iran, two more recalcitrant regimes, was quite another matter. They both declared they wanted to possess nuclear weapons, and U.S. diplomats feared that nuclear weapons in the hands of North Korea or Iran promised disaster.

The Democratic People's Republic of Korea had pursued a nuclear capability ever since its fratricidal war with South Korea and its ally, the United States. Most American officials regarded North Korea as a rogue state that did not keep its word; they argued for toughness. Others were willing to negotiate to achieve a nuclear-free Korean peninsula.

North Korea joined the nuclear nonproliferation treaty in 1985, but three years later, American reconnaissance satellites detected a nuclear program in North Korea. Despite opposition in Washington, by 1990 Donald P. Gregg, U.S. ambassador to Seoul, and Assistant Secretary of State Richard Solomon were working to improve relations with the North.

At the end of the Cold War, the United States unilaterally withdrew the nuclear weapons it stored in South Korea. In response, North Korea unilaterally agreed not to possess nuclear weapons and to stop reprocessing spent nuclear fuel. But by 1993, North Korea expelled the United Nations inspectors and threatened to withdraw from the nonproliferation treaty.

That threat gained North Korea high-level talks with the United States. Assistant Secretary of State for Political-Military Affairs Robert Gallucci began negotiating with North Korea. And that fall, Deputy Assistant Secretary Thomas Hubbard met with North Korea's United Nations delegates in New York. The American negotiators faced opposition from those in Washington and Seoul who favored tougher reactions.

While President Clinton pressed for sanctions, former President Jimmy Carter, a trained nuclear engineer, traveled to North Korea in June 1994 as a private citizen. Accompanied by former Ambassador Marion Creekmore and Dick Christenson, an interpreter from the State Department, Carter won a promise from President Kim Il Sung that North Korea would freeze nuclear arms production in exchange for ending the threat of sanctions. North Korea would accept nuclear reactors that did not produce weapons-grade plutonium and would receive oil to meet its energy needs. In addition, diplomatic steps included a visit to North Korea by Secretary Madeleine Albright in 2000.

President Clinton used Carter's achievement to reopen negotiations. Leon V. Sigal, a former member of the editorial board of *The New York Times* who is knowledgeable on North Korea, judged that "the Carter initiative was the turning point in nuclear diplomacy with North Korea." But Henry Kissinger and others condemned it as a "retreat."

The result was that the two governments, which distrusted each other, within four months concluded the "agreed framework" of October 1994, which froze the production of nuclear weapons. The North shut down its nuclear arms program, but every step was littered with barriers. And many still regarded North Korea as a state not to be trusted. Progress never seemed permanent.

In 2002, President Bush declared North Korea part of the "axis of evil." By linking North Korea with Iraq and Iran, Ambassador Gregg reportedly said, "The North Koreans were slapped in the face." But bilateral talks began with Assistant Secretary James A. Kelly representing the United States.

By early 2003, North Korea withdrew from the nonproliferation treaty, ended its freeze on nuclear production, and expelled the inspectors.

Christopher R. Hill, then assistant secretary for East Asian and Pacific affairs, was assigned to deal with the North Korean leaders. Hill concluded, "One day they withdrew from the Non-Proliferation Treaty, they withdrew from the safeguards that accompanied that, they kicked out the inspectors and within two months, just two months, they had turned this so-called research reactor into a bomb-making machine."

The Bush administration rejected bilateral talks. Instead, six-party talks, with North and South Korea, Russia, China, Japan, and the United States, began in 2003 and dragged on into 2007, when the United States unfroze all North Korean assets.

Hill proposed removing North Korea from the blacklist of state sponsors of terrorism if it abandoned its nuclear weapons program. In addition to the leaders in Pyongyang, he had to convince neoconservatives in Washington who opposed such "appeasement." Leon Sigal wrote, "Those ideologues equate diplomatic give-and-take with rewarding bad behavior."

In 2005, Ambassador Hill met alone with the North Koreans, despite American policy that frowned on talking with "the enemy." This policy set those who regarded talking with one's adversaries as appeasement against those who believed that diplomacy requires something more than talking with one's friends. George Kennan said, "We should be prepared to talk to the devil himself, if he controls enough of the world to make it worth our while."

In the spring of 2006, North Korea proposed bilateral talks, but Ambassador Hill was not allowed to follow up. On October 16, North Korea tested an underground plutonium device. Rejecting the advice of his more militant advisors, President Bush then authorized Hill to talk directly with the North Koreans. Hill explained firmly, "We are not going to accept North Korea as a nuclear state." A meeting in Berlin in January 2007 was so secret that Hill arranged to be invited to give a speech there as a cover for his visit. Otherwise, what was the Assistant Secretary for East Asian and Pacific Affairs doing in Germany?

That February, North Korea again agreed to give up its nuclear weapons program in exchange for removing the nation from the State Department's list of states sponsoring terrorism. It readmitted monitors to confirm the dismantling of the nuclear research complex at Yongbyon.

Israeli intelligence informed the United States that North Korea was helping Syria construct a nuclear reactor, and an Israeli air strike demolished Syria's reactor.

North Korea, in September 2008, reversed itself again and kicked the United Nations monitors out of its plutonium-making nuclear plant at Yongbyon. That destroyed the agreement that it would give up its nuclear weapons program in return for trade and energy benefits. American critics charged that North Korea was blackmailing to gain concessions, and North Korea complained that the United States had reneged on its promise to remove it from the terrorist blacklist. The United States teetered between the desires of North and South Korea.

Ambassador Hill had more work to do. In late September, he crossed the fortified demilitarized zone that divided the two halves of Korea and was driven to Pyongyang to negotiate with North Korea's leaders. After he returned to Seoul on October 11, the State Department removed North Korea from the blacklist of state sponsors of terrorism.

This inflamed another storm of controversy. The new agreement with North Korea permitted inspection of the acknowledged nuclear facility at Yongbyon, but verification at any additional sites would still require North Korean consent. Opponents of this agreement included officials in Vice President Cheney's office and in the State Department's verification office, as well as former UN Ambassador John Bolton.

The grueling game continued. North Korea reportedly detonated a nuclear device and again started plutonium production. And North Korea, in December 2009, refused to allow inspectors to take soil and air samples out of the country. American diplomats speculated that the Koreans hoped for better terms from the incoming Barack Obama administration.

On a three-day "exploratory" visit to Pyongyang that December, Stephen W. Bosworth, then the U.S. representative to North Korea on the International Energy Agency, brought an offer from President Obama to open a liaison office in North Korea. Afterward, Bosworth said that both sides understood the need to restart the six-nation talks and dismantle North Korea's nuclear weapons program. But no one was being optimistic, especially as North Korea's confrontation with the West became perilously unpredictable when the nation's President Kim Jong Il, died on a train of a heart attack on December 17, 2011, and was succeeded by his third son, Kim Jong Un, who was only in his twenties.

Toward the end of 2011, Glyn T. Davies replaced Bosworth as the U.S. representative to North Korea on the International Energy Agency. He brought cautious hopes of renewing the six-nation talks that had collapsed in 2008. Christopher Hill was named the U.S. ambassador to Baghdad, and Bosworth, a former dean of the Fletcher School of Tufts University, became a special envoy to North Korea. A year after President Kim's death, his son launched a long-range rocket capable of reaching the Philippines. American officials saw it as an act of defiance.

A "SLIPPERY SLOPE" IN IRAN

Iran, unlike North Korea, was not accused of having nuclear weapons. The fear there was, as Nicholas Burns put it, that "Iran is trying to develop the technology that would lead to a nuclear capability." Burns accused Iran of "cheating."

Iran had joined the nuclear nonproliferation treaty in 1968 and repeatedly denied that it was developing a nuclear weapon. But it enriched uranium and refused to give inspectors the access they needed to be sure that Iran was not working covertly toward building weapons.

The United States' strategy was to put worldwide pressure on Iran to stop all enrichment-related and reprocessing activities. This was difficult to accomplish because the United States had not had a diplomat stationed in Tehran since its embassy staff was taken hostage in 1979.

In July 2006, the UN Security Council decreed that Iran must suspend its enrichment program, and in December the council imposed sanctions, which were tightened the following March. This approach had its devotees— but did not appear to work.

In December 2007, the United States Intelligence Estimate judged that Iran had stopped its nuclear weapons program back in 2003 and had not restarted it as of mid-2007. But Nicholas Burns, who was assigned the lead in negotiating (if possible) with the Islamist leaders of Iran, cautioned, "They continued a ballistic missile program and very importantly, they continue this research in enrichment and reprocessing which could be an avenue, could be, towards the production of fissile material at their plant at Natanz in Iran."

Iran said its program was designed to produce peaceful nuclear energy, but the Bush administration repeatedly charged it was a cover for developing weapons. How should this uncertain but serious threat be dealt with? At one end of the spectrum of strategies was armed conflict. *The Washington Post* quoted Robert J. Einhorn, a former assistant secretary of state for nonproliferation, as saying, "Concerns about a slippery slope toward a military conflict with Iran have hurt U.S. efforts at diplomacy." President Bush said, "All options are on the table."

Burns anticipated toughening sanctions because, he said, "they refuse to negotiate and they refuse to slow down their nuclear efforts." In March 2008, the United Nations Security Council imposed a third set of sanctions on Iran. Accusations, denials, and threats shuttled back and forth. Iran proposed that the Middle East be made a nuclear-weapons-free zone, while the United States and Israel threatened military attacks to stop Iran's nuclear program.

Nicholas Burns' successor as undersecretary for political affairs, William J. Burns, a former assistant secretary for Near Eastern affairs, was sent to Geneva in the summer of 2008 to meet with the European Union's foreign policy head, Javier Solana, and Iran's nuclear negotiator, Saeed Jalili. William Burns' task was to intensify diplomatic efforts to stop Iran's enriching uranium. Although the meeting produced no substantive results, it did relax the Bush insistence that Iran stop enriching uranium before it could meet with American diplomats.

Nicholas D. Kristof, of *The New York Times,* wrote that documents prove that Iran made track 2 overtures, that is, informal back-channel approaches, to the United States in 2001–03 to begin settling a range of issues. Track 2 meetings were held in Paris and Geneva, he said, but "Bush administration hardliners aborted the process." It was another piece of the continuing puzzle.

The difficulty with Iran is how one comes to an agreement with a nation that insists it is not building a nuclear arsenal but that will not permit oversight to reassure a nervous world. Secretary of State Hillary Clinton made her suspicions clear: "I don't think there is any doubt that Iran is morphing into a military dictatorship with a sort of religious, ideological veneer."

"YOU ENCOUNTER PERIL, BUT YOU MAKE A DIFFERENCE"

Whether the men and women of the U.S. Foreign Service are trying to halt the proliferation of nuclear weapons or simply replacing lost passports, they belong to an organization that, history shows, repeatedly needs to be modified to do its job effectively "in response to the complex challenges of modern diplomacy."

The cacophony of recent studies and investigations suggests that the Foreign Service's shortcomings are fought over again and again because Americans are not paying attention. That has long been the Foreign Service's albatross. Glyn T. Davies, a second-generation ambassador, says, "We have no constituency really. Americans think diplomats are either sinister or baboons." Ambassador Charles R. Baquet III, who served in the Foreign Service for thirty years, believes that its real constituency is on the Hill, that a small number of people determine foreign policy. He wants more people beyond Washington to be involved.

On the other hand, Ambassador Philip Habib thought that the public was becoming more interested. He said, "Foreign policy is a matter of constant debate in the body politic. That was not always true, you know. Foreign policy in the old days was the reserve of a few."

The State Department has been trying to win the American public's attention and support. High-level diplomats now attract audiences as large as a thousand to foreign policy town meetings around the country. The Library of Congress Web site, under the title "Frontline Diplomacy," gives access to more than sixteen hundred diplomatic oral histories, donated by the Association for Diplomatic Studies and Training and created and mostly collected by Charles Stuart Kennedy. Kennedy, who was a career Foreign Service officer and a consul general for thirty years, has conducted more than nine hundred of these oral histories himself and collected another seven hundred interviews by others. The Library of Congress also contains oral histories from the various presidential libraries. And a separate collection has oral histories of hundreds of Foreign Service spouses. Altogether, they are a priceless treasure.

At its headquarters in Washington, D.C., the State Department, led by former Under Secretary R. Nicholas Burns, has created a display called the History of American Diplomacy. Although earlier generations, which mostly worked in "a culture of secrecy," might have regarded this as unseemly self-advertising, today the display is appreciated.

The presence of the U.S. Diplomacy Center in the lobby of the State Department's headquarters was a longtime dream of a few, including retired Ambassador Stephen Low. Stephen Estrada, director of the center, says it is intended to "bring diplomacy to life."

Even more important than such public relations projects is the power that the Foreign Service's consular arm possesses to sway the American public. That is where individual Americans have direct personal contact with the State Department and Foreign Service, on the visa line, in the passport office, and in answering calls for help. But both young vice consuls and their seniors sometimes seem unaware, or too busy, to grasp the impact of their decisions.

In one routine instance, a consular officer in Brazil rejected a request for a visa renewal for a young Brazilian in the middle of her college education in the United States. There was no question that she was going to return to Brazil; she had left her young child in Brazil with her mother. The student went to an American consul in another Brazilian city and was granted her renewal.

In the other case, an American-born student, whose parents are natives of Mexico and longtime U.S. citizens, invited her eighty-three-year-old grandmother in Mexico City to attend her graduation from college. They all were proud of the girl's achievement; she was the family's first to graduate from college. The consular office in Mexico City rejected the visa request from the grandmother, herself the mother of twelve children in Mexico. An appeal to Ambassador Carlos Pascual was denied. The grandmother did not attend the graduation.

In both these cases, consular officers acted with bureaucratic callousness and no appreciation of the effect of their decisions on the people involved or on the State Department and its Foreign Service. It seemed a poor way to build a constituency. Kathleen Stephens, looking back at her own consular career, says, "The amount of responsibility you get over people's lives is incredible."

Mexico was also trying unsuccessfully to control drug gangs. In March 2010, Lesley A. Enriquez, an American consulate worker (and American citizen), and her husband were both murdered in the border town of Ciudad

Juárez. Minutes later, the drug gangs killed the husband of another U.S. consular employee. This was the first time American officials were targeted. Although the antidrug campaign was funded with $1 billion, the U.S. Embassy appeared impotent.

Ambassador Diego C. Asencio, former assistant secretary in charge of the Bureau of Consular Affairs, has asserted that consular officers deal "with the very nature, character, and identity of the United States.... When an American has any dealings at all with the Department of State, it was usually through the consular end of the business." He warned new ambassadors this was "the area most likely to bite them in the rump."

The Foreign Service now has, in significant part, shifted its mission from passing information to advocacy. One historian has written that the diplomat's job now is to instruct "his political superiors and the articulate public in the proper course of action overseas." Reporting for reporting's sake is no longer adequate. Simply beating CNN with the news does not have much value. Ambassador Robert A. Bradtke says that Washington depends on the Foreign Service for "value added." Or, as Reno L. Harnish III, then the DCM in Stockholm and later ambassador to Azerbaijan, put it, "Information has changed to what we should be doing about it rather than just what is happening. The field has to recommend what can be done." Ambassador Jimmy J. Kolker said in summary, "We have redefined the role of the diplomat without telling ourselves."

One intriguing example of this new direction is a program that originated in 2010 when the World Health Organization and the National Institutes of Health sought to reduce the estimated four million deaths each year that strike the poor homes of the underdeveloped world from the use of inefficient cookstoves and biomass fuels (crop residue, charcoal, wood, and dung) for cooking and heating.

"For much of the developing world, preparing a meal is one of the most dangerous activities a woman can undertake," says Jacob Moss, director of the State Department's Cookstoves Initiative, which is part of the Global Alliance for Clean Cookstoves, led by the United Nations Foundation. Programs are already under way in Peru, Guatemala, South Africa, Mexico, and India.

In her confirmation hearing for Secretary of State in January 2009, Hillary Clinton summed up the challenge she saw facing the Foreign Service:

It is an outpost for American values that protects our citizens and safeguards our democratic institutions in times both turbulent and tame. State Department employees offer a lifeline of hope and help, often the only lifeline for people in foreign lands who are oppressed, silenced, and marginalized. We must not shortchange them or ourselves.

On taking office, Secretary Clinton was greeted by Steven Kashkett, vice president of the AFSA, representing the employees, and by Under Secretary William J. Burns, representing the officers. Their welcoming spirit was reminiscent of the attitude eight years earlier, when Secretary Colin Powell replaced Secretary Madeleine Albright, who had not totally won the department's enthusiasm. Kashkett voiced the staff's feeling of neglect and "the need to restore American diplomacy and American leadership abroad." In reply, Secretary Clinton promised "robust diplomacy and effective development." She declared, "Just as we would never deny ammunition to American troops headed into battle, we cannot send our civilian personnel into the field under equipped."

Secretary Clinton believes that "development" should be an equal partner with diplomacy and defense and insisted that she wanted US-AID strengthened. But she chided: ". . . we have to regain some credibility in order to regain the authorities and the resources that have drifted elsewhere." She said "migration" of authority to the Defense Department had occurred because it was more aggressive and agile. She concluded that USAID had to justify itself that "You encounter peril, but you make a difference."

New electronic forms called "connection technologies" made possible communication with people who cannot be reached by the older technologies. Among them, for example, are individuals in Iran and China. *The New York Times* reported, "Most of the news that reached the West from Iran came via YouTube and Twitter." The stream of innovation is unending, and social media are spreading around the globe. Youthful advocates in the State Department are already calling this "21st-century statecraft."

TWO SPECIAL ENVOYS

On her first afternoon in office, Secretary Clinton, with President Obama standing beside her, announced the appointment of two special envoys: Ambassador Richard C. Holbrooke, as special representative to Afghanistan and Pakistan, and Senator George J. Mitchell, as special envoy for the Middle East. Both men had built solid reputations as effective negotiators. The difference in their titles reflected the fine-tuning of Washington politics.

During an often controversial Foreign Service career, Richard Holbrooke seemingly had no problem, even enjoyed, dealing one-on-one with rogues like Ferdinand Marcos in the Philippines and Slobodan Milošević in Bosnia. In 1968, Holbrooke was a young member of the American delegation to the Paris peace talks on Vietnam. He served as ambassador to Germany and to the United Nations and twice as an assistant secretary of state. By 1995, he was the chief negotiator of the Dayton Peace Accords, which settled the Bosnian war.

He designed and executed the complex Dayton negotiations at Wright Patterson Air Force Base near Dayton, Ohio, ending three and a half years of bitter ethnic war among Serbs, Croats, and Muslims that was rooted in religious and nationalist rivalries. His success was based on imposing diplomatic leadership of the United States, backed by NATO force. U.S. intervention was initiated mainly by National Security Advisor Anthony Lake, but Holbrooke, Lake's rival, structured the negotiations to make success possible. He described the negotiations, which were in fact an uncertain success, as "a high-wire act without a safety net." (In the process of ending the war in Bosnia, the then Ambassador Robert C. Frasure; Colonel Samuel Nelson Drew of the National Security Council; and Joseph J. Kruzel of the Defense Department were killed.)

Holbrooke's assignment expanded to include Iran's government. Secretary Clinton said that the United States would not accept a nuclear-armed Iran and that U.S. absence from negotiations with Iran during the Bush administration had been a mistake. Holbrooke's brilliant, often abrasive diplomatic contributions ended with his death on December 13, 2010, at the age of sixty-nine. He had been stricken with a tear in his aorta three days earlier during a meeting with Secretary Clinton, and twenty-one hours of surgery could not save him. President Obama called him "simply one of the giants of American foreign policy." Ambassador Marc Grossman, a former director general of the Foreign Service, succeeded him.

Holbrooke had attempted to engage the Iranian government in a discussion of its nuclear plans and intentions. Receiving no response, he shifted to a more confrontational mode. Under Secretary William J. Burns shuttled among capitals to get agreement on a Security Council sanctions resolution. And in early 2010, Secretary Clinton bluntly told students at a women's college in Jeddah: "Iran is the largest supporter of terrorism in the world today."

Meanwhile, the Obama administration started building military strength in Afghanistan, following Frederick the Great's motto, "Diplomacy without arms is like music without instruments." Whether to add troops in Afghanistan became a heated foreign policy issue, with diplomats inside Obama's administration taking opposing sides. General James L. Jones, the national security advisor, voiced doubts about the proposed buildup.

The State Department also began recruiting hundreds of civilians to serve under Peter W. Galbraith, as a UN deputy. He had been the first U.S. ambassador to Croatia and was involved in exposing the gassing of the Kurds by Saddam Hussein. Galbraith reportedly had helped the Kurds gain control in an Iraq constitution over all new oil fields found in their territory. The United States wanted to hold all oil discoveries under the central Baghdad government.

When Lieutenant General Karl Eikenberry became the ambassador to Afghanistan, he strongly opposed a U.S. troop buildup and criticized President Hamid Karzai as "not an adequate strategic partner." Eikenberry worried that the buildup would only make the Afghans more dependent on the United States. He also recommended eliminating the enemy's sanctuaries in Pakistan.

Could the United States' huge effort in Afghanistan turn around this failed, corrupt nation, which *The New York Times*' Dexter Filkins called "one of the world's premier gangster-states"? Between 2001 and 2009, the international community invested $18 billion in trying to save Afghanistan. But the Taliban still managed to relaunch an insurgency in 2005.

In July 2011, Ryan C. Crocker, who had opened the embassy in 2002, returned as the sixth U.S. ambassador to Kabul in ten years. Paul D. Miller, former director for Afghanistan in the National Security Council, wrote, "The international community was effectively asking Afghans with no shoes to lift themselves up by their bootstraps."

George Mitchell, Secretary Clinton's other major appointment, had been a U.S. senator from Maine from 1980 to 1995, served as U.S. special envoy for Northern Ireland, and chaired the negotiations that led to the Belfast peace agreement. (He also led an investigation for Major League Baseball into the players' use of steroids.) Meaningful to his new assignment in the Middle East was the fact that his mother was an Arab emigrant from Lebanon. Mitchell regards himself as an Arab-American.

In a December 2009 interview, Mitchell summed up his expectations for the Palestinian-Israeli conflict:

The U.S. will play an active and sustained role in helping the parties to reach their shared objectives of the two-state solution. . . . We are committed to a viable, independent and contiguous Palestinian state and a Jewish state of Israel with secure and recognized borders.

By the spring of 2010, the Israelis and the Palestine Liberation Organization resurrected arm's-length talks for a four-month period. George Mitchell visited the area repeatedly to bring the two sides to this point and expected to provide for talks in Jerusalem and Ramallah.

As time went on, both the President and Secretary of State played visible and controversial roles trying to break up the gridlock on Israeli-Palestinian settlements fully aware of the dangers involving domestic U.S. politics.

President Obama also appointed as his representative to the United Nations Susan E. Rice, a young African-American woman who was a Rhodes Scholar and an assistant secretary of state. She was born in Washington, D.C., and her father, Emmett Rice, was an economist and a governor of the Federal Reserve System. She was invested in the protest against South African apartheid and had served as an advisor on Africa to President Clinton's National Security Council when the U.S. embassies in Tanzania and Kenya were bombed. She had been expected to succeed Hillary Rodham Clinton as Secretary of State in Obama's second term as President until, under domestic political pressure in 2012, she withdrew herself as a candidate.

On Secretary Clinton's first afternoon at the State Department in 2009, President Obama joined her there to underscore his commitment to the importance of diplomacy. He said America could no longer afford to drift or "cede ground to those who seek destruction." He promised the State Department and Foreign Service people who gathered there that "a new era of American leadership is at hand, and the hard work has just begun. You are going to be at the front lines of engaging in that important work."

Secretary Clinton made an introductory appearance the next day before applauding USAID employees. Francisco Zamora, vice president of USAID AFSA, greeted her with enthusiasm, but he warned, "There are too many actors currently involved in foreign assistance, causing much confusion and waste." He challenged her to create "a more empowered independent USAID."

Equally candid, Clinton admitted that USAID has been "decimated." She said, "It has half the staff it used to have." In 1990, it had 3,500 employees managing $5 billion a year, and by 2008 was down to 2,200 employees while handling $8 billion. Recently, to close this gap USAID had come to depend on for-profit contractors.

STORY WITHOUT END

The Obama administration took office in the face of violence in Kabul, extremism in Tehran, turmoil in Baghdad, and terrorism in Mumbai. Foreign policy never stands still, and the U.S. Foreign Service is constantly changing and evolving. Many of the men and women in this account have already moved on to new posts and new challenges. This story has no ending.

Vice President Joseph R. Biden Jr. arrived in Baghdad for his second visit to Iraq on the afternoon of September 15, 2009, and within three hours was the target of four mortar rounds aimed at the American embassy, where he was staying. He was unharmed, but two Iraqis died.

President Obama had been in office less than a year when he was awarded the Nobel Peace Prize. The citation honored "his extraordinary efforts to strengthen international diplomacy and cooperation between peoples." Since he had no time to have accomplished a great deal, it was presumed the award applauded the contrast with the previous administration.

Around the globe the new administration faced a number of crises. Its first Latin American test came in Honduras. Aware of President Manuel Zelaya's plans to remake Honduras' constitution, Secretary Clinton met with him in June 2009. A coup erupted when President Zelaya, son of a wealthy family, dismissed the leader of the armed forces, and Honduras's Supreme Court declared his proposed referendum illegal. At dawn on Sunday, June 28, 2009, the Honduran army, which had been built by the CIA, stormed the presidential palace in the capital of Tegucigalpa and sent President Zelaya, still in his pajamas, into exile in Costa Rica.

President Obama condemned the coup, and a number of neighboring countries withdrew their ambassadors. Leaders throughout Latin America called for Zelaya's peaceful return to office. In September, he stole back into Honduras, and with dozens of supporters settled in the Brazilian embassy, where they existed on takeout from Burger King.

Two months later, Deputy Assistant Secretary of State Craig Kelly and Zelaya agreed on a unity government and restored the planned elections. The election, on November 29, produced a new president, Porfirio Lobo, who was also a wealthy conservative. Lobo accompanied Zelaya and his family to the airport as they flew off to exile again, this time in the Dominican Republic. When President Lobo thanked Clinton for helping solve the crisis, the Honduran crowd booed.

By the end of 2010, Obama's policy of engagement, rather than isolation, brought a U.S. ambassador to Damascus for the first time since 2005, when the United States had protested Syria's support for Hezbollah, the militant Shiite group accused of assassinating Lebanon's prime minister. Robert S. Ford, a former ambassador to Algeria, was nominated for Damascus, but was blocked until Obama resorted to a recess appointment. In September 2011, Ambassador Ford's motorcade was attacked in Damascus and crowds besieged his office. He left in the face of threats to his life; Haynes Mahoney, the chargé d'affaires remained. In February 2012, the United States and European and Arab countries closed their Damascus embassies. The final seventeen staff, including six Marines, left the U.S. embassy and drove overland to Amman, Jordan.

Back in the United States, there were new versions of the usual infighting among various U.S. government entities dealing with foreign relations issues. And Obama's appointment of Harold Hongju Koh, dean of Yale Law School, as legal advisor of the State Department signaled a reversal of President Bush's harsh management of suspected terrorists in detention.

Secretary Clinton played up her own favored diplomatic buzzwords, "smart power," which she defined vaguely as "the intelligent use of all means at our disposal . . . a blend of principle and pragmatism." It was widely said "smart power" sounded better than "soft power," the Bush-era term. Clinton said, "With 'smart power,' diplomacy will be the vanguard of foreign policy." That sounded hopeful.

In January 2010, Secretary Clinton also spelled out a State Department policy of "internet freedom" devoted to access of information and freedom of communication among ordinary people. This was entirely appropriate to the United States' most treasured traditions.

After almost two years in office, Secretary Clinton summed up her view of American diplomacy. She identified the "global problems" that were challenging American leadership: violent extremism, worldwide recession, climate change, and poverty. She said they demanded collective solutions, "even as power in the world becomes more diffuse." To achieve this, she said she wanted to "elevate" diplomacy and development alongside defense.

To strengthen the State Department, Secretary Clinton pointed out, Congress had appropriated funds for 1,108 Foreign Service and Civil Service officers. And the USAID was hiring 1,200 new Foreign Service officers with development skills.

She launched the first Quadrennial Diplomacy and Development Review (QDDR), a wholesale review of State and USAID, to achieve "a more holistic approach to civilian power." The review also explored diplomatic and development strategies with key foreign partners.

Today, a U.S. ambassador operates, Clinton said, "as the CEO of a multi-agency mission." In addition to conducting traditional diplomacy, U.S.

diplomats must now bring in other government agencies and reach beyond governments to citizens. This was a new public-diplomacy strategy.

Less admirable was the failure of the State Department in 2010 to prevent the public disclosure of a quarter of a million confidential diplomatic cables. It was the most embarrassing miscue in the department's history and demonstrated the dangers hidden in the wonderland of the new technological revolution.

This disaster for the Foreign Service was apparently perpetrated by an Australian computer hacker and a twenty-three-year-old U.S. Army private, operating under the Web name WikiLeaks. They claimed they were "whistle-blowing" and saving the world. Although some people related this enterprise to freedom of information, in fact, it disrupted the privacy and security of diplomatic negotiations and endangered diplomats and their sources.

A former CIA general counsel called the harm done "just enormous." Dennis Blair, former U.S. director of national intelligence, said on TV, "If I were the intelligence chief of Iran, North Korea, these countries really trying to do harm to American interests, I've got a treasure trove there." He blamed the lack of real-time monitoring and security mechanisms.

WikiLeaks was doing what any terrorist or computer thief would be proud to do, revealing the communications of Foreign Service personnel. The guilty party was really the organization that enabled them to succeed in spreading confidential data around the globe. Defense Secretary Robert M. Gates said the U.S. government leaked like a sieve.

Ten months later, WikiLeaks released nearly 134,000 cables, and this time reports said the group was less careful about revealing the names of vulnerable people abroad. State Department spokesperson Victoria Nuland denounced WikiLeaks' "irresponsible, reckless and frankly dangerous actions."

Diplomats responded with anger and with what *The New York Times* described as "shudders." The White House condemned the disclosures of communications between the State Department and its embassies and consulates as "reckless and dangerous." The London *Sunday Times* called WikiLeaks "essentially an outlaw operation."

The subjects of the leaked cables ranged over North and South Korea, the failure of the United States to remove nuclear fuel from a Pakistani reactor, the United States' arm-twisting other nations to accept prisoners from the Guantánamo Bay prison, drug corruption in Afghanistan, Chinese official intrusion into Google's computer systems, Saudi support of al-Qaeda terrorists, and the U.S. failure to prevent Syria from supplying arms to Hezbollah. Cables named confidential sources. It was a huge embarrassment.

The cable leaks increased suspicion among diplomats who had to work together and depend on each other's confidences. Ambassador Anne W. Patterson admitted, for example, she had failed to persuade Pakistan to return to the United States enriched uranium that Pakistan regarded as insurance against India. Elizabeth Dibble, deputy chief of mission of the U.S. Embassy in Rome, was revealed to have called Italian Prime Minister Silvio Berlusconi "feckless, vain and ineffective." Shari Villarosa, head of the U.S. mission in Myanmar (Burma), called that nation's dictator Than Shwe "mad with power." The chief of staff to the German foreign minister resigned after WikiLeaks identified him as supplying the United States with an account of confidential negotiations. Bernard Kouchner, former foreign minister of France, complained that as a result of the WikiLeaks disclosures, "We will all terribly mistrust each other."

THE ARAB SPRING

The dangers in the Middle East were exposed on December 18, 2010, for all to see. It began in Tunisia when a man named Mohamed Bouazizi set himself on fire after police confiscated his roadside fruit stand. Demonstrations and violence spread throughout the region. There were many causes: unemployment, poverty, educated but dissatisfied youth, and rising food prices. Conservative and dictatorial rulers backed by the United States were overthrown. One university professor called the upheaval a "youthquake." It was significant that the first sites, Tunisia and Egypt, had no substantial oil revenues with which to buy off the protesters.

Tunisia's president fled to Saudi Arabia, ending his twenty-three years in power. In Egypt—where protestors stormed the fortresslike U.S. Embassy compound in Cairo—eighteen days of protests led to President Hosni Mubarak's condemnation to life in prison. Libya experienced heavy fighting before Muammar Qaddafi was killed. In Yemen, during months of protests and violence, hundreds of protesters attacked the American embassy. In Iran, five hundred protestors converged on the Swiss embassy, which was responsible for conducting relations with the United States. In Syria, the military massacred civilians. Syrian protesters also criticized Iran, warning that if they won power, Iran could lose its most effective regional ally.

So-called days of rage were staged throughout the region from Croatia to the People's Republic of China. Social media demonstrated the power of protesters to keep information flowing and provoke political change—especially among young people. The impact of the social media was immense.

TRAGEDY IN BENGHAZI

Violence struck the U.S. Foreign Service when four Americans were killed on Tuesday night, September 11, 2012, in Benghazi, Libya: Ambassador J. Christopher Stevens, fifty-two years old; Sean Smith, a veteran State Department information management officer; and two former Navy SEALs now serving as CIA security guards in Tripoli's U.S. embassy, Tyrone S. Woods of Portland, Oregon; and Glen A. Doherty, of Winchester, Massachusetts. Two other Americans and three Libyan security officers were wounded.

Paradoxically, Ambassador Stevens was passionately involved with the Libyan people. He supported the rebellion in Libya, and many Libyans revered him. A graduate of the University of California at Berkeley, he had been a Peace Corps volunteer in Morocco and developed a great interest in Arab culture and life in the "Arab street." His interest in the Arab people may well have been intensified because his mother was a member of the Chinook Indian Nation, skillful Native American negotiators and traders based at the mouth of the Columbia River.

In February 2011, the United States had closed down its embassy in Tripoli. And in April, Stevens had arrived in rebel-held Benghazi—the largest city in eastern Libya—and became the envoy to the Libyan opposition. A year later, in May 2012, he was appointed ambassador to Libya based in Tripoli. There, he had to use the residence as the chancery because, during the Arab Spring revolt, the original chancery had been burned down.

All that spring, the Benghazi mission was the scene of violence. Afterward, the accountability review board said, "At the time of the September attacks, Benghazi remained a lawless town."

Ambassador Stevens visited Benghazi on September 10, 2012, and the final tragedy at the Benghazi mission began with a surprise attack at about 9:30 P.M. on Tuesday, September 11. At that time, seven Americans were in the compound. Intelligence had not warned the mission, and the haphazard Libyan militia guarding the mission were inadequate. The attackers poured diesel fuel around the building and burned it. Ambassador Stevens and Sean Smith were asphyxiated.

By 11:30 P.M. the surviving Americans retreated to a nearby villa that was being used by the CIA. It came under sporadic fire. During the night, Libyan civilians found Stevens' body at the mission and took him to the hospital, where a doctor tried unsuccessfully to revive him.

The embassy in Tripoli flew a seven-person security team to Benghazi; they arrived at the CIA annex at about 5:00 A.M. At that time, without warning, those in the CIA villa were ambushed by intense, accurate gunfire and rocket-propelled grenades and mortar rounds. Woods and Doherty were killed. An hour and a half later, trucks loaded with heavily armed Libyans arrived and helped move the remaining Americans to the Benghazi airport. At dawn Wednesday, a plane flew them out to Tripoli and then to Ramstein Air Base in Germany.

Fifty Marines and two warships were rushed to Libya. Deputy Secretary of State William J. Burns joined a Libyan government memorial service in Tripoli on Thursday honoring the four dead Americans. President Obama lauded the Foreign Service and the CIA, declaring, "The brave Americans we lost represent the extraordinary service and sacrifices our civilians make every day around the globe."

Stevens' superiors at the State Department in Tripoli and Washington were blamed for not being prepared for the danger at Benghazi, and Congress was criticized for not supplying Foreign Service outposts with sufficient funds. Some Libyans attributed the outbreak of violence to a primitive video that disparaged the Prophet Muhammed. The video was said to have been made in the United States. Secretary Clinton called the video "disgusting and reprehensible."

That Wednesday morning at the State Department, President Obama thanked a closed meeting of the diplomatic workforce for their service and sacrifices. Whether or not the violence was related to the anniversary of the

9/11 attacks in the United States was difficult to determine. After a week, the White House labeled the assault on the Benghazi mission a "terrorist attack." To evaluate the security of the mission, Secretary of State Clinton created a five-person Accountability Review Board chaired by respected retired Career Ambassador Thomas R. Pickering and, as vice chairman, Admiral Michael Mullen, former chairman of the Joint Chiefs of Staff.

The emergency military force, the Africa Command's Commanders' In-Extremis Force, was not ready to react to this emergency. Instead, The Pentagon tried to send elite Delta Force commandos from Fort Bragg via Sicily. And they arrived too late.

The Libyan government prohibited American military action inside Libya, but the United States organized a secret command to strike those who had attacked in Benghazi and intercepted communications of the terrorist group Ansar al-Shariah, which had ties with al-Qaeda.

On December 18, Secretary Clinton's review board reported its findings on what had happened that night in Benghazi and made twenty-nine recommendations, of which five were classified, to improve security at U.S. "high risk, high threat" posts. Admiral Mullen said security at the Benghazi posts had been "grossly inadequate" for the attack that ensued.

In a letter to Senator John F. Kerry, chairman of the Senate Committee on Foreign Relations, Secretary Clinton accepted all twenty-nine recommendations. She said the State Department included nearly seventy thousand men and women in Washington and at more than 275 posts around the world, and she was responsible for all of them. She asked for more Marine Guards in high-risk situations. The same week as the attack in Benghazi, she pointed out, violent attacks were also made on U.S. embassies in Cairo, Sanaa, Tunis, and Khartoum.

In Egypt, where President Mohamed Morsi was a member of the Muslim Brotherhood, violence was extensive, and the U.S. Embassy at Cairo came under siege, even though Egypt was the second largest recipient of American foreign aid, after Israel, receiving $2 billion a year.

Violence also swept the fortified American embassy in Sanaa, Yemen. The American staff there had been evacuated, but five Yemenis were reported killed. And protests occurred in Morocco, Sudan, Iran, and Gaza. On February 1, 2013, a suicide bomber attacked a side entrance of the heavily guarded U.S. Embassy in Ankara, killing himself and a Turkish guard at the gate.

In Washington, four State Department officials were disciplined after

Benghazi, including the assistant secretary for diplomatic security, who resigned. The others were reassigned. Secretary Clinton noted that terrorists had killed sixty-five U.S. diplomatic personnel since 1977. "Diplomacy, by its very nature, must sometimes be practiced in dangerous places," said Deputy Secretary William J. Burns. But he warned, "We have to do better."

Better proved hard to do. As U.S. forces were cut back in Afghanistan, twenty-five-year-old Anne Smedinghoff of River Forest, Illinois, was one of five Americans killed on April 6, 2013. She had been in the Foreign Service only for the three years since she had graduated from the Johns Hopkins University. She was killed by a suicide bomber while she was accompanying the provincial governor, helping to donate books to a new school.

Totally disconnected from the Benghazi tragedy, Senator John F. Kerry, sixty-nine, of Massachusetts on February 1, 2013, replaced Hillary Clinton as Secretary of State. Over four years, she had visited 112 countries and traveled nearly a million miles. Once Susan Rice withdrew as a candidate, Kerry, who had received the Silver Star in the Vietnam War, had the field to himself. (Rice would become the national security advisor.)

Kerry had become involved in foreign affairs as a senator twenty-seven years earlier and become chairman of the Senate Foreign Relations Committee. Kerry's father had also been a member of the U.S. Foreign Service. Praising Secretary Clinton, John Kerry asked whether, in view of the previous eight years: "Can a man actually run the State Department?" Welcoming AFSA members replied with appreciative laughter.

50

The Ambassador

2011–13

How good is the U.S. Foreign Service? One can hear answers along the whole spectrum of approval and criticism. George Kennan approached the truth when he wrote, "The present service is, for the task at hand, just about the best that the American civilization of our day is capable of providing."

The Rogers Act in 1924 envisioned a professional Foreign Service, but President Hoover nibbled away at the principle of entrance only at the bottom and set up precedents for more interferences. The Great Depression and World War II also caused exemptions to the crucial rule of advancement on merit.

In 1945, the Foreign Service numbered 770 members; by the mid-1990s, it had swollen to nearly 10,000. At subordinate levels, "reforming" diplomats repeatedly made improvements, but at the top, tradition affected both the way ambassadors are chosen and how they did their job.

In the final year of President Obama's first term, the United States had 188 ambassadors, of which 116 (61.7%) were career officers and 59 (31.4%) political. Thirteen posts were vacant. Obama himself had made 153 career appointments and 71 political ones.

Although many political appointments over the years went to well-qualified candidates, the filling of some ambassadorial posts with inadequate political appointees damaged the Foreign Service's attractiveness as a lifetime professional career. The rise of the national security advisor and the involvement of other powerful Federal agencies into foreign policy also tended to undermine the role of the State Department and the Foreign Service abroad.

Charles W. Freeman, Jr., a notable if controversial former ambassador to Saudi Arabia who concerned himself with how the Foreign Service works, said: "The United States is now, to my knowledge, the only significant country, and it may well be on the way to being the only country, that continues to value amateurism over professionalism in diplomacy." He added, "I consider it absolutely shocking that... the United States still follows a 19th century practice with regard to appointments to the most senior diplomatic positions."

THE COST OF PATRONAGE AND CRONYISM

The value of able, experienced Foreign Service officers was demonstrated in January 1968, when the North Koreans captured the intelligence communications ship USS *Pueblo* and its crew. Months later, the former ambassador to Korea, Winthrop G. Brown, and James F. Leonard, his former deputy chief of mission and later ambassador to the United Nations, called on Under Secretary Nicholas Katzenbach with a peculiar proposal. Leonard said their experience showed that the Koreans had a very literal mindset. If the United States said *Pueblo* had been seized legitimately in North Korean waters, the United States could also say that that admission was a lie, and the Koreans would be satisfied and would release their prisoners. Incredible as this seemed to Western thinking, their advice worked. But it had required skillful Foreign Service officers with an intimate knowledge of Korean leaders' thinking. An inexperienced political appointee could not have achieved this.

Experienced American ambassadors are important for two reasons. He or she is the personal representative of the President of the United States and also usually functions as the responsible "chief of mission" abroad. But, it must be said, too often an ambassador is still the product of patronage, cronyism, or outright bribery.

President Nixon spoke on tape about Raymond Guest, a major donor to his campaign (and a polo player) who sought a diplomatic post. Nixon said, "I'm sure he is talking about a quarter of a million at least because he gave $100,000 last time in '65. . . . Now he can be ambassador to Brussels. . . .

Anybody who wants to be ambassador, wants to pay at least $250,000."
Guest had been named ambassador to Ireland in 1965 but did not receive
an ambassadorial appointment the second time.

Thirty of George W. Bush's largest fund-raisers were made ambassadors after the 2000 election. Susan R. McCaw, a socially active investment
banker, was assigned as ambassador to Austria in 2005 for, reportedly,
raising $1.7 million for Bush's campaign. Craig Roberts Stapleton, a real
estate executive and Bush's partner as an owner of the Texas Rangers baseball team, was given ambassadorships to the Czech Republic and France.

Although the Center for Strategic and International Studies (CSIS) did
not oppose the political appointment of ambassadors, it warned in 1998
that "the cost to the conduct of diplomacy is too high to sustain the current system of patronage." The CSIS report said coolly:

> As a result of much-publicized abuses in the appointment process,
> including the frequent requirement for sizable campaign contribu-
> tions, political appointees have been vilified by the media and the
> career service. Yet those with a distinguished record of public ser-
> vice or relevant expertise number among the most effective Ameri-
> can ambassadors, including Averell Harriman, Ellsworth Bunker,
> Arthur Burns, and Walter Mondale. The fault is not with political
> ambassadors per se, but with political ambassadors who lack the
> experience and expertise for representing the United States. There
> should be no room for them in America's diplomatic service. Be-
> cause of patronage and cronyism, the performance gap is often
> considerable, occasionally significant.

In past eras, ambassadorships depended on courtly skills, nobility manipulating nobility, deviousness countering deviousness, and adeptness
at gaining the ear of a king's mistress. One had to appear to be a gentleman. A British diplomat who began his career a century ago said that
diplomacy then was "war in lace."

That long-honored past has diminished. Now, a U.S. ambassador can
receive instantaneous instructions from Washington, or an assistant secretary of state can jet out and take over when a crisis detonates. For the most
troublesome problems, an envoy immersed in the politics and diplomacy of
the area will be ready to take charge. Ambassador William Attwood commented:

I think it's almost insulting to a man that you select as the President's personal representative to a country, who is steeped in that country, lives it day by day, and then at the slightest crisis nobody pays any attention to him; they send either the Secretary, or the Under Secretary, or Deputy Secretary over there to take care of it. This has been growing more and more in recent years, in the jet age.

Attwood's complaint is still valid. Forty-five years ago, the author of this book accompanied Secretary Dean Rusk on a tour of NATO countries, and in the fall of 2011, Secretary Hillary Clinton traveled to seven Near East countries. Problem solvers are still being sent out from Washington.

The current speeds of communication and transportation call for swift reactions and less-than-thoughtful responses. Haste is also generated by the public's immediate exposure to events through radio and television, and that can devalue analysis and decision making and leave the Foreign Service diplomat with little time for careful consideration. Television's Ted Koppel, on receiving the Cyrus R. Vance Award for Advancing Knowledge of Diplomacy, told a State Department audience that the twenty-four-hour news channel has "largely devolved into a desperate effort to be first with the obvious."

Another devastating change has been diplomats' increased vulnerability to violence. Ambassadors now travel in armored cars protected by a ring of armed guards; embassies and residences have been converted into reinforced-concrete forts. The number of American ambassadors who have been kidnapped or killed is shocking. To be appointed an ambassador these days is an honor in harm's way.

These alterations have not diminished the ambassador's role, but they have changed it tremendously. As "chief of mission," the ambassador commands a greater number and variety of personnel than ever before; and as the United States plays a larger part in the world, ambassadors acquire more complex responsibilities. Thomas R. Pickering, a seven-time ambassador and a respected under secretary of state, has experienced these changes from both abroad and Washington. Asked how the Foreign Service has changed over his forty-two-year career, he sees progress: "I believe the Foreign Service has increasingly emphasized and rewarded individual initiative and merit, and is playing a greater role in foreign policy formulation."

Anyone who presumes that everything is decided in Washington need only listen to the oral history in the Library of Congress of John Hugh Crimmins, who was ambassador to the Dominican Republic and Brazil:

> One of the basic points about policy and the execution of policy in what you call the trenches that impressed me enormously when I became chargé and chief of mission was the power of the ambassador in the field. It's really enormous. Enormous. . . . I think any ambassador worth his salt has no excuse for not being able to run a cohesive, tight operation.

Each new ambassador receives a letter from the President spelling out his or her authority. The ambassador has charge of all executive offices and personnel in country, except for those under command of an area military commander.

The ambassador has orders to report to the Secretary of State and the President "with directness and candor." And all executive branch personnel in country are supposed to keep their ambassador informed of all current and planned activities—in advance. But some ambassadors still complain that they do not know even how many CIA staff work from their embassy.

The Country Team, which the ambassador heads, includes all those in the various operating divisions of the embassy as well as representatives of the CIA, military, and as many as twenty-five other agencies of the United States government. A meeting of leaders of the Country Team who report directly to the ambassador can number more than a dozen. An embassy's employees can run in the hundreds. The chief of mission is responsible for the entire team.

The U.S. Office of Management and Budget estimates that today two-thirds of the staff who are hired in the United States and are stationed at diplomatic and consular posts are not State Department employees. Ambassador Brandon Grove, quoting John Kenneth Galbraith on his days in India, says, "The job of an ambassador is much like that of an airline pilot, there are hours of boredom and minutes of panic." A notorious case of this dichotomy occurred when armed FBI agents arrived in Aden in 2000 to run down the terrorists who had wrecked the destroyer USS *Cole*. The FBI special agent in charge clashed with Ambassador Barbara K. Bodine, until he was forced to return to New York.

Defense Secretary Robert M. Gates made a stir when he recommended that Congress increase the State Department budget and that the State Department be restored as the lead foreign policy agency. He said Congress denied State both resources and authority, and he wanted to reduce the damaging rivalry between State and Defense.

With the arrival of the Obama administration in 2009, more voices were lifted against the military assuming responsibilities that traditionally belong to civilians in a democracy. Thomas A. Schweich, a Republican who served in the State Department and the Foreign Service during George W. Bush's presidency, noted that generals and admirals headed the National Security Council and national intelligence and other government elements. He criticized the transfer of police work to the military in war-torn Iraq and Afghanistan. And he opposed The Pentagon's proposal to use twenty thousand U.S. soldiers to battle terrorists inside the United States. He went so far as to write, "We no longer have a civilian-led government."

Schweich opposed the "military takeover" of what had previously been civilian agencies at home. He criticized AFRICOM, the U.S. Africa Command that began in 2007 to manage military relations with fifty-three countries in Africa from a base in Stuttgart, Germany. AFRICOM was led by a four-star general with two deputies, one of whom, uniquely, is a civilian. Initially, that civilian deputy was Mary Carlin Yates, a senior State Department officer and former ambassador to Ghana. AFRICOM represented an effort to give civilians a role in the military-based organization.

POLITICAL VERSUS PROFESSIONAL

One crucial fact has not changed since the Constitution was adopted: an ambassador represents neither the State Department nor the Congress; he (and now she) is the personal representative of the President of the United States. (The Department of State is headed by a political appointee. Only once has a career Foreign Service officer served as Secretary of State: Ambassador Lawrence S. Eagleburger, a diplomat for more than forty years, was deputy secretary when Secretary James A. Baker resigned in 1992, and Eagleburger served as Secretary for six weeks.)

Of course, the United States has had politically appointed diplomats since its beginning, and the President today still chooses the ambassadors he wishes, with the consent of the Senate. The record shows that financial contributions do not promise superior diplomacy.

At first, American envoys came from the small circle of educated people known to the nation's leaders. The State Department was minuscule, and there was no system for developing careers. As the need for envoys increased, a political spoils system evolved. When that arrangement became foul enough, demands for reform sought to select diplomats and consuls based on merit. The spoils system was tempered but never eradicated.

An American ambassador is a professional who has climbed the Foreign Service ladder or a political appointee brought in from outside the State Department; each breed has its advocates. Some Presidents have demonstrated little faith in finding trustworthy and able representatives in the Washington bureaucracy. Others have preferred the abilities of men and women who have spent their adult lives working on the intricacies of foreign relations.

Ambassador Nicholas Burns believes the career Foreign Service is better off having to compete with talented political appointees for the best assignments. "The Foreign Service should not be afraid of competition," he says. Dan H. Fenn, who identified and screened ambassadors for President Kennedy and later was the founding director of the John F. Kennedy Presidential Library, believes that political appointees, chosen with care, often serve as the President's representative better than career appointees. For one thing, they have the President's ear.

India, for example, has had a splendid series of politically appointed U.S. ambassadors, including Chester Bowles, John Kenneth Galbraith, John Sherman Cooper, and Ellsworth Bunker. On the other hand, Søren Dyssegaard, retired minister-counselor of the Danish Foreign Ministry, wishes that the United States would send more professional career ambassadors to Copenhagen. He said he found that political appointees were on occasion unqualified or became best known for participating in Copenhagen's nightlife.

Generally, political appointees, because they are more likely to have had experience outside government, are more decisive and risk taking. They tend to know the political system better. They are also more likely to have the financial resources to afford the substantial expenses they are expected to cover at the more prestigious posts. And political appointees can relate more often to the political and social leaders in their host countries.

James Lilley was one who did not come up through the Foreign Service ranks; he had retired after working in the CIA for two decades. When Ronald Reagan and George H. W. Bush were elected in 1980, the transition team asked Lilley to name four positions he would like to have in the new administration. He was given his first choice: as a member of the National Security Council staff for East Asia. And after six months, he was appointed the director of the American Institute on Taiwan, where he kept the mainland Chinese leadership apprised of developments on Taiwan. He also met covertly with Ji Chaozhu, then a counselor at the Chinese Embassy in Washington, with whom he encouraged the Taiwan government to test openings to China.

Smith Hempstone, Jr., a conservative newspaperman in Chicago and Washington, was appointed ambassador to Kenya in 1989 and developed good relations with the local press. When he heard that a Kenyan minister had accused him of interfering in that country's affairs, Hempstone felt free to respond by saying, "You tell the minister if he doesn't stop telling lies about me, I'm going to start telling the truth about him." A career ambassador would have been reluctant to voice that blunt opinion.

A strong argument against political appointees is that they do not know how an ambassador works, while, obviously, a career Foreign Service officer has been exposed to a variety of models. Of course, the political appointee is also subject to the charge of being the product of patronage. The Foreign Service Act of 1980 says plainly, "Contributions to a political campaign should not be a factor in the appointment of an individual as a chief of mission." Nominees must reveal to Congress the amounts they and their family have donated. For a time, the American Academy of Diplomacy kept track of the price of attractive ambassadorial assignments but eventually gave up. Recently, some senior career Foreign Service officers have voiced disappointment (probably sardonic) that the "prices" of ambassadors are declining.

Career ambassadors can be overly cautious. Ambassador Brandon H. Grove, Jr., a former director of the Foreign Service Institute, recognized that career officers are part of a personnel system. He said, "Your home and the place to which you will return after three years in your assignment is the Department of State. And that can be inhibiting."

Grove also believed that career Foreign Service officers are more likely to be the target of those who disapprove of American foreign policies. On the other hand, as Joshua Kurlantzick of the Carnegie Endowment for International Peace pointed out, professional ambassadors are repeatedly assigned to go out and "solve the mess."

LITTLE ROOM AT THE TOP

Even though today some 50 or 60 percent of American chiefs of mission are products of the Foreign Service, only a small percentage of the men and women entering the Foreign Service can ever expect to become an ambassador. Ambassador Avis Bohlen, a career Foreign Service officer, put it candidly: "It's most frustrating when you get to the top and find out how few jobs there are." In her experience, "The effect is not so much on the quality of people coming in as how they carry out the work." And equally regrettable, as Robert A. Bradtke, ambassador to the Republic of Croatia, sees it, political appointees are getting "deeper into the system." They squeeze out career people at lower levels, which is not necessarily a good thing.

Political appointees gravitate toward the prestigious and comfortable missions in Europe. Exactly once in modern times has the most-sought-after assignment to the Court of St. James's in London gone to a career Foreign Service officer: Raymond G. Seitz, from 1991 to 1994. In contrast, at the lower end of the attractiveness of assignments was the embassy that Frederic L. Chapin opened in February 1961 as chargé at Fort Lamy (now N'Djamena), the capital of the impoverished, landlocked nation of Chad.

When Chad received its independence from France, Chapin and his three-member staff rented a small house and laid out the materials of the embassy on the dining room table between meals. They had no air-conditioning and one portable typewriter. The embassy safe stood by the bed of the administrative assistant's wife, who was acting as their secretary. Chapin served for several months, until Ambassador John A. Calhoun arrived.

Small and remote do not always mean disagreeable. Emil Skodon, who had led the embassy staff out of Kuwait, moved from serving as deputy

chief of the large embassy in Rome to ambassador in the capital of tropical Brunei, a city with fewer than thirty thousand people. There, he headed
a staff of five Foreign Service officers.

Ambassador Skodon's prime concerns were that Brunei remain both a
reliable source of oil and natural gas and a moderate Muslim nation. "We
do not assess that there is any credible domestic terrorism threat in Brunei," Skodon said. "However, there is a potential threat from regional terrorist groups. . . . In the past, Brunei has been identified as a potential part
of the Southeast Asia Islamic Caliphate that the terrorist group Jemaah
Islamiyah aims at establishing."

Ambassador Molly Bordonaro, a political appointee, seemed equally
happy on Malta, the tiny but strategic island in the middle of the Mediterranean. She said 30 percent of worldwide shipping goes though Maltese
waters and that it is the fifth largest ship registry in the world. She believed being a woman and a mother have helped her to be an ambassador.
She has reached out especially to Malta's young people, who often have
strong anti-American feelings. She played their music until 1:30 A.M., she
says with a smile; and she expanded the Fulbright program.

Political appointees' intimacy with the President can be a great advantage abroad. But it can also lead an ambassador into trouble. When Ambassador Melvin F. Sembler first arrived in Rome, an Italian reporter asked
him whether he spoke Italian. "No!" Sembler countered baldly. "I don't speak
Italian. I speak Bush." That won him attention but few friends.

J. Thomas Schieffer, U.S. ambassador to Japan, was a longtime friend
of President George W. Bush and made news when he sent the President
an out-of-channels cable warning that nuclear negotiations with North
Korea could damage relations with Japan.

In London, Ambassador Robert Tuttle, a Beverly Hills automobile dealer
and fund-raiser for George W. Bush, won himself unpleasant attention when
he told the BBC erroneously that the United States had not shipped suspected terrorists to Syria to be interrogated and tortured. An embassy
spokesperson had to issue a correction.

On Malta, Ambassador Bordonaro avoided such awkward incidents
by copying the White House. She says, "I have had no frustration getting
things done. Today, it is easy to copy people in the White House." Although
a career officer might hesitate to do that, Pamela Harriman in Paris was
also respected because she had access to President Clinton.

"CHARM SCHOOL"

The Foreign Service Institute has had in place since 1973 an ambassadorial seminar to prepare appointees, both career and noncareer. Spouses are invited to attend. The seminars began as one-day meetings and grew to two weeks. They came to include visits to a Special Forces base and to the CIA's headquarters in Langley, Virginia. The seminar is lightly called a "charm school," but it provides answers for questions the ambassador has probably never considered. For instance:

> If a group of businesspeople visit the mission, does the taxpayer pay
>   for the luncheon the ambassador gives for them?
> What is the ambassador's responsibility for the health care of lo-
>   cally hired embassy employees?
> Can an ambassador brief American correspondents and omit the
>   local press?
> Can a spouse use an official car to do shopping?
> During a crisis, when do you evacuate Americans from the mission?
> What are your responsibilities to the American community living
>   in country?
> When does an ambassador ask guidance from Washington?
> Are there times when an ambassador should not carry out instruc-
>   tions from Washington?

The Foreign Service Institute also offers incoming ambassadors and deputy chiefs of mission a two-day introduction to the International Cooperative Administrative Support Services system, which provides common support for all missions. And the National Security Executive Leadership Seminar exposes top-level officers to current strategic problems.

SUPPORT THE POLICY OR RESIGN

Ambassadors sometimes find that dealing with the State Department bureaucracy is more complicated than working with the leaders of their host country. Diplomats in the field and those in Washington may have very different perceptions of how a foreign policy problem should be handled.

Secretary of State Dean Rusk said, "There is no such thing as a complete set of facts. You are always looking through the fog of the future."

Some ambassadors advise others not to ask the department what they should do. Such inquiries produce delay and even resentment, and they can leave the ambassador powerless until instructions arrive. They say the ambassador is advised to tell the department what he or she intends to do by a deadline unless instructed differently. Thus, the ambassador writes his own instructions. Ambassador Richard C. Matheron used this technique successfully to prevent a break in relations when he was deputy chief of mission in Addis Ababa. He said; "I think a good diplomat can often lead the superiors in Washington to come to a position much faster if he or she takes the lead."

Before Ambassador William H. Sullivan, a veteran career Foreign Service officer, went out to Tehran in 1977, he met with President Jimmy Carter, who told him precisely what policies he wanted followed in Iran regarding the sale of military equipment to the shah, the acquisition of nuclear power plants from the United States, and collaboration between the CIA and SAVAK, the Iranian intelligence organization. Under Secretary Philip Habib had Sullivan write a memorandum for distribution within the department confirming the policies the President had spelled out. But Sullivan found that other State Department members were "totally unimpressed." They continued to tell Carter the policies they believed he should follow. As Ambassador William Attwood said of his experience in Guinea, "If the bureaucrats didn't want something to happen, it didn't happen."

SWITCHING POLICIES

American ambassadors represent a government that can change every four or eight years, and therefore they can find themselves supporting policies that can change when administrations change. American foreign policy making has been called "episodic."

Such disruption need not wait for an election. President Franklin D. Roosevelt's inner circle agreed with him that a lasting peace after World War II required a willingness to deal cordially with the Soviet Union. His sudden death on April 12, 1943, replaced his circle with Truman, Harriman, and James Byrnes, who favored being tough with the Russians. This had its own set of consequences, including the Cold War and the Vietnam War.

Another dramatic instance was the plan of George W. Bush's administration to place antiballistic interceptor missiles in Poland and radar for them in the Czech Republic to guard the West against possible strikes from Iran. Mark A. Pekala, then deputy assistant secretary of state, tried in 2007 to persuade the Eastern European leaders to accept the missiles and radars. But people in the two countries feared they would become targets, and powerful Russian opposition also blocked the $3.5 billion U.S. Missile Defense Shield Plan. Pekala and his colleagues finally did convince the Polish and Czech governments, and all twenty-six members of NATO eventually accepted the concept. (He was rewarded with the ambassadorship to Latvia.)

Then, in the fall of 2009, President Barack Obama's administration radically changed the Bush-era plan and decided to place the missiles on ships. Poland and the Czech Republic, which had risked agreeing to the United States' original call, showed signs of bafflement. And by year's end Prime Minister Vladimir V. Putin was warning that Russia would develop offensive weapons to overcome the U.S. missile shield.

Of course, no one asked whether the U.S. interceptor missiles could actually shoot down Iranian missiles. The New York Times said, "Missile defense has always been more about international politics than about new military technology." And in the United States, international politics can change every four years.

Ambassador Robert Murphy looked at the stress of "episodic" policy making this way:

A professional diplomat understands when he accepts government service that he is obedient to official policy, no matter how repugnant a particular line may be to him personally.... If an official is not willing to abide by this principle, it would be better for him not to enter the Foreign Service.

Murphy added that the only occasion in his long career when he felt he should have resigned in protest was the decision not to challenge the Russians' blockade of Berlin. That decision, he was convinced, led to the Soviet Union underestimating American determination and to the Korean War two years later.

Secretary Dean Rusk explained, "There is a delicate line between raising questions about policy and failing to support the policy.... When the

President has decided what policy shall be, an officer should support that policy or resign." He added, "My wife accuses me of having a capacity for accepting the inevitable. I've never quite known what the alternative is."

NEGOTIATORS' HALL OF FAME

One of the most valuable skills an ambassador can have is to be a capable negotiator. The art of negotiating requires the most basic human ingenuity. Ambassador Charles W. Freeman, Jr., wrote about Ambassador Arthur W. Hummel, "As a negotiator, one of his merits was his ability to maintain silence. Some recent studies have shown that the average American can only tolerate about seventeen seconds of silence. Not Art Hummel. He would sit there, poker-faced, and wait for the other side to say something."

An ambassador can be asked to negotiate a world-shaking international confrontation or some issue that is surprisingly small. When Ambassador Freeman set up the Liaison Office in Beijing, the Chinese wanted the right to raise the rent after five years. Freeman knew the Chinese claimed to have no inflation. So he negotiated with them to put into the lease a clause saying since there was no inflation in China, there would be no rent increases. They agreed.

Ambassador Philip Habib, himself a superb negotiator, made negotiating sound deceptively simple: "The function of mediation is to help narrow gaps and then bridge them."

A reason for his success, Ambassador Habib said, is that he was "very positive about most things. If you're a pessimist, you don't become a diplomat, because if you do, there's no way you're going to get ahead with the problems. You've got to be optimistic about the most ridiculous and difficult of problems." Habib holds a special and unconventional place in the Foreign Service legend. When he died, *The New York Times* said he was regarded as "the outstanding professional diplomat of his generation in the United States." Henry Kissinger called him "one of my heroes."

Habib believed he was an effective Middle East negotiator in part because his parents were Lebanese. He called himself "the youngest member of an immigrant family." Born in Brooklyn the son of a Lebanese neighborhood grocer, Habib studied agricultural economics and forestry, intending to become a forest ranger. He liked to say, "I learned how to tell the difference between the forest and the trees, which is important in diplomacy."

He passed the Foreign Service examinations in 1949, and as a skilled negotiator rose to become, in 1976, under secretary of state for political affairs, the highest career position.

Habib listed the modern American ambassadors who would man his Negotiators Hall of Fame. His pantheon included Cyrus Vance ("complete honesty"), Henry Kissinger ("capacity to conceptualize"), Averell Harriman ("capacity to understand the other guy's point of view"), David Bruce ("tough inner resiliency"), Ellsworth Bunker ("great presence"), and Henry Cabot Lodge ("a touch for the political"). Each one different, but each one effective.

A FOREIGN SERVICE CONVERSATION

Just as *The New York Times* judged Philip Habib "the outstanding professional diplomat of his generation," it is fair to nominate Ambassador George Frost Kennan as the surpassing intellectual Foreign Service officer of his generation. "I have always gone my own way intellectually" is the way he put it to me. Upon Kennan's death, Richard Holbrooke was all-encompassing; he wrote, "He was our greatest diplomat."

Kennan could see problems whole and unfiltered, whether the issue was the place of the Soviet Union in Europe or the place of the U.S. Foreign Service in the American bureaucracy. He did not always win the argument, but he shaped the discussion. He said, "Few were permitted to think large thoughts. It took a certain amount of arrogance on my part." Henry Kissinger said he "came as close to authoring the diplomatic doctrine of his era as any diplomat in our history."

Ambassador Kennan and I had not visited together for thirty-five years when I rang the bell of his yellow stucco home in Princeton, New Jersey, on a gray late-October morning. The frail elderly man came to the door, steadying himself with a cane in each hand. He had first joined the Foreign Service in 1926, when he was twenty-two, and he was now deep in his nineties, as alert and cordial as ever.

We sat and talked in a small room over the foyer. A silver bowl, the symbol of his Einstein Peace Prize, sat on a table nearby. Annelise, his Norwegian-born wife, stopped by and briefly discussed winterizing the windows.

We had much to talk about. I wanted to know why, to his mind, the Foreign Service still received so little public support. Virtually every other government department has significant support. Interior and Justice have a thousand roots, and Congress members are interested in those departments' affairs. But, Kennan felt, the State Department was on a cloud of its own: "It segregated itself, its mode of life." Kennan continued, "There is a total lack of knowledge of what the Foreign Service is meant to be." People depend on two sources for their knowledge of the Foreign Service, teachers and journalists. He said, "People who teach civics ought to include knowledge of institutions in relationships with other countries."

In his view, foreign affairs are conducted not by the whim of individuals but, more important, through institutions. Too often, he felt, the United States supports dictators instead of the institutions that would give our policies continuity. The dictators—he cited Stalin—always disappear. The institutions last.

He added thoughtfully, "There is a mutual contempt between journalism and diplomacy. Journalists say, What good is anything if you can't talk about it? And diplomats regard journalists as superficial; they touch a topic like the tips of a flower."

Ambassador Kennan had subjects he wanted to talk about, and leading them was the importance of the consular service. He had started his own career in the consular service, when the consular and diplomatic had just been "joined" by the Rogers Act. He added, "I would like to see restored the prestige of the old consular service. Today, I wonder whether joining the two services was a good thing."

Why did he switch to the diplomatic side? He answered with the story of the ambassador who explained, that: "My mother got tired of having her bags inspected at frontiers."

Although diplomacy requires change, change does not always ensure improvement. For example, he recalled, "It was most unfortunate that we got rid of the legation as distinct from the embassy. If I had my way, most posts abroad would be legations." When he was a young officer in the legation at Riga, "It had the same functions as an embassy but without the pretensions. . . . The ambassadorial position was reserved for relations between Great Powers." Since a President cannot see a hundred and fifty ambassadors, "It was better when there were a few important jobs that required ambassadors." The present system of appointing so many ambassadors is "all fraud."

"We are into an age of multinational diplomacy," he went on. "And I personally feel there ought to be a traveling ambassador to do the work that they send the Secretary of State to do. The Secretary should not spend months at a time rotating between the Palestinians and the Israelis. It is a misuse of the Secretary of State. The Secretary of State should have a certain amount of grandeur and be available to ambassadors who wish to call on him. I look back to when Mr. Stimson was Secretary of State, and he was available. Today, people want to see only the President." Kennan added that Secretary Hillary Clinton has said of her job, "You can either try to manage the building or manage the world; you can't try to do both."

Kennan said, "The National Security Council has become a second State Department. When it was set up, it was quite different." He named McGeorge Bundy as one who followed the original intention and "saw that the wheels were greased among the White House, The Pentagon, and the State Department." But Kissinger and Nixon made the National Security Advisor superior to the Secretary of State. Kennan said, "It was quite wrong."

That development debased respect for Foreign Service officers. "We were expected to have the same professional standards of dedication and discipline, of honor, as officers in the armed services." He would like more mingling between the Foreign Service and the armed services. The Foreign Service, he said, is not made up of "aristocratic sissies who attend tea parties and look down on other people."

Kennan admired the modern changes in Foreign Service demographics. "Education and character are the two great things," not race and class. "It is important to be brought up in a proper family. That makes a difference. You know how to behave, have some sensitivity to people. But they did not have to be wealthy families."

Kennan recollected that when he went to Moscow as minister-counselor, he advised Ambassador Averell Harriman that the embassy people had not had a vacation. Harriman said that they did not need one. Harriman did not respect what they did. Kennan bridled; he cited John Davies, who had parachuted into Bosnia, and another Foreign Service officer, who had jumped into the Philippines. Kennan himself had been a prisoner of war for nearly six months. He stressed that diplomats are not "effeminate mother's boys from wealthy families."

Someone should study "the real importance of chance in foreign affairs." In the 1920s, he was discouraged after a couple of years in Hamburg and wanted to quit. By chance, a colleague, future ambassador William Dawson, Jr., told him about a new language-training program. He signed up for Russian and became fluent, which set him on his life's course.

Kennan added that the Foreign Service was "abused and distorted" by the invasion of embassies by "oceans of civil service bureaucracy. . . . Nine out of ten are sent by departments for bureaucratic reasons of their own. Many are unprepared to live abroad. They are put in American ghettos and associate with each other." Kennan wanted to get rid of those "armies of people."

He believed the Foreign Service is also damaged when political appointments are made down to the level of the assistant secretary of state. The practice, he said, destroys the self-administration and discipline of the Foreign Service.

He felt that, in his experience, during crises the government in Washington did not know how to make best use of the Foreign Service. "In time of war, the government at home did not know what to do with the Foreign Service." And during the Great Depression, the State Department was "helpless in Washington. It had to stop admissions to the Foreign Service."

Diplomatic officers were "mishandled" during World War II. "Foreign Service officers had to report to draft boards and plead for themselves." The State Department refused to plead for them. "If they had closer ties with the military, this could have been avoided."

He admired Dean Acheson. "He didn't know anything about Europe, but he was highly honorable, a man of great dignity." He thought Rusk "colorless" and Kissinger "a politician and not fully American." Holbrooke was "remarkable"—of the caliber of secretaries of state.

During World War II, Kennan went home and saw FDR instead of the Secretary of State in order to clear up a dispute about the Azores. He said, "We had to go very high to get decisions. The State Department was too timid to do it themselves."

Did Kennan ever want to be Secretary of State? "At times I thought I might have done better than some."

Why did he quit the Foreign Service in 1953? "Foster Dulles fired me.

He called me in and said he had no place for me. He thought I was a Democrat because I worked for Acheson. I wasn't." After the Russians declared Kennan persona non grata in 1952 and Dulles would not give him another post, he retired. Eight years later, President Kennedy appointed him ambassador to Yugoslavia—an appointment that lasted barely two years.

Kennan believed that an ambassador should function inside the embassy with a core group of four or five civilians and the military attaché. "That core," he said, "has been lost" with the influx of people from so many other departments. He praised Pamela Harriman, ambassador to Paris and widow of Averell Harriman, as "a marvelous chief of mission; she set up a core." In contrast, he said, Averell Harriman, when ambassador in Moscow, operated with Churchill, Roosevelt, and Stalin "and paid little attention with anyone else."

Kennan wished there were "an invisible fence to protect those essential functions of the ambassador." The ambassador is, first of all, a means of communication, and "he lives in the country and tells his government what lies behind the language."

At quarter to twelve, at the end of a full morning of thoughtful talk, his wife, Annelise, came back into the room and helped him to his feet, and George Kennan excused himself and, with the aid of his two canes, went off to lunch.

Notes

Introduction: Closing Pandora's Box

1. "America's first line": U.S. Department of State, *Financial Report Fiscal Year 2007*, 5.
1. "became a necessity . . . There are temporary": François de Callières quote dates back to 1716.
3. "the American system": Bohlen, oral history interview by Mulhollan, 7.
3. Today, the United States: HR Fact Sheet, Bureau of Human Resources, Department of State.
3. "one of the best": Blake, Nelson Manfred, *Organization of American Historians*
3. "Diplomacy has always": Foreign Service Day 2005.

1: Making a Difference

7. Eddy was born: Eddy, "F.D.R. Meets Ibn Saud," 47.
8. "a daredevil who loved": Simmons and Alexander, *Through the Wheat*, 27.
8. "He was one": Patenaude, *Big Show in Bololand*, 92.
9. After lunch: Eddy, "F.D.R. Meets Ibn Saud," 26.
9. Eddy later said: ibid., 33–34, 42.
10. The son of a missionary: J. Paxton, "I Escaped over the Roof of the World"; for more on USS *Panay*, see chapter 31 of this book.
10. Consul General Paxton's party: V. Paxton, "American Nursing on the Roof of the World."
10. Two weeks after Paxton: Laird, *Into Tibet*, 82.
10. Mackiernan and Bessac tried: ibid., 153.
11. The terrain on the India side: V. Paxton, "American Nursing on the Roof of the World."
11. After their ten-week ordeal: ibid.; J. Paxton, "I Escaped Over the Roof of the World."

2: The Militiamen of Diplomacy: 1776–80

12. on March 3, 1776: Van Doren, *Benjamin Franklin*, 541.

12. "transact such business": Letter addressed to Silas Deane from Committee of Secret Correspondence, Philadelphia, dated March 2, 1776, in Delegates to Congress, *Letters of Delegates to Congress*.

12. Dean sailed from Chester: ibid.

13. He communicated in cipher: Hunt. *Department of State*, 37.

13. "Whether, if the Colonies": Letter addressed to Silas Deane from Committee of Secret Correspondence, Philadelphia, dated March 2, 1776, in Delegates to Congress, *Letters of Delegates to Congress*.

13. Deane was not above: Abernathy, "Commercial Activities of Silas Deane in France," 478.

14. "Friends of American Liberty": W. Williams, *Contours of American History*, 13.

14. Only William Bollan: ibid.

14. Committee of Secret Correspondence: E. Johnson, "Early History of the United States Consular Service," 20.

14. Franklin was its chair: Barnes and Morgan, *Foreign Service of the United States*, 6.

14. The Americans would need: Williams, *Contours of American History*, 14.

14. At first, efforts: Hunt, *Department of State*, 6.

14. At the end of 1775: Barnes and Morgan, *Foreign Service of the United States*, 11.

14. And the committee engaged: ibid.; Straus, *Under Four Administrations*, 50; Hunt, *Department of State*, 3.

14. Neither Deane nor Franklin: James, *Silas Deane*, 21.

14. On September 26: Van Doren, *Benjamin Franklin*, 563.

14. They were the colonies' first: E. Johnson, "Early History of the United States Consular Service," 23.

14. "Franklin was a natural": Schiff, *Great Improvisation*, 2.

15. "a handsome allowance": Barnes and Morgan, *Foreign Service of the United States*, 8.

15. Jefferson declined to join: Barnes and Morgan, *Foreign Service of the United States*, 11.

15. The first arms were shipped: Straus, *Under Four Administrations*, 36.

15. The other commissioner: Ellis, *Founding Brothers*, 13.

16. "an Act of violent Injustice": Clark, *Benjamin Franklin*, 241; also see Van Doren, *Benjamin Franklin*, 458.

17. In March 1777: McCullough, *John Adams*, 199.

17. Franklin made this estate: Van Doren, *Benjamin Franklin*, 635.

17. Although Franklin's French: Clark, *Benjamin Franklin*, 311; also see Van Doren, *Benjamin Franklin*, 631.

17. Britain's capable spymaster: R. Morris, *Peacemakers*, 10; Clark, *Benjamin Franklin*, 317; Van Doren, *Benjamin Franklin*, 582; McCullough, *John Adams*, 210.

18. In fact, codes: Barnes and Morgan, *Foreign Service of the United States*, 10.

18. Francis Dana was appointed: Hunt, *Department of State*, 5; Barnes and Morgan, *Foreign Service of the United States*, 17; Nordholt, *Dutch Republic and American Independence*, 65.

18. He and a Dutch banker: Nordholt, *Dutch Republic and American Independence*, 66.

19. "a forgotten man": R. Morris, *Peacemakers*, 355.

19. "a sort of militia": Nordholt, *Dutch Republic and American Independence*, 103.

19. "militia diplomatists": Hunt, *Department of State*, 12.

19. "militiamen of diplomacy": R. Morris, *Peacemakers*, 151.

19. The American commissioners: Van Doren, *Benjamin Franklin*, 588.

20. "Diplomacy can convert": Sicherman, "Benjamin Franklin," 6.

20. By year's end: Van Doren, *Benjamin Franklin*, 592.

20. This was the terrible winter: Van Doren, *Benjamin Franklin*, 593; Sicherman, "Benjamin Franklin," 7.

20. On February 5, 1778: Ginsburgh, "Between War and Peace" (Ph.D. dissertation), 132.

21. "But for his noble": Clark, *Benjamin Franklin*, 341.

21. "Your majesty may count": Clark, *Benjamin Franklin*, 342; also see Van Doren, *Benjamin Franklin*, 595.

21. The few American representatives: Barnes and Morgan, *Foreign Service of the United States*, 26.

21. The roots of consular duties: Harty, "Remarks at the Commonwealth Club, San Francisco" (speech).

21. "from our very beginnings": ibid.

21. Thomas Morris: Abernathy, "Commercial Activities of Silas Deane in France," 483; Barnes and Morgan, *Foreign Service of the United States*, 26; J., 1.

22. William Lee sided: Barnes and Morgan, *Foreign Service of the United States*, 26.

22. Thomas Morris died: C. Kennedy. *American Consul*, 7; Barnes and Morgan, *Foreign Service of the United States*, 27.

22. "I find that": E. Johnson, "Early History of the United States Consular Service," 24.

22. Franklin and Adams wrote: Barnes and Morgan, *Foreign Service of the United States*, 27; E. Johnson, "Early History of the United States Consular Service."

22. Deane carried a letter: Clark, *Benjamin Franklin*, 345.

22. Through Deane's yearlong: Brookhiser, *Gentleman Revolutionary*, 54.

22. John Jay: C. James, *Silas Deane*, 90.

23. "a gross injustice": ibid., 121.

23. "the most malicious enemy": Clark, *Benjamin Franklin*, 346.

23. Adams accepted Franklin's invitation: Van Doren, *Benjamin Franklin*, 600.

23. He had an explosive temper: McCullough, *John Adams*, 399.

23. Adams' crucial principle: Ferling, *John Adams*, 154.

23. "Adams was a conservative": ibid.

23. "As an American agent": Monaghan, *John Jay*, 170.

23. And the three Americans: Ferling, *John Adams*, 199.

24. "I wish Congress": Van Doren, *Benjamin Franklin*, 608.

24. Adams' harping became so infuriating: Clark, *Benjamin Franklin*, 348.

24. The American commissioners: Ferling, *John Adams*, 206.

24. "The King has no need": Monaghan, *John Jay*, 172.

24. When Lafayette returned: Clark, *Benjamin Franklin*, 350.

25. He would not discuss: ibid.

25. A committee chaired by: Hunt, *Department of State*, 12.

25. Adams had no forewarning: McCullough, *John Adams*, 225.

25. Adams set sail: Barnes and Morgan, *Foreign Service of the United States*, 18; Ferling, *John Adams*, 219.

25. Adams immediately paid: Ferling, *John Adams*, 219.

25. Vergennes, a starchy: R. Morris, *Peacemakers*, 191.

25. And he offended: McCullough, *John Adams*, 232.

25. The inactivity that Vergennes: Ferling, *John Adams*, 225–27.

26. Finding he was powerless: Barnes and Morgan, *Foreign Service of the United States*, 21.

26. Laurens' voyage was marred: ibid., 19.

26. "Since the foolish part": Quoted in Malone, *Jefferson and His Time*, 2: 627–28.

27. Adams secured aid: Nordholt, *Dutch Republic and American Independence*, 145.

27. Of Huguenot descent: Monaghan, *John Jay,* 95.

27. The tall, thin: ibid., 25.

27. But once it was adopted: ibid., 46, 68.

27. Jay was instructed: ibid., 132.

28. Conde de Floridablanca: ibid., 133; R. Morris, *Peacemakers,* 49; extension of remarks to House of Representatives, 66th Cong.

28. Floridablanca declined to provide: Monaghan, *John Jay,* 144.

28. "Your Excellency, I was": ibid., 147.

28. "Till now I have": Letter dated October 27, 1780, cited in Hunt, *Department of State,* 13.

28. He was mortified: Monaghan, *John Jay,* 152.

28. After a long year: ibid., 165.

29. John Adams perceived: Ferling, *John Adams,* 152.

29. Propaganda played a role: Van Doren, *Benjamin Franklin,* 672.

29. By June, Britain's unpopular: R. Morris, *Peacemakers,* 68.

3: "The Sword Was Sheathed": 1781–85

30. "But there is really": Letter dated August 6, 1779, quoted in Hunt, *Department of State;* also see Barnes and Morgan, *Foreign Service of the United States,* 6; W. Williams, *Contours of American History,* 14.

30. on January 10, 1781: Hunt, *Department of State,* 53.

30. Robert R. Livingston defeated: Monaghan, *John Jay,* 41; Hunt, *Department of State,* 17; Dangerfield, *Chancellor Robert R. Livingston of New York,* 140; W. Williams, *Contours of American History,* 89.

31. Livingston soon brought: Hunt, *Department of State,* 26; Dangerfield, *Chancellor Robert R. Livingston of New York,* 145.

31. When Livingston resigned: Barnes and Morgan, *Foreign Service of the United States,* 7; J. Kimball, *Short History of the U.S. Department of State,* 2.

31. The post of Secretary: Barnes and Morgan, *Foreign Service of the United States,* 8; Monaghan, *John Jay,* 244.

31. When Congress moved: Barnes and Morgan, *Foreign Service of the United States,* 8.

31. site of General Washington's farewell: W. Williams, *Contours of American History,* 9.

31. The solid block: Nordholt, *Dutch Republic and American Independence,* 159.

32. In response to: R. Morris, *Peacemakers,* 204; Ferling, *John Adams,* 235.

32. Adams returned to his house: Ferling, *John Adams,* 236.

32. Congress informed Adams: ibid., 237.

32. Instead of holding: ibid.; Dangerfield, *Chancellor Robert R. Livingston of New York,* 138.

32. He asked to be recalled: McCullough, *John Adams,* 266.

32. "to undertake nothing": Monaghan, *John Jay,* 173; Barnes and Morgan, *Foreign Service of the United States,* 20.

32. As Franklin had insisted: ibid., 17.

33. William Fitzmaurice, the Earl: Ferling, *John Adams,* 243.

33. to keep the United States: Van Doren, *Benjamin Franklin,* 668.

33. Adams proposed a treaty: Nordholt, *Dutch Republic and American Independence,* 205–07.

33. Laurens crossed the Channel: R. Morris, *Peacemakers,* 267; Ferling, *John Adams,* 244.

34. "Spain has taken four years": Monaghan, *John Jay,* 181.

34. Franklin's position was simple: Van Doren, *Benjamin Franklin,* 675.

34. Twenty-six-year-old Thomas Grenville: R. Morris, *Peacemakers,* 271.

34. Oswald took Grenville: ibid., 272.

34. The summer was filled: Monaghan, *John Jay*, 184.

34. "colonies or plantations . . . United States of America": Van Doren, *Benjamin Franklin*, 682.

35. Oswald wanted independence: Monaghan, *John Jay*, 199.

35. "The sword was sheathed": R. Morris, *Peacemakers*, 285.

35. Franklin met with Oswald . . . The commissioners, despite: H. W. Brands, *First American*, 616; Ferling, *John Adams*, 245.

36. This confirmed Jay's conviction: Van Doren, *Benjamin Franklin*, 682.

36. Oswald promised him: ibid., 683.

36. Expecting that Vergennes and Shelburne: Van Doren, *Benjamin Franklin*, 686.

37. "Commissioners of the United States": Ferling, *John Adams*, 242.

37. summoned Adams from Holland: ibid., 242.

37. Jay urged Oswald: Monaghan, *John Jay*, 205.

38. The commissioners did not: ibid., 206.

38. Henry Strachey, undersecretary: R. Morris, *Peacemakers*, 351; Barnes and Morgan, *Foreign Service of the United States*, 21.

38. Meanwhile, John Adams: Barnes and Morgan, *Foreign Service of the United States*, 19.

38. Adams and Jay found: Monaghan, *John Jay*, 186.

38. Negotiations followed for a week: ibid., 209.

38. The Americans gave up: R. Morris, *Peacemakers*, 362.

39. United States had the "right": McCullough, *John Adams*, 283.

39. It was finished: R. Morris, *Peacemakers*, 379–80; Ferling, *John Adams*, 252; Van Doren, *Benjamin Franklin*, 693.

40. "single indiscretion . . . this little misunderstanding": From a letter dated December 17, 1782, quoted in H. W. Brands, *First American*, 635.

40. the British believed: From a letter dated December 17, 1782, as discussed in Clark, *Benjamin Franklin*, 383; Ferling, *John Adams*, 254.

40. Franklin offered a model: Barnes and Morgan, *Foreign Service of the United States*, 21.

40. The two wily diplomats: H. W. Brands, *First American*, 636.

40. They recognized that what: Van Doren, *Benjamin Franklin*, 695.

40. In fact, Franklin asked: Dangerfield, *Chancellor Robert R. Livingston of New York*, 173–74.

40. At home, Secretary of State: ibid., 174.

40. He praised their results: ibid., 175.

40. "militiaman diplomats": Barnes and Morgan, *Foreign Service of the United States*, 21.

40. Vergennes directed Franklin: R. Morris, *Peacemakers*, 410; Clark, *Benjamin Franklin*, 384.

40. The agreed-to preliminaries: R. Morris, *Peacemakers*, 422.

40. Charles James Fox: ibid., 427.

41. The Peace Treaty of 1783: Combs, *Jay Treaty*, 4–5.

41. "I have never yet": From letter dated May 25, 1782, in R. Morris, *Peacemakers*, 438.

41. The peace treaty was ratified: Ammon, *James Monroe*, 43.

42. Adams traveled to Bath: Ferling, *John Adams*, 262.

42. Thomas Barclay, of Pennsylvania: Van Doren, *Benjamin Franklin*, 703.

4: Of Consuls, Commerce, and Confidence: 1784–1810

43. "the most beautiful bridge": C. James, *Silas Deane*; McCullough, *John Adams*, 313.

43. This was Jefferson's first: Ibid.

43. He never married again: Chernow, *Alexander Hamilton*, 312.

43. Jefferson brought with him: Malone, *Jefferson and His Time*, 2: 22; M. Kimball, *Jefferson*, 9; C. James, *Silas Deane*, 75.

43. Both Humphreys and Short: Malone, *Jefferson and His Time*, 2: 8.

44. "Reposing special trust": Hunt, *Department of State*, 264.

44. Jefferson was gracious: McCullough, *John Adams*, 111.

44. "wise and prudent Man": C. James, *Silas Deane*, 84.

44. Theirs was a strange: Ellis, *Founding Brothers*, 17.

44. They grew even closer: C. James, *Silas Deane*, 86.

44. It took two years: Malone, *Jefferson and His Time*, 2: 12.

45. He insisted she sail: Ellis, *American Sphinx*, 3.

45. She finally arrived: Malone, *Jefferson and His Time*, 3: 211; McCullough, *John Adams*, 372.

45. Hotel de Langeac: Van Doren, *Benjamin Franklin*, 19–29.

46. United States' neighbor, Spain: C. Kennedy, *American Consul*, 14.

46. Congress authorized Jay: Combs, *Jay Treaty*, 17.

46. Jefferson famously said: Malone, *Jefferson and His Time*, 2: 13; McCullough, *John Adams*, 330.

46. In May 1785: Malone, *Jefferson and His Time*, 2: 14.

47. Franklin finally left Passy: Van Doren, *Benjamin Franklin*, 723.

47. "The United States will never": From a letter dated May 10, 1785, quoted in H. W. Brands, *First American*, 647.

47. In 1784, the surprisingly: Pletcher, *Diplomacy of Involvement*, 14.

48. Although the Chinese never: Shaw, *Journals of Major Samuel Shaw*, 124–25.

48. Jay suggested that five: E. Johnson, "Early History of the United States Consular Service," 31.

48. "In this course Congress": ibid., 32.

48. These actions all emphasized: Combs, *Jay Treaty*, 15.

49. "He cannot dance": From letter to Judge Lee dated September 21, 1787, in R. Morris, *Peacemakers*, 451; also see McCullough, *John Adams*, 349.

49. The Adams family settled: Barnes and Morgan, *Foreign Service of the United States*, 25; Shackelford, *Thomas Jefferson's Travels*, 44.

49. On June 1, the young: Ferling, *John Adams*, 280; McCullough, *John Adams*, 335.

50. "They require to be": From letter dated September 28, 1787, quoted in Malone, *Jefferson and His Time*, 2: 55; also see McCullough, *John Adams*, 355; Shackelford, *Thomas Jefferson's Travels*, 45.

50. Adams, frustrated by: Barnes and Morgan, *Foreign Service of the United States*, 25.

50. Jefferson loved France: Malone, *Jefferson and His Time*, 2: 19.

51. Building on Adams's work: C. James, *Silas Deane*, 95.

51. American debt bred ill: Malone, *Jefferson and His Time*, 2: 187.

51. Comte de Montmorin: Monaghan, *John Jay*, 119.

51. On July 11: C. James, *Silas Deane*, 130.

52. Still, that November: Monaghan, *John Jay*, 626; Barnes and Morgan, *Foreign Service of the United States*, 36; Malone, *Jefferson and His Time*, 2: 200; E. Johnson, "Early History of the United States Consular Service," 36.

52. the French agreed: Malone, *Jefferson and His Time*, 2: 201.

52. President Washington appointed: E. Johnson, "Early History of the United States Consular Service," 39.

52. "The crowning achievement": Malone, *Jefferson and His Time*, 2: 199.

52. The consular convention: Barnes and Morgan, *Foreign Service of the United States*, 36; B. Powell, "Jefferson and the Consular Service."

52. He made the request: Malone, *Jefferson and His Time*, 2: 205.

53. On Sunday, July 12: ibid., 2: 225–26.

53. Jefferson watched the entry: ibid., 2: 226.

53. "Their hatred is stronger": From letter to Jay dated August 5, 1789, in ibid., 2: 227.

53. Jefferson said later: ibid., 2: 230.

53. John Marsden Pintard: B. Powell, "Jefferson and the Consular Service," 446.

53. By the end of August: ibid.

54. Under the law of April 14: "An Act concerning Consuls and Vice-Consuls," 2nd Cong, 1st sess., 1792, 254.

54. Salaries were provided: Barnes and Morgan, *Foreign Service of the United States*, 58; "An Act concerning Consuls and Vice-Consuls," 2nd Cong., 1st sess., 1792, 256.

54. It was not uncommon: C. Kennedy, *American Consul*, 22.

55. By 1830, there were: Barnes and Morgan, *Foreign Service of the United States*, 63.

55. Bordeaux in 1778: C. Kennedy, *American Consul*, 45.

55. letter that Secretary: Barnes and Morgan, *Foreign Service of the United States*, 65.

56. "if something is: Matthewson, "Jefferson and the Nonrecognition," 23.

57. on January 1, 1804: ibid., 35.

5: *Paying Off the Pirates: 1785–1805*

58. "indignation and impotence": From letter to Nathaniel Greene dated January 12, 1785, in C. James, *Silas Deane*, 27.

58. Adams thought that paying: ibid., 90.

59. on October 11, 1784: Wells, "Long-Time Friends," 3.

59. In June 1786, Barclay: C. Kennedy, *American Consul*, 15.

59. Accompanying Barclay in Marrakesh: Dur, "Conditions for Recognition."

59. Barclay appointed three Italians: C. Kennedy, *American Consul*, 15; Barnes and Morgan, *Foreign Service of the United States*, 30, 32.

59. "That it is inconsistent: Barnes and Morgan, *Foreign Service of the United States*, 33.

60. dey of Algiers demanded: Todd, *Life and Letters of Joel Barlow*, 118.

60. Jefferson was prepared: Morison, *John Paul Jones*, 400–01.

61. The United States paid $992,463.25: Todd, *Life and Letters of Joel Barlow*, 118.

61. In Paris in the summer: ibid., 118; Woodress, *Yankee's Odyssey*, 154.

61. In 1788, Barlow went: Woodress, *Yankee's Odyssey*, 115.

62. Barlow borrowed the dey's: ibid., 173; Ross, "Mission of Joseph Donaldson, Jr.," 433.

62. "That country is so": Adams, Message to Congress, June 23, 1797.

62. After many delays, Barlow: Woodress, *Yankee's Odyssey*, 186.

63. James Simpson, the U.S. consul: C. Kennedy, *American Consul*, 87; Wells, "Long-Time Friends," 4.

64. Eaton obtained Jefferson's permission: Zacks, *Pirate Coast*, 43.

64. The Marines, bayonets fixed: Moskin, *U.S. Marine Corps Story*, 37–38.

64. The very next day, *Constellation*: Zacks, *Pirate Coast*, 293

64. Joseph Pulis, a controversial: ibid., 249.

65. the United States finally: C. Kennedy, *American Consul*, 37.

6: *"One Nation as to Foreign Concerns": 1787–95*

66. "I have nothing": From letter dated August 5, 1787, quoted in C. James, *Silas Deane*, 126.

66. He left Paris: Shackelford, *Thomas Jefferson's Travels*, 75.

66. The delegates the states: Ellis, *Founding Brothers*, 8.

66. Jefferson asserted that the Senate: Hunt, *Department of State*, 106.

67. The executive's powers: Barnes and Morgan, *Foreign Service of the United States*, 37.

67. James Madison, the principal: Hunt, *Department of State*, 61.

67. he still wanted: Chernow, *Alexander Hamilton*, 260.

67. "To make us one": From letter dated December 16, 1786, in C. James, *Silas Deane*, 116.

67. On September 15, 1789: Hunt, *Department of State*, 67.

67. The department's name: Barnes and Morgan, *Foreign Service of the United States*, 39; Hunt, *Department of State*, 72–73.

67. the most important office: W. Williams, *Contours of American History*, 21.

67. Its secretary was responsible: Malone, *Jefferson and His Time*, 3: 167.

68. Jefferson left Paris: Malone, *Jefferson and His Time*, 2: 205.

68. His secretary, William Short: Shackelford, *Thomas Jefferson's Travels*, 160.

68. Jefferson landed at Norfolk: Malone, *Jefferson and His Time*, 2: 243.

68. En route, he learned: C. James, *Silas Deane*, 138n101.

68. He reached New York City: Malone, *Jefferson and His Time*, 2: 255.

68. he officially took charge: Barnes and Morgan, *Foreign Service of the United States*, 39.

68. it consisted of two: ibid., 81.

68. His principal clerks: Hunt, *Department of State*, 95.

68. George Taylor rather than: Malone, *Jefferson and His Time*, 2: 444; Hunt, *Department of State*, 95.

68. An act of July 1: Barnes and Morgan, *Foreign Service of the United States*, 40.

69. Under the Constitution, should: Monaghan, *John Jay*, 345.

69. Jefferson and Madison wanted: Combs, *Jay Treaty*, 31.

69. The U.S. Treasury Secretary: ibid., 49, 63.

69. In the end, Hamilton: Malone, *Jefferson and His Time*, 3: 157.

70. He warned that if: Malone, *Jefferson and His Time*, 2: 407.

70. "mistook cunning for wisdom": *American National Biography*.

70. Pinckney's Treaty, signed: *Dictionary of American Biography*.

70. Gouverneur Morris, whom Washington: Malone, *Jefferson and His Time*, 2: 310–15.

71. His instructions prohibited him: Combs, *Jay Treaty*, 90.

71. But he did propose creating: ibid., 96.

71. Making a recommendation: Malone, *Jefferson and His Time*, 2: 415.

71. "unsound and dangerous": Monaghan, *John Jay*, 347.

71. "I write to day": Quoted in Hunt, *Department of State*, 90.

72. Gouverneur Morris had come: Brookhiser, *Gentleman Revolutionary*, 97–98.

72. He now witnessed: ibid., 108.

72. After enduring repeated searches: ibid., 137.

72. On July 18, Morris: Morison, *John Paul Jones*, 412.

72. To save expense, Morris: ibid., 404.

73. Paine never forgave him: Brookhiser, *Gentleman Revolutionary*, 139.

73. In 1905, after a dedicated: Morison, *John Paul Jones*, 407–09.

73. The skittish Hamilton: Chernow, *Alexander Hamilton*, 301.

73. Washington wrote his warring: Jefferson, *Papers of Thomas Jefferson*, 24: 354; Malone, *Jefferson and His Time*, 2: 453n21.

73. "It accords with our": From letter to Morris dated November 7, 1792, quoted in Malone, *Jefferson and His Time*, 3: 42.

73. On April 22, President Washington: Chernow, *Alexander Hamilton*, 435–36.

74. "conspirators against human liberty": Malone, *Jefferson and His Time*, 3: 71.

74. But in practice: ibid., 149.

74. Redheaded Genêt: Combs, *Jay Treaty*, 114; Malone, *Jefferson and His Time*, 3: 81, 102.

74. The French government was pleased: Brookhiser, *Gentleman Revolutionary*, 161.

75. Chief Clerk George Taylor: Malone, *Jefferson and His Time*, 3: 147.

75. "Whatever logical powers": Ammon, *James Monroe*, 115.

75. The Republicans demanded: ibid., 110.

76. The convention voted: ibid., 120.

76. The Federalists were upset: Lord, *Dawn's Early Light*, 122.

76. Monroe obtained a passport: Ammon, *James Monroe*, 138.

7: "To Prepare for War Will Be Wise": 1793–1811

77. more than a hundred: Monaghan, *John Jay*, 363; Combs, *Jay Treaty*, 120.

77. Jay agreed to undertake: Monaghan, *John Jay*, 367.

78. Jay sailed from New York: ibid., 373; C. Kennedy, *American Consul*, 46.

78. His cordiality, his pro-British: Combs, *Jay Treaty*, 149–51.

78. "quietly rejoiced that": Monaghan, *John Jay*, 377.

78. "To continue to prepare": ibid., 378.

78. John Quincy Adams: McCullough, *John Adams*, 454.

78. Jay signed it, and Adams declared: Combs, *Jay Treaty*, 158.

78. "To use an Indian": Quoted in Monaghan, *John Jay*, 383.

79. many Americans believed: Malone, *Jefferson and His Time*, 3: xvii.

79. It was estimated that: Ammon, *James Monroe*, 348.

79. Jay had just been inaugurated: Monaghan, *John Jay*, 405.

79. Jay was hung: Combs, *Jay Treaty*, 162.

79. French Foreign Office: Malone, *Jefferson and His Time*, 3: 260.

79. In truth, the treaty: C. James, *Silas Deane*, 188–89.

80. "right of deposit": Malone, *Jefferson and His Time*, 3: 188.

80. Randolph protested and resigned: ibid., 263; Combs, *Jay Treaty*, 167; Ellis, *Founding Brothers*, 147; McCullough, *John Adams*, 457.

80. Charles Cotesworth Pinckney: McCullough, *John Adams*, 477.

80. Responding to the Jay Treaty: Ferling, *John Adams*, 336–39.

80. the strength to stop: McCullough, *John Adams*, 484.

80. the rumble of war: ibid., 478.

80. George Washington had announced: Ellis, *Founding Brothers*, 123.

81. John Quincy Adams: Ferling, *John Adams*, 389; Barnes and Morgan, *Foreign Service of the United States*, 113.

81. He sent to Paris: McCullough, *John Adams*, 483–85.

81. "The insults and injuries": From letter dated June 2, 1797, quoted in Malone, *Jefferson and His Time*, 3: 313.

81. On March 4, 1798: McCullough, *John Adams*, 495.

81. In June, John Marshall: ibid., 503; Malone, *Jefferson and His Time*, 3: 376–79.

81. The French Directory decreed: Malone, *Jefferson and His Time*, 3: 370.

81. French warships seized: Chernow, *Alexander Hamilton*, 553.

81. President Adams told Congress: Ferling, *John Adams*, 356.

81. the President saw himself: McCullough, *John Adams*, 500; Chernow, *Alexander Hamilton*, 553.

82. "Commander in Chief of all": Ferling, *John Adams*, 358–59.

82. Adams did not object: McCullough, *John Adams*, 504.

82. Virginia and Kentucky Resolutions: Commager, *Documents of American History*, 178–83.

82. Jefferson's assertion that the states: Chernow, *Alexander Hamilton*, 574.

82. specter of the "Quasi-War": McCullough, *John Adams*, 511–12.

82. After the XYZ insult: Malone, *Jefferson and His Time*, 3: 435.

82. "a total loss": Chernow, *Alexander Hamilton*, 599.

82. envoys shipped out: Robinson, *William R. Davie*, 332–37.

83. President became aware: Ferling, *John Adams*, 394; McCullough, *John Adams*, 539.

83. Washington City Orphan Asylum: W. Williams, *Contours of American History*, 10.

83. When Ellsworth and Davie: Robinson, *William R. Davie*, 337.

83. the proudest act: McCullough, *John Adams*, 567.

84. In its final form: Ferling, *John Adams*, 423.

84. Charles Pinckney, who had: Ferling, *John Adams*, 404.

84. Robert R. Livingston: Dangerfield, *Chancellor Robert R. Livingston of New York*, 309.

84. Lafayette welcomed Livingston: ibid., 311.

85. The dislike was mutual: Chernow, *Alexander Hamilton*, 466.

85. inventor Robert Fulton: Dangerfield, *Chancellor Robert R. Livingston of New York*, 405.

85. As Livingston settled: ibid., 340.

85. minister notify the French: ibid., 330.

86. Livingston sent a dispatch: Dangerfield, *Chancellor Robert R. Livingston of New York*, 363–65.

86. Each man was out: ibid., 365.

86. two Americans agreed: ibid., 375.

87. The treaty for Louisiana: ibid., 352–70.

87. On New Year's Day 1804: ibid., 384, 387.

87. Louisiana Purchase raised: Ellis, *Founding Brothers*, 241.

87. "The respect which one": Ammon, *James Monroe*, 235.

88. Monroe accused Livingston: ibid., 243.

88. in October, Armstrong reported: "Armstrong, John," entry in *Dictionary of American Biography*; Ammon, *James Monroe*, 244.

88. Monroe received instructions: ibid., 269.

89. Monroe went home: ibid., 270.

89. "Madison seldom left footprints": Ellis, *Founding Brothers*, 116.

89. on March 14, 1811: Ammon, *James Monroe*, 288.

89. He pressed: ibid., 297.

89. Madison's gamble led: ibid., 293.

89. His bluntness shocked: ibid.

89. Joel Barlow had been appointed: ibid., 295.

90. squeezed between the conflicting: Ammon, *James Monroe*, 298.

8: Drive for Identity and Respect: 1811–23

91. "If she wishes . . . The Russians have": Todd, *Life and Letters of Joel Barlow*, 268, 276, 278.

93. It did not matter much: P. Hill, "Who's in Charge?" (newsletter).

94. On April 1, 1812: Ammon, *James Monroe*, 305.

94. "resolved no longer": ibid., 305

95. But the French continued: ibid., 312.

95. The British minister cheerfully: ibid., 310.

95. Since the Senate felt: ibid., 315.

95. Richard Rush, son: ibid.

96. After Armstrong left Paris: C. Kennedy, *American Consul*, 48.

96. In the spring of 1813: Ammon, *James Monroe*, 319.

96. But in the end: Everett, "Eulogy on the Life and Character of John Quincy Adams."

97. On August 16, 1814: Lord, *Dawn's Early Light*, 30; Ammon, *James Monroe*, 330.

97. Stephen Pleasanton, John Graham: Lord, *Dawn's Early Light*, 73; Hunt, *Department of State*, 196.

97. They were later moved: Ammon, *James Monroe*, 197.

98. "many of the books": Clemmer, "Highlights in the Library's History."

98. Dr. William Thornton: Ammon, *James Monroe*, 334.

98. Monroe, determined, said: Lord, *Dawn's Early Light*, 203; Ammon, *James Monroe*, 335.

98. Much of the blame: "Armstrong, John," entry in *Dictionary of American Biography*.

99. The Treaty of Ghent: Lord, *Dawn's Early Light*, 317.

99. "The demonstration is satisfactory": Ammon, *James Monroe*, 344.

99. "the workshop in which": Nordholt, *Dutch Republic and American Independence*, 101.

100. "At the time of your appointment": C. Kennedy, *American Consul*, 38, 40; Goldberg, *Major Noah*, 111–12.

101. Noah left for home: ibid., 225.

101. Both sides continued: Ammon, *James Monroe*, 352.

102. Department of State numbered: Barnes and Morgan, *Foreign Service of the United States*, 81.

102. Both parts were exhaustive: ibid., 74–76.

102. Adams also reestablished: Bryson, *American Consular Officer in the Middle East*.

103. Poinsett informed the revolutionaries: Kissinger, *Age of Kennan, an American Life*, 562.

103. Only Graham spoke Spanish: Ammon, *James Monroe*, 428.

103. Much later, Jackson claimed: ibid., 417.

103. Jackson occupied Amelia Island: ibid.

104. They finally decided: ibid., 420.

104. "most important event": Quoted in Ammon, *James Monroe*, 445.

105. Both Anderson and Rodney: Robertson, "First Legations of the United States in Latin America."

105. Simon Bolivar, the "liberator": C. Kennedy, *American Consul*, 57.

106. A compromise in 1824: Ammon, *James Monroe*, 524.

106. foreign secretary, George Canning: ibid., 526.

107. "are henceforth not to": Ammon, *James Monroe*, 487–88.

107. "It seemed as if": ibid., 492.

9: An Early Professional: 1825–42

108. "amateurish foreign service": Shewmaker, "Review of *An American Consular Officer*."

109. "probably rank among": Bryson, *American Consular Officer*, 17.

109. A crowd of men: L. White, *Jacksonians*, 302; Van Buren, *Autobiography*, 231–32.

109. "wolves of the antechamber": L. White, *Jacksonians*, 303.

110. "When I left him": Van Buren, *Autobiography*, 270.

110. The United States gained: Lathrop, *Memories of Hawthorne*, 76.

110. By 1914, twenty-two consuls: Nevins, *Henry White*, 579.

111. As late as 1894: Lathrop, *Memories of Hawthorne*, 288.

111. by the 1890s: ibid., 290–91.

111. according to Dabney S. Carr: ibid., 87.

111. A noteworthy exception: ibid., 92.

111. Dr. Michael Meshaka: Bird, *Bible Work in Bible Lands*, 422.

112. These became causes célèbres: Bryson, *American Consular Officer*, 53.

112. Hodgson applied for: C. Kennedy, *American Consul*, 91.

112. "Secretary of Legation and Interpreter": Bryson, *American Consular Officer*, 60.

112. John Porter Brown: Barnes and Morgan, *Foreign Service of the United States*, 94.

113. "desires that you dissolve": Bryson, *American Consular Officer*, 78.

116. Hodgson and Margaret Telfair: C. Johnson, "William Brown Hodgson (1801–1871)," entry in *The New Georgia Encyclopedia*.

116. This experiment in professionalizing: C. Kennedy, *American Consul*, 98.

10: The Spoils System: 1829–48

117. surging spirit of expansion: LaFeber, *American Age*, 95.

117. His "rotation" began: Schlesinger, *Age of Jackson*, 46; L. White, *Jacksonians*, 5, 15.

118. "endless criminations and recriminations": U.S. Senate, Committee on Commerce, *Report Concerning Consular System*, 2.

118. "a fixed and uniform": ibid.; Barnes and Morgan, *Foreign Service of the United States*, 82.

118. Daniel Strobel, of South: C. Kennedy, *American Consul*, 74; Barnes and Morgan, *Foreign Service of the United States*, 83.

118. Strobel believed that: C. Kennedy, *American Consul*, 76; Barnes and Morgan, *Foreign Service of the United States*, 83.

118. Strobel wanted to: Barnes and Morgan, *Foreign Service of the United States*, 83.

119. To avoid an international: Van Buren, *Autobiography*, 354.

119. The Eaton affair caused: Schlesinger, *Age of Jackson*, 55; Van Buren, *Autobiography*, 375, 384, 396.

119. When Van Buren resigned: Barnes and Morgan, *Foreign Service of the United States*, 91.

119. When he differed: ibid., 91; Van Buren, *Autobiography*, 274; L. White, *Jacksonians*, 34.

120. voting against confirmation: Van Buren, *Autobiography*, 453; Schlesinger, *Age of Jackson*, 55.

120. "His Majesty also took": Van Buren, *Autobiography*, 457.

120. Aaron Vail, who had succeeded: Barnes and Morgan, *Foreign Service of the United States*, 91.

120. U.S. minister to Spain: ibid., 92; White, *Jacksonians*, 107.

120. "the worst consular system": C. Kennedy, *American Consul*, 76.

120. Among the duties stated: Barnes and Morgan, *Foreign Service of the United States*, 78.

121. Services for which: C. Kennedy, *American Consul*, 76.

121. responsibilities to report: Barnes and Morgan, *Foreign Service of the United States*, 80.

121. "According to the present": Barnes and Morgan, *Foreign Service of the United States*, 84; Select Committee to Report on the Consular System of the United States, *Report No. 714*, House of Representatives, 2.

121. "customs alone produce": Select Committee to Report on the Consular System, H. Rep. 714, 2.

121. President sent Livingston's report: Select Committee to Report on the Consular System, H. Rep. 714, 1; Barnes and Morgan, *Foreign Service of the United States*, 85.

121. "If the mission is": Barnes and Morgan, *Foreign Service of the United States*, 86–88.

122. in April 1838: Fuess, *Daniel Webster*, 29.

122. James Fenimore Cooper: C. Kennedy, *American Consul*, 73.

122. Nathaniel Hawthorne was: C. Kennedy, *American Consul*, 81.

123. Hawthorne was pleased: Barnes and Morgan, *Foreign Service of the United States*, 100, from Nathaniel Hawthorne, *The English Notebooks* (New York: Modern Language Association of America, 1941), 3.

123. old-fashioned American barbershop: Barnes and Morgan, *Foreign Service of the United States*, 101.

123. "For a man": Quoted in Barnes and Morgan, *Foreign Service of the United States*, 104.

123. James Buchanan, opened: C. Kennedy, *American Consul*, 82.

123. Hawthorne took pleasure: ibid., 83.

123. John M. Marston: ibid., 79.

123. William S. Sparks: ibid., 80.

123. Consul Joseph Binda: ibid.

124. Papal States in 1848: Nicholson, *United States and the Holy See*, 17–18.

124. first time a Pope: Nicholson, *United States and the Holy See*, 19–20;

125. undergo "radical changes . . . that while in the faithful": Select Committee to Report on the Consular System, H. Rep. 714, 1, 4, 8.

125. this bill died: Barnes and Morgan, *Foreign Service of the United States*, 86.

11: Expansion Westward: 1821–45

126. David G. Burnet: C. Kennedy, *American Consul*, 59–60.

127. "The great, fundamental": Fuess, *Daniel Webster*, 146.

127. Hawaii and the Pacific Ocean: Keliher, "Anglo-American Rivalry," 253.

127. "few calamities could": Storey, *Charles Sumner*, 42.

127. John C. Calhoun: Sellers, *James K. Polk, Continentalist*, 56.

127. in 1845, Congress passed: McCoy, *Polk and the Presidency*, 88; Larson, *In the Garden of Beasts*, 158.

128. Parrott and Jones were four: Moskin, *U.S. Marine Corps Story*, 61; C. Kennedy, *American Consul*, 61.

128. William A. Leidesdorff: C. Kennedy, *American Consul*, 62, 102, 242.

128. On October 11, 1845: Sellers, *James K. Polk, Continentalist*, 333.

129. "if the people": from letter dated October 17, 1845, in Sellers, *James K. Polk, Continentalist*, 334; also see LaFeber, *American Age*, 115; Connor and Faulk, *North America Divided*, 22.

129. Between 1830 and 1860: Barnes and Morgan, *Foreign Service of the United States*, 69–70.

129. Consular posts fanned out: C. Kennedy, *American Consul*, 71, 73.

129. In Africa, John Elmslie: ibid., 102.

129. United States bumped up: Keliher, "Anglo-American Rivalry," 228.

129. Samuel Simpson tried: C. Kennedy, *American Consul*, 103.

130. Havana, followed by Liverpool: Barnes and Morgan, *Foreign Service of the United States*, 97.

130. Its highly critical report: ibid., 86.

130. Consuls in Chinese ports: 30th cong., 1st sess., August 11, 1848, cited in C. Kennedy, *American Consul*, 112.

130. It was a primitive: Kennedy, *American Consul*, 117.

130. Consul Peter A. Brinsmade: ibid., 105.

130. Charles Bunker, of Nantucket: ibid., 106.

131. Terranova was found guilty: ibid., 108, citing Foster Rhea Dulles, *China and America: The Story of Their Relations Since 1784* (Westport, CT: Greenwood Press, 1981).

131. Caleb Cushing, of Massachusetts: Keliher, "Anglo-American Rivalry," 249.

131. the Treaty of Wanghai: LaFeber, *American Age*, 103; Barnes and Morgan, *Foreign Service of the United States*, 96.

132. He was acquitted: C. Kennedy, *American Consul*, 110, citing Dulles, *China and America*, 28

132. Fook li had the arrow: C. Kennedy, *American Consul*, 110.

132. charge of the State Department: Sellers, *James K. Polk, Continentalist*, 160, 184, 194, 214.

132. Secretary of State opposed: McCoy, *Polk and the Presidency*, 67.

132. "sometimes acts like": McCoy, *Polk and the Presidency*, 69.

132. "I need rest": From a letter dated November 18, 1844, in Sellers, *James K. Polk, Continentalist,* 272n14.

132. the "joint occupation": Sellers, *James K. Polk, Continentalist,* 235.

133. One problem was: ibid., 314.

133. He would play: ibid., 375.

133. Polk pointed out: McCoy, *Polk and the Presidency,* 72.

133. "I thought it was": Sellers, *James K. Polk, Continentalist,* 303; McCoy, *Polk and the Presidency,* 84–85.

133. fall of 1845: Sellers, *James K. Polk, Continentalist,* 357.

133. "by the prudence": From a letter dated December 2, 1845, quoted in ibid., 358.

134. But Polk was convinced: Sellers, *James K. Polk, Continentalist,* 369; Larson, *In the Garden of Beasts,* 229.

134. Ambassador McLane sensed: Sellers, *James K. Polk, Continentalist,* 382.

134. Andrew Jackson Donelson: ibid., 70; Barnes and Morgan, *Foreign Service of the United States,* 95.

134. spring of 1845: Sellers, *James K. Polk, Continentalist,* 225.

134. Donelson convinced Texas's secretary: ibid., 225–26.

134. General Zachary Taylor brought: ibid., 262.

135. The Senate ratified it: Fuess, *Daniel Webster,* 160; McCoy, *Polk and the Presidency,* 92–93.

135. Meanwhile, in case: Sellers, *James K. Polk, Continentalist,* 227; McCoy, *Polk and the Presidency,* 94.

12: War with Mexico: 1845–46

136. Congressman John Slidell, of Louisiana: Sellers, *James K. Polk, Continentalist,* 95, 336.

136. Polk wrote Slidell: ibid., 338.

136. "so feeble and degraded": ibid., 398.

136. Foreign Minister Manuel Pea: ibid.

136. "the Polk-Slidell policy": ibid., 400.

137. Because Mexican cavalry: C. Kennedy, *American Consul,* 66; Larson, *In the Garden of Beasts,* 241–42.

137. Polk signed the declaration: Connor and Faulk, *North America Divided,* 31, 38.

137. "all the powers": McCoy, *Polk and the Presidency,* 97.

137. U.S. Navy then "seized": Connor and Faulk, *North America Divided,* 87.

138. In January 1847: Moskin, *U.S. Marine Corps Story,* 63; Connor and Faulk, *North America Divided,* 93.

138. The question for Dimond: Polk, *Diary of James K. Polk,* 2: 179–180; McCoy, *Polk and the Presidency,* 125.

138. Dimond made a sketch: Polk, *Diary of James K. Polk,* 2: 195–97.

138. Congressman David Wilmot: Sellers, *James K. Polk, Continentalist,* 480.

138. The House narrowly passed: Connor and Faulk, *North America Divided,* 145.

138. The Whigs removed him: ibid., 160.

139. General Scott's army conquered: ibid, 130.

139. United States gained California: LaFeber, *American Age,* 212; Connor and Faulk, *North America Divided,* 168.

139. "to make war": LaFeber, *American Age,* 125.

140. basis of "popular sovereignty": LaFeber, *American Age,* 122.

140. The Bidlack-Mallarino Treaty: ibid., 124.

13: Consular Reform: 1853–65

141. "I believe that involuntary servitude": Pierce, Inaugural Address March 4, 1853.
141. organization called Young America: LaFeber, *American Age,* 133.
141. "wresting it from Spain": 33rd Cong., 2nd sess., House Executive Doc. No. 93, in Commager, *Documents of American History,* 333–35.
141. Northerners condemned this: LaFeber, *American Age,* 134; Barnes and Morgan, *Foreign Service of the United States,* 95.
142. the telegraph "decoupled": Howe, "What Hath God Wrought."
142. These advances in communication: Barnes and Morgan, *Foreign Service of the United States,* 80, 106.
142. Consular Reform Act: "An Act to Remodel the Diplomatic and Consular Systems of the United States," 34th Cong., 2nd sess., chapter 133, 1855, 619–26.
142. "If the President shall": "An Act to regulate the Diplomatic and Consular Systems of the United States," 34th Cong., 1st sess., chapter 127, 1856, 52.
142. This law directed: Barnes and Morgan, *Foreign Service of the United States,* 107; Hunt, *Department of State,* 334.
143. "the President will then": H. Adams, "Civil-Service Reform," 464.
143. to issue passports: Hunt, *Department of State,* 352.
143. large personnel turnover: C. Kennedy, *American Consul,* 83–84; Hunt, *Department of State,* 334; Barnes and Morgan, *Foreign Service of the United States,* 118.
143. Such inadequate salaries: Barnes and Morgan, *Foreign Service of the United States,* 121–22.
143. But provisions for salary: ibid., 123.
144. Patriotism for holidays: Emerson, *Journals* May–June 1846.

14: Japan's First American Consul: 1856–62

146. Harris was impressive: C. Kennedy, *American Consul,* 119.
146. Then, within hours: Shaw, *Journals of Major Samuel Shaw,* 77; C. Kennedy, *American Consul,* 119.
147. letter from the President: Shaw, *Journals of Major Samuel Shaw,* 160.
147. "attending seamen when they": Shaw, *Journals of Major Samuel Shaw,* 388; C. Kennedy, *American Consul,* 122.
148. Finally, the bearers entered: Shaw, *Journals of Major Samuel Shaw,* 534.
148. the crisis passed: Statler, *Shimoda Story,* 546.
148. July 29, 1858: Barnes and Morgan, *Foreign Service of the United States,* 97.

15: The Nation at War with Itself: 1861–65

150. President Jefferson Davis: Battle, Perrin, and Kniffin, "Charles J. Helm."
150. John T. Pickett: C. Kennedy, *American Consul,* 129.
151. Other consuls who joined: ibid.
151. Venice was surely: "America and the Holocaust," *The American Experience,* PBS. org.
151. William H. Seward: Taylor, *William Henry Seward,* 127.
151. "there is one part of my work: Goodwin *Team of Rivals,* 316.
151. "Governor Denied, there is : ibid.
151. Senator Charles Sumner: Storey, *Charles Sumner,* 189.
151. He believed the Union: ibid., 205.
151. The staff consisted of: Taylor, *William Henry Seward,* 142.

152. "from a state": Charles Francis Adams, "An Address on the Life, Character and Services of William H. Seaward" (1873), quoted in Barnes and Morgan, *Foreign Service of the United States,* 113.

152. "A Congressional delegation": Van Dyke, *Our Foreign Service,* 63.

153. "Very kind of you": Duberman, *Charles Francis Adams,* 257; Taylor, *William Henry Seward,* 143.

153. Charles Francis Adams was, it is fair: Roberts and Roberts, *Thomas Barclay,* 50.

153. He despised slavery: Duberman, *Charles Francis Adams,* 61.

154. "I am thankful": Duberman, *Charles Francis Adams,* 471n11.

154. But ever cautious: ibid., 267.

154. Adams had a minimal: Thayer, *Life and Letters of John Hay,* 1: 300; Roberts and Roberts, *Thomas Barclay,* 138.

154. Benjamin Moran, the Assistant: Duberman, *Charles Francis Adams,* 263.

154. Freeman H. Morse: C. Kennedy, *American Consul,* 136.

154. Henry S. Sanford: Duberman, *Charles Francis Adams,* 474 n. 52; 241.

155. most valuable propaganda coup: Clapp, *Forgotten First Citizen,* 159.

156. The British accepted: Duberman, *Charles Francis Adams,* 283.

156. Senator Sumner brought in: Storey, *Charles Sumner,* 222.

156. In February 1862: Milne, "Documents: The Lyons-Seward Treaty," 516; Dangerfield, *Chancellor Robert R. Livingston of New York,* 312.

156. With representatives from slaveholding: Goose, "'As a Nation, the English Are Our Friends,'" 1011.

156. Adams told Russell: Milne, "Documents: The Lyons-Seward Treaty," 517.

156. Under the Lyons-Seward: Storey, *Charles Sumner,* 223; Bancroft, *Life of William H. Seward,* 2: 344–45; C. Henderson, "Anglo-American Treaty," 308–19.

156. number of slaves brought: Milne, "Documents: The Lyons-Seward Treaty," 156.

157. Seward wrote Adams: E. Adams, *Great Britain and the American Civil War,* 275.

157. Seward took no action: Taylor, *William Henry Seward,* 190.

157. He no longer wanted: ibid., 216.

157. "For those fascinated": Goodwin, *Team of Rivals,* 599.

157. Mrs. H. S. Eggleston: Abernathy, "Commercial Activities of Silas Deane in France," 41.

158. George Perkins Marsh: D. Lowenthal, *George Perkins Marsh,* 235.

158. Renamed the CSS *Florida*: Duberman, *Charles Francis Adams,* 478n92; C. Kennedy, *American Consul,* 133, 139.

158. Captain James Dunwody Bulloch: C. Kennedy, *American Consul,* 137; Taylor, *William Henry Seward,* 166; Auchincloss, *Theodore Roosevelt,* 10; *Intelligence in the Civil War,* Office of Public Affairs, Central Intelligence Agency.

158. James De Long: Barnes and Morgan, *Foreign Service of the United States,* 117.

158. Henry Hotze, a former: Central Intelligence Agency, Office of Public Affairs, *Intelligence in the Civil War.*

159. "it dates the commencement": From letter dated April 4, 1862, in E. Adams, *Great Britain and the American Civil War,* 276.

159. "It would be superfluous": Quoted in Duberman, *Charles Francis Adams,* 311; also see Storey, *Charles Sumner,* 243; C. Kennedy, *American Consul,* 135; Taylor, *William Henry Seward,* 218.

159. "insolent threats of war"" From letter to Russell dated September 22, 1863, in Duberman, *Charles Francis Adams,* 314n53.

159. one final exposure: C. Kennedy, *American Consul,* 138.

160. That August, he announced: Barnes and Morgan, *Foreign Service of the United States,* 117.

160. As a lawyer: Clapp, *Forgotten First Citizen,* 58.

160. biography of John Charles Fremont: ibid., 107.

160. "If most of them": From *Evening Post* article dated May 25, 1853, quoted in ibid., 149.

160. The Bigelows settled: Clapp, *Forgotten First Citizen,* 154.

161. Lincoln and Seward dissuaded: ibid., 188.

161. Archduke Maximilian of Austria: Taylor, *William Henry Seward,* 230.

161. Bigelow assured him: Clapp, *Forgotten First Citizen,* 257.

161. Mexican firing squad executed: Taylor, *William Henry Seward,* 270.

162. Slidell was the more: Clapp, *Forgotten First Citizen,* 171.

162. He lost the lawsuit: ibid., 202.

163. Bigelow had the French: ibid.

163. George Perkins Marsh: D. Lowenthal, "Sabre-rattling American Intervention" (online review).

163. "the character of": D. Lowenthal, *George Perkins Marsh,* 230.

163. lengthy, thoughtful report: Clapp, *Forgotten First Citizen,* 219.

163. "I am quite convinced . . . the lawful spoils": Bigelow, "Consular System of the United States" (unpublished), 3; quotes from letter dated March 3, 1864, in Clapp, *Forgotten First Citizen.*

163. "It is not too": Bigelow, "Consular System of the United States" (unpublished), 34.

164. "Dayton died, supposedly": C. Kennedy, *American Consul,* 137; Clapp, *Forgotten First Citizen,* 220.

164. Bigelow expected to become: Clapp, *Forgotten First Citizen,* 240.

16: Public Trust, Private Property: 1866–85

166. President Johnson opened Alaskan: Pletcher, *Diplomacy of Involvement,* 38.

166. Baron Stoeckl helped: Nevins, *Hamilton Fish,* 251.

166. the baron kept $165,000: Taylor, *William Henry Seward,* 281.

166. rejected Seward's treaty: Pletcher, *Diplomacy of Involvement,* 68.

166. But Colombia's senate: Taylor, *William Henry Seward,* 280.

166. so Adams resigned: Nevins, *Hamilton Fish,* 553.

166. "wise discretion and cool": February 29, 1868, in Duberman, *Charles Francis Adams,* 330.

166. chose Hamilton Fish: Nevins, *Hamilton Fish,* 905.

167. Hunter had entered: ibid., 140, 863.

167. Sizable numbers of American: Alley, "Jim Felt Lucky," 414–17.

167. Fish proposed that all: Nevins, *Hamilton Fish,* 425.

167. Joint High Commission: ibid., 438, 442.

167. "the dingy quarters . . . the first great arbitration": ibid., 446, 448.

167. The treaty of Washington: ibid., 475–91.

168. sought the German and Swiss: ibid., 555.

168. John Meredith Read: ibid.

168. form of "public diplomacy": ibid., 520.

168. "indirect claims" were dropped: ibid., 550.

168. In 1865, American adventurers: ibid., 260.

168. Secretary Fish, no imperialist: ibid., 137, 216.

169. Grant called it: ibid., 268.

169. He even predicted: Storey, *Charles Sumner,* 345.

169. Major Raymond H. Perry: Nevins, *Hamilton Fish,* 276.

169. Babcock went back: ibid., 275–78.

169. And many Americans worried: ibid., 320.

169. But President Grant, appearing: ibid., 328.

169. Senator Sumner, loyal: ibid., 157.

169. he wanted to please: ibid.

169. In London, Motley, echoing: ibid., 161.

169. Benjamin Moran, the secretary: ibid., 205.

170. When Fish showed them: ibid.

170. Fish pleaded for leniency: ibid., 372–73.

170. very popular in London: ibid., 375.

170. State Department had to: ibid., 383.

170. poker to the "fast set": Dana, *Hospitable England in the Seventies,* 60.

170. In 1876, he resigned: Barnes and Morgan, *Foreign Service of the United States,* 138; Nevins, *Hamilton Fish,* 814.

170. attorney general, Edwards Pierrepont: Nevins, *Hamilton Fish,* 831.

170. Frederick Douglass, the African-American: ibid., 497.

170. Spanish island of Cuba: ibid., 177.

171. A landing party: ibid., 198.

171. wrote Fish that peaceful: ibid., 337.

171. Phillips protested and received: C. Kennedy, *American Consul,* 163.

171. When the governor said: Nevins, *Hamilton Fish,* 341; C. Kennedy, *American Consul,* 164.

171. Fish proposed an armistice: Nevins, *Hamilton Fish,* 302.

171. Fish instructed Sickles: ibid., 624.

171. "a marked change": ibid., 626.

172. Unknown to Fish: ibid., 635.

172. Fish reported these atrocities: ibid., 670–73.

173. Vice Consul Schmitt wisely brought: C. Kennedy, *American Consul,* 164–68.

173. The brutal Spanish military: ibid., 168.

173. The cantankerous Sickles: *Dictionary of American Biography.*

173. Cushing was a respected: *American National Biography.*

173. "the terrible evil": From Fish's letter dated December 24, 1873, in Nevins, *Hamilton Fish,* 694.

173. one of his grandsons: Nevins, *Hamilton Fish,* 916.

173. post–Civil War period: ibid., 639.

173. "convert a sacred public": H. Adams, "Civil-Service Reform," 450.

173. Grant should be applauded: ibid., 452.

174. Michael J. Cramer, Grant's brother-in-law: Barnes and Morgan, *Foreign Service of the United States,* 134.

174. Secretary Fish had to: Nevins, *Hamilton Fish,* 656.

174. Edward Rumsey Wing: Donald, *Lincoln,* 731.

174. notorious uncle, Ben Butler: Nevins, *Hamilton Fish,* 585.

174. Congress cut the number: Barnes and Morgan, *Foreign Service of the United States,* 131.

174. reorganized the department: ibid., 132.

174. given no training: C. Kennedy, *American Consul,* 146.

174. saddled with diverse responsibilities: ibid., 145.

175. "a minister of the": ibid., 150; Stillman, *Autobiography of a Journalist,* 1: 284.

17: The Long Bumpy Road to Professionalism: 1864–97

176. "I have only to": C. Kennedy, *American Consul,* 148; 687.

176. Few American ministers: Pletcher, *Diplomacy of Involvement,* 118.

176. In 1906, Congress created: *Diplomatic History,* vol. 27, no. 3.

177. S. Wells Williams: Pletcher, *Diplomacy of Involvement*, 107.

177. basis for importing Chinese: Taylor, *William Henry Seward*, 280.

177. died of pneumonia: *American National Biography*; also in Pletcher, *Diplomacy of Involvement*, 110.

177. Chinese government then bought: Pletcher, *Diplomacy of Involvement*, 139.

178. Vice Consul William N. Pethick: ibid.

178. The earliest trade: Griffis, *Corea, the Hermit Nation*.

178. treaty with Korea: Pletcher, *Diplomacy of Involvement*, 187.

178. Lucius H. Foote: ibid., 189.

179. In 1905, the United States: ibid., 222.

179. "Laura Stillman is one": C. Kennedy, *American Consul*, 153.

179. Despite Stillman's admirable record: ibid.

180. "The United States, knowing": ibid., 155.

180. Ottoman envoy in Washington: *Dictionary of American Biography*.

180. Secretary Fish finally spoke: Barnes and Morgan, *Foreign Service of the United States*, 138; Nevins, *Hamilton Fish*, 727.

180. Grant's "kitchen cabinet": Nevins, *Hamilton Fish*, 735, 761.

181. Grant gave Fish: ibid., 738.

181. Thus, Fish was able: Barnes and Morgan, *Foreign Service of the United States*, 139; Nevins, *Hamilton Fish*, 862.

181. Elihu Washburne had: Dana, *Hospitable England in the Seventies*, 153.

181. friends with Lincoln and Grant: *Dictionary of American Biography*.

181. Franco-Prussian War of 1870–71: Nevins, *Hamilton Fish*, 404.

181. Washburne was the only: Nevins, *Hamilton Fish*, 405; Barnes and Morgan, *Foreign Service of the United States*, 135–36.

181. "Washburne is entitled": Nevins, *Hamilton Fish*, 406.

181. "is removed to make . . . whether the entire diplomatic": *Report from the Joint Select Committee on Retrenchment*, Senate, 1–3, 17–18.

182. "Almost every consulate": From Keim's report, quoted in C. Kennedy, *American Consul*, 172.

183. "an utterly hopeless inebriate": ibid., 176.

183. From Cuba, Tweed and: Nevins, *Hamilton Fish*, 840–41, 649, 687.

184. By 1875, Secretary Fish: ibid., 785.

184. Grant vouched for: ibid., 794–803.

184. President Rutherford B. Hayes: ibid., 838.

184. "a tribute to the dominion": Henry James, Essay in London, 45.

185. Anthony M. Keiley: Barnes and Morgan, *Foreign Service of the United States*, 140–41.

185. "untenable and intolerable": Denza, *Diplomatic Law*, 38.

185. President Cleveland left: Barnes and Morgan, *Foreign Service of the United States*, 142.

185. American consul, Selah Merrill: *New York Times*, January 23, 1898.

185. in Jerusalem since 1856: Lathrop, *Memories of Hawthorne*, 52.

185. between 1882 to 1907: Goldman, "Holy Land Appropriated."

185. At the sultan's request: Straus, *Under Four Administrations*, 96.

185. "Had diplomacy been": Straus, *Letters 1888–1889* (online), entry for May 18, 1889.

185. "I only regret one": ibid.; "Hirsch, Solomon."

186. across the Pacific: Pletcher, *Diplomacy of Involvement*, 77.

186. harbor at Pago Pago: ibid., 82.

186. "A young man": Stevenson, *Footnote to History*, 42.

186. Shortly after Sewall arrived: ibid., 34.

187. Sewall was the only: Pletcher, *Diplomacy of Involvement*, 87.

187. "On the whole": From letter dated August 4, 1891, in ibid., 67; see also ibid., 76.

187. John S. Mosby: Nevins, *Hamilton Fish*, 393.

187. In 1876, Colonel Mosby: ibid., 844; see also *Dictionary of American Biography*.

188. David H. Bailey: Siepel, *Rebel*, 208.

188. George F. Seward: C. Kennedy, *American Consul*, 180.

188. George Seward be impeached: *Dictionary of American Biography*.

188. This became a public: Siepel, *Rebel*, 221.

188. "The women who get": ibid., 235–36.

189. In 1885, President Cleveland: C. Kennedy, *American Consul*, 178–82.

189. Charles J. Guiteau: *American National Biography*.

189. commercial information from abroad: Lathrop, *Memories of Hawthorne*, 49; W. Williams, *Contours of American History*, 82; Hunt, *Department of State*, 235.

190. Bureau of Trade Relations: Werking, *Master Architects*, 87; Hunt, *Department of State*, 238.

190. Essentially, the State Department: Werking, *Master Architects*, 200.

190. Office of Foreign Trade: ibid., 215.

190. He protested to the State Department: D. Lowenthal, *George Perkins Marsh*, 116.

190. the President could designate: Barnes and Morgan, *Foreign Service of the United States*, 146.

191. influential magazine *The Century*: "Consular Service and the Spoils System."

191. "goes to the wall . . . We have been well": ibid., 307, 309.

192. held in March 1896: Barnes and Morgan, *Foreign Service of the United States*, 150; C. Kennedy, *American Consul*, 178; Werking, *Master Architects*.

192. At this stage, reform: Leech, *In the Days of McKinley*, 139.

18: First Steps to Empire: 1898–99

195. Robert L. Beisner: Katzenbach, *Some of It Was Fun*, 33.

195. "ambivalent about the use": ibid., 37.

195. The new paradigm: ibid., 88.

195. Under this change: ibid., 90.

195. surge of American population: ibid., 74.

195. "a frontier of export": ibid., 76.

195. This early venture: ibid., 105.

196. David L. Gregg: Zimmermann, *First Great Triumph*, 285.

196. At first, the rivalry: Pletcher, *Diplomacy of Involvement*, 46.

196. Now, Hawaiian sugar: Zimmermann, *First Great Triumph*, 286.

196. John L. Stevens: Kinzer, *Overthrow*, 17, 30.

197. McKinley Tariff of 1890: Pletcher, *Diplomacy of Involvement*, 235.

197. succeeded by his sister Queen Liliuokalani: Kinzer, *Overthrow*, 9.

197. led by Sanford Dole: Blount, *Report of U.S. Special Commissioner James H. Blount*, 44.

197. Stevens made it clear: Kinzer, *Overthrow*, 28.

197. The next day: Coffman, *Nation Within*, 122; Kinzer, *Overthrow*, 29.

197. "to the superior force": Blount, *Report of U.S. Special Commissioner James H. Blount*, 29.

197. Blount declared that Stevens: Coffman, *Nation Within*, 142.

197. Henry Cabot Lodge: Zimmermann, *First Great Triumph*, 150.

197. "a substantial wrong": *Dictionary of American Bibliography*.

198. In a brief fight: Coffman, *Nation Within*, 235.

198. Queen Liliuokalani was arrested: ibid., 176.

198. Harold M. Sewall: ibid., 225.

198. On June 12, 1897: Coffman, *Nation Within,* 250, 256; Pletcher, *Diplomacy of Involvement,* 249–50.

198. The surprise treaty: Coffman, *Nation Within,* 257.

198. Queen Liliuokalani warned: ibid., 286.

199. Congress gave the Hawaiians: Zimmermann, *First Great Triumph,* 445.

199. "imperialism in its purest": ibid., 292.

199. Fitzhugh Lee, the bearded: Kellbach, "Maj. Gen. Fitzhugh Lee (1835–1905)," Spanish American War Centennial Web site.

199. On January 24: Leech, *In the Days of McKinley,* 164.

200. "want peace": Swanberg, *Citizen Hearst,* 143.

200. February 15, *Maine* exploded: Leech, *In the Days of McKinley,* 167. (According to Zimmermann, *First Great Triumph,* 233, 358, the number of casualties was 268.)

200. "claws under his gloves": Poncet, "U.S. Ambassador to Spain: Stewart L. Woodford."

200. The Spanish government retorted: Leech, *In the Days of McKinley,* 181.

200. Congress, on April 19: ibid., 189.

200. Two days later: Poncet, "U.S. Ambassador to Spain: Stewart L. Woodford."

200. McKinley ordered a blockade: Leech, *In the Days of McKinley,* 191.

201. Oscar F. Williams: C. Kennedy, *American Consul,* 198–99; 318.

201. cabled Consul Rounsevelle Wildman: ibid., 203; Zimmermann, *First Great Triumph,* 303; Pletcher, *Diplomacy of Involvement,* 276.

201. "Hong Kong McCulloch Wildman": Leech, *In the Days of McKinley,* 209.

202. E. Spencer Pratt: Zimmermann, *First Great Triumph,* 303; C. Kennedy, *American Consul,* 202–03.

202. "Tell Aguinaldo to come": C. Kennedy, *American Consul,* 202.

202. Aguinaldo rallied the Filipinos: Couttie, "War in the Philippines" (online).

202. Wildman supplied them: C. Kennedy, *American Consul,* 204.

202. Aguinaldo thought he had: Zimmermann, *First Great Triumph,* 304.

202. lost at sea: C. Kennedy, *American Consul,* 206.

202. On May 12: Leech, *In the Days of McKinley,* 219.

203. Teddy Roosevelt, who had surrendered: Auchincloss, *Theodore Roosevelt,* 11.

203. Philip C. Hanna: Kinzer, *Overthrow,* 44.

203. "rattle the Sultan's windows": Straus, *Under Four Administrations,* 124.

203. McKinley replaced Angell: ibid., 125, 128.

203. the press speculated: ibid., 127.

204. it took years: ibid., 142.

204. "As the Government": ibid., 145.

204. The Americans promised: Straus, *Under Four Administrations,* 146.

204. "If old Dewey": Leech, *In the Days of McKinley,* 323.

204. "the consent of the governed": Zimmermann, *First Great Triumph,* 236.

205. Fighting broke out: Couttie, "War in the Philippines" (online).

205. The prevailing attitude was: Zimmermann, *First Great Triumph,* 37.

205. The opponents of imperialism: Beisner, *Twelve Against Empire,* 224.

205. "a war of deliverance": ibid., 26.

205. The imperialists asserted: ibid., 231.

19: Three Diplomatic Friends: 1898–1905

207. Greeley lost badly: Duncan, *Whitelaw Reid,* 49.

207. William M. Evarts: ibid., 75.

207. "Going into diplomacy": Cortissoz, *Life of Whitelaw Reid,* 127.

208. French imports of American pork: Duncan, *Whitelaw Reid,* 124.

208. Reid's *Tribune* simply predicted: ibid., 144.

208. Seward made Hay: Thayer, *Life and Letters of John Hay,* 1: 280.

209. "that kicked over": Kluger, *Paper,* 154; O'Toole, *Five of Hearts,* 44.

209. President McKinley appointed Hay: Zimmermann, *First Great Triumph,* 83.

209. Henry White and American-born: Nevins, *Henry White,* 123; O'Toole, *Five of Hearts,* 289.

209. "I detest war": From letter to Thomas Stanton dated May 8, 1898, in Thayer, *Life and Letters of John Hay,* 2: 167.

209. when Queen Victoria seated: O'Toole, *Five of Hearts,* 293.

209. "It gives me exceptional": Thayer, *Life and Letters of John Hay,* 2: 173; O'Toole, *Five of Hearts,* 301.

210. "No serious statesman": Thayer, *Life and Letters of John Hay,* 2: 174.

210. Alvey A. Adee: W. Williams, *Contours of American History,* 41.

210. "quacking falsetto voice": Leech, *In the Days of McKinley,* 152.

210. "Our entering wedge": Gibson, *Hugh Gibson,* 75.

210. "the greatest Secretary": From letter dated February 18, 1910, in Roosevelt, *Letters,* 7: 48; also see Auchincloss, *Theodore Roosevelt,* 115.

212. nation's best-ever secretary of war: Ginsburgh, "Between War and Peace" (Ph.D. diss.), 224.

20: Practicing Imperialism: 1898–1905

213. October 1, 1898: Duncan, *Whitelaw Reid,* 124.

213. "with so large a half-breed": From an undated letter to McKinley, in Cortissoz, *Life of Whitelaw Reid,* 215.

214. Reid's cause was wrecked: Duncan, *Whitelaw Reid,* 198.

214. Emilio Aguinaldo led the struggle: Leech, *In the Days of McKinley,* 359.

214. "the muddle produced": ibid., 336.

214. The fighting was marked: Zimmermann, *First Great Triumph,* 405–07.

214. McKinley wanted: ibid., 387.

214. "the precise, arrogant": Leech, *In the Days of McKinley,* 406.

214. William Howard Taft: Zimmermann, *First Great Triumph,* 390.

215. Major Littleton Waller Tazewell: E. Morris, *Theodore Rex,* 99; Moskin, *U.S. Marine Corps Story,* 95.

215. "a howling wilderness": Zimmermann, *First Great Triumph,* 408–09.

215. "There is a moral": From Root's letter to Jessup dated September 20, 1930, in Jessup, *Elihu Root,* 1: 345.

215. Fourth of July 1902: Pletcher, *Diplomacy of Involvement,* 390.

215. During the decade after: Barnes and Morgan, *Foreign Service of the United States,* 154–55.

215. The consular corps: Zimmermann, *First Great Triumph,* 421.

216. White reached his post: Hendrick, *Life and Letters of Walter H. Page,* 77.

216. Phelps moved the legation: ibid., 82.

216. he and White pressed Congress: Nevins, *Henry White,* 63.

216. He devoted his new: Barnes and Morgan, *Foreign Service of the United States,* 145; Nevins, *Henry White,* 103.

216. "the present system . . . Consular Debauch": White, "Consular Reforms," 711, 712.

216. White was also appalled: ibid., 714.

217. White wanted to follow the British: ibid., 716.

217. "the absolute necessity . . . most of our diplomatic": ibid., 717, 718, 721.

217. "disgraceful . . . see much of": From letter to Mrs. White dated May 8, 1896, in Nevins, *Henry White,* 111, 112.
217. Boston Chamber of Commerce: Werking, *Master Architects,* 32.
218. By 1900, Senator Lodge: Zimmermann, *First Great Triumph,* 422.
218. The Lodge-Burton bill: Werking, *Master Architects,* 66.
219. "an exhibition of craven": From letter dated March 18, 1900, in Nevins, *Henry White,* 150.
219. Joseph H. Choate: Zimmermann, *First Great Triumph,* 449.
219. second Hay-Pauncefote Treaty: Leech, *In the Days of McKinley,* 513; Nevins, *Henry White,* 159.
220. in 1893 as chief: Barnes and Morgan, *Foreign Service of the United States,* 145.
220. In September, Secretary Hay: Dennett, *John Hay,* 292; Varg, *Open Door Diplomat,* 36.
221. "The truth is": Dennett, *John Hay,* 294.
221. "I would rather": From letter dated November 21, 1900, in Thayer, *Life and Letters of John Hay,* 2: 248.
221. Consul William Pethick: *New York Times,* December 21, 1901.
221. Although Rockhill doubted: Leech, *In the Days of McKinley,* 518–19.
221. In Peking the situation: Thayer, *Life and Letters of John Hay,* 2: 239.
222. When Conger went: Varg, *Open Door Diplomat,* 46.
222. "We have killed ten": Nevins, *Henry White,* 173.
222. "I notice that": Fitzpatrick, "Collapse of American Public Diplomacy," 2.
223. "I know of no": Leech, *In the Days of McKinley,* 526.
223. at Hay's suggestion: Jessup, *Elihu Root,* 1: 388.
223. After the Russo-Japanese War: Varg, *Open Door Diplomat,* 86.
224. his first loves: ibid., 125.
225. issue ended peacefully: ibid., 370–73; Phillips, *Ventures in Diplomacy,* 12.
225. "which every friend": Thayer, *Life and Letters of John Hay,* 2: 19; E. Morris, *Theodore Rex,* 239–40.
226. USS *Nashville* showed up: Zimmermann, *First Great Triumph,* 433.
226. "Uprising occurred tonight": Quoted in E. Morris, *Theodore Rex,* 289.
226. hundreds of U.S. Marines: Moskin, *U.S. Marine Corps Story,* 152.
226. The treaty contained: O'Toole, *Five of Hearts,* 370.
226. General Rafael Reyes: Zimmermann, *First Great Triumph,* 434; Thayer, *Life and Letters of John Hay,* 2: 319.
226. "I have a complaint": Thayer, *Life and Letters of John Hay,* 2: 319.
226. "a small body": *Diplomatic History,* vol. 35, n. 1, p. 55.
226. activist president was "liberating": E. Morris, *Theodore Rex,* 243.
227. Malay Hamid el Raisuli: in E. Morris, *Theodore Rex,* 324, the name given as Ahmed ben Mohammed el Raisuli.
227. Hay commended Gummer: Barnes and Morgan, *Foreign Service of the United States,* 183.
227. Lloyd C. Griscom: Schulzinger, *Making of the Diplomatic Mind,* 22.
227. "the liberal and progressive": From letter to Lodge, dated February 2, 1916, in Jessup, *Elihu Root,* 2: 7; see also E. Morris, *Theodore Rex,* 400.
228. "twisting the rope": From letters of Hay III, quoted in O'Toole, *Five of Hearts,* 320.
228. They would never see: Nevins, *Henry White,* 244.
228. "My doctor here says": Quoted in Thayer, *Life and Letters of John Hay,* 2. 101.
228. he died there: Thayer, *Life and Letters of John Hay,* 2: 409.
229. "so much to raise": From *New York Times,* July 7, 1905, p. 1.
229. "Ah me! The old": From letter dated July 1, 1905, quoted in Jessup, *Elihu Root,* 1: 448.

21: "The Main Object of Diplomacy": 1905–12

230. "I am extremely fond": From letter dated July 11, 1905, in Jessup, *Elihu Root,* 1: 448.

230. the oath of office: ibid., 1: 447.

230. "But I shall try": From letter dated September 9, 1905, quoted in ibid., 1: 448.

231. Root had an enormous: Werking, *Master Architects,* 94.

232. Choate invited him: Schulzinger, *Making of the Diplomatic Mind,* 56.

232. His main responsibilities: Phillips, *Ventures in Diplomacy,* 6–12.

232. "I replied with enthusiasm": ibid., 14.

232. In Peking, Phillips: ibid., 14, 16.

233. Then, Phillips maneuvered: ibid., 30–32.

233. Division of Far Eastern Affairs: Schulzinger, *Making of the Diplomatic Mind,* 56.

233. the "Tennis Cabinet": Phillips, *Ventures in Diplomacy,* 36–37.

233. third assistant secretary of state: ibid., 41.

233. Since Root detested: Jessup, *Elihu Root,* 2: 104.

233. executive orders Roosevelt gave: Plischke, *US Department of State,* 224.

233. before World War I: Schulzinger, *Making of the Diplomatic Mind,* 42.

233. "In view of": ibid, 42.

234. the only appropriate uniform: O'Toole, *Five of Hearts,* 382.

234. if you gain an inch: Werking, *Master Architects,* 102.

234. "tend to trade" Jessup, *Elihu Root,* 1: 590.

234. treaties Root signed: ibid., 1: 453.

234. After eighty years: Barnes and Morgan, *Foreign Service of the United States,* 162; Werking, *Master Architects,* 102.

235. Root and Carr drafted: ibid., 165.

235. By 1909, the United: *Good Government* 27, no. 3 (March 19, 1910).

236. Germans were selling: Werking, *Master Architects,* 120.

236. "Like the officers": ibid., 111.

236. A consul in Algeria: ibid.

236. If an unfit consular officer: ibid., 113.

236. "a lot of cheap": From letter dated September 29, 1907, in ibid., 122.

237. Root's energy, vision: Werking, *Master Architects,* 142.

237. Official Washington tended: Jessup, *Elihu Root,* 1: 470.

237. He hoped the elaborate: ibid., 1: 492.

238. "You had no business": Jessup, *Elihu Root,* 1: 533; E. Morris, *Theodore Rex,* 457.

238. purpose in taking office: Zimmermann, *First Great Triumph,* 442.

238. Charlemagne Tower, Jr.: *Dictionary of American Bibliography.*

238. Henry White encouraged: Nevins, *Henry White,* 210.

239. the Germans accepted arbitration: E. Morris, *Theodore Rex,* 191.

239. The blockade was lifted: Nevins, *Henry White,* 214.

239. Dr. Henry Watson Furniss: Justesen, "African-American Consuls Abroad."

239. Asylum, he said: Jessup, *Elihu Root,* 1: 558.

239. Three treaties were negotiated: ibid., 1: 526.

240. In October 1871: Kwok, *On the Occasion of the 130th Anniversary of the Los Angeles Chinese Massacre.*

240. 1884 law required visas: McKeown, "Ritualization of Regulation," 383.

240. Consul Wildman at Hong Kong: ibid., 386.

240. President Roosevelt asked: ibid.

240. Consul George Anderson: ibid., 394.

240. "a formidable competitor . . . Exactly so": From letter dated January 16, 1907, in Jessup, *Elihu Root*, 2: 8.

241. Under the Root-Takahira Agreement: Zimmermann, *First Great Triumph*, 472.

241. Willard Straight, the U.S.: Jessup, *Elihu Root*, 2: 37.

241. National Origins Act: ibid., 2: 34.

241. Kaiser Wilhelm II: Shirer, *Collapse of the Third Republic*, 112.

241. Germany, Austria-Hungary, France: E. Morris, *Theodore Rex*, 432.

241. Henry White, now: Nevins, *Henry White*, 268.

242. end of March 1906: ibid., 282.

242. "I think a man": From letter dated November 13, 1905, in Cortissoz, *Life of Whitelaw Reid*, 303.

242. On one hunting trip: Nevins, *Henry White*, 247.

242. 4 rue François-Premier: ibid., 285.

242. White expected to be: ibid., 298.

242. "for reasons unconnected": Barnes and Morgan, *Foreign Service of the United States*, 182.

243. more likely Helen Taft: Nevins, *Henry White*, 299; Auchincloss, *Theodore Roosevelt*, 113.

243. "Mr. Whitelaw Reid": Phillips, *Ventures in Diplomacy*, 47–48.

243. Permanent Court of Arbitration: Duncan, *Whitelaw Reid*, 242.

243. on December 15, 1912: Duncan, *Whitelaw Reid*, 243.

22: Warm-up for a World War: 1899–1914

246. "a declaration prohibiting": *Peace Conference at The Hague 1899* (government report).

246. Joseph H. Choate: Marshman, "Four Ages of Joseph Choate."

246. historian Fritz Stern: Stern, Remarks as honoree of the Leo Baeck Medal (printed program), 20.

246. Japan's "yellow menace": Tuchman, *Zimmermann Telegram*, 30–32; Berger, *Story of "The New York Times,"* 203.

247. Hale had also written: Tuchman, *Zimmermann Telegram*, 32–33, 45.

248. "a government of butchers": Cline, *United States and Mexico*, 144.

248. a "desperate brute": Tuchman, *Zimmermann Telegram*, 44.

248. William Canada, the American: ibid., 48.

249. The whole exercise: Moskin, *U.S. Marine Corps Story*, 158; Cline, *United States and Mexico*, 162; Tuchman, *Zimmermann Telegram*, 66.

249. He was unsuccessful: Cline, *United States and Mexico*, 172.

249. Lansing was the first: Foglesong, *America's Secret War Against Bolshevism*, 36.

249. At Santa Ysabel: Tuchman, *Zimmermann Telegram*, 95.

249. Pershing could not catch: From cable to Lansing dated March 20, 1916, in ibid., 95.

249. Henry P. Fletcher: American National Biography.

249. By 1910, the State: Hunt, *Department of State*, 220–21.

250. first resident diplomatic officer: Barnes and Morgan, *Foreign Service of the United States*, 180–81.

250. "that wild Indian": Grew, *Turbulent Era*, 77.

250. Ambassador Walter Hines Page: From letter dated June 5, 1914, in Hendrick, *Life and Letters of Walter H. Page*, 3: 84.

251. Bringing up to date: Barnes and Morgan, *Foreign Service of the United States*, 170.

251. In July 1916: ibid., 195.

252. "Let us either": *Congressional Record*, vol. 45, 2641–42, March 2, 1910, in Barnes and Morgan, *Foreign Service of the United States*, 175.

252. Only seven buildings: Barnes and Morgan, *Foreign Service of the United States*, 221–22.

252. Rogers was shocked: ibid., 184.

253. "In general, however": ibid., 185.

253. Frederic C. Penfield: ibid., 202–01.

253. Walter Hines Page, came: Hendrick, *Life and Letters of Walter H. Page*, 3: 2–3.

253. "the right stock . . . the right blood": ibid., 2: 131.

253. "already the land": ibid., 2; 142.

253. Page's faith in Anglo-American: Seymour, *American Diplomacy*, 256.

253. "self-conceived, if naive": Tuchman, *Zimmermann Telegram*, 131.

253. he wrote a confidential: Gerard, *My Four Years in Germany*, 430.

254. more bureaucracy-sensitive aides: Grew, *Turbulent Era*, 218.

254. But Gerard was appalled: Gerard, *My Four Years in Germany*, 78.

254. He preached that the United States: Schulzinger, *Making of the Diplomatic Mind*, 24.

254. Despite his efforts: American National Biography.

255. Germany competed for overseas: Tuchman, *Guns of August*, 329.

23: "Well, the Roof Has Fallen In": 1914–16

256. Frederic W. Wile: Berger, *Story of "The New York Times,"* 205.

256. Archduke Franz Ferdinand: Gerard, *My Four Years in Germany*, 106.

257. "my first and only": Crunden, *Hero in Spite of Himself*, 206.

257. "Situation in Europe": M. Sullivan, *Our Times*, 39.

257. Secretary Bryan also asked: From letter to Wilson dated July 29, 1914, in Hendrick, *Life and Letters of Walter H. Page*, 3: 125–26.

257. "this always solitary": ibid., 3: 126.

257. Ambassador Gerard in Berlin: Grew, *Turbulent Era*, 132.

257. Russia had mobilized: Tuchman, *Guns of August*, p. 56.

257. "towards stopping this dreadful": Gerard, *My Four Years in Germany*, 132.

257. "self-destructive madness": Kennan, *At a Century's Ending*, 18.

258. The embassy staff ran: Grew, *Turbulent Era*, 133.

258. "an end to those": ibid., 131.

258. At police headquarters, Grew: ibid., 136–37.

258. "Berlin is no longer": ibid., 137.

258. Hugh Gibson, the legation's: Whitlock, *Belgium*, 1: 86; Crunden, *Hero in Spite of Himself*, 275.

258. "this quiet post . . . wallowed in the luxury": Gibson, *Journal from our Legation in Belgium*, 3.

258. "Well, the roof . . . I would not be": Gibson, *Hugh Gibson*, 120, 121.

259. German ambassador notified: Tuchman, *Guns of August*, 122.

259. Ambassador Herrick stayed: Millis, *Road to War*, 74.

259. Since the Germans warned: Tuchman, *Guns of August*, 408.

259. The French appreciated: Mott, *Myron Herrick*, chapter 5.

259. "You only have to": Whitlock, *Belgium*, 1: 114.

259. Belgians' six infantry divisions: Tuchman, *Guns of August*, 105.

259. At five o'clock, Whitlock: Tuchman, *Guns of August*, 123; Gibson, *Journal from our Legation in Belgium*, 21.

259. The British diplomats: Gibson, *Journal from our Legation in Belgium*, 94.

259. This war would be fought: Pearton, *Diplomacy, War and Technology*, 132.

259. Warfare in the early twentieth century: ibid., 133.

259. withdrawn to Antwerp: Jouve, *Paris*, 18; Tuchman, *Guns of August*, 221–22.

259. Marquis of Villalobar: Whitlock, *Belgium*, 1: 143.

260. The king later thanked: *New York Times*, September 3, 1914.

260. They burned villages: Tuchman, *Guns of August*, 313; see also ibid., 173–74.

260. "that almost savage chant . . . became terrible, oppressive": M. Sullivan, *Our Times*, 28.

260. He was to stay: Millis, *Road to War*, 54.

260. Gibson and a driver left: Gibson, *Journal from our Legation in Belgium*, 125–49.

261. citizens of Ghent praised: ibid., 206–8; E. Powell, *Fighting in Flanders*.

261. king asked Gibson: Gibson, *Hugh Gibson*, 122–29; Moskin, *U.S. Marine Corps Story*, 14.

261. "I was astonished": Gibson, *Journal from our Legation in Belgium*, 280.

261. "Hoover had succeeded": Kennan, *Soviet-American Relations*, 2: 338.

262. expressing their gratitude: Whitlock, *Belgium*, 1: 417; Crunden, *Hero in Spite of Himself*, 281.

262. Americans lined up outside: Barnes and Morgan, *Foreign Service of the United States*, p. 190, from *Foreign Relations*, 1914 supplement, pp. 94–95.

262. He predicted that Britain's: Gerard, *My Four Years in Germany*, 206; Millis, *Road to War*, 56; Howard, *First World War*, 11.

263. Foreign Office asked Gérard: Gerard, *My Four Years in Germany*, 212.

263. kaiser refused to see: ibid., 219.

263. "disgustingly bad taste": Gerard, *My Four Years in Germany*, 318; Whitlock, *Belgium*, 2: 379.

263. He visited POW camps: Gerard, *My Four Years in Germany*, 160.

263. David R. Francis found: Barnes and Morgan, *Foreign Service of the United States*, 191; Francis, *Russia from the American Embassy*, 4.

263. "expectant legatees of a": Morgenthau, *All in a Life-Time*, 183–84.

264. Morgenthau's instructions were: Evans, *United States Policy and the Partition of Turkey*, 26.

264. Turks took over: Morgenthau, *Ambassador Morgenthau's Story*, 99–103, 108.

264. In March 1915: Pearton, *Diplomacy, War and Technology*, 146.

264. The hostages stayed: Morgenthau, *Ambassador Morgenthau's Story*, 157–68.

265. two million Armenians: ibid., 218.

265. And foreign service officers: Barnes and Morgan, *Foreign Service of the United States*, 192–93.

265. The department grew: ibid., 193.

265. "from the Department of": From letter dated September 22, 1914, in Hendrick, *Life and Letters of Walter H. Page*, 3: 146.

265. confidentially, Page said: From letter dated January 12, 1915, in ibid., 3: 220–21.

265. "There is only one": Hendrick, *Life and Letters of Walter H. Page*, 2: 8.

265. "You found the right": From letter dated January 12, 1915, in Hendrick, *Life and Letters of Walter H. Page*, 3: 215.

265. "So am I": M. Sullivan, *Our Times*, 219.

265. Page, reflecting the view: Hendrick, *Life and Letters of Walter H. Page*, vol. 1, ch. 13.

265. "the German military": From letter dated September 22, 1914, in ibid., 3: 141.

266. "Page is really": Hendrick, *Life and Letters of Walter H. Page*, 2: 348.

266. as too pro-German: From letter dated December 15, 1914, in ibid., 3: 198.

266. "If we are so": From Page's letter to House dated September 10, 1914, in ibid., 1: 7.

266. "The Kaiser did not": From letter to Page dated October 3, 1914, in ibid., 1: 9.

266. "The plain fact is . . . If the [German]": From Page's letter to House dated December 12, 1914, in ibid., 1: 12.

267. "German-Jewish bankers": Millis, *Road to War*, 116.

267. He described the civilians: From a note written in 1915 (undated), in Hendrick, *Life and Letters of Walter H. Page,* 2: 65–66.

267. "And when you take": From a 1915 letter to London, in ibid., 2: 117.

267. "The hate here": *American Diplomacy,* 134.

267. Wilson's diplomatic efforts: Seymour, *American Diplomacy,* 172.

267. war would not be brief: Hendrick, *Life and Letters of Walter H. Page,* 3: 234.

267. the identical dilemma: Seymour, *American Diplomacy,* 9.

267. two inconsistent wishes: Millis, *Road to War,* 253.

24: "Slaughterhouse Where Madness Dwells": 1915–17

268. 1,201 lives were lost: M. Sullivan, *Our Times,* 108.

268. Of 159 Americans aboard: From Page's letter to House dated July 21, 1915, in Hendrick, *Life and Letters of Walter H. Page,* 2: 25; see also M. Sullivan, *Our Times,* 108; Grew, *Turbulent Era,* 178.

268. They drew a zone: Millis, *Road to War,* 134.

269. "must declare war": From telegram dated May 8, 1915, in Hendrick, *Life and Letters of Walter H. Page,* 3: 239.

269. they walked listlessly: Hendrick, *Life and Letters of Walter H. Page,* 2: 1–3.

269. "There is such": ibid., 3: 241; Millis, *Road to War,* 178.

269. "We have five hundred": Gerard, *My Four Years in Germany,* 237; American National Biography; Tuchman, *Zimmermann Telegram,* 112.

269. "failure to act": From telegram dated May 11, 1915, in Hendrick, *Life and Letters of Walter H. Page,* 3: 243.

269. President's note that: Tuchman, *Guns of August,* 73; Grew, *Turbulent Era,* 195; Millis, *Road to War,* 70.

269. This message would force: Grew, *Turbulent Era,* 205.

269. "the Imperial Government": Gerard, *My Four Years in Germany,* 240.

269. The United States insisted: Grew, *Turbulent Era,* 208.

270. Page praised Wilson's handling: From an undated letter in Hendrick, *Life and Letters of Walter H. Page,* 2: 16.

270. "England in trying": Whitlock, *Belgium,* 1: 617–18.

270. Then, without warning: Massie, *Castles of Steel,* 543.

270. Germans, his "kinsmen": Hendrick, *Life and Letters of Walter H. Page,* 2: 236.

270. Whitlock immediately inquired: Whitlock, *Belgium,* 1: 447.

271. "We were haunted": Gibson, *Journal from Our Legation in Belgium,* 353.

271. "Have pity on her! . . . the whole proceeding": Whitlock, *Belgium,* 2: 5.

271. executed Edith Cavell: ibid., 2: 81–145; Gibson, *Journal from our Legation in Belgium,* 362.

271. "The storm of universal": Whitlock, *Belgium,* 2: 123.

272. In June 1940: Hunt, *Department of State,* 103.

272. The two overzealous Germans: Tuchman, *Zimmermann Telegram,* 90.

272. As Count Bernstorff recognized: Millis, *Road to War,* 242.

272. They were suspicious: Crunden, *Hero in Spite of Himself,* 310.

272. Admittedly, Whitlock too: ibid., 315.

272. "He is truculent": From letter to House dated February 7, 1916, in ibid., 316, 318.

272. "He is entitled": From letter dated February 7, 1916, in Crunden, *Hero in Spite of Himself,* 468.

273. Whitlock experienced more horrors: Whitlock, *Belgium,* 2: 478ff.; Tuchman, *Guns of August,* 315.

273. Herter returned shaken: Whitlock, *Belgium,* 2: 682.

273. Few of the men: ibid., 2: 753.

273. Although Bernstorff was able: Tuchman, *Zimmermann Telegram,* 71.

274. But President Wilson still: Hendrick, *Life and Letters of Walter H. Page,* 3: 273–78.

274. Germans claimed their U-boat: Millis, *Road to War,* 292.

274. He pocketed Lansing's note: Grew, *Turbulent Era,* 218.

274. Foreign Minister Jagow: Gerard, *My Four Years in Germany,* 324; Grew, *Turbulent Era,* 223.

274. Joseph C. Grew: Grew, *Turbulent Era,* 12.

274. "Do you come'. . . No, your Majesty": Gerard, *My Four Years in Germany,* 339.

274. "Whatever the result": Grew, *Turbulent Era,* 240.

275. "observe the rules": Millis, *Road to War,* 299.

275. It warned that if: Grew, *Turbulent Era,* 241.

275. The debate inside Germany: ibid., 244.

275. "America cannot be": From a February 1, 1916, speech, in Seymour, *American Diplomacy,* 260.

275. "the concerted action": From Wilson's address to the House on May 18, 1916, in Seymour, *American Diplomacy,* 262.

275. "diplomacy was bankrupt": Root, *Addresses on International Subjects,* 447.

275. "We are participants": From a May 27, 1916, speech, in Seymour, *American Diplomacy,* 175.

275. foreign policy "turning point": From letter addressed to House dated May 16, 1916, in ibid., 174.

276. "was speaking only": From Page's letter to House dated May 30, 1916, in ibid., 177.

276. Chancellor Bethmann-Hollweg: Tuchman, *Zimmermann Telegram,* 120.

276. fantastic idea to counter: ibid., 116.

276. He would seduce Mexico: ibid., 143.

276. Page and Wilson differed: Hendrick, *Life and Letters of Walter H. Page,* 3: 260.

276. "to get some American": From Wilson's letter to House dated July 22, 1916, in Seymour, *American Diplomacy,* 179.

276. Wilson said he had lost: Hendrick, *Life and Letters of Walter H. Page,* 2: 186.

276. "I think he is": Quoted in Hendrick, *Life and Letters of Walter H. Page,* 2: 188.

277. Page agreed to stay: Tuchman, *Zimmermann Telegram,* 161–62.

277. "Here is the opportunity": Carr, *Diary* (unpublished), 8–16.

277. "There is some latent": From entry dated December 13, 1916, in ibid.

278. David R. Francis: Francis, *Russia from the American Embassy,* 3.

278. growth of sales: Barnes, *Standing on a Volcano,* 183.

278. "By not talking": From letter to Wilson dated April 8, 1916, in ibid., 184.

278. "They are very aggressive": Barnes, *Standing on a Volcano,* 187–88.

278. Arthur T. Dailey: Kennan, *Soviet-American Relations,* 2: 330.

278. Russian intelligence suspected: ibid., 1: 39.

279. Russian army drilled recruits: Francis, *Russia from the American Embassy,* 11.

279. "One can attribute this . . . courage and enthusiasm": Kennan, *Soviet-American Relations,* 1: 40, 41.

279. Francis's first official visitor: Barnes, *Standing on a Volcano,* 186.

279. "the designing, usurious": ibid., 202.

280. by 1916 the Austrians: Tuchman, *Zimmermann Telegram,* 4.

280. "slaughterhouse where madness dwells": Millis, *Road to War,* 314.

280. neutrality was "intolerable": From letter to House dated November 24, 1916, in Seymour, *American Diplomacy,* 54.

280. "This was one": Grew, *Turbulent Era,* 252–53.

280. Grew repeated Wilson's desire: ibid., 259.

281. handed Grew a note: Millis, *Road to War*, 363–64; Grew, *Turbulent Era*, 294.

281. "buying a pig": Hendrick, *Life and Letters of Walter H. Page*, 2: 203.

25: "America in Armageddon": 1917–20

282. They were convinced that: Gerard, *My Four Years in Germany*, 364.

282. "a peace without victory": Auchincloss, *Woodrow Wilson*, 75; Seymour, *American Diplomacy*, 196.

282. German submarines would sink: Seymour, *American Diplomacy*, 199. ˙

283. an attack on humanity: ibid., 17.

283. "A promotion in the": Murphy, *Diplomat Among Warriors*, 8.

284. instructed Ambassador Gerard: Millis, *Road to War*, 392; Tuchman, *Zimmermann Telegram*, 151; Phillips, *Ventures in Diplomacy*, 75.

284. "Bernstorff has just been": Hendrick, *Life and Letters of Walter H. Page*, 2: 215; Millis, *Road to War*, 392.

284. "a hell-swept continent": From letter to Arthur W. Page dated March 25, 1917, in ibid., 2: 22.

284. Polo de Bernabe: Gerard, *My Four Years in Germany*, 35.

284. Bernstorff and a party: Tuchman, *Zimmermann Telegram*, 191.

285. "We want him": Millis, *Road to War*, 396.

285. several days to reach: Whitlock, *Belgium*, 2: 715.

285. Secretary Lansing telegraphed Villalobar: ibid., 2: 793; Millis, *Road to War*, 422.

286. China also had broken: Millis, *Road to War*, 436.

286. "a filthy hole": ibid, 436.

286. sent the "most secret": Tuchman, *Zimmermann Telegram*, 146.

286. to Eckhardt in Mexico: ibid., 147.

286. British Naval Intelligence intercepted: Hendrick, *Life and Letters of Walter H. Page*, 3: 338.

286. To decipher it: ibid., 3: 331–36; Tuchman, *Zimmermann Telegram*, 14.

287. March 3, Zimmermann admitted: Tuchman, *Zimmermann Telegram*, 183; Howard, *First World War*, 95.

287. Wilson asked a joint: M. Sullivan, *Our Times*, 266.

287. Published across the country: Seymour, *American Diplomacy*, 203; Tuchman, *Zimmermann Telegram*, 175.

288. state of war existed: Tuchman, *Zimmermann Telegram*, 196.

288. "a war against all": Seymour, *American Diplomacy*, 210.

288. he asserted that Germany: Commager, *Documents of American History*, Millis, *Road to War*, 437.

288. German woman singer collapsed: Millis, *Road to War*, 442.

288. "It's a great day . . . America in Armageddon": Millis, *Road to War*, 452.

288. British and American flags: Hendrick, *Life and Letters of Walter H. Page*, 2: 231.

288. King George V invited: ibid., 2: 240.

288. "I suppose I saw": May 4, 1917, in ibid., 2: 262–63c.

289. thirty-six destroyers "eventually": Hendrick, *Life and Letters of Walter H. Page*, 2: 278–79.

289. "The Germans are winning": From letter dated July 8, 1917, in ibid., 2: 289.

289. Morgenthau had the support: Fromkin, *Peace to End All Peace*, 319.

289. he told too many: Yale, "Ambassador Henry Morgenthau's Special Mission," 313.

289. Dr. Chaim Weizmann: Evans, *United States Policy and the Partition of Turkey*, 45; Yale, "Ambassador Henry Morgenthau's Special Mission," 315.

289. "Mr. Morgenthau never forgave": Yale, "Ambassador Henry Morgenthau's Special Mission," 320.

290. Colonel House warned: Evans, *United States Policy and the Partition of Turkey,* 55.

290. United States stayed aloof: ibid., 64.

290. The first assistance: Seymour, *American Diplomacy,* 222.

290. Third Assistant Secretary: Evans, *United States Policy and the Partition of Turkey,* 71–72.

290. dismayed to find it: Steel, *Walter Lippmann and the American Century,* 130.

290. take over the Inquiry: Schulzinger, *Making of the Diplomatic Mind,* 62.

290. The Inquiry worked day: *Diplomatic History,* vol. 35, no. 3, p. 464.

291. Wilson became their prophet: Seymour, *American Diplomacy,* 294–96.

291. "The Embassy now": From letter dated May 12, 1918, in Hendrick, *Life and Letters of Walter H. Page,* 2: 379.

291. more than a million: Howard, *First World War,* 124.

291. Irwin Laughlin, on one: Hendrick, *Life and Letters of Walter H. Page,* 2: 402.

291. He died at: *Dictionary of Amerian Biography.*

291. "The friend of Britain": Hendrick, *Life and Letters of Walter H. Page,* 3: 431.

292. "the restoration of peace": Seymour, *American Diplomacy,* 307–09.

292. Wilson said he would: Howard, *First World War,* 132.

292. Germany's military leaders: ibid.

292. House slept with it: Grew, *Turbulent Era,* 340–42.

293. "making strenuous efforts": ibid., 343.

293. a "magnanimous" peace: ibid., 344.

293. House struck back forcefully: Grew, *Turbulent Era,* 347.

293. Grew was named secretary: ibid., 356.

293. Christian Herter served: ibid., 388.

293. Then, suddenly, Grew, Straight: ibid., 369.

293. "so glorious a victory": From letter to House dated November 7, 1918, in Seymour, *American Diplomacy,* 395.

294. Allied leaders resented: Seymour, *American Diplomacy,* 367, 370.

294. Root emphasized that: Nevins, *Henry White,* 351.

294. Roosevelt left the hospital: Auchincloss, *Theodore Roosevelt,* 136; Straus, *Under Four Administrations,* 391–93.

294. Lodge wanted Germany: Nevins, *Henry White,* 355.

294. Countess Muriel Seherr-Thoss: ibid., 323–24.

295. "We have no idea": Ginsburgh, "Between War and Peace" (Ph.D. diss.), 313.

295. Many Republicans said: MacMillan, *Paris 1919,* 6.

295. "It is a definite": Nevins, *Henry White,* 380.

295. accepted Wilson's international organization: Seymour, *American Diplomacy,* 400.

295. Lodge insisted that: Nevins, *Henry White,* 400.

296. "Instead of men": Morgenthau, *All in a Life-Time,* 322.

296. "Diplomats were invented": MacMillan, *Paris 1919,* 145.

296. In Minsk, thirty-one Jews: Morgenthau, *All in a Life-Time,* 414.

296. The commissioners confirmed: ibid., 419.

296. On May 7, the peace: Nevins, *Henry White,* 448.

296. Ellis Loring Dresel: Craig and Gilbert, *Diplomats,* 131.

297. The severe peace terms: Howard, *First World War,* 139–43; Pearton, *Diplomacy, War and Technology,* 180.

297. On November 19, 1919: Ginsburgh, "Between War and Peace" (Ph.D. diss.), 335.

297. "Mr. White set up": Nevins, *Henry White,* 496.

297. "The Diplomatic Service . . . doing away with": H. White, "Baneful Influence of 'Politics'" (address), 6, 14, 1, 3.
298. Between the Civil War: ibid., 9–11.
298. "unless for some very . . . keep out of": ibid., 21, 12–13.
298. White wrote a report: Nevins, *Henry White*, 492.
299. Henry White died: ibid., 1.
299. "He was a great": ibid., 495.

26: The Russian "Terror": 1917–20

300. Francis knew no Russian: Barnes, *Standing on a Volcano*, 212.
300. he grasped the shocking: ibid., 218.
300. International Women's Day: Fromkin, *Peace to End All Peace*, 425.
300. shouting: "Bread! Bread!": Steffens, *Autobiography of Lincoln Steffens*, 2: 751.
300. A regiment mutinied: Francis, *Russia from the American Embassy*, 60.
300. They did not get: ibid., 63.
300. "This is undoubtedly": Francis, *Russia from the American Embassy*, 72.
301. "government by consent": Barnes, *Standing on a Volcano*, 229; Francis, *Russia from the American Embassy*, 91; Kennan, *Soviet-American Relations*, 1: 17.
301. "the United States recognizes": Barnes, *Standing on a Volcano*, 231; Francis, *Russia from the American Embassy*, 93.
301. "This afternoon the Ambassador": From letter dated March 22, 1917, in Houghteling, *Diary of the Russian Revolution*, 166.
302. "vastly strengthening to the": Francis, *Russia from the American Embassy*, 100.
302. "As I am six thousand": From letter to Jane Frances dated May 8, 1917, in Barnes, *Standing on a Volcano*, 232.
302. But North Winship: From letter dated March 20, 1917, in ibid., 237.
302. And the Root Commission: Francis, *Russia from the American Embassy*, 124; Kennan, *Soviet-American Relations*, 1: 22.
302. Kerensky appointed Lavr Kornilov: Barnes, *Standing on a Volcano*, 253.
303. He urged Francis: ibid., 263.
303. "Had the Provisional Government": Francis, *Russia from the American Embassy*, 141.
303. American ambassador was called: Phillips, *Ventures in Diplomacy*, 87.
303. morning of November 7: Kennan, *Soviet-American Relations*, 1: 72.
303. "Disgusting! But . . . the": Francis, *Russia from the American Embassy*, 187.
303. "Bolsheviki appear to have": Barnes, *Standing on a Volcano*, 268.
304. But he praised: From letter dated November 24, 1917, in Francis, *Russia from the American Embassy*, 190.
304. J. Butler Wright: Kennan, *Soviet-American Relations*, 1: 117.
304. Judson had been an observer: Kennan, *Soviet-American Relations*, 1: 42.
305. That would, he predicted: Foglesong, *America's Secret War Against Bolshevism*, 84.
305. Smith's ideas were received: ibid., 89.
305. British covertly supplied: Kennan, *Soviet-American Relations*, 1: 178–80; Foglesong, *America's Secret War Against Bolshevism*, 79.
305. "Russia will fairly swim . . . the black period": Kennan, *Soviet-American Relations*, 1: 156, 157.
306. Edgar G. Sisson: ibid., 1: 50–52.
306. President Wilson ordered Sisson: ibid., 1: 129.
306. department turned down: ibid., 1: 240.

306. obtain permission for Robins: ibid., 1: 232.

306. "It should not be thought": ibid., 1: 242–43.

307. French ambassador spoke up: ibid., 1: 336.

307. At midnight, Lenin telephoned: Barnes, *Standing on a Volcano*, 299.

307. but ordered to leave: Francis, *Russia from the American Embassy*, 218.

307. John K. Caldwell: Kennan, *Soviet-American Relations*, 1: 459.

307. arriving in April: Grew, *Turbulent Era*, 420.

308. Francis also recommended: Kennan, *Soviet-American Relations*, 1: 472.

309. Consul Macgowan's report: Graves, *America's Siberian Adventure*, 32.

309. The meeting failed: Kennan, *Soviet-American Relations*, 2: 159.

309. Czechs continued to fight: Barnes, *Standing on a Volcano*, 334.

310. A raging quarrel broke: Kennan, *Soviet-American Relations*, 2: 169.

310. Lansing concluded that Robins's: ibid., 2: 184.

310. DeWitt C. Poole: ibid., 1: 17.

310. primary American diplomat: Francis, *Russia from the American Embassy*, 320.

310. Robins' departure reduced: Kennan, *Soviet-American Relations*, 2: 297.

310. Trotsky repudiated diplomacy: Craig and Gilbert, *Diplomats*, 240–41.

311. In June, Francis reported: Foglesong, *America's Secret War Against Bolshevism*, 113.

311. Acting Secretary of State Polk: Kennan, *Soviet-American Relations*, 1: 375.

311. "We do not observe": Francis, *Russia from the American Embassy*, 241; Barnes, *Standing on a Volcano*, 340.

311. Germans, of course, protested: Kennan, *Soviet-American Relations*, 2: 257.

311. The British decided: ibid., 2: 263.

311. Lieutenant Hugh S. Martin: Foglesong, *America's Secret War Against Bolshevism*, 193.

311. Ambassador Francis endorsed: Kennan, *Soviet-American Relations*, 2: 55–57.

311. He had arrived: ibid., 2: 28.

312. Russians in the car: ibid., 2: 256.

312. "In my judgment": ibid., 2: 213.

312. he had grown concerned: ibid., 2: 212.

312. He now advocated: Message dated May 8 in Foglesong, *America's Secret War Against Bolshevism*, 196.

312. "inevitable a desperate conflict . . . the best answer": Kennan, *Soviet-American Relations*, 2: 221, 237.

313. The Americans explained: Foglesong, *America's Secret War Against Bolshevism*, 203.

313. Hugh Martin returned: Kennan, *Soviet-American Relations*, 2: 276.

313. Even though Siberia: ibid., 2: 365.

313. On June 23: ibid., 2: 373–75.

314. Consul Felix Cole: Foglesong, *America's Secret War Against Bolshevism*, 204.

314. these Czechs took over: Kennan, *Soviet-American Relations*, 2: 393.

314. The story was told: Moskin, *U.S. Marine Corps Story*, 141.

314. On July Fourth, at Vologda: Kennan, *Soviet-American Relations*, 2: 441.

314. Francis urged his government: Kennan, *Soviet-American Relations*, 2: 442.

314. "to guard the line": ibid., 2: 397; Foglesong, *America's Secret War Against Bolshevism*, 160.

315. No mention was made: Kennan, *Soviet-American Relations*, 2: 401.

315. Wilson's views "delusions": ibid., 2: 401–02.

315. In Tokyo, the general staff: ibid., 2: 411.

315. British and French seized: ibid., 2: 414.

315. Allied force from: ibid., 2: 426.

315. The British advanced: Foglesong, *America's Secret War Against Bolshevism*, 210.

315. The War Department objected: Francis, *Russia from the American Embassy*, 271.

316. The Japanese poured in: Foglesong, *America's Secret War Against Bolshevism*, 168.

316. "as far as": Graves, *America's Siberian Adventure*, 96.

316. a "strong man": Foglesong, *America's Secret War Against Bolshevism*, 179.

316. "Keep a stiff": Graves, *America's Siberian Adventure*, 160.

317. Twenty Americans with the YMCA: Francis, *Russia from the American Embassy*, 290.

317. Later, he was delighted: Kennan, *Soviet-American Relations*, 2: 458.

317. Using a false Norwegian: A. Krebs, "Norman Armour, 94, Dies," *New York Times* obituary on November 2, 1918.

317. information-gathering mission: Wadley, "Even One Is Too Many," (Ph.D. diss.), 4.

317. Courageously, Poole and Allen: Kennan, *Soviet-American Relations*, 2: 460.

318. Norwegian vice consul: ibid., 2: 467.

318. They took great risks: ibid., 2: 468.

318. At Archangel, Ambassador Francis: Barnes, *Standing on a Volcano*, 358.

318. Bolshevik Central Committee kept: Foglesong, *America's Secret War Against Bolshevism*, 118–23.

318. summer of 1921: Patenaude, *Big Show in Bololand*, 25–27.

319. widowed White Russian aristocrat: ibid., 342.

319. Consul Thornwell Haynes: Wadley, "Even One Is Too Many" (Ph.D. diss.), 5.

319. April 25, 1919: ibid.

319. Acting Secretary Polk tried: Foglesong, *America's Secret War Against Bolshevism*, 252.

320. After waiting two weeks: MacMillan, *Paris 1919*, 149.

320. Aboard ship, Wilson came: Barnes, *Standing on a Volcano*, 371.

320. "neither democracy nor Socialism": ibid., 386.

320. "Lenin is a fanatic": Dated January 22, 1919, in Francis, *Russia from the American Embassy*, 315.

320. U.S. government agents raided: Pfannestiel, "Soviet Bureau," 189–90.

320. In June 1919: Foglesong, *America's Secret War Against Bolshevism*, 229.

321. Bullitt had studied: W. Bullitt, *Bullitt Mission to Russia*, 2.

321. he wrote Colonel House: ibid., 15.

321. Roger C. Tredwell: ibid., 33.

321. armed with questions: Steffens, *Autobiography of Lincoln Steffens*, 2: 791.

321. The two Americans were: W. Bullitt, *Bullitt Mission to Russia*, 38.

321. "The destructive phase": ibid., 50.

321. Wilson never did: O. Bullitt, *For the President*, 8.

322. In his anger, Bullitt: W. Bullitt, *Bullitt Mission to Russia*, 96; Bullitt, *For the President*, 12.

322. He was severely criticized: O. Bullitt, *For the President*, 13.

322. "those conscientious, high-bred": Steffens, *Autobiography of Lincoln Steffens*, 2: 802.

322. "This testimony of course": From entry dated November 12, 1934, in Grew, *Turbulent Era*, 389.

322. "The Armistice had absolutely . . . the so-called submerged": Graves, *America's Siberian Adventure*, 144, 295, 192–93.

322. He was critical: ibid., 191.

323. Cossack leader Kolchak: MacMillan, *Paris 1919*, 82; Graves, *America's Siberian Adventure*, 301; Foglesong, *America's Secret War Against Bolshevism*, 185.

323. April 1, 1920: Graves, *America's Siberian Adventure*, 327.

323. civil war was over: Barnes, *Standing on a Volcano*, 386.

323. trade agreement with: Foglesong, *America's Secret War Against Bolshevism*, 291.

323. those who called: Graves, *America's Siberian Adventure*, 351.

27: The New Diplomacy of Oil: 1919–38

324. "dragged the Americans from": "State Department Begins Inquiry," *New York Times.*

324. Vice Consul Imbrie to death: Barnes and Morgan, *Foreign Service of the United States,* 228.

324. A Yale graduate: *History of the American Field Service in France,* section 1, "The Ambulance Sections," part 4.

325. He reported that men: Murray, "Report on Murder of Consul Imbrie" (unpublished), 9–10.

325. "the recrudescence of clerical": Ungar, "Pitch Imperfect."

325. "assume dictatorial powers": Murray, "Murder of Vice Consul Imbrie, Tehran, 1924," (letter to secretary of state); Zirinsky, "Blood, Power, and Hypocrisy," 276; Kamen, "Narcissus Is Now Greek and Roman."

325. declare himself His Majesty: Yergin, *Prize,* 270.

325. "Viewing the tragedy": Murray, "Murder of Vice Consul Imbrie, Tehran, 1924," (letter to Secretary of State).

326. "One of our greatest": Rockefeller, *Random Reminiscences of Men and Events.*

326. The United States competed: "Establishing the American Presence in the Middle East," *Multinational Oil Corporations and U.S. Foreign Policy* (government report), 1; Yergin, *Prize,* 194.

326. oil meant "mastery": Yergin, *Prize,* 12.

326. "The Great Game": Kinzer, *Overthrow,* 264.

326. Growing German interest: Yergin, *Prize,* 145.

326. Anglo-Persian Oil Company: ibid., 148.

326. acquired 51 percent: ibid., 164.

327. Palestine would be internationalized: Evans, *United States Policy and the Partition of Turkey,* 110.

327. The route to India: ibid., 115.

327. he insisted that Britain: ibid., 136.

327. Undeterred, the Americans formed: ibid., 139.

327. inexperienced men was "amazing": ibid., 145.

327. voluminous report recommending: King and Crane, *King-Crane Commission Report,* 26; Evans, *United States Policy and the Partition of Turkey,* 153.

327. a greater Syria: ibid., 34.

327. Mesopotamia, a separate Armenia: ibid., 51.

328. "the injustice of the Zionist . . . should be given up": ibid., 32.

328. Crane supported Hitler: Dodd, *Ambassador Dodd's Diary,* 11.

328. Dodd thought Crane: Diary entry dated October 4, 1933, in ibid., 42.

328. the king of Arabia: Yergin, *Prize,* 288.

328. tried to persuade: Kaplan, *Arabists,* 69–71.

328. British government prevented them: Fromkin, *Peace to End All Peace,* 534.

328. it was dismayed: Knee, "Anglo-American Relations in Palestine," 6.

328. Anglo-Persian Agreement: Fromkin, *Peace to End All Peace,* 457.

329. treaty with Soviet Russia: ibid., 488.

329. "Pursuing open doors": "Symposium: Fifty Years of William Appleman Williams," *Passport,* 10.

329. He urged that consulates: Evans, *United States Policy and the Partition of Turkey,* 171.

329. Turkish leaders could not: ibid., 174–77.

329. Mark L. Bristol: ibid., 178.

329. San Remo, Italy: Fromkin, *Peace to End All Peace,* 248, 410–11.

329. Robert Underwood Johnson: Evans, *United States Policy and the Partition of Turkey,* 282.

330. Turkish Petroleum Company: Yergin, *Prize,* 189.

330. government in Constantinople: Grew, *Turbulent Era*, 477.

330. The Russians fed arms: Evans, *United States Policy and the Partition of Turkey*, 289.

330. Congress passed an act: Yergin, *Prize*, 195.

330. Rear Admiral Bristol opposed: Evans, *United States Policy and the Partition of Turkey*, 259.

330. "Such Armenian reports": Bristol, "Armenian Issue Revisited" (letter), 2, 5.

330. Cornelius van H. Engert: Evans, *United States Policy and the Partition of Turkey*, 259.

330. Engert investigated the chaos: ibid., 252.

330. United States recognized: ibid., 262.

330. The Allies, led by: ibid., 276.

330. Arab forces fled: Stiller, *George S. Messersmith*, 257.

331. saying American policy: Evans, *United States Policy and the Partition of Turkey*, 265.

331. "By 1920, it seemed": B. Lewis, *What Went Wrong?*, 60.

331. But, added the division: From memo dated July 19, 1921, in Evans, *United States Policy and the Partition of Turkey*.

331. In January 1921: Evans, *United States Policy and the Partition of Turkey*, 329.

331. Robert W. Imbrie was: ibid., 338.

331. "the most authentic": ibid., 363.

331. The nationalist Turks defeated: ibid., 372.

332. "Diplomacy in Europe": Fromkin, *Peace to End All Peace*, 547; Evans, *United States Policy and the Partition of Turkey*, 375.

332. Lord George N. Curzon: Evans, *United States Policy and the Partition of Turkey*, 392.

332. under Allen Dulles: ibid., 396; Grew, *Turbulent Era*, 481–84.

332. conquered back in 1453: B. Lewis, *What Went Wrong?*, 4.

332. "It is surprising": Grew, *Turbulent Era*, 503.

332. "a simple, open, direct": ibid., 488.

332. Ambassador Child reasserted: ibid., 500.

332. military core of Persia: ibid., 529.

333. "Patience was the necessary": ibid., 553.

333. the Chester Concession: Craig and Gilbert, *Diplomats*, 206.

333. The straits were demilitarized: Evans, *United States Policy and the Partition of Turkey*, 403.

333. signed a treaty of amity: Grew, *Turbulent Era*, 600.

333. "avoid getting mixed up": From diary entry dated July 29, 1924, in ibid., 628.

334. a 20 percent share: Evans, *United States Policy and the Partition of Turkey*, 310.

334. Standard Oil of California won: "Establishing the American Presence in the Middle East," *Multinational Oil Corporations and U.S. Foreign Policy* (government report), 4.

334. reluctance the British understood: Abbasov, "Anglo-American Oil Controversy in Iran," 8.

334. State Department supported cooperation: Barnes, *Standing on a Volcano*, 12.

335. "There were different": quoted in Barnes, *Standing on a Volcano*, 13–14.

335. Grews sailed without incident: Grew, *Turbulent Era*, 710.

336. "The water nearly approached": ibid., 717.

336. Three days after: ibid., 717.

336. "In this country": From diary entry dated March 12, 1930, in ibid., 850.

336. Grew's most controversial task: Craig and Gilbert, *Diplomats*, 172–73.

336. "The practical and eminently": Grew, *Turbulent Era*, 917.

336. State Department had to: Yergin, *Prize*, 296.

337. Bert Fish, FDR's Florida: ibid., 292.

337. President Plutarco Calles, of Mexico: Grew, *Turbulent Era*, 667.

337. "the Bolshevik tendencies": Ritchie, "James Rockwell Sheffield" (thesis), 147.

337. recommended the use: From letter dated July 1, 1926, in ibid., 150.

338. President Lázaro Cárdenas: Yergin, *Prize*, 276.

338. "Japan could have done": Stiller, *George S. Messersmith,* 173–74.

338. The Mexican company, Pemex: Yergin, *Prize,* 279.

338. After Pearl Harbor: From Christopher Hill, interview by Montague.

28: "A Single Unified Service": 1920–45

339. "courtier diplomacy . . . aristocratic statecraft": Foglesong, *America's Secret War Against Bolshevism,* 3.

340. Harvey prudently volunteered: *American National Biography*; Pusey, *Charles Evans Hughes,* 2: 584–85.

340. "consuls performed 235,194": Barnes and Morgan, *Foreign Service of the United States,* 199.

340. "diplomacy ceases to be": Pearton, *Diplomacy, War and Technology,* 194.

341. handed to "outsiders": Grew, *Turbulent Era,* 386.

341. "He [Lansing] also said": From letter dated April 24, 1919, in ibid., 385–86.

341. "that the Diplomatic Service": From letter to Wright dated January 18, 1920, in ibid., 410.

341. "the ability of . . . the high Government": Grew, *Turbulent Era,* 410.

341. "But there is little": From diary entry dated January 27, 1920, in ibid., 425.

342. "the boys with": Lay, *Foreign Service of the United States,* 240; Committee on Foreign Affairs, 68th Cong., 1st sess.; Barnes and Morgan, *Foreign Service of the United States,* 207.

342. "For example, Leland Harrison": Heinrichs, "Bureaucracy and Professionalism" (chapter), 145.

342. "When I first went": Murphy, *Diplomat Among Warriors,* 444.

342. "We are far": Ilchman, *Professional Diplomacy in the United States,* 162, statement to the House Committee on Foreign Affairs.

343. asking for recommendations: Crane, *Mr. Carr of State,* 249.

344. colleges would produce "gentlemen": Schulzinger, *Making of the Diplomatic Mind,* 51.

344. "punctual, methodical, prudent": Heinrichs, "Bureaucracy and Professionalism" (chapter), 132–35.

344. "We shall have laid": Extension of remarks to House of Representatives, 66th Congress, p. 9186.

344. Secretary Lansing agreed: Ilchman, *Professional Diplomacy in the United States,* 153; Barnes and Morgan, *Foreign Service of the United States,* 203.

344. "The machinery of government": From letter dated January 21, 1920, in Barnes and Morgan, *Foreign Service of the United States,* 203.

344. "American diplomatic appointments": From p. 16 of the July 20, 1921, issue of *The New York Times,* as quoted in Ilchman, *Professional Diplomacy in the United States,* 157.

344. "wholly and unmixedly evil . . . primarily designed for": "American Universities, American Foreign Service and an Adequate Consular Law," by National Business League of America, 1909, p. 60.

345. "The European war came": Gullion, "Towards an Amalgamated Foreign Service?," 8.

346. "a man in a sweat": Heinrichs, "Bureaucracy and Professionalism" (chapter), 164.

346. Rogers's bill failed: Gullion, "Towards an Amalgamated Foreign Service?," 8.

346. Wilbur Carr would "bureaucratize": Heinrichs, "Bureaucracy and Professionalism" (chapter), 167.

346. Grew, Castle, and Hugh: ibid.; Grew, *Turbulent Era,* 471.

347. "find their way . . . people who talk": Heinrichs, "Bureaucracy and Professionalism" (chapter), 165.

347. "Low salaries are keeping": Crane, *Mr. Carr of State*, 254.

347. "The days of intrigue": Lay, *Foreign Service of the United States*, vii.

347. "I have seen some": Committee on Foreign Affairs, 67th cong., 4th sess., Hearing H.R. 12543, December 15, 1922.

347. "Mr. Chairman, this bill . . . fear of a dependent": ibid., December 19, 1922.

348. Davis said that his: From House Committee on Foreign Affairs, 68th Cong., 1st sess., p. 208, in Barnes and Morgan, *Foreign Service of the United States*, 201.

348. "We shall get rid . . . Shall our Government be": Hearing of 67th Cong., 4th sess., February 1923.

349. "We must have proper . . . That is too high": Hearing of 68th Cong., 1st sess., April 29–May 13, 1924.

351. American diplomacy was now: Schulzinger, *Making of the Diplomatic Mind*, 8.

351. "Record Shake-Up in Foreign . . . The greatest shake-up," *New York Times*, July 3, 1924.

351. Foreign Service School would develop new appointees. Calkin, *Women in the State Department*, 241–45.

352. "tend to bureaucratize": From diary entries dated May 26–June 6, 1924, in Grew, *Turbulent Era*, 619; Schulzinger, *Making of the Diplomatic Mind*, 117.

352. Grew pushed through: Grew, *Turbulent Era*, 621.

353. "The Rogers Act": From letter dated October 25, 1926, in ibid., 684.

353. Grew wrote a stiff: From letter dated November 29, 1926, in ibid., 686–87.

353. "the best young men": ibid.

353. In January 1925: Barnes and Morgan, *Foreign Service of the United States*, 213.

354. Foreign Service School graduated: ibid., 211.

354. "promotions and plums . . . neglected and robbed": From letter dated March 18, 1927, in Grew, *Turbulent Era*, 698.

354. "social diplomats . . . tea hounds": Grew, *Turbulent Era*, 699.

354. called for an investigation: Barnes and Morgan, *Foreign Service of the United States*, 214.

354. the Moses-Linthicum Act: ibid., 217; Stowell, "Moses-Linthicum Act on the Foreign Service."

355. career heads of mission: See table in Barnes and Morgan, *Foreign Service of the United States*, 364.

355. recently established standards: Barnes and Morgan, *Foreign Service of the United States*, 217–19.

29: Between World Wars: 1920–39

356. Ambassador Myron T. Herrick: Grew, *Turbulent Era*, 445.

356. "hostilities were suspended": Ginsburgh, "Between War and Peace" (Ph.D. diss.), 258.

357. many Americans felt: Abel, *Missiles of October*, 90.

357. Ambassador Hugh Gibson: U.S. Department of State, *Peace and War*, 9.

357. officers hobnobbed with Nazis: DeSantis, *Diplomacy of Silence*, 70.

357. approved Italy's invasion: ibid., 71–72.

358. his croquet parties: ibid., 71.

358. Roosevelt telephoned William Phillips: Phillips, *Ventures in Diplomacy*, 155.

358. his drunken pursuit: *Diplomatic History*, vol. 32, n. 5, p. 691; Berridge, *British Diplomacy in Turkey*, 79.

358. The young Welles passed: American National Biography.

359. "Through his dynamic": Phillips, *Ventures in Diplomacy*, 204.

359. Count Galeazzo Ciano: Craig and Gilbert, *Diplomats*, 522.

359. "an unhappy time": quoted in DeSantis, *Diplomacy of Silence,* 75.

360. Robert F. Kelley: Mayers, *George Kennan and the Dilemmas of US Foreign Policy,* 25.

360. "Hitler is finished": Dated January 30, 1933, in O. Bullitt, *For the President,* 23.

360. "The Japanese will have": O. Bullitt, *For the President,* 244.

360. "He may be regarded": ibid, 58.

361. U.S. minister in Riga: Kennan, *Memoirs,* 56.

361. department expert on: Mayers, *George Kennan and the Dilemmas of US Foreign Policy,* 10.

361. Kennan reverted to his: Kennan, *Memoirs,* 59–60.

361. "Dear Bill Buddha . . . and don't forget that": O. Bullitt, *For the President,* 97, 88.

361. "If we send men": From letter dated January 1, 1934, in O. Bullitt, *For the President,* 65.

362. "As you will": From letter dated January 7, 1934, in O. Bullitt, *For the President,* 75.

362. "No one in Europe": From letter dated April 8, 1935, in O. Bullitt, *For the President,* 110.

362. Moscow in June 1934: Herndon and Baylen, "Col. Philip R. Faymonville and the Red Army," 487.

362. "a man of absolutely": Cold War Interviews.

363. "I feel that it": From letter dated August 3, 1935, in O. Bullitt, *For the President,* 136.

363. "for I do not want": From letter dated August 14, 1935, in O. Bullitt, *For the President,* 137.

363. "Yet it must be": From letter dated April 20, 1936, in O. Bullitt, *For the President,* 154.

363. Kennan observed that: Kennan, *Memoirs,* 81.

363. Kennan early placed Bolshevism: Mayers, *George Kennan and the Dilemmas of US Foreign Policy,* 38.

363. "a terrible spectacle": Cold War Interviews.

363. xenophobic Soviet Union: Kennan, *Memoirs,* 71.

363. too close to the French: Murphy, *Diplomat Among Warriors,* 32.

363. in love with France: Craig and Gilbert, *Diplomats,* 657.

363. "Nobody, not even Lady": O. Bullitt, *For the President,* 160.

364. "By the end": Kennan, *Memoirs,* 81.

364. Joseph E. Davies: ibid., 82.

364. "For cat's sake": O. Bullitt, *For the President,* 212.

364. Bullitt came to see: ibid., 287.

365. Consular offices: Barnes and Morgan, *Foreign Service of the United States,* 230.

365. The board approved: ibid., 230.

365. Fewer than 5 percent: ibid., 234.

366. their social skills: Dodd, *Ambassador Dodd's Diary,* viii.

366. "a lot of dead wood": Craig and Gilbert, *Diplomats,* 655.

366. Frederic M. Sackett: "Frederic Moseley Sackett, 1868–1941," Sackett Family Association (online).

366. Senate took just two days: Dallek, *Democrat and Diplomat,* 190; Dodd, *Ambassador Dodd's Diary,* 3.

366. He wrote a paper: Dallek, *Democrat and Diplomat,* 103.

366. "one of the most": Dodd, *Ambassador Dodd's Diary,* 181.

366. "my objection is": From letter dated March 20, 1933, in Dallek, *Democrat and Diplomat,* 187.

367. "the most capable": "George S. Messersmith," *Fleetwood (PA) Area Historical Society* (online).

367. By 1930, he was: Stiller, *George S. Messersmith,* 24.

368. Secretary Stimson supported Messersmith: ibid., 31.

368. Dodd took a stroll: Dallek, *Democrat and Diplomat,* 197.

368. "adolescents in the great": From letter dated August 12, 1933, in ibid., 200.

368. Dodd warned FDR: Dallek, *Democrat and Diplomat*, 218.

368. Phillips rejected the boycott: ibid., 202.

368. And he cautioned: Craig and Gilbert, *Diplomats*, 151.

368. He told the department: From diary entry dated September 14, 1933, in Dodd, *Ambassador Dodd's Diary*, 36; Dallek, *Democrat and Diplomat*, 201–04.

368. The Nazis came: Dodd, *Ambassador Dodd's Diary*, 48.

368. They tapped Dodd's telephone: ibid., 56.

368. Dodd reported that some: From diary entry dated January 22, 1934, in ibid., 74.

369. "My final impression": From diary entry dated October 17, 1933, in ibid., 50.

369. "Ach, that is all": From diary entry dated March 7, 1934, in ibid., 89.

369. Hitler seemed convinced: Dallek, *Democrat and Diplomat*, 225–27.

369. "A unique triumvirate!" From diary entry dated March 7, 1934, in Dodd, *Ambassador Dodd's Diary*, 91.

370. He identified them: From diary entry dated January 17, 1936, in ibid., 300.

370. "The further I go": From diary entry dated March 22, 1934, in ibid., 92–93.

370. "of doubtful Cuban fame": From diary entry dated March 30, 1934, in ibid., 98.

370. "but be sure": From diary entry dated May 3, 1934, in ibid.

370. "the syphilis of all": Dallek, *Democrat and Diplomat*, 233.

370. Daniel A. Mulvihill: Dodd, *Ambassador Dodd's Diary*, 26.

370. Violinist Fritz Kreisler: ibid., 119.

370. Joachim von Ribbentrop's house: ibid., 131.

371. "I decided . . . that I": From diary entry dated July 13, 1934, in ibid., 126.

371. Dodd urged him: From diary entry dated September 19, 1934, in ibid., 166.

371. "The arms manufacturers": From diary entry dated September 9, 1934, in ibid., 167.

371. "Many of the young": ibid., 234.

371. "If we had entered": From letter dated May 9, 1935, in Dodd, letters, Great Britain / German Diplomatic Files; also see Dallek, *Democrat and Diplomat*.

371. "In two years Germany": From diary entry dated December 30, 1935, in Dodd, *Ambassador Dodd's Diary*, 292; Phillips, *Ventures in Diplomacy*, 174.

30: Early Aggressions: 1934–39

373. Breckinridge Long cabled: Cable Ambassador in Italy (Long) to Secretary of State, Rome, 13 September 1935.

373. shot and killed himself: *New York Times*, September 5, 1935.

374. "millions of colonists": U.S. Department of State, *Peace and War*, 278–83.

374. Jane Morrison Engert: J. Engert, *Tales from the Embassy*, 67–72.

374. Marrying a wealthy woman: ibid., 57–64.

374. Sara Morrison Cunningham: *New York Times*, July 28, 1972.

374. "a fine, death-dealing rain": Haile Selassie I, "Appeal to the League of Nations" (speech), 1.

375. people took refuge: J. Engert, *Tales from the Embassy*, 142.

375. Engert and his wife: ibid., 146.

375. Italian army arrived: U.S. Department of State, *Peace and War*, 28–32.

375. "courage and devotion to duty": J. Engert, *Tales from the Embassy*, 149.

375. Representative Edith Nourse Rogers; J. Engert, *Tales from the Embassy*, 150.

375. first American minister: Engert, "American Legation Under Fire," American Diplomacy .org, 1; Barnes and Morgan, *Foreign Service of the United States*, 228.

375. "can be designed": U.S. Department of State, *Peace and War*, 33–43.

376. Dodd and Mayer went: From diary entry dated March 7, 1936, in Dodd, *Ambassador Dodd's Diary*, 317–20.

376. "Germany's dictatorship is now": From letter dated April 1, 1936, in Dodd, letters, Great Britain / German Diplomatic Files.

376. But Hitler learned: Craig and Gilbert, *Diplomats*, 596–97.

376. He declared that Germany: Dallek, *Democrat and Diplomat*, 270.

376. "would be hopeless": ibid., 274.

376. "Dodd has many admirable": From letter dated December 7, 1936, in O. Bullitt, *For the President*, 196.

376. Dodd was by then: From letter dated November 23, 1937, in ibid., 233.

376. He criticized Counselor Mayer's: Dodd, *Ambassador Dodd's Diary*, 341.

377. Washington columnist Drew Pearson: From diary entry dated December 13, 1936, in ibid., 371.

377. "both truthless and ruthless": Dallek, *Democrat and Diplomat*, 296.

377. Dodd carried his protest: From diary entry dated May 29, 1937, in Dodd, *Ambassador Dodd's Diary*, 451.

377. Eric C. Windelin: Barnes and Morgan, *Foreign Service of the United States*, 229.

377. "a solid dictatorship": Dallek, *Democrat and Diplomat*, 286; from diary entry dated August 15, 1936, in Dodd, *Ambassador Dodd's Diary*, 341.

377. On Christmas 1936: From diary entry dated December 25, 1936, in Dodd, *Ambassador Dodd's Diary*, 374.

377. "Recently reports have come": From diary entry dated January 27, 1937, in ibid.

378. Bowers telephoned Secretary Hull: Bowers, *My Mission to Spain*, 100

378. Bowers judged that: ibid., 229–30.

378. Bowers favored the Republicans: ibid., 246.

378. When Hallet Johnson: ibid., 244.

378. "boiling mad": From address at the White House, January 15, 1937, cited in ibid., 255.

379. Bowers and his staff: Bowers, *My Mission to Spain*, 262.

379. "were unable to understand": ibid., 266.

379. "This Government will . . . These present warlike": From speech dated September 7, 1936, in U.S. Department of State, *Peace and War*, 331.

379. "I observed that while . . . a war against democracy": Bowers, *My Mission to Spain*, 290–91, 272.

380. Starting on March 16: ibid., 376.

380. Bowers was appalled: ibid., 384.

380. "To me the Munich": ibid., 392.

380. He wrote Roosevelt: ibid., 403.

380. But Britain and France: ibid., 409.

381. "civil war" in Spain: ibid., 415.

381. Bowers was sure: ibid., 416.

381. "With these views": ibid., 413.

381. as Hull explained: ibid.

381. "The marvelous fight . . . We have made": ibid., 414, 418.

381. called "astute, aristocratic": *Time*, December 18, 1944.

381. "known and confessed murderers": From diary entry dated November 13, 1935, in Dodd, *Ambassador Dodd's Diary*, 276.

382. "the kind of Ambassadors": Dallek, *Democrat and Diplomat*, 309.

382. "I am not so": From letter dated November 29, 1937, in Dodd, letters, Great Britain / German Diplomatic Files.

382. called on Dodd: From diary entry dated July 12, 1937, in Dodd, *Ambassador Dodd's Diary*, 422.

382. Messersmith had the chance: Stiller, *George S. Messersmith*, 102.

382. learn to swallow: ibid., 106.

382. The political leaders decided: ibid., 96.

382. Old Guard was still: ibid., 102.

382. State Department's operating budget: ibid., 104–09.

382. absurdity of spending $60: ibid., 107.

383. he and Sumner Welles: ibid., 116.

383. a confidential letter: From diary entry dated September 4, 1937, in Dodd, *Ambassador Dodd's Diary*, 427.

383. "All people are": From diary entry dated November 18, 1937, in ibid., 433.

383. "How our modern civilization": From diary entry dated December 14, 1937, in ibid., 438.

383. "violation of my understanding": From diary entry dated November 13, 1937, in ibid., 434; see also Dallek, *Democrat and Diplomat*, 314.

383. Hugh R. Wilson: O. Bullitt, *For the President*, 181; American National Biography.

384. good in the Fascist myth: Craig and Gilbert, *Diplomats*, 680.

384. "Good man . . . I have four boys": Beschloss, *Kennedy and Roosevelt*, 177, 162.

384. Kennedy asserted that: ibid., 174.

384. President did not want: ibid., 184.

385. Kennedy was sure Britain: Craig and Gilbert, *Diplomats*, 669.

385. Kennedy advised the powers: Conference report filed in House, H. Rep. 96–1432, 122.

385. America and the Jews: ibid.

385. Kennedy misjudged both: Craig and Gilbert, *Diplomats*, 680.

385. "He was clad": From letter dated March 3, 1938, in Wilson, Great Britain / German Diplomatic Files.

386. John Cooper Wiley: Stiller, *George S. Messersmith*, 122.

386. world conference on refugees: Stiller, *George S. Messersmith*, 124.

386. "that what took place . . . that I feared": From memo dated March 22, 1938, in H. Wilson, letters, Great Britain / German Diplomatic Files.

386. Hitler was gathering: Craig and Gilbert, *Diplomats*, 571.

387. Phillips later learned: Phillips, *Ventures in Diplomacy*, 221–22.

387. Messersmith said there was: Stiller, *George S. Messersmith*, 128.

387. Wilson, fearing Bolshevism: ibid., 129.

387. "a mass of seething": Morse, *While Six Million Died*, 223.

387. in Vienna protested: ibid., 224.

387. Their viciousness aroused anger: Stiller, *George S. Messersmith*, 127.

387. He said there would: Phillips, *Ventures in Diplomacy*, 224.

387. "challenge to modern civilization": November 15, 1938, in Morse, *While Six Million Died*, 232.

387. "A war which threatened": From January 4, 1939, speech, in U.S. Department of State, *Peace and War*, 447.

388. Kennan kept watch: Kennan, *Memoirs*, 102.

388. Chamberlain told the House: Shirer, *Rise and Fall of the Third Reich*, 611.

388. enabled Assistant Secretary Messersmith: Stiller, *George S. Messersmith*, 138.

388. On July 1: ibid., 142.

389. Messersmith ordered the roofs: ibid., 143.

31: "The Sands Are Running Fast": 1931–41

390. Johnson notified the department: Buhite, *Nelson T. Johnson,* 62; U.S. Department of State, *Peace and War,* 4.

391. Minister Johnson and Councilor: *New York Times,* February 1, 1932.

391. where, he liked to say: Buhite, *Nelson T. Johnson,* 137.

391. In 1925, Johnson came: ibid., 13.

391. Johnson predicted to Ambassador: From letter dated October 21, 1932, in ibid., 79.

392. Japan's "aggressive" policies: *Diplomatic History,* vol. 30, no. 2 (April 2006): 217–21.

392. Arthur R. Ringwalt: Barnes and Morgan, *Foreign Service of the United States,* 229; Kahn, *China Hands,* 33.

393. "We didn't have": Grew, *Turbulent Era,* 42.

393. That embassy at Heugasse: ibid., 81.

394. Grew was enthralled: ibid., 108.

394. Grew was offered: Grew, *Ten Years in Japan,* 17.

394. Stanley K. Hornbeck: American National Biography.

394. "The military are still": February 20, 1933, in Grew, *Ten Years in Japan.*

394. "Diplomatic agents nowadays": Grew, *Ten Years in Japan,* 96.

394. village of Kakizaka: ibid., 126.

395. waving American and Japanese flags: ibid., 127.

395. "It was a really": April 22, 1934, in ibid., 128.

395. "days of political intensity:" Grew, *Ten Years in Japan,* 128.

395. "swashbuckling temper . . . We would be": From letter dated December 27, 1934, in U.S. Department of State, *Peace and War,* 236; U.S. Department of State, *Peace and War,* 20.

395. shouting "Banzai Bambino": *Diplomatic History,* vol. 34, no. 2, p. 265.

395. "lovable, gentle, charming, courtly": Grew, *Ten Years in Japan,* 173.

396. disguised and walked out: ibid., 178.

396. tried by court-martial: ibid., 175.

396. O. Edmund Clubb: Kahn, *China Hands,* 31; Clubb, *Witness and I,* 48–49.

397. murdered in Shanghai: From telegram dated August 10, 1937, in U.S. Department of State, *Peace and War,* 374–75.

397. Bombers hit the foreign: Lilley and Lilley, *China Hands,* 25–26.

397. "I consider it desirable": From cable dated September 2, 1937, in U.S. Department of State, *Peace and War,* 379.

397. secretary authorized Leland Harrison: From cable dated September 28, 1937, in ibid., 380–83.

397. Americans were killed: Grew, *Ten Years in Japan,* 218.

397. "In modern times": *Time,* October 4, 1937.

397. Johnson prepared to return: Buhite, *Nelson T. Johnson,* 131.

397. Japanese bombers returned: *Time,* October 4, 1937.

398. Johnson had recommended: From letter to Stanley Hornbeck dated September 27, 1937, in Buhite, *Nelson T. Johnson,* 132.

398. Sir Robert Craigie: Grew, *Ten Years in Japan,* 223.

398. Hirota hoped that: ibid., 226.

398. The killing and looting: Lilley and Lilley, *China Hands,* 26.

398. "forming a mound . . . Nanking's streets were littered": Soong, "Writer Tells of Machine Gunning."

399. The Japanese strafed *Panay's:* Alley, "Jim Felt Lucky."

399. Atcheson, a doctor's son: Clubb, *20th Century China*, 98.

399. He did not know: Buhite, *Nelson T. Johnson*, 134.

399. "We must be prepared": From letter dated December 22, 1937, in ibid., 135.

399. Paxton, a missionary's son: Kahn, *China Hands*, 31.

400. Atcheson gave credit: Atcheson, "Report of the Second Secretary of Embassy in China," in *Papers Relating to the Foreign Relations of the United States, Japan*.

400. "The Government and people": From telegram dated December 13, 1937, in U.S. Department of State, *Peace and War*, 394–95.

400. Grew diplomatically thanked Hirota: Grew, *Ten Years in Japan*, 233ff.

400. Grew began to prepare: Grew, *Ten Years in Japan*, 234.

400. "a mistake . . . poor visibility": From Grew's cable sent December 14, 1937, in U.S. Department of State, *Peace and War*, 396–98.

400. The State Department planned: Yergin, *Prize*, 309.

400. Ambassador Dodd counseled: From diary entry dated December 14, 1937, in Dodd, *Ambassador Dodd's Diary*, 439.

401. he said, "two Japans": Grew, *Ten Years in Japan*, 236.

401. "But for a good . . . another similar incident": ibid., 237, 239.

401. Howard promised to warn: From letters dated July 11 and August 4, 1938, in Buhite, *Nelson T. Johnson*, 138.

401. "A Japanese-American war": Grew, *Ten Years in Japan*, 283.

402. "Time, I believe": April 10, 1940, in ibid.

402. "going hell-bent toward . . . vastly in the majority": August 1, 1940, in ibid.

403. They reached a compromise: Yergin, *Prize*, 313; Prange, *At Dawn We Slept*, 5.

403. Grew summarized his new: From cable dated September 12, 1940, in U.S. Department of State, *Peace and War*, 559–72.

403. "In general, the uses": ibid.

403. the situation is "hopeless": ibid., 672.

403. "January 27, 1941": Grew, *Ten Years in Japan*, 368; Yergin, *Prize*, 316.

403. "A member of": From cable dated January 27, 1941, in U.S. Department of State, *Peace and War*, 618–19.

403. Schuler complained that he: Kernan, "Schuler Files"; Thomas, "Pearl Harbor Remembered"; "Diplomat Frank Schuler, Jr., Dies"; "Frank A. Schuler, Jr., 88, U. S. Diplomat"; "Frank A. Schuler, Jr., 88, U. S. Diplomat in Japan."

404. "Roosevelt was still playing": Chace, "Winning Hand."

404. "double-crossed Japan by signing": June 23, 1941, in Grew, *Ten Years in Japan*, 396.

404. Welles and Stark had met: Prange, *At Dawn We Slept*, 165.

404. "full-blooded financial warfare": *Diplomatic History*, vol. 34, no. 1, p. 178.

405. He suggested that if: From memo by Wells dated July 24, 1941, in U.S. Department of State, *Peace and War*, 699–703.

405. Vichy French authorities: Yergin, *Prize*, 318.

405. "At last the United": Prange, *At Dawn We Slept*, 167.

405. "If the Japanese fail": Grew, *Ten Years in Japan*, 412.

405. bombers overflew Chungking: "USS *Tutuila*," from *Dictionary of American Fighting Ships*.

405. two-and-a-half-hour conversation: From August 18, 1941, in Grew, *Ten Years in Japan*, 419–21.

405. Ambassador Nomura delivered: U.S. Department of State, *Peace and War*, 130.

405. Roosevelt handed the Japanese: September 3, 1941, in ibid., 731–32.

406. "Prince Konoye repeatedly stressed": From Grew's memo dated September 6, 1941, in U.S. Department of State, *Peace and War*, 734.

406. belittled this detour: Yergin, *Prize*, 320.

406. Grew, in a report: September 29, 1941, in Grew, *Ten Years in Japan,* 437.

406. "progressive economic strangulation": ibid., 438.

406. "Let us not forget": September 30, 1941, in ibid., 446.

406. The embassy guard: October 19, 1941, in ibid., 459.

406. Japanese blocked heating oil: Yergin, *Prize,* 322.

406. "This is important": October 17, 1941, in Grew, *Ten Years in Japan,* 458.

406. Grew remained optimistic: October 27, 1941, in ibid., 462.

406. "on the record for": ibid, 462.

407. "But he warned that the United": November 3, 1941, in ibid., 469.

407. "The sands are running": ibid.

407. Grew was reassured when: Grew, *Ten Years in Japan,* 478.

407. Grew felt he was not: ibid., 471.

407. Tōjō's speech "utterly childish": December 1, 1941, in ibid., 484.

408. coded "triple priority" message: Grew, *Ten Years in Japan,* 497.

408. two hours before: Grew, *Report from Tokyo,* 3; M. Hill, *Exchange Ship,* 152–53.

32: "A Rattlesnake Posed to Strike": 1939–41

409. Ambassador William C. Bullitt: Stiller, *George S. Messersmith,* 143.

409. "Well, Bill, it's come": Beschloss, *Kennedy and Roosevelt,* 190.

409. "It's all over": ibid., 190.

410. "It's the end of": ibid.

410. Roosevelt comforted him: U.S. Department of State, *Peace and War,* 69–70.

410. "It would be our": From letter dated September 16, 1939, in O. Bullitt, *For the President,* 374.

410. "We in the Embassy": Phillips, *Ventures in Diplomacy,* 240–41.

410. he evidenced little sympathy: Mayers, *George Kennan and the Dilemmas of US Foreign Policy,* 73.

410. embassy and its staff: Kennan, *Memoirs,* 106.

410. "as a mass of inhuman . . . lust to dominate Europe": ibid., 112, 118.

410. Scholar Dean Rusk: Abel, *Missiles of October,* 82.

411. acting as a dissident: MacDonogh, *Good German,* 149.

411. Germany was unbeatable: U.S. Department of State, *Peace and War,* 520–22.

412. In Paris, the French: Murphy, *Diplomat Among Warriors,* 38.

412. "We are at one": May 14, 1940, in O. Bullitt, *For the President,* 416.

412. "any further pressure": From Phillips telegram sent June 1, 1940, in U.S. Department of State, *Peace and War,* 544; also see Phillips, *Ventures in Diplomacy,* 277–78.

412. "On this tenth day": From June 10, 1940, speech, in U.S. Department of State, *Peace and War,* 548.

412. "short of an expeditionary": U.S. Department of State, *Peace and War,* 77.

412. Ambassador Kennedy, in London: Beschloss, *Kennedy and Roosevelt,* 174.

412. British made it clear: O. Bullitt, *For the President,* 435.

412. Albert Einstein sent: Pearton, *Diplomacy, War and Technology,* 240.

413. Kennan brought them back: Kennan, *Memoirs,* 123.

413. Kennan warned against: ibid., 133.

413. Franklin Roosevelt appointed her: American National Biography.

413. She enjoyed two idyllic: Harriman, *Mission to the North,* 139.

413. State Department wanted: ibid., 214–15.

414. Captain Joseph A. Gainard: ibid., 229–45.

415. frightened local people: Harriman, *Mission to the North,* 246ff.

416. Germans burned Narvik's supply: ibid., 299.

416. "It seems to me": ibid., 321.

416. named assistant secretary: Morse, *While Six Million Died*, 38.

417. "an extreme nativist": "America and the Holocaust: People and Events: Breckinridge Long," *The American Experience*, PBS.org.

417. "eloquent in opposition": American National Biography—The War Diary of B. Long, February 6, 1938.

418. "a problem that ought": February 17, 1940, in Morse, *While Six Million Died*, 291.

418. "that these poor people": December 26, 1940, in ibid.

418. that prejudiced his application: Morse, *While Six Million Died*, 300.

418. a masked anti-Semitism: Schulzinger, *Making of the Diplomatic Mind*, 131ff.

419. transferred to Buenos Aires: Rafshoon, "Harry Bingham: Beyond the Call of Duty"; Harty, "Remarks at the Commonwealth Club, San Francisco."

420. "greatly agitated" young man: Telegram from Bern sent August 11, 1942

420. Elting, a Princeton graduate: *New York Times*, August 8, 2001.

420. passed Riegner's report: Elting, "Memorandum: Conversation with Mr. Gerhart M. Riegner"

420. persuaded Wise to refrain: Morse, *While Six Million Died*, 3–10.

420. personal letter to Welles. Morse, "How the Indifference of the U.S. State Department Aided The Nazi Murder Plot," *Heritage Vision* (online).

420. affidavits and personal accounts: Morse, *While Six Million Died*, 22.

420. Welles released Rabbi Wise: ibid.

421. "utter failure of certain": Morgenthau, "Secret Personal Report to the President," JewishVirtualLibrary (online); Morse, "How the Indifference of the U.S. State Department Aided The Nazi Murder Plot," *Heritage Vision* (online), 20.

421. "plain Anti-Semitism motivating": Morgenthau, "Secret Personal Report to the President," JewishVirtualLibrary (online).

421. "action be taken": January 25, 1944, in Morse, *While Six Million Died*, 313; Morse, "How the Indifference of the U.S. State Department Aided The Nazi Murder Plot," *Heritage Vision* (online).

421. "foolishly," according to journalist: Shirer, *Collapse of the Third Republic*, 802.

421. citing Gouverneur Morris: June 11, 1940, in O. Bullitt, *For the President*, 468.

422. "some fanciful reporting . . . hysteria about Communism": Shirer, *Collapse of the Third Republic*, 681; O. Bullitt, *For the President*, 448.

422. Murphy was startled: Vaughan, *FDR's 12 Apostles*, 6.

422. Murphy sent in reports: Murphy, *Diplomat Among Warriors*, 12–15.

422. Murphy watched the trial: ibid., 21–22.

422. The Germans stopped immediately: O. Bullitt, *For the President*, 477.

423. Countess Hélène de Portes: Shirer, *Collapse of the Third Republic*, 812–13; Murphy, *Diplomat Among Warriors*, 51–52.

423. "shrugged again and looked": Shirer, *Collapse of the Third Republic*, 836.

423. "the honor of France": ibid., 846.

423. "the French government will": From cable dated June 17, 1940, in U.S. Department of State, *Peace and War*, 553–54; Shirer, *Collapse of the Third Republic*, 857.

423. France's new leaders told: Shirer, *Collapse of the Third Republic*, 906–07.

423. January 7, 1941: O. Bullitt, *For the President*, 510.

423. When his accusations leaked: From memo dated April 23, 1941, in ibid., 514.

424. General Maxime Weygand: Murphy, *Diplomat Among Warriors*, 82.

424. most were inexperienced: ibid., 90–91.

424. J. Rives Child: Vaughan, *FDR's 12 Apostles*, 55.

425. Chiefs of missions took: Barnes and Morgan, *Foreign Service of the United States*, 242–45.

425. The training division: ibid., 252.

425. limits on the percentage: ibid., 254.

425. He agreed with Britain: From documents published in U.S. Department of State, *Peace and War*, 564–68.

425. endorse FDR for: Beschloss, *Kennedy and Roosevelt*, 17, 216.

425. "Your boys are not": ibid., 222.

426. Assistant Secretary Breckinridge Long: ibid., 222.

426. "I don't suppose": From diary entry dated May 12, 1943, in ibid., 252.

426. Admiral William D. Leahy: From letter dated December 20, 1940, in U.S. Department of State, *Peace and War*, 596.

426. "Never before since Jamestown": U.S. Department of State, *Peace and War*, 600.

426. "We must be": ibid., 607; the entire December 29, 1940, speech can be found in ibid., 599–608.

426. "When you see": From radio address dated September 11, 1941, in U.S. Department of State, *Peace and War*, 742.

427. Walter W. Orebaugh: Barnes and Morgan, *Foreign Service of the United States*, 247–50.

427. the Band of San Faustino: Orebaugh, *Guerrilla in Striped Pants*, 101.

427. Fighting with the partisans: ibid., 158.

428. On May 12, 1944: ibid., 218.

33: "A Very Tragic Moment": 1941–45

429. "This is a very": M. Hill, *Exchange Ship*, 157.

430. "We do not, we": Grew, *Ten Years in Japan*, 528.

431. evening poker game: M. Hill, *Exchange Ship*, 176.

431. leave Berlin immediately: Kennan, *Memoirs*, 136.

431. "Not until the end": ibid.

432. resented by Kennan: Mayers, *George Kennan and the Dilemmas of US Foreign Policy*, 56, 339n4.

432. determined to oppose: Phillips, *Ventures in Diplomacy*, 307.

432. Phillips advised President Roosevelt: ibid., 310.

432. "My mission failed": ibid., 327.

433. to be called Torch: Murphy, *Diplomat Among Warriors*, 96.

433. Hull and Welles feuded: Berridge, *British Diplomacy in Turkey*, 60.

433. "Don't tell anybody": Murphy, *Diplomat Among Warriors*, 102; Vaughan, *FDR's 12 Apostles*, 141.

433. "Nobody ever pays": Vaughan, *FDR's 12 Apostles*, 143.

433. "a secret agent": ibid., 150.

433. five small radio transmitters: Murphy, *Diplomat Among Warriors*, 109.

434. General Mark Clark: Vaughan, *FDR's 12 Apostles*, 164–76.

434. night of November 8–9: Murphy, *Diplomat Among Warriors*, 126; Vaughan, *FDR's 12 Apostles*, 208.

434. Darlan asked him: Vaughan, *FDR's 12 Apostles*, 211.

434. Charles W. Ryder: ibid., 213.

434. making his own decisions: Murphy, *Diplomat Among Warriors*, 127–34.

435. The twenty-year-old assassin: Vaughan, *FDR's 12 Apostles*, 207, 235.

435. "Nothing can take away": Vaughan, *FDR's 12 Apostles*, 240.

435. Ten of Murphy's vice consuls: ibid., 240–44.

435. prepared to invade Sicily: ibid., 221.

435. Murphy and Giraud persuaded: American National Biography.

435. de Gaulle was determined: Murphy, *Diplomat Among Warriors,* 178.

436. "regarding its role": Kennan, *Memoirs,* 163.

436. "I pointed out": Friedman, "Kodak's Nazi Connections."

437. "the farcical and near-tragic": Kennan, *Memoirs,* 173.

437. Bohlen and Kennan dined: ibid., 180–231.

437. "His integrity in": ibid., 233.

437. When the Warsaw uprising: ibid., 210.

437. Kennan believed that was: Cold War Interviews.

437. "He described to me . . . But I am not": Kennan, *Memoirs,* 212–13.

437. Churchill wanted to invade: Murphy, *Diplomat Among Warriors,* 190.

438. FDR was convinced: ibid., 227.

438. The summit: DeSantis, *Diplomacy of Silence,* 132–34.

438. After V-E Day, Murphy: Murphy, *Diplomat Among Warriors,* 263.

438. "Congratulations on the day": Kennan, *Memoirs,* 240–42.

34: Foreign Service for a New World: 1946–51

440. "talking to a stone": Kennan, *Memoirs,* 293.

440. in bed with the flu: Cold War Interviews.

441. He believed the American: DeSantis, *Diplomacy of Silence,* 174–75.

441. "At the bottom . . . World communism is": Kennan, *Memoirs,* 549, 557, 559.

441. Research by Hugh De Santis: De Santis, "Conflicting Images of the USSR," 478.

441. Roosevelt was "unrealistic": Cold War Interviews.

442. the "diplomacy of silence": De Santis, "Conflicting Images of the USSR," 484.

442. Barnes now pressed Washington: De Santis, "Conflicting Images of the USSR," 488.

442. generally regarded as: ibid., 489.

442. "iron curtain" divided Europe: ibid., 490.

442. "Balance of power": C. Freeman, interview by Kennedy.

442. His hope lay: Berridge, *British Diplomacy in Turkey,* 207.

443. Soviet power had limits: DeSantis, *Diplomacy of Silence,* 189.

443. local Communist parties: Kennan, *Memoirs,* 250.

443. "I did not believe": ibid., 464.

443. Loy Henderson judged: DeSantis, *Diplomacy of Silence,* 177.

443. Many U.S. diplomats shared: ibid., 188.

443. Soviet specialist Elbridge Durbrow: ibid., 195; Harry S. Truman Library, Oral History May 31, 1973 with Richard D. McKinzie, Washington, D.C.

443. deputy for foreign affairs: Kennan, *Memoirs,* 298.

443. chaired by Loy Henderson: Rusk, *As I Saw It,* 400.

444. in six weeks Britain: H. W. Brands, *Inside the Cold War,* 154.

444. cut Britain's national wealth: *Diplomatic History,* vol. 27, no. 1, p. 40.

444. Secretary Marshall asked him: Kennan, *Memoirs,* 325–26.

444. top-flight men like: Mayers, *George Kennan and the Dilemmas of US Foreign Policy,* 128.

444. its report, which formed: Kennan, *Memoirs,* 335.

444. "The Sources of Soviet": Kennan, *Memoirs,* 354ff.

444. "a great political force": ibid., 351.

445. "a strategic monstrosity": Mayers, *George Kennan and the Dilemmas of US Foreign Policy*, 114–15.

445. Kennan tried to make: Kennan, *Memoirs*, 365.

445. developments confirmed for him: ibid., 366–67.

445. It took more than: Rusk, *As I Saw It*, 354.

446. "virtually laws unto themselves": Kennan, *Memoirs*, 369.

446. "Personally, I appreciated": Murphy, *Diplomat Among Warriors*, 305.

446. "the ideal diplomat": American National Biography.

447. "Because of their wartime": Ginsburgh, "Challenge to Military Professionalism," 263.

447. The United States looked: Mayers, *George Kennan and the Dilemmas of US Foreign Policy*, 148–49, 155.

447. "the occupation forces": Takemae, *Inside GHQ,* 105.

447. He was an established: ibid., 151.

448. Atcheson was drowned: U. Alexis Johnson, interview by McKinzie, June 19, 1975 (transcript of tape-recorded interview), p. 5–6.

448. "Well, it can't": *Time*, August 25, 1947.

448. William J. Sebald: Takemae, *Inside GHQ*, 151.

448. MacArthur simply did not: Mayers, *George Kennan and the Dilemmas of US Foreign Policy*, 165.

448. "arrived in morning coats": W. Sullivan, *Obbligato*, 123.

448. went Marshall Green: Kennan, *Memoirs*, 383.

449. "had a violent prejudice": ibid., 382.

449. he showed the general: Ginsburgh, "Between War and Peace" (Ph.D. diss.), 388, 416, 437.

449. Far East was now: Moskin, "Our New Western Frontier," *Look*.

449. saw as "totalitarian practices": Kennan, *Memoirs*, 388.

449. James F. Byrnes: H. Brands, "Who Saved the Emperor?," 298.

449. Max W. Bishop: ibid., 294.

450. issue was essentially settled: ibid., 299.

450. imperial institution more democratic: ibid., 300.

450. try Hirohito as: ibid., 289.

450. debate over the retention: H. Brands, "Who Saved the Emperor?"; see also Hirohito, Emperor Imperial Rescript, January 1, 1946 (online).

450. MacArthur believed he: Mayers, *George Kennan and the Dilemmas of US Foreign Policy,* 166.

450. he admitted candidly: Kennan, *Memoirs*, 395.

450. United States still responsible: Mayers, *George Kennan and the Dilemmas of US Foreign Policy,* 170.

451. President Truman wanted: Sperber, *Murrow*, 132.

451. "the Zionist juggernaut": L. Henderson, interview by McKinzie, 104.

451. "I accused the Zionists": From letter to James R. Fuchs dated April 3, 1977, in E. Wright, interview by McKinzie.

451. "one of the most": H. W. Brands, *Inside the Cold War,* 188.

451. He was transferred to: E. Wright, interview with McKinzie, 47.

451. telegram to the State: Muccio, interview by Hess, 30–32.

451. A note reporting: Rusk, *As I Saw It*, 160.

452. invasion was a total surprise: ibid., 161.

452. "Aggression had been committed": Field, "Decision to Intervene," in *History of United States Naval Operations: Korea.*

452. "I had not been": Muccio, interview by Hess, 41.

452. The first unit: Montross and Canzona, *U. S. Marine Operations in Korea*, 105–06.

453. "MacArthur was a jackass": Whitman, "Architect of Postwar Policy."

35: The Foreign Service Catches Up: 1946–88

454. Positions were filled: Barnes and Morgan, *Foreign Service of the United States*, 255.

454. shortage of trained manpower: Murphy, *Diplomat Among Warriors*, 451.

455. Maximum salaries for ambassadors: Barnes and Morgan, *Foreign Service of the United States*, 259.

455. creation of the Foreign: Ruth A. Davis, interview by author, Virginia.

455. "These newer things. . . . In the Foreign Service": Battle, interview by McKinzie and Wilson, 36–37, 44.

456. Overseas missions included: Elder, *Information Machine*, 48.

456. Its report advised: Barnes and Morgan, *Foreign Service of the United States*, 267–68; Murphy, *Diplomat Among Warriors*, 452.

456. National Security Council: Rusk, *As I Saw It*, 524.

457. "Down in the government": Elder, *Information Machine*, 635

457. McGeorge Bundy, was trusted: ibid., 116.

457. The Rowe committee's results: Barnes and Morgan, *Foreign Service of the United States*, 271–72.

458. "The so-called Wriston Report": Bohlen, interview by Mulhollan, 9.

458. It would combine education: Letter to President of the Senate and Speaker of the House.

458. it would turn out: Schulzinger, *Making of the Diplomatic Mind*.

458. Ambassador Stephen Low: Low, interview by Kennedy, 58.

458. He told visitors: ibid., 58–59.

459. specialists and foreign nationals: Ruth A. Davis, interview by author, Virginia.

459. "I learned how": Tom C. Korologos, interview by author, Brussels.

459. Brandon Grove remembers: Davies, *China Hand*, 39–53.

460. Oral exams, which: Barnes and Morgan, *Foreign Service of the United States*, 283–84.

460. "contribute to the development . . . . They were protected": U.S. Department of State, *Diplomatic Immunity*.

460. These principles still hold: Denza, *Diplomatic Law*, 168.

461. the centuries-old principle of immunity: ibid., 212.

461. Both laws emphasized: ibid., 406.

461. British scholar Eileen Denza: ibid., 5.

461. Nikita Khrushchev blundered: "Estimate of Damage to U.S. Foreign Policy Interests" (government document).

462. more than one wife: Denza, *Diplomatic Law*, 322–25.

462. When the widow and: ibid., 34–35.

462. "A great change": Phillips, *Ventures in Diplomacy*, 460.

463. The USAID workforce: American Academy of Diplomacy, *Foreign Affairs Budget for the Future* (report), 18–19.

463. "fragmentation of foreign assistance": "AFSA Member Survey Results."

463. By 1952, this activity: Barnes and Morgan, *Foreign Service of the United States*, 289.

463. Knowledge was required: ibid., 297.

464. "You walk in": Habib, "The Work of Diplomacy," in conversation with Kreisler.

464. He nationalized the Canal: Rusk, *As I Saw It*, 187.

465. Suez Canal was vital: Murphy, *Diplomat Among Warriors*, 347.

465. "ill-conceived and pathetic": Matthews, "Foster Dulles and the Suez Crisis of 1956," 17.

465. KC-135 landed Murphy: Murphy, *Diplomat Among Warriors,* 399.

465. He arranged for: ibid., 408.

466. A decade earlier: Murphy, *Diplomat Among Warriors,* 375–418.

466. 1982 crisis in Lebanon: Shultz, *Turmoil and Triumph,* 44.

466. "getting to know people": John M. Evans, interview by author, Saint Petersburg.

466. more pressure on analysis: Burt and Robinson, *Reinventing Diplomacy in the Information Age,* 125.

467. This would not: *Washington Post,* July 25, 2004, p. C11.

467. delegate more decision making: Rusk, *As I Saw It,* 525.

467. "The idea that policy": ibid., 534.

467. The quantity of information: Burt and Robinson, *Reinventing Diplomacy in the Information Age,* 132–33.

467. the tragedy at Mogadishu: Davies, *China Hand,* 308.

467. "If . . . there had": Burt and Robinson, *Reinventing Diplomacy in the Information Age,* 129.

467. "to stick their necks": Rusk, *As I Saw It,* 527.

467. Rusk found this standard: Ted Sorensen, *Counselor,* 234.

468. "the world of diplomacy": Burt and Robinson, *Reinventing Diplomacy in the Information Age,* 113.

468. "The shift from": *Foreign Affairs,* vol. 76, no. 5, p. 6.

36: Diversity Comes to the Elite Service: 1922–2011

471. 66 percent males: "More Representative Foreign Service," *U.S. Diplomacy* (online).

471. Lucile Atcherson, of Columbus: Greenwald, "Life in Public Service," chap. 7 in *A Woman of the Times.*

471. She had the third: More Representative Foreign Service," *U.S. Diplomacy* (online).

471. "She is the first": *New York Times,* September 21, 1922.

472. "a clever woman": ibid., 516.

472. executive order in 1936: ibid., 526.

472. "The appointment of": Calkin, *Women in the State Department,* 161.

472. John Hay said: ibid., 24.

472. "their well-known inability": Van Dyke, *Our Foreign Service,* 75.

472. attitude that persisted: Schulzinger, *Making of the Diplomatic Mind,* 108.

472. Cecilia Kieckhoeder Jourdan: Calkin, *Women in the State Department,* 49; Gaddis, *George F. Kennan,* 50.

473. In 1922, Lillie Maie Hubbard: Calkin, *Women in the State Department,* 198.

473. "the most feasible": Calkin, *Women in the State Department,* 69.

473. three alternative strategies: ibid.

474. "It would only be . . . the inevitable tide": From Grew to Gibson, May 20, 1925, quoted in ibid., 70.

474. "We might as well": Diary entry dated January 19, 1925, in Grew, *Turbulent Era,* 646.

474. she said the best: Calkin, *Women in the State Department,* 76.

474. "My wife has already . . . I have the honor": Gibson, *Hugh Gibson,* 60, 61.

475. sent to Panama: Greenwald, "Life in Public Service," chap. 7 in *A Woman of the Times.*

475. accepted with regret: Calkin, *Women in the State Department,* 78.

475. "a ravishing orange skin-tight": *Time,* January 5, 1926.

475. "worse than useless": From telegram September 3, 1925, in Calkin, *Women in the State Department,* 78.

475. she resigned to join: ibid., 80; Gaddis, *George F. Kennan,* 78,

475. Frances Elizabeth Willis: Nash, "A Woman's Touch in Foreign Affairs?" 8.

475. "The minister left . . . Who is Willis?": Calkin, *Women in the State Department,* 166; Nash, "A Woman's Touch in Foreign Affairs?" 1.

476. She never pleaded discrimination: Nash, "A Woman's Touch in Foreign Affairs?," 11.

476. "I went into": ibid., 12.

476. first woman named: ibid., 5, 7.

476. While in Madrid: ibid., 6–7.

476. Executive Order 5189: Calkin, *Women in the State Department,* 89.

477. confusion and duplication: Barnes and Morgan, *Foreign Service of the United States,* 222.

477. G. Howland Shaw: Calkin, *Women in the State Department,* 96.

477. She was thrown clear: ibid., 97.

477. 207 women were appointed: A. Wright, "Breaking Through Diplomacy's Glass Ceiling," 58.

478. Clare Boothe Luce: "More Representative Foreign Service," *U.S. Diplomacy* (online).

478. The Foreign Service Act: McGlen and Sarkees, *Women in Foreign Policy,* 63.

478. Betty Ann Middleton: Gaddis, *George F. Kennan,* 108.

478. very narrow gateway: Calkin, *Women in the State Department,* 108.

478. Margaret Joy Tibbetts: McGhee, *Envoy to the Middle World,* 119.

479. But, by 1965: Calkin, *Women in the State Department,* 128.

479. "to provide greater justice": ibid., 135.

479. changes from within: ibid., 138.

479. After 1972, a female: R. Davis, "From the Queen of Sheba to Madeleine Albright and You" (speech), 8.

480. This made it unacceptable: Calkin, *Women in the State Department,* 148.

480. were known as "dragons": Laingen, interviewed by Kennedy, 6.

480. In contrast, more chiefs: ibid., 27.

480. "It was Roy": B. Atherton, interviewed by Weiss, 11–12.

480. "from day one": ibid., 12.

480. In August 1971: *New York Times,* July 28, 1989.

480. she was rejected: McGlen and Sarkees, *Status of Women in Foreign Policy,* 21.

481. "The savages in": ibid., 116; *Los Angeles Times,* February 13, 1972.

481. "We are going": McGlen and Sarkees, *Women in Foreign Policy,* 121.

481. District Court for: Petition for a Writ of Certiorari to the United States Court of Appeals, in the Supreme Court of the United States, October Term, 1985, p. 2.

481. engaged in sex discrimination: McGlen and Sarkees, *Women in Foreign Policy,* 64.

481. a number of changes: ibid., 17.

481. Twenty-six women who: ibid., 82.

481. only 7 percent: ibid., 83.

481. more than 200 women: *New York Times,* July 28, 1989.

481. "The class action": McGlen and Sarkees, *Women in Foreign Policy,* 176.

482. chief of mission assignments: Calkin, *Women in the State Department,* 176.

482. "Old male-dominant attitudes": ibid., 221.

482. "It used to be": R. Davis, "From the Queen of Sheba to Madeleine Albright and You" (speech), 2.

482. "Her intellectual courage": Calkin, *Women in the State Department,* 212.

482. "There's no job . . . Oh, even in": ibid., 157.

482. "At first I thought": R. Davis, "From the Queen of Sheba to Madeleine Albright and You" (speech), 8.

483. first African-American woman director: Susser and Rasmussen, "African-American Heritage."

483. "I was determined . . . The white, male": Vance, *Hard Choices*, 40, 41.

483. equal opportunity mandatory: McGlen and Sarkees, *Status of Women in Foreign Policy*, 20, 64.

483. women "agonizingly slow": McGlen and Sarkees, *Status of Women in Foreign Policy*, 20.

483. 1,006 women among 4,427: McGlen and Sarkees, *Women in Foreign Policy*, 76.

483. 6.9 percent (54 persons): ibid., 77.

483. women occupied 25 percent: A. Wright, "Breaking Through Diplomacy's Glass Ceiling," 54.

483. "Recruitment efforts suffered": McGlen and Sarkees, *Women in Foreign Policy*, 61; Commission on Civil Rights, *Equal Opportunity in the Foreign Service*, 9.

484. assigned to the political: McGlen and Sarkees, *Women in Foreign Policy*, 90.

484. Jeane Kirkpatrick became permanent: McGlen and Sarkees, *Status of Women in Foreign Policy*, 32.

484. "paid a price": D'Amico, "Review of *Her Excellency*."

484. "The Department has gone": Mak and Kennedy, *American Ambassadors in a Troubled World*, 48–49.

484. virtually "lily-white" U.S. Foreign: Krenn, *Black Diplomacy*, 43.

485. Bassett had studied: Susser and Rasmussen, "African-American Heritage"; Padgett, "Diplomats to Haiti and their Diplomacy," 276.

485. post in Haiti: Padgett, "Diplomats to Haiti and their Diplomacy," 276.

485. he returned home discouraged: Kremer, *James Milton Turner and the Promise of America*.

485. declined President Cleveland's offer: L. Davis, "Joseph Charles Price's Rejection."

485. When that imperialistic mission: Sears, "Frederick Douglass and the Mission to Haiti."

485. assigned to Cognac, France: Susser and Rasmussen, "African-American Heritage."

485. But by 1908: ibid.

486. James Carter, James Weldon: "More Representative Foreign Service," *U.S. Diplomacy* (online).

487. first secretary and consul: Krenn, *Black Diplomacy*, 46.

487. rank of career minister: Susser and Rasmussen, "African-American Heritage"; see also entry in *American National Biography*.

487. Edward R. Dudley: Krenn, *Black Diplomacy*, 19–20.

487. When Ambassador Dudley traveled: McGhee, *Envoy to the Middle World*, 120.

487. Terence A. Todman: interview by author, Washington, D.C.

488. "was concocted within": Krenn, *Black Diplomacy*, 52.

488. seventeen black FSOs: ibid., 145.

488. "the only bull": Manchester, *Last Lion*, 1: 34.

488. "As you know": January 1961, in Krenn, *Black Diplomacy*.

488. But in 1968: Susser and Rasmussen, "African-American Heritage."

488. only two black ambassadors: Krenn, *Black Diplomacy*, 147.

488. Rowan told this story: Rusk, *As I Saw It*, 383.

489. Ford Foundation in 1963: Krenn, *Black Diplomacy*, 147.

489. "that Washington is being . . . Support was my problem": ibid., 152, 157.

490. Terence Todman became: Krenn, *Black Diplomacy*, 166.

490. leaving no African-Americans: Susser and Rasmussen, "African-American Heritage."

490. He retired in 1993: Krenn, *Black Diplomacy*, 171.

490. Perkins then served: Susser and Rasmussen, "African-American Heritage"; Edward J. Perkins, interview by author, Aspen, CO.

490. nearly $4 million: Krenn, *Black Diplomacy*, 169.

490. "It is a racial": Makila James, in interview with author, Aspen, CO.
490. "The African slave trade": *Washington Post,* May 21, 1995.
490. James persevered; by 2005: M. James, "Standing Up."
491. end of 2005: Susser and Rasmussen, "African-American Heritage."
491. The overall picture: Krenn, *Black Diplomacy,* 130.
491. "I saw no one . . . My experience has": Bloch, "Women and Diplomacy."
491. Ambassador Edward J. Perkins: Rabby, "Blind Achieving Success in the Work Place" (letter).
492. by the mid-1970s: *Diplomatic History,* vol. 30, no. 1.
492. Christian A. Herter Award: Kessler, "Ex-Ambassador Criticizes Rice."
492. But health care: Eugene P. Sweeney, interview by author, Lisbon, Portugal.

37: China Hands: 1946–89

494. to Stilwell "at once": Clubb, *20th Century China,* 240.
494. Hurley distrusted the State: Kahn, *China Hands,* 123.
494. Colonel David D. Barrett: ibid., 116.
494. "selfish and corrupt": Kifner, "John Service, a Purged 'China Hand,' Dies at 89."
494. reported fully on Mao's: Davies, *China Hand,* 216.
495. "We should end": Service, *Lost Chance in China,* 165; quote in Kahn, *China Hands,* 131.
495. The Americans judged: Kahn, *China Hands,* 128.
495. Both sides were furious: ibid., 139.
495. orderly mind and: ibid., 64–65.
496. drew a pistol: ibid., 146.
496. threatened to destroy: ibid., 148.
496. a "narcissistic blowhard": Ji Chaozhu, *Man on Mao's Right,* 257.
496. "China is in": Kahn, *China Hands,* 3.
496. "He [Hurley] had come": Clubb, interview with McKinzie, 10.
497. He swore he would: Kahn, *China Hands,* 154.
497. Service left Yenan: ibid., 156.
497. Hurley convinced Roosevelt: J. Burns, *Roosevelt,* 590.
497. "the nightmarish quality": Kahn, *China Hands,* 158.
497. "a rock of strength": Kennan, *Memoirs,* 239.
498. Davis was awarded: See obituaries in *Washington Post* and *New York Times,* December 24, 1999.
498. "if ever again": CBS Radio on November 8, 1954, in Kahn, *China Hands,* 30.
498. Among those arrested: See Larsen's obituary in the May 4, 1988, *Washington Post.*
498. Service had given: Lumbers, " 'Staying Out of the Chinese Muddle,' " 128.
498. federal grand jury: Kahn, *China Hands,* 171.
498. was "recklessly indiscreet": Mirsky, "In the Service of Whose Country?"
498. General Order No. 1: Clubb, *20th Century China,* 257.
499. United States took sides: ibid., 260.
499. "the career men . . . destroy the Government": Kahn, *China Hands,* 175, 177, 178.
499. Secretary Byrnes came: *Time,* December 17, 1945.
499. failure of Marshall's mission: Clubb, *20th Century China,* 273.
499. John Leighton Stuart: Stuart, *Fifty Years in China.*
500. invading Japanese held Clubb: See Clubb's obituary, *New York Times,* May 11, 1989.
500. veteran FSO Fulton Freeman: Clubb, interview by McKinzie, 18.
500. Clubb arrived from Peking: Kahn, *China Hands,* 209.
500. since the Boxer Rebellion: ibid., 202; Clubb, interview with McKinzie, 19.

500. They were ushered out: Stuart, *Fifty Years in China,* 235.

500. Henry Luce finally recognized: Rowan, *Chasing the Dragon,* 182.

501. "the world's worst leadership": Clubb, *20th Century China,* 295.

501. Clubb dumped tons: Clubb, interview with McKinzie, 21, 23, 25.

501. Dean Acheson called "the Primitives": Whitman, "Architect of Postwar Policy, Acheson Advocated Containment of the Soviet Union"; W. Cohen, *Dean Rusk,* 44; Rusk, *As I Saw It,* 160.

501. "The unfortunate but inescapable": Kahn, *China Hands,* 205; see also Whitman, "Architect of Postwar Policy, Acheson Advocated Containment of the Soviet Union."

501. "there wasn't a thing": Battle, interview by McKinzie and Wilson, 33.

501. Congressman Walter H. Judd: Cold War Interviews.

503. "false loyalty to what": Myrdal, "Inherent Imperfections in Foreign Policy" (transcript of lecture), 4.

503. In 1963, Otepka: *New York Times,* April 20, 1969; also Rusk, *As I Saw It,* 562–63.

503. he stated under oath: Kahn, *China Hands,* 233.

503. Loyalty Review Board: ibid., 238.

503. "a completely loyal": ibid., 239–40.

504. Department of Defense objected: Kahn, *China Hands,* 272.

504. At age fifty-one: ibid., 243.

504. he be "terminated": ibid., 251.

504. "studied praise of Chinese": ibid.

504. *Foreign Service Journal* protested: ibid., 252–53.

505. "trying to put Communists": ibid., 258.

505. Dulles said if he: ibid., 261.

505. Davies bypassed the State: ibid., 284.

505. "weakened beyond real": ibid., 33.

505. "as we have heretofore": Quoted in Khan, *China Hands,* 34; also see ibid., 305.

505. "These Foreign Service officers": Kahn, *China Hands,* 295.

506. "will honor those Foreign": ibid., 299.

506. "For having been right . . . It remains essential": Tuchman, "Why Policy Makers Do Not Listen."

506. "It would be naive": Quoted in Kahn, *China Hands,* 305.

506. United States regarded: Karnow, *Vietnam,* 3.

506. ostensibly to recover Americans: Ministry of Foreign Affairs of the People's Republic of China, "Sino-U.S. Ambassadorial Talks."

507. Edward Rice recommended: Lumbers, "'Staying Out of the Chinese Muddle,'" 264.

507. "clouded in obscurity": quoted in ibid., 272.

507. "a dragon with": interview by Rostow, as quoted in ibid.

507. Starting in 1968, CIA: Lilley and Lilley, *China Hands,* 145; also see interview with Kissinger.

507. "a war on the": Lumbers, "'Staying Out of the Chinese Muddle,'" 276.

507. President Nixon cautiously: Mann, *About Face,* 22.

507. followed Lei Yang's interpreter: Ji Chaozhu, *Man on Mao's Right,* 241.

508. A second meeting: *Time,* February 2, 1970.

508. "These Warsaw talks": Karnow, *Vietnam,* 9; Mann, *About Face,* 23.

508. "After we'd been": Moskin, "Dangerous World of Walt Rostow," 29.

508. "We were fortunate": *New York Times* obituary February 1, 2007, quote from Henry Kissinger, "White House Years" 1979.

509. He emphasized the Soviet: Burr, *Negotiating U.S.-Chinese Rapprochement.*

509. Alexander M. Haig, Jr.: ibid.

509. "speaking the blunt": Memorandum of Conversation, Zhou Enlai and Haig, January 3,
      1972, p. 3.

509. Haig said the United: ibid., 5.

509. "unfortunately, most American . . . reinforce President Nixon's": ibid., 7.

509. "the image of": Memorandum of Conversation, Zhou Enlai and Haig, January 7, 1972, p. 13.

509. "not only a matter": ibid., 12.

509. "The Nixon trip": See Arts section, New York Times, February 13, 2011.

509. "give the Soviet Union": Kissinger, "Conversation with Orville Schell," 3.

509. Beijing over time replaced: Ji Chaozhu, Man on Mao's Right, 252.

509. In Beijing, Kissinger refused: Burr, Negotiating U.S.-Chinese Rapprochement.

509. "Until he became Secretary": Lilley and Lilley, China Hands, 154.

510. "the secret trip was": Cold War Interviews with Lord.

510. Secretary Rogers was left: Mann, About Face, 40.

510. Nelson Rockefeller in 1969: Low, interviewed by Kennedy, 31.

510. Secretary Dean Rusk: Rusk, As I Saw It, 197.

510. from a bilateral match: Diplomatic History vol. 27, no. 5 (November 2003), p. 656.

511. John Holdridge and Al: Lilley and Lilley, China Hands, 172–73.

511. "declared CIA officer": Mann, About Face, 64.

511. When Vance visited Beijing: Diplomatic History vol. 33, no. 4, p. 552.

511. Richard C. Holbrooke: Mann, About Face, 88.

511. Carter told him: ibid., 89.

511. finally closed its embassy: Lilley and Lilley, China Hands, 219.

511. Vance was shocked: Mann, About Face, 92.

512. "unofficial American Institute": Time, May 28, 1979.

512. He was saddled: Lilley and Lilley, China Hands, 242.

512. President Ronald Reagan supported: ibid., 248; Mann, About Face, 144.

512. Ji Chaozhu, the sophisticated: C. Freeman, interview by Kennedy.

512. In 1982, Haig resigned: Mann, About Face, 123–26.

512. He minimized the China-based: ibid., 128–33.

513. Dunlop said losing: Lilley and Lilley, China Hands, 274–79.

513. "the biggest exclusive club": Moskin, "Advise and Dissent."

513. as a young diplomat: Burr, Negotiating U.S.-Chinese Rapprochement; Moskin, "Advise and
      Dissent."

513. Bush's concern for: Lord, interview by Mann, in Mann, About Face, 178.

514. They finally walked: New York Times, February 27, 1989.

514. "What we are calling": Orville Schell, New York Times, April 16, 1989.

514. Brent Scowcroft criticized: Mann, About Face, 181.

514. "The Bush administration": Time, March 13, 1989.

514. Lord sent Scowcroft: Mann, About Face, 183.

514. On May 17: ibid., 187.

514. Lilley predicted to: Lilley and Lilley, China Hands, 308.

515. Americans back home: Mann, About Face, 192.

515. James Huskey was swept: Lilley and Lilley, China Hands, 315.

514. "He is a giant": ibid., 321.

515. asked for "physical protection": Thomas L. Friedman, New York Times, June 13, 1989.

515. Raymond Burghardt and McKinney: Mann, About Face, 202–04.

516. "not to engage in": Nicolas D. Kristoff, New York Times, June 26, 1990.

516. A new policy: Mann, About Face, 227, 240.

516. "Go home and tell": Lilley and Lilley, *China Hands*, 331.

516. "on the wrong side": Joint press conference on October 29, 1997, in Mann, *About Face*, 357.

38: Public Diplomacy: 1941–2012

517. "public diplomacy" bypasses: Denza, *Diplomatic Law*, 29.

517. "to promote the national": ibid.

517. has not been particularly: Myrdal, "Inherent Imperfections in Foreign Policy" (lecture in manuscript), 8.

518. "Public diplomacy creates": Daniel R. Russel, interview by author, The Hague, The Netherlands, May 23, 2005.

518. Radio, of course: Thomas Sorensen, *Word War*, 225.

518. "Television's ability to bring": Burt and Robinson, *Reinventing Diplomacy in the Information Age*, 20.

518. replace hierarchies with networks: ibid., 9.

518. "Ending the culture": Burt and Robinson, *Reinventing Diplomacy in the Information Age*, 12.

518. "In this world": ibid., 40.

518. "America's first practitioner": ibid., 41n89.

519. William Bayard Hale: Epstein, "German and English Propaganda," 2–12.

519. "Here speaks a voice": Thomas Sorensen, *Word War*, 10.

520. Office of War Information: Dizard, *Inventing Public Diplomacy*, 146.

520. But in 1946: Elder, *Information Machine*, 35.

520. By 1948, programs aiming: Thomas Sorensen, *Word War*, 23.

520. Public Law 402: Elder, *Information Machine*, 36.

520. end of 1952: *Diplomatic History*, vol. 27, no. 4, p. 551.

520. committee of the Daughters: Thomas Sorensen, *Word War*, 24.

520. "in the fields": Dizard, *Inventing Public Diplomacy*, 52.

521. "influencing the attitude": Grady, "Proposed New Program for USIE, Iran,"

521. "The program must": ibid.

521. The senator assailed him: Murrow, "Report on Senator Joseph R. McCarthy," *See It Now*, CBS-TV.

521. case of Beatrice Braude: Rosenfeld, "Lost Causes, Thwarted Dreams."

522. out of operations and propaganda: Elder, *Information Machine*, 199.

522. wary of foreign information: Thomas Sorensen, *Word War*, 45.

522. The new agency began: ibid., 47.

522. in 1979 cultural operations: Dizard, *Inventing Public Diplomacy*, 178.

522. At first, these USIS: ibid., 154.

522. The USIS centers worked: Thomas Sorensen, *Word War*, 66.

523. Some were burned: Dizard, *Inventing Public Diplomacy*, 180.

523. Satellites made live telecasts: Elder, *Information Machine*, 234.

523. But when Russian troops: Thomas Sorensen, *Word War*, 91.

523. "the cause of human": From Shultz's February 22, 1984, speech, in Burt and Robinson, *Reinventing Diplomacy in the Information Age*, 32 (see n66 for full bibliographic information on the speech).

523. "a call to the": "American and The World 1978," *Foreign Affairs*.

523. George V. Allen: Elder, *Information Machine*, 41; see also entry in *American National Biography*; Dizard, *Inventing Public Diplomacy*, 76; Thomas Sorensen, *Word War*, 104.

524. Kennedy and Murrow mobilized: Elder, *Information Machine*, 82.

524. "wars of national liberation": Dizard, *Inventing Public Diplomacy*, 84.

524. "We were required . . . influencing public attitudes": Thomas Sorensen, *Word War*, 238, 142.

524. persuasion—psychological warfare: Sperber, *Murrow*, 634.

524. USIA was seen as: Elder, *Information Machine*, 82.

524. Ed Murrow kept asking: "Public Diplomacy: A Strategy for Reform" (transcript of press conference), Council on Foreign Relations, 4.

524. "In the end": March 14, 1961, in Thomas Sorensen, *Word War*, 137.

524. Murrow, who had a global reputation: Elder, *Information Machine*, 178.

524. But Murrow understood: Thomas Sorensen, *Word War*, 141.

524. "To be persuasive": March 28, 1963, in ibid., 4.

525. USIA officer was assigned: Sperber, *Murrow*, 647–49.

525. "The commercial press": Elder, *Information Machine*, 2.

525. Propaganda was the government's: Dizard, *Inventing Public Diplomacy*, xiv.

525. condemned throughout Latin America: Moskin, *U.S. Marine Corps Story*, 607–15.

525. Henry Loomis, a former: Dizard, *Inventing Public Diplomacy*, 140.

525. Loomis returned in 1969: Dizard, *Inventing Public Diplomacy*, 140.

525. "honest journalism," Chancellor's term: Elder, *Information Machine*, 186.

525. especially crucial in reporting: ibid.

525. Two years later, JUSPAO: Thomas Sorensen, *Word War*, 282.

525. psychological-warfare and: *New York Times*, January 6, 2011.

526. Leonard H. Marks: See Marks' obituary, *New York Times*, August 16, 2006.

526. "There was an explosion": Glyn T. Davies, interview by author, London, England.

527. William P. Rogers: Dizard, *Inventing Public Diplomacy*, 108.

527. tension developed between: Thomas Sorensen, *Word War*, 65.

527. USIA to reorient itself: Dizard, *Inventing Public Diplomacy*, 211.

528. For three years: Feulner, "Regaining America's Voice Overseas: A Conference on U.S. Public Diplomacy," 26.

528. "the successor to": United States International Affairs Website

528. Senator Jesse Helms: Feulner, "Regaining America's Voice Overseas: A Conference on U.S. Public Diplomacy," 3; Dizard, *Inventing Public Diplomacy*, 213.

528. "undermine the President's": "Statement by the President: The Foreign Relations Revitalization Act of 1995 (S.908)," U.S. Senate.

528. "a reinvented Department": U.S. Department of State, "Fact Sheet Foreign Affairs Reorganization Dec. 30 (1998)."

528. USIS libraries were converted: Dizard, *Inventing Public Diplomacy*, 214.

528. They were called "crosswalkers": Krecke, "U.S.I.A.-State Integration: A Work in Progress."

528. Another 2,689 worked: *History of the Department of State During the Clinton Presidency (1993–2001)*, Bureau of Public Affairs, 13; U.S. Department State, "Fact Sheet Foreign Affairs Reorganization."

528. Ruth A. Davis: Krecke, "U.S.I.A.-State Integration," 6.

529. "I believe that": ibid., 8.

529. "The first thing": quoted in Feulner, "Regaining America's Voice Overseas: A Conference on U.S. Public Diplomacy," 1.

529. "American public diplomacy": quoted in ibid. 26.

529. "I devoted equal . . . I tried to counter": *Washington Post*, August 24, 2002.

529. the new Radio Sawa: Dizard, *Inventing Public Diplomacy*, 223.

530. "truly creative professionals": "Public Diplomacy: A Strategy for Reform" (transcript of press conference), Council on Foreign Relations, 6.

530. "Audiences may not agree": Tutwiler, "Public Diplomacy" (testimony before the House Appropriations Subcommittee on Commerce, Justice, State and the Judiciary).

530. "The country's best": Ungar, "Pitch Imperfect."
531. But a policy decision: Elder, *Information Machine*, 224.
531. removed from the VOA: Ungar, "Pitch Imperfect."
531. As of 1985, twelve USIS: Dizard, *Inventing Public Diplomacy*, 205.
531. gave Elsner $18,000: "U.S. Pays Former Employee $18,000 for Eleven Years in Czech Prison"; Dizard, *Inventing Public Diplomacy*, 205.
532. For years, USIS provided: Elder, *Information Machine*, 262.
532. Access is free: *State Magazine*, June 2009, 18.
532. "The focus of today's": Foreign Affairs Day, May 6, 2005.
532. "We have to go": Thomas C. Korologos, interview by author, Brussels, Belgium.
532. "excessive bureaucratic review . . . misplaced security concerns": Council on Foreign Relations, *Improving the U.S. Public Diplomacy Campaign in the War Against Terrorism*.
533. Foreign Service's job: William Imbrie, interview by author, Brussels, Belgium.
533. studies showed no improvement: *New York Times*, October 31, 2007.
533. "Those responsible for U.S.": Council on Foreign Relations, *Managing Secretary Rice's State Department*, 20–21.
533. "needs a major infusion": American Academy of Diplomacy, *Foreign Affairs Budget for the Future*, 15.

39: Diplomacy for American Dictators: 1953–89

534. "The American continents": Commager, *Documents of American History*, 236.
535. "We oppose aggression . . . The nature of democracy": Acheson, "Waging Peace in the Americas" (address), 3.
535. "traditional rulers of semi-traditional": Kirkpatrick, "Dictatorships and Double Standards."
535. "Lots of good": Kamane M. Romero, interview by author, Brussels, Belgium.
536. The United States appreciated: C. James, *Silas Deane*, 174.
537. Saudis contributed $32 million: Walsh, *Final Report of the Independent Counsel for Iran/Contra Matters*, 7.
537. "Our emissary should telephone": Secret cable from American Embassy Brunei to State Department, NSA, "Iran-Contra Affair 20 Years On," 10.
537. President Reagan authorized: Walsh, *Final Report of the Independent Counsel for Iran/Contra Matters*, 5.
537. "It's amateur hour": Shultz, *Turmoil and Triumph*, 785.
538. one American hostage: Walsh, *Final Report of the Independent Counsel for Iran/Contra Matters*, 1: 15–16.
538. He gave two reasons: Shultz, *Turmoil and Triumph*, 789.
538. State, not the NSC: ibid., 808; Walsh, *Final Report of the Independent Counsel for Iran/Contra Matters*, 1: 1.
538. "I would not break": Walsh, *Final Report of the Independent Counsel for Iran/Contra Matters*, 1: 7.
538. "So's your old man!": ibid., 1: 22, 38.
538. Secretary Shultz demanded: ibid., 1: 22.
538. first State Department document: ibid., 1: 24.
538. "But this snake": Shultz, *Turmoil and Triumph*, 784.
539. "not our system": Walsh, *Final Report of the Independent Counsel for Iran/Contra Matters*, 1: 13.
539. A Lebanese newspaper made: ibid., 1: 27, 29.

539. Shultz wrote that he: Shultz, *Turmoil and Triumph*, 811.

539. The public uproar: Walsh, *Final Report of the Independent Counsel for Iran/Contra Matters*, 1: 29.

539. confessed to Shultz: Shultz, *Turmoil and Triumph*, 845–46.

539. "continuing and unbelievable": Walsh, *Final Report of the Independent Counsel for Iran/Contra Matters*, 1: 1.

539. Four CIA officials: ibid., 1: 6.

539. "central aspects of Shultz's . . . Independent Counsel declined": ibid., 1: 1, 69.

540. "pleaded guilty to": Walsh, *Final Report of the Independent Counsel for Iran/Contra Matters*, 1: 25, 7.

540. "one of Washington's most": *Washington Post*, May 27, 2003, p. A1.

540. against his "gastronomic diplomacy": Kornbluh, "Negroponte File," May 26, 1983.

540. Meara admired the peasant: Meara, *Contra Cross*, 109.

540. "I didn't want": ibid., 98.

541. They talked until two: Gleijeses, *Shattered Hope*, 255.

541. "I came away": U.S. Department of State. *Foreign Relations of the United States*, vol. 4, document 20.

541. "It was perfectly clear": F. Lewis, "Ambassador Extraordinary."

541. El Pulpo: Oral History Thomas Cabot, Harry S Truman Library.

541. "For us there are": Dulles interview, Princeton University, cited in Kinzer, *Overthrow*, 215.

541. On January 16, 1954: U.S. Department of State, *Foreign Relations of the United States*, vol. 4, document 22.

541. In May, a secret: Gleijeses, *Shattered Hope*, 303; Holland, "Private Sources of U.S. Foreign Policy," 56.

541. Robert D. Murphy: Kinzer, *Overthrow*, 140.

542. "United Fruit Company expeditionary": ibid., 142.

542. William Pawley, a wealthy: Holland, "Private Sources of U.S. Foreign Policy," 43, 61.

542. pressed by Ambassador Henry: Murphy, *Diplomat Among Warriors*, 372.

542. "U.S. policy": R. White, "Rethinking Foreign Policy."

542. Arbenz drowned in his: Kinzer, *Overthrow*, 204.

543. He fired and Mein: M. Krebs, "Guatemala Critic" (telegram from embassy in Guatemala to Department of State).

000. the wife of the deputy: Ruge, "Foreign Service Life: Assignment Guatemala 1968: An Early Encounter with Terrorism," American Diplomacy.org.

543. In June 1990: Harrington, *Report on the Guatemala Review*, Intelligence Oversight Board, 28.

543. Colonel Julio Roberto Alpirez: ibid., 30

544. Robert G. Torricelli: *New York Times*, June 4, 1995.

544. voluminous, if cautious, report: Harrington, *Report on the Guatemala Review*, Intelligence Oversight Board.

544. "The human rights records": ibid., 3.

545. "Our Latin policies": "A More Representative Foreign Service," Association for Diplomatic Studies and Training.

546. coup overthrew Stroessner: *New York Times*, March 24, 1987, page 7A; *New York Times* article, December 22, 1987, page 4A; and *New York Times* editorial, March 26, 1987.

546. Earl E. T. Smith: *Communist Threat to the United States Through the Caribbean*, Subcommittee of the Committee on the Judiciary.

546. Smith later testified: ibid.; "Symposium: Fifty Years of William Appleman Williams," 24.

547. "the unsung hero": Rusk, *As I Saw It*, 232.

547. naval blockade versus: Abel, *Missiles of October,* 65.

547. Kennedy told him: ibid., 74.

547. Nicholas Katzenbach, prepared: ibid., 86.

548. "I don't know . . . No. Would you": Acheson, interview by Battle.

548. Chargé d'affaire, Cecil Lyon: Abel, *Missiles of October,* 104.

548. "Your President has done . . . You may tell": Acheson, in interview with Battle; Abel, *Missiles of October,* 105–06.

548. "Anything President Kennedy wants": Low, interview by Kennedy, 20.

548. "Wherever you are": ibid.

549. proposed exchanging the removal: *Diplomatic History,* vol. 33, no. 2, p. 261.

549. purpose of the boarding: Abel, *Missiles of October,* 161.

549. "We're eyeball-to-eyeball . . . I was always sorry": Moskin, "Dean Rusk."

549. "triumph of both": Rusk, *As I Saw It,* 229.

549. Only years later: BAS 10/62, p. 86.

549. "one mistake can make": Abel, *Missiles of October,* 198.

549. Operation Mongoose: Cold War Interviews with Samuel Halpern.

550. James Cason, a Dartmouth: *New York Times,* December 9, 2005.

550. Planning for Grenada: Moskin, *U.S. Marine Corps Story,* 736.

551. Sixty-three people, including: ibid., 731.

551. On October 25, ibid., 744.

551. UN General Assembly voted: Kinzer, *Overthrow,* 219–38.

551. Dana Gardner Munro: *Time,* July 7, 1930; see also obituary in *New York Times,* June 19, 1990.

552. By then, most Haitians: Padgett, "Diplomats to Haiti and their Diplomacy," 322, 324, 326.

552. Brian Dean Curran: Bogdanich and Nordberg, "Mixed U.S. Signals Helped Tilt Haiti Toward Chaos."

552. Reich called Clinton's support: ibid.

553. "assassinations, mob violence": ibid.

553. Bunker made seventy-five speeches: Schaffer, *Ellsworth Bunker,* 298.

554. Everett E. Briggs: Buckley, *Panama,* 148.

554. he was thwarted: ibid., 153.

554. Noriega had the Panamanian: Buckley, *Panama,* 88–89.

554. Delvalle fired General Noriega: ibid., 123.

554. Noriega short-circuited a military: ibid., 134.

554. "They were just throwing . . . ineptitude": ibid., 139.

555. Richard Cheney promised: ibid., 12.

555. "a bunch of Keystone": Kinzer, *Overthrow,* 253; Buckley, *Panama,* 212.

555. he turned himself over: Buckley, *Panama,* 244.

555. He was sentenced: Kinzer, *Overthrow,* 306.

556. "the best drug bust": Moskin, *U.S. Marine Corps Story,* 764.

556. But two years later: ibid., 766.

556. "the white elite": Buckley, *Panama,* 259–60.

40: Trujillo and Pinochet—Contrast in Violence: 1960–2004

557. "the underworld in epaulets": Davies, *Foreign and Other Affairs,* 47.

558. Farland, a former: Diederich, *Trujillo,* 10.

558. wartime FBI agent: Hevesi, "Joseph S. Farland," 92.

558. a coup against Trujillo: Diederich, *Trujillo,* 43.

558. said that the only: *Alleged Assassination Plots Involving Foreign Leaders,* 195.

558. "Dominicans put an end": ibid.

558. "the ingredients for": ibid., 199.

558. Two .38 caliber pistols: E. Simmons, "Dominican Adventure" (unpublished manuscript).

559. Trujillo's baby-blue Chevrolet: *Alleged Assassination Plots Involving Foreign Leaders*, 213; Simmons, "Military-Political Situation in the Dominican Republic," 218.

559. Trujillo stumbled out: Diederich, *Trujillo*, 113–21.

559. Trujillo was dead: ibid., 157–60.

559. His remark made headlines: ibid., 162–63.

560. John Calvin Hill: ibid., 246.

560. threatened Simmons with: E. Simmons, "Dominican Adventure" (unpublished manuscript).

561. On Sunday, April 25, army: A. Lowenthal, *Dominican Intervention*, 74.

561. Embassy supported the generals: U.S. Department of State, *Foreign Relations of the United States, 1964–1968*, vol. 32, p. 2.

561. generals ordered the air: A. Lowenthal, *Dominican Intervention*, 77–78.

561. Ambassador Bennett recommended: U.S. Department of State, *Foreign Relations of the United States, 1964–1968*, vol. 32, p. 2.

562. first combat-ready U.S. forces: Schaffer, *Ellsworth Bunker*, 139.

562. had been overruled: A. Lowenthal, *Dominican Intervention*, 151.

562. Carl Rowan, director: U.S. Department of State, *Foreign Relations of the United States, 1964–1968*. vol. 32, p. 2.

562. Secretary Rusk agreed: Rusk, *As I Saw It*, 373.

563. Helicopters blanketed the country: Schaffer, *Ellsworth Bunker*, 148.

563. ordered to support Balaguer: U.S. Department of State, *Foreign Relations of the United States, 1964–1968*, vol. 32.

563. he had coordinated: Crimmins, interview by Hewitt, 2.

563. Crimmins's purpose now: ibid., 4.

564. Later, they would: Bowers, *Chile Through Embassy Windows*, 298.

564. "The landing of . . . Our too great": ibid., 192, 315.

564. Salvadore Allende Gossens: Hove, "Arbenz Factor," 625.

564. When the demand: ibid., 628.

564. Senator Allende built: ibid., 661.

565. Korry, who openly disapproved: Korry's obituary, *New York Times*, January 30, 2003.

565. known as NSSM 97: Kornbluh, *Pinochet File*, 7–11.

565. Traditionally, Chile's congress chose: Boorstein, *Insider View*, 54.

565. sent Washington eighteen reports: Kornbluh, *Pinochet File*, 11.

565. "nothing more than paranoia": *New York Times Book Review*, May 13, 2007, 29.

565. Nixon instructed the CIA: Kornbluh, *Pinochet File*, 1; Kinzer, *Overthrow*, 178–79.

566. Once again, Nixon demonstrated: Hoffmann, "Kissinger Antimemoirs."

566. ordered not to tell: Kornbluh, *Pinochet File*, 13.

566. "American hand": *Covert Action in Chile, 1963–1973*, U.S. Senate, 4.

566. Track 2, closely held: ibid., 23.

566. "steps that President Frei . . . If necessary, General Schneider": Korry, "Situation Report" (secret report to Meyer and Kissinger).

566. By early October: Kornbluh, *Pinochet File*, 21.

566. Colonel Paul Wimert: *Covert Action in Chile, 1963–1973*, U.S. Senate, 45; Kornbluh, *Pinochet File*, 28; Kinzer, *Overthrow*, 183.

567. He died three days: Boorstein, *Insider View*, 68; Kornbluh, *Pinochet File*, 28.

567. unintended outcome forced: Boorstein, *Insider View*, 172.

567. The CIA later admitted: Kornbluh, *CIA Acknowledges Ties to Pinochet's Repression: Report to Congress Reveals U.S. Accountability in Chile*, Covert Action in Chile, 1963–1973, U.S. Senate, 11.

567. generals were to be: *Covert Action in Chile, 1963–1973*, U.S. Senate, 22; Boorstein, *Insider View*, 252.

567. "This I think was": Mak and Kennedy, *American Ambassadors in a Troubled World*, 61.

567. committee was known: *Covert Action in Chile, 1963–1973*, U.S. Senate, 34.

567. Korry contended that: ibid.

568. "But he just failed": Kornbluh, *Pinochet File*, 99.

568. Secretary of State William Rogers considered: Kornbluh, *Pinochet File*.

568. "We'll be very cool": From document 1, November 6, 1970, in Kornbluh, *Pinochet File*.

568. "ability to implement": Kissinger, "Policy Towards Chile" (top-secret letter).

568. "excess profits taxes": Kissinger, *Years of Upheaval*, 380.

568. Ambassador Korry dreamt up: Kornbluh, *Pinochet File*, 17–18.

568. CIA urged private groups: *Covert Action in Chile, 1963–1973*, U.S. Senate, 26.

568. "make the economy scream": ibid., 28.

568. CIA "heavily subsidized": *New York Times*, September 20, 1974, quoted in Boorstein, *Insider View*, 192.

568. "not a nut": *Covert Action in Chile, 1963–1973*, U.S. Senate, 22; Boorstein, *Insider View*, 87.

569. Chile's economy was chiefly: *Covert Action in Chile, 1963–1973*, U.S. Senate, 27.

569. U.S. Ambassador William Culbertson: Boorstein, *Insider View*, 23.

569. CIA began covert operations: Kornbluh, *Pinochet File*, 4.

569. in October 1967: Korry, "Ambassador Edward M. Korry in CEP," interview by Fermandois and Talavera, 14.

569. Chile's foreign indebtedness: Boorstein, *Insider View*, 27.

569. Chilean congress voted: *New York Times* editorial, July 19, 1971, quoted in ibid., 134.

569. U.S. government tried: Boorstein, *Insider View*, 100–01.

569. But most farm workers: ibid., 157.

569. "moved toward totalitarianism . . . The slide to chaos": Kissinger, *Years of Upheaval*, 384, 393.

569. "to aid the opposition": Seymour Hersh, *New York Times*, September 24, 1974, quoted in Boorstein, *Insider View*, 172.

570. "I reiterated assurances": From cable to Secretary of State sent October 12, 1973, in Kornbluh, *Pinochet File*, 173ff., document 4.

570. "We want to help": Kornbluh, *Pinochet File*, 201.

570. Foreign ministers of forty-three: *New York Times*, February 21, 1974.

570. authorized sending $10 million: *New York Times*, December 14, 1975.

570. "did not know . . . without our assistance": "Korry, Edward M., former U.S. Ambassador to Chile, Testimony of," Church Committee, 34, 40, 44.

570. "the idiots in the CIA . . . toy soldiers": Korry, "Ambassador Edward M. Korry in CEP," interviewed by Fermandois and Talavera, 23, 28.

570. "actively supported the military . . . These Cold War attitudes": CIA, *CIA Activities in Chile*, 2, 5.

571. On August 15, bombs: Kissinger, *Years of Upheaval*, 402.

571. carefully prepared coup: Boorstein, *Insider View*, 234.

571. Allende was killed: Aguilera and Fredes, *Chile*, 58; Kissinger, *Years of Upheaval*, 404–05.

571. American embassy reported: Kissinger, *Years of Upheaval*, 405.

571. La Moneda surrendered: Kornbluh, *Pinochet File*, 113.

571. Colonel Carlos Urrutia: ibid., 202.

571. "political mythology . . . implacable ideological hatred": Kissinger, *Years of Upheaval*, 374.

572. Thousands of Chileans: Kornbluh, *Pinochet File,* 161.

572. "However unpleasant they act": Kissinger, on October 1, 1973, in Bowers, *Chile Through Embassy Windows,* 201–03.

572. The DINA arranged: Jonathan Kandell, Pinochet's obituary, in *New York Times,* December 10, 2006.

572. Some were shot: Burbach, *Pinochet Affair,* 135, 141; Kornbluh, *Pinochet File,* 163.

572. Korry, Meyer, and Kissinger: Boorstein, *Insider View,* 249–50.

572. "have encountered worldwide skepticism . . . there is no evidence": *New York Times,* September 16, 1973, quoted in ibid., 250.

572. article in *Foreign Affairs:* Paul E. Sigmund's January 1974 article in ibid., 250.

572. William Colby, the CIA's director, revealed: *New York Times,* September 15, 1974, in ibid., 251.

573. That would require: *Diplomatic History,* vol. 34, no. 5, p. 823.

573. Vernon Walters, the CIA's: Kornbluh, *Pinochet File,* 213.

573. "maintaining and strengthening": ibid., 228.

573. That November, the: ibid., 323.

573. Operation Condor planned: ibid., 355, document 3.

574. "unpunished . . . to fully normalize": ibid., 405, 410.

574. Ambassador Harry Barnes: ibid., 423.

575. Scotland Yard officers: Burbach, *Pinochet Affair,* 102.

575. "Human rights were not": Kornbluh, *Pinochet File,* 487.

41: Dangerous Diplomacy: 1960–78

576. serve at "presence posts": Harry Thomas, interview by author, Washington, D.C.

576. "Statesmanship is in direct": Gardner, *Mission Italy,* 65.

577. "For a year": Douglas R. Smith, interview by author, Barcelona, Spain.

577. Armin H. Meyer: *New York Times* obituary, September 10, 2006.

577. Stanleyville on the Congo: Hoyt, *Captive in the Congo,* 40.

578. "a great avalanche": Oral history.

578. twenty-one new nations: Attwood, *Reds and the Blacks,* 15.

579. The ambassador had changed: Hoyt, *Captive in the Congo,* 62.

579. The Americans spent: ibid., 66.

579. "We now had": ibid., 67.

580. Hoyt agreed to send: ibid., 115.

580. President Jomo Kenyatta: Attwood, *Reds and the Blacks,* 203.

580. 1,300 Europeans in Stanleyville: ibid.

580. President Gbenye was using: ibid., 205.

580. The Americans despaired: Hoyt, *Captive in the Congo,* 155.

581. In early November: ibid., 188.

581. They heard rumors: Attwood, *Reds and the Blacks,* 192.

581. they would all be: Hoyt, *Captive in the Congo,* 191.

581. In Europe, a battalion: Attwood, *Reds and the Blacks,* 207.

581. Americans were moved: Hoyt, *Captive in the Congo,* 207.

581. Attwood was told: Attwood, *Reds and the Blacks,* 212.

582. from American C-130Es: U.S. Army Center of Military History, "Congolese Rescue Operation."

582. Eighteen had been killed: Hoyt, *Captive in the Congo,* xx.

582. Five more died: ibid., 225.

582. pilot told them: ibid., 220.

583. prime minister, Cheddi Jagan: Moskin, "Memo on a Marxist."

583. flew with Richard McCloy: Leger, *Haiti,* 126, 135, 136.

583. Viron P. Vaky: *Assassination of Representative Leo J. Ryan and the Jonestown, Guyana Tragedy,* U.S. House of Representatives.

583. The leaders in Jonestown: Mak and Kennedy, *American Ambassadors in a Troubled World,* 128.

584. Dwyer insisted that Ryan: *Assassination of Representative Leo J. Ryan and the Jonestown, Guyana Tragedy,* U.S. House of Representatives.

585. Dwyer was shot: Dwyer, *Report on CODEL Ryan's Visit to Jonestown and Subsequent Murder* (memo to Secretary of State).

585. Three members of the: *Assassination of Representative Leo J. Ryan and the Jonestown, Guyana Tragedy,* U.S. House of Representatives.

585. "He was tireless": Davies, *China Hand,* 210.

585. "He was a very": Mak and Kennedy, *American Ambassadors in a Troubled World,* 129.

585. Dwyer's daughter, who was: ibid., 133.

585. Although Ryan's staff criticized: "Nightmare in Jonestown," *Time,* December 4, 1978.

585. "As far as what": Dwyer, interview by Kennedy, 28.

42: Terrorists in the Embassies: 1968–2009

587. "Nothing prepares you": Under Secretary Bonnie R. Cohen, transcript, "Excerpts."

587. "Our diplomats are": R. Nicholas Burns, interview by author, Athens, Greece.

588. "I bridle a little . . . I didn't recall": Armitage, "Conversation with Former Deputy Secretary of State Richard Armitage," interview by Rose, 29.

588. "The 'war on terror' . . . Terrorism is not an": Brzezinski, "Terrorized by 'War on Terror.'"

588. "I spent many years": Talk by Ambassador Frank Calucci at Council on Foreign Relations, Washington, D.C., June 5, 2003.

589. Ten Americans, eleven FSNs: *Bombings of the US Embassies in Nairobi, Kenya and Dar es Salaam, Tanzania,* report of the accountability review boards, 1.

589. Forty-four were killed: Bushnell, "After Nairobi" (video transcript).

590. The damage to: *Bombings of the US Embassies in Nairobi, Kenya and Dar es Salaam, Tanzania,* report of the accountability review boards, 1.

590. Ambassador Bushnell had to: *New York Times,* August 13, 1998.

590. also participated in: *History of the Department of State During the Clinton Presidency (1993–2001),* Bureau of Public Affairs, 2, 7.

590. "We confronted a new": Bushnell, "After Nairobi," 3–4.

591. Accountability Review Board criticized: *Bombings of the US Embassies in Nairobi, Kenya and Dar es Salaam, Tanzania,* report of the Accountability Review Boards, 7.

592. Eighty-five people were injured: ibid., 1.

592. Osama bin Laden: Coll, *Ghost Wars,* 403.

592. correct these failures: *Bombings of the US Embassies in Nairobi, Kenya and Dar es Salaam, Tanzania,* report of the Accountability Review Boards, overview, 3.

594. Granville and his Sudanese: Jeffrey Gettleman, *New York Times,* January 2, 2008.

594. Leonhardy was released: *Time,* May 21, 1973.

594. embassy secretary, Antoinette Varnava: Cuddis, *George F. Kennan,* 100.

594. Soviet officers advising: J. Sullivan, *Embassies Under Siege,* 55–56.

595. "Ambassador Dubs was killed": ibid., ix.

595. Marines tried to turn: Moskin, *U.S. Marine Corps Story,* 721.

596. 2006, when Qaddafi said: "Daniel Williams in Cairo," *Washington Post*, May 16, 2006, A12.

596. Gene A. Cretz: *State Magazine*, September 2010, 30.

596. Outside the compound: *Time*, March 10, 1980, cited in Asencio, "Original Cheap Shot."

597. On October 30, 1979: J. Sullivan, *Embassies Under Siege*, 97–111.

597. Robert E. White: "U.S. Losses Ground in Central America," *New York Times*, July 9, 1980, A10.

598. "The city is progressively . . . incomprehensible and unacceptable": Shultz, *Turmoil and Triumph*, 70.

598. Habib needed months: ibid., 83.

598. "one of the unique": ibid.

599. United States pulled: Moskin, *U.S. Marine Corps Story*, 727–41.

600. "The State Department": from www.ojc.org/Higgins.

601. It was detonated: United Press International, August 13, 2001.

601. Karachi police in a: *Washington Post*, March 9, 1995.

602. The rocket launcher: CNN.com, September 13, 1995.

602. Among them were seven: *New York Times*, December 23 and 24, 1996.

604. International Red Cross: Danner, "Taking Stock of the Forever War," 9.

605. the United Nations took over: Resolution 1244.

605. Protestors ripped: McCormack, "Situation at U.S. Embassy Belgrade" (transcript of press briefing).

605. riot police moved slowly: *Washington Post*, February 22, 2008.

605. protected by fifteen-foot-high walls: *New York Times*, July 10, 2008, A11.

606. USS *Cole* in Aden: *New York Times*, September 18, 2008.

606. Solecki was in charge: Associated Press article in *New York Times*, February 2, 2009.

606. "Coping with increasing": J. Sullivan, *Embassies Under Siege*, xi.

43: A War Too Far—Vietnam: 1952–75

608. a "muddled hodgepodge . . . I could not think": Acheson, *Present at the Creation*, 673.

608. supported Ho Chi Minh's ambition: Barnet, *Intervention and Revolution*, 183.

608. Euro-centered colonialism won out: Toprani and Moss, "Filling the Three-Year Gap," 4–11.

608. British brought back: Karnow, *Vietnam*, 163.

608. France's role in Indochina's: Rusk, *As I Saw It*, 422.

609. Instead, North Vietnam set: Perkins, *Prudent Peace*, 40.

609. "Dulles was the reactionary's": Ji Chaozhu, *Man on Mao's Right*, 126.

609. Ambassador Frederick Reinhardt: *Diplomatic History*, vol. 30, no. 4.

609. Rusk did not want: W. Cohen, *Dean Rusk*, 183–84.

609. Rusk said that Diem: Rusk, *As I Saw It*, 432; Kross, "General Maxwell Taylor's Mission to Vietnam."

609. By 1963, eighteen thousand: Rusk, *As I Saw It*, 434.

609. "We must face": McNamara, *In Retrospect*, 52.

609. Afterward, Rusk confirmed: Rusk, *As I Saw It*, 437.

610. "the Saturday cable": ibid., 438.

610. President Kennedy himself: Kinzer, *Overthrow*, 151–69; McNamara, *In Retrospect*, 51–72.

610. Ambassador Lodge predicted: McNamara, *In Retrospect*, 85.

610. United States had actually: Hilsman, interview for *Vietnam*.

610. "We saw a world": McNamara, *In Retrospect*, 157–58.

610. "Unprovoked attack against": U.S. Department of State, *Foreign Relations of the United States*, 1, document 263.

611. "We believe that present": ibid., 1, document 271.

611. Contradictory reports soon started: U.S. Department of State, *Foreign Relations of the United States,* 1, document 276.

611. "An immediate and direct": ibid., 1, document 278.

611. Secretary McNamara replied: ibid.

611. "I recall there being": Read, second interview by Mulhollan, 2.

611. The Viet Cong attacked: Karnow, *Vietnam,* 424.

611. President Johnson began bombing: Rusk, *As I Saw It,* 449.

611. Barbara A. Robbins: Gaddis, *George F. Kennan,* 98.

612. Congress promptly assigned: "145: Statement by the President on the Bombing of the U.S. Embassy in Saigon."

612. "a catastrophic war": McNamara, *In Retrospect,* 195.

612. Under Secretary Ball opposed: M. White, "Going to War in Vietnam," *American Diplomacy.org.*

612. The conversations were brief: McNamara, *In Retrospect,* 196.

612. Every attempt crashed: Read, second interview by Mulhollan, 9–14.

612. They all favored: McNamara, *In Retrospect,* 197.

612. The North Vietnamese responded: ibid., 230; Karnow, *Vietnam, 497.*

613. On December 31, 1965: *Diplomatic History* vol. 31, no. 5 (November 2001), 836.

613. State Department's request: Karnow, *Vietnam,* 510.

613. base at Khe Sanh: Moskin, *U.S. Marine Corps Story,* 659; Prados, "Mouse That Roared," NSA, 17.

614. the end of January: Karnow, *Vietnam,* 536.

614. Ambassador Ellsworth Bunker: Schaffer, *Ellsworth Bunker,* 193, 172.

614. The commandos blew open: Zabecki, "Battle for Saigon," and North, "American Reporter Witnessed the VC Assault on the U.S. Embassy," on *History Net.*

614. Peter Arnett told the: North, "American Reporter Witnessed the VC Assault on the U.S. Embassy," on *History Net.*

615. "On the eve": Karnow, *Vietnam,* 550.

615. He sent a reassuring: Schaffer, *Ellsworth Bunker,* 195.

615. at 9:15 A.M.: North, "American Reporter Witnessed the VC Assault on the U.S. Embassy," on *History Net.*

615. General William C. Westmoreland: Moskin, *U.S. Marine Corps Story,* 66.

615. Four U.S. Army MPs: Karnow, *Vietnam,* 539–40.

615. Three days later: North, "American Reporter Witnessed the VC Assault on the U.S. Embassy," on *History Net.*

615. no longer supported President: Karnow, *Vietnam,* 559.

615. "Tet was the beginning": North, "American Reporter Witnessed the VC Assault on the U.S. Embassy," on *History Net.*

616. he recommended that: Karnow, *Vietnam,* 568.

616. "I shall not seek": W. Cohen, *Dean Rusk,* 311.

616. "the shape of": U.S. Department of State. *Foreign Relations of the United States,*

616. Eventually, two rectangular tables: F. Lewis, "Vietnam Peace Pacts Signed."

617. Bunker had expected: Schaffer, *Ellsworth Bunker,* 218.

617. Vietnamization "slow surrender": *Diplomatic History,* vol. 34, no. 3, p. 574.

618. "This may be": Perkins, *Prudent Peace,* 46.

618. Bunker thought the opposition: Walsh, *Final Report of the Independent Counsel for Iran/Contra Matters,* 1: 222.

618. defend Bunker against demands: ibid., 1: 235.

618. Kissinger played this: Karnow, *Vietnam,* 638–39.

618. "If you get rid . . . With all respect": *Diplomatic History,* vol. 34, no. 1, p. 220
618. "simply felt that they": Cold War Interviews.
619. "draft agreement was essentially": ibid.
619. "We warned them": "Vietnam Online," *American Experience* (transcript online), 9.
619. "savage and senseless": Karnow, *Vietnam,* 667.
620. "peace with honor": ibid., 669.
621. "You have a nation": *Time,* April 21, 1973.
622. By nightfall, after eighteen desperate hours: Karnow, *Vietnam,* 682.
622. At 3:45 A.M.: Mak and Kennedy, *American Ambassadors in a Troubled World,* 159–77.
623. airlifted from the Saigon embassy: Moskin, *U.S. Marine Corps Story,* 686.
623. "Our misjudgments of friend": McNamara, *In Retrospect,* 322
624. "for the United States": Diplomatic History, vol. 34, no. 3, p. 515.

44: Destiny and the Peacock Throne: 1951–81

626. "In short, armed intervention": Acheson, *Present at the Creation,* 507.
626. Shah Mohammad Reza Pahlavi: Kinzer, *All the Shah's Men,* 46.
626. Grady arrived in Iran: McGhee, *Envoy to the Middle World,* 219.
626. sole developer of oil: ibid., 186.
626. Significantly, Aramco agreed: ibid., 194–99.
627. McGhee was born: ibid., 322.
627. Much later, he served: ibid., 408.
627. Over three days: Acheson, *Present at the Creation.*
627. focusing on different issues: Battle, interview by McKinzie and Wilson, 52.
627. "I wanted to believe": McGhee, George, *Envoy to the Middle World,* 350.
628. Fearing that Britain: Acheson, *Present at the Creation,* 507.
628. Ambassador Grady cabled Washington: Shultz, *Turmoil and Triumph,* 98.
628. "a demagogue of considerable": Acheson, *Present at the Creation,* 501–04.
628. Acheson replaced Grady: Kinzer, *All the Shah's Men,* 117.
628. Chester Bowles succeed: Thacher, interview by Johnson.
628. Churchill-Eden government would not: McGhee, *Envoy to the Middle World,* 402–03; H. W. Brands, *Inside the Cold War,* 244.
628. Mossadegh said that gave: Kinzer, *All the Shah's Men,* 131.
629. "alternatives to Mussadig": Acheson, *Present at the Creation,* 685.
629. John Foster Dulles prophesied: Kinzer, *All the Shah's Men,* 158.
629. called Operation Ajax: H. W. Brands, *Inside the Cold War,* 282.
629. Kermit Roosevelt, chief: Kinzer, *All the Shah's Men,* 12–13.
629. Ambassador Henderson was thrilled: ibid.
630. "By the end": Bowden, *Guests of the Ayatollah,* 117; NSA, "Secret CIA History of the Iran Coup, 1953," xiii.
630. In December 1954: H. W. Brands, *Inside the Cold War,* 295, 298.
630. with intense hostility: Sick, *All Fall Down,* 7.
630. Iran was the world's: Yergin, *Prize,* 685.
630. economic and military aid: H. W. Brands, *Inside the Cold War,* 292.
630. "We were wrong": Laingen, interview by Kennedy, 8.
630. great oil revenues: C. Freeman, interview by Kennedy.
630. "We loved to see": Thacher, interview by Johnson.
631. "aftershocks of the dissolution": Armitage, "Conversation with Former Deputy Secretary of State Richard Armitage," interview by Rose, 26.

631. end of May 1972: Kissinger, *Years of Upheaval*, 868.

631. some State Department veterans: McGhee, *Envoy to the Middle World*, 72.

631. in exchange for: Oshinsky, *Conspiracy So Immense*, 20.

631. shah pressured the foreign: Kissinger, *Years of Upheaval*, 869.

631. Joseph S. Farland: Hevesi, "Joseph S. Farland, 92."

631. United States allowed him: Sick, *All Fall Down*, 14.

632. William H. Sullivan: Lilley and Lilley, *China Hands*, 113.

632. Ambassador Sullivan managed: Vance, *Hard Choices*, 317; W. Sullivan, *Mission to Iran*, 39.

632. He expected that: ibid., 64–72.

632. SAVAK, the Shah's secret: ibid., 96.

632. in nearby Afghanistan: Vance, *Hard Choices*, 324.

632. Ayatollah Khomeini, although: W. Sullivan, *Mission to Iran*, 199.

632. Dependents among the: ibid., 28.

632. American businesses cut back: Sullivan, J. *Embassies Under Siege*, 36–37.

632. "Our destiny is": Sick, *All Fall Down*, 60.

632. Cyrus Vance called in: ibid., 102.

632. telephoned the Shah directly: Vance, *Hard Choices*, 328; W. Sullivan, *Mission to Iran*, 171.

633. Strikes in the oil: Sick, *All Fall Down*, 78.

633. had to flee from: W. Sullivan, *Mission to Iran*, 174–76.

633. Sullivan replied bluntly: Vance, *Hard Choices*, 330.

634. The Iranian army platoon: W. Sullivan, *Mission to Iran*, 216–19.

634. His murder hastened: Yergin, *Prize*, 681.

634. By Christmas Day: Sick, *All Fall Down*, 128.

634. Brzezinski protested Vance's: Sick, *All Fall Down*, 95.

634. Ayatollah Khomeini urged: ibid., 10.

634. the mission was canceled: W. Sullivan, *Mission to Iran*, 222–26.

634. Brzezinski had persuaded: Sick, *All Fall Down*, 133.

634. Carter approved meetings: Bowden, *Guests of the Ayatollah*, 70.

635. They talked in: W. Sullivan, *Mission to Iran*, 215.

635. Sullivan brought the Shah: ibid., 230.

635. Secretary Vance told Sullivan: Vance, *Hard Choices*, 340.

635. "almost metaphysical rebellion": Kissinger, *Years of Upheaval*, 672.

635. Sullivan was convinced: W. Sullivan, *Mission to Iran*, 239–40.

635. "We must put": ibid., 232.

635. armed mob passed: Laingen, in interview with Kennedy, 10.

635. fought a battle nearby: W. Sullivan, *Mission to Iran*, 249–54.

635. Brzezinski reluctantly stopped: Sick, *All Fall Down*, 156.

635. "When the moment": ibid., 171.

636. The effect on American: Yergin, *Prize*, 698; Sick, *All Fall Down*, 168.

636. They attacked the residence: Laingen, interviewed by Kennedy, 58.

636. They destroyed documents: W. Sullivan, *Mission to Iran*, 263.

636. six Iranians who worked: J. Sullivan, *Embassies Under Siege*, 37.

636. accept revolutionary guards: Laingen, in interview with Kennedy, 48.

636. Americans had to establish: J. Sullivan, *Embassies Under Siege*, 39–40.

637. Sullivan urged the Shah: W. Sullivan, *Mission to Iran*, 277.

637. "one of the most": Vance, *Hard Choices*, 343–44.

637. shah was a friend: Sick, *All Fall Down*, 179.

637. Ambassador Sullivan flew out: Laingen, in interview with Kennedy, 48.

637. end of Sullivan's: Denza, *Diplomatic Law*, 41.

637. "used car lot": Laingen, in interview with Kennedy, 50.

637. Laingen was instructed: ibid., 49.

637. "We thought that": ibid., 53.

638. Marines again took charge: Laingen, in interview with Kennedy, 52, 57–58; see also Laingen, *Yellow Ribbon*, 8.

638. On October 22: There is some disagreement about this date. It is Sunday, October 21, in Sick, *All Fall Down*; October 22 in J. Sullivan, *Embassies Under Siege*, 46, and in Laingen, *Yellow Ribbon*, 9; and Tuesday, October 23, in Laingen, interview by Kennedy, 62 .

638. He was shocked: Laingen, interview by Kennedy, 62.

638. "We will do": ibid., 69.

638. Brzezinski sought out: J. Sullivan, *Embassies Under Siege*, 46.

638. angered the radical clerics: Laingen, *Yellow Ribbon*, 10.

639. Laingen raced up: Laingen, interview by Kennedy, 67.

639. reinforced with steel doors: J. Sullivan, *Embassies Under Siege*, 50.

640. He and Laingen ordered: Vance, *Hard Choices*, 373.

640. students in time painstakingly: Laingen, interview by Kennedy, 69.

640. No one knew whether: Kinzer, *Overthrow*, 202.

640. students had prepared well: Laingen, interview by Kennedy, 68; Bowden, *Guests of the Ayatollah*, 60.

640. She and her assistant: Laingen, interview by Kennedy, 71.

640. Kenneth Taylor was able: ibid., 77.

641. the last holdouts: Bowden, *Guests of the Ayatollah*, 79.

641. officials were unfamiliar: Vance, *Hard Choices*, 376.

641. "ought to deliberately": Sick, *All Fall Down*, 206.

641. seven hundred thousand barrels of oil: ibid., 212.

641. But Khomeini would not: Laingen, in interview with Kennedy, 71–72.

641. provisional government resigned: Sick, *All Fall Down*, 227.

642. Among the remaining hostages: Bowden, *Guests of the Ayatollah*, 199.

642. Khomeini proclaimed on American: ibid., 200.

642. President Carter worried: ibid., 136.

642. Soviet Union invaded Afghanistan: Vance, *Hard Choices*, 385–87.

642. "to disregard the growth": ibid., 396.

642. By mid-May 1988: Galster, "Afghanistan," NSA.

642. American diplomats believed: Gardner, *Mission Italy*, 251.

642. One more round: Cordovez and Harrison, *Out of Afghanistan*, overview and epilogue.

643. Foreign Minister, Sadegh Ghotbzadeh: Bowden, *Guests of the Ayatollah*, 361.

643. He was eventually executed: Laingen, interview by Kennedy, 76.

643. Moderates in Tehran: Bowden, *Guests of the Ayatollah*, 288, 292.

643. And Khomeini stood firmly: Laingen, *Yellow Ribbon*, 128.

643. By April 7, the hostages': ibid., 100.

643. He disagreed with U.S.: Bowden, *Guests of the Ayatollah*, 129–31.

644. William Belk was caught: Bowden, *Guests of the Ayatollah*, 263–67.

644. Political officer Michael Metrinko: W. Sullivan, *Mission to Iran*, 154.

644. survived for months: Sick, *All Fall Down*, 260.

644. "We must find": Laingen, *Yellow Ribbon*, 29, 44, 45.

644. "However secure your embassies": Laingen, interview by Kennedy, 89.

644. Vance opposed using force: Bowden, *Guests of the Ayatollah*, 211, 213.

644. Eight servicemen of: Sick, *All Fall Down*, 297–99; Laingen, *Yellow Ribbon*, 117; Bowden, *Guests of the Ayatollah*, 432–68.

645. Iran announced that: Laingen, *Yellow Ribbon,* 130–31.

645. "take and hold": Laingen, interview by Kennedy, 80.

645. The Iranians feared that: Laingen, *Yellow Ribbon,* 181.

646. a student took out: ibid., 246–47; Laingen, interview by Kennedy, 83.

646. For seventeen days: ibid., 83.

646. "We were released": ibid., 87.

646. two congressional committees: Bowden, *Guests of the Ayatollah,* 628.

45: Shuttling Salesman for Peace: 1947–83

647. "I didn't start . . . I really began": A. Atherton, interview by Mak, 277, 24, 29, 27.

648. became "very unhappy . . . I had a hard": Atherton, interview by Weiss, 1, 12.

648. Betty found a teaching: ibid. 12ff.

648. Ambassador Loy Henderson said: A. Atherton, interview by Mak, 47.

649. "I pointed out": L. Henderson, interview by McKinzie, 33.

649. Atherton said, was "nonsense": A. Atherton, interview by Mak, 62.

649. struggle between two: Miscamble, *George F. Kennan and the Making,* 8.

649. "My cook says": Mak and Kennedy, *American Ambassadors in a Troubled World,* 113.

650. "Never, ever should": ibid., 123.

650. victory in 1967: Rusk, *As I Saw It,* 390.

650. Security Council Resolution 242: A. Atherton, interview by Mak, 104.

650. rejected Atherton's letter: ibid., 110.

650. "because Pepsi hits": ibid., 113.

651. peace process stalled: A. Atherton, interview by Mak, 123.

651. They met with Sadat: ibid., 125.

651. secret meetings between Kissinger: Kissinger, *Years of Upheaval,* 205.

651. a baffling game: ibid., 208–16.

651. "Don't ever tell": Battle, interview by McKinzie and Wilson, 2–3

651. "Now, Atherton, I . . . Is that understood?": A. Atherton, interview by Mak, 137.

652. "a man of my": Kissinger, *Years of Upheaval,* 432.

652. He called the Soviet: ibid., 450–53.

652. Atherton was the first: ibid., 871.

652. not have "started something": ibid., 458.

652. Kissinger ordered weapons: ibid., 873, 885.

652. "the perilous dependence": Vance, *Hard Choices,* 23.

653. Then, as the Israelis: Kissinger, *Years of Upheaval,* 552.

653. Kissinger's first visit: ibid., 616.

653. a productive period: A. Atherton, interview by Mak, 144.

653. international conference at Geneva: Schaffer, *Ellsworth Bunker,* 304.

653. "In my view": Kissinger, *Years of Upheaval,* 803.

654. "That was the toughest . . . You stood up": A. Atherton, interview by Mak, 155, 154.

654. Kissinger had insisted precede: Kissinger, *Years of Upheaval,* 978.

655. Ellsworth Bunker, now eighty: ibid., 1049.

655. Kissinger believed that: ibid., 1083.

655. "Evidently the Deity": ibid., 1208.

656. "It took a while": A. Atherton, in interview with Mak, 175.

656. "Let every girl": Christopher Wren, *New York Times,* November 22, 1977.

657. "My job then": A. Atherton, interview by Mak, 181.

657. Sadat declared that there: ibid., 186.

658. Camp David Accords: Vance, *Hard Choices,* 227.

658. much of the discussion: A. Atherton, interview by Mak, 195.

658. "That was a dramatic": ibid., 200.

659. showing up "unnecessarily late": Oral History, Library of Congress, Battle.

660. conspired to focus: A. Atherton, interview by Mak, 218.

660. Egypt's international business: A. Atherton, interview by Mak, 211, and B. Atherton, interview by Weiss, 6.

660. Atherton was reappointed: A. Atherton, interview by Mak, 223.

661. "One of them": A. Atherton, interview by Mak, 234–35.

662. treated by Egyptian surgeons: ibid., 239.

662. "We shake the hand . . . President Sadat was murdered": David Shipler, *New York Times,* October 7, 1981.

662. Israel invaded Lebanon: Atherton, in interview with Mak, 245.

663. Habib came out of: Shultz, *Turmoil and Triumph,* 45.

663. "Well, you can't": B. Atherton, interview by Weiss, 27.

663. He and Harold Saunders: *Foreign Affairs,* vol. 819, p. 154

663. This team included: A. Atherton, interview by Mak, 284–85.

664. withholding a $100 million: *Foreign Affairs,* vol. 90, no. 1, p. 18.

664. "a peace process": *Diplomatic History* vol. 26, no. 4 (Fall 2002), p. 610.

664. The most intractable issues: John Lister, interview by author, Tel Aviv, Israel.

664. "a land of rumor": Edward S. Walker, Jr., interview by author, Tel Aviv, Israel.

46: *The Very Model of a Modern Foreign Service: 1970–2011*

665. 7,868 Foreign Service: State Department, Bureau of Human Resources, HR Fact Sheet, June 30, 2008.

665. "Marines go to": Lawrence P. Taylor, interview by author, Arlington, VA.

666. "The object of United": Cold War Interviews.

666. "We now realize": McGhee, *Envoy to the Middle World,* 12.

666. Russia, Belarus freed Zeltser: *New York Times,* February 15, 2009, p. 18; *New York Times,* July 1, 2009.

667. ambassador to Bangkok: William H. Itoh, interview by author, Aspen, CO.

667. Martinez felt he made: Hilarion Martinez, interview by author, Florence, Italy.

667. "Just as important": ibid.

668. "Not everyone has": Benjamin Garcia, interview by author, Aspen, CO.

668. "It is the only . . . You can't depend": Douglas R. Smith, interview by author, Barcelona, Spain

668. "Always . . . hold something": Low, interview by Kennedy.

668. "White men who didn't": Kathleen Stephens, interview by author, Lisbon, Portugal.

668. "generation and younger": R. Nicholas Burns, interview by author, Athens, Greece.

669. "We realized they are": E. Thomas Rowe, interview by author, Aspen, CO.

669. "Spouses are becoming": Janice Bay, interview by author, Washington, D.C.

670. "desperately unhappy . . . Going home to Washington": Jimmy J. Kolker, interview by author, Copenhagen, Denmark.

670. "Ambassadors have a": Virginia Morris, interview by author, Istanbul, Turkey.

671. In 1997, Robert Joseph: *New York Times,* March 21, 2007, pp. A1, 12.

671. "defend or implement . . . making the world": M. Wright, Letter to Secretary of State Colin Powell.

671. He acknowledged he had: *New York Times,* February 27, 2003.

671. John H. Brown: *New York Times*, March 12, 2003.

672. "This Secretary of State": *New York Times*, April 23, 1993.

672. "undermines what has": *Shafiq Rasul v. George W. Bush*, Amici Curiae, U.S. Supreme Court, p. 5.

672. American Foreign Service Association: Susan Reardon, interview by author, Washington, D.C.

672. Foreign Service officers know: Ruth A. Davis, interview by author, VA.

672. "Neither dissent affected . . . The Service tolerates": D. Jones, "Is There Life After Dissent?" 28, 29.

673. "After all, the evidence": D. Jones, "Is There Life After Dissent?" 30.

674. "To all hands: DON'T": National Security Agency Archives, 1971.

674. "Here in Decca": National Security Agency Archives, April 6, 1971.

674. "Our government has failed": ibid.

674. "deeply shocked at massacre . . . promptly, publicly, and prominently": National Security Agency Archives, March 29, 1971.

675. "taken over by": ibid.

675. State Department gave Blood: *Diplomatic History*, 2.

676. State Department had demanded: Kessler, "American Foreign Service Association Withdraws Award."

676. "I did it": John M. Evans, interview by author, Saint Petersburg, May 28, 2009.

676. "is untenable . . . That the invocation": Obama, letter to Secretary of State Condoleezza Rice, July 28, 2006.

677. "Many of us . . . If you do not": Avis Bohlen, interview by author, Paris, France.

677. "spent three miserable years": Mak and Kennedy, *American Ambassadors in a Troubled World*, 8.

677. "This is a career": Jimmy J. Kolker, interview by author, Copenhagen, Denmark.

678. "My friend who died . . . We put our families": R. Nicholas Burns, interview by author, Athens, Greece.

678. "I am part": Laingen, interview by Kennedy, 4.

678. "a decline in professional": A. Atherton, in interview with Mak, 290.

679. "I thought to myself": C. Freeman, interview by Kennedy.

679. "why things went well . . . define themselves not": ibid.

679. "had vested interest . . . have some mud": Oral History, Library of Congress.

679. "I'm out of": Edward S. Walker, Jr., interview by author, Tel Aviv, Israel.

679. "I felt at that": Kaplan, *Arabists*, 225.

680. "The best diplomacy": Obituary by Alden Whitman, *New York Times*, October 13, 1971.

680. More issues are global: "Overview of Foreign Policy Issues and Positions," appendix 1, memorandum written October 1976 for presidential candidate Jimmy Carter, in Vance, *Hard Choices*, 241–62.

680. in the West alone: Vance, *Hard Choices*, 424.

681. "The European Union is": Pfaff, "What's Left of the Union?" 28.

682. "If we don't regard": Rusk, *As I Saw It*, 503–04.

682. George Kennan, in particular: *Diplomatic History*, vol. 35, no. 1, p. 122.

682. Whether NATO would extend: *Diplomatic History*, vol. 34, no. 1, p. 199.

682. "not one inch eastward . . . We are the big": Douglas L. McElhaney, interview by author, Paris, France.

683. International Court of Justice: Phillips, *Ventures in Diplomacy*, 111.

684. "Developing countries must . . . holding it to effective": Vance, *Hard Choices*, 430, 434, 241–62, 461.

684. since World War II: Murphy, *Diplomat Among Warriors*, 452.

685. "We decided what": ibid., 447.

685. "The secretary of state": From *Atlanta Constitution*, June 27, 1982, quoted in Shultz, *Turmoil and Triumph*, 10.

685. "That prediction turned . . . Foreign Service officers": Shultz, *Turmoil and Triumph*, 33.

686. "You see, the Foreign": Bohlen, interview by Mulhollan, 7–8.

686. "I think the worst": Oral History, on-line, Library of Congress.

686. "The permanent career . . . In the hands of": Kissinger, *Years of Upheaval*, 434, 439.

686. "The U.S. Foreign Service": Kissinger, "Team of Heavyweights."

687. "extremely risk adverse": Rohatyn, "Discussion about the Life of Felix Rohatyn," interview by Rose.

687. increased by twenty-three: B. Cohen, "Excerpts from Testimony of Undersecretary of State for Management Bonnie R. Cohen."

687. "I thought the American . . . turn the American": *Washington Post*, September 13, 1995, A1.

688. "Americans have fallen . . . We will be unable": Gardner, "Who Needs Ambassadors?" (speech).

688. "Their efforts to secure": Council on Foreign Relations, *Secretary Colin Powell's State Department: An Independent Assessment* (task force report), 3.

689. a "record-breaking year": Anderson and Engel, "Record Year for Hiring at the State Department."

689. "a revolution in diplomatic . . . long-standing defects": Council on Foreign Relations, *Secretary Colin Powell's State Department: An Independent Assessment* (task force report), 2, 4.

47: The First and Second Iraq Wars: 1982–2011

690. "They are coming": Emil M. Skodon, interview by author, Rome, Italy.

690. Kuwait is small: ibid.

690. Inside the embassy compound: Levins, *Days of Fear*.

692. "By dictating this": J. Sullivan, *Embassies Under Siege*, 119.

692. Canadian embassy helped them: ibid., 125.

692. Iraqis there told him: Denza, *Diplomatic Law*, 22.

692. Its remaining eight diplomats: J. Sullivan, *Embassies Under Siege*, 114.

692. On January 17, 1991: Emil M. Skodon, interview by author, Rome, Italy; Levins, John, *Days of Fear*.

692. Edward W. Gnehm: Elizabeth Neuffer, *Boston Globe*, March 2, 1991.

692. tumultuous reshuffling for nearly: L. Henderson, interview by McKinzie, 22.

693. Henderson undertook the assignment: ibid., 24–25.

693. "We should have": ibid., 15.

693. "tattoo of blows": Cable to secretary, no. 639, sent November 24, 1952.

693. But once Mossadegh was overthrown: Sick, *All Fall Down*, 7.

694. William L. Eagleton: Kaplan, *Arabists*, 264–65.

694. soon despised Saddam Hussein: ibid., 268.

694. "a village thug": Mak and Kennedy, *American Ambassadors in a Troubled World*, 77.

695. "Ambassador Rumsfeld's visit": National Security Agency, document 35, dated December 26, 1983.

695. During Quainton's term: Denza, *Diplomatic Law*, 43.

697. Zbigniew Brzezinski flew: Cold War Interviews.

697. The United States sent: Mann, *About Face*, 138.

697. puritanical "students of Islam": Kinzer, *Overthrow*, 273.

697. "a tawdry season": Coll, *Ghost Wars*, 330.

698. Oakley replaced McWilliams: ibid., 205.

698. Valerie Plame Wilson: *Washington Post*, October 22, 2007, C1.

698. "I will go": *New Yorker*, October 18, 2004, quoted in Kinzer, *Overthrow*.

698. "I think the intelligence": Powell, "An Hour with General Colin Powell," interview by Rose.

699. State Department was blamed: *New York Times*, July 25, 2008.

699. "There was suspicion": Andrew E. Kramer, *New York Times*, June 19, 2008, 1.

699. Iraq could make: *New York Times*, July 1, 2009.

700. law permitting Iraqis: Alissa J. Rubin, *New York Times*, July 25, 2008.

700. Iraq was designated: Slavin, "Study Looks At Diplomats' Well-Being Status."

700. Special Inspector General: *New York Times*, October 29, 2008, 5.

700. case against five Blackwater: Risen, "Interference Seen in Blackwater Inquiry."

700. By 2007, 20 percent: *New York Times*, October 27, 2007, A1.

701. State Department ordered: *New York Times*, March 27, 2008.

701. "The U.S. Embassy": "Recruiting Locally Employed (LE) Staff to Serve in Iraq" (telegram, Department of State).

702. AFSA had not taken: Kessler, "Rice Orders That Diplomatic Jobs in Iraq Be Filled First"; M. Lee, "Rice Orders Baghdad Embassy Posts Filled."

702. 40 percent of the: R. Wright, "Stress Taking Toll on Foreign Service."

702. "a small but growing": American Foreign Service Association, "Telling Our Story" (e-mail).

702. Overall, in September 2007: Naland, "Nation Lacks Bench Strength for Diplomacy."

702. At the time: American Foreign Service Association, "Telling Our Story" (e-mail).

703. "that directed assignments into": *New York Times*, December 13, 2007, A26.

703. "We urge the Administration": Naland, "Between Iraq and a Hard Place" (e-mail).

703. "We're not weenies": American Foreign Service Association, untitled e-mail, October 2, 2008.

703. "At best, this is": Bullington, "From the Editor: Iraq, the Foreign Service, and Duty," *American Diplomacy.org*.

48: Fortress America: The Embassy: 2004–07

705. "Our footprint is so . . . We spend a lot": Combs, *Jay Treaty*.

706. Her job has no: Rowe, interview by author, June 2008.

707. "I think every day": Morison, *John Paul Jones*.

707. "a fascinating study": *New York Times*, February 24, 2010, C1.

707. Some of the results: Loeffler, "United States Embassies: America's Face Abroad," National Building Museum Web site.

707. "hardening sites . . . Diplomacy is the establishment": Asencio, "Original Cheap Shot."

708. "It does not make": B. Cohen, "Excerpts from testimony of Undersecretary of State for Management Bonnie R. Cohen."

708. "The important part": Powell, "An Hour with General Colin Powell," interview by Rose.

708. Marine Security Guard Battalion: Moskin, *U.S. Marine Corps Story*, 719–26.

708. group of Moroccan "tunnelers": Hunt, *Department of State*.

708. The Embassy of the Future: Center for Strategic and International Studies, *Embassy of the Future* (report).

709. built sixty-eight buildings: *State Magazine*, June 2009, 33.

709. In Jerusalem, seven years: *State Magazine*, June 2010, 12

709. "All non-employees are": Hunt, *Department of State*.

709. "We used to export": Armitage, "Conversation with Former Deputy Secretary of State Richard Armitage," interview by Rose, 30.

709. "If you don't have": Weigley, *American Way of War.*

709. Villa Taverna has been: Gardner, *Mission Italy,* 54.

710. that story apocryphal: ibid., 55.

710. said it was fact: See Albin Krebs's obituary of Luce in *New York Times,* October 10, 1987.

710. Ambassador Gardner opposed: Gardner, *Mission Italy,* 35.

710. "bribery and kickbacks": ibid., 313.

711. They discussed policy issues: ibid., 182.

711. Gardner also pressed: ibid., 253–54.

712. Italian government started withdrawing: *New York Times,* March 4, 2005.

712. The decision was widely criticized: Kamen, "Narcissus Is Now Greek and Roman."

712. "There is a war": Morison, *John Paul Jones.*

712. two McCarthy devotees: Kahn, *China Hands,* 257.

713. "I knew immediately . . . He drove me nuts": Morison, *John Paul Jones.*

714. Taylor objected: Oral History, Parsons, Truman Presidential Library; see also Parsons's obituary in *New York Times,* October 11, 1991.

715. They can confuse responsibility: Elder, *Information Machine,* 44.

716. forty-four U.S. agencies: Rusk, *As I Saw It,* 531.

717. Thomas M. Countryman: Moskin, *U.S. Marine Corps Story.*

717. Seeking a change after Cairo: ibid.

718. "Our job is to . . . That's how you": Morison, *John Paul Jones.*

718. "More and more": Barnes and Morgan, *Foreign Service of the United States.*

720. "tell the world about": Anne Callaghan, interview by author, Rome, Italy.

720. Paula S. Thiede: Paula S. Thiede, interview by author, Rome, Italy.

49: New Challenges for Modern Diplomacy: 1970–2012

722. Carol Laise, then director: Laingen, interviewed by Kennedy, 42.

723. AFSA delegation actually walked: Bleakley, "A.F.S.A. and the Foreign Service Act of 1980," 43.

723. "The State Department puts . . . It was a small": Virginia Morris, interview by author, Istanbul, Turkey.

724. Benjamin H. Read: Bleakley, "A.F.S.A. and the Foreign Service Act of 1980," 46; Vance, *Hard Choices,* 44.

724. "general apathy of most": Bleakley, "A.F.S.A. and the Foreign Service Act of 1980," 46.

724. an open political battle: *New York Times,* October 28, 1984.

724. "[The Act] Requires all": Conference report filed in House, H. Rep. 96–1432, 1.

725. Public Law 96-465: Foreign Service Act of 1980 (P.L. 96-465), 1.

726. The OIG study found: ibid., 1, 5.

726. "the senior glut": A. Atherton, in interview with Mak, 283.

726. It produced desperate: ibid.

726. Some officers with twenty: ibid., 286.

726. eliminated on the way: Eric S. Rubin, interview by author, Washington, D.C.

726. "When I came in . . . We are really stretched": ibid.

727. five under secretaries: "List of Ambassadorial Appointments," American Foreign Service Association, 3.

727. "hunter-gatherers of information . . . America's representatives abroad": ibid., 8.

727. "a crippled institution": United States Commission on National Security/21st Century, *Road Map for National Security*, x.

727. Among the specific recommendations: ibid. xi–xii.

727. "Confidence in the Department . . . is most in need": ibid., 52, 53, 61, 94.

727. It recommended shortening: ibid., 95.

727. ending the "blindfolding policy . . . completely counter to": ibid., 96.

728. analyses of diplomatic processes: Council on Foreign Relations, *Secretary Colin Powell's State Department* and *Secretary Powell's State Department*.

728. "non-partisan umbrella group . . . an organization weakened": ibid., foreword, executive summary.

728. "ludicrous" : Council on Foreign Relations, *Managing Secretary Rice's State Department*, 3.

728. 18.6 percent pay cut: ibid., 1.

728. The council said: Council on Foreign Relations, *Secretary Colin Powell's State Department*, 3.

728. The council judged: ibid., 17.

728. "a broken institution . . . the achievements have been": Council on Foreign Relations, *Secretary Powell's State Department*, executive summary, foreword.

728. number of persons taking: Janice Bay, interview by author, Washington, D.C.

729. The 2004 report said there: Council on Foreign Relations, *Secretary Powell's State Department*.

729. a parallel analysis: Council on Foreign Relations, *Managing Secretary Rice's State Department*.

729. appeal to fund: ibid., iv.

729. Thomas D. Boyatt: Boyatt, Testimony to Subcommittee of Senate Committee on Homeland Security and Government Affairs, 2; American Academy of Diplomacy, *Foreign Affairs Budget for the Future*, 3.

729. "America cannot be": "A Foreign Policy for the Global Age," *Foreign Affairs*, vol. 79, no. 6 (December 2000), pp. 22–39.

729. making leadership and management: Council on Foreign Relations, *Managing Secretary Rice's State Department*, 1.

729. The council criticized: ibid., 20.

730. "CA prides itself": ibid., 10.

730. a "huge success": ibid., 11.

730. diplomacy is "fundamentally flawed": HELP Commission, *Beyond Assistance* (report for Congress), 433.

730. most pressing Foreign Service: Council on Foreign Relations, *Managing Secretary Rice's State Department*, iv; 379.

730. number of unaccompanied: *State Magazine*, June 2010, 35.

730. To pay for this: Council on Foreign Relations, *Managing Secretary Rice's State Department*, iv.

730. "For better or worse": Naland, "New Foreign Service," 42.

731. "create a more secure": Council on Foreign Relations, *Managing Secretary Rice's State Department*, vi n1.

731. "Transforming the World": U.S. Department of State, *Financial Report Fiscal Year 2007*.

731. "a fundamental shift . . . driving more decision-making": Advisory Committee on Transformational Diplomacy, *Call to Action*, 1, 3, 6.

732. The 2025 working group: Advisory Committee on Transformational Diplomacy, *Final Report of the State Department*, 4.

732. Nearly half voiced: Kashkett, "AFSA Opinion Poll Results Highlight Disturbing Trends."

732. Christopher R. Hill: From a conference hearing held on March 25, 2009.

732. "is simply not . . . to publicly embarrass": *Foreign Affairs*, (January/February 2009), pp. 148–151.

733. "militarization" and "staff up": Chas Freeman, "Debt, Defense and Diplomacy" (speech).

733. "The Foreign Service is": quoted in McGlen and Sarkees, *Women in Foreign Policy*.

733. "but by patient long-term": Foreign Affairs Day, Washington, D.C., May 6, 2005.

733. to a "hot spot": R. N. Burns, "Global Challenges and Opportunities in U.S. Foreign Policy" (speech), 6.

734. two additional echelons: Herbst, prepared statement before subcommittees of the House Committee on Armed Services.

734. grandiose and "ludicrously ambitious": Easterly, "Foreign Aid Goes Military!," 51.

734. By 2008, two years: Herbst, "Briefing on Civilian Stabilization Initiative," U.S. Department of State.

734. "I am here": *Washington Post,* February 15, 2008.

734. "with inadequate diplomatic . . . critical personnel shortages": American Academy of Diplomacy, *Foreign Affairs Budget for the Future,* introductory letter, foreword, 2.

736. But, paradoxically, the prolonged: ibid., 319.

736. Its weapons program: ibid.

736. "diplomatic marathon of negotiations . . . These steps marked": R. N. Burns, "America's Strategic Opportunity with India," 4.

736. Despite opposition in Washington: Sigal, *Disarming Stranger,* 26.

737. In response, North Korea: ibid., 32.

737. That threat gained: ibid., 65.

737. Carter won a promise: ibid., 157.

737. North Korea would accept: CNN.com, October 4, 1999.

737. diplomatic efforts included: *Foreign Affairs,* vol. 86, no. 5, p. 81.

737. President Clinton used Carter's: Sigal, *Disarming Stranger,* 162.

737. "the Carter initiative": ibid., 132–33.

737. But Henry Kissinger: ibid., 165.

737. concluded the "agreed framework": ibid., 78.

737. The North shut down: ibid., 190.

737. many still regarded: ibid., 231.

738. "One day they withdrew": C. Hill, "Newsmaker Interviews," interview by Warner, 5.

738. "We should be prepared": Moskin, "Our Foreign Policy Is Paralyzed."

738. not allowed to follow: Sigal, "Turnabout Is Fair Play," 32.

738. President Bush then authorized: ibid.

738. "We are not going": Hill, "Update on the Six-Party Talks" (speech).

738. That February, North Korea: Hill, interview by Montagne, 4.

739. Israeli intelligence informed: Sigal, "Efforts for a Nuclear-Free North Korea Are Bearing Fruit," 54.

739. American critics charged: *New York Times,* September 24–25, 2008.

739. removed North Korea from: Cooper, "U.S. Declares North Korea Off Terror List."

739. North Korea reportedly detonated: *New York Times,* December 11, 2009.

740. He brought cautious: *New York Times,* December 18, 2009.

740. American officials saw it: *New York Times,* December 12, 2012, 1.

740. "Iran is trying": R. N. Burns, "Burns on Bringing India in from the Cold, and Isolating Iran," interview by McMahon.

740. This approach has its: *New York Times,* March 14, 2010

740. "They continued a ballistic": N. Burns, "Tony Jones Talks to US Undersecretary of State Nicholas Burns."

741. "Concerns about a . . . they refuse to negotiate": *Washington Post*, September 1, 2006.

741. "Bush administration hardliners": *New York Times*, April 29, 2007;

741. "I don't think": "Frances Perkins and the German-Jewish Refugees, 1933–1940," 16.

742. "We have no constituency": Glyn T. Davies, interview by author, London.

742. Ambassador Charles R. Baquet: Charles R. Baquet III, interview by author, Aspen, CO.

742. "Foreign policy is": Habib, "Work of Diplomacy."

743. "bring diplomacy to life": Linn, "Coming Attraction."

744. Although the antidrug: *New York Times*, March 14, 2010.

744. U.S. embassy appeared impotent: *State Magazine*, November 2010, 18.

744. "with the very nature . . . the area most likely": Asencio, interview by Kennedy, 9–10, 3.

744. "his political superiors": Schulzinger, *Making of the Diplomatic Mind*, 124.

744. "Information has changed": Reno L. Harnish III, interview by author, Stockholm, Sweden.

744. "We have redefined": Jimmy J. Kolker, interview by author, Copenhagen, Denmark.

745. "It is an outpost": Clinton, "Transcript," 26–27.

745. "the need to restore": Clinton and Kashkett, "Text of Remarks at Welcome Ceremony for Secretary Clinton," 2.

745. "robust diplomacy and effective . . . Just as we": *Council on Foreign Relations*, Washington D.C., July 15, 2009, Department of State.

745. "21st-century statecraft": E. Kennedy, "Ambassador Carlton J. H. Hayes' Wartime Diplomacy."

746. He designed and executed: Foreman, *World on Fire*, 201.

746. His success was based: Geist, "Nazi Conspiracy and Aggression, Volume IV, Document No 1769-PS" (deposition), 6.

746. "a high-wire act without": ibid., 18.

746. In the process: Cohen, "Taming the Bullies of Bosnia."

747. "simply one of the": *New York Times*, December 14, 2010, pp. A1, 33.

747. "Iran is the largest": *New York Times*, February 17, 2010.

747. "Diplomacy without arms": Geist, "Nazi Conspiracy and Aggression, Volume IV, Document No 1769-PS" (deposition), 28.

747. The United States wanted: *New York Times*, November 12, 2009.

747. "not an adequate strategic": *New York Times*, January 26, 2010.

747. "one of the world's": *Foreign Affairs*, vol. 90, no. 1, p. 43.

747. "The international community" ibid., 62.

748. "The U.S. will play": Mitchell, "Interview with Middle East Bulletin."

748. George Mitchell visited: *New York Times*, March 8, 2010, A5.

748. played visible and controversial: *New York Times*, September 5, 2010, A1.

749. "cede ground to those . . . a new era": "President Obama Delivers Remarks to State Department Employees," *Washington Post*.

750. He was unharmed: *New York Times*, September 16, 2009.

750. In September, he stole: *Washington Post*, June 29, 2009, 1; *New York Times*, September 27, 2009, 6.

750. Craig Kelly and Zelaya: *New York Times*, November 10, 2009.

750. When President Lobo thanked: *New York Times*, December 31, 2010, A8.

751. "the intelligent use": Council on Foreign Relations, Washington, D.C., July 15, 2009 Department of State.

751. "With 'smart power'": *New York Times*, January 13, 2009,

751. policy of "internet freedom": Foreign Affairs, vol. 90, no. 1, p. 30, 40.

752. harm done "just enormous": Glenn Kessler, *Washington Post*, November 29, 2010.

752. "If I were": Tony Blair, interview with Charlie Rose, Charlie Rose.com, November 30, 2010.

752. "irresponsible, reckless and . . . reckless and dangerous": *New York Times*, November 28, 2010, A1.

752. "essentially an outlaw operation": *London Sunday Times*, April 11, 2010.

753. Anne W. Patterson admitted: *New York Times*, December 1, 2010, 1.

753. "feckless, vain and ineffective": *New York Times*, December 3, 2010, A15.

753. "We will all terribly": *New York Times*, December 4, 2010, A7.

755. trucks loaded with heavily: *New York Times*, November 2, 2012, A4.

755. William J. Burns joined: *New York Times*, September 20, 2012.

755. "The brave Americans": *New York Times*, September 12, 2012. Article on "Cairo."

755. "disgusting and reprehensible": *New York Times*, December 13, 2012.

756. labeled the assault: *New York Times*, September 20, 2012.

756. Benghazi and intercepted: Eric Schmitt, *New York Times*, October 2, 2012.

50: The Ambassador: 2011–13

758. "The present service": ibid., 211.

759. "The United States is . . . I consider it": Charles Freeman, interview by Kennedy.

760. Thirty of George W.: Spire, "Diplomats" (paper presented at International Studies Association), 3.

760. Susan R. McCaw: ibid., 2.

760. Craig Roberts Stapleton: Department of State biography.

760. "the cost to the": Council on Foreign Relations, *Secretary Colin Powell's State Department*, 3.

760. "As a result": Burt and Robinson, *Reinventing Diplomacy in the Information Age*, 46–47.

760. "war in lace": Cleveland, Mangone, and Adams, *Overseas Americans*, 67.

761. Haste is also: Burt and Robinson, *Reinventing Diplomacy in the Information Age*, 125.

761. "I believe the Foreign": Honley, "Classic 'Field Diplomat,'" 39.

762. FBI special agent: Craig Whitlock, *Washington Post*, May 4, 2008, A1.

763. "We no longer": Schweich, "Taking Command."

764. "The Foreign Service should": R. Nicholas Burns, interview by author, Athens, Greece.

764. Søren Dyssegaard, retired minister-counselor: Dyssegaard, interview by author.

764. more likely to have: Spire, "Diplomats" (paper presented at International Studies Association), 7.

765. "You tell the minister": ibid., 8; see also *New York Times*, November 30, 2006.

765. "Contributions to a political": Foreign Service Act of 1980, section 303(3).

766. "deeper into the system": Robert Bradtke, interview by author, London.

766. Chapin served for several: Mak and Kennedy, *American Ambassadors in a Troubled World*, 62.

767. Ambassador Skodon's prime concerns: Skodon, interview by author, Rome.

767. she expanded the Fulbright: Molly Bordonaro, interview by author, Malta.

767. J. Thomas Schieffer: Glenn Kessler, *New York Times*, October 26, 2007, A8.

767. embassy spokesperson had to: Ewen MacAskill, *Guardian*, December 27, 2005; Colin Brown, *Independent*, December 27, 2005.

767. "I have had no": Molly Bordonaro, interview by author, Malta.

768. If a group of: Mak and Kennedy, *American Ambassadors in a Troubled World*, 37–49.

768. two-day introduction to: *State Magazine*, July 2010, 42.

768. Executive Leadership Seminar: *State Magazine*, December 2010, 30.

769. "There is no such": Moskin, "Dean Rusk," 16.

769. "I think a good": Mak and Kennedy, *American Ambassadors in a Troubled World*, 81.

769. They continued to tell: W. Sullivan, *Mission to Iran*, 20–23.

769. "If the bureaucrats didn't": Mak and Kennedy, *American Ambassadors in a Troubled World*, 85.

770. showed signs of bafflement: *Newsweek,* September 28, 2009, 22.

770. Vladimir V. Putin was: *New York Times,* December 30, 2009, A6.

770. "Missile defense has always": David Sanger and William J. Broad, *New York Times,* September 18, 2009.

770. "A professional diplomat": Murphy, *Diplomat Among Warriors,* 316–17.

770. "There is a delicate": Rusk, *As I Saw It,* 474.

771. "My wife accuses me": Moskin, "Dean Rusk," 16.

771. "As a negotiator": Charles Freeman, interview by Kennedy.

771. So he negotiated: ibid.

771. "The function of mediation . . . very positive": Habib, "Work of Diplomacy."

771. "the youngest member . . . a touch for the": Habib, "Work of Diplomacy."

773. "It segregated itself . . . You can either try": "Frances Perkins and the German-Jewish Refugees, 1933–1940," 10.

AFSA Memorial List

Memorial Plaques in the State Department lobby honor Foreign Service members who lost their lives in the line of duty. (Names are listed in the order in which they were inscribed.)

WILLIAM PALFREY—*Lost at Sea—1780*

JOEL BARLOW—*Exposure—Zarnowice, 1812*

RICHARD C. ANDERSON—*Yellow Fever—Cartagena, Colombia, 1823*

NATHANIEL G. INGRAHAM, JR.—*Fever—Tampico, Mexico, 1824*

HARRIS E. FUDGER—*Murdered—Bogotá, Colombia, 1825*

JAMES A. HOLDEN—*Lost at Sea—1827*

JOHN S. MEIRCKEN—*Lost at Sea—1832*

WILLIAM SHALER—*Cholera—Havana, Cuba, 1833*

WILLIAM S. SPARKS—*Cholera—Venice, Italy, 1849*

THOMAS T. TURNER—*Epidemic—Bahia, 1849*

THOMAS I. MORGAN—*Yellow Fever—Rio De Janeiro, 1850*

HARDY M. BURTON—*Yellow Fever—St. Thomas, 1852*

GEORGE R. DWYER—*Coast Fever—Mozambique, 1854*

BEVERLY L. CLARKE—*Tropical Fever—Guatemala, 1860*

ISAAC S. MCMICKEN—*Yellow Fever—Acapulco, Mexico, 1860*

GEORGE TRUE—*Smallpox—Funchal, 1862*

EDWARD W. GARDNER—*Lost at Sea—1863*

CHARLES G. HANNAH—*Yellow Fever—Demerara, 1864*

ABRAHAM HANSON—*African Fever—Monrovia, Liberia, 1866*

HIRAM R. HAWKINS—*Epidemic—Tumbez, Peru, 1866*

ALLEN A. HALL—*Epidemic—La Paz, Bolivia, 1867*

H. E. PECK—*Yellow Fever—Haiti, 1867*

JAMES WILSON—*Yellow Fever—Venezuela, 1867*

JAMES H. MCCOLLEY—*Yellow Fever—Callao, 1869*

WILLIAM STEDMAN—*Yellow Fever—Santiago, Cuba, 1869*

CHARLES E. PERRY—*Epidemic—Aspinwall, Colombia, 1872*

THOMAS BIDDLE—*Epidemic—Guayaquil, 1875*

JOHN F. FLINT—*Drowned Saving Life—La Union, El Salvador, 1875*

PHILIP CLAYTON—*Yellow Fever—Callao, 1877*

HENRY H. GARNET—*African Fever—Monrovia, 1882*

JESSE H. MOORE—*Yellow Fever—Callao, 1883*

DAVID T. BUNKER—*Yellow Fever—Demerara, 1888*

VICTOR F. W. STANWOOD—*Murdered—Madagascar, 1888*

WILLIAM D. MCCOY—*Fever—Monrovia, Liberia, 1893*

JOHN R. MEADE—*Yellow Fever—Santo Domingo, 1894*

ALEXANDER L. POLLOCK—*Yellow Fever—San Salvador, 1894*

FREDERICK MUNCHMEYER—*Yellow Fever—San Salvador, 1895*

JOHN B. GORMAN—*Malignant Malaria—Matamoros, Mexico, 1896*

ALBERT S. WILLIS—*Malaria—Honolulu, Hawaii, 1897*

ROUNSEVELLE WILDMAN—*Lost at Sea—1901*

THOMAS T. PRENTIS—*Volcanic Eruption—Martinique, 1902*

AMEDEE TESTART—*Volcanic Eruption—Martinique, 1902*

THOMAS NAST—*Yellow Fever—Guayaquil, 1902*

WILLIAM F. HAVEMEYER—*Cholera—Bassorah, Turkey, 1904*

PHILIP CARROLL—*Fever—Manzanillo, Mexico, 1906*

BENJAMIN H. RIDGELY—*Exhaustion—Mexico City, 1908*

ARTHUR A. CHENEY—*Earthquake—Messina, 1908*

JOHN W. GOURLEY—*Smallpox—Ciudad Juárez, Mexico, 1910*

THEODORE C. HAMM—*Smallpox—Durango, Mexico 1914*

ROBERT N. MCNEELY—*Lost at Sea—1915*

CHARLES P. MCKIERNAN—*Smallpox—Chungking, China, 1916*

CHARLES F. BRISSEL—*Cholera—Baghdad, 1916*

ALFRED L. M. GOTTSCHALK—*Lost at Sea—1918*

MADDIN SUMMERS—*Exhaustion—Moscow, 1918*

JOHN D. O'REAR—*Smallpox—La Paz, Bolivia, 1918*

LUTHER K. ZABRISKIE—*Smallpox—Aguas Calientes, Mexico, 1921*

CARL R. LOOP—*Saving Life—Catania, 1923*

MAX D. KIRJASSOF—*Earthquake—Yokohama, Japan, 1923*

PAUL E. JENKS—*Earthquake—Yokohama, Japan, 1923*

CLARENCE C. WOOLARD—*Epidemic—Cape Haitien, Haiti 1923*

ROBERT W. IMBRIE—*Murdered—Tehran, Persia, 1924*

WILLIAM T. FRANCIS—*Yellow Fever—Liberia, 1929*

WILLIAM I. JACKSON—*Drowned Attempting to Save Life—Matanzas, Cuba, 1930*

JOHN T. WAINWRIGHT—*Drowned Attempting to Save Life—Matanzas, Cuba, 1930*

G. RUSSELL TAGGART—*Hurricane—Belize, British Honduras, 1931*

J. THEODORE MARRINER—*Murdered—Beirut, Syria, 1937*

JOHN M. SLAUGHTER—*Earthquake—Guayaquil, 1942*

THOMAS C. WASSON—*Shot by Sniper—Jerusalem, 1948*

DOUGLAS S. MACKIERNAN—*Killed by Gunfire—Tibet, 1950*

ROBERT LEE MIKELS—*Burned Attempting to Save Life—Pusan, Korea, 1951*

DAVID LEBRETON, JR.—*Drowned Saving Lives—Tunis, 1953*

WILLIAM P. BOTELER—*Killed by Grenade—Nicosia, Cyprus, 1956*

ROBERT A. MCKINNON—*Tropical Disease—Ouagadougou, 1961*

BARBARA A. ROBBINS—*Killed in Bombing of Embassy—Saigon, Vietnam, 1965*

JOSEPH W. GRAINGER—*Murdered—Vietnam, 1965*

JOSEPH R. RUPLEY—*Killed by Gunfire—Caracas, Venezuela, 1965*

DOLPH B. OWENS—*Vietnam, 1960*

JACK J. WELLS—*Plane Crash—Vietnam, 1965*

NORMAN L. CLOWERS—*Viet Cong Ambush—Vietnam, 1966*

WILLIAM D. SMITH III—*Vietnam, 1966*

DON M. SJOSTROM—*Laos, 1967*

JOHN R. MCLEAN—*Laos, 1967*

ROBERT K. FRANZBLAU—*Shot While Evacuating Refugees—Vietnam, 1967*

DWIGHT HALL OWEN, JR.—*Killed by Communist Forces—Vietnam, 1967*

CARROLL H. PENDER—*Landmine Explosion—Vietnam, 1967*

FREDERICK J. ABRAMSON—*Shot During Viet Cong Ambush—Vietnam, 1968*

THOMAS M. GOMPERTZ—*Killed in Tet Offensive—Vietnam, 1968*

JOHN T. MCCARTHY—*Died from Gunshot Wound—Vietnam, 1968*

KERMIT J. KRAUSE—*Killed in Tet Offensive—Vietnam, 1968*

JEFFREY S. LUNDSTEDT—*Killed in Tet Offensive—Vietnam, 1968*

ROBERT R. LITTLE—*Killed in Tet Offensive—Vietnam, 1968*

STEPHEN H. MILLER—*Vietnam, 1968*

HUGH C. LOBIT—*Shot by Sniper—Vietnam, 1968*

RICHARD A. SCHENK—*Landmine Explosion—Vietnam, 1968*

MICHAEL MURPHY—*Viet Cong Ambush—Vietnam, 1968*

JOHN GORDON MEIN—*Shot by Guatemalan Rebels—Guatemala, 1968*

GEORGE B. GAINES—*Died from Gunshot Wounds—Vietnam, 1969*

ROBERT P. PERRY—*Murdered by Palestinian Terrorists—Jordan 1970*

DAN A. MITRIONE—*Assassinated by Uruguayan Rebels—Uruguay, 1970*

CLEO ALLEN NOEL, JR.—*Assassinated by Palestinian Terrorists—Sudan, 1973*

GEORGE CURTIS MOORE—*Assassinated by Palestinian Terrorists—Sudan, 1973*

EVERETT D. REESE—*Killed in Action—Vietnam, 1955*

THOMAS W. RAGSDALE—*Died While a Prisoner of War—Vietnam, 1967*

DONALD V. FREEMAN—*Shot During Hostile Fire—Vietnam, 1967*

ALBERT A. FARKAS—*Pulmonary Embolism Following Sniper Wound—Vietnam, 1968*

ROBERT W. BROWN, JR.—*Shot During Hostile Fire—Vietnam, 1968*

ROBERT W. HUBBARD—*Killed While Trying to Escape Viet Cong—Vietnam, 1968*

JOSEPH B. SMITH—*Landmine Explosion—Vietnam, 1970*

RUDOLPH KAISER—*Viet Cong Ambush—Vietnam, 1972*

JOHN PAUL VANN—*Helicopter Crash—Vietnam, 1972*

JOHN S. PATTERSON—*Kidnapped and Murdered—Mexico, 1974*

RODGER P. DAVIES—*Shot by Sniper—Cyprus, 1974*

JAMES C. MARSHALL—*Killed in Tet Offensive—Vietnam, 1968*

STEVEN A. HAUKNESS—*Killed in Tet Offensive—Vietnam, 1968*

CHARLES W. TURBERVILLE—*Killed in Bomb Blast—Cambodia, 1971*

JOHN PATRICK EGAN—*Kidnapped and Killed by Insurgents—Argentina, 1975*

CHARLES MCMAHON—*Rocket Attack—Vietnam, 1975*

DARWIN L. JUDGE—*Rocket Attack—Vietnam, 1975*

THOMAS OLMSTEAD—*Pancreatitis—Cambodia, 1975*

FRANCIS E. MELOY, JR.—*Assassinated by Terrorists—Beirut, 1976*

ROBERT O. WARING—*Assassinated by Terrorists—Beirut, 1976*

ADOLPH DUBS—*Kidnapped and Killed by Terrorists—Kabul, 1979*

STEVEN J. CROWLEY—*Shot by Mob—Islamabad, 1979*

BRYAN L. ELLIS—*Burned Attempting to Save Life—Islamabad, 1979*

CHARLES ROBERT RAY—*Assassinated by Terrorists—Paris, 1982*

ROBERT C. AMES—*Killed in Bombing of Embassy—Beirut, 1983*

THOMAS R. BLACKA—*Killed in Bombing of Embassy—Beirut, 1983*

PHYLISS N. FARACI—*Killed in Bombing of Embassy—Beirut, 1983*

TERRY L. GILDEN—*Killed in Bombing of Embassy—Beirut, 1983*

KENNETH E. HAAS—*Killed in Bombing of Embassy—Beirut, 1983*

DEBORAH M. HIXON—*Killed in Bombing of Embassy—Beirut, 1983*

FRANK J. JOHNSTON—*Killed in Bombing of Embassy—Beirut, 1983*

JAMES F. LEWIS—*Killed in Bombing of Embassy—Beirut, 1983*

MONIQUE LEWIS—*Killed in Bombing of Embassy—Beirut, 1983*

WILLIAM R. MCINTYRE—*Killed in Bombing of Embassy—Beirut, 1983*

ROBERT V. MCMAUGH—*Killed in Bombing of Embassy—Beirut, 1983*

WILLIAM R. SHEIL—*Killed in Bombing of Embassy—Beirut, 1983*

ALBERT N. VOTAW—*Killed in Bombing of Embassy—Beirut, 1983*

GEORGE TSANTES—*Killed by Gunshot—Athens, 1983*

LEAMON R. HUNT—*Murdered by Guerillas—Rome, 1984*

KENNETH G. CRABTREE—*Killed in Bombing—Namibia, 1984*

DENNIS WHYTE KEOGH—*Killed in Bombing—Namibia, 1984*

A. A. SCHAUFELBERGER III—*Shot by Insurgents—San Salvador, 1983*

CHARLES F. SOPER—*New Delhi, 1983*

MICHAEL RAY WAGNER—*Killed in Bombing of Embassy—Beirut, 1984*

KENNETH V. WELCH—*Killed in Bombing of Embassy—Beirut, 1984*

CHARLES F. HEGNA—*Killed by Gunmen on Plane—Tehran, 1984*

WILLIAM L. STANFORD—*Killed by Gunmen on Plane—Tehran, 1984*

ENRIQUE CAMARENA—*Killed by Drug Traffickers—Guadalajara, 1985*

VIRGINIA WARFIELD—*Automobile Accident—New Delhi, 1983*

BOBBY JOE DICKSON—*Shot by Gunmen—San Salvador, 1985*

THOMAS T. HANDWORK—*Shot by Gunmen—San Salvador, 1985*

PATRICK R. KWIATKOWSKI—*Shot by Gunmen—San Salvador, 1985*

GREGORY H. WEBER—*Shot by Gunmen—San Salvador, 1985*

LAURENCE A. STEINHARDT—*Plane Crash—Ottawa, 1950*

WILLIAM F. BUCKLEY—*Kidnapped and Killed by Terrorists—Beirut, 1985*

WILLIAM E. NORDEEN—*Car Bombing—Athens, 1988*

ARNOLD L. RAPHEL—*Airplane Explosion—Pakistan, 1988*

HERBERT M. WASSOM—*Airplane Explosion—Pakistan, 1988*

MATTHEW K. GANNON—*Airplane Bombing—Scotland, 1988*

RONALD A. LARIVIERE—*Airplane Bombing—Scotland, 1988*

DANIEL E. O'CONNER—*Airplane Bombing—Scotland, 1988*

JAMES N. ROWE—*Shot by Communists—Philippines, 1989*

JOHN A. BUTLER—*Shot in Crossfire—Grenada, 1989*

GLADYS D. GILBERT—*Plane Crash—Ethiopia, 1989*

ROBERT W. WOODS—*Plane Crash—Ethiopia, 1989*

THOMAS J. WORRICK—*Plane Crash—Ethiopia, 1989*

FREDDIE R. WOODRUFF—*Drive-by Shooting—Georgia, 1993*

BARBARA L. SCHELL—*Helicopter Crash—Iraq, 1994*

BARRY S. CASTIGLIONE—*Died in Ocean Rescue—El Salvador, 1992*

GARY C. DURELL—*Ambushed by Terrorists—Pakistan, 1995*

JACQUELINE K. VAN LANDINGHAM—*Ambushed by Terrorists—Pakistan, 1995*

SAMUEL NELSON DREW—*Automobile Accident—Bosnia, 1995*

ROBERT C. FRASURE—*Automobile Accident—Bosnia, 1995*

JOSEPH J. KRUZEL—*Automobile Accident—Bosnia, 1995*

RONALD H. BROWN—*Plane Crash—Croatia, 1996*

LEE F. JACKSON—*Plane Crash—Croatia, 1996*

STEPHEN C. KAMINSKI—*Plane Crash—Croatia, 1996*

LESLIANNE SHEDD—*Plane Crash—Comoros, 1996*

NATHAN ALIGANGA—*Nairobi Embassy Bombing—Kenya, 1998*

JULIAN LEOTIS BARTLEY, SR.—*Nairobi Embassy Bombing—Kenya, 1998*

MOLLY HUCKABY HARDY—*Nairobi Embassy Bombing—Kenya, 1998*

KENNETH R. HOBSON II—*Nairobi Embassy Bombing—Kenya, 1998*

PRABHI G. KAVALER—*Nairobi Embassy Bombing—Kenya, 1998*

MICHELLE O'CONNOR—*Nairobi Embassy Bombing—Kenya, 1998*

SHERRY LYNN OLDS—*Nairobi Embassy Bombing—Kenya, 1998*

UTTAMLAL TOM SHAH—*Nairobi Embassy Bombing—Kenya, 1998*

SETH JOHN FOTI—*Plane Crash—Bahrain, 2000*

PHILIP THOMAS LINCOLN, JR.—*Automobile Accident—China, 1996*

J. KIRBY SIMON—*Carbon Monoxide Poisoning—Taiwan, 1995*

NANCY FEREBEE LEWIS—*Pesticide Poisoning—Egypt, 1993*

PASQUAL MARTINEZ—*Hotel Fire—Russia, 1991*

ROBERT B. HEBB—*Plane Crash—Honduras, 1989*

EDWARD R. CHENEY—*Plane Crash—Philippines, 1976*

GARNETT A. ZIMMERLY—*Plane Crash—Philippines, 1976*

BRUCE O. BAILEY—*Plane Crash—Vietnam, 1972*

LUTHER A. MCLENDON, JR.—*Plane Crash—Vietnam, 1972*

LIVINGSTON LORD SATTERTHWAITE—*Helicopter Crash—Greenland, 1959*

WILLIAM DALE FISHER—*Plane Crash—Ethiopia, 1961*

GUSTAV CRANE HERTZ—*Died of Malaria While Held Captive—Vietnam, 1967*

ROSE MARIE ORLICH—*Killed in an Earthquake—Nicaragua, 1972*

RICHARD AITKEN—*Automobile Accident—Sudan, 1981*

PHILIP ROBERT HANSON—*Plane Crash—Togo, 1981*

JAMES DAVID MARILL—*Automobile Accident—Cameroon, 1986*

ROBERT ROBERTS—*Carbon Monoxide Poisoning—Israel, 1987*

MARIE D. BURKE—*Murdered in Home—United Kingdom, 1989*

THOMAS P. DOUBLEDAY, JR.—*Malaria—Liberia, 1993*

JAMES T. LEDERMAN—*Automobile Accident—Egypt, 1994*

BARBARA J. GREEN—*Terrorist Attack—Pakistan, 2002*

LAURENCE M. FOLEY—*Terrorist Attack—Jordan, 2002*

JERRY V. COOK—*Automobile Accident—Madagascar, 1978*

RICHARD A. COULTER—*Automobile Accident—Iran, 1975*

HOWARD V. FUNK, JR.—*Automobile Accident—Kenya, 1972*

OSCAR C. HOLDER—*Plane Crash—Nepal, 1962*

SIDNEY B. JACQUES—*Plane Crash—Nepal, 1962*

JAMES MOLLEN—*Terrorist Attack—Iraq, 2004*

EDWARD J. SEITZ—*Rocket Attack—Iraq, 2004*

JOHN FRANCIS O'GRADY—*Plane Crash—Australia, 1960*

BARBARA C. HEALD—*Rocket Attack on U.S. Embassy—Iraq, 2005*

KEITH E. TAYLOR—*Rocket Attack on U.S. Embassy—Iraq, 2005*

STEPHEN E. SULLIVAN—*Terrorist Attack—Iraq, 2005*

DAVID E. FOY—*Terrorist Attack—Pakistan, 2006*

MARGARET ALEXANDER—*Helicopter Crash—Nepal, 2006*

DORIS KNITTLE—*Murdered by Servant—Afghanistan, 1970*

HENRY W. ANTHEIL, JR.—*Plane Exploded in Midair—Estonia, 1940*

STEVEN THOMAS STEFANI IV—*Killed by Bomb—Afghanistan, 2007*

JOHN MICHAEL GRANVILLE—*Vehicle Ambush—Sudan, 2008*

BRIAN DANIEL ADKINS—*Murdered in Home—Ethiopia, 2009*

FELIX RUSSELL ENGDAHL—*Accidental Fall in POW Camp—Hong Kong, 1942*

THOMAS W. WALDRON—*Died of Cholera—Macau, 1844*

EDMUND ROBERTS—*Died of Dysentery—Macau, 1844*

VICTORIA J. DELONG—*Earthquake—Haiti, 2010*

DALE J. GREDLER—*Heart Attack / Lack of Medical Facilities—Indonesia, 2010*

TERRENCE L. BARNICH—*Roadside Bomb—Iraq, 2009*

EUGENE F. SULLIVAN—*Black Water Fever— Ethiopia, 1972*

SHARON S. CLARK—*Cerebral Malaria—Nigeria, 2010*

ANNE T. SMEDINGHOFF—*Roadside Bomb— Afghanistan, 2013*

JOHN CHRISTOPHER STEVENS—*Terrorist Attack—Libya, 2012*

SEAN PATRICK SMITH—*Terrorist Attack—Libya, 2012*

GLEN A. DOHERTY—*Terrorist Attack—Libya, 2012*

TY WOODS—*Terrorist Attack—Libya, 2012*

RAGAEI SAID ABDELFATTAH—*Suicide Bomber—Afghanistan, 2012*

JOSEPH GREGORY FANDINO—*Line of duty— Vietnam, 1972*

FRANCIS J. SAVAGE—*Terrorist bomber— Vietnam, 1967.*

Bibliography

BOOKS

Abel, Elie. *The Missiles of October: The Story of the Cuban Missile Crisis, 1962.* London: MacGibbon and Kee, 1969.

Acheson, Dean. *Present at the Creation: My Years in the State Department.* New York: W. W. Norton, 1969.

Adams, Ephraim Douglass. *Great Britain and the American Civil War.* New York: Russell and Russell, 1958.

Aguilera, Pilar, and Ricardo Fredes, eds. *Chile: The Other September 11.* Melbourne: Ocean Press, 2003.

Ammon, Harry. *James Monroe: The Quest for National Identity.* Charlottesville: University Press of Virginia, 1990.

Attwood, William. *The Reds and the Blacks: A Personal Adventure.* New York: Harper and Row, 1967.

Auchincloss, Louis. *Theodore Roosevelt.* New York: Times Books / Henry Holt, 2001.

———. *Woodrow Wilson.* New York: Viking, 2000.

Bancroft, Frederic. *The Life of William H. Seward.* Vol. 2. New York: Harper and Brothers, 1900.

Barnes, Harper. *Standing on a Volcano: The Life and Times of David Rowland Francis.* Saint Louis: Missouri Historical Society Press, 2001.

Barnes, William, and John Heath Morgan. *The Foreign Service of the United States: Origins, Development, and Functions.* Washington, D.C.: Historical Office, Department of State, 1961.

Barnet, Richard J. *Intervention and Revolution: The United States in the Third World.* New York: World Publishing, 1968.

Beisner, Robert L. *Twelve Against Empire: The Anti-Imperialists, 1898–1900.* Chicago: Imprint Publications, 1992. First published 1968 by McGraw-Hill.

Berger, Meyer. *The Story of "The New York Times," 1851–1951.* New York: Simon and Schuster, 1951.

Bergeron, Paul H. *The Presidency of James K. Polk.* Lawrence: University Press of Kansas, 1987.

Berridge, G. R. *British Diplomacy in Turkey, 1583 to the Present: A Study in the Evolution of the Resident Embassy*. Leiden, The Netherlands: Martinus Nihoff, 2009.

Beschloss, Michael R. *Kennedy and Roosevelt: The Uneasy Alliance*. New York: W. W. Norton, 1980.

Bird, Isaac. *Bible Work in Bible Lands: Events in the History of the Syria Mission*. Philadelphia: Trustees of the Presbyterian Board of Publication, 1872. Available online at http://archive.org/details/bibleworkinbible00bird.

Blinken, Vera. *Vera and the Ambassador: Escape and Return; Donald and Vera Blinken*. Albany: State University of New York Press, New York, 2008.

Boorstein, Edward. *Allende's Chile: An Inside View*. New York: International Publishers, 1977.

Bowden, Mark. *Guests of the Ayatollah: The First Battle in America's War with Militant Islam*. New York: Atlantic Monthly Press, 2006.

Bowers, Claude G. *Chile Through Embassy Windows: 1939–1953*. New York: Simon and Schuster, 1958.

———. *My Mission to Spain: Watching the Rehearsal for World War II*. New York: Simon and Schuster, 1954.

Brands, H. W. *The First American: The Life and Times of Benjamin Franklin*. New York: Doubleday, 2000.

———. *Inside the Cold War: Loy Henderson and the Rise of the American Empire, 1918–1961*. New York: Oxford University Press, 1991.

Bridges, Hal. *Iron Millionaire: Life of Charlemagne Tower*. Philadelphia: University of Pennsylvania Press, 1952.

Brookhiser, Richard. *Gentleman Revolutionary: Gouverneur Morris, The Rake Who Wrote the Constitution*. New York: Free Press, 2003.

Bryson, Thomas A. *An American Consular Officer in the Middle East in the Jacksonian Era: A Biography of William Brown Hodgson, 1801–1871*. Atlanta: Resurgens Publications, 1979.

Buckley, Kevin. *Panama: The Whole Story*. New York: Simon and Schuster, 1991.

Buhite, Russell D. *Nelson T. Johnson and American Foreign Policy Toward China, 1925–1941*. East Lansing: Michigan State University Press, 1968.

Bullitt, Orville H. *For the President: Personal and Secret; Correspondence Between Franklin D. Roosevelt and William C. Bullitt*. Boston: Houghton Mifflin, 1972.

Bullitt, William C. *The Bullitt Mission to Russia: Testimony before the Committee on Foreign Relations United States Senate*. New York: B. W. Huebsch, 1919.

Burbach, Roger. *The Pinochet Affair: State Terrorism and Global Justice*. London: Zed Books, 2003.

Burns, James MacGregor. *Leadership*. New York: Harper and Row, 1978.

———. *Roosevelt: The Soldier of Freedom*. New York: Harcourt Brace Jovanovich, 1970.

Burt, Richard, and Olin Robinson. *Reinventing Diplomacy in the Information Age*. Washington, D.C.: Center for Strategic and International Studies, 1998.

Calkin, Homer L. *The Women in the State Department: Their Role in American Foreign Affairs*. Washington, D.C.: Department of State, 1978.

Chace, James. *Acheson: The Secretary of State Who Created the American World*. New York: Simon and Schuster, 1998.

Chapman, Peter. *Bananas: How the United Fruit Company Shaped the World*. New York: Canongate, 2007.

Chernow, Ron. *Alexander Hamilton*. New York: Penguin, 2004.

Choate, Joseph H., Henry Van Dyke, Edward Cary, William Dean Howells, and George Haven Putnam. *John Bigelow: Memorial Addresses Delivered before The Century Association, March 9, 1912*. New York: The Century Association, 1912.

Clapp, Margaret. *Forgotten First Citizen: John Bigelow.* Boston: Little, Brown, 1947.

Clark, Ronald W. *Benjamin Franklin: A Biography.* New York: De Capo, 1983.

Cleveland, Harlan, Gerard J. Mangone, and John Clarke Adams. *The Overseas Americans.* New York: Arno Press, 1980. First published 1960 by McGraw-Hill.

Cline, Howard F. *The United States and Mexico.* Cambridge, MA: Harvard University Press, 1953.

Clubb, O. Edmund. *Twentieth Century China.* New York: Columbia University Press, 1964.

———. *The Witness and I.* New York: Columbia University Press, 1975. Available online at Google Books.

Cockcroft, James D., ed. *Salvador Allende Reader.* Melbourne: Ocean Press, 2000.

Coffman, Tom. *Nation Within: The Story of America's Annexation of the Nation of Hawai'i.* Kāne'ohe, Hawai'i: Tom Coffman / EPICenter, 1998.

Cohen, Warren I. *Dean Rusk.* The American Secretaries of State and Their Diplomacy, vol. 19. Totowa, NJ: Cooper Square Publishers, 1980.

Coll, Steve. *Ghost Wars: The Secret History of the CIA, Afghanistan, and bin Laden, from the Soviet Invasion to September 10, 2001.* New York: Penguin, 2004.

Combs, Jerald A. *The Jay Treaty: Political Battleground of the Founding Fathers:* Berkeley: University of California Press, 1970.

Commager, Henry Steele, ed. *Documents of American History.* 3rd edition. New York: F. S. Crofts, 1943.

Connor, Seymour V., and Odie B. Faulk. *North America Divided: The Mexican War, 1846–1848.* New York: Oxford University Press, 1971.

Cordovez, Diego, and Selig S. Harrison. *Out of Afghanistan: The Inside Story of the Soviet Withdrawal.* New York: Oxford University Press, 1995. See esp. overview and epilogue.

Cortissoz, Royal. *The Life of Whitelaw Reid.* London: Thornton Butterworth, 1921.

Craig, Gordon A., and Felix Gilbert, eds. *The Diplomats, 1919–1939.* 1953. Reprint, Princeton, NJ: Princeton University Press, 1981.

Craig, Gordon A., and Francis L. Loewenheim, eds. *The Diplomats, 1939–1979.* Princeton, NJ: Princeton University Press, 1994.

Crane, Katherine E. *Mr. Carr of State.* New York: St. Martin's Press, 1960.

Crunden, Robert M. *A Hero in Spite of Himself: Brand Whitlock in Art, Politics and War.* New York: Alfred A. Knopf, 1969.

Dallek, Robert. *Democrat and Diplomat: The Life of William E. Dodd.* New York: Oxford University Press, 1968.

Dana, Richard Henry. *Hospitable England in the Seventies: The Diary of a Young American, 1875–1876.* Boston: Houghton Mifflin, 1921.

Dangerfield, George. *Chancellor Robert R. Livingston of New York, 1746–1813.* New York: Harcourt, Brace, 1960.

Davies, John Paton, Jr. *China Hand: An Autobiography.* Philadelphia: University of Pennsylvania Press, 2012.

———. *Foreign and Other Affairs: A View from the Radical Center.* New York: W. W. Norton, 1964.

Dennett, Tyler, *John Hay: From Poetry to Politics.* New York: Dodd, Mead, 1933.

Denza, Eileen. *Diplomatic Law: A Commentary on the Vienna Convention on Diplomatic Relations.* 2nd ed. Oxford: Oxford University Press, 1998.

Department of State. *Foreign Affairs Manual,* vol. 3, section 4820. Available online at http://www.state.gov/m/a/dir/regs/fam/.

DeSantis, Hugh. *The Diplomacy of Silence: The American Foreign Service, the Soviet Union, and the Cold War, 1933–1947.* 1980. Reprint, Chicago: University of Chicago Press, 1983.

Diederich, Bernard. *Trujillo: The Death of the Goat*. Maplewood, NJ: Waterfront Press, 1990. First published 1978 by Little, Brown.

Dizard, Wilson P., Jr. *Inventing Public Diplomacy: The Story of the U.S Information Agency*. Boulder, CO: Lynne Rienner Publishers, 2004.

Dodd, William Edward. *Ambassador Dodd's Diary, 1933–1938*. Edited by William E. Dodd, Jr., and Martha Dodd, with an introduction by Charles A. Beard. New York: Harcourt, Brace, 1941.

Donald, David Herbert. *Lincoln*. London: Jonathan Cape, 1995.

Duberman, Martin B. *Charles Francis Adams, 1807–1886*. Boston: Houghton Mifflin, 1960.

Duncan, Bingham. *Whitelaw Reid: Journalist, Politician, Diplomat*. Athens: University of Georgia Press, 1975.

Elder, Robert E. *The Information Machine: The United States Information Agency and American Foreign Policy*. Syracuse, NY: Syracuse University Press, 1968.

Ellis, Joseph J. *American Sphinx: The Character of Thomas Jefferson*. New York: Alfred A. Knopf, 1997; Vintage Books, 1998.

———. *Founding Brothers: The Revolutionary Generation*. New York: Alfred A. Knopf, 2000.

Ellsworth, Harry Allanson. *One Hundred Eighty Landings of the United States Marines, 1800–1934*. Washington, D.C.: History and Museums Division, Headquarters, US Marine Corps., 1974.

Engert, Jane Morrison. *Tales from the Embassy: The Extraordinary World of C. Van H. Engert*. Westminster, MD: Eagle Editions, 2006.

Evans, Laurence. *United States Policy and the Partition of Turkey, 1914–1924*. Baltimore: Johns Hopkins Press, 1965.

Ferling, John. *John Adams: A Life*. New York: Henry Holt, 1996.

Foglesong, David S. *America's Secret War Against Bolshevism*. Chapel Hill: University of North Carolina Press, 1995.

Foreman, Amanda. *A World on Fire: An Epic History of Two Nations Divided*. London: Allan Lane, 2010.

Forrestal, James. *The Forrestal Diaries*. Edited by Walter Millis. New York: Viking, 1951.

Francis, David R. *Russia from the American Embassy, April, 1916–November, 1918*. New York: Charles Scribner's Sons, 1921.

Fromkin, David. *A Peace to End All Peace: The Fall of the Ottoman Empire and the Creation of the Modern Middle East*. New York: Avon Books, 1990. First published 1989 by Henry Holt.

Fuess, Claude Moore. *Daniel Webster*. Vol. 2, *1830–1852*. Boston: Little, Brown, 1930.

Gaddis, John Lewis. *George F. Kennan: An American Life*. New York: Penguin, 2011.

Gara, Larry. *The Presidency of Franklin Pierce*. Lawrence: University Press of Kansas, 1991.

Gardner, Richard N. *Mission Italy: On the Front Lines of the Cold War*. New York: Rowman and Littlefield, 2005.

Gerard, James W. *My Four Years in Germany*. New York: George H. Doran, 1917.

Gibson, Hugh. *Hugh Gibson, 1883–1954: Extracts from His Letters and Anecdotes from His Friends*. Edited by Perrin C. Galpin. New York: Belgian American Educational Foundation, Inc., 1956.

———. *A Journal from Our Legation in Belgium*. Garden City, NY: Doubleday, Page, 1917.

Ginsburgh, Robert N. "Between War and Peace." Ph.D. diss., Harvard University, 1948.

Gleijeses, Piero. *Shattered Hope: The Guatemalan Revolution and the United States, 1944–1954*. Princeton, NJ: Princeton University Press, 1991.

Goldberg, Isaac. *Major Noah: American-Jewish Pioneer*. Philadelphia: Jewish Publication Society of America, 1936.

Goodwin, Doris Kearns. *Team of Rivals: The Political Genius of Abraham Lincoln*. New York: Simon and Schuster, 2005.

Graves, William S. *America's Siberian Adventure, 1918–1920*. New York: Peter Smith, 1931.

Grew, Joseph C. *Report from Tokyo: A Message to the American People.* New York: Simon and Schuster, 1942.

———. *Ten Years in Japan.* New York: Simon and Schuster, 1944.

———. *Turbulent Era: A Diplomatic Record of Forty Years, 1904–1945.* 2 vols. Edited by Walter Johnson. Boston: Houghton Mifflin, 1952.

Griffis, William Elliot. *Corea, the Hermit Nation.* New York: Charles Scribner's Sons, 1894.

Grove, Brandon. *Behind Embassy Walls: The Life and Times of an American Diplomat.* Columbia: University of Missouri Press, 2005.

Harriman, Florence Jaffray. *Mission to the North.* New York: J. B. Lippincott, 1941.

Hart, John Mason. *Revolutionary Mexico.* Berkeley: University of California Press, 1987.

Hendrick, Burton J. *The Life and Letters of Walter H. Page.* 3 vols. New York: Doubleday, Page, 1922–25. See esp. vol. 1, chap. 13, "Germany's First Peace Drives." Available online at Google Books.

Hill, Max. *Exchange Ship.* New York: Farrar and Rinehart, 1942.

History of the American Field Service in France: "Friends of France," 1914–1917, Told by Its Members. Boston: Houghton Mifflin, 1920. See esp. section 1, "The Ambulance Sections," part 4. Available online from Google Books.

Houghteling, James L., Jr. *A Diary of the Russian Revolution.* New York: Dodd, Mead, 1918. Available online at http://archive.org/details/diaryofrussianre00houg.

Howard, Michael. *The First World War.* Oxford: Oxford University Press, 2002.

Hoyt, Michael P. E. *Captive in the Congo: A Consul's Return to the Heart of Darkness.* Annapolis, MD: Naval Institute Press, 2000.

Hunt, Gaillard. *The Department of State: Its History and Functions.* New Haven, CT: Yale University Press, 1914.

Ilchman, Warren Frederick. *Professional Diplomacy in the United States, 1779–1939: A Study in Administrative History.* 1961. Reprint, Chicago: University of Chicago Press, 1974.

James, Coy Hilton. *Silas Deane: Patriot or Traitor?* East Lansing: Michigan State University Press, 1975.

Jefferson, Thomas. *The Papers of Thomas Jefferson.* Vol. 24, *1 June to 31 December 1792.* Edited by John Catanzariti. Princeton, NJ: Princeton University Press, 1990.

———. *The Writings of Thomas Jefferson.* Edited by Paul Leicester Ford. Vol. 4, *1784–1789.* New York: G. P. Putnam's Sons, 1894.

Jessup, Philip C. *Elihu Root.* 2 vols. New York: Dodd, Mead, 1938.

Ji Chaozhu. *The Man on Mao's Right: From Harvard Yard to Tiananmen Square; My Life Inside China's Foreign Ministry.* New York: Random House, 2008.

Jouve, Daniel. *Paris: Birthplace of the USA.* Paris: Grund, 1995.

Kahn, E. J., Jr. *The China Hands: America's Foreign Service Officers and What Befell Them.* New York: Viking, 1975.

Kaplan, Robert D. *The Arabists: The Romance of an American Elite.* New York: Free Press, 1995.

Karnow, Stanley. *Vietnam: A History.* New York: Viking, 1984; Penguin, 1984.

Katzenbach, Nicholas deB. *Some of It Was Fun: Working with R.F.K. and L.B.J.* New York, W. W. Norton, 2008

Kennan, George F. *At a Century's Ending: Reflections, 1982–1995.* New York: W. W. Norton, 1997.

———. *Memoirs, 1925–1950.* Boston: Little, Brown, 1967.

———. *Soviet-American Relations, 1917–1920.* Vol. 1, *Russia Leaves the War.* Princeton, NJ: Princeton University Press, 1956.

———. *Soviet American Relations, 1917–1920.* Vol. 2, *The Decision to Intervene.* Princeton, NJ: Princeton University Press, 1958.

Kennedy, Charles Stuart. *The American Consul: A History of the United States Consular Service, 1776–1914.* Contributions in American History, no. 139. Westport, CT: Greenwood Press, 1990.

Kimball, Marie. *Jefferson: The Scene of Europe, 1784–1789.* New York: Coward-McCann, 1950.

Kinzer, Stephen. *All the Shah's Men: The American Coup and the Roots of Middle East Terror.* Hoboken, NJ: John Wiley and Sons, 2003.

——. *Overthrow: America's Century of Regime Change from Hawaii to Iraq.* New York: Times Books / Henry Holt, 2006.

Kissinger, Henry. *Years of Upheaval.* Boston: Little, Brown, 1982.

Kluger, Richard. *The Paper: The Life and Death of "The New York Herald Tribune."* New York: Alfred A. Knopf, 1986.

Kornbluh, Peter. *The Pinochet File: A Declassified Dossier on Atrocity and Accountability.* New York: New Press, 2003.

Kremer, Gary R. *James Milton Turner and the Promise of America: The Public Life of a Post–Civil War Black Leader.* Columbia: University of Missouri Press, 1991.

Krenn, Michael L. *Black Diplomacy: African Americans and the State Department, 1945–1969.* Armonk, NY: M. E. Sharpe, 1999.

Kurlansky, Mark. *Cod: A Biography of the Fish That Changed the World.* New York: Penguin, 1997.

LaFeber, Walter. *The American Age: US Foreign Policy at Home and Abroad, 1750 to the Present.* New York: W. W. Norton, 1989.

Laingen, L. Bruce. *Yellow Ribbon: The Secret Journal of Bruce Laingen.* Washington, D.C.: Brassey's (US), 1992.

Laird, Thomas. *Into Tibet: The CIA's First Atomic Spy and His Secret Expedition to Lhasa.* New York: Grove Press, 2002.

Larson, Erik. *In the Garden of Beasts.* New York: Crown Publishers, 2011.

Lathrop, Rose Hawthorne. *Memories of Hawthorne.* New York, 1897. Available at http://www .gutenberg.org/ebooks/6926.

Lay, Tracy Hollingsworth. *The Foreign Service of the United States.* New York: Prentice-Hall, 1925.

Leech, Margaret. *In the Days of McKinley.* New York: Harper and Brothers, 1959.

Leger, J. N. *Haiti: Her History and Her Detractors.* New York: Neale Publishing, 1907.

Levins, John. *Days of Fear.* London: Motivate Publishing, 1997.

Lewis, Bernard. *What Went Wrong? The Clash Between Islam and Modernity in the Middle East.* New York: Harper Collins, Perennial, 2003.

Lilley, James. *China Hands: Nine Decades of Adventure, Espionage, and Diplomacy in Asia.* With Jeffrey Lilley. New York: Public Affairs, 2004.

Lord, Walter. *The Dawn's Early Light.* New York: W. W. Norton, 1972.

Lowenthal, Abraham F. *The Dominican Intervention.* Cambridge, MA: Harvard University Press, 1972.

Lowenthal, David. *George Perkins Marsh: Prophet of Conservation.* Seattle: University of Washington Press, 2000.

——. *George Perkins Marsh: Versatile Vermonter.* New York: Columbia University Press, 1958.

MacDonogh, Giles. *A Good German: Adam von Trott zu Solz.* Woodstock, NY: Overlook Press, 1992.

MacMillan, Margaret. *Paris 1919.* New York: Random House, 2001.

Mak, Dayton, and Charles Stuart Kennedy. *American Ambassadors in a Troubled World: Interviews with Senior Diplomats.* Westport, CT: Greenwood Press, 1992.

Malone, Dumas. *Jefferson and His Time.* Vol. 2, *Jefferson and the Rights of Man.* Boston: Little, Brown, 1951.

——. *Jefferson and His Time.* Vol. 3, *Jefferson and the Ordeal of Liberty.* Boston: Little, Brown, 1962.

Manchester, William. *The Last Lion: Winston Spencer Churchill.* Vol. 1. New York: Dell Publishing, 1989.

Mann, James. *About Face: A History of America's Curious Relationship with China, from Nixon to Clinton.* New York: Vintage Books, 2000.

Massie, Robert. *Castles of Steel: Britain, Germany, and the Winning of the Great War at Sea.* New York: Random House, 2003.

Mayer, Martin. *The Diplomats.* Garden City, NY: Doubleday, 1983.

Mayers, David. *George Kennan and the Dilemmas of US Foreign Policy.* New York: Oxford University Press, 1988.

McCoy, Charles A. *Polk and the Presidency.* Austin: University of Texas Press, 1960.

McCullough, David. *John Adams.* New York: Simon and Schuster, 2001.

McGhee, George. *Envoy to the Middle World: Adventures in Diplomacy.* New York: Harper and Row, 1983.

McGlen, Nancy E., and Meredith Reid Sarkees. *The Status of Women in Foreign Policy.* New York: Foreign Policy Association, 1995.

———. *Women in Foreign Policy: The Insiders.* New York, Routledge, 1993.

McNamara, Robert S. *In Retrospect: The Tragedy and Lessons of Vietnam.* New York: Random House, 1995.

Meara, William R. *Contra Cross: Insurgency and Tyranny in Central America, 1979–1989.* Annapolis, MD: Naval Institute Press, 2006.

Millis, Walter. *Road to War: America, 1914–1917.* Boston: Houghton Mifflin, 1935.

Miscamble, Wilson D. *George F. Kennan and the Making of American Foreign Policy, 1947–1950.* Princeton, NJ: Princeton University Press, 1992.

Monaghan, Frank. *John Jay: Defender of Liberty Against Kings and Peoples, Author of the Constitution and Governor of New York, President of the Continental Congress, Co-author of the Federalist, Negotiator of the Peace of 1783 and the Jay Treaty of 1794, First Chief Justice of the United States.* New York: Bobbs-Merrill, 1935.

Montross, Lynn, and Nicholas A. Canzona. *U.S. Marine Operations in Korea, 1950–1953.* Vol. 1, *The Pusan Perimeter.* Washington, D.C.: Headquarters, U.S. Marine Corps, 1954.

Morgenthau, Henry. *All in a Life-Time.* In collaboration with French Strother. Garden City, NY: Doubleday, Page, 1922.

———. *Ambassador Morgenthau's Story.* Ann Arbor, MI: Gomidas Institute Books, 2000. First published 1919 by Doubleday, Page.

Morison, Samuel Eliot. *History of United States Naval Operations in World War II.* Vol. 3, *The Rising Sun in the Pacific, 1931–April 1942.* Boston: Little, Brown, 1948.

———. *John Paul Jones: A Sailor's Biography.* Boston: Little, Brown, 1959.

Morris, Edmund. *Theodore Rex.* New York: Random House, 2001.

Morris, Richard B. *The Peacemakers: The Great Powers and American Independence.* New York: Harper and Row, 1965.

Morse, Arthur D. *While Six Million Died: A Chronicle of American Apathy.* New York: Random House, 1967.

Moskin, J. Robert. *The U.S. Marine Corps Story.* 3rd edition. New York: Little, Brown, 1992.

Mott, T. Bentley. *Myron Herrick: Friend of France.* Garden City, NY: Doubleday, Doran, 1929.

Murphy, Robert. *Diplomat among Warriors.* Garden City, NY: Doubleday, 1964.

Neff, Donald. *Fallen Pillars: US Policy towards Palestine and Israel Since 1945.* Washington, D.C.: Institute for Palestine Studies, 1995. Chapter one excerpted online at http://www.washingtonpost.com/wp-srv/style/longterm/books/chap1/fallenpillars.htm.

Nevins, Allan. *Hamilton Fish: The Inner History of the Grant Administration.* New York: Dodd Mead, 1936.

———. *Henry White: Thirty Years of American Diplomacy*. New York: Harper and Brothers, 1930.

Nicholson, Jim. *The United States and the Holy See: The Long Road*. Rome: Trenta Giorni Società Cooperativa, 2004.

Nordholt, Jan Willem Schulte. *The Dutch Republic and American Independence*. Translated by Herbert H. Rowen. Chapel Hill: University of North Carolina Press, 1982.

North Atlantic Treaty Organization. *NATO Handbook*. Brussels: NATO Office of Information and Press, 2001.

O'Sullivan, Christopher D. *Sumner Welles, Postwar Planning, and the Quest for New World Order, 1937–1943*. New York: Columbia University Press, 2003. Available online at http:// www .gutenberg-e.org/osc01/.

O'Toole, Patricia. *The Five of Hearts: An Intimate Portrait of Henry Adams and His Friends, 1880–1918*. New York: Clarkson Potter, 1990.

Orebaugh, Walter W. *Guerrilla in Striped Pants: A US Diplomat Joins the Italian Resistance*. With Carol Jose. New York: Praeger, 1992.

Oshinsky, David M. *A Conspiracy So Immense: The World of Joe McCarthy*. New York: Free Press, 1983.

Patenaude, Bertrand M. *The Big Show in Bololand: The American Relief Expedition to Soviet Russia in the Famine of 1921*. Stanford, CA: Stanford University Press, 2002.

Pearton, Maurice. *Diplomacy, War and Technology since 1830*. Lawrence: University Press of Kansas, 1984.

Perkins, John A. *The Prudent Peace: Law as Foreign Policy*. Chicago: University of Chicago Press, 1981.

Persico, Joseph E. *Roosevelt's Secret War: FDR and World War II Espionage*. New York: Random House, 2001.

Phillips, William. *Ventures in Diplomacy*. Boston: Beacon Press, 1952.

Pletcher, David M. *The Diplomacy of Involvement: American Economic Expansion across the Pacific, 1784–1900*. Columbia: University of Missouri Press, 2001.

Plischke, Elmer. *US Department of State*. Santa Barbara, CA: Greenwood Press, 1999.

Polk, James K. *The Diary of James K. Polk during His Presidency, 1845–49*. Vol. 2. Chicago: A. C. McClurg, 1910.

Powell, E. Alexander. *Fighting in Flanders*. New York: Charles Scribner's Sons, 1914. Available online at http://archive.org/details/fightinginflande00powe.

Prange, Gordon W. *At Dawn We Slept: The Untold Story of Pearl Harbor*. New York: McGraw-Hill, 1981.

Pusey, M. J. *Charles Evans Hughes*. 2 vols. New York: Macmillan, 1951.

Raymond, Henry J. *The Life and Public Services of Abraham Lincoln together with His State Papers*. New York: Derby and Miller, 1865.

Roberts, Priscilla H., and Richard S. Roberts. *Thomas Barclay (1728–1793) Consul in France, Diplomat in Barbary*. Bethlehem, PA: Lehigh University Press, 2008.

Robinson, Blackwell P. *William R. Davie*. Chapel Hill: University of North Carolina Press, 1957.

Rockefeller, John Davis. *Random Reminiscences of Men and Events*. New York: Doubleday, Page, 1909.

Roosevelt, Theodore. *Letters*. Vol. 7, *The Days of Armageddon, 1909–1914*. Selected and edited by Elting E. Morison. Cambridge, MA: Harvard University Press, 1954.

Root, Elihu. *Addresses on Government and Citizenship*. Collected and edited by Robert Bacon and James Brown Scott. Cambridge, MA: Harvard University Press, 1916.

———. *Addresses on International Subjects*. Collected and edited by Robert Bacon and James Brown Scott. Cambridge, MA: Harvard University Press, 1916.

——. *The Military and Colonial Policy of the United States*. Cambridge, MA: Harvard University Press, 1916.

Rowan, Roy. *Chasing the Dragon: A Veteran Journalist's Firsthand Account of the 1949 Chinese Revolution*. Guilford, CT: Lyons Press, 2004.

Rusk, Dean. *As I Saw It*. As told to Richard Rusk. Edited by Daniel S. Papp. New York: W. W. Norton, 1990.

——. *The Winds of Freedom: Selections from the Speeches and Statements of Secretary of State Dean Rusk, January 1961–August 1962*. Edited by Ernest K. Lindley. Boston: Beacon Press, 1963.

Schaffer, Howard B. *Ellsworth Bunker: Global Troubleshooter, Vietnam Hawk*. Chapel Hill: University of North Carolina Press, 2005.

Schiff, Stacy. *A Great Improvisation: Franklin, France, and the Birth of America*. New York: Henry Holt, 2005.

Schlesinger, Arthur M., Jr. *The Age of Jackson*. Boston: Little, Brown, 1945.

Schulzinger, Robert D. *The Making of the Diplomatic Mind: The Training, Outlook, and Style of United States Foreign Service Officers, 1908–1931*. Middletown, CT: Wesleyan University Press, 1975.

Sellers, Charles. *James K. Polk, Continentalist, 1843–1846*. Princeton, NJ: Princeton University Press, 1966.

Service, John S. *Lost Chance in China: The World War II Despatches of John S. Service*. Edited by Joseph W. Esherick. New York: Random House, 1974.

Seymour, Charles. *American Diplomacy During the World War*. 2nd edition. Baltimore: Johns Hopkins Press, 1942.

Shackelford, George Green. *Thomas Jefferson's Travels in Europe, 1784–1789*. Baltimore: Johns Hopkins University Press, 1995.

Shaler, William. *Algiers, Political, Historical, and Civil*. Boston: Cummings, Hilliard, 1826.

Shaw, Samuel. *The Journals of Major Samuel Shaw, The First American Consul at Canton*. Salisbury, NC: Documentary Publications, 1970. First published 1847 by Wm. Crosby and H. P. Nicholas.

Sherer, Carroll Russell. *A Great Adventure: Thirty Years in Diplomatic Service*. Self-published, 2007.

Shirer, William L. *The Collapse of the Third Republic: An Inquiry into the Fall of France in 1940*. New York: Simon and Schuster, 1969.

——. *The Rise and Fall of the Third Reich*. New York: Simon and Schuster, 1960.

Shultz, George P. *Turmoil and Triumph: My Years as Secretary of State*. New York: Charles Scribner's Sons, 1993.

Sick, Gary. *All Fall Down: America's Tragic Encounter with Iran*. New York: Random House, 1985.

Siepel, Kevin H. *Rebel: The Life and Times of John Singleton Mosby*. New York: St. Martin's Press, 1983.

Sigal, Leon V. *Disarming Stranger: Nuclear Diplomacy with North Korea*. Princeton, NJ: Princeton University Press, 1998.

Simmons, Edwin H., and Joseph H. Alexander. *Through the Wheat: The U.S. Marines in World War I*. Annapolis, MD: Naval Institute Press, 2007.

Sorensen, Ted, *Counselor: A Life on the Edge of History*. New York: Harper Collins, 2008.

Sorensen, Thomas C. *The Word War: The Story of American Propaganda*. New York: Harper and Row, 1968.

Sperber, A. M. *Murrow: His Life and Times*. New York: Feundlich Books, 1986.

Stahr, Walter *Seward: Lincoln's Indispensable Man*. New York: Simon and Schuster, 2012.

Statler, Oliver. *Shimoda Story*. New York: Random House, 1969.

Steel, Ronald. *Walter Lippmann and the American Century*. Boston: Little, Brown, 1980.

Steffens, Lincoln. *The Autobiography of Lincoln Steffens.* Vol. 2. New York: Harcourt, Brace, 1931.

Stevenson, Robert Louis. *A Footnote to History: Eight Years of Trouble in Samoa.* Honolulu: University of Hawaii Press, 1996.

Stiller, Jesse H. *George S. Messersmith: Diplomat of Democracy.* Chapel Hill: University of North Carolina Press, 1987.

Stillman, William J. *The Autobiography of a Journalist.* 2 vols. Boston: Houghton Mifflin, 1901.

Storey, Moorfield. *Charles Sumner.* American Statesmen series, vol. 30. Boston: Houghton Mifflin, 1900.

Straus, Oscar S. *Under Four Administrations: From Cleveland to Taft.* Boston: Houghton Mifflin, 1922.

Stuart, John Leighton. *Fifty Years in China.* New York: Random House, 1954. Available online at http://archive.org/stream/fiftyyearsinchin012639mbp#page/n0/mode/1up.

Sullivan, Joseph G., ed. *Embassies Under Siege: Personal Accounts of Diplomats on the Front Line.* An Institute for the Study of Diplomacy Book. Washington, D.C.: Brassey's, 1995.

Sullivan, Mark. *Our Times: The United States, 1900–1925.* Vol. 3, *Pre-War America.* New York: Charles Scribner's Sons, 1930.

———. *Our Times: The United States, 1900–1925.* Vol. 5, *Over Here, 1914–1918.* New York: Charles Scribner's Sons, 1933.

Sullivan, William H. *Mission to Iran.* New York: W. W. Norton, 1981.

———. *Obbligato, 1939–1979: Notes on a Foreign Service Career.* New York: W. W. Norton, 1981.

Swanberg, W. A. *Citizen Hearst: A Biography of William Randolph Hearst.* New York: Charles Scribner's Sons, 1961.

Takemae, Eiji. *Inside GHQ: The Allied Occupation of Japan and Its Legacy.* New York: Continuum, 2002.

Taylor, John M. *William Henry Seward, Lincoln's Right Hand.* New York: Harper Collins, 1991.

Thayer, William Roscoe. *The Life and Letters of John Hay.* 2 vols. Boston: Houghton Mifflin, 1915.

Todd, Charles Burr. *Life and Letters of Joel Barlow, LL.D., Poet, Statesman, Philosopher.* New York: Burr Franklin, 1972.

Tuchman, Barbara W. *The Guns of August.* New York: Ballantine Books, 1994. First published 1962 by Macmillan.

———. *The Zimmermann Telegram.* New York: Ballantine Books, 1985. First published 1958 by Macmillan.

Van Buren, Martin. *Autobiography.* House Document 819, 66th Cong., 2nd sess., vol. 93, part 1. Washington, D.C.: Government Printing Office, 1920.

Vance, Cyrus. *Hard Choices: Critical Years in America's Foreign Policy.* New York: Simon and Schuster, 1983.

Van Doren, Carl. *Benjamin Franklin.* New York: Viking, 1938.

Van Dyke, Frederick. *Our Foreign Service: The "ABC" of American Diplomacy.* Rochester, NY: Lawyers Cooperative Publishing, 1909. Available at http://www.archive.org/bookreader/print.php?id=ourforeignservic00vandandserver=ia341019.

Varg, Paul A. *Open Door Diplomat: The Life of W. W. Rockhill.* Urbana: University of Illinois Press, 1952.

Vaughan, Hal. *FDR's 12 Apostles: The Spies Who Paved the Way for the Invasion of North Africa.* Guilford, CT: Lyons Press, 2006.

Walsh, Lawrence E. *Final Report of the Independent Counsel for Iran/Contra Matters.* Vol. 1. Washington, D.C.: United States Court of Appeals for the District of Columbia, August 4, 1993. See esp. chap. 24–26 and executive summary. Available online at http://www.fas.org/irp/offdocs/walsh/index.html.

Weigley, Russell F. *The American Way of War: A History of United States Military Strategy and Policy.* New York: Macmillan, 1973.

Werking, Richard Hume. *The Master Architects: Building the United States Foreign Service, 1890–1913.* Lexington: University Press of Kentucky, 1977.

White, Leonard D. *The Jacksonians: A Study in Administrative History.* New York: Macmillan, 1954.

Whitlock, Brand. *Belgium: A Personal Narrative.* 2 vols. New York: D. Appleton, 1919.

Williams, William Appleman. *The Contours of American History.* London: Verso, 1961.

Woodress, James. *A Yankee's Odyssey: The Life of Joel Barlow.* Philadelphia: J. B. Lippincott, 1958.

Yergin, Daniel. *The Prize: The Epic Quest for Oil, Money, and Power.* New York: Free Press, 1991.

Zacks, Richard. *The Pirate Coast: Thomas Jefferson, the First Marines, and the Secret Mission of 1805.* New York: Hyperion, 2005.

Zimmermann, Warren. *First Great Triumph: How Five Americans Made Their Country a World Power.* New York: Farrar, Straus and Giroux, 2002.

ARTICLES

Abbasov, Mamed. "The Anglo-American Oil Controversy in Iran 1919–1924." *Journal of Azerbaijani Studies* (Khazar University, Baku, Azerbaijan) 1, no. 4 (1998): 1–18.

Abernathy, Thomas P. "Commercial Activities of Silas Deane in France." *American Historical Review* 39, no. 3 (April 1934): 477–85.

Adams, Henry Brooks. "Civil-Service Reform." *North American Review* 109, no. 225 (October 1869): 443–76, http://ebooks.library.cornell.edu/n/nora/.

"AFSA Member Survey Results." *Vanguard* (USAID, Washington, D.C.) 3, no. 1 (February 2009).

Alley, Norman. "Jim Felt Lucky." *Collier's.* February 12, 1938.

Anderson, Michael G., and Veda Engel. "Record Year for Hiring at the State Department." *State Magazine.* January 2000. 22–23.

Asencio, Diego C., with Susan Morrisey Livingstone. "The Original Cheap Shot." *World Affairs* 146 (1983).

Barr, Cameron W. "A Day of Terror Recalled." *Washington Post.* November 27, 2004. A20.

Bennett, Brian. "Hill, Christopher, Dealmaker." *Time.* April 3, 2008.

Bird, Jerri. "Arab-Americans in Israel: What 'Special Relationship'?" *Foreign Service Journal* 79, no. 6 (June 2002): 42–50.

Bleakley, Ken. "A.F.S.A. and the Foreign Service Act of 1980." *Foreign Service Journal.* June 2003. 42–46.

Bloch, Julia Chang. "Women and Diplomacy." *Ambassadors Review.* Council of American Ambassadors. Fall 2004.

Bogdanich, Walt, and Jenny Nordberg. "Mixed U.S. Signals Helped Tilt Haiti Toward Chaos." *New York Times.* January 29, 2006.

Brands, Hal. "Who Saved the Emperor? The MacArthur Myth and U.S. Policy Toward Hirohito and the Japanese Imperial Institution, 1942–1946." *Pacific Historical Review* (University of California Press) 75, no. 2 (May 2006): 271–305.

Brzezinski, Zbigniew. "Terrorized by 'War on Terror.'" *Washington Post.* March 25, 2007.

Burns, R. Nicholas. "America's Strategic Opportunity with India: The New U.S.-India Partnership." *Foreign Affairs* (Council on Foreign Relations, New York). November–December 2007.

———. "R. Nicholas Burns, Under Secretary for Political Affairs, Questions and Answers with Rob Wiley. State Magazine. September 2007. 13–23.

Bushnell, Prudence. "After Nairobi: Recovering from Terror." *Foreign Service Journal* 77, no. 7–8 (July–August 2000).

Camp, Dick, Jr. "And a Few Marines: Colonel William A. Eddy." *Leatherneck, Magazine of the Marines*. April 2004. 46–49.

Carlson, C. A. "Scholars Wrangle with Visa System in a Post 9/11 World." *Weillcornellmedicine* (Weill Cornell Medical College and Weill Cornell Graduate School of Medical Sciences, New York). Fall 2005. 16–17.

Carlson, Peter. "His Diplomatic Coup: Getting Them on the Record." *Washington Post*. May 19, 2007. C01.

Chace, James. "The Winning Hand." *New York Review of Books*. March 11, 2004. 17–20.

Clemmer, Dan. "Highlights in the Library's History." *State Magazine*. September 1998. 52.

Clinton, Hillary. "Transcript: Senate Confirmation Hearing: Hillary Clinton." *New York Times*. January 13, 2009.

Cohen, Roger. "Taming the Bullies of Bosnia." *New York Times Magazine*. December 17. 1995.

"The Congo: That Man, C'est Moi." *Time*. August 14, 1964. http://www.time.com/time/magazine /article/0,9171,897236,00.html.

Cooper, Helene. "U.S. Declares North Korea Off Terror List." *New York Times*. October 12, 2008. A1–22.

Craig, Gordon A. "Nazis Rise to Power Made Little Impression." *New York Times*. January 30, 1983.

D'Amico, Francine. "Review of *Her Excellency: An Oral History of American Women Ambassadors*." *Oral History Review* 23, no. 2 (Winter 1996): 104–107.

Danner, Mark. "Taking Stock of the Forever War." *New York Times Magazine*. September 11, 2005.

"David Franks: Vindication of an American Jewish Patriot." *American Jewish Historical Society Newsletter*. Spring 2004.

Davis, Lenwood G. "Joseph Charles Price's Rejection of Position as Minister Resident and Consul General of the United States to Liberia." *Journal of Negro History* 63, no. 3 (July 1978): 231–32.

Dawson, Horace G., Jr. "First African-American Diplomat." *Foreign Service Journal* 70, no. 1 (January 1993): 42–45.

De Santis, Hugh. "Conflicting Images of the USSR: American Career Diplomats and the Balkans, 1944–1946." *Political Science Quarterly* 94, no. 3 (Autumn 1979): 475–94.

"Diplomat Frank Schuler, Jr., Dies; Warned of Hostile Japan in '30s." *Washington Post*. May 5, 1996.

Dur, Philp F. "Conditions for Recognition." *Foreign Service Journal* 62, no. 3 (September 1985): 44–46.

Easterly, William. "Foreign Aid Goes Military!" *New York Review of Books* 55, no. 19 (December 4, 2008): 51–58.

Farmer, Paul. "Who Removed Aristide?" *London Review of Books*. April 15, 2004.

"Frances Perkins and the German-Jewish Refugees, 1933–1940." *American Jewish History* (American Jewish Historical Society). March 2001. http://francesperkinscenter.org/refugees .html.

"Frank A. Schuler, Jr., 88, U. S. Diplomat in Japan." *Chicago Tribune*. May 7, 1996.

"Frank A. Schuler, Jr., 88, U. S. Diplomat." *Washington Times*, May 6, 1996.

Friedman, John S. "Kodak's Nazi Connections." *The Nation*. March 26, 2001.

Garnham, David. "Foreign Service Elitism and U.S. Foreign Affairs." *Public Administration Review* 35, no. 1 (January–February 1975): 44–51.

Ginsburgh, Robert N. "The Challenge to Military Professionalism." *Foreign Affairs* (Council on Foreign Relations, New York) 42, no. 2 (January 1964): 255–68.

Gleijeses, Piero. "A Brush with Mexico." *Diplomatic History* 29, no. 2 (April 2005): 223–54.

Goldman, Shalom. "The Holy Land Appropriated: The Careers of Selah Merrill, Nineteenth Century Christian Hebraist, Palestine Explorer, and U. S. Consul in Jerusalem." *American Jewish History*. June 1997.

Goose, Van. "'As a Nation, the English Are Our Friends': The Emergence of African American Politics in the British Atlantic World, 1772–1861." *American Historical Review* 113, no. 4 (October 2008): 1003–28.

Gullion, Edmund A. "Towards an Amalgamated Foreign Service?" *American Foreign Service Journal* 26, no. 1 (January 1949).

Hafner, Lutz. "The Assassination of Count Mirbach and the 'July Uprising' of the Left Socialist Revolutionaries in Moscow, 1918." *Russian Review* 50 (1991): 324–44.

Heinl, Nancy Gordon. "America's First Black Diplomat." *Foreign Service Journal* 50, no. 8 (August 1973): 20–22.

Henderson, Conway W. "The Anglo-American Treaty of 1862 in Civil War Diplomacy." *Civil War History* (Kent State University Press) 15, no. 4 (December 1969).

Herndon, James S., and Joseph O. Baylen. "Col. Philip R. Faymonville and the Red Army, 1934–43." *Slavic Review* 34, no. 3 (September 1975): 483–505.

Hevesi, Dennis. "Joseph S. Farland, 92, Envoy Who Helped in Kissinger Ruse, Dies." *New York Times*. February 1, 2007.

Hickey, Donald R. "America's Response to the Slave Revolt in Haiti, 1791–1806." *Journal of the Early Republic* 2, no. 2 (Winter 1982): 361–79.

Hill, Peter P. "Who's In Charge?" *Society for American Historians of Foreign Relations Newsletter*, December 2001.

Hoffmann, Stanley. "The Kissinger Antimemoirs." *New York Times Book Review*. July 3, 1983, 1.

Holbrooke, Richard. "The Paradox of George F. Kennan." *Washington Post*. March 21, 2005, A19.

Holland, Max. "Private Sources of U.S. Foreign Policy: William Pawley and the 1954 Coup d'Etat in Guatemala." *Journal of Cold War Studies* 7, no 4 (Fall 2005): 36–73.

Honley, Steven Alan. "A Classic 'Field Diplomat': Thomas R. Pickering." *Foreign Service Journal* 79, no. 6 (June 2002): 36–41.

Hove, Mark T. "The Arbenz Factor: Salvador Allende, U. S.-Chilean Relations, and the 1954 Intervention in Guatemala." *Diplomatic History* 31, no. 4, (September 2007): 623–63.

Howe, Daniel Walker. "What Hath God Wrought." *Newsletter of Foreign Policy Research Institute* (Philadelphia) 13, no. 5 (August 2008).

James, Makila. "Standing Up." *State Magazine*. February 2008. 20–21.

"James Rives Childs, 95, Former Ambassador, Dies." *Washington Post*. July 17, 1987.

Johnson, Emory R. "The Early History of the United States Consular Service 1776–1792." *Political Science Quarterly* 13, no. 1 (March 1898): 19–40.

Jones, David. "Is There Life After Dissent?" *Foreign Service Journal* 79, no. 6 (June 2002): 26–31.

Jusserand, J. J. "The School for Ambassadors" (presidential address delivered to the American Historical Association in St. Louis, December 28, 1921). *American Historical Review* 27, no. 3 (April 1922): 426–64.

Justesen, Benjamin R. "African-American Consuls Abroad, 1897–1909." *Foreign Service Journal* 81, no. 9 (September 2004): 72–76.

Kamen, Al. "Narcissus Is Now Greek and Roman." *Washington Post*. March 4, 2005. A19.

Kantor, Jodi. "Back on World Stage, a Larger-Than-Life Holbrooke." *New York Times*. February 8, 2009.

Kashkett, Steve. "AFSA Opinion Poll Results Highlight Disturbing Trends." AFSANEWS (American Foreign Service Association). January 2008.

Keliher, Macabe. "Anglo-American Rivalry and the Origins of U.S China Policy." *Diplomatic History* 31, no. 2 (April 2007): 227–57.

Kennan, George F. "Diplomacy Without Diplomats?" *Foreign Affairs* (Council on Foreign Relations, New York) 76, no. 5 (September–October 1997): 198–212.

Kennedy, Emmet. "Ambassador Carlton J. H. Hayes' Wartime Diplomacy: Making Spain a Haven from Hitler." *Diplomatic History* 36, no. 2 (April 2012): 237–60.

Kernan, Michael. "The Schuler Files." *Washington Post.* January 26, 1977.

Kessler, Glenn. "American Foreign Service Association Withdraws Award to U.S. Envoy for Referring to the Armenian Genocide as Genocide." *Washington Post.* June 9, 2005. A19.

———. "Ex-Ambassador Criticizes Rice: Envoy Unhappy with State Department's Treatment of Gays." *Washington Post.* December 5, 2007. A27.

———. "Foreign Affairs Panel Calls for Overhaul of State Dept." *Washington Post.* December 9, 2007. A29.

———. "Rice Orders That Diplomatic Jobs in Iraq Be Filled First." *Washington Post.* June 21, 2007. A11.

Kifner, John. "John Service, a Purged 'China Hand,' Dies at 89." *New York Times.* February 4, 1999.

Killgore, Andrew I. "A Letter from U. S. Diplomats to George W. Bush." *New York Review of Books* 51, no. 18 (November 18, 2004).

King, Laura. "Ground Is Shifting Underneath Diplomacy with Pakistan." *Los Angeles Times.* March 31, 2008.

Kirkpatrick, Jeane J. "Dictatorships and Double Standards." *Commentary.* November 1979.

Kissinger, Henry A. "The Age of Kennan." *New York Times Book Review.* November 10, 2011. 1.

———. "Team of Heavyweights." *Washington Post.* December 5, 2008. A25.

Knee, Stuart. "Anglo-American Relations in Palestine 1919–1925: An Experiment in Realpolitik." *Journal of American Studies of Turkey* 5 (1997): 3–18.

Kornbluh, Peter. "Still Hidden: A Full Record of What the US Did in Chile." *Washington Post.* October 24, 1999.

Kralev, Nicholas. "Gates Seen Reversing Rivalry with State." *Washington Times.* April 17, 2008.

———. "Rice Urges More Ambassador Powers." *Washington Times.* April 18, 2008.

Kraut, Alan M., Richard Breitman, and Thomas W. Imhoof. "The State Department, the Labor Department, and German Jewish Immigration, 1930–1940." *Journal of American Ethnic History* (University of California Press) 3, no. 2 (Spring 1984). http://80-www.jstor.org.library.nysoclib.org/stable/view/27500316.

Krebs, Albin. "Norman Armour, 94, Dies; Served as an Assistant Secretary of State." *New York Times.* September 29, 1982.

Krecke, Dave. "U.S.I.A. State Integration: A Work in Progress." *State Magazine.* December 2000.

Kross, Peter. "General Maxwell Taylor's Mission to Vietnam." *Vietnam Magazine.* February 2005.

Kurlantzick, Joshua. "Conservatives' Secret Love Affair with the State Department: The Fixers." *New Republic.* January 25, 2007.

Lee, Christopher, "Overseas Security Advisory Council Turns 20." *Washington Post.* December 6, 2005. A27.

Lee, Matthew. "Rice Orders Baghdad Embassy Posts Filled." Associated Press, June 21, 2007.

Lewis, Flora. "Ambassador Extraordinary: John Peurifoy." *New York Times Magazine.* July 18, 1954.

———. "Vietnam Peace Pacts Signed; America's Longest War Halts." *New York Times.* January 28, 1973.

Linn, Priscilla R. "Coming Attraction," *State Magazine.* May 2009. 14–15.

Lippman, Thomas W. "The Day F. D. R. Met Saudi Arabia's Ibn Saud." *The Link* (Americans for Middle East Understanding, New York) 38, no. 2 (April–May 2005): 2–16. www.ameu.org.

Low, Stephen. "Telling Our Story: The National Museum of American Diplomacy." *State Maga-zine.* September 2004. 82–83.

Lukacs, John. "America's Venice." *American Heritage Magazine* 52, no. 3 (April 2001).

Lumbers, Michael. "'Staying Out of the Chinese Muddle': The Johnson Administration's Response to the Cultural Revolution." *Diplomatic History* 31, no. 2 (April 2007): 259–294.

MacFarquhar, Neil. "For State Department, Blog Team Joins Muslim Debate." *New York Times.* September 22, 2007.

Marshman, D. M., Jr. "The Four Ages of Joseph Choate." *American Heritage Magazine* 26, no. 3 (April 1975).

Martin, William J., II, Roger I. Glass, John M. Balbus, Francis S. Collins. "A Major Environmental Cause of Death." *Science* 334 (14 October 2011): 180–81.

Matthews, John P. C. "Foster Dulles and the Suez Crisis of 1956." *American Diplomacy,* September 14, 2006. http://www.unc.edu/depts/diplomat/item/2006/0709/matt/matthews_suez.html.

Matthewson, Tim. "Jefferson and the Nonrecognition of Haiti." *Proceedings of the American Philosophical Society* 140, no. 1 (March 1996): 22–48.

Mayer, Jane. "The Hidden Power: The Legal Mind behind the White House's War on Terror." *New Yorker.* July 3, 2006.

McKeown, Adam. "Ritualization of Regulation: The Enforcement of Chinese Exclusion in the United States and China." *American Historical Review* 108, no. 2 (April 2003): 377–403.

Milne, A. Taylor. "Documents: The Lyons-Seward Treaty of 1862." *American Historical Review* 38 (October 1932): 511–25.

Mirsky, Jonathan. "In the Service of Whose Country?" *Opinion Asia.* December 14, 2009.

"Mohammed Mossadegh: Person of the Year 1951." *Time.* January 7, 1952. www.time.com/rtime.subscriber/personoftheyear/archives/stories/1951.html

Moskin, J. Robert. "Advise and Dissent." *Town and County.* March 1987. 154–242.

———. "The Dangerous World of Walt Rostow." *Look.* December 12, 1967. 27–31.

———. "Dean Rusk: Cool Man in a Hot World." *Look.* September 6, 1966. 18–21.

———. "Memo on a Marxist." *Look,* July 17, 1962. 66–68.

———. "Our Foreign Policy Is Paralyzed." *Look.* November 19, 1963. 25–27.

———. "Our New Western Frontier." *Look.* May 30, 1967. 36–54.

Naland, John K. "Nation Lacks Bench Strength for Diplomacy." *Federal Times.* November 26, 2007.

———. "The New Foreign Service." *Foreign Service Journal* 84, no. 3 (February 2007): 41–47.

Nash, Philip. "A Woman's Touch in Foreign Affairs? The Career of Ambassador Frances E. Willis." *Diplomacy and Statecraft* 13, no. 2 (June 2002): 1–20.

"Nightmare in Jonestown." *Time.* December 4, 1978.

Norris, Robert S., and Hans M. Kristensen. "The Cuban Missile Crisis: A Nuclear Order of Battle, October and November 1962." *Bulletin of Atomic Scientists* 12 (October 2012): 85–91.

"Odor of Oil (continued)." *Time.* September 16, 1935.

Padgett, James A. "Diplomats to Haiti and their Diplomacy." *Journal of Negro History* 25, no. 3 (July 1940): 265–330.

Paxton, J. Hall, interview by Milton Lehman, "I Escaped Over the Roof of the World." *Saturday Evening Post.* April 29, 1950.

Paxton, Vincoe M. "American Nursing on the Roof of the World." *American Journal of Nursing* 50, no. 11 (November 1950): 698–701.

Pfaff, William. "What's Left of the Union?" *New York Review of Books* 52, no. 12 (July 14, 2005): 26–29.

Pfannestiel, Todd. "The Soviet Bureau: A Bolshevik Strategy to Secure U.S. Diplomatic Recognition through Economic Trade." *Diplomatic History* 27, no. 2 (April 2003): 171–192.

Powell, Burt E. "Jefferson and the Consular Service." *Political Science Quarterly* 21, no. 4 (December 1906): 626–38.

"President Obama Delivers Remarks to State Department Employees." *Washington Post*. January 22, 2009.

Prettiman, C. A. "The Many Lives of William Alfred Eddy." *Princeton University Library Chronicle* 53, no. 2 (Winter 1992).

Rafshoon, Ellen "Harry Bingham: Beyond the Call of Duty." *Foreign Service Journal* 79, no. 6 (June 2002): 16–25.

Risen, James. "Interference Seen in Blackwater Inquiry." *New York Times*. March 3, 2010.

Robertson, William Spence. "The First Legations of the United States in Latin America." *Mississippi Valley Historical Review* 2, no. 2 (September 1915): 183–212.

Rogers, Kenneth N., Jr. "Medals Awarded by the United States Department of State." *Journal of the Orders and Medals Society of America*, 59, no. 3 (May–June 2008).

Rosenfeld, Megan. "Lost Causes, Thwarted Dreams: Beatrice Braude and the Long Shadow of McCarthyism." *Washington Post*. December 31, 1982. D1.

Ross, Frank E. "The Mission of Joseph Donaldson, Jr., to Algiers, 1785–97." *Journal of American History* 7, no. 4 (December 1935): 422–33.

Rubin, Barry. "Anglo-American Relations in Saudi Arabia 1941–45." *Journal of Contemporary History* 143, no. 2 (April 1979): 253–67.

Schweich, Thomas A. "Taking Command." *Washington Post*. December 21, 2008. B1–5.

Sciolino, Elaine, and William J. Broad. "Report Raises New Doubts on Iran Nuclear Program." *New York Times*. November 16, 2007.

Sears, Louis Martin. "Frederick Douglass and the Mission to Haiti, 1889–1891." *Hispanic American Historical Review* 21, no. 2 (May 1941): 222–38.

Shewmaker, Kenneth E. "Review of *An American Consular Officer in the Middle East in the Jacksonian Era: A Biography of William Brown Hodgson, 1801–1871* by Thomas A. Bryson." *American Historical Review* 85, no. 1 (February 1980): 211.

Sigal, Leon V. "Efforts for a Nuclear-Free North Korea Are Bearing Fruit." *Global Asia* 3, no. 1.

———. "Primer—North Korea, South Korea, and the United States: Reading between the Lines of the *Cheonan* Attack." *Bulletin of Atomic Scientists* 12 (September–October 2010): 35–44.

———. "Turnabout Is Fair Play." *Foreign Service Journal* 84, no. 7–8 (July–August 2007): 30–35.

Simmons, Edwin H. "Military-Political Situation in the Dominican Republic." (Declassified from Secret). *ONI Review* 17, no. 5 (May 1962): 218–26.

Slany, William Z. "American Diplomacy in the 20th Century." *State Magazine*. January 2005. 25–27.

Slavin, Barbara. "Study Looks At Diplomats' Well-Being Status." *USA Today*. June 15, 2007. 10A.

"Smyrna's Ravagers Fired on Americans." *New York Times*. September 18, 1922.

Soong, Norman. "Writer Tells of Machine Gunning by Japanese Planes and Launch." Reported from aboard the USS *Oahu*, Shanghai, December 17, 1937. *New York Times*. December 18, 1937.

"State Department Begins Inquiry." *New York Times*. July 20, 1924.

Steinfels, Margaret O'Brien. "Death and Lies in El Salvador: The Ambassador's Tale." *Commonweal*. October 26, 2001.

Stowell, Ellery C. "The Moses-Linthicum Act on the Foreign Service." *American Journal of International Law* 25, no. 3 (July 1931): 516–20.

Susser, Marc J., and Kathleen B. Rasmussen. "The African-American Heritage." *State Magazine*. February 2006, 28–32.

"Symposium: Fifty Years of William Appleman Williams *Tragedy of American Diplomacy*: An

Anniversary, a Discussion, and a Celebration." *Passport* (Society for Historians of American Foreign Relations) 40, issue 2, (September 2009): 8–36.

Thomas, Helen. "Pearl Harbor Remembered." *Seattle Post-Intelligencer.* December 7, 2003.

Toprani, Anand, and Richard A. Moss. "Filling the Three-Year Gap: Nixon, Allende, and the White House Tapes, 1971–73." *Passport, the Newsletter of the Society for Historians of American Foreign Relations* (Columbus, Ohio) 41, no. 3 (January 2011): 4–11.

Tuchman, Barbara. "Why Policy Makers Do Not Listen." *Foreign Service Journal* 50, no. 3 (March 1973): 18–21.

Twelve ex-ministers of the United States. "The Consular Service and the Spoils System." *Century Illustrated Monthly Magazine* 48, issue 2 (June 1894): 306–11, http://ebooks.library.cornell.edu /c/cent/.

Ungar, Sanford J. "Pitch Imperfect." *Foreign Affairs* (Council on Foreign Relations, New York), May–June 2005.

"U.S. Pays Former Employee $18,000 for Eleven Years in Czech Prison." *Agence France Presse* (English). October 18, 1991.

Vitalis, Robert. "Black Gold, White Crude: An Essay on American Exceptionalism, Hierarchy, and Hegemony in the Gulf." *Diplomatic History* 26, no. 2 (Spring 2002).

White, Henry. "Consular Reforms." *North American Review* 159, no. 457 (December 1894): 711–21, http://ebooks.library.cornell.edu/n/nora/.

White, Robert E. "Rethinking Foreign Policy: Lessons from Latin America." *Commonweal.* June 4, 1999.

Whitman, Alden. "Architect of Postwar Policy, Acheson Advocated Containment of the Soviet Union." *New York Times.* October 13, 1971. Obituary.

Wolgemuth, Kathleen Long. "Woodrow Wilson's Appointment Policy and the Negro." *Journal of Southern History* 24, no. 4 (November 1958): 457–71.

Wright, Ann. "Breaking Through Diplomacy's Glass Ceiling." *Foreign Service Journal* 82, no. 10 (October 2005): 53–62.

Wright, Robin. "Stress Taking Toll on Foreign Service." *Washington Post.* June 20, 2007. A17.

Yale, William. "Ambassador Henry Morgenthau's Special Mission of 1917." *World Politics* (Yale Institute of International Studies) 1, no. 3 (April 1949): 308–20.

Zirinsky, Michael P. "Blood, Power, and Hypocrisy: The Murder of Robert Imbrie and American Relations with Pahlavi Iran, 1924." *International Journal of Middle East Studies* (Cambridge University) 18 (1986): 275–92.

GOVERNMENT DOCUMENTS

"An Act concerning Consuls and Vice-Consuls." 2nd Cong., 1st sess., 1792. 254–57. April 14, 1792.

"An Act in Addition to the Several Acts Regulating the Shipment and Discharge of Seamen, and the Duties of Consuls." 26th Cong., 1st sess., July 20, 1840, 394–97.

"An Act to Execute Certain Treaty Stipulations Relating to Chinese." 47th Cong., 1st sess., 1882. Chap. 126.

"An Act to Regulate the Diplomatic and Consular Systems of the United States." 34th Cong., 1st sess., 1856. Chap. 127. 52–65.

"An Act to Remodel the Diplomatic and Consular Systems of the United States." 34th Cong., 2nd sess., 1855. Chap. 133. 619–26.

Adams, John. Message to Congress, June 23, 1797. Avalon Project, Yale Law School, 2004.

Advisory Committee on Transformational Diplomacy. *A Call to Action.* U.S. Department of State, January 2008.

———. *Final Report of the State Department* in 2025 Working Group.

Alleged Assassination Plots Involving Foreign Leaders: An Interim Report of the Select Committee to Study Governmental Operations with Respect to Intelligence Activities. 94th Cong., 1st sess., November 20, 1975. Rep. 94–465. Washington, D.C.: Government Printing Office. http://www .aarclibrary.org.

"Bolshevik Propaganda." Subcommittee of the Committee on the Judiciary. 65th Cong., 3rd sess., February 11, 1919–March 10, 1919. S. Res. 439 and 469. Washington, D.C.: Government Printing Office, 1919.

Blount, James H. *Report of U.S. Special Commissioner James H. Blount to U.S. Secretary of State Walter Q. Gresham Concerning the Hawaian Kingdom Investigation.* July 17, 1893. Executive documents of the House of Representatives, 53rd Cong., 3rd sess., 1894–95.

The Assassination of Representative Leo J. Ryan and the Jonestown, Guyana Tragedy. Report of a Staff Investigative Group to the Committee on Foreign Affairs. House. May 15, 1979.

Boyatt, Thomas D., Testimony to Subcommittee of Senate Committee on Homeland Security and Government Affairs. Washington, D.C. August 1, 2007.

Burchfield, Charles Hays. "Powell Announces $1 Million U.S. Grant for Minority Diplomats." International Information Programs, Department of State, Washington, D.C. May 20, 2002.

Burns, R. Nicholas. "Statement before the House Committee on International Relations," Washington, D.C. May 18, 2005. [belgrade.usembassy.gov/policy/kosovo/050519.html]

———. "United States Policy Toward Iran." Opening Statement before the House International Relations Committee, Washington, D.C. March 8, 2006.

Burr, William, ed. *Negotiating U.S.-Chinese Rapprochement.* National Security Archive Electronic Briefing Book no. 70. 2002. www.gwu.edu/~nsarchiv/NSAEBB/NSAEBB70/.

Central Intelligence Agency. *CIA Activities in Chile.* Washington, D.C. September 18, 2000. www .cia.gov/cia/reports/chile/.

———. Office of Public Affairs. *Intelligence in the Civil War.* Washington, D.C. https://www.cia .gov/library/publications/additional-publications/civil-war/Intel_in_the_CW1.pdf (last updated January 3, 2012).

Clinton, Hillary, and Steven Kashkett. "Text of Remarks at Welcome Ceremony for Secretary Clinton." Department of State, Washington, D.C., January 22, 2009. Afsanet-request@listserv .afsa.org.

Cohen, Bonnie R. "Excerpts from Testimony of Undersecretary of State for Management Bonnie R. Cohen before the Senate Task Force on Function 150, September 17, 1998." Washington, D.C. Appendix D to Source 561.

Committee on Foreign Affairs, 67th Cong., 4th sess., Hearing H.R. 12543.

Communist Threat to the United States Through the Caribbean. Subcommittee of the Committee on the Judiciary. Senate. August 27 and 30, 1960. Washington, D.C.: Government Printing Office.

Congressional Research Service, Library of Congress, *The U.S. Government and the Vietnam War, Executive and Legislative Roles and Relationships, Part I, 1945–61.* Page 310. Washington, D.C.: Government Printing Office, 1984.

Council on Foreign Relations. *Improving the U.S. Public Diplomacy Campaign in the War Against Terrorism.* Task Force Report. New York. No date.

———. *Managing Secretary Rice's State Department: An Independent Assessment.* Task Force Report. Washington, D.C., June 2007.

———. *Secretary Colin Powell's State Department: An Independent Assessment.* Task Force Report. Washington, D.C. March 19, 2003.

———. *Secretary Powell's State Department: An Independent Assessment.* Task Force Report. Washington, D.C. November 2004.

Covert Action in Chile, 1963–1973: Staff Report of the Select Committee to Study Governmental Operations with Respect to Intelligence Activities. U.S. Senate. Washington, D.C. December 18, 1975.

Delegates to Congress. *Letters of Delegates to Congress, 1774–1789. Volume 3: January 1, 1776–May 15, 1776.* 1776. Washington, D.C.: Library of Congress, 1976–1996). memory.loc.gov/amen /amiaw/lwdg.html

Department of State, *History of the Department of State During the Clinton Presidency (1993–2001)* Management and Organizational Change. Office of the Historian, Bureau of Public Affairs, Department of State. Washington, D.C.

Department of State, HR Fact Sheet. Bureau of Human Resources. Washington, D.C.: Department of State, June 30, 2008.

Diplomatic Immunity. Prepared by the U. S. Department of State, Office of the Legal Adviser, January 13, 1997.

Dwyer, Richard A. *Report on CODEL Ryan's Visit to Jonestown and Subsequent Murder.* Memo from American embassy, Georgetown, to secretary of state. Washington, D.C. November 22, 1978.

"Establishing the American Presence in the Middle East." *Multinational Oil Corporations and U.S. Foreign Policy: Report to the Committee on Foreign Relations, United States Senate, by the Subcommittee on Multinational Corporations.* Washington D.C.: Government Printing Office, January 2, 1975. Chap. 1.

"Estimate of Damage to U.S. Foreign Policy Interests: From Net of Listening Devices in U.S. Embassy Moscow." Washington, D.C. October 2, 1964. *Foreign Relations of the United States, 1964–1968.* Volume 14, Soviet Union. February 21, 2001.

"Events Leading Up to World War II, 1931–1944." 1931. 78th Cong., 2nd sess. House document no. 541. Washington, D.C.: Government Printing Office, 1944.

Extension of remarks to House of Representatives, 66th Cong., November 19, 1919. Appendix to the *Congressional Record,* p. 9186.

"Fact Sheet: North Korea's Nuclear Weapons Program." Center for Defense Information, Washington, D.C. No date.

Foreign Service Act of 1980. 96th Congo., 2nd Sess., September 29, 1980. H. Rept. 96–1432. http://thomas.loc.gov.

Galster, Steve. "Afghanistan: The Making of U.S. Policy, 1973–1990." *Afghanistan: Lessons from the Last War.* Volume 2, National Security Archive, The September 11th Sourcebooks. George Washington University, Washington, D.C. October 9, 2001.

Geist, Raymond H. "Nazi Conspiracy and Aggression Volume IV, Document No 1769-PS." Disposition given at United States embassy, Mexico, Federal District, August 28, 1945. Avalon Project , Yale Law School, New Haven.

Grady, Henry F. "Proposed New Program for USIE, Iran." American embassy, Tehran, July 6, 1950.

Haass, Richard N. "Planning Policy in Today's World: Remarks at the Kennan Institute, 2003 Annual Dinner." Washington, D.C., May 22, 2003.

Harrington, Anthony C. *Report on the Guatemala Review.* Intelligence Oversight Board. Washington, D.C. June 28, 1996. http://www.ciponline.org/iob.htm.

Hearing of 67th Cong., 4th sess., February 1923.

Hearing of 68th Cong., 1st sess., April 29–May 13, 1924.

Helping to Enhance the Livelihood of People around the Globe (HELP) Commission. *Beyond Assistance.* Report for Congress. Washington, D.C., December 2007.

Herbst, Ambassador John E. "Briefing on Civilian Stabilization Initiative." Department of State, Washington, D.C. February 14, 2008.

———. Prepared Statement before subcommittees of the House Committee on Armed Services, Washington, D.C. February 26, 2008.

A History of the American Consulate at Vladivostok, 1875–1948. Manuscript by E. M. Duncan, May 29, 1992, U.S. Consulate, Vladivostok, Russia.

Jackson, Andrew. "Message from the President of the United States, in relation to the Consular Establishment of the United States." 22nd Cong., 2nd sess., March 2, 1833. 5–29.

Kimball, John C. *A Short History of the U.S. Department of State, 1781–1981*. Department of State Publication 9166. Washington, D.C. January 1981.

Kissinger, Henry A., "Policy Towards Chile." Top Secret letter from the National Security Council to secretaries of state and defense and directors of Office of Emergency Preparedness and of Central Intelligence. National Security Council, Washington, D.C. November 9, 1970.

Kornbluh, Peter. *CIA Acknowledges Ties to Pinochet's Repression: Report to Congress Reveals U.S. Accountability in Chile*. Chile Documentation Project, National Security Archive. September 19, 2000.

———, ed. "The Negroponte File." National Security Archive Electronic Briefing Book no. 151, parts 1 and 2. April 12, 2005.

Kornbluh, Peter, and John Dinges, "Lifting of Pinochet's Immunity Renews Focus on Operation Condor." National Security Archive, pp. 1–9. Washington, D.C. June 10, 2004.

Korry, Edward. "Permit Me Three Quick Comments," Secret cable from Santiago to John Hugh Crimmins, Department of State, Washington, D.C. August 11, 1970.

———. "Situation Report." To Assistant Secretary Meyer and Henry Kissinger. Secret Sensitive Eyes Only. Santiago, Chile to Washington, D.C. September 21, 1970.

Krebs, Max V. (deputy chief of mission). "Guatemala Critic." Telegram from embassy in Guatemala to Department of State. August 23, 1968.

Lake, Anthony (assistant to the president for national security affairs). "Intelligence Oversight Board Terms of Reference: Guatemala." Memorandum to Anthony S. Harrington, chairman of the Intelligence Oversight Board. The White House, Washington, D.C. April 10, 1995.

Lakhdar Boumediene v. George W. Bush. Amici Curiae. U.S. Supreme Court. Nos. 06-1195 and 06-1196. June 12, 2008.

Letters to Delegates to Congress: Volume 3, January 1, 1776–May 15, 1776. U.S. Congressional Documents and Debates, 1775–1875. Letter addressed to Silas Deane from Committee of Secret Correspondence, Philadelphia, dated March 2, 1776.

McCormack, Sean. "The Situation at U.S Embassy Belgrade." Transcript of press briefing at 5:18 P.M., U.S. Department of State, Washington, D.C. February 21, 2008.

"Memo from Assistant Secretary of State Breckinridge Long to State Department Officials Dated June 26, 1940, Outlining Effective Ways to Obstruct the Granting of U.S. Visas."

Memorandum of Conversation. Prime Minister Zhou Enlai and Brigadier Alexander M. Haig, Jr. Peking [Beijing], China. January 3, 1972. National Security Archive Electronic Briefing Book no. 70.

Memorandum of Conversation. Prime Minister Zhou Enlai and Brigadier Alexander M. Haig, Jr. Peking [Beijing], China. January 7, 1972. National Security Archive Electronic Briefing Book no. 70.

Murray, W. Smith. "Murder of Vice Consul Imbrie, Tehran, 1924." Secret and highly confidential letter from the second secretary of legation in charge of consulate to the secretary of state. Washington, D.C., October 2, 1924. http://www.h-net.org/`bahai/docs/imbrie.htm.

———. "Report on Murder of Consul Imbrie to the Department of State." Teheran, Persia, August 10, 1924.

National Security Archive. "The Secret CIA History of the Iran Coup, 1953." Electronic Briefing

Book no. 28. George Washington University, Washington, D.C. http://www.gwu.edu/~nsar-chiv/NSAEBB/NSAEBB28/index.html.

Obama, Barack. Letter to Secretary of State Condoleezza Rice. July 28, 2006.

Office of Inspector General, U.S. Department of State and the Broadcasting Board of Governors. *Memorandum Audit Report: Department of State's Foreign Service "Up-or-Out" Promotion Service*. Report no. AUD/PR-02-27, Washington D.C. August 2002.

Papers Relating to Foreign Affairs Accompanying the Annual Message of the President to the Second Session, Thirty-eighth Congress. Part 3, Washington, D.C.: Government Printing Office, 1865.

Paul, James A. "Oil Companies in Iraq: A Century of Rivalry and War: Global Policy Forum, UN Security Council, November 2003.

Peace Conference at The Hague 1899: General Report of the United States Commission. Delivered to John Hay, secretary of state, The Hague, July 31, 1899. Avalon Project, Yale Law School, http://avalon.law.yale.edu/19th_century/hag99-04.asp.

Petition for a Writ of Certiorari to the United States Court of Appeals, in the Supreme Court of the United States, October term, 1985. No. 85–50.

Prados, John. "The Mouse That Roared: State Department Intelligence in the Vietnam War." NSA, Washington, D.C. No date. www.gwu.edu/~nsarchiv/NSAEBB/NSAEBB121/prados.htm

"Recognizing Iran as a Strategic Threat: An Intelligence Challenge for the United States." Staff Report of the House Permanent Select Committee on Intelligence. Subcommittee on Intelligence Policy. Washington, DC. August 23, 2006.

"Recruiting Locally Employed (LE) Staff to Serve in Iraq." Telegram, Department of State. 2007.

Report Concerning Consular System, dated February 16, 1831. Committee on Commerce. 21st Cong., 2nd sess., February 16, 1831. S. Rep. 57. 1–13.

Report from the Joint Select Committee on Retrenchment. 40th Cong., 2nd sess., in the Senate, July 2, 1868.

Report of the Congressional Committees Investigating the Iran-Contra Affair. U.S. Congress. Washington, D.C. House Select Committee to Investigate Covert Arms Transactions with Iran and Senate Select Committee on Secret Military Assistance to Iran and the Nicaraguan Opposition. 1987.

Schoenfeld, Ambassador Rudolf E. "Communist Party Strength in Guatemala." Secret letter to secretary of state's special assistant for intelligence. Guatemala City. February 13, 1953. www.mtholyoke.edu

Secret cable from American embassy, Brunei, to State Department. August 4, 1986. "The Iran-Contra Affair 20 Years On." National Security Archive. www.gwu.edu/~nsarchiv/NSAEBB/NSAEBB210/index.htm.

Select Committee to Report on the Consular System of the United States. June 17, 1846. 29th Cong., 1st sess., H. Rep. 714. Accompanying HR 489.

Shafiq Rasul v. George W. Bush. Amici Curiae. U.S. Supreme Court. Nos. 03-334 and 03-343.

"Statement by the President: The Foreign Relations Revitalization Act of 1995 (S.908)." U.S. Senate. July 31, 1995.

Stroock, Thomas F. Secret cable 04268 to secretary of state. From Guatemala City to Washington, D.C. May 10, 1991.

Tutwiler, Margaret DeB. (undersecretary for public affairs). "Public Diplomacy: Reaching Beyond Traditional Audiences." Testimony before the House Appropriations Subcommittee on Commerce, Justice, State and the Judiciary. Washington, D.C., February 4, 2004.

U.S. Army Center of Military History. "The Congolese Rescue Operation (November 1964)." http://www.army.mil/cmh-pg/documents/AbnOps/TABE.htm.

U.S. Department of State. "Diplomacy for the '70's: A Program of Management Reform for the Department of State," Washington, D.C.: Government Printing Office, 1970.

———. "Fact Sheet Foreign Affairs Reorganization Dec. 30 (1998)." http://fas.org/news/usa/1998/12/98123003_tlt.html.

———. *Financial Report Fiscal Year 2007: Transforming the World through Diplomacy.* Washington, D.C. November 15, 2007.

———. *Foreign Relations of the United States, 1952–1954.* Vol. 4, *The American Republics,* Guatemala Compilation. Washington, D.C.: Government Printing Office, 1983.

———. *Foreign Relations of the United States, 1964–1968.* Vol. 1, *Vietnam, 1964,* and Vol. 2, *Vietnam, January–June 1965.* Washington, D.C.: Government Printing Office, 1992. http://www.state.gov/www/about_state/history/vol_i/index.html and http://www.state.gov/www/about_state/history/vol_ii/index.html.

———. *Foreign Relations of the United States, 1964–1968.* Vol. 4, *Vietnam, September 1968–January 1969.* Washington, D.C.: Government Printing Office, 1998.

———. *Foreign Relations of the United States, 1964–1968.* Vol. 32, *Dominican Republic, Cuba, Haiti, Guyana.*

———. "Note on U.S. Covert Action Programs." *Foreign Relations of the United States, 1964–1968,* Vol. 12, *Western Europe,* April 16, 2001. Pp. xxxi–xxxv.

———. *Peace and War: United States Foreign Policy, 1931–1941.* Publication 1983. Washington, D.C.: Government Printing Office, 1943.

———. "Reorganization Plan and Report. III. The Public Diplomacy and Public Affairs Missions." http://.www.fas.org/irp/offdocs/pdd-68-dos.htm.

———. *Reports of the Consuls of the United States.* Vol. 23, *July–September 1887,* Bureau of Foreign Commerce. "Report of Rule Letcher, consul, Rio Grande do Sul, March 31, 1887." Washington, D.C.: Government Printing Office, 1887.

———. "The Seizure of the Saudi Arabian Embassy in Khartoum." Intelligence Memorandum. June 1973. Reprinted in *Foreign Relations of the United States, 1969–1976.* Vol. E-6, *Documents on Africa,* 1073–1076. State Department, Washington, D.C.

Wells, Sherrill B. "Long-Time Friends: A History of Early U.S.-Moroccan Relations 1777–1787." Washington, D.C.: Office of the Historian, U.S. Department of State, no date.

Wright, Mary Ann. Letter to Secretary of State Colin Powell. From Ulaanbaatar, Mongolia. March 19, 2003. www.govexec.com.

INTERVIEWS, ORAL HISTORIES, AND SPEECHES

Acheson, Dean. Oral history interview by Lucius D. Battle. April 27, 1964. Interview JFKOH-DGA-01. John F. Kennedy Presidential Library and Museum, Boston, MA. http://www.jfklibrary.org/Asset-Viewer/Archives/JFKOH-DGA-01.aspx.

———. "Waging Peace in the Americas" (address). September 19, 1949. http://avalon.law.yale.edu/20th_century/decad063.asp.

Armitage, Richard. "A Conversation with Former Deputy Secretary of State Richard Armitage," Interview by Charlie Rose. June 13, 2006. *Charlie Rose* television show. http://www.charlierose.com/view/interview/358.

Asencio, Diego C. Interview by Charles Stuart Kennedy. Beginning September 11, 1986. Foreign Affairs Oral History Collection of the Association for Diplomatic Studies and Training. "Frontline Diplomacy," Manuscript Division, Library of Congress, Washington, D.C. http://memory.loc.gov/cgi-bin/query/D?mfdip:1:./temp/~ammem_hUEz::.

Atherton, Alfred Leroy, Jr. Oral history interview by Dayton Mak. Beginning summer 1990. Foreign Affairs Oral History Collection of the Association for Diplomatic Studies and Training. "Frontline Diplomacy," Manuscript Division, Library of Congress, Washington, D.C. http://memory.loc.gov/cgi-bin/query/D?mfdip:2:./temp/~ammem_GBBJ::.

Atherton, Betty Wylie. Interview by Mary Louise Weiss. Beginning October 2, 1987. Foreign Affairs Oral History Collection of the Association for Diplomatic Studies and Training. "Frontline Diplomacy," Manuscript Division, Library of Congress, Washington, D.C. http://memory.loc.gov/cgi-bin/query/D?mfdip:1:./temp/~ammem_eA2d::.

Battle, Lucius D. Oral history interview by Richard D. McKinzie and Theodore A. Wilson, June 23, 1971. Harry S Truman Library and Museum, Independence, MO. http://www.trumanlibrary.org/oralhist/battle.htm.

Bohlen, Charles E. Oral history interview by Paige Mulhollan. November 20, 1968. Oral History Collection, Lyndon Baines Johnson Presidential Library, Austin, TX.

Burns, R. Nicholas. "Burns on Bringing India in from the Cold, and Isolating Iran." Interview by Robert McMahon. August 2, 2007. Council on Foreign Relations, New York. http://www.cfr.org/india/burns-bringing-india-cold-isolating-iran/p13975.

———. "Global Challenges and Opportunities in U.S. Foreign Policy." Remarks to Council on Foreign Relations, Washington, D.C. February 25, 2008.

Clubb, O. Edmund. Oral history interview by Richard D. McKinzie. June 26, 1974. Harry S Truman Library and Museum, Independence, MO.

Cold War Interviews. Includes interviews with Zbigniew Brzezinski; Henry Kissinger; John Negroponte; George Kennan; John Service; John Paton Davies, Jr.; Winston Lord; Roger Hilsman; Samuel Halpern; and Helmut Sonnenfeldt. National Security Archive, George Washington University, Washington, D. C. http://www.gwu.edu/~nsarchiv/coldwar/interviews/.

Crimmins, John Hugh. Interview by Ashley C. Hewitt, Jr. Beginning May 10, 1989. Foreign Affairs Oral History Collection of the Association for Diplomatic Studies and Training. "Frontline Diplomacy," Manuscript Division, Library of Congress, Washington, D.C. http://memory.loc.gov/service/mss/mssmisc/mfdip/2005%20txt%20files/2004cri01.txt.

Davis, Ruth A. "From the Queen of Sheba to Madeleine Albright and You." Speech given at the International Career Advancement Program, Aspen, CO. August 23, 1997.

Dwyer, Richard A. Interview by Charles Stuart Kennedy. Beginning July 12, 1990. Foreign Affairs Oral History Collection of the Association for Diplomatic Studies and Training. "Frontline Diplomacy," Manuscript Division, Library of Congress, Washington, D.C. http://memory.loc.gov/cgi-bin/query/D?mfdip:1:./temp/~ammem_WEGV::.

Everett, Edward. "Eulogy on the Life and Character of John Quincy Adams Delivered at the Request of the Legislature of Massachusetts in Faneuil Hall." Boston, MA. April 15, 1848.

Feulner, Edwin J., Chair. "Regaining America's Voice Overseas: A Conference on U.S. Public Diplomacy." Heritage Foundation, Washington, D.C., January 13, 2004. http://www.heritage.org/research/lecture/regaining-americas-voice-overseas-a-conference-on-us-public-diplomacy.

Freeman, Charles W., Jr. Oral history interview by Charles Stewart Kennedy. April 14, 1995. Library of Congress.

———. "America in the World: Magoo at the Helm." Remarks to the Washington World Affairs Council Summer Institute on International Affairs, Washington, D. C., June 23, 2008.

———. "Debt, Defense and Diplomacy: Foreign Policy Dilemmas before the President-Elect." Remarks to the State Association of County Retirement Systems, Costa Mesa, CA, November 13, 2008.

Gardner, Richard N. "Who Needs Ambassadors?" Speech to the American Society of International Law, Washington, D.C., March 29, 1996.

Habib, Phillip C. "The Work of Diplomacy." Conversation with Harry Kreisler. May 14, 1982. Conversations with History series, Institute of International Studies, University of California, Berkeley. http://conversations.berkeley.edu/content/philip-habib.

Haile Selassie I (emperor of Ethiopia). "Appeal to the League of Nations." Geneva, June 1926.

Harty, Maura (assistant secretary of state for consular affairs). "Remarks at the Commonwealth Club, San Francisco." March 30, 2005. http://www.passportsusa.com/law/legal/testimony/testimony_2250.

Henderson, Loy W. Oral history interview by Richard D. McKinzie, June 14 and July 5, 1973. Harry S. Truman Library and Museum, Independence, MO. http://www.trumanlibrary.org/oralhist/hendrson.htm.

Hill, Christopher. Interview by Renee Montagne. March 7, 2007. *Morning Edition*. National Public Radio News. Washington, D.C.

——. "Newsmaker Interviews." Interview by Margaret Warner. *News Hour with Jim Lehrer*. August 9, 2005. http://www.pbs.org/newshour/bb/international/july-dec05/hill_8-09.html.

——. "Update on the Six-Party Talks." Talk at Center for Strategic and International Studies, Washington, D.C. July 1, 2008.

Hilsman, Roger. Interview for *Vietnam, A Television History Program*, WGBH-TV, Boston. May 18, 1981. http://openvault.wgbh.org/catalog/vietnam-c3d5d3-interview-with-roger-hilsman-1981.

"Historic Meeting of a Saudi King and an American President." Press release, Royal embassy of Saudi Arabia, Washington, D.C., c. 1999. [No date given but article refers to 1945 meeting 54 years previous.]

Holbrooke, Richard. "Robert C. Frasure Memorial Lecture." Embassy of the United States, Tallinn, Estonia. April 1, 1998.

Johnson, U. Alexis. Oral history interview by Richard D. McKinzie. June 19, 1975. Harry S. Truman Library and Museum, Independence, MO. http://www.trumanlibrary.org/oralhist/johnsona.htm.

Jones, Megan. Interviewed by J. Robert Moskin, Venice, Italy, June 2008.

Kaiser, Philip. Oral history interview by Niel M. Johnson. June 8 and 11, 1987. Harry S. Truman Library and Museum, Independence, MO. http://www.trumanlibrary.org/oralhist/kaiserp.htm.

Kissinger, Henry. "Conversation with Orville Schell." Transcript. Asia Society Center on U.S.-China Relations, New York, January 20, 2007.

Korry, Edward M. "Ambassador Edward M. Korry in CEP." Interview by Joaquín Fermandois and Arturo Fontaine Talavera. October 18–21, 1996. Center for Public Studies, Santiago, Chile. www.cepchile.cl/dms/archivo_1146 . . . /rev72.korryinterv_ing.pdf.

Laingen, L. Bruce. Interview by Charles Stuart Kennedy. 1993. Foreign Affairs Oral History Collection of the Association for Diplomatic Studies and Training. "Frontline Diplomacy," Manuscript Division, Library of Congress, Washington, D.C. http://memory.loc.gov/cgi-bin/query/D?mfdip:1:./temp/~ammem_TPi8:: .

Latourette, Kenneth S. "Peter Parker: Missionary and Diplomat." Speech to the Yale Medical Society, New Haven, CT., November 5, 1935. [See online under Parker.]

Ledsky, Nelson. "U.S. Organizer of 1980 Boycott Talks About Politics and the Olympics." Interview by Kenan Aliyev, Azerbaijani Service, no date. htp://www.phayul.com/news/article.aspx?id=20144&t=1.

Low, Stephen. Interview by Charles Stuart Kennedy. Beginning December 5, 1997. Foreign Affairs Oral History Collection of the Association for Diplomatic Studies and Training. "Frontline Diplomacy," Manuscript Division, Library of Congress, Washington, D.C. http://memory.loc.gov/cgi-bin/query/D?mfdip:5:./temp/~ammem_wquY::.

Mitchell, George. "Interview with Middle East Bulletin." December 1, 2009. http://middleeast/progress.org/2009/12/progress-requires-patience-compromise-courageous leadership.

Moose, Richard M. Interview for *Vietnam, A Television History Program*, WGBH-TV, Boston. October 23, 1981. http://openvault.wgbh.org/catalog/vietnam-b44658-interview-with-richard-m-moose-1981

Muccio, John J. Oral history interview with Jerry N. Hess. February 10 and 18, 1971. Truman Library and Museum, Independence, MO. http://www.trumanlibrary.org/oralhist/muccio .htm.

Myrdal, Gunnar. "Inherent Imperfections in Foreign Policy." Lecture, St. Louis, Missouri, April 20, 1965.

Powell, Colin. "An Hour with General Colin Powell." Interview by Charlie Rose. November 17, 2005. *Charlie Rose* television show. http://www.charlierose.com/view/interview/654.

"Public Diplomacy: A Strategy for Reform." Transcript of press conference. Council on Foreign Relations, New York, July 30, 2002.

Read, Benjamin H. Oral history interview 2 by Paige E. Mulhollan. March 1970. Oral History Collection, Lyndon Baines Johnson Presidential Library, Austin, TX. http://www.lbjlib.utexas .edu/johnson/archives.hom/oralhistory.hom/ReadB/ReadB.asp.

Robins, Raymond. *Statement of Recommendations Concerning the Russian Situation: American Economic Cooperation with Russia*. Washington, D.C., July 1, 1918.

Rohatyn, Felix. "A Discussion about the Life of Felix Rohatyn." Transcript 2840. Interview by Charlie Rose, with Elizabeth Rohatyn and Hugh Carey, Paris, France, December 21, 2000. *Charlie Rose* television show.

Rowe, E. Thomas. Interview by J. Robert Moskin, Aspen, CO., September 1991.

Seward, William, "The Irrepressible Conflict." Speech given in Rochester, New York, October 25, 1858. http://www.nyhistory.com/central/conflict.htm.

Sigal, Leon V. "How Not to Build Trust—or Get One's Way—with North Korea." Typescript. Talk to Korea Society, September 22, 2006.

Skodon, Emil M. Interview by J. Robert Moskin, By e-mail, August 2007.

"Statement by the President on the Bombing of the U.S. Embassy in Saigon." March 30, 1965. American Presidency Project, University of California, Santa Barbara. http://www.presidency .ucsb.edu/ws/?pid=26847.

Stern, Fritz. Remarks as honoree of the Leo Baeck Medal. Printed Program of Tenth Annual Dinner. Leo Baeck Institute, New York, November 14, 2004.

Thacher, Nicholas G. Oral history interview by Niel M. Johnson. May 28, 1992. Harry S. Truman Library and Museum, Independence, MO. http://www.trumanlibrary.org/oralhist/thachern .htm.

Tull, Theresa A. Interview by Charles Stuart Kennedy. Beginning November 9, 2004. Foreign Affairs Oral History Collection of the Association for Diplomatic Studies and Training. "Frontline Diplomacy," Manuscript Division, Library of Congress, Washington, D.C. http://memory .loc.gov/cgi-bin/query/D?mfdip:2:./temp/~ammem_1emz::.

Urquhart, Brian "Reflections of a Life in War and Peace," Conversation with Henry Kreisler. March 19, 1966. Conversations with History series, Institute of International Studies, University of California, Berkeley. http://conversations.berkeley.edu/content/sir-brian-urquhart.

White, Henry. "The Baneful Influence of 'Politics' upon Our Foreign Relations." Address before the National Convention of the United States, Navy League of the United States, Washington, D.C., 1916.

———. "Diplomacy and Politics." Address before the American Historical Association, Washington, D.C., 1915.

Wilson, Joseph C. IV. "A Diplomat's Odyssey." In conversation with Harry Kreisler. May 27, 2004. Conversations with History series, Institute of International Studies, University of California, Berkeley. http://conversations.berkeley.edu/content/joseph-wilson.

Wright, Edwin M. Oral history interview by Richard D. McKinzie. July 26, 1974. Harry S. Truman Library and Museum, Independence, MO. http://www.trumanlibrary.org/oralhist/ wright.htm.

ONLINE SOURCES

1867 Alaska Treaty with Russia. March 30, 1867. http://www.nelson.com/nelson/school/discov ery/cantext/usa/1867sewa.htm.2001.

"America and the Holocaust: People and Events: Breckinridge Long." *The American Experience.* PBS.org.

Austin, Heather W. "Valeriano Weyler y Nicolau." Spanish American War Centennial. http:// www.spanamwar.com/Weyler.htm.

Bullington, James R. "From the Editor: Iraq, the Foreign Service, and Duty." American Diplomacy.org. October 2, 2007.

Bushnell, Prudence. "Nairobi." Video transcript. http://www.usdiplomacy.org/accessibility /transcript/Bushnell.html.

Couttie, Robert. "The War in the Philippines." Spanish American War Centennial http://www .spanamwar.com/Philippines.htm.

Engert, Jane M. "American Legation Under Fire: Addis Ababa, 1936." Excerpt from biography. American Diplomacy.org. http://www.unc.edu/depts/diplomat/item/2006/1012/enge/engert_ corn.html.

"Frederic Moseley Sackett, 1868–1941." Sackett Family Association. http://www.sackettfamily. info/fredericgallery.htm.

"George S. Messersmith, 1883–1960." *Fleetwood (PA) Area Historical Society,* including letter to Under Secretary of State William Phillips, June 26, 1933, Berlin. http://www.fleetwoodpa.org /messersmith_george/messersmith_george.htm.

"Helmut Hirsch Exhibit." Brandeis [University] Libraries Special Collections Helmut Hirsch Exhibit.

Hirohito, Emperor Imperial Rescript. January 1, 1946. http://www.chukai.ne.jp/~masago/ningen .html.

"Hirsch, Solomon." Jewish Encyclopedia.com (text from *Jewish Encyclopedia*, 1906). http://www .jewishencyclopedia.com/articles/7745-hirsch-solomon.

Kellbach, John. "Maj. Gen. Fitzhugh Lee." Spanish American War Centennial. http://www.span amwar.com/Leebiop.htm.

Kennedy, Robert C. "The Big Thing." Article on purchase of Alaska in *Harper's Weekly.* http:// www.nytimes.com/learning/general/onthisday/harp/0420.html, 2001.

Kross, Peter. "The Assassination of Ngo Dinh Diem." HistoryNet.com.

Kwok, Munson. *On the Occasion of the 130th Anniversary of the Los Angeles Chinese Massacre: A Statement of Remembrance.* Chinese American Museum, Los Angeles, 2001.

"List of Ambassadorial Appointments." American Foreign Service Association. Updated March 30, 2012. http://www.afsa.org.

Loeffler, Jane Canter "United States Embassies: America's Face Abroad." National Building Museum, Washington, D.C. http://www.nbm.org/blueprints/fall96/page6/page6/htm.

Lowenthal, David. "Sabre-rattling American Intervention." Book review. Posted on H-Diplo online discussion network. December 23, 2009.

McSherry, Patrick. "Battle of Manila Bay—May 1, 1898." Spanish American War Centennial. http://www.spanamwar.com/mbay.htm.

Möise, Edwin E. "The Vietnam Wars, Section 9, The Negotiations." http://www.clemson.edu /caah/history/Faculty Pages/EdMoise/viet9.html.

"A More Representative Foreign Service." U.S. Diplomacy. http://www.usdiplomacy.org/history /service/representative.php.

Morgenthau, Henry. "Secret Personal Report to the President." Washington, D.C., January 16, 1944. Jewish Virtual Library. http://www.jewishvirtuallibrary.org/jsource/Holocaust/mor grep.html.

Morse, Arthur D. "How the Indifference of the U.S. State Department Aided the Nazi Murder Plot." *Heritage Vision*, 2005–2008. http://paperpen.com/heritage/350/look/look1.htm.

Museum of the City of San Francisco. "Thomas O. Larkin's Letters to the Secretary of State about the Gold Discovery." http://www.sfmuseum.org/hist6/larkin.html.

North, Don. "An American Reporter Witnessed the VC Assault on the U.S. Embassy." *History Net*. http://www.historynet.com/magazines/vietnam/3025836.html?page=2&c=y.

Olson, Robert K. "Ambassador Henry Grady and Indian Independence." American Diplomacy. http://americandiplomacy.org.

Overseas Security Advisory Council, Global Security News and Reports. http://www.osac.gov.

Poncet, Jose. "The U.S. Ambassador to Spain: Stewart L. Woodford." Spanish American War Centennial. http://www.spanamwar.com/Woodford.htm.

Ruge, Helga. "Foreign Service Life: Assignment Guatemala 1968: An Early Encounter with Terrorism." American Diplomacy.org.

Sicherman, Harvey. "Benjamin Franklin: American Diplomacy Traditions."American Diplomacy.org, 2007.

United States Commission on National Security/21st Century. *Road Map for National Security: Imperative for Change; The Phase III Report*. February 15, 2001.

U.S. Military Police. "The Tet Offensive—1968." http://home.mweb.co.za/re/redcap/tet.htm.

U.S. Naval Ships History. "Gainard DD-706." http://navyhistory.com/destroyer/Gainarddd706.html.

"Vietnam Online." Transcript. *American Experience*. PBS. http://www.pbs.org./wgbh/amex/vietname/series/pt_09.html.

White, Mark. "Going to War in Vietnam: George Ball's Dissent in the 1960s." American Diplomacy.org. http://www.unc.edu/depts/diplomat/item/2007/0406/whit/white_ball.html.

Zabecki, David T. "Battle for Saigon." *History Net*. http://www.historynet.com/magazines/vietnam/3030136.html?showAll=y&c=y

MISCELLANEOUS SOURCES

American Academy of Diplomacy. *A Foreign Affairs Budget for the Future*. Washington, D.C., October 2008.

American Foreign Service Association. "Telling Our Story." E-mail, October 17, 2007.

"American Universities, American Foreign Service and an Adequate Consular Law." National Business League of America, 1909.

Atcheson, George, Jr. "Report of the Second Secretary of Embassy in China to the Secretary of State, Shanghai, December 21, 1937." *Papers Relating to the Foreign Relations of the United States, Japan: 1931–1941*. Vol. 1, pp. 532–41. Washington, D.C.: Government Printing Office, 1943.

Battle, Perrin, and Kniffin. "Charles J. Helm." *Kentucky: A History of the State*. 7th edition, Campbell Co., 1887. http://www.rootsweb.com/~kygenweb/kybiog/campbell/helm.cj.txt.

Bigelow, John. "Consular System of the United States." Report to the secretary of state. Paris, February 28, 1864. Papers of John Bigelow. New York Public Library.

Bombings of the US Embassies in Nairobi, Kenya and Dar es Salaam, Tanzania on August 7 1998. Report of the accountability review boards. http://www.fas.org/irp/threat/arb/board.

Bradley, General Omar N., (chairman of the Joint Chiefs of Staff). "Memorandum to the Secretary of Defense (Johnson)." Appendix 3, November 18, 1949. In Cyrus Vance, *Hard Choices*, pp. 498–500.

Breitman, R. "American Diplomatic Records Regarding German Public Opinion during the Nazi Regime." International Conference at Yad Vashem, Israel, 10–13 February 1995. http://www.zupdom.com/icons- multimedia/ClientsArea/HoH/LIBARC/LIBR.

Bristol, Mark L. "The Armenian Issue Revisited." Letter to Dr. James L. Barton, 28 March 1921, on board USS *St. Louis*. Available at Web site of Assembly of Turkish American Associations, pp. 1–7.

Burns, Nicholas. "Tony Jones Talks to US Undersecretary of State Nicholas Burns." December 5, 2007. *Lateline* television show, Australian Broadcasting Corporation, Canberra, Australia. http://www.abc.net.au/lateline/content/2007/s2110889.htm.

Camp, Dick, Jr. "Leatherneck: And a Few Marines—Colonel William A. Eddy." http://www.ar amcoexpats.com/Articles/Community/Annuitants-And-Former-ExPats/1430.aspx.Aramco ExPats Corporation 4 May 2004.

Carr, Wilbur J. *Diary*. Wilbur J. Carr Papers. Manuscript Division, Library of Congress, Washington, D.C.

Center for Strategic and International Studies. *The Embassy of the Future*. Final Report. Washington, D.C., 2007.

Dodd, William E. Letters to and from. American Embassy, Berlin, 1935–1937. Great Britain / German Diplomatic Files, box 32. Franklin D. Roosevelt Presidential Library.

Eddy, William A. Documents on life of . . . USMC (Deceased) from History and Museums Division, Headquarters United States Marine Corps. June 16, 2003.

——. "F.D.R. Meets Ibn Saud." 1954. Vista, CA: Selwa Press, 2005, pp. 1–47.

——. Press release obituary. Department of Information, Headquarters, United States Marine Corps. May 4, 1962.

Elting, Howard, Jr. "Memorandum: Conversation with Mr. Gerhart M. Riegner, Secretary of World Jewish Congress." August 10, 1942. Geneva.

Engert, Cornelius van H. Papers. Special Collections, Georgetown University Libraries, Washington, D.C.

Epstein, Jonathan A. "German and English Propaganda in World War I." New York: CUNY Graduate Center / New York Military Affairs Symposium (NYMAS), December 1, 2000.

Fall of Saigon Marine Association. *Ambassador Graham Martin Saigon, April 29–30, 1975*, pp. 1–26. http://www.fallofsaigon.org/martin.htm.

Field, James A., Jr. "The Decision to Intervene." Part 1 of chapter 3 in *History of United States Naval Operations: Korea*. Washington, D.C.: Department of the Navy.

Fitzpatrick, Kathy R. "The Collapse of American Public Diplomacy." United States Information Agency Alumni Association Survey, Quinnipiac University, Hamden, CT, 2008.

"Francis M. Dimond." *National Cyclopaedia of American Biography*. Vol. 9. Ann Arbor, MI: University Microfilms, 1967. First published 1899 by James T. White.

"The German Request for Free Passage through Belgium." Kaiserlich Deutsche Gesandschaft in Belgien-Brüssel, August 2, 1914. World War I Document Archive.

Gilbert, Prentiss. Prentiss Bailey Gilbert Papers, 1910–1939. Rochester, University of River Campus Libraries. http://www.lib.rochester.edu/index.cfm?.

Ginsburgh, Robert N. "Between War and Peace." Ph.D. diss., Harvard University, 1948.

Great Britain / German Diplomatic Files, box 32. Franklin D. Roosevelt Presidential Library. Letters to and from Ambassador Joseph Grew, the American embassy, Tokyo, 1933–36. www .fdrlibrary.marist .edu/pst/box32/t301b07.html.

Greenwald, Marilyn S. "A Life in Public Service." Chap. 7 in *A Woman of the Times: Journalism, Feminism, and the Career of Charlotte Curtis*. Athens: Ohio University Press, 1999. Available at http://www.nytimes.com/books/first/g/greenwald-times.html?.

Harriman, Florence Jaffray. "Women in American History." Encyclopaedia Britannica Online.

Heinrichs, Waldo H., Jr. "Bureaucracy and Professionalism in the Development of American Career Diplomacy." *Twentieth-Century American Foreign Policy*. Edited by John Braeman, Robert H. Bremner, and David Brody. Columbus: Ohio State University Press, 1971.

Jacobs, Matthew. "The Quintessential American Diplomat." *American Diplomacy*, book review. http://www.unc.edu/depts/diplomat/AD_Issues/amdipl_14/Jacobs_briggs.html.

Johnson, Charles J., Jr. "William Brown Hodgson (1801–1871)." *The New Georgia Encyclopedia*. University of Georgia Press, 2009.

Jue, Stanton. "Anson Burlingame, An American Diplomat." *American Diplomacy*. September 2011.

King, Henry Churchill, and Charles R. Crane. *The King-Crane Commission Report, August 28, 1919*. Published in *Editor and Publisher*, 55, no. 27, (December 2, 1922). http://www.hri.org /docs/king-crane/.

Kopp, Harry W. "International Affairs Forum Interviews Harry W. Kopp." Center for International Relations, June 18, 2009. http://www.ia-forum.org/Contents/ViewInternalDocument .cfm?ContentID=6929.

"Korry, Edward M. former U.S. Ambassador to Chile, Testimony of." Church Committee, Volume 7, Covert Affairs. December 4, 1975.

Lee, Matthew. "Diplomats Reclaim Foreign Policy Roles." Associated Press News, August 22, 2007.

Mendez, Antonio J. "A Classic Case of Deception: CIA Goes Hollywood." https://www.cia.gov/ library/center-for-the-study-of-intelligence/1-15.

Ministry of Foreign Affairs of the People's Republic of China. "Sino-U.S. Ambassadorial Talks." 1999–2005. fmprc.gov.cn/eng/ziliao/3602/3604/t18054.htm.

Murrow, Edward R. "A Report on Senator Joseph R. McCarthy." *See It Now*, CBS-TV, March 9, 1954. http://en.wikipedia.org/wiki/Edward_R._Murrow.

Naland, John (president, American Foreign Service Association). "Between Iraq and a Hard Place." E-mail message, November 5, 2007.

Neumann, Carynn E. "Diplomatic Security (DS), United States Bureau." *Espionage Encyclopedia*. http://www.faqs.org/espionage/De-Eb/Diplomatic-Security-DS-United-States-Bureau.html.

"North Korea Nuclear Weapons Program." Federation of American Scientists. November 16, 2006.

Olson, Russ, "You Can't Spit on a Foreign Policy." September 2000 newsletter, Society for Historians of American Foreign Relations. http://www.shafr.org/newsletter/2000/sep/spit.htm.

Pickering, Thomas R. *Report of Accountability Review Board—Benghazi*. Department of State. December 18, 2012, pp. 1–39. (unclassified)

Rabby, Rami. "The Blind Achieving Success in the Work Place." Letter. National Federation of the Blind, 1995.

Ridges, Peter. "Notes from Italy: The Oversized Embassy." *California Literary Review*, November 6, 2007. http://calitreview.com/280/print.

Ritchie, Albert, II. "James Rockwell Sheffield: A Biographical Essay." Bachelor of Arts thesis, American Studies Department, Yale University, 1961.

Schmidt, Elizabeth. "Oscar F. Williams (1843–1909)." *Epitaph Newsletter*. Mount Hope Cemetery, Rochester, New York, Spring 1989.

Schumaker, James. "Petrograd, Potatoes and Ambassador David Francis." *American Diplomacy*, September 2010.

Simmons, Edwin Howard. "Dominican Adventure." Unpublished manuscript. Alexandria, VA., November 11, 2006, pp. 1–19, plus attachment, prepared at the request of author.

———. "Report from the Dominican Republic: Excerpts from the Transcript of a Debriefing by Lt. Col. Edwin H. Simmons, USMC, Returning U.S. Naval Attaché, Ciudad Trujillo. Declassified from Secret. *ONI Review*, January 1961, pp. 518–29.

Sommers, William. "Washington Irving: Sunnyside to Spain." *American Diplomacy*, June 2012.

Spire, Lorna Lloyd. "Diplomats: A Breed Apart or Anyone Goes? The Question of Political Appointees as Heads of Mission." Paper presented to International Studies Association, San Diego, March 2006.

Straus, Oscar. *Letters 1888–1889*, Constantinople. Via Internet.

"Treaty of Reciprocity between the United States of America and the Hawaiian Kingdom." 1875. Supplemented by Convention of December 6, 1884.

Vicary, Elizabeth Zoe. "William Alexander Leidesdorff." *American National Biography*. Oxford University Press, 2000. Available online at: http://www.anb.org/articles/10/10-00979.html.

Voorhees, David William. "John Romeyn Brodhead." In *American National Biography*. Vol. 3. New York: Oxford University Press, 1999.

Wadley, Patricia Louise. "Even One Is Too Many: An Examination of the Soviet Refusal to Repatriate Liberated American World War II Prisoners of War." Ph.D. dissertation. Texas Christian University, May 1993.

Warder Cresson. Jewish Virtual Library. 2009. www.jewishvirtuallibrary.org/jsource/biography /Cresson.html.

Williams, Jonathan. "Williams, Jonathan MSS." Lilly Library, Indiana University, Bloomington, Indiana.

Wilson, Hugh R. Letters to and from American embassy, Berlin, March–November 1938. Great Britain / German Diplomatic Files, box 32. Franklin D. Roosevelt Presidential Library. http:// www.fdrlibrary.marist.edu/pst/box32/t301b07.html

Acknowledgments

A project of this size and range requires the participation of many people, and I appreciate the contributions of all those who helped make this book possible.

The dedication of five people was indispensable. Foremost was Gail I. Job, who has shared her skills and judgment with me almost continually since 1975. No one could have accomplished more than she over the dozen years that we organized and researched this book.

Originally, the book was suggested to me by Ambassador A. Leroy Atherton, Jr., when he was the director general of the U.S. Foreign Service. Roy, a superb diplomat, was my Harvard College classmate—and my friend for more than fifty years. He and his wife, Betty, also made key contacts for me in the Foreign Service and the State Department.

At the other end of the journey, André Bernard, close friend and splendid editor, read the manuscript and suggested countless improvements.

Michael V. Carlisle, my respected literary agent and friend, always believed in the project and made certain that the manuscript became a published book.

Lynn C. Goldberg contributed not only the support of a loving wife but also of an incomparable professional book publicist. (I do not know how we can thank our devoted English springer spaniel, Talley, but she deserves it, too.)

Among the members of the Foreign Service who contributed generously of their time and thought by agreeing to interviews are Jeffrey J. Anderson; Diego Asencio; William Attwood; Charles R. Baquet III; Anne Barbaro; Janice Bay; Ruth Blaukopf; Avis Bohlen; Michele T. Bond; Molly Bordonaro; Tobin J. Bradley; Robert Bradtke; R. Nicholas Burns; Frankie Calhoun; Anne T. Callaghan; Laura Camerani; J. Michael Cleverley; Thomas M. Countryman; Glyn T. Davies; Ruth A. Davis; Kelly Degnan; James E. Donegan; Gordon Duguid; John P. Dwyer; Brinelle Elaine Ellis; Roderick Engert; John M. Evans; Yael Fedboy; Lauri Fitz-Pegado; Claude Fohlen; Norval E. Francis, Jr.; Benjamin Garcia; Richard N. Gardner; Peggy A. Gennatiempo; Brandon Grove; Giovanni Guasina; D. Brent Hardt; Reno L. Harnish III; William C. Harrop; Robert A. Hartung; William J. Haugh; John E. Herbst; Heather Hodges; Richard Holtzapple; Carolyn Huggins; William Imbrie; William H. Itoh; Makila James; Megan James; Clifton M. Johnson; Steven Kashkett;

Craig A. Kelly; Ian Kelly; George F. Kennan; Charles Stuart Kennedy; Scott F. Kilner; John M. Koenig; Jimmy J. Kolker; Tom C. Korologos; L. Bruce Laingen; Stephen Low; Samuel W. Lewis; John Lister; Hugo Llorens; Clare Boothe Luce; Alan W. Lukens; Hilarion Martinez; Douglas McElhaney; Sherwood McGinnis; Virginia Morris; John Naland; R. James Nicholson; Jerome J. Octgen; Edward L. Peck; Mark Pekala; Edward J. Perkins; Thomas R. Pickering, Anthony C. E. Quainton; Susan Reardon; Kenneth N. Rogers; Kamane M. Romero; Peter F. Romero; Richard A. Roth; Edward M. Rowell; Eric S. Rubin; Dean Rusk; Daniel Russel; Stephen A. Schlaikjer; Rockwell A. Schnabel; Andrew J. Schofer; Kyle Scott; Melvin F. Sembler; Leon V. Sigal; Emil M. Skodon; William Z. Slany; Douglas R. Smith; Kathleen Stephens; Eugene P. Sweeney; Clyde D. Taylor; Elia E. Tello; Paula Thiele; Harry Thomas; Matthew A. Thompson; Terrance A. Todman; Edward S. Walker, Jr.; and Warren Zimmermann.

The staff of the undersecretary for political affairs, including Maren C. Brooks, Cattlin Hayden, and Anneliese L. Reinemeyer, guided me through the State Department bureaucracy.

Others who contributed possibilities among foreign policy issues and sources included William B. Arthur; Louis Auchincloss; Captain John T. Beaver, USN; Abraham Ben Zvi and Itamar Rabinovich of Tel Aviv University; Richard A. Clarke, former special advisor to the President for cyberspace security; M. Richard Duque, of the French Foreign Service; Søren and Birgit Dyssegaard, of the Danish Foreign Service; Dan H. Fenn, Jr.; Joseph V. Genovese; Major General Robert Ginsburgh and his wife Gail; Robert Guidin and Steven Honley, of the *Foreign Service Journal*; W. Gregory Gallagher, librarian of The Century Association; the former dean Allan E. Goodman, of Georgetown University School of Foreign Service; Master Sergeant Thurman Lawrence, (USMC); Professor Bernard Lewis, of Princeton; Margaret E. Mahoney; William J. Martin II, of the National Institutes of Health; Susan Reardon; Sister Kathleen Ross, former president of Heritage University in Washington State; Professor E. Thomas Rowe, of the University of Denver; Arthur M. Schlesinger, Jr.; Brigadier General Edwin Simmons (USMC); and his wife Frances; and Captain Rolf Yngve (USN); as well as the staffs of the Library of Congress and the New York Society Library.

Among others who helped in various essential ways were Michael Adair; Michael Briggs; Maurizio Caprara, of *Corriere della Sera*; Matt and Phyllis Clark; Elizabeth Dwyer; Jane Engert; Daniel Jouve; Mark, David, and Nancy Moskin; James R. and Jill Sheffield; Woodrow A. Wickham; and Carl Wohlleben.

In these days of ever-changing digital technology, I also thank these computer experts for recovering hours of lost work and solving mysterious high-tech puzzles: Alex Marx, Danny Oquendo, Nicolas I. Held, Bruce Stark, Keith Brown, Rey Clarke, and Daniel Seligman.

And once Thomas Dunne decided to publish this book, I was helped extensively by my editor Rob Kirkpatrick and Nicole Sohl, of Thomas Dunne Books, and by freelancers Nancy Johnson, who prepared the bibliography; Julie Gutin, who developed the notes; and Vincent Virga, who skillfully researched the pictures. Writing this book has certainly not been a solo flight.

Index

About the Author

J. Robert Moskin has written nine books. His prize-winning history, *The U.S. Marine Corps Story,* now in its third edition, is generally regarded as the definitive work on the subject. His award-winning *Among Lions* told the story of the battle for Jerusalem in 1967. *Mr. Truman's War* recalled the final months of World War II and the beginning of the postwar era.

An editor of *Look* magazine for nineteen years—the final five as its foreign editor, Moskin reported from the world's trouble spots: the Middle East; Berlin; East Asia; Korea; Europe, east and west; Cuba; and, three times, from the Vietnam War. On his third Vietnam wartime trip, he interviewed North Vietnamese leaders in Hanoi.

He has reported on the State Department and the U.S. Foreign Service since the days when John F. Kennedy was President and Dean Rusk was Secretary of State. Moskin and *Look* photographer James Hansen were the only media people to accompany Secretary and Mrs. Rusk on a tour of NATO countries. Moskin interviewed Ambassador George F. Kennan at the Institute for Advanced Studies in 1963—and again not long before his death in 2005.

For this history of the U.S. Foreign Service, Moskin conducted more than a hundred interviews around the globe. The suggestion that he write this book was made to him by Ambassador A. Leroy Atherton, when he was the director general of the Foreign Service. Although this was an independent enterprise, Moskin had unstinting cooperation from members of the Foreign Service in Washington and abroad.

Moskin received grants for this history from the John D. and Catherine T. MacArthur Foundation, and the Una Chapman Cox Foundation, the Association for Diplomatic Studies and Training, the Delavan Foundation, and the DACOR Bacon House Foundation.

He has served as the editorial director of the Aspen Institute and the Commonwealth Fund, a major philanthropic foundation. And he was a senior editor of *Collier's* and the *World Press Review,* the managing editor of the *Woman's Home Companion,* and editor at large of the *Saturday Review.*

Moskin's work has received the following recognition: Distinguished Service Award of the Marine Corps Combat Correspondents Association for 1978 and 1999; General Oliver P. Smith Award of the Marine Corps Heritage Foundation; Distinguished Service Award of the Marine Corps Historical Foundation; National Jewish Book Award (for *Among Lions*); Citation for Excellence of the Overseas Press Club; best magazine reporting from abroad, of the Overseas Press Club; National Headliners Award, for best feature writing; and for best magazine writing, the Page One Award of the Newspaper Guild of New York; and the Sidney Hillman Foundation Award.

Moskin has degrees in American history from Harvard and Columbia universities. During

World War II, he served in the U.S. Army in the southwest Pacific. He and his wife of twenty-seven years, Lynn Goldberg, live in New York City and Tyringham, Massachusetts. He and his first wife, the late Doris Moskin, have three children, Mark, David, and Nancy, and three grand-children. For more detail, see his Web site: www.jrobertmoskin.com.